BIBLIOGRAPHY OF VIRGINIA HISTORY
SINCE 1865

THE UNIVERSITY OF VIRGINIA INSTITUTE
for Research in the Social Sciences
Institute Monograph No. 5

The University of Virginia
Institute for Reseach in the Social Sciences

PUBLICATIONS OF
THE UNIVERSITY OF VIRGINIA
INSTITUTE FOR RESEARCH IN THE
SOCIAL SCIENCES

PUBLISHED STUDIES
  A STATISTICAL STUDY OF VIRGINIA (1928)
  PUBLIC AND PRIVATE WELFARE, ROANOKE, VIRGINIA (1928)*
  COUNTIES IN TRANSITION: A STUDY OF COUNTY PUBLIC AND PRI-
    VATE WELFARE ADMINISTRATION IN VIRGINIA (1929)
  RURAL DEPOPULATION IN CERTAIN TIDEWATER AND PIEDMONT
    AREAS OF VIRGINIA (1929)
  RESEARCH IN THE SOCIAL SCIENCES: ITS FUNDAMENTAL METHODS
    AND OBJECTIVES (1929)†
  LIFE INSURANCE IN VIRGINIA (1929)
  RURAL AND URBAN LIVING STANDARDS IN VIRGINIA (1929)
  FORT LEWIS: A COMMUNITY IN TRANSITION (1930)
  BIBLIOGRAPHY OF VIRGINIA HISTORY SINCE 1865 (1930)
  PROBLEMS IN CONTEMPORARY COUNTY GOVERNMENT (1930)

FOR EARLY PUBLICATION
  LABOR IN THE INDUSTRIAL SOUTH
  SURVEY OF CRIMINAL JUSTICE IN VIRGINIA
  WORKMEN'S COMPENSATION AND AUTOMOBILE LIABILITY INSURANCE
    IN VIRGINIA
  CURRENCY, CREDIT AND CRISES IN VIRGINIA SINCE 1860
  REGIONALISM IN FRANCE

STUDIES IN PROGRESS
  THE DISTRIBUTION OF THE TAX BURDEN IN VIRGINIA
  VIRGINIA JAIL AND POLICE COURT SYSTEM
  A PSYCHOLOGICAL AND SOCIAL STUDY OF THE POPULATION OF CER-
    TAIN AREAS OF THE BLUE RIDGE
  THE COMMODITY COOPERATIVE IN THE SOUTH
  STATE SUBSIDIES IN VIRGINIA
  LABOR AND LABOR CONDITIONS IN VIRGINIA

  *Published by The City Planning and Zoning Commissions, Roa-
noke, Virginia.
  †Published by The Macmillan Company, New York.

BIBLIOGRAPHY OF VIRGINIA HISTORY SINCE 1865

BY

LESTER JESSE CAPPON
Research Associate in History

Under the Direction of
DUMAS MALONE
Sometime Richmond Alumni
Professor of History

THE INSTITUTE FOR RESEARCH
IN THE SOCIAL SCIENCES
UNIVERSITY, VIRGINIA
1930

THE MICHIE COMPANY, PRINTERS
CHARLOTTESVILLE, VA

FOREWORD

THE history of Virginia since the Civil War has attracted relatively slight attention on the part of historians. They have been interested rather in the more glamorous life of former days and in the extraordinary achievements and exploits of her earlier statesmen and soldiers. Many have doubtless felt that with Appomattox the glory of the Old Dominion faded. Virginia's slow recovery from the travail of war and social readjustment has not been spectacular. National interest in the New South, which has so markedly increased, has not been focused upon her, but rather upon states where the race problem has been more acute or the rise of industry more revolutionary. In no other Southern commonwealth has the transition to modern times been effected more gradually, or, we venture to claim, with smaller sacrifice of traditional values.

Even a casual glance at the closely-printed pages of this book will, however, dispel any illusions about the limitations of recent Virginia history as a field of historical investigation. Those who have been responsible for this undertaking have themselves been surprised to discover what rich materials are available for this single state, the later history of which may have seemed to the casual observer relatively uneventful. In economic development, education, and literature, if not in politics, Virginians have done more in these latter years than they themselves may have known. And in the doing they have contributed to American history a chapter of unspectacular heroism and unostentatious attainment in the face of much quiet tragedy and many now-forgotten failures, the ghosts of which the painstaking bibliographer has disturbed.

Feeling that a guide was needed for a field yet imperfectly charted, we originally planned that the compiler of this bibliography should do for the whole South what he has yet been able to do only for Virginia. The limitation of the scope of the work has been considerably due to the embarrassing thoroughness with which Dr. Cappon proceeded upon his laborious task. It soon appeared that years would be required to cover even a few of the Southern states, so it was decided to concentrate attention upon the commonwealth wherein our chief interest lay. By so doing we hoped to aid all workers in recent Virginia history, and in particular to provide a background for the investigations undertaken by other groups associated with the Insti-

for Research in the Social Sciences at the University of Virginia, and those who may succeed them.

Both in scope and arrangement this compilation differs greatly from Dr. Earl G. Swem's *A Bibliography of Virginia* (1916-17). While covering a more restricted period, it has been limited to no single collection, even so notable a collection as the Virginia State Library. Working nearly three years in Washington, New York, Cambridge, and other centers in both North and South, as well as in Virginia, Dr. Cappon has listed and evaluated materials bearing on every phase of the history of the state during the years he has covered. How thoroughly he has done his work, the following pages will abundantly disclose. He has included manuscript materials, though relatively few of these for the period since the Civil War are available in public collections. With great care he has arranged his titles topically, for the convenience of the investigator. Of the source materials listed by him, the following among many are deserving of special note: the annual reports of the Virginia railroads, the pamphlets on the public debt of the state, the so-called "boom literature" (Part III, Sections 2-3), the catalogues of institutions of learning, the minutes of religious organizations, and the works of Virginia men of letters—which were included because of the growing recognition of the importance of contemporary literature to the social historian.

That this elaborate inventory of materials will stimulate investigation of the recent history of Virginia, and will further the growing movement to preserve manuscripts and printed works bearing upon this and every other period of her life, I am confident. Since the credit will all go, as it should go, to Dr. Cappon, I can afford to say that his book will prove invaluable to anyone who may use it. I know of no comparable work dealing with any other American state.

DUMAS MALONE.

TABLE OF CONTENTS

PREFACE

THIS Bibliography has been compiled primarily as a guide to students of research. The word "history" was interpreted in its broadest sense to include every phase of man's activity and thought, and most of the entries consist of the raw material from which formal history is written. Serious effort was put forth throughout the work to approach completeness so far as practicable and to keep the fundamental criterion of useability in mind. Hence the grouping of material under certain general topics; the inclusion of descriptive and critical notes on individual items; the repetition of certain entries which are concerned with more than one general topic; and in the case of specific details, it is hoped that the index will be found adequate.

The reader will note that the material under each topic is divided into several groups of historical sources. In distinguishing between source material and secondary works, the prevailing character of the subject-matter of each entry determined its classification. In Part X, the phrase "Virginia Men of Letters" was broadly interpreted to include native Virginians, writers who lived for a considerable period in Virginia, or who were influenced by family or other connections in the state.[1]

Because of the abundance of material, some arbitrary lines had to be drawn in the exclusion of certain kinds of publications. Therefore, articles in periodicals, except for some reprints, were eliminated; the various publications and documents of the Commonwealth of Virginia were not analyzed, because Dr. Earl G. Swem's invaluable *Bibliography of Virginia*[2] contains that information through the year 1916, and a supplementary volume on the period since that date is in preparation. Of the numerous works on the southern states which include material on Virginia, the majority were not listed because they fall more properly into a bibliography on the South as a whole, recently begun by the present compiler.

The Virginiana in the Library of Congress, used as the basis of the Bibliography, as well as the invaluable collection in the Virginia State Library at Richmond, were checked and rechecked as being most essential to this compilation. Material in other libraries was

---

1. For explanatory notes on certain technical details, see below, pp. xvii-xviii.
2. Cf. item **36** in the present work.

added and, in most cases, checked with that already compiled, but their catalogues and shelf-lists were examined mainly to find additional works. Thus, for example, the library of Randolph-Macon College, Ashland, Virginia, was visited primarily to obtain a record of material on the Methodist Episcopal Church, South. A key to the libraries consulted will be found following the preface.

To Dr. Dumas Malone, who conceived the idea and general plan of the Bibliography, I wish to express my appreciation of his advice and generous assistance in the development of the project. Among the many librarians, without whose coöperation the work could not have been carried on, I am especially indebted to Mr. Wilmer L. Hall, Assistant Librarian of the Virginia State Library, who gave me unrestricted access to the archives and helpful suggestions on the form of the compilation; to Mr. Harry Clemons, Librarian of the University of Virginia, and Miss Marjorie Carver in charge of the Virginiana at the University, for their untiring interest and aid; and to Dr. Earl G. Swem, Librarian of the College of William and Mary, who gave me numerous valuable suggestions from his vast experience as a bibliographer, on the arrangement and presentation of materials. Finally, I am grateful to Miss Helen H. Brooke of the Library of Congress for her careful and painstaking work of proof-reading which eliminated many serious errors, and to Miss Ruth Ritchie for her patience and efficiency in completing the index. For the faults and short-comings of the Bibliography, the compiler alone must assume responsibility.

LESTER J. CAPPON.

University of Virginia,
  15 May 1930.

LIBRARIES

BP	Boston Public Library, Boston, Mass.
BRE	Bureau of Railway Economics, Washington, D. C.
H	Harvard University, Widener Library, Cambridge, Mass.
HB	Harvard School of Business Administration, Boston, Mass.
HL	Harvard Law School, Cambridge, Mass.
ICC	Interstate Commerce Commission, Washington, D. C.
LC	Library of Congress, Washington, D. C.
McC	McCormick Agricultural Library, 679 Rush St., Chicago, Ill.
NYP	New York Public Library, New York City
RM	Randolph-Macon College, Ashland, Va.
USAg	U. S. Department of Agriculture, Washington, D. C.
USC	U. S. Department of Commerce, Washington, D. C.
USE	U. S. Bureau of Education, Washington, D. C.
USF	U. S. Forest Service, Washington, D. C.
USG	U. S. Geological Survey, Washington, D. C.
USH	U. S. Public Health Service, Washington, D. C.
USHy	U. S. Public Health Service, Hygienic Laboratory, Washington, D. C.
USL	U. S. Department of Labor, Washington, D. C.
USM	U. S. Bureau of Mines, Washington, D. C.
UT	Union Theological Seminary, Richmond, Va.
V	Virginia State Library, Richmond, Va.
VB	Virginia Baptist Historical Society, Richmond University, Richmond, Va.
VD	Virginia Diocesan Library, 110 West Franklin St., Richmond, Va.
VMI	Virginia Military Institute, Lexington, Va.
VPI	Virginia Polytechnic Institute, Blacksburg, Va.
VU	University of Virginia, Charlottesville, Va.
WL	Washington and Lee University, Lexington, Va.
WM	College of William and Mary, Williamsburg, Va.

EXPLANATORY NOTES

Government departments are alphabetized by catch-word, not by first word of title.

In the collations Roman numerals indicate volumes; Arabic numerals indicate separate pamphlet numbers.

In Part VI, a date in parenthesis in the collation indicates the year when the school was established.

A hyphen and the sign / indicate *inclusive* dates, the latter denoting a twelvemonth other than a calendar year.

A repeated entry is listed in the index under its original number.

Abbreviations

Access. no	accession number
adv.	advertisements
agric.	agricultural
A. M. E.	African Methodist Episcopal Church
Bapt.	Baptist
bd.	board
bus.	business school
ca. (circa)	approximately
cf.	compare
C. H.	court house
Co.	county
co.	company
co-ed.	co-educational
col.	colored
col. & prep.	college & preparatory
comp.	compiled, compiler
co-ord.	co-ordinate college for women
diagr.	diagram(s)
doc.	document
ed.	edited by, edition, editor
elem.	elementary
enl.	enlarged
engin. col.	engineering college
et al.	and another (others)
f°.	folio
facsim. (s)	facsimile(s)
ff.	following
fold.	folded
front.	frontispiece
ibid.	same
illus.	illustrated
incl.	including
incompl.	incomplete

indust.	industrial
irreg.	irregularly
jr. col.	junior college
l.	leaf (leaves)
Luth.	Lutheran
M. E., So.	Methodist Episcopal Church, South
milit.	military
mimeog.	mimeographed
ms. (s)	manuscript(s)
nar.	narrow
n. d.	no date of publication given
non-sect.	non-sectarian
n. p.	no place of publication given
numb.	numbered
obl.	oblique
p.	page(s)
period.	periodical
p. l.	preliminary leaf (leaves)
pl.	plate(s)
P. O.	post office
port. (s)	portrait(s)
prep.	preparatory
Presbyt.	Presbyterian
print.	printed
Prot. Episc.	Protestant Episcopal Church
pseud.	pseudonym
pt.	part
pub.	published by, publisher
q. v. (*quod vide*)	refers to an item listed elsewhere
rev.	revised
Rom. Cath.	Roman Catholic
r. r.	railroad
ry.	railway
ser.	series
soc.	society
stenog.	stenographic school
tel. & tel.	telephone and telegraph
typew.	typewritten
unp.	unpaged
v.	volume
var. pag.	varied pagination
V. M. I.	Virginia Military Institute
vol. (s)	volume(s)
V. P. I.	Virginia Polytechnic Institute
4°.	quarto
8°.	octavo
12°.	duodecimo
16°.	sexdecimo

PART I. BIBLIOGRAPHIES AND INDEXES

1. BERCAW, LOUISE O. Dairying in Virginia. Some references on the early development of the industry. Comp. in the library, Bur. of agricultural economics, U. S. Dept. of agriculture . . . Washington, D. C., Aug. 3, 1926.

> 5 l. typew. 4°.   **USAg**

2. ———. Development of commercial fruit-growing in Virginia. List of references . . . Bur. of agricultural economics, U. S. Dept. of agriculture. Washington, D. C., Feb. 21, 1925.

> 5 l. typew. 4°.   **USAg**

3. CALENDAR of Virginia state papers and other manuscripts . . . preserved in the Capitol at Richmond . . . Richmond, 1875-93.

> 11 v. 4°. Imprint varies.
> v. XI: Jan. 1, 1836-Apr. 15, 1869; H. W. Flournoy, ed.

4. CONVERSE, HENRY A. Indexes to the Virginia and West Virginia reports: By Henry A. Converse . . . Edited by Howard Bayne . . . With a memoir of the author by his brother James B. Converse. Richmond, West, Johnston, 1881.

> xxii p., 1 l., 359 p. 8°.   **LC, V, VU**

5. A DIGEST of the decisions of the Supreme courts of appeals of Virginia and West Virginia reported in vols. 1-118 Virginia reports . . . , vols. 1-77 West Virginia reports . . . , vols. 1-86 Southeastern reporter to . . . 1915. Comp. under the American digest classification scheme . . . by members of the editorial staff of the American digest system . . . St. Paul, Minn., West, 1906-16.

> 7 v. 8°.   **LC, V, VU**

6. [GORDON, ARMISTEAD C.] A bibliography of the published writings of Armistead C. Gordon, . . . 1923. [Staunton, Va., Priv. print. for the author by McClure, 1923]

> 8 p. 8°. 80 copies only.   **H, LC, VU**

7. GUTHRIE, JAMES H. Index to the Virginia law register, vols. I-X, with a list of leading articles, and tables of cases reported in full and of cases digested . . . Lynchburg, Va., Bell [1906]

> 386 p. 8°. (v. I-X; May, 1895-Apr., 1905)   **VU**

8. HALL, WILMER L. . . . A bibliography of taxation in Virginia since 1910, comp. by Wilmer L. Hall, assistant state librarian. Richmond, Bottom, 1926.

> 38 p. 8°. (In Virginia. State library. *Bulletin*, XVI, 1).
> Almost all the books listed are in the State library.

9. HOLT, GUY. A bibliography of the writings of James Branch Cabell . . . Philadelphia, Centaur, 1924.

> 73, [9] p. front. 8°. (The Centaur bibliographies of modern American authors. [no. 3])
> Contents: First editions (description of title-pages); Cabell's contributions to books and to periodicals; some criticism in periodicals and in books.

10. HURST, SAMUEL N. A complete alphabetical, analytical, chronological annotated digest of all the reported decisions of the Supreme court of appeals of Virginia, Special court of appeals, High court of chancery, and General court, from Jefferson's reports to 92 Virginia reports, 1730-1896, by Sam N. Hurst . . . assisted by Hon. Randal M. Brown . . . Pulaski City, Va., Hurst, 1897-1902.

> 8 v. 8°. v. 6-8 pub. in Luray, Va., by Hurst & Co.
> **LC, V**: 1-8; **VU**: 3-8

11. ———. A complete alphabetical, analytical, chronological annotated digest of all the reported decisions of the Supreme court of appeals of Virginia from 93 Virginia reports to 99 Virginia reports, 1896-1902, together with a complete subject-index, table of cases, table of statutes cited or construed, and table of cases explained, criticised, or overruled, by Sam N. Hurst . . . Supplement to Virginia digest. Vol. I. Luray, Va., Hurst, 1902.

> 2 p. l., 960 p. 8°.   **LC, VU**

12. ———. A complete index to all the reported decisions of the Supreme court of appeals of Virginia, Special court of appeals, High court of chancery, and General court, from Jefferson's reports to 99 Virginia reports, 1730-1902; with a complete table of cases, list of statutes cited or construed, &c.: being also an index to "Hurst's Virginia digest." . . . In two parts. Luray, Va., Hurst [1902]

> 2 p. l., 1231 p., 1 l., [1233]-1376 p. 8°.   **LC, VU**

13. ———. A complete annotated criminal digest of all the reported decisions of the Supreme court of appeals of Virginia and West

Virginia from the first organization of the old General court of Virginia to 97 Virginia and 46 West Virginia . . . Pulaski City, Va., Hurst, 1900.

1 p. 1., viii, 795, [1] p., 1 1., 217, [1] p., 1 1. 8°.   LC, V, VU

14. ———. Index and directory of Virginia law: being a complete index to the Virginia law register (I to XIX) the code and acts of Virginia (1887 to 1914) the constitution of Virginia and a complete directory of annotations in the "Trinity set," L. R. A., Virginia reports annotated, and Virginia law register with methods and costs of obtaining charters, rules of practice, canons of ethics, court calendar and official directory and complete tables of statutes amended or repealed, statutes and constitution construed, decisions overruled, questioned, or decided by divided court, addresses before Virginia State bar association, leading articles in Virginia law journal, forms, fees, etc. . . . Pulaski, Va., Hurst, 1914.

xii, 1039 p. 12°.   LC, V, VU

15. JOHNSON, MERLE D. A bibliographic check-list of the works of James Branch Cabell, 1904-1921 . . . New York, Shay, 1921.

27, [1] p. 12°.   BP, LC, NYP

"First editions" arranged chronologically by date of publication. An epistolary preface, by James Branch Cabell.

16. KENNEDY, JOHN P. Calendar of transcripts, including the annual report of the Dept. of archives and history. John P. Kennedy, state librarian. Richmond, Bottom, 1905.

iv, 5-658, xliv p. 4°.

Check-list of bound MSS. and transcripts forming part of the collection in the Virginia state library.

17. MARTIN, WILLIAM B. An index to the Virginia reports, from Jefferson to vol. 91, both inclusive, with a total of cases reported, and of Virginia cases cited, in those volumes. By William Bruce Martin, judge of the court of law and chancery, of the city of Norfolk, Va., Richmond, Va., Randolph, 1896.

2 p. 1., 1065 p. 8°.   LC, V, VU

First pub. in 1881, covering Virginia reports from Jefferson to 33 Grattan (688 p.); supplement pub. in 1889, covering Virginia reports, 75-84 (336 p.); 1903 supplement covering Virginia reports, 92-100.

18. MATTHEWS, JAMES M. Digest of the laws of Virginia of a criminal nature. Illustrated by judicial decisions. To which is prefixed the new constitution of Virginia . . . 2d ed., Richmond, Va., Randolph & English, 1871.

376 p. 8°.   HL, V, VU

19. MATTHEWS, JAMES M. [*Ibid.*] . . . 3d ed., rev., and enl. Richmond, Randolph & English, 1890.

3 p. l., 421 p. 8°.   LC, V

20. MICHIE, THOMAS J. The encyclopedic digest of Virginia and West Virginia reports; being a complete encyclopedia and digest of all the Virginia and West Virginia case law up to and including vol. 103 Virginia reports and vol. 55 West Virginia reports; under the editorial supervision of Thomas Johnson Michie. Charlottesville, Va., Michie, 1905-07.

13 v. 8°.   HL, LC, V, VU

21. ———. . . . Complete encyclopedia and digest of all the Virginia and West Virginia case law from vol. 104 to vol. [121] Virginia reports, both inclusive, and from vol. 56 to vol. [79] West Virginia reports, both inclusive . . . vol. XIV-[XVII] —supplement. Charlottesville, Va., Michie, 1909-19.

4 v. 8°.   HL, LC, V, VU

22. ———. . . . Cumulative supplement; being a complete encyclopedia and digest of all the Virginia and West Virginia case law from vol. 104 to vol. 129 Virginia reports, both inclusive, and from vol. 56 to vol. 87 West Virginia reports, both inclusive . . . Charlottesville, Va., Michie, 1922-23.

6 v. 8°.   HL, LC, VU

23. ———. . . . Supplement, being a complete encyclopedia and digest of all the Virginia and West Virginia case law from vol. 130 to vol. [147] Virginia reports, both inclusive, and from vol. 88 to vol. [104] West Virginia reports, both inclusive . . . Charlottesville, Va., Michie, 1925-28.

4 v. 8°.   HL, LC, VU

24. ———. An index-digest to vols. 92-99 Virginia reports (both inclusive) and vols. 1 and 2 Virginia decisions . . . Charlottesville, Va., Michie, 1902.

500 p. 8°.   LC, V, VU

25. MINOR. MRS. KATE P., *et al.* . . . A list of newspapers in the Virginia state library, Confederate museum and Valentine

museum. Comp. by Mrs. Kate Pleasants Minor . . . and
Miss Susie B. Harrison . . . under the direction of Earl G.
Swem . . . Richmond, Va., 1912.

> 3 p. l., p. [285]-425. 8°. (In Virginia. State library. *Bulletin,* V, 4)
> 3 indexes: by library; titles, by states, alphabetically; chronological,
> 1723-1911.

26. NEW YORK. PUBLIC LIBRARY. List of works in the New York
public library relating to Virginia. [New York, 1907]

> 71 p. 8°. (Reprint from its *Bulletin,* Feb.-Apr., 1907)
>   **BP, H, LC, NYP**

27. NEWMAN, CAROL M. Virginia literature; a dissertation presented
to the faculty of the University of Virginia as a part of the requirements for degree of Ph.D. June, 1903. [n. p., n. d.]

> 69 p. 8°.   **H, V, VU**
> Contains a check-list of Virginia writers (Virginians who published
> books between 1607 and 1901).

28. PATTON, JOHN S. The Byrd library. A collection of Virginiana
in the library of the University of Virginia, founded on the Alfred Henry Byrd gift. Comp. by John S. Patton, librarian, with
a prefatory note by Robert Lewis Harrison. Charlottesville,
University of Virginia, 1914.

> 45 p. 8°.   **NYP, V, VU**
> Alphabetical list, by authors.

29. PAUL, MRS. KATHERINE S. A partial list of Virginia authors
and their works. Comp. for the use of the Committee on Virginia authors of the board of World's fair managers . . .
[n. p., 1892].

> 60 p. 8°.   **LC, V**

30. [RICHARDSON, CARRIE W.] [Bibliography of the writings and
addresses of Edwin A. Alderman, in the University of Virginia.
July, 1926].

> 16 l. typew. 4°.   **VU**

31. ROYALL, WILLIAM L. A digest of the decisions of the Supreme
court of appeals of Virginia, contained in Grattan's reports, vols.
1 to 21 . . . New York, Diossy, 1873.

> vi, 472 p. 8°.   **LC, V**

32. THE SOUTHEASTERN REPORTER. . . . Digest of decisions of
the Supreme court of appeals of Virginia and West Virginia, and

Supreme courts of North Carolina and South Carolina, and the Supreme court and Court of appeals of Georgia, reported in the Southeastern reporter, vols. 1- ; with a table of constitutions, codes and statutes construed, and a table of cases digested. St. Paul, West, 1895-19—

8°. (National reporter system digests. Key number system. Southeastern series; in progress)
HL: I-CXXXV, 1887-1927; **LC**: I-CXL, 1887-1928; **VU**: I-LV.

33. . . . SOUTHEASTERN REPORTER DIGEST. [Virginia ed.] Including cases reported in vols. 1- Southeastern reporter 82- Virginia reports and also . . . state reports . . . together with an index-digest of vols. 1- Virginia . . . edited by the editorial staff of the American digest system. St. Paul, West, 1925-

8°. (Key number system. In progress)
LC, VU: I-CXXV (S. E. report., LXXXII-CXL); index-digest, I-LXXXII.

34. STANARD, WILLIAM G. The Virginia archives . . . Washington, Govt., 1904.

p. 645-664. 8°. (Reprint from Amer. hist. assoc., *Annual report,* 1903, I)

35. SWEM, EARL G. A bibliography of the conventions and constitutions of Virginia, including references to essays, letters and speeches in the Virginia newspapers . . . Richmond, Va., 1910.

p. [355]-441. 8°. (In Virginia. State library. *Bulletin,* III, 4)

36. ———. . . . A bibliography of Virginia . . . Richmond, Bottom, 1916-17.

2 v. 8°. (In Virginia. State library. *Bulletin,* VIII, 2-4; X, 1-4)
Pt. I: Titles of books in the Virginia state library which relate to Virginia and Virginians; titles of books written by Virginians, and of those printed in Virginia; with index. Pt. II: Titles of printed official documents of Virginia, 1776-1916; with index.
An invaluable guide to Virginiana.

37. ———. . . . A contribution to the bibliography of agriculture in Virginia; ed. by Earl G. Swem, assistant state librarian, from the manuscript of N. F. Cabell. Richmond, Bottom, 1918.

35 p. 8°. (In Virginia. State library. *Bulletin* XI, 1-2)

38. ———. . . . A list of manuscripts recently deposited in the Virginia state library by the state auditor . . . Richmond, Bottom, 1914.

32 p. 8°. (In Virginia. State library. *Bulletin,* VII, I)

39. ———. . . . A list of manuscripts relating to the history of agriculture in Virginia, collected by N. F. Cabell, and now in the Virginia state library . . . Richmond, Bottom, 1913.

20 p. 8°. (In Virginia. State library. *Bulletin,* VI, 1)

40. ———. . . . Maps relating to Virginia in the Virginia state library and other departments of the commonwealth, with the 17th and 18th century atlas-maps in the Library of Congress . . . Richmond, Bottom, 1914.

2 p. l., p. [37]-263. 8°. (In Virginia. State library. *Bulletin,* VII, 2-3)
Arranged chronologically; includes maps in atlases, geological survey reports, periodicals, railroad pamphlets, etc.

41. THOMAS, ELLA M. Virginia women in literature, a partial list . . . 1902. Richmond, Johnson, 1902.

61 p. 8°.   **V, VU**
Comp. for the Charleston exposition. "The names are of those who were born in Virginia, or of those who were adopted by her long enough to be looked upon as belonging to her." [p. 3.]

42. U. S. LIBRARY OF CONGRESS. BIBLIOGRAPHY, Div. of. References on the boundary controversies between Virginia (and West Virginia) and Maryland. [Washington, D. C.] Sept. 14, 1914.

9 l. typew. 4°.   **LC, V**

43. UNIVERSITY OF VIRGINIA. . . . University bibliography 1922- Charlottesville, The University [1924–

8°. (*University of Virginia record.* Extension series)
"Published under the auspices of the Research committee."
Annual, except the first, which covers 1922-24.
LC: 1922/24-27/28: **NYP:** 1924/25, 26/27; **USAg:** 1925/26-27/28; **USE:** 1924/25; **V:** 1925/26-27/28; **VU:** 1922/24-27/28.

44. VIRGINIA. AGRICULTURAL EXPERIMENT STATION, Blacksburg. . . . Index to preceding bulletins . . . Blacksburg, Va. [1897]

1 p. l., p. [131]-140. 8°. (Its *Bulletin,* 83, new ser., VI, 12)
BP, LC, NYP, USAg, V, VPI

45. VIRGINIA HISTORICAL SOCIETY, Richmond. Catalogue of the manuscripts in the collection of the Virginia historical society, and also of some printed papers. Comp. by order of the Executive committee. Richmond, Jones, 1901.

2 p. l., 120 p. 8°.   LC, NYP, V

46. VIRGINIA NEWSPAPERS in public libraries. [Library of Congress, Virginia historical society, and Virginia state library] Part I. [Richmond, 1901-03]

8°. (In *Virginia magazine of history and biography,* VIII, 337-346; IX, 1-11, 130-138, 289-297, 411-414; X, 225-229, 421-422) No more pub.

47. VIRGINIA POLYTECHNIC INSTITUTE, Blacksburg. . . . Research and publication completed and in progress. 1923/26- [Blacksburg, 1927-

8°. (In its *Bulletin,* XX, 2; XXII, 3; in progress)
H, LC, NYP, USE, V, VPI: 1923/26-27/28.

48. VIRGINIA. STATE LIBRARY, Richmond. . . . Check-list of Virginia state publications 1926-   Richmond, Bottom, 1927-

8°. (In its *Bulletin,* XVI, 4; XVII, 2; in progress)
A list of the publications received by the Virginia state library and the State law library, not a complete catalog of all printed Virginia documents issued.

49. ———. ———. Legislative reference lists [of books in the Virginia state library] . . . Richmond, Va. [1908?-

8°. H: 1910, 12; LC: 1910, 12; NYP: 1907/08, 10, 12, 14, 16; USC: 1912; USL: 1912; V: 1908, 10, 12; VU: 1910.
Comp. to assist the legislature.

50. WEGELIN, OSCAR. A bibliography of the separate writings of John Esten Cooke . . . Metuchen, N. J., Print. for C. F. Heartman, 1925.

20 p. incl. front. (port.) facsims. 8°. (Heartman's historical series, no. 43) 51 copies printed.   BP, H, LC

51. WILLIAMS, JOHN W. Index to enrolled bills of the General assembly of Virginia, 1776 to 1910. Comp. by John W. Williams, clerk of the House of delegates and keeper of the rolls. Richmond, Bottom, 1911.

1155 p. 8°.   LC, NYP, V, VU, WM

PART II. ECONOMIC

1. BIBLIOGRAPHY

52. [1] BERCAW, LOUISE O. Dairying in Virginia . . . Washington, D. C., Aug. 3, 1926.

53. [2] ————. Development of commercial fruit-growing in Virginia . . . Washington, D. C., Feb. 21, 1925.

54. [8] HALL, WILMER L. . . . A bibliography of taxation in Virginia since 1910 . . . Richmond, 1926.

55. [37] SWEM, EARL G. . . . A contribution to the biliography of agriculture in Virginia . . . Richmond, 1918.

56. [39] ————. . . . A list of manuscripts relating to the history of agriculture in Virginia . . . Richmond, 1913.

57. [44] VIRGINIA. AGRICULTURAL EXPERIMENT STATION, Blacksburg. . . . Index to preceding bulletins . . . Blacksburg [1897]

58. [47] VIRGINIA POLYTECHNIC INSTITUTE, Blacksburg. . . . Research and publication completed and in progress. 1923/26— [Blacksburg, 1927—

2. AGRICULTURE

Government Publications and Documents

59. ALFALFA: instructions adapted to southern New Jersey, Delaware, southern Maryland, Virginia . . . Washington, Govt., 1920.

6 p. 8°. (U. S. Dept. of agriculture. *Dept. circular,* 115)

60. ALWOOD, WILLIAM B. Enological studies. The chemical composition of American grown grapes in Ohio, New York, and Virginia. Washington, Govt., 1911.

35 p. incl. tables. 8°. (U. S. Dept. of agriculture. Bur. of chemistry. *Bulletin,* 145; rev. *Enological studies,* 4)

61. AMHERST COUNTY AGRICULTURAL ADVISORY COUNCIL. Five year program for Amherst County . . . Agronomy; livestock; horticulture; agricultural engineering; boys' and girls' club work.

Virginia polytechnic institute and the U. S. Dept. of agriculture
co-operating. Blacksburg, Va., Extension division, 1926.

18 p. 8°.   USAg

Recommendation offered to the people of the county.

62. APPOMATTOX COUNTY AGRICULTURE ADVISORY BOARD. Five year
program for Appomattox County . . . 1925 . . . Virginia . . . polytechnic institute and the U. S. Dept. of agriculture co-operating. Extension division, John R. Hutchison, director . . . Blacksburg, Va. [1926]

14 p. 8°.   USAg

63. AUGUSTA COUNTY AGRICULTURAL ADVISORY COUNCIL. A five year
agricultural program for Augusta County . . . Virginia polytechnic institute and the U. S. Dept. of agriculture co-operating.
Blacksburg, Va., Extension division, 1926.

42 p. 8°.   USAg

64. BENNETT, HUGH H. Soils of the Shenandoah River terrace: a
revision of certain soils in the Albemarle area of Virginia. Washington, Govt., 1912.

16 p. illus., table. 8°. (U. S. Dept. of agriculture. Bur. of soils.
Circular, 53)

65. BONSTEEL, JAY A. . . . Soils of eastern Virginia and their
uses for truck crop production . . . Washington, Govt., 1922.

70 p. plates, fold. maps. 8°. (U. S. Dept. of agriculture. *Dept. bulletin,*
1005)

Contribution from the Bur. of soils.

66. BRODELL, ALBERT P. Cost of producing Virginia dark fire-cured
and bright tobacco. Charlotte and adjacent counties. Crop year
1922-23. Preliminary report 1923-24. Washington, 1923-24.

1 p. l., 11 p. mimeog. 4°.   USAg

67. CAMPBELL COUNTY AGRICULTURAL ADVISORY BOARD. Five year
agricultural program for Campbell County . . . Virginia polytechnic institute and the U. S. Dept. of agriculture co-operating.
Blacksburg, Va., Extension division, 1926.

18 p. 8°.   USAg

68. CAROLINE COUNTY AGRICULTURAL ADVISORY COUNCIL. Five year
program of agricultural development for Caroline County . . .

Virginia polytechnic institute and the U. S. Dept. of agriculture
co-operating. Blacksburg, Va., Extension division, 1925.

15 p. 8°.   **USAg**

69. A DESCRIPTIVE catalogue of the soils of Virginia so far identified
in the soil survey. Washington, Govt., 1913.

21 p. map, table, diagr. 8°. . (U. S. Dept. of agriculture. *Dept. bulletin,*
46)

70. ESSEX COUNTY AGRICULTURAL ADVISORY COUNCIL. Program for
developing Essex County's agriculture as worked out in 1925 by
the . . . council and D. H. Crosby . . . Virginia . . .
polytechnic institute and the U. S. Dept. of agriculture co-operating.
Blacksburg, Va., Extension division [1926?]

17 p. 8°.   **USAg**

71. EZEKIEL, MORDECAI, *et al.* . . . Factors affecting returns
from the dairy enterprise in the Shenandoah Valley. Preliminary
report based on conduct of the dairy enterprise on 188 farms in
Rockingham and Augusta counties, Virginia. By Mordecai Ezekiel and J. J. Vernon. U. S. Dept. of agriculture, Bur. of agricultural economics, and Virginia experiment station, Div. of agricultural economics, co-operating. Washington, Govt., 1926.

17 p. mimeog. 4°.   **USAg**

72. FUNK, WARREN C. . . . An economic study of small farms
near Washington, D. C. . . . Washington [Govt.] 1920.

19 p. illus., diagrs. 8°. (U. S. Dept. of agriculture. *Dept. bulletin,*
848)

Study of 152 farms on which each operator devoted most of his time
to supervision and labor. Farms located in Fairfax County and adjoining territory.

73. GOULD, H. P. Orchard fruits in the Piedmont and Blue Ridge
regions of Virginia and the South Atlantic states. Washington,
Govt., 1908.

102 p. plates (incl. 2 maps) 8°. (U. S. Dept. of agriculture. Bur.
of plant industry. *Bulletin,* 135)

74. GRAYSON COUNTY AGRICULTURAL ADVISORY BOARD. Five year
agricultural program for Grayson County . . . Virginia polytechnic institute and the U. S. Dept. of agriculture co-operating
Blacksburg, Va., Extension division, 1927.

29 p. 8°.   **USAg**

75. HALIFAX COUNTY AGRICULTURAL ADVISORY COUNCIL. Five year agricultural program for Halifax County . . . by . . . David T. Painter. Virginia polytechnic institute and the U. S. Dept. of agriculture co-operating. Blacksburg, Va., Extension division 1926.

20 p. 8°.   USAg

76. HUTCHISON, JOHN R. Our agricultural problem . . . Virginia polytechnic institute, Extension service. Blacksburg, Va., 1926.

39 p. 8°.   USAg

77. KEITHLY, K. A. . . . Co-operative marketing of livestock and wool in Virginia, by K. A. Keithly, representing the U. S. Bur. of markets and crop estimates and the Virginia Div. of markets of the state Dept. of agriculture. [Richmond, 1922]

5 numb. l. f°.   USAg

78. McNESS, GEORGE T., *et al.* Improvement of Virginia fire-cured tobacco. By George T. McNess, E. H. Mathewson, and B. G. Anderson. Washington, Govt., 1907.

40 p. illus., tables 8°. (U. S. Dept. of agriculture. Bur. of soils. *Bulletin,* 46)

79. MANNY, T. B. . . . What farmers say about marketing Eastern shore potatoes and what farmers suggest for better marketing . . . A preliminary report. U. S. Dept. of agriculture, Bur. of agricultural economics, in co-operation with University of Maryland and Virginia agricultural experiment station. Washington, D. C., Nov., 1928.

12 p. mimeog. 4°.   USAg

80. MECKLENBURG COUNTY AGRICULTURE ADVISORY BOARD. Five year agricultural program for Mecklenburg County . . . Virginia . . . polytechnic institute and the U. S. Dept. of agriculture co-operating . . . Blacksburg, Va., Extension division, 1926.

20 p. 8°.   USAg

81. MOUNT WEATHER OBSERVATORY, Bluemont, Va. Bulletin . . . vols. 1-6. Washington, Govt., 1908-14.

6 v. plates, diagrs. 8°.   LC, USAg, V
Charles F. Marvin, chief. v. 1-4 prepared under the direction of Willis L. Moore, chief of U. S. Weather bur., Dept. of agriculture.
Discontinued. Later contributions from members of the staff of the

observatory are published in the *Monthly weather review,* and in supplements.

82. ———. . . . Summary of the free air data at Mount Weather for the three years, July 1, 1907 to June 30, 1910. By the Aerial section—William R. Blair in charge . . . [Washington, Govt., 1911]

39 p. diagrs. 4°. **LC**

83. NORFOLK, VA. INDUSTRIAL COMMISSION. Agriculture and food production in and around Norfolk, Virginia, and its tributary territory; tidewater Virginia and eastern North Carolina . . . issued by the Industrial commission (official) of the city of Norfolk, Va. . . . [Norfolk, Va., Burke & Gregory, *ca.* 1912]

71 p. illus. 8°.
Description by counties, with separate section on Norfolk and the "Garden of Tidewater." Very enthusiastic in tone.

84. POLLARD, THOMAS. The hog: the varieties to raise, general management, and diseases; by Dr. Thomas Pollard, commissioner of agriculture of Virginia. Richmond, Frayser, 1878.

77 p. 8°. **V, VU**

85. ———. Sheep husbandry for Virginia . . . Richmond, Va., Walker, 1881.

142 p. 8°. (Pub. with the *5th Annual report* of the commissioner of agriculture of Virginia) **V**
Based partly upon former treatises on sheep; written to urge every farmer to own sheep.

86. PULASKI COUNTY, VA. BOARD OF AGRICULTURE. A five year program for the agricultural development of Pulaski County, Virginia. Prepared by the . . . county Board of agriculture, Virginia polytechnic institute, and U. S. Dept. of agriculture cooperating. Blacksburg, Va., Extension division, 1927.

22 p. illus. 8°. **USAg**

87. ROCKBRIDGE COUNTY AGRICULTURAL ADVISORY BOARD. Five year agricultural program for Rockbridge County . . . Virginia polytechnic institute and U. S. Dept. of agriculture co-operating. Blacksburg, Va., Extension division, 1926.

16 p. 8°. **USAg**

88. RUNNER, G. A. The so-called tobacco wireworm in Virginia. Washington, Govt., 1914.

30 p. illus., tables. 8°. (U. S. Dept. of agriculture. *Dept. bulletin,* 78)
Bibliography, p. 29-30.

89. SCARBOROUGH, W. S. . . . Tenancy and ownership among Negro farmers in Southampton County, Virginia . . . Washington [Govt.] 1926.

27 p. map. 8°. (U. S. Dept. of agriculture. *Dept. bulletin,* 1404)
Contribution from Bur. of agricultural economics. Reveals conditions among Negro farmers in a selected district where plantation organization has largely disappeared and the Negro farmers enjoy a large measure of independence.

90. SHAFFER, B. E. Packing and loading basket apples. Virginia Dept. of agriculture, Div. of markets. Richmond, Va., 1928.

[4] p. 8°.   USAg

91. SMYTH COUNTY AGRICULTURAL ADVISORY COUNCIL. A five year agricultural program for Smyth County . . . Virginia polytechnic institute and U. S. Dept. of agriculture cooperating. Blacksburg, Va., Extension division [1926]

20 p. 8°.   USAg

92. STANTON, T. R. Cereal experiments in Maryland and Virginia. Washington, Govt., 1916.

51 p. illus., map, tables. 8°. (U. S. Dept. of agriculture. *Dept. bulletin,* 336)

93. ———. Fall-sown grains in Maryland and Virginia. Washington, Govt., 1917.

23 p. illus., tables. 8°. (U. S. Dept. of argriculture. *Farmers' bulletin,* 786)

94. The 28-HOUR law: Decision of the Circuit court of appeals for the fourth circuit, reversing decision of the District court for the Eastern district of Virginia, in a case involving violation of the 28-hour law (act of June 29, 1906; 34 Stat. 607). Washington, Govt., 1909.

10 p. 8°. (U. S. Dept. of agriculture. Office of the Solicitor. *Circular,* 21)
The 28-hour law regulates the transportation and care of animals in interstate commerce.

95. U. S. AGRICULTURE, Dept. of. MARKETS, Bur. of. Marketing of peanuts in the Virginia-North Carolina section, season of 1919-20. Washington, D. C., 1920.

13 p. mimeog. f°. **USAg**

96. ———. ———. SOILS, Bur. of. [Soil surveys in Virginia, 1901-1918] Washington, Govt. [1903-22]

17 v. 8°. **USAg**

Surveys (with dates of pub.): Accomac and Northampton counties (1920); Albemarle area (1903); Appomattox County (1905); Bedford area (1903); Campbell County (1911); Chesterfield County (1908); Fairfax and Alexandria counties (1917); Frederick County (1916); Hanover County (1906); Henrico County (1914); Leesburg area (1904); Louisa County (1906); Montgomery County (1908); Norfolk area (1904); Pittsylvania County (1922); Prince Edward area (1903); Yorktown area (1906).

97. ———. ———. WEATHER BUR. CLIMATOLOGICAL SERVICE. Virginia section. Climatological data. Vol. 1- ; 1891-19— Richmond, 1891-19—

4°. monthly.

USAg: VI, 12; VII, 1-2, 5; VIII, 2-5, 10-11; IX, 1, 3-12; X, 1-8, 11-12; XI-XIX, 6; XXIV-XXIX; (1896-1909, 14-19). **V**: V-IX, XVI-XXXIV; (1895-99, 1906-24).

98. ———. CENSUS, Bur. of the. Fourteenth census of the United States: 1920 . . . Bulletin . . . Agriculture: Virginia. Statistics for the state and its counties. Prepared under the supervision of William Lane Austin, chief statistician for agriculture . . . [Washington, Govt., 1921]

48 p. incl. map, tables. 4°.

99. ———. RAILROAD ADMINISTRATION. Norfolk & Western railway. Agricultural dept. Livestock bulletin: Roanoke, Va. Nov. 1, 1918; Dec. 1, 1918; Jan. 1, 1919. [n. p., n. d.]

4 p. tables. **V**

Livestock for sale, exchange, or wanted; descriptive list with names of owners and addresses.

100. ———. ———. Virginia. The Old Dominion welcomes the homemaker and offers unexcelled opportunities for success on the farm. Issued by the U. S. Railroad administration, Agricultural section . . . [Washington, Adams, 1919?]

32 p. illus., fold. map. 8°. **LC, NYP, USAg**

Agricultural resources and products described by sections; with attractive illustrations.

101. VIRGINIA. Annual reports of officers, boards and institutions of the commonwealth of Virginia . . . Richmond, Va. [1866-19—

tables. 8°.

H: 1872/73, 73/74; LC: 1866/67, 69/70, 71/72-84, 85/86-1904, 06-14, 16-24/25; NYP: 1866, 69-1925; USC: 1880-1902; V: 1866-1928; VU: 1869/70, 71-1928; WM: 1866, 71/72-99, 1901-03, 06-22/23, 24/25-26/27.
For analysis of these reports, to 1916, see E. G. Swem, *Bibliography of Virginia*, II, *passim.* **[36]**
Include reports of the board and dept. of agriculture, 1889-19—

102. ———. AGRICULTURAL EXPERIMENT STATION, Blacksburg. Announcement . . . [Blacksburg, Va., 1888].

7 p. 8°.   USAg

103. ———. ———. Annual report. [1st-] 1889/90-19— Lynchburg, Va. [etc.] 1891-19—

8°. Report year ends June 30.
BP: 1889/90-92/93, 94/95-1905/06, 11/12, 13/14, 15/16-18/19; LC: 1889/90-90/91, 93/94-97/98, 1905/06-07/08, 17/18-18/19; NYP: 1890/91-93/94, 96/97-97/98, 99/1900-00/01, 02/03-05/06, 07/08, 09/10-11/12, 13/14-18/19; USAg: 1889/90-1905/06, 07/08-18/19; V: 1889/90-93/94, 95/96, 97/98-1905/06, 07/08-08/09, 11/12-13/14, 16/17-18/19; VPI: 1889/90-1926/27.

104. ———. ———. Bulletin no. 1- ; Sept., 1899-19— Blacksburg [Blacksburg, 1927—

illus., plates. 8°. monthly; part irreg.
First series ends with no. 11, 1891; new series begins with no. 12, Jan., 1892, under heading Virginia agricultural and mechanical college. Agricultural experiment station.
BP: 2-5, 7, 9-36, 38, 39, 41-175, 181-187, 189-193, 195-198, 200-211, 214-219, 229-240, 249-257; LC: 2-12, 17-18, 20, 22, 24, 26, 32, 35, 36, 38-43, 45-46, 50-52, 55-56, 58, 61-64, 68-70, 72-208, 261, 262 (1889-1914, 28); NYP: 2-5, 9-47, 50-63, 65-240, 242-247, 249-259; USAg: 1-264 (1889-1929); USC: 88, 91-94, 98-99, 101, 105-107, 121-122, 127-130, 132-134, 137, 139, 143-149, 154, 155 (1899-1905); USH: 250, 256; USHy: 85 (rev.), 103, 123; USL: 194 (1911); V: 2-5, 7-47, 50-247, 249, 251-263 (1889-1928); VPI: 1-264; VU: 189-190, 192, 201-232, 237-240 (1910-23).

105. ———. ———. Circular no. 1-8; 1908-09. [n. p., 1908-09]

illus. 8°. No more pub.
H: 7; NYP: 1-2, 4-8; USAg: 1-8; V: 1-8; VPI: 1-8; VU: 2, 5, 7, 8.

106. ———. ———. Technical bulletin no. 1- ; April, 1915—
Blacksburg, Va., 1915—

    illus. 8°. Issued irreg.
    LC: 11 (1916); **NYP:** 1-8, 10-33 (1915-27); **USAg:** 1-20, 22, 24-34, 36
(1915-29); **USHy:** 28 (1925); **V:** 1-32; **VPI:** 1-36 (1915-29); **VU:** 23,
24, 26-34.

107. ———. ———. HORTICULTURE, ENTOMOLOGY, AND MYCOLOGY
DEPT. Circular no. 1- ; [189-?-19-?] Blacksburg, Va. [189-?-
19-?]

    8°. **NYP:** 7 (1900).

108. ———. ———. PLANT PATHOLOGY, Laboratory of. Scientific paper no. 1- ; 1908— [Blacksburg, Va., 1908—

    8°. Issued irreg. Reprinted from various periodicals.
    USAg: 11, 13, 19, 20, 65; **VPI:** 1-75 (1908-29).

109. ———. AGRICULTURE, Commissioner of. Crop, stock, labor,
. . . report . . . Comp. from special correspondents by
Thomas Pollard, commissioner of agriculture. Richmond, Frayser, 1878-79.

    8°.   **NYP:** June, 1879; **V:** June, 1878; **VU:** 1878, 79.
    Information given by counties.

110. ———. AGRICULTURE, Dept. of. Analyses and valuation of fertilizers . . . [Richmond, 1883-85]

    tables. 8°.   **USAg:** Jan., 1885; **V:** Jan.-July, 1883.

111. ———. AGRICULTURE AND IMMIGRATION, Dept. of. Analysis
of fertilizers . . . [Richmond, 1904?-

    8°. (In its *Bulletin,* 18-21 (1904); 24-27 (1905); 31-33 (1906); 36-37
(1907); 38, 39, 42, 43, (1908); 45-48 (1909); 50, 52-54 (1910); 56-61
(1911); 63, 65, 67, 69 (1912); 75, 77, 80, 82 (1913); 86-87, 89-90, 92
(1914); 95, 100 (1915).)

112. ———. ———. . . . Annual report of the commissioner and
the Board of agriculture and immigration. 1st- ; 1877-19—
Richmond, 1877-19—

    illus., tables. 8°. Report year ends Sept. 30.
    Title varies: Annual report of the commissioner of agriculture; Re-
port of the state board of agriculture; etc.
    Admin. report is printed separately, 19-?—
    Commissioners: Thomas Pollard, 1877-8-?; Randolph Harrison, 188-
?-87/88?; Thomas Whitehead, 1888/89-97/98; George W. Koiner, 1898/
99-19—
    HB: 1923/25; **LC:** 1881, 91/92, 93/94-97/98, 99/1900-04/05, 06/07-15/

16, 17/18-21/23; **NYP**: 1879/80-82/83, 89/90-90/91, 92/93-95/96, 1901/02, 03/04-15/16, 23/25; **USAg**: 1877-1927/28; **USG**: 1878; **V**: 1878-81, 87, 89/90, 94/95-95/96, 1903/04-19/20, 21/22-26/27; **VU**: 1901/02, 03/04-05/06, 09/10.

113. VIRGINIA. AGRICULTURE AND IMMIGRATION, Dept. of. Bulletin. Old ser., no. 1-[?]; 1889-[9-?]; new ser., no. 1- ; 1901— . Richmond, 1889-19—

> illus. 8°. monthly. Includes *Year book,* 1913-
> **LC**: 8, 35, 37-38, 49-70, 73-95, 97, 99-114, 126, 138, 183, 184, 196, 207, 229, 241; **NYP**: 12, 22, 27-28, 31, 34, 36-111, 113-213, 215-240; **USAg**: old ser., 1, 5; new ser., 1-28, 30-51, 53-256; **USC**: 34, 49, 55, 148, 172, 183; **USHy**: 66; **V**: 1-21, 23-27, 50-51, 53-54, 56-61, 63-71, 73-83, 85-95, 97-108, 120-125, 127-137, 139-147, 149-182, 184-195, 197-230, 232-250; **VU**: 57, 78, 104, 170, 179, 189, 190, 192, 193, 197, 203-206; **WM**: 84, 104, 138, 183, 218, 229.

114. ———. ———. Farmers' bulletin, no. 1-27; 1904-18. Richmond, 1904-[18?]

> illus. 8°. Issued irreg.
> **LC**: 7-13, 15-25; **NYP**: 1-6, 11-13, 16, 19-26; **USAg**: 1-27; **V**: 1-4, 6-13, 15, 17-25; **VU**: 1-4, 6.

115. ———. ———. . . . . Hand-book of Virginia. By the commissioner of agriculture . . . Richmond [1876-19—

> illus., ports., maps, tables, diagrs. 8°. Issued irreg.
> Title varies: Abbreviated hand-book of Virginia; Virginia: a handbook; Virginia: information for the homeseeker and investor; Virginia: a synopsis . . .; Virginia to-day, opportunities for the homeseeker; etc.
> **BP**: 1881, 89, 93, 1910; **LC**: 1876, 79, 85, 86, 89, 93, 97, 1906, 07, 09-11, 15, 19, 23, 26; **NYP**: 1881, 85-86, 89, 93, 1905-06, 10-11, 15, 19, 23; **USAg**: 1885-86, 89, 93, 1906-07, 09-11, 15, 19, 23, 26; **USC**: 1897; **USG**: 1881, 85-86, 93, 1919, 23; **USL**: 1923; **V**: 1879, 81, 85-86, 89, 93, 1905-06, 09, 11, 13, 15, 19, 23, 26; **VU**: 1879, 81, 89, 93, 1906-07, 09, 11, 15, 19, 23, 26; **WM**: 1909, 19.

116. ———. ———. Leaflet, no. 1-8; 1913-21. [n. p.] 1913-21.

> 8°.   **USAg**: 1-8.

117. ———. ———. Report of the committee on analytical and agricultural chemistry (Messrs. Gaines and Koiner) to the State board of agriculture, Jan. 8, 1895. [Richmond, 1895?]

> 8 p. 8°.   **V**

118. ———. ———. The story of Virginia products that excel . . . George W. Koiner, commissioner. [Richmond, Va., 1927]

> [28] p. illus. 8°.   **NYP, USAg, V**

119. ——. ——. Virginia. A synopsis of the geology, geography, climate and soil of the state, together with its resources of mines, forests and fields, its flocks and its herds. Also selections from the press . . . Accompanied by statistics of its educational, religious and social system; to which is added a collection of maps showing its transportation facilities, and the location of its cities and principal towns. Pub. by the State board of agriculture. Richmond, Fergusson, 1889.

116 p. 1 l., [12] p. front. (fold. map) illus. 8°.

LC, NYP, USAg, V, VU

120. ——. ——. Virginia farms for sale listed by the owners with the Dept. of agriculture and immigration . . . George W. Koiner, commissioner. [Richmond, 1919—

8°.   **NYP:** 1919; **USAg:** 1919; **V:** 1926, 28.

121. ——. ——. Virginia: information for the homeseeker and investor . . . G. W. Koiner, commissioner. [Richmond, 1907]

72 p. front., illus., fold. map. 8°.   **LC, USAg, V, VU**

Resources and products of the state described; with letters from northern and western farmers who have settled in Virginia.

122. ——. ——. Virginia to-day, opportunities for the homeseeker. Richmond, Va., Dept. of agriculture and immigration [1923]

27 p. illus. 8°.   **LC, NYP, USAg, USG, USL, V, VU**

G. W. Koiner, commissioner.

123. ——. ——. Year book . . . 1913— Richmond, 1913—

illus., tables. 8°. (Its *Bulletin,* 84, 96, 109, 115, 126, 138, 148, 172, 183, 196, 207, 218, 229 [*q. v.,* **113**])

124. ——. ——. DAIRY AND FOOD DIVISION. Annual report. 1st-[15th?] 1908/09-23/25. Richmond, Va., 1910-25.

illus., plates. 8°.

First report covers period June 1, 1908-Mar. 1, 1909. First and second reports pub. also as nos. 8 and 14, respectively, of the *Bulletin* of this division. No report pub., 1919/20. Division abolished, 1926.

HB: 1914/15-15/16; **LC:** 1908/09-09/10; **NYP:** 1908/09-10/11, 14/15-23/25; **USAg:** 1908/09-20/21; **USC:** 1908/09-10/11, 16/17-17/18; **V:** 1908/09-23/25.

125. ——. ——. ——. Bulletin, no. 1-88; 1908-25. Richmond, Va., 1908-25.

illus. (incl. plans, plates) 8°.

LC: 1-33, 53, 69, 77, 81, 84-88; **NYP:** 1-88; **USAg:** 1-83; **USC:** 9-11, 20, 76, 77; **V:** 1-31, 33-73, 76, 81, 84, 86-88.

126. VIRGINIA. AGRICULTURE AND IMMIGRATION, Dept. of. DAIRY
AND FOOD DIVISION. Circular, no. 1-[68?]; 1908-[19?] Richmond, Va., 1908-[19?]

   8°. no. 2 is a broadside.
   NYP: 38-40, 42; **USAg:** 1-50, 52-58, 60-68.

127. ——. ——. ——. Quarterly report . . . Sept./Dec., 1908-
[1916?] Richmond, Va., 1908-[16?]

   8°. (In its *Bulletin*, 1, 5, 30, 33, 36, 39-40, 44, 46, 52, 54, 56, 58, 60, 62)
   None pub., Mar. 31, 1909-Mar. 1, 1913.

128. ——. ——. ——. Ten reasons why a dairy farm in Virginia pays better than in any other state. [Richmond, Bottom,
1915]

   40 p. illus. 8°.   **LC, USAg, V**

129. ——. ——. ——. War bulletin, no. 1-[?]; May 15, 1917-
[18?]   Richmond, Va., 1917-[18?]

   8°. (In its *Bulletin,* 20, 23, 24)

130. ——. ——. MARKETS, Div. of. A brief outline of the work
of the Division of markets . . . showing activities engaged
in since its establishment by the 1916 legislature. C. W. Koiner,
commissioner; B. C. Moomaw, jr., director. [n. d.]

   7 l. mimeog. 4°.   **USAg**

131. ——. ——. ——. . . . Bulletin, no. 1- ; April, 1923—
Richmond, Va., 1923—

   8°.   **USAg, V:** 1, 2, (Apr., Sept., 1923).

132. ——. ——. ——. . . . Co-operative agricultural business
organizations in Virginia. Richmond, Aug. 25, 1921.

   5 numb. l. mimeog. f°.   **USAg**

133. ——. ——. ——. List of Virginia apple growers . . .
[n. p.] 1918.

   Pub. in co-operation with the U. S. Bur. of markets.   **USAg**

134. ——. ——. ——. Recommended standards for grading,
packing, and inspection of Virginia apples, season 1926. Richmond [1926]

   16 p. 8°.   **USAg**

135. ——. ——. ——. . . . Report . . . to the commissioner of agriculture . . . [1917?—] Richmond, Va. [1917?—

   mimeog. 4°. biennial   **USAg:** 1921/23, 25/27, 27/28.

136. ——. ——. ——. Rules and regulations for grading, packing and inspection of Virginia apples, effective Aug. 1, 1927. Richmond, Va. [1927]

16 p. 8°. **USAg**

137. ——. ——. ——. Special report on inspection work . . . 1922-25. Richmond, 1924-[26?]

mimeog. f°. **USAg**

138. ——. ——. STATISTICS, Div. of agricultural. Bulletin, no. 1- ; 1924— Richmond, 1924—

8°. **HB**: 3; **LC**: 1-5; **NYP**: 1-5; **USAg**: 1-4; **V**: 1-5; **WM**: 1, 5.

139. ——. ——. ——. Survey bulletin, no. 1- ; Feb., 1926— Richmond, Va., 1926—

illus. 8°. **LC**: 1-2; **NYP**: 1-2; **USAg**: 1-2; **V**: 1.

140. ——. ——. ——. Virginia farm statistics, 1923— Comp. jointly by the U. S. Dept. of agriculture, Bur. of agricultural economics, and Virginia Dept. of agriculture, Div. of agricultural statistics . . . Richmond, Bottom, 1924—

illus., tables, diagrs. 8°. (Its *Bulletin,* 1-5 [*q. v.,* **138**])
HB: 1925; **LC**: 1923-27; **NYP**: 1923-27; **USAg**: 1923-26; **V**: 1923-27; **WM**: 1923, 27.

141. ——. ——. TEST FARM, State, Saxe, Charlotte County. Bulletin, no. 1-7; 1901/02-08. Richmond, 1902-08.

illus. 8°. (In Dept. of agriculture and immigration. *Annual report,* 1902-08)

142. ——. CROP PEST COMMISSIONERS, Board of. Circular, [1st ser.] no. 1-69 [190-? - 06?]; new ser., Oct., 1906-[?] Blacksburg, Va. [190-? -19-?]

illus. 8°. **LC**: 32, 42, 45, 49; new ser., 1-5. **NYP**: 32, 42, 44-45, 52-53; new ser., 1-8, 10-11. **USAg**: 7, 23, 27, 44-45, 48, 52-53, 65, 68-69; new ser., 1-9. **V**: 27, 31-32, 42, 44-45, 49, 52; new ser., 1-9 (1903-14). **VU**: 45; new ser., 2-5.

143. ——. ——. Quarterly bulletin, vol. 1-8; Apr., 1919-26. Blacksburg, Va., 1919-26.

illus., 8°. Includes *Biennial report* of State entomologist and plant pathologist. Board abolished, 1926.
LC: I, 1, 2; **NYP**: I-VI; **USAg**: I-IV; **V**: I-VIII, 1; **VU**: V, 3, 4.

144. ——. ——. Report of the state entomologist and plant pathologist on the San José scale and the administration of the

crop pest law.   1st-[15th?] ; 1895/96-19[24/25?]   Richmond,
1896-19[25?]

illus. 8°. biennial.
H: 1900/01; **LC**: 1899/1901-15/17; **NYP**: 1900/01-22/23; **USΛg**:
1895/96-1918/19; **V**: 1900/01-16/17; **VU**: 1901/03-07/09.

145. VIRGINIA. CROP PEST COMMISSIONERS, Board of. Report on
the inspection of Roanoke County for the San José scale, by William W. Alwood, state entomologist and pathologist. Blacksburg,
Va., 1901.

35, [1] p. incl. tables, fold. map. 12°.   **USAg**

146. ———. LAWS, STATUTES, etc. Extracts from Virginia crop
pest law . . . approved May 9, 1903. [n. p., 1903?]

[4] p. 8°.   **USAg**

147. ———. ———. Fertilizer law . . . [n. p., 1915]

7 p. 8°.   **USAg**

148. ———. ———. Rules and regulations governing the agricultural seed law . . . approved March 16, 1910. [n. p., 1910]

[2] p. 8°.   **USAg**

149. VIRGINIA POLYTECHNIC INSTITUTE, Blacksburg. Holstein-Frie-
sians. Virginia state record cows. All breeds. All ages. [Blacks-
burg, 1918]

8 p. 8°.   **USAg**

150. VIRGINIA. TRUCK EXPERIMENT STATION, Norfolk. Bulletin,
no. 1- ; 1909— Norfolk, 1909—

8°. quarterly; irreg., previous to Oct., 1913.
Pub. in co-operation with the Virginia Agricultural experiment station
and the Dept. of agriculture and immigration.
NYP: 1-61 (1909-27); **USAg**: 1-61; **V**: 1-61; **VU**: 1-43; **WM**: 1-25.

151. ———. ———. Circular, no. 1-[?] ; Feb. 18, 1909-[?]   Norfolk, Va. [1909- ?]

8°.   **USAg**: 1-2.

152. ———. VETERINARIAN, State. Annual report. 1st-[?] ; 1896-
19[-?]   Richmond, 1896-19[-?]

8°.   **NYP**: 1897; **USAg**: 1896-97, 1907-10; **V**: 1896.

153. ———. ———. Special report . . . on foot and on mouth
disease in Virginia: its cause, how spread among cattle, other
ruminants and swine, and its control and eradication. Richmond,
Saunders, 1916.

38 p. front. (port.) plates. 8°.   **LC, USAg**

Dr. J. G. Ferneyhough, state veterinarian.
Submitted to the State live stock sanitary board.

154. ———. WEIGHTS AND MEASURES, Bur. of. . . . First annual report . . . for the year ending Sept. 30, 1925 . . . Richmond, Bottom, 1925.

54 p. incl. tables. 8°. No more pub. **V**
Bureau abolished, 1926, and duties transferred to Div. of markets of the Dept. of agriculture and immigration.

155. WILEY, H. W. Record of experiments in the production of sugar from sorghum in 1889 at . . . Morrisville, Va. . . . Washington, Govt., 1890.

112 p. incl. tables, fold. plan. 8°. (U. S. Dept. of agriculture. Div. of chemistry. *Bulletin,* 26)

Other Source Material

156. AGRICULTURAL SOCIETY OF ALBEMARLE. [Papers; 1722-1879]
MSS. bound in f°. vol. **V**
Extracts from printed works copied on loose sheets; letters from individuals dealing with agricultural questions; essays read before the society.

157. AMERICAN WHITE ORPINGTON CLUB. 1911 annual year book of the . . . club. Richmond, Mutual print. [1911?]
47 p. 8°. **V**
A poultry club.

158. AMERICAN WOOL AND COTTON REPORTER. Sheep breeding and wool growing in Virginia, prepared by the American wool, cotton, and financial reporter. Frank P. Bennett, ed. [Boston] Norfolk & western railroad co. [*ca.* 1894]
36 p. illus. 8°. **LC**
The sheep industry as a profitable undertaking for Virginia farmers; prepared for distribution among them. Contains letters from livestock men in support of the proposition.

159. BARBOUR B. JOHNSON. Address . . . before the annual meeting of the Virginia state agricultural society, Oct. 27, 1875. [n. p., 1875?]
16 p. 8°. **LC, V, VU**
Sheds some light upon economic conditions in rural Virginia and the South since the Civil War.

160. BECK, THOMAS. "Glenara" for sale. A beautiful country seat and stock farm, located in Fauquier County, Va., near Marshall. [n. p., 18- ?]
16 p. incl. illus., front. 8°. **LC**

161. BERKELEY, C. N. Why is Virginia poor? An illustrated work. Setting forth the plans, operations, and results of farming in Virginia . . . Richmond, Va., Baughman, 1884.

41 p. illus., plates. 8°.   LC, USAg, V
A pessimistic picture of Virginia agriculture since 1865; discusses the ignorance of the Virginia farmer. Contains advertising to attract immigrants.

162. BUELL, P. B. Northern Virginia: grain, fruit, and blue grass farms for sale. [Herndon, Fairfax County, Va., 19- ?]

[8] p. 16°.   LC
List of farms, with brief descriptions.

163. CAMPBELL, JOHN L. Extract from the reports of Professors John L. Campbell and John R. Procter, upon the Glenwood estate. [Richmond] Richmond press, 1910.

23 p. charts. 8°.   V

164. CASSELMAN & CO., *firm.* "The farmer's friend," the Virginia land agency of Richmond, Casselman & co., 812 E. Main St., Richmond, Va. Richmond [1905?]

48 p. illus. 8°.   V
The propagandist introduction is followed by a list of farms for sale, with a brief description of each.

165. CATO, MARCUS PORTIUS, *Censorius.* Cato's Farm management. Eclogues from the *De re rustica* of M. Portius Cato, done into English, with notes of other excursions in the pleasant paths of agronomic literature, by a Virginia farmer . . . [Chicago, Donnelley] 1910.

60 p. 1 l. 12°.   H, USAg
Preface signed: F. H. [*i. e.,* Fairfax Harrison]

166. ———. Roman farm management; the treatises of Cato and Varro done into English, with notes of modern instances, by a Virginia farmer. New York, Macmillan, 1913.

xii p. 1 l., 365 p. 8°.   LC, V, VU
Preface signed: F. H. [*i. e.,* Fairfax Harrison]
Contains some references to Virginia agriculture.

167. CHESAPEAKE & OHIO RAILWAY CO. INDUSTRIAL DEPT. Country life in Virginia, 1912. Richmond [1912?]

132 p. (incl. adv.) illus., plates, map. 8°.   V
"The[se] pages aim to state accurately and concisely Virginia's rich agricultural opportunities and natural advantages," especially in the territory along the C & O ry. Contains list of farms, with locations and prices.

168. ———. REAL ESTATE DEPT. Country life in Virginia. In the sunny southland where there are opportunities for everybody. Richmond, Va. [1911]

> 95, [1] p. illus. 8°. Advertisements in back.   **USAg**
> Includes list of farms for sale, and testimonials.

169. COLE, E. F. Fruit packing and marketing. An address delivered before the fruit growers of Patrick County, by E. F. Cole, in co-operation with the Land and industrial dept. of the Danville & western railway co. [Danville, Va., Waddill, 1912]

> 16 p. 8°.   **USAg**

170. CULPEPER AND ADJOINING COUNTIES FAIR ASSOCIATION. [1st-] annual premium list [1921?—] [n. p., 1912?—

> 8°. Advertisements interspersed.   **V:** 4th, 1924.

171. CURLES NECK farm on the James River, Virginia. Virginia sporting estate of Cornelius K. Billings. [Description] [New York?] 1917.

> 90, [9] p. illus., map, plan, 4°,   **H**

172. CURRY, JABEZ L. Address before the Virginia state agricultural society . . . Delivered in the hall of the House of representatives on the 25th of October, 1874 . . . Richmond, Fergusson, 1875.

> 13 p. 8°.   **NYP, USAg**

173. DANVILLE TOBACCO ASSOCIATION. President's annual report . . . 1908. Danville, Va. [190-? - ?]

> 16°.   **USAg:** 1906, 09; **V:** 1908.

174. DAVIS, WESTMORELAND. Remarks made upon the organization of the Virginia dairymen's association. Blacksburg, Dec. 22, 1907. [Blacksburg, Va., 1907]

> [10] p. 8°.   **USAg, V**

175. DESCRIPTION of 100,000 acres of land in Giles, Craig, Monroe, and Bland counties, Virginia. Philadelphia, 1871.

> 23 p. fold. maps. 8°.   **V**
> Land offered for sale by agents of the owners.

176. DRINKARD, ALFRED W., jr. Some neglected phases of our orchard industry. [n. p., n. d.]

> 14 p. 8°.   **V**

177. DUNNINGTON, F. P., *et al.* Lectures, delivered before the Albemarle agricultural society, by Prof. F. P. Dunnington [on "The mineral food of plants"], Prof. W. M. Thornton [on "Roadmaking"], and Dr. J. R. Page [on "Worn-out lands and their improvement"]. Charlottesville, Chronicle, 1881.

50 p. 8°.   **USAg, V, VU**

178. EASTERN SHORE OF VIRGINIA PRODUCE EXCHANGE, Onley, Va. By-laws . . . rev. ed., adopted Apr. 24, 1914. [Onley, Va., 1914]

46 p. 16°.   **USAg**

179. ———. Telegraphic code of the Eastern Shore of Virginia produce exchange. Onley, Va., General Office [1911—

24°.   **LC**: 1913, 17; **USAg**: 1911.

180. ELMWOOD NURSERIES, Hallsboro, Va. . . . For spring of 1899. Supplement to our spring catalogue, 1898. Notice to our friends and customers. [n. p., 1898?]

11 p. illus. 8°.   **V**
Prices and description of fruits, vegetables, and flowers.

181. FARMERS' CONVENTION OF VIRGINIA. Proceedings of the . . . convention . . . held at Richmond, Va., April 15-16, 1885. [n. p., 1885?]

49 p. 8°.   **V**

182. FARMERS' COUNCIL OF VIRGINIA AND NORTH CAROLINA. Constitution . . . Petersburg, Va. [1873?]

8 p. 8°.   **V**
An organization "in which the entire farming and mercantile classes can have a voice and representation."

183. FISHER, THOMAS J. A description. That splendid estate and ancient country seat of the Alexander family, known as Abington. Situate[d] in Alexandria County, Va., . . . opposite Washington City. To be sold at public auction, on Thursday, May 19, 1881. [Washington, D. C.? 1881?]

10 p. 8°.   **LC**

184. FOUR-STATE CONFERENCE. Abstract of proceedings . . . on the potato situation. [1st- ; 1928—] Richmond, Va. [pub. by the Virginia Commission on conservation and development] 1929—

illus., tables, diagrs. 8°.   **USAg**: 1928.

Conference embraces Maryland, Virginia, and the Carolinas.
1928 session also known as Norfolk potato conference.

185. FULLERTON, WILLIAM. An address delivered before the Piedmont agricultural society on the 19th . . . October, 1876, at Culpepper [*sic*], Virginia . . . [n. p., 1876?]

34 p. 8°. BP, LC, USAg, V, VU

Stresses the value of scientific farming and reveals indirectly the backwardness of Virginia agriculture during reconstruction.

186. GAMMACK, FREDERICK S. How to know the best layers in a flock of hens. How to build an inexpensive poultry house . . . Hampton, Va., Hampton normal and agricultural institute, 1920.

19 p. illus. 8°. USAg

187. HAMPTON NORMAL AND AGRICULTURAL INSTITUTE, Hampton, Va. Notes on agriculture. Hampton, Va., The Institute, 1904.

98 p. illus. 8°. USAg

188. ———. [Report of meeting of the Farmers' conference held in conjunction with the Hampton ministers' conference and the Hampton summer school for teachers, June 22-25, 1920] 1920.

mimeog. 4°. USAg

189. HARRIS, L. W., *firm*. Virginia farms, "The land of heart's delight." Suburban homes, timber and mineral lands, alfalfa lands, tobacco, oyster shores. For sale by L. W. Harris, real estate and loans . . . Richmond, Va. [Richmond, Va., n. d.]

41, [1] p. plates. 8°. V

190. HENRICO FARMERS CLUB. By-laws . . . Richmond, 1884.

11 p. 12°. V

Organized, Aug., 1884.

191. HOOD, W. T., & CO., *firm*. Descriptive catalogue of fruit and ornamental trees, grape vines, small fruits, shrubs, plants, etc., cultivated and for sale by W. T. Hood & co., Richmond, Va. [Richmond, n. d.]

61 p. 8°. V

192. IMBODEN, JOHN D. Virginia, the home for the northern farmer. Three letters . . . to Horace Greeley. New York, Taylor, 1869.

16 p. 8°. V

Written by the domestic agent of immigration for Virginia to the ed-

itor of the New York *Tribune,* and printed therein. Contains some statistics on prices, wages, etc.

193. JETER, W. H., & CO., *firm.* . . . Catalogue of Virginia
farms . . . for sale by W. H. Jeter & co., real estate brokers,
Richmond, Va. No. 2 edit. [Richmond? n. d.]

> 40 p. plates. 8°.   V

194. JOHNSON, LUCIUS E. Address . . . before the Virginia
state farmers' institute, Roanoke, Virginia, Jan. 12, 1911. [Roa-
noke, Va., Stone, 1911]

> 22 p., 1 l. 12°.   H, LC, USAg, V
> Confidence expressed for the future of Virginia agriculture.

195. KNIGHT, THOMAS M. Introducing Thomas Phosphate in old
Virginia. Wheat, grass, and legumes. Charleston, S. C., Coe-
Mortimer [n. d.]

> 31 p. illus. 8°.   V

196. LEE, BAKER P. Address . . . before the Chesapeake agricultural fair association at Cape Charles City, Va., 30 Oct.,
1888. Richmond, Murphy, 1888.

> 8 p. 8°.   V

197. MASSIE, EUGENE C. Address . . . upon the Torrens system of land registration, at the annual meeting of the Virginia
Board of trade, held at Roanoke, Va., Aug. 30-31, 1905. Pub.
in pursuance of a resolution of the board. Richmond, Va., Whittet & Shepperson, 1905.

> 16 p. 8°.   LC, V
> Proposal to substitute the Torrens system for the cumbersome Vir-
> ginia system.

198. ———. Reform of our land laws. Address before Virginia
state bar association, Aug. 8, 1905 . . . Richmond, Waddey,
1905.

> 20 p. 8°.   LC, V
> Concerning the Torrens system of land registration.

199. MECKLENBURG COUNTY AGRICULTURAL FAIR. Premium list
. . . [n. p., 19—?—

> 8°. Held at Chase City, Va., 1912, 14.   V: 1912, 14

200. NEWMAN, CLIFFORD L. Making soil and crops pay more.
. . . Richmond, Va., Virginia-Carolina chemical co., 1918.

> [8], 135 p. illus. 8°.   H, LC, NYP, USAg

201. NORFOLK AGRICULTURAL AND INDUSTRIAL FAIR ASSOCIATION. List of premiums, rules and regulations . . . [1st-] ; 1920— Norfolk fair grounds, Norfolk, Va. . . . [n. p., 1920—

    illus. 8°. Advertisements interspersed.   **VU**: 3d, 4th (1922, 23).

202. NORFOLK & WESTERN RAILWAY CO. AGRICULTURAL AND INDUS-TRIAL DEPT. Opportunities in Virginia and North Carolina along the Norfolk & western railway. [Roanoke, 1915]

    32 p. illus. 4°.   **USAg**

203. ———. ———. Virginia, an ideal home for all; a descriptive handbook and catalogue of farms for sale along the N. & W. rail-way lines . . . [Roanoke, Va., Stone, 1907?]

    100 p. illus., map, plan, music. 4°.   **NYP**
    Advertisements interspersed.

204. ———. ———. Virginia and North Carolina; their agricultural and industrial possibilities. [Roanoke, Union, 1917]

    [14] p. illus. fold. 4°.   **USAg**

205. ———. ———. Virginia, the home of the apple. [n. p., 1911]

    32 fold. p. illus. 8°.   **USAg**
    The possibilities of fruit culture in Virginia.

206. ———. ———. Where industries thrive. Roanoke, Va. [1913]

    96 p. port., map. 4°.   **BRE, NYP**
    Description of agriculture and manufacturing along the N. & W. ry. in Virginia and neighboring states.

207. PAGE, JOHN R. Report of experiments in corn culture on the Experimental farm of the University of Virginia, for 1876. Charlottesville, Chronicle, 1876.

    16 p. tables. 8°.   **VU**

208. ———. Report of experiments in corn, wheat, and grass culture on the Experimental farm of the University of Virginia . . . Charlottesville, Chronicle [187-?- ?]

    tables. 8°.   **VU**: 1879/80, 84/85.

209. ———. Report of experiments in wheat and beet culture on the Experimental farm of the University of Virginia. 1878. Charlottesville, Chronicle, 1878.

    31, [1] p. 8°.   **VU**

210. PAGE, JOHN R. Report of experiments in wheat culture on the Experimental farm of the University of Virginia, for 1876—[?] Charlottesville, Chronicle, 1876—[?]

tables. 8°.   **USAg:** 1876; **VU:** 1876, 77.

211. ———. Report of John R. Page, . . . professor of agriculture, zoölogy and botany, in the University of Virginia. Charlottesville, Chronicle, 1885.

85, [1] p. 8°.   **VU**
Report on the work of the school of agriculture, including the research of the experiment stations.

212. PATRONS OF HUSBANDRY. VIRGINIA STATE GRANGE. Minutes of the 1st- annual meeting of the Virginia state grange . . . Richmond, Lewellen [1873?—

8°.   **USAg:** 1886, 95; **V:** 1873, 75, 76.

213. PENINSULA HORTICULTURAL SOCIETY. Transactions . . . 1st- ; 1888-19— Dover, Del., 1888-19—

8°.   **LC:** 19th (1906); **V:** 1st-10th (1888-97).

214. PIEDMONT AGRICULTURAL SOCIETY. Annual fair . . . 1st- [?] ; [1872?- ?] at Culpeper, Va. Baltimore [etc., 1872?- ?]

8°.   **LC:** 6-8th (1877-79).

215. ———. Annual report of the president . . . 1876. [n. p., 1876?]

8 p. 8°.   **LC**
Signed: S. S. Bradford.

216. RAGLAND, ROBERT L. Cultivation and curing of fine yellow and shipping tobacco from the plant-bed to market . . . Pub. by request of the Commissioner of agriculture. [n. p., n. d.]

15 p. 8°.   **USAg, VU**

217. ———. Major Ragland's instructions how to grow and cure tobacco, especially fine yellow. Carefully rev. by him and introducing the latest and best experience in this line . . . Richmond, Va., Southern fertilizing co. [1885]

36 p. illus. 8°.   **LC**

218. ———. On the cultivation and curing of tobacco and more particularly of fine yellow tobacco. Richmond, Va., 1872.

15 p. 16°.   **USAg**

219. ———. Tobacco from the seed to the salesroom. Richmond, Va., 1880.

22 p. 8°.   USAg

219a. ———. Tobacco; how to raise it and how to make it pay. Hyco, Va., 1895.

33 p. 4°.   USAg

220. RICHMOND, VA. CHAMBER OF COMMERCE. An answer to objections to the Torrens system. Richmond, 1906.

39 p. 8°.   V

Members of the Virginia bench and bar discuss the advantages to individuals and to the state of adopting the Torrens system of land registration.

221. RICHMOND GRAIN EXCHANGE. By-laws of the Richmond grain exchange as amended and adopted Mar. 4, 1908. [Richmond] Saunders, 1908.

33 p. 16°.   LC

222. RICHMOND SPECIAL HORSE SALE CO. Special spring sale of high class horses at auction, Southern stock yards, Richmond, Va. . . . Conducted by Smyth bros.-McCleary-McClellan co., H. E. Kline, Joseph Lassiter, representing the Richmond special horse sale co. [Richmond, 1909-10]

2 v. 8°.   **V**: Apr. 27-29, 1909; Apr. 26-28, 1910.

223. ROANOKE INDUSTRIAL AND AGRICULTURAL ASSOCIATION. Premium list, rules and regulations of the great Roanoke fair . . . 1904. Roanoke, Va., 1904.

64 p. 8°.   NYP

224. ROSSER, THOMAS L. Address . . . before the District agricultural fair, Staunton, Va., Oct. 15, 1886. Charlottesville, Chronicle, 1887.

16 p. 8°.   VU

Opportunities in rural Virginia and the South for agriculture; comparison with those in the West.

225. SARG, JAMES F. A new dairy industry; preparation and sale of artificial mothers' milk "Normal infants' milk" by James Fred. Sarg . . . Black Forest farm, Kempsville, Va., U. S. A. . . . Norfolk [Va.] Barron, 1896.

162 p. illus. 12°.   LC

226. SCHERER, PAUL. The business of farming in Virginia; a study of some of our agricultural resources . . . Roanoke, Stone [1902]

32 p. 8°.   LC

Issued by the Norfolk & western railway co.

227. ———. Virginia; a home for the farmer . . . Issued by Norfolk & western railway co. . . . [Roanoke, Va., Stone, *ca.* 1898]

64 p. 8°.   LC, USAg

228. SHENANDOAH VALLEY APPLE LANDS CO. The story of apple growing for profit in the Waynesboro fruit section of the Shenandoah Valley in Virginia, by H. M. Magie. Waynesboro, Va., 1911.

16 p. illus., map. 8°.   USAg

229. SOUTHERN FARM AGENCY, Lynchburg, Va. Farms in southside and middle Virginia. [Lynchburg? 1921?]

32 p. illus. 12°.   USAg

List of farms, with brief descriptions.

230. ———. Rappahannock Valley farms; finest alfalfa lands in the east . . . [Lynchburg? 19-?]

28 p. illus. 8°.   USAg

List of farms for sale with descriptions.

231. ———. Supplement to *Virginia and the Carolinas* **[232]** . . . Farms, country seats, game preserves, Georgia sea islands and lands in all parts of the South . . . [Lynchburg, Va., 19-?]

15 p. illus. 8°.   LC

232. ———. Virginia and the Carolinas illustrated. Lynchburg, Va., Southern farm agency [189-?]

16 p. illus. 8°.   LC

At head of title: Southern railway—Supplement.

233. SOUTHERN FERTILIZING CO., Richmond, Va. Cotton: its production and movement in the United States; movement and consumption in Great Britain and on the continent; with some account of its production, &c., in India, Brazil and Egypt, and the outlook for 1875. Presented by the Southern fertilizing co., Richmond, Va. Richmond, Va., Clemmitt & Jones [1875]

20 p. incl. tables. 8°.   LC, USAg

Discusses the bright outlook for American cotton for 1875; cotton manufacturing in U. S. and the South; with statistics.

234. ———. 1877. Cotton prospects. An examination of the points of advantage peculiar to the cotton-growing interest in the Southern states . . . Richmond, Va., Clemmitt & Jones [1877]

29 p. 8°.   **LC, V**

Discusses the revival of the cotton industry in the South since the Civil War.

235. ———. Figures that meet the low prices of wheat. So much appropriate plant-food never before offered for so little money. [Richmond? 1883?]

24 p. 8°.   **V**

236. ———. Grain: a comparison between the cereal production of the United States and other countries . . . with some observations on the drift of the grain question in this country, and the ability of Virginia to continue a wheat grower with profit. The Southern fertilizing co., Richmond, Va. Richmond, Va., Clemmitt & Jones [1875]

28 p. incl. tables. 8°.   **LC**

To reveal Virginia's capacity for diversified products, including wheat.

237. ———. The position tobacco has ever held as the chief source of wealth to Virginia . . . by the Southern fertilizing co. . . . Richmond [1876]

22 p. 8°.   **LC, USAg**

How Virginia and North Carolina are competing with Kentucky and Tennessee for standard tobacco; the value of European markets. Contains also an historical sketch of the industry in Virginia.

238. ———. Some observations on the analysis and valuation of commercial fertilizers. [Richmond, 187-?]

15 p. 8°.   **V**

239. ———. . . . Some points relating to grain . . . Richmond [1876]

38 p. 8°.   **V**

240. ———. Tobacco in Virginia and North Carolina. Some observations in connection with the several types of tobacco now produced in these two states (including Dr. Voelcker's examina-

tion of our fine yellow tobacco) and on the introduction of a new
type, namely cigar tobacco. Richmond, Va., 1877.

31 p. fold. map. 8°.   USAg

241. SOUTHERN FERTILIZING CO., Richmond, Va. Tobacco: the
outlook in America for 1875; production, consumption and movement in the United States, the German empire, Hungary, Turkey,
Cuba, Brazil, Japan, and the other tobacco-growing countries;
with some observations on farm labor in the South, and a general
statement of the agriculture of the United States. Presented by
the Southern fertilizing co., Richmond, Va. Richmond, Va.,
Clemmitt & Jones [1875]

1 p. l., 32 p. incl. tables. 8°.   LC
Includes statistics of the industry in the U. S., especially Virginia
and North Carolina; discusses the value of the Negro as an agricultural
laborer.

242. SOUTHERN RAILWAY CO. Homes of the early presidents, and
present day opportunities for homes and agriculture in northern
Virginia . . . [Philadelphia, Edgell, 1913]

1 p. l., 5-64 p. illus. 4°.   H, LC, USAg, V, VU

243. SOUTHERN SETTLEMENT AND DEVELOPMENT ORGANIZATION. Virginia dept. Some agricultural information about Virginia. Charlottesville [1914]

[36] p. nar. 8°.   USAg

244. SOUTHERN TIMBER AND LAND CO. Facts about southeast Virginia, no. 2. Its climate, soil, agriculture, markets, transportation and opportunities for investments. With list of farms and
other properties for sale by the Southern timber and land co., inc.,
126 N. Sycamore St., Petersburg, Va. [1907]

79 p. illus. 8°.   V

245. SOUTHSIDE VIRGINIA AGRICULTURAL AND INDUSTRIAL EXHIBIT,
inc. Premium list of the . . . annual exhibition . . .
Petersburg, Va. [19-?—

8°.   V: 1915.

246. STATE FARMERS' ALLIANCE OF VIRGINIA. Proceedings of the
1st- annual session . . . [1888?—] Petersburg, Va. [etc.,
1888?—

8°.   V: 3rd, Aug. 19-21, 1890, at Lynchburg.

247. SURRY COUNTY NEGRO FARMERS' FAIR ASSOCIATION. Catalogue
of the 1st- annual exhibition of the Surry County Negro farm-

ers' fair, Lebanon Baptist church, Surry County, Va. . . .
1915— [n. p., 1915—

8°. V: 1915, 16.

248. TUTTLE, ALBERT H. Education and agriculture. An address
delivered before the Virginia State board of agriculture, Oct. 31,
1888 . . . [n. p., n. d.]

17 p. 8°. VU

249. UNIVERSITY OF VIRGINIA. CONFERENCE FOR THE STUDY OF
PROBLEMS OF RURAL LIFE. . . . Rural life conference held at
the University of Virginia summer school . . . 1st- ; 1908—
Charlottesville, Va., The University [1908—

plates. 8°. (University of Virginia. *Alumni bulletin*) **H:** 1911-15;
LC: 1909, 10, 12, 19; **NYP:** 1910-13, 16, **V, VU:** 1908-19.

250. VAIDEN, V. Agricultural development and vocational education. Address delivered at the Virginia bankers' convention at
Old Point Comfort, Va., June 19, 1914. [n. p., 1914]

p. 23-32. 8°. USAg

251. VIRGINIA AGRICULTURAL ADVISORY COUNCIL. A five year program for the development of Virginia's agriculture worked out
by the Virginia agricultural advisory council. [Richmond] 1924.

103 p. incl. illus., tables, diagrs. 8°. **LC, NYP, USAg, V, VU, WM**
Council organized to better conditions on farms and in homes by
closer co-operation of all agricultural organizations: 34 listed; includes
reports of sub-committees.

252. VIRGINIA ANGORA CO. Charter, by-laws, location, information
[etc.] Boston, Mudge, 1880.

38 p. 8°. **NYP**
Organized to raise goats and other livestock in the mountain region
of Virginia, and to erect mills to utilize the products therefrom.

253. VIRGINIA-CAROLINA CHEMICAL CO. CROP BOOK DEPT. [Agri-
cultural pamphlets. Richmond, Va., 1915—

illus. 8°-12°. **NYP, USAg, V**
Separate pamphlets on citrus fruits and truck crops; corn; cotton;
grasses for hay and pasture; orchards and good fruits; peanuts; strawberries and other berries; tobacco; vegetables and truck crops; wheat,
oats, rye, barley, and rice. With advertisements of "V-C" fertilizers.

For the annual reports, etc., of the *Virginia Carolina chemical co.,* see
below, § 3: RESOURCES AND INDUSTRY **[486-502]**

254. VIRGINIA CROP IMPROVEMENT ASSOCIATION. Annual report
. . . 1st- ; 1921/22— [Blacksburg, Va.] 1922—
8°. 4th report (1926) not pub.   **USAg:** 1st-3d, 1921/22-23/24.

255. ———. . . . Manual of seed certification . . . [March,
1926] Blacksburg, Va. Pulaski, Va., Smith [1926]
30 p. 8°.   **USAg**

256. VIRGINIA DAHLIA SOCIETY. Annual exhibition . . . [n. p.,
19-?—
8°.   **V:** 1927.

257. VIRGINIA FRUIT GROWERS, inc. Annual report . . . 1st-
[1910/11?—] Staunton, Va., McClure [1911?—
$._{0}8$ **USAg:** 1910/11-12/13; **V:** 1910/11-12/13.
Successor to Shenandoah Valley fruit growers' association.

258. VIRGINIA LAND AGENCY, Petersburg, Va. Established 1865.
[Petersburg, Va., Griffin & Jervis, 1886]
32 p. 8°.   **BP**

259. VIRGINIA REAL ESTATE ASSOCIATION. Proceedings of the . . .
association . . . 1st- ; 1903— [Charlottesville, Va., 1903—
8°.   **LC, V:** 1903.

260. VIRGINIA STATE AGRICULTURAL SOCIETY. Officers, rules, regulations, and schedule of premiums for the fair . . . [1st- ;
186-?—] Richmond [186-?—
8°. Advertisements interspersed.   **LC:** 1877; **V:** 1876, 86, 91, 93.
Title varies: Virginia state agricultural and mechanical society,
1891, 93.

261. ———. Souvenir of Virginia state agricultural society fair,
held at Richmond, Va., Oct. 31 and Nov. 1 and 2, 1883. [Rich-
mond? 1883]
12 p. 4°.   **V**
Views of Richmond.

262. VIRGINIA STATE CHAMBER OF COMMERCE. [Documents on ag-
riculture] Richmond, 1926-27.
nar. 8°.   **H, NYP, V**
Agriculture doc., no. 1: "Climate of Virginia" (1927); *Commerce doc.,*
no. 7: "Hampton Roads for apple exports" (1926).

263. VIRGINIA STATE DAIRYMEN'S ASSOCIATION. Proceedings of the
1st- annual convention . . . 1908— Richmond, 1908—

8°. (6th-12th, 1913-19, arc in Virginia. Dept. of agriculture and immigration. Dairy and food div. *Bulletin,* 32, 45, 64, 70, 73, 79)
LC: 1913; NYP: 1913-19; USAg: 1913-19, 22; V: 1914-19, 27.

264. VIRGINIA STATE FAIR ASSOCIATION, inc. Premium list . . .
1st- ; 1906— Richmond, Va., 1906—
8°. V: 1906, 09, 13-16, 26-27.

265. ———. Program and merchants' guide, annual exposition
. . . 1st- ; 1906— Richmond, 1906—
8°. V: 1906.

266. VIRGINIA STATE FARMERS' INSTITUTE. . . . Annual session
. . . Official program . . . 1st- [1904?—] Roanoke
[etc., 1904?—
8°. USAg: 2d, 3d, 5th, 9th (1905, 06, 08, 12); V: 1905-06, 09, 11;
VU: 1909.

267. VIRGINIA STATE GRANGE. [Circulars. 1874-75] [1874-75]
8° (Include report of Executive committee [1874?]) V
See also *Patrons of husbandry. Virginia state grange.* **[212]**

268. VIRGINIA STATE HORTICULTURAL SOCIETY. Bulletin . . .
vol. I, no. 1- ; [July?] 1913— Crozet, Va., 1913—
8°. Title changed to *Virginia fruit,* beginning with V, 2; 1917—
LC: I, 5 (Nov., 1913). NYP: I, 3, 5; II, 3-5; III, 3-5; IV, 2; V, 2;
(1913-17). USAg: I, 4-IV, 4; V, 1-2. V: II (1914). VU: IV, 1
(1916).

269. ———. Fruit growing in Virginia; brief information of the
sections of the state where commercial orcharding has proved
successful. Pub. from information collected by A. W. Drinkard,
jr., and Walter Whately. [Charlottesville, Va.] 1911.
47, [1] p. fold. map. 8°. USAg

270. ———. Report . . . 1st- annual session of the Virginia
state horticultural society . . . 1896/97-19— Bedford, City,
Va. [etc.] 1897-19—
illus., plates, port., fold. map. 8°.
Title varies slightly.
LC: 1898/99, 1900-02, 06-08, 10-11, 13-14, 26; NYP: 1900-02, 12-20,
22-26; USAg: 1897/98-1903, 06-08, 10-26; V: 1904-14, 26; VU: 1911, 13-26.

271. VIRGINIA STATE POMOLOGICAL SOCIETY. Charter, constitution,
and by-laws. Chartered, Aug., 1886, Charlottesville, Va. Print.
at office of the Fruit and grape grower. [Charlottesville, 1886]
14 p. 16°. USAg, V

272. VIRGINIA STOCK FARM CO. Inaugural announcement of the Virginia stock farm company . . . [Roanoke, Va., Stone, 1908]

124 p. front., illus. 8°.   **USAg**

273. [WALKER FAMILY ACCOUNT BOOKS. Walker's Creek, Rockbridge County, Va., 1865-91]

4 v. MSS. f°.   **McC**

The 4 vols. cover the following years, respectively: [I] 1865-70; [II] 1871-76; [III] 1870-81; [IV] 1881-91.

Reveal prices of farm products, merchandise, etc., and shed light upon contemporary economic conditions.

274. [WALKER FAMILY DIARY. Walker's Creek, Rockbridge County, Va., 1865-19—

8 v. MSS. note books. 4°. and f°.   **McC**

Earlier vols. of the diary date back to the 18th cent. Since 1865 the record has been kept by: James A. Walker, 1865-Mar. 23, 1897; M[argaret] D. W[alker], 1897-1924, in progress.

Reveals the every-day life of a representative family of the county; contains material on agriculture, farm business, social life of the community, religious activity (Presbyterian), notes on education, but little on politics.

275. [WEST SALEM LAND CO., West Salem, Va. Letter of George Allen, president of the company, to William E. Pettee. July 24, 1891]

1 l. MS. 4°.   **NYP**

276. [WOODS, S. B.] Wilton. [Charlottesville, 19 -?]

[8] p. illus. 8°.   **LC**

Advertisement of a country estate in Albemarle County.

Secondary Works

277. ARNOLD, BENJAMIN W. . . . History of the tobacco industry in Virginia from 1860 to 1894 . . . Baltimore, Johns Hopkins, 1897.

86 p. 8°. (Johns Hopkins university. *Studies in historical and political science* . . . 15th ser., I-II)

Study of the industry from the stand-points of planter and manufacturer; with some discussion on organization within the industry, and the pros and cons of the American tobacco co.

278. BITTING, SAMUEL T. . . . Rural land ownership among the Negroes of Virginia with special reference to Albemarle County. [Charlottesville, Va., Michie, 1915]

110 p., 1 l. 8°. (University of Virginia. *Phelps-Stokes fellowship papers,* II)

Economic condition of the rural Negro fully treated; reveals enormous gains of Negroes in farm ownership.

279. GEE, WILSON, *et al.* Rural depopulation in certain tidewater and piedmont areas of Virginia. By Wilson Gee . . . and John J. Corson, 3d. Pub. by the Institute for research in the social sciences, University [of] Virginia. [Charlottesville, Va.] Michie, 1929.

x, 104 p. map, tables, diagrs. 8°. (University of Virginia. Institute for research in the social sciences. *Institute monograph,* 3) **LC, V, VU**

Valuable study of migrants and non-migrants, whites and Negroes, their social origins, present occupations, etc.; based upon first-hand investigation in the region and analysis of census statistics.

280. GEE, WILSON. . . . Some of the best things in rural Virginia . . . Charlottesville, Va., The University [1926]

55, [1] p. illus. 8°. (*University of Virginia record.* Extension series, X, 9) **LC, USAg, V, VU, WM**

"The University of Virginia and the U. S. Dept. of agriculture cooperating."

Reveals the commendable work being done in social and economic welfare for various districts of rural Virginia.

281. The GRACCHUSSARY rhyme book. Richmond, Va., 1916.

32 p. col. illus. 4°. **V**

"To teach children the simple truths about farming . . ."

282. HULVEY, CHARLES N. . . . The laws of Virginia as they pertain to the farmer. [Charlottesville] University of Virginia, 1924.

83 p. 8°. (*University of Virginia record.* Extension series [VIII, 11; July, 1924]) **USAg, V, VU**

283. HUTCHINSON, JOHN A. Land titles in Virginia and West Virginia, including tax sales, deeds, forfeitures, ejectment, adverse possession, boundaries and surveys, unlawful detainer, claims for improvements, authentication of deeds, etc. . . . Cincinnati, Clarke, 1887.

xiii, 368 p. 8°. **LC**

284. LAPSLEY, N. A. Virginia fertilizer and feeding stuffs funds. A review of the statutes creating these funds and a discussion of the leading decisions of federal and state courts on the subject of state inspection laws. By a member of the Virginia Dept. of agriculture. [Richmond? 1914?]

18 p. 8°.   V

285. McMAHON, JOHN R., ed. How these farmers succeeded. New York, Holt, 1919.

261 p. illus. 8°.   LC, USAg, V
ch. 8 (p. 107-125) on Henry C. Stuart of Virginia.

286. MORRISON, ALFRED J. The first Virginia state fair and its organizer, Gen. Richardson. Richmond, 1913.

2 col. (From Richmond *Virginian,* Sunday, Oct. 12, 1913)   **USAg**

287. PRICE, HARVEY L., *et al.* Virginia supplement . . . [New York, *ca.* 1923]

16 p. illus. 12°.   **LC**
"Principal soils and crops of Virginia," by H. L. Price; "Tobacco in Virginia," by M. Ferguson. Elementary treatments.

288. STEVENS, WAYNE M. The Eastern shore of Virginia produce exchange. A detailed study of its history, organization, operative methods, and accounting system . . . [n. p., 191-?]

111 numb. 1. illus. 4°.   **USAg**
Contains MS. amendments to Oct. 1, 1917.

Periodicals

289. AGRICULTURAL and industrial outlook; pub. by the Chesapeake & Ohio railway co. Vol. 1- Richmond, Va. [191-?—

illus., maps. f°. Issued irreg.
NYP: VI, 3-4; VII, 1; (1917-23).

290. ALLISON & ADDISON'S hand book of the garden, seed catalogue, and almanac . . . Richmond, Allison & Addison [186-?—

8°.   **V:** 1868-70.

291. AMERICAN BREEDER and planter; pub. in the interest of agriculture. Vol. 1-[?] Richmond, Va., 1880-[?]

8°. monthly.
Frank G. Ruffin, jr., ed.
USAg: I, 6-7 (Jul.-Aug., 1880); **V:** I, 1-2, 5.

292. AMERICAN FRUIT grower. Vol. 1-8, no. 2; Sept., 1915-Aug., 1917. Charlottesville, Va., 1915-17.

illus. 4°. monthly.
Title varies: Virginia fruit grower and farmer.
Combined with *The Fruit grower,* Sept., 1917, as XXVIII, 16 (pub. in Chicago).
NYP: III, 2-VIII, 2 (Apr., 1916-Aug., 1917); **USAg:** I, 1-3-VIII, 2 (1915-17).

293. CRENSHAW planters warehouse almanac . . . Comp. by John C. Goode. Richmond, Richmond press [190-?—
8°. **V:** 1909/10.

294. THE FARMER; devoted to agriculture, horticulture, the mechanic arts, and household economy. Vol. 1-2. Richmond, Va., 1866-67.

fronts. (ports.) illus. 8°. No more pub.
LC: II; **USAg:** I-II; **V:** I (imperf.), II.

295. The FARMERS' gazette and industrial index; devoted to agriculture, mechanic arts, and industrial interests of the South . . . vol. 1-3; Mar., 1869-Feb., 1871[?] Richmond, Va., 1868-[71?]

8°. monthly.
BP: I-III (imperf.) **USAg:** I, 9-11; II, 3-4, 6-12; III, 1-6, 8. **V:** I, 4; III.

296. JOURNAL of agriculture; pub. and controlled by the Executive committee, Virginia state agricultural society. Jan.-Dec., 1879. Richmond, 1879.

8°. monthly. No more pub. ?
Contains proceedings of the society, premiums at annual fairs, etc.
NYP; USAg; V: I, 1, 4-6, 8, 10-11; **VU:** I, 1.

297. MODERN farming. Vol. 1-23; 1888-May 1, 1909 [?] Richmond, Va., 1888-19[09?]

4°. monthly.
Title varies: Southern tobacconist and modern farmer, 1888-1907.
LC: XX-XXIII. **NYP:** IX-XVI (imperf.), XVIII-XXIII. **USAg:** X, 38, 50-XI, 49; XII-XIV, 20, 22-XVI, 11, 14-33; XVII-XX, 9; XXI-XXIII; (1898-1909). **V:** XIX, 5-6, 8-XX, 9 (1906-07).

298. The MONTICELLO farmer and grape grower . . . Charlottesville, Va. [18 -?]

monthly. **V:** Oct., 1883.
Devoted to the interests of farmers, grape-growers, stockraisers, and manufacturers of Piedmont Virginia.

299. The SOUTHERN PLANTER; devoted to practical and progressive agriculture, trucking, live-stock, and fireside. New series, vol. 1- ; 1867-19— Richmond, Va., Southern Planter pub. co., 1867-19—

> illus. 4°. and f°. monthly and semi-monthly.
> Title varies: Southern planter and farmer, 1868-81.
> **USAg:** XXVIII-XC (1867-81, Jul., 1882-1929). **V:** XXVIII-LXXVII (1867-1916, imperf.); LXXVIII-XC (1917-29). **VU:** XXXVII, 1, 7, 10; XXXIX, 1-3, 5, 7-12; XL, 2, 6, 8 (1876-79); LXXI, 4 (Apr., 1910); LXXX, 4 (Apr., 1919); LXXXVIII, 11 (June, 1927).

300. THE SOUTHERN PROGRESS; a magazine of opportunity and patriotism. Vol. 1- ; July, 1912— Richmond, Va., 1912—

> illus. f°. monthly.
> Nos. not pub.: XII, 3-XIV, 3 (Mar., 1918-Mar., 1919), and XVII, 3-6 (Sept.-Dec., 1920).
> **NYP:** IV, XI-XXXV (imperf.). **USAg:** I, 1-3; II, 4-5; III, 1-3; VI-IX, 5; X, 1-5; XI, 1-2 (1912-17). **V:** I-II, 4; III, 1; V, 3-6; X-XI, 5; XIV, 4; XVII, 1; XVIII, 1, 6; XIX, 1-3; XXIII, 6; XXIV, 2; XXVI, 2-6; XXVII-XXX; XXXI, 1-3, 5-6; XXXII, 1-4; XXXIII, 3-6; XXXIV; (1912-29).

301. The SOUTHLAND journal; in the interest of farms, schools, and roads. No. 1-[43?]; [1920?-21?] Petersburg, Va. [1920?-21?]

> illus. 4°. weekly. Ceased pub. with no. 43 ?
> **USAg:** 17-43, May 17, 1920-Jan. 21, 1921.

302. TRI-STATE tobacco grower. Vol. 1-6, no. 2; 1921-26. Raleigh, N. C. Pub. by the Tobacco growers' co-operative association of Virginia, North Carolina, and South Carolina, 1921-26.

> illus. f°. monthly. No more pub.
> **USAg:** I, 3, 4, 6-VI, 2; **WM:** IV-V (imperf.).

303. [VIRGINIA-CAROLINA CHEMICAL CO.] Almanac . . . [n. p., 19 -?]

> 12°.   **V:** 1907.

304. VIRGINIA FARM journal, an illustrated magazine for progressive Virginia farmers. Vol. 1, no. 1-4[?]; Dec. 15, 1903-March, 1904[?] Alexandria, Va., 1903-[04?]

> illus. f°. monthly. Probably ceased pub. with Mar., 1904.
> **USAg:** I, 1-4.

305. VIRGINIA FARMER. Vol. 1- ; [1897/98?-19—] Emporia, Va., 1897?-19—

> illus. f°. monthly.   **USAg:** XVIII, 1, 3, (Sept., Nov., 1914).

306. VIRGINIA FRUIT; pub. by the Virginia state horticultural society. Vol. 1- ; 1913— Richmond, 1913—

8°. Issued 5 times a year.
Pub. as the *Bulletin* of the society, to V, 2, Mar., 1917. (*q. v.* **[268]**)
LC: I, 5 (Nov., 1913). **NYP**: I, 3, 5; II, 3-5; III, 3-5; IV, 2; V, 2; VI, 1; VII, 2; (1913-19). **USAg**: I, 4-IV, 4; V, 1-4, 7-8; VI, 2, 8; VII, 2; VIII, 2; IX, 2; X, 2; XI, 2, 5; XII, 2; (Aug., 1913-Mar., 1924). **V**: II, XIV. (1914, 26). **VU**: IV, 1 (1916).

307. VIRGINIA HIGHWAY motor transport and tractor review, a magazine designed to create interest in improvement of highways in Virginia, the development of the motor transport idea, and the use of tractors on farms of the Old Dominion. Vol. 1, no. 1- ; Nov., 1919— Richmond, Va., 1919—

illus. 4°. monthly. **V**: I, 4-5 (1919-20).

308. V. P. I. agricultural journal; pub. . . . by the Agricultural club of the College of agriculture [Virginia polytechnic institute] vol. 1-2, no. 4; Dec., 1906-June, 1908. Blacksburg, Va., 1906-08.

plates. 8°. bi-monthly. No more pub.
V: I, 2 (Feb., 1907); **VPI**: I-II, 4 (1906-08).

309. VIRGINIA REAL ESTATE DIRECTORY . . . Richmond, 19[2-?]—

8°. semi-annual.
Includes list of brokers and salesmen licensed.
LC: June, 1927. **V**: June, 1925, and supple.; same for 1926 and 27.

310. VIRGINIA REAL ESTATE JOURNAL. Vol. 1-[?]; [1880?-] Richmond, Va. [1880?- ?]

monthly? **V**: III, 3 (1882).

311. VIRGINIA REAL ESTATE JOURNAL . . . Richmond, Va. [19-?—

monthly? **V**: Aug., 1923.

312. VIRGINIA REALTOR. Pub. . . . by the Virginia realty publishing co., vol. 1- ; April, 1926— Richmond, 1926—

illus. 4°. monthly.
Official organ of the Virginia real estate association.
V: I, 1-8 (Apr.-Nov., 1926); II, 4-12; III, 1; (1927-28).

For further references on Agriculture, see Pt. III, § 2: *Description and Travel,* and § 3: *Population, Race Relations, etc.* See also Pt. VI, under titles *Hampton normal and agricultural institute,* and *Virginia polytechnic institute.*

3. Resources and Industry

Government Publications and Documents

313. Ashe, William W.   Examination of, and report on, . . .
acre tract [of forest land] . . . in . . . Virginia.   1909-10.
MSS.   USF
13 reports on lands in various counties of Virginia, with names of
owners.

314. ——. . . . Short-leaf pine in Virginia.   The increase in
its yield by thinning.   Richmond, Bottom, 1913.
44 p. plates (incl. front.) 8°.   USAg, USF,V
Virginia Dept. of agriculture and immigration in co-operation with
the U. S. Forest service.

315. Baker, Hugh P.   Notes on general conditions of natural timber along the Rappahannock River, and reference to success of
a catalpa-chestnut plantation at Belmont, Lancaster County, Va.
[n. d.]
MSS.   USF

316. Barrows, J. S.   Mine sampling and chemical analyses of coals
tested at the U. S. fuel-testing plant, Norfolk, Va., in 1907.
Washington, Govt., 1908.
23 p. 8°. (U. S. Geological survey. *Bulletin*, 362)

317. Campbell, M. R.   Geology of the Big Stone Gap coal field of
Virginia and Kentucky.   Washington, Govt., 1893.
106 p. plates. 8°. (U. S. Geological survey. *Bulletin*, 111)

318. Clark, W. B.   The eocene deposits of the middle Atlantic slope
in Delaware, Maryland, and Virginia.   Washington, Govt., 1896.
167 p. plates. 8°. (U. S. Geological survey. *Bulletin*, 141)

319. Darton, N. H.   Economic geology of Richmond, Va., and vicinity . . .   Washington, Govt., 1911.
48 p. plates. 8°. (U. S. Geological survey. *Bulletin,* 483)

320. Fontaine, W. M.   The Potomac formation in Virginia.   Washington, Govt., 1896.
149 p. plates. 8°. (U. S. Geological survey. *Bulletin*, 145)

321. [Forest tracts:] Examination of, and report on, . . .
acre tracts of . . . [owner's name] in . . . county, Va.
[190-?]
MSS.   USF

Reports by: W. von Bayer, J. F. Bond, W. Bradfield, N. C. Brown, R. C. Bryant, E. E. Carter, A. K. Chittenden, E. D. Clark, W. T. Cox, J. H. Foster, H. S. Graves, W. B. Greeley, G. Griswold, G. M. Homans, R. S. Hosmer, L. Margolin, H. G. Merrill, L. S. Murphy, A. B. Patterson, F. W. Reed, T. H. Sherrard, W. D. Sterrett, D. Tierney, W. B. Willey, A. W. Williamson, K. W. Woodward.

322. GROVER, N. C. Surface water supply of Middle Atlantic states, 1906 (. . . Potomac, James, Roanoke . . . River drainages); N. C. Grover, district hydrographer. Washington, Govt., 1907.

100 p. plates. 8°. (U. S. Geological survey. *Water-supply paper* 203)

323. GROVER, N. C., *et al.* Report of progress of stream measurements for the calendar year 1905, Part III, . . . Potomac, James, Roanoke . . . River drainages by N. C. Grover and J. C. Hoyt. Washington, Govt., 1906.

128 p. plate. 8°. (U. S. Geological survey. *Water-supply paper*, 167)

324. ———. Surface water supply of the New-Kanawha River basin, W. Va., Va., and N. C.; N. C. Grover, chief hydraulic engineer; A. H. Horton and G. C. Stevens, district engineers. Washington, Govt., 1925.

iv, 281 p. plates. 8°. (U. S. Geological survey. *Water-supply paper*, 536)

325. HILDEBRAND, SAMUEL F., *et al.* Fishes of Chesapeake Bay, by Samuel F. Hildebrand and William C. Shroeder. Washington, Govt., 1927.

368 p. illus. 8°. (U. S. Dept. of commerce. Bur. of fisheries. *Bulletin*, XLIII, pt. 1)

326. KNOWLTON, F. H. Fossil wood and lignite of the Potomac formation. Washington, Govt., 1889.

72 p. plates. 8°. (U. S. Geological survey. *Bulletin*, 56)

327. [LYNCHBURG, VA.] An armor plant for the United States. Lynchburg, Virginia . . . [Lynchburg, Pub. by the city] Bell print., 1917.

15 p. 8°.   VU

328. MANUFACTURES of Virginia and West Virginia . . . Census of 1905 . . . Washington, Govt. [190-?]

43 p. 4°. (U. S. Dept. of commerce. Bur. of the census)

329. MARSHALL, R. B. Results of spirit leveling in Delaware, District of Columbia, Maryland, and Virginia, 1896 to 1909, inclusive . . . Washington, Govt., 1910.

74 p. 8°. (U. S. Geological survey. *Bulletin,* 434)

330. ———. Results of spirit leveling in Virginia, 1900 to 1913, inclusive. Washington, Govt., 1914.

68 p. plate. 8°. (U. S. Geological survey. *Bulletin,* 562)

331. MAURY, MATTHEW F. Physical survey of Virginia. Geographical position of; its commercial advantages, and national importance. (Preliminary report) by M. F. Maury, . . . professor of physics, Virginia military institute, Lexington, Va. . . . December, 1868. Richmond, Nye, 1868.

[92] p. fold. maps. 8°.

332. ———. Physical survey of Virginia. Her resources, climate and productions. Preliminary report. No. II. By M. F. Maury, with notes and additions by his son [Richard L. Maury] July 1, 1877. Pub. by direction of the Board of immigration. Richmond, Va., Randolph, 1878.

142 p., 1 l. col. fold. map. 8°.
Geographic and economic conditions described by counties.

333. PARKER, N. H., *et al.* The Potomac River basin: Geographic history, rainfall and stream flow, pollution, typhoid fever, and character of water; relation of soils and forest cover to quality and quantity of surface water; effect of industrial wastes on fishes; by H. N. Parker, Bailey Willis, R. H. Bolster, W. W. Ashe, and M. C. Marsh. Washington, Govt., 1907.

364 p. plates. 8°. (U. S. Geological survey. *Water-supply paper,* 192)

334. PEYTON, JEANNIE S. State forestry laws. Virginia. Washington, Govt., 1915.

6 p. 4°. (U. S. Forest service. *Forestry laws leaflets,* Misc. S-8)

USAg, USF

335. ROGERS, WILLIAM B. A reprint of annual reports and other papers on the geology of the Virginias. By the late William Barton Rogers . . . New York, Appleton, 1884.

xv, 832, p. fold. plates (part col.) fold. map, charts. 8°.

BP, LC, USG, V, VU, WM

336. SIMMONS, ROGER, E. . . . Wood-using industries in Virginia. . . . [n p.] American forestry association, 1912.

88 p. plates. 8°.

Virginia Dept. of agriculture and immigration in co-operation with U. S. Forest service.

A report of practical economic value to manufacturers.

337. STERRETT, W. D. Forest management of loblolly pine, in Delaware, Maryland, and Virginia. Washington, Govt., 1914.

59 p. illus., map, tables. 8°. (U. S. Dept. of agriculture. *Dept. bulletin,* 11)

338. STONE, RALPH W. . . . Coal resources of the Russell Fork basin in Kentucky and Virginia. Washington, Govt., 1908.

127 p. illus., plates (part fold.) maps (incl. 2 in pocket) diagrs. 8°. (U. S. Geological survey, *Bulletin,* 348)

339. THOM, WILLIAM T. The Negroes of Litwalton, Va.: a social study of the "oyster Negro." Washington, Govt., 1901.

p. 1115-1170. 8°. (In U. S. Bur. of labor. *Bulletin,* 37)

Study of a typical Negro community engaged in the oyster industry.

340. U. S. CONGRESS. HOUSE. PUBLIC LANDS, Committee on. . . . Shenandoah and other national parks . . . Report. (To accompany H. R. 11287) . . . [Washington, Govt., 1926]

11 p. 8°. (69 Cong., 1 sess. House. *Report,* 1160)   LC, USAg

Submitted by Mr. Abernethy. Includes report of Southern Appalachian national park commission, April 8, 1926.

341. ———. ———. SENATE. PUBLIC LANDS AND SURVEYS, Committee on. . . . Shenandoah and Great Smoky Mountain national parks . . . Report. (To accompany S. 4073) . . . [Washington, Govt., 1926]

8 p. 8°. (69 Cong., 1 sess. Senate. *Report,* 824)   LC, V

Submitted by Mr. Stanfield. Report of commission appointed by the Secretary of the interior.

342. ———. FISHERIES, Bur. of. . . . Condition and extent of the oyster beds of James River, Virginia . . . Washington, Govt., 1910.

2 p. l., [3]-83 p. 2 fold. charts. 8°. (Dept. of commerce and labor. Bur. of fisheries. *Document,* 729)

George M. Bowers, commissioner. Report by H. F. Moore on the examination of the oyster beds, at the request of the Virginia Commission of fisheries. "Confined to statements of fact and a short discussion of several obvious avenues of application."

343. U. S. FISHERIES, Bur. of.   Fisheries of Maryland and Virginia. Washington, Govt., 1925.

  1 p. 8°. (Its *Statistical bulletin*, 745)   USC

344. ———. FOREST SERVICE.   Forest policy advocated for Virginia. 1914. [n. p., 1914?]

  Clipping file.   USF

345. ———. ———.   Virginia to make a study of forest conditions. [n. p., 190-?]

  mimeog. 4°. Letter file.   USF

346. ———. ———.   Virginia's place in forestry. 1914. [n. p., 1914?]

  Clipping file.   USF

347. ———. MINES, Bur. of.   Analyses of Virginia coals. Washington, Govt., 1925.

  79 p. illus. 8°. (Its *Technical paper,* 365)

348. [101] VIRGINIA.   Annual reports of officers, boards and institutions of . . . Virginia . . . Richmond, Va. [1866-19—

  Include reports of the Commission of fisheries, 1875—   ; also, Bur. of labor and industrial statistics, 1898—

349. [112] ———. AGRICULTURE AND IMMIGRATION, Dept. of. Annual report . .   Richmond, 1877-19—

350. ———. CONSERVATION AND DEVELOPMENT, State commission on.   A publicity program for the development of the state of Virginia . . . Richmond, Bottom, 1927.

  [8] p. incl. diagr. 8°.   V

351. ———. FISHERIES, Commission of. . . . Oyster records. Distances and bearings of numbered corners of public grounds from shore stations, depth of water, description of shore stations, &c.   Report of the survey of the natural oyster rocks, beds, and shoals . . . Signed [by] John T. Wilkins, fish commissioner of Virginia. Jan. 1, 1894. [Richmond? 1894]

  16 v. 8°.   V
  Records for the following counties: Accomac, Essex, Gloucester, Isle of Wight, Lancaster, Mathews, Middlesex, Nansemond, Norfolk, Northampton, Northumberland, Princess Anne, Richmond, Warwick, Westmoreland, York.

352. ———. ———. Report . . . [1st- ; 187-? -19—] Richmond 18[7-?]-19—

> 8°. Report year ends Sept. 30. Biennial, 1919/21-
> **H:** 1871, 74/75-83, 99/1900-02/03, 06/07-10/11; **LC:** 1878/79, 90/91, 1900/01, 02/03, 04/05, 08/09, 10/11-16/17, 18/19-24/25; **NYP:** 1874/75-78/79, 81/82-83; **USC:** 1879/80-81/82, 83/84-84/85, 91/92-92/93, 94/95, 99/1900-02/03, 04/05, 06/07-12/13; **V:** 1875/76-76/77, 78/79, 81/82-83, 1904/05-05/06, 10/11-15/16, 18/19, 19/21, 22/23-25/27; **VU:** 1877.

353. ———. FORESTER, State. Administrative report. 1st- ; 1915— Charlottesville, Va. [1916—

> illus. 8°. 1st report covers period Mar.-Dec., 1915.
> Begin. 1920, the reports are issued as Bulletins of the dept. (*q. v.* [357])
> **H:** 1915-24/25; **LC:** 1915-20/21, 24/25; **NYP:** 1915-24/25; **USAg:** 1915-24/25; **USG:** 1918/19, 20/21, 22/23; **V:** 1915, 16/17, 18/19, 20/21, 22/23; **VU:** 1915-26; **WM:** 1918/19, 20/21.

354. ———. ———. Circular, no. 1- ; [19-? - ?] Charlottesville, Va. [19-?—

> 8°. **V:** 27,

355. ———. ———. Forestry leaflet, no. 1- ; 1915— Charlottesville, Va., 1915—

> illus. 8°.
> **USF:** 1-3, 6, 8, 9, 19; **USG:** 19 (1918); **V:** 1-3, 8-9, 19; **VU:** 1-19.

356. ———. ———. [Pamphlets and posters on forest fires, etc.] Charlottesville [*ca.* 1916]

> broadsides. **H**

357. ———. ———. Virginia forestry publications, no. 12- ; 1917— Charlottesville, 1917—

> illus. plates. 8°. Issued irreg. 1-11 not pub.
> Title varies: Bulletin of state forester, 1917-22.
> **BP:** 26 (1922); **H:** 12-19, 21-22, 24, 28-37, 39; **HB:** 12-15, 19; **LC:** 12-20, 22, 26, 28-38 (1917-25); **NYP:** 1-5, 8, 10-26, 28-38; **USAg:** 12-39; **USF:** 12-38; **USG:** 12-15, 17, 21, 24-26, 28-30, 32-39; **USM:** 17, 18; **V:** 12-19, 21, 24, 26, 28-37, 39; **VU:** 1-39; **WM:** 12, 15-19, 26, 34, 37.

358. ———. GAME AND INLAND FISHERIES, Commission of. . . . Game survey, season . . . 1921— Richmond, 1921—

> 8°. Season ends Feb. 1. **V:** 1921, 23.

359. ———. ———. Report . . . 1st- ; 1916/17— Richmond, 1917—

> plates. 8°. Report year ends June 30. 1st-5th, 1916-21, are annual; 1922/23- are biennial.

Title varies: State dept. of game and inland fisheries, 1916-26.
LC: 1916/17-20/21, 24/25-25/26; **NYP**: 1923/25-26/27; **USAg**: 1916/17-22/23; **V**: 1920/21, 22/23, 24/25, 26/27.

360. VIRGINIA. GAME AND INLAND FISHERIES, Commission of. Statement showing the operation of the Department . . . , Mar. 1, 1921-Mar. 1, 1925. [Richmond, 1925]

[4] p. tables. 12°.   **V**
McDonald Lee, commissioner.

361. ———. GEOLOGICAL SURVEY. Administrative report. 1st-6th; 1908/09-18/19. Charlottesville, 1910-20.

6 v. maps. 8°. biennial. No more pub.
Title varies: Administrative report of the state geologist.
·HB: 1908/09-18/19; **LC**: 1908/09-18/19; **USC**: 1908/09, 10/11; **USAg**: 1912/13, 18/19; **USG**: 1908/09-18/19; **V**: 1912/13-16/17; **VU**: 1908/09-18/19.

362. ———. ———. . . . Bulletin, no. 1-3, 1A-3A, 4-14, 15A, 16- ; 1905— [Richmond, Va.] 1905—

illus., plates, maps, diagrs. 8°. Issued irreg.
No. 1-3 have at head of title: Virginia Dept. of agriculture and immigration. Geological survey of Virginia. Thomas L. Watson, geologist in charge. Geological series, bulletin.
HB: 1-3, 1A, 4-5, 7-14, 15A, 16-26; **LC**: 1-3, 1A-3A, 4-14, 15A, 16-27, 30; **NYP**: 1-3, 1A, 2A, 4-14, 15A, 16-30; **USAg**: 1-3, 1A-3A, 4-14, 15A, 16-31; **USC**: 2-3, 1A-3A, 4-9, 12, 14, 15A, 18; **USG**: 1-3, 1A-3A, 4-14, 15A, 16-31; **V**: 1-3, 1A-3A, 4-14, 15A, 16-31; **VU**: 1-3, 1A-3A, 4-14, 15A, 16-31 (1905-27); **WM**: 1A-3A, 4-14, 15A, 16, 18-25, 28, 30.

363. ———. ———. . . . Report on the mineral production of Virginia . . . 1908-12. Charlottesville, University of Virginia, 1909-13.

4 v. illus., plates, maps (part fold.) tables (part fold.) diagrs. 8°. 1908, 11, 12, are annual; 1909/10, biennial. No more pub.
1908-11 are its *Bulletin*, 1A, 6, 8. [**362**].

364. ———. GOVERNOR, 1874-76 (James L. Kemper). Correspondence of the governor of Virginia with the governor of Maryland and the authorities of Accomac County, Va.; also, the opinion of the attorney-general of Virginia in relation to recent difficulties in the waters of the Pocomoke . . . Richmond, Walker, 1874.

38 p. 8°.   **LC, V**
Concerning rights in the oyster industry of the Pocomoke.

365. ———. ———, 1926— (Harry F. Byrd). Virginia: the home of industry as well as the birthplace of presidents. Gov. Byrd's glowing but conservative review of the industrial and banking progress of the state . . . Richmond, Va., State conservation and development commission [1927]

> 7, [1] p. incl. port., map, tables. 8°.   **V**
> Reprint from *Manufacturer's record,* Nov. 11, 1926.

366. ———. INDUSTRIAL COMMISSION. Annual report . . . 1st- ; 1918/19— Richmond, 1920—

> tables, diagrs. 8°. Report year ends June 30. Biennial, 1921/23-
> **HL**: 1918/19-21/23; **LC**: 1918/19-23/25; **NYP**: 1918/19-26/27; **USL**: 1918/19-26/27; **V**: 1918/19-26/27; **VU**: 1919/20; **WM**: 1919/20.

367. ———. ———. Bulletin, no. 1- ; Dec., 1918— Richmond, 1919—

> 8°. Issued irreg.; part monthly.
> **HL**: 5 (July, 1920); **LC**: 1; **NYP**: 1-2, 5-7 (1918-22); **USL**: 1, 4-7; **V**: 1-2, 5-6.

368. ———. ———. Opinions of the Industrial commission . . . vol. 1- ; 1919— Richmond, Va., 1921—

> 8°. annual.
> **HL**: 1920-25; **LC**: 1919-25; **NYP**: 1919-27; **USL**: 1919-27; **V**: 1919-28; **VU**: 1919-28; **WM**: 1920-24, 26.

369. ———. LABOR AND INDUSTRY, Bur. of. Annual report . . . 1st- ; 1898/99— Richmond, 1899—

> plates, ports., tables. 8°. Report year irreg.
> Called Bur. of labor and industrial statistics, 1898/99-1921/23; a branch of the Dept. of labor and industry, 1927-
> 1st report covers the years 1898 and 1899; 25 and 26th annual reports, 1921/23, issued in combined report.
> **H**: 1925/26; **HB**: 1917/18, 21/23, 24/25-26/27; **HL**: 1901/02-03/04, 05/06-08/09, 10/11-11/12, 15/16-18/19, 20/21-21/23, 24/25-25/26; **LC**: 1898/99, 1900-25/26; **NYP**: 1898/99, 1900-26/27; **USAg**: 1898/99-1905/06, 09/10, 11/12-12/13, 18/19, 24/25-26/27; **USG**: 1916/17-26/27; **USL**: 1898/99-1926/27; **V**: 1898/99-1919/20, 21/23-26/27; **VU**: 1913/14, 24/25.

370. ———. LAWS, STATUTES, etc. Compilation of the laws of Virginia relating to oysters. Comp. by the Commission of fisheries . . . Richmond [19—

> 8°.   **NYP**: 1901, 02 supple.; **V**: 1910.

371. ———. ———. Compilation of the laws of Virginia relating to oysters, fish, clams, and crabs. 1906. Sections of the code and acts of the General assembly. Comp. by the Auditor of public accounts. Richmond, Bottom, 1906.

> 76 p. 8°.   **V**

372. VIRGINIA. LAWS, STATUTES, etc. Dog law, as amended by the General assembly of 1920. Issued by the Commissioner of game and inland fisheries. [Richmond? 1921?]

5 p. 8°.   USHy

373. ———. ———. Game laws of Virginia, issued by the Secretary of the commonwealth. Richmond, Bottom, 1906.

16 p. 16°.   V

374. ———. ———. Laws of the state of Virginia for the preservation of oysters and to obtain revenue for the privilege of taking them within the waters of the commonwealth; also, forms of licenses and reports of inspectors, commissioners, treasurers, and clerks, of fees, fines, forfeitures, and taxes. 1882. Pub. by the Auditor of public accounts. Richmond, 1882.

34 p. 8°.   V

375. ———. ———. Laws of Virginia relating to fisheries of tidal waters . . . Pub. by the Commission of fisheries . . . Richmond, Bottom [19—

16°. Laws of 1918 comp. by Lewis H. Machen, director of Legislative reference bur.; 1926 comp. by W. W. Rowell, clerk of Commission of fisheries.

LC: 1918, 26, 27 supple. A; V: 1916, 18, 21, 26, 27 supple. A, 28.

376. ———. ———. Laws of Virginia relating to game, inland fish, and dogs. Comp. by the Dept. of game and inland fisheries. Richmond [19—

16°.   V: 1916, 18, 20, 23, 24, 26.

377. ———. ———. The Virginia fish and game protective association to the people of Virginia; with the laws of this commonwealth relating to fish and game. Richmond, Clemmitt & Jones, 1878.

20 p. 8°.   V

378. ———. ———. Water power, an act providing for the supervision of the development of the waters of the commonwealth through the State corporation commission, including the licensing of the erection of dams. Chap. 424, Acts of assembly, 1928, approved Mar. 24, 1928 . . . [Richmond, 1928]

11 p. 8°.   V

379. VIRGINIA MILITARY INSTITUTE. Semi-annual report of the superintendent of the Virginia military institute, enclosing the report of a geological and mineral examination of a portion of the James River iron-belt, by M. McDonald, professor of geology. Richmond, Frayser, 1879.

23 p. front. (fold. map) 8°. USE, USG, V
Francis H. Smith, supt.

380. VIRGINIA. PENITENTIARY, State. INDUSTRIAL DEPT. Catalogue no. 2. [Furniture and equipment manufactured] [n. p., 19-?]

20 p. illus. 4°. V
"Actual photographic reproductions with descriptions and prices."

381. ———. WATER POWER AND DEVELOPMENT COMMISSION. Water power, a potential factor in Virginia's development . . . A discussion of Virginia's economic condition, her resources, by the . . . commission, J. R. Horsley, director, A. W. Drinkard, jr., [and] W. Giles . . . Richmond, 1925.

32 p. illus., map, tables. 8°. NYP, USC, USG, V, WM
Appendix: Act authorizing creation of Water power and development commission . . . Approved Mar. 20, 1924.

382. WRIGHT, C. L. Briquetting tests at the United States fuel-testing plant, Norfolk, Va., 1907-08. Washington, Govt., 1909.

41 p. plates. 8°. (U. S. Geological survey. *Bulletin,* 385)

Other Source Material

383. An ACCOUNT of the ALLEGHANY SPRINGS, in Montgomery County, Va., with an elaborate analysis of the water, and well authenticated cases establishing their efficacy in the treatment of a large class of prevalent and obstinate chronic complaints . . . Lynchburg, Bryant & Browne, 1872.

47 p. 12°. VU

384. An ACCOUNT of the HOT SPRINGS, Bath County, Va., and an analysis of the waters, with a brief notice by Prof. J. L. Cabell, M.D., of the University of Virginia, resident physician, of the effects of thermal baths in cases of gout, rheumatism, diseases of the liver, etc. S. C. Tardy & Thos. R. Price & co. Richmond, Clemmitt & Jones, 1872.

48 p. 12°. H
Ed. of 1875: 109 p. V

385. An ACCOUNT of the MEDICINAL properties of the Healing Springs. Richmond, Hammersley, 1868.

28 p. fold. map. 12°. BP

386. The ALLEGHANY SPRINGS, Montgomery Co., Va.; and elaborate analysis of the water, with well authenticated cases, establishing their efficacy in the treatment of a large class of . . . chronic complaints: together with some notice of their locality, facility of access and means of accommodation. Philadelphia, Merrihew, 1874.

> 60 p. 12°.   V

387. APPALACHIAN POWER CO., Bluefield, W. Va. Hydroelectric power in the southwest Virginias. Bluefield, W. Va., Appalachian power co. [ca. 1913]

> 23, [1] p. illus. (incl. map) 4°.   LC
> Electric power developed from the New River.

388. ARMSTRONG, W. N. Oyster industries in Virginia. [n. p., 1879]

> 12 p. 8°.   V
> Decline of the industry in the James River and lower Chesapeake Bay; conditions which endanger it; and the remedy.

389. [BAILEY, JOHN M., *receiver*] To the stockholders of the Virginia, Tennessee, and Carolina steel and iron company. New York, Feb. 13, 1893. [New York, 1893]

> 31 p. 8°.   V
> Detailed statement of the company's finances since its inception in 1890.

390. BAYLOR, J. B. Oyster industry; the oyster interests of Virginia and Connecticut compared. Richmond, Whittet & Shepperson, 1892.

> 30 p. 8°.   V
> Series of letters written for the Richmond *Dispatch* and the *Times,* 1892-93, contrasting the decline of the industry in Virginia with its advance in Connecticut.

391. BLUE RIDGE IRON CO. Prospectus. Ores. "Brown hematite." "Manganese." Luray, Va., 1889.

> 35 p. map. 8°.   BP

392. [BOWLES, B. F.] [Day book of B. F. Bowles, merchant. Goochland Court House, Va., 1860-76]

> MS. book. f°.   LC
> Reveals prices of merchandise during the period.

393. BOYD, CHARLES R. Resources of south-west Virginia, showing the mineral deposits of iron, coal, zinc, copper and lead. Also the

staples of the various counties, methods of transportation, access,
etc. . . . New York, Wiley, 1881.

xiv, 321 p. incl. front., diagrs. plates, fold. map. 8°.
An account of conditions, not a statement of opinions. Counties
described: Montgomery, Pulaski, Wythe, Smyth, Washington, Giles,
Bland, Tazewell, Russell, Scott, Lee, Wise, Dickenson, Buchanan,
Floyd, Carroll, and Grayson, Va.; Ashe and Alleghany, N. C.

394. BUENA VISTA PLASTER & MINING CO., Plasterco P. O., Va.
Plaster or gypsum, its uses. Land plaster, best and cheapest im-
prover of land . . . Plasterco P. O., Washington County,
Va. [1899?]

16 p. 8°.   V

395. CAMPBELL, JOHN L. Geology and mineral resources of the
James River valley, Virginia. U. S. A. . . . New York,
Putnam, 1882.

1 p. l., 119 p. fold. map (in pocket) diagrs. 8°.
                            BP, LC, NYP, USG, V, VU

396. CAMPBELL, JOHN L., and H. D. Report on the Snowden slate
quarries of the Virginia slate mining company, Staunton, 1884.

4 p. 2 fold. maps. 8°.   **USG**
Reprint from *The Virginias* (*q. v.* **[557]**), V, 162-163, Oct., 1884.

397. CENTRAL VIRGINIA MINING & MANUFACTURING CO. Mining
property: 4 gold mines located in the counties of Orange and
Louisa, Virginia. Incorp., June, 1878. New York, 1878.

20 p. fold. map. 8°.   V

398. CHESAPEAKE & OHIO RAILWAY CO. INDUSTRIAL DEPT. Industrial sites along the Chesapeake & Ohio railway . . . Lynchburg, Brown-Morrison [n. d.]

128 p. illus., maps. 4°.   **NYP, V**

399. COMMITTEE ON NEW INDUSTRIAL TOWNS. A self-owning town.
A report to . . . [the] Newport News shipbuilding & dry
dock company regarding a co-partnership scheme for Hilton [Va.]
[New York, 1918]

19 p. 12°.   **BP**

400. DANVILLE & NEW RIVER RAILROAD COMPANY (projected).
Charter, president's report, resolutions of stockholders, etc., etc.
Line of road, when completed across the Blue Ridge,—110 miles
—penetrating the richest mineral region of Virginia. Iron, copper, coal, etc., etc., in abundance. Danville, Va., Waddel, 1881.

23 p. 8°.   **NYP**

401. A DESCRIPTION of the Healing springs, Bath County, Virginia. Richmond [1886]

29 p. 8°.   BP

402. DUNLOP, JAMES N. The promotion and encouragement of manufacture, the mechanic and useful arts; an address delivered before the Virginia mechanics' institute, in the hall of the Young men's Christian association, May 18, 1888. Richmond, Whittet & Shepperson, 1889.

32 p. 12°.   V

403. ELIZABETH IRON CO. To capitalists. Report of the Elizabeth iron company of Augusta County, Virginia, U. S. [n. p., 1873?]

32 p. 8°.   LC

Reports on the ore, furnace, and iron works, and the value of Kanawha coal for furnace use.

404. ELLINGER, WILLIAM. Letter on the oyster question of Virginia. By W. Ellinger, Fox Island, Virginia, 1894. Baltimore, Friedenwald [1894?]

21 p. 8°.   V

How the oyster supply is endangered and how the state may deal with the problem.

405. [EUBANK, JOHN L.] An account of the medicinal properties of the Healing Springs, Bath Co., Va. . . . Richmond, Va., Hammersley, 1868.

28 p. fold. map. 12°.   LC

406. FARMERS' ALLIANCE CO-OPERATIVE MANUFACTURING CO. [Prospectus and] charter. Iron Gate, Alleghany County, Va. New Market, Va. [1890?]

8 p. 8°   V

407. FARROW, EDWARD S. Mineral resources of Bland County in southwestern Virginia . . . New York, Hudson terminal building, 1911.

37 p. illus. 8°   LC, USG

408. FAUQUIER WHITE SULPHUR SPRINGS, Virginia. Season of 1882. Under the management of F. Tenney & co. . . . [Washington? 1882?]

8 p. 8°.   LC

409. FAUQUIER WHITE SULPHUR SPRINGS, Fauquier County, Va. . . . H. Cabell Maddux, manager . . . Baltimore, Guggenheimer, Weil, 1888.

15 p. illus. 8°.   **LC**
Ed. of 1891: Warrenton, Va. 8 p.   **NYP**

410. FISHER, HOWELL. Report on the agricultural and mineral resources of Virginia and West Virginia, and more particularly on the extent, quality, and value of the coal and iron deposits situated along the line of the Chesapeake & Ohio railroad, showing the advantage of that region for successful mining and manufacturing industry . . . New York, Wynkoop & Hallenbeck, 1870.

24 p. 8°.   **BP, NYP, USG, V**
Ed. of 1871.   **V**
Ed. of 1872.   **USG**

411. FRAZIER & RANDOLPH, Rockbridge Alum Springs, Va. Analysis of the Rockbridge Alum Springs, in Virginia; with some account of their history, and the properties of the water, in letters of eminent physicians and other gentlemen . . . Frazier & Randolph, proprietors. [n. p., 1867]

36 p. front. (fold. map) 12°.   **LC, V**

412. [GALLAGHER, CHARLES] The London and Virginia gold, silver, and copper mine. [New York, 1881]

3 l. 4°.   **V**
On jacket: For sale, the London & Virginia gold, silver, and copper mine of Buckingham County, Va. Prospectus . . .

413. GEOLOGICAL and analytical report of the kaolin mines near Staunton, Augusta County, Virginia. New York, Bryant, 1866.

12 p. 8°.   **V**
Examinations made for northern manufacturers.

414. GRISWOLD, GEORGE. Examination of 700 acre tract of Virginia Beach development company, in Princess Anne County, Va. Oct., 1902.

MS.   **USF**

415. HAUPT, HERMAN, *et al.* Report of Gen. Herman Haupt, chief engineer, and of Prof. J. P. Lesley, geologist, to the Shenandoah valley railroad co. Philadelphia, Review print., 1871.

31 p. fold. maps. 8°.   **HB**
Route of the railroad and resources of the adjacent country.

416. HEALING SPRINGS, Bath County, Virginia. [Cincinnati, Proctor & Collier, 19-?]

10 p. illus. 12°.   LC

417. HINSDALE, WILLIAM R. Roaring Run iron ore property. Botetourt and Alleghany counties, Va. Owned by Harry L. Horton, New York City. Report by William R. Hinsdale, consulting engineer. New York, 1911.

[3]-50, [1] p. front. (map) illus. 2 fold. maps. 4°.   USG

418. The HOMESTEAD, Hot Springs, Va. [Chicago, Ill., E. H. Clark advertising agency, ca. 1915]

[20] p. illus., fold. col. pl. 8°.   LC
Cover-title: Virginia Hot Springs.

419. HOT SPRINGS, Bath County, Virginia, with some account of their medicinal properties, and an analysis of the waters, with cases of cure of gout, rheumatism, diseases of the liver . . . Richmond, Clemmitt & Jones, 1871.

96 p. 8°.   LC
Pub. by S. C. Tardy and Thomas R. Price & co., owners.

420. HOTCHKISS, JEDEDIAH. The Shenandoah iron, lumber, mining and manufacturing company of Virginia; a report on its charter, lands, iron ores, and other minerals, timber, water-powers, iron-works, and other improvements and commercial facilities . . . Staunton, Va., Spectator, 1878.

56, 15 p. 2 maps. 8°.   V

421. IMBODEN, J. D. The coal and iron resources of Virginia. Their extent, commercial value, and early development. A paper read before a meeting of members of the legislature and prominent citizens in the Capitol at Richmond, Feb. 19, 1872 . . . Richmond, Clemmitt & Jones, 1872.

28, [1] p. 8°.   LC, VU

422. JAMES RIVER COAL CO. Description of Virginia carbonate found on lands of the James River coal company. New York, Baker & Godwin, 1874.

8 p. 8°.   V
With extracts from the New York press.

423. JAMESTOWN PORTLAND CEMENT CORP. . . . Stockholders' agreement. Old Colony trust company, depositary . . . [n. p., 1911?]

9 p. 4°.   HB

424. JONES, MERIWETHER. Report on the Richmond coal field. April 1916.

13 l. typew. 5 blueprints, by W. F. Hobart. 4°.

V: Access. no. 13859

425. JORDAN's White Sulphur Springs, Frederick County, Virginia . . . Winchester, Times, 1871.

16 p. 8°. **LC**

426. LETTER to Charles E. Hellier, Esq., on the character and conditions of the timber situation in Wise, Dickenson, and Buchanan counties of Virginia. [n. d.]

MSS. **USF**

Report on "one of the few, almost absolutely virgin forest areas of good timber left in the Eastern United States."

427. LEVERING, JAMES H. Report: canalization of the Potomac River and coal reduction plant to operate a gas engine actuated power station, prepared for Hon. Howard Sutherland, Hambleton & company, investment bankers, New York, Philadelphia, Baltimore, and Washington . . . [Washington, D. C., 1924]

20 numb. l. 8°. **LC**

Plan to develop hydro-electric power in the Potomac.

428. McALLISTER, JOSEPH T. Historical sketches of Virginia Hot Springs, Warm Sulphur Springs and Bath County, Virginia . . . [Salem, Va., Salem print., 1908]

51 p. 12°. **H, LC, V**

429. [McCORMICK, CYRUS H.] [Personal papers of the Cyrus H. McCormick family, 1865-*ca.* 1910]

MSS. **McC**

Material on Virginia includes papers on the reaper business; social and economic conditions during reconstruction and afterward; religious activity, especially of the Presbyterian church (including the question of the re-union of the church, North and South); education, especially concerning Washington and Lee university.

430. McCORMICK REAPER CO. [Records, 1865-1902]

MSS. **McC**

Letters received: about 100,000 pieces (loose letters) arranged chronologically, among which are some on the business in Virginia. *Letters sent out*: letterpress copy-books, bound; 165 v. on period 1865-84 (800 to 1,000 p. per v.); about 400,000 pieces covering period 1865-1902. Arranged chronologically and indexed by town and state; include all business of the company in Virginia.

431. McCreath, Andrew S. The iron ores of the Valley of Virginia. [n. p., 1883?]

> 10 p. 8°.   **V**
>
> Reprint from Amer. institute of mining engineers, *Transactions,* June, 1883.
>
> Examination of ores made at request of Shenandoah Valley and Norfolk & western railroad companies.

432. ———. The mineral wealth of Virginia tributary to the lines of the Norfolk & western and Shenandoah Valley railroad companies . . . Harrisburg, Pa., Hart, 1884.

> ix, [1], 157 p. 2 fold. maps, diagrs, 8°.   **BP, LC, USG, V, VU**
>
> Based upon personal investigation and field work. Advantages, particularly to the ironmaster, are stressed.

433. ———. The mineral wealth of Virginia tributary to the lines of the Shenandoah Valley and Norfolk & western railroad companies . . . Harrisburg, Pa., Hart, 1883.

> v, 105 p. illus. 8°.   **USG, V**

434. McCreath, Andrew S., *et al.* Geological and chemical report on a portion of the Virginia and Tennessee coal and iron company's property, embracing about 15,000 acres along the Clinch Valley division of the Norfolk & western railway, Wise County, Va., by Messrs. Andrew S. McCreath and E. V. D'Invilliers. [Abingdon, Va.? 1892]

> iv, 67 p. fold. map (in pocket) diagrs. 8°.   **USG, V**
>
> typew. copy: 46 p. 4°.   **HB**

435. ———. Mineral resources of the upper Cumberland Valley of south-eastern Kentucky and south-western Virginia. Tributary to the proposed Cumberland Valley extensions of the Louisville & Nashville railroad. By Andrew S. McCreath and E. V. D'Invilliers. Louisville, Ky., Courier journal, 1888.

> 152 p. fold. map, diagrs. 8°.   **USG, V**

436. ———. The New River-Cripple Creek mineral region of Virginia, by Andrew S. McCreath and Edward V. D'Invilliers. Harrisburg, Pa., Harrisburg pub., 1887.

> xi p. 1 l., 171 p. plates, maps (1 fold.) 8°.   **HB, LC, NYP, USG, V**
>
> Pub. for gratuitous distribution to invite attention to the advantages of this mineral region in southwestern Virginia; emphasis upon iron resources and development.

437. MASSANETTA mineral springs, Harrisonburg, Va. Baltimore, Friedenwald [1885?]

12 p. 8°. **V**

Advertising the health-restoring properties of these springs; with testimonials.

438. MAURY, MATTHEW F. [Letter book, 1868-69]

MSS. 4°. **LC**

The letters reveal Maury's untiring efforts to arouse interest in developing Virginia's resources, encouraging immigration, improving transportation, and thus to establish the foundations of future prosperity.

439. ———. The resources of the coal field of the upper Kanawha, with a sketch of the iron belt of Virginia, setting forth some of their markets and means of development . . . Baltimore, Sherwood, 1873.

44 p. 8°. **BP, H, USG, V**

Favorable report on the possibilities of the region.

440. The MEDICINAL properties of the Healing Springs, Bath County, Virginia, together with a few certificates of cure of diseases of the skin, rheumatism . . . William B. Bishop, proprietor. Richmond, Baughman [1878]

16 p. illus.(on cover) 8°. **V**

441. [MERCHANTS' account books. Shenandoah Valley of Virginia, 1865-*ca.* 1900]

MSS. 8°.-f°. **McC**

Reveal prices of a wide variety of merchandise during the period and, indirectly, something of contemporary economic conditions.

442. MERRIMAC ANTHRACITE COAL CORP. A prospectus setting forth salient features of the coal lands of the Price Mountain tract controlled by Merrimac anthracite coal corporation . . . [East Aurora, N. Y., The Roycrofters, *ca.* 1922]

2 p. l., 7-28 p. illus. (incl. map) 4°. **LC**

Attractive booklet containing the history and operations of the corporation, sketches of officers, engineer's report, etc. The coal lands are in Montgomery County, Va.

443. MONTEZUMA DEVELOPMENT AND TRUST CO. Charter, approved Feb. 14, 1888, as amended Jan. 14, 1892 . . . [n. p., n. d.]

4 p. 8°. **V**

444. MOORMAN, JOHN J. Virginia White Sulphur Springs, with the analysis of its waters, the diseases to which they are applicable,

and some account of society and its amusements at the Springs
. . . Baltimore, Kelly, Piet, 1869.

27 p. plan. 12°.   LC
Ed. of 1877: Baltimore, Sun. 31 p.   V

445. MORRIS, GOUVERNEUR. Report on a portion of property of the
Virginia & Tennessee coal and iron company, made to Baltimore
trust and guarantee company . . . dated Big Stone Gap, Mar.
21, 1894.

7 p. typew. 4°.   V: Access. No. 13817

446. MORTON, J. H., *et al.* Reports on the Stringfellow gold mine of
Fauquier County, Va., made by Prof. J. H. Morton, New York,
Capt. J. G. Riley, San Francisco, Prof. F. M. Endlich, Smithso-
nian institute. Brooklyn, N. Y., Baker, 1879.

16 p. 8°.   V

447. NEW RIVER RAILROAD, MINING & MANUFACTURING CO. Iron
ores and other minerals from the New River in Virginia . . .
Philadelphia, U. S. Centennial exhibition, 1876.

6 p. front. (fold. map) 8°.   V
Catalogue of iron ores, limestone, and coal from this region, with
chemical analyses.

448. NEWPORT NEWS SHIPBUILDING & DRY DOCK CO., Newport News,
Va. At the gateway to the sea. The story of a great shipbuilding
plant at Hampton Roads . . . Newport News, Va., Newport
News shipbuilding & dry dock co., 1921.

72 p. 8°.   VU

449. ———. Beating swords into plowshares; the romance of business boasts no more spectacular chapter than the 1917-1918 meta-
morphosis from a peace to a wartime footing . . . [Newport
News, Va., Newport News shipbuilding & dry dock co., *ca.* 1926]

30 p. 4°.   H, VU

450. ———. Description of the works . . . [New York, Evening post, 1907]

16 p. illus. 8°.   NYP, V

451. ———. Floating harbor equipment. [Newport News, Va.,
Newport News shipbuilding & dry dock co., *ca.* 1927]

31, [1] p. illus. 4°.   LC
Advertising the steel docks, floats, ferries, etc., equipped by this company.

452. ———. Newport News shipbuilding & dry dock company to the Central trust company of New York. Mortgage. Dated Apr. 15, 1890. New York, Burgoyne [1890]

 16 p. 8°.   **HB**

453. NORFOLK CREOSOTING CO. Creosoted timber; its preparation and uses. Norfolk creosoting co. Norfolk, Va. . . . Philadelphia, Heywoods, 1900.

 92 p. incl. front., illus. 16°.   **HB, LC**

454. NOTES on the pine trees of lower Virginia and North Carolina. [n. p., n. d.]

 22 p. 8°.   **V**

455. OYSTER CONVENTION, Richmond, Va. Proceedings of the convention called to consider and discuss the oyster question, held at the Richmond Chamber of commerce, Richmond, Va., Jan. 12, 1894, with papers issued in calling the convention. Richmond, Fergusson, 1894.

 47 p. 8°.   **LC, USAg**
 To devise methods of reviving and improving the oyster industry; problems of ownership of beds and their protection.

456. PIEDMONT GOLD BELT CHARTERED CO. Prospectus . . . Richmond, Va., 1896.

 10 p. 8°.   **V**
 To develop the gold resources of Buckingham County, Va.

457. PORTSMOUTH BUSINESS MEN'S ASSOCIATION. Pound nets, public revenue, and the people. Portsmouth, Va. [1910]

 8 p. 8°.   **V**
 A movement to prevent the obstruction of migration of food and fish in the bays and rivers of Virginia.

458. [POWER, R. B.] Moore house and Temple farm, Yorktown, Virginia. [189-?]

 4 p. mimeog., map. 4°.   **LC**
 Advertisement of property for hotel site, with opportunities for oyster planting, etc.

459. QUARLES, B. M. An account of the medicinal properties of the Healing Springs, Bath Co., Va. . . . B. M. Quarles, agent . . . Richmond, Va., Clemmitt & Jones, 1873.

 24 p. 12°.   **LC, V**

460. REPORT on lands in the counties of Wise and Buchanan, Virginia, and McDowell, West Virginia. Philadelphia, Murphy, 1882.

8 p. 8°.   LC

Timber and mineral lands advertised, with letters of surveyors and county clerks.

461. RICHMOND & DANVILLE RAILROAD CO. Catalogue of the minerals and woods of the regions of the states of Virginia, North and South Carolina, and Georgia, traversed by the lines of the Richmond & Danville railroad company, displayed in its exhibits . . . Richmond, Va., Baughman, 1889.

1 p. l., ii, [3]-34 p. 8°.   HB, LC, NYP

462. RICHMOND CEDAR WORKS, Richmond, Va. [Circulars] [n. p., 1925]

4°.   HB

463. RICHMOND GRANITE CO., Richmond, Va. Dressed granite monuments, sarcophagi, etc. Made for the trade, by the Richmond granite company at their quarries, Richmond, Va. . . . Philadelphia, Henry, 1879.

126 p. illus. 8°.   LC

Contains 243 designs, with dimensions.

464. RICHMOND ICE CO. [Circulars] [n. p., 1927]

4°.   HB

465. RIDGWAY, THOMAS S. Geological report upon the iron ore, coal, and other mineral deposits found along the line of the Chesapeake & Ohio railroad . . . New York, Pub. for the Chesapeake & Ohio railroad co., 1872.

[3]-26 p. 8°.   BP, LC, NYP, V, WM

466. ROANOKE ROOFING & METAL CORNICE CO. Roanoke roofing and metal cornice co., manufacturers of architectural sheet metal work . . . [Illustrated catalogue] [Roanoke, Va., *ca.* 1893]

108 p. incl. illus., tables. 8°.   LC

467. ROCK ENON springs and baths, Frederick County, Virginia. Washington, D. C., Judd, 1878.

12 p. illus., map. 8°.   LC

Ed. of 1880: Washington, Judd & Detweiler. 24 p.   LC

Ed. of 1883: [Washington, McGill] 16 p. illus.   LC

Ed. of [1889?]: [Washington, McQueen & Wallace] 22 p. A. S. Pratt, proprietor.   LC

468. ROCKBRIDGE Alum Springs. [Philadelphia, 189-?]

46 p. illus. 12°.　　　　　　　　　　　　　　　　　　　　　LC

The Springs as a health and pleasure resort; contains testimonials on the quality of the water.

469. ROCKBRIDGE CO., inc. Prospectus and memorandum of the Rockbridge company. [New York? 188-?]

7, 16 p. 8°.　　　　　　　　　　　　　　　　　　　　　　　V

Company formed to develop mineral, timber, and agricultural lands in the valleys of the James and North rivers, Va.

470. ROYAL LAND COMPANY OF VIRGINIA. The Royal land com'y of Virginia: its purposes and charters: its anthracite coal, iron ore, other minerals and timber lands: and its narrow-gauge railroads from Chesapeake Bay to Pittsburg[h] and the West. Their condition, advantages and prospects as a security for its first mortgage seven per cent. gold bonds. With information in relation to the bituminous and anthracite coals, hematite, specular and magnetic iron ores . . . Richmond, Clemmitt & Jones, 1877.

4 p. l., 79, 56 p. fold. profile, fold. maps. 8°.　　　　　　USG, V

471. ST. JOHN, I. M. Notes on the coal trade of the Chesapeake & Ohio railroad in its bearing upon the commercial interest of Richmond, Va. . . . [n. p., 1878]

8°.　　　　　　　　　　　　　　　　　　　　　　　　　　　　BP

472. SCHUBERT, ELMER A. Development of chemical industries along the Norfolk & western railway; natural resources; developed and undeveloped, paper read before symposium, National exposition of chemical industries, . . . Sept. 27, 1917 . . . Roanoke, Va., Union print. [1917]

11 p. 8°.　　　　　　　　　　　　　　　　　　　　　　　USG

473. SEARS, H. M. The Natural Bridge national forest. A chapter of Virginia history . . . [Washington] 1925.

11 p. mimeog., map. 4°.　　　　　　　　　　　　　　　　USAg

474. SHALER, NATHANIEL S. Preliminary report concerning the resources of the country adjacent to the line of the proposed Richmond & southwestern railway . . . Cambridge [Mass.] Wheeler, 1880.

v, 54 p. fold. map. 4°.　　　　　　　　　　　　　　　　BRE, HB

475. ————. Report on the resources of the country traversed by the Virginia, Kentucky & Ohio railroad, and the Paris, George-

town & Frankfort railroad, in the states of Virginia and Kentucky.
Cambridge, Mass., Wheeler, 1881.

18 p. 8°.   BP, BRE

476. . . . SHENANDOAH ALUM SPRINGS! Shenandoah County,
Va. . . . Analysis, by Professor J. W. Mallet . . . Also
description of springs and testimonials . . . Mt. Jackson, Va.,
Valley farmer book and job office, 1878.

15 p. 12°.   LC
Ed. of 1883: [Peoria, Ill., Franks] 9 p.   LC

477. SKETCHES of the gold fields of eastern Virginia. By those familiar with them. Richmond, 1895.

16 p. 16°.   V
"To the public," by L. P. Routt. Reports, by Robert F. Morris and
John S. Fleming.

478. SOUTHWESTERN VIRGINIA, inc. Power in southwestern Virginia.
A great mountain empire served by the Appalachian power company, Bluefield, W. Va. [Wytheville, Va.? 1919?]

16 p. illus. 8°.   V

479. SWEET CHALYBEATE SPRINGS, Alleghany County, Virginia.
B. F. Eakle, manager. [Sweet Chalybeate, Va., 1901?]

24 p. incl. illus., map. 16°.   LC
Ed. of [19-? Richmond, Hill] [24] p. illus.   LC

480. TOBACCO trade of the city of Richmond, Va. Constitution and
by-laws . . . Richmond, Hill, 1893.

12 p. 8°.   V
An association of tobacco merchants and manufacturers.

481. VIRGINIA & CAROLINA COAST RAILROAD CO. . . . Report of
J. T. Odell. Apr. 26, 1905. [n. p., 1905]

7 p. 4°.   BRE
Favorable report on the natural resources and industrial interests
owned by the company which may assure the success of the railroad just
established. Mainly timber resources.

482. VIRGINIA & KENTUCKY COAL FIELDS CORP. Preliminary memorandum . . . [Issued by] William Salomon & co., bankers,
New York, Mar. 19, 1906. [n. p., 1906]

50 p. 4°.   HB
Corporation to be formed to acquire coal lands or mineral rights in
Buchanan, Dickenson, and Tazewell counties, Va.

483. [VIRGINIA & TENNESSEE COAL & IRON CO.] Description of Virginia property of the Virginia & Tennessee coal and iron company. Mar. 2, 1896.

5 p. typew., map. 4°.   **V:** Access. no. 13819

484. VIRGINIA ANTHRACITE COAL CO. . . . Prospectus. [Richmond, Va? 1903?]

vii p. 4°.   **HB**
Contains statements of development and financial plan.

485. VIRGINIA-CAROLINA CHEMICAL CO., Richmond, Va. Annual statement. 1st- ; [1895/96?-19—] [New York? 1896?-19—

4°. Report year ends May 31.
Title varies: Financial statement.
Includes balance sheets of the Southern cotton oil co.
HB: 1900/01-27/28; **LC:** 1910/11-21/22, 23/24, 26/27-27/28; **NYP:** 1903/04, 08/09, 10/11, 14/15-18/19, 22/23-23/24, 26/27; **USG:** 1922/23.

486. ———. [Cases concerning the Virginia-Carolina chemical company as a "fertilizer trust." U. S. Supreme court. Transscript of record. Oct. term, 1906. Washington, 1906?]

Reprints. 8°.   **H**

487. ———. Consolidated balance sheet of the Virginia-Carolina chemical company, and its subsidiary companies, at close of quarter ending . . . , including the Southern cotton oil company, at close of quarter ending . . . Richmond, 1904—

16°. **HB:** Dec. 15, 1904 & Mar. 15, 1905; **NYP:** Sept. 15, 1904 & Aug. 31, 1904.

488. ———. Deposit agreement . . . [New York, 1924]

2 v. 4°.   **HB:** Mar. 3.

489. ———. List of common and preferred stockholders . . . [n. d.]

115 l. typew. 4°.   **HB**
Includes addresses and number of shares.

490. ———. List of preferred stockholders . . . of 300 shares and over . . . 1908—

typew. copies. 4°.   **HB:** Oct. 2, 1908; another undated.

491. ———. Reorganization of the Virginia-Carolina chemical company; plan and agreement, dated Aug. 10, 1925. [Richmond, 1925]

73 p. incl. table. 4°.   **HB, NYP**

492. VIRGINIA-CAROLINA CHEMICAL CO., Richmond, Va. . . . Report of the Board of directors to the stockholders . . . [Richmond? 1896?-19—

4°.   LC: 1913; May, 1923.

493. ———. [Report of the president] . . . [Richmond? 19-?—

4°.   HB: July 19, 1911.

494. ———. Virginia-Carolina chemical company and Central trust company of New York. Trust agreement, dated Oct. 1, 1902. [n. p., 1902]

48 p. 4°.   HB

495. ———. Virginia-Carolina chemical company and Guaranty trust company of New York, trustee. Trust agreement. Dated Nov. 1, 1920 . . . [n. p., 1920]

56 p. 4°.   HB

496. ———. Virginia-Carolina chemical company and the Equitable trust company of New York, trustee. Trust agreement . . . Dated May 15, 1914 . . . New York, Young [1914]

ix, 115 p. 8°.   HB

497. ———. Virginia-Carolina chemical company and the Equitable trust company of New York, trustee. Trust agreement . . . Dated July 1, 1922 . . . [n. p., 1922?]

117 p. 4°.   HB

498. ———. Virginia-Carolina chemical company, The Consumers chemical corporation, Messrs. Blair & company and Hallgarten & company, and preferred shareholders of the Consumers chemical corporation. Agreement . . . Dated April 1, 1913. New York, Hecla [1913]

18 p. 4°.   HB

499. ———. Virginia-Carolina chemical company to Central trust company of New York, trustee. First mortgage. Dated Nov. 2, 1908. New York, Young [1908]

x, 172 p. 8°.   HB

500. ———. Virginia-Carolina chemical company to Central union trust company of New York, trustee. Indenture, dated June 1, 1922. $35,000,000 gold bonds. [n. p., 1922]

252 p. 4°.   HB

501. [253] ———. CROP BOOK DEPT. [Agricultural pamphlets. Richmond, Va., 1915—

502. VIRGINIA-CAROLINA SUPPLY CO. Catalogue D. Plumbers' and steam-fitters' supplies . . . Norfolk, Virginia-Carolina supply co., 1908.

4 p. l., 11-464 p. illus. 4°.   **NYP**

503. VIRGINIA COAL PRODUCTS CORP. [Circulars] [n. p., 1916]

4°.   **HB**

504. VIRGINIA CONSOLIDATED MILLING CO., Petersburg, Va. Handbook of information in reference to the Virginia consolidated milling company . . . Collected and published under the direction of the . . . company . . . Petersburg, Va., Buchanan, 1903.

527, [47] p. 8°.   **LC**
Contains agreement of merger between the Matoaca manufacturing company and the Emporia land & investment company, whereby the Virginia consolidated milling company came into existence; also other official papers and documents.

505. ———. Mortgage or deed of trust. Virginia consolidated milling company . . . to International trust company of Boston, Mass. . . . Dated Aug. 7, 1903 . . . [n. p., 1903?]

23 p. 8°.   **HB**

506. VIRGINIA CONSTRUCTION CO. Report of the president and directors, with accompanying documents, as submitted to stockholders in annual meeting at Richmond, Va., July 16, 1889. [n. p., 1889?]

8 p. tables. 8°.   **V**
Company engaged in construction work on railroads.

507. VIRGINIA ELECTRIC RAILWAY AND DEVELOPMENT CO. James River construction company. Contract for dams, canal and power house. May, 1899. Richmond, Waddey, 1899.

35 p. 4°. p. 3-6, 32-34, omitted.   **NYP**

508. VIRGINIA FISH AND GAME PROTECTIVE ASSOCIATION. An address to the people of Virginia . . . with the proceedings of the . . . association and the laws of this commonwealth in relation to fish and game. Pub. by order of the association. Richmond, Clemmitt & Jones, 1877—

8°. Title varies.   **LC, VU**: 1877; **H, NYP, V, VU**: 1878.

509. VIRGINIA FISH AND GAME PROTECTIVE ASSOCIATION. Quarterly bulletin, vol. 1- ; [1915?—] Richmond, Va. [1915?—
illus. 4°.   **USAg:** III-V, 3; Jan., 1918-Nov., 1920.

510. VIRGINIA HARDWOOD LUMBER CO., Tazewell, Va. [Circulars]
[n. p., 1928]
4°.   **HB**

511. VIRGINIA HOT SPRINGS. [n. p., 1905]
[16] p. 12°.   **H**

512. VIRGINIA HOT SPRINGS CO. Report . . . Richmond [18-?—
8°. Report year ends Oct. 31.
HB: 1894; 1897 (typew.).

513. VIRGINIA IRON, COAL & COKE CO. Annual report. 1st- ;
1902/03— [Roanoke, Va., 1903—
8°. Report year ends June 30.
Reports for 1902/03-04/05 include reports of Virginia & southwestern railway co. **[1003]**
    BRE: 1902/03-13/14; **HB:** 1902/03-23/24; **LC:** 1904/05-05/06, 07/08-10/11; **NYP:** 1904/05, 06/07-09/10, 13/14-26/27.

514. VIRGINIA LEAD & ZINC CORP., Richmond, Va. [Circular] [n. p., 1916?]
4°.   **HB**

515. ———. Report of J. S. Grasty, July 5, 1916, on the Holladay mine. [Charlottesville, 1916]
14 p. plates, plans. 8°.   **USG**

516. VIRGINIA MINES DEVELOPMENT CO., inc. [Circular, May, 1916]
[n. p., 1916]
4°.   **HB**
Established for gold mining in Goochland County.

517. VIRGINIA PYRITES MINING CO. Prospectus of the . . . company, incorporated April, 1891. [Richmond, 1891?]
8 p. 8°.   **V**
"Property of the company located in Louisa County, Va. . . ."

518. VIRGINIA SHIPBUILDING CORP., Alexandria, Va. [Notes on financial status, etc., and tentative balance sheet as of Nov. 30, 1919]
11 l. MSS. 16°. 12 l. typew. 4°.   **HB**

519. VIRGINIA STATE CHAMBER OF COMMERCE. [Documents on natural resources] Richmond, 1925-27.

    nar. 8°.   H, NYP, V

    Industry doc., no. 1: "Minerals of Virginia . . ." (1927). *Miscell. doc.,* no. 2: "Shenandoah national park in Virginia" (1925); no. 12: "National forests in Virginia . . ." (1926).

520. ———. Virginia industrial survey; specifications for local industrial surveys, 1928. Richmond, Virginia State chamber of commerce [1928]

    16 p. typew. 4°.   V

521. VIRGINIA STEEL, IRON & SLATE CO., Richmond, Va. Prospectus . . . [Richmond? 1890?]

    15 p. 8°.   V

    Operations to be carried on near Howardsville, Albemarle County.

522. VIRGINIAN RAILWAY CO. . . . List of coal operations on Virginian railway and connections, showing mine numbers, location, post office address, and names of sales agents. Issued Nov. 20, 1924. [Norfolk? 1924]

    7 p. incl. map. 4°.   BRE

523. . . . The WALLAWHATOOLA water, the finest acidulated water in America. This health giving fountain is near Millboro depot, Bath County, Va. Baltimore, Lipscomb [187-?]

    12 p. 12°.   VU

    Analyses of the water, and testimonials.

524. WARM SULPHUR SPRINGS, Bath County, Virginia. [Warm Springs, Va., 1896]

    15 p. incl. illus. 16°.   LC

    Ed. of 1884.   H

525. WARREN, GEORGE H., *et al.* A report upon the drainage of the lowlands of the Chickahominy River, by George H. Warren, assisted by John R. Haswell and Newton B. Wade . . . June 1912.

    27 p. typew., illus., diagr. (blue-print) 4°.   V: Access. no. 8.

526. WATSON, THOMAS L., *et al.* . . . Mineral resources of Virginia . . . Lynchburg, Va., Bell, 1907.

    xxxi, 618 p. illus., plates (part fold.; incl. maps) fold. tables, diagrs. 8°.

    At head of title: The Virginia Jamestown exposition commission.

    Bibliographies interspersed. "Cement and cement materials," by R.

S. Bassler, p. 86-167; "Clays," by Heinrich Ries, p. 167-187; "Iron," by
R. J. Holden, p. [402]-491.
A valuable survey of the state's mineral wealth and its development;
authoritative and scholarly; economic factors are stressed.

527. WEEKS, JOSEPH D.   The iron ores of the James River valley,
Virginia . . . New York, Williams, 1881.

[8] p. illus., tables. 8°.   LC
Reprint from the *Iron age,* Mar. 3 & 10, 1881.
Discussion of the exploitation of the ores, tests, and possibilities of
development.

528. ———. Notes of a trip through the James River valley . . .
Pittsburg[h], National iron and steel pub. co., 1881.

1 p. l., 105-110 p. 8°.   LC, V
Paper read before the Engineers' society of western Pennsylvania,
Feb. 22, 1881.
Iron resources and works of this region; economic problems involved
in their development.

529. [273] [WALKER family account books.   Walker's Creek,
Rockbridge County, Va., 1865-91]

Secondary Works

530. [277] ARNOLD, BENJAMIN W. . . . History of the tobacco industry in Virginia from 1860 to 1894 . . . Baltimore, 1897.

531. EBY, JAMES B.   The geology and coal resources of the coal-
bearing portions of Wise and Scott counties, Virginia . . .
[Lynchburg, Va., Bell, 1924]

iv, [2], 102 p., 1 l. illus. (maps) diagrs. 8°.
Thesis (Ph.D.), Johns Hopkins university, 1922. Pub., with additional matter, as Virginia Geological survey, *Bulletin,* 24 (1923).

532. FROEHLING, HENRY, *et al.*   A handbook on the minerals and
mineral resources of Virginia.   Prepared for the Virginia Commission to the St. Louis exposition, by [Henry] Froehling &
[Andrew] Robertson, chemists and economic geologists, Richmond, Va.   Richmond, Va. [Salem, Salem print., 1904]

viii, 159 p. plates. fold. map. 80°.   BP, LC, NYP, USC, USG, V
Based mainly upon geological survey reports, bulletins, etc.

533. HUBBARD, GEORGE D., *et al.*   Notes on the geology of Giles

County, Va., by George D. Hubbard and Carey G. Croneis. Oberlin, Ohio, 1926.

[70] p. fold. map. 8°. (Oberlin college. *Laboratory bulletin,* 48)
LC

534. LAMBETH, WILLIAM A. Notes on the geology of the Monticello area, Virginia . . . [n. p.] 1901.

22 p. fold. map, diagr. 8°.   USG, V, VU
Thesis (Ph.D.), University of Virginia.

535. LONSDALE, JOHN T. . . . Geology of the gold pyrite belt of the northeastern piedmont, Virginia . . . University, Va., 1927.

xii, p., 1 l., 110 p. illus., tables, diagrs., plates (incl. fold. map in pocket) 8°.
Thesis (Ph.D.), University of Virginia. Also pub. as Virginia Geological survey, *Bulletin,* 30.

536. NEWMAN, OLIVER P. . . . Great Falls of the Potomac . . . Newspaper article by Mr. O. P. Newman, giving a history of the water-power rights of the Great Falls of the Potomac. [Washington, Govt., 1911]

9 p. 8°. ([U. S.] 61 Cong., 3 sess. Senate. *Doc.,* 790)   LC, V

537. ROBERTS, JOSEPH K. The geology of the Virginia Triassic . . . Charlottesville, Va., Michie, 1928.

1 p. l., v-xii, 205 p. illus., plates (incl. maps, 4 fold.) 8°.
Thesis (Ph.D), Johns Hopkins university, 1922. Pub. also as Virginia Geological survey, *Bulletin,* 29.
Contains description of the coal and building stone resources of eastern Virginia and the piedmont.

538. SKEEN, LYMAN. The bacterial flora of the Charlottesville and University of Virginia water supply . . . Richmond, Hoen [1901?]

14 p. charts. 8°.   H, V, VU
Thesis (Ph.D), University of Virginia, 1901.

539. WHITE, A. F. Composition of the waters of Rockbridge County, Virginia, and their relation to the geological formations. Winchester, Va., Norton, 1906.

38 p. fold. map. 8°.   USG

540. WRIGHT, FRANK J. . . . . Physiography of the upper James

River basin in Virginia . . . Charlottesville, University of Virginia, 1925.

v, [1] p., 1 l., 67 p., 1 l. illus., plates, 2 fold. maps (1 in pocket) 8°. Thesis (Ph.D.), Columbia University, 1925. Also pub. as Virginia Geological survey, *Bulletin,* 11.

Periodicals

541. [289] AGRICULTURAL and industrial outlook; pub. by the Chesapeake & Ohio railway co. Richmond, Va. [191-?—

542. APPALACHIAN mines and industrial record. Vol. 1- ; [1908? —] Johnson City, Tenn. [1908?]-09; Roanoke, Va., 1910—
4°. monthly. v. 5 issued as new ser., v. 1 (1910)
LC: II-III, 2 (Jan.-Sept., 1909); V, 1-3 (Jan.-June, 1910)

543. [294] The FARMER; devoted to agriculture, horticulture, the mechanic arts, and household economy. Richmond, 1866-67.

544. [295] The FARMERS' gazette and industrial index; devoted to agriculture, mechanic arts, and industrial interests of the South . . . Richmond, 1868-[71?]

545. GAME and fish conservationist, vol. 1- ; Sept., 1920— Richmond, Va., Pub. by the Dept. of game and inland fisheries, 1920—
illus. 4°. bi-monthly.
USAg: I, 1-5; II-III, 6 (1920-24); IV-VIII (1925-29). **V:** II, 2-4, 6; III, 1-3; IV, 4; V, 1-6; VI, 1-6; VII, 2-6; VIII, 1-2 (1922-28).

546. [298] The MONTICELLO farmer and grape grower . . . Charlottesville, Va. [18-?]

547. NEWS letter, Virginia. Forestry dept., no. 1- ; June, 1923— University of Virginia, University, Va., 1923—
typew. mimeog. 4°.   **VU:** 1, 3 (June, 1923, Feb., 24)

548. The OYSTERMAN and fisherman; devoted to sea food and allied industries. Vol. 1- ; [1903?—] Hampton, Va. [The Oysterman pub. co., [1903?—
illus. 4°. monthly.
Title varies: The Oysterman . . .
LC: VI, 1-4, 6-12; VII-XII; (1908/09-14/15). **NYP:** III-IV (imperf.), V-XIII. **USC:** VI-XII (imperf.). **V:** VIII-XIII (imperf.).

549. PRO QUERENTE; "P. Q.", a journal devoted to the lawyer, mer-

chant, manufacturer, and jobber. Vol. 1- ; [1899?-19—]
Richmond, Va. [1899?-19—

8°. monthly.   V: III, 1, 5, 7 (Jan., May, July, 1901).

550. RICHMOND MERCANTILE and manufacturing journal. Vol. 1- ;
1883— Richmond, Va., 1883—

illus. f°. monthly.
Richard E. Frayser, ed.
V: I-XIII, 3, 5-6, 8-10; XIV, 1-2, 5, 9, 12; XV, 4; (1883-96).

551. RICHMOND TRADE journal . . . Richmond, Va., Richmond
trade journal co. [1892?—

W. H. Rowland, ed.
V: II, 2-3, 6-8, 10, 12-13, 15-16; July 21-Dec. 22, 1892.

552. SOUTHERN HOMESEEKER and investor's guide. Vol. 1-10; no.
1; 1909/10-18. Roanoke, Va., pub. by the Norfolk & western
railway co., Agricultural and industrial dept., 1909-18.

illus. 4°. quarterly. No more pub.
NYP: I, 2-X, 1 (June, 1909-June, 1918).

553. [300] The SOUTHERN PROGRESS; a magazine of opportunity
and patriotism. Richmond, 1912-17.

554. VIRGINIA FOREST warden. The Virginia Forest service, Conservation and development commission, University of Virginia.
Vol. 1- ; 1927/28— Charlottesville, Va., 1927—

illus. 4°. Issued irreg.
V: I, 1-6 (Feb., 1927-Sept., 1928); VU: I.

555. VIRGINIA MANUFACTURER. Vol. 1-2[?] Buchanan, Va., 1890-
91[?]

No more pub.?   Engin. Soc. Lib., N. Y. City: II.

556. The VIRGINIA STENOGRAPHER. Vol. 1- ; 1895— Pub. by the
Richmond stenographers' association, Richmond, Va., 1895—

8°. monthly.   NYP: I, 1-4 (May-Aug., 1895).

557. The VIRGINIAS, a mining, industrial & scientific journal, devoted to the development of Virginia and West Virginia. Ed.
and pub. by Jed. Hotchkiss . . . Vols. 1-6; 1880-85. Staunton, Va., 1880-85.

6 v. illus. (incl. ports.) maps. f°.
Merged into the *Industrial South,* of Richmond, Va.
H, LC: I-VI; NYP: I-V; USG, V: I-VI.

Directories

558. CHESAPEAKE & OHIO RAILWAY CO. . . . Official industrial guide and shippers' directory . . . [Richmond? C & O railway co., 19—

> illus. 4°. Advertisements interspersed.
> Issued by General freight dept.
> **BRE**: 1912-13; **LC, NYP**: 1906; **V**: 1907.

559. VIRGINIA. LABOR AND INDUSTRY, Bur. of. Complete list of industrial and mercantile establishments in the state of Virginia, as to cities, towns, and counties, with addresses . . . Richmond, Va. [1920?]

> 68 p. 8°.   **USL**

560. ———. ———. . . . Industrial directory . . . Richmond, Va. [1920?—

> 8°.   **H, HB, LC, NYP, USAg, USC, USG, USL**: 1925; **V**: 1920-25.

> For further references on Resources and Industry, see Pt. II, § 7: *Urban and County Development;* also Pt. III, § 2: *Description and Travel,* and the Directories.

4. TRANSPORTATION AND COMMUNICATION

Government Publications and Documents

561. CRAIGHILL, WILLIAM P. The James River and Kanawha canal or central water line of Virginia. Report of the examination and survey of the Kanawha River, from the falls to the Ohio River. By William P. Craighill . . . to the third session of the Forty-second Congress of the U. S. Richmond, Clemmitt & Jones, 1873.

> 12 p. 8°.   **LC**
> p. 4-12: A preliminary report by E. Lorraine.

562. CRAIGHILL, WILLIAM P., *et al.* Reports of the U. S. engineers [William P. Craighill, W. G. Turpin, and W. R. Hutton] on the survey of the James River and Kanawha canal, and on the advantages of the central water line, as a national work. Richmond, Gary, 1871.

> 104 p. 8°.   **V**
> Also pub. as U. S. 41 Cong., 3 sess. House. *Exec. doc.,* 110.

563. CRUMP, W. W. Speech before the Senate Committee on roads and international navigation, on the application of Mr. Reuben

Ragland for an amendment to the charter of the Petersburg railroad company, Feb. 13, 1873. Richmond, Clemmitt & Jones, 1873.

42 p. 8°. **VU**

564. DANIEL, PETER V., jr. Free railroad laws. Argument . . . on Senate bill no. 46, "To authorize the formation of railroad corporations, and to regulate the same." [Richmond, Va.] Clemmitt & Jones [1872]

32 p. 8°. **BRE**
Objections to unrestricted and general laws incorporating railroads in Virginia.

565. DISMAL SWAMP CANAL CO. Annual report . . . [1866—] Norfolk, Va. [1866—

8°. Report year ends Sept. 30. **LC**: 1868, 69.
See also Virginia. Public works, Board of. *Annual report* **[711]**

566. ———. Memorial and other papers of the Dismal Swamp canal company to the Senate and House of representatives of the U. S. . . . Dec., 1877. [n. p., 1877?]

13, 17 p. 12°. **V**

567. DUKE, RICHARD T. The James River and Kanawha canal. Speech . . . in the House of representatives, Feb. 13, 1873. Washington, 1873.

14 p. 8°. **LC, VU, WM**
A plea in behalf of the completion of the canal by means of federal aid; with an historical sketch of the canal and its value to the country as a whole.

568. ELLIS, THOMAS H. Letters from [Thomas H. Ellis] the president of the James River and Kanawha company on the condition and affairs of the company. Richmond, Enquirer, 1867.

43 p. 8°. **V, WM**
Addressed to the Richmond *Enquirer,* in answer to criticisms in the *Times* and *Examiner.*

569. HARAHAN, WILLIAM J. Testimony . . . before the Interstate commerce commission, Dec. 4, 1925, opposing the lease of the Virginia railway to the Norfolk & western railway and giving the reasons therefor. [n. p., 1925]

12 p. 8°. **BRE, ICC**

570. HARRIS, JAMES M. The James River and Kanawha canal. Report on lockage, & cost of construction, and the practicability of locks and dams on the New River. By James M. Harris, engineer and superintendent James River & Kanawha co. Richmond [Va.] Clemmitt & Jones, 1874.

23 p. 8°.   **LC, V**

571. HUGHES, R. W. The Virginia central water-line. Speech of Mr. R. W. Hughes of Virginia, upon the proposed completion of the water-line through that state by the national government, delivered before the Committee on commerce of the House of representatives, Jan. 17, 1873. [n. p., 1873?]

8 p. 8°.   **VU, WM**

572. JAMES RIVER & KANAWHA CO. . . . Annual report of the president and directors to the stockholders . . . 1st-46th; 1835-79/80. Richmond, 1837-80.

tables. 8°. Report year ends in Oct.
32d report is for 1865/66.
BRE: 1867/68-77/78; **V:** 1868/69-73/74, 75/76-77/78; **VU:** 1874/75-77/78; **WM:** 1865/66.
See also: Virginia. Public works, Board of. *Annual report* **[711]**

573. ———. Convict labor on canal repairs; at a meeting of the Board of directors . . . held at the office of the company in Richmond, . . . Dec. 21, 1877 . . . [Richmond? 1878?]

7 p. 8°. No title-page.   **VU**

574. ———. Proceedings of the stockholders . . . Richmond, Va., 1837-80.

8°. (In its *Annual report* **[572]**)

575. ———. Report [to the Board of public works of Virginia by the president of the James River & Kanawha company, Jan. 5, 1867] [n. p., 1867?]

17 p. 8°.   **WM**

576. ———. . . . To the bondholders . . . Office of the James River & Kanawha company, Richmond, Mar. 13, 1878. [Signed: John W. Johnston, president] [n. p., 1878?]

[2] p. 8°. No title-page.   **VU**

577. ———. Transportation to the seaboard. The central route from the Mississippi River to the Atlantic Ocean, by the Ohio, Kanawha and James rivers. Richmond, Clemmitt & Jones, 1874.

55 p. tables. 8°.   **BRE, LC, VU**
Pub. by order of the president and directors of the James River & Kanawha co.

578. JEFFERSON MEMORIAL AND INTERSTATE GOOD ROADS CONVENTION, Charlottesville, Va.   Proceedings of the . . . convention, held at Charlottesville, Va., April 2, 3, and 4, 1902.   Washington, Govt., 1902.

> 60 p. plates (incl. front.) diagr. 8°. (U. S. Dept. of agriculture. Office of public road inquiries.   *Bulletin,* 25)
>
> Martin Dodge, director.

579. JOHNSTON, JOHN W.   Communication to the Board of public interests of the city of Richmond, from John W. Johnston, president, James River & Kanawha company [and] Buchanan & Clifton Forge railway company.   [n. p., 1879]

> 12 p. 8°.   VU
>
> The interest of Richmond in the speedy opening up and development of the James Valley.

580. LORRAINE, E.   The central water-line from the Ohio River to the Virginia capes, connecting the Kanawha and James rivers, affording the shortest outlet of navigation from the Mississippi basin to the Atlantic.   Richmond, Va., Gary & Clemmitt, 1868.

> 95 p. map, tables. 8°.   **BP, BRE, LC, NYP, V, WM**
>
> "Comp. and pub. by order of the president and directors of the James River & Kanawha co., at the request of prominent citizens of the western states."   Shows need of water transportation between East and West for all year traffic.   Contains also a history of the company and the revival of the project after the Civil War.
>
> 2d ed.:   1869.   96 p.   **BP, V, WM**

581. LOUISVILLE, KY. COUNCIL.   NORFOLK COMMITTEE.   Our ocean highway.   The importance of a connection with the Atlantic seaboard and the city of Louisville.   Report of the Norfolk committee [on rail connections] to the General council.   Louisville, Bradley & Gilbert, 1868.

> 12 p. 8°.   **WM**

582. MARYLAND. COURT OF APPEALS.   Opinion of the Court of appeals of Maryland, delivered by Associate Judge Miller, in the case of the commonwealth of Virginia vs. the state of Maryland, the Chesapeake & Ohio canal company and others.   April term, 1870.   Annapolis, Colton, 1870.

> 31 p. 8°   **LC**
>
> Judgment settling the claims of creditors against the Chesapeake & Ohio canal co.

583. NORFOLK, VA. COUNCIL. Charters, franchises, ordinances, resolutions, etc., of various companies composing the Virginia railway
& power company, the Bay shore terminal company, and the Norfolk heat, light & power company. Norfolk, 1912.
8°   H

584. ———. DOCK COMMISSIONERS, Board of. Report on the development of a municipal terminal near Sewall's Point in the port of
Norfolk, by B. F. Cresson, jr. Norfolk, 1917.
47 p. 8°.   H

585. ———. HARBOR COMMISSIONERS. Report . . . [Norfolk?
18—
8°.   V: 1876-78.

586. ———. ——. Rules and regulations for the port of Norfolk
and Portsmouth, and port warden lines of the harbor . . .
Norfolk, Va., Virginian print., 1879.
31 p. 8°.   V

587. OULD, ROBERT. Speech before the Senate Committee on roads
and internal navigation, on the application of Mr. Reuben Ragland
for an amendment to the charter of the Petersburg railroad company, Feb. 15, 1873. Richmond, Clemmitt & Jones, 1873.
30 p. 8°.   NYP, VU

588. PUBLIC ROADS of Virginia: mileage and expenditures in 1904.
Washington, Govt., 1906.
4 p. table. 8°. (U. S. Dept. of agriculture. Bur. of public roads. *Circular*, 44)

589. RICHMOND, VA. Memorial to the Congress of the U. S., asking an appropriation for the removal of obstructions and deepening
the channel of James River, in Virginia. Richmond, Evening state
journal, 1870.
6 p. 8°.   LC, WM
A memorial in behalf of the council and citizens of Richmond, signed
by Wm. C. Dunham and others.

590. ———. COUNCIL. JAMES RIVER IMPROVEMENT COMMITTEE.
Annual report . . . to the Council of the city of Richmond
. . . Richmond [1871?—
tables, diagrs. 8°.
Includes engineer's report, and other documents.
LC: 1878; **NYP**: 1878/79; **V**: 1871, 78; **VU**: 1875, 77, 78.

591. ———. JOINT COMMITTEE OF CITY COUNCIL AND CHAMBER OF COMMERCE. Improvement of the James River, Va.; its value to commerce and necessity as a work of both national and local importance . . . [Richmond, 1899?]

    13 p. 8°.   V

592. ———. PORT COMMISSION. Brief by the Richmond Port commission on the deepening and straightening of the James River at a hearing before Henry C. Jewett, lieut.-col., Corps of engineers, district engineer, at Richmond, Va., on June 6, 1928. [Richmond, 1928]

    1 p. l., 1-38 numb. l., 39-46 numb. l. incl. tables. typew. 4°.   V

593. ———. PUBLIC WORKS, Dept. of. Preliminary survey of the James River harbor, by the Dept. of public works to the City council committee on dock, river, and harbor. Richmond, Va., 1925.

    28 p. plans. 8°.   V

594. TERRY, WILLIAM. James River and Kanawha canal and improvement of New River. Speech . . . in the House of representatives, Feb. 13, 1873 . . . [Washington, Congressional Globe, 1873?]

    7 p. 8°.   WM

595. TOMKINS, CALVIN. Address of Hon. Calvin Tomkins, commissioner of docks of the city of New York, and remarks from others before the Public docks committee, Norfolk City council, July 19, 1912. With map of the port of Norfolk and ordinance creating a "Dock and belt line commission," defining its duties and powers, etc. Printed pursuant to resolution of the Norfolk City council. [Norfolk, 1912]

    1 p. l., 12 p. fold. map. 8°.   LC
    Advice to the City council on how it may best develop the port of Norfolk.

596. U. S. ADVISORY BOARD ON HARBOR OF NORFOLK AND PORTSMOUTH. Report of the U. S. Advisory board, (Commodore Thos. H. Stevens, U. S. N., chairman) upon the subject of improving the harbor of Norfolk and Portsmouth. Norfolk, Va., Landmark, 1877.

    11 p. 8°.   LC

597. ———. CIRCUIT COURT, 4th circuit. East. dist. of Virginia. Argument for the James River & Kanawha company in the suit of

Eugene Davis *et al. v.* James River & Kanawha company and the state of Virginia on the demurrer to the bill in the Circuit court of the city of Richmond. Richmond, 1867.

 16 p. 8°.   **V**
 Signed: Ould & Carrington, of the counsel for the company.
 Suit involving bonds of the company, assumed by the state.

598. U. S. CIRCUIT COURT, 4th circuit. East. dist. of Virginia. Bolling W. Haxall *v.* James River & Kanawha company, Richmond & Alleghany railroad company, *et al.* [Richmond? 1880?]

 26 p. 4°.   **V**
 Involves the transfer of the works, property, and franchise of the James River & Kanawha co. to the railroad.

599. ———. ———. ———. The Southern Bell telephone and telegraph company, appellant, *v.* City of Richmond, appellee. Appeal from Circuit court of the U. S. for the eastern district of Virginia, at Richmond. Transcript of record. Record filed, Mar. 1, 1900. [n. p., 1900?]

 118 p. 8°.   **V**

600. ———. ———. West. dist. of Virginia. . . . Baltimore & Ohio railroad company *v.* S. B. Allen, auditor of public accounts of Virginia, *et al.* Demurrers and answers of defendants. 1883. [n. p., 1883?]

 11 p. 8°.   **V**
 Regarding taxation of and attempted invasion by Winchester & Potomac railroad, Winchester & Strasburg railroad, Strasburg & Harrisonburg railroad, and Valley railroad—all subsidiaries of the Baltimore & Ohio.

601. ———. COMMERCE, Dept. of. SECRETARY, Office of the. AERONAUTICS BRANCH. Airway bulletin . . . Washington, Govt. [192-?—

 8°.   **USC**
 no. 68: Virginia; no. 128: West Point, Va.; no. 189: Richmond, Va. (municipal airport); no. 205: Richmond, Va. (Charles Field); no. 267: Richmond, Va. (Richmond air junction).

602. ———. CONGRESS. HOUSE. COMMERCE, Committee on. The James River and Kanawha canal or central water line of Virginia. Report of the Committee of commerce . . . submitted Feb. 13, 1873. Washington, D. C., Gibson, 1873.

 15 p. 8°.   **LC, WM**
 Proposition of Virginia and West Virginia to turn over this public work to the U. S. for completion.

603. ——. ——. ——. ——. Ship-canal . . . Report . . .
on sundry bills for the construction and improvement of interior
lines of navigation. Feb. 13, 1873. [Washington, 1873?]

28 p. 8°.   **WM**

Includes a report on the James River and Kanawha canal.

604. ——. ——. ——. RIVERS AND HARBORS, Committee on.
Lake Drummond canal. Hearings on the subject of the acquisition of the Lake Drummond (Dismal Swamp) canal, Virginia and
North Carolina. . . . Apr. 14, 1924. Washington, Govt.,
1924.

53 p. 8°. (68 Cong., 1 sess.)   **LC**
S. Wallace Dempsey, N. Y., chairman.

605. ——. ——. SENATE. COMMERCE, Committee on. Dismal
Swamp canal. Hearing before the Committee on commerce, U. S.
Senate . . . Apr. 17, 1912 . . . Washington, Govt., 1912.

48 p. 8°   **LC**
Knute Nelson, chairman.
Concerning the proposition that the U. S. purchase the Dismal
Swamp canal.

606. ——. ——. ——. LIBRARY, Committee on the. . . .
Mount Vernon memorial highway . . . Report. (To accompany S. 1369) . . . [Washington, Govt., 1928]

7 p. incl. tables. 8°. (70 Cong., 1 sess. Senate. *Report,* 469) Calendar
no. 481.   **LC**
Submitted by Mr. Fess.

607. ——. DISTRICT COURT. Georgia. Southern dist. Central
railroad & banking company of Georgia, Richmond & Danville railroad company. Decisions of the U. S. Court for the Southern district of Georgia. Savannah, Ga., Morning news, 1892.

60 p. 8°.   **BRE**
Suit involving the lease of the Central railroad of Georgia by the
Richmond & Danville.

608. ——. ENGINEER DEPT. . . . James River and Kanawha
canal. Letter from the secretary of war, in answer to a resolution
of the House, of Feb. 3, relative to the survey of the James River
and Kanawha canal. [Washington, Govt., 1871]

104 p. 8°. (U. S. 41 Cong., 3 sess., 1870-71. House. *Exec. doc.,* 110)
                                                                        LC, WM
Report of examination of part of western section of the canal and
proposed extension.

609. U. S. ENGINEER DEPT. . . . National road from the Aqueduct bridge to Mount Vernon, Va. Letter from the secretary of war, transmitting, with a letter from the chief of engineers, a report of a survey for a national road from the Aqueduct bridge to Mount Vernon, Va. Washington, Govt., 1890.

19 p. fold. plates (incl. maps) 8°. (U. S. 51 Cong., 1 sess. House. *Exec. doc.,* 106)   **LC**

Report of Lieut. Col. Peter C. Hains, with appended report of B. F. Mackall. Contains charter of the Mount Vernon avenue assocciation, p. 17-19.

610. ———. ———. . . . Newport News Middle Ground Bar, Virginia. Letter from the secretary of war, transmitting, with a letter from the chief of engineers, reports of examination of channel across Newport News Middle Ground Bar, with a view to obtaining a depth of 35 feet and suitable width between Old Point and Newport News, Va. . . . [Washington, Govt., 1910]

17 p. 2 fold. charts. 8°. (61 Cong., 2 sess. House. *Doc.,* 550) **LC, V**

Reports by Majs. J. E. Kuhn and M. M. Patrick, with indorsements by Board of engineers for rivers and harbors. Dated Jan. 17, 1910.

611. ———. ———. . . . Norfolk-Beaufort Inlet waterway, Virginia and North Carolina. Letter from the secretary of war, transmitting, with a letter from the chief of engineers, report of examination and survey of inland waterway from Norfolk, Va., to Beaufort Inlet, N. C. [Washington, Govt., 1906]

20 p. fold. map. 8°. (59 Cong., 2 sess. House. *Doc.,* 84)   **LC**

Report of a special board of engineers, Smith S. Leach, C. A. F. Flagler, and G. P. Howell, accompanied by report of the Board of engineers for rivers and harbors.

612. ———. ———. . . . Norfolk harbor, Virginia, and approaches thereto. Letter from the secretary of war, transmitting, with a letter from the chief of engineers, reports on preliminary examination and survey of Norfolk harbor . . . with a view to obtaining a depth of 35 feet and suitable width from deep water in the sea via Elizabeth River and the Southern Branch to the navy-yard; also between Lamberts Point and Pinners Point . . . also the Southern Branch of the Elizabeth River above the navy-yard . . . [Washington, Govt., 1910]

40 p. 2 fold. charts. 8°. (61 Cong., 2 sess. House. *Doc.,* 551)   **LC**

Reports by Majs. J. E. Kuhn and M. M. Patrick, with indorsements by Board of engineers for rivers and harbors. Dated Jan. 17, 1910.

613. ———. ———. . . . Norfolk harbor, Va., in the vicinity of Craney Isand. Letter from the secretary of war transmitting report from the chief of engineers on preliminary examination and survey of Norfolk harbor, Va., with a view to providing an anchorage basin in the vicinity of Craney Island . . . [Washington, Govt., 1928]

36 p. incl. tables. fold. plate. 8°. (70 Cong., 1 sess. House. *Doc.*, 143)
LC

614. ———. ———. . . . Norfolk harbor, Virginia. Letter from the acting secretary of war, transmitting, with a letter from the chief of engineers, report of examination of the three branches of Elizabeth River at Norfolk Harbor, Virginia. [Washington, Govt., 1906]

8 p. fold. map. 8°. (59 Cong., 1 sess. House. *Doc.*, 373) LC
Contains report of Capt. E. E. Winslow, together with the endorsement of the Board of engineers for rivers and harbors, signed: D. W. Lockwood.

615. ———. ———. . . . Norfolk harbor, Virginia. Letter from the secretary of war, transmitting, with a letter from the chief of engineers, report of examination of Norfolk harbor, Virginia, from deep water in Hampton Roads to the navy-yard. [Washington, Govt., 1906]

10 p. fold. map. 8°. (59 Cong., 1 sess. House. *Doc.*, 381) LC
Contains report of Capt. E. E. Winslow, together with endorsement of Board of engineers for rivers and harbors, signed: R. L. Hoxie. Dated Jan. 17, 1906.

616. ———. ———. . . . Potomac River at Alexandria, Va. Letter from the secretary of war, transmitting, with a letter from the chief of engineers, reports of examination and survey . . . [Washington, Govt., 1908]

8 p. fold. map. 8°. (60 Cong., 2 sess. House. *Doc.*, 1253) LC, V

617. ———. ———. . . . Potomac River at Mount Vernon, Va. Letter from the acting secretary of war, transmitting, with a letter from the chief of engineers, reports of examination and survey of Potomac River at Mount Vernon, Va. . . . [Washington, Govt., 1908]

8 p. 8°. (60 Cong., 1 sess. House. *Doc.*, 654) LC, V
A. Mackenzie, chief of engineers.

618. U. S. ENGINEER DEPT. . . . Report of examination and survey of Nansemond River, Virginia . . . [Washington, Govt., 1909]

    7 p. 8°.   **V**

619. ———. ———. . . . Reports on the construction of the piers of the aqueduct of the Alexandria canal across the Potomac River at Georgetown. Washington, 1873.

    49 p. fold. plates. 4°.   **BP**

620. ———. ———. CHIEF OF ENGINEERS (Brig. Gen. A. A. Humphreys) Annual report upon the improvement of rivers and harbors in Maryland, Virginia, West Virginia, and North Carolina, in charge of William P. Craighill . . . being Appendix F of the Annual report of the Chief of engineers for 1878. Washington, Govt., 1878.

    ix, 445-499 p. 8°.   **LC, VU**

621. ———. ———. ———. Report upon the third subdivision of the central transportation route, from the Ohio or Kanawha River to tide-water in Virginia, in charge of William P. Craighill . . . being Appendix V of the Annual report of the Chief of engineers for 1877. Washington, Govt., 1877.

    671-815 p. 8°.   **VU**

622. ———. ———. RIVERS AND HARBORS, Board of engineers for. . . . The ports of Baltimore, Md., Washington, D. C., and Alexandria, Va. Prepared by the Board of engineers for rivers and harbors, War dept., in co-operation with the U. S. Shipping board. Washington, Govt., 1926.

    xi, 395 p. fold. front., 11 plates, 3 fold. maps, 6 fold. plans, tables, diagrs. 8°. (Port series, 16)   **H, LC, WM**
    At head of title: War dept. Corps of engineers, U. S. Army and U. S. Shipping board.

623. ———. ———. ———. . . . The ports of Norfolk, Portsmouth, and Newport News, Va. Prepared by the Board of engineers for rivers and harbors, War dept. in co-operation with the U. S. Shipping board. Washington, Govt., 1927.

    viii, 282 p. fold. front., 9 plates, fold. map, fold. plans, tables, diagrs. 8°. (Port series, 15)   **H, LC, V, VU, WM**
    At head of title: War dept. Corps of engineers, U. S. Army and U. S. Shipping board.

624. ———. INTERSTATE COMMERCE COMMISSION. . . . [Tentative valuation reports of Virginia railroads to the . . . commission . . . 1921-28]

mimeog. 4°.-f°. Complete files in: **BRE, ICC**

Reports are filed with the governor of Virginia and kept by the State corporation commission.

625. ———. ———. . . . [Valuation reports of Virginia railroads . . . 1918—] Washington, Govt., 1918—

8°. (In its *Report,* vols. 75, 84, 97, 103, 106, 108, 110, 114, 116, 119, 121, 125, 127, 130, 133-135, 137, 141, in progress)

See index to each vol. for cases involving Virginia roads.

626. ———. ———. SAFETY, Bur. of. [Reports of the director of the Bureau of safety upon accidents which occurred on railroads in Virginia . . . Washington [19-?—

mimeog. 4°.; printed 8°. **BRE, ICC**

627. ———. ———. VALUATION, Div. of. Report on the cost of reproduction new and cost of reproduction less depreciation of the Norfolk southern railroad company and leased corporations, *viz.*: the Atlantic & North Carolina railroad company, Carthage & Pinehurst railroad company. [Philadelphia, Presidents' conference committee, 1916]

38 p. fold. map. 8°. **BRE, ICC**

Printed by general secretary for committees' use, but not published.

628. ———. ———. VALUATION ORDER, NO. 20. [Corporate histories of Virginia railroads, sent in response to Valuation order, no. 20 . . . 1916—

typew. var. sizes; some as charts. **BRE**; complete file in: **ICC**

Contain history of organization and operation of each subsidiary and consolidated interstate railroad.

629. ———. RAILROAD ADMINISTRATION. [Agreements between the director general of railroads and the various Virginia railroads . . . 1918-20.

typew. and print. l. 4°. **BRE, ICC**

Filed separately under name of railroad.

630. ———. ———. [Final settlements between the director general of railroads and the various Virginia railroads . . . 1920-24]

print. forms and typed l. 4°. **BRE, ICC**

631. U. S. Railroad administration. . . . Virginian railroad. Rules and regulations of the operating dept. Effective Dec. 1, 1918. [Roanoke, Va., Stone, 1918?]

    1 p. l., 174 p. illus. (part col.) 16°.   **BRE, V**

632. ———. ———. . . . Walker D. Hines, director general of railroads. Richmond, Fredericksburg & Potomac railroad company, and Guaranty trust company of New York, as trustee. Equipment trust agreement. Equipment trust, no. 65. Dated Jan. 15, 1920. [n. p., 1920]

    40 p. 4°.   **BRE**

633. ———. ———. . . . Walker D. Hines, director general of railroads. Washington southern railway company, and Guaranty trust company of New York, as trustee. Equipment trust agreement. Equipment trust, no. 78. Dated Jan. 15, 1920. [n. p., 1920]

    40, 4 p. 8°.   **BRE**
    Amendment of Sept. 1, 1920; 34 p. at end.

634. ———. Supreme court. . . . The City of Richmond, petitioner, v. The Southern Bell telephone & telegraph company . . . Brief for appellee or respondent. [n. p., 1898?]

    100 p. 8°. (Oct. term, 1898)   **V**

635. ———. ———. . . . The Southern Bell telephone & telegraph company v. the City of Richmond . . . Supplemental brief for appellant. [n. p., 1900?]

    12 p. 8°. (Oct. term, 1900)   **V**
    Suit involving the extent of power granted to this public utility by the state.

636. ———.———. . . . State corporation commission of Virginia v. Atlantic coast line railway, the Chesapeake & Ohio railway, the Chesapeake western railway, the Louisville & Nashville railroad, the Norfolk & western railway, and the Southern railway . . . Appeals from Circuit court of U. S. for the Eastern district of Virginia. 6 cases heard together. [n. p., n. d.]

    178 p. 8°. (Oct. term, 1908)   **V**
    Suit in which the railroads challenged the right of the State corporation commission to determine and alter intrastate rates.

637. ———. Treasury dept. . . . Dismal Swamp canal . . . Letter from the secretary of the Treasury in reference to the interest of the government in the Dismal Swamp canal company. [Washington, 1878]

> 89 p. fold. map. 8°. (45 Cong., 2 sess. House. *Exec. Doc.,* 19)   LC
> Includes memorials of the company to Congress, reports, financial statements, etc.; legislation of Virginia, North Carolina, and the U. S. respecting the company.

638. ———. ———. . . . Rules and regulations governing anchorage grounds in Hampton Roads and the harbors of Norfolk and Newport News. June 20, 1918. Washington, Govt., 1918.

> 12 p. incl. map. 4°.   LC

639. ———. WAR DEPT. James River and Kanawha canal. Letter from the Secretary of war . . . [Washington, 1871]

> 104 p. 8°. (41 Cong., 3 sess. House. *Exec. doc.,* 110)   BRE
> Report of survey for completion of the project.

640. ———. ———. Letter from the Secretary of war, transmitting a communication from the Chief of engineers . . . and accompanying copy of report from Lieut. Col. William P. Craighill, Corps of engineers, upon a survey of James River, Virginia. Mar. 31, 1882. [Washington, Govt., 1882]

> 20 p. 8°. (47 Cong., 1 sess., *Exec. doc.,* 147)   V

641. ———. ———. Norfolk harbor, Virginia. Channels in the southern and eastern branches of Elizabeth River. Letter from the Secretary of war . . . Mar. 24, 1924. [Washington, Govt., 1924]

> 27 p. fold. maps. 8°. (68 Cong., 1 sess., *Doc.,* 226)   V

642. ———. ———. . . . Rules and regulations governing anchorage grounds in Hampton Roads and the harbors of Norfolk and Newport News, Virginia, including regulations to govern the use and navigation of said waters by vessels, other than common carriers, carrying explosives. Oct. 18, 1921. Washington, Govt., 1921.

> 14 p. incl. chart. 4°.   LC

643. [101] VIRGINIA. Annual reports of officers, boards, and institutions of . . . Virginia . . . Richmond, Va. [1866-19—

> Include reports of the State highway commissioner, 1906/07—

644. ———. ATTORNEY GENERAL. . . . In the matter of application of the Norfolk & western railway company to acquire con-

trol by lease of the Virginia railway company. Brief on behalf
of the commonwealth of Virginia and its State corporation commission . . . Richmond [1926]

2 p. l., 63 p. 8°.   BRE
At head of title: Before the Interstate commerce commission.
Finance docket, no. 4943.

645. VIRGINIA. AUDITOR. [Blank form of circular letter accompanying a statement, showing the amount of gross income received by
each railroad company as apportioned . . . to defray the . . .
expenses of the office of Railroad commissioner] [Richmond,
1880]

21 p. 4°. No title-page.   NYP

646. ———. ———. Value of property of railroad companies. Nov.
22, 1881. By John E. Massey, auditor of public accounts. [Rich-
mond? 1881?]

fold. table.   V

647. ———. CIRCUIT COURT OF ALBEMARLE. Thomas S. Leath *v.*
Chesapeake & Ohio railway company. October (1902) term of
the Circuit court of Albemarle. Stenographer's transcript.

649 p. typew. small 4°.   V

648. ———. CORPORATION COMMISSION, State. Annual report.
1st- ; 1903— Richmond, 1904—

8°. Report year ends Dec. 31.
Continuation of *Annual report* of Railroad commissioner [712]
BP: 1903, 05-15; **BRE**: 1903-27; **H**: 1903-15; **HB**: 1903-27; **HL**:
1903-28; **LC**: 1903, 05-27; **NYP**: 1903-27; **USAg**: 1913-16, 18-23, 25-27;
USC: 1903-14, 19 (pt. 2), 20, 21 (pt. 2), 22-26; **USG**: 1913-26; **V**: 1903-
28; **VU**: 1903-27; **WM**: 1903-20, 23-27.

649. ———. ———. . . . . Application of the Chesapeake & Potomac telephone company of Virginia for revision of rates. Order and opinion of July 31, 1926. Richmond, Bottom, 1926.

135 p. incl. tables, diagrs. 8°.   V
At head of title: Virginia State corporation commission, Case no. 2557.

650. ———. ———. Circular, no. 1- ; 1903— Richmond, 1903—

8°. no. 28 supersedes no. 8, which supersedes no. 2.
LC: 8 (1911); **NYP**: 28 (1920); **V**: 2 (1903), 8 (1911), 28 (1920);
VU: 28.

651. ———. ———. Constitutional provisions, statutes, and public
regulations governing railroads and other common carriers in

the state of Virginia . . . Comp. and issued by the State
corporation commission. Richmond, 1905—

8°. **BRE**: 1911; **HB**: 1905; **LC**: 1905; **NYP**: 1905; **USM**: 1917; **V**:
1905, 07-08, 10-11, 22.

652. ———. ———. . . . Mileage, class, and commodity rates
applicable to steam railroads in Virginia. As authorized by the
Commission, and in force . . . [Richmond, Bottom, 1910?—

8°. Running title: Freight tariff.
BRE: 1909, 14, 15; **LC**: 1909, 14, 15; **USAg**: 1914; **V**: 1909, 10, 13-14.
Rates for each railroad tabled separately.

653. ———. ———. . . . Mileage freight rates and passenger
rates applicable to steam railroads in Virginia, as authorized by
the Commission and in force Dec. 31, 1912. Richmond, Bottom,
1913.

98 p. 8°.   **V**

654. ———. ———. . . . Mileage freight rates applicable to
steam railroads in Virginia, as authorized by the Commission and
in force Dec. 31, 1915. Richmond, Bottom, 1916.

122 p. 8°.   **V**

655. ———. ———. . . . (Motor vehicle) Annual report . . .
to the State corporation commission . . . for the year ending
Dec. 31 . . . [Richmond, Bottom, 19—

12 p. incl. forms. 4°.   **V**
"This form of annual report is designed for all auto transportation
companies . . ."

656. ———. ———. Opinion and order of the State corporation commission of Virginia in the matter of the motion of the attorney
general of Virginia to increase the assessment for taxation for
1907 upon the roadbeds and tracts of the Atlantic coast line railroad company, the Chesapeake & Ohio railway company, Norfolk
& western railway company, Louisville & Nashville railroad company, Seaboard air line railway, Southern railway company, Wash-
ington-Southern railway company, decided by the commission the
23d day of October, 1907. Richmond, Bottom, 1908.

8 p. 8°.   **V**
Negative decision by the commission.

657. ———. ———. Opinions and orders of the State corporation
commission of Virginia in the proceedings to prescribe a maxi-

mum passenger rate of 2 cents per mile, and proceedings to put
into effect a single uniform freight classification. Decided, April
27, 1907. Richmond, Bottom, 1907.

44 p. 8°.   BRE, V

658. VIRGINIA. CORPORATION COMMISSION, State. [Protest against
the consolidation of the Richmond, Fredericksburg & Potomac railroad company with any other system] April 21, 1922.

1 l. mimeog. 4°.   BRE

659. ———. ———. Rules and regulations relating to storage, demurrage and car service in Virginia. Prepared and prescribed by
the State corporation commission . . . Richmond, Bottom,
1904—

8°.   BRE: 1904, 08; HB: 1904; LC: 1908; NYP: 1908; V: 1908.

660. ———. ———. Schedule of routes and distances from the courthouses in the state of Virginia to the penitentiary, reformatories,
and state hospitals . . . July 1, 1911. Richmond, Bottom,
1911.

47 p. 8°.   V

661. ———. ———. Statement of taxable values of public service
corporations in cities, towns, and counties, as assessed by the
State corporation commission for the year . . . Richmond,
Bottom [190-?—

8°.   LC: 1919; USG: 1919; V: 1907, 16.

662. ———. ———. Statement showing the assessed value of railroad, electric railway and canal property in Virginia, and the tax
extended thereon for the year . . . Richmond, 1888-19—

8°. Comp. by the Board of public works, 1888-1902; by the State corporation commission, 1903—
LC: 1888-1902; V: 1888-1905, 07-11.

663. ———. ———. Statement showing the assessed value of telegraph, telephone, express, steamboat, steamship, and sleeping car
properties in the commonwealth of Virginia, and the tax extended
thereon for the year . . . Richmond, Bottom, 1903—

8°.   LC: 1914; NYP: 1922; V: 1903-11.

664. ———. ———. Statement showing the assessed value of water,
heat, light, and power properties in the commonwealth of Vir-

ginia, and the tax extended thereon for the year . . . Richmond, Bottom [19-?—

    8°.   **V**: 1910.

665. ——. ——. . . . . Tariffs, rules, and classification governing express companies. Prescribed by the State corporation commission of Virginia . . . Richmond, Bottom [190-?—

    4°.   **BRE**: 1908; **V**: 1908, 12, 14, 15.

"Applicable to express traffic between points within the state of Virginia."

666. ——. ——. Virginia classification no. 1. To take effect Oct. 15, 1907. Being a classification of freight applicable to the railroad lines doing business in Virginia, as ordered. Prepared and issued by order of State corporation commission, R. T. Wilson, clerk. Richmond, Mitchell & Hotchkiss, 1907.

    var. pag. 4°.   **BRE, V**

667. ——. ——. Virginia classification no. 1, effective Oct. 1, 1907 (revised to Dec. 31 . . .) Being a classification of freight applicable to the railroad lines doing business in Virginia, as ordered . . . Richmond [1913?—

    var. pag. 4°.   **USAg**: 1915; **BRE**: 1913-14; **V**: 1913-15.

668. ——. ——. Virginia classification no. 1. Supplement no. 2 (including supplement no. 1) - ; 1907— Being a classification of freight applicable to the railroad lines doing business in Virginia, as ordered . . . Richmond, 1907—

    var. pag. 4°.

BRE: 2 (1907); **LC**: 6 (1911); **NYP**: 7 (1912); **V**: 2-9 (1907-15).

Each supplement supersedes wholly, or in part, the preceding one.

669. ——. General assembly. A brief statement of the interest of the commonwealth of Virginia in the Richmond, Fredericksburg & Potomac railroad company and some reasons why the same should continue to have the care and protection of the state. To the governor and members of the General assembly of Virginia, in session, January, 1908. [Richmond? 1908?]

    10 p. 8°.   **V**

Signed: A. R. Holladay, John B. Purcell, Frank W. Christian, committee.

670. ——. ——. Joint resolution memorializing the Interstate commerce commission in regard to a reduction in freight rates. [Richmond? 1922]

[3] p. 4°.   **BRE**
Reprinted in *Congressional record,* LXII, 2661 (Feb. 10, 1922)

671. VIRGINIA. GENERAL ASSEMBLY. Maximum car limit bill. Stenographic report of statement made by representatives of the railway companies in Virginia, and by representatives of the conductors' and brakemen's organizations, at hearings before committees of the General assembly of Virginia, at the 1914 session, on the Maximum car limit bill . . . [Richmond? 1914]

144 p. 8°.   **BRE, LC, V**
The bill as introduced prohibited railway companies from handling more than 50 cars in one freight train.

672. ———. ———. Memorial of the General assembly of Virginia to the Congress of the U. S. relative to water communication between the Atlantic and Mississippi. Richmond, Clemmitt & Jones, 1870.

7, [1] p. 8°.   **H, LC, V, WM**
Proposal to connect the waters of the James and Greenbrier rivers and improve the Greenbrier, New, and Kanawha rivers.

673. ———. ———. HOUSE. ROADS COMMITTEE. Argument delivered Feb. 12, 1904, before House committee on roads and internal navigation . . . , by Egbert G. Leigh, jr., president of the Richmond Chamber of commerce, on house bill no.——— "In relation to the assessment for taxation of the rolling stock of railway corporations." . . . [Richmond? 1904]

16 p. 8°.   **V**

674. ———. ———. ———. ———. Full crew bill. Stenographic report of statements made by representatives of railway companies in Virginia and by representatives of the brakemen's organization at hearings before the Roads committee of the General assembly of Virginia, at the 1914 session, on the full crew bill . . . [Richmond? 1914]

231 p. 8°.   **BRE, V**
The bill as introduced requires railway companies to provide additional employees in train service. Bill was introduced in the Senate, and did not reach the floor of the House.

675. ———. ———. ———. ———. Maximum car limit and full crew bills; statment of N. D. Maher . . . before the Roads committee of the House of delegates, 1914 session of the Virginia legislature. [Roanoke? Va., 1914]

8 p. 8°.   **LC, V**

676. ———. ———. SENATE. Speech made in the Senate of Virginia by Harry F. Byrd on Mar. 20, 1923, on the pay-as-you-go road plan *versus* the bond road plan. Harrisonburg, Va. [n. d.]

15 p. 8°.   **V**

677. ———. GOVERNOR, 1918-22 (Westmoreland Davis). Address of His Excellency, Westmoreland Davis, Governor of Virginia, and the Hon. Rosewell Page, second auditor of Virginia before the convention of the Virginia good roads association, held in Richmond, Va., Jan. 14, 15, and 16, 1919. Richmond, Bottom, 1919.

15 p. 8°.   **V**

678. ———. ———. How to get good roads in Virginia . . . [by Westmoreland Davis] [n. p., 1919?]

14 p. 8°.   **V**

679. ———. HAMPTON ROADS PORT COMMISSION. Hampton Roads, an asset of Virginia. Portsmouth, Va., 1925.

71 p. 8°.   **V**

A clear statement of the significance of this waterway to Virginia; its value as a source of revenue and a factor in national defence. Includes text of duties of the commission.

680. ———. ———. Minutes of public hearing before the . . . commission on: 1. Proposed merger of the Chesapeake & Ohio railway with the Nickel Plate (Van Sweringen) system. 2. Proposed lease of the Virginian railway by the Norfolk & western railway. At Council chamber, Norfolk, Va., June 2, 1925. [n. p., 1925?]

46 p. 8°.   **V**

681. ———. ———. . . . . Report, 1922/23-26 . . . [Portsmouth, Printcraft, 1923-26]

tables, fold. plans. 8°.   **LC:** 1926; **V:** 1922/23, 26.

Succeeded by *State port authority* of Virginia **[710]**

Prior to the first report, a Commission on the development of Hampton Roads issued a report, pub. as *Doc.,* 5, Virginia General assembly, 1922; House of delegates.

682. VIRGINIA. HARBOR COMMISSIONERS, port of Norfolk and Portsmouth, Board of. Harbor commissioners' rules and regulations for the port of Norfolk and Portsmouth, and port warden lines of the harbor . . . Norfolk, 1879.

1 p. l., [3]-31 p. 8°.   **V**

683. ———. ———. Report. 1875/76- [?] Norfolk, 1876- [?]

8°. Report year irreg.
LC: 1875/76-77/78, 79/80-81/82; **V:** 1875/76-77/78.

684. ———. HIGHWAY COMMISSION, State. Annual report . . . 1st- ; 1906/07— Richmond, Bottom, 1907—

plates, fold. maps, fold. diagrs. 8°.
Report year ends Sept. 30.
LC: 1906/07-15/16, 17/18-24/25; **NYP:** 1906/07-07/08, 09/10-10/11, 13/14, 16/17-19/20, 23/25-27/28; **USAg:** 1906/07-18/19, 21/22-24/25; **USC:** 1907/08-10/11; **USG:** 1917/18; **V:** 1906/07-15/16, 17/18-20/21, 22/23-25/27; **VU:** 1920/21-21/22.

685. ———. ———. . . . Bridge specifications. 1926. Richmond, Bottom, 1926.

1 p. l., 185 p. incl. illus., tables. 8°.   **LC, V**

686. ———. ———. Bulletin . . . 1914— Richmond, Bottom, 1914—

8°. monthly?
LC: Aug., 1915; **USAg:** Aug., 1915; **V:** Sept., 1914; Aug., Sept., Dec., 1915; Sept., 1916.

687. ———. ———. . . . General specifications for steel highway bridges. 1909. Richmond, Va., Waddey, 1909.

32 p. 8°.   **USAg, NYP**

688. ———. ———. . . . Numbers and description of routes in the state highway system . . . Oct. 1, 1926. Richmond, 1926.

10 p. 8°.   **V**

689. ———. ———. Virginia state highway commission. Specifications. Jan. 1, 1926. Richmond, Bottom, 1925.

153 p. incl. tables, forms. 8°.   **LC, V**
Hand-book on materials and construction of highways.

690. ———. LAWS, STATUTES, etc. An act in relation to the disposition of the interest of the State in the James River & Kanawha company. Approved, Feb. 12, 1872. [n. p., 1872]

3 p. 8°.   **WM**

691. ——— . ———. An act to amend and re-enact the Act entitled "An Act to incorporate the Virginia canal company, and to transfer the rights and franchises of the James River & Kanawha company thereto," passed Mar. 29, 1861. Approved, Feb. 3, 1866. [n. p., 1866?]

62 p. 8°.   WM

692. ———. ———. An act to authorize the Virginia & Tennessee railroad to borrow money. Passed Jan. 19, 1866. [n. p., 1866?]

12 p. 8°.   BRE

Includes extracts from minutes of the Board of directors.

693. ———. ———. An act to establish a state highway commission together with an act creating the state convict road force. July, 1906. Richmond, 1906.

8 p. 8°.   USAg

694. ———. ———. An act to incorporate the Norfolk & great western railroad company, passed Feb. 6, 1867. [n. p., 1867?]

ii p. 8°.   WM

695. ———. ———. . . . A bill to require the erection, installation, maintenance, and operation by certain railroad companies of automatic warning devices, at certain grade crossings . . . [Richmond? 1922]

4 p. 8°. (Virginia. General assembly. Senate. *Bill,* 241)   BRE

696. ———. ———. Charter of the Farmville & Powhatan railroad company. 1895. [n. p., 1895?]

6 p. 8°.   V

697. ———. ———. Compilation of laws respecting the Richmond & Petersburg railroad co. passed by the General assembly of Virginia. Richmond, Gary, 1874.

38, 4 p. 8°.   BRE

698. ———. ———. A compilation of the statute laws governing common carriers in the state of Virginia, so far as such carriers are subject to the jurisdiction of the Railroad commissioner, and defining the powers and duties of commissioner. Code of 1887 in operation May 1, 1888. Richmond, Goode, 1888.

20 p. 8°.   BRE

699. ———. ———. Extracts from general road laws as enacted by the General assembly, sessions 1904, 1906, 1908, 1910, 1912, and 1914. Richmond, Va. [1914]

56 p. 8°.   USAg

700. VIRGINIA. LAWS, STATUTES, etc. Motor vehicle law. Statutes of Virginia relating to regulation, supervision and control of motor vehicle carriers. Comp. and pub. by the Motor vehicle commissioner with all amendments to June 22, 1926 . . . Richmond, Bottom, 1926.

12 p. 8°.   LC, V

701. ———. ———. Motor vehicle laws of Virginia. Chap. 149-continuing the office of motor vehicle commissioner. Chap. 474-to regulate the operation of vehicles on public highways. As amended by . . . acts of assembly, 1926. Richmond, Bottom, 1926.

51 p. 8°.   V
Ed. of 1928: 47 p.   V

702. ———. ———. Road laws of Virginia, as enacted by the General assembly, session 1904 to . . . , inclusive. Comp. and issued by the State highway commission . . . Richmond, Bottom [1910?—

8°.   NYP: 1904/16, 04/26; V: 1904/10, 04/16, 04/18, 04/22, 04/26.

703. ———. ———. . . . Road laws of . . . Virginia [extracts] Printed by authority of the General assembly. Richmond, O'Bannon, 1888.

16 p. 8°.   V

704. ———. ———. . . . State, state aid, general road, motor, and traffic laws. As enacted by General assembly, sessions 1904 [to] . . . 1926. [Richmond, Bottom, 1926]

169 p. 8°.   LC, V

705. ———. ———. Virginia State highway commission. Laws providing state aid for the permanent improvement of public roads as enacted by the General assembly, sessions 1906, 1908 and 1910. Richmond, Capitol [1910]

20 p. 8°.   V

706. ———. LEGISLATIVE REFERENCE BUREAU. Road laws of the American states. A digest collected by Lewis H. Machen, director of the Legislative reference bureau of Virginia. Richmond, Bottom, 1919.

> 154, p. incl. tables. 8°.   **BP, LC, NYP, V**
> Topical arrangement of laws, by states.

707. ———. MOTOR VEHICLE COMMISSIONER. Annual report. 1924/25. Richmond, 1925.

> tables. 8°. Report year ends June 30.   **LC, V**
> Superseded by *Annual report* of Div. of motor vehicles, Dept. of finance **[709]**

708. ———. ———. List of standard make automobiles, showing style of car, model and weight, for the years 1919-1926 . . . together with tables of license fees on basis of weight . . . Richmond, Bottom, 1926.

> 36 p. 4°.   **V**
> With Supplement, no. 1.

709. ———. MOTOR VEHICLES, Div. of. Annual report. 1st- ; 1925— Richmond, Bottom, 1925—

> 8°.   **V:** 1st, 2d (1925, 27).
> At head of title: Virginia. Dept. of finance. Div. of motor vehicles.
> Continues *Annual report* of Motor vehicle commission **[707]**

710. ———. PORT AUTHORITY, State. Annual report. 1926/27— Richmond, 1928—

> 8°. Report year ends June 30.   **LC, USAg, V:** 1926/27.
> Successor to Hampton Roads port commission **[681]**

711. ———. PUBLIC WORKS, Board of. Annual reports of the internal improvement companies of the state of Virginia, to the Board of public works . . . Richmond, Va. [1816-95?]

> tables. 8°.
> **BP:** 1873; **BRE:** 1866-76; **HB:** 1866-76; **LC:** 1866-76; **NYP:** 1866-76; **V:** 1866-76, 89, 93, 95; **VU:** 1867-76; **WM:** 1867-72.
> For railroad reports after 1876, see Virginia. Railroad commission. *Annual report* **[712]**

712. ———. RAILROAD COMMISSIONER. . . . Annual report of the Railroad commissioner of the state of Virginia. [1st-26th] 1877-1901/02. Richmond, Walker, 1877-1902.

> 26 v. fold. map. 8°. Report year irreg.
> Cont. in the reports of the State corporation commission **[648]**
> **BP:** 1893; **BRE:** 1877-1901/02; **H:** 1877-1901/02; **HB:** 1877-83, 85-1901/02; **HL:** 1877-87, 89-1901/02; **LC:** 1877-1901/02; **McC:** 1878; **NYP:**

1877-1901/02; **USC**: 1880-81, 83-1901/02; **V**: 1877-1901/02; **VU**: 1878-81, 86-87, 89-1901/02; **WM**: 1883-84, 86, 88-89, 91-93, 95-99, 1900-01/02.

713. VIRGINIA. RAILROAD COMMISSIONER. Schedule of routes and distances from each courthouse in each county and city of Virginia to the cities of Richmond, Williamsburg, and Staunton . . . Rev. June 1, 1882. [Richmond, 1882]

23 p. 8°.   **V**

714. ————. SPECIAL COMMITTEE in relation to settlements made with the Chesapeake & Ohio canal co., 1877. Reports of the Special committee . . . by Gen. B. T. Johnson, as attorney for the state of Virginia, and his subsequent settlements with the Board of public works. Richmond, Walker, 1877.

98 p. 8°.   **BRE, ICC, V**
John E. Massey, chairman.

715. ————. SUPREME COURT OF APPEALS. . . . Commonwealth of Virginia v. Richmond & Petersburg railroad company. Petition for rehearing. [Richmond? 1878?]

47 p. 8°.   **BRE**
Concerning the taxation of the railroad company by the state and local governments.

716. ————. ————. . . . Commonwealth of Virginia v. The Richmond, Fredericksburg & Potomac railroad company. Brief of Samuel W. Williams, attorney general for the commonwealth. [Richmond, 1910?] [1]

6 p. 8°.   **V**

Other Source Material

717. ALBEMARLE & CHESAPEAKE CANAL CO. Annual report of the president and board of directors to the stockholders . . . Norfolk, Va. [18-? -19-?]

8°.   **LC**: 1872/73; **NYP**: 1876/77, 99/1900-00/01.

718. ALEXANDRIA & FREDERICKSBURG RAILWAY CO. Annual report to the Interstate commerce commission . . . 1888-90.

3 v. print. forms, MSS. 4°.   **ICC**

---

1. For other briefs, petitions, etc., of cases involving Virginia railroads, see the bound volumes of pamphlets (in **V**) under title *Virginia briefs,* which include railroad lawsuits.

719. ————. Response on behalf of the Alexandria & Fredericksburg
railway company, to the address of Peter V. Daniel, Esq., president of the Richmond, Fredericksburg & Potomac railroad company. [n. p., n. d.]

    11 p. 8°.   **V**

    A sarcastic reply to Pres. Daniel, who opposed the extension of the
road to Richmond.

720. ALEXANDRIA & WASHINGTON RAILWAY CO. Annual report to
the Interstate commerce commission . . . 1888-90.

    3 v. print. forms, MSS. 4°.   **ICC**

    Consolidated into Washington southern railway co., 1890 **[1078-1081]**

721. ALLEGHANY CAR TRUST. Agreement of association. [New
York, 1881?]

    12 p. 8°. Dated Mar. 1, 1881.   **HB**

    Formed "for the purpose of buying, selling and leasing rolling stock to
be sold or leased to the Richmond & Alleghany railroad co. . . ."

722. AMERICAN TELEPHONE & TELEGRAPH CO. Virginia. Constitutional provisions, general statutes and session laws relating to telegraph and telephone corporations. In effect Jan. 1, 1905. . . .
New York, 1905.

    xxxvi, 5-117 p. 8°.   **LC**

723. ASSOCIATED RAILWAYS OF VIRGINIA & THE CAROLINAS. Agreement . . . [n. p., 1887?]

    10 p. 8°.   **BRE, HB**

    Piedmont air line, Atlantic coast line, Seaboard air line, and subsidia-
ries; agreement to regulate competition.

724. ATLANTIC & DANVILLE RAILWAY CO. Annual report to the Interstate commerce commission . . . 1891-19——

    print. forms, MSS. 4°. In progress.   **ICC**

725. ————. Annual report to the stockholders . . . [Norfolk?
188-? -19——

    8°. In progress.   **NYP:** 1895-98.

    Chartered, 1882; re-organized, 1894; leased to Southern railway co.,
1899.

726. ————. . . . Lease [to Southern railway company] For a
term to expire July 1, 1949. [n. p., 1899]

    34 p. 4°. Dated Aug. 31, 1899.   **BRE**

727. ATLANTIC & DANVILLE RAILWAY CO. [Mileage report [1] to the Interstate commerce commission . . . 1890]

print. form, MS. 4°.   ICC

728. ———. Second mortgage. The Atlantic & Danville railway company to the Trust company of America, trustee. Dated Apr. 1, 1903. Norfolk, Va., Barron [1903]

81 p. 8°.   BRE, LC

729. ATLANTIC COAST LINE ASSOCIATION. Annual report to the Interstate commerce commission . . . 1888-99.

12 v. print. forms, MSS. 4°.   ICC
Consolidated into Atlantic coast line railroad co.

730. ———. By-laws for the government of the Atlantic coast line association and the companies forming the same. Adopted May 11, 1887. Richmond, Waddey, 1887.

21, v p. 8°.   V

731. ATLANTIC COAST LINE RAILROAD CO. Annual report to the Interstate commerce commission . . . 1900—

print. forms, MSS. 4°. In progress.   ICC

732. ———. . . . Annual report to the stockholders . . . 1899/1900— Richmond, Va., 1900—

8°. Report year ends June 30, 1899/1900-15/16; Dec. 31, 1916— in progress.
Formed by consolidation of Atlantic coast line railroad co. of Virginia, Norfolk & Carolina railroad co., and others.
1900 is 66th report, continuing series of Atlantic coast line railroad co. of Virginia.
BP: 1902/03, 09/10; **BRE:** 1899/1900-28; **H:** 1901/02-06/07; **HB:** 1901/02-05/06, 07/08-17; **ICC:** 1899/1900-28; **LC:** 1899/1900-26; **NYP:** 1899/1900-14/15, 20-22; **V:** 1901/02-14/15, 19, 21-27.

733. ATLANTIC COAST LINE RAILROAD CO. OF VIRGINIA. Annual report to the stockholders . . . 1898/99. Richmond, 1899.

8°. Report year ends June 30.   BRE, LC, NYP
Formed by consolidation of Richmond & Petersburg railroad co. [899-901] and Petersburg railroad co. [862-863], 1899.

734. ATLANTIC, MISSISSIPPI & OHIO RAILROAD CO. . . . Act of incorporation, meeting of commissioners, joint meeting of stock-

---

1. "Mileage reports" to the I. C. C. from certain intrastate roads are in accordance with the form issued as *Circular,* 11.

holders, and meeting of subscribers . . . Lynchburg, Va. 1870.

24 p. 8°.   **BRE**

735. ———. . . . Annual report of the president and directors . . . 1870/71-80/81. [Lynchburg, Va., 1871-81]

11 v. 8°.

Formed by consolidation of the Norfolk & Petersburg **[823-824]**, the South side **[879]**, and the Virginia & Tennessee railroad companies **[1006]**; sold under foreclosure, 1881, and succeeded by Norfolk & western railroad co. **[841-844]**

ICC: 1872/73, 78/79-79/80; **LC:** 1870/71-73/74, 76/77-79/80; **NYP:** 1871/72-72/73, 77/78-80/81; **V:** 1872/73.

736. AUTOMOBILE CLUB, Richmond. Historical tours of Virginia . . . [Richmond, Whittet & Shepperson, 1925]

80 p. illus. (incl. maps) 4°.   **LC, V, WM**

20 routes outlined, with mileage and points of interest.

737. BALTIMORE & VIRGINIA RAILROAD CO. [Project report [1] to the Interstate commerce commission . . . 1912, 14-18]

print. forms, MSS. 4°.   **ICC**

738. BALTIMORE & VIRGINIA STEAMBOAT CO. Annual report to the Interstate commerce commission . . . 1923—

print. forms, MSS. 4°. In progress.   **ICC**

739. ———. Annual report . . . to the stockholders . . . 1923— [Baltimore? 1923—

8°. In progress.   **ICC:** 1923-25.

Operates certain steamer lines purchased from Maryland, Delaware & Virginia railway co., sold under foreclosure, 1923.

740. BANK OF NORTH AMERICA & TRUST CO. The Virginia railway equipment trust. Series D. Lease of equipment. Dated May 1, 1923. Bank of North America & trust company, as trustee, to the Virginian railway company. Trust agreement . . . [n. p., 1923?]

28 p. 4°.   **HB**

741. BANKERS TRUST CO., New York. . . . Bankers trust company, trustee, with Virginia & southwestern railway company.

---

1. "Project reports" to the I. C. C. from certain roads planned or under construction are in accordance with the form issued as *Circular*, 12.

Contract of conditional sale of equipment. Series E. [n. p., 1911?]

31 p. 8°. Dated Nov. 1, 1911.   BRE, HB

742. BANKERS TRUST CO., New York. . . . Bankers trust company, trustee, with Virginia & southwestern railway company. Contract of conditional sale of equipment. Series F. [n. p., 1913?]

28 p. 8°. Dated June 16, 1913.   BRE

743. BLACKFORD, CHARLES M. Legal history of the Virginia midland railway co., and of the companies which built its lines of road. Being an accurate compilation of the more important laws, decrees, deeds, contracts and other proceedings necessary to a true understanding of its properties, rights, powers, and franchises. . . . Pub. by order of the company. Lynchburg, Va., Bell, 1881.

2 p. l., 240 p. 8°.   BRE, VU

744. [BOOTH, EDWIN G.] Address to the stockholders of the R. F. & P. R. R. co. Richmond, Va., Dec. 12, 1876. [Richmond? 1876?]

xvi, 56 p. 8°.   BRE, VU

"Review and criticism of the Response of the president of the Richmond, Fredericksburg & Potomac R. R. co. to certain resolutions of enquiry adopted by the Senate of Virginia on the 15th of January, 1876 . . ."

745. BOYKIN, MAURY. Plan for projecting an Atlantic coastal trunk line railroad through Norfolk. May 1, 1923. [n. p., 1923]

16 p. map. 8°.   BRE

746. BRAXTON, ALLEN C. The Virginia state corporation commission . . . [Lynchburg? 1904?]

18 p. 8°. Reprint from *Virginia law register,* X, 1 (May, 1904)   V

Importance and value of the commission in state regulation of railroads.

747. BROWN, J. W. One of Virginia's lost opportunities [James River and Kanawha canal. 1911?]

4 p. typew. 4°.   V: Access. no. 88.

Copy of article pub. in Richmond *Times-dispatch,* Feb. 19, 1911.

748. BUCHANAN & CLIFTON FORGE RAILWAY CO. . . . Annual report . . . to the stockholders . . . , together with the proceedings of the stockholders . . . Richmond, Clemmitt & Jones, 1877-78.

2 reports, in 43d and 44th *Annual reports,* respectively, of the James River & Kanawha co. **[572]**
Succeeded by Richmond & Alleghany railroad co. **[868-875]**

749. BYRD, HARRY F. Speech . . . to the Virginia good roads convention at Richmond, Va., Apr. 9, 1925. [n. p., 1925?]

12 p. 8°. **V**
Ways and means of financing the construction of the state highway system during 1926 and 1927.

750. The CASE of the foreign bondholders and the Atlantic, Mississippi & Ohio railroad co.: the answer of the company and accompanying documents; correspondence between Gen. William Mahone, president, and John Collinson, agent of the company; also Gen Mahone's letter to Capt. Tyler, who presided over the meeting of foreign bondholders in London, &c., &c. Richmond, Va., 1876.

69 p. 8°. **VU**

751. CHARLOTTESVILLE & ALBEMARLE RAILWAY CO. Annual report of the president . . . Charlottesville, Va. [1903?—

8°. In progress. **HB:** 1918, 19, 22; **VU:** 1922.
Electric railway; chartered, 1903.

752. CHESAPEAKE & OHIO CANAL CO. Annual report of the president and directors . . . Washington [etc.] 1829-[19-?]

tables (part. fold.) 8°. Report year ends June.
BRE: 1874/75-76/77; **LC:** 1866/67-72/73.

753. ———. Report of the president to the Board of directors . . . Baltimore [18- ? -19-?]

8°. Report year ends Dec. 31. **LC:** 1871.

754. CHESAPEAKE & OHIO RAILWAY CO. Annual report to the Interstate commerce commission . . . 1888-19—

print. forms, MSS. 4°. In progress. **ICC**

755. ———. . . . Annual report . . . to the stockholders . . . 1868/69— Richmond, Va. [1869?-19—

8°. Report year ends June 30. In progress.
Organized as Chesapeake & Ohio railroad co. in 1868; a consolidation of the Virginia central and the Covington & Ohio railroad cos.; reorganized in 1878 as Chesapeake & Ohio railway co.
BP: 1879/80, 82/83, 97/98-99/1900; **BRE:** 1868/69, 72/73-74/75, 76/77-79/80, 82/83, 86/87, 89/90-1927/28; **H:** 1868, 98/99-1909/10, 16/17; **HB:**

1899/1900-16/17, 20/21; **ICC**: 1874/75, 84/85-86/87, 88/89-91/92, 94/95-1927/28; **LC**: 1868/69, 74/75, 80/81, 82/83-86/87, 88/89-1909/10, 15/16; **NYP**: 1870/71, 72/73-73/74, 76/77, 78/79-79/80, 82/83-84/85, 86/87, 88/89-1926/27; **V**: 1888/89-1906/07, 13/14-16/17.

756. CHESAPEAKE & OHIO RAILWAY CO. Central trunk line to, the West. A statement showing the superiority of the Chesapeake & Ohio railroad as a short, constant and economical line of communication between the Atlantic seaboard cities and those of the Ohio and Mississippi valleys and the Pacific coast; with an account of the present condition and prospects of the enterprise. February, 1870. New York, Fisk & Hatch [1870]

    28 p. front. (fold. map) 8°.   **BRE**

757. ———. Chesapeake & Ohio railroad co. A statement of its present condition as presented to the receiver by its officers; also of the character and condition of the suits now pending for the foreclosure of mortgages. [Richmond? Va., 1875?]

    62 p. 8°.   **BRE, V**

758. ———. History of the Chesapeake & Ohio railroad with a map showing its connection with the Pacific railroad, resources of the country, legislation of Virginia and West Virginia. Richmond, Nye, 1868.

    16 p. 8°.   **NYP**

759. ———. Notes on the coal trade of the Chesapeake & Ohio railroad, in its bearing upon the commercial interests of Richmond, Va. 1878. [n. p., 1878?]

    12 p. 8°.   **NYP, VU**

760. CHESAPEAKE & POTOMAC TELEPHONE CO. OF VIRGINIA. Annual report to the Interstate commerce commission . . . 1914—

    print. forms, MSS. 4°. In progress.   **ICC**

761. ———. Annual report . . . to the stockholders . . . [Richmond? 1905?—

    8°. In progress.   **ICC**: 1914-17, 21-28.

    Incorp. in 1905 as Southern Bell telephone & telegraph co. of Virginia; name changed in 1912.

762. COLEMAN, GEORGE P. Address . . . A brief summary of highway construction, by the president of the Virginia good roads association; delivered in Richmond, Va., Sept. 3, 1923. [n. p., 1923?]

8 p. 8°   V
On cover: "Vote for bonds and have good roads now."

763. COMMERCIAL TRUST CO. The Virginian railway equipment trust. Series C. Lease of equipment. Dated Apr. 1, 1920. Commercial trust company to the Virginian railway company. Agreement . . . [n. p., 1920?]

23 p. 4°.   HB

764. CONTINUOUS water line communications between the Mississippi and the Atantic. Memorial of the Louisville and Cincinnati commercial conventions, to the Congress of the U. S., on the opening of a complete system of continuous water communications between the Mississippi River and the Atlantic Ocean. Richmond, Clemmitt & Jones, 1873.

42 p. 8°.   LC, WM
Advantages of water over rail transportation, and of the James River-Kanawha route over the Great Lakes.

765. COVERDALE, W. H., & CO. Traffic report on the Virginian railway. [n. p., 1912?]

36 p. maps, tables, charts. typew. 4°.   HB
Dated Apr. 15, 1912.

766. DANVILLE & NEW RIVER RAILROAD CO. Annual report to the Interstate commerce commission . . . 1888-90.

3 v. print. forms, MSS. 4°.   ICC
Chartered, 1873; operation begun, 1881; purchased by Richmond & Danville railroad co., 1890. **[876-895]**

767. [400] ———. Charter, president's report, resolutions of stockholders, etc. . . . Danville, Va., 1881.

768. DANVILLE & WESTERN RAILWAY CO. Annual report to the Interstate commerce commission . . . 1891-19—

print. forms, MSS. 4°. In progress.   ICC
Reorganization of Danville & New River railroad co. **[766]**; controlled by Southern railway co.

769. DELAWARE, MARYLAND & VIRGINIA RAILROAD CO. Annual report to the Interstate commerce commission . . . 1888-19—

print. forms, MSS. 4°. In progress.   ICC
Incorp. in Del., 1883; controlled by Pennsylvania railroad co. since 1917.

770. DELAWARE, MARYLAND & VIRGINIA RAILROAD CO. Annual report . . . to the stockholders . . . [New York? etc., 188-? -19—

8°. **ICC:** 1921-26 (included in reports of Pennsylvania railroad co.). In progress.

771. DIGGS, ISAAC, *et al.* Virginia corporation digest. A collection of the case and statute law of Virginia on corporations, including railroad, municipal and other corporations, with notes and references. By Isaac Diggs and Ben T. Barret . . . Richmond, Picot, 1907.

2 p. 1., 957 p., 1 1, 142 p. 8°.   **LC**

772. DUNN, A. C. Second report of A. C. Dunn, chief engineer, upon the survey and location of the Richmond & Newport News railway. Richmond, Examiner, 1867.

42 p. 8°.   **BRE, V**

773. EAST TENNESSEE & VIRGINIA RAILROAD CO. Annual report . . . to the stockholders . . . Knoxville, Tenn. [1865-69]
80°.   **BP:** 1866; **LC:** 1866/67.
Consolidated with East Tennessee, Virginia & Georgia railroad co., 1869.

774. EAST TENNESSEE, VIRGINIA & GEORGIA RAILWAY CO. Annual report to the Interstate commerce commission . . . 1888-95.

8 v. print. forms, MSS. 4°.   **ICC**
Merged in Southern railway co. 1894.

775. ———. Annual report . . . to the stockholders . . . [Knoxville, Tenn., 1870-95]

26[?] v. 8°.
Consolidation of East Tennessee & Virginia and East Tennessee & Georgia railroad cos., 1869; reorganized, 1886.
BRE: 1871, 73-74, 76-79, 86-88, 93; **ICC:** 1879, 85-90, 93; **LC:** 1870-80, 84-87, 91-94; **NYP:** 1870, 73, 75-80, 83-86, 93.

776. FARMERS' LOAN & TRUST CO., New York. The Virginian railway equipment trust. Series E. Lease of equipment. Dated July 1, 1925. The Farmers' loan & trust company, as trustee, to the Virginian railway company. Trust agreement . . . [n. p., 1925?]

31 p. 4°.   **HB**

777. FARMVILLE & POWHATAN RAILROAD CO. Annual report to the Interstate commerce commission . . . 1890-1905.

16 v. print. forms. MSS. 4°. ICC

Organized, 1884; sold under foreclosure, 1905, and reorganized as Tidewater & western railroad co.

778. ——. $1,000,000 first consolidated mortgage. 1895. [n. p., 1895?]

24 p. 4°. V

779. FREDERICKSBURG & GORDONSVILLE RAILROAD CO. First mortgage sinking fund gold bonds of the Fredericksburg & Gordonsville railroad company of Virginia. Seven per cent. interest per annum, payable the 1st of May and November, in gold, free from U. S. government tax. Principal payable 30 years from Nov. 1, 1869. New York, Arthur, 1869.

44 p. map. 8°. NYP

780. FREDERICKSBURG & RAPPAHANNOCK RAILROAD CO. [Project report to the Interstate commerce commission . . . 1910, 12]

print. forms, MSS. 4°. ICC

781. FREEMAN, JOHN C. The situation of Richmond and its commercial opportunities; address delivered at the 4th annual convention, Atlantic deeper waterways association. Richmond, Oct. 17-20, 1911. [n. p., 1911?]

9 p. 8°. V.

Significance of the inland waterway project from Maine to Florida, as affecting Richmond.

782. [FRENCH, S. BASSETT] Central water line of Virginia. [Richmond? Va., 1873]

19 p. 8°. LC

Argument in behalf of the James River and Kanawha canal to connect the East and West; water v. rail carriage.

783. GARRETT, JOHN W. Reply of John W. Garrett, president of the Baltimore & Ohio railroad company, to the communication of A. P. Gorman, president of the Chesapeake & Ohio canal company, May 5, 1877. . . . Baltimore, Sun, 1877.

18 p. 8°. LC, VU

784. GORDON, JAMES, & CO. A letter from James Gordon & company of Norfolk, Va., on direct trade between Europe and Norfolk, to Gen. M. W. Ransom of North Carolina. Norfolk, Va., Wilson, 1873.

27 p. 8°.   VU

785. GREAT FALLS & OLD DOMINION RAILROAD CO. Annual report to the Interstate commerce commission . . . 1908-12.

5 v. print. forms, MSS. 4°.   ICC

786. ———. Annual report . . . to the stockholders . . . [Washington, D. C., 1900?—

8°.   LC: 1911.
Electric railway; chartered, 1900; succeeded by Washington & Old Dominion railway co., 1912. **[1073-1074]**
Report for 1911 pub. as U. S. 62 Cong., 2 sess. House. *Doc.*, 507.

788. GUARANTY TRUST CO. OF NEW YORK. Guaranty trust company of New York, trustee, with Virginia & southwestern railway company. Contract of conditional sale of equipment. Series G. Dated Mar. 2, 1914. [n. p., 1914?]

28 p. 8°.   BRE, HB, V

789. [HAMPTON ROADS] Norfolk Ledger-dispatch, vol. 97, no. 127; Dec. 31, 1924. Hampton Roads port development edition. Norfolk, 1924

28 p. illus. f°. With photogravure section.   V

790. HUNSDON, CARY. Virginia's road problem. Mar. 23, 1923. (2d print.) [Richmond ? 1923]

16 p. 8°.   V
Bond issue *v.* pay-as-you-go policy to build state highways, and why the latter is preferable in Virginia.

791. JAMES RIVER IMPROVEMENT CO. Report and documents. Improvement of James River. Jan. 26, 1874. [n. p., 1874?]

22 p. 8°.   VU

792. JOHNSON, LUCIUS E. Address delivered before the Committee on corporations of the Constitutional convention [of Virginia] By Lucius E. Johnson, general manager, Norfolk & western railway. [Roanoke] 1902.

30 p. 8°.   ICC
In opposition to the establishment of the State corporation commission with wide powers over railroad rates, etc.

793. ———. Taxation of the Norfolk & western railway in the state

of Virginia.   A statement for the information of the public, prepared by Lucius E. Johnson, president . . . Roanoke, Va.,
Stone [1915]

    11 p. 8°.   V

794. Loree, L. F.   Report on the Virginian railway.   1912.

    16 p. typew. fold. maps. 4°.   HB

    Dated Mar. 27, 1912, and addressed to the National city bank, Lee
Higginson & co., and Kissel, Kinnicutt & co. Report on route of the
railroad, equipment, and resources of adjacent territory.

795. Lyons, James.   James River and Kanawha canal.   The work's
transcendant importance.   How it shall be completed to the waters
of the Ohio or Kanawha.   The views of Hon. James Lyons, Richmond, Dec. 27, 1872.   [n. p., 1872]

    6 p. 8°.   LC, V

    Written to E. S. Gregory, editor of the Petersburg *Appeal*.

796. McAdams, Thomas B.   Address: "Financing our highways,"
at the annual banquet, 11th annual convention, Virginia good roads
association . . . Richmond, Jan. 19, 1922.   [Richmond?
1922]

    7, [1] p. 8°.   USAg

797. Mahone, William.   [Letter of William Mahone to John
Goode, jr., April 15, 1870. n. p., 1870?]

    18 p. 8°.   WM

    Concerning Mahone's management of the consolidated railroad line
from Norfolk to Bristol, and the rates charged.

798. Maryland, Delaware & Virginia railway co.   Annual report to the Interstate commerce commission . . . 1905-24.

    20 v. print. forms, MSS. 4°.   ICC

799. ———.   Annual report . . . to the stockholders . . .
[n. p., 1905-24]

    20 v. 8°. -4°.   Report year ends Dec. 31.

    Formed by consolidation of the 2 railroads of the same name, in Mary-
land and Delaware; succeeded by the Baltimore & eastern and Maryland
& Delaware coast railroads.

    Operated ferries between Virginia and Maryland.

    BRE: 1905-24; **ICC:** 1905-24; **LC:** 1906, 10, 13; **NYP:** 1905-10, 15,
17-18.

800. MITCHELL, BROADUS. Richmond's transportation facilities: a crisis . . . [Richmond, Va., News-Leader, 1918?]

15 p. 4°.   V

Concerning improvement of the James River from Richmond to its mouth.

801. MEMORIAL of the delegates to the National board of trade on the subject of the James River and Kanawha canal, reported in the Cincinnati Chamber of commerce, and approved March, 1870. Cincinnati, Wrightson, 1870.

11 p. 8°.   WM

802. MONROE, THOMAS M. Remarks of Thomas M. Monroe, of Dubuque, Iowa, before the National board of trade, at its meeting in December, 1868, in the city of Cincinnati, on the subject of continuous water communication between the valley of the Mississippi and the Atlantic seaboard. Richmond, Gary, Clemmitt & Jones, 1869.

24 p. 8°.   WM

803. NATIONAL BOARD OF TRADE. Report of the committee on the National board of trade on a continuous water line of transportation through Virginia. Richmond, Gary, Clemmitt & Jones, 1869.

42 p. incl. tables. 8°.   BP, LC, NYP, WM

Signed by J. J. Porter and others.

Revival and extension of the James River and Kanawha project.

804. NATIONAL CITY CO., New York. The Virginian railway. A few impressions. [New York, 1916?]

21 p. incl. illus. 12°.   BRE

Physical characteristics of the railroad and its handling of coal.

805. ———. The Virginian railway; traffic development and operating economies. New York [1917]

29 p. illus. 8°.   BRE, HB

806. NEW ENGLAND-VIRGINIA CONFERENCE. New England and Virginia. Joint meeting of the 4th annual New England-Virginia conference with the New England council . . . Poland Spring, Maine, and Crawford House, White Mountains, New Hampshire, Sept. 16-18, 1927. [Concord, N. H., Rumford, 1927?]

27 p. 8°.   USC, V, VU

Addresses by: William S. Rossiter, chairman; J. Gordon Bohannan, vice chairman; LeRoy Hodges, Virginia State chamber of commerce.

807. NEWPORT NEWS & HAMPTON RAILWAY, GAS & ELECTRIC CO. Agreement . . . with Pennsylvania company for insurance on lives and granting annuities. Dated Jan. 31, 1916. [n. p., 1916]

   4 p. 8°.   HB

808. ———. Annual report to the Interstate commerce commission . . . 1914-18.

   5 v. print. forms, MSS. 4°.   ICC

809. ———. Annual report . . . to the stockholders . . . [n. p., 1914?—

   8°. In progress.   **BRE:** 1921; **HB:** 1915-23.
   Successor to Newport News & Old Point railway & electric co., 1914.
   [813-815]

810. ———. . . . To Maryland trust company, trustee. First and refunding mortgage. Dated Feb. 2, 1914 . . . Baltimore, King [1914]

   iv, 81 p. 4°.   HB

811. NEWPORT NEWS & OLD POINT RAILWAY & ELECTRIC CO. Annual report to the Interstate commerce commission . . . 1912-14.

   3 v. print. forms, MSS. 4°.   ICC
   Chartered, 1898; succeeded by Newport News & Hampton railway, gas & electric co., 1914. **[807-810]**

812. ———. . . . General mortgage five per cent. 40-year gold bonds. Agreement. Dated Feb. 9, 1909. Alexander Brown & sons, Baltimore; Brown brothers & company, . . . depositaries and committee. New York, Evening Post [1909]

   8 p. 4°.   HB

813. ———. General mortgage. Newport News & Old Point railway & electric company to Maryland trust company, trustee. [n. p., 1901?]

   40 p. 8°.   HB
   Dated Feb. 28, 1901.

814. NEWPORT NEWS & YORKTOWN RAILWAY CO. [Project report to the Interstate commerce commission . . . 1910-11]

   print. forms, MSS. 4°.   ICC

815. NORFOLK, ALBEMARLE & ATLANTIC RAILROAD CO. Annual report to the Interstate commerce commission . . . 1891.

1 v. print. forms, MSS. 4°.   ICC
Reorganized as Norfok, Virginia Beach & southern railroad co., 1896.
[857-858]

816. ———. [Mileage report to the Interstate commerce commission . . . 1892-95]

print. forms, MSS. 4°.   ICC

817. NORFOLK & CAROLINA RAILROAD CO. Annual report to the Interstate commerce commission . . . 1889-94.

6 v. print. forms, MSS. 4°,   ICC
Chartered in 1887 and 1888 as Chowan & southern railroad co.; name changed in 1889; consolidated into Atlantic coast line railroad co., 1899.
[731-732]

818. ———. Annual report . . . to the stockholders . . . 1890/91-98/99. [Norfolk, Va., 1891-99]

9 v. 8°. Report year ends June 30.
LC: 1896/97; **NYP**: 1892/93, 94/95, 96/97, 98/99; **V**: 1890/91-94/95.

819. NORFOLK & CAROLINA TELEPHONE & TELEGRAPH CO. Annual report to the Interstate commerce commission . . . 1914—

print. forms, MSS. 4°. In progress.   ICC
Incorp. in 1902.

820. NORFOLK & GREAT WESTERN RAILROAD CO. Proceedings of the . . . annual meeting of the stockholders . . . [1st- ? ; 1867 - ?] Richmond [1868? - ?]

8°.   **WM**: 3d (1869).
Proceedings for 1869 contain a letter from Com. M. F. Maury.

821. NORFOLK & OCEAN VIEW RAILROAD & HOTEL CO. Annual report to the Interstate commerce commission . . . 1888-89, 91, 93-94.

5 v. print. forms, MSS. 4°.   ICC
Chartered, 1879; reorganized as Norfolk & Ocean View railway co., 1898; merged in Norfolk railway & light co., 1901.

822. ———. [Mileage report to the Interstate commerce commission . . . 1890, 95-1901]

print. forms, MSS. 4°.   ICC

823. NORFOLK & PETERSBURG RAILROAD CO. . . . Annual report
. . . to the stockholders . . . Petersburg, Va. [1859?-70]

8°. BRE: 1869; **V**: 1867; **WM**: 1869.

Chartered, 1851; consolidated into Atlantic, Mississippi & Ohio railroad
co., 1870. **[734-735]**

824. ———. Special report of the president and directors . . .
31 May 1866. Norfolk, Va., Daily Old Dominion, 1866.

iv, 12 p. 8°. **V**

Brief review of past and present conditions of the road, by Pres. William Mahone, with reference to proposed consolidation with the South
side railroad co.

825. NORFOLK & PORTSMOUTH BELT LINE RAILROAD CO. Annual report to the Interstate commerce commission . . . 1899-19—

print. forms, MSS. 4°. In progress. **ICC**

Chartered, 1898.

826. NORFOLK & PORTSMOUTH TRACTION CO. Annual report . . .
to the stockholders . . . [n. p., 1907—

tables, map. 4°. **HB**: 1907-09.

Electric railway. Formed by consolidation of Norfolk, Portsmouth &
Newport News co. (chartered 1900 and 1902) with Port Norfolk electric railway co., and others, 1906.

827. NORFOLK & SOUTHERN RAILROAD CO. Annual report to the Interstate commerce commission . . . 1891-1907.

17 v. print. forms, MSS. 4°. **ICC**

Organized, 1891, as successor to the Norfolk southern and the Albemarle & Pantego railroad cos.; consolidated with others into the Norfolk & southern railway co., 1907.

828. ———. Annual report . . . to the stockholders . . .
[New York, 1891?-1907]

8°. BRE: 1903/04-04/05; **HB**: 1899/1900, 01/02; **ICC**: 1898/99; **LC**:
1893/94, 96/97, 98/99; **NYP**: 1893/94-1901/02, 03/04.

829. ———. First general mortgage five per cent. 50-year gold
bonds. Norfolk & southern railroad company to Guaranty trust
company of New York. First general mortgage, dated Nov. 15,
1904. Supplemental mortgage, dated Nov. 21, 1904. [n. p.,
1904?]

67, 12 p. 4°. **HB**

830. Norfolk & Southern railroad co. First mortgage. Norfolk
& southern railroad company to Atlantic trust company, trustee.
June 2, 1891. Deed of Norfolk, Virginia Beach & southern railroad. [n. p., 1891?]
    40 p. 8°.   HB

831. ———. $1,000,000 Norfolk & southern railroad company first
general mortgage 5 per cent. 50-year gold bonds. Dated July 1,
1904 . . . [Pittsburgh, Elite, 1904?]
    [4] p. 4°.   HB

832. ———. [Organization and title papers. n. p., 1891?]
    232 p. 8°.   BRE

833. Norfolk & southern railway co. Annual report to the Interstate commerce commission . . . 1907-10.
    4 v. print. forms, MSS. 4°.   ICC
    Successor to Norfolk & southern railroad co.; reorganized as Norfolk
southern railroad co., 1910. **[845-851]**

834. ———. Norfolk & southern railway company to Manhattan
trust company, trustee. Collateral trust indenture, securing
$2,750,000, three-year six per cent. collateral trust notes. Dated
Oct. 1, 1907. New York, Evening Post [1907?]
    28 p. 4°.   HB

835. ———. Reorganization committee. . . . Plan and agreement . . . New York, Evening Post [1908]
    12 p. fold. map. 4°.   HB

836. Norfolk & Virginia Beach railroad co. Annual report to
the Interstate commerce commission . . . 1888-90.
    3 v. print. forms, MSS. 4°.   ICC
    Chartered, 1882; consolidated into Norfolk, Albemarle & Atlantic rail-
road co., 1891. **[815-816]**

837. Norfolk & Washington air line railway co. [Project report to the Interstate commerce commission . . . 1906-10]
    print. forms, MSS. 4°.   ICC

838. Norfolk & Washington, D. C. steamboat co. Annual report to the Interstate commerce commission . . . 1915—
    print. forms, MSS. 4°. In progress.   ICC

839. [———.] [Description of route and service between Washington and Norfolk. New York, Mathews-Northrup, 190-?]
    32 p. illus., map. 12°.   H

840. NORFOLK & WESTERN RAILWAY CO. [Agreement, mortgages, etc., 1900—

    Pamps. 8°.-4°.   HB, NYP

841. ———. Annual report to the Interstate commerce commission . . . 1888-19—

    print. forms, MSS. 4°. In progress.   ICC
    Organized, 1881, as successor to the Atlantic, Mississippi & Ohio railroad co. [734-735], with title Norfolk & western railroad co.; reorganized, 1896, as Norfolk & western railway co.

842. ———. Annual report of the board of directors to the shareholders . . . 1st- ; 1881— Philadelphia and New York [1882-19—

    8°.-4°. Report year ends Dec. 31, 1881-96, and 1916— ; ends June 30, 1896/97-1915/16. In progress. Title varies.
    [1st ser.] 1881-95; [2d ser.] 1896-19—
    BP: 1894, 95, 96/97, 98/99, 1900/01-13/14, 15/16-18; **BRE:** 1881-1928; **H:** 1885-86, 91-92, 95-1915/16, 18; **HB:** 1882-1928; **ICC:** 1881-1928; **LC:** 1881-87, 89-1926; **NYP:** 1881-1928; **V:** 1881-1928.

843. ———. Norfolk & western railroad. [Norfolk, Va.? 1882]

    15 p. map. 8°. (Reprint from *Industrial review,* June, 1882)   **BP**

844. ———. The Shenandoah Valley route. [Time table] November, 1896. New York, 1896.

    8°.   **NYP**

845. NORFOLK SOUTHERN RAILROAD CO. Annual report to the Interstate commerce commission . . . 1910—

    print. forms, MSS. 4°. In progress.   ICC
    Chartered, 1910, as successor to the Norfolk & southern railway co. [833-835]

846. ———. Annual report . . . to the stockholders . . . 1st- ; 1910/11— [Norfolk, Va., 1911—

    map. 4°. Report year ends June 30. In progress.
    BRE: 1910/11-27/28; **HB:** 1910/11-27/28; **ICC:** 1910/11-27/28; **LC:** 1910/11-13/14, 16/17; **NYP:** 1910/11-11/12, 13/14-14/15, 21/22-26/27.

847. ———. Circular and plan of organization. Dated May 26, 1890. [n. p., 1890]

    11 p. 8°.   **NYP**

848. ———. Income mortgage. [D. T. Hoag and U. S. Grant, jr.] [n. p., 1881?]

    20 p. 8°. Dated Dec. 31, 1881.   **NYP**

849. NORFOLK SOUTHERN RAILROAD CO. Norfolk southern railroad, Atlantic & North Carolina railroad, Carthage & Pinehurst railroad. Comments on the federal valuation reports. Engineering and land divisions by F. L. Nicholson, chief engineer. [Philadelphia? 1914?]

33 p. 8°.   HB

850. ————. Report on cost of reproduction new and cost of reproduction less depreciation of the Norfolk southern railroad company and leased corporations, *viz.*: the Atlantic & North Carolina railroad company, the Carthage & Pinehurst railroad company. [Philadelphia, Office of General secretary, President's conference committee, 1916]

38 p. map. 8°.   NYP

851. ————. Report on Norfolk southern railroad company and leased lines, Atlantic & North Carolina railroad, Carthage & Pinehurst railroad, as of June 30, 1914. Engineering. [Philadelphia? 1914?]

38 p. fold. map. 8°.   HB

852. NORFOLK TERMINAL & TRANSPORTATION CO. Annual report to the Interstate commerce commission . . . 1926—

print. forms, MSS. 4°. In progress.   ICC
Controlled by the Chesapeake & Ohio railway co.

853. NORFOLK TERMINAL RAILWAY CO. Annual report to the Interstate commerce commission . . . 1912-16, 18—

print. forms, MSS. 4°. In progress.   ICC
Incorp., 1910.

854. ————. Mortgage. Norfolk terminal railway company to Guaranty trust company of New York. Dated May 20, 1911. Operating agreement . . . Supplemental operating agreement . . . [n. p., 1911?]

45, 33, 12 p. fold. map. 8°.   HB

855. ————. [Project report to the Interstate commerce commission . . . 1911]

print. form. MS. 4°.   ICC

856. [NORFOLK TIDEWATER TERMINAL] Agreement between carriers at Norfolk and Norfolk tidewater terminal. [Tentative agreement, June 12, 1925] [Norfolk? 1925]

12 l. mimeog. f°.   BRE

857. NORFOLK, VIRGINIA BEACH & SOUTHERN RAILROAD CO. Annual report to the Interstate commerce commission. . . . 1897-1900.

> 4 v. print. forms, MSS. 4°. ICC
>
> Successor to Norfolk, Albemarle & Atlantic railroad co. **[815-816]**; purchased by and merged in Norfolk & southern railroad co., 1899. **[827-832]**

858. ———. [Mileage report to the Interstate commerce commission . . . 1896]

> print. form, MS. 4°. ICC

859. ORANGE, ALEXANDRIA & MANASSAS RAILROAD CO. Proceedings of the . . . annual meeting of the stockholders . . . 1st-[6th?] 1867-[72?] Alexandria, Va., Gazette, 1867-[72?]

> 6 v. ? 8°. HB: 1st-2d (1867-68).
>
> Formed by consolidation of Orange & Alexandria and the Manassas Gap railroad cos.; consolidated with Lynchburg & Danville railroad co. to form Washington City, Virginia midland & great southern railroad co., 1872. **[1076-1077]**

860. ORANGE & ALEXANDRIA RAILROAD CO. Proceedings of the . . . annual meeting of the stockholders . . . Alexandria, Va., Gazette [185-?-67?]

> 8°. HB, ICC: 1866.
>
> Chartered, 1848; consolidated into Orange, Alexandria & Manassas railroad co., 1867.

861. ORANGE & FREDERICKSBURG RAILROAD CO. Annual report to the Interstate commerce commission . . . 1925-26.

> 2 v. print. forms, MSS. 4°. ICC
>
> Successor to Potomac, Fredericksburg & Piedmont railroad co., 1925; succeeded by Virginia central railway co., 1927. **[1023]**

862. PETERSBURG RAILROAD CO. Annual report to the Interstate commerce commission . . . 1888.

> 1 v. print. forms, MSS. 4°. ICC
>
> Chartered, 1830; consolidated with Richmond & Petersburg railroad co., 1898, **[899-901]** and became Atlantic coast line railroad co. of Virginia, 1899. **[733]**

863. ———. Annual report . . . to the stockholders . . . [n. p., 18-? -98]

> 8°. NYP: 1882-84, 89-98.

864. PETERSBURG TELEPHONE CO. Annual report to the Interstate commerce commission . . . 1914—

    print. forms, MSS. 4°. In progress.   ICC

865. PIEDMONT RAILROAD CO. Proceedings of the stockholders . . . embracing the reports of the president, auditor, and superintendent at their 4th, 5th, and 6th annual meetings . . . Richmond, Gary & Clemmitt, 1867.

    71 p. 8°.   BRE, ICC, NYP
    Chartered, 1862; leased to and virtually owned by the Richmond & Danville railroad co. **[876-895]**

866. PRESIDENT'S CONFERENCE COMMITTEE. Eastern group cost data. Tunnels and subways. Account 5. [Nov. 14, 1916] [n. p., 1916?]

    14 l., incl. fold. table. blue-prints. 4°. (*Eastern group pamphlet,* 66)
                                BRE
    Tunnels on the Virginian railway.

867. PROCEEDINGS of the convention held for establishing direct trade between Norfolk and Liverpool; and for completing the connections of Norfolk with the Ohio and Mississippi rivers, and the Pacific coast, held in the city of Norfolk on the 14th, 15th, and 16th days of October, 1868. Norfolk, Journal, 1868.

    49 p. 8°.   WM

868. RICHMOND & ALLEGHANY RAILROAD CO. Agreement for the reorganization of the Richmond & Alleghany railroad company. Dated Jan. 15, 1885. [n. p., 1885?]

    11 numb. l. 4°.   BRE, HB, NYP

869. ———. Agreement for the reorganization of the Richmond & Alleghany railroad co. Dated Feb. 17, 1885. [n. p., 1885?]

    numb. l. 4°.   NYP

870. ———. Annual report to the Interstate commerce commission . . . 1888-89.

    2 v. print. forms, MSS. 4°.   ICC
    Chartered, 1878; merged into Chesapeake & Ohio railway co., 1890. **[754-755]**

871. ———. Annual report . . . to the stockholders . . . 1st-[9th?] 1880/81-[89?] Richmond, 1881-[90?]

    10 v. 8°. Report year ends Sept. 30.
    BRE: 1880/81, 82/83, 85/86-86/87; **ICC:** 1884/85-87/88; **LC:** 1883/84, 85/86-86/87; **NYP:** 1880/81, 83/84-86/87; **V:** 1880/81.

872. ———. . . . . Bill praying for appointment of receivers, Petitions of receivers, and Orders of Circuit court of the city of Richmond, etc. . . . Richmond [1881]

    409 p. 4°.   NYP

873. ———. Charter, title deeds, and first mortgage of the Richmond & Alleghany railroad company. [New York, Tompkins, 1880?]

    55 p. 8°.   BRE, HB, V
    Mortgage dated Mar. 5, 1880.

874. ———. Henry Whelen and Samuel Shethar, trustees, and Richmond & Alleghany railroad company. Lease and contract. Series B. Dated Sept. 2, 1881. [New York, 1881?]

    10 p. 8°.   HB
    Concerning the lease of rolling-stock by the Alleghany car trust. [721]

875. ———. . . . . Second mortgage. Supplementary mortgage. Contract for consolidation with Ohio central railroad and Atlantic & northwestern railroad. Manchester water power mortgage. New York, Penfield, 1882.

    75, v. p. 8°.   HB

876. RICHMOND & DANVILLE RAILROAD CO. Agreement between the Richmond & Danville railroad company and the Atlanta & Charlotte air-line railway company. Dated Mar. 26, 1881. [n. p., 1881]

    23 p. 8°.   BRE

877. ———. Agreement between the Richmond & Danville railroad company, the Georgia Pacific railway company, and Central trust company of New York, trustee. Dated Dec. 14, 1882. [n. p., 1882?]

    13 p. 8°.   V
    For co-operation in handling the traffic of the two railroads.

878. ———. Agreement between the Richmond & Danville railroad company and the Southern express company. Dated May 29, 1888. [n. p., 1888]

    11 p. 8°.   BRE
    Concerning the control of all express business on the railroad and its subsidiaries.

879. ———. Agreement between the Richmond & Danville railroad company and Union palace car company . . . [n. p., 1889]

    10 p. 8°. Dated Jan. 25, 1889.   BRE

880. RICHMOND & DANVILLE RAILROAD CO.   Annual report to the Interstate commerce commission . . .   1888-94.

> 7 v. print. forms, MSS. 4°.   ICC
> Chartered, 1847; reorganized as part of the Southern railway co., 1894.
> **[981-984]**

881. ———. Annual report . . . to the stockholders . . . [Richmond? 1848?-93?]

> 8°.-4°.   Report year ends Sept. 30.
> 1865/66 is 19th report.
> **BP:** 1868/69; **BRE:** 1865/66-90/91; **HB:** 1867/68, 70/71, 73/74, 75/76-80/81, 90/91; **LC:** 1870/71, 73/74, 75/76-79/80, 82/83, 84/85, 86/87-90/91; **NYP:** 1872/73, 78/79-90/91; **V:** 1873/74-75/76, 78/79, 80/81-83/84, 89/90.

882. ———. Auditor's report . . .   [Richmond? 18-? -93?]

> 8°.   Report year ends Sept. 30.
> **LC:** 1887/88; **V:** 1880/81.

883. ———. By-laws and organization for conducting business of the Richmond & Danville railroad, as approved by the Board of directors, Aug. 18, 1875. Philadelphia [1875]

> 30 p. 8°.   BRE, V

884. ———. Charter of the Richmond & Danville railroad company, Mar. 9, 1847, and subsequent acts of the General assembly of Virginia concerning that company. Richmond, Va., Jones, 1885.

> 42 p. 8°.   BRE, V

885. ———. . . . Consolidated mortgage to Central trust company of New York. Dated Oct. 22, 1886. [n. p., 1886?]

> 23 p. 8°.   HB, NYP, V

886. ———. Cost of transportation. [Appendix to 30th annual report . . . being a supplementary report of the general superintendent, T. M. R. Talcott . . .] Richmond, Clemmitt & Jones, 1878.

> 30 p. tables. 8°.

887. ———. Deed from the Richmond & Danville railroad company to the Central trust company of New York, trustee, dated Feb. 1, 1882, to secure an issue of $4,000,000 of debenture bonds. Richmond, Jones, 1886.

> 15 p. 8°.   V

888. ———. Deed. The Richmond & Danville railroad company to Isaac Davenport, jr., and George B. Roberts. [n. p., 1874?]

15 p. 8°. Dated Oct. 5, 1874. **BRE, HB**

889. ———. Equipment sinking fund five per cent. mortgage of the Richmond & Danville railroad company to the Central trust company of New York, trustee . . . Dated Sept. 3, 1889 . . . [New York? 1889?]

40 p. 8°. **HB**

890. [———.] Lease of the Georgia Pacific railway to the Richmond & Danville railroad company. Dec. 19, 1888. [n. p., 1888?]

29 p. 8°. **V**

891. ———. [Leases and agreements. 1874-91]

bound in 1 v. 8°. **HB**

892. ———. President's report for the year . . . [n. p., 18-? -93?]

8°. Report year ends Sept. 30.

HB: 1876/77-77/78, 79/80, 83/84; **V**: 1880/81.

893. ———. Report of special investigating committee . . . Dec. 8, 1875. [Philadelphia, 1875]

28 p. 8°. **V**

894. ———. The Richmond & Danville railroad company to Central trust company of New York. Supplemental agreement. Consolidated five per cent. gold bonds, secured by mortgage. Dated Oct. 22, 1886. [New York, 1886]

7 p. 8°. **NYP**

895. ———. Sale of the state's interest in the Richmond & Danville railroad company. Report of the committee appointed under a resolution of the House of delegates to examine into the sale and transfer of the state's stock . . . Richmond, Clemmitt & Jones, 1873.

39 p. 8°. **V, VU**

896. RICHMOND & EASTERN RAILWAY CO. [Project report to the Interstate commerce commission . . . 1916-17]

print. forms, MSS. 4°. **ICC**

Project abandoned.

897. RICHMOND & MECKLENBURG RAILROAD CO. Annual report to the Interstate commerce commission . . . 1888-19—

print. forms, MSS. 4°. In progress.   ICC
Chartered, 1880; leased to Southern railway co., 1898— **[981-984]**

898. ———. . . . Richmond & Mecklenburg railroad company to Virginia trust company as trustee. First mortgage . . . [n. p., 1898?]

25 p. 8°. Dated Nov. 1, 1898.   HB

899. RICHMOND & PETERSBURG RAILROAD CO. Annual report to the Interstate commerce commission . . . 1888.

1 v. print. forms, MSS. 4°.   ICC
Chartered, 1836; consolidated with Petersburg railroad co., 1898, **[862-863]** and became Atlantic coast line railroad co. of Virginia, 1899. **[733]** Operated by Atlantic coast line association after 1888. **[729-730]**

900. ———. Annual report . . . to the stockholders . . . [Richmond? 18-?]-98.

8°. **BRE**: 1865-70, 76-79, 89; **ICC**: 1879; **NYP**: 1875-77, 79, 82, 84-86, 90-92, 94-98.

901. ———. Proceedings of the stockholders . . . at their general meeting, and reports made by the president, directors and superintendent, to the stockholders . . . Richmond [1854?-98]

8°. Report year irreg.
LC: 1869, 78/79, 96/97-97/98; **NYP**: 1868, 74; **V**: 1865.

902. RICHMOND & RAPPAHANNOCK RIVER RAILWAY CO. Annual report to the Interstate commerce commission . . . 1914-16.

3 v. print. forms, MSS. 4°.   ICC
Incorp., 1912; dissolved, Dec., 1917.

903. RICHMOND & SOUTHWESTERN RAILWAY CO. . . . Annual report . . . to the stockholders . . . [1st- ; 1898/99?-19—] [n. p., 1899? -19—

tables. 8°. Report year ends June 30. In progress.
HB: 11th-18th (1908/09-15/16).

904. ———. Charters and statutes [issued by Virginia and Kentucky] Boston. Priv. print., 1881.

24 p. 8°.   HB

905. ————. Prospectus and reports upon the Richmond & south-western railway company. [Richmond? Va.] Priv. print., 1880.

25 p. 2 maps (1 fold.) 4°. **BRE, LC**

Includes synopsis of charter, table of comparative distances, reports on natural resources, terminal facilities, etc.

906. RICHMOND & TRANS-ALLEGHANY NARROW GAUGE RAILWAY CO. . . . Charter. Approved Feb. 20, 1874. Richmond, Va., 1874.

8 p. 8°. **V**

907. RICHMOND & WEST POINT TERMINAL RAILWAY & WAREHOUSE CO. Annual report . . . to the stockholders . . . [Richmond? 1881? -93?]

13 v. 8°.-f°. Report year ends Nov. 30.

Chartered, 1880; dissolved, 1894; property acquired by Southern railway co. **[981-984]**

BRE: 1881/82-84/85, 86/87-89/90; **ICC**: 1888/89-89/90; **LC**: 1881/82, 82/83, 86/87-90/91; **NYP**: 1881/82-84/85, 86/87-89/90; **V**: 1889/90.

908. ————. Plan and agreement for the reorganization of the Richmond & West Point terminal railway & warehouse company, Richmond & Danville railroad company and system, East Tennessee, Virginia & Georgia railway company and system. Dated May 1, 1893. Drexel, Morgan & co., depositaries. [n. p.] 1893.

49 p. tables. 4°. **BRE, HB, NYP**

909. ————. Report of the treasurer . . . [Richmond? 18 - ?-93?]

8°. **V**: 1888.

910. ————. Richmond & West Point terminal railway & warehouse company and its subordinate companies, including the Richmond & Danville railroad company and system, East Tennessee, Virginia & Georgia railway company and system. Plan of reorganization as modified. Dated Feb. 20, 1894 . . . [New York, 1894]

15 p. 4°. **BRE, HB, NYP**

911. ————. . . . To all depositors under the plan and agreement for the reorganization of the Richmond & West Point terminal railway & warehouse company, and its subordinate companies, including the Richmond & Danville railroad company and system, East Tennessee, Virginia & Georgia railway company and

system, dated May 1, 1893, with the modification heretofore
adopted. [New York, 1894]

2 l. f°.   NYP

912. RICHMOND & WEST POINT TERMINAL RAILWAY & WAREHOUSE
CO. To the holders of securities of the Richmond & West Point
terminal railway & warehouse company and of its auxiliary corporations. [New York? 1892?]

28 p. l. tables. 4°. Dated Mar. 1, 1892.   HB

913. ———. To the stockholders . . . [April 14, 1888] [New
York, 1888?]

10 p. 8°.   BRE
Ed. of 1887.   V

914. ———. [Trust deeds, agreements, etc., 1874-91]

bound in 1 v. 8°.   HB

915. RICHMOND & YORK RIVER RAILROAD CO. Annual report . . .
to the stockholders . . . [Richmond, 1866-74?]

8°. **BRE**: 1866, 69/70-70/71, 1872/73; **HB**: 1868/69-69/70 (1 rep.);
LC: 1867.
Chartered, 1853; restored after Civil war; succeeded by Richmond,
York River & Chesapeake railroad co., 1874. **[947-949]**

916. ———. Statement by Alexander Dudley, president. Feb. 20,
1868. [Richmond, 1868]

7 p. 8°.   BRE
Showing the present condition and future prospects of the road.

917. RICHMOND CHAMBER OF COMMERCE. Conference for trade expansion with Central and South American countries. Proceedings . . . Richmond, Va., Whittet & Shepperson, 1914—

8°.   USC: 1914.

918. ———. James River from the head of tide to Hampton Roads
as a national waterway. Richmond, Johns, 1886.

12 p. fold. maps, diagr. 8°.   V
Deepening of the James River channel as essential to Richmond's
commerce and industry.

919. RICHMOND, FREDERICKSBURG & POTOMAC RAILROAD CO. Annual report to the Interstate commerce commission . . . 1888-
19—

print. forms, MSS. 4°. In progress.   ICC
Chartered, 1834; controlled by Richmond-Washington co.

920. ———. Annual report . . . [to the stockholders] Richmond [183-?-19—

8°. Report year ends June 30. In progress. Report for 1866 is 34th. Title varies: Annual meeting of the stockholders.

BRE: 1866, 70, 72, 76-77, 79-80, 88-1928; **H**: 1899, 1906-08, 12/13; **HB**: 1866, 67, 91, 93, 97-1928; **ICC**: 1902-28; **LC**: 1876, 78-81, 84-86, 88-89, 91, 93-94, 96-1900, 12/13; **NYP**: 1865-67, 69, 70, 73-89, 91-1900, 04-17; **V**: 1866-67, 75-84, 87-1927; **WM**: 1869.

921. ———. Charter . . . , and other acts in relation to said company. Richmond, Jones, 1881.

31 p. 8°.   NYP

922. ———. Consolidated gold mortgage. The Richmond, Fredericksburg & Potomac railroad company to the Central trust company of New York, trustee. Dated Apr. 1, 1890 . . . [n. p., 1890]

27 p. 8°.   HB

923. ———. Consolidated gold mortgage. The Richmond, Fredericksburg & Potomac railroad company to the Central trust company of New York, trustee. Dated Apr. 1, 1903. [n. p., 1903]

38 p. 8°.   HB

924. ———. Report of the president and directors of the Richmond, Fredericksburg & Potomac railroad company in response to resolutions at an adjourned meeting of the stockholders on Apr. 3, 1878. Richmond, Clemmitt & Jones, 1878.

26 p. 8°.   BRE, V

925. ———. Response of the president of the Richmond, Fredericksburg & Potomac railroad company to certain resolutions of inquiry adopted by the Senate of Virginia on 15 Jan. 1876, in relation to that company, and referred to the Board of public works. [n. p., n. d.]

23 p. 8°.   V

926. ———. Review and criticism of the response of the president of the Richmond, Fredericksburg & Potomac railroad company . . . **[925]** [n. p., n. d.]

56 p. 8°.   V, VU

927. RICHMOND, FREDERICKSBURG & POTOMAC RAILROAD CO. Richmond, Fredericksburg & Potomac railroad; historical and geographical. [n. p., 1912]

17 p. illus., map. 8°.   BRE, HB, V
How the railroad serves eastern Virginia; points of interest along
the route.

928. ———. . . . Rules and regulations governing clerical employees. Effective July 1, 1921. [Richmond, 1921]

14 p. 16°.   BRE

929. ———. Rules governing employees of the Richmond, Fredericksburg & Potomac railroad company and Washington southern railway company. In effect July 1, 1914. Richmond, Adams, 1914.

127 p. illus. 16°.   BRE

930. ———. [Treasurer's report . . . Richmond [18 -?-19—

8°. Report year ends June 30.   NYP: 1891/92.

931. RICHMOND, FREDERICKSBURG & POTOMAC AND RICHMOND & PETERSBURG CONNECTION RAILROAD CO. Annual report to the Interstate commerce commission . . . 1889-1919.

31 v. print. forms, MSS. 4°.   ICC
Chartered, 1866; abandoned, 1919.

932. RICHMOND-NEW YORK STEAMSHIP CO. Annual report to the Interstate commerce commission . . . 1920-25.

5 v. and circular. print. forms, MSS. 4°.   ICC

933. RICHMOND PASSENGER & POWER CO. An ordinance to authorize the construction and operation of a street railway within the limits of the city of Richmond by the Richmond passenger & power co. [n. p., 19-?]

31 p. 8°.   LC
Text of proposed ordinance. The company was chartered in 1900.

934. ———. Richmond passenger & power company to Atlantic trust company. Debenture mortgage. Dated July 1, 1900. New York [1900]

37 p. 4°.   BRE

935. ———. Richmond passenger & power company to Merchants' trust company. Consolidated mortgage. Dated Jan. 1, 1900. New York, Evening Post [1900]

37 p. 4°.   BRE, HB

936. RICHMOND, PETERSBURG & CAROLINA RAILROAD CO. [Mileage report to the Interstate commerce commission . . . 1899]

> print. form, MS. 4°.   **ICC**
> Succeeded by Seaboard air line railway co., 1900. **[964-965]**

937. RICHMOND RAILROAD CLUB. Official proceedings . . . vol. 1- ; 1902— [Richmond, Va., 1902—

> illus., diagrs. 8°. monthly, except June to Aug.
> Meetings suspended in 1917, "until after peace has been declared."
> No more pub.?
> **BRE**: X-XVI (1911-17); **H**: IX, 9; XI, 8-XVI, 5 (1910, 12-17);
> **HB**: IX-X, XII-XVI, 7 (1909-17); **LC**: XII-XIV (1912-15); **NYP**:
> II, 3-9; III, 1, 3-5, 7-9; IV, 2-9; V, 1-3, 5-10; VI, 1-6, 8-9; VIII, 3-9;
> IX-XVI (1903-17); **V**: XI-XIII (1912-14).

938. RICHMOND RAILWAY & ELECTRIC CO. . . . Orders for motormen and conductors of Richmond railway & electric company. Richmond, Va., June 1, 1893. Richmond, Va., Waddey, 1893.

> 27 p. 16°.   **LC**
> At head of title: No. 2.

939. RICHMOND TERMINAL RAILWAY CO. Agreement between Richmond terminal railway company and Atlantic coast line railroad company and Richmond, Fredericksburg & Potomac railroad company and the First national bank of Richmond, Virginia, trustee. For joint use and operation of passenger terminals at Richmond, Virginia. Dated Jan. 1, 1922. [New York, Court, 1922]

> 26 p. 8°.   **BRE**

940. ———. Annual report to the Interstate commerce commission . . . 1919—

> print. forms, MSS. 4°. In progress.   **ICC**
> Incorp., 1916.

941. ———. [Terminal report[1] to the Interstate commerce commission . . . 1918]

> print. form, MS. 4°.   **ICC**

942. ———. . . . Points on which information will be desired at the next general meeting of the above company, to be held in the city of Richmond, on May 31, 1888. New York [1888]

> 20 p. 8°.   **BRE, NYP**
> 13 points concerning the financing of certain Virginia and southern railroads.

---

1. "Terminal reports" to the I. C. C. from certain terminal railroads are in accordance with the form issued as *Circular,* 13.

943. RICHMOND TERMINAL RAILWAY CO. Richmond terminal organization. Extracts from the plan. [New York, 1893]
8 p. tables. 4°. Dated May 1, 1893. **BRE, HB**

944. RICHMOND TRACTION CO., Richmond, Va. [Letter to Middendorf, Oliver & company, Baltimore, Md. Jan. 30, 1900]
3 p. typew. 4°. **HB**
Why the company did not increase its dividend.

945. RICHMOND, WASHINGTON & CHESAPEAKE RAILWAY CO. [Project report to the Interstate commerce commission . . . 1912]
print. form, MS. 4°. **ICC**

946. RICHMOND-WASHINGTON HIGHWAY CORP. Annual report . . . to the stockholders . . . 1st- ; 1913— Richmond [1913?—
4°. **V: 2d (1914).**

947. RICHMOND, YORK RIVER & CHESAPEAKE RAILROAD CO. Annual report to the Interstate commerce commission . . . 1888-94.
7 v. print. forms, MSS. 4°. **ICC**
Successor to Richmond & York River railroad co., 1874 **[915-916]**; consolidated into Southern railway co., 1894. **[981-984]**

948. ———. Annual report . . . to the stockholders . . . [n. p., 1874?-94]
21 v. 8°. **BRE: 1874-76.**

949. ———. To the bondholders and stockholders [in regard to reorganization] [New York, 1894]
3 p. f°. **BRE**

950. ROANOKE & BENT MOUNTAIN RAILWAY CO. [Project report to the Interstate commerce commission . . . 1910-11]
print. forms, MSS. 4°. **ICC**

951. ROANOKE & MOUNT AIRY SOUTHERN RAILROAD CO. [Project report to the Interstate commerce commission . . . 1911-13]
print. forms, MSS. 4°. **ICC**

952. ROANOKE & SOUTHERN RAILWAY CO. Annual report to the Interstate commerce commission . . . 1890-96.
7 v. print. forms, MSS. 4°. **ICC**
Chartered, 1887; merged into Norfolk & western railway co., 1896.
[840-842]

953. ————. First mortgage. Deed of trust or mortgage. The Roanoke & southern railway company to the Mercantile trust & deposit company of Baltimore, trustee. Dated Mar. 16, 1892. Philadelphia, Allen, Lane & Scott [1892]

   54 p. 8°.   **HB, NYP**

954. ROANOKE TELEPHONE CO., Roanoke, Va. Annual report to the Interstate commerce commission . . . 1922.

   1 v. print. forms, MSS. 4°.   **ICC**

955. ROANOKE TRACTION & LIGHT CO. [Circulars . . . 1908?]
   4°.   **HB**
   Chartered, 1908; controls Roanoke railway & electric co.

956. ROARING FORK RAILROAD CO. [Mileage report to the Interstate commerce commission . . . 1907—

   print. forms, MSS. 4°.   **ICC**
   Chartered, 1904.

957. ROBERTS, GEORGE B. Extracts from the testimony of George B. Roberts, president Alexandria & Fredericksburg R. R. co., and from the cross examination of Peter V. Daniel, president Richmond, Fredericksburg & Potomac R. R. co. Phonographically reported by John P. Green. Philadelphia, Helfenstein & Lewis, 1871.

   28 p. 8°.   **BRE**
   Project of getting a through route from the North to southern sea-board cities, via R. F. & P. R. R.

958. ROBINSON, CONWAY. Communication of Aug. 7, 1878, from Conway Robinson, to Moncure Robinson and Thomas A. Biddle, proxies for stockholders in the Richmond, Fredericksburg & Potomac railroad company, residing in Great Britain and Pennsylvania. [n. p., 1878?]

   1 p. l., [19]-28 p. 8°.   **BRE**

959. ————. Views of Conway Robinson upon questions before an adjourned meeting of the stockholders in the Richmond, Fredericksburg & Potomac R. R. co. on the third day of April, 1878. [n. p., 1878]

   11 p. 8°.   **BRE, HB, VU**
   The value of resuming steamboat communication between Washington and Richmond, by the Railroad co.

960. ROBINSON, MONCURE, *et al.* Report of Moncure Robinson and
Thomas A. Biddle, proxies, to stockholders of the Richmond,
Fredericksburg & Potomac railroad company, residing in Great
Britain and Pennsylvania. [Philadelphia? 1878?]

16 p. 8°.   **BRE, VU**

961. RUFFIN, FRANK G. Advantages of the James River in Virginia for shipbuilding . . . Richmond, Waddey, 1883.

26 p. tables. 8°.   **V**
Addressed to the shipbuilders of Glasgow to interest them in developing this industry in the James River.

962. ――――. Petition concerning the Richmond & Alleghany and
the Chesapeake & Ohio railways. To the General assembly of
Virginia. [n. p., n. d.]

7 p. 8°.   **V**
Objections to the railroad rates.

963. RURAL ROAD IMPROVEMENT LEAGUE. Manual . . . [1916]
[n. p., 1916?]

12 p.   **V**
Contains history, constitution, by-laws, etc. Chartered, 1914.

964. SEABOARD AIR LINE RAILWAY CO. Annual report to the Interstate commerce commission . . . 1900―

print. forms, MSS. 4°. In progress.   **ICC**
Successor to Richmond, Petersburg & Carolina railroad co. **[936]**;
merged into Seaboard air line system.

965. ――――. Annual report . . . to the stockholders . . .
1st- ; 1900/01― [Norfolk, etc.] 1901―

tables. 8°. (1904-07); 4°. (1901-03, 08―)
Report year ends June 30. In progress.
BRE: 1900/01-27/28; **H**: 1900/01-15/16; **HB**: 1909/10-13/14; **ICC**:
1900/01-27/28; **LC**: 1900/01-15/16; **NYP**: 1900/01-15/16; **V**: 1906/07.

966. SEABOARD & ROANOKE RAILROAD CO. Annual report to the Interstate commerce commission . . . 1888-1900.

13 v. print. forms, MSS. 4°.   **ICC**
Formed, 1849, by consolidation of Seaboard & Roanoke railroad co.
of Virginia with Roanoke railroad co. of North Carolina; consolidated
into Seaboard air line railway co., 1900.

967. SEAY, GEORGE J. The railroads and the people; address . . .
before the Richmond Chamber of commerce, Mar. 25, 1909. Richmond, Va. [1909]

31 p. 8°.   **V**

968. SEGAR, JOSEPH. Letter . . . [to Col. B. M. Joncs, chief engineer, Norfolk & great western railroad] on the great thoroughfares and their national aspects. Oct. 1, 1868. [Richmond? 1868?]

    8 p. 8°.   **WM**
    Reprint from Richmond *Whig,* Dec. 2, 1868.

969. SHAW, C. P. Address on the question of good county roads; delivered at the annual meeting of the Virginia Board of trade, Roanoke, Va., Aug. 30-31, 1905 . . . Richmond, Whittet & Shepperson, 1905.

    11 p. 8°.   **V**
    Reveals the backwardness of Virginia's highway policy.

970. SHENANDOAH IRON & COAL CO.'S RAILROAD. [Mileage report to the Interstate commerce commission . . . 1908-16]

    print. forms, MSS. 4°.   **ICC**

971. ——. [Project report to the Interstate commerce commission . . . 1906]

    print. form, MS. 4°.   **ICC**

972. SHENANDOAH LUMBER CO.'S RAILROAD. [Project report to the Interstate commerce commission . . . 1907]

    print. form, MS. 4°.   ·   **ICC**
    Charter dissolved.

973. SHENANDOAH VALLEY RAILROAD CO. Agreement between the Pennsylvania railroad company, the Cumberland Valley railroad company, the Shenandoah Valley railroad company. Dated June 13, 1883. For interchange of traffic, etc. Philadelphia, Allen, Lane & Scott, 1883.

    9 p. 8°.   **NYP**

974. ——. Annual report to the Interstate commerce commission . . . 1888-91.

    3 v. print. forms, MSS. 4°.   **ICC**
    Chartered, 1867; merged into Norfolk & western railroad co., 1890.
    [841-844]

975. ——. Annual report . . . to the stockholders . . . [1st-10th? 1881-90?] Philadelphia, 1882-[90?]

    10 v. 8°. **BRE:** 1884, 86; **ICC:** 1883, 87; **LC:** 1884; **NYP:** 1884-86.

976. SHENANDOAH VALLEY RAILROAD CO. First mortgage bonds of the Shenandoah Valley railroad (Valley division) . . . General information of the character and resources of the country traversed by the road. Philadelphia, Times, 1879.

50 p. illus. 8°.   HB

977. ———. Plan and agreement appointing purchasing committee for the reorganization of the Shenandoah Valley railroad. Dated Aug. 5, 1890. [n. p., 1890]

17 p. 8°.   HB

978. SMITH, HENRY C. Pilotage . . . [Articles by Dr. Henry Clay Smith in answer to critics of the Pilot association and the Hampton Roads commission. Crewe, Va.? 1921?]

3 nos. Reprints from *Nottoway record*, Crewe, Va., Oct. 14, Nov. 11, Dec. 9, 1921.
Directed especially against Gov. Westmoreland Davis, Rep. Ewell, and the *Southern planter*.

979. SOUTH SIDE RAILROAD CO. . . . Annual report . . . to the stockholders . . . Petersburg, Va. [185-? -70?]

8°.   **BRE:** 1869; **NYP:** 1869; **V:** 1866-67; **WM:** 1869.
17th report is for 1866.
Consolidated into Atlantic, Mississippi & Ohio railroad co., 1870.
[734-735]

980. SOUTHALL, JAMES C. Cheap transportation. Delivered before the American cheap transportation association, in Richmond, Virginia, Dec. 2, 1874 . . . Richmond, Clemmitt & Jones, 1875.

39 p. 8°.   LC
The James River and Kanawha canal route as a path of cheap transportation; a plea to finish the work, by means of federal aid.

981. SOUTHERN RAILWAY CO. Annual report to the Interstate commerce commission . . . 1895-19—

print. forms, MSS. 4°. In progress.   ICC
Chartered, 1894, as successor to Richmond & West Point terminal railway & warehouse co. **[907-914]**

982. ———. . . . Annual report . . . to the stockholders . . . 1st- ; 1894/95— [Washington, D. C., 1895—

8°. Report year ends June 30, 1895-1917; Dec. 31, 1918— ; in progress.
BP: 1904/05, 06/07-10/11, 12/13, 14/15; **BRE:** 1894/95-1928; **H:** 1894/95-1928; **HB:** 1909/10-16/17, 18-21; **ICC:** 1894/95-1928; **LC:** 1894/95-1919, 21-26; **NYP:** 1894/95-1928; **V:** 1895/96-1910/11, 13/14-16/17; **WL:** 1894/95-97/98, 99/1900, 01/02-11/12, 13/14, 15/16-16/17, 18.

983. ———. Component railways of the Southern system in Virginia. [May 1, 1922]

1 p. typew. 4°.   **BRE**

984. ———. Proceedings at the . . . annual meeting of the stockholders. 1st- ; 1894-19— [Richmond, 1894-19—

4°. In progress.   **BRE**: 1914; **LC**: 1914, 28.

985. The SOUTHSIDE consolidation act . . . one line, one railroad, one company, one management from the seaboard to Cumberland Gap; papers, letters, and speeches . . . relating to the measure. Richmond, Nye, 1867.

35 p. maps. 8°.   **HB, V**

986. STEVENS, JOHN G. Report on the Richmond & Alleghany railroad company . . . [New York, 1881?]

40 p. 8°. Dated Dec. 21, 1880.   **HB**
Information on the present condition and future prospects of the railroad.

987. SWEM, EARL G., comp. [Annual reports of turnpike companies, railroads, electric lines, canals, steamboat lines, and telegraph companies, operating in Virginia, as reported to the Virginia Board of public works, the Railroad commissioner, and the State corporation commission, 1865-19—

p. 1023-1044. 8°. (In his *Bibliography of Virginia*, II [36])

988. [TAZEWELL COUNTY, VA.] County bond issues for road improvement. Correspondence between Messrs. George E. St. Clair, L. E. Johnson, and D. H. Barger, relative to county bond issues for road improvement, originating from letter written by Mr. St. Clair to Mr. Johnson . . . [n. p., 1911?]

33 p. 8°.   **USAg**

989. [———.] Tazewell County. Road bond issue [of] $625,000. [Tazewell, Va., Clinch Valley news, 1911]

8 p. 12°.   **VU**
Contains official statement of resources of the county, the form of bonds, and authority for their issue.

990. TECHNICAL ADVISORY CORP., New York. Report of investigation with reference to improving the James River, submitted to the Committee on dock, river, and harbor of the Common council

acting for the city of Richmond, Va. [pt. 1]   Technical advisory
corporation, consulting engineers, New York.   [n. p., 1924]

182 p. plates, maps, fold. plans, tables, diagrs. 8°.   **V, VU**
In 5 parts, each with separate title-page: Pt. 2: Report of investigations with reference to new industries for Richmond. Pt. 3: Report
. . . with reference to Richmond's industrial advantages. Pt. 4: Report . . . with reference to Richmond's industrial handicaps. Pt.
5: Report . . . with reference to Richmond's industrial possibilities; a plan for industrial improvement.

991. THE TIMES-DISPATCH, Richmond, Va. A menace to Virginia's
commerce . . . 1922. [Richmond, 1922]

23 p.   **V**
Proposed revision of freight rates in the South: general advance in
rates to and from Virginia points.

992. VALLEY RAILROAD CO. Annual report to the Interstate commerce commission . . . 1888-1909.

22 v. print. forms, MSS. 4°.   **ICC**
Chartered, 1866; controlled by Baltimore & Ohio railroad co.

993. ———. . . . Annual report . . . to the stockholders
. . . 1st-[?] 1871/72-[19-?]   Salem, Va. [etc.] 1872-
[19-?]

8°. Report year ends Sept. 30.
ICC: 1872/73; **LC**: 1871/72-72/73.

994. VIRGINIA AIR LINE RAILWAY CO. Annual report to the Interstate commerce commission . . . 1908-12.

5 v. print. forms, MSS. 4°.   **ICC**
Chartered, 1906; merged into Chesapeake & Ohio railway co. [754-
759]

995. ———. [Project report to the Interstate commerce commission
. . . 1907]

print. form, MS. 4°.   **ICC**

996. ———. Virginia air line railway company to the Franklin
trust company. First mortgage. Dated May 1, 1907. New
York, Burgoyne [1907]

42 p. 8°.   **BRE**

997. VIRGINIA & CAROLINA COAST RAILROAD CO. Annual report to
the Interstate commerce commission . . . 1906-07.

2 v. print. forms, MSS. 4°.   **ICC**
Formed by consolidation of Suffolk & Carolina railway co. with oth-

ers, 1905; consolidated with Norfolk & southern railroad co. **[827-832]** and others, to form Norfolk & southern railway co. **[833-835]**

998. ———. Statement . . . Rudolphe Kleybolte & company, bankers . . . [New York? 1905]

8 p. map. 4°.   **BRE**
Financial aspects of the incorporation of the road; also its timber resources.

999. The VIRGINIA & KENTUCKY RAILROAD, connecting Bristol-Goodson with Cumberland Gap. Its value as part of a through line of railway from the power waters of the Ohio and the central waters of the Mississippi rivers, to the Virginia seaboard: and to the industrial interests of Virginia . . . By Robert W. Hughes, president of the company . . . [n. p., 1867]

14 p. 8°.   **HB**

1000. VIRGINIA & KENTUCKY RAILWAY CO. Annual report to the Interstate commerce commission . . . 1907-16.

10 v. print. forms, MSS. 4°.   **ICC**
Chartered, 1892, as Gladeville railroad co.; name changed to above, 1902; receivership appointed, 1914.

1001. ———. [Mileage report to the Interstate commerce commission . . . 1903-05]

print. forms, MSS. 4°.   **ICC**

1002. VIRGINIA & SOUTHWESTERN RAILWAY CO. Annual report to the Interstate commerce commission . . . 1899-19—

print. forms, MSS. 4°. In progress.   **ICC**
Chartered, 1899; control acquired by Southern railway co., 1906. **[981-984]**

1003. ———. Annual report . . . to the stockholders . . . 1st- ; [1899?-19—] [Washington, D. C.? 1899?-19—

8°. Report year ends June 30. In progress.
Reports for 1902/03-04/05 pub. with *Annual reports* of the Virginia iron, coal & coke co. **[513]**
BRE: 1902/03-04/05, 08/09-15/16; **ICC:** 1908/09-16/17; **LC:** 1910/11, 12/13-15/16; **NYP:** 1904/05, 08/09-15/16.

1004. ———. . . . Mortgage, $2,000,000. Morton trust company, trustee. Dated Sept. 18, 1902 . . . [New York, 1902]

29 p. 8°.   **BRE**

1005. VIRGINIA & SOUTHWESTERN RAILWAY CO. . . . Virginia & southwestern railway company to the Standard trust company of New York, trustee. First consolidated mortgage. [New York, 1908?]

50 p. 4°. Dated Apr. 29, 1908.   HB

1006. VIRGINIA & TENNESSEE RAILROAD CO. Annual report of the president and directors . . . Lynchburg, Va. [1849?-70]

tables (part fold.) 8°. Report year ends Sept. 30.
Chartered, 1849; consolidated, 1870, with Atlantic, Mississippi & Ohio railroad co. **[734-735]**
BRE: 1865, 68/69; **LC:** 1868/69; **NYP:** 1868/69; **V:** 1869/70; **WM:** 1868/69.

1007. ———. President's report . . . Lynchburg [18-? -70?]

8°.   WM: 1868 & suppl.

1008.. VIRGINIA & TENNESSEE TELEPHONE CO. Annual report to the Interstate commerce commission . . . 1915-16.

2 v. print. forms, MSS. 4°.   ICC
Merged into Chesapeake & Potomac telephone co. of Virginia. **[760-761]**

1009. VIRGINIA ANTHRACITE COAL & RAILWAY CO. Annual report to the Interstate commerce commission . . . 1909-11.

3 v. print. forms, MSS. 4°.   ICC
Chartered, 1902; merged into Norfolk & western railway co., 1911. **[840-842]**

1010. ———. [Mileage report to the Interstate commerce commission . . . 1904-06, 08]

print. forms, MSS. 4°.   ICC

1011. VIRGINIA BLUE RIDGE RAILWAY CO. [Mileage report to the Interstate commerce commission . . . 1916—

print. forms, MSS. 4°.   ICC

1012. ———. [Project report to the Interstate commerce commission . . . 1915]

print. form, MS. 4°.   ICC

1013. VIRGINIA CAR SERVICE ASSOCIATION. . . . Annual report for the fiscal year . . . [1st- ; 1890/91?—] [Richmond, Va.? 1891?-19—

8°. Report year ends June 30.
ICC: 16th-17th (1905/06-06/07); **V:** 13th (1902/03).

1014. ———. . . . Hand-book, 1907. Richmond, Va., 1907.

45 p. 8°.   ICC

1015. ———. . . . Revised car service rules. Effective Dec. 15, 1902. Superseding all previous car service rules and instructions to agents. Richmond, Dietz, 1902.

15 p. 16°.   V

1016. VIRGINIA-CAROLINA & SOUTHERN RAILWAY CO. Annual report to the Interstate commerce commission . . . 1909-12.

4 v. print. forms, MSS. 4°.   ICC
Merged into Virginia-Carolina railway co., 1912.

1017. ———. [Project report to the Interstate commerce commission . . . 1906-07]

print. forms, MSS. 4°.   ICC

1018. VIRGINIA-CAROLINA RAILWAY CO. Annual report to the Interstate commerce commission . . . 1901-19.

19 v. print. forms, MSS. 4°.   ICC
Chartered, 1900; merged into Norfolk & western railway co., 1919.
[840-842]

1019. ———. [Project report to the Interstate commerce commission . . . 1898, 1900]

print. forms, MSS. 4°.   ICC

1020. VIRGINIA CENTRAL RAILROAD CO. . . . Annual report . . . to the stockholders . . . Richmond, Va. [1836?-68]

32 v., ? 8°. 31st report is for 1866.
BRE: 1866-67; **NYP**: 1867; **V**: 1866.
Chartered, 1836, as Louisa railroad co.; consolidated with Covington & Ohio railroad co., 1868, to form Chesapeake & Ohio railroad co. **[755-758]**

1021. ———. Contract of the Virginia central railroad company for completing the Covington & Ohio railroad. Richmond, 1867.

7 p. 8°.   BRE

1022. ———. Proceedings of the called meeting of the stockholders . . . held in . . . Richmond, May 22, 1867. Richmond, Enquirer, 1867.

16 p. 8°.   V

1023. Virginia central railway co. Annual report to the Interstate commerce commission . . . 1927—
> print. forms, MSS. 4°. In progress.   ICC
> Successor to Orange & Fredericksburg railroad co., 1927. **[861]**

1024. Virginia claim conference. Freight claims. Suggestions
of interest to the shipping public. [n. p.] Virginia claim conference, 1910.
> 7 p. illus. 8°.   ICC

1025. Virginia electric & power co. Annual report to the stockholders . . . [Richmond, 1925—
> 8°. In progress.   **BRE:** 1925; **V:** 1925-26.
> Successor to Virginia railway & power co., 1925. **[1046-1049]**

1026. [507] Virginia electric railway & development co.
James River construction company . . . Richmond, 1899.

1027. Virginia good roads association. Questions and answers
on highway financing, construction, and maintenance. [n. p.,
n. d.]
> 14 p. 8°.   V
> The state's road program for 1924-25 and plans for the years immedi-
> ately following.

1028. ———. Report of committee on legislation, adopted by the
State good roads convention, held in Richmond, Va., Oct. 10 and
11, 1895. [Washington, Govt., 1895]
> 6 p. 8°. (U. S. Dept. of agriculture. Office of road inquiry. *Circular,*
> 18)   **USAg**
> State highway program proposed.

1029. Virginia good roads convention, Richmond, Va. . . .
Proceedings of the . . . convention, held in Richmond, Virginia, Oct. 18, 1894 . . . Washington, Govt., 1895.
> 62 p. 8°. (U. S. Dept. of agriculture. Office of road inquiry. *Bulletin,*
> 11)   **BP, NYP, USAg, V**

1030. ———. Programme of the Virginia good roads convention
held in Richmond . . . Oct. 18, 1894. Roanoke, 1894.
> 38 p. 8°.   **USAg**

1031. Virginia historic highway association. Bulletin, vol. 1,
no. 1- ; 1924— Lynchburg, Va., 1924—
> 8°.   **V: I-**

1032. VIRGINIA LUMBER & BOX CAR CO.'S RAILROAD. [Mileage report to the Interstate commerce commission . . . 1918-28]

    print. forms, MSS. 4°.   **ICC**
    Abandoned, 1928.

1033. ———. [Project report to the Interstate commerce commission . . . 1916-17]

    print. forms, MSS. 4°.   **ICC**

1034. VIRGINIA MIDLAND RAILWAY CO. Annual report to the Interstate commerce commission . . . 1888-98.

    11 v. print. forms, MSS. 4°.   **ICC**
    Formed, 1881, as successor to Washington City, Virginia midland & great southern railroad co. **[1076-1077]** and controlled by Richmond & Danville railroad co. **[876-895]**; merged into Southern railway co., 1898. **[981-984]**

1035. ———. Annual report . . . to the stockholders . . . [Alexandria, Va.? 1881-98]

    18 v. 8°. Report year ends Sept. 30.
    BRE: 1881, 83/84-84/85; **ICC**: 1881-85/86; **LC**: 1884/85; **NYP**: 1881-84/85.

1036. ———. Proceedings of the . . . annual meeting of the stockholders . . . 1st-[18th?] 1881-[98?] Alexandria, Va., Gazette, 1881-[98?]

    18 v. 8°.   **LC, NYP**: 1881-84.

1037. ———. Report to the stockholders of the Virginia midland railway company, reorganized by consent and agreement of creditors of each class. Feb. 1, 1881. [Alexandria, Va., Gazette, 1881]

    126, 80 p. front. (fold. map) 8°.   **BRE, HB, LC**
    Includes proceedings of first general meeting of stockholders, report on physical condition of the road, and statement of liabilities.

1038. ———. Virginia midland railway company to Central trust company of New York. General mortgage. Dated Apr. 15, 1886. [n. p., 1886?]

    15 p. 8°.   **HB**

1039. ———. The Virginia midland railway company to the Central trust company of New York, trustee. Income mortgage and deed of trust. Dated Nov. 29, 1881. New York, Francis & Lutrel, 1881.

    23 l. 4°.   **NYP**

1040. VIRGINIA MIDLAND RAILWAY CO. The Virginia midland railway company to Robert T. Baldwin, J. Wilcox Brown, and Robert Garrett, trustees. Serial mortgage . . . [n. p., 1881?]

41 p. 8°. Dated Mar. 1, 1881.   HB

1041. VIRGINIA NORTHERN DEVELOPMENT & RAILROAD CO. [Project report to the Interstate commerce commission . . . 1900]

print. form, MS. 4°.   ICC

1042. VIRGINIA NORTHERN RAILROAD CO. [Mileage report to the Interstate commerce commission . . . 1904-06]

print. forms, MSS. 4°.   ICC
Road abandoned and rails taken up.

1043. VIRGINIA ORE & LUMBER CO.'S RAILROAD. [Mileage report to the Interstate commerce commission . . . 1906, 08-16]

print. forms, MSS. 4°.   ICC
Official name of the company: Fayerdale ore & lumber corp.

1044. VIRGINIA PASSENGER & POWER CO. Annual report of the president, board of directors and stockholders . . . [Richmond, Va., 190-? -09?]

fold. map, 8°. Report year ends Dec. 31.   V: 1903.
Public utility company of Richmond and Manchester; chartered, 190-?; succeeded by Virginia railway & power co. **[1046-1049]**

1045. [VIRGINIA PILOT ASSOCIATION] The Virginia pilots, their relation and value to commerce, the ports and commonwealth during peace and war . . . [Norfolk, Va., 1922]

1 p. l., [140] p. 8°.   V

1046. VIRGINIA RAILWAY & POWER CO. Annual report . . . to the stockholders . . . Richmond, Fergusson, 1910-25.

15 v. 4°. Report year ends June 30, 1910-20; Dec. 31, 1921-24.
Chartered, 1909; successor to Virginia passenger & power co. **[1044]** became Virginia electric & power co., 1925, **[1025]**
BRE: 1909/10, 11/12-24/25; **NYP:** 1909/10-10/11, 14/15; **USG:** 1914/15, 18/19, 20/21-23/24; **V:** 1909/10-24.

1047. ———. In the matter of modifications of the street railway franchises in Richmond. Argument presented to Sub-committee on streets, of the Richmond City council, on Jan. 10, 1910. [Richmond, 1910?]

24 p. 8°.   V

1048. ———. Petition and draft of ordinance, presented to the Council of the city of Richmond, Nov. 2, 1914. [Richmond? 1914?]

90 p. facsim. 4°.   **V**
Asking the Council to extend the franchise of the company.

1049. ———. Report of light and power service of the Virginia railway & power company, Richmond, Va. By W. J. Norton, G. F. Sever, and C. F. Lacombe. [Richmond? 1915]

18 p. 4°.   **V**

1050. VIRGINIA ROAD BUILDERS ASSOCIATION. Constitution and by-laws . . . Nov. 23, 1911. [Richmond?] 1911.

24°.   **NYP**

1051. VIRGINIA SEABOARD & WESTERN RAILROAD CO. [Project report to the Interstate commerce commission . . . 1902]

print. form, MS. 4°.   **ICC**

1052. VIRGINIA SOUTHERN RAILROAD CO. Annual report to the Interstate commerce commission . . . 1905—

print. forms, MSS. 4°. In progress.   **ICC**
Chartered, 1902.

1053. VIRGINIA STATE CHAMBER OF COMMERCE. Commerce documents, nos. 1-11. Richmond, 1924-28.

11 pams. nar. 8°.   **NYP, V**
1. Hampton Roads, Virginia's greatest asset. (1924) 2. Itinerary of New England visit to Virginia, week of Oct. 27, 1924. (1924) 3. New England-Virginia economic union. (1924) 4. Itinerary of Pan-American visit to Virginia, May 11-14, 1925. (1925) 5. Itinerary of Maine visit to Virginia, Feb. 19, 1926. (1926) 6. Itinerary of Latin American (journalists) visit to Virginia, Apr. 14-16, 1926. (1926) 7. Hampton Roads for apple exports. (1926) 8. . . . 9. Itinerary of all-British Virginia visit in the U. S., May-June, 1927. (1927). 10. Commercio americano. (1928) 11. Itinerary of Middle western visit to Virginia, May 11-14, 1928. (1928).

1054. VIRGINIA STEAMSHIP CO. Annual report to the Interstate commerce commission . . . 1921-22.

2 v. print. forms, MSS. 4°.   **ICC**
Company dissolved.

1055. VIRGINIA TARIFF BUREAU. Proposed form of tariff applying from eastern cities and interior eastern points to southern points. [n. p., 1909]

7 p. incl. tables. 4°.   **ICC**

144   BIBLIOGRAPHY OF VIRGINIA HISTORY

1056. Virginia western coal & iron co. [Project report to the Interstate commerce commission . . . 1897]

print. form, MS. 4°.   ICC

1057. Virginian & western railway co. Virginian & western railway company, mortgagor, the Virginian railway company, guarantor, and Central union trust company of New York, trustee. First mortgage of Virginian & western railway company. Dated Mar. 1, 1922. New York, Evening post [1922?]

125 p. 4°.   HB

1058. Virginian railway co. Annual report to the Interstate commerce commission . . . 1907—

print. forms, MSS. 4°. In progress.   ICC
Incorp., 1904, as Tidewater railway co.; name changed to above, 1907.

1059. ———. Annual report . . . to the stockholders . . . 1st- ; 1909/10— New York, 1910—

8°. Report year ends June 30. In progress.
BRE: 1909/10-27/28; **HB:** 1909/10-27/28; **ICC:** 1909/10-27/28; **LC:** 1909/10-10/11, 12/13; **NYP:** 1909/10-11/12, 13/14-15/16; **V:** 1909/10-27/28.

1060. ———. Description of Virginian railway's coal pier at Sewall's Point, Hampton Roads, Norfolk, Va. Oct. 15, 1911. Norfolk, Va., Donaldson-Ackiss [1915]

15, [2] p. illus., fold. map, tables. 16°.   HB

1061. ———. Indenture . . . between the Virginian railway company . . . and Norfolk & western railway company . . . [n. p., 1925]

34 p. 4°. "Proof—Subject to correction . . ."   HB

1062. ———. [Project report to the Interstate commerce commission . . . 1896-98]

print. forms, MSS. 4°.   ICC

1063. ———. Stockholders of the Virginian railway company and H. H. Rogers, William R. Coe, Adrian H. Larkin, Godfrey M. Hyams, George H. Church, trustees. Stock trust agreement. Dated Oct. 1, 1919. [n. p., 1919?]

14 p. 8°.   HB

1064. ————. The Virginian railway company to the Central trust company of New York. First mortgage. Dated May 1, 1907. [New York, Burgoyne, 1907?]

55 p. 4°. HB

1065. ————. The Virginian railway company to the Equitable trust company of New York, vendor and trustee. Equipment trust agreement securing five per cent. gold notes. Dated Nov. 1, 1908. New York, Burgoyne [1908?]

35 p. 4°. HB

1066. ————. Virginian railway company to the Farmers' loan & trust company. First mortgage. Dated May 1, 1912. New York, Evening post [1912?]

100 p. 4°. H, HB

1067. ————. The Virginian railway. A few impressions. Compliments of Kissel, Kinnicutt & company, bankers, . . . New York. [New York? n. d.]

[21] p. illus. obl. 4°. HB
Description of yards, bridges, loading facilities, terminals, etc.

1068. VIRGINIAN TERMINAL RAILWAY CO. Annual report to the Interstate commerce commission . . . 1914—

print. forms, MSS. 4°. In progress. ICC
Incorp., 1907; leased by Virginian railway co. since 1913.

1069. ————. [Mileage report to the Interstate commerce commission . . . 1910-13]

print. forms. MSS. 4°. ICC

1070. ————. [Project report to the Interstate commerce commission . . . 1907-09]

print. forms, MSS. 4°. ICC ·

1071. WASHINGTON, ALEXANDRIA & MT. VERNON RAILWAY CO. Annual report to the Interstate commerce commission . . . 1908-11.

4 v. print. forms, MSS. 4°. ICC
Electric railway. Chartered, 1890, as Alexandria & Fairfax passenger railway co.; name changed to above, 1896; reorganized, 1910, as Washington-Virginia railway co. [1082-1083]

1072. ————. . . . . Report to the stockholders . . . [Washington, D. C., 1897?-1910?]

8°. LC: 1907, 08.

1073. WASHINGTON & OLD DOMINION RAILWAY CO. Annual report to the Interstate commerce commission . . . 1912—

print. forms, MSS. 4°. In progress.   ICC
Electric railway. Incorp., 1911; successor to Great Falls & Old Dominion railway co. **[785-786]**

1074. ———. Report . . . to the stockholders . . . [Washington, D. C., 1911—

8°. In progress.   LC: 1911-12.
Report for 1911 pub. as U. S. 62 Cong., 2 sess. House. *Doc.,* 506.

1075. WASHINGTON, ARLINGTON & FALLS CHURCH RAILWAY CO. Annual report to the Interstate commerce commission . . . 1908-11.

4 v. print. forms, MSS. 4°.   ICC
Electric railway. Chartered, 1891 and 1892, as Washington & Arlington railway co.; reorganized under above name, 1894; leased to Washington, Alexandria & Mt. Vernon railway co., 1908 **[1071-1072]**; became Washington-Virginia railway co., 1911. **[1082-1083]**

1076. WASHINGTON CITY, VIRGINIA MIDLAND & GREAT SOUTHERN RAILROAD CO. Annual report . . . to the stockholders . . . [Baltimore? 1873?-81?]

9 v. 8°.   **BRE:** 1874; **ICC:** 1874-75.
Formed, 1872, by consolidation of Orange, Alexandria & Manassas **[859]** and Lynchburg & Danville railroad cos.; succeeded by Virginia midland railway co., 1881. **[1034-1040]**

1077. ———. Proceedings of the . . . annual meeting of the stockholders . . . 1st-[9th?] 1873-[81?] Baltimore [etc.] 1873-[81?]

9 v. 8°.   **HB:** 2d-3d (1874-75).

1078. WASHINGTON SOUTHERN RAILWAY CO. Annual report to the Interstate commerce commission . . . 1890-1920.

31 v. print. forms, MSS. 4°.   ICC
Chartered, 1890, as consolidation of Alexandria & Fredericksburg railway co. **[718-719]** and Alexandria & Washington railway co. **[720]**; merged into Richmond, Fredericksburg & Potomac railroad co., 1920. **[919-930]**

1079. ———. Annual report . . . to the stockholders . . . [n. p., 1890?-1918?]

29 v. ? 8°. Report year ends June 30.
BRE: 1902/03-06/07, 09/10-17/18; **HB:** 1913/14; **ICC:** 1903/04-17/18; **NYP:** 1912/13; **V:** 1903/04-17/18.

1080. ———. First (gold) mortgage. Washington southern railway company to the Safe deposit & trust company of Baltimore, trustee. Dated June 1, 1903 . . . [n. p., 1903]

35 p. 8°. **HB**

1081. ———. Proceedings of the . . . annual meeting of the stockholders . . . [1st-28th? 1891?-1918?] [n. p., 1891?-1918?]

28 v. ? 8°. **HB:** 1907; **V:** 1904-18.

1082. WASHINGTON-VIRGINIA RAILWAY CO. Annual report to the Interstate commerce commission . . . 1911-27.

17 v. print. forms, MSS. 4°. **ICC**
Electric railway. Chartered, 1910; merged with Washington, Alexandria & Mt. Vernon railway co. **[1071-1072]** and Washington, Arlington & Falls Church railway co. **[1075]**; succeeded by Arlington & Fairfax railway co. and Mt. Vernon, Alexandria & Washington railway co., 1927.

1083. ———. Annual report . . . [to the stockholders] [Washington, D. C., 1911-27?]

19 v. 8°. **BRE:** 1915/16; **LC:** 1911, 12.
Report for 1911 pub. as U. S. 62 Cong., 2 sess. House *Doc.*, 501; 1912 as U. S. 62 Cong., 3 sess. House. *Doc.*, 1318.

1084. WINDOW, RICHARD R. A few facts with 368 questions and answers . . . 19th ed., with maps and other additions. [Newark?] 1891.

2 p. l., 59, [1] p. illus. (incl. maps) 16°. **LC, NYP**
Guide book to places in Virginia reached by the Old Dominion steamship lines; with some information on transportation charges, accommodations, etc.

Secondary Works

1085. BAKER, JOSEPH B. The Virginian railway; the release of a great domain. [New York? 1912]

58 p. front., fold. map, illus., fold. plate. 8°. **BRE, HB**
Survey of the construction and operation of the railway, and its economic significance.

1086. CONNOR, JOHN V. A descriptive analysis of the Chesapeake & Potomac telephone company; a study in public utility operations, methods and policies . . . Washington, D. C., 1926.

iii, [1], 5-80 p. 8°. **H, LC, V**
Thesis (Ph.D.), Catholic university of America, 1926.
A clear, concise, account, based upon experience in the company, personal investigation, and reports.

1087. DUNAWAY, WAYLAND F. . . . History of the James River & Kanawha company . . . New York, Columbia university, 1922.

> 251 p. 8°. (Columbia university, *Studies in history, economics and public law*, CIV, 2, whole no. 236)
> Pub. also as thesis (Ph.D.), Columbia university, 1923.
> A scholarly study of the company and its commercial significance.

Periodicals

1088. CHESAPEAKE & Ohio and Hocking Valley employes' magazine. Vol. 1, no. 1- ; Feb. 1914— Richmond, Va., 1914—

> illus. 8°.-4°. monthly. Discont. pub., Apr., 1918-Mar., 1920.
> Title varies: Chesapeake & Ohio employes' magazine, Feb., 1914-Nov., 1923. Successor to Safety first bulletin. **[1092]**
> **BRE:** I-XIV (1914-29); **H:** III, 7-V, 2 (1916-18); **ICC:** IV-V (imperf.), VI-XIV; **NYP:** II, 1-3, 5-11; III-IV; V, 2-XV (1915-28); **V:** VIII, 2-XIV, 5.

1089. NORFOLK & western magazine; pub. by the Norfolk & western railway co. Vol. 1- ; 1923— Roanoke, Va., 1923—

> 8°. monthly.
> **BRE:** I-VII (1923-29); **V:** I, 6-12; II; III, 1-3, 6, 11-12; IV-VII.

1090. The PILOT. Vol. 1- [?] New York [1891?- ?]

> illus., maps. 8°.-4°. monthly.
> R. F. Day, ed. "Issued by the Old Dominion steamship co."
> **LC:** X-XVIII (1900/01-08/09); **NYP:** I, 7; IV, 11; X-XV, 4, 6-12; XVI, 1, 3-8, 10-12; XVII-XIX, 11; XX, 1-5, 8, 10-12; XXI, 1-4, 6-12; XXII, 1-4, 6. (1892, 95, 1900-07, 10-13)

1091. PUBLIC service bulletin; pub. by the Virginia state corporation commission. Vol. 1, no. 1- ; Sept., 1918— Richmond, 1918—

> 4 col. news sheet. f°. monthly.   **V:** I, 1.
> "Published for free distribution for the purpose of informing the taxpayers of Virginia concerning the work of the State corporation commission."

1092. SAFETY first bulletin; pub. by the Chesapeake & Ohio railway co. Nos. 1-38; Jan., 1913-Jan., 1916. Richmond, Va., 1913-16.

> 38 nos. illus. 4°.   **BRE:** 1-38.
> Became Chesapeake & Ohio employes' magazine, Feb., 1914. **[1088]**

1093. [301] The SOUTHLAND journal; in the interest of farms, schools, and roads. Petersburg, Va. [1920?-21?]

1094. The VESTIBULE . . . [Vol. 1- ? ; 189-? - ?] Norfolk, Va., S. W. Bowman [189-? - ?]

    illus. 8°. monthly.   **LC:** Jan.-Dec., 1895.
    Pub. under the direction of the Seaboard air line railway.

1095. [307] VIRGINIA highway motor transport and tractor review . . . Richmond, Va., 1919—

Directories

1096. ATLANTIC COAST LINE RAILROAD CO. TRAFFIC DEPT. Industrial and shippers' guide. [n. p., n. d.]

    447 p. illus., maps. 4°.   **Univ. N. C.**
    Descriptions and directories by states served by the railroad.

1097. [558] CHESAPEAKE & OHIO RAILWAY CO. . . . Official industrial guide and shippers' directory . . . [Richmond? 19—

1098. CHESAPEAKE & OHIO RAILWAY DIRECTORY, containing an illustrated history and description of the road, together with improvements and connections already completed and those in contemplation; also, the names of the merchants, manufacturers, professional men, and farmers, with post office addresses in the counties of Elizabeth City, Warwick, York, James City, New Kent, Charles City, King William, Henrico . . . together with a description of the surface, soil, average value of lands, county and city officers, and other useful and valuable information. Comp. by J. H. Chataigne. 1881. [n. p., *ca.* 1881]

    379 p. 8°.   **NYP, V**

1099. NORFOLK & WESTERN RAILWAY. . . . Industrial, shippers' and buyers' official guide, for the use of the company's patrons and others seeking information relative to its territorial resources . . . [New York? 1900—

    illus. 4°. Advertisements interspersed.
    LC: 1900; **USAg:** 1916; **V:** 1905, 16; **VU:** 1916.

For further references on Transportation and Communication, see Pt. II, § 7; *Urban and County Development;* also Pt. III, § 2: *Description and Travel.*

5. LABOR

Government Publications and Documents

1100. RICHMOND, VA. EMPLOYMENT BUREAU, Public. Annual report . . . [1st- ; 1915—] Richmond, 1916—

> tables. 8°. (Dept. of public welfare)
> Title varies: Annual summary, 1926—
> **LC**: 1915, 16, 19-22; **NYP**: 1915-17, 19; **V**: 1915-16, 19-21, 23, 25-27; **VU**: 1919-20, 22-24.

1101. ———. ———. Clearance bulletin, no. 1- Richmond [192-?—
> 8°.   **V**: 28-32 (Oct., 1927-Apr., 1928).

1102. ———. ———. Monthly employment bulletin . . . Richmond [1920?—

> 8°. **H**: Aug.-Oct., Dec., 1920; Jan.-Oct., 1921. **V**: May, June, Sept., Dec., 1920; Jan.-Mar., June-Nov., 1921; Jan.-June, Aug.-Dec., 1922; 1923-24; Jan.-Mar., May-Dec., 1925; 1926; Jan., Mar.-Aug., Oct.-Dec., 1927; Jan.-Feb., Apr.-Dec., 1928; Jan.-Mar., 1929.

1103. U. S. SHIPBUILDING LABOR ADJUSTMENT BOARD. . . . Decision as to wages, hours and other conditions in the shipyards of the Newport News shipbuilding & dry dock company by Shipbuilding labor adjustment board. Mar. 7, 1918. [Washington? 1918]

> 3, 4 numb. l. 8°.   **LC**
> Autographed from typewritten copy.
> "Exhibit A: Minimum wage scale for journeymen, specialists, helpers and laborers in specified crafts in the employ of Newport News shipbuilding & dry dock company"—4 numb. l. (at end).

1104. ———. CHILDREN'S BUREAU. . . . Child labor and the work of mothers on Norfolk truck farms . . . Washington, Govt., 1924.

> iv, 27 p. front. 8°. (*Bureau publication,* 130)
> At head of title: U. S. Dept. of labor. James J. Davis, secretary. Children's bureau. Grace Abbott, chief.
> Investigation planned and carried on under general supervision of Ellen N. Matthews; field work directed by Ethel M. Springer. Exposes conditions of child labor and great educational handicap of the children.

1105. ———. WOMEN'S BUREAU. . . . Hours and conditions of work for women in industry in Virginia. March, 1920. Washington, Govt., 1920.

32 p. incl. tables. 8°. (Its *Bulletin,* 10)
At head of title: U. S. Dept. of labor. Women's bureau. Mary Anderson, director.
Investigation directed by Miss Agnes L. Peterson, assisted by Mrs. Ethel L. Best, Miss Helen Bryan, and Miss Agnes H. Campbell; report prepared by Miss Mary N. Winslow.

1106. [101] VIRGINIA. Annual reports of officers, boards and institutions of . . . Virginia . . . Richmond, Va. [1866-19—

Include reports of the Bur. of labor and industrial statistics, 1898-19—

1107. [366] ——. INDUSTRIAL COMMISSION. Annual report . . . Richmond, 1920—

1108. [367] ——. ——. Bulletin, no. 1- . . . Richmond, 1919—

1109. ——. ——. [Miscellaneous leaflets. Richmond, 1919—

8°.-4°. & broadsides.
Include "Eight months of workmen's compensation in Virginia," by R. H. Tucker, chairman of the Industrial commission; also placards on workmen's compensation, and formsheets of the Commission for use by employers and employees in case of accident, etc.

1110. [368] ——. ——. Opinions of the Industrial commission . . . Richmond, Va., 1921—

1111. [369] ——. LABOR AND INDUSTRY, Bur. of. Annual report . . . Richmond, 1899—

1112. ——. LAWS, STATUTES, etc. Acts concerning coal mines and safety of employes, creating a department and inspector of mines under the Bur. of labor and industrial statistics, approved Mar. 13, 1912. Richmond, Bottom, 1912.

16 p. 8°. **USM**

1113. ——. ——. The child labor laws . . . Bur. of labor and industrial statistics, Commissioner's office. [Richmond?] 1922.

8 p. 16°. **V**

1114. VIRGINIA. LAWS, STATUTES, etc. Labor laws of the commonwealth of Virginia. Bur. of labor and industrial statistics . . . Richmond, Bottom, 1920—

forms. 16°.-8°.
John Hirschberg, commissioner of labor, and Howard T. Colvin, assistant commissioner, 1920; John H. Hall and H. W. Furlow, respectively, 1924. Comp. by Legislative reference bur., 1924.
H: 1924; HB: 1920, 24; HL: 1924; LC: 1920, 24; NYP: 1920, 24; USC: 1924; USG: 1924; USL: 1920, 24; V: 1920, 24; VU: 1924; WM: 1924.

1115. ———. ———. Workmen's compensation law of Virginia, as amended by the . . . General assembly . . . Richmond, Bottom, 1918—

8°. At head of title: Industrial commission . . .
1923 ed. includes the Vocational rehabilitation law; 1924 ed. includes annotations, court decisions construing the act and formal rules of the Industrial commission.
H: 1920; HL: 1920, 22-24; LC: 1918, 20, 22, 24, 26, 28; NYP: 1920; 23-24; USL: 1918, 20, 22, 24, 26, 28; V: 1918-28; VU: 1923.

1116. ———. LEGISLATIVE REFERENCE BUREAU. Summary of workmen's compensation laws in the U. S. and territories. Comp. by Howard Colvin, chief clerk of the Legislative reference bureau of Virginia. Richmond, Bottom, 1916.

44, [1] p. 8°.   V

1117. ———. WORKMEN'S COMPENSATION, Commission on. . . . Communication from the governor transmitting the report of the Virginia Commission on workmen's compensation . . . Jan. 1, 1918. [Richmond, 1918]

32 p. 8°.   USL

1118. ———. ———. . . . Tentative draft of a bill providing for workman's compensation in Virginia, prepared and submitted by the Commission under authority of a joint resolution agreed to by the General assembly of Virginia, Feb. 5, 1916 . . . [n. p., 1916]

20 p. 8°.   USL

Other Source Material

1119. AMERICAN FEDERATION OF LABOR. VIRGINIA BRANCH. Minutes of joint meeting of Executive board of Virginia federation of labor and Farmers educational and co-operative union, held in Richmond, Nov. 11, 1911. [n. p., 1911?]

[15] p. 16°.   USL

1120. ———. ———. Minutes of the meeting of the Executive board of the Virginia federation of labor, held in Richmond, Aug. 8, 1911. [n. p., 1911?]

> 11 p. 16°.   USL

1121. ———. ———. Proceedings of the . . . annual session . . . [Roanoke, etc., 1896?-19—

> 8°. 17th report pub. in *Virginia federation of labor journal,* July, 1912.
> [1135]
> NYP: 1915, 20-22, 24; USL: 1911, 14-16, 18-26; V: 1902, 04-05, 07-11.

1122. [BOARD OF ARBITRATION in the controversy between the Southern railway company, etc., and the International brotherhood of maintenance of way employees] Arbitration, pursuant to agreement dated Nov. 3, 1913, of the wage dispute between Southern railway company, Northern Alabama railway company, and Virginia & southwestern railway company, and their employes of the Maintenance of way department. Dec. 17, 1913. [Washington? D. C., 1914?]

> vii, 21 p. 8°.   LC, USL
> Hilary A. Herbert, chairman.

1123. HATCHER, ORIE L. The Virginia bureau of vocations for women. [n. p., 1919?]

> 7, [1] p. 8°.   V
> Purposes of the bureau; its aid to women workers.

1124. LIBERTY MUTUAL INSURANCE CO. The cost of compensation insurance in Virginia, describing the Virginia workmen's compensation act and discussing methods which produce compensation insurance at cost. Boston, Liberty mutual insurance co. [*ca.* 1918]

> 32 p. 12°.   LC

1125. McKELWAY, A. J. Child labor in Virginia. New York City [1914?]

> 12 p. illus. 8°. (National child labor committee. *Pamphlet,* 171)
>   USL
> Conditions of child labor that need to be remedied; uniform child labor law advised.

1126. MASON, LUCY R. The shorter day and women workers . . . Richmond, Va., Virginia league of women voters, 1922.

> 26 p. 8°.   LC, NYP, USL, V
> Arguments in favor of a 9-hour (and ultimately an 8-hour) day for women workers in Virginia; advantages to employers and employees, with testimony of leading men in industry.

1127. MEREDITH, WYNDHAM R. The social problem; its supposed and real solutions. An address delivered before the Society of the alumni of Richmond college . . . June 22, 1887. [n. p., 1887?]

21 p. 8°.   V

Discussion of labor problems and how the status of the laborer may be improved; attack upon socialistic ideas.

1128. MINOR, JAMES F., comp. The workmen's compensation laws of Virginia and West Virginia, together with rules of procedure and other information. Compiled, annotated, and indexed by James F. Minor. Charlottesville, Michie, 1919.

xci, 691 p. 8°.   LC

1129. RICHMOND EXCHANGE FOR WOMEN'S WORK. Annual report . . . [Richmond, Va. ? 1884?—

8°.   V: 25th, 27-31st, 34th (1908, 10-14, 17).

Secondary Works

1130. BUCK, JABOB L. Hampton studies of occupations for men. Studies prepared in order to aid students of Hampton Institute in choosing their vocations. Cambridge, Mass., Harvard university, 1926.

[3], 87, [9] p. typew. 4°.   H

Thesis (Ed.M.), Harvard university, 1926.

Analysis of occupations filled by Negroes, according to the census of 1920, to show nature of work and preparation required; also a letter from a successful worker in each occupation.

1131. PINCHBECK, RAYMOND B. . . . The Virginia Negro artisan and tradesman . . . Richmond, Va., Byrd, 1926.

146 p. 8°. (University of Virginia. *Phelps-Stokes fellowship papers,* VII)

A scholarly study showing, among other things, the effect of the change from slavery to freedom; also a statistical study of Negroes in various occupations since 1890, the urban trend of Negro artisans, and the importance of trade schools.

Periodicals

1132. [1088] CHESAPEAKE & Ohio and Hocking Valley employes' magazine . . . Richmond, Va., 1914—

1133. MILLER & RHOADS monthly record; pub. by and for the employees of the Miller & Rhoads store. Richmond, Va., 1910 -[12?]

3 v. 8°. No more pub.?
Publication of matters of interest to the employes of the department store.
V: I, 1-2, 4-6; II, 1, 3-9, 11-12; III, 1-6.

1134. SPLINTERS. Pub. by employes of E. I. du Pont de Nemours & co. Hopewell, Va., 1917-18.

2 v. 8°. semi-monthly, Jan.-June, 1917; monthly, Aug.-Nov., 1918.
No more pub.   V: I, & II, except nos. 1-2.
Pub. in the interest of the employes of the powder and allied products co.; reveals industrial and social conditions in the plant and community during period of the World war.

1135. VIRGINIA federation of labor journal; official organ of the Virginia federation of labor. Vol. 1, no. 1-   ; Jan., 1912— Richmond, Southern print., 1912—

4°. monthly.   V: I-II, 6 (1912-June, 1913).
Howard T. Colvin, ed.

6. FINANCE, BANKING, INSURANCE, ETC.

Government Publications and Documents

1136. ALLEN, HENRY C. Speech . . . in the House of delegates, Mar. 19, 1879, on the settlement of the public debt. Richmond, Goode, 1879.

15 p. 8°.   VU
By a re-adjuster.

1137. COCHRAN, ALEXANDER B. Speech . . . in vindication of his course on the funding bill, delivered in the Senate of Virginia, Feb. 8, 1873 . . . Richmond, Enquirer, 1873.

14 p. 8°.   VU

1138. DAVIS, CHARLES H. . . . A plan for the organization of a rural banking system in the state of Virginia . . . Washington [Govt.] 1913.

32 p. 8°. ([U. S.] 62 Cong., 3 sess. Senate. *Doc.*, 1006)
Presented by Mr. Fletcher, president of the Southern commercial congress.   H, LC, USAg, V
Plan to foster co-operation among the farmers.

1139. DONOHOE, STEPHEN R. Communication from Hon. S. R. Donohoe [auditor of public accounts] setting forth his views in reference to the segregation of taxes. In response to a joint resolution requesting him to address the General assembly on the subject of tax reform. Read before the Senate and House of delegates . . . Jan. 26, 1915. [Richmond, 1915]

    4 p. 8°.   V

1140. FEDERAL RESERVE BANK OF RICHMOND. Exhibits supplementing the first report of the operations of the Federal reserve bank of Richmond [by] William Ingle. [Richmond? 1916?]

    8°.   V

1141. ———. General business and agricultural conditions in the 5th federal reserve district. By Caldwell Hardy, chairman and federal reserve agent. Richmond, Mar. 31, 1922. [Richmond? 1922]

    [8] p. tables. 8°.   V

1142. ———. Questions and answers on the federal reserve system, ed. by Chas. A. Peple . . . Richmond, Va., Federal reserve bank of Richmond, 1926.

    xi, 178 p. front., fold. form. 12°. (2d ed.)   LC, V

1143. ———. Report . . . [1st-] 1914/15— [Richmond? 1916—

    8°.   LC: 1914/15 & suppl., 1918.

1144. ———. Review of the operations of the Federal reserve bank of Richmond from date of organization to the close of the year 1915. [By William Ingle, chairman of the Board. Richmond, 1916]

    18 p. 8°.   LC, USAg, V

1145. FREEMAN, DOUGLAS S. Tax reform in Virginia. The co-operation of the press essential to the enactment of better laws. The work of the Tax commission. An address before the Virginia press association . . . July 12, 1911, by Douglas S. Freeman, secretary of the State tax commission . . . Richmond, Va., State tax commission, 1911.

    18 p. 8°.   LC, V
    Virginia's tax problems outlined.

1146. HEARD, JAMES L. Taxation as affecting municipalities. An address delivered before the Virginia league of municipalities, by James Lindsey Heard, of the Norfolk bar. Nov. 10, 1914. Issued by the Legislative reference bureau of Virginia. Richmond, Va., Bottom, 1915.

    15 p. 8°.   **V**

1147. HENRY, WILLIAM W. Speech . . . [in the House of delegates] on the debt of Virginia, delivered 2d and 4th February, 1878. [n. p., 1878?]

    20 p. 8°. No title-page.   **VU**

    In opposition to the "Barbour bill" and repudiation of the state debt.

1148. HOWE, SAMUEL T. Tax commissions of certain states. An extract from a paper prepared . . . for the Annals of the American academy of political and social science . . . Issued by the Legislative reference bureau of Virginia. Richmond, Bottom, 1915.

    14 p. 8°.   **V**

1149. HUGHES, ROBERT W. The coupon and tax question. May a state be enjoined from collecting her taxes by a federal court[?] If she can be at all, then under what circumstances? Opinion of Hon. Robert W. Hughes, U. S. district judge for the eastern district of Virginia, sitting alone, in Circuit court, 15th May, 1883, in a case from the western district of Virginia. [Richmond? 1883]

    14 p. 8°.   **V**

1150. HUGHES, DENVER & PECK, special counsel. Argument in the support of the right of the U. S. to hold the coin and bullion claimed by the Bank of Virginia, the Farmers' bank, and the Exchange bank, all of Richmond, Va. Washington, 1866.

    22 p. 8°.   **H, NYP**

1151. ISAACS & CO., William B., *firm*, Richmond, Va. Petition of William B. Isaacs & company, of Richmond, Va., representatives of certain banks in Richmond, praying for the restoration of certain coin belonging to them, now in the Treasury of the U. S. [Washington, 1877]

    94(?) p. 8°. (U. S. 45 Cong., 2 sess. *Miscell. doc.,* 5)

                    V (copy probably incompl.)

1152. JOHNSON, BRADLEY T. Report on the public debt of Virginia to the Senate, by Bradley T. Johnson, senator from the city of Richmond. 100,000 copies of this pamphlet are being circulated. You will not lack company if you read it. Ashland, Va., Robbins & Holderby, 1889.

> 24 p. 8°. p. 5-24 a reprint of Virginia Senate, *Doc.*, 24, sess. of 1877/78.
> **V**
> At head of title: Old Virginia never tires. [Preface] signed by Richard M. Smith.

1153. LAMB, JAMES C. The Virginia coupon cases. Arranged and reported by James C. Lamb, ed. [of] the Virginia law journal. . . . Richmond, Fergusson, 1885.

> 63 p. 8°.   **V**

1154. MAHONE, WILLIAM. Attitude of the re-adjusters of Virginia concerning the state debt, free schools, a free ballot, and a fair count. Speech delivered in the Senate of the U. S., Mar. 28, 1881. Washington, 1881.

> 39 p. table. 8°.   **H, NYP, V**

1155. MASSEY, JOHN E. Speech of Mr. Massey, of Albemarle, on the bill to prevent counterfeit, or improperly obtained coupons from being received in payment of taxes, debts, dues, and demands due the state. Delivered in the Virginia House of delegates, Feb. 8, 1875. Richmond, Fergusson & Rady, 1875.

> 14 p. 8°.   **V**

1156. MEREDITH, WYNDHAM R. Digest of acts and extracts from acts in relation to the public debt of Virginia, with references to, and a list of decisions thereon . . . Pub. by the Sinking fund commissioners. Richmond, Goode, 1886.

> 147 p. 8°.   **V**

1157. MOORE, C. LEE. Review of tax legislation in Virginia, extra session, 1915. By . . . the auditor of public accounts. Reprint from Richmond *Times-dispatch*. Issued by Legislative reference bureau of Virginia. Richmond, Bottom, 1915.

> [3]-15 p. 8°.   **NYP, V**

1158. MORRISSETT, CARLISLE H. Address to the commissioners of the revenue by C. H. Morrissett, state tax commissioner. Delivered in 1926 at Roanoke, May 24; Bristol, May 25; Danville, May

27; Norfolk, May 28; Harrisonburg, June 2; Fredericksburg, June 4; and Richmond, June 9. Richmond, Bottom, 1926.

14 p. 8°. LC, V

Clear account of tax reform (especially segregation) in Virginia, as accomplished by the General assembly in 1925.

1159. PAGE, THOMAS W. Address on tax reform, made before the General assembly of Virginia, Jan. 15, 1915. [n. p., 1915?]

19 p. 8°. VU

1160. RICHMOND, VA. COMMITTEE REPRESENTING RICHMOND. A natural and economic territory for a federal reserve district, with Richmond as the location of the bank. Respectfully submitted to the Reserve bank organization committee . . . Richmond [1914?]

57 p. maps. 4°. NYP, V

Brief prepared by George J. Seay.

1161. ROYALL, WILLIAM L. Statement of William L. Royall, of Richmond, Va., concerning state banking systems, before the Committee on banking and currency, House of representatives, on . . . Dec. 19, 1896. Washington, Govt., 1897.

36 p. 8°. H, LC, NYP

1162. RUFFIN, FRANK G. Communication from [Frank G. Ruffin] the second auditor relative to funding the public debt. [Richmond, 1884]

8 p. 8°. V

1163. ———. Examination into the merits of the reported proposition of the British bondholders, said to be their substitute for the Riddleberger act. By . . . the second auditor of Virginia. Richmond, Johns, 1886.

16 p. 8°. V

Spirited attack upon the alleged proposal to settle claims of foreign bondholders against the state.

1164. ———. Examination of Judge Robert W. Hughes' decision in the case of John P. Faure v. The Commissioners of the sinking fund of Virginia . . . Richmond, Johns & Goolsby, 1884.

24 p. 8°. V

Submitted to the General assembly of Virginia.

1165. RUFFIN, FRANK G. Facts, thoughts, and conclusions in regard to the public debt of Virginia. Richmond, Johns & Goolsby, 1885.

64 p. 8°.   V, VU

Bitter denunciation of Republican financial policy during reconstruction, by a Democrat.

1166. ———. A further examination into the political and official record of Hon. Robert W. Hughes . . . being a replication to his reply to my examination of his decision in the case of Jno. P. Faure *v*. The Commissioners of the sinking fund . . . Richmond, Goolsby, 1884.

26 p. 8°.   V

1167. SANDS, WILLIAM H. Paper submitted to the Tax commission by William H. Sands, examiner of records of the 10th circuit. Subjects: Equalization, segregation, reduction of taxation, and remedy . . . [Richmond, 1914]

15 p. 8°.   V

1168. STEARNES, ORREN L. Tax segregation and tax reform. By [a] member of the House of delegates from Roanoke County. [Richmond? 1915]

31 p. 8°.   V

Arguments in favor of complete segregation.

1169. TALIAFERRO, WILLIAM B. Speech . . . delivered in the House of delegates, Mar. 18-19, 1879, on the settlement of the public debt. Richmond, Goode, 1879.

16 p. 8°.   VU

Opposed to repudiation of the debt.

1170. THOMAS, ALSEN F. Taxation; an address before Legislative committee on tax revision at Lynchburg, June 27, 1914 . . . [Brookneal, Va., Star, 1914]

23, [1] p. 8°   LC, V

Faults of the existing system of taxation, and remedies proposed.

1171. TURNER, Z. Funding the state debt. Speech in the House of delegates . . . Mar. 24 & 27, 1871. [Richmond? 1871]

16 p. 8°.   V

1172. U. S. CIRCUIT COURT, 4th circuit. East. & West. districts of Virginia. [Coupon cases, involving the public debt of Virginia and the state's creditors]

Too numerous to list, these cases, 1865-80, are reported in *The Federal cases,* I-XXX, *passim;* since Feb., 1880, in the *Federal reporter,* I- , *passim.* Some were also printed as separate pamphlets (to be found especially in **V**).

1173. U. S. CONGRESS. HOUSE. CLAIMS, Committee on. . . . Payment of certain monies advanced by Maryland and Virginia . . . Adverse report. (To accompany S. 5252.) [Washington, Govt., 1909]

15 p. 8°. (60 Cong., 2 sess. House. *Report,* 2318)   **LC, V**
Submitted by Mr. Miller.

1174. ——. ——. ——. ——. Virginia and Maryland claim. Evidence before the Committee on claims of the House of representatives on Senate bill 5252, 60th Congress, 1st session . . . Dec. 16, 1908. Statements of Hon. Charles C. Carlin . . . Hon. John W. Daniel . . . and Hon. Isidor Rayner . . . Washington, Govt., 1909.

19 p. 8°.   **LC**
James M. Miller, chairman.
On verso of title-page: "An act to provide for the payment of certain moneys advanced by the states of Virginia and Maryland to the U. S. government to be applied toward erecting public buildings for the federal government in the District of Columbia."

1175. ——. ——. ——. JUDICIARY, Committee on the. Public debt of Virginia. Hearings before the Committee on the judiciary, House of representatives . . . on H. J. res. 74. Apr. 24, 1912. Washington, Govt., 1912.

26 p. 8°.   **LC**
Henry D. Clayton, chairman.
Speech of Mr. Hamilton, of West Virginia, upon House joint resolution 74, expressing the sense of Congress that the government should pay that part of the public debt of Virginia, existing at the time of the separation of West Virginia therefrom.

1176. ——. ——. SENATE. CLAIMS, Committee on. . . . Payment of certain moneys advanced by Virginia and Maryland to

U. S. . . . Report. (To accompany S. 5252.) [Washington, Govt., 1908]

35 p. 8°. (60 Cong., 1 sess. Senate. *Report,* 480)   LC
Calendar, no. 509. Submitted by Mr. Martin.
Includes Senate *Report,* 1787, 49 Cong., 2 sess. (Committee on claims); and the joint resolution of the General assembly of Virginia approved Mar. 5, 1888, transferring a certain claim of Virginia against the U. S. government to the Mt. Vernon avenue association.

1177. U. S. Supreme court. Commonwealth of Virginia *v.* state of West Virginia. [Briefs, arguments, exhibits, etc. before the Supreme court of the U. S.] [Richmond, etc., 1907-15?]

8°.   H, LC, NYP, V
A large number of the documents are listed in E. G. Swem, *Bibliography of Virginia,* II, *passim.* **[36]**

1178. ———. ———. [Coupon cases, involving the public debt of Virginia and the state's creditors]

These cases are reported in *U. S. Reports.* The test case was *Poindexter v. Greenhow* (114 U. S. 270).

1179. [101] Virginia. Annual reports of officers, boards, and institutions of . . . Virginia . . . Richmond, Va. [1866-19—

Include reports of the auditor of public accounts, 1865— ; the second auditor on the condition of the public debt, the literary fund, and commissioners of the sinking fund, 1871/72— ; the state accountant, 1912/13— ; the treasurer, 1865—

1180. ———. Reports of officers and institutions as to estimated needs for next two fiscal years, made in response to joint resolution agreed to Jan. 11, 1912 . . . [Richmond, 1912]

22 p. 8°.   V

1181. Virginia, *plaintiff.* Proceedings in the equity suit of the commonwealth of Virginia *v.* the state of West Virginia, with an appendix. Comp. by Clarke W. May, attorney general. Charleston [W. Va., Tribune print., etc.] 1907-11.

5 v. 8°.   H, LC, NYP, V
v. II-IV, by William G. Conley, attorney general; v. III, pt. 1, "contains matter previously printed in . . . I & II."
I-II: Record of suit. III: Record, pt. 1; being proceedings in the Supreme court prior to referring of the cause to a special master. Record, pt. 2; being the evidence taken and proceedings had before the special master, Charles E. Littlefield, at Richmond, Va., Nov. 16, 1908 to

July 2, 1909. IV: Appendix to the record; being certain public acts of the legislatures of Virginia and West Virginia and of Congress, etc. V: Names of residents of West Virginia and others holding or owning bonds, registered stock, or deferred certificates of Virginia.

1182. VIRGINIA. ACCOUNTANCY, State board of. Examination, Virginia State board of accountancy . . . [Richmond, Va., 19—

8°. **V:** 1924-27.
Examination held in Richmond every Oct.

1183. ———. ACCOUNTANT, State. Annual report . . . Richmond, 19—

8°. Report year ends Sept. 30.
LC: 1914/15-25/26; **NYP:** 1920/21-25/26; **USC:** 1913/14, 15/16-20/21; **V:** 1912/13, 15/16, 17/18-22/23, 24/25-25/26; **VU:** 1925/26.
See also *Annual reports* of officers [etc.] of Virginia **[1179]**

1184. ———. ———. Comparative cost of local government. Statement of receipts and disbursements of the counties of Virginia . . . 1923/24— Richmond, 1925—

tables. 8°.
LC: 1923/24-24/25; **NYP:** 1923/24-25/26; **V:** 1923/24-25/26; **VU:** 1924/25-25/26; **WM:** 1924/25.

1185. ———. ———. Method of keeping accounts of county treasurers and form of report of county audit. Richmond, Va., 1920.

30 p. tables. 8°. **V**

1186. ———. AUDITOR OF PUBLIC ACCOUNTS. Account book of money paid to state officials . . . [1866-80]

3 v. MSS. **V:** Access. nos. 293-295.
1866-70 (568 p.); 1871-78 (303 p.); 1878-80 (135 p.).

1187. ———. ———. Account of taxes paid by state banks, 1862-68.

193 p. f°. MSS. **V:** Access. no. 296.

1188. ———. ———. Circular of the auditor of public accounts to assessors of land . . . January, 1925. [Richmond, Bottom, 1924]

20 p. 8°. **V**
"Re-assessment of land and lots and improvements thereon—laws," p. 8-20.

1189. VIRGINIA. AUDITOR OF PUBLIC ACCOUNTS. Circular to the commissioners of revenue on their powers and duties regarding the assessment of taxes on persons, personal property, money, incomes, real estate . . . Richmond, Bottom, 1920—

8°.   LC: 1925; NYP: 1925; V: 1925; VU: 1920, 25.

1190. ———. ———. Compilation of, and references to, the statutes which authorize payments to officers and others out of the state treasury for services and expenses in criminal and other cases, etc. . . . Comp. and issued for use of judges, clerks of courts, and other officers. Richmond, 19—

8°.   V: 1914, 17.

1191. ———. ———. . . . . Duties of county treasurers and laws relating to: collection of levies, payment of warrants drawn upon county, school and road funds, annual settlement with board of supervisors and county school board . . . 1928. Richmond, 1928.

61 p. 8°.   V

1192. ———. ———. [Instructions to commissioners of the revenue, based upon the revised tax law of 1865. Alexandria, 1865]

8 p. 8°.   LC

L. W. Webb, auditor of public accounts.
Includes the duties of the commissioners and the text of the Act of 1865.

1193. ———. ———. [List of insolvent capitation and property taxes for the year 1881. Richmond? 1881?]

8°.   V

Series of lists, by counties, with the number from each: Charles City (1); Franklin (2); Frederick (5); Goochland (3); Greene (3); Hanover (3); Isle of Wight (1); King George (3); Lee (3); Mecklenburg (1); Prince Edward (1); Richmond (2); Westmoreland (3).

1194. ———. ———. Report . . . [1865/66-19—] Richmond [1866-19—

tables (part. fold.) 8°. Report year ends Sept. 30.
Title varies slightly.
BP: 1878/79; H: 1911/12, 13/14-14/15; HB: 1922/23; LC: 1865/66, 71/72, 75/76-76/77, 83/85, 89/90-1922/23, 24/25-25/26; NYP: 1871/72-75/76, 82/83-83/85, 89/90-90/91, 92/93-98/99, 1900/01-03/04, 05/06-26/27; USAg: 1875/76-76/77, 86/87-89/90, 92/93-1900/01, 02/03-16/17, 18/19-26/27; USC: 1879/80-88/89, 90/91-92/93, 1909/10-16/17; V: 1865/66,

69/70, 76/77-77/78, 80/81-81/82, 85/86, 93/94-1927/28; **VU**: 1913/14, 19/20, 21/22; **WM**: 1865/66, 70/71-71/72.

See also *Annual reports* of officers [etc.] of Virginia **[1179]**

1195. ———. ———. Report of the second auditor on the condition of the public debt of Virginia, of the Literary fund, and the report of the Commissioners of the sinking fund . . . Richmond, 1872—

    8°. Report year ends Sept. 30.

    HB: 1912/13, 18/19-21/22; **LC**: 1870/71-74/75, 76/77-79/80, 81/82-89/90, 92/93-94/95, 96/97, 98/99-1922/23, 24/25-25/26; **NYP**: 1870/71, 72/73-79/80, 81/82-1926/27; **USC**: 1873/74, 79/80-1914/15, 16/17-18/19, 20/21-22/23, 24/25.

    See also *Annual reports* of officers [etc.] of Virginia **[1179]**

1196. ———. ———. Reports of guaranty, trust, indemnity, and fidelity companies . . . Richmond [19—

    4°   **NYP**: 1905.

1197. ———. ———. Reports of life insurance companies, &c. . . . [1893?]-1905. Pub. by the auditor of public accounts . . . [Richmond [1894?]-1906.

    8°.-4°. Report year ends Dec. 31.

    BP: 1893, 95, 97, 1901, 04; **H**: 1893, 95, 97-99, 1901; **LC**: 1893, 95-1905; **NYP**: 1893-1900, 05; **USC**: 1893, 97-98, 1901, 04; **V**: 1893, 96-1905.

    For subsequent reports, see Virginia. Bur. of insurance. *Annual report.* **[1231]**

1198. ———. ———. State licenses issued by commissioners of the revenue: schedule of cost. Pub. by the auditor of public accounts . . . Richmond, Bottom, 192—

    tables. 8°.   **LC, NYP**: 1924; **V**: 1926.

1199. ———. ———. Statement showing results to counties and cities under operation of Weaver-Buchanan bill. House bill, no. 8 . . . [Richmond, Va.] 1915.

    [4] p. tables f°.   **V**

    Effects of partial tax segregation upon the revenues of counties; statistics by counties.

1200. ———. ———. Supplement. Roster of Confederate pensioners of Virginia showing payments . . . to all pensioners enrolled under the several acts of Assembly . . . Richmond, 19—

    8°.   **LC**: 1909/10, 12, 26; **V**: 1908-17, 19-23, 25-26.

1201. VIRGINIA. AUDITOR OF PUBLIC ACCOUNTS. Taxation. Report of the efforts of the Auditor of public accounts to enforce a compliance with tax laws and result of investigations by grand juries of the tax assessments of 1912, together with the tentative plan for segregation of the subjects of taxation proposed by the auditor. Richmond, Bottom [19-?]

    89 p. 8°.   **VU**

1202. ———. ———. [?] [Vouchers and orders of the court for artificial limbs. 1867-68]

    MSS., 6 bundles (300 per bundle).   **V**
    Compensation for disabled ex-Confederate soldiers.

1203. ———. ———. [?] [Vouchers for constitutional convention, 1867-68]

    MSS.   **V**

1204. ———. ———. [?] [Vouchers for pay of officers of the state government. 1785-1868]

    MSS., 355 bundles.   **V**

1205. ———. CORPORATION COMMISSION, State. List of foreign corporations authorized to do business in Virginia as of Apr. 1, 1928 . . . [Richmond, 1928]

    26 p. 8°.   **V**
    For earlier years, see its *Annual report,* 1903— **[648]**

1206. ———. ———. Methods and costs of obtaining charters in Virginia . . . Richmond, Bottom, 1911.

    17 p. 8°. (Its *Circular,* 8 **[650]**)

1207. ———. ———. Rules of practice and procedure in cases and proceedings before the . . . commission. Adopted Oct. 6, 1903. [Richmond, 1903]

    6 p. 8°.   **V**

1208. ———. ———. BANKING DIVISION. Comparative statement showing the condition of incorporated state banks . . . [Richmond, 19—

    typew. mimeog. 4°.
    H: Nov. 17, 1919, Nov. 15, 1920, 1921-27.

1209. ———. ———. ———. A report of building and loan associations in Virginia, made to the State corporation commission.

Comp. by M. E. Bristow, chief examiner of banks, as of Apr. 30, 1926 (average date). Richmond, Oct. 30, 1926. [Richmond, 1926]

8 p. 8°.   **V**

1210. ———. ———. ———. Statement . . . showing the condition of incorporated state banks . . . and national banks in Virginia. No. 1- ; 1909/10— [Richmond, 1910—

8°.   **LC**: 3-8 (1910-11); **V**: 1-34 (1910-16).

C. C. Barksdale, chief examiner.

1211. ———. ———. ———. Statements showing the condition of the incorporated state banks at the close of business . . . 1st- ; 1903/04— Richmond, 1905—

8°. No separate reports pub. for 1905 and 1906.

1904-09 contain also statutes of Virginia regulating or affecting state banks, in force on Jan. 1, 1905, and Sept. 1, 1909.

BP: 5th, 7-8th, 10-15th (1916-24); **H**: 1910, 12-19, 23-26; **HB**: 1904, 07, 10-15, 17, 26-27; **LC**: 1904, 07, 09-12, 14, 16, 24-25, 27; **NYP**: 1904, 08, 10-27; **USAg**: 1922-23; **USC**: 1904, 08, 10-12; **V**: 1904, 07-20, 22-25; **WM**: 1924.

For further references on the State corporation commission, see above, § 4: *Transportation and Communication* **[648-668]**

1212. ———. Excise, State board of commissioners of. Minutes . . . Mar. 17, 1890 to Dec. 16, 1893.

23 p. f°. MSS.   **V**: Access. no. 363.

1213. ———. General assembly. House. Appropriations, Committee on. Report . . . to the House of delegates as required by the following resolution: Resolution to go into effect on or before the 10th day of February, 1914. [n. p., n. d.]

44 p. 8°.   **V**

Amounts asked for and amounts appropriated to every department of state government and to every state institution.

1214. ———. ———. ———. Finance, Committee on. Report of House Committee on finance in relation to public debt, taxation, etc. [Richmond? 1878]

10 p. 8°.   **LC**

William B. Taliaferro, chairman.

1215. ———. ———. ———. ———. Report of the Committee on finance in response to a resolution of House of delegates calling for

a statement of the precise and comprehensive amount of the public debt on the 1st day of Dec., 1878 . . . [Richmond?
1878?]

> 2 sheets.   V

1216. VIRGINIA. GENERAL ASSEMBLY. TAX REVISION, Joint committee on. . . . Report of the Joint committee on tax revision, 1914. Richmond, Va. [1914]

> viii, 298 p. fold. diagr. 8°.
> Committee appointed in 1914 to report on all questions pertaining to
> assessment and collection of taxes and methods of appropriating and
> expending revenue on the state. Report covers whole field of taxation;
> with recommendations.

1217. ———. GOVERNOR. . . . Budget, 1920/22— [Richmond]
1920—

> tables. f°.
> Submitted to the General assembly by the governor.
> **BP:** 1920/22; **H:** 1920/22; **LC:** 1920/22-28/30; **NYP:** 1920/22-
> 24/26, 28/30; **V:** 1920/22-28/30; **VU:** 1920/22-26/28; **WM:** 1920/22-
> 28/30.

1218. ———. ———. . . . Classifications and instructions for the
preparation of budget estimates . . . 1920-22. [Richmond,
1919]

> 15 p. fold. forms. 8°.   **LC, V**
> "Virginia budget law", 1920-22, p. [14]-15.

1219. ———. ———. . . . Communication from the governor
submitting the budget bill, being a tentative bill for all proposed
appropriations of the budget, submitted by the governor of Virginia to the presiding officer of each house of the General assembly of Virginia in accordance with the provisions of the budget law (section 8, chap. 64, Acts of Assembly, 1918, pp. 118-120)
. . . [Richmond] 1920—

> 8°. **LC:** 1920/22-28/30; **NYP:** 1920/22-26/28, suppl. to 26/28; **V:**
> 1920/22-28/30; **VU:** 1920/22-26/28; **WM:** 1920/22-26/28.

1220. ———. ———, 1874-78 (James L. Kemper). Correspondence
of the governor with the agent of the American bond-funding
and banking association. Richmond, 1874.

> 10 p. 8°.   V
> Plan to recapitalize the state debt by issue of new bonds.

1221. ———. ———, 1922-26 (E. Lee Trinkle). Distinctive features of the Virginia budget system . . . An address delivered before the Governors' conference, White Sulphur Springs, W. Va., Dec. 14-16, 1922. Richmond, Va., Press of Virginia state penitentiary [1922]

15 p. 8°.   LC, V

1222. ———. ———. (———). A plea for principle; shall the federal government control the credit of the states? A communication from E. Lee Trinkle, governor of Virginia, to her senators and representatives in Congress. Richmond, 1922.

24 p. 8°.   V
Concerning the taxation of bonds, securities, etc.

1223. ———. ———, 1926— (Harry F. Byrd) Chart showing the amounts authorized for expenditure by the commonwealth of Virginia from all sources during the year ending Feb. 29, 1928, for the several activities of the state government. [Richmond, 1926]

chart. 24 x 30 cm.   V

1224. ———. ———. (———). Repeal of the state tax on land and personal property. Statement by Gov. Harry F. Byrd on the repeal of the 25 cents state tax on land and personal property, showing the effect upon each locality, and based upon actual and not estimated returns. Tables prepared by C. H. Morrissett, state tax commissioner, and the State corporation commission. Richmond, Bottom, 1927.

12 p. incl. tables. 8°.   V
"Comparative statement of assessed values of the properties of public service corporations as assessed by the State corporation commission, . . .", p. 9-11; "Explaining an act relating to county budget systems," by J. H. Bradford, budget director, p. 11-12.

1225. ———. ———. (———). The tax situation in Virginia, a statement showing the effect of new tax laws . . . Richmond, Bottom, 1927.

6 p. incl. tables. 8°.   V

1226. [365] ———. ———. (———). Virginia: the home of industry . . . Richmond, Va. [1927]

1227. ———. ———. BUDGET, Div. of the. Directions for the preparation of county budget estimates. Prepared by J. H. Bradford, director of the budget . . . Richmond, Va., Bottom, 1927.

8 p. 8°.   V.

1228. VIRGINIA. GOVERNOR. BUDGET, Div. of the. State financial procedure in Virginia. By J. H. Bradford . . . 1928. Richmond, Div. of purchase and printing, 1928.

15, [2] p. 8°.   **LC, V, VU**

1229. ———. INSURANCE, Bur. of. Annual report of the commissioner of insurance . . . 1906/07— Richmond, 1907—

8°. Report year ends April 30.
Preceded by Virginia. Auditor of public accounts. *Reports of life insurance companies, &c.* **[1197]**
 H: 1908/09-19/20; **HB**: 1906/07-26/27; **LC**: 1906/07-26/27; **NYP**: 1906/07-26/27; **USAg**: 1911/12, 14/15-20/21; **USC**: 1906/07-09/10, 11/12-13/14, 15/16-19/20; **V**: 1906/07-10/11, 12/13, 15/16, 18/19, 20/21, 24/25-26/27; **VU**: 1920/21-26/27.

1230. ———. ———. Bulletin, no. 1-2; Oct. & Dec., 1909. Richmond, 1909.

2 nos. 4°. No more pub.   **V**

1231. ———. ———. . . . List of fire and marine, life, industrial, sick benefit, fidelity, surety, casualty and miscellaneous insurance companies and fraternal orders and associations authorized to write business in Virginia for the year ending . . . Richmond, 192—

8°.   **V**: 1926/27.

1232. ———. ———. Statistical tables of fire, marine, life, and miscellaneous insurance companies . . . [n. p., 19—

8°.   **H**: 1915; **NYP**: 1915-16; **V**: 1915.

1233. ———. JUDGES. Report of county and corporation judges in response to circular of governor of Virginia of Nov. 10, 1871, calling for certain statistical information. Richmond, Schaffter, 1871.

ii, 84 p. 8°.   **LC, V**
Report of county taxes, rates, court expenses, etc.

1234. ———. LAWS, STATUTES, etc. Abstract of the laws of Virginia in relation to insurance companies: also, forms of power of attorney appointing agent, agent's bond, report of taxes, annual statement, &c. [Richmond, 187—

8°.   **LC**: 1878; **WM**: 1872.
Issued by the auditor of public accounts, William F. Taylor.

1235. ———. ———. Abstract of the laws of . . . Virginia in relation to insurance, guaranty, fidelity, indemnity and trust companies . . . Comp. by the auditor of public accounts. Richmond, 19—

8°. **LC:** 1905; **USAg:** 1915, **V:** 1905.

1236. ——. ——. An act . . . entitled "An Act to provide a plan of settlement of the public debt," approved Mar. 28, 1879. [Richmond? 1879]

7 p. 12°. **NYP**

1237. ——. ——. An act for assessment of taxes on persons, property, incomes, and licenses, and imposing taxes thereon for the support of the Government and free schools, and pay the interest on the public debt. Approved Apr. 22, 1882. [n. p., n. d.]

50 p. 8°. **V**

1238. ——. ——. An act to incorporate the Virginia international land, loan & trust company. Approved Mar. 23, 1870. [Richmond] 1870.

8 p. 8°. **HB**

1239. ——. ——. An act to levy an excise tax upon the public utility corporations of the state; to segregate and make them liable to taxation by the state alone; to fix the method and rate of such taxation; and to repeal all state taxes upon the real and personal property of the state. By O. L. Stearnes, member of House of delegates from Roanoke County. [Salem, Va., Salem print., 1915]

28 p. 8°. **V**

1240. ——. ——. An act to put into effective operation the provisions of the constitution relating to the creation, appointment and organization of the "State corporation commission," its jurisdiction, powers, functions and duties; the qualification of the members and officers thereof, their appointment and salaries, the location of its offices, and places and times of its public sessions; its writs, processes, orders, findings and judgments; appeals from its orders, findings and judgments, and its expenses, etc. Approved Apr. 15, 1903. [Richmond? 1903?]

24 p. 8° **V**

1241. ——. ——. A bill to establish a bureau of banking under the control of the State corporation commission, to provide for the appointment of a commissioner of banking, to regulate the business of banking in this state, to declare certain acts to be crimes and to provide penalties for the violation of the provision herein contained. Richmond, Co-operative press, 1909.

29 p. 8°.   V

1242. VIRGINIA. LAWS, STATUTES, etc. A bill: To revise, simplify, arrange and consolidate into one act the general tax and revenue statutes of the commonwealth, and be designated and cited as "The Tax code of Virginia." [n. p., 1928?]

495 p. 8°. ("Senate bill, no. 1")   VU

1243. ———. ———. Compilation of the laws relating to the sale, redemption, and re-sale of lands, lots, etc., delinquent for the non-payment of the taxes, levies, interest, costs, charges, etc., thereon. Issued by the auditor of public accounts, May 20, 1926. Richmond, Bottom, 1926.

46 p. 8°.   V

1244. ———. ———. Confederate pension law of Virginia, comp. by the auditor of public accounts . . . Richmond, Bottom, 19—

8°.   V: 1908, 12, 16.

1245. ———. ———. . . . . Foreign corporations. Constitutional provisions and statutes of Virginia relating to domestication by foreign corporations, with the entrance fee to be paid at the time certificate of authority to do business in Virginia is secured from the State corporation commission and the registration fee to be paid annually thereafter. Comp. and issued by the State corporation commission with all amendments . . . Richmond, Bottom, 19—

8°.   LC: 1914, 26; V: 1914, 24, 26.
R. T. Wilson, clerk of the commission, 1926.

1246. ———. ———. Gasoline tax law. Statute of Virginia providing for a tax on motor vehicle fuels, as amended by the General assembly, session of 1928. Comp. and issued by the Div. of motor vehicles . . . Richmond, 1928.

14 p. 8°.   V

1247. ———. ———. . . . . Income tax law of 1926. Issued by State tax commission, 1926. Richmond, Bottom, 1926.

34 p. 8°.   LC,V

1248. ———. ———. Laws in relation to commissioners and collectors of the public revenue, etc., now in force, containing suggestions to and forms for clerks of courts. Pub. by the auditor of public accounts. Richmond, Walker, 1873-[82?]

8°. **NYP:** 1873, 81-82; **V:** 1873-74, 78, 81-82; **VU:** 1881-82.

1249. ———. ———. . . . . Laws relating to insurance, guaranty, trust, indemnity, fidelity, security and other like companies. Comp. and pub. by the Bur. of insurance. Joseph Button, commissioner of insurance. Richmond, Bottom, 1906.

89 p. 8°. **V**

1250. ———. ———. The lien law of Virginia. Code of Virginia, chap. CX, with all the amendments thereto from 1887 to Mar. 5, 1900, as to vendors' lien, the lien of mechanics, and others. Richmond, Ackerly, 1900.

7 p. 8°. **LC, V**

1251. ———. ———. The Riddleberger bill, as passed by the General assembly at the session of 1879-80, and vetoes by the governor. Printed by order of the Senate. [Richmond? 1880]

15 p. 8°. **V**

1252. ———. ———. The Riddleberger debt law . . . Approved Feb. 14, 1882. [n. p., 1882?]

10 p. 8°. **NYP, V**
With a statement of the public debt of Virginia.

1253. ———. ———. State tax commission and segregation acts. Chap. 147—tax commission act; chap. 576—segregation act; chap. 188—examiners of records, and commissioners of revenue act. Reprinted from Acts of Assembly, session 1926. Richmond, 1926.

59 p. 8°. **V**

1254. ———. ———. Statutes of Virginia relating to banks [trust companies] and the banking business, with amendments as enacted by General assembly . . . Comp. by State corporation commission. Banking division . . . Richmond, Bottom, 19—

8°. **H:** 1924, 26; **HB:** 1922, 24, 26 suppl.; **LC:** 1912; **NYP:** 1905, 10, 20, 24, 26; **USC:** 1912; **V:** 1910, 12, 14, 20, 22, 24, 26 suppl.; **WM:** 1924.

1255. ———. ———. Tax bill of 1890, with the general provisions of the code of Virginia in relation to the duties, &c., of the commissioners of the revenue and the county and city treasurers. [Richmond? 1890]

118 p. 8°.   H, LC, USC, V

1256. VIRGINIA. LAWS, STATUTES, ETC. The tax code of Virginia, with all amendments enacted at the session of the General assembly of 1928. Pub. by the Dept. of taxation of . . . Virginia. Richmond, Div. of purchase and printing, 1928.

xxvii, 290 p. 8°.   V

1257. ———. ———. . . . Tax laws of Virginia . . . Richmond, 1865-19—

8°. Title varies.
Issued by the auditor of public accounts.
HB: 1920; **HL**: 1918, 22; **LC**: 1865, 90, 98, 1905, 08, 10, 12, 14-16, 18-19, 24, 26; **NYP**: 1912, 15-16, 18-20, 22, 24, 26, 28; **USC**: 1906, 10, 12, 14, 16, 18, 20; **V**: 1890, 98, 1900, 05, 08, 10-15, 18, 24, 26; **VU**: 1916; 20, 26; **WM**: 1922.

1258. ———. ———. The Virginia banking act; an act to revise, collate, and codify into one act the general statutes of the commonwealth relating to banks and banking. Chap. 507, Acts of assembly, 1928, approved Mar. 27, 1928. Reprinted from the Acts. [Richmond, 1928]

37 p. 8°.   V

1259. ———. ———. Virginia corporation law. Constitutional provisions and statutes of Virginia relating to issuing, amending and taxing charters of corporations. Comp. by the State corporation commission . . . Richmond, 19—

8°. **HB**: 1916, 24, 26; **LC**: 1905-06, 09-10, 14, 18, 20, 26; **NYP**: 1905, 10, 14, 20, 22; **USC**: 1905, 10; **V**: 1905, 08, 10, 26; **VU**: 1926, 28.

1260. ———. ———. Virginia insurance laws . . . comp. and pub. by the Bur. of insurance of Virginia . . . Richmond, Bottom, 19—

8°. Title varies.
HB: 1924; **NYP**: 1914-15, 18; **USAg**: 1914; **V**: 1906, 10, 14, 19, 24 & suppl.

1261. ———. ———. Virginia pension law, 1926. Issued by auditor of public accounts, Apr. 15, 1926. Richmond, Bottom, 1926.

15 p. 8°.   LC, V

1262. ———. ———. Virginia securities law as amended by the General assembly of Virginia of 1928, with titles to sections inserted and with index. Issued by the Securities division of the State corporation commission . . . Richmond, 1928.

32 p. 8°.   V

1263. ———. LEGISLATIVE REFERENCE BUREAU. Extracts from messages and addresses of governors of Virginia, regarding taxation, 1893-1914. Comp. by Lewis H. Machen, director of Legislative reference bureau of Virginia. Richmond, Bottom, 1915.

1 p. l., 3-34, [1] p. 8°.   V

1264. ———. ———. Extracts from the proceedings of the Conference on taxation of the sixteenth conference for education in the South. Richmond, Va., Apr. 17-18, 1913. Issued by the Legislative reference bureau of Virginia. Richmond, Bottom, 1914.

27 p. 8°.   V

1265. ———. ———. A summary of tax systems, boards, and methods of equalization of the several states. Comp. by Lewis H. Machen, director of the Legislative reference bureau of Virginia. Richmond, Bottom, 1915.

29 p. 8°.   LC, V
A condensation of portions of a bulletin recently issued by the U. S. Bur. of the census, supplemented by reference to bulletins of the New York tax reform association.

1266. ———. PURCHASING AGENT, State. Report . . . 1924/26— Richmond, Bottom, 1926—

tables. 8°. biennial.   LC, V: 1924/26.
Succeeded by Div. of purchase and printing, 1927.

1267. ———. SINKING FUND, Commissioners of the. [Report]
See above, Virginia. Auditor of public accounts. *Report of the second auditor* . . . **[1195]**

1268. ———. SUPREME COURT OF APPEALS. Coleman's administratrix *v.* The Piedmont & Arlington life insurance company. Notes of argument by A. R. Blakey, of counsel for appellee. [n. p., 1879]

10 p. 8°.   V

1269. ———. ———. Piedmont & Arlington life insurance company *v.* McLean, etc. Notes of argument by A. R. Blakey, of counsel for the appellant. [Richmond, 1879]

20 p. 8°.   V

1270. Virginia. Supreme court of appeals. Piedmont & Arlington life insurance company *v.* McLean, etc. Reply to defendant's brief. [n. p., n. d.][1]

7 p. 8°.   V

1271. ——. Tax board, State. Circular, no. 1-[16?] [Richmond? 1915-18?]

8°.   HL: 11, 14; **NYP:** 1-6-7, 11, 13-16; **V:** 1, 6-7, 11, 13-14, 16.

1272. ——. [Tax books] [Land tax books, Virginia counties. 1865-1927]

MS. books.
Presumably covering all Virginia counties.[2]   V

1273. ——. [——] [Personal tax books, Virginia counties. 1865-1927]

MS. books.
Presumably covering all Virginia counties.[2]   V

1274. ——. Tax commission, State. Circular of instructions to commissioners of the revenue, 1927 . . . Richmond, Bottom, 1927.

7 p. 8°.   V

1275. ——. ——. Important circular of instructions to commissioners of the revenue. Issued . . . July 2, 1927. Richmond, Bottom, 1927.

[5] p. 8°.   V

1276. ——. ——. List of corporations organized or doing business in Virginia. 1919— Richmond, 1919—

8°. (Its *Bulletin,* 16-   **[1281]** issued subsequently by the Dept. of taxation)

1277. ——. ——. Report to the General assembly of Virginia by the Tax commission appointed to make an investigation of the system of assessment, revenue and taxation now in force in this state.

1. For other briefs of cases involving Virginia finance, banking, insurance, etc., see the bound volumes of pamphlets (in **V**) under title *Virginia briefs.*
2. Beginning 1928, counties are no longer required to deposit copies of land tax and personal tax books with the State tax commissioner (successor to the Auditor of public accounts), since segregation of these taxes has become effective.

William Hodges Mann, chairman . . . Richmond, Va. [Richmond press] 1911.

xlviii, 369, p. 8°.   **LC, NYP, USC, V, VU, WM**

1278. ———. [———?] Reports of collateral inheritance tax. 1877-78.
MSS., 50 pieces.   **V:** Access. no. 13208.

1279. ———. ———. . . . Statement of rates of county and district levies . . . 1916-17. [Richmond?] 1917-18.

2 nos. 8°.   **NYP**
Later years issued in its *Bulletin.* **[1281]**

1280. ———. TAX COMMISSION, 1914. [Papers, including minutes of meetings, accounts, correspondence, hearings, receipts, reports, vouchers, warrants, etc.]

MSS.   **V:** Access. nos. 13788-13816.

1281. ———. TAXATION, Dept. of. Bulletin . . . no. 1- ;
1916— Richmond, 1916—

8°. Issued irreg.
Nos. 1-32 (1916-24) issued by State tax board; nos. 33-43 (1925-27) by State tax commission; nos. 44- (1927—) by Dept. of taxation.
HL: 12, 21, 23, 27; **LC:** 2, 12, 16-17, 23, 25-37, 41-43; **NYP:** 2, 12, 16-17, 19-44; **USAg:** 37; **V:** 1, 2, 9-10, 12, 16-17, 19-44; **VU:** 31; **WM:** 23.

1282. ———. ———. Report . . . 1916/17— Richmond, 1918—
tables. 8°. biennial.
Issued by State tax board, 1916/17; by State tax commission (in its *Bulletin,* 37, 41-43 **[1281]**), 1926-27.
LC: 1916/17, 24/25-26/27; **NYP:** 1916/17, 24/25-26/27; **USAg:** 1924/25; **V:** 1916/17, 24/25-26/27.

1283. ———. TREASURER. Annual report . . . Richmond [1866-
19—
tables. 8°. Report year ends Sept. 30.
BP: 1886/87-87/88, 97/98-98/99; **H:** 1911/12; **LC:** 1871/72-74/75, 87/88, 92/93-1925/26; **NYP:** 1866/67, 73/74-79/80, 82/83, 87/88-99/1900, 02/03-26/27; **USC:** 1873/74, 98/99-1913/14, 15/16, 18/19-20/21; **V:** 1865/66, 67/68-68/69, 74/75, 80/81-82/83, 95/96-96/97, 1900/01, 02/03, 05/06, 07/08-14/15, 16/17-17/18, 19/20-26/27.
See also *Annual reports* of officers [etc.] of Virginia **[1179]**

1284. WAREHOUSE book and account of state revenue, 1861 to Mar., 1872.

MSS. f°.   **V:** Access. no. 349.

1285. WEST VIRGINIA, *defendant*. Virginia *v.* West Virginia. Argument Hon. Reverdy Johnson in the Supreme court of the U. S., delivered in behalf of the defendant, . . . May 8, 1867 . . . Washington, Globe, 1867.

18 p. 8°.   BP, NYP

1286. ———. ATTORNEY-GENERAL. Debt suit, Virginia *v.* West Virginia; joint resolutions by West Virginia legislature creating commission; opinions of U. S. Supreme court; briefs on final hearing; master's report. [n. p., 1913]

xxxii, 564, 193, xv, [4] p. fold. table. 8°.   H, NYP, V

1287. ———. ———. Proceedings in the Virginia debt case; including the opinion of the Supreme court of U. S., rendered Nov. 10, 1913. Charleston, W. Va., 1913.

viii, 259, p. 8°.   V

1288. ———. DEBT COMMISSION. Report of the New Virginia debt commission, Feb. 8, 1919. [Charleston? 1919]

10 p. 8°.   LC, V

John J. Cornwell, chairman.

Reply to resolutions of the Virginia legislature as to whether an agreement was reached between the commissions of Virginia and West Virginia.

1289. ———. ———. Virginia *v.* West Virginia; a statement of the negotiations between the Virginia and West Virginia debt commissions at the New Hotel Willard, Washington, D. C., Mar. 4, 1914, embracing the proposition submitted by West Virginia, the reply of Virginia thereto, and the rejoinder of West Virginia. [n. p., n. d.]

19 p. 8°.   V

1290. ———. GENERAL ASSEMBLY. SENATE. FINANCE COMMITTEE. Report . . . [on the subject of Virginia's public debt and the share which it is equitable for West Virginia to bear and pay] Charleston, W. Va., Dec. 22, 1873. [Charleston, Walker, 1873?]

44 p. tables. 8°.   V, VU

1291. ———. ———. ———. ———. The Virginia debt. Report . . . Charleston, W. Va. [1903?]

5 p. 8°.   V

1292. ———. GOVERNOR (Henry D. Hatfield). Special message of His Excellency, Henry D. Hatfield, governor, to the Legislature of West Virginia, Feb. 5, 1915, together with the report of the Virginia debt commission, made pursuant to the requirements of a joint resolution of the Legislature adopted Feb. 21, 1913 . . . Printed by order of the commission. [Charleston, W. Va., Tribune, 1915]

116 p. 8°.   LC, NYP, V
John W. Mason, chairman of the West Virginia commission.

1293. ———. ———. Special message of Gov. Hatfield to Legislature of 1917 on subject of the Virginia debt. [Charleston, W. Va., Tribune, 1917]

58 p. 8°.   LC, NYP, V
An appendix to the governor's special message on the same subject to the Legislature of 1915.

1294. WILLIAMS, CHARLES U. Present financial status of Virginia: with some suggestions as to the importance and means of restoring the credit of the state. Richmond, Goode, 1877.

23 p. 8°.   V, VU
By a member of the Finance committee of the Virginia House of delegates; with the minority report of the Committee, regarding taxation and the public debt.

Other Source Material

1295. The ADJUSTMENT COMPANY. To holders of the West Virginia debt. Baltimore, 1893.

22 p. tables. 8°.   V
Brief history of the debt and factors involved in bringing about a settlement.

1296. AMERICAN INSTITUTE OF BANKING. RICHMOND CHAPTER. Year book . . . [Richmond? 19—

8°.   V: 1910.

1297. AMERICAN NATIONAL BANK, Richmond, Va. Tempus fugit. [Richmond, Dietz, ca. 1913]

40 p. 12°.   V
Contains list of officers and board of directors of the bank.

1298. BENNOCH, FRANCIS.   Report of Mr. Francis Bennoch on Virginia.   Sept., 1880.   London [Wertheimer, Lea & co.] 1880.
8 p. 8°.   LC, NYP, VU
Report on economic conditions (especially financial) of Virginia, on behalf of foreign bondholders, after a personal investigation.

1299. BONDHOLDERS' COMMITTEE, New York.   Agreement, dated May 19, 1890.   Between . . . Bondholders' committee and creditors of Virginia . . .   [New York, 1890]
6 p. 8°.   NYP

1300. ———.   Plan and proposition for the adjustment of the debt of Virginia, dated Nov. 28, 1890 . . .   [New York, 1890]
7 p. 8°.   NYP

1301. ———.   Settlement of the debt of the state of Virginia, under the bondholders' agreement of May 12, 1890, the "Plan and Proposition" of Nov. 28, 1890, and the Act of the Legislature of Virginia, approved Feb. 20, 1892.   Showing the award made to the depositing security holders by Hon. Edward J. Phelps, John Henry Daniell, and S. N. Braithwaite, committee of distribution.   [New York, 189-?]
70 p. tables. 8°.   LC

1302. ———.   The Virginia debt settlement.   History of the bonds . . .   [New York? 1890?]
20 p. 8°.   NYP, V
S. G. Ellis, Secretary of the Committee.
Statement by the Committee appointed under an agreement "to consummate such a compromise as creditors (of the State) accept."

1303. BROWN, J. WILLCOX.   [Article on the state debt of Virginia. Pub. in the Richmond *Times-dispatch*, Feb., 1913]
3 p. typew. 4°.   V

1304. ———.   Financial relief that might have been.   [Richmond] 1911.
7 p. typew. 4°.   V: Access. no. 87.
Copy of article pub. in the Richmond *Times-dispatch*, 1911.

1305. ———.   State debt of Virginia.   [Richmond] 1911.
3 p. 4°.   V: Access. no. 89.
Copy of article pub. in the Richmond *Times-dispatch*, Feb. 21, 1911.

1306. The CASE of William D. Coleman . . . Baltimore, Foster, 1878.

110 p. 8°.   **V, VU**

Involving the Sinking fund commission and the public debt of Virginia.

1307. CATON, JAMES R., & H. B. Synopsis of the corporation law of the state of Virginia. Alexandria, Ramey, 1903.

16 p. 16°.   **BP**

1308. CHITTENDEN, LUCIUS E. Three letters addressed to the Treasurer of Virginia, occasioned by the measures proposed in the Legislature of that state, in the session of 1872, involving the repudiation of the principal or interest of the bonds of the commonwealth of Virginia. Washington, Gibson, 1872.

41 p. 8°.   .   **BP**

1309. [CLERGYMAN, *signed*] Repudiation is theft . . . forcible adjustment highway robbery. [n. p., 187-?]

16 p. 8°.   **NYP**

1310. COLLINSON, JOHN. Virginia state debt. Report of Mr. John Collinson and Mr. E. R. Leland, to the Council of foreign bondholders, and the Funding association of the U. S. A. (ltd.), on the funding act, 1879; with appendix of documents. [London, Wertheimer, Lea & co., n. d.]

29 p. 8°.   **VU**

1311. CONFERENCE TO CONSIDER THE QUESTION OF TAX REFORM, Richmond, Va. Proceedings . . . at Hotel Richmond, Richmond, Virginia, Jan. 20 and 21, 1914. Richmond, Whittet & Shepperson, 1914.

67, [1] p. 8°.   **NYP, V, VU**

Under the auspices of the Richmond Chamber of commerce.

1312. CORPORATION OF FOREIGN BONDHOLDERS, London. Annual general report of the Council . . . London [187-? - ?]

8°.   **NYP**: 1873(?), 76-79, 81.

Contains information on the Virginia state debt.

1313. [771] DIGGS, ISAAC. Virginia corporation digest . . . Richmond, 1907.

1314. ELAM, W. C.   Mahone and Virginia!   An open letter to Hon. John Paul, from Col. W. C. Elam.   [n. p., n. d.]

15 p. 8°.   V

1315. FACTS about West Virginia's share of the debt; also a compilation of what has occurred in either state respecting it.   [n. p., 1882?]

9 p. 8°.   V
Argument over the proposition that West Virginia pay one-third of the debt.

1316. FULKERSON, ABRAHAM.   [Notes for speeches made by Abraham Fulkerson on the repudiation of the state debt.   1879]

MSS.   **V**: Access. no. 13750.

1317. ———.   [Speech of Abraham Fulkerson at Abingdon, Va. n. d.]

19 p. MSS.   **V**: Access. no. 93.
Speech on the state debt.

1318. GARNETT, CHRISTOPHER B., *et al.,* comp.   The business man's code of Virginia laws, containing a compilation of such statutes as every business man needs and should have access to . . . containing, also, forms, precedents, explanations, and the constitution of Virginia; comp. and ed. by Christopher B. Garnett and Robert N. Pollard . . . Pulaski, Va., Smith, 1907.

2 p. l., 634, p. 8°.   **LC, V**

1319. GERMAN-AMERICAN BANKING & BUILDING CO., Richmond, Va. Constitution of the German-American banking & building company.   (Perpetual)   Richmond, Randolph & English, 1890.

16 p. 12°.   V

1320. GREGORY, J. M.   Judge J. M. Gregory, of Chesterfield County, Virginia, re-writes his letter in Chesterfield *Chronicle* of Apr. 24, 1898, by request of the Populist club of Swansboro, Va. . . . [n. p., 1898]

29 p. 12°.   V
Concerning the state bank bill, and why the Populists cannot support the money platforms of either the Republican or the Democratic party.

1321. [HAAS, T. N.] [Communication to the daily *News-record,* Harrisonburg, Virginia, concerning taxation. Sept. 17, 1925]

    12 l. typew. f°.   V

    Copy of article pub. in the Harrisonburg daily *News-record,* Sept. 19, 1925.

    On the necessity of equalizing taxation.

1322. Is Virginia bankrupt? [n. p., 187-?]

    34 p. 8°.   VU

    I. Thomas Branch & co., bankers and commission merchants.—II. Paper, nos. 1-4, signed "B. T. J." [*i. e.,* Bradley T. Johnson] Reprinted from Richmond *Dispatch.*—III. Edmund Pendleton on the state debt and funding bill. Botetourt County, Jan. 6, 1875. Reprinted from Richmond *Dispatch.*

1323. [JOHNSON, BRADLEY T.] The public debt of Virginia and the attempt to repeal the funding bill. [n. p., 1872?]

    16 p. 8°.   V, VU, WM

    Arguments in support of the funding bill.

1324. [792] JOHNSON, LUCIUS E. Address delivered before the Committee on corporations of the Constitutional convention [of Virginia] . . . [Roanoke] 1902.

1325. [793] ———. Taxation of the Norfolk & western railway in the state of Virginia . . . Roanoke [1915]

1326. LEE, ROBERT E. [Letter (to J. Willcox Brown, Dec. 23, 1868), declining to go into the life insurance business]

    2 p. typew. MS. (copy)   V: Access. no. 91.

    A brief explanation of his own letter, to which this was a reply, is added by Mr. Brown (dated Mar. 18, 1913).

1327. [1124] LIBERTY MUTUAL INSURANCE CO. The cost of compensation insurance in Virginia. Boston [*ca.* 1918]

1328. LIFE INSURANCE COMPANY OF VIRGINIA. Non-participating premium rates ordinary and intermediate, together with tables of loans and surrender values. Richmond, Va. [1908]

    211 p. tables. 16°.   H

1329. LOUISA FARMERS' LIFE INSURANCE CO., Louisa, Va. Constitution and by-laws . . . (Annual catalogue, 1902-03). [Louisa, Va., Louisa County news, 1902]

    16 p. 8°.   V

    Organized, May, 1894.

1330. LYONS, JAMES. The funding bill; is it constitutional? The opinion of the Hon. James Lyons in the negative. Richmond, Whittet & Shepperson, 1878.

15 p. 8°.   V, VU

1331. McNEILL, WARREN A. Probable incidence of the gasoline tax. [1925]

7 l. tables, diagrs. typew. photostat. f°.   V

"This is a slight revision of a study published in the *Times-dispatch*, Richmond, Va., Sunday, Nov. 22, 1925."

1332. MAHONE, WILLIAM. Re-adjuster-Republican debt settlement unhinged by Bourbon legislation . . . [Petersburg, Va., 1885]

4 p. 8°.   BP

1333. [MARSHALL, WILLIAM] Whose repudiation? [London, 188-?]

16 p. 8°. No title-page.   NYP

1334. [MASON, JAMES M.] The facts about West Virginia's equitable proportion of the debt incurred by Virginia, before she was divided. [n. p., 1874?]

23 p. 8°.   V

Preface signed: J. M. Mason, Charleston, W. Va.

A West Virginian's account of the early period of the debt controversy. He was a creditor of Virginia.

1335. MASSEY, JOHN E. Autobiography of John E. Massey; ed. by Elizabeth H. Hancock. New York and Washington, Neale, 1909.

312 p. front. (port.) 8°.

Memoirs of the "Father of readjustment"; intimate information on the debt controversy, with quotations from contemporary newspapers.

1336. MEDICAL SOCIETY OF VIRGINIA. LEGISLATIVE COMMITTEE. The relation of the medical profession to the public health. Richmond, Va., 1909.

22 p. 12°.   V

Reasons why Virginia physicians should be exempt from a license tax

1337. MERCHANTS & PLANTERS SAVINGS BANK, Richmond, Va. Charter, constitution and by-laws. . . . Chartered Mar., 1867 . . . Richmond, Examiner, 1867.

14 p. 16°.   V

1338. MINOR, RALEIGH C. The law of tax titles in Virginia . . .
[Charlottesville] Anderson bros., University of Virginia, 1898.

    viii, [2], 188 p. 8°.   LC, V

1339. MOSS, W. W. Address on the need of a state bank examiner
[in Virginia]. Delivered at the annual meeting of the Virginia
Board of trade, Roanoke, Va., Aug. 30-31, 1905. Richmond,
Whittet & Shepperson, 1905.

    8 p. 8°.   V

1340. MUTUAL ASSURANCE SOCIETY. Constitution, rules and regulations of the Mutual assurance society against fire on buildings of
the state of Virginia . . . Richmond, Wynne, 1866.

    23 p. 12°.   McC

1341. ——. Constitution, rules and regulations of the . . .
society . . . , as amended and revised July 11th, 1898. Incorporated 1794. Richmond, Jones, 1898.

    36 p. 16°.   V

1342. MUTUAL BUILDING FUND ASSOCIATION. Constitution and by-
laws . . . (organized Feb. 29, 1876), Lexington, Va. Richmond, Guide & News, 1876.

    22 p. 16°.   McC

1343. PAGE, THOMAS W. The future of tax reform in Virginia.
Prepared for the Richmond "Times-Dispatch" . . . [Rich-
mond, n. d.]

    8°.   VU

1344. PETERSBURG LAND BANK COMMITTEE. Argument presented to
the Federal farm loan board for the establishment of a Federal
land bank at Petersburg, Va. Presented by Petersburg land bank
committee representing the Chamber of commerce and the city
. . . [Petersburg? Va.] 1916.

    81 p. 20 maps (fold.) tables, diagrs. 8°.   H, NYP, V, VU
    William H. Mann, chairman.

1345. The PUBLIC debt of Virginia. [n. p., 1888?]

    6 l. 4°.   LC
    Summary history of the debt and the embarrassing financial condi-
tion of Virginia since the Civil war.

1346. REAL ESTATE BANK OF VIRGINIA. Communication from the Real estate bank of Virginia to the General assembly [of Virginia] of 1st January, 1873. [Norfolk? 1873?]

9 p. 8°.   WM,
Basis of the organization and how the bank can relieve the financial strain of the state.

1347. REYNOLDS, C. M. Virginia defended. A letter to a British bondholder, by Hon. C. M. Reynolds, treasurer of the state. [n. p., 1880]

broadside. 44 x 26 cm.   V
Concerning the state debt.

1348. RICHMOND NEWS-LEADER. The fee system in Virginia, with suggestions for improvements in the existing laws . . . Richmond, Va., 1925.

66 p. tables. 8°. (The *Richmond News-Leader* reprints, 1)   V
"Being a compilation of editorials appearing in the Richmond News-Leader, 1924-25."
Appendix: Report of the State fee commission for 1922, p. 51-66.

1349. ROCKBRIDGE BUILDING FUND ASSOCIATION, Lexington, Va. Constitution and by-laws of the Rockbridge building fund association, organized Oct. 31, 1866. Lexington, Letcher, Leech & Burgess, 1868.

32 p. 16°.   McC

1350. ROCKINGHAM HOME MUTUAL FIRE INSURANCE CO., North River, Va. Constitution and by-laws of the . . . company. Incorporated 1869. Rev. 1902 . . . [n. p., 1902?]

14, [4] p. 16°.   V

1351. ROCKINGHAM NATIONAL BANK. Facts and figures; scenes and views. Harrisonburg and Rockingham County, Virginia. [Harrisonburg, 1913?]

12 l. illus. obl. 24°.   NYP

1352. ROYALL, WILLIAM L. The president's relations with Senator Mahone and repudiation. An attempt to subvert the Supreme court of the U. S. New York, Hale, 1882.

48 p. 12°.   NYP, V, VU
Reveals the influence of the debt question in Virginia politics and subsequently in national relations.

1353. ————. Some reminiscences . . . New York and Washington, Neale, 1909.

> 210 p. 12°.
> Life in Richmond after the Civil war as experienced by the author; a conservative's account of financial conditions.

1354. RUFFIN, FRANK G. Essay on the inspection laws of Virginia. [n. p., 1869]

> 16 p. 8°.   **BP, VU**
> Analysis of these tax laws.

1355. [SCOTT, JOHN] During the war and after the war. Warrenton, Va., Caldwell & Frank [1896?]

> 1 p. l., 59 p. 1 l., 13 p. 8°.   **LC, V**
> Ed. of [1900?] 5 p. l., 97 p. front. (port.) 12°.   **V**
> Pt. 2 has title: *The coupon controversy;* the Virginia debt question and the struggle in the courts.

1356. SHANDS, WILLIAM R. The Virginia blue sky law. Address . . . before the Virginia state bar association at Hot Springs, Va., Aug. 12, 13, 14, 1925. Richmond, Richmond press, 1926.

> 23 p. 8°.   **V**

1357. SHEWMAKE, OSCAR L. The uniform small loan law and its operation on Virginia . . . 2d ed. Richmond, Va., Virginia industrial lenders assoc., 1926.

> 26 p. 12°.   **WM**

1358. SOUTHEASTERN BUILDING & LOAN ASSOCIATION, Norfolk, Va. . . . Agents' instruction book. Norfolk, Va., 1895.

> 14 p. 16°.   **LC**

1359. [STAUNTON LIFE INSURANCE CO., Staunton, Va.] Coupon policy forms. [Staunton, 1894]

> [8] p. 6 fold. forms. nar. 8°.   **LC**

1360. STUART, ALEXANDER H. Address . . . to the people of Augusta County [Virginia], reviewing the state debt of Virginia. How it was incurred, legislation in regard to it, and how it can be paid. Staunton, Va., Spectator, 1877.

> 12 p. 8°.   **VU**
> Reprint from Staunton *Spectator,* June 19, 1877.

1361. THORNTON, SIR EDWARD, *et al.* Virginia state debt. Report to the Council of foreign bondholders of negotiations conducted at Richmond by the Right Hon. Sir Edward Thornton . . . and Mr. S. N. Braithwaite, on behalf of the English bondholders. London, The Council of foreign bondholders, 1887.

> 67 p., 1 l. 3 fold. tables. 8°.   LC, V

1362. . . . To the treasurer of the commonwealth of Virginia. [Richmond? 1872]

> 24 p. 8°.   LC
> Series of letters, signed "Adirondack," upon the finances of Virginia; warning against possible repudiation of the state debt.

1363. [TYLER, NATHANIEL] What is our true policy? It is herein considered: by a Virginian . . . Richmond, Gary & Clemmitt, 1866.

> 76 p. 8°.   LC
> Copyrighted by Nathaniel Tyler.
> Proposed application of a plan of real estate loan associations to Virginia.

1364. VIRGINIA ALBERENE CORPORATION. Mortgage and deed of trust. Dated Mar. 1, 1922. Virginia alberene corporation to the Pennsylvania company for insurances on lives and granting annuities, trustee . . . Philadelphia, Allen, Lane & Scott [1922?]

> 72 p. 8°.   HB

1365. ———. [*Ibid.*, dated May 1, 1925]

> 95 p. 8°.   HB

1366. VIRGINIA ASSOCIATION FOR THE COMMON GOOD. Showing Virginia's total revenues and disbursements for the fiscal years, 1911-1921 . . . Comp. and based upon State auditor's reports. Richmond, Va., 1922.

> blue-print.   V

1367. ———. Statement showing capital invested in Virginia. In national and state institutions (including regional reserve banks), manufacturing, mining, jobbing and retail business, and Virginia's agricultural wealth, as compared with other southern states . . . Richmond, Va., 1922.

> diagr. (blue-print) 61½ x 63 cm.   V
> T. M. Wortham, statistician.

1368. VIRGINIA BANKERS' ASSOCIATION. Proceedings of the . . .
annual convention . . . [1st- ; 1894?-19—] [Richmond,
1894?-19—

> plates, ports. 8°.
> H: 1923; **LC**: 1913, 15-16, 21-28; **NYP**: 1908, 10-19, 21-22, 25, 28;
> **V**: 1903-16, 21-28.

1369. ———. Program of the . . . annual convention . . .
[Richmond? 18-? -19—

> 8°.   **V**: 1925, 27-28.

1370. ———. Report of the agricultural committee . . . [Rich-
mond, 19—

> 12°.   **USAg**: 1918, 20.

1371. VIRGINIA FIRE & MARINE INSURANCE CO. Historical sketch of
the Virginia fire & marine insurance company, together with valuable hints to insurers, fire insurance explained, statement of
condition of company, etc. Richmond, Clemmitt & Jones, 1879.

> 120 p. 12°.   **V**
> Contains list of agencies in Virginia.

1372. VIRGINIA SENTIMENT on question of abolishing internal-
revenue tax and removal of duties on iron ores, soft coal, coke,
etc. [n. p., 1887?]

> 13 p. 8°.   **LC**
> Reveals feeling of industrial districts and mining regions against the
> internal-revenue tax and in favor of a higher tariff.

1373. VIRGINIA STATE CHAMBER OF COMMERCE. [Documents on fi-
nance] Richmond, 1925-28.

> nar. 8°.   **H, NYP, V**
> *Civics doc.,* no. 2: "Virginia budget system" (1925). *Finance doc.,*
> no. 1: "Tax conditions in Virginia" (1925); no. 2: "Virginia revenues
> and expenditures" (1925); no. 3: "Tax administration in Virginia and
> other states" (1925); no. 4: "Tax needs in Virginia" (1925). *Miscell. doc.,*
> no. 5: "First year 5-5 program, 1924-28" (1925); no. 10: "Second year
> 5-5 program, 1924-28" (1926); no. 14: "Third year 5-5 program . . ."
> (1927); no. 18: "Fourth year 5-5 program . . ." (1928).

1374. VIRGINIA TRUST CO., Richmond. Address of the president at
the annual meeting of the stockholders . . . [Richmond?
19—

> 8°.   **V**: Jan. 20, 1926.

1375. ———. [Statement of condition] Richmond, Va. [19—

> 12°.   **V**: 1928.

1376. [A VIRGINIAN] An investigation of the act of the General assembly for the funding of the public debt, approved Mar. 30, 1871. By a Virginian. [n. p., 1871?]

> 7 p. 8°.   VU
> Argument, based upon constitutional grounds, against funding the debt.

1377. [WEST VIRGINIA COMMITTEE, New York] Virginia deferred certificates, commonly known as "West Virginia certificates." [New York, Cole, 1885]

> 10 p. 8°.   NYP

1378. WEST VIRGINIA DEBT agreement. Agreement under which the certificates will be deposited. Committee: John Crosby Brown, chairman [et al.] [New York? 1898]

> 4 p. 8°.   V
> Committee: John C. Brown, chairman, J. Kennedy Tod, George Coppell, Clarence Cary. Advisory board: Thomas F. Bayard, W. Pinkney Whyte, Edward J. Phelps, George G. Williams. Depository: Brown bros. & co., New York. Secretary of committee: Robert L. Harrison. Counsel: Cary & Whitridge, New York.

1379. WILLIAMS, ASHBY. Corporation laws of Virginia (being an Act concerning corporations, which became a law May 21, 1903; with amendments contained in acts 1904, 1906, and 1908; and other general acts relating to corporations) together with abstracts of the decisions of the courts, and a full collection of forms . . . Roanoke, Va., Stone, 1909.

> xxii, 282 p. 8°.   LC, V

1380. WISE, HENRY A. Address at West Point, Va., Dec. 29, 1874, to the Knights of Pythias, on their invitation. [Richmond, 1875]

> 18 p. 8°.   V
> A plea against the payment of the debt of the old state of Virginia (before the separation of West Virginia), by the present commonwealth.

1381. WOODHULL, MAXWELL V. Outlines of a plan for the refunding and management of the debt of Virginia. Copyright, 1888, by Maxwell Van Zandt Woodhull. Washington, D. C., Judd & Detweiler, 1888.

> 7 p. 8°.

Secondary Works

1382. CUNNINGHAM, RICHARD E. Fifty years of service, 1870-
1920. Richmond, Va., National state & city bank [1920]

> 44 p. incl. front., illus (incl. ports.) 8°.   **H, LC, NYP**
> Sketch of the history and organization of the bank, by the vice-
> president.

1383. DANFORTH, JOHN B., *et al.* Historical sketch of the Mutual
assurance society of Virginia, Richmond, Va., from its organization in 1794 to 1879, comp. by John B. Danforth and Herbert A.
Claiborne. Richmond, Jones, 1879.

> 2 p. l., 153 p. incl. tables. 8°.   **V**
> Annals of the company, based upon its record and documents.

1384. JACKSON, E. HILTON. Is Virginia entitled to compensation
for the cession of the Northwest territory to the national government? Paper read by Mr. E. Hilton Jackson of Washington,
D. C., before the Virginia state bar association at the Hotel Chamberlin, Old Point, Va., Aug. 6th, 7th, 8th, 1912. Richmond,
Richmond press [*ca.* 1913]

> 36 p. 8°.   **LC, V**
> Historical aspects of the question are discussed and the issue raised in
> connection with Virginia's debt controversy with West Virginia.

1385. MAGRUDER, FRANK A. . . . Recent administration in Virginia . . . Baltimore, Johns Hopkins, 1912.

> vii p., 1 l., 11-204 p. 8°. (Johns Hopkins university, *Studies in histori-
> cal and political science* . . . XXX, 1)
> A study, based mainly upon government documents, of the state's ex-
> pansion in administration along economic, educational, and political
> lines, since the constitutional convention of 1902.

1386. PEARSON, CHARLES C. The readjuster movement in Virginia
. . . New Haven, Yale university; [etc.] 1917.

> viii p., 1 l., 191 p. fold. maps. 8°. (Yale historical publications.
> *Miscellany,* IV)
> Scholarly study of Virginia's debt controversy and its relation to
> national forces, showing the interplay of conservatism, aristocracy, and
> democracy.

1387. ROYALL, WILLIAM L. History of the Virginia debt controversy. The Negro's vicious influence in politics. . . . Richmond, Va., West, 1897.

> 111 p. 12°.   **BP, LC, NYP, V, VU**
> Virginia's financial struggle and the readjustment movement told from

the conservatïve point of view; the author writes, in part, from personal experience.

1388. SNAVELY, TIPTON R. . . . The taxation of Negroes in Virginia . . . [Charlottesville, Va., Michie, 1916]

> 97 p. incl. illus. (map) tables, diagrs. 8°. (University of Virginia. *Phelps-Stokes fellowship papers,* III)
> Unbiased study showing especially inequalities in taxation, delinquency, and political effects of the tax system.

1389. SYDENSTRICKER, EDGAR. A brief history of taxation in Virginia . . . Issued by the Legislative reference bureau of Virginia. Richmond, Bottom, 1915.

> 66 p. 8°.
> A clear account, covering the entire history of the state, to 1914, based upon tax records, acts, reports, and other documents.

1390. VIRGINIA HIGH-SCHOOL LITERARY & ATHLETIC LEAGUE. . . . State tax commission . . . Pub. by the University [of Virginia] [Charlottesville, Surber-Arundale, 1924]

> 129 p. incl. tables. 8°. *University of Virginia record.* Extension series, VIII, 6, Feb., 1924)   **USE, V, VU**
> Reprints of articles on taxation and tax reform.

Periodicals

1391. The BI-MONTHLY guild. A journal devoted to the interests of beneficial organizations. v. 1-18, ; [1890?]-1907; Richmond, Va.[H. T. Ezekiel, etc., 1890?]-1907.

> illus. (incl. ports.) 4°. monthly. No more pub.
> LC: XII-XVIII, 2; Feb., 1901-Apr., 1907.
> Concerned particularly with insurance; reveals also contemporary social conditions.

1391a. FEDERAL RESERVE BANK OF RICHMOND. Monthly review, business and agricultural conditions. Richmond, Va. [1921?—
> monthly.   **HB**: 1921-28.

1392. The INSURANCE advocate; devoted to life, fire, and marine insurance . . . Richmond, Va., 1870-[?]
> monthly?   **V**: I (1870).
> William P. Gretter, ed.

1393. The INSURANCE advocate . . . Vol. 1-[5?] Richmond, Va., 1876-[80?]
> monthly?   **NYP**: 1876, 78-80.

1394. The RICHCHAP. Richmond chapter, American institute of banking. Vol. 1-   [1913?—   ] Richmond, Va. [1913?—

> illus. 8°. monthly?
> V: XV, 2-8; **XVI**, 1-6; (1927/28-28/29).

Directory

1395. VIRGINIAS and Carolinas insurance directory . . . Louisville, Ky., The Insurance field, 19—

> 12°.   **LC**: 1912/13.

> For further references on Finance, Banking, Insurance, etc., see Pt. II, § 7: *Urban and County Development;* also Pt. IV, § 3: *Local Government.*

7. URBAN AND COUNTY DEVELOPMENT

Government Publications and Documents

> See Pt. IV, § 3: *Local Government*—Government Publications and Documents.

Other Source Material: (a) Urban Development

Abingdon, Va.

1396. WILMER, ARTHUR P., ed. Abingdon, Virginia: a sketch of its history and attractions. An educational center and delightful residential town . . . situated in a country unsurpassed for combined mineral and agricultural wealth . . . Lynchburg, Va. [n. d.]

> 24 p. illus. 8°.   **LC**
> Emphasis upon coal and iron resources.

Alexandria, Va.

1397. ALEXANDRIA HOSPITAL. Annual report . . . 1st- ; [1872/73?-19—] Alexandria [1873?-19—

> 8°. Report year ends Jan. 31.   **LC**: 1906/07.
> Financial and administrative report.

1398. ALEXANDRIA WATER CO. . . . Annual report . . . [n. p., 1865?-19—

> nar. 8°. Report year ends June 30.
> HB: 1922/23; NYP: 1866/67, 70/71-76/77, 78/79.

1399. CALLAHAN, CHARLES H. The memorial to Washington; an historic souvenir . . . [Alexandria, Local memorial committee of Alexandria, *ca.* 1923]

> 128 p. col. front., illus., col. pl., ports., fold. map. 4°.   **LC, V, WM**
> Concerning the nature and purpose of the Washington masonic national memorial association and the monument being erected at Alexandria.

1400. FREEMASONS. ALEXANDRIA-WASHINGTON LODGE, NO. 22. The lodge of George Washington and his masonic neighbors. [Washington, D. C., Roberts, 1920]

> [50] p. incl. illus., ports., plan, facsim. 8°.   **LC, V, VU**
> On cover: A memorial to Washington, the mason, to be erected at Alexandria, Va.

1401. JACKSON, EUGENE B. . . . The romance of historic Alexandria . . . A complete guide to the old city with explanation and map of markers. Rev. & enl. edit. Alexandria, Wade, 1923.

> 4 p. l., 73 p. illus. (incl. ports.) map. 8°.   **BP, LC, NYP, V, VU**

1402. The WASHINGTON HERALD. Progressive Alexandria. 1910. The Washington herald. [Washington, 1910]

> 20 p. illus. f°.   **LC**
> Alexandria edition of the *Herald,* portraying the city's economic and social progress.

1403. WASHINGTON MONUMENT ASSOCIATION, Alexandria, Va. . . . Memorial medallions struck at the Philadelphia mint by order of Congress to aid in erecting a monument to Washington as a citizen, in his home town. Alexandria, Va., Washington monument association [1902?]

> [15] p. illus. 16°.   **LC**

1404. WEDDERBURN, ALEXANDER J. Historic Alexandria, Va., past

and present. Souvenir Virginia ter-centennial, 1907. Endorsed
by City council and Chamber of commerce. [n. p., 1907]

92 p. illus. 8°.   LC, V
Hand-book for the Jamestown exposition.

1405. ———. . . . Souvenir Virginia ter-centennial of historic
Alexandria, Va., past and present . . . [Alexandria, *ca.*
1907]

[96] p. illus. obl. 8°.   H, LC, V

Appomattox C. H., Va.

1406. APPOMATTOX LAND CO. Prospectus . . . Washington,
Gibson, 1890.

11 p. 12°.   LC
Company organized to develop real estate in Appomattox Court
House, through historic interest in the place.

Bristol, Va.-Tenn.

1407. HISTORICAL and descriptive review of the industries and resources of the city of Bristol-Goodson, Tenn. and Va., including
many sketches of its public spirited men, and enterprising business establishments. New York [Bristol, Tenn.] Empire pub.,
1885.

86 p. front., illus., ports. 8°.   V
A publication using superlatives extensively to portray the advantages
and possibilities of the city.

1408. ISAACS, I. J., comp. The city of Bristol, Virginia-Tennessee,
its interests and industries; comp. under the auspices of the Board
of trade. Also a series of comprehensive sketches of representative business enterprises. . . . Bristol, King, 1915.

88 p. illus. 8°.   LC, NYP
Commercial and industrial progress of the city since 1900; a typical
board of trade pamphlet.

Buena Vista, Va.

1409. BUENA VISTA, Virginia. [New York, Southern pub., 189-?]

46 p. incl. illus. 4°.
Descriptive pamphlet.

1410. Facts worth knowing about Buena Vista. Giles County [Virginia]   [New York, 1890]

    24 p. map. 12°.   **NYP**

Charlottesville, Va.

1411. Albemarle club of colonial dames. A historical guide to Albemarle County, including Monticello, the University of Virginia, and Charlottesville . . . Pub. under auspices of the Albemarle club of colonial dames and the Albemarle chapter, Daughters of the American revolution. Charlottesville, Michie, 1924.

    64 p. illus., fold. map (front.) 12°.   **VU**
    Advertisements in back.

1412. American legion. Virginia. Charlottesville & Albemarle post, no. 74. All aboard; a farcical musical comedy . . . [Program] Jefferson theatre, May 12 & 13, 1924. [Charlottesville, Va., Surber-Arundale, 1924]

    [30] p. 4°. Advertisements interspersed.   **VU**

1413. Bibb, A. P., & co. Piedmont Virginia: with notice of Charlottesville, the central city of the Old Dominion. [Resources of Albemarle County, Va.] Charlottesville, Jeffersonian [1893?]

    77 p. illus. 8°.   **NYP**

1414. Charlottesville Chamber of commerce. Charlottesville in Albemarle County, Virginia . . . Charlottesville, Michie [1926?]

    [12] p. illus. nar. 8°.   **VU**
    Advertising the resources, activities, etc., of the city.

1415. Charlottesville home-coming committees. The pageant "The light of Albemarle," and official program. Albemarle home-coming celebration. Charlottesville, Virginia, Nov. 1-2-3-4, 1922. [Charlottesville, Surber-Arundale, 1922]

    [56] p. illus., map. 4°.   **VU**
    Includes notes on the resources of the county.

1416. Charlottesville public health & nurse association. Annual reports of officers and committees . . . [n. p., 19—

    12°.   **V:** [1909/10]

1417. The GEORGE ROGERS CLARK statue. [The unveiling of the monument to George Rogers Clark by Robert Aitken, a gift to the University of Virginia from Paul Goodloe McIntire, Charlottesville, Nov. 3, 1921] [Charlottesville? Va., 1921?]

16 p. illus. 8°.   **LC, NYP, VU**

Addresses by Albert Lefevre, Edwin A. Alderman, and Archibald Henderson.

1418. MONTICELLO HOTEL, Charlottesville, Va. A word-picturelogue thru beautiful, historic Charlottesville. Charlottesville, Va., Monticello hotel [*ca.* 1928]

16 p. illus. 8°.   **LC, V, VU**

Brief description of Monticello and other historic estates and the University of Virginia.

1419. The UNVEILING of the Lewis-Clark statue at Midway park in the city of Charlottesville, Virginia, Nov. 21, 1919 . . . being a record of the exercises attending the unveiling; ed. by W. M. Forrest. [Charlottesville] The city of Charlottesville, 1919.

36 p., 1 l. front. 8°.   **LC, NYP, V, VU**

"The Lewis and Clark expedition: an historical discourse," by A. C. Gordon, p. 13-36.

1420. WALKER, ALBERT E., comp. The Daily progress, historical and industrial magazine, Charlottesville, Virginia: "The Athens of the South." Ed. and comp. by Albert E. Walker. Charlottesville, Va., Progress pub. [1906]

46, [1] p. illus. f°.   **BP, VU**

Advertisements in back.

Danville, Va.

1421. ART work of Lynchburg and Danville, Virginia . . . Chicago, Gravure illus. co., 1903.

13 p. illus., 64 pl. f°.   **V**

Description of the cities' industries, residential districts, parks, etc.; beautifully illustrated.

1422. DANVILLE, VA. COMMITTEE OF 40 TO INVESTIGATE THE DANVILLE RIOT. Danville riot, Nov. 3, 1883. Report of Committee of

40 with sworn testimony of 37 witnesses, &c. Richmond, Johns & Goolsby, 1883.

47 p. 8°.   NYP, V, WM

Committee appointed by the citizens of Danville.

1423. DANVILLE GENERAL HOSPITAL. Annual report of the Danville general hospital . . . and the Ladies benevolent society . . . Danville [18-? -19—

8°.   V: 1907-13.

1424. The DANVILLE REGISTER & THE BEE. Industrial survey of Danville trading territory, 1928. City of Danville and Pittsylvania, Henry, Halifax, Patrick, and Franklin counties, Virginia; Rockingham, Caswell, and Person counties, North Carolina. Danville, Va., The Danville register & the bee [1928]

f°.   V

1425. DANVILLE TRACTION & POWER CO. [Circulars . . . 1912] [n. p., 1912]

4°.   HB

1426. LEVY, ERNEST C. Bacteriological report of mechanical filtration plant at Danville, Virginia . . . Pittsburgh, Pittsburgh filter manufacturing co., 1905.

6 p., 1 l. 8°.   H, LC

1427. POLLOCK, EDWARD. Illustrated sketch book of Danville, Virginia; its manufactures and commerce . . . [Danville, Waddill] 1885.

212 p. illus. 8°. Advertisements interspersed.   LC, V

Contains a description of each important firm.

1428. PORTER, DUVAL, ed. Men, places and things, as noted by Benjamin Simpson [*pseud.*] Ed. by Duval Porter. 1st ed. [Danville, Va.] Dance bros., 1891.

400 p. 8°.   LC, V

Pt. 1: *Autobiography,* is a rather disunified account, humorously told, of Simpson's experiences as a newspaper man in Washington, D. C., and Virginia during the 'seventies and 'eighties. Pt. 2: *Miscellaneous.* Pt. 3: *The City of Danville,* with an account of its history during the 'eighties, its government, schools, churches, newspapers, representative men.

Pt. 1 was reprinted, with some omissions and additions, Richmond, 1904, under title: *Adventures of an office seeker.*

1429. RIDDICK, J. HUDSON. The Danville riot; an address, Nov. 10, 1883. Baltimore, 1884.

8 p. 8°.   V

Reprint from *Virginia Star*, Richmond, Nov. 29, 1883. A plea, by a Negro minister, for education of the Negro, and decrying the race prejudice that caused the riot.

Fort Monroe, Va.

See below, *Hampton* and *Norfolk, Va.*

Fredericksburg, Va.

1430. [BORST, ADDISON] Fredericksburg, Va., and vicinity. The home of Washington, Mary, the mother of Washington, Richard Henry Lee, and their descendants. New York, University pub., 1876.

24 p. 12°.   LC, NYP, V

Contains brief description of economic and social conditions in the mid-seventies.

1431. FREDERICKSBURG AND ADJACENT NATIONAL BATTLEFIELDS ME-MORIAL PARK ASSOCIATION. Fredericksburg . . . park association. Fredericksburg, Virginia. 1899. Fredericksburg, Va., Free lance, 1899.

[1], 27 p. fold. map. 8°.   LC, V

Historical sketch of the association, embracing the charter and all state legislation, memorial of the G. A. R., and United Confederate veterans' endorsement, and proposed national legislation.

1432. FREDERICKSBURG and Fredericksburgers. [Fredericksburg, Va., 1903?]

[85] p. illus. 8°.   LC, V

Hand-book of the city's resources and activities.

1433. FREDERICKSBURG CHAMBER OF COMMERCE. Fredericksburg, Virginia, America's most historic city. Ed. by L. J. Houston, jr., city manager. Fredericksburg, Va., 1924.

12 p. illus., map. 8°.   LC, NYP, V

Resumé of political, economic, and social factors of the city; also places of historic interest.

1434. FREE LANCE, Fredericksburg, Va. The Free lance-Star historical and industrial number, portraying the glorious past and future possibilities of Fredericksburg, Virginia; ed. and comp. by Albert E. Walker. Fredericksburg, Va., Free lance-Star pub. [*ca.* 1907]

> 40 p. illus. f°.   LC, NYP, V
>
> Supplement to the Free lance-Star.

1435. HOWISON, ROBERT R. Fredericksburg: past, present and future. New ed. with supplement by Robert Reid Howison . . . Fredericksburg, Va., Adams, 1898.

> 80 p. 12°.   LC
>
> Delivered as a lecture for the benefit of the Fredericksburg library and lyceum association in 1880. Supplement contains a description of the monuments and memorials that are preserved, and a brief summary of economic and social conditions in the 'nineties.
>
> 1st ed., 1880: 52 p.   NYP, V

1436. KISHPAUGH, ROBERT A. America's most historic city, Fredericksburg; a guide to its points of interest . . . Fredericksburg, Va., R. A. Kishpaugh, 1912.

> 32 p. illus. 12°.   LC
>
> Ed. of 1915.   NYP
>
> Ed. of [*ca.* 1922]   LC

Hampton, Va.

1437. [BETTS, CHARLES W.] Visitors' hand book of Old Point Comfort, Va., and vicinity, including Fortress Monroe, town of Hampton, National home for d.[isabled] v.[olunteer] s.[oldiers], National cemetery and Hampton normal and agricultural institute. Ed. of 1883. [anon.] Hampton, Press of the Hampton institute, 1883.

> 52 p. plates. 24°.   H, LC
>
> Ed. of 1885 (3d): 84 p.   BP, NYP
>
> Ed. of 1891 (5th): 104 p.   LC, V
>
> Ed. of 1893: 114, [1] p.   LC

1438. [CUMMING, JAMES M.] Confederate memorial day in Hampton, May 24, 1894. Hampton, Va., Hampton weekly news [1894]

> [4], 40 p. ports. obl. 16°.   H

1439. HAMPTON BOARD OF TRADE. Hampton illustrated, a brief
. . . sketch of Hampton, Va., and its surroundings. Akron,
Ohio, Werner, 1892.

   39 p. obl. 16°.   NYP

1440. HAMPTON MONITOR. Special industrial and Jamestown ter-
centennial exposition number, exploiting the multifarious advantages of Hampton, Virginia. Aug., 1907. Hampton, 1907.

   56 p. f°.   NYP

1441. HEALTH, comfort, pleasure, scenic surroundings, Hygeia Hotel,
the seaside resort of America. [New York, Putnam, 189-?]

   29 p. 12°.   NYP

1442. [KIMBERLY, W. H.] Souvenir of Old Point Comfort and environs. New York, Albertype co., 1889.

   1 p. l., 16 plates. obl. 24°.   LC
   Ed. of 1895: [4] p. 21 plates. obl. 12°.   H

1443. OLD POINT COMFORT. Hotels Hygeia and Chamberlin. George
A. Keeler, manager. [Philadelphia, Art press, n. d.]

   [8] p. illus., map. 8°.   H

1444. OLD POINT COMFORT, Va. Fort Monroe. National home for
disabled volunteer soldiers. Album of views. National cemetery. Hampton normal and agricultural institute. Town of Hampton. [Hampton, Va., Print. off. Normal school] 1883.

   1 p. l., 16 plates. obl. 48°.   LC, NYP

1445. [PHOEBUS, HARRISON] A monograph on Old Point Comfort,
Virginia. Philadelphia, Allen, Lane & Scott [1876]

   22 p. incl. front. map., fold. plan. 12°.   LC
   Proprietor's advertisement of Hygeia hotel.
   Ed. of [1880]: 32 p.   BP

1446. [PLECKER, W. A.] Climate and health at Old Point Comfort,
Virginia. Issued by the Hotel Chamberlin, G. F. Adams, manager.
[n. p., 1904]

   15 p. 12°.   LC

1447. VIEWS of Fortress Monroe and vicinity. Fort Monroe, Va.,
W. Baulch, 1892.

   16 plates. 24°. No title-page.   LC

Harrisonburg, Va.

1448. HARRISONBURG DAILY NEWS. Rockingham County. Its past and present, illustrated ed. [Harrisonburg] pub. by the Harrisonburg daily news [19-?]

illus. f°.   **VU**

1449. HISTORIC Harrisonburg . . . [Roanoke, Va., Stone, *ca.* 1908]

[12] p. illus. obl. 8°.   **LC**
"Arranged for the Men's organ committee of the Presbyterian church in Harrisonburg, Virginia." Contains views of the city, with brief notes.

1450. [1351] ROCKINGHAM NATIONAL BANK. Facts and figures; scenes and views. . . . [Harrisonburg, 1913?]

Lexington, Va.

1451. [1342] MUTUAL BUILDING FUND ASSOCIATION. Constitution and by-laws . . . Richmond, 1876.

1452. [1349] ROCKBRIDGE BUILDING FUND ASSOCIATION, Lexington, Va. Constitution and by-laws . . . Lexington, 1868.

1453. UNITED DAUGHTERS OF THE CONFEDERACY. MARY CUSTIS LEE CHAPTER, Lexington, Va. Historic Lexington. [n. p., 1907?]

unp. illus. 4°.   **V**

Liberty, Va.

1454. POLLOCK, EDWARD. Sketch-book of Liberty, Virginia. Its people and its trade. Liberty, Va., Bedford index, 1887.

143 p. illus. 12°.   **LC, V**
Advertisements interspersed.

Lynchburg, Va.

1455. [1421] ART work of Lynchburg and Danville, Virginia . . . Chicago, 1903.

1456. COLORED ORPHAN ASYLUM & INDUSTRIAL SCHOOL, Lynchburg. Report . . . [n. p., 18-? -96?]

8°.   **USC:** 1891, 95-96.

1457. HELPER, HINTON A. Centennial souvenir of Lynchburg, Va. New York, South pub. [1886]

96 p. sq. 16°.   NYP

1458. [327] LYNCHBURG, VA. An armor plant for the United States, Lynchburg, Virginia . . . [Lynchburg] 1917.

1459. LYNCHBURG CHAMBER OF COMMERCE. Lynchburg in old Virginia. The city of industry and opportunity. [Lynchburg] Pub. by the Publicity and advertising committee of the Chamber of commerce [191-?]

48 p. 8°.   VU

1460. ODD FELLOWS HOME OF VIRGINIA, Lynchburg. Charter, bylaws, and forms of application for admission, Odd Fellows home of Virginia. Lynchburg, Va., 1910. [Richmond, Va., Pohlig, 1910?]

22 p. 16°.   V

1461. POLLOCK, EDWARD, ed. Sketch book of Lynchburg, Va. Its people and its trade . . . Pub. by E. Pollock and S. C. Judson. E. Pollock, comp. and ed. Lynchburg, Va., Virginia job print., 1887.

176 p. illus. 8°. Advertisements interspersed.   LC
The publishers claim one merit for the book, "its fidelity to fact . . ."

Manassas, Va.

1462. The MANASSAS JOURNAL. Historical, pictorial, educational, industrial and anniversary edition . . . v. 17, no. 1; May 19, 1911. [Manassas, Va., The Manassas journal pub. co., 1911]

4, 40 p. illus. f°.   LC, V

Manchester, Va.

1463. BURGWYN, COLLINSON P. Report of Col. C. P. E. Burgwyn, civil engineer, on the natural advantages and water-power facilities of the city of Manchester and the county of Chesterfield, with accompanying maps. Manchester, Leader, 1888.

8 p. maps. 8°.   ·   V

1464. MANCHESTER BOARD OF TRADE. The city of Manchester, Virginia. [Manchester?] 1896.

> 20 p. illus. 8°. Advertisements interspersed.   **LC**
>
> "A brief summary of her past; some facts and figures about her present, with a glance at her prospects for the future."

1465. TRI-CITY SYSTEM. Richmond, Manchester, and Petersburg, Virginia: trolley rides in cities and country. [n. p., n. d.]

> 36 p. fold., illus., maps. obl. 8°. fold.   **LC**
> Interurban transportation advertising.

1466. **[1044]** VIRGINIA PASSENGER & POWER CO. Annual report . . . [Richmond, Va., 190-? -09?]

1467. **[1046]** VIRGINIA RAILWAY & POWER CO. Annual report . . . to the stockholders . . . Richmond, Fergusson, 1910-25.

Newport News, Va.

1468. BETTER NEWPORT NEWS ASSOCIATION. Report on municipal survey of Newport News, Va. 1919. By D. A. Calhoun. Issued by the Better Newport News association, Newport News, Va., 1919.

> 281 p. maps, plans, tables, diagrs. 4°.   **VU, WM**
>
> A programme of progress affecting all phases of the city's life, as proposed after a study by various experts.

1469. DAILY PRESS, Newport News, Va. Nov. 23, 1913. Booster edition . . . "Newport News thirty years ago . . . Newport News to-day." [Newport News, Va., 1913]

> 60 p. illus. f°. (*Daily press*, XIX, 275)   **V**

1470. [FERRY, B. A., & co.] The harbor of a thousand ships . . . Newport News, Virginia . . . [Newport News, Va., Newport News, print., 1921?]

> 191 p. illus. 8°.   **V, VU**
>
> Description of the city's government, business houses, harbor, etc.

1471. HAMPTON ROADS MARITIME EXCHANGE. Annual . . . Norfolk, Va. [192-?—

illus. 8°.

H: 1925; **NYP**: 1922, 25-27; **USC**: 1922, 25-28; **VU**: 1925; **WM**: 1925.

Descriptions of the port cities of Hampton Roads; their commercial and industrial activity.

1472. [807] NEWPORT NEWS & HAMPTON RAILWAY, GAS & ELECTRIC CO. Agreement . . . [n. p., 1916]

(See also items, **808-810**)

1473. [811] NEWPORT NEWS & OLD POINT RAILWAY & ELECTRIC CO. Annual report to the Interstate commerce commission . . . 1912-14.

(See also items, **812-813**)

1474. [814] NEWPORT NEWS & YORKTOWN RAILWAY CO. [Project report to the Interstate commerce commission . . . 1910-11]

1475. NEWPORT NEWS CHAMBER OF COMMERCE. Names of officers, directors, standing committee, and annual report . . . [Newport News, Va., 1909?—

8°. **USAg**: 1911/12; **USC**: 16th (1923/24).

1476. NEWPORT NEWS LIGHT & WATER CO. Annual report of the directors . . . [n. p., 19—

8°. **HB**: 1921, 22.

1477. [448] NEWPORT NEWS SHIPBUILDING & DRY DOCK CO. At the gateway to the sea . . . Newport News, Va., 1921.

(See also items, **449-452**)

1478. NEWPORT NEWS, Va. [Newport News, Morton, 1902]

18 plates. obl. 8°. **LC**

Views of the city.

1479. OLD DOMINION LAND CO. Annual report . . . [New York, 18-?-19—

8°. Report year ends Sept. 30. Title varies slightly.

LC: 1891/92-92/93, 94/95, 96/97-1905/06; **NYP**: 1895/96-96/97.

1480. OLD DOMINION LAND CO.   Newport News, Virginia.   Issued by the Old Dominion land co., Newport News, Va.   [Lynchburg, Va., Bell, 1915?]

> 2 p. l., 3-31, [1] p. illus. 8°.   **NYP**

> For further references on Newport News, see *Norfolk, Va.*

Norfolk, Va.

1481. BOUTWELL, W. R.   Virginia tourist . . . Norfolk, Va., Gatling print., 1892.

> 125 p. incl. plates, port. obl. 24°.   **LC**
> "Containing . . . curious and practical features of Norfolk, and Portsmouth, Old Point Comfort, Hampton, and Newport News . . ." A guide-book and souvenir. "Principally the wealthier class will read it [!] . . ."

1482. EBERLE, FRANK, ed.   The story of Norfolk.   City of great opportunities.   The coming metropolis of the new South . . . Norfolk, Va., Board of trade, 1908.

> [54] p. illus. 4°.   **BP, NYP, V**
> An elaborate pamphlet, well illustrated; pub. "to follow up the exploitation given to Norfolk during the [Jamestown] Exposition period."

1483. [1471] HAMPTON ROADS MARITIME EXCHANGE.   Annual . . . Norfolk, Va. [192-?—

1484. HOSPITAL ST. VINCENT DE PAUL.   Annual report . . . [1st- Norfolk, 1857?-19—

> illus. 8°.   **VU**: 71st (1927).

1485. ILLUSTRATED standard guide to Norfolk and Portsmouth and historical events of Virginia 1607 to 1907.   Jamestown exposition ed.   Norfolk, Va., Standard lithographing and publishing co. [*ca.* 1907]

> 134 p. illus., fold. map. 12°.   **LC, VU**
> Advertisement interspersed.

1486. JOHNSON, ELEANOR S.   Norfolk, its historical features . . . [Norfolk, Va., Nusbaum book & news co., *ca.* 1904]

> [6]-24 p. plates. 8°.   .   **NYP**

1487. Jones, Cary W. General and commercial guide to Norfolk and Portsmouth . . . E. Pollock, ed. [Norfolk, Va., Pollock & Barcroft] 1886.

179 p. illus. 8°.   LC

1488. ———. Norfolk as a business centre; its principal industries and trades . . . Norfolk, Va., Virginia job presses, 1880.

163 p. illus., fold. plates, fold. map. 8°.   LC, V
The author's feeling of "pardonable pride in the City's Prosperity and Growth" is very evident. Largely advertising matter.
Ed. of 1881: 191 p., 1 l., 7 p.   LC, V
Ed. of 1882: 162 p.   LC, V
Ed. of 1884: 182, [1] p.   LC, V

1489. Keiley, C[harles] R. A little light on Norfolk. Written . . . for the city of Norfolk . . . [Norfolk? 1916?]

24 p. plates. 8°.   NYP, V
Pamphlet advertising the city's progress.

1490. Manufacturers' record. Norfolk's industrial and commercial prosperity. [Baltimore, 1907]

xx p. f°. (Reprint from *Manufacturers' record,* Apr. 11, 1907)   V

1491. Mayo, W. R. Address of welcome delivered by Capt. W. R. Mayo, president of Norfolk Chamber of commerce, to the Virginia Board of trade, at its second annual meeting, Norfolk, Va., Aug. 25, 1904. Richmond, Whittet & Shepperson, 1904.

8 p. 8°.   V

1492. [826] Norfolk & Portsmouth traction co. Annual report . . . to the stockholders . . . [n. p., 1907—

1493. Norfolk Board of trade & business men's association. Charter and by-laws . . . Norfolk, 19—

8°.   NYP: 1907, 13.

1494. ———. Information about Norfolk, Portsmouth, Berkley, Virginia, and vicinity . . . [Norfolk, 1905]

40 p. incl. illus., maps, tables. 16°.   LC, V
Describing "the three cities whose industrial growth and common commercial interests bid fair to result, through civic union, in what may be called Greater Norfolk." Statistical tables in back.
Ed. of 1907: [47] p. illus., maps. 12°.   V

1495. NORFOLK BOARD OF TRADE & BUSINESS MEN'S ASSOCIATION. New facts and figures about Norfolk, Va. Norfolk, 1899.

    54 p. 8°.   **USAg**

1496. ———. Norfolk and Hampton Roads graphically shown and described. [Norfolk, 1909]

    [2], 15 [1] p. illus., plates, maps. 8°.   **BP, NYP**

1497. NORFOLK CHAMBER OF COMMERCE. Annual report of the Norfolk Chamber of commerce and Board of trade . . . , 1st- ; [1915?—] Norfolk [1915?—

    4°.   **NYP**: 7th (1921).

1498. ———. The city by the sea. Facts and figures about Norfolk. No 2. Issued by the Chamber of commerce. Norfolk, Va. [Green, Burke & Gregory] 1903.

    xvi, 7-45 p. front. (map) 8°. Advertisements in back.   **LC**

    Norfolk as a commercial city, and how it may develop manufacturing. Ed. of 1893.   **V**

1499. ———. Constitution and by-laws . . . Norfolk, Brown, 1902.

    15 p. 12°.   **NYP**

1500. ———. 1896. Norfolk, Va., port and city. Facts and figures of its trade, commerce and manufactures. Comp. by Samuel R. Borum, secretary, Chamber of commerce. [Norfolk, 1896]

    77, [11] p. incl. illus., map. 8°.   **LC, NYP, V**
    Advertisements in back.

    Description of the city and its life is supplemented by statistics and proud reflections upon its accomplishments.

1501. ———. Facts and figures about Norfolk, Va. Comp. and issued by the Chamber of commerce, 1890. Norfolk, Va., Green, Burke & Gregory, 1890.

    60 p. 8°. Advertisements interspersed.   **LC, V**
    Ed. of 1897: 32 p.   **NYP**

1502. ———. Industrial and commercial Norfolk; its rail and water transportation, belt line facilities, factory sites, market accessibility and labor. Norfolk, Va. [1921?]

    16 p. illus. 8°.   **V**

1503. ———. Norfolk, Virginia, central Atlantic port. Norfolk, Barron, 1914.

> 60 p. illus. (incl. maps). 12°.   **LC, USC**
> Advertising Norfolk's economic prosperity.

1504. ———. Pictures in maritime Dixie: Norfolk, Va., port and city; the Chamber of commerce book. By A. M. Norfolk, Engelhardt, 1893.

> 204 p. illus. 8°.   **LC, V**

1505. ———. Shipper's information on the port of Norfolk, U. S. A., on Hampton Roads, unequalled for efficient and economical handling of export and import traffic. Norfolk [192-?]

> 16 p. illus. 8°.   **V**

1506. [453] NORFOLK CREOSOTING CO. Creosoted timber . . . Philadelphia, 1900.

1507. NORFOLK EMANCIPATION ASSOCIATION. Emancipation celebration; souvenir program booklet. 1863, sixty-second anniversary, 1925 . . . Norfolk, Va., W. Smith, under auspices of Norfolk emancipation ass'n., 1925.

> [24] p. illus. (incl. ports.) 8°   **LC, V**
> Includes advertisements, of Negroes.
> A Negro organization interested in the social progress of the colored race.

1508. NORFOLK, ITS HISTORY, geography, and civic development. A hand-book for teachers of the third grades. Norfolk, Va. [192-?]

> 84 p. 8°.   **H**

1509. NORFOLK MERCHANTS' & MECHANICS' EXCHANGE. Report of the president and directors . . . for the year ending Oct. 31, 1869. . . . Norfolk, Journal, 1870.

> 89, ii p. tables. 8°.   **WM**
> Chartered, Dec. 1, 1868. Report reveals economic progress of Norfolk and Portsmouth.

1510. NORFOLK, VIRGINIA . . . the gateway of the South. Historical Norfolk, by Kenton F. Murray . . . The Norfolk of to-day, by Charles P. Sapp . . . Philadelphia, Sheldon, 1904.

> 8°.   **V**

1511. VIRGINIA CLUB, Norfolk. Officers and members. Constitution and by-laws. Norfolk [18—? - ?]

16°. **NYP:** 1891.

1512. NOWITZKY, GEORGE I. Norfolk; the marine metropolis of Virginia, and the sound and river cities of North Carolina. A narrative . . . Norfolk, Va., and Raleigh, N. C., G. I. Nowitzky, 1888.

v, 216 p. 12°. **H, LC, NYP, V, VU**

Detailed description in rather florid language, and historical narrative "gleaned from undisputed authority." No "puffs" were promised to advertisers.

1513. SOCIETY OF THE SOUTHERN INDUSTRIAL CLASSES, Norfolk. Report . . . to the trustees of the John F. Slater fund and the General education board . . . Hampton, Va. [18-? - 19—

8°. **USAg:** 1902/03-04/05, 06/07, 08/09.

1514. [1358] SOUTHEASTERN BUILDING & LOAN ASSOCIATION, Norfolk. . . . Agents' instruction book. Norfolk, Va., 1895.

1515. SQUIRES, WILLIAM H. Guide to Norfolk, Va., Portsmouth, Virginia Beach, Ocean View, Old Point Comfort, Hampton, Newport News and vicinity. Comp. and pub. by W. H. T. Squires . . . Norfolk, Va., Barron [1915]

45 p. illus. (incl. maps) nar. 8°. **BP, LC, NYP, VU**

1516. TIDEWATER cities of Hampton Roads, Virginia. 1907. [Norfolk? 1907?]

25 p. illus. 8°. **V**

A little hand-book of Norfolk, Portsmouth, Newport News, Hampton, and Old Point Comfort, for visitors to the Jamestown exposition, 1907.

1517. WESTON, EDMUND B., et al. The Norfolk, Virginia, filter plant. Test of a mechanical filter installed by the New York Filter manufacturing company, . . . for the East Providence water company . . . Reports by John H. Appleton, Gardner T. Swarts, and Edmund B. Weston. Providence, Snow & Farnham, 1900.

42, [1] p. plates, plans. 8°. **BP**

1518. WILCOX, DELOS F.   A report upon the proposed modification in the rates of fare and franchise provisions affecting the street railway lines in the city of Norfolk, as presented to the Norfolk city council by the Virginia railway & power co., in March 1913 . . . Made at the direction of the Committee on light, heat and trolley service of the Chamber of commerce of Norfolk, Virginia, inc. . . . Rendered May 20, 1914. [Norfolk, Burke & Gregory, 1914]

2 p. l., 70 p. 8°.   **LC, NYP, V**

1519. WITHIN the capes of Virginia, showing the advantages and attractions of Norfolk, Portsmouth, Newport News, Hampton. Richmond, Va., Monitor, 1898.

41 p. 8°.   Advertisements in back.   **LC**
". . . Main object is to promote the interest of the community, attract the capitalist and investor to the point of investigation, and secure the settler." Includes sketches of the Seaboard air line and Chesapeake & Ohio railroads.

Old Point Comfort, Va.

See above, *Hampton* and *Norfolk, Va.*

Petersburg, Va.

1520. BISHOP, CARTER R.   "The cockade city of the Union." Petersburg, Virginia. [Petersburg?] 1907.

16 p. map. 8°.   **V**
Written for the Council of the city.

1521. DAILY INDEX-APPEAL.   Fiftieth anniversary number, 1865-1915. Sunday, Sept. 5, 1915. Petersburg, Va., 1915.

8, 52, 14 p. illus., ports., diagrs., map. f°.   **BP**

1522. [JONES, THOMAS W.]   Miniatures, Petersburg, Virginia. Cincinnati, Beckwith [*ca.* 1905]

24 views. 16°.   In portfolio.   **LC**

1523. KERNODLE, LOUISE N.   Guide-book of the city of Petersburg, with views and map of the city. Richmond, Central pub. co. [*ca.* 1916]

80 p. illus., map. 8°.   Advertisements in back.   **LC, V**

1524. MANN, H. C. Historic Petersburg. Illustrated by H. C. Mann. [n. p., *ca.,* 1907]

24 p. illus. 8°.   V

Issued for the Jamestown exposition.

1525. PETERSBURG ARMOR PLANT COMMITTEE. Argument presented to the Secretary of the navy for the establishment of the government armor plant in the vicinity of Petersburg, Virginia; presented by the Petersburg armor plant committee, representing the city of Petersburg and the Chamber of commerce of Petersburg, inc., Sept., 1916. [Washington, D. C., National capital press, 1916]

63 p. 8 fold. plans. 8°.   BP, H, LC, NYP, VU

1526. PETERSBURG BENEVOLENT MECHANIC ASSOCIATION. Charter, constitution, and by-laws. Origin, Jan. 4, 1825; revised Oct., 1900. Petersburg, Va., Fenn & Owen, 1900.

36 p. 16°.   V

1527. PETERSBURG CHAMBER OF COMMERCE. Annual report of the president . . . [Petersburg? 19-?—

8°.   V: 1911-13.

1528. ———. The city of Petersburg, Virginia. The book of its Chamber of commerce. By A. M. . . . Petersburg, Va., Engelhardt, 1894.

116 p. illus., ports. 4°.   BP, V

The city's business interests and progress; with brief descriptions of individual firms and offices.

1529. ———. A little book for keeps; Petersburg, a Virginia leader: 1907. Petersburg [1907?]

32 p. illus. 16°.   V

Economic and social activity of the city; a pocket edition.

1530. [1344] PETERSBURG LAND BANK COMMITTEE. Argument presented to the Federal farm loan board for the establishment of a Federal land bank at Petersburg, Virginia. [Petersburg? Va.] 1916.

1531. PETERSBURG MUSICAL ASSOCIATION. A brief history, the charter, and the constitution and by-laws of the . . . association . . . March, 1890. Petersburg, Va., Fenn & Owen, 1890.

31, [1] p. 8°. BP

1532. ———. Musical convention, ninth, and seventh music festival held in Petersburg, Va., May 26-30, 1890. [Petersburg, Fenn & Owen] 1890.

unp. ports. 4°. BP

1533. [864] PETERSBURG TELEPHONE CO. Annual report to the Interstate commerce commission . . . 1914—

1534. POLLOCK, EDWARD. Historical and industrial guide to Petersburg, Virginia. Petersburg, Beckwith, 1884.

248 p. illus., map. 8°. LC, V, VU
Advertisements interspersed.

1535. [1465] TRI-CITY SYSTEM. Richmond, Manchester, and Petersburg, Virginia: trolley rides . . . [n. p., n. d.]

1536. VIRGINIA land agency, Petersburg, Va. Established 1865. [Griffin & Jervis, Petersburg, Va., 1886]

32 p. 8°. BP
Organized to encourage immigration.

1537. VISIT of William Howard Taft . . . and Mrs. Taft on the occasion of the unveiling of a monument . . . at Fort Mahone. May 19, 1909. [Petersburg, Franklin, 1909]

unp. illus., ports. 4°. V

1538. WOMAN'S CLUB, Petersburg. Club calendar . . . [n. p., 19—

8°. V: 1924/25.

Portsmouth, Va.

1539. POLLOCK, EDWARD. Sketch book of Portsmouth, Virginia. Its people and its trade. Portsmouth, Va., E. Pollock, 1886.

287 p. illus., fold. map, fold. plates. 16°. LC, V
Advertisements interspersed.

Emphasis upon commerce and transportation in the section on the *post bellum* period.

1540. PORTSMOUTH, BERKLEY & SUFFOLK WATER CO. OF PORTS-
MOUTH. [Circular] [n. p., 1904]

4°.   HB

1541. [457] PORTSMOUTH BUSINESS MEN'S ASSOCIATION. Pound
nets, public revenue, and the people. Portsmouth, Va. [1910]

For further references on Portsmouth, see above, *Norfolk, Va.*

Richmond, Va.

1542. AMERICAN ILLUSTRATING CO., Richmond. Pen and sunlight
sketches of Richmond, the most progressive metropolis of the
South . . . Richmond, Va., The American illustrating company [1910?]

   1 p. l., [37]-165, [2] p. illus. 4°.   LC, V
Written to illustrate Richmond's prosperity; separate descriptions of
business firms, stores, etc.; excellent illustrations.

1543. [1296] AMERICAN INSTITUTE OF BANKING. RICHMOND CHAP-
TER. Year book . . . [Richmond, 19—

1544. [1297] AMERICAN NATIONAL BANK, Richmond. Tempus
fugit. [Richmond, *ca.* 1913]

1545. AMERICAN SOCIETY OF MECHANICAL ENGINEERS. Souvenir of
the convention of the American society of mechanical engineers, at
Richmond, Va., Nov. 11-14, 1890. By the citizens and the local
members of the society. [Richmond, Va., 1890]

   1 l., 31 plates. obl. 24°.   NYP
On cover: Richmond illustrated.

1546. ANDERSON, WILLIAM A. Address . . . upon the laying
of the cornerstone of the equestrian statue of Stonewall Jackson,
in Richmond, Virginia, on June 3, 1915, at the request of the Stonewall Jackson monument corporation. [n. p., 1915?]

   12 p. 8°.   V

1547. BROCK, R[OBERT] A. Richmond as a manufacturing and trading centre; including a historical sketch of the city . . . Richmond, Jones & Cook, 1880.

   92 p. illus., plates, fold. map. 8°.   BP, H, LC, NYP, V
Advertisements in back. Contains statistical tables.

1548. BURFORD, WILLIAM B., pub. Richmond, Virginia; illustrated. Indianapolis, Burford, 1891.

17 p. illus. f°.   V
Pictures of the city; the text is only incidental

1549. BURGESS, MRS. MARY A. History of the battle fields around the city of Richmond, and how to reach them. Distance from the city and full information concerning them. M. A. Burgress, pub., Richmond, Va., 1905.

24 p. map. 16°.   V

1550. ———. . . . Richmond guide book; sketches and views of Richmond, Virginia, supplemented by sketches of Williamsburg, Jamestown, Yorktown. Description and map, historic battlefields. Location given of all pictures in book. Richmond, Va., M. A. Burgess, 1909.

87 p. front. (fold. map) illus. 16°.   LC, V
Revised and largely rewritten from her *Sketches and views, points of interest* (1903).

1551. ———. Sketches and views, points of interest, Richmond, Virginia . . . Richmond, Va., M. A. Burgess, 1903.

92 p. illus. (incl. port.) map. 16°.   LC
Ed. of 1907.   V

1552. BURTON, PETER J. Police court pictures at Richmond, Virginia. Richmond, 1892.

84 p. 12°.   V
Vivid picture of the court and reproduction of typical scenes that took place in it.

1553. CEREMONIES incident to laying of corner stone of new city hall, Apr. 5, 1887. Richmond, Waddey, 1887.

38 p. illus. (front.) 4°.   V

1554. CEREMONIES of the unveiling of the monument to John Tyler, tenth president of the U. S., Hollywood cemetery, Richmond, Virginia, Oct. 12, 1915. [Richmond? 1915]

[7] p. illus. (incl. port.) 8°.   BP, LC, V, VU

1555. CHESAPEAKE & OHIO HOSPITAL ASSOCIATION, Richmond. Report of the Board of governors . . . Richmond [18-? -19—

8°.   USC: Dec., 1902.

1556. CHESTERFIELD LAND & IMPROVEMENT CO., Richmond. Report on terminal, dock, and manufacturing facilities, by C. P. E. Burgwyn, engineer of James River improvement. Boston, 1888.

13 p. fold. maps. 8°.   **V**

1557. CHESTERMAN, WILLIAM D. Guide to Richmond and the battlefields . . . Richmond, Goode, 1881.

68 p. incl. plates, map. 16°.   **H, LC, NYP, V**
Ed. of 1884: 64 p. incl. plates, map.   **BP, LC, NYP, V**
Ed. of 1890: 77 p. illus. (Hill print.)   **LC**
Ed. of 1894: 73 p. illus. (Hill print.)   **NYP, V**

1558. ———. Richmond, Virginia. An outline of its attractions and industries . . . Richmond, Jones, 1888.

24 p. 8°.   **NYP**

1559. CHISHOLM BROS., pub. [Souvenir of the city of Richmond] Portland, Me. [1888?]

fold. plate. 18 x 157 cm.   **V**

1560. CHRISTIAN, GEORGE L. Address . . . the occasion being the presentation of a silver service by the Richmond Chamber of commerce to Tazewell M. Carrington on his retirement as president of the Chamber . . . Jan. 5, 1914. [n. p., 1914?]

14 p. 8°.   **V**

1561. CITY of Richmond, of historic fame, of great commercial prestige. [Richmond, 1905]

40 p. illus. 4°.   **V**
Brief review of the city's industry and social life, followed by descriptions of business firms.

1562. CLARK, E. C., pub. Historic Richmond and vicinity. Richmond, 1920.

sheet, 43 x 72 cm., printed on both sides.   **V**
Shows points of interest, and the defense of Richmond.

1563. CLASSIFIED list of contributors to the Jefferson Davis monument fund, Richmond, Va., to June 20, 1896. [n. p., n. d.]

16 p. 16°.   **V**
Includes also a classified list of contributors from June 20, 1896, to June 2, 1897.

1564. CLUVERIUS, THOMAS J. My life, trial and conviction. Richmond, Dudley, 1887.

    112 p. 16°.   **H, LC, V**
    Account of a Richmond murder trial by the accused and convicted.
    Enl. ed. of 1887: 128 p.   **H, LC**
    Enlarged ed. contains an account of the execution of the murderer.

1565. COMMONWEALTH CLUB, Richmond. Officers and members . . . Constitution and by-laws . . . [Richmond, 189-? -19—

    16°.   **H**: 1903; **LC**: 1897; **NYP**: 1892, 97, 1903; **V**: 1897.
    Organized "for the promotion of social intercourse and for the purpose of maintaining a library and reading room."

1566. COMMUNITY RECREATION ASSOCIATION, Richmond. Report . . . [Richmond? 19—

    8°. Report year ends Apr. 1.   **V**: 1924/25.

1567. CONFEDERATE SOLDIERS' & SAILORS' MONUMENT ASSOCIATION. Report of committee on ceremonies incident to unveiling of monument, Richmond, Va., May 30, 1894. [n. p., 1894]

    21 p. 8°.   **V**

1568. ———. Souvenir, unveiling soldiers' and sailors' monument, Richmond, Virginia, May 30, 1894. Richmond, Hill, 1894.

    25, [41] p. incl. illus. (part col.) ports. 8°.   **LC, V**
    Advertisements interspersed.
    Contains report on the work of the association.

1569. COOK, MRS. A. F. In and about Richmond. [Richmond, Whittet & Shepperson, 192-?]

    30 p. illus., front. (port.) map. 16°.   **V**
    Includes a description of Mrs. Cook's cafeteria.

1570. "COUSIN TOMMIE" (T. J. Cluverius) A parody. By a Richmond lady, respectfully dedicated to the counsel for the Commonwealth. Richmond, Johnston, 1885.

    8 p. 12°.   **V**
    A poem concerning the Cluverius murder case, in defence of the victim.

1571. DAUGHTERS OF THE AMERICAN REVOLUTION. VIRGINIA. COMMONWEALTH CHAPTER, Richmond. Commonwealth chapter, Daughters of the American revolution. Organized Feb. 2, 1902. Richmond, Va. [Richmond] Dietz [1912?]

    [16] p. 12°.   **V**

1572. [EVANS, EDWARD S.] The official encyclopaedic guide to Richmond and vicinity, including battlefields. Richmond, Richmond press, 1906.

> 160 p. front., plates, fold. map. 12°.   **LC, V**
> Advertisements in back.

1573. EZEKIEL, HERBERT T. The recollections of a Virginia newspaper man . . . Richmond, Va., H. T. Ezekiel, 1920.

> 124, [10] p. front. (port.) 8°.   **H, LC, NYP, V**
> Events and incidents in Richmond during the last quarter of the 19th cent., told in familiar style.

1574. FIREMEN'S RELIEF ASSOCIATION, Richmond. The Richmond. Virginia, Fire department, its organization and equipment, with an account of its precursors from the initial organization of "effective friendship" in 1816 . . . Richmond [Hill] 1894.

> 8 p., 1 l., 9-64 p. front., illus., plates, ports. 8°.   **V**
> Includes a sketch of the department in the mid-'nineties, and of the chief of the force. Advertisements in back.

1575. FOREST LAWN CEMETERY, Richmond. Forest lawn cemetery, Richmond, Virginia. Richmond, Va. [1924?]

> 8°.   **V**

1576. [FREEMAN, DOUGLAS S.] This year—Richmond! An authentic tourists' guide to "The gateway of the South" and points of historical interest in and around the city of Richmond . . . Richmond, Dietz, 1927.

> 47 p. incl. illus., double map. 12°.   **V**
> "Distributed by the Automobile club of Richmond." Includes advertisements.

1577. [781] FREEMAN, JOHN C. The situation of Richmond and its commercial opportunities . . . [n. p., 1911?]

1578. FREEMASONS. KNIGHT TEMPLARS. RICHMOND COMMANDERY, NO. 2. General orders . . . Richmond, Va., Apr. 24, 1909 . . . Attend a stated conclave of your commandery in the asylum, in the Masonic temple . . . Apr. 27, at 8 P. M. . . . Officers . . . [and] members. [Richmond, 1909]

> [4] p. 8°.   **V**

1579. ———. ———. Richmond-Randolph Lodge, no. 19. Programme of exercises to be observed by . . . [the] lodge . . . , in laying the corner stone of the Alexander Whittaker memorial chapel and Sunday school room. Held in church yard of St. John's P. E. church, Richmond, Virginia, . . . Oct. 19, '07, at 4:30 o'clock. Richmond, Whittet & Shepperson [1907]

10 p. illus. 8°.   V

1580. A full account of the great calamity, which occurred in the capitol at Richmond, Virginia, Apr. 27, 1870, with a list of killed and wounded. Richmond, Ellyson & Taylor, 1870.

32 p. 8°.   BP, LC, NYP, V, VU

By an eye-witness who gathered testimony from others in the catastrophe.

1581. Garnett, Theodore S. J. E. B. Stuart (major-general) commander of the cavalry troops, Army of northern Virginia, C. S. A.; an address delivered at the unveiling of the equestrian statue of Gen. Stuart, at Richmond, Virginia, May 30, 1907. . . . New York & Washington, Neale, 1907.

61 p. front. (port.) plates. 8°.   LC, V, VU

The introduction, by the publishers, gives the setting for the speech and a few facts about the ceremony.

1582. [1319] German-American banking & building co., Richmond. Constitution of the . . . company. Richmond, 1890.

1583. Have a look at our city. [n. p., 1922]

[108] p. plates (post card views) 4°.   V

Advertisements interspersed.

1584. Hermitage country club, Richmond. The Hermitage country club. 1916-17. Constitution and by-laws. [n. p., 1916?]

20 p. 16°.   V

1585. Hill monument association, Richmond. Souvenir, Hill monument unveiling, May 30, 1892. [Richmond, 1892]

41, [7] p. illus. (incl. port.) 12°.   LC

Advertisements interspersed.

Monument to Ambrose P. Hill, 1825-65.

1586. [Holmes, James T.] Richmond revisited by a federal, 1865-1905, Columbus, Ohio. Columbus, O., Berlin, 1905.

    36 p. 8°.   LC, NYP, V

    Richmond of 1865 and 1905 contrasted.

1587. Home for needy confederate women, Richmond. History of the Home for needy Confederate women, 1900-04 . . . Richmond, Hill [n. d.]

    64 p. incl. adv. 8°.   V

    Contains list of officers and their reports, list of beneficiaries, brief sketch of the institution, and letters from leading men praising its work.

1588. Hotel Richmond [and] Hotel William Byrd, Richmond. Convention city advantages of Richmond, Virginia . . . [n. p., n. d.]

    10 p. illus. fold. 4°.   V

1589. Illustrated greetings from Richmond, Va. Cincinnati, Ohio, 1901.

    100 views on 25 1. incl. cover-title. 4°.   V

    Made for George S. Cook, Richmond, Va.

1590. Jefferson realty corp. Certificate of incorporation . . . [Richmond?] 1905.

    18 p. 4°.   V

1591. The Jefferson, Richmond, Virginia. [Baltimore & Richmond, Hoen, 189-?]

    10, [2] p. illus. 12°.   LC

    Description of the new Jefferson hotel.

1592. [579] Johnston, John W. Communication to the Board of public interests of the city of Richmond . . . [n. p., 1879]

1593. Joynes, L[evin] S. Yellow fever: liability of Richmond to the disease, and the need of preventive measures. [Richmond, 1878?]

    23 p. 8°. (Reprint from *Virginia medical monthly*, Nov., 1878)   V, VU

1594. Juvenile protective society of Virginia. Memorial to the honorable council of the city of Richmond in behalf of the erring children of the city, aided by the juvenile division of the Police court. [Richmond, 1913]

    8 p. 8°.   V

1595. KERNODLE, MRS. LOUISE W. Guide book of the city of Richmond . . . with views and map of the city, also description and map of battlefields . . . Richmond, Va., Central pub. co., 1914.

> 2 p. l., [9]-57 p. front., illus. fold. map. 12°.   LC
> Ed. of 1916: 80 p. incl. front. etc.   LC, V
> Ed. of 1916: 92 p. front. etc.   LC
> Eds. of 1919 & 1921.   V
> Eds. of 1920 & 1925.   NYP
> Ed. of 1924: 127 p. incl. front. etc.   LC
> Ed. of 1926: 127 p. incl. front. etc.   LC
> Advertisements interspersed.

1596. LADIES' HOLLYWOOD MEMORIAL ASSOCIATION, Richmond. Our Confederate dead; this souvenir is authorized by the Ladies' Hollywood memorial association of Richmond, Virginia . . . [Richmond, Whittet & Shepperson] 1916.

> 24 p. 2 pl. (incl. front.) 12°.   LC
> Ed. of 1896.   V

1597. LAND & THOMPSON, pub. Historical and descriptive review of the industries of Richmond, 1884. Commerce, trade and manufactures, manufacturing advantages, business and transportation facilities, together with sketches of the principal business houses and manufacturing establishments . . . Richmond, Va., Land & Thompson, 1884.

> 168 p. illus. 4°.   LC, V

1598. LEIGH, EGBERT G., jr. Address of E. G. Leigh, jr., president [of] Richmond Chamber of commerce, at the banquet . . . May 22, 1906. [Richmond, 1906]

> 12 p. 8°.   V
> What the Chamber has accomplished for the city during 40 years, and plans for the future.

1599. [McCARTHY, CARLTON] Walks about Richmond. A story for boys, and a guide to persons visiting the city, desiring to see the principal points of interest, with an index showing the exact location of each point mentioned . . . Richmond, Va., McCarthy & Ellyson, 1870.

> vii, 9-175 p. 4 plates (incl. front.) port. 16°.   BP, LC, NYP, V

1600. McLean, Francis H., *et al.* . . . Survey of the social agencies of Richmond, Va., by Francis H. McLean . . . and Miss Hilda K. Mills . . . [n. p.] Amer. association for organizing family social work, 1923.

159 p. 8°.   V

1601. Magdalen association, Richmond. Annual report. [1st-? ; 1875?- ?] Richmond [1875?- ?]

8°.   LC: 24th (1898).

A social welfare organization.

1602. Male orphan asylum, Richmond. Charter, constitution and by-laws . . . Richmond, Va., Walthall, 1902.

23 p. 8°.   V

1603. ———. Proceedings of the . . . annual meeting . . . Richmond, [1874?-19—

illus., plates. 8°.   LC: 52d (1898).

1898 contains annual reports of the president and superintendent.

1604. Marshall, Hudson S. Address delivered at the opening of the building of the Confederate memorial institute at Richmond, Virginia, on May 3, 1921 . . . [n. p., 1921]

21 p. 8°.   V, VU

1605. Masonic home of Virginia, Richmond. Annual report . . . 1st- [1891?-19—] Richmond, Va. [1891?-19—

8°.   V: 19-24th (1909-14).

1606. ———. Charter and by-laws of the Masonic home of Virginia. Incorporated Jan. 7, 1890, sess. acts, 1889/90, p. 43, as amended. Richmond, Va., Fergusson, 1909.

22 p. 16°.   V

1607. A memorial of the 6th annual reunion of the United Confederate veteran association and the laying of the corner stone of the Jefferson Davis monument, Richmond, Virginia, June 30, July 1-2, 1896. [Richmond, Va., 1896]

unp. illus., plates, map. 4°.   V

1608. Memorial of unveiling of Lee's statue, Richmond, Va., May 29, 1890. Richmond, Jones, 1890.

15 p. 8°.   NYP

1609. [1337] MERCHANTS & PLANTERS SAVINGS BANK, Richmond. Charter, constitution and by-laws . . . Richmond, 1867.

1610. MILLHISER, CHARLES. Various addresses of interest to the community, delivered by Charles Millhiser: On the return of resolutions, To the women of Beth Ahabah, To the men of Beth Ahabah, Our rabbi, The Jefferson club. [Richmond?] 1923.

17, 8, 10, 3, 17 p. 8°.   **LC, NYP**

Reveal social life among the Jews in Richmond.

1611. MOORE, JOSIAH S. Reminiscences, letters, poetry, and miscellanies. Richmond, Flanhart, 1903.

viii, 785 p. front. (port.) 8°.   **LC, V, VU**

Portrayal of economic, religious, and social life in Virginia, especially in Richmond, 1865-1900. Contains poems by the author.

1612. MOORE STREET INDUSTRIAL INSTITUTION, Richmond. Annual report of the Board of managers . . . 1st- [1875/76?—] Richmond [1876?—

8°.   **BP:** 23d (1897/98).

1613. ———. Moore St. industrial institution . . . established in 1875 for the industrial eduction of colored youths. [Descriptive circular] Richmond, 18—

illus. 4°.-8°.   **BP:** 1885, 88; **H:** [1889?]

1614. MOORE STREET MISSIONARY INDUSTRIAL SOCIETY, Richmond. A plan for helping destitute children. Dated Richmond, Va., Mar. 23, 1875. [n. p., 1875]

4 p. 8°.   **BP**

This society developed into the Moore St. industrial institution.

1615. MORRISON, ANDREW, comp. The city on the James; Richmond in history . . . Richmond [18-?]

163 p. 8°.   **NYP**

1616. ———. The city on the James. Richmond, Virginia. The Chamber of commerce book. Ed. by Andrew Morrison. Richmond, Va., Engelhardt, 1893.

316 p. incl. front., illus., ports. 8°.   **H, LC, NYP, V**

Treats in detail all phases of Richmond's development, with emphasis upon economic factors; with statistical tables.

1617. MORRISON, ANDREW, comp. Richmond, Virginia, and the new South. Richmond & Chicago [188-?]

    163 p. illus. 8°.   V

    A hand-book describing the city in the 'eighties.

1618. MURPHY, DANIEL. Richmond, Va. A guide to and description of its principal places and objects of interest. Richmond, Va., Randolph & English, 1881.

    69. [1] p. front., plates, fold. maps. 8°.   LC, V

    A matter-of-fact account of economic and social conditions.

1619. NEW album of Richmond views. [n. p., 1888?]

    10 p. 8°.   V

1620. The NEW Richmond. Rise of the city since the war left it ruined. More prosperous than ever. Great industries established and business growing. New York, 1902.

    16 p. 8°. mounted clippings from the New York *Sun,* Oct. 19, 1902.

                                              NYP

1621. NEW YORK news letter. Richmond number. Sept.-Oct., 1901. [New York, 1901]

    32 p. 8°.   NYP

1622. NURSES' SETTLEMENT, Richmond, Va. INSTRUCTIVE VISITING NURSE ASSOCIATION. Report . . . Richmond [1902?-

    8°.   V: 1914-20

    Report for 1914 contains a short history of the Nurses' settlement. Combined with Social workers of the Nurses' settlement, 1914.

1623. ———. SOCIAL WORKERS. Yearbook . . . Richmond [19—

    8°.   V: 1915.

1624. OLD DOMINION HOSPITAL, Richmond. Rules and regulations of the Old Dominion hospital, adopted by the Woman's board of managers and the faculty of the Medical college of Virginia, June, 1896 . . . Richmond, Hill, 1896.

    9 p. 8°.   V

1625. PICTURESQUE Richmond: Richmond, Virginia, and her suburbs. Richmond, Hill, 1891.

    [98] p. incl. plates & adv. illus. 4°.   V

    Written to reveal the city's progress since 1865.

1626. POINDEXTER, CHARLES. Richmond: an illustrated handbook and guide, with notices of the battle-fields. Richmond, Va., Hill, 1896.

112 p. illus., port., plates, maps. 16°.   **BP, LC, NYP, V**

1627. ———. Richmond: an illustrated hand-book of the city and battle fields, with historic sketch and maps. . . . Richmond, Va., Hermitage press., 1907.

126 p. illus., 2 fold. maps (incl. front.) 16°.   **LC, NYP, V, VU, WM**

1628. REAL ESTATE TRUST CO., Richmond. Documents in evidence: Richmond post office. [Richmond, 1903?]

[30] p. 8°.   **V**

Arguments concerning the location of a new post office on the west side of the city.

1629. RETAIL GROCERS' ASSOCIATION OF RICHMOND, inc., ed. Old Virginia cooking; Retail grocers' association of Richmond, incorporated, editors. Richmond, Va. [Richmond press, *ca.* 1910]

159 p. 8°. Advertisements interspersed.   **LC**

Cook book as a form of advertising of the association.

1630. RETREAT FOR THE SICK, Richmond. . . . Annual report . . . Richmond [1880?-19—

8°.   **V**: 1887, 89-91, 93-98, 1902, 06-09.

1631. ———. Constitution and by-laws . . . [Richmond, 1904?]

18 p. 16°.   **V**

1632. RICHMOND. Brooklyn, N. Y. [19—?]

24 phot. obl. 8°.   **H, V**

Views, with descriptive matter.

1633. RICHMOND AMATEUR BASE BALL COMMISSION. Constitution, rules and by-laws . . . New York, Amer. sports pub. [1912]

16°. (Spalding's athletic library. Auxiliary series)   **NYP**

1634. RICHMOND ART CLUB. Art movement. [n. p., 1914]

10 p. 8°.   **V**

1635. RICHMOND ASSOCIATED CHARITIES. Annual report of the president and general secretary . . . [Richmond? 1906?—

8°.   **V**: 16-18th (1921-23).

1636. RICHMOND ASSOCIATED CHARITIES. Bulletin . . . vol. 1, no. 1- ; Dec., 1906— Richmond, 1906—

   8°.   **V**: I, 1.

1637. RICHMOND CHAMBER OF COMMERCE. The advantages of Richmond, Virginia, as a manufacturing and trading centre, with notes for the guidance of tourists on the lines of transportation running from Richmond. [By George Watson James] Richmond, Pub. under the auspices of the trade committees of the Chamber of commerce and Commercial club, 1882.

   64 p. 3 fold. maps (incl. front.) 8°.   **BP, H, LC, NYP, V**
   Written to attract northern and eastern capital to the South.

1638. ——. Annual report . . . Richmond [18-? -19—
   8°. **BP**: 1890/91; **H**: 1900-06, 08, 11-15; **NYP**: 1883/84, 1911; **USAg**: 1889/90-92/93, 98-1901, 03-05, 07, 10-18; **USC**: 1889/90-92/93, 1910-15; **V**: 1890/91-92/93, 1901-06, 10-14.

1639. [917] ——. Conference for trade expansion . . . Proceedings . . . Richmond, 1914—

1640. ——. Constitution, by-laws, officers and list of members . . . Richmond, Jones, 1887.
   16 p. 12°.   **V**

1641. ——. Industrial, commercial and financial advantages of Richmond . . . Virginia. [Richmond, Chamber of commerce, 192-?]
   12 p. illus., map. 4°. fold.   **V**

1642. [1311] [——] Conference to consider the question of tax reform, Richmond, Va. Proceedings . . . Richmond, 1914.

1643. ——. Report of the president . . . Richmond [18-? -19—
   8°. Title varies.
      LC: 1899-1905, 07, 10-14; **NYP**: 1902-06, 08-10, 12-19, 23; **USC**: 1899-1901, 19; **V**: 1891-93, 99-1906, 10-14.

1644. ——. Report of the Special committee on the Richmond Chamber of commerce and its traffic bureau. Submitted by Col. John B. Purcell, chairman, for consideration of the Board of directors, June 8, 1905. [Richmond, 1905]
   unp. 16°.   **V**

1645. ———. Report on the trade and commerce of Richmond, Va., . . . with other statistics and documents . . . Comp. for the Richmond Chamber of commerce, by P. G. Coghlan, secretary. Richmond, Fergusson & Rady, 187—

8°. Report for 1871 includes "several years preceding."
LC: 1871; V: 1871, 72/73.

1646. ———. Richmond, the capital city of Virginia. [Richmond, 1907?]

[32] p. illus. 8°.   LC, VU
Emphasis upon industrial and social features, with some statistics.

1647. ———. . . . Richmond, the capital of Virginia. [Richmond, Va., Chamber of commerce, 1923]

24 p. illus., map. 8°.   V
On cover: Richmond . . . city of prosperity and opportunity.

1648. ———. Richmond, Virginia, the city on the James; the book of its Chamber of commerce and principal business interests. Richmond, Engelhardt, 1902-03.

165 p. illus. (incl. map, ports.) f°.   NYP

1649. [———] Richmond, Virginia. "Down where the South begins." [Richmond, 192-?]

32 p. illus., map. 4°.   V

1650. [———] Richmond, Va.: its growth, attractions, advantages . . . [Richmond, Whittet & Shepperson, 1901]

22 p. 16°.   NYP

1651. ———. . . . Richmond, Virginia, yesterday and today. Compliments of the city of Richmond and the Chamber of commerce of Richmond, Va., 1914. [Richmond, Whittet & Shepperson, 1914]

69 p. illus. 8°.   H, LC
Ed. of 1912.   NYP
Ed. of 1913.   H, LC, V
Economic material well organized; contains statistics.

1651a. ———. Statement of the advantages and fitness of Richmond, Va. as a location for a government armor factory. For presentation to the Armor factory board. U. S. Navy dept., by the Richmond Chamber of commerce, 1897.

11 p. 2 fold. charts. 8°.   LC

1652. RICHMOND CHAMBER OF COMMERCE. AIR PORT COMMITTEE. Proposed Richmond air port. Report and recommendations . . . [Richmond, 1926]

20 p. 8°.   V

1653. ———. TRAFFIC MANAGER. Annual report . . . Richmond, Va. [1895?-19—

8°.   V: 1896, 1900, 10-13, 21.

1654. RICHMOND CLUB, Richmond, Va. Constitution, by-laws, officers and members of the . . . club. Richmond, Fergusson & Rady, 1869—

16°.   V: 1869, 73.

Established to promote social intercourse and provide a reading-room.

1655. RICHMOND CLUB OF PRINTING HOUSE CRAFTSMEN. Richmond club of printing house craftsmen; its history and mission. Supplemented by "Reminiscences of 35 years of printing in Richmond," by August Dietz . . . Richmond [1921]

8°.   V

1656. RICHMOND EVENING JOURNAL. Richmond and Virginia. [Richmond] 1915.

64 p. illus., ports. f°. (*Richmond evening journal*, II, 9; June 15, 1915)
BP, NYP

1657. [1129] RICHMOND EXCHANGE FOR WOMAN'S WORK. Annual report . . . [Richmond, Va.? 1884?—

1658. RICHMOND GUN CLUB. Eighth annual tournament, July 4, 1908. [Richmond, Va., 1908]

unp. 8°.   V

1659. RICHMOND HORSE SHOW ASSOCIATION. Seventh annual exhibition, Oct. 8-12, 1907. Official catalogue . . . Richmond, Va., 1907.

96 p. 8°.   V

1660. [464] RICHMOND ICE CO. [Circulars] [n. p., 1927]

1661. RICHMOND ILLUSTRATED in albertype. New York, Wittemann [1888]

1 p. l., 36 plates. obl. 24°.   **LC**

1662. RICHMOND MOZART ASSOCIATION. Constitution and by-laws of the Richmond Mozart association, organized Apr. 28, 1876. Incorporated Dec. 16, 1876. Richmond, Clemmitt & Jones, 1877.

16 p. 16°. V

1663. [933] RICHMOND PASSENGER & POWER CO. An ordinance to authorize the construction and operation of a street railway . . . [n. p., 19-?]

(See also items, 934-935)

1664. [938] RICHMOND RAILWAY & ELECTRIC CO. . . . Orders for motormen and conductors . . . Richmond, 1893.

1665. RICHMOND STREET guide; where to go, how to get there. Pub. by Central publishing co. Richmond, Va. [1924]

40 p. 12°. Advertisements interspersed. V

1666. [944] RICHMOND TRACTION CO. [Letter to Middendorf, Oliver & company, Baltimore, Md. . . . 1900]

1667. RICHMOND UNIVERSITY. Illustrated Richmond. Souvenir, guide, and official map . . . with guide to points of interest Pub. by Saunders & Bowers for Richmond college [ca. 1908]

[11] p. plates. 8°. V

Contains an historical sketch of Richmond college.

1668. RICHMOND, VIRGINIA, 1907. The capital metropolis and historic centre of the Old Dominion. [Richmond, Hermitage, 1907]

16 p. illus. 4°. BP, NYP, V, VU

1669. The RICHMOND VIRGINIAN. Land book and industrial edition, Dec. 22, 1916. Richmond, Va., 1916.

14, 14, 14, 8 p. f°. WM

1670. ROBERTSON, JOHN C. Pure water and better fire protection for Richmond. Richmond, Va., Whittet & Shepperson, 1902.

14 p. 8°. V

1671. ST. ELIZABETH'S HOSPITAL, Richmond. Clinics and collected papers. Vol. 1- ; 1922— St. Louis, Mosby, 1922—

illus. 8°. No more pub.? LC, NYP, V

Pt. I: Some features of management of St. Elizabeth's hospital, p. 17-31.

1672. SANDS, OLIVER J. What is before us! An address to the Credit men's association of Richmond, Va. . . . 1921. [Richmond, Va., Fergusson, 1921?]

    10 p. nar. 8°.   **V**
    Concerning the economic depression of 1921.

1673. SAUNDERS, CLYDE W., *et al.* Illustrated Richmond; souvenir, guide, and official map, containing elaborate list of Richmond views, with guide to points of interest, hotels, clubs, theatres, etc., and comprehensive historical sketch. [Richmond, Va.] Pub. by C. W. Saunders and C. W. Bowers for the Rchmond news co. [*ca.* 1908]

    [46] p. illus., fold. map. 8°.   **LC, NYP**

1674. SCOTT, W. W., *et al.* The capitol of Virginia and of the Confederate States: being a descriptive and historical catalogue of the public square and buildings, and of the statuary, paintings and curios therein. By W. W. Scott and W. G. Stanard. Richmond, Goode, 1894.

    23 p. 4°.   **BP, LC**

1675. SHELTERING ARMS FREE HOSPITAL, Richmond. [Report] Richmond, Va. [19-?—

    8°.   **V: 1905.**

1676. SNAPSHOTS at Richmond, Va., U. S. A. By the business man, editor, preacher, doctor, photographer . . . [Richmond, Hill, 1895]

    128 p. illus. 8°. Advertisements interspersed.   **BP, NYP, V**
    Various economic activities discussed by important business men.

1677. SOCIETY FOR THE PREVENTION OF CRUELTY TO ANIMALS, Richmond. . . . Report . . . [Richmond, 19-?—

    8°.   **V: 1911, 14-15, 25/26.**

1678. SOME events of interest about Richmond. 1924. Richmond, Fergusson [1924]

    15 p. 16°.   **V**

1679. SOUVENIR, Lee monument unveiling, May 29, 1890. [Richmond, Hill, 1890]

    96 p. illus., ports. 12°.   **V**

1680. SOUVENIR of the unveiling of the Richmond Howitzer monument at Richmond, Va., Dec. 13, 1892; address by Leigh Robinson . . . [n. p.] 1893.

> 98 p. front. 8°.   **V**

1681. [990] TECHNICAL ADVISORY CORP., New York. Report of investigation with reference to improving the James River . . . [n. p., 1924]

1682. THOMAS J. (STONEWALL) JACKSON MONUMENT CORP. Ceremony of laying the corner stone for the equestrian statue of Lieut.-Gen. Thomas Jonathan (Stonewall) Jackson, C. S. A., Richmond, Va., June 3, 1915, one o'clock P. M., intersection of Monument Avenue and Boulevard. Richmond, Mitchell & Hotchkiss [1915]

> 12 p. 8°.   **V**

1683. [1465] TRI-CITY SYSTEM. Richmond, Manchester, and Petersburg, Virginia: trolley rides . . . [n. p., n. d.]

1684. The TUESDAY CLUB, Richmond. Fourth annual May music festival, May 3, 4, & 5, True reformer's opera hall, 1909. Richmond, Va., 1909.

> 34 p. 8°.   **V**
>
> A Negro festival.

1685. UPSHUR, JOHN N. Medical reminiscences of Richmond during the past forty years. [n. p., 1906?]

> 24 p. 12°.   **V**
>
> Development of health agencies and medical organizations since 1865, with brief sketches of leading physicians.

1686. VIEWS of Richmond, Va. [Richmond, West, Johnston, 1884]

> 2 v. plates. obl. 16°.   **LC**

1687. [1025] VIRGINIA ELECTRIC & POWER CO. Annual report to the stockholders . . . [Richmond, 1925—

1688. [VIRGINIA HISTORICAL PAGEANT] [Pamphlets, clippings, etc., Virginia historical pageant, May 22-28, 1922. Richmond, Va.]

> var. pag. & size.   **V**

1689. VIRGINIA HOME FOR INCURABLES, Richmond. Report . . . Richmond [1895?-19—

> 8°. Incorp., Mar. 1, 1894.   **LC:** 1899; **V:** 1903.

1690. VIRGINIA ILLUSTRATING CO., Richmond. Richmond, Virginia, 1917 . . . Richmond [1917?]

[37]-184 p. incl. illus., plates, ports. 8°.   **V**

"A glance at her history; a review of her progress; . . . a description of her business enterprises . . ." etc.

1691. [1044] VIRGINIA PASSENGER & POWER CO. Annual report . . . [Richmond, 190-? -09?]

1692. [1046] VIRGINIA RAILWAY & POWER CO. Annual report . . . to the stockholders . . . Richmond, 1910-25.

(See also items, **1047-1049**)

1693. [261] VIRGINIA STATE AGRICULTURAL SOCIETY. Souvenir . . . [Richmond? 1883]

1694. [1374] VIRGINIA TRUST CO., Richmond. Address of the president at the annual meeting . . . [Richmond? 1926?]

(See also item, **1375**)

1695. VISITOR'S guide to Richmond and vicinity; embracing a sketch of the city; social statistics and notices of all places in and about the city of interest to the tourist . . . Richmond, Bates, 1871.

50 p. 4 plates (incl. front.) fold. plan. 16°.   **BP, H, LC, NYP**

1696. WALTHALL, DAVID K. History of Richmond lodge, no. 10, A. F. & A. M. Richmond, Ware & Duke, 1909.

198, xvi p. front. (port.) plates. 8°.   **V, WM**

Chronology of the lodge by decades, taken directly from the records and amounting to a source book.

1697. WALTHALL, ERNEST T. Hidden things brought to light. [n. p.] 1908.

48 p. illus. 12°.   **V**

Changes in the physical appearance and life of Richmond during the second half of the 19th century.

1698. WEAVER, CLARENCE E., comp. Sketches of Richmond, Virginia, U. S. A. Who's who and what's what, industrial, commercial, financial, historical, educational, biographical . . ·. Richmond, Va., Central pub. co. [*ca.* 1924]

223 p. incl. front., illus., ports. 8°.   **LC, V**

Contains "editorial sketches" of men and industries.

1699. WEBER, GUSTAVUS A. Report on housing and living conditions in the neglected sections of Richmond, Virginia, prepared by Gustavus A. Weber, secretary Society for the betterment of housing and living conditions in Richmond. Richmond, Va., Whittet & Shepperson, 1913.

80 p. incl. tables. plates, plan. 8°. **BP, LC, V, VU**

Report based upon returns made by volunteers in a house to house investigation, upon personal observations by the secretary, and analysis of laws and regulations; with discussion of means for betterment of conditions.

1700. WEDNESDAY CLUB, Richmond. Thirteenth annual music festival of the Wednesday club . . . 1906. Richmond, Whittet & Shepperson, 1906.

47 p. ports. 8°. **V**

1701. WESTMORELAND CLUB, Richmond. . . . Constitution and rules of the Westmoreland club, Richmond, Va. Club house, no. 601, Grace St., Richmond, 1880.

32 p. 8°. **V**

1702. ———. The constitution, by-laws, and house rules of the Westmoreland club of Richmond, Va. With a list of the officers and members. Also, its history and some account of its peculiar treasures . . . Richmond, 1909.

66 p. 16°. **WM**

1703. ———. Fiftieth anniversary, Jan. 29, 1927. Westmoreland club, Richmond, Virginia. [Richmond? 1927]

[6] p. f°. Illus. on covers. **V**

1704. ———. [Register of members . . . n. p., 19-?—

12°. **V**: 1912, 22, 25, 28.

1705. WOMAN'S CLUB, Richmond. Annual report . . . 2d- ; 1896-19— Richmond, Va., 1896-19—

illus., plates. 12°. Report year ends in March.

1896 is 2d report; 1st report never pub.

H: 1918/19; **LC**: 1907/08; **V**: 1896-1909/10, 11/12-15/16, 18/19-21/22, 23/24 25/26.

1706. ———. Constitution and by-laws . . . 1919-20. [Richmond? 1919?]

19 p. 12°. **V**

1707. WOOD, HENRY W. Optimism and progress. Address . . . before the Chamber of commerce, Richmond, Va., Mar. 25, 1909. [Richmond?] Pub. by the Chamber of commerce [1909]

16 p. 8°.   V

On the advantages of consolidating Richmond and Manchester.

1708. [WOOD, JAMES P.] The industries of Richmond. Her trade, commerce, manufactures and representative establishments. Richmond, Metropolitan pub., 1886.

144 p. illus. 8°.   NYP

1709. YOUNG MEN'S BUSINESS ASSOCIATION. Business facts about Richmond, Va. Richmond, Monitor, 1897.

21 l. map. obl. 24°.   NYP

Roanoke, Va.

1710. LUMSDEN, L. L., *et al.* Paratyphoid fever. Roanoke, Va. By L. L. Lumsden, A. W. Freeman, and W. B. Foster. May 30, 1913. Washington, Govt., 1913.

10 p. 8°. (U. S. Public health service. *Health report reprint*)
USH, USHy

1711. NOLEN, JOHN. Remodeling Roanoke; report to the Committee on civic improvement . . . [Roanoke, Va., Stone, 1908?]

40 p. illus. (57 p.) fold. map. 8°.   BP, H, LC

1712. ———. Replanning small cities; six typical studies. New York, Huebsch, 1912.

218 p. front., plates, plans. 8°.   H, LC
p. 9-30 on Roanoke, Va.

1713. PICTURESQUE Roanoke; being a series of reproductions from photographic views, taken in the city of Roanoke, Virginia, and the vicinity thereof, especially for this work . . . Roanoke, Va., Stone, 1902.

1 p. l., [32] p. of illus., 1 l. 4°.   LC

1714. POWELL, EDWARD A. The beckoning land . . . [Roanoke, Va., 1914?]

[5]-34 p. incl. illus., 4 col. plates. col. front. 4°.   H, LC, V
A description of Roanoke, Va., and the surrounding country.

1715. ROANOKE BOOSTER CLUB. Roanoke, Va., a city of enterprise, energy, and progress. [Roanoke] Pub. under the auspices of the Association of commerce, 1922.

48 p. incl. illus., plates. 8°.   LC

An attractive pamphlet; with historical sketch.

1716. ROANOKE CHAMBER OF COMMERCE. Roanoke industrial survey for Chamber of commerce of Roanoke, Va. [Roanoke, n. d.]

8°.   VU: I.

1717. ———. Roanoke, Virginia: its location, climate, and water supply; its manufacturing, commercial, and educational advantages, and general desirability as a place of residence. Comp. and ed. under auspices of Jamestown exposition committee, by E. B. Jacobs, secretary . . . [Roanoke, Va., 1907?]

32 p. illus. 8°.   LC, VU

How Roanoke typifies the development of the new South.

1718. ROANOKE GAS & WATER CO. Annual report . . . 1st- ; 1890— Roanoke, Va. [1891?-19—

8°. Report year ends Dec. 31.   V: 13th (1902).

1719. ROANOKE GAS LIGHT CO. First mortgage. Roanoke gas light company to Philadelphia trust company. Dated Feb. 1, 1926. Philadelphia, Allen, Lane & Scott [1926]

69 p. 8°.   HB

1720. ROANOKE HOSPITAL ASSOCIATION. Annual report . . . 1st- ; 1900— [Roanoke, 1901?—

plates. 8°. Report year ends Dec. 31.   LC: 7th (1906).

1721. ROANOKE WATER WORKS CO. [Circulars] [n. p., 1919-25]

4°.   HB

1722. SMITH, F. P. A synopsis of Roanoke and her wonderful prosperity . . . Roanoke, Va., Yager [1891]

50 p. port. 16°.   LC

1723. TAYLOR, FRANK H. The city of Roanoke, Virginia. As it appears in the year 1890 . . . New York, Giles [1890]

48 p. illus. obl. 24°.   LC

Outline of the city's development, with an introduction on the "industrial invasion" of the South by northern capital.

1724. TAYLOR, EWART & CO. The Roanoke water works company and the territory it serves . . . [n. p., 1925?]

    18, [1] p. map (front.) illus. 8°.   **HB**

    Brief description of Roanoke and her industry.

1725. TERRY & POPE, pub. Roanoke, Virginia, in 1891. Its investment opportunities. Its manufacturing advantages. Its transportation service. Its trade facilities. Its home attractions . . . Roanoke, Va., Hammond, 1891.

    21 p. 16°.   **LC**

1726. WOOD, GEORGE P. . . . The methods used in the official survey of Roanoke, Virginia . . . [Roanoke? 1892]

    [5]-19, [1] p. incl. diagrs. 8°.   **LC**

    At head of title: Transactions of the Association of engineers of Virginia.

    Contains suggestions for improved platting in the city.

Salem, Va.

1727. CITIZEN'S EXECUTIVE COMMITTEE, Salem, Va. Salem and the Roanoke valley: a circular of information.—Location, railroad facilities, business interests . . . Issued by the Citizen's executive committee. Salem, Va., Times-register print., 1884.

    68 p. 8°.   **BP, LC, NYP**

1728. SALEM IMPROVEMENT COMMITTEE. Salem, Virginia: its attractions and advantages. 2d revised edition. Lynchburg, Bell, 1890.

    32 p. illus., plate. 8°.   **BP, NYP**

1729. SALEM, VIRGINIA, county seat of Roanoke County; something of her past history and future prospects. Salem, Va., Salem print. [1907?]

    32 p. illus. fold. 4°.   **USAg**

Staunton, Va.

1730. BEAUTIFUL Thornrose cemetery, Staunton, Virginia. 1907. [Staunton, Beverly, 1907]

    94 p. illus. 8°.   **V**

    Organization of the company, description of grounds, Confederate memorial, etc.

1731. The DISPATCH AND NEWS, Staunton, Va. The Dispatch and news historical and industrial number, 1761-1906; Staunton, the queen city; ed. and comp. by Albert E. Walker. Staunton, Va., Augusta print. [1906]

    1 p. l., 46 p. illus. (incl. ports., map) f°.　　　　　　　**LC, NYP**

1732. GORDON, ARMISTEAD C. Staunton, Virginia: its past, present and future. With illustrations from photographs by Edmund Berkeley. New York, South pub. [188-?]

    74 p., 1 l. map. obl. 16°.　　　　　　　　　　　　　　**BP, LC**

1733. HOTCHKISS, JEDEDIAH. The city of Staunton, Augusta County, Virginia, and the surrounding country, their condition, resources, and advantages, and the inducements they offer to those seeking homes or places for business, investments, etc. . . . Staunton, Strasburg, 1878.

    48 p. illus., map. 8°.　　　　　　　　　　　　　　**LC, NYP, V**
    Reliable statistics quoted.

1734. STAUNTON DEVELOPMENT CO. Prospectus of the . . . company. Staunton, Va., 1890.

    7 p. 8°.　　　　　　　　　　　　　　　　　　　　　　**V**
    A land and improvement company.

1735. [1359] [STAUNTON LIFE INSURANCE CO.] Coupon policy forms. [Staunton, 1894]

1736. [YOST, SAMUEL M.] Beautiful Thornrose. Staunton, Va., Valley print., 1911.

    [24] p. illus. 8°.　　　　　　　　　　　　　　　　　　**V**
    Description of Thornrose cemetery.

Suffolk, Va.

1737. CEREMONIES attending the unveiling of the monument erected by Col. Thomas W. Smith, at Suffolk, Va., to the memory of the Confederate dead, . . . Nov. 14, 1899, including incidents, addresses, description of the monument, etc. Suffolk, Herald, 1890.

    26 p. 8°.　　　　　　　　　　　　　　　　　　　　**V, VU**

1738. POLLOCK, EDWARD. Sketch book of Suffolk, Va. Its people and its trade . . . Portsmouth, Va., Fiske & Purdie, 1886.

    144 p. illus. 16°. Advertisements interspersed.　　　**LC, V**
    A typical industrial and trade review.

1739. [1540] PORTSMOUTH, BERKLEY & SUFFOLK WATER CO. [Circular] [n. p., 1904]

1740. VIRGINIA-PILOT AND NORFOLK LANDMARK. Suffolk progress edition of the Virginia-pilot and Norfolk landmark. July, 1914. [Norfolk. 1914]

> 28 p. illus. f°.   **V**
> A typical newspaper review of the city's activities.

Washington, D. C.—Virginia suburbs.

1741. GORDON, F. R. Views of beautiful Fort Myer heights, adjoining the capital of the U. S. . . . [Washington, Advertiser, 19-?]

> 13, [3] p. illus. 8°.   **LC**
> Ft. Myer as a suburban development.

1742. [LATIMER & CLEARY, Washington, D. C.] Plan of the town Abington Park, Alexandria County [Va.] with description—views on the environs, etc. [Washington? 1874?]

> 10 p. 8°.   **LC**
> Prospectus of a Washington suburb.

1743. ROSEMONT DEVELOPMENT CO., Washington, D. C. Rosemont . . . suburb. [n. p., 1913]

> 16 p. incl. illus. 8°.   **LC**
> Description of the "only absolutely fully improved suburb of Washington, D. C."

West Point, Va.

1744. BAGBY, BATHURST B. . . . Changes in a small town brought about by the Health department, by B. B. Bagby, M.D., West Point, Virginia . . . Washington, Govt., 1924.

> 4 p. 8°. (U. S. Public health service. Public health reports. *Reprint,* 821, from XXXVIII, 10, Mar. 9, 1923, p. 456-458)   **LC, USH, USHy**
> An account of the present sanitary conditions in West Point. Originally pub. in *Virginia medical monthly,* XLIX, 9; Dec., 1922.

1745. [BROOKS, S. A.] Claims of the South for settlement. [n. p., 187-?]

> 8 p. fold. map. 8°.   **LC**
> The advantages of West Point, terminus of the Richmond & York River railroad.

1746. OLD DOMINION INDUSTRIAL CORP., West Point, Va. Information about Westpoint, Va. A coming city of America. An inland deep sea port. Truck farms, fruit and nut orchards . . . Richmond, Va., Whittet & Shepperson [n. d.]

[16] p. fold. illus. 8°.   **V**

1747. WEST POINT, Virginia, and King William County. 1888. Richmond, Waddey, 1888.

36 p. fold. map. 8°. Advertisements in back.   **LC, NYP, V**

Prepared by H. I. Lewis, I. Diggs, and T. P. Bagley, committee; reveals contemporary economic and social conditions.

Williamsburg, Va.

1748. SPENCER, JOHN B. An illustrated historical sketch of Jamestown, Williamsburg and Yorktown . . . [Petersburg, Va., Franklin, 1907]

[48] p. illus. obl. 8°.   **LC**

Cover-title: Souvenir guide, Jamestown, Williamsburg and Yorktown, 1607-1907.

1749. WILLIAMSBURG BUSINESS MEN'S ASSOCIATION. Facts about Williamsburg and vicinity . . . Richmond, Whittet & Shepperson, 1900.

49 p. illus., map. 8°.   **H, WM**

Winchester, Va.

1750. The CENTENNIAL celebration at Winchester, Va., July 4, 1876 . . . 1776. Winchester, News office, 1876.

31 p. 8°.   **VU**

1751. MORGAN, JOHN T. Address . . . on the unveiling of the monument to the unknown Confederate dead, delivered at Winchester, Virginia. June 6, 1879. Washington, D. C., Globe, 1879.

24 p. 8°.   **LC, VU**

1752. RICHARDS, LUTHER A. Some points of interest in and near historic Winchester, Virginia . . . [Winchester, Va.] Eddy press [1908]

32 p. illus. 8°. Advertisements in back.   **LC**

2d ed. [*ca.* 1909] 38 p.   **LC**

1753. WINCHESTER BOARD OF TRADE. In the garden of the Old Dominion. A little talk with the pleasure and health seeker about Winchester in the valley of the Shenandoah. Winchester [Eddy press] 1900.

12 l. illus. sq. 24°.   NYP

1754. WINCHESTER CHAMBER OF COMMERCE. Winchester, the queen city of the valley of Virginia . . . [Lynchburg, Bell, 1924]

64 p. illus., fold. map. 8°.   V, VU

Yorktown, Va.

1755. [CLOS, JEAN H.] Yorktown country club. Yorktown, Va. [*ca.* 1924]

[30] p. front., illus. (incl. ports., maps) 4°.   LC
"Written and designed by Jean Henri Clos."

1756. [1748] SPENCER, JOHN B. An illustrated historical sketch of . . . Yorktown . . . [Petersburg, 1907]

1757. STEVENS, JOHN A. Yorktown centennial handbook; historical and topographical guide to the Yorktown peninsula, Richmond, James River and Norfolk . . . New York, For the author, by Coffin & Rogers, 1881.

124 p. incl. illus., ports., maps. 8°.   LC, NYP, V, VU
Includes a description of the Yorktown centennial association and notes on economic and social conditions.

Other Source Material: (b) County Development

1758. [1411] ALBEMARLE CLUB OF COLONIAL DAMES. A historical guide to Albemarle County . . . Charlottesville, 1924.

1759. ALBEMARLE COUNTY, VA. COUNTY COMMISSIONER. Handbook descriptive of Albemarle County, including city of Charlottesville. Ed. by Walter Whately . . . [n. p., 1907]

33 p. 8°.   VU

1760. [ALEXANDER, CHARLES, *et al.*] Mecklenburg County, Virginia; its history, resources and advantages; the place for homes,

health, happiness, and inviting business prospects. Come and see!
. . . [n. p.] 1907.

16 p. 8°.   NYP, V

Publication prepared by Charles Alexander, H. F. Hutcheson, and
Thomas D. Jeffress.

Ed. of 1909.   LC

1761. ALEXANDRIA COUNTY, VA. BOARD OF SUPERVISORS. A brief
history of Alexandria County, Virginia; its wealth and resources,
great and growing industries, educational and social advantages
. . . Pub. under authority of the county Board of supervisors
by C. G. Boteler, Crandal Mackey, M. E. Church, W. S. Hoge,
jr., C. B. Haller, committee. Falls Church, Va., Newell [1907]

56 p. illus., fold. map. 8°.   LC, NYP, V

Advertisements in back.

1762. AMHERST COUNTY, VA. BOARD OF SUPERVISORS. Facts of
interest about Amherst County . . . April, 1907. [n. p.,
1907]

15 p. 16°.   V

1763. BAKER, W. W. Description of Chesterfield County, Va.
[n. p., 1888?]

15 p. 24°.   NYP

1764. BEDFORD the richest in natural resources of the counties in
piedmont Virginia, offers homes to the grazers, the dairyman,
the vinticulturist, the fruit-grower, the stock-raiser, the tobacco
planter, and all others in search of cheap homes in an unsurpassed
climate, with every natural advantage . . . [Bedford, Va.]
Bedford index print. [1893?]

1 l., 48 p. 8°.   BP, H, NYP, V

Advertisements in front and back.

1765. BOYD, CHARLES R. Grayson County, Virginia, by C. R. Boyd,
state geologist (ex-officio). Economic: ores, stones, etc. Analysis, agricultural products: timber, soils, manufactures, transportation, summaries. Scientific: geology, mineralogy. Independence, Va., Brown, 1897.

2 p. l., [2]-42 p., 1 l. fold. map. 8°.   USG

Emphasis upon mineral resources.

1766. BRUNSWICK COUNTY, VA. BOARD OF SUPERVISORS. Brunswick County, Virginia. Information for the homeseeker and investor. Prepared under the supervision of the Hon. I. E. Spatig, as authorized by the Board of supervisors of Brunswick County, Virginia, July 23, 1906. Comp. by Marvin Smithey. Richmond, Va., Williams, 1907.

> 48 p. illus. 8°. Advertisements in back.   **LC, NYP, V, VU**
> On cover: Jamestown exposition, 1607-1907.

1767. [1463] BURGWYN, COLLINSON P. Report . . . on the natural advantages . . . of the . . . county of Chesterfield . . . Manchester, 1888.

1768. CAROLINE COUNTY, VA. BOARD OF SUPERVISORS. A handbook of Caroline County, Virginia. Pub. by authority of the Board of supervisors of the county. 1907. Bowling Green, Va., Echo pub., 1907.

> 14 p. fold. map. 8°.   **LC, V**
> Information "to meet numerous inquiries from persons seeking homes in Virginia."
> Ed. of 1888: Caroline sentinel print.: 6 l. map.   **NYP**

1769. CARRINGTON, JOHN C. Charlotte County, Virginia: historical, statistical, and present attractions . . . Richmond, Va., Hermitage, 1907.

> 5 p. l., 7-142 p. incl. illus., plates. 8°.   **LC, V**
> Contains many letters from local and state officials and from residents, to sustain the statements regarding the resources and development of the county. Pub. under auspices of the county Board of supervisors.

1770. CHESTERFIELD COUNTY, Virginia. [n. p., 1915?]

> 29 p. illus. 8°.   **H, LC**
> A descriptive sketch of the county.

1771. [CLAIBORNE, J. G., comp.] Franklin County, Virginia, historical and industrial . . . past—present—future . . . [Rocky Mount, Va., County news print., 1926]

> 44 p. illus. (incl. ports.) f°.   **V**
> Issued as a supplement to the *County news*, Rocky Mount, Va.

1772. [――――] Nelson County, Virginia, historical and industrial; past, present, future . . . [Lynchburg, Brown-Morrison, 1925]

    40 p. illus., map, facsim. f°.   **V, WM**

    Issued as supplement to the *Nelson County times,* Lovingston, Va.

1773. COCKE, WILLIAM B. Sussex County, Virginia, the homeseeker's paradise. A guide to homeseekers and investors . . . Comp. principally by Commissioner William B. Cocke, Booker, Va. Richmond, Va., Williams, 1907.

    19, [12] p. illus. 8°.   **V, VU**

1774. COVINGTON, VA. CHAMBER OF COMMERCE. Alleghany County, Virginia: its resources and industries. Issued by the Chamber of commerce of Covington, Va. . . .Roanoke, Va., 1907.

    32 p. fold. front., illus. 8°.   **LC, V, VU**

1775. Cox, T. B. Chesterfield County, Virginia. Its history and present condition. Prepared under the supervision of the Hon. John B. Watkins, as authorized by the Board of supervisors of the county, Aug., 1906. Comp. by T. B. Cox. Richmond, Va., Williams, 1907.

    45 p. illus. 8°.   **V, VU**

1776. CRAIG COUNTY, VA. BOARD OF TRADE. Craig County, Virginia. Information concerning formation, description, mineral and agricultural resources, educational advantages, streams and water power, timber lands, mineral springs, resorts, and other natural advantages. Roanoke, Va., Stone [n. d.]

    16 p. illus. nar. 8°.   **LC**

1777. The CULPEPER exponent. "Anniversary number, 1881-1909, exploiting the multifarious advantages of Culpeper, Virginia . . . " [Culpeper, 1909]

    16 p. illus. f°. (*Culpeper exponent,* XXIX, 11)   **V**

1778. CUMBERLAND COUNTY, a county of sunshine and flowers, of happy homes and contented people. [n. p., 1907]

    [12] p. 16°.   **V**

1779. [DAVENPORT, ISAAC, jr.] Petition [to Congress by citizens of the county of Henrico, Virginia, relative to the payment of rents, etc. on private property used by the U. S. army for various purposes after the surrender of the Confederate army, April, 1865] [n. p., 1870?]

　　4 p. 8°.　　　　　　　　　　　　　　　　　　　　　　　　LC

　　Isaac Davenport, jr., first signer.

1780. A DESCRIPTION of Henrico County, Virginia, 1888. Richmond, Murphy, 1888.

　　8 p. 8°.　　　　　　　　　　　　　　　　　　　　　　　NYP, V

1781. FAIRFAX COUNTY, VA. BOARD OF SUPERVISORS. . . . Industrial and historical sketch of Fairfax County, Virginia . . . Prepared and pub. under authority of the county Board of supervisors by the following committee: M. D. Hall, S. R. Donahoe, Franklin Williams, jr., J. S. Pearson, M. E. Church. [Falls Church, Newell] 1907.

　　95 p. incl. front., illus., fold. map. 8°.　　　　　　NYP, V, VU

1782. FARRAR, F. R. Amelia County, Virginia; an outline of the soil, productions, minerals, etc. Richmond, Waddey, 1888.

　　16 p. 8°.　　　　　　　　　　　　　　　　　　　　　　　　　V

1783. FAUQUIER COUNTY, Virginia. Historical notes. Pub. as a supplement to the map of Fauquier County. Warrenton, Va., 1914.

　　45 p. 8°.　　　　　　　　　　　　　　　　　　　　　　　　　V

　　Signed: H. C. G.

1784. FOSTER & HENDERSON, *firm*. Loudoun County, Virginia; its social, agricultural and manufacturing advantages, as detailed in a series of letters, written by Fenton M. Henderson, and published in the *Democratic mirror*, Leesburg, Va. 1868. [Leesburg, Va., 1868]

　　8 p. 12°.　　　　　　　　　　　　　　　　　　　　　　　　　V

1785. FRANCIS, W. P. Smyth County, Virginia. Information concerning transportation, mountains, streams, water powers, and places of interest, elevations, and the mineral waters. Richmond, Va., Fergusson, 1888.

　　16 p. 24°.　　　　　　　　　　　　　　　　　　　　　　　NYP

1786. GAINES, RICHARD V. Hand-book of Charlotte County, Virginia. Its history, physical characteristics, climatic conditions, social, moral and religious advantages, statistical and other information, with letters from prominent citizens showing its desirability as a home, and the inducements it offers to the industrious and intelligent farmer and mechanic. Richmond, Va., Waddey, 1889.

68 p. illus., map. 8°.   NYP, USAg,V
Comp. by the county commissioner.

1787. [GREGORY, EDWARD D., comp.] The Peaks of Otter, Virginia. [Photographs by F. H. Richardson] [Roanoke, Stone, 1900]

32 p. illus. 16°.   H, LC
Describes localities in Bedford County, Va.

1788. HANDBOOK of Mecklenburg County . . . Danville, Va., Boatwright, 1901.

19 p. illus. 12°. Advertisements in back.   LC, NYP
Describes resources of the county; why lands are for sale.   !

1789. HANOVER COUNTY, Virginia. Historical and industrial. Past—present—future. Pub. by the Herald-progress, Ashland, Va. 1720-1926. [Ashland, 1926]

[32] p. incl. illus. f°.   V, VU, WM
Advertisements interspersed.

1790. HARRIS, FINDLAY. Virginia, Washington County, its location, climate, resources, attractions and advantages . . . Comp, by the request of the Board of supervisors of Washington County, by Findlay Harris, editor *Abingdon Virginian,* Abingdon, Va., 1907. [Bristol, Tenn., King, 1907]

46 p. illus., map. 8°.   V

1791. [1448] HARRISONBURG DAILY NEWS. Rockingham County . . . [Harrisonburg, 19-?]

1792. HENRICO COUNTY, VA. BOARD OF SUPERVISORS. Henrico County, Virginia: a hand-book embracing an outline of its history and a description of its resources and advantages as a home. Issued by order of the Board of supervisors. Richmond, Va., Whittet & Shepperson, 1893.

46 p. illus., map. obl. 4°.   LC, NYP

1793. HEUSER, H. M., comp. A short historical and physical description of Wythe County, Virginia . . . Pub. by order of the Board of supervisors for distribution at the Jamestown tercentennial exposition, 1907. [Wytheville, Va., 1907?]

35 p. illus. 8°.   **V**

1794. HISTORICAL Hanover County, Virginia, 1720 . . . 1926. [Ashland, Va., Herald-progress, 1926]

[32] p. illus. (incl. ports.) f°.   **LC**

Advertisements interspersed.

Portraying the economic and social progress of Hanover County; includes a sketch of Randolph-Macon college.

1795. [1733] HOTCHKISS, JEDEDIAH. The city of Staunton, Augusta County, Virginia, and the surrounding country . . . Staunton, 1878.

1796. KING WILLIAM COUNTY, VA. COUNTY COUNCIL. King William County, Virginia . . . Comp. and presented by County council, . . . King William Court House, Va. [Richmond, Carrett & Massie, 1925]

60 p. illus., map. 8°.   **V, WM**

1797. The LOUDOUN mirror . . . Leesburg, Va., Nov. 5, 1909. [Leesburg, 1909]

14 p. illus. f°. Illustrated supplement.   **V**

"A modest review of our leading men and enterprises."

1798. LOUISA COUNTY, VA. COUNTY COMMISSIONER. Description of Louisa County; Jesse J. Porter, county commissioner to represent the Louisa exhibit at the Richmond exposition. [Louisa, Va., Louisa news & farmer, 1888]

8 p. 8°.   **NYP, V**

Includes a farmer's statement of his sales of farm products, 1887-88.

1799. [MECKLENBURG COUNTY, Va.] South hill enterprise, industrial progress, Mar. 2, 1922.

2 sections. illus. f°.   **V**

1800. MONTGOMERY COUNTY, VA. BOARD OF SUPERVISORS. Montgomery County, Virginia. Jamestown exposition souvenir. [n. p., 1907]

    16 p. illus. 8°.   **LC, V**

    Contains articles on the resources of the county, by members of the V. P. I. faculty.

1801. MORRISON, ALFRED J. . . . Halifax County, Virginia: a handbook prepared under the direction of the Board of supervisors . . . Richmond, Va., Waddey, 1907.

    93, [3] p. front. (fold. map.) illus. 12°.   **LC, NYP, V, VU, WM**

    Pt. I: descriptive. Pt. II: historical.

1802. [MORRISON, E. M.] Isle of Wight County. 1608-1907. [Norfolk? Va., 1907]

    72 p. illus., plates. nar. 8°.   **LC, NYP, V, VU, WM**

    Comp. for distribution at the Jamestown exposition. Advertisements in back. Includes description of contemporary conditions.

1803. MORRISON, R. F. Rappahannock [County] . . .; photographs by William H. Lewis . . . [Washington] Washington herald, 1926.

    8 p. l., 20 numb. l. illus. 8°.   **LC**

    Mounted newspaper clippings.

1804. MUSTARD, HARRY S. . . . Outline of rural health administration in Rockbridge County, Virginia, by H. S. Mustard, assistant surgeon, U. S. Public health service . . . Washington, Govt., 1920.

    22 p. incl. 1 illus., forms. 8°. (U. S. Public health service. Public health reports. *Reprint,* 613, from **XXXV**, 40; Oct. 1, 1920; p. 2309-2328)
                                  LC, USAg, USH, USHy, USL

    Organization, publicity, and activities of the rural health campaign in Rockbridge County, 1919-20, with results and summary of conclusions. Contains "exhibits" of placards, letters, and general publicity material used.

1805. NORFOLK COUNTY, its history and development; the leading county of Virginia. Apr. 16, 1907. [n. p., 1907]

    23 p. 12°.   **LC, V**

1806. PATRICK COUNTY, VA. BOARD OF SUPERVISORS. Patrick County, Virginia; its resources and advantages. 1907 . . . [Roanoke, Stone, 1907?]

    15 p. 16°.   **V**

1807. PRINCE EDWARD COUNTY for a home in Virginia. Richmond, Va., Johns, 1888.

46 p. illus., tables. 8°. NYP, V

1808. PULASKI COUNTY, VA. COMMISSION, JAMESTOWN EXPOSITION, 1907. Pulaski County, Virginia. A historic and descriptive sketch designed to show forth the natural advantages, resources and general adaptability of the banner county of southwest Virginia, to agriculture, cattle raising, and also commercial and industrial enterprises. Pub. under the direction of the Committee in charge of the Pulaski County exhibit at the Jamestown exposition held at Norfolk, Va., 1907. Pulaski, Va., Southwest pub. [1907]

96 p. illus. 8°. LC, USAg, V

1809. REID, J. A. Handbook of Madison County, Virginia. [n. p., 188-?]

4 p. 12°. NYP

1810. RIVES, W. C. Historic Dinwiddie County, Virginia; or, The last long camp. Pub. by order of the Jamestown exhibit committee of Dinwiddie Co., Va. [Petersburg, Franklin, 1907]

12 p. incl. plates, fold. map. 8°. H, V, VU

1811. SEAMON, W. H. Albemarle County, Virginia. A handbook giving a description of its topography, climate, geology, minerals, fruits, plants, history, educational, agricultural and manufacturing advantages, and inducements the county offers the industrious and intelligent farmer and manufacturer. Ed. by W. H. Seamon, Crozet, Va. . . . Pub. by William H. Prout, Charlottesville. Charlottesville, Va., Jeffersonian, 1888.

110 p. illus. 8°. NYP, V, VU

1812. SHEFFEY, JOHN P. General resources and advantages of Smyth County, in the most attractive section of Appalachian Virginia . . . Printed by order of the Board of supervisors, in the year of the Jamestown exposition, 1907. [Richmond, Va., Stone, 1907]

63, [1] p. illus. 16°. V

On cover: Handbook of Smyth County, Virginia, 1907; Exposition number.

1813. [SHENANDOAH COUNTY, Va.] Shenandoah herald, Aug. 20, 1926. Greater Shenandoah County edition.

illus. f°. (*Shenandoah herald,* CIX, 34) V

1814. SHOWELL, VIRGINIA. Essex sketches; an appreciation . . . Baltimore, Thomas & Evans, 1924.

85 p. illus. 8°. V, WM

Rural life and social conditions among the older families of the county, interwoven with historical incidents.

1815. SKETCH and map of Southampton County, Virginia. Prepared by the Exposition committee, 1888. [Richmond] Richmond Dispatch, 1888.

8 p. map. 12°. NYP

1816. WALKER, B. H., comp. King and Queen County, Virginia. Information for the home-seeker and investor. Prepared under the supervision of W. H. Walker, as authorized by the Board of supervisors . . . , Aug., 1906. Comp. by B. H. Walker, Stevensville, Va. Richmond, Picot, 1906.

32 p. illus. 8°. Advertisements in back. LC, V

Contains little specific information.

1817. WALMSLEY, JAMES E. The shadow of the mighty peaks; a historical pageant of Bedford County, Virginia . . . Presented May 17, 1922, under the auspices of the Bedford County pageant committee. Bedford, Va., Bedford print. [1922]

[9], 4-38 p. front., plates. 8°. V

1818. [1747] WEST POINT, Virginia, and King William County . . . Richmond, 1888.

1819. WISE COUNTY, her industries, resources, and prominent men. [Norton, Va., 1920]

28 p. illus., ports. f°. (*Crawford's weekly:* industrial edition. Norton, Va., Oct., 1920. Bruce Crawford, ed.) V

Secondary Works

1820. BOHANNON, A. W. Old Surry. Thumb-nail sketches of places of historic interest in Surry County, Virginia . . . [Petersburg, Va., Plummer, 1927]

74 p. front. 8°. VU

Contains scattered notes on the period since 1865.

1821. BRADLEY, J. H.   Official history of the Norfolk fire department from 1740 to the present day, illustrating and describing the equipment of the fire department to-day.   Gathered from official sources compiled by J. H. Bradley under the supervision of Martin J. Ryan, chief.   [Norfolk?] 1897.

[52] p. illus., plates. obl. 8°.   V

Advertisements interspersed.

"The statements . . . are compiled from Department sources, and verified by actual reports and memoranda kept in the department archives."

1822. BROCKETT, FRANKLIN L.   The lodge of Washington.   A history of the Alexandria Washington lodge, no. 22, A. F. and A. M. of Alexandria, Va.   1783-1876.   Comp. from the original records of the Lodge . . . Alexandria, Va., French, 1876.

xvi, [17]-220 p. illus., plate, 3 ports. 8°.   **BP, LC, V, VU**

1823. CATLETT, CLAY M., *et al.* . . . An economic and social survey of Augusta County, by Clay Catlett [and] Elliott G. Fishburne; a laboratory study in the School of rural social economics of the University of Virginia.   [Charlottesville] University of Virginia, 1928.

x, 168 p. plates. 8°. (*University of Virginia record.* Extension series, XII, 7; Jan., 1928)

Virginia county surveys, ed. by Wilson Gee, X.

1824. CAVANAGH, CATHERINE F.   The awakening of Alexandria. [n. p., 1909?]

p. [426]-431. illus. 8°.   (Reprint from the *New age,* May, 1909)

Improvements in the city's condition since 1865.

1825. CHILDS, BENJAMIN G. . . . The Negroes of Lynchburg, Virginia . . . Charlottesville, Va., Surber-Arundale, 1923.

57 p. diagrs. 8°. (University of Virginia. *Phelps-Stokes fellowship papers,* V)   **LC, NYP, USL, V, VU, WM**

An investigation of the social and economic status of the Negroes of Lynchburg, showing their development and influence upon the growth of the city.

1826. CHRISTIAN, GEORGE L.   The Capitol disaster.   A chapter of reconstruction in Virginia . . . [Richmond] Richmond press [1915]

46 p. illus., 2 plates. 8°.   **H, LC, NYP, V, WM**

A sketch of the reconstruction government of Virginia and its corruption; also extracts from a contemporary pamphlet, Richmond, 1870; "A full account of the great calamity which occurred in the Capitol at Richmond . . ." **[1580]**

1827. ———. Sketch of the origin and erection of the Confederate memorial institute at Richmond, Virginia, prepared by Hon. George L. Christian . . . at the request of the Board of lady managers . . . [Richmond, 1921]

32 p. front., port. 8°.   **LC, V, WM**
Ed. of 1923.   **V**

1828. [1382] CUNNINGHAM, RICHARD E. Fifty years of service, 1870-1920. Richmond, Va., National state & city bank [1920]

1829. [1383] DANFORTH, JOHN B., *et al.* Historical sketch of the Mutual assurance society of Virginia . . . Richmond, 1879.

1830. DECK, PATRICK A., *et al.* . . . An economic and social survey of Loudoun County, by Patrick A. Deck [and] Henry Heaton; a laboratory study in the James Wilson school of economics of the University of Virginia. [Charlottesville] University of Virginia, 1926.

2 p. l., [3]-132 p. plates. 8°. (*University of Virginia record*. Extension series, X, 10; June, 1926)
Virginia county surveys, ed. by Wilson Gee, VII.
Includes "Historical sketch of Loudoun County," by Henry P. White, p. [9]-24.

1831. DETWILER, SADIE C., *et al.* Fairfax County geography supplement, by Sadie C. Detwiler [*et al.*] . . . Fairfax County school board. University, Va., 1925.

24 p. 4°.   **VU, WM**

1832. FEREBEE, ENOCH E., *et al.* . . . An economic and social survey of Princess Anne County, by E. E. Ferebee [and] J. Pendleton Wilson, jr.; a laboratory study in the James Wilson school of economics of the University of Virginia. [Charlottesville] University of Virginia, 1924.

96 p. plates. 8°. (*University of Virginia record*. Extension series, VIII, 9; May, 1924)
Virginia county surveys, ed. by Wilson Gee, II.

1833. FULLER, MABEL C., *et al.* Pittsylvania County geography supplement, by Mabel C. Fuller [*et al.*] . . . University, Va., Pittsylvania County school board, 1925.

32 p. 4°.   **VU, WM**

1834. GEE, WILSON, ed. [Economic and social surveys of Virginia counties; laboratory studies in the School of rural social economics of the University of Virginia. Charlottesville, University of Virginia, 1922—

plates. 8°. In progress. (In *University of Virginia record.* Extension series, *passim*)

[1] *Albemarle County,* by Wilson Gee, *et al.* (Oct., 1922). [2] *Princess Anne County,* by Enoch E. Ferebee and J. Pendleton Wilson (May, 1924). [3] *Fairfax County,* by Lehman Nickell and Cary J. Randolph (Aug., 1924). [4] *Rockingham County,* by John S. Peters and W. F. Stinespring (Sept., 1924). 5. *King and Queen County,* by Joseph R. Mundie (July, 1925). 6. *Clarke County,* by Paul L. Warner (Aug., 1925). 7. *Loudoun County,* by Patrick A. Deck and Henry Heaton (June, 1926). 8. *Giles County,* by Francis A. Snidow and F. W. McComas (Feb., 1927). 9. *Northampton County,* by Clarence W. Holland, jr., N. L. Holland, and W. W. Taylor (Nov., 1927). 10. *Augusta County,* by Clay M. Catlett and Elliott G. Fishburne (Jan., 1928). 11. *Wise County,* by Ralph E. Kennedy (May, 1928).

Based upon personal investigation and reliable statistics, these surveys form invaluable pictures of contemporary economic and social life, from an objective point of view.

1835. GEE, WILSON, *et al.* . . . An economic and social survey of Albemarle County [by] Wilson Gee, A. L. Bennett, Elizabeth Fahrney, Mabel Nussman, P. B. Barringer, Ottie Craddock, Odie Mayhew, C. F. Whitmore. [University, Va.] University of Virginia, 1922.

111 p. plates. 8°. (*University of Virginia record.* Extension series, VII, 2; Oct., 1922)

Virginia county surveys, ed. by Wilson Gee, I.

1836. GILKESON, REBECCA. A brief social and economic survey of Augusta County, Virginia, 1880-1910. [Chicago] 1913.

44 l. 4°. Reproduced from typed copy.   **NYP**

Thesis, University of Chicago, 1913.

1837. GILLIAM, ROSA, *et al.* Campbell County geography supplement, by Rosa Gilliam [*et al.*] . . . University, Va., Campbell County school board, 1925.

28 p. 4°.   **WM**

1838. GOOD, VIRGINIA, *et al.* Rockingham County geography supplement, by Virginia Good [*et al.*] . . . University, Va., Rockingham County school board, 1924.

27 p. 4°.   **WM**

1839. HETZEL, SUSAN R. The building of a monument; a history of the Mary Washington associations and their work . . . Lancaster, Pa., Wickersham, 1903.

3 p. l., 255 p. plates, ports. (incl. front.) facsim. 8°.   **LC, V**

History of the Mary Washington monument at Fredericksburg and the work of the associations.

1840. HOFFER, FRANK W. Counties in transition. A study of county public and private welfare administration in Virginia. The Institute for research in the social sciences, University, Va. [Charlottesville, Michie] 1929.

xiv, 255 p. tables. 8°. (*Institute monograph,* 2)

1841. ———. Public and private welfare, Roanoke, Virginia . . . Pub. by the Roanoke city planning and zoning commissions, the Roanoke Community fund, and the Roanoke Chamber of commerce as a part of a comprehensive city study. June, 1928. [Roanoke, Stone] 1928.

142 p. illus., maps, plans. 4°. (University of Virginia. Institute for research in the social sciences)

A detailed study of social agencies in Roanoke, their work and accomplishments, principles and policies; based upon personal interviews with officers of the agencies and upon their records.

1842. HOLLAND, CLARENCE W., *et al.* . . . An economic and social survey of Northampton County, by C. W. Holland, jr., N. L. Holland, W. W. Taylor; a laboratory study in the School of rural social economics of the University of Virginia. [Charlottesville] University of Virginia, 1927.

x, 146 p. plates. 8°. (*University of Virginia record.* Extension series, XII, 5; Nov., 1927)

Virginia county surveys, ed. by Wilson Gee, IX.

1843. [HOLLYWOOD CEMETERY, Richmond, Va.] Historical sketch of Hollywood cemetery, from the 3d of June, 1847, to 1st Nov., 1875. Prepared by a committee appointed for that object, on the 4th . . . May, 1875 . . . Richmond, Baughman, 1875.

41, [1] p. 8°.   **LC, V, WM**

1844. HODGES, LE ROY. Petersburg, Virginia, economic and municipal, by Le Roy Hodges . . . preface by W. Jett Lauck . . .
Petersburg, Va., Issued by the Chamber of commerce of Petersburg, 1917.

> 166 p. incl. tables, charts, diagrs. fold. maps. 8°.
> A scholarly descriptive and analytical study based upon reliable
> sources.

1845. KENNEDY, RALPH, E. . . . An economic and social study
of Wise County . . . ; a laboratory study in the School of rural social economics of the University of Virginia. [Charlottes-
ville] University of Virginia, 1928.

> 147 p. plates. 8°. (*University of Virginia record.* Extension series, XII,
> 11; May, 1928)
> Virginia county surveys, ed. by Wilson Gee, XI.

1846. KNIGHT, CHARLES L. . . . Negro housing in certain Virginia cities . . . Richmond, Va., William Byrd press, 1927.

> 158 p. illus. 8°. (University of Virginia. *Phelps-Stokes fellowship pa-
> pers,* VIII)
> A scientific study of Negro living conditions in Richmond, Lynchburg,
> and Charlottesville, revealing pointedly the need for improvement in these
> districts.

1847. MILLER, MRS. LENA K., *et al.* Albemarle County geography
supplement, by Mrs. Lena K. Miller [*et al.*] . . . University,
Virginia, Albemarle County school board, 1925.

> 32 p. 4°.   **WM**

1848. MUNDIE, JOSEPH R. . . . An economic and social survey
of King and Queen County . . . ; a laboratory study in the
James Wilson school of economics of the University of Virginia.
[Charlottesville] University of Virginia, 1925.

> 5 p. l., [9]-98 p. plates. 8°. (*University of Virginia record.* Extension
> series, IX, 10; July, 1925)
> Virginia county surveys, ed. by Wilson Gee, V.

1849. NICKELL, LEHMAN P., *et al.* . . . An economic and social
survey of Fairfax County, by Lehman Nickell [and] Cary J. Randolph; a laboratory study in the James Wilson school of economics
of the University of Virginia. [Charlottesville, Va.] University
of Virginia [1924]

> 127 p. plates. 8°. (*University of Virginia record.* Extension series,
> VIII, 12; Aug., 1924)
> Virginia county surveys, ed. by Wilson Gee, III.

1850. PETERS, JOHN S., *et al.* . . . . An economic and social survey of Rockingham County, by J. S. Peters [and] W. F. Stinespring; a laboratory study in the James Wilson school of economics of the University of Virginia. [Charlottesville] University of Virginia, 1924.

131 p. plates. 8°. (*University of Virginia record.* Extension series, IX, 1; Sept., 1924)

Virginia county surveys, ed. by Wilson Gee, IV.

1851. SANDERS, H. R., *et al.* Loudoun County geography supplement . . . by H. R. Sanders [*et al.*] . . . University, Va., Loudoun County school board, 1925.

27 p. 4°. **WM**

1852. SNIDOW, FRANCIS A., *et al.* . . . . An economic and social survey of Giles County, by Francis A. Snidow [and] F. W. McComas, jr. . . . [Charlottesville] University extension division [1927]

2 p. l., p. [411]-516. plates. 8°. (*University of Virginia record.* Extension series, XI, 8; Feb., 1927)

Virginia county surveys, ed. by Wilson Gee, VIII.

1853. WARNER, PAUL L. . . . An economic and social survey of Clarke County . . . ; a laboratory study in the James Wilson school of economics of the University of Virginia. [Charlottesville] University of Virginia, 1925.

127 p. plates. 8°. (*University of Virginia record.* Extension series, IX, 12; Aug., 1925)

Virginia county surveys, ed. by Wilson Gee, VI.

Includes historical sketch of the county, by Henry W. Carpenter, p. 11-22.

For historical accounts of Virginia cities and counties, see Pt. VIII: *Local History.*

Periodicals

1854. The CAVALIER. An illustrated news-magazine, issued every Saturday. v. 1-v. 2, no. 1; Oct. 10, 1903-Jan. 2, 1904. Richmond, Va., J. G. A. Montague & co., 1903-04.

2 v. illus. (incl. ports.) 4°. No more pub. **LC, V**

J. G. A. Montague, ed.

1855. The CAVALIER. Fortress Monroe, Va. v. 1-v. 2, no. 16; 1905-June, 1906. Fortress Monroe, Va., 1905-06.

    2 v. illus. 8°. semi-monthly. No more pub.   **NYP**
    Mildred B. Pierce, ed.

    Contains historical articles and news of contemporary social life in the region of Old Point Comfort.

1856. The IDEA, a rebell yell. v. 1-4; July, 1906-Oct. 8, 1910. [Lynchburg, Va.] 1906-10.

    16°. monthly.   **LC: I-IV.**
    Publication suspended, May, 1907-Dec., 1908.

    Pub. to expose and undermine political corruption and immorality, first in Lynchburg, then in Richmond and elsewhere in Virginia.

1857. The IDEA: a sign of the times. v. 1-2; Lynchburg, Va. [1906?-08?] v. 3-5; 1908-10. Richmond, Va., 1908-10.

    8°. weekly. No more pub.   **V: III-V, 4.**
    A. A. Yoder, ed. and pub.

    A news magazine, especially on affairs in Richmond.

1858. JOURNAL of commerce. v. 1-[?]; 1904-[?] Richmond, Va., 1904-[?]

    monthly.   **V: I.**

1859. [1133] MILLER & RHOADS monthly record . . . Richmond, Va., 1910-[12?]

1860. [549] PRO QUERENTE; "P. Q.", a journal devoted to the lawyer, merchant, manufacturer, and jobber. Richmond [1899?-19—

1861. RICHMOND, v. 1-   ; 1914— Richmond, Va., Pub. by the Richmond Chamber of commerce, 1914—

    f°. monthly.
    NYP: II, 7-8; III, 4; V, 6, 12; VI, 2-4, 6-12; VII, 1, 3-7, 9-11; VIII, 4-5; IX-XVI (1916-28/29). **V:** VIII, 7-XV (1922-28/29).

1862. [550] RICHMOND MERCANTILE and manufacturing journal. Richmond, 1883—

1863. RICHMOND MODES and manners. v. 1, no. 1-   ; Aug., 1926— Richmond, Va., 1926—

    illus. 4°. bi-monthly.
    Miss Elizabeth Lee, ed.
    V: I-III, 5 (Aug., 1926-Apr., 1929).

1864. [551] RICHMOND TRADE journal . . . Richmond, Va. [1892?—

1865. RICHMOND'S young men. 1905-08; new ser., v. 1, no. 1- ; Apr., 1928— Richmond, Va., Pub. by the Y. M. C. A., 1905-08; 1928—

illus., adv. 4°. Issued irreg. (part weekly)
V: 1905-08; new ser., I, 1-4; II, 5 (1928-29).

1866. ROANOKE. v. 1, no. 1- ; [Nov., 1911?—] Roanoke, Va., Pub. by the Chamber of commerce, 1911—

illus. 4°. monthly.
BP: I, 6; II, 1 (Apr., Oct., 1912). V: I, 6.

1867. The TRAIL . . . Pub. by the First troop of Boy scouts, Winchester, Virginia . . . v. 1- ; Oct. 22, 1917— [Richmond, 1917—

illus. (part col.) 4°.   LC: I (Oct. 22, 1917).

1868. The VIGILANT; Pub. by the Norfolk police division. v. 1, no. 1- [Aug., 1923—] [Norfolk, Va., 1923—

8°. monthly.   NYP: III, 6; IV, 6 (Jan., 1926 & '27).
Contains *Annual report* of the division.

1869. [310] VIRGINIA REAL estate journal. [Richmond, Va. [1880? -?]

1870. [311] VIRGINIA REAL estate journal. Richmond, Va. [19-?—

1871. [312] VIRGINIA REALTOR. Richmond, 1926—

1872. VIRGINIA UTILITY news. nos. 1- ; Mar. 17, 1928— Richmond, Va., 1928—

leaf. 42 x 20. 5 cm. monthly.   V: 1-12 (Mar., 1928-Feb., 1929).
Pub. by the Virginia Committee on public utility information.

1873. WHAT'S going on in Richmond, a weekly magazine of advance information. v. 1, no. 1-11; Apr. 10-June 24, 1922. Richmond, Va., 1922.

11 nos. illus. 8°. weekly. No more pub.   **V**

Directories

Alexandria, Va.

1874. ALEXANDRIA, Virginia, directory . . . Alexandria and Richmond, Va., Hill directory co. [187-? -19—

plans. 8°.

Title varies: Richmond's directory of Alexandria, Va., 1876-89, 99-1907; Barrett's directory of Alexandria, Va., 1908; Alexandria, Virginia, directory, 1910—

Preceded by Chataigne's directory of Alexandria and Fredericksburg. [1877]

LC: 1876/77, 81/82, 87/88-88/89, 99-1908, 10-21, 23-24, 26, 28; NYP: 1910, 21, 24.

1875. BOYD'S business directory and guide, to the cities of Washington, Georgetown and Alexandria . . . Washington, D. C., Boyd's directory co. [186-? -19—

illus. 8°.   BP: 1867, 79, 98, 1903, 07; LC: 1867, 72.

1876. BOYD'S directory of Washington, Georgetown, and Alexandria . . . Washington, D. C., 1870-71.

2 v. plans. 8°.   LC

1877. CHATAIGNE'S directory of Alexandria and Fredericksburg . . . together with a complete business directory of the counties of Alexandria, Fairfax, Fauquier, Loudoun, Prince William and Spotsylvania . . . [Alexandria, Va.] J. H. Chataigne [ca. 1876-8-?]

8°.   LC: 1876/77, 81/82, 87/88-88/89; NYP: 1881/82.

Title varies: Chataigne's Alexandria city directory, 1876-81; *ibid.,* 188—

Continued as Richmond's directory of Alexandria, Va.

1878. . . . DIRECTORY of rural residents . . . in the vicinity of Richmond, Manchester, Petersburg, and Alexandria . . . Norfolk [190—

4°.   LC: 1905.

Alexandria County.

1879. ALEXANDRIA County, Virginia directory . . . [Washington, D. C., Ideal print., 19—

8°.   LC: 1912.

W. G. Collins, ed.

Arlington County.

1880. ARLINGTON County in a "nutshell" . . . Clarendon, Va., The Nutshell co. [19—

24°.   **LC:** 1925.

A classified business directory.

1881. ARLINGTON County, Virginia . . . directory and year book, 1924— Rosslyn, Va., Colonial print. [*ca.* 1924—

8°.   **LC:** 1924.

Bristol, Va.-Tenn.

1882. BRISTOL, Va.-Tenn. directory [v. 1- ; 1901/02—] Richmond, Va. [etc.] Hill directory co., [1901—

8°. Title varies: Hill directory co.'s directory of Bristol, Tenn.-Va., 1901/02; Bristol, Va.-Tenn. directory, 1903/04—

   LC: 1901/02, 03/04, 05/06, 08/09, 13/14, 15/16, 17/18, 21, 25, 27; **NYP:** 1901/02-10/11.

1883. CUMBERLAND TELEPHONE & TELEGRAPH CO. Telephone directory . . . [of] Bristol, Va.-Tenn. [etc.] Bristol, 19—

8°.   **NYP:** June & Oct., 1916.

Charlottesville, Va.

1884. CHARLOTTESVILLE, Va. directory . . . Richmond, Va., Hill directory co., 1902—

8°.   **LC:** 1904/05; **NYP:** 1902/03-06/07; **VU:** 1904/05.

1885. DIRECTORY and list of Albemarle county farmers . . . containing a general and business directory of Charlottesville and other valuable information, including a guide to the streets of Charlottesville and a list of farmers of Albemarle County, Virginia . . . Richmond, Va., Hill directory co., 19—

8°.   **VU:** 1910/11, 14/15.

1886. OFFICIAL building code and builder's directory, Charlottesville, Va. 1924. Charlottesville, Michie, 1924.

96 p. 8°. Advertisements in front and in back.   **VU**

1887. TURNER'S annual directory for the city of Charlottesville, Va. . . . [v. 1-] 1888/89— Yonkers, N. Y., E. F. Turner [*ca.* 1888—

8°.   **LC:** 1888/89.

Clifton Forge, Va.

1888. DAVIES' city directory, Clifton Forge, Va. for 1914— [v. 1-] Clifton Forge, Va., A. B. Davies [*ca.* 1914—

8°.   **LC**: 1914.

Danville, Va.

1889. CHESAPEAKE & POTOMAC TELEPHONE CO. Telephone directory [of] Lynchburg, Bedford City, Danville and Chatham, Va. . . . [Lynchburg, Va., 19—

8°.   **NYP**: May, Oct., 1913-1916.

1890. OFFICIAL directory of the members of the Council and officers of the city of Danville, Va. . . . Danville [Boatwright] 1908.

[8] p. 16°.

1891. RICHMOND'S Danville directory. . . . Issued bi-annually. Washington, D. C., Richmond & co., 19—

8°.   **LC**: 1902/03-06/07, 17, 21, 27; **NYP**: 1902/03, 04/05-06/07.

Fairfax County.

1892. FAIRFAX County, Va., directory . . . William G. Collins, ed. . . . [Falls Church, Newell, *ca.* 1906—

illus. 8°.   **LC**: 1906.

Fredericksburg, Va.

1893. [1877] CHATAIGNE'S directory of Alexandria and Fredericksburg . . . [Alexandria, Va., *ca.* 1876-8-?]

1894. CHESAPEAKE & POTOMAC TELEPHONE CO. Telephone directory [of] Richmond, Ashland, Fredericksburg, Gordonsville, Louisa, Waverly and Williamsburg, Va. [Richmond, Chesapeake & Potomac telephone co., 19—

8°. June 1, 1914— include West Point.
NYP: May 15, Oct. 15, 1913; Jan. 15, June 1, 1914; Feb., June, 1915; June, Sept., 1916; June, Sept., 1917. **V**: May, 1913; June, Nov., 1914.

Hampton, Va.

See below, *Newport News, Va.*

Hanover County.

1895. BERNARD, R. S.   Directory of the counties of Hanover, Chesterfield, Amelia, Dinwiddie, Greensville, and Brunswick.   Comp.
. . . by R. S. Bernard, Madison Run, Orange County, Va.
1896.   Richmond, Ware & Duke, 1896.
    287 p. 8°.   **V**

1896. DANIEL, W. J.   Directory of Hanover County, Va., 1906.
Richmond, Va., Walthall [1906]
    unp. 8°.   **V**

Hopewell, Va.

1897. HOPEWELL and City Point, Virginia, directory, 1916— v. 1-
Richmond, Va., Hill directory co. [*ca.* 1916—
    8°.   **LC:** I-II (1916-17).

Lexington, Va.

1898. The CITY of Lexington, Virginia, 1923— v. 1- [Lexington, *ca.* 1922—
    8°.   **LC:** 1923.

Lynchburg, Va.

1899. [1889] CHESAPEAKE & POTOMAC TELEPHONE CO.   Telephone
directory [of] Lynchburg . . . [Lynchburg, Va., 19—

1900. LYNCHBURG, Virginia, directory . . . Lynchburg and Richmond [etc.] Hill directory co. [187-? -19—
    8°. Title varies: Walsh's Lynchburg, Virginia, city directory, Pub.
    by Walsh directory co., *ante* 1912.
        LC: 1897/98, 1907-24, 26-28; **NYP:** 1897/98-99/1900, 02, 04-08, 11;
    V: 1879/80, 1922-26.

1901. OFFICIAL building code and builder's directory, Lynchburg,
Va. Lynchburg, Cleland, Nov., 1922.
    112 p. fold. map. (front.) 8°.   **VU**
    Advertisements interspersed.

Manchester, Va.

1902. HADDOCK's directory of Manchester, Va., and suburbs, for
1893/94, to which is appended a business directory of Chesterfield
County.   T. M. Haddock & co.   [*ca.* 1893]

   206 p. 8°.   **V**

   For further references on Manchester, see below, *Richmond, Va.*

Newport News, Va.

1903. CHATAIGNE's Peninsula directory, 18—   Containing besides
a general and business directory of Newport News, Hampton,
Chesapeake City and Old Point, a list of post offices in Virginia
. . . [Richmond, Va.]   Chataigne directory co.   [189-? -19—

   8°.   **LC**: 1896/97-1914/15, 17-20, 23, 25, 27.

1904. CHESAPEAKE & POTOMAC TELEPHONE CO. OF VIRGINIA.   Telephone directory [of] Norfolk, Portsmouth, Newport News,
Hampton, . . . [Smithfield] Suffolk, [Va.] . . . Elizabeth City, N. C. [Norfolk, Va.? 19—

   8°.   **NYP**: Aug., 1913; Nov., 1914-1916.

1905. HILL's directory co.'s (incorporated) Newport News, Kecoughtan, Hampton, Phoebus and Old Point, Va., city directory
. . . Richmond, Va. [etc.] Hill directory co.   [18? -19—

   8°.   Title varies.

   LC: 1896/97-1914/15, 17-20, 23, 25, 27; **NYP**: 1900, 12.

Norfolk, Va.

1906. CHATAIGNE's directory of Norfolk, Va. . . . [Richmond,
Va.] Chataigne directory co.   [187-?-1896]

   fold. plans. 8°.

   Title varies: Norfolk and Portsmouth directory . . . comp. by
Chataigne & Boyd, 1872/73; *ibid.,* comp. by Sheriff & Chataigne, 1874/75;
Sheriff & co.'s Norfolk and Portsmouth directory . . . comp. by B.
R. Sheriff, 1875/76; Chataigne's directory of Norfolk and Portsmouth,
1883-88; Chataigne's directory of Norfolk, Portsmouth and Berkley, 1889-
189—

   BP: 1877/78, 86, 1908; **LC**: 1872/73-75/76, 80/81, 82/83, 83/84, 85-86,
88-92/93, 94, 95/96-96/97; **V**: 1883/84, 89; **WM**: 1889, 91/92.

1907. [1904] CHESAPEAKE & POTOMAC TELEPHONE CO. OF VIR-
GINIA. Telephone directory [of] Norfolk, Portsmouth . . .
[etc.]   [Norfolk, Va.? 19—

1908. HILL directory co's incorporated Norfolk and Portsmouth (Virginia) city dircetory . . . 1897-19— Norfolk, Va., Hill directory co. [*ca.* 1897-19—

fold. maps. 8°.

Title varies: J. L. Hill printing co.'s directory of Norfolk, Portsmouth and Berkley, Va., 1897-1901; Hill directory co.'s directory of Norfolk, Portsmouth and Berkley, 1902; etc.

BP: 1908; **LC**: 1897-1901, 03-20/21, 22-24, 27-28; **NYP**: 1898, 1900, 02-11, 13-16, 18, 20/21-27; **V**: 1902, 03/04, 12-13, 23-24; **VU**: 1902, 03.

1909. JEWISH social directory . . . a compendium of names and addresses of members of the Jewish communities of Baltimore, Washington, Norfolk and Richmond, and a list of officers of the prominent Jewish institutions . . . Baltimore, Md., Greater Baltimore pub. co. [190—

illus. 8°.   **LC**: 1908, 09, 11.

1910. NORFOLK city and business directory, for 1866. To which is added a business directory of Portsmouth . . . Baltimore, Webb & Fitzgerald, 1866.

128, 72 p. 8°.   **LC, NYP**

1911. NORFOLK city directory for [1870—] Norfolk, Va., J. F. Milligan & A. J. Dalton [1870—

8°.   **LC**: 1870, 72.

1912. The NORFOLK VIRGINIAN annual for the year 1884 . . . Norfolk, Va., M. Glennan [1883]

8 p. 1., 18 1. front., illus. 8°.   **LC**

Contains statistics of Norfolk for 1883 and almanac for 1884. Advertisements interspersed.

1913. The RICHMOND and Norfolk society blue book including Petersburg and other suburban towns. New York City, Dau pub., 19—

8°.   **LC**: 1909, 12, 15; **NYP**: 1906; **VU**: 1906.

1914. YOUNG & co.'s business and professional directory of Richmond, Norfolk, Petersburg, and surrounding towns. Richmond, Va., Williams [189-? -19—

8°.   **V**: 1899, 1900.

Orange County.

1915. WOOLFOLK, C. W. Directory of the counties of Orange, Louisa, Albemarle, Culpeper, and Spotsylvania. Comp. and for sale by C. W. Woolfolk, Orange, Va. W. J. Daniel, Bibb's, Va. 1895. [Richmond, Va., Ware & Duke, 1895]

    1, 267 p. 8°.   V

1916. ———. Orange County directory . . . 1894. Lynchburg, Va., Bell, 1894.

    60 p. 8°.   V

Petersburg, Va.

1917. CHATAIGNE's Petersburg directory . . . [Petersburg? Va., 18-? -19—

    8°. Comp. by J. H. Chataigne, to 1903; by Hill directory co., 1903/04—
    LC: 1879/80; **NYP**: 1899/1900, 01/02, 03/04, 05/06, 07/08, 09/10, 11/12, 15/16, 21; **V**: 1870/71, 72/73, 76/77, 79/80, 86/87, 88/89, 91/92, 93/94, 95/96, 99/1900, 03/04, 05/06, 07/08, 24.

1918. DIRECTORY and gazetteer of city of Petersburg, 1877-78, including a history of the city . . . ed. and pub. by Campbell & co., Petersburg, Va. Richmond, Cary, 1877.

    4 p. l., 174 p. 8°.   V
    Contains a sketch of the history of Petersburg, by Edward S. Gregory, p. [1]-67.

1919. [1878] . . . DIRECTORY of rural residents . . . in the vicinity of . . . Petersburg . . . Norfolk [190—

1920. PETERSBURG city directory. Petersburg, Va., Webb & Fitzgerald 186—

    8°.   **NYP**: 1866.

1921. SHERIFF & co. Petersburg directory: containing the names of the citizens, a complete business directory, and a list of all the streets, lanes, alleys, &c. Also the state and city governments, with a complete list of all the post offices in Virginia, West Virginia, and North Carolina. Comp. by Benj. R. Sheriff. Petersburg, Va., 187—

    8°.   **V**: 1870/71, 76/77.

1922. [1914] YOUNG & CO.'s business and professional directory of . . . Petersburg, and surrounding towns. Richmond, Va. [189-? -19—

Portsmouth, Va.
See above, *Norfolk, Va.*

Richmond, Va.

1923. [1894] CHESAPEAKE & POTOMAC TELEPHONE CO. Telephone directory [of] Richmond, Ashland [etc.] [Richmond, 19—

1924. [1878] . . . DIRECTORY of rural residents . . . in the vicinity of Richmond, Manchester . . . [etc.] Norfolk [190—

1925. DUDLEY, DEAN & CO. Richmond directory, containing a general directory of the citizens, a business directory, city record, court record, &c. . . . 1870. Richmond, Va., West & Johnston, 1870.

> xv, [1], 214 p. front. (fold. map) 8°.   **LC. NYP, V**
> Advertisements interspersed.
> Pub. this year only, as a rival of the Boyd directory, which began in 1868.

1926. [1909] JEWISH social directory . . . of Jewish communities of . . . Richmond . . . Baltimore [190—

1927. [1913] RICHMOND and Norfolk society blue book . . . New York City, 19—

1928. RICHMOND, Virginia, directory . . . Richmond, Va., Hill directory co. [1819-19—

> 12°.-8°. Title varies: The city of Richmond business directory and city guide, 1866; Boyd's directory of Richmond city, 1869/70; Sheriff & Chataigne's Richmond city directory, 1874/75; Sheriff & co.'s Richmond city directory, 1876/77; Chataigne & Gillis Richmond city directory, 1877/78; Chataigne's Richmond city directory, 1879/80; J. L. Hill printing co.'s directory of Richmond, 1897; J. L. Hill printing co's directory of Richmond and Manchester, Va., 1899-1904; Greater Richmond directory, 1905-10; Richmond, Virginia, directory, 1911—
> 1883/84 no. contains a reprint of the first directory pub. of Richmond, 1819.
> **BP**: 1882/83, 1909; **LC**: 1866, 69-1928; **NYP**: 1866, 69, 98, 1900-07, 09-27; **V**: 1866, 69/70-76/77, 79/80-95/96, 98, 1902-14; **VU**: 1877/78; **WM**: 1921.

1929. RICHMOND SOCIETY blue book. Elite family directory. Club membership. 1904. New York, Dau [*ca.* 1904]

84 p. 8°.   **V**

1930. RICHMOND TIMES almanac, weather forecasts, and book of facts for the office, home, and farm . . . Richmond, Va., Times [189-? -19—

8°. quarterly.   **LC:** 1898, 1901; **V:** 1898-1901.

1931. RICHMOND TIMES-DISPATCH. Classified business and professional directory and blue book. Richmond, 19—

8°.   **V:** 1917.

1932. SEVENTH ST. CHRISTIAN CHURCH, Richmond, Va. WOMAN'S COUNCIL. WELFARE DEPT. Directory of social agencies of Richmond, Va. 1917—   [Richmond, Va., 1917—

16°.   **V:** 1917, 24.

1933. SOUTHERN BELL TELEPHONE & TELEGRAPH CO. Official directory Richmond telephone exchange . . . Petersburg telephone exchange . . . Richmond, Southern Bell telephone & telegraph co. [189-? -19—

8°.   **LC:** 1898.

1934. VIRGINIA FEDERATION OF BUSINESS AND PROFESSIONAL WOMEN'S CLUBS. Directory of business and professional women in Richmond, Va. [Richmond? 19—

12°.   **V:** 1921.

1935. [1914] YOUNG & CO.'s business and professional directory of Richmond . . . and surrounding towns. Richmond, Va. [189-? -19—

Roanoke, Va.

1936. DIRECTORY of the city of Roanoke . . . Roanoke, Va., Stone [189—

8°.   **LC:** 1898/99.
J. W. Beard, comp.

1937. JEWISH blue book of Roanoke, Virginia. Roanoke, 1924.

60 p. illus. 8°. Advertisements interspersed.   **LC**
Contains some information on Jewish society.

1938. ROANOKE, Virginia, directory, 1913—   v. 1-   [Richmond] Hill directory co. [*ca.* 1913—

    8°. **LC:** 1913-21/22, 22-24, 26-28; **NYP:** 1916, 19/20, 23-24, 26; **V:** 1922-27.

1939. WALSH's Roanoke, Virginia, city directory . . . Charleston, S. C., Walsh directory co., 19—

    8°.   **LC:** 1904; **NYP:** 1902, 10, 12.

Salem, Va.

1940. . . . DIRECTORY of the town of Salem, Virginia . . . Salem, Va., M. J. Anderson, 19—

    8°.   **LC:** 1925.

Staunton, Va.

1941. STAUNTON, Va. . . . city directory. Richmond, Va., Hill directory co. [1903?—

    8°. **LC:** 1904/05-06/07, 10/11, 12/13, 14/15, 19/20, 22/23, 24, 27; **NYP:** 1904/05 ; **V:** 1922/23.

1942. TURNER's annual Staunton directory for 18— . . . New York, Pub. by the Turner directory co. [188-? - ?]

    8°.   **McC:** 1888/89, 90/91.

Suffolk, Va.

1943. SUFFOLK, Virginia, city directory . . . Asheville, N. C., Piedmont directory co., inc. [1911?—

    8°.   **LC:** II, IV, VII (1912/13, 20/21, 27/28).
    E. H. Miller, comp.

Tazewell, Va.

1944. POLK, R. L., & CO. R. L. Polk & co.'s Blucfield directory, including Graham, Pocahontas, Princeton and Tazewell, 1910/11— . . . v. 1- Pittsburgh, Pa., R. L. Polk & co. [*ca.* 1910—

    8°. **LC:** 1910/11, 12/13, 15/16, 17/18, 19/20, 21/22, 23/24, 25/26, 27/28; **NYP:** 1910/11.

Washington, D. C.—Virginia suburbs.

1945. NELSON's suburban directory of Maryland and Virginia towns adjacent to the District of Columbia, 1912/13— [v. 1-] Washington, D. C., J. C. Nelson [*ca.* 1912—

    8°.   **LC**: I-VI, XII (1912/13-17/18, 23); **NYP**: 1912/13, 17/18.

1946. POLK's Washington suburban directory of Maryland and Virginia towns adjacent to the District of Columbia . . . 1927/28— Washington, D. C., New York [etc.]   R. L. Polk & co. [*ca.* 1927—

    8°.   **LC, V**: 1927/28.

For further references on Washington, D. C., see above, *Alexandria, Va.*

Williamsburg, Va.

1947. [1894] CHESAPEAKE & POTOMAC TELEPHONE CO. Telephone directory [of] . . . Williamsburg, Va. [Richmond, 19—

Winchester, Va.

1948. RANDALL's business directory of Hagerstown, Md., Winchester, Va., Martinsburg, W. Va. . . . [etc.] Hagerstown, Md., J. C. Randall, 18—

    8°.   **LC**: 1898/99.

1949. WINCHESTER, Virginia, city directory [v. 1- ; 1918/19—] Asheville, N. C., Piedmont directory co. [1918—

    8°.   **LC**: IV-V (1921/22, 27).
    E. H. Miller, comp.

For further references on Urban and County Development, see Pt. IV, § 3: *Local Government;* also Pt. VI, § 3: *Elementary and Secondary Schools.* See also Pt. VIII: *Local History.*

8. PUBLIC WELFARE AND REGULATION

Government Publications and Documents

1950. CLARK, TALIAFERRO. . . . Trachoma: a survey of its prevalence in the mountain sections of Virginia and West Vir-

ginia, by Taliaferro Clark, surgeon, U. S. Public health service
. . . Washington, Govt., 1914.

31 p. incl. map. 8°. (U. S. Public health service. Public health reports. *Reprint,* 198, from XXIX, 23; June 5, 1914)

LC, USH, USHy, V

1951. CUMMING, HUGH S. Investigation of the pollution and sanitary conditions of the Potomac watershed, with special reference
to self-purification and the sanitary condition of shellfish in the lower
Potomac River . . . Plankton studies by W. C. Purdy and
hydrographic studies by Homer P. Ritter. Washington, Govt.,
1916.

231 p. plates. 8°. (U. S. Public health service. Hygienic laboratory.
Bulletin, 104)   USH, USHy

1952. ———. Investigation of the pollution of tidal waters of
Maryland and Virginia, with special reference to shellfish-bearing
areas. Washington, Govt., 1916.

199 p. 8°. (U. S. Public health service. *Bulletin,* 74)   USH, USHy

1953. DRAINAGE ditches covered economically. Concrete pipe manu-
factured and laid cheaply in Emporia, Va. Mar. 13, 1925. Washington, Govt., 1925.

8 p. 8°. (U. S. Public health service. Public health reports. *Reprint*)

USH, USHy

1954. GRUBBS, SAMUEL B. . . . Extra-cantonment zone sanitation, Newport News, Va., and vicinity, by S. B. Grubbs, surgeon,
U. S. Public health service . . . Washington, Govt., 1918.

13 p. 8°. (U. S. Public health service. Public health reports. *Reprint,*
457, from XXXIII, 10; Mar. 8, 1918; p. 308-318)   LC, USH, USHy, V

1955. NEGRO REFORMATORY ASSOCIATION OF VIRGINIA. . . . Annual report to the Board of trustees . . . [n. p., 189-? -19—
8°.   V: 1897/98, 1908/09, 15/16.

1956. ———. . . . Biennial report to the General assembly of
Virginia . . . 1st- ; 1900/01— [Hanover, Va., 1901—
8°. Report year ends May 20.
NYP: 1900/01, 03/05, 07/09-10/12, 14/15-16/17; V: 1914/15.

1957. ———. Report of the acting superintendent and executive
committee for the year ending May 20, 1909. Richmond [1909]
13 p. plates. 8°.   NYP, V

1958. PRISON ASSOCIATION OF VIRGINIA. Address . . . to citizens and officials of the state. Richmond, Ezekiel, 1904.

[11] p. 8°.   **V**

Work of the association in reforming minors. Contains text of Act of Mar. 8, 1904, regarding commitment of minors to the association.

1959. ———. Biennial report . . . Richmond, Va. [189-? -19—

8°. **LC**: 1898/99; **V**: 1890/91-96/97, 99/1900, 01/02, 04/05, 06/07, 08/09, 10/11, 12/13.

Report for 1898/99 contains statistics of the Laurel industrial school.

1960. ———. Charter, constitution, by-laws, and organization . . . Richmond, Va., Ezekiel [1890-19—

8°.   **V**: 1890, 1902.

1961. ———. Report of the president of the Prison association of Virginia, as delegate to the National conference of charities and corrections at Detroit, May 28 to June 3, 1902. [Richmond, Ezekiel, 1902]

14 p. 8°.   **V**

Recommendations for improvements in Virginia's system of prison life and occupation.

1962. [101] VIRGINIA. Annual reports of officers, boards, and institutions of . . . Virginia . . . Richmond, Va. [1866-19—

Include reports of the State board of charities and corrections and Dept. of public welfare, 1908/09— ; State epileptic colony, 1909/10— ; Dept. of health, 1909— ; Commissioner of State hospitals for the insane, 1903/04— ; Eastern and Western state hospitals 1865/66— ; Central state hospital, 1870— ; Southwestern state hospital, 1886/87— ; Institution for the deaf, dumb, and blind, 1866— ; Virginia home and industrial school for girls, 1914/15—

1963. ———. BLIND, Commission for the. Report . . . [Staunton, etc., 1923—

tables. 8°. Report year ends Sept. 30.

Annual, 1922/23; biennial, 1923/25—

LC: 1st-2d (1922/23-23/25); **V**: 1922/23-23/25.

1964. ———. ———. Virginia commission for the blind; we help the blind to help themselves. Headquarters office, 608 National bank building, Charlottesville, Va. . . . [Charlottesville? 1922?]

7, [1] p. 16°.   **V**

Signed (on last page): L. L. Watts.

1965. ———. BLIND, Legislative commission for the. Report . . . 1920-21. [n. p., *1922?*]

12 p. 8°.   **V**

Succeeded by the permanent Commission for the blind, 1922.

1966. ———. CENTRAL STATE HOSPITAL, Petersburg. Annual report . . . 1st- ; 1870— Richmond and Petersburg [1871-19—

8°. Report year ends Sept. 30.

Original name: Central lunatic asylum for colored insane, located at Richmond; moved to Petersburg, 1885.

BP: 1870/71, 72/73-73/74; **LC**: 1873/74-74/75, 76/77, 78/79-81/82, 1900/01-03/04, 05/06-18/19, 21/22-25/26; **NYP**: 1870/71-71/72, 81/82-84/85, 87/88-96/97, 98/99-99/1900, 06/07-16/17, 18/19; **USC**: 1879/80-1909/10, 14/15-17/18; **V**: 1899/1900, 02/03-09/10, 11/12-26/27; **VU**: 1914/15-26/27.

See also: Virginia. *Annual reports of . . . institutions . . .* **[1962]**

1967. ———. CHARITIES AND CORRECTIONS, State board of. Annual report . . . 1908/09-20/21. Richmond, Bottom, 1909-21.

8°. Report year ends Sept. 30.

Succeeded by State board of public welfare. *Biennial report* **[2023]**

BP: 1913/14-18/19; **H**: 1909/10-18/19; **HL**: 1909/10, 11/12, 14/15-18/19, 20/21; **LC**: 1908/09-20/21; **NYP**: 1908/09-20/21; **USC**: 1908/09-10/11, 12/13-18/19; **USHy**: 1912/13, 16/17-17/18; **V**: 1908/09-20/21; **VU**: 1908/09-19/20.

See also: Virginia. *Annual reports of officers, boards . . .* **[1962]**

1968. ———. ———. The jail; a pressing social problem . . . Richmond, Bottom, 1913.

8 p. 8°. Reprint from *Annual report* of State board of charities and corrections, 1913.   **USL, V**

1969. ———. ———. Mental defectives in Virginia: a special report of the State board of charities and corrections to the General assembly of 1916 on weak-mindedness in the state of Virginia, together with a plan for the training, segregation and prevention of the procreation of the feeble-minded. Richmond, Bottom, 1915.

123 p. front., illus., plates, tables, diagrs. 8°.

1970. ———. ———. Probation manual with analysis of the probation laws of Virginia. Richmond, Bottom, 1918.

19 p. incl. forms. 8°.   **HL, NYP, USL, V, VU**

1971. VIRGINIA. CHARITIES AND CORRECTIONS, State board of. The problem of the feeble-minded. Richmond, Bottom, 1913.

19 p. 8°.   V

Reprint from *Annual report* of State board of charities and corrections, 1913.

1972. ———. ———. Why Virginia needs prison farms for misdemeanants . . . [n. p., 1916?]

8 p. 8°. Reprint from *Annual report* of State board of charities and corrections, 1916.   NYP, V, VU

Advantages of a prison farm to the prisoners and to the state.

1973. ———. ———. The work of the State board of charities and corrections. General statement from the Annual report for the year ending Sept. 30, 1914, filed with the governor by J. T. Mastin, secretary. Richmond, 1915.

15 p. 8°.   USL

1974. ———. CHILDREN'S CODE COMMISSION. Digest of bills, submitted to the General assembly of Virginia . . . [n. p., 1921]

25 p. 8°.   V

1975. ———. CONFERENCE OF BOARDS OF VISITORS OF VIRGINIA STATE INSTITUTIONS, Richmond. First conference . . . called by Hon. Westmoreland Davis, governor of Virginia, Thursday, Jan. 23, 1919. Hall of House of delegates. [Richmond? 1919]

[3] p. 16°.   V

1976. ———. CONSTITUTIONAL CONVENTION, 1901-02. Extracts of the Journal and documents from the Constitutional convention of Virginia 1901-02 touching the question of intoxicating liquors. Printed in pursuance of . . . resolution agreed to by the Senate, Feb. 21, 1912. [Richmond, 1912?]

109 p. 8°.   V

1977. [660] ———. CORPORATION COMMISSION, State. Schedule of routes and distances from courthouses in the state of Virginia to the penitentiary, reformatories, and state hospitals . . . Richmond, 1911.

1978. ———. DEAF AND BLIND, SCHOOL for the, Staunton. . . .
Report . . . Richmond and Charlottesville [1867-19—

plates. 8°. Report year ends Sept. 30.

Title varies: Report of the Board of visitors of the Institution for the
deaf and dumb and the blind . . ., 1867- [?]

Annual 1867-1902 (?); biennial, 1903/05 (?)—

H: 1866/67, 71/72-73/74, 1912/13; **LC**: 1866/67, 70/71-71/72, 73/74,
1911/12-16/17; **NYP**: 1866/67-68/69, 70/71-80/81, 82/83, 85/86, 96/97-
1912/13, 15/16-16/17; **USC**: 1914/15, 16/17; **USL**: 1915/17; **V**:
1880/81-81/82, 1901/02-14/15.

See also: Virginia. *Annual reports of . . . institutions . . .*
[1962]

1979. ———. ———. Superintendent's outline of rules for teachers
and officers of the Virginia school for the deaf and the blind.
1910. [Richmond? 1910?]

26, [6] p. 16°. **V**

1980. ———. ———. Superintendent's rules for the employees of
the Virginia school for the deaf and the blind. [Richmond?
1910?]

16, [1] p. 16°. **V**

1981. ———. DEAF AND BLIND CHILDREN (COLORED), State school
for, Newport News. . . . Annual report of the superintendent of the . . . school [under white management] . . .
Hampton, Va., Houston, 1909—

illus. 8°. Report year ends Sept. 30. **V**: 1st (1908/09).

1982. ———. ———. By-laws . . . adopted by the Board of
visitors, Mar. 28, 1908. [n. p., 1908]

16 p. 16°. **H**

1983. ———. DENTAL EXAMINERS, State board of. Official list of
registered dentists in the state of Virginia. Fredericksburg, Va.
[190-?—

8°. **LC, V**: May 1, 1910.

1910 includes also the law regulating the practice of dentistry, approved Mar. 12, 1906.

1984. ———. EASTERN STATE HOSPITAL, Williamsburg. Annual report . . . Richmond [1866-19—

8°. Report year ends Sept. 30.

Original name: Eastern lunatic asylum.

H: 1870/71, 72/73, 80/81; **LC**: 1868/69, 72/73-73/74, 97/98-1910/11,

13/14-25/26; **NYP**: 1872/73, 78/79; **USC**: 1890/91-1902/03, 04/05-09/10, 11/12-18/19, 20/21; **V**: 1868/69, 72/73, 1901/02, 03/04-04/05, 06/07, 09/10, 11/12-12/13, 14/15-22/23, 24/25-27/28; **VU**: 1901/02-02/03, 04/05-08/09, 10/11, 12/13, 14/15, 16/17, 18/19-22/23, 25/26, 27/28; **WM**: 1872/73, 1925/26.

See also: Virginia. *Annual reports of . . . institutions . . .*
[1962]

1985. VIRGINIA. EPILEPTICS AND FEEBLE-MINDED, State colony for, Madison Heights. Biennial report . . . Richmond, 1921—

8°. Report year ends Sept. 30.

Continuation of *Annual report* of State epileptic colony, 1st-10th, 1909/10-18/19, and Colony for feeble-minded, 1st-6th, 1913/14-18/19; the latter first opened to pupils in 1914.

Annual, 1909/10-18/19; biennial, 1919/21—

LC: 1911/12-23/25; **NYP**: 1926/27; **USC**: 1914/15; **USL**: 1912/13-18/19; **V**: 1911/12-13/14, 17/18, 23/25-27/28; **VU**: 1910/11-12/13, 14/15-15/16, 19/21-25/26, 27/28.

See also: Virginia. *Annual reports of . . . institutions . . .*
[1962]

1986. ———. HEALTH, Dept. of. Annual report . . . Richmond, 1872-19—

tables (part fold.) 8°. Report year ends June 30.

Title varies: State board of health. Biennial, 1923/25-

BP: 1872/73; **H**: 1909/10-10/11, 12/13-13/14; **LC**: 1872/73-73/74, 1908/09, 10/11-20/21, 22/23, 24/25-26/27; **NYP**: 1871/72, 1907/08-14/15, 16/17-26/27; **USAg**: 1908/09-12/13, 14/15-17/18, 20/21-22/23; **USH**: 1904/05, 08/09-20/21, 22/23, 25/26-27/28; **USHy**: 1904/05, 09/10-26/27; **USL**: 1911/12-16/17, 23/25-26/27; **V**: 1905/06, 08/09-14/15, 16/17-17/18, 20/21-26/27; **VU**: 1908/09, 20/21.

See also: Virginia. *Annual report of officers, boards . . .* **[1962]**

1987. ———. ———. Annual report . . . for the year ending Sept. 30, 1915. Advance report . . . Richmond, 1916.

[5]-58 p. 8°.   **LC**

1988. ———. ———. Foes of health and their conquest. Richmond, 1916.

var. pag. 8°. (Selected bulletins, 1912-15)   **V, VU, WM**

1989. ———. ———. New talks on the prevention of disease. Selected numbers of the Virginia health bulletin . . . [Richmond, 1912?]

2 p. l., [424] p. incl. illus., diagrs. 8°. **V, VU**

21 nos. of the *Virginia health bulletin*, 1908-12, to which are prefixed a general title-page and table of contents.

1990. ———. ———. Popular talks on preventable diseases. [Richmond, Va., 1908-09]

var. pag. 8°. (Selected numbers of the *Virginia health bulletin*, I, 1908-09) **V, VU**

1991. ———. ———. . . . . Sanitary survey of the schools of Orange County, Va. Report of an investigation by the Virginia State board of health, the Dept. of education of the University of Virginia, and the Virginia State dept. of education, by Roy K. Flannagan, M.D., director of inspections, Virginia State board of health. Washington, Govt., 1914.

28 p. plates, map. 8°. (U. S. Bur. of education. *Bulletin,* (1914), 17, whole no. 590)

1992. ———. ———. . . . Sewage disposal for suburban and country homes . . . Washington, Govt., 1926.

1 p. l., 41 p. incl. illus., tables. 8°. (U. S. Public health service. Public health reports. *Supplement,* 58) **LC, NYP, USH, USHy, USL**
Reprint from *Virginia health bulletin,* XVII, 6, June, 1925.

1993. ———. ———. Virginia health bulletin. Vol. 1-12; 1896-1908. New ser., vol. 1- ; 1908/09— Richmond, 1896-1908; 1908-19—

illus., plates. 8°. monthly.

BP: new ser., VII (1915). **H:** new ser., I, 1-3; III, 5, 7-8, 10-11; IV, 1, 2, 6, 9-11, & ext. 1-2; V, 2-6, 9-12, & ext. 2-3, 5-6; VI, 1-12, & ext. 1, 3, 5-7; VII, 1-2, & ext. 1, 3; XI, 6; (1908-19); XVII, ext. 12 (Nov., 1925). **HL:** X, 3, & suppl. (1918). **LC:** new ser., II-IV, VI-VIII, X-XIX (imperf.); (1910-12, 14-16, 18-27); reprints, 1908-16, 20-28. **NYP:** new ser., II, IV, VII, VIII, 1-9, 11-12; X, 1-10, 12; XI, 1-8; XII, XIII, 1-9, 11-12; XIV-XIX; (1910-27). **USAg:** new ser., I, 1-2, 4-18; II, III, 1-4, 6, 10-11; IV, 5-6, 8, 10; V, VI, 1-7, 9-10; VII-IX; (1908-17). **USH:** new ser., II, IV-VII, VIII (incompl.), IX-XX, 6. **USHy:** new ser., I, 1-4, 6, 8, 12-14; II, III, 1-6, 10-11; IV, 1-8, 10-12; V, 1-3, 10-12; VI, 1-7, 9-11; VII, 1-2, 4-6, 8-10, 12; VIII, IX, 1, 3-4, 6-12; X, 1-2, 5, 8, 10-12; XI, 3; XII-XVIII; (1908-27). **USL:** new ser., I, 3, 6, 9; II, 12; III, 1-2, 5, 8-12; IV, 1-2, 5, 7-12; V-XI; XII-XVI (lacking some ext. nos.). **V:** I, 1-2, 4, 10-11; II, 1, 3, 7; III, 4, 5, 12; IV, 5, 7-11; V, 1, 3, 6-12; VI, 1-7, 9-10, 12; VII, 1-2, 4-6; VIII, 1-4, 6-19; IX, 1-9; X, 1-10;

XI, 1-9; XII, 1-3; (1896-1908). New ser.: I, 1, 3-18; II-III; IV, 1-3,
5-12; V-VI; VII, 1-2, 4-5, 7-12; VIII, 1-9, 11-12, & ext. 2; IX, 1-4, 8-11;
X-XVI; XVII, 2-4, 12; XVIII-XXI; (1908-29). **VU**: new ser., I-IV,
VI-XX (1908-12, 14-28). **WM**: new. ser., I-II, X, XII-XVIII (1908-
10, 18, 20-26).

1994. VIRGINIA. HEALTH, Dept. of. CHILD WELFARE, Bur. of.
Help for midwives. Bur. of child welfare, State board of health,
co-operating with Children's bureau, Dept. of labor, U. S. A. Richmond, Va., 1924.

50 p. 16°.   **USHy, USL, V, VU**

1995. ———. ———. VITAL STATISTICS, Bur. of. [New family series, nos. 1-5] [Richmond, 1921-25].

5 nos. 16°. Nos. 1-3 and 5 issued by the Bur. of child welfare, co-
operating with the U. S. Children's bureau.

1. The new family (1921). 2. Feeding the new family (1922).
3. Bread for the new family (1924 ?). 4. Eugenics in relation to the new
family, and law on racial integrity (1924). 5. The new family and
race improvement (1925).

LC: 1-4; **NYP**: 1-4; **USHy**: 1-2; **USL**: 1-5; **V**: 1-5; **VU**: 1-2, 4.

1996. ———. HOME AND INDUSTRIAL SCHOOL FOR GIRLS, Chesterfield County. Annual report . . . 1st- ; 1914/15— Richmond, 1915—

plates. 8°. Report year ends Sept. 30.

HL: 1918/19, 22/23; **USC**: 1914/15, 18/19; **USL**: 1914/15-18/19,
22/23-23/25; **V**: 1914/15-18/19, 22/23-23/25, 26/27.

1997. ———. INDUSTRIAL SCHOOL FOR COLORED GIRLS, Peake. . . .
Annual report . . . [1st- ; 1915/16?—] [Peake? Va.,
1916?—

illus. 8°. Report year ends Mar. 1.

H: 5th (1919/20); **HL**: 1915/16, 17/18-19/20; **USE**: 1925/26; **USL**:
1917/18-24/25; **V**: 1915/16-26/27; **WM**: 1920/21.

1998. ———. INSANE, State hospitals for the. Report of the commissioner of State hospitals for the insane . . . [1st- ;
1903/04?—] Richmond [1904?—

8°. Report year ends Sept. 30.

LC: 9th-15th (1911/12-17/18).

1999. ———. ———. Rules and regulations for the State hospitals
for the insane . . . Richmond, Whittet & Shepperson, 1905.

20 p. 12°.   **LC**

2000. ———. LABOR AND INDUSTRIAL STATISTICS, Bur. of. Prison leaflets, no. 1-   [Richmond, Penitentiary print. [1921?—

8°.   V: 1.

No. 1. Address by Hugh Frayne on the state use system.

2001. ———. LAWS, STATUTES, etc. Act creating and by-laws governing the State board of charities and corrections, Virginia. Richmond, Bottom, 1908.

14 p. 8°.   V

2002. ———. ———. By-laws of Western lunatic asylum, Virginia Regulations. Code of Virginia, chap. 85. Of lunatic asylums and the care of insane persons and their estates. [Richmond? 1870]

36 p. 8°.   V

2003. ———. ———. A compilation of laws relating to the Virginia penitentiary, Dec. 30, 1904. Richmond, Williams, 1905.

64 p. 8°.   V-

2004. ———. ———. The laws and by-laws governing the registration and examination of nurses and licensed attendants in Virginia . . . [Richmond? 192—

8°.   V: 1922, 27.

2005. ———. ———. Laws concerning jails . . . [Issued by the Virginia State board of charities and corrections] Richmond, 19—

8°.   HL: 1919.

2006. ———. ———. Laws of Virginia relating to the insane, feeble-minded and inebriate. Comp. by C. H. Morrissett, director Legislative reference bureau. Sept., 1920. Richmond, Bottom, 1920.

40 p. 8°.   V

2007. ———. ———. . . . . Layman prohibition law, in effect June 16, 1924 . . . Richmond, Bottom, 1924.

90 p. 8°.   V

2008. ———. ———. . . . . Layman prohibition law (as amended) in effect June 17, 1928. Richmond, Div. of purchase and printing, 1928.

107 p. incl. forms. 8°.   LC, V

2009. VIRGINIA. LAWS, STATUTES, etc. Liquor laws of Virginia, including also federal laws relating to interstate shipments. Annotated by Morton L. Wallerstein. Issued from the office of the attorney general of Virginia, as of Dec. 31, 1915. Richmond, Bottom, 1916.

 80 p. 8°.   **HL, LC, V, VU**

2010. ——. ——. The poor laws of Virginia . . . Richmond, Bottom, 1909.

 14, [1] p. 16°.   **V**
 Issued by the State board of charities and corrections.

2011. ——. ——. The public welfare and juvenile laws of Virginia, with rules, regulations, and policies of administration. Issued by the State board of public welfare . . . Richmond, Bottom, 192—

 8°. Title varies.
 Prepared by Arthur W. James, special agent, in 1926.
 H: 1926; **HL:** 1922; **LC:** 1922, 26; **NYP:** 1922, 26; **USL:** 1922, 26;
 V: 1922, 23, 26; **VU:** 1922, 26; **WM:** 1926.

2012. ——. ——. Summary and analysis of the juvenile laws in Virginia, by Hon. James Hoge Ricks, judge of the Juvenile and domestic relations court of Richmond, Va. Rev. and issued by the State board of charities and corrections. Richmond, Penitentiary print., 1921.

 51 p. 8°.   **LC, NYP, VU**
 Ed. of 1915.   **USL, V**
 Ed. of 1918.   **HL**

2013. ——. ——. Virginia laws for the suppression of vice. Comp. by the Virginia Committee on training-camp activities, Richmond . . . 1917. Richmond, Bottom, 1917.

 14 p. 1 l. 8°.   **H, HL, NYP, USHy, VU**

2014. ——. LEE CAMP SOLDIERS' HOME, Richmond. Report of the Board of visitors. . . . 1895— Richmond, 1896—

 tables. 8°. Report year ends Dec. 31.
 USC: 1903; **V:** 1895-1926.

2015. ——. LEGISLATIVE REFERENCE BUREAU. Extracts from liquor laws of prohibition states. Comp. under the direction of Lewis

Machen, director of the Legislative reference bureau of Virginia. Richmond, Bottom, 1916.

264 p. 8°.   LC, V

A compilation "helpful to the members of the Legislature of Virginia in framing their own prohibition measure."

2016. ———. MOTION PICTURE CENSORSHIP, Div. of. Report . . . 1922/24— [Richmond, 1924?—

8°.   V: 1922/24-26/27; VU: 1922/24.

Called State board of censors, to 1927.

2017. ———. PENITENTIARY. Annual report of the Board of directors . . . Richmond [1866-19—

8°. Report year ends Sept. 30.

HL: 1910/11-25/26; NYP: 1874/75, 76/77, 78/79, 80/81, 82/83, 87/88, 89/90-91/92, 93/94-98/99, 1900/01-04/05, 06/07-09/10, 11/12-20/21; USC: 1873/74-74/75, 77/78, 79/80-1914/15, 16/17-18/19; V: 1874/75-82/83, 1902/03-05/06, 08/09, 10/11-25/26.

2018. ———. ———. Communication from the Board of directors relative to the late fire at the penitentiary. Richmond, Va., 1878.

6 p. 8°.   VU

2019. ———. POOR, Overseers of the. Reports . . . 1820-1900.

MSS.; 50 bundles (200 per bundle)   V: Access. no. 13199.

2020. ———. PROHIBITION, Commissioner of. Annual report . . . 1st- ; 1916/17— Richmond, 1918—

tables (part fold.) 8°.

Signed by the attorney general, Div. of prohibition enforcement.

LC: 1st-8th (1916/17-25/26); NYP: 1916/17-21/23, 25/27; V: 1916/17-27/28.

2021. ———. ———. Statement of J. Sidney Peters, commissioner of prohibition of Virginia, in reply to hostile criticisms of the Dept. of prohibition. Richmond, 1919.

23 p. 8°.   LC, NYP, V

Charges against prohibition agents answered.

2022. ———. PUBLIC WELFARE, State board of. The disappearance of the county almshouse in Virginia. Back from "over the hill." By Arthur W. James, special agent, the State board of public welfare. Richmond, Bottom, 1926.

83 p. incl. illus., maps, fold. plan. 8°.   LC, NYP, USL, V, VU, WM

2023. VIRGINIA. PUBLIC WELFARE, State board of. Report . . . 1921/23— Richmond, 1923—

plates, tables, diagrs. 8°. Report year ends Sept. 30.

Supersedes State board of charities and corrections. *Annual report.* [1960] Became Dept. of public welfare, 1927.

HL: 1921/23-24/25; LC: 1921/23-25/26; NYP: 1921/23-26/27; USL: 1921/23-26/27; V: 1921/23-26/27; VU: 1921/23, 24/25-26/27.

See also: Virginia. *Annual reports of officers, boards* . . . [1962]

2024. ———. QUARANTINE COMMISSION. Elizabeth River district. Report of the medical officer of quarantine . . . [Norfolk, 187-? - ?]

8°. Report year ends Dec. 20.   NYP: 1877-78.

2025. ———. SOUTHWESTERN STATE HOSPITAL, Marion. Annual report . . . 1st- ; 1886/87— Richmond, 1887—

8°. Report year ends Sept. 30.

Called Southwestern lunatic asylum, 1886-1893.

LC: 1897/98, 1900/01-04/05, 08/09, 10/11-11/12, 13/14-25/26; NYP: 1895/96; USC: 1886/87-88/89, 92/93-1904/05, 07/08-08/09, 14/15, 18/19; V: 1888/89, 1900/01, 03/04-04/05, 06/07, 12/13, 14/15, 25/26-26/27.

See also: Virginia. *Annual reports of . . . institutions . . .* [1962]

2026. ———. TUBERCULOSIS COMMISSION. Report . . . 1915. Printed by order of the governor. Richmond, Bottom, 1916.

73 p. 8°.   V

2027. ———. WESTERN STATE HOSPITAL, Staunton. Annual report . . . Richmond, Va. [1866-19—

8°. Report year ends Sept. 30.

Called Western lunatic asylum previous to 1894.

H: 1869/70-72/73, 79/80, 81/82; LC: 1873/74, 1901/02-25/26, 27/28; McC: 1877/78; NYP: 1869/70, 73/74, 75/76, 78/79-79/80, 83/84; USC: 1899/1900-01/02, 07/08, 14/15-15/16; V: 1865/66-68/69, 1917/18-27/28; VU: 1867/68-68/69, 71/72-72/73, 88/89, 90/91, 95/96-97/98, 99/1900, 02/03-05/06, 07/08-11/12, 14/15-25/26, 27/28.

See also: Virginia. *Annual reports of . . . institutions . . .* [1962]

2028. ———. ———. Card of the democratic steward [J. W. Blackburn] of the Western lunatic asylum in relating to the investigation of that institution in April, 1889. [n. p., n. d.]

8 p. 8°.   V

2029. ——. ——. Management of the Western lunatic asylum, Staunton, Va. [Staunton? 1891]

    [8] p. 8°.   LC

Other Source Material

2030. ANDERSON, ARCHER. Address on the opening of Lee Camp soldiers' home. May 20, 1885 . . . Richmond, Pub. by R. E. Lee camp, no. 1, 1885.

    12 p. 8°.   LC, V

2031. BUFFALO LITHIA SPRINGS, Va. Buffalo Lithia Springs, Mecklenburg County, Virginia. Remarks on the medicinal properties and uses of these waters, with opinions of medical men as to their virtues, together with reports of cases, illustrative of their effects in various forms of chronic disease. Thos. F. Goode: proprietor. Resident physician, William B. Towles . . . Richmond, Clemmitt & Jones, 1878.

    54, [1] p. 8°.   LC
    Ed. of [1879?] 80 p.   V

2032. BUFORD, EDWARD P. Replies to editorials and correspondence on prohibition in the Brunswick *Times-gazette*. [Lawrenceville, Va., 1923?]

    17 p. 8°.   V
    Opposition of a Virginian to federal prohibition and the rôle played by some of the clergy in attempted enforcement.

2033. CABELL, ROYALL E. The issues involved in statewide prohibition. A speech delivered . . . before a mass meeting of the people of Richmond, held in the Academy of music . . . , May 14, 1914. Norfolk, Va. [1914]

    22 p. 8°.   V

2034. CHILDREN'S HOME SOCIETY OF VIRGINIA. Report . . . 1910. [n. p., 1910?]

    16 p. illus. 8°.   V

2035. DREWRY, WILLIAM F. Care and condition of the insane in Virginia. Dr. William F. Drewry. superintendent of the Virginia state hospital for the insane. [Richmond, Va.? 1908]

    [8] p. 8°.   V
    Paper read at 35th national conference of charities and correction, Richmond, Va., May, 1908.

2036. DREWRY, WILLIAM F. The present status of epileptics in Virginia. Petersburg, Fenn & Owen [1901]

    12 p. 8°.   V

2037. GARNETT, ALEXANDER Y. Observations on the sanitary advantages of tidewater Virginia, embracing Virginia Beach as a winter health resort . . . Philadelphia, Dornan, 1887.

    16 p. 8°.   NYP, WM
    Reprint from Amer. climatological assoc., *Transactions,* May 31, 1887.

2038. GUILD, MRS. JUNE P., comp. Manual for Virginia social workers, compiled from the Virginia code and the U. S. statutes, by June Purcell-Guild . . . [Richmond] The Richmond, Virginia, Council of social agencies, 1926.

    73, [6] p. 12°.   LC, USL, V

2039. GUNDRY HOME AND TRAINING SCHOOL FOR THE FEEBLE-MINDED AND EPILEPTIC, Falls Church, Va. [Circular of information] [n. p., n. d.]

    8 p. 16°.   USL

2040. The HOT SPRINGS of Virginia. Bath County, Va. [J. A. August & co.] Richmond, Va., Baughman [187-?]

    24 p. 12°.   H, LC

2041. JOHNSTON, GEORGE B. Value to the public of state medical societies. Presidential address, Medical society of Virginia, Hot Springs, Sept. 1, 1897 . . . [Richmond, Va., 1897]

    9 p. 8°.   LC
    Reprint from *Medical register* . . . Sept. 15, 1897.

2042. [1336] MEDICAL SOCIETY OF VIRGINIA. LEGISLATIVE COMMITTEE. The relation of the medical profession to the public health. Richmond, 1909.

2043. NATIONAL HOME, D.[isabled] V.[olunteer] S.[oldiers], Hampton, Va. Photogravures. Brooklyn, N. Y., Albertype co. [*ca.* 1900]

    15 illus. 12°.   V

2044. PRESBYTERIAN ORPHANS' HOME, Lynchburg, Va. Bulletin
. . . vol. 1- [Lynchburg, 1914?—

4°. monthly.

V: X; XI, 1-10, 12; XII-XIII; XIV, 1-10, 12; XV; XVI, 1-2, 4, 6-7,
9-12; XVII, 2-3; (1923-29).

2045. SMYTH, JOHN H. Negro delinquent children in Virginia . . .
[Speech by] president of the Negro reformatory association of
Virginia, at the 25th National conference of charities and correc-
tion. New York, May 24, 1898. [n. p., 1898?]

[9] p. 12°. USL, V

Concerning the work of the Negro reformatory association of Virginia.

2046. THOMAS, ALSEN F. The crisis; an address delivered by ex-
Senator A. F. Thomas before the Prohibition and evangelical asso-
ciation, Purcellville, Virginia, Aug. 10, 1910. [Lynchburg, Va.,
Bell, 1910]

16 p. 8°. LC

An attack upon the liquor traffic and the abuses of privileged corporations in Virginia.

2047. VIRGINIA ANTI-TUBERCULOSIS ASSOCIATION. Annual report
. . . [Richmond, 19-?—

8°. V: 1927.

2048. ———. How to be healthy, wealthy, and wise. 1921. [Rich-
mond? 1921?]

[8] p. illus. 8°. V

Distributed by the Richmond Health dept.

2049. ———. Lost: 5,000 men and $25,000,000 in Virginia during
1909. [Richmond, 1910?]

24 p. 8°. V

In support of an appeal to the General assembly of Virginia for an increased appropriation for the Catawba tuberculosis sanatorium.

2050. VIRGINIA ASSOCIATION OF WORKERS FOR THE BLIND. Proceedings of the . . . annual convention . . . [1st- ; 1920—]
[n. p., 1920—

8°. VU: 2d (1921).

2051. VIRGINIA CHILD WELFARE CONFERENCE, Richmond. The child in Virginia; hand-book and programme, May 22-25, 1911. [Richmond? 1911]

14 p. illus. 8°.   **V, VU**

Object of the conference: "A better crop of boys and girls."

2052. ———. . . . Virginia and the welfare of her children; addresses and discussions, Child welfare conference, Richmond, Va., May 22-25, 1911, held under auspices of State conference of charities and correction. Dr. Roy K. Flannagan, pres. . . . Richmond, 1911.

129, [4] p. 8°.   **NYP, USL, V**

2053. VIRGINIA CONFERENCE OF CHARITIES AND CORRECTION. Proceedings . . . [1st- ; 1903?—] Newport News, Richmond [etc., 1903?—

illus., diagrs. 8°. Issued irreg.

Title varies: Virginia state conference of social work, 192- ?

H: 10-11th (1913); **HL:** 1915, 17, 21; **LC:** 1913, 17, 21; **NYP:** 1913, 15-17, 21; **USC:** 1913; **USHy:** 1917; **USL:** Jan. & Dec., 1913, 17; **V:** 1903-04, 06, 09, 11, 13-17, 21; **VU:** 1909, 11, 13, 17, 21.

2054. ———. Program . . . [Richmond, 1903?—

8°.   **V:** 7th (1909).

2055. VIRGINIA CONFERENCE OF SOCIAL WORK. . . . Mental hygiene; child welfare . . . Richmond, Bottom, 1924.

40 p. 8°.   **V, VU**

Address at 1924 session of Virginia conference of social work; issued as a bulletin of the State board of public welfare.

2056. VIRGINIA COUNCIL OF RURAL AGENCIES. Community life campaign Apr. 23-May 20, 1922. "Build a better community." A handbook for the use of county councils, speakers and workers in the Community life campaign. [Pulaski, Smith, 1922]

49 p. 8°.   **USAg, USE, VU**

2057. The VIRGINIA SOCIAL HYGIENE ASSOCIATION. Organized April 13-14, 1915, in Richmond, Va., for the purpose of making a determined and persistent warfare against the social evil. [Richmond] 1915.

16 p. 16°.   **V**

2058. VIRGINIA STATE FIREMEN'S ASSOCIATION. Proceedings and minutes of the . . . annual convention . . . [1st- ; 1887?— Portsmouth, Va., etc., 1887?-19—

8°.   **NYP:** 23d-27th (1909-13).

Secondary Works

2059. DAVIS, DANIEL W. The life and services of Rev. Wm. Washington Browne, founder of the Grand fountain u. o. of true reformers . . . written by D. Webster Davis . . . with an introduction by Rt. Rev. Benjamin F. Lee . . . [Richmond, Va.] Mrs. M. A. Browne-Smith [1910]

x, 11-192 p. front., plates, ports. 8°.   **LC, V**

Treats of the temperance and reform movement among the Negroes of the South, with emphasis upon the work in Virginia by Rev. Browne. A simple narrative revealing the forces for betterment among the Negroes during the latter part of the 19th century.

2060. LEVY, ERNEST C., *et al.* Certain conclusions concerning typhoid fever in the South, as deduced from a study of typhoid fever in Richmond. [By] E. C. Levy . . . and Allen W. Freeman . . . Richmond, 1908.

39 p. maps, diagrs. 8°.   **V**

Reprint from *Old Dominion journal of medicine and surgery,* VII, 5; Nov., 1908.

2061. [1385] MAGRUDER, FRANK A. . . . Recent administration in Virginia . . . Baltimore, 1912.

2062. PIDGEON, MARY E. . . . The laws of Virginia as they affect women and children . . . Charlottesville, Va., University of Virginia, 1926.

29 p. incl. illus. 8°. (*University of Virginia record.* Extension series, X, 12; Aug., 1926)   **H, USL, V, VU**

2063. THOMPSON, S. H. The life of John R. Moffett, by Rev. S. H. Thompson, . . . president of Scottsburg [Va.] normal college . . . Salem, Va., Pub. by Mrs. Pearl Moffett, 1895.

xii, 269 p. front., ports, plates. 12°.   **LC, V**

Temperance reform in Danville, led by J. R. Moffett, a Baptist clergyman.

Periodicals

2064. AMERICAN issue. Virginia ed. v. 1- ; Mar. 28, 1908—
[Chicago, The Anti-saloon league, 1908—
   illus. f°. semi-monthly.
   J. C. Jackson, ed., Mar., 1908- (?)
   Supersedes the *Civic sentinel.* **[2065]**
   LC: I-II (1908-09). **NYP**: II, 19; III, 16, 18, 20-22; (1909-10). **V**:
III (Mar., Aug., 1910); VII, 21; VIII, 3-33; IX, 1-6; (1928-29).

2065. The CIVIC sentinel. Official organ of the Virginia anti-saloon
league. v. 1-7; 1901-Jan., 1908. Richmond, Va., Anti-saloon
league of Virginia, 1901-08.
   7 v. illus. f°. monthly.   **LC**: I, 2-VII, 9.
   Title varies: The Christian federation, 1901-Mar., 1904.
   Editors: C. H. Crawford, 1901-03; J. W. West, Mar.-Apr., 1903; G.
   B. Moore, 1903-04; E. J. Richardson, 1904-07; R. H. Bennett, 1907-08.
   Superseded by the *American issue,* Virginia ed. **[2064]**

2066. PUBLIC welfare . . . published monthly by the [Virginia]
State board of public welfare . . . v. 1, no. 1- ; Jan.,
1923— Richmond, Va., 1923—
   4°. bi-monthly, 1923-26; monthly, 1927—
   Arthur W. James, ed.
   Title varies: The X-Ray, I-III (1923-26).
   LC: I, 1-5, 7-12. **NYP**: I, 2-12; III, 1, 3-12; IV-V; (1923/24-28).
   V: I, 1, 3, 5, 8-12; III, 1-8, 10-12; IV, 1-8, 10-12; V, 1-3; VI, 4-12; VII,
1-2; (1923-29). **VU**: IV, 4, 6, 9-12; V, 1-2; VI, 4, 6-7, 9, 11-12; (1926-28).

2067. The TIDEWATER trail. A chronicle for groups of service
women in this community who can be depended upon to promote
all movements looking toward the betterment of life. v. 1- ;
[1927?—] Norfolk, Va. [1927?—
   illus. 8°. monthly?
   V: II, 17-27; June, 1928-Apr., 1929.

2068. The VIRGINIA CHILDREN's home finder; published quarterly by
the Children's home society of Virginia in the interest of homeless,
destitute, and dependent children. v. 1, no. 1- ; May, 1920—
Richmond, Va., 1920—
   illus. 4°. quarterly in May, Aug., Nov., and Feb.
   V: V-IX (1924/25-28/29); **VU**: VIII, 3 (Nov., 1927).

2069. The VIRGINIA GUIDE, published at the Virginia school for the deaf and blind. v. 1-   [18-? -19—   ] Staunton, Va. [18-? -19—

f°. bi-weekly.

V: XXXV, 1-19; XXXVI, 1-18; XXXVII, 1-19; XXXVIII, 1-19; XXXIX, 1-19; XL, 1-18; XLI, 1-19; XLII, 1-19 (1915-16); XLIII, 8-19; XLIV, 1-18; XLV, 1-17; XLVI, 1-17; XLVII, 1-10, 12-17; XLVIII, 1-18; XLIX-L, 17; LI, 1-8, 10-14; LII, 1-11; LIII, 1-10; LIV, 1-9; LV, 1-6 (1929). **VU**: XLIX, 5, 7-9, 11, 13-16 (1922/23) ; L, 1-2, 8, 10, 13, 17; LI, 2, 6-8, 12, 14; LII, 1-2, 5-8, 11.

For further references on Public Welfare and Regulation, see Pt. II, § 7: *Urban and County Development;* also Pt. IV, § 3: *Local Government.* See also, Pt. II, § 3, for items on health resorts and hot springs.

PART III. GENERAL SOCIAL CONDITIONS

1. BIBLIOGRAPHY

See above, Pt. I: *Bibliography.*

2. DESCRIPTION AND TRAVEL

Government Publications and Documents

2070. GANNETT, HENRY. . . . A gazetteer of Virginia . . .
Washington, Govt., 1904.

> 159, iii p. 8°. (U. S. Geological survey. *Bulletin,* 232)
> A general description of the state precedes the gazetteer.

2071. RICHMOND, WESTMORELAND, LANCASTER, AND NORTHUMBER-
LAND COUNTIES, VA. BOARD OF IMMIGRATION. The Northern Neck
of Virginia as a home for immigrants, by the Board of immigration . . . New York, Schmidt & Curtius, 1872.

> 16 p. map. 12°.   **V**

2072. TOCHMAN, G. Emigration to the U. S. Organization of the
State board of immigration in the state of Virginia. Statistical
disclosure of agricultural wealth of the "North", "West" and
"South" of the U. S. State of Virginia: its climate, soil, productions, natural advantages over other states of the Union, &c. Issued and published by Gen. G. Tochman, European general state
agent of immigration for the state of Virginia: for the use, information and protection of emigrants seeking homes in the U. S., and
the capitalists seeking profitable investments in lands and public
works of the state . . . Nov., 1869. 2d. ed. . . . New
York, Batchelar, 1869.

> 31 p. 8°.   **V**

2073. [340] U. S. CONGRESS. HOUSE. PUBLIC LANDS, Committee
on. . . . Shenandoah and other national parks . . . Report . . . [Washington, 1926]

2074. [341] ———. ———. SENATE. PUBLIC LANDS AND SURVEYS, Committee on. . . . Shenandoah and Great Smoky Mountain national parks . . . Report . . . [Washington, Govt., 1926]

2075. ———. JAMESTOWN TER-CENTENNIAL COMMISSION. . . . Final report of the Jamestown ter-centennial commission. Message from the President of the U. S., transmitting the final report . . . embodying reports of various officers of the Jamestown exposition, held at Norfolk, Virginia, in 1907 . . . Washington, Govt., 1909.

 160 p. plates (1 fold.) plans. 8°. (60 Cong., 2 sess. Senate. *Doc.,* 735)

                  LC, USAg, V
 George B. Cortelyou, chairman.

2076. VIRGINIA. AGRICULTURE AND IMMIGRATION, Dept. of. Along highways in old Virginia. Dept. of agriculture and immigration. Geo. W. Koiner, commissioner, Richmond, Va. . . . [Richmond? 1925?]

 23, [1] p. incl. illus., map. 8°.   LC, V, VU
 An attractive pamphlet giving points of interest and scenic beauty along Virginia highways.

2077. [115] ———. ———. . . . Hand-book of Virginia . . . Richmond [1876-19—

2078. ———. IMMIGRATION, Board of. The state of Virginia to the people of Great Britain. [n. p., 1866]

 1 l., [3]-8 p. 8°. 1500 copies printed.   V
 Signed by James Galt, James Black, B. B. Haxall, Board of immigration.

 Brief description of what Virginia has to offer to immigrants; includes text of "Act to promote and encourage immigration into the State of Virginia, Mar. 3, 1866."

2079. ———. ———. . . . Virginia: a brief memoir for the information of Europeans desirous of emigrating to the New World . . . Richmond, Va., Nye, 1868.

 16 p. 8°.   LC, NYP
 Signed: G. Tochman, European agent of immigration for Virginia. At head of title: For circulation in Great Britian and in the U. S.

 "This memoir was [also] published in the German language in the *Virginia Staats Zeitung,* and 10,000 extra copies of the issue of the paper containing it, had been secured, and partly already sent to Europe for circulation in Germany."

2080. VIRGINIA. IMMIGRATION, Board of. Virginia: a geographical and political summary, embracing a description of the state, its geology, soils, minerals and climate; its animal and vegetable productions; manufacturing and commercial facilities; religious and educational advantages; internal improvements, and form of government. Prepared and pub. under the supervision of the Board of immigration, and by authority of law. Richmond, Va., Walker, 1876.

iv p., 2 l., [3]-319, [1] p. incl. illus., tables, fold. maps. 8°.

BP, LC, USC, USG, V, VU, WM

Comp. by Jedediah Hotchkiss.

Ed. of 1898.   **NYP**

2081. ——. IMMIGRATION, Commissioner of. Report of the commissioner . . . to the State board of agriculture, Apr. 9, 1890. Richmond, Waddey, 1890.

8 p. 8°.   **V**

Charles Grattan, commissioner.

Concerning the progress of immigration in Virginia and the reasons for its slowness.

2082. ——. LAWS, STATUTES, etc. Public parks, an act providing for the condemnation of lands and buildings for use as a public park or for public park purposes. Reprinted from the Acts of the assembly, chap. 410, Act. of 1928. [Richmond, 1928]

40 p. 8°.   **V**

2083. ——. WORLD'S FAIR MANAGERS, Board of. Organization, by-laws, plan of work, local and general . . . including an official directory of the Board of managers, officers of the Board, and Auxiliary board, and of the officers of the Columbian exposition at Chicago. 1892. [n. p., 1892?]

55 p. 12°.   **V**

Other Source Material

2084. ADDRESSES delivered at the Pan-American exposition, Buffalo, N. Y., on Virginia-day, Aug. 23, 1901. Pub. by the Richmond Chamber of commerce. Richmond, Va., 1901.

48 p. 12°.   **NYP, V**

"Address," by J. H. Tyler, governor of Virginia.—"The physical and industrial resources of Virginia," by Joseph Bryan.—"Education in Virginia," by G. M. Miles.

2085. AMMEN, S[AMUEL] Z. History and description of the Luray Cave . . . Including explanations of the manner of its formation, its peculiar growths, its geology, chemistry, &c. . . . The whole so arranged as to serve as a guide . . . Baltimore, Borst, 1880.

    18 p. front. (fold. map) illus., plates. 8°.   LC

    3d ed., 1882: 48 p.   LC, NYP

    5th ed., 1886: 47 p.   LC, V

    Ed. of 1890.   V

2086. [ARGYLL, JOHN G., 9th duke of] A trip to the tropics and home through America. By the Marquis of Lorne. London, Hurst and Blackett, 1867.

    1 p. l., xii, 355, [1] p. front. 8°.   LC, NYP

Contains notes on conditions in Virginia after the Civil war; extracts from letters written while the author was travelling.

2087. ATLANTIC COAST LINE RAILROAD CO. Nation's garden spot is that part of Virginia, North Carolina and South Carolina, Georgia, Alabama, and Florida traversed by the Atlantic coast line . . . Wilmington, Atlantic coast line [1906?]

    48 p. illus., map. 8°.   V

Some of the information given is of doubtful authenticity.

2088. ATLANTIC, MISSISSIPPI & OHIO RAILROAD. . . . Southern excursionist's guide-book to cheap and pleasant summer homes in the mountains of Virginia, on the line of the Atlantic, Mississippi & Ohio railroad . . . Lynchburg, Va. [Petersburg, Ege] 1879.

    48 p. illus. 16°. Advertisements in back.   LC

2089. BALL, EMMA R. Washington's home and the story of the Mount Vernon ladies' association of the Union. [Richmond, Va., Whittet & Shepperson, *ca.* 1912]

    [18] p. illus., plates. 16°.   LC, V

    Signed: Mrs. Charles B. Ball.

Brief account of the accomplishments of the association.

2090. BARRIE, ROBERT, *et al.* Cruises, mainly in the Chesapeake, by Robert Barrie and George Barrie, jr. Philadelphia, Franklin, 1909.

    7 p. l., 3-276 p. front., plates, fold. map. 8°. Reprinted in part from various periodicals.   LC, V

2091. BEALE, E[DWIN] I.   Highways and byways of the Virginia peninsula, a book of information; designed as a hand-book for the use of tourists and all others interested in the history, soil, and topography of the peninsula.   Newport News, Va.   The author [1907]

 2 p. 1., [2]-58, [2] p. front., illus., plates. 12°.   **LC**

Some account of economic development since 1880.

2092. BEAUTIES of the C & O from the mountains to the sea.   [Philadelphia, Jordan, 1897]

 [24] p. illus. 8°.   **LC**

2093. The BEAUTIFUL Luray caverns, Luray, Virginia   . . .   Luray, Va., Kauffman [ca. 1913]

 [28] p. of illus. 8°.   **LC**

2094. BEYER, EDWARD.   Album of Virginia; or, illustrations of the Old Dominion.   [n. p., n. d.]

 40 plates. obl. f°.   **NYP**

2095. [1413] BIBB, A. P., & co.   Piedmont Virginia: with notice of Charlottesville   . . .   Charlottesville [1893?]

2096. The BOOK of the Shenandoah Valley.   [Harrisonburg, Va., Shenandoah council, no. 205, n. d.]

 122 p. 8°.   **VU**

2097. BROWN, MRS. MARY C.   Nature undergound; the Endless Caverns, in the heart of the historic Shenandoah Valley, by Mary Mitchell Brown, illustrated in line and colour by John Richard Flanagan.   New Market, Va.   [ca. 1921]

 [35] p. illus. (part mounted, col.) 4°.   **LC, NYP, VU**

Description of the caverns, preceded by an historical sketch of the Valley.

2098. BRUCE, THOMAS.   Southwest Virginia and Shenandoah Valley.   An inquiry into the causes of the rapid growth and wonderful development of southwest Virginia and Shenandoah Valley, with a history of the Norfolk & western and Shenandoah Valley railroads   . . .   Richmond, Hill, 1891.

 vii, [3], 259 p. 8°.

Written to reveal the progress of this region during the 'seventies and 'eighties.

2099. CAVERNS of Luray. Baltimore, 1893.

49 p. 12°. **H**

Eds. of 1889 and 1890. **H**

2100. CHAPMAN, GORDON S. Touring Virginia with the National editorial association. 1925. Sandersville, Ga. [1925]

62 p. illus. 8°. **VU**

Travelogue of the N. E. A., with notes on economic and social conditions in tidewater and piedmont Virginia and in the Valley.

2101. CHESAPEAKE & OHIO RAILROAD CO. From ocean to ocean. A trip through the historic and picturesque regions of the Virginias via the Chesapeake & Ohio route. Cincinnati, O., 1888.

31 p. illus. f°. **BRE**

2102. ———. Virginia in black and white . . . Washington, D. C., Passenger dept. Chesapeake & Ohio [1893]

64 p. incl. front., illus. fold. map. 12°. **LC, NYP**

Virginia summer resorts advertised.

2103. CHESAPEAKE & OHIO RAILWAY CO. As we speed. [Buffalo, N. Y., n. d.]

[12] p. illus. 8°. **H**

Description of Virginia along the route of the C & O.

2104. ———. Route and resorts of the Chesapeake & Ohio railway. [Richmond, Baughman, 1900]

80 p. illus., plan. 8°. **NYP**

Advertisements in back.

2105. ———. Route, resorts, and resources of the Chesapeake & Ohio railway of Virginia and West Virginia. Richmond, Baughman, 1879.

4, 48 p. map, illus. 8°. **H, HB**

2106. ———. To the mountains and the sea-shore through the battlefields of Virginia . . . [Cincinnati] 1885.

[120] p. illus., fold. map. 4°. **BRE**

2107. ———. A trip through the historic and picturesque regions of the Virginias via the Chesapeake & Ohio route. [Cincinnati, 188-?]

16 l. illus. f°. **NYP**

2108. [CHESAPEAKE & OHIO RAILWAY CO.] Virginia hot springs. [New York?] 1903.

    22 p. 12°.   **H**

    Ed. of 1904: 8 l.   **NYP**

    Ed. with n. d. [Washington, D. C.?] 20 p.   **V**

2109. ———. Virginia mountains and sea shore. Issued by the Passenger dept. [Chesapeake & Ohio railway co.] Bits of scenery and morsels of information for the summer. [Chicago, Poole, 1891]

    35, [1] p. illus., plates. obl. 8°.   **LC**

2110. ———. The Virginias, past and present. Issued by the Chesapeake & Ohio railway co., Passenger dept. [Chicago, Poole] 1900.

    48 p. illus. (incl. map) 12°.   **LC**

    Points of interest for tourists; resorts, hotels, etc.

2111. ———. REAL ESTATE DEPT. Country life in Virginia . . . [Richmond, Va.] C & O railway co. [1911]

    95, [1] p. illus., map. 8°.   **USAg**

2112. CHESTERMAN, WILLIAM D. The James River tourist. A brief account of historical localities on James River. Prepared by W. D. Chesterman. Pub. by L. B. Tatum, supt. of the Virginia steamboat co. Richmond, Dispatch steam print., 1878.

    51, 57-69 p. front., illus., plates, maps. 12°.   **BP, LC, V**

    Ed. of 1879: 1 p. l., 5-53, [1] p.   **LC**

    Eds. of 1881 and 1886.   **BP**

    Ed. of 1889: 91 p.   **LC, NYP, V**

2113. CHICKERING, J. W. Ninovag Luray (Lure) Pelovepolöl fa L. D. Benton. [New York, 189-?]

    8 p. 16°. (Beale's *Volapuk leaflets*, 5)   **NYP**

    Concerning the Luray Caverns.

2114. A CHRISTMAS holiday tour to Old Point Comfort, over the Pennsylvania railroad. [n. p., 1891?]

    16 p. map. 8°.   **NYP**

2115. COLONIAL Virginia. Some historic points on line of the Chesapeake & Ohio railway. [T. H. Gurney, General passenger agent, Richmond, Va., n. p., n. d.]

    [14] p. illus. fold. 4°.   ·   **VU**

2116. CUMBERLAND VALLEY RAILROAD CO. Rural resorts and summer retreats along the line of the Cumberland valley railroad, including picnic parks and pleasure places. [Philadelphia, Allen, Lane & Scott] 1881.

> 53 p. illus. 8°.   LC
>
> Emphasis upon Shenandoah Valley; with interesting engravings.

2117. DESCRIPTION of the Natural Bridge, Va., and its history. Philadelphia, Packard, Butler & Partridge [188-?]

> 42 p. plates. 8°.   LC, NYP
>
> Ed. of 1886.   BP
>
> Ed. of 1887.   V
>
> Ed. of 1889: 61 p.   V

2118. [DINWIDDIE, MARSHALL L.] Mt. Vernon, former home [of] George Washington. [Mt. Vernon on the Potomac, Ye olde Mt. Vernon inn, *ca.* 1921]

> [12] p. illus. (incl. port.) obl. 8°.   LC
>
> Description of the rooms and furnishings; with historical notes.

2119. [DOUGHTY, FANNY A.] Days at Mount Vernon. A collection of authentic incidents in modern times. Boston, Todd, 1879.

> 26 p. plates. 8°.   LC
>
> Distinguished visitors to Mt. Vernon, and some amusing incidents.

2120. EAST TENNESSEE, VIRGINIA & GEORGIA RAILWAY CO. From the mountains to the Gulf. A tour of the regions traversed by the East Tennessee, Virginia & Georgia railway and its connections. Written by Frank H. Taylor . . . New York [1891?]

> [52] p. illus., fold. map. 8°. Advertisements in back.   BRE
>
> Contains some material on social and economic conditions in Virginia.

2121. EASTERN SHORE of Virginia, a description of its soil, climate, industries, development and future prospects. Baltimore, Harlem paper co., 1891.

> 8 p. 8°.   V

2122. The EIGHTH wonder of the world. Luray caverns on the Norfolk & western railroad. Lawrance ed. [Richmond, Waddey, 189-?]

> 8 p. obl. 48°.   NYP

2123. ENDLESS CAVERNS, wonderful and spectacular, New Market, Virginia, in the heart of the Shenandoah Valley. [n. p., *ca.* 1912]

29 p. col. illus. 12°.   LC

2124. FIVE views of nature's playground, southwestern Virginia. [n. p., n. d.]

folder, col. illus., map. f°.   V

2125. FREEMAN, EDWARD A. Some impressions of the U. S. . . . New York, Holt, 1883.

x p., 1 l., 304 p. 12°.   LC, V

Scattered notes on Virginia, and on the Negro, from observations made in 1881-82.

2126. GRAND CAVERNS; wonders of the subterranean world, Grottoes, Va. [Chicago, Rand, McNally, 1926]

[10] p. illus. (part col.) 8°.   LC

2127. The GROTTOES of the Shenandoah, consisting of the Weyer and the Fountain caves . . . Augusta County, Va. Lighted by a grand system of incandescent electric lights . . . [Ed. by] A. W. Howison. Staunton, Va., Valley Virginian print., 1889.

28 p. illus., plates, map. 8°.   BP

2128. HALE, MRS. LOUISE C. We discover the Old Dominion . . . ; drawings by Walter Hale. New York, Dodd, Mead, 1916.

5 p. l., 374, p. front., plates, map. 8°.   BP, LC, NYP, V, VU

A garrulous account of travels through Virginia, with personal incidents and bits of history interspersed.

2129. HALL, EDWARD H. Jamestown, a sketch of the history and present condition of the site of the first permanent English settlement in America . . . New York, The American scenic and historic preservation society, 1902.

30 p. incl. map. front., plates. 12°.   BP, H, LC, V

2130. HALL, JOHN L. Introductory address delivered . . . at the Jamestown celebration, held May 13, 1895. [n. p., 1895?]

8 p. 8°.   WM

2131. HARRISON, FAIRFAX. Looking to the future in Virginia: address at the annual re-union of Confederate veterans at Fisher's Hill, Va. Aug. 7, 1915 . . . [n. p., 1915?]

6 p. 8°.   **LC, VU**

On the future development of Virginia in light of her recent progress.

2132. HAWTHORNE, HILDEGARDE. Rambles in old college towns . . . with drawings by John Albert Seaford. New York, Dodd, Mead, 1917.

5 p. l., 364 p. front., plates. 8°.   **H, LC, V**

Contains descriptions, in conversational style, of the University of Virginia and William and Mary college, with bits of history interspersed.

2133. HENKEL, DAVID S. A description of the New Market endless caverns . . . New Market, Va., Henkel & co., 1880.

36 p. 16°.   **LC**

2134. [HILLYARD, M. B.] Virginia; its climate, soil, productions, manufacturing industries, and mineral wealth. Published by the Norfolk & western railroad company, for gratuitous distribution in the interest of emigration to the state of Virginia. Baltimore, Record print. [189-?]

36 p. 8°.   **BP, LC, NYP, V**

Reprint of the author's *New South*, p. 64-93.

2135. HISTORICAL, industrial, and statistical review and mailing and shipping guide of Tennessee [and Virginia] New York [etc.] 1887.

unp. illus. 8°.   **H**

2136. HOGE, PEYTON H., *et al.* The travels of ego and alter; an epistolary narrative of a tramp through the Old Dominion. By Peyton H. Hoge and Howard R. Bayne. Richmond, West, Johnston, 1879.

48 p. 8°.   **V, WM**

Conditions in the 'seventies, contrasted with those before the Civil war.

2137. HOTALING, MRS. H. C. Carry me back to ol' Virginia: editor-

ial correspondence, by Mrs. H. C. Hotaling of Minnesota delega-
tion, National editorial association. Richmond, Va., 1925.

[64] p. illus. 8°.   **WM**

A travelogue shedding light upon contemporary economic and social
conditions in Virginia. (Cp. with **[2100]**)

2138. HOTEL ALPIN, Hot Springs, Virginia, on the Chesapeake &
Ohio railway. L. C. Alpin, proprietor. New York, South pub.
[19-?]

16 p. illus. 16°.   **LC**

2139. HUTCHINS, FRANK, *et al.* Houseboating on a colonial waterway, by Frank and Cortelle Hutchins; illustrated with many photographs by the authors. Boston, Page, 1910.

xii, 299 p. front., plates, ports. 8°.   **BP, LC, NYP, V, VU**

A readable travalogue of a voyage up the James River to Richmond,
with historical notes interspersed.

2140. ———. Virginia: the Old Dominion, as seen from its colonial
waterway, the historic river James, whose every succeeding turn
reveals country replete with monuments and scenes recalling the
march of history and its figures from the days of Captain John
Smith to the present time. By Frank and Cortelle Hutchins. With
a map and 54 plates, of which six are in full color, from photographs by the authors. Boston, Page, 1921.

xii, 299 p. plates (incl. front.) fold. map. 8°.   **BP, LC, NYP, V, WM**

Originally pub. in 1910, under title: *Houseboating on a colonial waterway.*
[2139]

2141. INGERSOLL, ERNEST. Through the Shenandoah Valley; the
chronicle of a leisurely journey through the uplands of Virginia
. . . Issued by the Passenger dept. of the Shenandoah Valley
railroad company . . . Roanoke, Va. New York, 1886.

55 p. illus., fold. map. 12°.   **BRE, H, NYP**

A florid description of the Valley.

2142. ———. To the Shenandoah and beyond: the chronicle of a
leisurely journey through the uplands of Virginia and Tennessee,
sketching their scenery, noting their legends, portraying social and
material progress, and explaining routes of travel . . . With
illustrations by Frank H. Taylor. New York, Leve & Alden, 1885.

3 p. l., [5]-125, [1] p. front. (fold. map) illus. 8°.   **BP, LC, NYP, V**
Ed. of 1886.   **LC**

2143. The INTERMONT hotel, Covington, Virginia. Health and pleasure resort . . . [Richmond, Va., Hill, 189-?]

[16] p. incl. cover-title, illus. nar. 16°. **LC**

2144. JAMES RIVER garden club, Richmond. Historic gardens of Virginia, compiled by the James River garden club, edited by Edith Tunis Sale . . . Richmond, Va., William Byrd press [*ca.* 1923]

355 p. col. front., plates (part col.) plans. 8°.

Descriptions of famous gardens in all parts of the state, with their historic background. Beautifully illustrated.

2145. [JAMESTOWN EXPOSITION, 1907] Commemorating the event of the first permanent English settlement in America, 1607, Jamestown exposition, Apr. 26-Nov. 30, 1907. [Norfolk, Va., Barron, 1907?]

16 p. plates, port. 12°. **NYP, V**

2146. ———. Glimpses of the Jamestown exposition and picturesque Virginia. Original photographs graphically reproduced, depicting the most unique exposition ever held on American soil . . . A scenic panorama of the Old Dominion . . . Chicago, Laird & Lee, 1907.

176 p. of illus. front. (diagr.) 12°. **LC, NYP**

2147. ———. Guide to historic Virginia and the Jamestown centennial . . . Chicago, Laird & Lee, 1907.

142 p. 16°. **WM**

Contains brief description of the centennial and a general itinerary for visitors.

2148. ———. Jamestown Aeronautical congress, Norfolk, Va., Apr. 26 to Nov. 30, 1907. New York, Dept. of congresses and special events, Jamestown exposition [1907]

11 l. illus. (plans) 8°. **NYP**

2149. ———. Jamestown exposition on Hampton Roads, 1907 . . . Rules and regulation governing the system of awards. Newport News, Franklin print. [n. d.]

4 p. 8°. **V**

2150. ———. Jamestown ter-centennial exposition, Norfolk, Va., Apr. 26 to Nov. 30, 1907. [St. Louis, Curran, 1906]

8 p. 16°. **NYP**

2151. [JAMESTOWN EXPOSITION, 1907] Official catalogue with maps, illustrations of grounds and exhibits. Jamestown ter-centennial exposition . . . [Norfolk, Va., Jamestown official publication co., 1907]

70 p. illus., fold. map. 8°.   LC

2152. ————. . . . Official classification of exhibit departments . . . Norfolk, Tidewater pub., 1907.

63 p. 8°.   H, V

2153. ————. . . . Official guide of the Jamestown ter-centennial exposition, held at Sewell's Point on Hampton Roads, near Norfolk, Va., Apr. 26-Nov. 30, 1907. Comp. and ed. by W. H. Bright. Norfolk, Va., Hess, 1907.

112 p. front. (fold. plan) illus., plates. 8°.   LC
Advertisements interspersed.

2154. ————. See! See! See! Guide to Jamestown exposition, historic Virginia, and Washington . . . Washington, D. C., Adams, 1907.

66 p. illus., plates. 8°.   LC

2155. JAMESTOWN OFFICAL PHOTOGRAPH CORP., Norfolk, Va. Historical Virginia photographs and official views of the Jamestown exposition . . . Catalogue no. 2. Norfolk, Barron [n. d.]

20 p. 16°.   V

2156. ————. The Jamestown exposition illustrated; photographs made with Goerz lenses by Jamestown official photograph corporation . . . Published by Jamestown official photograph corporation . . . the trade supplied by American news company . . . New York, Blanchard, 1907.

[40] p. of illus. 4°.   LC

2157. ————. The Jamestown exposition photo-gravures. [Brooklyn, N. Y., Albertype co., ca. 1907]

24 illus. (2 fold.) on 22 l. 4°.   V

2158. ————. Scenes at the Jamestown exposition, with historic sites in old Virginia . . . Pub. by Jamestown official photograph corporation . . . the trade supplied by American news company . . . New York, Blanchard [1907]

[128] p. illus. obl. 12°.   LC, V

2159. JARVIS' Mount Vernon and Arlington album. [Washington, D. C., J. F. Jarvis, 1893]

    12 p. obl. 16°.   LC

2160. JEFFERSON CLUB ASSOCIATION, St. Louis. The pilgrimage to Monticello, the home and tomb of Thomas Jefferson by the Jefferson club of St. Louis, Mo., Oct., 10 to 14, 1901. St. Louis, Curran, 1902.

    2 p. l., [3]-78 p. front., plates, ports. 8°.   LC, NYP, V

    Record of the celebration, speeches, unveiling of a monument, etc.

2161. JETT, DORA C. In tidewater Virginia. [Richmond, Whittet & Shepperson, 1924]

    156 p. illus., plates. 12°.   BP, NYP, V, VU, WM

    Descriptions of many old Virginia homesteads.

2162. [JOHNSTON, ELIZABETH B.] Visitors' guide to Mount Vernon . . . 5th ed., rev. and improved. Washington, D. C., Gibson [1878?]

    61 p. front., illus. 16°. Advertsements in back.   LC, NYP

    Description of the mansion, its furnishings, and the estate. Contains list of officers of the Mt. Vernon ladies assoc.

    Eds. of 1886, 89, 91.   NYP

2163. JONES, JOHN E. Mount Vernon, the home of Washington . . . Washington, D. C., U. S. press association, 1915.

    44 p. front., illus., plates, ports. 8°.   LC

    A readable description of interesting details at Mt. Vernon, with historical notes interspersed.

2164. [KEEFER, JOSEPH I.] Mt. Vernon and its surroundings . . . Washington, D. C., J. I. Keefer [ca. 1906]

    1 p. l., 54 p. illus. 12°.   LC

2165. KEIM, DE B[ENNEVILLE] R. A guide to the Potomac River, Chesapeake Bay and James River, and an ocean voyage to northern ports. A series of interesting and instructive excursions by water from Washington . . . Washington, D. C., By the compiler [ca. 1881]

    80 p. front. (fold. map) illus. 12°.   LC

2166. ———. Washington and Mount Vernon, what to see, and how

to see it. A sightseer's guide . . . 30th ed. The text of this
guide is revised to date. Washington [*ca.* 1893]

80 p. illus., maps, diagr. 12°.   **LC**

29th-33d eds. pub. in 1893.

2167. KELLOGG, JOHN B. Mount Vernon, and what may be seen
there: or, The orphans' excursion to the home of Washington; being a description in verse of the more important relics of the mansion, the beautiful scenery, and the various objects of interest about
the place . . . Washington, D. C., C. W. Brown, 1884.

16 p. 8°.   **LC**

2168. KERBEY, JOSEPH O. On the war path; a journey over the historic grounds of the late Civil war, by Maj. J. O. Kerbey . . .
Chicago, Donohue, Henneberry, 1890.

301 p. illus. 8°.   **LC, VU**

Written in journalistic style, the narrative affords some incidental in-
sight into economic and social conditions in eastern Vrginia at the end
of the 'eighties.

2169. KING, JOHN T. . . . Guide to Baltimore & Ohio railroad
. . . [Baltimore, 1874?]

100 p. illus., plates, port. 12°.   **LC**

Advertisements interspersed. Contains information on hotels, train
connections, historic homes of the Shenandoah Valley, etc.

2170. LITTLETON, MAUD W. Monticello, by Mrs. Martin W. Littleton. [n. p., 1912?]

[59] p. illus., plates, ports. 8°.   **H, LC, NYP, VU**

History of the Jefferson estate and the movement for making it national property. Pt. 2 contains letters to Mrs. Littleton from men in
public life who favor the acquisition of Monticello by the U. S. government.

2171. [LURAY CAVERNS CORP., Luray, Va.] The beautiful caverns
of Luray, Luray, Virginia. In the Shenandoah Valley, three miles
of subterranean splendor, brilliantly lighted by electricity . . .
[Luray, Va., *ca.* 1906]

15, [1] p. illus. 12°.   **LC**

Ed. of 1923.   **VU**

2172. LURAY CAVERNS, on the Norfolk & western railway. [n. p.,
1898?]

[12] p. 12°.   **LC**

Eds. of [1900?] and [190-?] 15 and 16 p., respectively.

2173. McAllister, Joseph T. Appalachian tours in the Virginias
. . . Virginia Hot Springs, Va., McAllister pub., 1913.

32 p. illus., maps. 4°. **H, V**

2174. Maddux, Martin. Orkney Springs, Shenandoah County,
Virginia. Open from June 1st to December 1st annually. Martin
& H. Cabell Maddux, proprietors. Baltimore, Friedenwald [1884]

24 p. incl. plates. 8°. **LC**
Description of the resort and surroundings, rates of board, etc., with
testimonials.
Ed. of 1886: 48 p. **LC**

2175. [Mason, Otis T.] The caverns of Luray. Reprinted from
the official report of a visit to the Luray Caverns, in Page County,
Virginia, under the auspices of the Smithsonian institution, July
13th and 14th, 1880 . . . [n. p., Shenandoah Valley railroad
co.? 1882?]

13, [1] p. illus., map. 8°. **BP, H, LC, NYP**
Slight abridgement of the original report, printed in the Smithsonian
institution, *Report for 1880*, p. 449-460.

2176. The Mayflower's log . . . Virginia development number. Washington, D. C., 1926.

illus. 4°. (The . . . *Log*, II, 9; Sept., 1926) **V**
Articles on Virginia's progress and development, by leading men of
the state.

2177. [Mohler, J. L.] A description of Weyer's Cave, in Augusta
County, Va. Staunton, Valley Virginian, 1881.

1 p. l., [5]-15 p. illus. 8°. **LC, NYP**
Signed: J. L. Mohler.

2178. [1418] Monticello hotel, Charlottesville, Va. A word-
picturelogue thru beautiful, historic Charlottesville. Charlottesville
[ca. 1928]

2179. Mount Vernon ladies' association of the union. An
illustrated handbook of Mount Vernon, the home of Washington.
[Washington?] L. W. House [ca. 1899]

[48] p. illus. 8°. **LC**
Ed. of 1905. **LC**

2180. MOUNT VERNON LADIES' ASSOCIATION OF THE UNION. An illustrated handbook of Mount Vernon, the home of Washington . . . copyright . . . by the Mount Vernon ladies' association. Phila[delphia] Beck [*ca.* 1921]

32 p. illus. (part col.) map. 8°.   LC

Ed. of [*ca.* 1928] 34 p.   LC

Detailed description of buildings and furnishings of the estate; with list of officers of the Mt. Vernon ladies' association since its foundation.

2181. The NATURAL BRIDGE of Virginia and its environs.   [n. p.] 1890.

1 p. 1., 16 numb. 1. 16 plates. obl. 8°.   LC, V

2182. The NATURAL BRIDGE, Rockbridge co., Va.   [n. p., 188-?]

16 p. 24°.   LC, NYP, V

2183. NEWTON, JOSEPH. Emigration to Virginia, (east) "or the Old Dominion state." (3d ed.) Report from Joseph Newton on his second visit to Virginia. London, Virginian land agency [1871]

[3]-52 p. 8°.   LC

Describes very favorably the sections and counties of Virginia, to attract English emigrants. Contains *Notes* of the author's first visit to Virginia (1869), and extracts from the letter of an English settler in Virginia, and from the English press.

2184. NORFOLK & VIRGINIA BEACH RAILROAD CO. The Princess Anne hotel, Virginia Beach, Va. . . . [New York, Hosford & sons, 1888]

16 p. illus., map. obl. 24°.   LC

Virginia Beach as a pleasure resort.

2185. NORFOLK & WESTERN RAILROAD CO. Through Virginia over the Norfolk & western railroad. Roanoke, Va., Passenger dept., Norfolk & western railroad, 1887.

66, [4] p. illus., table. 12°.   V

The illustrations are of more value than the text.

2186. ――――. . . . Tourists and excursionists guide book to summer homes in the mountains of Virginia, on the line of the Norfolk & western railroad . . . Philadelphia, 1882.

80 p. illus., map. 16°. Advertisements in back.   BRE

Leading places along the way described, with accommodations for tourists.

2187. ———. Virginia summer resorts. Buffalo, N. Y., Art-printing works of Matthews, Northrup & co., 1889.

> 2 p. l., 7-42, [2] p. illus. 12°.   **LC**
> Map on back cover. Springs and resorts open for the season.
> Ed. of 1891: 66 p.   **LC**

2188. NORFOLK & WESTERN RAILWAY CO. Reference book of the Norfolk & western railroad co. . . . Outlining the present condition of progress in mining, manufactures and agriculture and the undeveloped resources of those portions of the state of Virginia traversed by its lines. [New York, Giles, 188-?]

> 94 p. illus., map. nar. 12°. (Norfolk & western railway. Virginia resorts. *Pamphlet,* 4)   **LC, V**

2189. ———. . . . The Shenandoah Valley . . . N[ew] Y[ork], Crawford [189-?]

> 17 l. illus., port. obl. 24°. (Norfolk & western railway. Virginia resorts. *Pamphlet,* 9)   **LC**

2190. ———. Virginia summer resorts. Roanoke, Va. [1902]

> 46 p. incl. illus., map. 8°. folder.   **LC, NYP**

2191. [OLD DOMINION STEAMSHIP CO.] . . . Old Dominion line. Along the historic James River. [New York?] 1902.

> 19, [5] p. incl. illus., map. nar. 8°. (Old Dominion series, 2)   **LC**
> Comp. by R. F. Day. Describes points of interest from Norfolk to Richmond.

2192. ———. Old fields revisited; or, Hunting health and history in Virginia . . . New York [Leve & Alden's publication dept.] 1884.

> 32 p. illus., plates, maps. 8°.   **NYP, V**
> Picturesque narrative of fictitious characters who visited the James Valley in the mid-'eighties; also some notes on the Blue Ridge.

2193. ORKNEY SPRINGS CO. History of Orkney Springs, Shenandoah County, Va. . . . Mt. Jackson, Va., Valley farmer book and job office, 1877.

> 16 p. illus. 16°.   **LC**
> Hotel accommodations, rates, etc.

2194. PANGBORN, JOSEPH G. Picturesque B & O [Baltimore & Ohio railroad] Historical and descriptive. Subscription ed. Chicago, Knight & Leonard, 1883.

288 p. illus. 4°.   BP

2195. PARROTT, CARYL S. A descriptive reading on Virginia . . . Philadelphia, Rau, 1890.

2 p. l., 785-800 p. 12°.   LC

Brief descriptions and historical notes of the capitol, Old Point Comfort, Luray Inn., etc.; to accompany lantern slides.

2196. PENNSYLVANIA RAILROAD CO. Pennsylvania tours. A June pleasure trip to Gettysburg, Luray Caverns, the Natural Bridge, Richmond, and Washington . . . [Philadelphia, Allen, Lane & Scott] 1888.

39 p. 12°.   NYP

2197. ———. Tours to Old Point Comfort, Richmond, and Washington. [Philadelphia, Allen, Lane & Scott, 1896]

18 p. map. 16°.   NYP

2198. POLLARD, EDWARD A. The Virginia tourist. Sketches of the springs and mountains of Virginia; containing an exposition of fields for the tourist in Virginia; natural beauties and wonders of the state; also accounts of its mineral springs; and a medical guide to the use of the waters, etc., etc. . . . Illustrated by engravings from actual sketches. Philadelphia, Lippincott, 1870.

277 p. front. (fold. map) plates. 12°.

Narrative of a tour, wth some notes on economic and social conditions in western Virginia.

2199. PORTERFIELD, G. T. Season of 1905, Mountain Lake, Giles County, Virginia. 4,500 feet above tide. [Roanoke, Stone, *ca.* 1905]

20, [4] p. illus. 16°.   LC

Description of the natural beauty and advantages of this resort.

2200. POTOMAC GARDENS, inc., Washington, D. C. Potomac gardens, in the Mount Vernon estate of George Washington; the suburb beautiful of the world's most beautiful city. Washington, D. C., Potomac gardens, inc. [*ca.* 1915]

[22] p. illus. (incl. plan) 8°.   LC

2201. The POTOMAC RIVER from Great Falls to Point Lookout . . . [Washington, 1878]

    3 fold. 1. fold. map. 12°.   **LC**

    A descriptive leaflet, copyrighted by J. B. Philip and J. P. Anderson.

2202. PROCTER, JOHN R. Big Stone Gap, Virginia. New York, J. J. Little, 1890.

    32 p. maps, illus., plates. 4°.   **LC**

    Contains a 4-page reprint on the "great future of Big Stone Gap" from the Big Stone Gap *Herald,* May 15, 1890; also a full page advertisement of the sale of lots on June 2d by the Big Stone Gap improvement co. Geological maps by J. B. Hoeing.

2203. PROTESTANT EPISCOPAL CHURCH IN THE U. S. GENERAL CONVENTION, 1898. The pilgrimage to Jamestown, Va., of the bishops and deputies of the General convention of the Protestant Episcopal church in the U. S. . . . Oct. 15, 1898. New York, De Vinne, 1898.

    32 p. plates (incl. front.) 8°.

2204. PUGH, JAMES A. Southside Virginia . . . [Roanoke, Va.? Norfolk & western railroad co., 1891?]

    15 p. 8°. (Reprint from Roanoke *Daily times,* June 21, 1891)   **V**

    A "write-up" of the region east of the Blue Ridge, by the president of the Virginia press association.

2205. RAILROAD scenery in Virginia. Staunton, Cave of Fountains, and Elliott's Knob, as seen through a city girl's spectacles. Richmond, Va., 1874.

    24 p. 8°.   **BP**

2206. REAVIS, JOHN R. Mount Vernon avenue. A national memorial highway from Washington to Mt. Vernon. With some account of the natural and historical attractions along its proposed route . . . Washington, D. C., Pub. under the auspices of the Mt. Vernon avenue assoc., 1888.

    35 p. illus. 8°.   **LC**

2207. REEDS, CHESTER A. The Natural Bridge of Virginia and its environs . . . a guide to Natural Bridge including a description and discussion of the origin and development of this striking geographical feature. New York, Nomad pub., 1927.

    62 p. incl. front., illus. 8°.   **LC, NYP, V**

2208. RHODES, THOMAS L. The story of Monticello, as told by Thomas L. Rhodes . . . to Frank B. Lord. Washington, D. C., American pub., 1928.

94 p. front., illus., 8°.   **LC, NYP, V**

By the superintendent of Monticello for almost 40 years. Chapters on the first sale of the estate, its decline, and its purchase by the Thomas Jefferson memorial foundation.

2209. RICHMOND & ALLEGHANY RAILROAD CO. The Richmond & Alleghany railroad in Virginia. Description of the lands, climate, mineral and other resources of the counties along its line; and the Hand-book of Virginia . . . Richmond, Va. [1881?]

[193]-216 p., 4 1., 189 p. 8°.   **BRE, NYP**

The *Hand-book of Virginia,* by the Commissioner of agriculture of Virginia, 3d ed., 1881, has separate title-page. Cf. [115]

2210. ———. Up the James River; or, a trip to the mountains of Virginia . . . New York, Leve & Alden [1885?]

32, [6] p. illus. 12°.   **V**

Brief descriptions of industry and resources, with sections on Richmond, Lynchburg, and Clifton Forge.

2211. ———. Virginia industrial exposition held under the auspices of the First regiment Virginia volunteers . . . Richmond, Va., Johns & Goolsby, 1881.

8 p. 8°.   **HB**

Contains prospectus and rules and regulations of the exposition.

2212. RICHMOND & DANVILLE RAILROAD CO. "Bon Air." Its attractions for summer residents; its enjoyable resources for excursionists. [New York, Aldine press, 1882]

13, [1] p. incl. front., illus. fold. plan. 24°.   **LC**

Advertisement of Bon Air resort near Richmond, controlled by Bon Air land & improvement co.

2213. ———. Country homes near the nation's capital . . . [Philadelphia, Allen, Lane & Scott, 1888]

14 p. 12°.   **LC**

Scenic attractions and points of interest along the railroad in Fairfax and Loudoun counties.

2214. ———. The summer of 1882 among the health resorts of northeast Georgia, upper South Carolina, western North Carolina, and Virginia. [3d ed.] [New York, Aldine press, 1882]

3 p. l., 56 p. front., illus. 4°. LC

2215. ———. Where to spend the summer and how to reach the resorts of Virginia, western North Carolina and Georgia, via the Piedmont air line, Richmond & Danville raiload. [New York, Crawford, 1886?]

78 p. illus., plates, fold. map. 12°. BRE

2216. RILEY, E[LIHU] S., jr. To Pen-Mar, and the caverns of Luray. A guide book . . . Annapolis, Md., Daily record print., 1882.

40 p. illus. 8°. LC

2217. SAXBY, H. Historic C & O. An interesting trip through the historic and picturesque regions of the Virginias, via the Chesapeake & Ohio route. [n. p., 189-?]

19 l. f°. NYP

2218. SCHARF, J[OHN] T. Orkney Springs, Shenandoah County, Virginia. Its attractions as a summer resort. Its baths, hotels, cuisine, amusements, scenery . . . and the medicinal virtue of its waters . . . Philadelphia, Everts, 1890.

30 p. illus. 8°. LC

2219. The SEVENTH wonder of the world . . . [n. p., 18-?]

[4] p. 8°. LC
Natural Bridge, Va.

2220. SHENANDOAH NATIONAL PARK. NATIONAL CONFERENCE ON STATE PARKS. Fifth national conference on state parks, May 25-28, 1925, at Skyland . . . in the heart of the proposed Shenandoah national park . . . [Announcement] Washington, D. C., Judd & Detweiler [1925]

23 p. illus., fold. plate. 8°. LC

2221. SHENANDOAH VALLEY & OHIO RAILROAD CO. A glance at the country through which it passes between tidewater and the Ohio River, a distance of 300 miles. New York, Sackett, 1874.

24 p. map. 8°. BP

2222. The SHENANDOAH VALLEY of Virginia railroad development. Agricultural and industrial progress. Magnificent scenery. The wonderful Luray Caverns . . . [Staunton, Va., Valley Virginian, 1881]

clipping from *Valley Virginian,* May 19, 1881. f°.   **NYP**

2223. SHENANDOAH VALLEY RAILROAD CO. Through the Shenandoah Valley. Caverns of Luray, Natural Bridge, grottoes of the Shenandoah, and the chronicle of a leisurely journey through the uplands of Virginia. Issued by the Passenger dept. . . . New York, Giles [1890?]

76 p. illus., fold. map. 12°.   **BP, H, LC, NYP, V**

2224. SKYLAND, situated on high plateau in the Blue Ridge near grand old Stony Man Peak, overlooking famous Shenandoah Valley. 3,500 feet in the blue. Washington, D. C., Judd & Detweiler, 1912.

1 p. l., [5]-37 p. illus. 8°.   **LC**
Ed. of 1917: 72 p.   **LC**
Ed. of 1919: 80 p.   **LC**

2225. SLATER, WILLIAM. Virginia: containing valuable information to those who think of emigrating there . . . London, Kitto, 1872.

viii, 54 p. front. (map) 8°.   **NYP**

2226. SMITH, EDWARD E. Our Virginia; a description of Virginia for young people . . . drawings by Frederic H. Spigel. Richmond, Va., States pub. [*ca.* 1923]

3 p. l., 122 p. illus. 8°.   **LC, V, WM**
"A story of and pictures about what we are now doing."

2227. SNOWDEN, WILLIAM H. Some old historic landmarks of Virginia and Maryland described in a hand-book for the tourist over the Washington, Alexandria & Mount Vernon electric railway . . . Philadelphia, Lippincott, 1894.

71 p. plates, ports., facsim. 8°.   **LC, NYP**
Incidental information on conditions in the late 19th cent.
2d ed., 1901: Alexandria, Ramey print.; 100 p.   **LC**
3d ed., 1902: 122 p.   **H, LC, NYP**
5th ed., 1904: 124 p.   **V**

2228. SOUTHERN RAILWAY CO. Virginia, the territory of the Southern railway, in piedmont, the Valley, middle and tidewater sections of the "Old Dominion." [Washington, D. C., Southern railway, 1904]

sheet. 16½ x 69½ cm. fold.   LC

2229. SOUTHWESTERN VIRGINIA, inc. See southwestern Virginia. [n. p., n. d.]

folder. illus., map.   V

2230. SQUIER, LOUISE S. Sketches of southern scenes . . . New York, Pratt, 1885.

203 p. front., illus. 8°.   BP, H, LC, V, VU

Narrative, written in a dispassionate manner, of a tour through Virginia in the 'eighties, by a citizen of Brooklyn, N. Y.

2231. STANARD, MARY N. Jamestown and the Association for the preservation of Virginia antiquities. By Mary Newton Stanard, historian A. P. V. A. [Richmond, Va., Print. for the Society by W. E. Jones, 1903?]

8 p. plate. 8°.   LC, VU, WM

Preservation of historical remains at Jamestown by the Association.

2232. [STANDARD OIL CO. OF NEW JERSEY] Know your own state . . . Virginia. [New York, *ca.* 1925]

44, [4] p. illus. (incl. maps) 8°.   LC, V

Points of interest in Virginia for auto tourists.

2233. STANSBURY, CHARLES F. The lake of the Great Dismal, by Charles Frederick Stansbury, with a preface by Don Marquis. New York, Boni, 1925.

xv, 238 p. fold. front. (map) plates, port. 8°.   LC, VU

A well written description of the region, with quotations from preceding writers and indirect reference to economic conditions.

2234. The STATE of Virginia: its geological formation: climate: productions: industries, etc., with a report of its leading educational institutions. Birmingham, International agency, 1873.

46 p. 8°.   VU

2235. [STONE PRINTING & MANUFACTURING CO., Roanoke, Va.] Peaceful scenes: descriptive handbook for travelers over the Norfolk & western railway, containing a brief reflection of the historic

points of interest, and pleasure resorts along the line, together
with a statement of the existing industrial conditions . . .
[Roanoke, Va., Stone] 1898.

130 p. illus. 8°.   (Norfolk & western railway. Virginia resorts.
Pamphlet, 13)   **LC**

2236. STONER, WINIFRED SACKVILLE-. Old Jamestown; a glance at
its history, past and present. [Norfolk, Donaldson] 1904.

14 p. illus. (on front cover) 8°.   **LC**
Concerning the work done to restore Jamestown.

2237. SWANSON, CLAUDE A. Addresses by . . . [the] governor of Virginia, Jamestown Island, May 13, 1907. Jamestown
exposition, June 12, 1907. Richmond, Bottom, 1907.

15 p. 8°.   **V**

2238. TOURISTS' guide for pleasure trips to the summer resorts, sea
bathing and watering places convenient to Baltimore and its vicinity. Baltimore, Hagadorn, 1878.

59 p. front., illus. 24°.   **LC**
Includes Virginia resorts along the Chesapeake.

2239. TOURISTS' illustrated guide to the summer resorts and watering places of East Tennessee and Virginia. Knoxville, Whig &
chronicle print., 1878.

64 p. fold. maps. 8°.   **BP**

2240. TRAVEL, entertainment, and enterprise. Norfolk, Va., Norfolk, Portsmouth & Newport News co. [1903]

32 l., map. obl. 16°.   **NYP**

2241. TUCKER, HENRY S. Address . . . at the opening of the
Jamestown exposition, the ter-centennial celebration of the found-
ing of the first permanent settlement of the English people in
America, on Hampton Roads, Virginia, Apr. 26, 1907. [Norfolk,
Burke & Gregory, 1907]

22 p. 8°.

2242. VALLANDIGHAM, EDWARD N. Delaware and the Eastern
Shore; some aspects of a peninsula pleasant and well beloved . . .
with 80 illustrations. Philadelphia and London, Lippincott, 1922.

3 p. l., 5-329, [1] p. front., plates, fold. map. 8°.   **LC, NYP, V**
Historical and descriptive, with emphasis upon the life of the people.

2243. VALLEY LAND & IMPROVEMENT CO., Luray, Va. The Caverns of Luray. The property of the Valley land & improvement company, Luray, Va. . . . An illustrated guide-book. Philadelphia, Allen, Lane & Scott, 1890.

47 p. map. 8°.   NYP

Ed. of 1893: 50 p.   NYP

2244. VAN HAREN, ETHEL. Mount Vernon mansion, Virginia . . . [San Francisco, *ca.* 1925]

[8] p. illus. 12°.   LC

Brief description of the estate.

2245. VIRGINIA BEACH, Princess Anne County, Virginia. [n. p., 189?-]

[14] p., incl. illus. 12°.   LC

Attractions of the Beach as a pleasure resort.

2246. VIRGINIA BOARD OF TRADE. Report of the president . . . 1st- ; 1903— Richmond, 1903—

8°. Submitted at annual meeting of the Board.

V: 2d (1904).

2247. [VIRGINIA EXPOSITION, 1888] Catalogue of the exhibit of relics and antiquities at the Virginia exposition, Oct. 3-Nov. 21, 1888. Richmond, Jones, 1888.

36 p. 8°.   VU

2248. VIRGINIA MIDLAND RAILWAY. Excursion guide of the Virginia midland railway . . . The Virginia springs, western North Carolina and north Georgia summer resorts. [New York, Aldine press, 1882]

x, 54 p. incl. front., illus., fold. map. 8°.   LC

2249. ———. Summer resorts and points of interest of Virginia, western North Carolina, and north Georgia . . . New York, Crawford, 1884.

95, [5] p. illus., plates, fold. table. 8°.   BP, V

2250. VIRGINIA NAVIGATION CO. Afloat on the James. New York, Giles [*ca.* 1895]

84 p. illus. 12°. **NYP, V**

Description of attractive places of the past and present along the James River.

Ed. of [1897] 84 p. **LC**

Ed. of [1903] 85, [10] p. (Richmond, Dietz) **LC, NYP, V**

Ed. of [1914] 81 p. (Richmond, The Company) **LC**

2251. VIRGINIA STATE CHAMBER OF COMMERCE. . . . Annual report of the managing director . . . Year 1 . . . 1924— Richmond, 1925—

nar. 8°. **NYP:** 1, 3 (1924, 26).

2252. ——. [Documents on state development and the programme of the State chamber of commerce] Richmond, 1925-28.

nar. 8°. **H, NYP, V**

Miscell. doc., no 1: "Constitution and by-laws [of the State chamber of commerce]" (1925); no. 2: "President's report for 1924, presenting 1925 budget" (1925); no. 3: "Shenandoah national park in Virginia" (1925); no. 6: "Accomplishments and objectives [of the State chamber of commerce]" (1925); no. 8: "In old Virginia" (1925); no. 12: "National forests in Virginia. Vacation opportunities" (1926); no. 13: "President's report for 1926, presenting 1927 budget" (1927); no. 15: "Itinerary of Old Northwest. George Rogers Clark visit to Virginia, Nov. 17-19, 1927" (1927); no. 16: "Virginia, old Northwest territory. George Rogers Clark," By R. W. Moore (1927); no. 17: "President's report for 1927, presenting 1928 budget" (1928).

2253. ——. Virginia: historic shrines and scenic attractions, accessible by Virginia historic highway tour. Comp. by the Virginia historic highway association. Lynchburg, Va. [1925]

80 p. illus., maps. 8°. **V**

Guide-book for automobile tourists.

2254. VIRGINIA, TENNESSEE & GEORGIA AIR LINE. The scenic attractions and summer resorts along the railways of the Virginia, Tennessee & Georgia air line, the Shenandoah Valley RR., the Norfolk & western RR., and the East Tennessee, Virginia & Georgia RR. . . . New York, Aldine press, 1883.

80 p. front., illus., maps. 4°. **LC**

2255. WARNER, CHARLES D. On horseback. A tour in Virginia, North Carolina and Tennessee. With notes of travel in Mexico and California . . . Boston & New York, Houghton, Mifflin, 1888.

3 p. l., [3]-331 p. 12°. BP, H, LC, V, VU

Sheds some light upon *post bellum* conditions in Virginia.

2256. WASHINGTON & OHIO RAILROAD CO. The Washington & Ohio railroad. A glance at the country through which it passes, between Washington, D. C., and the Ohio River, a distance of 325 miles. Philadelphia, Collins, 1873.

100 p. 8°. BRE, LC

Includes description of northern and western Virginia.

2257. WASHINGTON CITY, VIRGINIA MIDLAND & GREAT SOUTHERN RAILROAD CO. An account descriptive of the Washington City, Va. midland, and great southern railroad, and of the terminal and intervening cities, towns and counties upon its line . . . Lynchburg, Virginia book and job print., 1874.

71, [3] p. 8°. BRE

2258. WAYLAND, JOHN W. Art folio of the Shenandoah Valley . . . with historical and descriptive sketches; author and publisher: John W. Wayland . . . Harrisonburg, Va. [*ca.* 1924]

[114] p. illus. 4°. LC, NYP, V, VU, WM

2259. ———. A bird's-eye view of the Shenandoah Valley, with map . . . Staunton, McClure, 1924.

15 p. incl. map. 8°. NYP, V, VU, WM

This sketch originally prepared for the United commercial teachers of America.

2260. ———. Historic landmarks of the Shenandoah Valley, beauty and history in the footsteps of Washington, Stonewall Jackson, and Robert E. Lee; author and publisher: John W. Wayland. Harrisonburg, Va. [*ca.* 1924]

[47] p. illus. 4°. LC, NYP, V, VU, WM

Historic spots and modern places of interest briefly described and beautifully illustrated.

2261. ———. . . . . Scenic and historical guide to the Shenandoah Valley; a handbook of useful information for tourists and students . . . Dayton, Va., Ruebush [*ca.* 1923]

2 p. l., 100, [3] p. illus. 8°. LC, NYP, V, VU

2262. WEDDERBURN, ALEXANDER J. Mt. Vernon avenue . . . from the capitol by Grant's statue, Lincoln memorial, over the Memorial bridge, by Arlington, through Alexandria to the tomb of Washington. Pub. by authority Mt. Vernon avenue ass'n. Prepared by Alex. J. Wedderburn. [Washington, D. C., Art pub. co., *ca.* 1913]

[48] p. illus. obl. 8°.   LC

2263. ——. Mount Vernon guide. [2d rev. and improved ed.] Alexandria, Va., Office of Our fireside, 1876.

28 p. illus., 12°.   LC

2264. WISE, KATE E., ed. The Wise guide to historic places in Virginia, 1607-1907 . . . Hampton, Va., Virginian print. [*ca.* 1907]

3 p. l., [11]-125 p. illus., plates. 16°.   LC

Guide-book to tidewater Virginia; published especially for visitors to the Jamestown exposition.

2265. [YOUNG, WILLIAM H.] Journal of an excursion, from Troy, N. Y., to Gen. Carr's headquarters at Wilson's landing, (Fort Pocahontas) on the James River, Va., during the month of May, 1865. By one of the party. Troy, N. Y., Priv. print., 1871.

59 p. 8°.   LC, NYP

Interesting account of conditions in the lower James Valley and Richmond immediately after the cessation of hostilities between North and South; reveals, to some extent, the aftermath of the war.

2266. [ZIMMERMAN, THOMAS C.] The Caverns of Luray, Page County, Va., at Luray station, Shenandoah Valley railroad . . . (Editorial correspondence Reading, Pa., Times and dispatch, June 25th, 1881) One of the greatest natural curiosities in the world— some of its attractions—how it was discovered. [Washington? 1881]

6 p. illus. 8°.   LC

Signed: T. C. Z.

Secondary Works

2267. CAMERON, WILLIAM E. Geography of Virginia. [New York, American book co., 1904]

14 p. illus. (incl. col. map) 4°.   LC

2268. CHANDLER, JULIAN A., *et al.* . . . Virginia, by Julian A. C. Chandler . . . and William L. Foushee . . . New York, Macmillan, 1902.

> viii p., 1 l., 59 p. front. (fold. map) illus. 8°. (Tarr and McMurry geographies. Supplementary vol.) **LC, V**

2269. DAVIS, JANE E. Jamestown and her neighbors on Virginia's historic peninsula . . Richmond, Garrett & Massie [*ca.* 1928]

> ix p., 1 l., 99 p. front., illus. (map) plates, plan. 8°.
> **H, LC, NYP, V, VU**
> "Some of the chapters . . . were included in a book called *Round about Jamestown* . . ." (1907), rev. and enlarged. Contains scattered notes on events since 1865, and on contemporary conditions.

2270. EARLE, SWEPSON. The Chesapeake Bay country . . . Baltimore, Md., Thomsen-Ellis, 1923.

> 510, [2] p. incl. col. front., plates (part col.) ports., map (facsim.) col. fold. map. 8°.
> Historical and descriptive, based upon observations during the author's travels and upon preceding accounts.

2271. [GEOGRAPHY of the Virginias and Carolinas. New York, American book co., *ca.* 1896]

> 14 p. illus., maps. 4°. **LC**

2272. GLASS, E[DWARD] C. Geography of Virginia . . . New York [etc.] American book co. [*ca.* 1898]

> 15-22 p. illus., map. 4°. **LC**

2273. HENNING, JULIA R. Geography of Virginia . . . Richmond, Va., Johnson, 1893.

> 2 p. l., 19, [1] p. 8°. **LC**
> 2d. ed., 1894: 32 p. **LC, V, WM**
> Ed. of 1904. **V**

2274. HOTCHKISS, JED[EDIAH] Geography of Virginia. Richmond, Va., Hoen, 1877.

> 146 p. illus., maps. f°. **VU**

2275. ———. Geography of Virginia, a supplement to the Eclectic series of geographies . . . [Cincinnati] Van Antwerp, Bragg, 1878.

> 16 p. illus., map. f°. **LC, VU**
> Condensed from the author's *Geography of Virginia.* **[2274]**

2276. KERN, MARGARET E. The trail of the three notched road . . . ; silhouette sketches by Margaret Eugénie Kern, map drawn by J. W. Townes, jr. Richmond, Va., William Byrd press, 1928.

> 96 p., 1 l. illus. (incl. plans) double map. 8°.   **LC, VU**
>
> Trail and road leading from Powhatan's Village (east of Richmond) to Staunton. Includes notes on events and incidents since 1865.

2277. KING, GRACE E. Mount Vernon on the Potomac; history of the Mount Vernon ladies' association of the Union . . . New York, Macmillan, 1929.

> xiii, 491 p. front., plates, ports. 8°.
>
> A detailed account of the work of the association, based upon the official records. Part II treats of the period 1874-1927; the restoration of Mt. Vernon through the untiring efforts of the association.

2278. LANCASTER, ROBERT A. Historic Virginia homes and churches . . . with 316 illustrations. Philadelphia & London, Lippincott, 1915.

> xviii, 527 p. incl. illus., plates, front. 8°.   **BP, LC, V, VU, WM**

2279. LOSSING, BENSON J. The home of Washington and its associations, historical, biographical, and pictorial. New ed., rev., with additions . . . Illustrated by numerous engravings, chiefly from original drawings by the author . . . New York, Townsend, 1866.

> 2 p. l., [7]-376 p. front., illus. (incl. plans, facsims.), plates, ports. 8°
> **LC**
>
> First ed., 1859, issued under title: *Mount Vernon and its associations*.

2280. ———. The home of Washington; or, Mount Vernon and its associations, historical, biographical, and pictorial . . . Illustrated by numerous engravings chiefly from original drawings by the author, engraved by Lossing & Barritt. Pub. by subscription only. New York, Virtue & Yorston [*ca.* 1870]

> 2 p. l., [11]-446 p. front., illus. (incl. ports., facsims.) 8°.   **LC, NYP**
>
> The text is essentially that of the first ed. (1859), with additions resulting from the author's visit to Mt. Vernon in 1870.

2281. ———. Mount Vernon, and its associations. Descriptive. Historical and pictorial . . . With 160 illustrations. Engraved on steel and wood, chiefly from original drawings by the author. Cincinnati, Yorston [*ca.* 1886]

1 p. l., 448 p. front., illus. 8°.   **LC**
Ed. of [1882]: 2 p. l., 11-446 p., 1 l.   **NYP**

2282. LOWTHER, MINNIE K. Mount Vernon, Arlington, and Woodlawn; history of these national shrines from the earliest titles of ownership to the present, with biographical sketches, portraits, and interesting reminiscences of the families, who founded them . . . Washington, D. C., Potter, 1922.

xi, [1], 83 p. incl. front., illus. 8°.   **LC**

2283. McGEE, W. J. Geography of Virginia. A supplement to Maury's Manual of geography . . . New York, University pub., 1904.

18 p. illus. (incl. maps) 4°.   **LC, NYP**

2284. MAURY, [MATTHEW F.] Geography of Virginia. A supplement to Maury's Manual of geography. [New York, University pub., 1878]

8 p. illus., map. 4°.   **LC**
Ed. of [1882]: 10 p. incl. col. map.   **LC**

2285. MEAD, EDWARD C. Historic homes of the South-West mountains, Virginia; . . . with 23 illustrations and a map. Philadelphia & London, Lippincott, 1899.

3 p. l., 5-275 p. front., 2 plates, fold. map. 8°. **BP, LC, NYP, V, VU**
Contains notes on conditions and changes of ownership of the homes since 1865; historic houses in Albemarle County included.

2286. MONSEES, CARL H. The historic peninsula of Delaware, Maryland and Virginia . . . Snow Hill, Md. [*ca.* 1927]

1 p. l., 15 plates, fold. map. 4°.   **LC, V**
"The places herein pictured are described in *The Chesapeake Bay country*, by Swepson Earle [**2270**], and *The entailed hat,* by Geo. Alfred Townsend."

2287. OFFICIAL blue book of the Jamestown ter-centennial exposition, A. D. 1907. The only authorized history of the celebration . . . Norfolk, Va., Colonial pub. co. [*ca.* 1909]

viii, 806 p. incl. illus., plates., ports. f°. **BP, NYP, V, VU, WM**

2288. PAGE, THOMAS N. Mount Vernon and its preservation, 1858-1910; the acquisition, restoration, and care of the home of Wash-

ington by the Mount Vernon ladies' association of the Union for
over half a century . . . [New York, Knickerbocker press,
ca. 1910]

> xi, 84 p. front., plates, ports. (part col.) 12°.   **BP, LC, V**

2289. PATTON, JOHN S., *et al.* Monticello and its master, by John S.
Patton and Sallie J. Doswell. Charlottesville, Va., Michie [*ca.*
1925]

> 78 p. incl. front. (port.) illus. 12°.   **H, LC, NYP, V, VU**
> Advertisements in back.
> Ch. XI is concerned with the Thomas Jefferson memorial foundation,
> which purchased Monticello.

2290. PLECKER, WALTER A.   The climate of tidewater Virginia
. . . [New York? 1907?]

> 11, [1] p. 12°.   **V**
> Reprint from *New York medical record*, Aug. 27, 1907.

2291. SMITH, EDWARD E.   The state of Virginia . . . Boston,
New York [etc.] Ginn [*ca.* 1923]

> 34 p. illus., map. 4°.   **LC, V**
> Supplement to *New geography*, bk. 2, of the Freye-Atwood geograph-
> ical series.

2292. SURFACE, GEORGE T.   Studies on the geography of Virginia
. . . [Philadelphia] 1907.

> [53] p. fold. map. 8°.   **BP, H, LC, NYP, VU**
> Thesis (Ph.D.), University of Pennsylvania, 1907.
> Chapters on geographic influence upon economic history, physiogra-
> phy of Virginia, climate and boundaries, racial and regional study of pop-
> ulation, Virginia trade and commerce; all based upon reliable source ma-
> terial.

2293. TOWNSEND, GEORGE A. Monticello and its preservation, since
Jefferson's death, 1826-1902. Correspondence of George Alfred
Townsend, "Gath". [Washington, D. C., Gibson, 1902]

> 56 p. front., plate, port. 8°.   **BP, H, LC, VU, WM**

2294. TRAVELERS' PROTECTIVE ASSOCIATION OF AMERICA. VIRGINIA
DIVISION. . . . Historical review of the T. P. A. since date of
organization. Industrial and commercial history of Virginia
. . . [n. p., 1913]

> 176 p. illus. (ports.) 4°.   **V**

2295. WILSTACH, PAUL. Jefferson and Monticello . . . Garden
City, N. Y., Doubleday, Page, 1925.

> 3 p. l., vii-xiii, 258 p. front., plates, ports, plans, facsim. 8°.
> Chs. 14-15 on Monticello from 1826 to 1925, and Jefferson's neighbor-
> hood to-day.

2296. ———. Mount Vernon, Washington's home, and the nation's
shrine . . . Garden City, N. Y., Doubleday, Page, 1916.

> xvi, [4]-301, [1] p. front., plates, ports., map, plan, facsims. 8°.
> Authentic history of Mt. Vernon, well written; with an account of the
> estate since Washington's death.

2297. ———. Potomac landings, by Paul Wilstach . . . photographs by Roger B. Whitman and others. Garden City, N. Y., and
Toronto, Doubleday, Page, 1921.

> xii p., 1 l., 376 p. front. (fold. map) plates, ports. 8°.
> Ch. 18 is a description of the river as the author found it.

Periodicals

2298. The JAMESTOWN bulletin. v. 1-4, v. 5, no. 1-5; June 16, 1904-
May, 1909. Norfolk, Va. [The Woman's Jamestown association,
etc.] 1904-09.

> 5 v. illus. 4°. monthly.
> No numbers issued Aug.-Dec., 1904, Feb.-Mar., 1905.
> Ed. by Mrs. F. A. Walke, *et al.*
> Devoted to the interests of the Jamestown exposition.
> **BP**: I-II; III, 1-9, 11-12; IV, 2, 5-7, 10; V, 1-4. **LC**: I-V, 5. **NYP**:
> I-II; III-IV (imperf.); V, 1-5. **V**: I-V, 5.

2299. . . . JAMESTOWN magazine . . . v. 1-2; June, 1906-
Dec., 1907. Norfolk, Va., A. Hess [1906]-07.

> 2 v. illus. (incl. ports.) 8°. monthly.
> Official organ of the Jamestown exposition.
> **LC**: I-II. **NYP**: I, 1, 4, 6-7, 9-12. **VU**: I, 2-12. **WM**: I; II, 2.

2300. The JAMESTOWN ter-centennial. A magazine devoted to the
interests of the Jamestown exposition, 1907. Richmond, Va.,
Walsh & Via, 1904-[?]

> 8°.   **V**: I, 1-3 (May-Aug., 1904).

2301. [1090] The PILOT. Vol. 1- [?] New York [1891?- ?]

2302. The SOUTHERN homeseeker and investor's guide. [v. 1- .?]
Roanoke, Va., Norfolk & western railway [19-? - ?]
8°. quarterly.   **V**: 1914-17.

2303. The SOUTHLAND magazine. A magazine for the South.
[v. 1- ; 1903?—   ] Norfolk, Va. [1903?—
Issued irreg.   **NYP**: VI-VIII; 1908-10 (imperf.).

2304. VIRGINIA first in the heart of the nation; published by Virginia
State chamber of commerce. v. 1, no. 1- ; Spring, 1926—
Richmond, Va., 1926—
    illus. 4°. quarterly.
    Contains attractive articles on the state's progress and development;
well illustrated.
    H: I-III (1926/27-28). **V**: I-III. **VU**: I, 1-3; II-III.

    For further references on Description and Travel, see above, Pt. II, § 4:
    Transportation and Communication.

3. POPULATION, RACE RELATIONS, IMMIGRATION

Government Publications and Documents

2305. DU BOIS, WILLIAM E. The Negroes of Farmville, Virginia:
a social study . . . [Washington, Govt., 1898]
    p. 1-38. 8°. (In U. S. Bur. of labor. *Bulletin*, 14; Jan., 1898)
    Study of Negro life in a town where conditions typified those of the
Negro in Virginia in general.

2306. FRISSELL, HOLLIS B., *et al.* . . . Dietary studies of Negroes in eastern Virginia in 1897 and 1898. By H. B. Frissell
. . . and Isabel Bevier . . . Washington, Govt., 1899.
    45 p. plates. 8°. (U. S. Dept. of agriculture. Office of experiment
stations. *Bulletin*, 71)
    Studies confined to families living in the Dismal Swamp region. Value
of conclusions lessened by very limited number of studies made.

2307. [1955] NEGRO REFORMATORY ASSOCIATION OF VIRGINIA. . . .
Annual report . . . [n. p., 189-? -19—
    See also items **[1956-1957]**

2308. [2071] RICHMOND, WESTMORELAND, LANCASTER, AND NORTH-
UMBERLAND COUNTIES, VA. BOARD OF IMMIGRATION. The North-
ern Neck of Virginia as a home for immigrants . . . New
York, 1872.

2309. [89] SCARBOROUGH, W. S. Tenancy and ownership among
Negro farmers in Southampton County, Virginia . . . Washington, 1926.

2310. [339] THOM, WILLIAM T. The Negroes of Litwalton, Va.:
a social study of the "oyster Negro." Washington, 1901.

2311. [2072] TOCHMAN, G. Emigration to the U. S. . . .
New York, 1869.

2312. [115] VIRGINIA. AGRICULTURE AND IMMIGRATION, Dept. of.
. . . Hand-book of Virginia . . . Richmond [1876-19—

2313. [1995] ———. HEALTH, Dept. of. VITAL STATISTICS, Bur.
of. [New family series . . . Richmond, 1921-25]
   no. 4: Eugenics in relation to the new family, and law on racial integrity (1924).

2314. [2078] ———. IMMIGRATION, Board of. The state of Virginia to the people of Great Britain. [n. p., 1866]
   See also items [2079-2081]

Other Source Material

2315. BRUCE, PHILIP A. . . . The plantation Negro as a freeman; observations on his character, condition, and prospects in
Virginia . . . New York [etc.] Putnam, 1889.
   ix, 262 p. 8°. (Questions of the day, LVII)
   Frank statement of opinion based upon personal observation and con-
   tact with the Negro.

2316. BUFORD, PATTIE. [Three series of letters and a magazine article giving an account of her work among the Negroes in Virginia]
[New York, 1880?-82]
   4 pts. in 1 v. 8°.   **BP**

2317. COLORED STATE FAIR, Richmond, Va.   Catalogue and premium list . . . Richmond, Va., Oct. 24-29, 1910. [Richmond, 1910]

26 p. 8°.   **V**

2318. HAMPTON NEGRO CONFERENCE. Annual report, Hampton Negro conference.   no. 2- ; July, 1898-19—   Hampton, Va., Hampton institute press [1898]-19—

illus. 8°.

The report of the first conference, July, 1897, is contained in the *Southern workman,* XXVI, 9; Sept., 1897.

Title varies: Hampton Negro conference, 1898-1901; Proceedings of the Hampton Negro conference, 1902-04; Annual report, Hampton Negro conference, 1905—   (printed as numbers of the *Hampton bulletin*)
LC: 2-16 (1898-1912); **V**: 1903, 09-10, 12.

2319. JAMES RIVER VALLEY IMMIGRATION SOCIETY. Chartered Aug. 11, 1888. Officers . . . directors . . . Richmond, Baughman, 1888.

18 p. 12°.   **NYP**

2320. JORDAN, BOOKER L.   Practical talk to agents of the Southern aid society of Va. (incorporated), rev.— July, 1909, by B. L. Jordan . . . Richmond, Va., Mitchell, 1909.

4 p. l.,[7]-56 p. front., plates, ports. 16°.   **LC**

An interesting publication, presumably by Negroes, with instructions to insurance agents of the Society.

2321. KNIGHTS OF PYTHIAS, E. & W. H. VIRGINIA GRAND LODGE (COLORED).   Proceedings . . . [1st- ; 1892?— n. p., 1892?—

8°.   **V**: 11th (1902).

2322. LANGSTON NATIONAL MONUMENT, HISTORICAL AND EMANCIPATION ASSOCIATION OF VIRGINIA.   Souvenir journal of the 35th national emancipation celebration, at Culpeper, Va., Thursday, Sept. 22d, 1898, under auspices of the Langston national monument, historical and emancipation association, of Virginia (incorporated) . . . Comp. by Rev. Robt. B. Robinson . . . [Alexandria? Va., M. L. Robinson? 1898]

20 p. ports. 8°.   **LC**

2323. [438] MAURY, MATTHEW F. [Letter book, 1868-69]

2324. [1610] MILLHISER, CHARLES. Various addresses of interest to the community . . . [*viz.,* the Jews of Richmond] [Richmond?] 1923.

2325. MITCHELL, JOHN, jr. Sketch of the life of George Williams, jr. [colored], founder of Virginia industrial, mercantile, building and loan association. Embracing also the charter, prospectus, as well as some of the advantages obtained by those who hold stock in the association. By the editor of the "Richmond planet" . . . [Richmond? 1891?]

  21 p. 12°.   **V**
  A Negro company.

2326. [1507] NORFOLK EMANCIPATION ASSOCIATION. Emancipation celebration . . . Norfolk, 1925.

2326a. ODD-FELLOWS, Grand united order of. VIRGINIA. DISTRICT GRAND LODGE. Report of the 20th annual session . . . of the District grand lodge of Virginia, held in Pine St. A. M. E. church, Suffolk, Va., Sept. 18 . . . [to] 20, 1900. Recorded, compiled, and arranged by M. V. P. Wm. M. T. Forrester, district grand secretary. Richmond, Va., 1900.

  84 p. 8°.   **V**

2327. PATTESON, CAMM. The young bachelor; with an appendix, containing an essay on "The destiny of the Negro in America" . . . Lynchburg, Va., Bell, 1900.

  119 p. front. (port.) 12°.   **LC, VU**
  Object of the author is, in part, "to describe the state of *quasi* war which existed for nearly ten years after . . . [the Civil war]" The appendix treats the Negro problem in a dispassionate manner, from a southern point of view.

2328. POLISH EMIGRATION LAND CO. IN VIRGINIA. By-laws, charter, prospectus, and *odezwa* [announcement] (in Polish language) of the Polish emigration land co. in Virginia. Washington, P. L. Schriftgiesser, 1870.

  35 p. 24°.   **LC**
  A rare pamphlet of "boom literature" to attract immigrants to Virginia, with special reference to land in Amherst, Bedford, and Rockbridge counties.

2329. [1429] RIDDICK, J. HUDSON.   The Danville riot . . .
Baltimore, 1884.

2330. ROYALL, WILLIAM L.   A reply to "A fool's errand, by one of
the fools."   New York, Hall, 1880.

> 95 p. 8°.   **BP, NYP, V**
>
> An attempt to correct certain misrepresentations concerning the atti-
> tude of the South towards the Negro after the Civil war, and the gen-
> eral character of social conditions in Virginia and the South.

2331. [2045] SMYTH, JOHN H.   Negro delinquent children in Virginia . . . [n. p., 1898?]

2332. [SOUTHERN SETTLEMENT SOCIETY]   Plan of the Southern settlement society, incorporated by the State of Virginia, 1874. [n. p.,
n. d.]

> 8 p. 8°.   **VU**

2333. STATE IMMIGRATION CONVENTION, Richmond, Va.   Proceedings of the State immigration convention, held under the auspices
of the Virginia agricultural and mechanical society, at the Chamber
of commerce assembly room, Richmond, Virginia, Oct. 16-17, 1894.
Richmond, Va., Whittet & Shepperson, 1895.

> 85, [2] p. 8°.   **LC, USC, V**
>
> At this convention the Immigration association of Virginia was formed.

2334. [247] SURRY COUNTY NEGRO FARMERS, FAIR ASSOCIATION.
Catalogue of the . . . annual exhibition . . . [n. p.,
1915—

2335. [1684] The TUESDAY CLUB, Richmond.   Fourth annual May
music festival . . . Richmond, 1909.

2336. UNITED ORDER OF TRUE REFORMERS.   GRAND FOUNTAIN OF
VIRGINIA.   Minutes of the . . . annual session.   Richmond,
Va., Reformer print. [1881?-19—

> illus. 8°.   **V**: 25th, 28th (1905, 08).
>
> A Negro lodge.

2337. ———. ———.   The revised constitution of the United order of
true reformers, of the state of Virginia. [Richmond? Va., *ca.*
1887]

> 36 p. 16°.   **LC**

2338. ———. ———. ROSEBUD DEPT. Minutes of the Reformers union rosebud nursery convention, Southern grand division . . . Convened in True reformers' hall, Richmond, Va. [n. p., 1906?—

illus., ports. 8°.   **V**: 2d, 4th (1907, 09).

Negro lodge for improving the status and character of the race.

2339. [258] VIRGINIA LAND AGENCY, Petersburg, Va. Established 1865. [Petersburg, 1886]

2340. WILLIAMS, DANIEL B. Emancipation address. Our duties and how to discharge them. Delivered in the town hall of Salem, Va., Jan. 2, 1893, under the auspices of the Emancipation club of Salem, with which was joined the Emancipation club of Roanoke, Va. . . . [n. p., 1893?]

28 p. front. (port.) 12°.   **V**

Secondary Works

2341. [278] BITTING, SAMUEL T. . . . Rural land ownership among the Negroes of Virginia . . . [Charlottesville, 1915]

2342. BROWN, WILLIAM H. . . . The education and economic development of the Negro in Virginia . . . [Charlottesville, Va., Surber-Arundale, 1923?]

150 p., 1 l. illus. (maps) diagr. 8°. (University of Virginia. *Phelps-Stokes fellowship papers,* VI)

Impartial, scholarly study, showing the improvement of the Negro economically and socially. Chs. 4-9 on the period since 1860.

2343. [1825] CHILDS, BENJAMIN G. . . . The Negroes of Lynchburg, Virginia . . . Charlottesville, 1923.

2344. DOGGETT, ALLEN B., jr. . . . Three Negro communities in tidewater Virginia . . . Hampton, Va., Normal and agricultural institute, 1912.

46 p. illus. 8°. (*Hampton bulletin,* XIX, 4)

Describes economic and social conditions in Little Forks community, Nansemond County; in Ebenezer community, Southampton County; and in Ruthville community, Charles City County.

2345. Ezekiel, Herbert T., *et al.* History of the Jews of Richmond, 1769-1917, by Herbert T. Ezekiel and Gaston Lichtenstein. Richmond, Ezekiel, 1917.

374 p. 8°.   BP, LC, NYP, VU, WM

Most of the material on the period since 1865 is in the form of annals, which reveal the social activities of the Jews.

2346. ———. World war section of The history of the Jews of Richmond, by Herbert T. Ezekiel and Gaston Lichtenstein. Richmond, Va., Ezekiel, 1920.

2 p. l., p. [381]-443. 8°.   LC, NYP, V

Based upon contemporary records and source material gathered during and immediately after the war. Includes lists of Richmond Jews who served in the war; a soldier's diary; and brief articles on war activities in Richmond.

2347. [279] Gee, Wilson, *et al.* Rural depopulation in certain tidewater and piedmont areas of Virginia. By Wilson Gee . . . and John J. Corson, 3d . . . [Charlottesville] 1929.

2348. [1846] Knight, Charles L. . . . Negro housing in certain Virginia cities . . . Richmond, 1927.

2349. McAllister, Joseph T. Humor in ebony . . . Virginia Hot Springs, Va., Homestead news stand [*ca.* 1911]

44 p. illus. 8°.   LC, V

Stories and anecdotes of Negro life and character in Virginia.

2350. McConnell, John P. Negroes and their treatment in Virginia from 1865 to 1867 . . . Pulaski, Va., B. D. Smith [*ca.* 1910]

3 p. l., 126 p. 8°.   H, LC, V, VU

Portrays the political and racial antagonism resulting from the reconstruction acts.

2351. Morton, Richard L. The Negro in Virginia politics, 1865-1902 . . . [Charlottesville? Va., 1919]

1 p. l., [5]-199 p. fold. maps. 8°. (University of Virginia. *Phelps-Stokes fellowship papers,* IV)

Thesis (Ph.D), University of Virginia, 1918.

Unbiased account; economic factors discussed chiefly in connection with state finance.

2352. [1131] Pinchbeck, Raymond B. . . . The Virginia Negro artisan and tradesman . . . Richmond, 1926.

2353. SCHURICHT, HERMANN. History of the German element in Virginia . . . Baltimore, Kroh, 1898-1909.

2 v. in 1. port. 8°.

Vol. II on the 19th century contains valuable material on German immigration, rural life, patriotic celebrations, industry, etc. The author is biased very perceptibly and his history is not always accurate.

2354. [1388] SNAVELY, TIPTON R. . . . The taxation of Negroes in Virginia . . . [Charlottesville, 1916]

2355. SURFACE, GEORGE T. Racial and regional study of the Virginia population . . . [New York, 1907]

p. 285-291. 8°. (In Amer. geographical society. Bulletin, XXXIX, 5; May, 1907)

Printed also in the author's Studies on the Geography of Virginia. **[2292]**

2356. TAYLOR, ALRUTHEUS A. The Negro in the reconstruction of Virginia . . . Washington, D. C., Association for the study of Negro life and history [ca. 1926]

iv, 300 p. 8°.

The story of reconstruction in Virginia rewritten to give proper perspective and emphasis to the part played by the Negro. Sheds new light upon this controversial period of the state's history.

Periodicals

2357. The FREEDMAN'S friend. [v. 1- ; 1909?—] Cambria, Va., Printed by the Christianburg industrial institute press [1909?—

8°. quarterly.   LC: XIII, 2 (1921).

2358. The SOUTHERN workman. v. 1- [1873?-19—] Hampton, Va., Hampton institute press [1873?-19—

illus. 8°.-4°. monthly.

Founded by Gen. Samuel C. Armstrong in 1872 and published by the Hampton normal and agricultural institute.

Title varies: The Southern workman and Hampton school record, ante 1900.

The magazine is "devoted to the interests of undeveloped races." Provides a forum for discussion of ethnological, sociological, and educational problems.

BP: XV-LVIII (1886-1929). H: I-LVIII (1873-1929). LC: II-IV, VI-LVIII (1873-75, 77-1929). NYP: V, 10; VIII, 4; IX, 12; X,

1-5; XIII, 7-12; XIV, 8-9; XV, 2-7, 9-10, 12; XVI, 1-6; XVIII, 2; XIX-XX; XXI, 1-11; XXII, 1-11; XXIII-LVIII; (1876, 79-81, 86-87, 89-1929). **USAg:** XXVIII-LVIII (1899-1929). **USE:** XXIV-XXXVIII (1895-1909). **USL:** XXIX, XXXI-LIV (1900, 02-25). **V:** XXIII-LVIII (1894-1929). **VU:** XL, 2; XLI-XLVI; XLVIII-LVIII; (Feb., 1911; 1912-17, 19-29). **WM:** XLV-LVI (1916-25).

For further references on Population, Race Relations, and Immigration, see above, Pt. II, § 7: *Urban and County Development;* also Pt. III, § 2: *Description and Travel.* See also, Pt. VI, § 3, under title: *Hampton normal and agricultural institute.*

4. SOCIAL LIFE AND CUSTOMS

Government Publications and Documents

2359. CRAIGHILL, WILLIAM P. Annual report upon building monument at Yorktown, Va., by William P. Craighill, lieutenant-colonel of engineers, U. S. A. . . . Washington, Govt., [18-? -?]

fold. maps. 8°.   **V:** 1882, 83.

2360. U. S. CONGRESS. HOUSE. RULES, Committee on. Public ownership of Monticello. Hearings before the Committee on rules of the House of representatives on S. Con. res. 24, . . . July 24, 1912 . . . Washington, Govt., 1912.

78 p. 8°.   **LC**

Robert L. Henry, chairman.
Statement of Mrs. Martin W. Littleton of New York City.

2361. ———. ———. ———. ———. Purchase of Monticello. Hearings on H. J. res. 390, H. J. res. 418, and a substitute therefor. Washington, Govt., 1915.

16 p. 8°.   **LC**

Text of resolutions and substitute statements of Jefferson M. Levy and Mrs. Martin W. Littleton, Feb. 23, 1915, with certain correspondence.

2362. ———. ———. SENATE. LIBRARY, Committee on the. Public ownership of Monticello. Hearing before the Committee on the Library, U. S. Senate, 62d Congress, 2d session, on S. J. res. 92, a joint resolution providing for the purchase of the home of Thomas

Jefferson, at Monticello, Virginia . . . Washington, Govt., 1912.

    57 p. 8°.   **LC, NYP**
    George P. Wetmore, chairman.
    Statement of Mrs. Martin W. Littleton of New York, July 9, 1912.

2363. ——. ——. ——. PUBLIC BUILDINGS AND GROUNDS, Committee on. Purchase of Monticello. Hearing before the subcommittee of the Committee on public buildings and grounds, U. S. Senate, 64th Congress, 2d session, on S. J. res. 153, a bill directing the secretary of the Treasury to acquire by purchase the estate known as Monticello, in the state of Virginia, including the former home of Thomas Jefferson and lands surrounding the same, being about 700 acres, said property being located in Albemarle County, Va. Jan. 9, 1917 . . . Washington, Govt., 1917.

    26 p. 8°.   **LC**
    Claude A. Swanson, chairman.

2364. ——. YORKTOWN CENTENNIAL COMMISSION. General programme of ceremonies at the dedication of the Yorktown monument. Washington, Govt., 1881.

    [3] p. 8°.   **LC**

2365. ——. ——. [Invitation to the Yorktown centennial celebration . . . New York, Amer. bank note co., 1881]

    1 l. 8°.   **LC**

2366. ——. ——. Official programme of the Yorktown centennial celebration. Oct. 18 . . . [to] 21, 1881 . . . Pub. by authority of the . . . commission, by F. T. Wilson. Washington, 1881.

    xiv, 154 p. illus. 8°.   **LC, NYP**

2367. ——. ——. Report of the . . . commission in accordance with a joint resolution of Congress, approved Mar. 3, 1881, providing for the erection of a monument at Yorktown, Va., commemorative of the surrender of Lord Cornwallis. Washington, Govt., 1883.

    169 p. plates. 8°. (U. S. 47 Cong., 2 sess. Senate. *Report,* 1003)
                                                 LC, NYP

2368. VIRGINIA. COMMISSION ON CELEBRATION OF THE 300TH AN-NIVERSARY OF THE FIRST LEGISLATIVE ASSEMBLY IN AMERICA. 300th anniversary of the first law-making body on the western hemisphere, which convened at Jamestown, July 30, 1619. Celebration held . . . Aug. 15, 1919. [n. p., 1919?]

[8] p. illus., facsim., ports. 4°.   **V**

2369. ———. GENERAL ASSEMBLY. Order of exercises and addresses at the celebration of the 300th anniversary of the first law making body on the western hemisphere which convened at Jamestown, July 30, 1619. House of delegates. Richmond, Aug. 15, 1919. Jamestown, 1619-1699. Williamsburg, 1699-1780. Richmond, 1780-1919. [Richmond? 1919?]

35 p. front., illus., plates (1 col.) ports., fascism. 8°.   **LC, NYP, V**

2370. ———. ———. GENERAL HENRY LEE, Committee on reinterring the remains of. Report of the committee appointed under act of the General assembly approved Mar. 12, 1912, for the purpose of reinterring the remains of General Henry Lee—"Light-horse Harry" Lee—at Lexington, Virginia. Richmond, Va., Whittet & Shepperson [1913?]

[8] p. illus., ports. 8°.   **LC, V**
Hugh A. White, chairman.

2371. ———. GETTYSBURG MONUMENT COMMISSION. Ceremonies attending the dedication of the Virginia memorial on the battlefield of Gettysburg, Friday, June 8, 1917, at two o'clock. [Richmond, Va., Waddey, 1917]

48 p. front., plates, ports. 4°.   **LC, NYP, V, VU**

2372. ———. GOVERNOR, 1906-10 (Claude A. Swanson). Proclamation. 100th anniversary of the birth of Jefferson Davis, June 3, 1908. [Richmond, 1908]

broadside & port. 8°.   **V**

2373. ———. MOUNT VERNON, Board of visitors to. Report . . . Richmond [18-?-19—

front., port., maps. 8°.   **LC, NYP, V, VU**: 1901.
See also: Virginia. *Annual reports* of officers, boards and institutions . . . of Virginia, 1874-75, 90-93, 95. **[101]**

Other Source Material

2374. ALDERMAN, EDWIN A.   Virginia, by Edwin Anderson Alderman.   New York, Scribner's, 1916.

> 3 p. l., 57 numb. l. front. (5 port.) 12°.   **LC, NYP, USE, V**
> "An address delivered in response to the toast 'Virginia' at the banquet given by the citizens of Petersburg, Virginia, to the president of the U. S. and the governor of Pennsylvania, on May 19, 1909."

2375. [ALLAN-OLNEY, MARY]   The new Virginians, by the author of 'Junia' [etc.]   . . .   Edinburgh and London, Blackwood, 1880.

> 2 v. 8°.   **LC, VU**
> Realistic picture of life in rural Virginia, near the Blue Ridge, in the 'seventies; written in the form of letters.

2376. [AMERICAN SCENIC AND HISTORIC PRESERVATION SOCIETY]   . . .   Monticello, Virginia.   Statements on both sides of the controversy concerning the proposed public ownership of the home of Thomas Jefferson.   Albany, N. Y., 1914.

> p. 517-541.   8°.   (In its *19th annual report*, 1914, Appendix F)
>   **LC, NYP, V**

2377. ANDREWS, MRS. MARIETTA M.   Memoirs of a poor relation; being the story of a post-war southern girl and her battle with destiny, by Marietta Minnigerode Andrews   . . .   New York, Dutton [*ca.* 1927]

> 3 p. l., ix-xiv p., 3 l., 3-455 p. front., plates, ports. 8°.   **H, LC, NYP, VU**
> Written in entertaining style, the narrative reveals economic and social conditions among some of the leading families of Virginia during the latter decades of the 19th century.

2378. AVARY, MRS. MYRTA L.   Dixie after the war; an exposition of social conditions existing in the South, during the twelve years succeeding the fall of Richmond.   By Myrta Lockett Avary   . . .   With an introduction by General Clement A. Evans; illustrated from old painting, daguerreotypes and rare photographs.   New York, Doubleday, Page, 1906.

> 5 p. l., [ix]-x, 435 p. front. plates, ports. 8°.   **LC, NYP, V, VU**
> A southern woman's experiences and observations in Virginia and South Carolina during reconstruction; also material by other participants.

2379. BALTIMORE AGRICULTURAL AID SOCIETY. Report of the secretary of the Baltimore agricultural aid society. Dec. 23, 1865. Baltimore, Murphy, 1865.

23 p. 8°.   LC, V

Relief for the stricken people of the South, especially of Virginia, with letters from county agents on the benefits derived from the Society's work.

2380. [159] BARBOUR, B. JOHNSON. Address before the annual meeting of the Virginia agricultural society, Oct. 27, 1875. [n. p., 1875?]

2381. BARRY, HERBERT. Our individual responsibility as to national preparedness. Address . . . in Madison Hall, University of Virginia, Charlottesville, Va., Apr. 15, 1916. New York [National security league, 1916]

18 p. 8°.   BP

2382. BEALE, CYRUS W., comp. Kappa alphas in Richmond, Virginia; some Virginia Kappa alphas, 1915 . . . including biographical sketch of Kappa alphas in Richmond with summary of chapter membership, vicinity Kappa alphas, members of active chapters in Virginia, and a state Kappa alpha reference list . . . [Richmond, Whittet & Shepperson] 1915.

73 p., 1 l. 8°.   LC, V

2383. BENSON, C[ORNELIUS] H. "Yank and "Reb"; a history of a fraternal visit paid by Lincoln post, no. 11, G. A. R., of Newark, N. J., to Robt. E. Lee camp, no. 1, Confederate veterans and Phil. Kearney post, no. 10, G. A. R. of Richmond, Va., Oct. 15 to Oct. 18, inclusive. By Comrade C. H. Benson . . . Newark, Neuhut, 1884.

124 p. 12°.   LC, V

Reveals the forces at work for the restoration of amity between North and South; with some light on economic and social conditions in Virginia.

2384. BLOW, MRS. A. A. An address delivered before the Daughters of the American revolution at their congress held in Washington, D. C., April, 1905, by Mrs. A. A. Blow, of Virginia, chairman John Smith monument committee of the Association for the preservation of Virginia antiquities. [n. p., n. d.]

8 p. 8°.   LC, V, VU

2385. BLUE RIDGE ROD AND GUN CLUB, inc. Charter, members, by-laws and rules . . . Washington, [D. C.] 19—

front., illus. 12°. **LC**: 1909, 16.

2386. BRADLEY, ARTHUR G. Other days, recollections of rural England and old Virginia, 1860-1880, by A. G. Bradley. London, Constable, 1913.

xi, 427, [1] p. front. (port.) 8°. **H, LC, NYP, V, VU**

Valuable light on social conditions in Virginia during the 'seventies, from the observations of an Englishman on the plantations and in the mountains.

2387. BRECKINRIDGE, WILLIAM C. "The ex-Confederate, and what he has done in peace." An address delivered before the Association of the Army of northern Virginia at the meeting held in Richmond, Va., Oct. 26, 1892, by Hon. Wm. C. P. Breckinridge . . . Printed by order of the association. Richmond, Hill, 1892.

22 p. 8°. **H, LC, V**

An exaggerated sketch of the extent to which the South was rebuilt, economically and educationally, by the early 'nineties.

2388. CLAIBORNE, JOHN II. Seventy-five years in old Virginia; with some account of the life of the author and some history of the people among whom his lot was cast,—their character, their condition, and their conduct before the war, during the war and after the war . . . New York & Washington, Neale, 1904.

xvi, [17], 360 p. 2 port. (incl. front.) 8°.

Describes conditions in Virginia and North Carolina after the Civil war.

2389. The CONFEDERATE dead. Memorial day at Elmwood cemetery, Norfolk, Virginia . . . June 18, 1884. Norfolk, Va., Norfolk landmark [1884?]

19 p. 8°. **V**

2390. CONFEDERATE leaders and other citizens request the House of delegates [of Virginia] to repeal the resolution of respect to Abraham Lincoln, the barbarian . . . [n. p., 1928]

16 p. 8°. **VU**

Letters from Virginians requesting that the resolution to honor the birthday of Lincoln be repealed and expunged from the records of the Virginia House of delegates.

2391. [CONFEDERATE MEMORIAL ASSOCIATION] . . . The South's battle abbey. Atlanta, Ga., Respress co. [1896?]

[3]-32 p. 8°.   LC

Pamphlet promoting the campaign to raise money for the erection of a Confederate memorial institute, as proposed by Charles B. Rouss. Cf. G. L. Christian, *Sketch of the origin and erection of the Confederate memorial institute at Richmond, Virginia* . . . (1921) **[1827]**

2392. CRINGAN, MRS. JOHN W. Instruction in cooking: with selected receipts . . . Richmond, Hill, 1895.

323 p. front., diagr. 8°.   V

2393. CURRY, J[ABEZ] L. Lessons of the Yorktown centennial. Address of the Hon. J. L. M. Curry, . . . delivered in Richmond, on 22d October, 1881, by request of the City council. Richmond, Dispatch steam print., 1881.

24 p. 8°.   LC, NYP, V

The address is prefaced by resolutions of the Richmond Common council in preparation for the centennial; also by a brief description and programme of the celebration.

2394. DAUGHTERS OF THE AMERICAN REVOLUTION. VIRGINIA. Proceedings of the . . . Virginia state conference . . . [Wytheville, etc., 1897?-19—

8°. **LC:** 13th, 26-28th, 30th-31st (1909, 22-24, 26-27); **V:** 2d-4th, 8th-21st, 23d-30th (1898-1900, 04-17, 19-26); **VU:** 14th, 16th (1910, 12); **WM:** 27-28th (1923-24).

2395. [DAVIDSON papers] [Papers of James D. Davidson and his son, Charles A., of Lexington, Va., 1865-85]

MSS.   McC

As a result of the wide law practice of the Davidsons, the MSS. contain information on legal, economic and general social conditions; some papers on political matters and a few on religious activity; some information on reconstruction in Virginia. The Davidsons were interested in the development of transportation in the state; they were agents for insurance companies and had a trustee interest in Washington and Lee University and in the Western state hospital at Staunton.

2396. DOVE, JOHN. The Virginia text-book: containing a history of Masonic grand lodges, and the constitution of Masonry, or Ahiman rezon: together with a digest of the laws, rules, and regulations of the Grand lodge of Virginia; also, a complete compilation of the illustrations of Masonic work, as drawn from

Preston, Webb, Read, and others . . . 3d. Ed. Richmond, Goode, 1866.

xii, [13]-380 p. front. (port.) illus. 12°.   **V**
4th ed., 1877.   **WM**
5th ed., 1889.   **WM**

2397. FLEMING, MARY E. Emergency helps for housekeepers and others, by Mrs. G. W. Fleming. Lynchburg, Bell, 1906.

231 p. 12°.   **LC, V**

2398. [1431] FREDERICKSBURG AND ADJACENT NATIONAL BATTLE-FIELDS MEMORIAL PARK ASSOCIATION. Fredericksburg . . . park association . . . Fredericksburg, 1899.

2399. FREEMASONS. VIRGINIA. GRAND LODGE. Proceedings of the . . . grand annual communication . . . Richmond [1778?-19—

ports. 16°-8°. Title varies slightly.
LC: 108-109th, 114-115th, 120th-123d, 130-136th, 138-150th (1885-86, 91-92, 97-1900, 08-14, 16-28); **NYP:** 1866, 68-73, 76-80, 83-1903, 05-28; **V:** 1864-66, 67-68, 72, 74-75, 77-83, 85-97, 99-1903, 05-14, 16-18, 20-24, 26.

2400. ——. ——. ——. Proceedings of the special communication of the most worshipful Grand lodge of Virginia at Yorktown, on the 17th and 18th days of October, 1881. Richmond, Goode, 1881.

77 p. 8°.   **LC, NYP**

2401. ——. ——. ——. Report of the Special committee on Masonic temple association, adopted . . . Dec. 15, 1899. [n. p., n. d.]

14 p. 8°.   **V**
Plans to build a Masonic temple in Richmond.

2402. ——. ——. GRAND ROYAL ARCH CHAPTER. Proceedings . . . [n. p., 18-?- ?]

8°.   **NYP:** 1866-69, 71-75; **V:** 1866, 68-77.

2403. ——. ——. KNIGHTS TEMPLAR. GRAND COMMANDERY. Proceedings of the annual assembly . . . Richmond [18-?-19—

8°.   **NYP:** 1868-69, 71, 73, 75, 77, 86-91; **V:** 1877-81, 92 94-95.

2404. FREEMASONS. VIRGINIA. MERIDIAN LODGE, NO. 284. Year book . . . [n. p., 19—

    8°.   V: 1920.

2405. FUNERAL obsequies [Gen. Robert E. Lee's] Oct. 15, 1870. Order of procession . . . [n. p., 1870?]

    broadside. 25½ x 20½ cm.   V

2406. GLOUCESTER MONUMENT ASSOCIATION. Proceedings . . . at the unveiling of the monument at Gloucester Court House, Virginia . . . West Point, Va., 1890.

    34 p. 8°.   WM

2407. GOSSON, LOUIS C. Post-bellum campaigns of the blue and gray, 1881-1882 . . . Trenton, N. J., Naar, Day & Naar, 1882.

    192 p. front. 12°.   LC, V

An account of a visit to Richmond, Va., by the members of Aaron Wilkes post, no. 23, G. A. R., and of return visit to Trenton, N. J., by members of several Confederate organizations of Richmond. Reveals the restoration of good feeling between North and South.

2408. GRACE EPISCOPAL CHURCH, Richmond, Va. LADIES' AID SOCIETY. The kitchen queen. Richmond, Va., West, Johnston, 1893.

    72 p. 12°.   V

A cook book issued by the Society.

2409. GRAND ARMY OF THE REPUBLIC. DEPT. OF MASSACHUSETTS. JOHN A. ANDREW POST, NO. 15, Boston. The old stars and stripes of the Richmond Grays, and the "Grays" in the Confederate army. [Boston? 1887?]

    12 numb. l. 8°.   LC, V

The introduction relates how the John A. Andrew post was received by the ex-Confederates during the G. A. R. visit to Richmond; reveals growing amity between North and South.

2410. ——. DEPT. OF NEW JERSEY. AARON WILKES POST, NO. 23, Trenton. On to Richmond! by Post no. 23, G. A. R., Dept. of New Jersey, and its friends, Oct. 16. 1881. Bishop W. Mains.

pub. Illustrated by Joseph W. Phillips. Trenton, N. J., Murphy, 1881.

81 p. plates. 12°. **LC**

An account which throws considerable light upon contemporary social conditions in Richmond and vicinity and reveals the cordiality between the soldiers of former contending armies.

2411. HAMMOND, E. M. Address . . . delivered at the University of Virginia, July 1, 1890. [Charlottesville] Jeffersonian print. [1890]

11 p. 8°. **V**

Preaches loyalty to the South in a spirit characteristic of the old school of conservatives.

2412. [HAMPTON NORMAL AND AGRICULTURAL INSTITUTE] Lynching: a national menace. The white South's protest against lynching. [Hampton, 1919]

17 p. 8°. **LC**

Includes a "press symposium" of leading southern newspapers opposed to lynching.

2413. [HUNTER McGUIRE MEMORIAL ASSOCIATION] Ceremonies and addresses attending the presentation of a statue of Hunter Holmes McGuire by the Hunter McGuire memorial association, and its acceptance by the state, at Richmond, Va., Jan. 7, 1904. Pub. under the auspices of R. E. Lee camp, no. 1, Confederate veterans, Richmond, Va. [1904?]

3-30 p. plate. 4°. **V**

2414. INAUGURATION of the Jackson statue. Introductory address of Governor Kemper, and oration, by Rev. Moses D. Hoge, D.D., . . . Oct. 26, 1875. Richmond, Walker, 1875.

23 p. 8°. **H, LC, V, VU**

Reveals the promotion of reconciliation between North and South.

2415. INDEPENDENT ORDER OF G.[OOD] S.[AMARITINES] AND D. [AUGHTERS] OF S.[AMARIA] STATE GRAND LODGE, NO. 6. Minutes of annual session . . . [n. p., 1873?-19—

8°. **V:** 34th (1906).

2416. INTERNATIONAL ORDER OF GOOD TEMPLARS. VIRGINIA. GRAND LODGE. Proceedings of the annual session . . . Franklin, Va. [etc., 1868?-19—

8°. **NYP:** 11th, 23d (1878, 90).

2417. JONES, JOHN W. Army of northern Virginia memorial volume. Comp. by Rev. J. William Jones . . . at the request of the Virginia division of the Army of northern Virginia association. Richmond, Randolph & English, 1880.

347 p. 8°.   BP, LC, V, VU

Contains the proceedings of the Lee memorial meeting and of the annual meetings and reunions (1st-9th) of the Virginia division of the Army of northern Virginia association.

2418. KNIGHTS OF DAMON OF VIRGINIA. Constitution, by-laws, rules of order and general laws for the government of the grand lodge, Knights of Damon, and the order in general under the control and government of Knights of Damon of Virginia. Comp. by Sir J. C. Randolph . . . Richmond, Va., Reformer print., 1904.

32 p. 8°.   V

2419. KNIGHTS OF PYTHIAS. VIRGINIA. GRAND LODGE. Proceedings . . . 1st- ; 1868— [n. p., 1868—

8°.   V: 1st-9th, 35th, 39th (1868-77, 1903, 07).

2420. LEE, ELIZABETH. Virginia: past and present . . . Richmond, Waddey, 1895.

3 p. l., 9-78 p. 12°.   H, LC, V, VU

Personal experiences, 1865-95 (chs. 8-11), revealing in a limited way economic and social conditions; told as reflections rather than facts, with a touch of pathos, not bitterness.

2421. LEE MEMORIAL ASSOCIATION. Ceremonies connected with the inauguration of the mausoleum and the unveiling of the recumbent figure of General Robert Edward Lee, at Washington and Lee university, Lexington, Va., June 28, 1883. Oration of John W. Daniel . . . Historical sketch of the Lee memorial association. Lynchburg, Va., Bell, 1883.

83 p. 8°.

"Historical sketch of the Lee memorial association, by W. Allan," p. [3]-19.

2422. LEE MONUMENT ASSOCIATION. Organization of the Lee monument association, and the Association of the Army of northern Virginia, Richmond, Va., Nov. 3d and 4th, 1870. Richmond, Randolph & English, 1871.

52 p. front. (port.) 8°.   BP, LC, NYP, V

2423. LORTON, HETH. Address by Mr. Heth Lorton, treasurer Virginia Cincinnati, delivered before a special meeting of the Society of the Cincinnati in the state of Virginia on Dec. 15, 1905, in Richmond, Virginia . . . [Richmond, 1905]

7 p. 8°.   **BP, H, LC**

2424. McDONALD, JAMES J. Life in old Virginia: a description of Virginia, more particularly the tidewater section, narrating many incidents relating to the manners and customs of old Virginia so fast disappearing as a result of the war between the states, together with many humorous stories . . . Ed. by J. A. C. Chandler. Norfok, Va., Old Virginia pub. co., 1907.

vii, 374 p. front. (port.) plates. 8°.   **H, LC, V, VU**

Chs. 16-21, in part, on the *post bellum* period; an account of some observations in eastern Virginia, 1865-90.

2425. The MANASSAS battlefield Confederate park (incorporated) Prince William County, Virginia . . . the South's proposed memorial to valor and in the interest of American history. Washington, D. C. [*ca.* 1921]

20 p. illus. 8°.   **LC, V**

2426. MARSHALL, CHARLES. Address delivered before the Lee monument association, at Richmond, Virginia, Oct. 27, 1887, on the occasion of laying the corner-stone of the monument to General Robert E. Lee . . . Published by request. Baltimore, Murphy, 1888.

59 p. 8°.   **BP, H, LC, NYP, V**

2427. MAURY, MATTHEW F. [Papers, 1866-68]

vols. XXV & XXVI. 4°. MSS.   **LC**

On general economic and social conditions in Virginia during the late 'sixties; mostly letters on the aftermath of the Civil war and the first efforts to recuperate.

2428. MONTICELLO ASSOCIATION, Charlottesville, Va. . . . Minutes of the 1st- meeting of the Monticello association. [1913— n. p., 1913—

fronts., illus., port. 8°.

Title varies: Minutes of the first meeting of the original members of the Monticello graveyard association, 1913; Minutes of the . . . annual meeting of the members . . ., 1914.

No report pub. for 1918.

H: 8-10th, 12-13th (1921-23, 25-26); LC: 1st-12th (1913-17, 19-25); V: 1913-22; VU: 1913, 15-27.

2429. MOORE, CARRIE P. The way to the heart, hints to the inexperienced; a collection of tested Virginia recipes . . . Richmond, Va., Whittet & Shepperson, 1905.

155 p. 8°.   **LC, V**

2430. MOORE, SALLIE A. Memories of a long life in Virginia, by Mrs. John H. Moore . . . Staunton, Va., McClure [1920]

183 p. front., plate, ports. 12°.   **LC, V**

Scattered notes on social conditions in Virginia after the Civil war.

2431. MOUNT VERNON LADIES' ASSOCIATION OF THE UNION. Act of incorporation for the purchase of Mount Vernon. Constitution and by-laws. [New York, 1872]

14 p. 8°.   **NYP**

2432. ———. Annual report . . . Washington, D. C. [etc.] 1858-19—

8°. Reports issued irreg., 1858-70; beginning with 1872, issued annually.

Title varies: Proceedings of the council; Report; Minutes . . .

LC: 1866/67, 70, 72/73, 76-1927; **NYP**: 1871/72-72/73, 85, 89-90, 98, 1900; **V**: 1867, 70, 71/72, 79, 81-1901, 03-28; **VU**: 1927, 28.

2433. ———. Charter, constitution and by-laws of the Mount Vernon ladies' association of the Union. [Washington?] 1924.

24 p. 8°.   **LC**

2434. ———. Constitution and by-laws . . . [n. d.]

10 l. front. (port.) f°. MS.   **V**

2435. ———. Washington's home and the story of the Mount Vernon ladies' association of the Union. Richmond, Va., Whittet & Shepperson [n. d.]

18 p. front.., illus. 12°.   **V**

2436. NATIONAL SOCIETY OF COLONIAL DAMES OF AMERICA. VIRGINIA. Celebration of the 300th anniversary of the first legislative assembly in America . . . July 30, 1919. [n. p., 1919?]

19 p. 8°.   **V**

2437. ———. ———. The Colonial dames of America in the state of Virginia. [n. p., 1900]

4 l. with pasted clippings, illus. 8°.   **VU**

2438. ———. ———. The constitution and officers of the Society . . . [including the constitution and by-laws of the Society of the colonial dames of America in the state of Virginia, instituted . . . 1892] Richmond, West, Johnston, 1893.

30 p. 16°. **V**

2439. ———. ———. [List of officers and members] . . . Richmond [18-?-19—

8°. **NYP**: 1894, 97; **VU**: 1908.

2440. ———. ———. [Report to the state societies of "work accomplished, and undertaken, from June 1, 1908 to June 1, 1909"] [n. p., 1909?]

4 l. 4°. **V**

2441. ———. ———. The Society of the colonial dames of America in the state of Virginia. 1913. Richmond, Va., Mitchell & Hotchkiss, 1913.

208 p. 8°. **LC, V**

Contains list of members and register of ancestors.

2442. ———. ———. The unveiling of a tablet, erected by the Colonial dames of America in the state of Virginia, to the founders of the college of William and Mary. Oct. 22, 1901. [Richmond, Jones, 1901?]

47 p. 8°. **LC, V**

Includes an address by Col. William Lamb, p. 11-45.

2443. ODD-FELLOWS, Independent order of. VIRGINIA. GRAND LODGE. Proceedings . . . [n. p., 18-? -19—

8°. **V**: 1868-78, 83, 86-89, 91-94, 96-1902, 04-07, 09-15.

2444. ORDER OF EASTERN STAR OF VIRGINIA. Proceedings of the grand chapter . . . Richmond, 19—

plates (ports.) 8°. **V**: 1904-08.

2445. ORDER OF FIRST FAMILIES OF VIRGINIA, 1607-1620. Statutes, 1923-24. [Milwaukee, Hammersmith-Kortmeyer co., 1924]

15, [1] p. 16°. **LC, V**

Constitution and by-laws of the Society.

2446. PALMER, BENJAMIN M. The present crisis and its issues. An address delivered before the literary societies of Washington and

Lee university, Lexington, Va., 27 June 1872 . . . Pub. at the request of the societies and also of the Board of trustees of the university. Baltimore, Murphy, 1872.

28 p. 8°.   LC, USE, V

Economic and social problems confronting Virginia and the South, as a result of the Civil war.

2447. PARKER, DAVID B. A Chautauqua boy in '61 and afterward; reminiscences by David B. Parker, second lieutenant, 72d New York, detailed superintendent of the mails of the Army of the Potomac, U. S. marshal, district of Virginia, chief post office inspector; ed. by Torrance Parker; introduction by Albert Bushnell Hart . . . Boston, Small, Maynard [ca. 1912]

xxvi, 388 p. front., plates, ports., facsims. 8°.   LC, V

Some account of conditions in Virginia after the Civil war; delightfully told.

2448. PARKER, WILLIAM W. Forty years a doctor. An address delivered before the Society of alumni of the Medical college of Virginia, April 9, 1891. [n. p., 1891]

15 p. 8°. (Reprint from *Virginia medical monthly.* June, 1891)   V

2449. PATRIOTIC ORDER SONS OF AMERICA OF VIRGINIA. Lee birthplace memorial committee composed of the State executive committee, Patriotic order sons of America of Virginia. F. W. Alexander, secretary, Oak Grove, Va. . . . [n. p., n. d.]

[12] p. illus., ports. nar. 8°.   V

2450. [2327] PATTESON, CAMM. The young bachelor . . . Lynchburg, 1900.

2451. PEIRPONT, FRANCIS H. Gov. Peirpont's address to the people of Virginia. May 19, 1865. [Washington, McGill & Witherow, 1865?]

16 p. 8°.   V

Economic and political conditions in Virginia at the close of the Civil war; the status of reconstruction in the state.

2452. [PHILLIPS, JAMES J.] . . . Trial and conviction of James Jeter Phillips for the murder of his wife. Richmond, Vore, 1868.

96 p. front. (port.) 12°.   LC, V

At head of title: The Drinker's Farm tragedy.

2453. POLLARD, EDWARD A. Memoir of the assassination of Henry Rives Pollard. Prepared by his brother, Edward A. Pollard. Lynchburg [Va.] Schaffter & Bryant, 1869.

32 p. 8°.   H, LC

2454. POLLARD, HENRY R. Address . . . before the Oakwood memorial association . . . May 7, 1910. Richmond, Whittet & Shepperson [1910?]

16 p. 8°.   V

On the spirit of the Confederacy.

2455. [POLLOCK, GEORGE F.] Story of the sylvan play and Indian pageant and pow-wow at Stony Man camp, Skyland, Va. [Washington, D. C., Judd & Detweiler, *ca.* 1916]

1 p. 1., 28 1. incl. illus., plates. obl. 8°.   LC

Cover-title: The wedding of Wetona.

Indian pow-wow as summer entertainment at Skyland, Stony Man camp.

2456. [1428] PORTER, DUVAL, ed. Men, places, and things . . . [Danville, Va.] 1891.

2457. PRYOR, SARA A. My day; reminiscences of a long life, by Mrs. Roger A. Pryor . . . New York, Macmillan, 1909.

ix, 454 p. front., plates, ports. 8°.

Conditions in Virginia after the Civil war interestingly related, chs. 26-29.

2458. ———. Reminiscences of peace and war, by Mrs. Roger A. Pryor . . . Rev. and enl. ed. New York, Macmillan [etc.] 1905.

xviii, 418 p. front., plates, ports., double map. 8°.

Contains valuable material on *post bellum* conditions in Richmond and vicinity, chs. 24-26; readable and reliable.

2459. [1629] RETAIL GROCERS' ASSOCIATION OF RICHMOND, inc., ed. Old Virginia cooking . . . Richmond [*ca.* 1910]

2460. RIVES, WILLIAM C., jr. An address delivered before the Society of alumni of the University of Virginia, July 1, 1869 . . .

Pub. by order of the Society. Richmond, Gary, Clemmitt & Jones, 1869.

34 p. 8°.   LC, VU

A sane, objective discussion of the social changes wrought by the Civil war and what Virginia has done since 1865 to rebuild; the obligations of her people towards her.

2461. ROSSER, ELIZABETH W. Housekeepers' and mothers' manual. By Mrs. Thomas L. Rosser. Richmond, Va., Waddey, 1895.

viii, 9-604 p. 8°.   LC

A cook book.

2462. SCHOFIELD, JOHN M. Forty-six years in the army, by Lieutenant-General John M. Schofield. New York, Century, 1897.

xvi p., 1 l., 577 p. front. (port.) 8°.

Ch. 21 on reconstruction in Virginia—showing Gen. Schofield's opposition to the radical measures of Congress.

2463. SMITH, MRS. MARY S., comp. Virginia cookery-book, comp. by Mary Stuart Smith. New York, Harper, 1885.

xvii, 352 p. 12°.   BP, LC, USAg

2464. SMITH, PRESLEY A. Boyhood memories of Fauquier, by P. A. L. Smith. Richmond, Va., Old Dominion press, 1926.

163 p., 1 l. front., plates. 8°.   LC, NYP, V

Reveals something of social conditions in rural Virginia in the decades immediately following the Civil war.

2465. SOCIETY OF THE CINCINNATI. VIRGINIA. Banquet to the General society of the Cincinnati, given by the Society of the Cincinnati in the state of Virginia, upon the occasion of the triennial meeting, at Richmond, Virginia, May 10, 1905. [New York, Dempsey & Carrol, 1905]

7 l. plates. 4°.   V

2466. ———. ———. By-laws . . . adopted . . . [Richmond? 19—

4°.   BP, H, LC: 1905; V: 1912.

2467. ———. ———. Circular letter of the Society of the Cincinnati, in the state of Virginia, June 22, 1907. [n. p., 1907]

38 p. 8°.   H, LC

Contains copy of the Society's circular letter of Dec. 15, 1905, showing wherein the Institution of the Society has not been, and is not followed.

2468. ———. ———. [Correspondence of the Correspondence committee of the Virginia society . . . referring to the Virginia
resolutions of Dec. 15, 1905] [Richmond, 1906]

16 p. 4°.   BP

2469. ———. ———. Minutes of the annual meeting . . . [Rich-
mond, 178-?-19—

8°.   **LC:** 1913-15; **V:** 1909-11, 14-18, 20-27.
The Virginia society was founded in 1783.

2470. ———. ———. [Preambles and resolutions adopted, Dec. 15,
1905] [New York, 1905]

[4] p. 4°.   H

2471. ———. ———. Roster of the Society . . . [Richmond?
18-? -19—

8°. **LC:** 1907/08, 12/13-13/14, 15/16; **V:** 1907/08-08/09, 10/11, 12/13-
13/14, 15/16, 17/18, 19/20-21/22, 23, 25, 27; **VU:** 1912/13.

2472. Society of Virginia of the District of Columbia. Society
register, the Society of Virginia of the District of Columbia; containing a brief history of its organization, a biography of its elective officers, its constitution and by-laws and a roster of its membership, corrected for the fiscal year, Oct. 31, 1925 . . . F. C.
Baggarly, ed. Washington, D. C., The Society [ca. 1926]

127 p. incl. plates, ports. 8°.   **LC, VU, WM**

2473. Sons of Confederate veterans. Virginia. Hand-book of
the Virginia division, Sons of Confederate veterans, containing
general orders 1-2-3, compiled by Headquarters Virginia division
. . . Richmond, Va. [1922]

40 p. illus. (port.) 8°.   **LC, V, VU**
Advertisements in back.

2474. ———. ———. Minutes of the annual meeting . . . [Rich-
mond, Whittet & Shepperson, 1896?-19—

8°.   **V:** 1903, 05-06, 08-09.

2475. ———. ———. R. E. Lee camp, no. 1. Action of R. E. Lee
camp, no. 1, Sons of Confederate veterans, and R. E. Lee camp,
no. 1, C. V., in regard to Barnes' Brief history of the U. S., with

review of the history by Rev. J. William Jones. Richmond, Va.,
1895.

> 14 p. 8°.   VU
> Charges of injustice and bias against the South.

2476. SONS OF THE AMERICAN REVOLUTION. VIRGINIA SOCIETY.
Constitution and by-laws, officers, members, revolutionary ancestors, and state and national numbers, officers of the national society. Editors: Robert A. Brock [and] Benjamin B. Minor.
Richmond, Jones, 1897.

> 22, [2] p. 8°.   V
> Ed. of 1913.   V

2477. ———. ———. Year book . . . [Richmond, Va., 19—

> 8°.   V: 1901, 24.

2478. STILES, ROBERT. Address at the dedication of the monument
to the Confederate dead, University of Virginia, June 7, 1893.
Richmond, Taylor & Taylor, 1893.

> 28 p. 8°.   V

2479. A SOUVENIR of New Haven, Connecticut, fraternally dedicated
to the Richmond Light infantry blues battalion of Richmond, Virginia, by the Second company Governor's Foot Guard, upon the occasion of their visit to New Haven, Sept. 9, 10, 11, 1908. [n. p.,
1908?]

> 137 p. illus. 8°.   V
> Reveals something of the restoration of amity between North and
> South.

2480. STUART, ALEXANDER H. [Miscellaneous papers and letters,
1865-67]

> MSS.   LC
> Include 5 letters to Frank Taylor, 1867. Comments on the bad po-
> litical and social conditions in Virginia after the Civil war.

2481. SUTHERLIN, WILLIAM T. Address before the Mechanics' association of Danville, Va., Mar. 11, 1867 . . . Richmond, Enquirer, 1867.

> 29 p. 8°.   LC, V
> A plea for the development of Virginia through the efforts of her
> young men and the securing of immigrants.

2482. TEMPLE, LUCY L. Home made candies, with lessons . . . Richmond, Va. [1909?]

29 p. 8°.   V

2483. [TUCKER, JOHN R.] Opinion concerning the charter of the Mount Vernon ladies' association. [n. p.] 1885.

8°. No title-page.   LC

Relation of the state of Virginia to the association through the rights granted in the charter.

2484. TYLER, DAVID G. Address of welcome to the Confederate veterans . . . Delivered at the auditorium, Richmond, Va., June 1, 1915, 25th reunion, United Confederate veterans. [Richmond, 1915]

7 p. 8°.   LC, V, VU

2485. TYLER, LYON G. Address of President Lyon G. Tyler, on the occasion of the celebration by William and Mary college and the A. P. V. A. of the first settlement of Jamestown. May 13, 1895. [Richmond, Va., Printed for private distribution by J. H. Whitty, 1895]

[2], 2-6 p. fold. map. 8°.   H, LC, NYP, V

2486. UNITED CONFEDERATE VETERANS. A memorial of the sixth annual reunion of the United Confederate veterans association and the laying of the cornerstone of the Jefferson Davis monument . . . [Richmond, Va., 1896]

unp. plates, map. obl. 8°.   V, VU

2487. ———. Official souvenir, 25th reunion United Confederate veterans, June 1-2-3, 1915, Richmond, Va. Comp. by J. H. Bradley, Richmond, Va., Jones [1915]

64 p. illus., ports. 4°.   V

2488. ———. Speeches at Richmond reunion, May 30 to June 3, 1907, of Gen. Stephen D. Lee, . . . Col. Robert E. Lee, jr., and Col. J. W. Daniel. [n. p., 1907?]

23 p. 8°.   V

2489. ———. VIRGINIA DIVISION. A. P. HILL CAMP, NO. 6, Petersburg, Va. Roster and historical sketch of A. P. Hill camp . . . Organized Dec. 16, 1887. Petersburg, Va. [n. d.]

63 p. 8°.   V

2490. UNITED CONFEDERATE VETERANS. VIRGINIA DIVISION. GRAND CAMP. Proceedings of the . . . annual meeting of the Grand camp Confederate veterans, department of Virginia. Richmond [1888?-19—

col. fronts. 8°.
16th has imprint: Pulaski, Va., 1904.
17th-18th, 1904-05, issued together.
LC: 7-14th, 16-28th, 37-39th (1894-1901, 03-15, 24-26); **NYP:** 1912-15; **V:** 1894-1916, 20, 24; **VU:** 1898.

2491. ——. ——. ——. COMMITTEE ON CONFEDERATE MONUMENT, Richmond. Report of committee on ceremonies incident to the unveiling of the soldiers' & sailors' monument, at Richmond, Va., May 30, 1894. [Richmond, 1894]

21 p. 8°.   LC

2492. ——. ——. ——. HISTORY COMMITTEE. Official report . . . Richmond, Hill [189-? -19—

8°.   **V:** 1899, 1901-03.
American history told from the Confederate point of view.

2493. UNITED DAUGHTERS OF THE CONFEDERACY. VIRGINIA DIVISION. Minutes of the 1st- annual convention . . . [n. p., 1896?-19—

8°.   **LC:** 13th-22d (1908-16); **V:** 1900-26.

2494. ——. ——. Virginia leads. [n. p.] 1916.

31 p. 12°.   V
List of events and incidents in which Virginia was first; an expression of exaggerated state pride and patriotism.

2495. ——. ——. Year book . . . [n. p., 19-?—

8°.   **V:** 1917-18.

2496. ——. ——. ALBEMARLE CHAPTER. Constitution and bylaws . . . Charlottesville, Va., 1915.

12 p. 16°.   VU

2497. ——. ——. ALLEGHANY CHAPTER, NO. 62, Covington. Souvenir program. Unveiling of Confederate monument, Covington, Va., Sept. 15, 1911. [Roanoke, Stone, 1911]

[12] p. col. illus. 12°.   V

2498. UNIVERSITY OF VIRGINIA. CIVIC CLUB. An investigation of conditions in the Ragged Mountains of Virginia, conducted by the Civic club of the University of Virginia. Charlottesville, Va., The Civic club, 1912.

26 p. 8°.   H, LC, V, VU

Degraded economic and social conditions among the backward people of the Ragged Mountains, "mentally isolated in the midst of an advanced and cultured civilization."

2499. VIRGINIA FEDERATION OF WOMEN'S CLUBS. 1907-1908. Organized 1907. [Lynchburg, Bell, 1907?]

32 p. 12°.   V

2500. ———. Year book . . . 1907/08— [n. p., 1908—

8°.   USL: 1913/14; V: 1907/08.

2501. VIRGINIA FUNERAL DIRECTORS' ASSOCIATION. Proceedings of the 1st- annual convention . . . Richmond [1888?-19—

8°.   LC: 19th, 29th (1906, 16).

2502. VIRGINIA LEAGUE OF WOMEN VOTERS. Virginia cookery book; traditional recipes. Richmond, Va. [ca. 1921]

192 p. 8°. Advertisements included.   NYP

2503. VIRGINIA STATE CHAMBER OF COMMERCE. Golfing in Virginia. Richmond, Va., 1928.

nar. 8°. (Its *Miscell. Doc.,* 19)   H, NYP, V

2504. VIRGINIA STATE FEDERATION OF POST OFFICE CLERKS. . . . Annual convention . . . [1st- ; 1921?—] [n. p., 1921?—

4°.   V: 6-8th (1926-28).

2505. The VIRGINIANS, New York. . . . Constitution and by-laws and list of officers and members . . . [New York, 1889?-19—

12°. LC: 1903/04-08/10, 12/13-13/14, 15/16, 17/18, 19/20; NYP: 1908/10, 12/13-13/14; V: 1907/08-08/10, 12/13-13/14, 19/20; VU: 1912/13.

Founded in 1889, "to conserve interest and pride in Virginia's history, to celebrate the anniversaries of great events in Virginia's annals . . ."

2506. WATSON, WALTER A. . . . Notes on southside Virginia, by Walter A. Watson, edited by Mrs. Walter A. Watson, under the direction of Wilmer L. Hall, assistant state librarian. Richmond, Bottom, 1925.

> 3 p. 1., 5-346 p. 8°. (In Virginia. State library. *Bulletin,* XV, 2-4)
> Contains excerpts from Watson's diary, 1888-1916, on life in Virginia and in Washington, D. C.

2507. WISE, JOHN S. . . . Memorial address of Hon. John S. Wise, at New Market, Va., May 12, 1898. Delivered at the unveiling of a monument to the memory of the southern soldiers and V. M. I. cadets who fell in the battle of New Market, May 15, 1864. [New Market, Va., Henkel, 1898]

> 14, [2] p. 8°.   LC, NYP, V

2508. WOODMEN OF THE WORLD. HEAD CAMP, JURISDICTION "L". Proceedings of the seventh biennial session convention Head camp, Jurisdiction "L", embracing the states of Virginia, West Virginia, Maryland, Delaware, and the District of Columbia, held at Roanoke, Va., Mar. 14-15, 1911. [n. p., 1911?]

> 44 p. ports. 8°.   V

2509. YOUNG MEN'S CHRISTIAN ASSOCIATION. VIRGINIA. Report of the annual convention . . . 1st- [1875?-19—] Staunton, Va. [etc., 1875?-19—

> 8°.   VU: 3d, 4th, 11-25th (1877-78, 87-1902).

2510. ——. ——. Year book, containing proceedings of the . . . state convention . . . Richmond [1877?-19—

> 8°.   VU: 28th (1904/05).

2511. ——. ——. STATE EXECUTIVE COMMITTEE. The riddle of the boy and some clues to the answer; a brief study of boy-development and an outline of a practical program of work. Prepared at the request of the Co-operative educational association and issued by the State executive committee, Virginia Young men's Christian associations, as a part of the Citizens' reading course. [n. p., 19—]

> 15 p. illus., ports., map. 8°.   USE, V

2512. [YORKTOWN CENTENNIAL ASSOCIATION] The centennial anniversary of the surrender of Lord Cornwallis, and the British forces under his command on the 19th day of October, 1781, virtually the closing of the struggle for American independence, to be appro-

priately celebrated on the field of Yorktown, Va., in October, 1881.
New York, American bank note co., 1880.

17 p. 8°.   **LC, NYP, VU**

2513. YORKTOWN centennial illustrated. Boston, 1881.

f°.   **NYP**

2514. YORKTOWN centennial, 1781-1881. Wilcox silver plate co.
[n. p., 1881]

14 p. ports. 4°.   **NYP**

2515. YORKTOWN, VA. MEETING PREPARATORY TO A NATIONAL CEN-
TENNIAL CELEBRATION. Proceedings of the meeting at Yorktown,
preparatory to a national centennial celebration of the surrender of
Lord Cornwallis, with correspondence had in pursuance thereof.
Richmond, Frayser, 1879.

19, [1] p. 8°.   **LC**

2516. ———. ———. Yorktown. An appeal to the country for a national centennial celebration of the surrender of Lord Cornwallis.
Norfolk, Va., Virginian print, 1879.

8 p. 8°.   **LC**

Secondary Works

2517. BUCKLEY, WILLIAM. Buckley's history of the great reunion
of the North and the South and of the blue and the gray, by William Buckley; an impartial, non-political account of the beginning
of reconciliation . . . in the U. S. . . . [Staunton, Mc-
Clure, *ca.* 1923]

244 p. front., plate, ports. 8°.   **LC, V, VU**

An "account of the very important and noble part taken in the reunion by the veterans of the 28th New York regiment of infantry volunteers, and the 5th Virginia infantry regiment."—Pref.

2518. [280] GEE, WILSON. . . . Some of the best things in rural Virginia . . . Charlottesville [1926]

2519. GREEN, BENNETT W. Word-book of Virginia folk-speech
. . . Richmond, Jones, 1899.

435 p. 8°.   **BP, LC, V**
Ed. of 1912: 530 p.   **LC, V, VU, WM**

The word-book, with definitions, is preceded by "Some Virginia folk
sayings" and "Virginia counties." At end of book is a list of Indian
place-names, with their meanings.

2520. HARWOOD, WALTER R.   History of Richmond lodge no. 45 of Benevolent & protective order of Elks, by W. R. Harwood, secretary.   Aug. 25, 1915.

4 p. typew. 4°.   **V**: Access. no. 13821.

2521. [HEITMANN, JOHN]   A history and manual of the Independent order of Odd fellows; the history of Odd fellowship in Virginia, with an introduction by Edmund H. Allen . . . Accotink, Va., Committee on publications, Accotink lodge, no. 75, I. O. O. F. [*ca.* 1927]

4 p. l., [7]-219 p. incl. illus., tables. plate, ports. 8°.   **LC, V**
Preface signed: John Heitmann, Archibald U. Turner, William G. Adam, Andy D. Yates, Ernest B. Herdener.

2522. A HISTORY of the monument erected by the U. S. government to commemorate the close of the Revolutionary war, at Yorktown, Oct. 19, 1781.   Being a narrative of its inception, construction, completion, and official examination.   Philadelphia, Dewey & Eakins, 1890.

26 p. front., plate, phot. 8°.   **LC**

2523. [2277] KING, GRACE E.   Mount Vernon on the Potomac; a history of the Mount Vernon ladies' association of the Union . . . New York, 1929.

2524. LICHTENSTEIN, GASTON.   George Washington's lost birthday. History of Meridian lodge; also other articles written at various times, by Gaston Lichtenstein.   Richmond, Va., William Byrd press, 1924.

115 p. front. (facism.) illus., ports. 8°.   **LC, V**

2525. LINDSAY, JAMES H.   The McCue murder.   Complete story of the crime and the famous trial of the ex-mayor of Charlottesville, Virginia . . . Charlottesville, Progress pub. [1904]

192 p. illus. 8°.   **LC, V**

2526. [2279] LOSSING, BENSON J.   The home of Washington and its associations, historical, biographical, and pictorial . . . New York, 1866.

See also items **[2280-2281]**

2527. [2285] MEAD, EDWARD C.   Historic homes of the South-West mountains, Virginia . . . Philadelphia & London, 1899.

2528. MOORE, JOSIAH S., ed. History and by-laws of Henrico union lodge, no. 130, A. F. & A. M., Richmond, Virginia, with a list of officers and members. Richmond, Jones, 1905.

179 p. front., ports. 8°.   **V**

2529. ———. History and by-laws of Richmond royal arch chapter, no. 3, A. F. & A. M., Richmond, Virginia, with a list of officers and members . . . Richmond, Williams, 1911.

194 p. 8°.   **V**
Includes brief notes on the lodge since 1865.

2530. OWEN, BENJAMIN P., jr. Historical sketch of Manchester lodge, no. 14, A. F. & A. M. . . . Richmond, Picot, 1907.

132 p. illus. 8°.   **V**
Scattered information from the records of the lodge on the development and activity of the organization since 1865.

2531. PAGE, THOMAS N. The Old Dominion: her making and her manners. New York, Scribner's, 1908.

ix, 394, p. 8°.
Chs. 6-7 on the period since the Civil War. The narrative is based upon secondary accounts, to which the author adds his own opinions; very readable, but not to be regarded as serious history.

2532. PATTON, JOHN S. Virginia clubs in historic homes. Baltimore, Sun, 1911.

6 l. pasted clippings, illus. 8°. (From the Baltimore *Sun,* Jan. 1, 1911)
          VU
Historic sketches of the Colonnade club (University of Virginia), Redland club, and Stone tavern.

2533. [2289] PATTON, JOHN S., et al. Monticello and its master, by John S. Patton and Sallie J. Doswell. Charlottesville [ca. 1925]

2534. RADY, CHARLES P. History of Richmond Randolph lodge, no. 19, A. F. & A. M. From A. L., Oct. 29, 5787, A. D., 1787, to A. L., Oct. 29, 5887, A. D., 1887. By Charles P. Rady, historian of the lodge. Richmond, Fergusson, 1888.

vii, 50, [4] p. illus., plate. 8°.   **V**
Leading events under the various worshipful masters, as recorded in the papers of the lodge.

2535. SMITH, WILLIAM R. History of the Baptist home for aged women, Richmond, Va. Richmond, Jenkins, 1922.

> 60 p. front., plates, ports. 12°. **V**
>
> A strictly chronological account of the Home from its beginning in 1881, stressing the yearly meetings of the organization.

2536. SNODGRASS, CHARLES E. History of Loge Française, no. 53, A. F. & A. M. Richmond, Gillis & Baptist, 1874.

> 44 p. 8°. **V**
>
> A chronology, containing brief notes from the records of the lodge, 1865-74.

2537. THOMAS JEFFERSON MEMORIAL FOUNDATION, inc. The story of Thomas Jefferson memorial foundation, dedicated to the preservation of Monticello, the home of Thomas Jefferson situated at Charlottesville, Virginia . . . [New York, Thomas Jefferson memorial foundation, *ca.* 1926]

> [12] p. illus. nar. 4°. (*The Monticello papers,* 4B) **LC**

2538. UNITED CONFEDRATE VETERANS. JOHN BOWIE STRANGE CAMP. Memorial history of the John Bowie Strange camp . . . together with brief sketches of the Albemarle chapter of the United daughters of the Confederacy, and the R. T. W. Duke camp, Sons of Confederate veterans . . . Charlottesville, Michie, 1920.

> viii, 330 p. ports. (incl. front.) 8°. **VU**
>
> Includes ceremonies at the unveiling of Confederate monuments, and memorial day exercises.

2539. [2295] WILSTACH, PAUL. Jefferson and Monticello . . . Garden City, N. Y., 1925.

> See also items [2296-2297]

Periodicals

2540. [1391] The BI-MONTHLY guild . . . v. 1-18 . . . Richmond, Va. [1890?]-1907.

2541. [1854] The CAVALIER. An illustrated news-magazine . . . v. 1-v. 2, no. 1 . . . Richmond, Va., 1903-04.

2542. [1855] The CAVALIER. Fortress Monroe, Va. v. 1-v. 2, no. 16 . . . Fortress Monroe, Va., 1905-06.

2543. The CRITIC . . . v. 1, no. 1- Richmond, Va., 1888—

illus. f°. weekly. Advertisements in back.

W. C. Trueman, ed., June 11, 1888—

None issued, Dec. 30, 1888-Dec. 28, 1889.

A humor magazine, containing also articles on genealogy, fashions, etc.

LC: I, 27-III, 64 (Nov. 19, 1888-Mar. 15, 1890).

2544. The CRUCIBLE. An organ for the promotion of a better understanding of Germany by the people of the U. S. v. 1; Dec. 5, 1914-May 15, 1915. Richmond, Va., The Crucible publishing co. [1914-15]

384 p. 4°. weekly. No more pub.   **LC, V**

C. L. Droste, ed.

Nos. 20 and 24 include supplements (unpaged).

Official organ of the German-American alliance of Virginia, Feb.-May, 1915.

2545. The MASONIC review; devoted to the interests of legitimate masonry. v. 1, no. 1- [?] March, 1894-[?] Richmond, Va., 1894-[?]

8°. monthly.   **V: I, 1.**

2546. ROUGH ASHLAR. Published monthly and devoted exclusively to the interests of the masonic fraternity. v. 1, no. 1- [May, 1891?—] Richmond, Va. [1891?—

8°. monthly.   **V: III (1893/94).**

2547. SONS OF THE REVOLUTION. VIRGINIA SOCIETY. . . . Quarterly magazine . . . v. 1- ; Jan., 1922— Richmond, Va., Sons of the revolution in state of Virginia, 1922—

illus., plates, ports., facsim. 8°.

Quarterly, v. 1-4 (1922-25); semi-annual, v. 5- (1926—

G. W. James, jr., ed., 1922—

BP: I-IV. LC: I-IV; VI, 1; (1922-25, Jan./July, 1928). **V**: I-VII.
WM: I-III.

2548. SOUTHERN advertising journal, pub. monthly in the interest of advertising . . . v. 1- ; Dec., 1908— Richmond, Va., R. S. Freeman, 1908—

illus. 8°.   **LC**: I (1908/09).

2549. The VIRGINIA club woman . . . v. 1, no. 1- ; Sept./Oct., 1928— [Richmond? Va., 1928—

illus. 4°. bi-monthly.
Official organ of the Virginia federation of women's clubs.
V: I, 1, 3-4 (1928/29); **VU:** I, 1-2.

2550. VIRGINIA masonic journal. v. 1, no. 1- ; July, 1906—
[Richmond, Va.] 1906—

8°. **V:** I-VII; VIII, 1-6, 9, 12; IX, 1-9, 11-12; X; XI, 1-2, 4-6; XII-
XXIV; (1906/07-28/29).

2551. VIRGINIA Odd fellow. v. 1-25; [1893?]-1917. New ser.,
v. 1- ; 1918— Richmond, Va. [1893?]-19—

illus. f°. monthly.
"Official organ of the Grand lodge, Grand encampment, and Rebekah
assembly of Virginia."
LC: XIII-XXV (1905-17); new ser., I-II (1918-19). **V:** XIX-XXV,
new ser., VIII-XII (1925-29).

Directories

2552. BUSINESS and professional directory of eastern Virginia.
[n. p., 19—

8°.   **V:** 1903/04.

2553. BUSINESS directory of the principal cities and villages of Virginia . . . Richmond, Va., B. Bates; Petersburg, Va., J. B.
Ege [18—

8°.   **LC:** 1873-74.
Fitzgerald & Dillon, comp.

2554. CHATAIGNE's Virginia business directory and gazetteer . . .
Comp. by J. H. Chataigne & co. Richmond, Va., 18—

8°.   **V:** 1880/81, 84/85, 88/89, 90/91, 93/94; **WM:** 1893/94.

2555. DELAWARE state and peninsula directory . . . Wilmington, Del., W. Costa & co., 1891—

fold. map. 8°.   **LC:** 1891.
Includes Eastern Shore of Virginia.

2556. The DELAWARE state and peninsula directory. (Eastern shores of Maryland and Virginia.) . . . 1899/1900— [v. 1]- Wilmington, Del., The Delaware state publishing co. [*ca.* 1899—

fold. map. 8°.   **LC:** 1899/1900.

2557. EASTERN SHORE herald almanac, Eastville, Va., 19—

8°.   **V:** 1916-17, 19-20, 22.

Contains "Northampton County official directory."

2558. FARM and household almanac for Virginia and North Carolina, for the year 1891. R. K. Bowle's calculations, made expressly for this almanac. Richmond, Va., Hill [1890]

63 p. 12°.   **V**

2559. HILL's southern almanac . . . Richmond, Va., Virginia fire & marine insurance co. [etc., 18-? -19—

illus. 12°.

Title varies: Illustrated southern almanac, 1900, 02; Virginia and North Carolina southern almanac, 1904; Hill's Virginia and North Carolina southern almanac, 1905-08.

LC: 1894-1917, 21-23; **V:** 1893-1924.

2560. RICHARDSON's Virginia and North Carolina almanac for the year of our Lord . . . Calculated by David Richardson, of Louisa County, Va. [1866- ?]

8°.   **V:** 1866-67, 71.

2561. VIRGINIA business directory and gazetteer . . . Richmond, Va., Hill directory co., 1877-19—

8°. Title varies.

LC: 1877/78, 80/81, 84/85, 88/89-90/91, 93/94, 97/98, 1906, 11, 17; **NYP:** 1917; **V:** 1877/78, 97/98, 1906, 11, 17; **VU:** 1877/78; **WM:** 1897/98, 1911, 17.

2562. [559] VIRGINIA. LABOR AND INDUSTRY, Bur. of. Complete list of industrial and mercantile establishments in . . . Virginia . . . Richmond, Va. [1920]

2563. [560] ———. ———. . . . Industrial directory . . . Richmond, Va. [1920?—

2564. [309] VIRGINIA real estate directory . . . Richmond [192-?—

2565. VIRGINIA state business directory, 1871-72; containing a new map of the state, together with its state government, post offices, brief sketches of its principal cities and villages; a large list of farmers; history of the several states and territories, etc. Andrew Boyd & co. Richmond, 1871.

675 p. fold. map. 8°.   Advertisements interspersed.   **VU**

2566. The VIRGINIAN'S pictorial annual . . . for 1884 [Norfolk? 1884?]

unp. illus. 8°.   Advertisements interspersed.   **LC**
An almanac.

2567. The WARROCK-RICHARDSON Virginia and North Carolina almanack for the year of our Lord . . . Richmond, Va., Goode [1865—

12°.   **LC**: 1865-89; **V**: 1865, 67-90.
Title varies: Warrock's Virginia and North Carolina almanack, 1865-73; Warrock's edition of Richardson's almanack.

Calculated by David Richardson of Louisa County, 1865-73; by R. K. Bowles of Louisa County, 1874—

For further references on Social Life and Customs, see above, Pt. II, § 7: *Urban and County Development;* also Pt. III, §§ 2 and 3: *Description and Travel* and *Population, Race Relations, Immigration,* respectively.

PART IV. POLITICAL AND CONSTITUTIONAL

1. BIBLIOGRAPHY

2568. [3] CALENDAR of Virginia state papers and other manuscripts . . . Richmond, 1875-93.

2569. [4] CONVERSE, HENRY A. Indexes to the Virginia and West Virginia reports . . . Richmond, 1881.

2570. [5] A DIGEST of the decisions of the Supreme courts of appeals of Virginia and West Virginia . . . to 1915. St. Paul, 1906-16.

2571. [7] GUTHRIE, JAMES H. Index to the Virginia law register, vols. I-X, with a list of leading articles . . . Lynchburg, Va. [1906]

2572. [10] HURST, SAMUEL N. A complete . . . annotated digest of all the reported decisions of the Supreme court of appeals of Virginia [etc.] 1730-1896 . . . Pulaski City, Va., 1897-1902.

See also, items **11-14.**

2573. [17] MARTIN, WILLIAM B. An index to the Virginia reports, from Jefferson to vol. 91 . . . Richmond, 1896.

2574. [18] MATTHEWS, JAMES M. Digest of the laws of Virginia of a criminal nature . . . 2d ed., Richmond, 1871.

2575. [19] ————. [*Ibid.*] . . . 3d ed. . . . Richmond, 1890.

2576. [20] MICHIE, THOMAS J. The encyclopedic digest of Virginia and West Virginia reports . . . Charlottesville, 1905-07.

See also, items **21-24.**

2577. [31] ROYALL, WILLIAM L. A digest of the decisions of the Supreme court of appeals of Virginia, contained in Grattan's reports, vols. 1-21 . . . New York, 1873.

2578. [32] The SOUTHEASTERN REPORTER. . . . Digest of de-

cisions of the Supreme court of appeals of Virginia and West
Virginia [etc.] . . . reported in the Southeastern reporter,
vols. 1- . . . St. Paul, 1895-19—

2579. [33] . . . SOUTH EASTERN REPORTER digest. [Virginia ed.]
Including cases reported in vols. 1- South eastern reporter
82- Virginia reports . . . St. Paul, 1925—

2580. [35] SWEM, EARL G. A bibliography of the conventions
and constitutions of Virginia . . . Richmond, 1910.

2581. [42] U. S. LIBRARY OF CONGRESS. BIBLIOGRAPHY, Div. of.
References on the boundary controversies between Virginia (and
West Virginia) and Maryland. [Washington, D. C.] 1914.

2582. [51] WILLIAMS, JOHN W. Index to enrolled bills of the
General assembly of Virginia, 1776 to 1910 . . . Richmond,
1911.

2. STATE GOVERNMENT

Government Publications and Documents

2583. BOUNDARY LINE BETWEEN MARYLAND AND VIRGINIA, Board
of arbitrators to adjust the. Boundary line between the states of
Maryland and Virginia, before the Hon. Jeremiah S. Black, Hon.
Wm. A. Graham, and Hon. Chas. I. Jenkins, arbitrators upon the
boundary line. Wm. J. Robertson, R. T. Daniel, counsel for the
state of Virginia. Richmond, Clemmitt & Jones, 1875.

 21 p. 8°.   **V**

2584. ———. . . . Communication from the governor of Virginia transmitting report of the Commissioners to arbitrate the
boundary line between Virginia and Maryland . . . [Rich-
mond, 1877]

 61 p. 8°. (Virginia. General assembly. 1876-77. House. *Doc.*, VI)
               BP, LC, V
 No title-page.

2585. ———. Opinions and award . . . Washington, M'Gill &
Witherow [1877]

 97 p. 8°.   **LC, USG, V**
 Opinion and award, by J. S. Black and C. J. Jenkins; Minority opinion, by J. B. Beck.

2586. BOUNDARY LINES BETWEEN VIRGINIA AND MARYLAND, 1870-74, Commission on. Report and journal of proceedings of the joint commissioners to adjust the boundary line of the states of Maryland and Virginia. Authorized by the act of 1872, chapter 210. Annapolis, Mills & Colton, 1874.

344 p. 8°.　　　　　　　　　　　**H, LC, NYP, USG, V, VU**

Includes report of the Maryland commissioners, Dec. 30, 1873; abstract of the Maryland statement, by I. D. Jones; journal of proceedings (at their joint meetings) of the Virginia and Maryland commissioners; statments of the Maryland case and the Virginia case; etc.

2587. BURKE, ROBERT E. Contested-election case—Wise *v.* Young. Speech of Hon. R. E. Burke, of Texas, in the House of representatives . . . Apr. 25, 1898. [Washington, Govt., 1898?]

20 p. 8°.　　　　　　　　　　　**LC**

Involving the 2d Congressional district of Virginia.

2588. CHILTON, WILLIAM E. . . . State claims Northwest Territory. Address of William E. Chilton of West Virginia in the Senate of the U. S. on Apr. 10, 1912, and Address of Gov. Claude A. Swanson of Virginia on "Virginia day" delivered at the Jamestown exposition, June 12, 1907 . . . Washington, Govt., 1912.

30 p. 8°. ([U. S.] 62 Cong., 2 sess. Senate. *Doc.,* 948)　**H, LC, V**

2589. CRUMPACKER, EDGAR D. Contested-election case, Thorp *v.* Epes. Speech of Hon. E. D. Crumpacker, of Indiana, in the House of representatives . . . Mar. 22, 1898. Washington [Govt.] 1898.

16 p. 8°.　　　　　　　　　　　**LC**

Involving the 4th Congressional district of Virginia.

2590. GARNETT, CHRISTOPHER B., *et al.,* comp. The business man's code of Virginia laws, containing a compilation of such statutes as every business man needs and should have access to . . . containing also, forms, precedents, explanations, and the constitution of Virginia; comp. and ed. by Christopher B. Garnett and Robert N. Pollard . . . Pulaski, Va., Smith, 1907.

2 p. l., 634 p. 8°.　　　　　　　　　　　**LC, V**

2591. GOODE, JOHN, jr. Contested-election case of Platt *v.* Goode. Speech of Hon. John Goode, jr., of Virginia, delivered in the U. S.

House of representatives, July 26, 1876. Washington, Polkinhorn, 1876.

20 p. 8°.   VU

2592. GOODE, JOHN, jr. . . . Contested-election case of John T. Stovall, contestant, *v.* George C. Cabell, contestee . . . Washington, Polkinhorn, 1882.

70 p. 8°. (In U. S. 47 Cong., 2 sess. House)   LC, V

Signed: John Goode, of counsel for contestee.

2593. GOODE, J. THOMAS. Contested-election case of J. T. Goode *v.* J. F. Epes, from the fourth Congressional district of Virginia. Washington, Govt., 1893.

305 p. 8°.   LC

2594. HANK, JOSIAH D. Annotations to vols. 75 to 105, Virginia reports—both inclusive . . . Charlottesville, Va., Michie, 1907.

1005 p. 8°.   LC, V

2595. HAY, JAMES. Election contest—Thorp *v.* Epes. Speech . . . in the House . . . March 23, 1898. Washington [Govt.] 1898.

20 p. 8°.   LC

2596. HAYES, JAMES M., jr., *et al.*, comp. Tabulated statement of apportionment for representation in the House of delegates and Senate of Virginia and Congress of the U. S. . . . printed for use of joint committee . . . comp. by James M. Hayes and John W. Williams . . . Richmond, 1920.

19 p. 8°.   V

2597. HILL, BEN H. Political position and record of William Mahone. Remarks of Hon. Ben H. Hill, of Georgia, in the U. S. Senate, March 14, 1881. [Washington, Polkinhorn, 1881?]

4 p. 8°.   V

2598. HULL, JOHN A. Richard A. Wise *v.* W. A. Young. Contested election from the Second Virginia district. Remarks of Hon. J. A. T. Hull, of Iowa, in the House of representatives . . . Mar. 10, 1900. Washington [Govt.] 1900.

4 p. 8°.   LC

2599. JONES, ISAAC D. Report of Hon. Isaac D. Jones upon the boundary line award between Maryland and Virginia, to the governor of Maryland. Annapolis, Colton, 1878.

    8 p. 8°. (Maryland. General assembly. Senate. *Doc.,* N)   **NYP**

2600. JORGENSEN, JOSEPH. Contested election House of representatives, 45th Congress. Wm. E. Hinton, jr., contestant, *v.* Joseph Jorgensen, contestee. Answer of Joseph Jorgensen. Richmond, Va., "Guide and news" print., 1877.

    24 p. 8°.   **LC**

2601. LANGSTON, JOHN M. Contested-election case of John M. Langston *v.* E. C. Venable, from the fourth Congressional district of Virginia. Washington, Govt., 1889.

    1197 p. 8°.   **LC**

2602. LASSITER, FRANCIS R. Francis R. Lassiter ads. C. E. Wilson. Contested election. 4th [Congressional] district of Virginia. In the House of representatives, 57th Congress. Brief for contestee . . . [n. p., 1901 ?]

    89 p. 8°.   **LC**

2603. MARYLAND. BOUNDARY LINE BETWEEN . . . MARYLAND AND VIRGINIA, Commissioner for surveying and marking the. Report . . . to the governor of Maryland, Jan. 16, 1884. Annapolis, Young, 1884.

    23 p. 8°.   **VU**

2604. ———. BOUNDARY LINE BETWEEN MARYLAND AND VIRGINIA IN TANGIER AND POCOMOKE SOUNDS, Commissioner on the part of Maryland, for relocating and remarking of the. Report . . . [Baltimore] 1898.

    28 p. plates, map. 8°.   **BP, NYP, V**

2605. ———. CONSERVATION COMMISSION. Joint report of engineers on re-locating and re-marking Maryland-Virginia boundary line across Tangier and Pocomoke sounds. December, 1916. [Baltimore, Thomas & Evans, 1917]

    35 p. plates, fold maps. 8°.   **LC, USG**

    Signed: Fred. E. Ruediger, engineer, Commission of fisheries of Virginia. Swepson Earle, engineer, Conservation commission of Maryland.

2606. MARYLAND. GENERAL ASSEMBLY. JOINT COMMITTEE TO ADJUST AND MARK EASTERN SHORE BOUNDARY, 1867. Report of the commissioners appointed by the legislatures of Maryland and Virginia to run and mark the division line between Maryland and Virginia, on the Eastern Shore of Chesapeake Bay. Printed by authority. Annapolis, Thompson, 1868.

36 p. 8°.   BP, V

2607. ———. GOVERNOR, 1874-76 (James B. Groome). Correspondence of the governor of Maryland with the governor of Virginia in relation to the recent difficulties in the waters of the Pocomoke. Annapolis, Advertiser, 1876.

32 p. 8°.   NYP

2608. MASSEY, JOHN E. . . . Papers and testimony in the contested election case of John E. Massey v. John S. Wise, from the state of Virginia at large. [Washington, Govt., 1884]

2 v. 8°. (U. S. 84 Cong., 1 sess. House. *Miscell. doc.,* 27)   V

2609. MATHEWS, EDWARD B., *et al.* Report on the location of the boundary line along the Potomac River between Virginia and Maryland in accordance with the Award of 1877, by Edward B. Mathews, state geologist of Maryland, Wilbur A. Nelson, state geologist of Virginia. Baltimore, 1928.

v, 48 p. front., plate, map, 6 fold. charts. 8°.   LC, VU

2610. MORRISSETT, CARLISLE H. Notes on statutes [of Virginia] subsequent to the Code of 1919. Richmond, Bottom, 1921.

[2], 106 p. 8°.   HL, VU

2611. ———. Proposed amendments to the constitution of Virginia. A statement pointing them out and explaining them . . . [Richmond, 1928]

30 p. 8°.   V

2612. ———. Virginia statutes of 1924; an address by C. H. Morrissett, director of the State legislative reference bureau, before the Virginia state bar association, Winchester, July 3, 1924. Richmond, Bottom, 1924.

67 p. 8°.   LC, V

2613. OTEY, PETER J. Extract of speech in the House of representatives, July 19, 1897; Effect of federal legislation on state affairs. Washington, Govt., 1897.

    16 p. 8°.   V

2614. PAUL, JOHN. Contested-election case of John Paul *v.* Thomas W. Harrison from the seventh Congressional district of Virginia . . . Washington, Govt., 1921.

    2 v. 8°.   LC

2615. PLATT, JAMES H. Virginia politics. Speech of Hon. James H. Platt, of Virginia, delivered in the House of representatives, Apr. 6, 1872. Washington, Rives & Bailey, 1872.

    14 p. 8°.   LC

A bitter attack upon the Democratic party of Virginia, which the author charges with deception in regaining control of affairs in that state in 1870.

2616. THORNTON, WILLIAM M. . . . John Warwick Daniel. Address delivered at the unveiling of Ezekiel's statue of Senator Daniel, at Lynchburg, Va., May 26, 1915, by William M. Thornton . . . Washington, Govt., 1915.

    16 p. 8°. ([U. S.] 64 Cong., 1 sess. Senate. *Doc.,* 17)   LC, V, VU

Sketch of the life of this distinguished Virginian, with brief quotations from his speeches to illustrate his attitude on public questions.

2617. TUCKER, JOHN R. Contested-election case of Platt *v.* Goode. Speech of Hon. John Randolph Tucker of Virginia, in the House of representatives, July 26, 1876. Washington [Govt.] 1876.

    19 p. 8°.   VU

2618. ———. Counting the electoral votes. Speech of Hon. John Randolph Tucker, of Virginia, in the House of representatives, . . . Jan. 23, 1877. Washington, 1877.

    51 p. 8°.   H, VU

Concerning the Hayes-Tilden election.

2619. ———. Elections by the People must be free from the power and presence of the standing army! Speech . . . delivered in the House of representatives, . . . Apr. 4, 1879 . . . Washington, Polkinhorn, 1879.

    16 p. 8°. (Reprint from *Congressional record,* IX, pt. 1, 237-243)

                                                   NYP, VU

2620. U. S. Congress. House. Elections no. 2, Committee on.
. . . Contested election case of John M. Parsons, contestant, *v.*
Edward W. Saunders, contestee, from the fifth Congressional dis-
trict of Virginia. Arguments of counsel before Committee on elec-
tions no. 2. J. H. Carrico . . . Hon. A. J. Montague, Hon.
John M. Thurston, attorneys for contestant. Hon. Edward W.
Saunders, as contestee. Washington, Govt., 1910.

224 p. 8°. (U. S. 61 Cong., 1 sess.)   LC, V

2621. ——. ——. ——. ——. O'Ferrall *v.* Paul. Papers and
testimony in the contested election case of C. T. O'Ferrall *v.* John
Paul, from the seventh Congressional district of Virginia. Jan. 9,
1884. Washington, Govt., 1884.

808 p. 8°.   V

2622. ——. ——. ——. Reconstruction, Committee on. . . .
Test oath in Virginia. Papers relative to the test oath in Virginia
. . . [Washington, 1869]

29 p. 8°. (41 Cong., 2 sess. House. *Miscell. doc.*, 8)   LC

Consists of papers laid before the Committee in the matter of the admission of Virginia to representation in Congress, etc.

2623. ——. ——. Senate. Privileges and elections, Committee on. . . . Report [of] the committee . . . who were
directed by the Senate to inquire into the alleged massacre of colored men at Danville, in the state of Virginia, on the 3d day of November last. May 27, 1884. [Washington, Govt., 1884?]

lxxv, 1298 p. 8°. (48 Cong., 1 sess. *Report,* 579)   V

2624. ——. District court. Virginia (Eastern dist.) Bankruptcy rules of the District court of the U. S. for the Eastern district of Virginia. January, 1928. Washington, Govt., 1928.

1 p. 1., 17 p. 8°.   LC

2625. ——. ——. ——. Rules of the District court of the U. S.
for the Eastern district of Virginia. January, 1928. Washington,
Govt., 1928.

viii, 27 p. 8°.   LC

2626. ——. Supreme court. Boundary line between Virginia and
Tennessee. Bill and exhibits in chancery. [Washington? 1886]

13 p., 1 l., 99 p. 8°.   V

2627. ———. WAR DEPT. Letter of the Secretary of war, communicating a corrected copy of the constitution framed by the Virginia convention, as furnished by Brevet Maj.-Gen. J. M. Schofield, commanding the First military district. [Washington, Govt., 1868]

26 p. 8°. (U. S. 40 Cong., 2 sess. Senate. *Exec. doc.,* 54) **V**

2628. [101] VIRGINIA. Annual reports of officers, boards, and institutions of . . . Virginia . . . Richmond, Va. [1866-19—

Include Annual report of Attorney general, 1865/66—

2629. ———. AMENDMENTS TO THE CONSTITUTION, Commission to suggest. The constitution of Virginia. Report of the Commission to suggest amendments to the constitution to the General assembly of Virginia. To be submitted to the extra session March, 1927. Richmond, Bottom, 1927.

xii, 82 p. 4°. **LC, NYP, V, VU, WM**

Robert R. Prentis, chairman.

Contains parallel texts of the state constitution as of March, 1927, and with the proposed amendments.

2630. ———. ———. . . . . Minutes of meetings; constitution of Virginia, report of Commission. Appendix: Stenographer's transcript: Public hearing; Report of Drafting committee of Commission. [Richmond, Va., 1927]

29 l., 1-44, xii, 82, 45-50 p., 241, 1 l., 128 p. 4°. **V**

Bound as arranged by the Comission.

Official papers of the Commission, with autograph signatures.

2631. ———. ———. Report of Drafting committee . . . [Richmond, 1927]

128 p. 4°. **V**

"Constitution with proposed amendments" and "Constitution as at present (for comparison)", in parallel columns.

2632. ———. ———. Suggested amendments to the constitution of Virginia. Summary of the Report of the Commission to suggest amendments to the constitution. Richmond, Bottom, 1927.

31 p. 8°. **LC, NYP, V, VU, WM**

Robert R. Prentis, chairman.

Explanation of the various amendments proposed and their significance in promoting economy and efficiency in the state government.

2633. VIRGINIA. ATTORNEY-GENERAL. Alphabetical summary of opinions of attorneys-general and of constitutional and statutory provisions relating to the compatibility of offices, state, federal, county, city and town. Comp. by Morton L. Wallerstein, law clerk. Office of the attorney-general of Virginia. Richmond, Bottom, 1915.

19 p. 8°.   HL, LC, V

2634. ——. ——. Annual report . . . Richmond [1866-19—

8°. Report year ends Sept. 30, 1865/66-88/89; Dec. 31, 1890-19—

H: 1915; HL: 1903-28; LC: 1872/73, 94, 1903-19, 21-26; NYP: 1903-06, 11-17, 19-27; V: 1880/81-81/82, 1903-27; VU: 1920.

2635. ——. ——. Jones *et al. v.* Virginia State board of canvassers, no. 189 in prohibition. Selden *et al. v.* same, no. 190 in equity. Argument of William A. Anderson, attorney-general of Virginia, before the Supreme court of the U. S., in the Virginia suffrage cases . . . Final argument Apr. 4th and 5th, 1904. [n. p., 1904]

48 p. 8°. (U. S. Supreme court. Oct term, 1903)   V

2636. ——. ——. Digest of opinions rendered by attorneys-general of Virginia, 1883-1915, inclusive. Office of Jno. Garland Pollard, attorney-general of Virginia. Richmond, Bottom, 1916.

131 p. 8°.   HL, LC, NYP, V, VU

"Explanatory note" signed: Morton L. Wallerstein.

2637. ——. ——. Executive continuance in office until a successor is constitutionally qualified; correspondence and opinion. [Richmond, 1868?]

16 p. 8°.   V

Opinion of the attorney-general, James Neeson.

2638. ——. ——. Qualifications for voting on enabling act. An opinion by the attorney-general of Virginia. Richmond, Bottom, 1914.

8 p. 16°.   LC

John Garland Pollard, attorney-general.

2639. ——. AUDITOR. . . . List of judges and officers in counties and cities . . . comp. and issued by auditor of public accounts, Jan. 1, 1928. Richmond, Bottom, 1928.

22 p. 8°.   LC

2640. ———. ———. List of judges, treasurers, sheriffs, and other officers in the state of Virginia . . . Pub. by the auditor of public accounts. Richmond [189-?-19—

16°. LC: 1899, 1915, 21; V: 1899, 1904, 15, 20, 22, 24, 26, 28.

2641. [1203] ———. ———. [?] [Vouchers for constitutional convention, 1867-68]

2642. ———. BOUNDARY LINE BETWEEN VIRGINIA AND MARYLAND, Commissioner relative to the. Report to the governor of the Virginia Commissioner relative to the boundary line between Virginia and Maryland. Printed pursuant to a joint resolution. Richmond, O'Bannon, 1888.

2 p. l., 594, [1] p. 4°. V

2643. ———. BOUNDARY LINES, Commission on, 1870-74. Documents relating to the western and southern boundary of the states of Maryland and Virginia. Richmond, Clemmitt & Jones, 1874.

80 p. 8°. V

2644. ———. ———. Final report of the Virginia Commissioners on the Maryland and Virginia boundary to the governor of Virginia. Richmond, Walker, 1874.

221 p. 8°. BP, H, LC, NYP, V

Contents: Report.—Memoranda of a journal of the Virginia Commissioners: Correspondence.—Journal of the joint commission of Maryland and Virginia.

2645. ———. ———. Report and accompanying documents of the Virginia commissioners appointed to ascertain the boundary line between Maryland and Virginia. Richmond, Walker, 1873.

146, 314 p. plate. 8°. BP; H, HL (maps wanting); LC, NYP, V

Contents: A. Statement on the part of the Commissioners of Maryland.—B. Statement on the part of the Commissioners of Virginia.—C. Appendix (314 p.) Depositions taken by the Commissioners of Maryland and Virginia.

"Maps to accompany the Report of the Commissioners on the boundary line between Virginia and Maryland"; bound separately: 2 p. l., 9 fold. maps. 8°.

2646. ———. ———. . . . The report of the commissioners on boundary lines between the state of Virginia, and the states of

372   BIBLIOGRAPHY OF VIRGINIA HISTORY

Maryland, North Carolina and Tennessee, read in the Senate, Jan. 17, 1872. [Richmond, 1872]

2 p. 1., [3]-22 p. 8°. ([Virginia. General assembly, 1871-72] Senate doc.)   BP, HL, LC, NYP, V

2647. VIRGINIA. CITIZENS' COMMITTEE ON CONSOLIDATION AND SIMPLIFICATION IN STATE AND LOCAL GOVERNMENTS. Report . . . Submitted to the governor of Virginia in accordance with Act of General assembly of 1926. Richmond, Bottom, 1927.

19 p. 8°.   LC, V

William T. Reed, chairman.

The organization of the state and local governments in 1926 and a detailed exposition of the proposed re-organization.

2648. ———. CODE, Commission to revise the. Report of the Commission to revise the code, submitted to the General assembly . . . , Feb. 2, 1916. Richmond, 1916.

4 p. 8°.   V

2648a. ———. ———. Report of the Commission to revise the Code of Virginia, submitted to the General assembly, session 1918. Richmond, Bottom, 1917.

x, 2177 p. 8°.   V

2649. ———. CONSTITUTION. Constitution of Virginia. [Richmond, 1867?]

33 p. 8°.   V

2650. ———. ———. Constitution of Virginia, framed by the convention which met in Richmond, Virginia, the third day of December, 1867. Richmond, State journal print. [n. d.]

70 p. 8°.   V

Includes also election ordinance; congressional apportionment; First military district, *General orders,* 61, 65 **[3184]**; official memoranda.

2651. ———. ———. Constitution of Virginia . . . Richmond, State journal print. [n. d.]

36 p. 8°.   V

2652. ———. ———. The constitution of Virginia, framed by the convention which met in Richmond, Virginia, on Tuesday, December 3, 1867. Passed April 17, 1868. Richmond, New nation pub., 1868.

    41 p., 1 l. 8°.   **BP, H, LC, NYP, V**

    Corrected ed., 1868: 37 p.   **V**

2653. ———. ———. Die constitution von Virginien, passirt in der am Dienstag den 3ten Dezember 1867, zu Richmond, Va., zusammengetretenen convention. Angenommen am 17ten April, 1868. Richmond, Va., Virginia staatszeitung, 1868.

    48 p. 8°.   **V**

2654. ———. ———. Constitution of Virginia. [Printed pursuant to a resolution adopted by the General assembly on the 9th day of December, 1876. Richmond? 1876]

    33, [1] p. 8°.   **LC, V**

2655. ———. ———. Constitution [as ratified by vote of the people, July 6, 1869, with subsequent amendments] [Richmond? 1883?]

    22 p. 8°.   **NYP, V**

2656. ———. ———. The constitution of Virginia, an annotated ed., by Armistead R. Long . . . Together with a reprint of the previous constitutions of Virginia. Lynchburg, Va., Bell, 1901.

    xvi p., 1 l., 194 p. 8°.   **H, LC, V**

2657. ———. ———. The constitution of the state of Virginia, adopted by the convention of 1901-2. Published by authority. Richmond, 1902.

    x, 87 p. 8°.   **H, HL, LC, NYP, USAg, USC, V, VU**

2658. ———. ———. Constitution of Virginia. Richmond, Bottom, 1912.

    68 p., 1 l. 16°.   **LC, NYP, V**

    "Amendments ratified at election in November, 1912" (1 l.) laid in. Ed. of 1908: 79 p.   **BP**

2659. ———. ———. Constitution of Virginia . . . Richmond, Bottom, 1915.

    150 p. 16°.   **H, HL, LC, NYP, V, VU**

2660. ———. ———. Draft of the constitution of Virginia as finally adopted by the convention and referred to the Committee on final revision and adjustment of the various provisions of the constitution that may be agreed upon, and upon the schedule. Richmond, O'Bannon, 1902.

55 p. 8°.   LC

2661. VIRGINIA. CONSTITUTION. Proposed amendments to the constitution . . . agreed to by the General assembly of 1926 and . . . to be published for three months prior to the next general election. [Richmond, Bottom, 1926]

13 p. 8°.   V

2662. ———. ———. Proposed amendments to the constitution of Virginia. Agreed to by the General assembly of Virginia at the regular session of 1926 and the extra session of 1927. Pub. in pursuance of section 196 of the constitution and an act of the General assembly of Virginia approved Apr. 18, 1927. Richmond, Bottom, 1927.

70 p. 8°.   LC, NYP, V

2663. ———. CONSTITUTIONAL CONVENTION, 1867-68. Address of the conservative members of the late state convention to the people of Virginia. [n. p., n. d.]

8 p. 8°.   V

2664. ———. ———. The debates and proceedings of the Constitutional convention of the state of Virginia, assembled at the city of Richmond, Tuesday, Dec. 3, 1867: being a full and complete report of the debates and proceedings of the convention, together with the reconstruction acts of Congress and those supplementary thereto, the order of the commander of the First military district assembling the convention, and the new constitution. Official: W. H. Samuel, phonographic reporter. Richmond, New nation pub., 1868.

750 p. 8°.   H, LC, NYP, V

2665. ———. ———. Documents of the Constitutional convention of the state of Virginia. Richmond, New nation pub., 1867 [1868]

310 p. tables (1 fold.) 8°.   H, HL, LC, NYP, V

2666. ———. ———. Journal of the Constitutional convention of the state of Virginia, convened in the city of Richmond, Dec. 3, 1867, by an order of General Schofield, dated Nov. 2, 1867, in pursuance of the act of Congress of Mar. 23, 1867. Richmond, New nation pub., 1867 [1868]

391 p. 8°.   BP, H, HL, LC, NYP, V

2667. ———. ———. Protest of the conservative candidates from the city of Richmond, against the confirmation of the proceedings at the election on the 23d and 24th days of October, 1867. Richmond, Va., Oct. 31, 1867.

3 p. 8°.   V

Addressed to Maj.-Gen. Schofield and signed by Thomas J. Evans, Alexander H. Sands, N. A. Sturdivant, Marmaduke Johnson, William Taylor.

2668. ———. ———. Reply of Maj-Gen. Schofield to the protest of the conservative candidates from the city of Richmond, against the confirmation of the proceedings at the election on the 23d and 24th days of October, 1867. Richmond, Va., Nov. 7, 1867.

5 p. 8°.   V

2669. ———. CONSTITUTIONAL CONVENTION, 1901-02. An ordinance to provide for the registration of voters under this constitution, and prior to the year nineteen hundred and four (1904) [Richmond, 1902]

24 p. 8°. (In its *Journal,* 1901-[02])   LC, NYP

2670. ———. ———. Journal of the Constitutional convention of Virginia. Held in the city of Richmond, beginning June 12th, 1901. Printed by authority. Richmond, O'Bannon, 1901-[02]

574, [473], x p., 1 l., 87 p. 8°.   H, LC, NYP, V, VU

2671. ———. ———. Report of the proceedings and debates of the Constitutional convention, state of Virginia. Held in the city of Richmond June 12, 1901, to June 26, 1902 . . . Richmond, Va., Hermitage press, 1906.

2 v. 8°.   H, HL, LC, NYP, V, VU, WM

J. H. Lindsay, ed. and comp.

2672. ———. ———. [Resolutions of the Constitutional convention of 1901-02. n. p., n. d.]

8°.   V: 1-294 (incompl.).

2673. VIRGINIA. CONSTITUTIONAL CONVENTION, 1901-02. COMMIT-
TEE UPON FINAL REVISION AND ADJUSTMENT . . . Report of
the Committee upon final revision and adjustment of various provisions of the constitution, and upon the schedule. [n. p., n. d.]
96 p. 4°.   V

2674. [1207] ——. CORPORATION COMMISSION, State. . . .
Rules of practice and procedure in cases and proceedings before
the . . . commission . . . [Richmond, 1903]

2675. ——. ECONOMY AND EFFICIENCY, Commission on. . . .
Report of the Commission on economy and efficiency to the General assembly, Jan. 9, 1918. [Richmond, Richmond press, 1918]
67 p. 3 fold. diagrs. 8°.   H, LC, NYP, V
P. H. Drewry, chairman.

A survey of the various departments and boards of the state government, exposing the weaknesses and deficiencies of the system; consolidation recommended, and a budget system.

2676. ——. EXAMINERS OF APPLICANTS FOR ADMISSION TO THE
BAR, Board of. Virginia bar examinations, from June, 1910, to
most recent examination. Richmond, Appeals press [n. d.]
90 p. 8°.   V
See also items **[33 , 33]**

2677. ——. GENERAL ASSEMBLY. Attendance book . . . [1874,
81, 82 (and extra sess., 82), 83/84, 85/86, 87/88, 89/90-97/98]
MSS.   V

2678. ——. ——. . . . . A description of the seal and flag;
joint resolution adopted by the General assembly, Jan., 1912.
Richmond, Bottom, 1912.
[4] p. illus. 8°.   V

2679. ——. ——. List of members of the Senate and House of
delegates of Virginia . . . Richmond [18-? -19—
16°. BP: 1897/98; H: 1916; LC: 1901/02, 04, 16; V: 1897/98, 1901
(extra sess.), 04, 06, 12, 18, 26, 28; VU: 1908.

2680. ——. ——. Manual of the Senate and House of delegates
. . . Richmond [18-? -19—
16°. H: 1908; LC: 1897/98, 99/1900, 01/02-16, 26-28; NYP: 1885/86
(Senate), 91/92-1901/02, 08, 10, 14-28; USC: 1899/1900, 01/02-14, 16; V:
1876/77-77/78, 85/86, 87/88, 89/90, 91/92, 93/94, 1910-20; VU: 1910.

2681. ———. ———. A register of the General assembly of Virginia 1776-1918 and of the constitutional conventions, by Earl G. Swem . . . and John W. Williams . . . Richmond, Bottom, 1918.

x, 450 p. 8°. BP, H, LC, NYP, V, WM
Pub. also in Virginia. State library. *14th annual report,* 1916-17. **[330-]**

2682. ———. ———. Rules of the Senate and House of delegates of Virginia . . . Richmond [18-? -19—

16°. Pub. in the *Journals* of the Senate **[2693]** and of the House of delegates **[2690]**

2683. ———. ———. AUDITING COMMITTEE. Report of the Auditing committee of the legislature of Virginia for the year 1911. To which is added the report for the year 1910; and all made in conformity to section 68 of the Constitution . . . Richmond, Va., The auditing committee, 1911.

31 p. 8°. V

2684. ———. ———. INAUGURATION OF GOV. WILLIAM H. MANN, Committee on. Inauguration of Gov. Wm. H. Mann, hall of the House of delegates, Feb. 1, 1910. [Richmond? 1910]

4 l. illus., plates (ports.) 8°. V

2685. ———. ———. INAUGURATION OF GOV. H. C. STUART, Committee on. Inauguration of Gov. H. C. Stuart, Feb. 2d, 1914 . . . [Richmond? 1914]

10 l. incl. pl., ports. 4°. LC, V
Committee on the part of the Senate: Edward Echols, John R. Saunders, A. C. Harman, *et al.* Committee on the part of the House: Edwin P. Cox (speaker), W. W. Baker, Chas. W. Grant, *et al.*

2686. ———. ———. INAUGURATION OF GOV. E. LEE TRINKLE, Committee on. Inauguration of Gov. E. Lee Trinkle, . . . Feb. 1, 1922. [Richmond, Waddey, 1922]

12 l. incl. col. front., plates, ports. 8°. V

2687. ———. ———. INAUGURATION OF GOV. HARRY F. BYRD, Committee on. Ceremonies incident to the inauguration of Harry Flood Byrd, governor of Virginia, . . . Feb. 1, 1926. [Richmond, 1926]

14 l. incl. plates, ports. 8°. V

2688. VIRGINIA. GENERAL ASSEMBLY. REDISTRICTING THE STATE, Joint committee for. Plan agreed upon by the Joint committee for redistricting the state into districts for the Senate and House of delegates on the basis of a population of 2,306,351 . . . Richmond, 1921.

15 p. 8°.   V

2689. ———. ———. HOUSE OF DELEGATES. House bills . . . [Richmond? 1866-19—

8°. **NYP:** 1907; **V:** 1866/67, 74/75, 78/79-79/80, 81/82, 87/88, 89/90, 95/96, 97/98, 99/1900, 01/02, 19-20, 22-24, 26-28; **VU:** 1873-77/78.

2690. ———. ———. ———. Journal [1] . . . Richmond [1865-19—

8°. **BP:** 1864/65, 69, 69/70-70/71, 74, 74/75-75/76, 1915 (extra sess.); **HL:** 1912-14, 19-23; **LC:** 1865-67, 69/70-1928; **McC:** 1874; **NYP:** 1865-67, 69-1920, 22-28; **V:** 1865/66-1928; **VU:** 1870/71, 72/73, 74-1928; **WM:** 1869/70-71/72, 74-79, 81/82-93/94, 1902-04, 10-16, 18-22, 26, 28.

2691. ———. ———. ———. Report of the Special committee of the House of delegates, to investigate the charges against Hon. Alexander Mahood, judge of the 14th Judicial circuit of Virginia, together with the testimony taken by the Committee. Richmond, Schaffter, 1871.

51 p. 8°.   V

2692. ———. ———. SENATE. Senate bills . . . [Richmond? 1866-19—

8°. **NYP:** 1907; **V:** 1870/71, 77/78, 83/84, 85/86, 87, 91/92, 95/96, 99/1900, 02/04, 06-28; **VU:** 1876/77-79.

2693. ———. ———. ———. Journal [1] . . . Richmond [1865-19—

8°. **BP:** 1866/67, 69/70-70/71, 74-74/75; **HL:** 1912-15, 19-23; **LC:** 1865-67, 69/70-1928; **McC:** 1874; **NYP:** 1866/67-1928; **V:** 1865-1928; **VU:** 1865, 66/67, 69/70-70/71, 74-1928; **WM:** 1869/70-71/72, 74-78/79, 81/82, 83/84-87, 89/90-91/92, 93/94, 99/1900-04, 10-28.

2694. ———. GOVERNOR. Executive papers of Virginia. 1866-77; Feb., Mar., 1878; June-Dec., 1879; 1881; June-Dec., 1882; 1883-98.

MSS.   V

---

1. The documents appended to the *Journals,* 1865-1916, are analyzed in E. G. Swem, *Bibliography of Virginia,* II, 569 ff. **[36]**

2695. ———. ———. Messages . . . [Richmond, 1865-19—

8°. **BP**: 1874, 89; **LC**: 1867, 72, 75, 77, 1912, 14-15, 18, 20, 24, 26; **NYP**: 1865-67, 70-72, 74-77, 81, 87, 89, 91-96, 98, 1902-04, 08-18, 22-26; **V**: 1865-67, 69-72, 74-79, 81-1928.

See also the *Journals* of the Senate [2693] and of the House of delegates [2690]

2696. ———. ———. [Separate messages, proclamations, etc. Richmond, etc., 1865-19—

8°. **BP**: Dec. 2, 1874; Dec. 6, 1889; 1898. **H**: June 19, 1865; Mar. 27, 1874; Jan. 10, 1912; Jan. 14, 1920. **NYP**: Mar. 8, 1870; Jan. 13, 1873; Nov. 26, 1903. **USC**: Feb., 1902. **V**: 1865, 70, 74, 77, 78, 81, 82, 91, 99, 1902, 04, 06, 08, 10, 12, 14, 15, 16, 18, 20, 22, 23, 24, 26, 28. **VU**: Feb. 1, 1918; Mar. 3, 1922; Jan. 13, 1926.

See also the documents appended to the *Journals* of the Senate [2693] and of the House of delegates [2690]

2697. ———. GOVERNOR, 1869-73 (Gilbert C. Walker). Messages and official papers of Hon. G. C. Walker, governor of Virginia, during the years 1869 . . . [to] 1873. Richmond, Schaffter, 1871 [1874?]

167 (*i. e.*, 165), [117] p. front. (port.) 8°. **H, V, VU**

2698. [364] ———. ———, 1874-76 (James L. Kemper). Correspondence of the governor of Virginia with the governor of Maryland and the authorities of Accomac County, Va. . . . Richmond, 1874.

2699. ———. ———, 1898-1902 (J. Hoge Tyler). Letters and public papers of Gov. J. Hoge Tyler, 1898-1902. [n. p., 19—]

194 p. front. (port.) 8°. **LC, V**

2700. ———. ———, 1906-10 (Claude A. Swanson). Addresses, messages, and proclamations of Claude A. Swanson . . . 1906-10. Richmond, Bottom, 1910.

158 p. 8°. **LC, NYP, V**

2701. ———. ———, 1922-26 (E. Lee Trinkle). . . . Report on the state personnel situation in Virginia to the General assembly January, 1926. By E. Lee Trinkle, governor. Richmond, Bottom, 1926.

149 p. incl. tables. 8°. ([General assembly, 1926] Senate. [*Doc.*] 1)
LC, NYP, V, VU

2702. VIRGINIA. GOVERNOR, 1926— (Harry F. Byrd). Address
. . . on the subject of simplification of government in Virginia.
Delivered before the General assembly of Virginia, . . . Feb.
3, 1926. Richmond, Bottom, 1926.

    10 p. 8°.   **NYP, V**

2703. ——. ——. ——. The constitution of Virginia. A discussion of the amendments proposed to the constitution of Virginia
. . . Election, June 19, 1928. [Richmond, Bottom, 1928]

    24 p. 8°.   **V**

2704. ——. ——. ——. A discussion of the amendments proposed to the constitution of Virginia . . . Proposal no. 1.
Election, June 19, 1928. [Richmond, 1928]

    8 p. 8°.   **V**

2705. ——. ——. ——. A discussion of the amendments proposed to the constitution of Virginia . . . Proposal no. 2.
Election, June 19, 1928. [Richmond, 1928]

    10 p. 8°.   **V**

2706. ——. ——. ——. A discussion of the amendments proposed to the constitution of Virginia . . . Proposals 3, 4, and
5. Election, June 19, 1928. [Richmond, 1928]

    6 p. 8°.   **V**

2707. ——. ——. ——. A discussion of the plan to increase governmental efficiency by vesting in the governor the authority to be
"business manager" of Virginia's government. [Richmond, 1927]

    8 p. 8°.   **NYP, V**

2708. ——. ——. ——. Inaugural address of Harry Flood Byrd,
governor, delivered before the General assembly and the people of
Virginia . . . Feb. 1, 1926. Richmond, Bottom, 1926.

    17 p. 8°.   **V**

2709. ——. ——. ——. Looking forward; an address on governmental re-organization and the future outlook for Virginia . . .
Richmond, Bottom, 1927.

    15 p. 8°.   **V**
    Delivered before the Farmers' 4H. club of Madison County, July 15,
1927.

2710. ——. ——. ——. Program of progress. An address, by Harry Flood Byrd, governor. Delivered before the General assembly of Virginia, Jan. 16, 1928 . . . Richmond, Bottom, 1928.

14 p. 8°. ([General assembly, 1928] Senate. *Doc.,* 5) **LC, V**

2711. ——. ——. ——. Reorganization of the government of Virginia. Address of Harry F. Byrd, governor. Delivered before the General assembly of Virginia, extra session, . . . Mar. 16, 1927. Richmond, Bottom, 1927.

12 p. 8°. ([General assembly, 1927] House. *Doc.,* 1) **LC, V**

A concise, summary statement of surveys of the state government, made by various commissions with a view to simplification and consolidation; suggested amendments to the constitution; the financial condition of the state.

2712. ——. ——. ——. Virginia's business government, an address by Harry Flood Byrd, governor, delivered before the General assembly of Virginia convened in regular session, Jan. 11, 1928 . . . Richmond, Bottom, 1928.

48 p. 8°. ([General assembly] Senate. *Doc.,* 1) **NYP, V**

2713. ——. LAWS, STATUTES, etc. . . . An act for protection of labels, trademarks, &c. Approved Apr. 30, 1903. [n. p., 1903?]

5 p. 8°. **V**

2714. ——. ——. . . . An act to reorganize the administration of the state government. Adopted at the extra session of the General assembly of Virginia, 1927. Reprinted from Acts of assembly. Richmond, Bottom, 1927.

24 p. 8°. **LC, NYP, V**

Running title: The reorganization of the state government.

2715. ——. ——. Acts and joint resolutions (amending the Constitution) of the General assembly. Session . . . [Richmond, 18-? -19—

8°. **V**: 1893/94, 1922-24, 26, 27 (extra sess.), 28.

2716. ——. ——. Acts of the General assembly of Virginia . . . Richmond [1865-19—

8°. **BP:** 1866/67, 69/70-72/73, 74 77/78, 79/80, 81/82, 83/84-85/86, 87/88; **H:** 1866/67, 69/70-72/73, 74-77/78, 79/80, 81/82, 83/84-85/86, 87/88, 1902/03 (extra sess.); **HL:** 1865/66-67, 69/70-1926, 27 (extra);

LC: 1865-1928; **McC**: 1866/67, 70/71, 74, 74/75, 83/84, 84 (extra), 87/88, 89/90; **NYP**: 1865-93/94, 95/96-1928; **USAg**: 1865/66-66/67, 79/80, 84 (extra), 85/86, 91/92-1928; **USC**: 1887/88, 89/90-1928; **USL**: 1918-28; **V**: 1865-1928; **VU**: 1865-1928; **WM**: 1865/66-66/67, 69/70-72/73, 74-79/80, 81/82, 83/84-89/90, 91/92-97/98, 1901 (extra), 01/02-04, 06-28.

2717. VIRGINIA. LAWS, STATUTES, etc. Amendments to election laws, 1908. [Richmond? 1908?]

    8 p. 8°.   LC, V

2718. ———. ———. An annotated pocket code of Virginia: embracing such parts of the code of 1887, and the subsequent acts of the General assembly, as an attorney usually needs in his practice; with a general index to code and acts, which is an index to all the code of 1887 and all subsequent acts, and an index to local acts, which is an index to said code and acts so far as relating to particular counties, cities, towns, &c.; to which is added the U. S. bankruptcy law, By Sam N. Hurst . . . Published pursuant to legislative authority. Pulaski City, Va.: Hurst & co., 1898.

    498 p. 12°.   LC, NYP, V, VU
    2d ed., 1905: vii, [1], 691 p.   LC, V, VU
    3d ed., 1913: vii, [1], 921 p.   LC, V, VU
    4th ed., 1920: xxii, 1051 p.   LC, V, VU
    5th ed., 1928: 1442 p.   LC, V, VU

2719. ———. ———. . . . Code of Virginia: including legislation to Jan. 1, 1874. Prepared by George W. Munford. Published for the state of Virginia, pursuant to law, under the direction of R. F. Walker, supt. of public printing. [3d ed.] Richmond, Goode, 1873.

    xix, 1646, [1] p. 8°.   LC, NYP, V, VU, WM
    Authorized by Acts of Mar. 25 and Apr. 2, 1873. This is a compilation, not a revision.

2720. ———. ———. The Code of Virginia: with the Declaration of independence and the Constitution of the U. S.; and the constitution of Virginia. Published pursuant to an act of the General assembly of Virgina, approved May 21, 1887 . . . Richmond, Goode, 1887.

    xvi, 1177 p., 1 l. 8°.   LC, USAg, V, VU
    Revised by E. C. Burks, Waller R. Staples, and John W. Riely, as provided for in an act approved Mar. 18, 1884.

2721. ———. ———. ———Howard's index to the Code of Virginia of 1887. By Overton Howard. Richmond, Va., West, Johnston, 1895.

    203 p. 8°.   **V**

2722. ———. ———. ———Supplement to the Code of Virginia: being a compilation of all acts of a general and permanent nature passed by the General assembly since Mar. 15, 1887; to which are added references to decisions construing or affecting the Code of 1887, and subsequent legislation; including also references to all local public acts, passed during the same period, affecting particular counties, cities or towns of the commonwealth. By Jno. Garland Pollard . . . Richmond, Hill, 1898.

    vi p., 1 l., 514 p. 8°.   **LC, NYP, V, VU**

2723. ———. ———. Code of Virginia as amended to adjournment of General assembly, 1904, together with all other statutes of a general and permanent nature then in force, including tax bill, annotated constitution of Virginia, Constitution of the U. S., Declaration of independence, Articles of confederation, published by authority of the General assembly. Edited by Jno. Garland Pollard of the Richmond bar . . . St. Paul, Minn., West, 1904.

    2 v. 8°.   **LC, V, VU**

2724. ———. ———. Code of Virginia, with the Declaration of independence, the Constitution of the U. S., the constitution of Virginia . . . annotated . . . Pub. by authority of the commonwealth of Virginia under an act approved Mar. 8, 1918. Richmond, Bottom, 1919.

    2 v. 8°.   **HL, LC, NYP, USC, USL, V, VU, WM**

    "The statutes of this state of a general nature have been revised and codified but three times since the year 1819. These codifications consist of the codes of 1849, 1887 and the present code. There have been other publications called codes, to-wit: The codes of 1860, 1873 and 1904, and . . . supplements of the last mentioned . . . They were mere compilations of statutes by private persons . . ."

    Ed. of 1924: cvi, 2048 p.   **HL, LC, USAg, USC, V, VU, WM**
    Supplements . . . , comp. by John G. Pollard: 1922, 26, 28.
                              HL, LC, NYP, USC, V, VU, WM

2725. ———. ———. The Code of Virginia (pleading and practice)

an abridgment of the Virginia Code of 1924 for the student of
Virginia pleading and practice. Charlottesville, Va., Michie, 1927.

1 p. l., p. 1505-1824. 8°.   **LC, V, VU**

2726. VIRGINIA. LAWS, STATUTES, etc. A compilation of the laws
of a general and permanent nature passed by the General assembly
of Virginia, at its session of 1899-1900, exclusive of the tax laws
published by the auditor of public accounts . . . Richmond,
Hill, 1900.

184 p. 8°. (With Virginia. Laws, statutes, etc. *Supplement to the
code of Virginia,* 1898 **[2722]**)

2727. ———. ———. Extracts from Virginia election laws, also the
electoral board and registration laws. Richmond [18? -19—

8°. **H:** 1906; **LC:** 1906; **V:** 1881, 83, 87, 89, 90, 92, 1900, 04, 06, 12,
16, 20, 24, 26 suppl.

2728. ———. ———. General laws of the commonwealth of Virginia, as in force July 1, 1923, with the Constitution of the U. S.,
the constitution of Virginia, and annotations as stated in the
preface, edited by C. H. Morrissett . . . Charlottesville, Va.,
Surber-Arundale, 1923.

cxviii, 2177 p. 8°.   **HL, LC, NYP, V**

2729. ———. ———. General laws of Virginia. 1887-94. A compilation of laws of a general and permanent nature passed since
the adoption of the Code of 1887, including tax and license laws.
By Jno. Garland Pollard, of the Richmond bar. Richmond, Va.,
Hill [1894]

2 p. l., 290, p. 8°.   **USAg, V**
Ed. of 1896.   **USAg**

2730. ———. ———. Joint resolution proposing an amendment to
section 46, article IV of the constitution. [Richmond? 1907?]

3 p. 8°.   **NYP**

2731. ———. ———. . . . Laws relating to the powers and duties of the state accountant. In effect June 18, 1922. [Richmond,
1922]

8°.   **NYP**

2732. ———. ———. The negotiable instruments law of Virginia.
As enacted by the General assembly of Virginia, session 1897-98.
Richmond, Waddey, 1898.

24 p. 8°.   **V**

2733. ———. ———. An official pocket Code and form book for justices of the peace, mayors, sheriffs, constables, notaries, and other officials, containing all the statutory law of Virginia pertaining to their duties up to and including acts, 1928, and over 200 up-to-date legal forms for the practical discharge of their various duties, by Sam N. Hurst . . . Appalachia, Va., Hurst & co., 1928.

> 619 p. 12°.   LC
> "Published pursuant to legislative authority."

2734. ———. ———. An ordinance to provide for the registration of voters . . . prior to the year 1904. [n. p., n. d.]
> 24 p. 8°.   LC
> Includes list of registration boards, by counties.

2735. ———. ———. Pollard's code biennial, 1908; containing all statutes of a general and permanent nature passed by the General assembly of Virginia at its sessions of 1906 and 1908, also annotations to the Code of Virginia, 1904, and the constitution and tax bill; ed. by Jno. Garland Pollard . . . Richmond, Va., Waddey, 1908.

> xxvii, 759 p. 8°.   LC, V, VU
> Ed. of 1912: liv, 399 p.   LC, V, VU

2736. ———. ———. Pollard's supplement to the code of Virginia, containing all statutes of a general and permanent nature passed by the General assembly at its sessions of 1906, 1908 and 1910. Also annotations to the Code of Virginia, 1904, and the constitution and tax bill. Edited by Jno. Garland Pollard . . . Richmond, Va., Waddey, 1910.

> 1027 p. 8°.   HL, LC, V, VU
> "This work is intended to bring down to date the Code of 1904."

2737. ———. ———. . . . . Powers and duties of the boards of supervisors . . . Issued by auditor of public accounts. 1928. Richmond, Div. of purchaser and printing, 1928.

> 175 p. incl. tables, forms. 8°.   LC

2738. ———. ———. Primary election laws of Virginia in effect Jan. 1, 1915, with a summary of the opinions rendered by Jno. Garland Pollard, attorney-general. Issued by B. O. James, secretary of the commonwealth. Richmond, Bottom, 1915.

> 22 p. 8°.   LC, V

BIBLIOGRAPHY OF VIRGINIA HISTORY

2739. VIRGINIA. LAWS, STATUTES, etc. Provisions of the laws of
Virginia relating to commissioners in other states, territories, &c.
[n. p., 1881]

5 p. 8°. V

2740. ———. ———. Virginia election laws, also the Electoral board
and registration laws . . . Richmond, Bottom [19—

8°. H: 1912, 16; **LC:** 1912, 16, 24; **V:** 1912, 16; **VU:** 1916.

2741. ———. LEGISLATIVE REFERENCE BUREAU. [Bulletins, 1914-
18 . . . Richmond, Bottom, 1914-18]

8°. V

2742. ———. ———. Legislation in Virginia 1914. Comp. by Lewis
Machen, director of the Legislative reference bureau of Virginia.
Richmond, Bottom, 1915.

13 p. 8°. LC, NYP, V

Condensed analysis of affirmative work of a general nature accomplished by the legislature of 1914; arranged topically.

2743. ———. ———. Legislation in Virginia. Extra session 1915.
Prepared by Hon. Lewis Machen, chairman of the Committee on
legislation and law reform of the Virginia state bar association,
for its annual meeting, Aug. 4, 5, and 6, 1915. Richmond, Richmond press, 1915.

31 p. 8°. V

2744. ———. ———. Notes on statutes subsequent to the Code of
1919. By C. H. Morrissett, director of the Legislative reference
bureau. Richmond, Bottom, 1921.

1 p. l., 106 p. 8°. H, LC, NYP, V, VU

2745. ———. SECRETARY OF THE COMMONWEALTH. Annual report . . . Richmond [1865-19—

plates. 8°. Report year ends Sept. 30.
H: 1910/11, 26/27; **LC:** 1902/03-16/17, 18/19-20/21, 22/23-26/27;
NYP: 1902/03-27/28; **USC:** 1902/03, 04/05-18/19, 22/23; **USL:** 1926/27;
V: 1902/03-11/12, 13/14-14/15, 18/19-20/21, 22/23-26/27; **VU:** 1902/03,
04/05-10/11, 12/13-13/14, 17/18, 20/21, 22/23, 25/26.

For Reports prior to 1902/03, see Virginia. General assembly. Senate.
Documents, appended to *Journal.* **[2693]**

2746. ———. SIMPLIFICATION AND ECONOMY OF STATE AND LOCAL

GOVERNMENT, Commission on. Report . . . to the General
assembly of Virginia January, 1924. Richmond, Bottom, 1924.

233 p. tables (1 fold.) 8°.   LC, NYP, V, VU, WM

In 3 parts: (1) History and general principles (including what former commissions have done); (2) Recommendations; (3) Summary and
conclusions. A valuable study of the state government.

2747. ———. SUPREME COURT OF APPEALS. Cases decided in the
Supreme court of appeals of Virginia . . . 1866/67— [v. 58-]
Richmond [1867-19—

8°. Title varies: Reports of cases decided . . .

Reporters: P. R. Grattan, 1866/67-83, v. 17-33 [v. 58-74]; James M.
Matthews, 1881/82, v. 1 [v. 75]; George W. Hansbrough, 1881/83-93/95,
v. 1-15 [v. 76-90]; Martin P. Burks, 1895-1916 (29 v.) [v. 91-119];
Thomas J. Michie, 1916/17— [v. 120-   ] in progress.

HL: 1895-1928; LC: 1881-1928; NYP: 1916/17-17/18; V: 1866/67-
1928; VU: 1866/67-1928.

2748. ———. ———. Rules of the Supreme court of appeals of the
state of Virginia. Revised and adopted June 25, 1869 . . .
Richmond, Va., 1869.

22 p. 8°.   V

2748a. ———. [———] Virginia appeals. Decisions of the Supreme
court of appeals of Virginia . . . Vol. 1. From Mar. 1, 1907,
to Feb. 29, 1908. Richmond, 1907-08.

xiv, 906 p. 8°.   V, VU

Editors: Wm. W. Scott and Maury B. Watts.

2749. ———. [———] Virginia appeals; the earliest report of all
current decisions of the Supreme court of appeals, 1921-24. v.
24-32. Richmond, Va., 1921-[24]

8°.   HL

2750. ———. ———. Virginia reports, Jefferson—33 Grattan. 1730-
1880. Annotated under the supervision of T. J. Michie. Charlottesville, Va., Michie co., 1901.

8°.   LC

Contents: Reports of cases . . . by P. R. Grattan.—v. 24-25,
From Nov. 1, 1873-Mar. 1, 1875. [Reprint]

2751. ———. UNIFORM STATE LAWS, Commissioners on. Report,
 . . . 1915. Richmond, 1915.

8°.   HL

2752. WADDILL, EDMUND, jr.   Edmund Waddill, jr., contestant, *v.* Geo. D. Wise, contestee.   Contested election from the third Congressional district of Virginia, before the House committee on elections of the 51st Congress.   Reply brief for contestant . . . Richmond, Jones, 1889.

36 p. 8°.   V

2753. WALKER, JAMES A.   Contested-election case.   Thorp *v.* Epes. Speech . . . in the House of representatives . . . Mar. 22, 1898.   Washington [Govt.] 1898.

20 p. 8°.   LC

2754. WHYTE, [WILLIAM] P.   Boundary line between the states of Maryland and Virginia.   Before the Board of arbitrators.   Synopsis of argument made by Mr. Pinkney Whyte, of counsel for Maryland, Aug. 26, 1876.   [Baltimore? 1876?]

36 p. 8°.   LC, V, WM

In support of Maryland's claim to the Potomac River and all the islands in it, to the southwestern bank of that river.

2755. WILSON, C. E.   Contested election case of C. E. Wilson, contestant, *v.* F. R. Lassiter, contestee, for the seat in the 57th Congress of the U. S. from the fourth Congressional district of Virginia.   Brief for contestant . . . [n. p., 1901?]

60 p. 8°.   LC

Other Source Material

2756. [BAGBY, GEORGE W.]   1860-1880.   John Brown and William Mahone.   An historical parallel foreshadowing civil trouble.   Richmond, Va., Johnston, 1880.

23 p. 16°.   V

Signed: Edmund Ruffin's shade.

Relation of Virginia politics to national politics, and the antagonism between Democrats and Republicans.

2757. BELL, JOHN W.   Memoirs of Gov. William Smith of Virginia.   His political, military and personal history.   New York, Moss, 1891.

xvi p., 2 l., 461 p. front., illus., plate., port., facsim., diagr. 8°.

H, LC, V

Contains some reprints of letters on politics after 1865 and brief notes on the political life of the period.

2758. BRAXTON, A[LLEN] C. Address of Hon. A. C. Braxton, chairman of the Committee on corporations, Constitutional convention, in support of the majority report. Delivered . . . Feb. 4, 1902. Richmond, Hill, 1902.

32 p. 8°. V

2759. ———. The legitimate functions and powers of constitutional conventions with special note on Virginia convention of 1901. By A. Caperton Braxton . . . Lynchburg, Va., Bell, 1901.

30 p. 8°. LC, V
Reprint from *Virginia law register,* June, 1901.

2760. BUMGARNER, SIMEON C. Bumgarner's pocket code of Virginia, for magistrates; a compilation of the Virginia law, of a general and permanent nature, applicable in his court; together with all necessary forms and procedure, of general and permanent use; to which is added "a guide to notaries"; forms for the use of constables, and with a compilation of the Virginia law pertaining to the collection of debts, for the use of merchants and other business men, including a list of reliable attorneys in every town in the state of Virginia. Ed. and comp. by S. C. Bumgarner . . . Harrisburg, Pa., Pub. house of United evangelical church, 1914.

309 p. 12°. LC, V

2761. BUREAU OF MUNICIPAL RESEARCH, New York. Organization and management of the state government of Virginia; a report on a survey made for the governor and his Committee on consolidation and simplification, prepared by the New York Bureau of municipal research, January, 1927. Richmond, Bottom, 1927.

156 p. fold. table, fold. diagrs. 8°. LC, NYP, USAg, V
An exposition of the state government, with proposals to increase its efficiency; concentration of power and responsibility in the governor is emphasized.

2762. CARY, HUNSDON. Some observations on political parties in Virginia . . . [Richmond, 1921]

27 p. 8°. H, V, VU
Historical sketch of parties in Virginia, followed by a suggestion to the Republicans: to oppose Negro suffrage.

2763. [1307] CATON, JAMES R., & H. B. Synopsis of the corporation law of . . . Virginia. Alexandria, 1903.

2764. CHAMBERLAYNE, JOHN H. Why despair? An address delivered before the Society of alumni of the University of Virginia, July 1, 1880 . . . Richmond, Goode, Pub. by the Society, 1880.

21 p. 8°.   VU

Discussion of political conditions during the *post bellum* period.

2765. CHARACTERISTIC facts in the business and political career of General William Mahone. [n. p., 188-?]

16 p. 8°.   V

By an opponent of Mahone's.

2766. [1826] CHRISTIAN, GEORGE L. The Capitol disaster. A chapter of reconstruction in Virginia . . . [Richmond, 1915]

2767. CONVENTION OF THE COLORED PEOPLE OF VIRGINIA, 1865. . . . Proceedings of the Convention of the colored people of Va., held in the city of Alexandria, Aug. 2, 3, 4, 5, 1865. Alexandria, Va., Cowing & Gillis, 1865.

24 p. 8°.   H, LC

Reports, resolution, and speeches, directed especially towards the rights of the Negro to citizenship and suffrage; expressed in moderate terms.

2768. DABNEY, ROBERT L. A defence of Virginia, and through her, of the South, in recent and pending contests against the sectional party . . . New York, Hale, 1867.

356 p. 12°.   BP, H, LC, NYP, V

2769. DANIEL, JOHN W. Speeches and orations of John Warwick Daniel, comp. by his son, Edward M. Daniel. Lynchburg, Bell, 1911.

2 p. l., 9-787 p. front. (port.) 8°.   LC, NYP, V, VU

Shed light on contemporary politics in Virginia.

2770. [2395] [DAVIDSON papers] [Papers of James D. Davidson and his son, Charles A., of Lexington, Va., 1865-85]

2771. DEAD calumnies against General Mahone, ex[h]umed again by democratic hyenas, here buried once more! Other democratic falsehoods met and exposed! [n. p., 188-?]

8 p. 8°.   V

Broadsides and pamphlets inserted.

2772. DEMOCRATIC PARTY. VIRGINIA. The primary plan adopted by the Democratic state convention at Richmond, Virginia, June 10, 1904. [Richmond? 1904]

7 p. 8°. LC

2773. ———. ———. Virginia Democratic state organization. Adopted at the state convention at Norfolk, Va., May 3, 1900. [Richmond, Saunders, 1900]

[4] p. 8°. V

2774. ———. ———. STATE CENTRAL COMMITTEE. A reply to sundry charges brought by General William Mahone against the Democratic party of Virginia . . . Richmond, Waddey, 1899.

68 p. 8°. V

Concerning the corruption of the Republican party and its mishandling of affairs in Virginia.

2775. DOYLE, R. DEVEREUX. Some political writings . . . Norfolk, Green, Burke & Gregory, 1893.

34 p. 8°. V, VU

A Virginian's opinions in opposition to increasing federal control and to the protective tariff; with some light on political conditions in Virginia in the 'eighties and 'nineties.

2776. EQUAL suffrage. Address from the colored citizens of Norfolk, Va., to the people of the U. S. Also an account of the agitation among the colored people of Virginia for equal rights. With an appendix concerning the rights of colored witnesses before the state courts. New Bedford, Mass., Anthony & sons, 1865.

26 p. 8°. H, LC

2777. EQUAL SUFFRAGE LEAGUE OF VIRGINIA. Virginia state laws concerning women. Richmond, Whittet & Shepperson [1910?]

16 p. 12°. V

"Questions by Catherine Waugh McCulloch."

2778. ———. Year book . . . 1st- ; 1910— Richmond, 1910—

12°. V: 1910, 16; VU: 1916.

2779. GILMER, JOHN H. Substance of the argument submitted in the Senate of Virginia, Feb. 17, 1866, in explanation and support

BIBLIOGRAPHY OF VIRGINIA HISTORY

of the various bills reported in relation to Negro evidence. Richmond, Allegre & Goode, 1866.

11 p. 8°.   H

2780. GILMER, JOHN H. War of races. By whom it is sought to be brought about. Considered in two letters, with copious extracts from the recent work of Hilton [*sic*] R. Helper, by John H. Gilmer. Richmond, 1867.

16 p. 8°.   H, LC, V

A passionate attack upon a Resolution of the people of Albemarle County, Va., to co-operate with the Republican party in maintaining unconditionally the Union. A warning to both whites and Negroes against the Republicans.

2781. [GLENNAN, MICHAEL] A review of a Reply to a paper, which included the sketch of two lives. Norfolk, Va., 1883.

25 p. 8°.   LC

The "Reply" was by William Lamb, and the controversy between the two men an outgrowth of the Mahone campaign in Virginia politics. "An explanation" signed: M. Glennan.

2782. GOODE, JOHN. Recollections of a lifetime, by John Goode, of Virginia. New York & Washington, Neale, 1906.

x p., 1 l., [13]-266 p. front. (port.) 8°.   BP, H, LC, V, VU, WM

The experiences of a Virginia Democrat in law and politics, in Virginia and in Congress, during the second half of the 19th century. Includes discussion on reconstruction in Virginia, the state debt, the election of 1876, and, in some detail, the author's work as president of the Constitutional convention of 1901-02.

2783. GOOLRICK, CHARLES O. The short ballot; a discussion of the question from the affirmative view . . . [Richmond, Va., 1928]

12 p. 8°.   V

2784. GORDON, JAMES L. The protection of the suffrage; an address delivered before the Society of the alumni of the University of Virginia . . . July 2, 1890. Charlottesville, 1891.

23 p. 8°.   V, VU

2785. [GOVERNORSHIP of Virginia. Campaign of 1921. Pamphlets, clippings, campaign literature of E. Lee Trinkle and Henry W. Anderson, candidates for the office. Richmond, etc., 1921]

var. pag. & size.   V

2786. GREELEY, HORACE. Horace Greeley's views on Virginia, and what he knows about the South—slave-breeding—mixed schools— miscegenation—making sectional war—Kansas and the South— favoring secession—letting "the erring sisters go"—confiscation, rapine, and ravage—slave insurrections—supporting General Butler's New Orleans order—the Ku-Klux trials, &c., &c., &c. [Washington? 1872]

8 p. 8°.   LC, V

Extracts from Greeley's articles in the New York *Tribune,* to expose his political views.

2787. HANNA, J. MARSHALL. The acts of kings: a Biblical narrative of the acts of the first and second kings of the first province, once Virginia. Including the doings of the first and second tycoons of the city of Richmond, from the surrender to the present time . . . New York, G. W. Carleton; London, S. Low, 1868.

74 p. illus. 12°.   H, LC, V, VU

A satire on the official acts of Generals Schofield and Stoneman, in Richmond, 1867-68.

2788. HARDAWAY, W. O. Constitutional and law reform. A compilation of articles by W. O. Hardaway and Walter H. Saunders with a report of the proceedings of the Roanoke conference and other matter, reprinted from the Roanoke evening world. Edited by Charles I. Stewart. [Salem, Va., Sentinel, 1895?]

82 p. 8°.   V

2789. HARLOW, B. F., comp. Delinquent and forfeited lands; acts of the legislatures of Virginia and West Virginia, constitutional provisions, and decisions of the Court of appeals respecting same . . . Lewisburg, W. Va., 1877.

175 p. 8°.   HL, V

2790. HAWKINS, R. W. [Letters of R. W. Hawkins to Charles Spaithe. Nov. 13, 14, and 18, 1881]

MSS.   NYP

On Virginia politics.

2791. HUGHES, ROBERT W. A chapter of personal and political history. An appeal from the sectional to the national Whigs. [Norfolk? 1881?]

14 p. 8°.   V, VU

Judge Hughes defends his shift from the Democratic to the Republican party after the Civil war.

2792. HUGHES, ROBERT W. Opening of the presidential campaign
in Virginia. Great speech of Col. Robert W. Hughes, delivered at
Abingdon, Va., on Wednesday evening, the 29th day of May,
1872. [n. p., 1872]

    11 p. 8°.   LC

A vigorous attack upon Horace Greeley and his political record with
reference to the South; secondarily, an attack upon the party in Virginia supporting Greeley instead of Grant.

2793. ——. Papers showing the political course of R. W. Hughes,
the Republican candidate for governor, before and since the fall of
the southern Confederacy in 1865; prefixed by a biographical
sketch. Richmond, Gillis, 1873.

    32 p. 8°.   LC, VU

Portraying Hughes' consistent policy in support of the Union (after
the Civil war) and of conciliation with the Federal government.

2794. ——. A reply to a pamphlet assailing his political and official conduct, by Robert W. Hughes, a citizen of Virginia. [n. p.,
1884?]

    44 p. 8°.   V, VU

Involving the Virginia debt question and Judge Hughes' stand against
repudiation. Appended is Hughes' correspondence concerning the coupon cases.

2795. ——. Speech . . . before the Republican state convention at Lynchburg, Va., July 31, 1873. [Lynchburg, Lynchburg
evening press, 1873]

    12 p. 8°.   VU

Lauding the Republican principles and platform.

2796. HURST, SAM N. An annotated constitution of Virginia: ex-
hibiting under one view and at a glance . . . both the old and
new constitutions, and the changes made by the new; and annotated with all the Virginia decisions construing the old provisions
of the new constitution, and with important decisions of sister
states and the Supreme court of the U. S. touching the new provisions; with an appendix giving ordinances for the registration of
voters and the extension of charters, and the statutes authorizing
the constitution . . . Luray, Va., Hurst, 1903.

    xviii, 241 (*i. e.*, 242) p. 8°.   HL, LC, NYP, V

2797. [HUTTON, FRANCIS B.] Endorsements of Judge Francis B. Hutton for judge of the Supreme court of appeals of Virginia. [n. p., 1914]

26 p. 8°.   V

2798. LANGSTON, JOHN M. From the Virginia plantation to the national capitol; or, The first and only Negro representative in Congress from the Old Dominion. John Mercer Langston . . . Hartford, Conn., American pub. co., 1894.

x, 11-534 p. front., plates, ports. 8°.   LC, V, VU

The Negro in Virginia education and politics. The author, writing in the third person, is obviously proud of his achievements, gained through "self-reliance, the secret of success."

2799. LYBROOK, A. M. Mahoneism unveiled! The plot against the people exposed. Judge Lybrook, the readjuster senator from Patrick [County] tears the mask from Mahone. Other interesting campaign facts . . . [n. p., 1882?]

16 p. 8°.   V

2800. McILWAINE, RICHARD. Suffrage. An address before the Conference of Democratic members of the Constitutional convention of Virginia. Jan. 6, 1902. [n. p., 1902]

1 p. l., 4 p. 8°.   NYP

2801. MACHEN, LEWIS H. The work of the [Virginia] legislature of 1908. A report read . . . before the Virginia state bar association . . . Aug. 5, 1908. Richmond, Richmond press [1908]

24 p. 8°.   V

2802. MAHONE, WILLIAM. The Barbour dynasty contrasted with the "Mahone dynasty"; a reply to Hon. John S. Barbour's Pungoteague letter. [n. p., 1887?]

13 p. 8°.   V

2803. —— [?] [Letter of Mahone to Maj. T. J. Brady. Feb. 27, 1888]

MS.   NYP

On Virginia politics.

2804. ——. The vital Virginia issues; a speech by General Wil-

liam Mahone, Republican nominee for governor of Virginia. Delivered at Abingdon, Va., Sept. 23, 1889. [n. p., 1889?]

18 p. 8°.   V

Discussion of such subjects as free ballot, value of the Negro, the
Democratic record, free trade and protection, labor, need for home markets, etc.

2805. MARINE RAILWAY & COAL CO., inc., Alexandria, Va., defendant. Action of ejectment brought by the U. S. to recover a par-
cel of land made, in the course of river and harbor improvement,
out of the submerged soil of the Potomac River. [Briefs and
other records, 1916— Washington, D. C.? 1916—

var. pag. 8°.   LC

2806. [MARSHALL, A. J.] [Address] to the voters of Rappahannock, Fauquier, Madison and Culpepper [sic] counties, composing the seventeenth Senatorial district of Virginia, as appointed
by the constitution adopted in Alexandria, in the month of April,
1864. [n. p., 1865?]

51 p. 8°.   LC

Signed: A. J. Marshall, Warrenton, Va.
A discussion of the political situation and a warning against "Black
Republican" control.

2807. [MARTIN, THOMAS S.] [Miscellaneous pamphlets . . .
for re-election of Thomas S. Martin to the U. S. Senate, 1911]

12°.-f°.   V, VU

Include a copy of the *Thomas S. Martin rally*, pub. in Charlottesville, Aug.
7, 1911.

2808. [197] MASSIE, EUGENE C. Address . . . upon the Torrens system of land registration . . . Richmond, 1905.

2809. [198] ———. Reform of our land laws . . . Richmond, 1905.

2810. MAYO, JOSEPH. Virginia abstractions. An address before
the Society of alumni of the Virginia military institute. Delivered July 3, 1873. By Col. Joseph Mayo . . . Richmond,
Clemmitt & Jones, 1873.

20 p. 8°.   LC

By a "die-hard" advocate of state rights, who passionately defends
Virginia's position in the Civil war and opposes reconciliation with the
national government.

2811. MEEKINS, GEORGE W. A week in Hepsidam; being the first and only true account of the mountain, men, manners, and morals thereof . . . Richmond, Gary, 1879.

66 p. 8°.   VU
A satire on Virginia politics, the state debt, etc.

2812. MEMORIAL in regard to the admission of Virginia. Read in the Senate, Jan. 12, 1870. [Washington, Judd & Detweiler, 1870]

4 p. 8°.   BP, LC
Signed: Isaac P. Baldwin [etc.]

2813. MEMORIAL of Col. John B. Baldwin, of Staunton, Virginia. [Staunton, Va., Staunton spectator, 1874]

46 p. 8°.   VU
Sketches of his political life.

2814. MINOR, RALEIGH C. To the members of the Constitutional convention [on the advantages of plural voting]. Charlottesville, 1901.

8 p. 8°.   V, VU

2815. MOSBY, [JOHN S.] *et al.* Letters [of John Singleton Mosby and John Tyler, jr.] [n. p., 1876]

8 p. 8°. (Reprint from New York *Herald,* Aug. 12, 1876)
      H, LC, VU
In support of Hayes and Wheeler in the presidential campaign of 1876.

2816. MUNFORD, BEVERLEY B. Random recollections. [n. p., Priv. print.] 1905.

3 p. l., 238 p. 8°.   H, V
Sheds some light upon politics in Virginia during and after reconstruction, and upon education; by a conservative Democrat, opposed to the re-adjusters.

2817. NEW YORK. UNION LEAGUE CLUB. . . . Report of the proceedings of the conference at Richmond, June 11th and 12th, 1867. [New York] Club house, 1867.

13 p. 8°.   BP, H, LC
Caption title: The mission to Virginia; report of the president. Includes the report of John Jay, one of the delegates of the Club. Conference was called to harmonize the factions in the Republican party of Virginia.

2818. O'FERRALL, CHARLES T.   Forty years of active service; being some history of the war between the Confederacy and the Union and of the events leading up to it, with reminiscences of the struggle and accounts of the author's experiences of four years from private to lieutenant-colonel and acting-colonel in the cavalry of the Army of northern Virginia . . . New York & Washington, Neale, 1904.

> 367 p. front. (port.) 8°.
>
> Pt. II: The author's official life—an account of state politics in the 'seventies and 'eighties, with emphasis upon the debt controversy; also of southern issues in Congress during the 'nineties. The author aims to write "in the spirit of a fraternal Union of the two sections of our once divided but now re-united land."

2819. PEOPLE'S PARTY. VIRGINIA. People's party of Virginia. For lieutenant-governor Edmund R. Cocke, of Cumberland. Platform. Address to the party [by the Committee to determine a line of policy for the party. 1897]   [n. p., 1897?]

> 4 p. 8°.   V

2820. PIDGEON, MARY E.   Hand-book of election law for the Virginia voter. Pub. by the University of Virginia. Charlottesville, Michie, 1925.

> 31 p. 8°. (*University of Virginia record.* Extension series, IX, 7; Mar., 1925)   **V, VU**

2821. ——, *et al.* . . . The short ballot proposal in Virginia, compiled by Mary Elizabeth Pidgeon and Elizabeth Jeffries Heinrich . . . Charlottesville, Va., The University [1926]

> 2 p. 1., p. [181]-302. 8°. (*University of Virginia record.* Extension series, XI, 5; Nov., 1926)   **H, LC, NYP, USE, V, VU, WM**
>
> Contains arguments pro and con regarding the short ballot; also comments of Virginia editors.

2822. POLLARD, EDWARD B.   The subjection of woman according to St. Paul. An address before the Equal suffrage league of Richmond, Va. [n. p., 1914]

> [14] p. 8°.   V
>
> On progressive interpretation of Scripture—in favor of woman's suffrage.

2823. POLLARD, HENRY R.   Memoirs and sketches of the life of

Henry Robinson Pollard; an autobiography. Richmond, Va.,
Lewis [ca. 1923]

> xiv p., 2 l., 443 p. incl. tables. front., plate, ports., facsim. 8°. **LC, V**
> A simple narrative of the author's active life in Virginia law and pol-
> itics for over 50 years. Much of the story is based upon recollections, en-
> livened by numerous incidents.

2824. PUTNAM, HARRINGTON. The Virginia ideal in contrast with
the Prussian theory of the state; address of Harrington Putnam,
. . . at the commencement of Washington and Lee university,
Lexington, Va., June 12, 1917.

> 3-16 p. 8°.   **LC**

2825. REDMOND, J. J. Fifty years after; or, The second fall of
Richmond, Virginia. Chapter II. [n. p., 1909?]

> [8] p. 8°.   **V**
> Concerning corruption in Virginia government at the beginning of the
> 20th century.

2826. REPUBLICAN CONGRESSIONAL COMMITTEE, Washington, D. C.
[Letter to] Dr. R. A. Wise, Williamsburg, Va., from D. B. Henderson, secretary Repub. cong. com., in reply to inquiry touching
the attitude of the Committee towards the nominees of the Coalitionists in Virginia . . . Aug. 24, 1882. [n. p., 1882]

> 4°. sheet, printed on one side.   **V**

2827. REPUBLICAN PARTY. VIRGINIA. . . . Campaign text book
. . . [1909] Issued by authority of the Republican state executive committee . . . [Roanoke, Va., Hammond, 1909]

> 77, [2] p. 8°.   **H**

2828. ———. ———. Proposed plan of organization of the Republican party of Virginia, submitted by the State executive committee. [Roanoke, Va., Stone, 1905]

> 8 p. 8°.   **H**

2829. REPUBLICAN STATE COMMITTEE. VIRGINIA. Address of the
Republican state committee to the people of Virginia. Sept. 11,
1871. Richmond, Va., Gillis, 1871.

> 15 p. 8°.   **BP**
> Signed: Ro. W. Hughes, chairman.

2830. REPUBLICAN STATE COMMITTEE. VIRGINIA. Anything to beat Mahone! the acme of Bourbon statesmanship . . . [Campaign letter] [Richmond? 1885]

    4 p. 8°.   BP
    Signed: Wm. Mahone, chairman.

2831. ———. ———. Democratic hostility to popular education . . . [Campaign letter] [Richmond? 1885]

    4 p. 8°.   BP
    Signed: Wm. Mahone, chairman.

2832. ———. ———. To the Congress of the U. S., Jan. 14, 1870 [in regard to the admission of Virginia and the condition of the loyalists] [Richmond, 1870]

    4 p. 8°.   BP

2833. [220] RICHMOND CHAMBER OF COMMERCE. An answer to objections to the Torrens system Richmond, 1906.

2834. [ROBERTSON, JOHN] Opuscula. Seria ac jocosa. Found in the Scrutoir of an ultra octogenarian . . . [n. p.] Printed for the publisher, 1870—

    71 p. 12°.   LC, V, VU
    Pt. I, p. 3-7, is a satire on Republican reconstruction in Virginia.

2835. RUFFIN, FRANK G.[1] An appeal to the 31,527 readjuster democrats of Virginia. [Richmond? 1883?]

    15 p. 8°.   V
    Part of the campaign against William Mahone.

2836. ———. . . . Mahoneism unveiled! The great plot to sell out Virginians to the Republican party exposed . . . [n. p., 1882?]

    16 p. 8°.   V

2837. [2462] SCHOFIELD, JOHN M. Forty-six years in the army. New York, 1897.

2838. SEGAR, JOSEPH E. Address . . . on the war, the union, and the restoration of peace, delivered on the occasion of a complimentary serenade to him, at the Monumental hotel, Richmond, on the night of June 22, 1865 . . . [Richmond, 1865]

    7 p. 8°.   LC
    Exultation of a unionist over the end of the Civil war and the promises of law and order under Gov. Peirpont of Virginia.

---

1. See also items **1162-1166**.

2839. ———. Address . . . to the voters of the Norfolk district (From the Norfolk Day book.) [Washington, 1876]

    8 p. 8°. **LC**

Decries the Democratic record of secession and rebellion and advocates the development of Virginia's natural resources.

2840. SOUTHALL, JAMES C. Speech . . . in the so-called "convention", . . . Feb. 24 [1868] in favor of the adoption of the minority report of the Committee on the elective franchise. [n. p., n. d.]

    32 p. 8°. **V**

2841. [STATE CONSERVATIVE COMMITTEE] State conservative committee, June 23, 1869. Rumors are afloat that Gen. Canby will insist on exacting from all elected, the "iron-clad oath". [n. p.] 1869.

    Broadside. 13½ x 10½ in. **H**

A sworn statement, in MS., is appended, that this broadside was posted in the Manassas hotel several days prior to the election held July 6, 1869.

2842. A STATEMENT in behalf of the candidacy of Hon. G. T. Garnett, for re-election as judge of the Thirteenth judicial circuit [of Virginia] [n. p., 1906?]

    20 p. 8°. **V**

2843. STUART, ALEXANDER H. A narrative of the leading incidents of the organization of the first popular movement in Virginia in 1865 to re-establish peaceful relations between the northern and southern states, and of the subsequent efforts of the "Committee of nine" in 1869, to secure the restoration of Virginia to the union, by Alex. H. H. Stuart. Richmond, Va., Jones, 1888.

    72 p. 8°.

A clear, concise account of Stuart's part in effecting a restoration of Virginia to the union in accord with the opinions of the conservative southern Democrats.

2844. SWANSON, CLAUDE A. [Pamphlet] issued in behalf of the candidacy of Senator Claude A. Swanson to succeed himself in the U. S. Senate, consisting of editorials . . . favoring his election in the primary, or commending his administration as governor, and his public record. Alexandria, Barrett [1911]

    31 p. 8°. **V, VU**

2845. [Swanson-Davis campaign for U. S. senator, 1922. Pamphlets in support of Westmoreland Davis and of Claude A. Swanson. 1922]

var. pag. & size.   **V, VU**

2846. Thomas, Alsen F. The Virginia constitutional convention and its possibilities . . . Lynchburg, Va., Bell, 1901.

77 p. 12°.   **LC, NYP, V**

A clear discussion of the problems to be met by the convention of 1901-02, including a pointed section on the question of Negro suffrage and the Negro in politics.

2847. [Tibbets, Luther C.] Spirit of the South; or, Persecution in the name of the law, as administered in Virginia. Related by some victims thereof. Also its effects upon the nation and its general government. Washington, D. C., Pub. for the trade and the people, 1869.

76 p. 8°.   **BP, H, LC, NYP**

An account of various law suits involving Luther C. Tibbets, a union man, and of his persecutions by the Ku-Klux Klan.

2848. Tucker, John R. Virginia legislation of 1926. Address . . . before the Virginia state bar association at Hot Springs, Virginia, Aug. 4, 1926. Richmond, Richmond press, 1926.

27 p. 8°.   **V**

2849. Tunstall, Robert B. The Virginia bar: its conditions and its needs. Address . . . [by] president of the Virginia state bar association . . . Aug. 12, 1925. With open letter and appendix to the members of the bar of Virginia . . . Pub. by Virginia state bar association. Richmond, Va., Richmond press [1925]

29 p. 8°.   **NYP, V**

2850. ———. Wanted: a constitutional convention . . . An address delivered before the Lynchburg bar association, May 26, 1924 . . . [Charlottesville, Michie, 1924]

19 p. 8°. (Reprint from *Virginia law register,* new ser., X, 3; July, 1924)   **V, VU**

2851. [VIRGINIA. Campaign of 1887. Hon. William Mahone. Washington, etc., 1884-87]

66 pamphlets, etc. 8°. LC

Volume of campaign literature of the Republican party in Virginia, made up of pamphlets, broadsides, leaflets, newspaper clippings, etc., bound together. Includes material on the debt question and the readjuster movement.

2852. VIRGINIA decisions. A collection of Virginia cases not officially reported . . . Charlottesville, Va., Michie, 1902.

2 v. 8°. LC, V, VU

2853. VIRGINIA INSTITUTE OF CITIZENSHIP AND GOVERNMENT, Charlottesville. The Virginia institute of citizenship and government, University, Virginia . . . [Charlottesville] University extension [1927]

163 p. 8°. (*University of Virginia record*. Extension series [XI, 12])
LC, NYP, V, VU, WM

Program and addresses at meeting of the Institute, concerned with efficient government in Virginia.

2854. VIRGINIA STATE CHAMBER OF COMMERCE. Virginia citizenship creed. Richmond, Va., 1925.

nar. 8°. (Its *Civics doc.*, 1) H, NYP, V

2855. [VIRGINIA UNION ASSOCIATION] Address of the loyal Virginians to their friends in the North. [Alexandria, Va., 1865]

7 p. 8°. BP, LC

Signed: S. Ferguson Beach, Lysander Hill, W. J. Cowing, corresponding committee. Dated: Alexandria, Va., June 30, 1865.

An appeal to the North to support the unionist cause in Virginia.

2856. VIRGINIA Supreme court reporter. An advance report of all current decisions of the Supreme court of appeals of Virginia. Digest of vol. 1 [-3], with tables of cases reported, cases cited, and statutes cited. Richmond, Va., Jones & Powell [1900-01]

3 v. 8°. LC: II; V: I-III.

Comp. by H. Stewart Jones and T. Norment Powell.

2857. [WOOD, T. W.] An address to intelligent, patriotic voters. [Richmond, Va., July 18, 1898] [Richmond? 1898?]

24 p. 8°. V

Arguments against the adoption of the gold standard of coinage.

Secondary Works

2858. ANDERSON, HENRY W. Political conditions in Virginia. An address . . . before the school of present day politics conducted by the College of William and Mary and the Times-dispatch, at Richmond [Va.] Mar. 6, 1928. [Richmond? 1928]

54 p. 8°.   H, VU

Political affairs in Virginia, especially since the Constitutional convention of 1901-02; the recent reform movement in state government.

2859. BARTON, R[OBERT] T. Pleading and practice in the courts of chancery. 3d ed. . . . Charlottesville, 1926.

2 v. 8°.   HL

2860. BRAGG, GEORGE F. The hero of Jerusalem; in honor of the 100th anniversary of the birth of General William Mahone of Virginia, by the Rev. George F. Bragg . . . Baltimore, Md. (A page in the Mahone legislature of 1881-82.) [Baltimore? 1926]

27, [1] p. incl. port. 8°.   LC, V

A review of Mahone's political career—a tribute to his policies and actions in the "readjuster" movement. Contains also a reprint of the Republican platform of 1884 and a condensed statement of the platform of the state convention of 1885.

2861. BRENAMAN, J[ACOB] N. A history of Virginia conventions . . . With constitution adopted by convention of 1867-68, and constitution adopted by convention of 1901-02 appended. Richmond, Hill, 1902.

122, x p., 1 l., 87 p. 8°.

Based almost entirely upon primary sources; with emphasis upon the convention of 1901-02 and the predominant issue of suffrage.

2862. BURKS, MARTIN P. Notes on the property rights of married women in Virginia . . . Lynchburg, Va., Bell, 1893.

viii, 87 p. 8°.   LC, V
Ed. of 1894.   HL

2863. CALDWELL, FREDERICK P. The Virginia and West Virginia judicial dictionary-digest, words and phrases; being a compilation of all words, phrases and maxims which have been defined, construed, interpreted or applied in Virginia and West Virginia cases and in the codes of those states, combined with a digest of Virginia and West Virginia cases and principles of law as therein applied. Prepared by the editorial staff of the publishers and under the supervision of Fred. P. Caldwell . . . Cincinnati, O., Anderson [ca. 1922-23]

6 v. 8°.   HL, LC

2864. CARLIN, LEO. Equity procedure embodying the principles of pleading and practice applicable to courts of equity, and containing many precedents of general practical utility, designed especially to meet the demands of practice in Virginia and West Virginia . . . being a thorough revision of Hogg's Equity procedure. Cincinnati, O., 1921.

2 v. 8°.   HL

2865. CHANDLER, JULIAN A. . . . Representation in Virginia . . . Baltimore, Johns Hopkins, 1896.

83 p. 8°. (Johns Hopkins university. *Studies in historical and political science,* 14th ser., VI-VII)

Concerned with representation in the state legislature only. Chap. VII treats "The present system of representation," through the re-apportionment of 1891; East-West sectionalism in Virginia regarded as basic factor in the struggle over representation.

2866. DANIEL, JOHN W. The law and practice of attachment, under the code of Virginia; and of bail and injunction in analogous cases wherein attachment is not available—with a variety of all necessary forms. Also: the law of attachment under the new code of West Virginia, with explanatory references to the context . . . Lynchburg, Schaffter & Bryant; Philadelphia, Johnson; [etc., etc.] 1869.

viii, 304 p., 1 l. 8°.   HL, LC, V
Ed. of 1891.   HL
Ed. of 1903.   HL, NYP

2867. DAVIS, R. B., jr., comp. Virginia laws made plain; laws and legal forms prepared for the use of farmers, mechanics and business men . . . [St. Joseph, Mo., Combe print., ca. 1913]

100 p. 8°.   LC, V
"Presented by First national bank, Carlville, Virginia."

2868. ECKENRODE, HAMILTON J. . . . The political history of

Virginia during reconstruction . . . Baltimore, Johns Hopkins, 1904.

128. p. 8°. (Johns Hopkins university. *Studies in historical and political science*, 22d ser., VI-VIII)

A well balanced study of political reconstruction in Virginia, to 1870, based upon reliable source material. The author presents the advantages and disadvantages of the outcome to both whites and Negroes.

2869. Fox, WILLIAM F. Civil government of Virginia; a text-book for schools, based upon the constitution of 1902 and conforming to the laws enacted in accordance therewith . . . New York and Chicago, Richardson, Smith & co. [1904]

176 p. 12°.   LC, V

2870. ———. Manual of Virginia civil government, to accompany a chart of Virginia civil government. New York and Chicago, Franklin pub. [1899]

144 p. 12°.   LC

A text-book; contains text of Virginia state constitution.

2871. GRAYBILL, WILLIAM M. Charts of the governments of the U. S., and of the state of Virginia . . . Roanoke, Va., Bell, 1887.

sheet. 39 x 35½ cm.   LC

Parallel charts to compare the departments of government and their functions, in Virginia and the U. S.

2872. GREGORY, GEORGE C., comp. Forms for Virginia and West Virginia annotated; including statutory, common law and equity, commercial, corporation and criminal forms. 2d ed., by M. P. Caldwell, assisted by the Publisher's editorial staff. Charlottesville, 1925.

xlvii, 1390 p. 8°.   HL

2873. HANK, JOSIAH D., comp. . . . Virginia laws made plain; laws and legal forms prepared for the use of business men, farmers, and mechanics . . . Kansas City, Mo., Bankers law pub. co. [*ca.* 1923]

100 p. 8°.   LC, V

"Presented by Carlville trust company, Carlville, Virginia."

2874. HARRISON, T[HOMAS] W. Wills and administration; a discussion of the devolution of a decedent's estate and the procedure

for the distribution thereof, for Virginia and West Virginia . . .
Charlottesville, 1927.

    2 v. 8°.   HL

2875. HUBBARD, L. C. Francis H. Peirpont and the restored government of Virginia. . . . May, 1918.

    93 p. typew. 4°.   V

    Thesis (A. M.), Richmond college, 1918.

    Based mainly upon Peirpont MSS. and documentary sources, the account is an "appreciation" of the governor's work in Virginia and West Virginia.

2876. HUGHES, RAY O. Elementary community civics. Virginia ed.
. . . Boston, New York [etc.] Allyn and Bacon [*ca.* 1923]

    xx, 516, 25 p. front., illus. 12°.   LC, V

    "Virginia supplement": p. 449-514, based upon F. A. Magruder, *Recent administration in Virginia* **[1385]**

2877. HURST, SAM N. A complete encyclopedia of Virginia law, being a concise but comprehensive alphabetical presentation of the present common and statute law, civil and criminal, of the commonwealth based on the monumental works of Dr. John B. Minor; the works, brochures, and notes of Judge Martin P. Burks and Professors Charles A. Graves, William M. Lile, and Raleigh C. Minor, and other treatises, textbooks, expositions, and repositories of Virginia law, modernized to date by recent Virginia and other decisions, the Code of Virginia 1919, and subsequent acts of the General assembly including acts, 1922, with complete practical revised forms adapted to the present law . . . Pulaski, Va., Richmond, Va., Hurst & co., 1922.

    2 v. 8°.   HL, LC, VU

2878. ———. A new guide for justices of the peace of Virginia, commonwealth's attorneys, and other county and district officers of the state, in the discharge of their respective duties, together with useful forms for the practical performance of the same; as well as a manual for attorneys-at-law, as to all matters of a civil or criminal nature, cognizable by or appertaining to the courts of a single justice or the county courts of Virginia . . . [Richmond, Va., Hill, 1893]

    xiv, 801 p. 8°.   V

2879. [JOHNSON, WILLIAM B.] The loves of Jonathan and Virginia. By Boswell [*pseud.*] . . . Philadelphia, 1873.

vii, 9-120 p. 12°.   **LC, V, VU**

A southern view of the union; the history of Virginia in verse. Bk. VI on "Reconciliation or Reconstruction."

2880. [JONES, JOHN W.] Virginia's next governor, Gen. Fitzhugh Lee . . . New York, Cheap pub. co. [1885]

31 p. 12°.   **LC, V**

A sketch of Lee's life, military service, and political views, especially as regards the state debt and state rights. Campaign literature.

2881. LEE, HOWARD B. Criminal trial in the Virginias. Charleston, W. Va., 1926.

[9], 691 p. 8°.   **HL**

2882. McBAIN, HOWARD L. Government and politics in Virginia . . . Richmond, Va., 1916.

viii, 230 p. 8°.   **LC**

A text-book, well written and illustrated.

Ed. of 1920: viii, 230 p.   **VU**

Ed. of 1922: viii, 332 p.   **LC, NYP, V, WM**

2883. ———. How we are governed in Virginia . . . Richmond, Va., Hermitage press, 1908.

155 p. front., illus. 12°.   **LC, USE, V**

A text-book for the 6th or 7th grade; the activities of the state government presented in an intimate and personal way.

2884. McDANEL, RALPH C. The Virginia constitutional convention of 1901-1902. Baltimore, Johns Hopkins, 1928.

vii, 166 p. 8°. (Johns Hopkins university. *Studies in historical and political science,* ser. XLVI, 3)

Favorable opinion expressed as to the personnel and accomplishments of the convention. Contains chapters on suffrage, the state corporation commission, the departments of government, and amending the constitution.

2885. [McRAE, SHERWIN] Virginia state capitol. An historical account of the erection of the capitol, and the review of the question of its preservation; also a brief account of the acquisition of the public square. [Richmond, 1871]

8 p. 8°. (Reprint from *Old Dominion magazine,* July 15 [*i. e.,* Aug. 15] 1871)   **V**

2886. **[1385]** [MAGRUDER, FRANK A.] Recent administration in Virginia . . . Baltimore, 1912.

2887. MASSIE, EUGENE C. The Torrens system; a manual of the uniform land registration act of Virginia. Richmond, 1916.

xvii, 206 p. 8°.   HL

2888. MATTHEWS, JAMES M. A guide to commissioners in chancery, with practical forms for the discharge of their duties, adapted to the statute law of Virginia . . . 2d ed. rev. and enl. Richmond, Va., Randolph & English, 1871.

xi, 254 p. 8°.   V

2889. [MINOR, JOHN B.] Synopsis of the law of crimes and punishments in Virginia. 2d ed. Richmond, 1869.

284 p. 8°.   HL

2890. ———. Synopsis of the practice of the law in Virginia in civil cases. [n. d.—19th cent.]

682 fol. MSS. 8°.   HL

2891. **[1338]** MINOR, RALEIGH C. The law of tax titles in Virginia . . . [Charlottesville] 1898.

2892. **[2351]** MORTON, RICHARD L. The Negro in Virginia politics, 1865-1902 . . . [Charlottesville? 1919]

2893. MUNFORD, GEORGE W. Historical synopsis of the changes in the laws and constitution of Virginia. [n. p., 1873?]

30 p. 8°.   V

From the *Code of Virginia,* 1873, ed. by G. W. Munford **[2719]**

2894. NATIONAL WOMAN'S PARTY. How Virginia law discriminates against women. [n. p., n. d.]

12 p. 12°.   HL

2895. ———. Legal position of women in Virginia. [n. d.]

44 p. multig. f°.   HL

2896. PAGE, ROSEWELL. Government in Virginia . . . Richmond, Williams, 1924.

5 p. l., [5]-189 p. 12°.   LC, NYP, V, VU, WM

Government and administration in Virginia briefly described; a kind of reference book for the general reader.

2897. PHILLIPS, LOUIS C. The law of instructions to juries in Virginia, with a collection of forms in civil and criminal cases, approved by the Supreme court of appeals of Virginia . . . Newport News, Va., Abbe. [*ca.* 1908]

lv, 708 p. 8°.   **LC, V**

2898. PIDGEON, MARY E., ed. . . . The convention and the primary; prepared for Virginia high school literary and athletic league . . . Charlottesville, Va., The University [1925]

106 p. 8°. (*University of Virginia record.* Extension series, X, 3; Nov.,
1925)   **LC, NYP, VU**
Contains brief notes on the Virginia primary.

2899. [2062] ———. . . . The laws of Virginia as they affect women and children . . . Charlottesville, 1926.

2900. ———. . . . Virginia citizenship, a correspondence course for club use including bibliography . . . Charlottesville, The University, 1922.

28 p. incl. diagrs. 8°. (*University of Virginia record.* Extension series,
VII, 3; Nov., 1922)   **USE, VU**

2901. PULLIAM, DAVID L. The constitutional conventions of Virginia from the foundation of the commonwealth to the present time . . . Richmond, West, 1901.

180 p. 8°.   **BP, H, HL, LC, V, VU**
Written on the eve of the convention of 1901-02, this account ends
with the legislative act authorizing the convention and the proposed
amendments to the constitution, to remedy the evils of the previous convention (1867).

2902. ROBERTSON, ALEXANDER F. Alexander Hugh Holmes Stuart, 1807-1891; a biography . . . Richmond, Va., William Byrd press [*ca.* 1925]

xix, 484 p. front., plate, ports. 8°.   **H, LC, V, VU**
Reveals Stuart's activity in politics and education in Virginia after
1865. No bibliography, but many excerpts from his correspondence and
an appendix of some of his important writings.

2903. SAMS, C[ONWAY] W. A brief comparison of the most important statutes of the codes of Virginia of 1873 and 1887, being especially those referred to in "Minor's Institutes of common and statute law." Richmond, West, Johnston & co., and Randolph & English, 1888.

viii, 160 p. 8°.   **V**

2904. ———. A treatise of the law of attachment and bail in Virginia and West Virginia . . . Richmond, Randolph, 1896.

3 p. l., [ix]-x p., 1 l., 459 p. 8°. **HL, V**

2905. SANDS, ALEXANDER H. History of a suit in equity as prosecuted and defended in the Virginia state courts and in the U. S. circuit courts . . . 2d ed. Richmond, Va., Randolph & English, 1882.

viii p., 2 l., 760, lx p. 8°. **V**

1st ed., 1854.

2906. SHEPARD'S Virginia citations and annotations. A compilation of citations of all Virginia and West Virginia reports; the U. S. Supreme court reports; the federal reporter; notes of the lawyers' reports annotated; including all Virginia cases cited in the Southeastern reporter (Virginia cases), together with key number annotations. Also citations of constitutions, codes and all subsequent laws and rules of court. First ed., 1913. New York, Frank Shepard co. [*ca.* 1912]

227 p. 8°. **LC, V**

2907. SMITH, A. MEADE. Commissioners in chancery in Virginia; comprising a digest of the statute law governing commissioners, under the code of Virginia, 1887, which went into effect May 1, 1888, with explanatory comments and references, forms and tables . . . Richmond, West, Johnston, 1888.

208 p. 8°. **V**

2908. SMITH, MARGARET V. A few notes upon the history of the constitution or form of government of Virginia from the foundation of the colony to the present time. Glens Falls, Glens Falls pub. [*ca.* 1901]

144 p. 16°. **BP, V**

2909. SMITHEY, ROYALL B. The civil government of Virginia; for the use of schools. New York, Cincinnati [etc.] American book co. [1898]

175 p. 12°. **LC, USE, V, VU, WM**

Ed. of 1904: 204 p. 8°. **LC, V**

A text book, with questions at the end of each chapter, and text of Virginia constitution in back.

2910. SOUTHEASTERN REPORTER. South eastern reporter blue book. Complete tables giving volume and page of the South eastern reporter where every case in the following state reports may be found: Georgia, vols. 77-161, Georgia appeals [vols.] 1-35, North Carolina [vols.] 96-191, South Carolina [vols.] 25-136, Virginia [vols.] 82-144, West Virginia [vols.] 29-101. 12th ed. A cumulation of the tables formerly published in the South eastern reporter, vols. 1-135. St. Paul, West, 1927.

[1033] p. 8°.   Various pagings.   **LC**

2911. TURPIN, JOHN B. John E. Massey; a memorial address . . . Charlottesville, Va., Old Dominion print. [1904]

19 p. port. 12°.   **LC**

Sketch of the life of Rev. Massey, including his part in Virginia politics, especially with reference to the readjuster movement.

2912. WHEALTON, LOUIS N. The Maryland and Virginia boundary controversy (1668-1894) . . . [New York] Leon [1904]

55, vi p. 3 maps (1 fold.) 8°.

Thesis (Ph.D.), Johns Hopkins university.

Based upon official documents and reliable source material. Chaps. 6 and 7 treat of the settlement by arbitration, 1860-84, and fishery rights and oyster troubles, 1884-94, respectively.

2913. WILLIAMS, DANIEL B. A sketch of the life and times of Capt. R. A. Paul. An authentic and abbreviated history of his career from boyhood to the present time; containing a reliable account of the politics of Virginia from 1874 to the present time . . . Richmond, Va., Johns & Goolsby [*ca.* 1885]

68 p. front. (port.) 8°.   **LC, V**

A pro-readjuster's account of the political life and services of R. A. Paul, a freedman, in the readjuster and Republican party.

Periodicals

2914. [1856] The IDEA, a rebel yell. Vols. 1-4; July, 1906-Oct. 8, 1910. [Lynchburg, Va.] 1906-10.

2915. WOMAN voter of Virginia. Vol. 1, no. 1- ; Feb., 1927— Richmond, Pub. by the Virginia league of women voters, 1927—

illus. 8°.   quarterly.

V: I, 1, 4 (Feb., July, 1927); II, 1 (Oct., 1927).

Directory

2916. VIRGINIA constitutional convention directory, 1901. Pub. by
J. L. Hill print. co., Richmond, Va. [1901]

93 p. 16°. **V**

For further references on State Government, see above, Pt. II, § 6: *Finance, Banking, Insurance,* especially for items on the state debt controversy. See also Pt. VI, § 4: *Professional and Learned Societies.*

3. LOCAL GOVERNMENT

Government Publications and Documents

2917. ALEXANDRIA, VA. AUDITOR. Annual statement of the finances
of the city . . . , the mayor's message, with department reports for the fiscal year . . . ; revenue and license laws and
official directory. Alexandria [18-?-19—

8°. Report year ends May 31.
LC: 1877/78-80/81, 82/83-1910/11; **NYP:** 1880/81-1905/06, 07/08-
18/19; **V:** 1885/86-1914/15; **WM:** 1924.

2918. ———. COUNCIL. Celebration of the first centennial of the
municipal government of the city of Alexandria, Virginia, Mar.
9, 1880. Pub. by order of the City council. Alexandria, Va.,
Gazette, 1880.

49 p. 8°. **LC, NYP**

2919. ———. ———. Remonstrance to the Congress of the U. S.,
against the bill to annex the city and county of Alexandria to the
District of Columbia. [Alexandria, Va., Turner, 1865]

14 p. 8°. **LC**
Drawn up by a Committee appointed by the mayor and City council;
showing the advantages of remaining as part of Virginia, as per the cession of 1846.

2920. ———. MAYOR. Annual message . . . to the City council . . . Alexandria [18—

8°. **NYP:** 1877/78; **V:** 1883.

2921. ———. ———. Circular and accompanying papers of Hon. K.
Kemper, mayor of Alexandria. To the bondholders and other
creditors of the city. Alexandria, 1878.

25 p. 8°. **LC, NYP**
Plan to adjust the debt of the city.

2922. ALEXANDRIA, VA. ORDINANCES, ETC. Acts and joint resolutions of the City council of Alexandria . . . Alexandria, 1881.
8°.   LC: Aug. 1, 1880-Sept. 15, 1881.

2923. ———. ———. The charter and laws, of the city of Alexandria, Va., and an historical sketch of its government. Pub. by the City council. Alexandria, Va., Gazette, 1874.
163 p. 8°.   LC, NYP
Revised by William F. Carne.

2924. AUGUSTA COUNTY, VA. TREASURER. Report . . . [Staunton? 19-?—
NYP: 1912/13 (clipping from Staunton *Daily leader,* Oct. 1, 1913).

2925. BRISTOL, VA.-TENN. Report of the city clerk (auditor) and treasurer, . . . [etc.] [Bristol? 18-?-19—
8°.   NYP: 1900/01.

2926. CHARLOTTESVILLE, VA. Blank proposal and advertisement . . . Street improvement bonds. Apr. 15, 1903. [Charlottesville, 1903?]
2 l. 8°.   NYP

2927. ———. Taxes on licenses, city of Charlottesville. For the year commencing May 1, 1912. [Charlottesville] Michie [1912]
26 p. 8°.   V

2928. ———. AUDITOR. . . . A comparative statement of assessed values, estimated receipts, estimated expenditures, actual receipts, actual expenditures, and distribution of incidental expenditures . . . Sept. 1, 1906-Sept. 1, 1911, and a statement of the bonded debt, floating debt, sinking fund, and assets and liabilities of the city, Sept. 1, 1911. Issued under resolution of the Council, Oct. 12, 1911. [Charlottesville, 1912]
unp. 8°.   V

2929. ———. GAS WORKS, Supt. of city. Annual report . . . [n. p., 19—
8°.   V: 1909-11.

2930. ———. ORDINANCES, ETC. The code of Charlottesville, Va., containing the charter as amended and re-enacted as a whole . . . and the general ordinances of the city in effect Sept. 1, 1909.

Comp. by E. I. Carruthers, assisted by H. D. Jarman.   Charlottesville, Michie, 1909.

319 p. 8°.   **V, VU**

2931. ———. ———. Licenses . . . [required in various occupations, and taxes thereon]   [Charlottesville]   Michie [1909?]

23 p. 8°.   Arranged by subject.   **V**

2932. ———. ———. Ordinances governing water-works, sewer system, plumbers, and plumbing . . . [n. p., 189-?-19—

8°.   **V:** 1895, 1909.

2933. ———. WATER AND SEWERAGE, Supt. of. Annual report
. . . [Charlottesville? 19—

8°.   **V:** 1908-11.

2934. ———. WATER WORKS. Contract and specification for trench-
ing and pipe-laying. 1885. [n. p., n. d.]

38 p. 4°.   **VU**

2935. DANVILLE, VA. AUDITOR. Annual report of the city auditor
. . . [Danville, 18-?-19—

8°.   Report year ends Apr. 30.

LC: 1898/99-1903/04, 05/06-15/16, 21/22; **NYP:** 1898/99-1903/04,
06/07-19/20, 26/27; **V:** 1897/98-1927.

2936. ———. CORPORATION COURT. Was Rev. J. R. Moffett mur-
dered? Clark *v.* Commonwealth. D. M. no. 43Z. From the Corporation court of the city of Danville. Richmond, Va., Taylor &
Dalton [1892?]

192, 2 p. 8°.   **V**

2937. ———. ENGINEER, City. Annual report . . . [Danville,
18-?-19—

8°.   Report year ends Apr. 30.

NYP: 1909/10-14/15; **V:** 1904/05-14/15.

2938. ———. HEALTH DEPT. A summary of the municipal department of health, Danville, Va. May 1, 1913 to Apr. 30, 1914.
Danville, Townes, 1914.

20 p. table. 8°.   **V**

2939. ———. MAYOR. Annual report . . . [Danville, 18-?-19—

8°.   **V:** 1905; **WM:** 1925.

Report for 1905 includes reports of all city officials.

2940. DANVILLE, VA. ORDINANCES, ETC. Charter and ordinances of the city of Danville, Virginia. Pub. by order of the Council. Danville, Va., Townes, 1907.

    258 p. 8°.   **HL, V**

2941. ———. ———. Constitutional provisions, charter and general ordinances of the city of Danville, Virginia, 1923. Danville, Townes, 1923.

    284, [18] p. 8°.   **V**

2942. ———. ———. Tax ordinance for the fiscal year . . . Danville, Va. [18-?-19—

    8°.   **V**: 1892, 95-13/14, 22/23-28.

2943. ———. WATER DEPT. Annual report of the Water and Light departments . . . Danville, Va. [18-?-19—

    plates. 8°. Report year irregular.

    Title varies: Annual reports of the superintendent of the city water, gas and electric light works . . .

    LC: 1899/1900, 04/05; **NYP**: 1903-13/14; **V**: 1905/06-07/08.

2944. ESSEX COUNTY, VA. Financial statement. Receipts and expenditures . . . [n. p., 19—

    8°.   **NYP**: 1911, 12.

2945. FALLS CHURCH, VA. Report of the financial transactions . . . [n. p., 19—

    8°.   **V**: 1911-13.

2946. FREDERICKSBURG, VA. CITY MANAGER. Annual report on the fiscal affairs . . . Fredericksburg [1914?—

    8°. **H**: 1913/14, 16, 20, 22, 26-27; **LC**: 1913/14-26; **NYP**: 1913/14-27; **V**: 1915-27; **WM**: 1923-27.

2947. ———. ———. Acts of incorporation and general ordinance of Fredericksburg, Va. Approved, May 19, 1899. Fredericksburg, printed by order of the City council, 1899.

    112 p. 8°.   **V**

2948. ———. ORDINANCES, ETC. The general ordinance of the corporation of Fredericksburg, made and passed by the mayor and commonalty of the town of Fredericksburg. Pub. by authority of the mayor and Council. Fredericksburg, White, 1871.

    1 p. l., xi, 45 p. 8°.   **LC**

2949. ———. ———. [Ordinances of Fredericksburg, Va., with an historical preface, and a list of mayors. Fredericksburg? 1881]

124 p. 12°.   V

Preface contains brief notes on the city since 1865.

2950. HAMPTON, VA. ORDINANCES, ETC. Ordinances of the town of Hampton, Virginia. Hampton, Va., Palmer, 1897.

[3], 55 p. 12°.   V

Ed. of 1904 (for 1902): 120 p.   V

2951. ISLE OF WIGHT COUNTY, VA. Statement showing financial condition . . . Isle of Wight [19—

8°.   NYP: 1913/14.

2952. LEXINGTON, VA. Charter of the town of Lexington. Approved Apr. 28, 1874. [n. p., n. d.]

16 p. 8°.   VU

2953. ———. COUNCIL. Charter and general ordinances of the town of Lexington, Virginia. Lexington, Va., 1892.

xi, 148 p. 8°.   HL, McC

2954. LYNCHBURG, VA. Official reports of the city of Lynchburg . . . Lynchburg, Va. [18-?-1915?

tables. 8°. Report year ends Jan. 31.

Continued by City manager, *Annual report* . . . [2958]

NYP: 1895/96, 1901/02-14/15; V: 1904/05-14/15.

2955. ———. Report . . . [Vol. 1-   ; 1921— Lynchburg, 1921—

mimeog. 4°. monthly.

NYP: I-XI, XIII-XVI (1921-25/26, 26/27-28).

2956. ———. Supplement to the Code of the city . . . together with the reports of the city officers for year ending . . . Lynchburg, Va. [18-?-19—

8°. Report year ends Jan. 31.

NYP: 1893, 95-96, 98, 1901-16, 22/23.

2957. ———. CHARTERS. Charter of the city of Lynchburg, Va., including the city manager form of government and constitutional and legislative provisions. [Lynchburg, Va.?] 1923.

92 p. 8°.   H

2958. LYNCHBURG, VA. CITY MANAGER. Annual report of the city of Lynchburg, Va. . . . Lynchburg, 1916—

illus., maps, tables, diagrs. 4°.
Report year ends Jan. 31.
Continuation of *Official reports* of the city of Lynchburg . . .
[2954]
NYP: 1923/24-27; **V**: 1922/23-27; **VU**: 1915/16; **WM**: 1923/24-27.

2959. ———. COUNCIL. . . . Resources and advantages of Lynchburg, Virginia, and tributary country. Prepared and pub. by order of the City council of Lynchburg. Lynchburg, Virginian, 1872.

16 p. fold. map. 8°.   **LC, NYP, USAg, USG, V**

2960. ———. ———. FINANCE COMMITTEE. Finances of the city of Lynchburg . . . Lynchburg, Va. [19—

4°.   **NYP, V**: 1914/15-17/18.

2961. ———. ———. STANDING COMMITTEE. Report . . . Lynchburg, Va. [186-?-19—

8°.   **NYP**: 1868/69, 75/76, 77/78, 81/82-86/87, 88/89-90/91.

2962. ———. ENGINEERING DEPT. . . . Standard specifications for the construction of improved pavements and appurtenances. H. L. Shaner, city engineer . . . [Lynchburg, Va., Bell] 1912.

135 p. incl. diagrs. 8°.   **NYP**

2963. ———. HEALTH DEPT. Report . . . Vol. 1- [1910?-19—] [Lynchburg, 1910?-19—

8°.   **NYP**: X, 2 (Feb., 1919); XII, 1-6 (Feb.-July, 1926).

2964. ———. ORDINANCES, ETC. The Code of the city of Lynchburg, Virginia, containing the charter as amended to date, the constitutional and legislative provisions of the state relating to cities, and the general ordinances of the city enacted as a whole . . . Pub. by order of the City council. Lynchburg, Bell [18-?-19—

8°.   **NYP**: 1887; **V**: 1905, 15.

2965. ———. ———. The Code of the city of Lynchburg, Virginia. Containing the constitutional and legislative provisions of the state relating to cities. The charter of the city as amended to date and the act governing the city manager plan of city government, and the general ordinances of the city enacted as a whole, 1923. Rev. by Mayo C. Brown. Pub. by order of the City council. Lynchburg, Bell, 1923.

vii, 426 p. incl. illus., tables, diagrs. 8°.   **V**

Appendix contains a short historical sketch of Lynchburg.

2966. ———. ———. The general ordinances, passed 12th August, 1880, and the city charter approved 3rd March, 1880 . . . Rev. & arranged by Chas. M. Blackford, city attorney. Lynchburg, Bell, 1880.

167, xxvi, p. 8°.   **McC, USC, V**

2967. ———. ———. Ordinances imposing taxes on licenses and real and personal property . . . Lynchburg [19—

8°.   **USC**: 1912; **V**: 1906-07.

2968. ———. WATER DEPT. Report of superintendent of water works . . . [Lynchburg, 18-?- ?]

8°.   **NYP**: 1890/91.

2969. MANCHESTER, VA. Advertisement and blank proposal . . . Four per cent. refunding bonds . . . Mar. 24, 1905. [Manchester? 1905?]

2 l. 8°.   **NYP**

2970. ———. Statement of receipts and disbursements . . . [Manchester, 19-?-10]

8°. Title varies slightly.   **LC**: 1903/04-09/10.

2971. ———. CHARTERS. The charter and ordinances of the city of Manchester. Published by authority of the Council of the city of Manchester. Manchester, 1904.

8°.   **USC**

2972. ———. COUNCIL. COMMITTEE OF INDUSTRIES. Manchester, Virginia, offers special inducements to manufacturers, a profitable field for investors. [Richmond, Anderson, 191-?]

[15] p. illus. nar. 8°.   **LC, VU**

Ed. of 1907.   **V**

2973. ———. HEALTH, Board of. Annual report . . . Manchester, Va. [19-?—

8°.   **LC, USC**: 1905-08; **V**: 1906, 08.

2974. NEWPORT NEWS, VA. Budget of the city . . . for the fiscal year . . . [n. p., 19—

8°. Report year ends Dec. 31.   **VU**: 1926.

2975. ———. ORDINANCES, ETC. The ordinances of the city of Newport News (in force July 1, 1900) with the charter as amended, and an appendix . . . Comp. & pub. by order of the Council. Newport News, Franklin, 1900.

viii, 283 p. 8°.   **V**

2976. ———. ———. The ordinances of the city of Newport News from the incorporation of the city to Sept. 1, 1908. Comp. by Samuel R. Buxton. Newport News, Franklin [1908]

164, x p. 8°.   **V**

2977. NORFOLK, VA. Finances of the city of Norfolk, Virginia. [Norfolk, 19-?—

8°. **H**: 1909/10; **LC**: 1907/08-09/10, 11/12-16/17, 18/19, 22; **NYP**: 1910/11-12/13, 26; **V**: 1907/08-16/17, 21-24.

2978. ———. New loan. $460,000 . . . four per cent. bonds. July 1, 1902. [n. p., 1902]

1 l. 4°.   **NYP**

2979. ———. BEAUTIFYING THE CITY, Commission on. Norfolk lawns and how to grow them. Issued by the Commission on beautifying the city. Norfolk, Va. [Vogue print.] 1918.

27, [4] p. illus., plate. 8°.   **LC, NYP, USAg**

2980. ———. ———. Report . . . 1st- ; 1908/11— Norfolk, Va. [1912?—

8°. Report period varies.
H: 1st-3d (1908/11-13/15); **LC, NYP**: 1912/13-13/15.

2981. ———. CHARTERS. Charter of the city of Norfolk, Virginia. Approved . . . Norfolk, Va. [18-?-19—

8°. **H**: 1908, 14, 18, 19; **LC**: 1882, 84, 1906, 08, 18, 19; **NYP**: 1908, 19; **USC**: 1908; **V**: 1906, 08, 14, 19; **VU**: 1914.

2982. ———. ———. The charter and the general ordinances of the city of Norfolk. (Passed prior to Jan. 1, 1920.) Codified, supplemented and rev. by Herbert G. Cochran, special assistant city attorney. In collaboration with R. W. Peatross, city attorney.

Pub. by authority of ordinance of the Council, passed Apr. 6, 1920. Effective Apr. 14, 1920. [Norfolk, 1920?]

xviii, 1026 p. 8°.   H, HL, LC, NYP, V, WM

Lettered on cover: Norfolk city code. 1920.

2983. ———. ———. Proposed charter of the city of Norfolk, prepared by the Charter commission of said city. [Norfolk, Minter-Moore print., 1917]

64 p. 8°.   H, LC, NYP, V

2984. ———. CITY MANAGER. Budget for 1918/19— [Norfolk? 1918?—

4°.   **LC**: 1918/19-22; **NYP**: 1923; **V**: 1918/19-19/20, 21.

Continuation of *Budget,* issued by the City council, Committee on finance **[2990]**

2985. ———. CIVIL SERVICE COMMISSION. Rules of the . . . commission. [n. p., n. d.]

2 l. 4°.   **NYP**

2986. [583] ———. COUNCIL. Charters [etc.] of various companies composing the Virginia railway & power company [*et al.*] . . . Norfolk, 1912.

2987. ———. ———. City of Norfolk, Virginia . . . [Norfolk, Va., 1924]

80 p. front., illus., tables, diagrs. 4°.   **NYP, V, WM**

Pub. by authority of the City council "to acquaint the people of Norfolk with things concerning their own city that . . . may be regarded as certain evidence that a firm foundation for the development of Metropolitan Norfolk has been laid." Improvements under city-manager government as reflected in economic and social conditions.

2988. ———. ———. Proceedings of the City council of Norfolk city, in committee of the whole council, May 22nd and 25th, 1911, in reference to the water question. [Norfolk, 1911]

97 p. 8°.   **LC**

2989. ———. ———. Rules of order . . . [Norfolk, 19—

16°.   **LC, NYP, V**: 1915.

2990. ———. ———. COMMITTEE ON FINANCE. Budget . . . for

422   BIBLIOGRAPHY OF VIRGINIA HISTORY

appropriations for accounts of various departments of the city of
Norfolk. [Norfolk, Va., 19-?-18]

8°. & f°. **LC**: 1915/16-17/18; **NYP**: 1911/12-15/16; **V**: 1911/12-
13/14, 15/16, 17/18.

Succeeded by Norfolk City manager. *Budget* . . . **[2984]**

2991. NORFOLK, VA. COUNCIL. COMMITTEE ON FINANCE. Report
. . . to the City council. [Norfolk, Va., 19—

8°.   **H**: 1911-12; **HL**: 1912-13; **NYP**: 1910, 12-14; **V**: 1912-14.

2992. ———. ———. SPECIAL COMMITTEE ON CHEAPER GAS. Report
of the Special committee of the City council to effect cheaper gas.
Aug. 28, 1916. With report of the sub-committee, the Baltimore
plan, and report of Willard F. Hine, consulting engineer, on "Fair
rate for gas in the city of Norfolk, Virginia," Aug. 25, 1916.
[Norfolk, 1916]

16 p. 8°.   NYP

2993. ———. COUNCILS. Stenographer's minutes. City of Norfolk
investigation into the "water option", before a committee of the
Councils, Jan. 21, 1897. Norfolk, Barron [1897]

1 p. l., 86 p. 8°.   NYP

2994. ———. ———. POLICE FORCE INVESTIGATING COMMITTEE. Report . . . concerning the charges of Mayor Lamb, in his annual message, against the Police commissioners and police force
of the city of Norfolk, Va. [Norfolk, Wise] 1885.

15 p. 8°.   NYP

2995. [584] ———. DOCK COMMISSIONERS, Board of. Report on
the development of a municipal terminal . . . Norfolk, 1917.

See also items **585-586, 595-596.**

2996. ———. ENGINEER, City. Report . . . Norfolk [19—

8°. Report year ends June 30.   **NYP**: 1913/15.

2997. ———. ———. Report of W. T. Brooke, city engineer, to
Councils of the city of Norfolk, Va., on water works situation.
Jan. 28, 1901. Norfolk, Barron, 1901.

23 p. 8°.   NYP

2998. ———. FIRE DEPT. Report of the chief . . . [Norfolk?
18-?-19—

8°.   **H**: 1898-99.

2999. ———. HEALTH, Board of. Report . . . [Norfolk? 18-?-?]

8°.   LC: 1874-75.

3000. ———. HEALTH DEPT. Statement of mortality, vital statistics . . . and local meteorology . . . Norfolk [189-?-19—

f°.-4°. monthly.

NYP: Feb.-Dec., 1895; Jan.-Dec., 96; Jan.-Aug., Oct.-Dec., 97; Feb., Mar., May, Aug., Sept., 98; Aug.-Sept., 99; Aug., 1900; Dec., 01; Jan., 02.

3001. ———. IMPROVEMENT AND DEVELOPMENT OF . . . NOR-FOLK, Special commission on. Report of the Commission . . . to the honorable Select and Common councils, May, 1880. Norfolk, Va., 1880.

36 p. 8°.   V

Report on streets, sanitary conditions, sewage, etc.

3002. [83] ———. INDUSTRIAL COMMISSION. Agriculture and food production in and around Norfolk, Virginia . . . [Norfolk, 1912]

3003. ———. ———. Norfolk, Virginia . . . commercial, industrial, historical, geographical, social. Issued by . . . the Industrial commission of the city of Norfolk, Va. . . . Comp. by B. A. Banks. [Norfolk, Tidewater print.] 1910.

80 p. incl. illus., map. 8°.   BP, LC, NYP

Ed. of 1909.   NYP, V

"Norfolk is a genuine city of opportunity, and to let these opportunities be known is the main object of this compilation." A readable pamphlet.

3004. ———. ———. Norfolk, Virginia, "The sunrise city by the sea." . . . [Norfolk, Va.] The Industrial commission, 1912.

77 p. illus., maps, fold. plan. 8°.   NYP

Ed. of 1914: 84 p.   H, NYP, V, VU

3005. ———. MAYOR. Message of . . . mayor of the city . . . to the Select and Common councils, together with municipal reports . . . Norfolk [18-?-19—

8°. Report year varies.

H: 1874, 77, 81, 98, 99, 1926; LC: 1872/73, 77-1900/01; NYP: 1877-84, 86-89, 89/91-1900/01; V: 1873, 78, 98-1900/01.

3006. NORFOLK, VA. ORDINANCES, ETC. Building ordinances, city of Norfolk, Virginia. [Norfolk, Atlantic coast print.]   1918.

320 p. 12°.   H, LC, V

3007. ———. ———. An ordinance imposing taxes on property, persons and licenses for the payment of interest on the city debt and to meet the general appropriations for the year . . . [Norfolk, 19—

8°. Report year ends June 30.
LC: 1915; **NYP:** 1910-15; **USC:** 1909; **V:** 1911, 12-15, 17, 19-20.

3008. ———. ———. An ordinance imposing taxes on the shares of stock of the capital of banks, banking associations, trust and security companies, and licenses for the payment of interest on the city debt, and to meet the general appropriations, for the period . . . [Norfolk, 19—

8°. Report year ends June 30.
HL: 1911-12; **LC:** July-Dec., 1919; **NYP:** 1919/20, 21/22-22/23.

3009. ———. ———. An ordinance, making appropriations for the 8th or Berkley Ward, for the fiscal year beginning July 1, 1910, and ending June 30, 1911, and regulating the payment of same. Approved, Apr. 7, 1910. [Norfolk, 1910]

3 p. 8°.   NYP

3010. ———. ———. Ordinance making appropriations for the fiscal year . . . and regulating the payment of money out of the city treasury. Norfolk [19—

8°. Report year ends June 30.
HL: 1911/12-12/13; **NYP:** 1910/11-15/16, 19-22; **V:** 1912/13-13/14.

3011. ———. ———. An ordinance with reference to salaries of certain officers and employees of the city of Norfolk, and providing for additional employees in certain departments. [Norfolk, 1912?]

7 p. 8°.   HL, NYP, V

3012. ———. ———. Ordinances imposing licenses, May 1, 1928-Apr. 30, 1929, . . . for payment of interest on the city debt . . . [n. p., 1928]

46 p. 8°.   BP

3013. ———. ———. The ordinances of the city of Norfolk; to which is appended the charter of the city. Pub. by authority of the Councils. 1875. Norfolk, Landmark, 1875.

208 p. 8°. **HL, USC, V**

3014. ———. ———. The ordinances of the city of Norfolk and acts of Assembly of Virginia relating to the city government, with an appendix. 1885. Norfolk, Va., Landmark, 1885.

239 p. 8°. **LC, USC, V**

Ordinances, comp. by Charles G. Elliott, have special title-page.

3015. ———. ———. The ordinances of the city of Norfolk, with the amended charter and an appendix containing special ordinances, acts of the Assembly of Virginia relating to the city government, etc. 1894. Norfolk, Barron, 1894.

viii, 381 p. 8°. **LC, NYP, USC, V**

3016. ———. ———. The ordinances of the city of Norfolk, Va. (date of enactments including May 29, 1902.) With the amended charter, acts of Assembly relating to city government and an appendix. Comp. by H. N. Poulson and R. E. Steed. Under the supervision of Walter H. Taylor, city attorney, and the Ordinance committee of the councils. Pub. by authority of the councils, as per ordinance adopted July 1, 1902. Norfolk, Va., Burke & Gregory, 1902.

vii, [9]-932 p. 8°. **LC, NYP, USC, V**

3017. ———. ———. Ordinances relating to the Board of health of the city of Norfolk, Va. Comp. by H. N. Poulson and R. E. Steed, 1902. [Norfolk, Va., 1902]

8°. **USC**

3018. ———. ———. Plumbing ordinance, city of Norfolk, Virginia. [Norfolk, Atlantic coast print.] 1918.

72 p. 4°. **H, LC, V**

3019. ———. ———. The revised ordinances of the city of Norfolk, to which are prefixed the original charter of the borough, and the amended charter of 1845 creating the borough into a city, and a collection of acts and parts of acts of the General assembly, relating to the city. Pub. by authority of the councils. 1866. Norfolk, Va., Old Dominion, 1866.

190 p. 8°. **LC, NYP, V**

3020. NORFOLK, VA. ORDINANCES, ETC. Supplement to the Norfolk city code, 1920, including ordinances of a general nature passed prior to Jan. 1, 1924. Comp. by Edmund S. Ruffin, jr., and John D. Corbell. [Norfolk? 1924]

iii, 180 p. 8°.   V, WM

3021. ———. PLAYGROUND COMMISSION. Annual report . . . [1st-   ] 1913— Norfolk, 1913—

illus., plates. 8°.
LC: 1st-2d (1913-14); **NYP**: 1913-14; **V**: 1913-15.

3022. ———. PUBLIC SAFETY DEPT. FIRE DIV. Annual report . . . Norfolk [19—

8°. Report year ends June 30.   **NYP**: 1912/13.

3023. ———. STREET, SEWER & DRAIN COMMISSIONERS BOARD. . . . Regulations governing plumbing, house drainage, and the ventilation of house sewers, Norfolk, Va. Norfolk, Wise, 1883.

12 p. 12°.   **NYP**

3024. ———. TRAFFIC COMMISSION. Report on traffic conditions and public transportation service in the city of Norfolk, Virginia, 1926 . . . Part[s] 1-4. [Norfolk, Va.] Traffic commission [1926]

4 pts. in 1 v. 4°.   **NYP**

3025. ———. WATER COMMISSIONERS. Contract [and specifications for the structures upon the Norfolk water works] Feb., 1871. [Norfolk, 1871]

63 p. 4°.   **NYP**

3026. ———. ———. Minority report of I. Walker Truxtin, member of the Water commission. May 8, 1911. [Norfolk? 1911?]

4 p. 8°.   V
Concerning competition with the Norfolk County water co.

3027. ———. WATER DEPT. . . . Annual report . . . [1st- ; 1875-19—   ] Norfolk [1875?-19—

8°. **LC**: 23d-32d (1896/97-1905/06); **NYP**: 1876, 87/88, 89/90-99/1900, 01/02-05/06; **V**: 1901/02-05/06.

3028. ———. ———. Report and plans of the Hon. W. J. McAlpine for a supply of water for the city of Norfolk. Feb., 1871. Norfolk, Va., Journal, 1871.

48 p. 8°. **BP, NYP, V**

3029. ———. ———. The Water department of the city of Norfolk, 1894. [Norfolk, Va., Barron, 1894]

15 p. 8°. **LC**

Contains ordinances, rules, regulations, etc.

3030. PETERSBURG, VA. Proposals for $75,000 3½ per cent. forty-year street paving and improvement bonds . . . [n. p., 1901]

2 l. 4°. **NYP**

3031. ———. COUNCIL. Report of the city of Petersburg, Virginia, for the period Sept. 15, 1920 to June 30, 1923, being a complete report of the city government under the council-manager plan. Petersburg, Va., Plummer, 1923.

87 p. 8°. **H, LC, NYP, V, VU, WM**

3032. ———. HEALTH DEPT. Report . . . [Petersburg, 19—

8°. **NYP:** 1923-24; Nov., 1926; Sept., Nov., 1927. **USC:** 1917. **V:** 1923-24, 27-Jan., 29.

3033. ———. ———. Statistical reports . . . Petersburg, Va. [19—

8°. **USC:** 1900-12, 15-16; **V:** 1920/22.

3034. ———. ORDINANCES, ETC. Charter and ordinances of the city of Petersburg, prepared and revised by John C. Armistead, Sept., 1869. Petersburg, Va., Ege, 1869.

128 p., 1 l. 8°. **V**

Pub. by direction of the Common council.

3035. ———. ———. Code of the city of Petersburg, Virginia, of 1912. Containing ordinances of a general nature in force July 1, 1911, the charter of 1875, as amended . . . Revised and codified . . . by Bernard C. Syme. [n. p., 1912]

552 p. 8°. **V**

3036. ———. ———. Ordinances for imposing and collecting taxes on licenses and taxes for the exercise of certain privileges within the city of Petersburg . . . [Petersburg? 19—

8°. **V:** 1912, 13.

3037. PETERSBURG, VA. TREASURER, City. Annual report . . .
[Petersburg, Va.? 19—

    8°.   V: 1910-11.

3038. PORTSMOUTH, VA. ACCOUNTANT-AUDITOR. Finances of the
city of Portsmouth, Va., for the fiscal year ended Dec. 31, 1909.
Reported by William H. Gleason, accountant-auditor, Chicago.
[Portsmouth, Fiske, 1910]

    63 p. 8°.   NYP, V

3039. ——. MAYOR. . . . Mayor's annual message, together
with municipal reports . . . Portsmouth [18-?-19—

    8°. **H**: 1915-18, 20, 22-23, 25-26; **NYP**: 1885/86, 89/90, 95/96-96/97,
98/99-1904/05, 06-12, 20-22; **V**: 1905-11, 15-24.

3040. ——. ORDINANCES, ETC. An ordinance fixing duties of the
city surveyor and the inspector of plumbing and establishing
plumbing regulations for the city of Portsmouth, Va. Portsmouth,
Fiske, 1896.

    28 p. 12°.   NYP

3041. ——. ——. Ordinances for imposing and collecting taxes on
licenses, real estate, personal property, and banks . . . Portsmouth, Va. [19—

    8°.   NYP: 1908/09; V: 1912.

3042. ——. ——. Ordinances of the city of Portsmouth, Virginia.
Pub. by order of the City council. Portsmouth, Va., Fiske, 1905.

    [166] p. 8°.   HL, V
    Ed. of 1906: 23 p.   NYP

3043. ——. ——. Supplementary city ordinances. 1896-1902.
[Portsmouth, 1902]

    22 p. 8°.   NYP

3044. POTOMAC, VA. ORDINANCES, ETC. Charter, rules of order and
ordinances of the town of Potomac, Arlington County, Va. Comp.
by Walter U. Varney . . . [n. p.] Pub. by authority of Council, 1924.

    3 p. l., 220, [21] p. 16°.   V

3045. PRINCESS ANNE COUNTY, VA. HEALTH, Board of. Rules and regulations of the Board of health . . . Norfolk, Va., Burke & Gregory, 1906.

19 p. 8°.   **V**

3046. RICHMOND, VA. Annual city reports . . . Richmond, Va. [18-?-19—

8°. Include annual message of mayor, reports of the auditor, collector, treasurer, board of health, etc.

BP: 1872/73-76/77; **LC:** 1872/73-78/79, 80/81-82/83, 84/85, 86-1921; **NYP:** 1872/73-74/75, 76/77, 79/80, 81/82-82/83, 84/85, 93, 95-1914, 16-24; **V:** 1872/73-96, 98-1926.

3047. ——. Blank proposal and advertisement . . . Refunding bonds. Richmond [19—

8°.   **NYP:** Dec. 9, 1904; May 17, 1905; June 7, 1906.

3048. ——. ACCOUNTANT, Special. Annual report . . . Richmond [19—

8°.   **LC:** 1911/12.

3049. ——. ——. The answer of the Special accountant (Carlton McCarthy) to the two (three?) opinions of the city attorney (Hon. H. R. Pollard) which was refused a place in the picture, with some additions, etc., etc. . . . Richmond, Va., Whittet & Shepperson, 1903.

33 p. 8°.   **V**

Regarding the disposition of the city's sinking-fund.

3050. ——. ——. The bonded debt of the city of Richmond: its past, present, and future. A paper read before a Special joint committee of the City council composed of the Committee on finance and the Commissioners of the sinking-fund . . . By Carlton McCarthy, special accountant of the city, . . . Sept. 23, 1903. Also two opinions of the city attorney, Hon. H. R. Pollard, delivered to the same committee. Richmond, Va., Pub. by authority . . . of the committee, 1903.

73 xiv, p. 8°.   **USC, V**

3051. ——. ADMINISTRATIVE BOARD. Annual report . . . 1st- ; 1913— Richmond, Va. [1914?-19—

8°.   **LC:** 1913; **NYP:** 1913-15; **V:** 1914.

3052. RICHMOND, VA. ADMINISTRATIVE BOARD. Report . . . in reference to the lease of the city gas works. Richmond, 1915.

20 p. 16°.   V

3053. ———. ADVISORY ARCHITECT. Report of advisory architect [Alfred C. Bossom] on designs submitted in the competition for the selection of an architect and the procuring of a design for the proposed new municipal building. Richmond, William Byrd press, 1914.

14 p. 8°.   V

3054. ———. ALMSHOUSE, City. Duties of orderlies . . . Rules and regulations. Richmond, Evening news [n. d.]

broadsides.   BP

3055. ———. ———. OUTDOOR POOR, Dept. of. Annual report of the superintendent of the city almshouse, Dept. of outdoor poor, Shockoe Hill cemetery and City hospital. Richmond, Evening news [18-?- ?]

8°. Report year ends Jan. 31.   BP: 1873/74.

3056. ———. AUDITOR. Annual report . . . Richmond [18-?-1919]

8°. Report year ends Jan. 31.

Succeeded by *Annual report* of Comptroller, 1919/20— **[3061]**

BP: 1901-02; H: 1910/11, 17/18-18/19; LC: 1897/98-1918/19; NYP: 1881/82-83/84, 86/87-90/91, 93/94-1902/03, 04/05-17/18; USC: 1910/11-13/14, 15/16-16/17; V: 1903/04, 06/07, 10/11, 12/13, 16/17.

3057. ———. BUILDING INSPECTOR. Annual report . . . [1st-] 1907— Richmond, Va., 1908—

8°.   H: 1912-14; LC: 1907, 12-21; VU: 1920-24.

3058. ———. CHARTERS. Amendments to the city charter, 1912. An act to amend and re-enact sections 19, 19d, 26, 28, 29, 30 . . . (Approved Feb. 9, 1912) . . . Richmond, 1912.

8°.   USC

3059. ———. ———. The charter of the city of Richmond . . . Richmond, [18-?-19—

8°. BP: 1906; H: 1919; NYP: 1898, 1906, 15, 16, 19; V: 1898, 1906, 19, 26; VU: 1906.

3060. ———. COLLECTOR. Annual report of the city collector. Richmond [18-?-19—

8°. Report year ends Jan. 31.
LC: 1900, 02/03-04/05.

3061. ———. COMPTROLLER. Annual report . . . 1919/20— Richmond, 1920—

tables (part fold.) 4°. Report year ends Jan. 31.
Continuation of *Annual report* of the Auditor [**3056**].
H: 1919/20-26/27; **LC:** 1919/20-26/27; **NYP:** 1922/23, 24/25-25/26.

3061a. ———. ———. Statement of cash receipts and disbursements . . . 1922/23— [Richmond, 1923—

f°. Report year ends Jan. 31. **LC:** 1922/23.
Autographed from typew. copy.

3062. ———. COUNCIL. Franchises granted by the City council of Richmond, Virginia, as contained in the Code of 1885 and as ordained since 1885 to Dec. 31, 1899 . . . Richmond [1899?]

247 p. 8°. **V**

3063. ———. ———. Manual . . . [Richmond, 18-?-19—

12°. **NYP:** 1896; **V:** 1920-22.

3064. ———. ———. Rules for the government of the new Council of the city of Richmond. [Richmond, 1877]

17 p. 8°. **BP**

3065. ———. ———. CITY SEAL, Committee on. Report of the Committee . . . , recommending a new design. Adopted Sept. 9, 1872. [n. p., 1872?]

7 p. 8°. **H, WM**

3066. ———. ———. EXTENSION OF CITY LIMITS, Sub-committee on. Report . . . Summary of statistical facts and comparisons. Richmond, Flanhart, 1902.

17 p. tables. 8°. **V**

3067. ———. ———. FINANCE COMMITTEE. Statement of the financial condition of the city of Richmond . . . Dec. 1, 1908. Richmond, 1908.

12 p. 12°. **NYP**

3068. RICHMOND, VA. COUNCIL. POOR, Committee on relief of the. A general city hospital and the new colored almshouse. A statement presented for consideration to the Committee on relief of the poor, by councilman Ennion G. Williams, Feb. 19, 1907. [Richmond] Richmond press [1907]

10 p. 8°.   V

3069. ———. ———. ———. Reply of Dr. Ennion G. Williams to the statements of Mr. Marx Gunst in opposition to plan to build a city hospital. Richmond, Flanhart, 1907.

9 p. 8°.   V

Reveals inadequacy of present city home and the great need for a better hospital for the poor.

3070. ———. ———. PRINTING AND CLAIMS, Committee on. Notice of contracts awarded for the book and job printing, stationery, blank books, and other forms of binding and ruling, padding, numbering, etc., and for the city advertising for the year 1911. Richmond, Saunders, 1911.

10 p. 8°.   V

3071. ———. ———. SPECIAL COMMITTEE TO INVESTIGATE THE HEALTH DEPT. Report . . . Richmond, Va., 1906.

13 p. 8°.   V

3072. ———. ———. STREETS, Committee on. Report of the Committee on streets, and the ordinance granting certain rights to the Southern Bell telephone & telegraph company. Recommended to the Council for adoption, June 21, 1901. [Richmond? 1901?]

18 p. 8°.   V

3073. ———. ———. WATER COMMITTEE. Description of the waterworks at Richmond, Virginia. By C. E. Bolling, supt., 1832-1889. Richmond, Waddey, 1889.

7 p. front., plate. 8°.   NYP

3074. ———. ———. ———. Proposals, contract and specifications for hydraulic pumping machinery. [Richmond, 1880]

26 p. illus. 4°.   NYP

Contains MS. notes.

3075. ——. ——. ——. Report of the Water committee appointed by Joint committee on water and finance . . . [Richmond, 1895]

7 p. 8°. **NYP**

3076. ——. ——. ——. Report on the mode of supplying Church Hill[1] with water, and on the extension of the works, by Joseph J. Heindl. Mar. 4, 1871. Richmond, Evening news, 1871.

21 p. 8°. **LC, NYP**
Contains a brief article on sources of taxation for the estimated outlay.

3077. ——. ——. ——. Report to the Water committee on the investigation of the effect of trades wastes on the water of James River at Richmond, by Ernest C. Levy. Richmond, Saunders, 1905.

28 p. incl. front. (map) tables. 8°. **V**
Concerning pollution of the water by waste from mills along the river.

3078. ——. ELECTRICAL DEPT. Annual report . . . 1915-18. Richmond, 1916-19.

4 v. 8°. **LC:** 1915.
Continued by *Annual report* of Dept. of public utilities, 1919— **[3110]**

3079. [1100] ——. EMPLOYMENT BUREAU, Public. Annual report . . . Richmond, 1916—

See also items **1101-1102.**

3080. ——. ENGINEER, City. Annual report . . . Richmond [18-?-19—

8°. **H:** 1887, 89, 91-97, 99-1900, 03; **LC:** 1898, 1900-17; **V:** 1901-02, 05-09.

3081. ——. ——. Estimated costs of suggested improvements of roadways, sidewalks, alleys, and sewers within the present corporate limits of the city of Richmond, Va. Comp. to Jan. 1, 1904 . . . Richmond, Flanhart, 1904.

35 p. f°. **V**

3082. ——. ——. Trees of the city [of Richmond] 1904. By W. E. Cutshaw, city engineer. Richmond, Va., Flanhart, 1904.

18 p. 8°. **V**

---

1. Church Hill is a section of the city of Richmond.

3083. RICHMOND, VA. FIRE DEPT. Annual report . . . Richmond [18-?-19—

plates. 8°. Report year ends Dec. 31.

H: 1899; **LC:** 1898, 1900-21; **NYP:** 1903, 15-17, 23-25; **USC:** 1913-15, 17; **V:** 1900, 05, 07.

3084. ——. FIRE PREVENTION, Bur. of. Annual report . . . Richmond [19—

8°.   **LC:** 1921-23, 25.

3085. ——. GAS WORKS, Supt. of city. Annual report . . . Richmond [18-?-1918]

tables. 8°.

Continued by *Annual report* of Dept. of public utilities, 1919— **[3110]**
LC: 1901-03, 05-07, 12, 14; **NYP:** 1903-04; **V:** 1873-96, 98-1923.

3086. ——. HEALTH, Bur. of. Annual report . . . 1st-   ; 1919— Richmond, 1919—

8°.   **NYP, V:** 1919.

Prior to 1919 issued as report of Health dept. **[3087]**; in Dept. of public welfare, 1919—

3087. ——. HEALTH DEPT. Annual report. 1st-   ; 1871— Richmond, 1872-19—

maps, tables (part fold.) diagrs. 8°.

Title varies: Annual report of the Board of health of the births, marriages and deaths, 1871-81; Annual report of the Board of health, 1882-86; Annual report of the Health dept., 1887-19—

BP: 1872, 89, 99; **H:** 1907-10, 12-18; **LC:** 1871-87, 92-1921; **NYP:** 1871, 76, 79-84, 86, 98, 1904-18, 20-21; **USAg:** 1908-20; **USC:** 1890, 92-1900, 02-17; **V:** 1872, 76, 79-80, 85, 97-98, 1900, 02-03, 06-12, 14, 16-18, 20-22; **VU:** 1909, 20-24.

3088. ——. ——. The extermination of mosquitoes (by E. C. Levy . . .) Pub. by the Health dept. of the city of Richmond, Va. . . . Richmond, Va., 1908.

14 p. illus. 8°.   H, **LC, USAg, V**

3089. ——. ——. Monthly bulletin. Vol. 1-[?] July, 1907— [?] [Richmond, 1907-1-?]

illus. 8°.

Successor to Richmond Health dept. *Monthly report* **[3090]**

H: I, 5-IV, 1 (Nov., 1907-July, 1910); **LC:** I-III; **NYP:** III-IV, 6; **USAg:** I-III; **V:** II-IV, 7.

3090. ———. ———. Monthly report . . . Richmond, Va. [189-?-1906]

8°. **NYP:** Sept.-Dec., 1895; 1896; Jan.-May, July-Dec., 1897; Jan., 1898; Jan.-July, 1899; Jan.-Mar., 1900; Jan.-Sept., 1901; Jan.-Sept., 1902; Jan.-June, 1903; Jan.-Aug., 1904.

Continued as Richmond Health dept. *Monthly bulletin,* 1907-[1-?]
[3089]

3091. ———. ———. [Pamphlets] Richmond, 1913-15.

var. pag. 8°.-16°.   **V**

Articles on pure food, sanitation, etc.

3092. ———. ———. Richmond health bulletin, no. 1- ; July, 1918— [Richmond, 1918—

8°. quarterly.

H: 1; **NYP:** 1-3; **V:** 1.

3093. ———. JUVENILE & DOMESTIC RELATIONS COURT. 1st- Annual report . . . 1916— Richmond, 1917—

8°.   **V, VU, WM:** 6th (1921).

3094. ———. MAYOR. Annual message and accompanying documents of the mayor to the City council. [Richmond, 18-?-19—

8°. **BP:** 1877; **H:** 1906-11, 13-19; **NYP:** 1893-94, 1909-11, 13-16; **V:** 1873-96, 98-1926.

3095. ———. ORDINANCES, ETC. Building code of the city of Richmond, Va. Approved, Jan. 13, 1922. [Richmond, 1922]

179 p. incl. tables. 12°.   **V, VU**

Prepared by the Commission on revision of the building code.

Ed. of 1916: 246 p.   **NYP**

3096. ———. ———. [Building ordinances. Richmond, 1908-09]

var pag. 8°.   **H**

3097. ———. ———. Certain resolutions and ordinances of the Council of the city of Richmond . . . Richmond [1900—

8°.   **H:** 1910/12; **LC:** 1910/12-12/14; **V:** 1898/1900-00/02.

3098. ———. ———. The charter and ordinances of the city of Richmond, with the amendments to the charter. Pub. by authority of the Common council of the city of Richmond. Richmond [1867- ?]

8°. **BP:** 1869, 75; **LC:** 1867; **NYP:** 1867, 69; **USC:** 1885; **V:** 1867.

3099. RICHMOND, VA. ORDINANCES, ETC. The charter and the general ordinances of the city of Richmond. Comp. by the city attorney by authority of a joint resolution of the Council . . . approved Mar. 9, 1908, and adopted as Richmond city code 1910 by the ordinance approved Oct. 25, 1910, entitled "An ordinance arranging and consolidating into a code the general ordinances of the city of Richmond in force Sept. 1, 1910." [Richmond] Capitol print., 1910.

748 p. 8°.   **H, LC, NYP, USC**
Henry R. Pollard, city attorney.
Ed. of 1915.   **USC**
Ed. of 1916.   **H**

3100. ———. ———. The charter of the city of Richmond, approved May 24—amended July 11, 1870; and the city ordinances, passed since the late edition of the ordinances in 1869. Pub. by authority of the Council . . . Richmond, Evening news, 1871.

95 p. 8°.   **HL, LC, NYP, V**

3101. ———. ———. Compilation of statutes, ordinances, resolutions . . . for the construction, maintenance, and operation of street railways, electric light and power properties by Virginia railway & power company and Richmond & Henrico railway company, within the corporate limits of Richmond, as they existed on and after Nov. 5, 1914. Comp. for Committee on streets of the Council of Richmond, by Virginia railway & power company. 1915. [Richmond? 1915]

785 p. 8°.   **V**

3102. ———. ———. Extract from Richmond city code. 1924 (as amended to May 1, 1927) chap. 10. Concerning the levying of taxes and the assessment of licenses. Richmond, Williams, 1927.

52 p. 8°.   **V**

3103. ———. ———. Franchises granted by the City council of Richmond, as contained in the Code of 1885 and as ordained since 1885 to Dec. 31, 1899. Printed by authority of joint resolution approved Oct. 6, 1899. Richmond, 1900.

247 p. 8°.   **V**

3104. ———. ———. Ordinance to authorize construction and operation of street railway by Citizens' rapid transit company. [Richmond? n. d.]

20 p. 4°.   **V**

3105. ———. ———. Ordinance to authorize construction and operation of street railway by Richmond passenger & power company. [Richmond? n. d.]

unp. 8°. **V**

3106. ———. ———. Ordinances of the Council of the city of Richmond . . . [frequently including the city charter] [Richmond, 1867-19—

8°. **BP:** 1874/76; **H:** 1910, 12/14; **HL:** 1869, 75; **NYP:** 1875, 79, 85, 99, 1906, 10/12; **V:** 1867, 69, 70/71, 74-76, 78-80, 82/84, 85/86-86/88, 98/1900-06/08, 10, 12/14-24/26.

3107. ———. POLICE DEPT. Annual report of the chief of police . . . [1st- ; 1871—] Richmond [1871?-19—

8°. [1st ser.] 1871-94; [new ser.] 1895-19—

LC: 1879/80, 81/82-85, 98-99, 1901-04, 06, 10, 12, 15-21; **NYP:** 1899-1916, 24-25; **VU:** 1924.

3108. ———. PUBLIC BUILDINGS, Supt. of. Preliminary report on heating and ventilating the capitol building at Richmond, Va., by Joseph J. Heindl, supt. . . . [Richmond, 1876]

[8] p. 8°. **NYP**

3109. ———. PUBLIC CHARITIES, Supt. of. Annual report . . . 1st- ; 1896-19— Richmond, Va., 1897-19—

tables. 8°.

Issued by the Dept. of public welfare of Richmond.

LC: 3d, 7-9th, 12th (1898, 1902-04, 07); **VU:** 1921-22.

3110. ———. PUBLIC UTILITIES, Dept. of. Annual report . . . 1919— Richmond, 1920—

tables. 8°.

Continues the annual reports of the Electrical dept. **[3078]** and the Supt. of city gas works **[3085]** and water works **[3118]**

LC: 1919-21; **NYP:** 1922; **V:** 1919-27.

3111. ———. PUBLIC WELFARE, Dept. of. Annual report . . . Richmond [19—

tables. 8°. Report year ends Dec. 31.

V: 1926; **VU:** 1921-24.

3112. ———. ———. Monthly bulletin . . . [Richmond? 19—

8°. **NYP:** Feb., 1921.

3113. RICHMOND, VA. PUBLIC WORKS, Dept. of. Annual report of the director. Richmond [19—

8°.   **NYP**: 1922-23; **V**: 1924-27.

3114. ———. ———. SURVEYS, Bur. of. . . . Report of the geodetic and topographic survey of Richmond, Virginia, as executed in 1921-1922 by the R. H. Randall co., topographic engineers, under the supervision of the Bureau of surveys . . . [Richmond?] 1923.

83 p. incl. tables. charts, diagr., maps, plate. 8°.

H, NYP, USG, V, WM

3115. ———. SINKING FUND, Commissioners of the. Statements of the bonded debt and sinking funds . . . 1922/23— Richmond, 1923—

f°. Report year ends Jan. 31.   **LC**: 1922/23.
Autographed from typew. copy.

3116. ———. STREET CLEANING DEPT. Annual report . . . Richmond, Va. [19—

tables, diagrs. 8°.   **LC**: 1902-04, 06-12, 14.

3117. ———. TREASURER. Annual report . . . Richmond [18-?-19—

8°. **LC**: 1899/1900-00/01, 02/03-04/05, 06/07-15/16; **NYP**: 1896/97, 98/99-1904/05, 06/07-16/17; **V**: 1872/73-95/96, 97/98-1922/23.

3118. ———. WATER WORKS. Annual report of the superintendent . . . Richmond, Va. [18-?-19—

8°. Report year ends Dec. 31.
Continued as *Annual report* of Dept. of public uitilities, 1919— **[3110]**
    LC: 1897, 1900-17; **NYP**: 1871/72-74/75, 85-1900, 02-07, 09-14; **V**: 1883, 88-89, 93, 1900-03, 05-07.

3119. ROANOKE, VA. Annual reports of the official departments . . . [1st ser.? 18-?-1904?] [new ser.?] 1st-   ; 1905— [Roanoke, 18-?-1905? 1906—

8°. Title varies: Official reports of the city of Roanoke, Va. . . ., 1905.
    LC: 1905-12, 15; **NYP**: 1892/93, 1905, 07-08, 10-13; **V**: 1892/93, 1905-12, 18.

3120. ———. CHARTERS. Charters and general ordinances of the city of Roanoke, Virginia. Also special ordinances and curative acts pertaining to the issue of bonds . . . Comp. and arranged by W. E. Thomas, clerk of Council. Pub. by order of the City council. Roanoke, 1898.

x p., 1 l., 412 p. 8°.   **USC, V**

3121. ———. CIVIC IMPROVEMENT, Committee on. Sanitary Roanoke. Report to the Committee on civic improvement, by C. E. Emerson, jr., and Ezra B. Whitman, civil and sanitary engineers, Baltimore, Md. Presented to the city of Roanoke by the Woman's civic betterment club of Roanoke, Virginia. [Roanoke, Stone, 1907]

118 p. 12°.   **VU**

3122. ———. COUNCIL. Manual . . . [Roanoke, Va., 18—
8°.   **NYP:** 1902/03.

3123. ———. ———. Rules for the government of the Board of aldermen and Common council . . . Rev. by Joint standing committee on ordinances . . . Adopted . . . Oct. 24, 1904. [Roanoke? 1904?]

26 p. 16°.   **V**

3124. ———. FIRE DEPT. Annual report of the chief. Roanoke, Va. [19—
8°.   **LC:** 1907; **NYP:** 1912.

3125. ———. ORDINANCES, ETC. Charters and general ordinances . . . Also special ordinances and curative acts pertaining to the issue of bonds; special ordinances under which private rights have vested or private liabilities have been imposed . . . Comp. & arranged by W. E. Thomas, clerk of Council. [Roanoke] Pub. by order of City council, 1898.

x p., 1 l., 412 p. 8°.   **V**

3126. ———. ———. City of Roanoke, Virginia. An ordinance to provide regulations governing the erection of buildings in this city. Comp. by the Engineers' association of Virginia. Approved June 23, 1894. Roanoke, Stone, 1894.

20 p. 8°.   **NYP**

3127. ROANOKE, VA. ORDINANCES, ETC. Code of the city of Roanoke, Virginia, containing constitutional provisions relative to cities and towns, charters of the town of Big Lick, the town of Roanoke, and the charters of the city of Roanoke, various amendments thereto, and a compilation of all statutory provisions relating to cities and towns of the commonwealth, and the general ordinances of the city; rev. by C. B. Moomaw and C. A. McHugh. Pub. by order of the City council. [Roanoke, Union print., 1909]

2 p. l., [7]-583 p. 8°.   LC, NYP, USC, V

3128. ———. ———. Ordinance imposing taxes on licenses; also upon real estate and personal property . . . Roanoke [18-?-19—

8°.   USC: 1911; V: 1908-09.

3129. ST. PAUL, VA. ORDINANCES, ETC. Ordinances and by-laws of St. Paul, Wise County, Virginia. Together with certain general laws relating to the government of towns. [n. p., 1915]

59 p. 8°.   V

3130. ———. ———. Town of St. Paul, Wise County, Virginia. Ordinances and by-laws of said town, and order incorporating said town, setting forth the metes and bounds thereof . . . [n. p., 1911?]

59 p. 8°.   V
Established in 1911.

3131. SALEM, VA. Blank proposal and circular . . . Gold refunding bonds. Mar. 10, 1900. [Salem, 1900]

2 l. 8°.   NYP

3132. STAUNTON, VA. CITY MANAGER. Annual report of the city of Staunton, Virginia. [Staunton, Va., 1909?—

plates, tables (part fold.) diagrs. 8°.
Report year ends Mar. 31.
NYP: 1909-09/10, 11/12-12/13, 14/15-15/16, 17/18-20/21, 24/25-26/27;
V: 1911/12, 14/15, 17/18-20/21, 24/25-26/27; WM: 1925/26.

3133. ———. ORDINANCES, ETC. Charter and general ordinances of the city of Staunton, 1885. Staunton, Stoneburner & Prufer, 1885.

vii, 158 p. 8°.   McC

3134. ———. ———. The charter and general ordinances of the city of Staunton. Codified, arranged, and published under the authority of the [City] council . . . 1897. Staunton, Shultz, 1897.

203 p. 8°.   V

3135. ———. ———. The code of the city of Staunton, Virginia, containing the charter and general laws and ordinances. Staunton, Shultz, 1910.

279 p. 8°.   V

3136. [599] U. S. CIRCUIT COURT, 4th circuit. East. dist. of Virginia. The Southern Bell telephone and telegraph company, appellant, *v.* City of Richmond, appellee . . . [n. p., 1900?]

3137. [634] ———. SUPREME COURT. . . . The City of Richmond, petitioner, *v.* The Southern Bell telephone & telegraph company . . . [n. p., 1898?]

See also item **635.**

3138. [2639] VIRGINIA. AUDITOR. . . . List of judges and officers in counties and cities . . . Richmond, 1928.

See also item **2640.**

3139. ———. ———. . . . Powers and duties of the boards of supervisors [of the counties] . . . Richmond, Div. of purchase and printing, 1928.

175 p. 8°.   V

3140. [2647] ———. CITIZENS' COMMITTEE ON CONSOLIDATION AND SIMPLIFICATION IN STATE AND LOCAL GOVERNMENTS. Report . . . Richmond, 1927.

3141. [661] ———. CORPORATION COMMISSION, State. Statement of taxable values of public service corporations in cities, towns, and counties . . . Richmond [190-?—

3142. ———. GENERAL ASSEMBLY. Investigation of charges against James H. Woolfolk, judge of county court of Louisa . . . [n. p., 1884?]

79 p. 8°.   V

Charges by members of the bar and citizens of Louisa County, on grounds of incompetency and improper conduct.

3143. VIRGINIA. GENERAL ASSEMBLY. HOUSE. COURTS OF JUSTICE, Committee for. Investigation of charges against Hon. W. W. Newman, judge of the county court of Hanover County, by the Committee for courts of justice of the House of delegates of the General assembly of Virginia, session 1883-84. Richmond, Derr, 1884.

56 p. 8°.   V

3144. ——. ——. ——. ——. Investigation of Judge W. W. Newman, county judge of the County of Hanover, Virginia . . . in obedience to a resolution of the House of delegates, adopted Jan. 11, 1884.

unp. typew. 4°.   V
Copy of *Proceedings,* evidence, etc.

3145. ——. GOVERNOR, 1874-76 (James L. Kemper). Message . . . to the Senate [of Virginia] giving his reasons for withholding his assent to the bill "to provide a charter for the city of Petersburg." Richmond, 1874.

6 p. 8°.   NYP, VU

3146. ——. ——, 1926— (Harry F. Byrd). County government. [Richmond, Bottom, 1926]

14 p. 8°.   V
Virginia's county government compared with that in certain representative states, and proposed reforms.

3147. [1233] ——. JUDGES. Report of county and corporation judges . . . Richmond, 1871.

3148. WEST POINT, VA. Blank proposal and circular . . . Water bonds . . . Oct. 8, 1903. [West Point, 1903]

2 l. 8°.   NYP

3149. WESTMORELAND COUNTY, VA. COUNTY COURT. Fee books of the clerk of the county court. 1860-67, 71-78.

MSS.   V

3150. WINCHESTER, VA. COUNCIL. Report of committee . . . upon the relations of the city and the Council to the Handley board and fund . . . [Winchester, Eddy, 1900]

39 p. 8°.   NYP

3151. ——. ORDINANCES, ETC. Act of incorporation (as amended) and general ordinances, revised and re-arranged, 1901. Winchester, Va. [n. d.]

8°.   HL

3152. ——. ——. Revised ordinances of the city of Winchester, together with the city charter, and other acts of the General assembly relating to cities and towns. Winchester, Winchester news, 1875.

1 p. l., 88, xv, [1] p. 8°.   NYP

Other Source Material

3153. BUREAU OF MUNICIPAL RESEARCH, New York. County government in Virginia; report on a survey made for the governor and his Committee on consolidation and simplification, prepared by the New York Bureau of municipal research, Jan., 1927. Richmond, Bottom, 1928.

100 p. diagrs. 8°.   LC, USAg, V, WM

3154. ——. Norfolk, Virginia; report on a survey of the city government. Prepared by the Bureau of municipal research, New York, Sept.-Dec., 1915. [n. p., 1916?]

529 p. fold. charts. 8°.   H, V

3155. ——. Richmond, Virginia; report on a survey of the city government. Prepared for the Civic association of Richmond by the Bureau of municipal research, New York, 1917. [New York, 1918?]

viii, 965 p. incl. plans, tables, diagrs., forms. 8°.   H, LC, V

3156. ——. Summary of recommendations, including chapter on organization from Report of a survey of the city government of Richmond, Va. Prepared for the Civic association of Richmond . . . , 1917. [New York, 1918?]

80 p. chart. 8°.   H, LC, V

Advocating centralization of authority and responsibility in the mayor for management of all administrative departments.

3157. CIVIC ASSOCIATION OF RICHMOND, Va. An administrative survey for Richmond. [Richmond, 1915]

7 p. nar. 8°. (Its *Bulletin,* 2)   NYP

3158. CIVIC ASSOCIATION OF RICHMOND, Va. How to obtain a government that fixes responsibility. [Richmond, 1915]

8 p. 8°.   V

3159. DEMOCRATIC nominating convention of the Eighth Congressional district of Virginia, held Aug. 28, 1878, at the city of Alexandria, Va. Reported by E. W. Grant. [Washington, D. C.] Washington post, 1878.

31 p. 8°.   VU

3160. [ELECTION broadsides. Roanoke, Va., Nov. 7, 1911]

var. sizes.   H

3161. GAINES, ELIZABETH V. County government in Virginia. Richmond, Virginia League of women voters [19-?]

8 p. 8°.   V, VU

3162. GLASS, R. H. Reply of R. H. Glass, editor of the Petersburg post, to the malicious pamphlet of William E. Hinton, jr. . . . also a card from R. H. Glass, jr. Petersburg, Harrison, 1878.

20 p. 8°.   VU
Excerpts from the *Post,* showing Hinton's political conduct.

3163. HINTON, WILLIAM E., jr. Extract from a speech . . . delivered at the Academy of music, Petersburg, Va., Nov. 4, 1878, in which he denounces R. H. Glass, editor "Daily post". Petersburg, Ege, 1878.

8 p. 8°.   VU
A conservative's statement of political conditions and antagonism between conservatives and radicals in Petersburg.

3164. HODGES, LE ROY. Graphic argument for city-manager government. July 16, 1917. Petersburg, Va., 1917.

[4] p. diagrs. 4°. (Petersburg Bur. of governmental research. *Bulletin,* 1, July 16, 1917)   NYP, V

3165. ———. Reorganization of municipal government in Virginia. [Washington, 1915]

[4] p. diagrs. 4°. (The Southern commercial congress. Bur. of economics and public efficiency. *Bulletin,* 3, July 15, 1915)   V

3166. HOLSINGER, S. D. General manager plan of government of Staunton, Va. [Staunton? 190-?]

12 p. 8°.   NYP

3167. HUNDLEY, GEORGE J. The Petersburg charter and governor's veto. Substance of the speech . . . delivered in the Senate of Virginia, Mar. 13, 1874. [n. p., n. d.]

10 p. 8°.   VU

Attack upon the governor for opposing political restrictions upon the Negroes of Petersburg.

3168. KEMPER, JAMES L. Letter from Governor Kemper: The Petersburg charter, the political situation considered, principles and aims of the conservative party, our relations with the Federal government. Apr. 11, 1874. [n. p., n. d.]

4 p. 8°.   V

3169. LEAGUE OF VIRGINIA MUNICIPALITIES. . . . Annual convention . . . Containing minutes of the meetings and the addresses . . . [1st- ; 1906?— n. p., 1906?—

8°.   H: 6th (1911); V: 3d-6th, 10th (1908-11, 15).

3170. ———. Articles of association . . . [n. p., n. d.]

5 p. 16°.   V

3171. ———. Program for the . . . annual meeting. [n. p., 1906?—

8°.   LC: 6th (1911).

3172. MANCHESTER ANTI-CONSOLIDATION LEAGUE. Fellow citizen, consolidation concerns you! Whatever of ill there is in it will fall upon you! The Manchester anti-consolidation league in preparing and submitting to you this pamphlet, are [sic] contending for your interests as much as theirs. We earnestly urge you to read therefore, and consider it thoughtfully. [Weymouth, Meister & Smethie, n. d.]

14 p. 8°.   V

Opposing a movement for consolidation of Manchester into Richmond.

3173. NEWPORT NEWS and commission government (supplement). [Newport News, Franklin print., ca. 1915]

8 p. 8°.   LC

3174. NORFOLK CHAMBER OF COMMERCE. For a better form of government for the city of Norfolk, Virginia. Norfolk [Virginia specialty co.] 1915.

[2], 23 p. nar. 8°.   V

Conclusions of the Charter commission after a year's investigation, and recommendations favoring a city-manager form of government.

3175. A POLITICAL cancer; being an abridged history of the Norfolk County conspiracy, and an incidental personal controversy. [Norfolk?] Pub. by the Democratic executive committee of Norfolk County, Va., Jan., 1904.

16 p. 8°. (Reprint from Lynchburg *Daily news*)   V

Controversy between Carter Glass and R. C. Marshall over political conditions in Norfolk County.

3176. SUPPLEMENT containing the names of those white voters who paid to the treasurer of the city of Richmond the capitation tax for 1879 between April 30 and Sept. 1, 1880 . . . [Richmond] Dispatch press [1880]

19 p. 8°.   V

Secondary Works

3177. CROSBY, JOHN. The Staunton plan. [New York, 1909]

29 p. nar. 16°. (Reprint from *Municipal journal and engineer,* Dec. 29, 1909; with an addendum)   **NYP**

3178. NUCKOLS, ROBERT R. A history of the government of the city of Richmond, Virginia, and a sketch of those who administer its affairs . . . Richmond, Williams, 1899.

140, [2] p. incl. front., illus., plates. 8°.   **H, LC, USC, V, VU**

Brief historical sketch of each department of the city government.

Periodical

3179. VIRGINIA municipal review. Vol. 1-   ; Jan., 1924— Richmond, Review pub. co., 1924—

illus. ports., tables, charts. 4°. monthly.

Official publication of the League of Virginia municipalities.

H: II, 2-9, 11-12; III, 1-7, 10-12; IV-V (1925-28). **NYP:** III, 1-8, 10-12. **V:** I-VI. **VU:** I; II, 1, 3-12; III-V. **WM:** I.

Directories

See above, Pt. II, § 7: *Urban and County Development—Directories.*

PART V. MILITARY

Bibliography

See above, Pt. I : *Bibliography*.

Government Publications and Documents

3180. LULL, EDWARD P. History of the U. S. Navy yard at Gosport, Virginia (near Norfolk) . . . for the Bur. of yards and docks, Navy dept. Washington, Govt., 1874.

64 p. 8°.   **H, LC**

Conclusion contains an outline of the condition of the yard in the early 'seventies.

3181. SWANSON, CLAUDE A. Why America is in the war. Speech . . . in the Senate of the U. S., Tuesday, Feb. 26, 1918. [Washington, Govt., 1918]

18 p. 8°.   **V**

3182. U. S. CONGRESS. SENATE. NAVAL AFFAIRS Committee on. Naval training station on Hampton Roads, Virginia. Hearing before the Committee on naval affairs, U. S. Senate, on the bill (S. 6708) authorizing and directing the secretary of the navy to contract for the purchase of a lot of land on Hampton Roads, Virginia, and the buildings, structures, piers, and improvements thereon, for the use of the Navy department of the U. S. as a naval training station and a coaling station, and for other governmental purposes. Washington, Govt., 1908.

39 p. 8°.   **LC**

3183. ———. WAR DEPT. FIRST MILITARY DISTRICT. Circulars . . . 1867-70. [Richmond, 1867-70]

var. pag. 8°.

V: nos. 1-13 (Apr.-Oct., 1867); June-Dec., 1869 (9 nos.); Jan., 1870 (4 nos.).

3184. ———. ———. ———. General orders . . . Richmond, 1867-70.

var. pag. 8°.

McC: no. 61 (official memo., I-V)—May 21, 1869. **V**: 1867—nos. 1-

3, 5-6, 8-9, 11-12, 15-16, 28, 31, 34, 36-40, 42, 47-48, 51, 64-65, 68, 77, 83; 1868—nos. 13, 15-16, 21-54, 56-70, 72-155; 1869—nos. 1-24, 26-83, 92-144; 1870—nos. 1-15.

3185. ———. ———. ———. General orders and circulars, headquarters First military district, 1869. [Index] Richmond, Asst. adjutant-general's office, 1870.

9 p. 8°.   V

3186. ———. ———. ———. [Letter from Brevet Major General Ed. R. S. Canby to B. W. Giles] Richmond, Va., June 26, 1869.

4 p. 8°.   V

3187. ———. ———. ———. [Letter from Brevet Major-General E. R. S. Canby to General W. T. Sherman (with accompanying papers) concerning reconstruction and the test oath] Richmond, Va., Aug. 23, 1869.

5 p. 8°.   V

3188. ———. ———. ———. [Memoranda . . . Richmond, 1869]

var. pag. 8°.

V: May 10, June 19, 24; July 6; Aug. 18, 28; Sept. 24, 25; Nov. 25; Dec. 20.

3189. ———. ———. ———. Memoranda [containing] copies of the opinions of the commanding general of the First military district and the attorney general of the U. S. on the subject of the exaction of the oath of July 2, 1862, under the act of Congress of Mar. 2, 1867, and the acts supplementary thereto, from all persons elected to the legislature or to office, at the election of July 6, 1869, in the state of Virginia, and the principal correspondence with various citizens on that subject. [n. p., 1869?]

22 p. 8°.   V

3190. ———. ———. ———. Official memoranda [consisting of acts and resolutions of Congress relating to reconstruction] [Richmond, 1869]

20 p. 8°.   V

3191. ———. ———. ———. Registration districts. [Richmond? 1869]

5 p. 8°.   V

3192. ———. ———. ———. Roster of troops serving in the First military district . . . Richmond, Assistant adjutant-general's office, 1867-69.

12°. **V**: Mar., 1867; Jan., Mar., June, Nov., Dec., 1868; Jan., Feb., Sept.-Dec., 1869.

3193. [101] VIRGINIA. Annual reports of officers, boards, and institutions of . . . Virginia . . . Richmond, Va. [1866-19—

Include reports of the Adjutant-general, 1865-19—

3194. ———. ADJUTANT-GENERAL. Militia of Virginia. General organization; divisions and brigades. [Richmond, 1871?]

12 p. 8°.   **V**

3195. ———. ———. Regulations for the Virginia volunteers. Richmond, O'Bannon, 1896.

276 p. 16°.   **V**

3196. ———. ———. Report . . . Richmond [18-?-19—

fold. tables. 8°.

Report year ends in Oct., to 1918; biennial, 1922/23—

LC: 1874, 90/91-93/94, 95/96, 98/99-1903/04, 05/06-15/16, 17-24/25; **NYP**: 1895/96-1925/27; **V**: 1879/80-80/81, 97/98-98/99, 1900/01-01/02, 04/05-25/27; **VU**: 1919.

See also: Virginia. Annual reports of officers . . . **[3193]**

3197. ———. ———. Report of the adjutant-general of the commonwealth of Virginia. Part two. The selective service May 20, 1917-Dec. 31, 1918. Richmond, Bottom [1919]

72 p. incl. form. 8°.   **LC, VU**

Includes "Roster of district boards, local boards, government appeal agents, medical advisory boards, and legal advisory boards in the state of Virginia as constituted by the President under the provisions of the act of May 18, 1917, and the selective service regulations": p. [51]-70.

3198. ———. ———. Roster commissioned officers Virginia volunteers, 1871-1920. Comp. and issued by Jo Lane Stern, adjutant-general of Virginia. Richmond, Bottom, 1921.

viii, 292 p. 8°.   **LC, V, WM**

3199. ———. ———. Uniform of the Virginia volunteers. General orders, May 1, 1886. [Richmond, 1886?]

30 p. 16°.   **V**

3200. VIRGINIA. ADJUTANT-GENERAL. The uniform of the volunteer militia of Virginia. Prescribed by the commander-in-chief, May 1, 1883. Richmond, Walker, 1883.

     13 p. 8°.   **V**

3201. ———. ———. Virginians who lost their lives in the World war. Reprinted from Annual report adjutant-general of Virginia for year ending Dec. 31, 1920. [Richmond? 1921]

     52 p. 8°.   **LC**

3202. [1200] ———. AUDITOR. Supplement. Roster of Confederate pensioners of Virginia . . . Richmond, 19—

3203. [1202] ———. ———. [?] [Vouchers and orders of the court for artificial limbs. 1867-68]

3204. ———. DEFENSE, Council of. Legal handbook for guidance of soldiers and sailors; prepared by Lewis H. Machen, chairman, Legal committee, Virginia Council of defense. Richmond, Va., Appeals press, 1918.

     29 p. 16°.   **LC, V**

3205. [1244] ———. LAWS, STATUTES, ETC. Confederate pension law of Virginia . . . Richmond, Bottom, 19—

3206. ———. ———. [Laws for the organization and government of the] volunteer militia of Virginia. [Richmond? 1882]

     14 p. 8°.   **V**
     James McDonald, adjutant-general.

3207. ———. ———. The military laws of Virginia (as in force July 1, 1925). With index. Official. Pub. by William Wilson Sale, the adjutant-general under the direction of E. Lee Trinkle, governor and commander-in-chief. Comp. by C. H. Morrissett, director of the Legislative reference bureau. Richmond, Bottom, 1925.

     45 p. 8°.   **HL, LC**

3208. [2013] ———. ———. Virginia laws for the suppression of vice . . . Richmond, 1917.

3209. ———. ———. Virginia volunteer militia. [Richmond, 1882?]

     14 p. 8°.   **V**
     Issued by the Adjutant-general.

3210. [2014] ———. LEE CAMP SOLDIERS' HOME, Richmond. Report of the Board of visitors . . . Richmond, 1896—

3211. ———. MILITARY RECORDS, Secretary of Virginia. Report . . . Richmond, 1910-[17?]

8°. Dept. abolished, Mar., 1917.
LC: 1909-10; **NYP:** 1910-11; **V:** 1909.

3212. ———. MILITIA. Constitution and by-laws of the First regiment Virginia volunteers, of Richmond city. Richmond, Dispatch, 1872.

30 p. 16°. **V**

3213. ———. SELECTIVE SERVICE SUPERVISION, Dept. of. Roster of district boards, local boards, government appeal agents, medical advisory boards, and legal advisory boards, in the state of Virginia . . . and the selective service regulations . . . Rev. ed., July 1, 1918. [Richmond] Hill, 1918.

37 p. 8°. **V**
Printed also in Virginia. Adjutant-general. *Report . . . Part two. The selective service* . . . **[3197]**

3214. ———. WAR HISTORY COMMISSION. Publications, no. 1- ; April, 1919— [Richmond? 1919—

8°. **V:** 1-3.

3215. ———. ———. Publications of the Virginia War history commission [Source vols.] . . . Richmond, Pub. by order of the Executive committee, 1923-27.

7 v. illus. 8°. **BP, H, LC, NYP, V, VU,WM**
Arthur K. Davis, ed.
I: Virginians of distinguished service of the World war (1923). II: Virginia war history in newspaper clippings (1924). III: Virginia war letters, diaries, and editorials (1925). IV: Virginia war agencies, selective service and volunteers (1926). V: Virginia military organizations in the World war; with supplement of distinguished service (1927). VI: Virginia communities in war time. 1st ser. (1926). VII: *Ibid.* 2d ser. (1927).
An invaluable collection of source material (and calendars thereto) of Virginia's part in the World war. Objective presentation of the material was sought throughout.

3216. ———. ———. [Statement of the present status of the work of the Virginia War history commission. Richmond, 1927]

[4] p. 4°. **V**
Dated: June 15, 1927.

3217. VIRGINIA. WAR HISTORY COMMISSION. . . . Supplement
. . . nos. 1-4. [Richmond, 1921]

4 nos. 8°.   **V**

Reprint from *Virginia magazine of history and biography*, XXIX, 65-96,
193-224, 305-336, 449-496 (Jan.-Oct., 1921).

1. [Calendar of] source material from Virginia counties. 2. [Calen-
dar of] source material from Virginia cities. 3. Calendar of military histories, narratives, and reports. 4. Lists and calendars of source material.

3218. ———. WAR MEMORIAL COMMISSION. . . . Report . . .
Richmond, Bottom, 19—

8°.   **V:** 1926, 28.

Other Source Material

3219. AMERICAN LEGION. RICHMOND POST, NO. 1. "Lest we forget." Official program, Armistice day, Nov. 11, 1918-Nov. 11,
1921. [Richmond, Whittet & Shepperson, 1921]

[36] p. incl. adv. ports. 4°.   **V**

3220. ———. ———. WOMEN'S AUXILIARY. Official guide and
souvenir of the first anniversary of the signing of the armistice
. . . Richmond, Nov. 10-15. [Richmond, Williams, 1919]

48 p. incl. adv. illus., ports., map. 4°.   **V**

3221. ———. VIRGINIA DEPT. . . . Proceedings of the 1st-
. . . state convention of the American legion . . . 1919—
[n. p., 1919—

8°.   **NYP:** 1st-7th (1919-25); **V:** 1922-27.

3222. [2030] ANDERSON, ARCHER. Address on the opening of
Lee Camp soldiers' home. May 20, 1885 . . . Richmond,
1885.

3223. ASTON, ANDREW C. "Lest we forget." [Roster of] 3rd battalion, 317th infantry. [Richmond, Dietz, 1919?]

23 p. 8°.   **V**

3224. BATCHELDER, ROGER. Camp Lee described and photographed
by Roger Batchelder . . . with photographs taken by the
author under the official authorization of the Committee on public information and the War department, and with the endorse-

ment of the authorities of Camp Lee. Boston, Small, Maynard &
co. [*ca.* 1918]

66, [2] p. incl. front. (plan) illus. 16x24½cm. **H, LC, V**

3225. [CABELL, JULIAN M.] A brief sketch of Base hospital no. 41,
by the commanding officer. [Washington, D. C., 1925]

29 p. illus. (incl. ports.) 8°. **LC, V, VU**
The Base hospital located at the University of Virginia.

3226. COBB, WALTER W., ed. The final roster, a roster of the soldiers who saw service in the great war from Nottoway County,
Va. Ed. by Walter Westray Cobb, captain infantry R. C., U. S.
army. [Lynchburg, Va., Bell, *ca.* 1920]

240 p. 8°. **LC, V**

3227. [DOUGLAS, BENJAMIN L.] "Lest we forget." Manassas
memories of the Hartford city guard army manoeuvres, Manassas,
Virginia, Sept. 3-11, 1904 . . . Hartford, Conn., Gaines,
1904.

34 p. 8°. **LC**

3228. [GEISINGER, JOSEPH F.] ed. History of U. S. army Base
hospital no. 45 in the great war (Medical college of Virginia
unit). Richmond, William Byrd, 1924.

3 p. l., [9]-352 p., 1 l. front., illus., plates, ports. (part fold.) fold.
maps. 8°. **LC, V, VU, WM**
Written by individual members of the hospital, generally interesting
and well illustrated. Most of the history is concerned with activity in
France; the concluding chapter describes the return to Richmond.

3229. HISTORY of the 318th infantry regiment of the 80th division,
1917-1919. [Richmond, William Byrd, 1919]

189 p., 1 l. illus. (incl. ports., maps) 4°. **LC, V**
Although the "record, compiled since [Nov., 1918] . . ., has been
written largely from memory," it affords a clear conception of the stress
of the war period. War preparations and training in Virginia are de-
picted in chs. 1-2.

3230. MAHONE'S BRIGADE. Second reunion . . . held on the
anniversary of the battle of the Crater . . . Norfolk, July 31,
1876. Norfolk, Landmark, 1876.

13 p. 8°. **V**

3231. [2043] NATIONAL HOME, D. V. S., Hampton, Va. Photo-
gravures. Brooklyn [*ca.* 1900]

3232. RICHMOND GRAYS. [Papers, 1872-82]
MSS. 17 pieces.   **V**: Access. no. 19824.

3233. ———. Record book, 1871-77.
MSS.   **V**

3234. ———. Co. A, 1ST REG. VIRGINIA INFANTRY. Minutes
. . . Jan.-Mar., 1911.
18 l. typew. 4°.   **V**: Access no. 19825.

3235. RICHMOND LIGHT INFANTRY BLUES. R. L. I. blues; speech of
Gen. H. A. Wise, war roll, roll of honorary members, and present
roll of the company. 1874. Richmond, Clemmitt & Jones, 1874.
30 p. col. front. 4°.   **V**

3236. ROSTER of Company D and brief history of the First battalion,
318th infantry, 80th division, American expeditionary forces,
France. [n. p., 1920?]
[20] p. incl. illus. 4°.   **V**

3237. SCHWARTZ, LEON. A short history of the battalion. First
battalion, 320th infantry. [Troyes, Grande imprimerie de Troyes,
1919?]
3 p. l., 71 p. 16°.   **V**

3238. SHAW, ARTHUR F. Company "K", 317th infantry; being a
history of its activities and a record of its personnel, September,
1917, to June, 1919. [Grand Rapids, Mich., White] 1919.
118 p. incl. plates (ports.) 4°.   **V**

3239. [2465] SOCIETY OF THE CINCINNATI. VIRGINIA. Banquet
to the General society of the Cincinnati, given by the Society of
the Cincinnati in the state of Virginia, . . . May 10, 1905.
[New York, 1905]
See also items **2466-2471**.

3240. [SWAIM, ROGER D.] ed. "When we fit for General Grant";
light battery A, Massachusetts field artillery, in the manoeuvres
at Manassas, Virginia, September, 1904. Cambridge, Riverside
press, 1906.
5 p. l., 54 p. front. (port.) plate, fold. map (in pocket) 8°.   **BP, LC**

3241. VIRGINIA ARTILLERY. PEGRAM BATTALION. Annual reunion of Pegram battalion association . . . Richmond [Va., 18-?—
8°.   LC, NYP, V: 1886.
Typical reminiscences of Civil war battles, revealing, however, the loyalty of the *post bellum* South to the Union.

3242. VIRGINIA MILITARY INSTITUTE, Lexington. Record of service in the World war of V. M. I. alumni and their alma mater, comp. by the historiographer of the Virginia military institute. [Richmond, Richmond press] 1920.
1 p. l., vii, [3]-445 p. 8°.   H, LC, NYP, V
Joseph Reid Anderson, historiographer.

3243. VIRGINIA NATIONAL GUARD. The Year book of the Virginia national guard, 1923— Richmond, Pub. by the Virginia guardsman, Whittet & Shepperson, 1923.
illus., ports. 4°. No more pub.   V: 1923.

3244. VIRGINIA POLYTECHNIC INSTITUTE, Blacksburg, Va. Virginia polytechnic institute in the World war. Blacksburg, Va., V. P. I., 1927.
167 p. illus., front. 16°.   USE, VPI
Record of V. P. I.'s services at home and abroad, with quotations from speeches, letters, reports, etc.

3245. VIRGINIA's own in the world's war; brief history of 80th, 29th, and 42d divisions . . . Richmond [*ca.* 1919]
[4] p. 8°.   LC

3246. VIRGINIA's roll of honor. [Richmond, National pub. co., 1919?]
30 l. ports. 4°.   V
Alphabetical list of men from Virginia who "made the supreme sacrifice on foreign soil" during the World war.

3247. WISE, JENNINGS C. Memorandum of argument for the retention of Camp Lee, Petersburg, Va., before the Military affairs committee, U. S. House of representatives. By Munn, Anderson & Munn, Jennings C. Wise, Esq., representing the Chamber of commerce of the city of Petersburg, Va., May 18, 1921. Washington, Roberts [1921?]
22 p. 8°.   V

Secondary Works

3248. AMERICAN LEGION. VIRGINIA DEPT. History of the American legion, Department of Virginia, 1919-1924. Including history of individual posts and roster of membership as of Aug. 1, 1924. Richmond, Va., William Byrd [1925?]

> 192 p. front., plates, ports. 8°.   **NYP, V, VU**
> Prepared and issued by "Legion year book committee." Includes chronology of each post of the Virginia dept.

3249. BLACKFORD, CHARLES M. Annals of the Lynchburg Home guard . . . Prepared by request by Charles M. Blackford, jr., M.D., chairman, assisted by the . . . committee . . . Pub. by the company. Lynchburg, Va., Rohr, 1891.

> 185 p. front., plate, ports. 12°.   **BP, LC, NYP, V, VU**
> The Lynchburg Home guard was enrolled as Co. G, 11th regiment, Virginia infantry, during the Civil war; in 1914 it formed Co. E of the 1st regiment of Virginia infantry.
> Pt. III deals with "the reorganization of the Company and its history since the [Civil] war."

3250. [2517] BUCKLEY, WILLIAM. Buckley's history of the great reunion of the North and the South and of the blue and the gray . . . [Staunton, *ca.* 1923]

3251. [2346] EZEKIEL, HERBERT T., *et al.* World war section of The history of the Jews of Richmond . . . Richmond, 1920.

3252. RICHMOND HOWITZERS. A sketch of the Richmond howitzers and their historic home. Organized Nov. 9, 1859. Reorganized Apr. 10, 1871. Pub. by the Richmond howitzers. [Richmond] Hill, 1903.

> 40 p. illus. 4°.   **V**

3253. WORTHAM, T. M. The Virginia militiaman. Paper read by Capt. T. M. Wortham, Virginia field artillery, before the Field artillery association of Virginia. Richmond, Dietz, 1909.

> 19 p. 8°.   **V**
> Concerning the character of the personnel of the Virginia militia.

Periodicals

3254. The AMERICAN legion directory, Richmond district. Richmond post, no. 1, North Richmond post, no. 38, South Richmond

post, no. 137, American legion auxiliary (to Richmond post, no. 1)
[1st-   ] 1922—   [Richmond, 1922—

illus. (incl. ports.) 8°.   **LC, V**: 1st (1922).

3255. The BAYONET; official publication of Camp Lee. Vol. 1-   ;
Oct. 5, 1917— Camp Lee, Va., 1917—

illus. f°. weekly.   **LC**: I-III (Oct. 5, 1917-May 30, 1919).
Official publication of the 80th division, National army, Oct., 1917-
May, 1918.

Absorbed in 1918 Camp Lee edition of *Trench and camp* **[3264]**
No number issued for Feb. 14, 1919.

3256. The COME-BACK; published by soldiers for soldier-patients at
the port of debarkation. Vol. 1-   ; Jan. 11, 1919-[?] Newport
News, Va., 1919-[?]

illus. f°. weekly.   **LC**: I-III (Oct. 5, 1917-May 30, 1919).
Newport News and Hampton edit. "Especially devoted to Camp
Stuart debarkation hospital and Debarkation hospital 51 at Hampton.,
Va."

3257. D-BARKER. no. 1-94; Jan. 17-May 6, 1919. Hampton, Va.,
Debarkation hospital no. 51, 1919.

2 v. illus. 8°.-f°. daily (except. Sun. or Mon.)   **LC**
Nos. 1-4 (Jan. 17-21) have title: The Advance sheet.
No more pub.

3258. GEE aitch 43. no. 1-89; May 7-Aug. 17, 1919. Hampton, Va.,
1919.

2 v. illus. 8°. No more pub.?   **LC**
"Published every day, except Monday, and devoted to the interests of
General hospital no. 43, Hampton, Va."
Title varies: The Orphan, May 7-18, 1919; Gee aitch 43, May 20-Aug.
17, 1919.

3259. HAMPTON ROADS bulletin. Vol. 1-3; [1919?-21] Hampton
Roads, Va., U. S. Naval training station [1919?-21]

illus. f°. daily. No more pub.
LC: III, nos. 135-139, 141-158, 160-181, 183-186, 188-192, 223-224, 226-
235, 249-282, 284, 286-290, 292-300, 302-305, 307-311 (1921).

3260. HEADS up. Debarkation hospital no. 52. Vol. 1-[2?] [Rich-
mond college, Va., 1918-19?]

illus. 8°. 6 nos. a week.
LC: II, 67-82 (Mar. 19-Apr. 5, 1919). **V**: I, 1-7, 10, 12; II, 1-84;
(1918-19).

3261. KEEP the cadence. Vol. 1; Oct. 24, 1919-Jan. 24, 1920. National soldiers' home, Va., 1919-20.

[72] p. illus. 4°. weekly. No more pub.   **L'C**
"Published . . . in the Educational department print shop and devoted to the interests of General hospital no. 43, National soldiers' home, Va., and vicinity."

3262. NAVY life. May, 1918—   Norfolk, Va., 1918—

illus. 4°. monthly.
Title varies: Norfolk naval recruit, May-July, 1918; Navy life, Aug., 1918—
Pub. from May, 1918 to Mar., 1919 by the enlisted personnel at the Naval training station, naval operating base, Hampton Roads, Va.
LC: May, 1918-Apr., 1919; July-Aug., Oct.-Nov., 1919; Jan., 1920.

3263. "O. D." Third corps area. Fort Eustis, Virginia. Vol. 1- ; 1925— Prepared by the men of the Citizen's military training camp . . . Pub. by Military training camps association of the U. S. . . . Chicago, Ill., 1925—

illus., ports. 4°. annual. Advertisements in back.
V: I-III (1925-27); **VU:** III.

3264. TRENCH and camp . . . Edition for Camp Lee, Petersburg, Va. Vol. 1; [Oct. 8? 1917]-July 22, 1918 [Richmond, 1917]-18.

1 v. illus. f°.   **LC**
"Published under auspices of National war work council, Y. M. C. A. of the U. S."
"Printed . . . by courtesy of the News leader."
Merged into the *Bayonet* **[3255]**

3265. The VIRGINIA guardsman. Published by the Military board of Virginia. Vol. 1- ; [1921?-] Richmond, Va. [1921?—

illus., ports., plans, tables, diagr. f°. monthly.
V: VI-IX (1926-29).

3266. The VIRGINIA volunteer, a periodical of preparedness, published monthly. Vol. 1, no. 1- ; [Apr.] 1917-[?] Richmond, Va., 1917-[?]

8°. monthly.   **V:** I, 2-6/7 (1917).

3267. WAR history commission news letter, no. 1- ; July 15, 1919-[?] Richmond, 1919-[?]

f°. Issued irreg.   **V:** 1-7 (1919).

For further references on Military history, see above, Pt. III, § 4: *Social Life and Customs.* See also Pt. VI, § 2, under title: *Virginia military institute.*

PART VI. EDUCATIONAL

1. Bibliography

3268. [30] [Richardson, Carrie W.] [Bibliography of the writings and addresses of Edwin A. Alderman, in the University of Virginia. July, 1926]

3269. [43] University of Virginia. . . . University bibliography 1922— Charlottesville [1924—

3270. [47] Virginia polytechnic institute, Blacksburg. . . . Research and publication completed and in progress. 1923/26— [Blacksburg, 1927—

2. General Works

Government Publications and Documents

3271. Charlottesville, Va. Public library. Books in the . . . library. A brief catalogue prepared by Ella W. Johnson, secretary of the Library board. [n. p., n. d.]
100 p. 8°.   **V**

3272. Falls Church, Va. Public library. . . . Catalogue of books. [Washington, 1902]
1 p. l., 16 p. 8°.   **LC**

3273. Newport News, Va. Public library. Annual report . . . [Newport News, Va., 19—
8°.   **LC**: 1925

3274. Norfolk, Va. Public library. Annual report. [1st- ; 1904?—] Norfolk [1905?—
8°.   **LC**: 1907-09; **NYP**: 1904, 07-09, 27; **V**: 1907-09.
Report for 1907 accompanied by an historical sketch by the librarian, W. H. Sargeant.

3275. ———. ———. [Catalogue. 1908?]
116 p. typew. 4°. No title-page.   **V**

3276. NORFOLK, VA. PUBLIC LIBRARY. The charter, constitution, by-laws and regulations of the Norfolk public library of Norfolk, Virginia. Norfolk, Burke & Gregory, 1907.

14 p. 12°.   BP, LC, V
Ed. of 1898: 20 p.   NYP

3277. ———. ———. . . . Finding list. Fiction by titles. Norfolk, Burke & Gregory, 1904.

vi, 40 p. 8°.   BP, LC, NYP, V

3278. PETERSBURG, VA. WILLIAM R. MCKENNEY FREE LIBRARY. Annual report. 1st- [1924/25?—] Petersburg, Va. [1925?—
8°. Report year ends June 30.
V: 3d (1926/27).

3279. RICHMOND, VA. CITY GOVERNMENT LIBRARY. Catalogue, City government library . . . : authors, titles, subject . . . Richmond, Flanhart, 1904.

26 p. 8°.   **V**

3280. ———. PUBLIC LIBRARY. Annual report . . . 1st- ; 1922/24— Richmond, 1924—
8°. Report year ends Dec. 31.
1st Annual report covers period, Nov. 16, 1922-Dec. 31, 1924.
NYP, V: 1st-4th (1922/24-27); **VU:** 1927-28.

3281. ———. ———. Catalogue of the Richmond circulating library, no. 18 North 3d Street . . . Richmond, Baughman, 1879.

[59] p. 12°.   **V**

3282. U. S. EDUCATION, Bur. of. Circulars of information . . . 1870— Washington, Govt., 1870—
plates, maps, tables. 8°.
Circulars on Virginia: 1887, no. 1; 1888, no. 1.   **H, USE**

3283. [101] VIRGINIA. Annual reports of officers, boards, and institutions of . . . Virginia . . . Richmond, Va. [1866-19—
Include reports of the second auditor on the condition of the . . . literary fund . . ., 1871/72— ; the superintendent of public instruction, 1870/71— ; the superintendent of public printing, 1870/71— ; the State library, 1903/04—

3284. ———. EDUCATION COMMISSION. . . . Report of the Virginia Education commission to the General assembly of the commonwealth of Virginia. 1912. Richmond, Bottom, 1912.

102 p. maps. 8°. ([Virginia. General assembly] Senate. *Doc.,* III)

USE, V, VU

3285. ———. ———. A tentative report to the Virginia Education commission on a mill tax for the educational system of the state. By Chas. G. Maphis, secretary. Charlottesville, Va., Michie, 1910.

29 p. 8°. **USE, V**

Printed also in Virginia. General assembly, 1912. Senate. *Doc.,* III, 64-80. **[3284]**

"Exhibit A: Extracts from letters of university presidents and others, regarding a mill tax for educational institutions," p. [19]-29.

3286. ———. ———. . . . Virginia public schools, a survey of a southern state public school system. By the Virginia Education commission, Harris Hart, president, and the Virginia Survey staff, Alexander J. Inglis, director . . . Yonkers-on-Hudson, N. Y., World book co., 1920-21.

2 v. illus., plates, tables. 8°. (Educational survey ser. [VII-VIII])

Contents: pt. 1. Reports of the Education commission and Survey staff.—pt. 2. Educational tests.

3287. ———. ———. Virginia public schools, Education commission's report to the assembly of Virginia. Survey staff's report to the Education commission. Richmond, Va., Waddey, 1919.

400 p. incl. tables, diagrs. plates. 8°.

H, LC, NYP, USE, V, VU, WM

3288. ———. EDUCATION, State board of. . . . Annual report of the superintendent of public instruction of . . . Virginia, with accompanying documents. School year 1911-1912. Richmond, Bottom, 1914.

48 p. incl. tables. 8°. **LC**

At head of title: Supplement to Feb. number, 1914, of *Virginia journal of education.*

3289. ———. ———. Bulletin . . . Vol. 1- ; 1918— Richmond, 1918—

tables, diagrs., charts. 8°. quarterly.

H: III, 1; VI, 1; VII, 1, suppl. 1; (1920, 23-24). LC: I, 1; II, 1; IV, 2; VI, 1-2; VII, 1 &' suppls. 1, 3-8; VIII, 1-2; IX, 1 (suppls. 1, 3), 2; X, 2; (1918-19, 21, 23-26). NYP: II, 1. USAg: II, 3; IX, 1. USE:

I, 1; II, 1, 2 (suppl. 4), 3; III, 1-2, 4; IV, 1 (suppls. 1, 3), 2, 4 & suppl.
2; V, 1, 4; VI, 1 (suppl. 1), 2; VII, 1 (suppls. 1, 3-8), 4; VIII, 1 (suppl.
2); IX, 1 (suppls. 3, 6); X, 1 (suppl. 1), 2 (suppl.). **USL**: II, 3; IX,
1. **V**: I-IV; V, 1-2, 4; VI, 1-4; VII-VIII (some suppls. wanting); IX,
1-3; X-XI, 2; (1918-25/26, 27-27/28). **VU**: I, 1; II, 1-2; III, 1; IV, 1
& suppl. 2; V, 4; VI, 2; VII, 1, suppls. 1-8, 10; VIII, 1 & suppl.; IX, 1.
WM: II, 2; V, 4; IX, 1 (suppl. 6).

3290. VIRGINIA. EDUCATION, State board of. Circular . . .
[Richmond, 18-?-19—

> 8°. **H:** 4 (1886) [new ser.?], 133 (1896), 256 (1904); **USE**: 83, 84,
> 89 (186-?, 1873) [old ser.?]; **V**: 139 (1896), 256, 268 (1904-05).

3291. ——. ——. . . . . Circular of information concerning
certification of teachers. [Richmond? Va., 1914]

> 15 p. 8°.   **USE**

3292. ——. ——. Counting the cost. Richmond, Bottom, 1915.

> 19 p. ports., plate. 8°.   **V, VU**
> A brief survey of various efforts in Virginia to improve public educa-
> tion and the methods of financing it.

3293. ——. ——. Illiteracy in Virginia. Some facts which cannot be overlooked. Prepared by E. R. Chesterman, secretary of the
State board of education. Pub. by the Dept. of public instruction. Richmond, Bottom, 1914.

> 21, [1] p. illus. 8°.   **USC, USE, V, VU**

3294. ——. ——. List of books for rural school libraries in the
state of Virginia, issued by the Dept. of public instruction . . .
Richmond, Va., 1909—

> 8°.   **USE**: 1909; **V**: 1909, 11, 20, 22; **VU**: 1909.
> Ed. of 1909 contains text of the law: p. [3]-4.

3295. ——. ——. Memorial day annual, 1912. The causes and
outbreak of the war between the states, 1861-1865. For use as a
source book of contemporary authorities. Pub. by the Dept. of
public instruction at the request of the Confederate memorial literary society. Richmond [Richmond press] 1912.

> 94 p. incl. front., port. 8°.

3296. ——. ——. Regulations, etc., of the Board of education
. . . [Richmond? 1871]

> 8 p. 8°.   **USE**

3297. ——. ——. . . . . Regulations for the examination of teachers and topical outlines of subjects required. Issued by the Dept. of public instruction. Richmond, Bottom, 1917.

22 p. 8°. **USE**

At head of title: . . . Form E—no. 18, 1917. Commonwealth of Virginia. State board of education.

Supplement to *Virginia journal of education,* Mar. 1, 1917.

3298. ——. ——. . . . . Report of the superintendent of public instruction. [Richmond? 1870]

11 p. 8°. **LC, NYP, USE, VU**

Report transmitting "Outline plan of public instruction for the state of Virginia."

W. H. Ruffner, supt.

3299. ——. ——. The school fair in Virginia. Suggestions for organizing and conducting . . . [Richmond, 1913]

8°. **NYP**

3300. ——. ——. Virginia school report: . . . of the superintendent of public instruction . . . 1st- ; 1870/71-19— Richmond, 1871-19—

plates, ports., maps, plans (part fold.) tables (part fold.) 8°.

Report year ends July 31, except Aug. 31, 1871-74.

Reports issued annually, 1871-74, 1911/12— ; biennial, 1874/76-1910/11.

Title varies: Virginia school report, 1871; First annual report of the superintendent of public instruction, . . . 1871.

Issued as *Bulletin* of State board of education, 1918— **[3289]**

Superintendents: W. H. Ruffner, 1871-81; R. R. Farr, 1882-85; J. L. Buchanan, 1886-89; J. E. Massey, 1890-97; J. W. Southall, 1898-1905; J. D. Eggleston, 1906-12; R. C. Stearnes, 1913-18; Harris Hart, 1919—

BP: 1870/71-72/73, 76/77, 79/80-81/82, 86/87, 89/90-90/91, 94/95; **H**: 1870/71-1927/28; **LC**: 1870/71-76/77, 78/79, 80/81, 84/85-85/86, 91/93-1914/15, 16/17-17/18, 20/21-26/27; **McC**: 1873/74-74/75; **NYP**: 1870/71-95/97, 99/1901-14/15, 16/17-17/18; **USAg**: 1870/71-74/75, 84/85, 99/1900-00/01, 03/04-04/05; **USE**: 1870/71-1911/12, 13/14-14/15, 16/17-22/23, 25/26-26/27; **V**: 1870/71-1927/28; **VU**: 1870/71-1925/26; **WM**: 1870/71-81/82, 83/84-1916/17, 19/20-26/27.

See also: Virginia. *Annual reports of officers, boards, and institutions* . . . **[3283]**

3301. ——. ——. AGRICULTURAL EDUCATION, Div. of. Record book for supervised home practice in agriculture . . . [Richmond, Bottom, 1926]

26 p. incl. forms. 4°. **V**

3302. VIRGINIA. EDUCATIONAL SYSTEM OF VIRGINIA, Commission to survey the. Public education in Virginia; report to the Educational commission of Virginia of a survey of the public educational system of the state, by M. V. O'Shea, director. Richmond, Bottom, 1928.

vii, 634 p. tables, diagrs. 8°.

3303. ———. ———. Report . . . submitted to the General assembly, Jan., 1928 . . . Richmond, Bottom, 1928.

35 p. 8°. ([Virginia. General assembly] House. *Doc.,* 4)
BP, LC, USE, V, VU, WM

3304. ———. ———. . . . Report . . . to be submitted to the General assembly, Jan., 1928. Part[s] one [and two] Confidential. [Richmond, 1927]

2 v. 8°.   **V**

3305. ———. GOVERNOR, 1870-74 (Gilbert C. Walker). Letter of Governor Walker on the public school system. Richmond, 1870.

iii p. 12°.   **USE**

3306. ———. ———, 1926— (Harry F. Byrd). The educational system of Virginia. An address by Harry Flood Byrd, governor. Delivered before the General assembly of Virginia, Jan. 16, 1928 . . . Richmond, Bottom, 1928.

10 p. 8°. ([General assembly, 1928] Senate. *Doc.,* 6)   **LC, USE, V**

3307. ———. LAW, Dept. of. LEGISLATIVE DRAFTING, Div. of. Analysis of changes in school code. [Richmond, 1928]

14 p. 8°.   **V**

3308. ———. LAWS, STATUTES, ETC. Amendments to school laws (Acts of assembly, 1916) and to regulations of the State board of education. Pub. as a supplement to Virginia school laws, 1915, by order of the State board of education. Richmond, Bottom, 1917.

24 p. 8°.   **H, USE, VU**

3309. [———. ———.] . . . Changes in the school law. [Richmond? 1896?]

18 p. 8°.   **USE**
John E. Massey, state supt.

3310. ———. ———. Review of the school law, by the superintendent of public instruction (being a supplement to his annual report). [Richmond? 1871?]

28 p. 8°. **USE**

W. H. Ruffner, state supt.

3311. ———. ———. Virginia school laws enacted by the General assembly . . . Richmond [1878-19—

8°. Issued by the Dept. of public instruction and the State board of education.

Title varies: School law of Virginia . . .

Ed. of 1904 "contains the provisions of the new state constitution on education . . ."

Issued as nos. of *Bulletin* of State board of education **[3289]** after 1923.

H: 1878, 92, 1903, 10, 15, 20, 23, 28; **LC:** 1883, 92, 1901, 03, 07, 15; **NYP:** 1883, 1910, 15; **USAg:** 1907, 15; **USE:** 1878, 83, 92, 1901, 03, 07, 08, 10, 15, 20, 23; **V:** 1883, 92, 1901, 03, 05, 07, 10, 15 & suppl., 23; **VU:** 1907, 10, 15, 20, 23; **WM:** 1907, 10, 15, 20, 23.

3312. ———. MEDICAL EXAMINERS, Board of. Proceedings of the medical examining board of Virginia, . . . Richmond, Va. Fredericksburg, Va. [1903?— ; Roanoke, 1917—

tables. 8°. semi-annual. **LC:** 1915-24; **V:** 1915-28.

3313. ———. PUBLIC PRINTING, Supt. of. Annual report . . . Richmond [18-?-19—

8°. Report year ends Sept. 30.

LC: 1873/74, 1906/07, 14/15-17/18, 19/20-23/25; **NYP:** 1908/09-13/14, 16/17; **USC:** 1879/80-1901/02, 04/05, 06/07-10/11; **V:** 1904/05-08/09, 10/11-15/16, 18/19, 20/21-23/25, 26/27.

See also: Virginia. *Annual reports of officers, boards, and institutions* . . . **[3283]**

3314. ———. STATE LIBRARY, Richmond. Annual report . . . 1st- ; 1903/04— Richmond, 1904—

8°. Report year ends June 30.

BP: 1st-18th (1903/04-20/21); **H:** 4-18th, 20th, 21st-24th (1906/07-20/21, 22/23, 23/25-27/28); **LC:** 1903/04-20/21, 22/23, 23/25-26/27; **McC:** 1920/21; **NYP:** 1903/04-27/28; **USC:** 1903/04-05/06, 07/08-09/10; **V:** 1903/04-27/28; **VU:** 1903/04-27/28; **WM:** 1903/04-05/06, 07/08-14/15, 16/17-20/21, 22/23, 25/26.

3315. ———. ———. Books for the blind in the Virginia State library. (October, 1912) [Richmond, Va., Bottom, 1912]

[4] p. 8°. **V**

3316. Virginia. State library, Richmond. Bulletin. Vol. 1-   ;
Jan., 1908—   Richmond, 1908—

> 8°. quarterly. None pub., 1922-23.
> Include finding lists of books in the State library, bibliographies, lists
> of mss., maps, etc. See items **25, 35-40, 48-49.**
> **BP:** I; III, 1, 3; IV-X; XII, 1-2; XIII-XV; (1908, 10-17, 19, 20-25.
> **H:** I-XVII (1908-28). **HL:** III, 1-4. **LC:** I-XVII. **NYP:** I-XVI.
> **USAg:** IV, 2-4; VI, 1; XI, 1-4. **USC:** IV, 2-4. **USG:** VII, 2-3; IX,
> 1-3. **V, VU:** I-XVII. **WM:** I-II, IV-X.

3317. ———. ———. Catalogue of the Virginia State library, 1877
. . . Richmond, Gary, 1877.

> 369 p. 8°.   **V, VU, WM**
> Arranged alphabetically.

3318. ———. ———. Education in Virginia. A brief list of selected books, etc., in the Virginia State library, compiled for the
use of the Commission to survey the educational system of Virginia. [Richmond, 1927]

> 9 numb. 1. 4°.   **V**
> Autographed from typewritten copy.

3319. ———. ———. Leaflet, nos. 1-11 [*i. e.,* 10] May, 1904-Feb.,
1905. [Richmond, 1904-05]

> 10 nos. 8°. monthly. No more pub.   **V:** 1, 3-10.

3320. ———. ———. Regulations of the Virginia State library.
Richmond, Richmond press, 1907.

> 10 p. 16°.   **LC, V**

3321. ———. ———. Statistics of Virginia libraries . . . Compiled by Virginia State library, Library extension division. [Rich-
mond, Bottom, 1924—

> 8°.   **LC:** 1923; **V:** 1923-24, 26, 27/28.

3322. ———. ———. Virginia State library. Class in library science. Schedule, class 1906-07. [Richmond, 1906]

> 15 p. 12°.   **V**

3323. ———. ———. Traveling libraries division. . . . Report . . . By F. B. Berkeley, chief; John P. Kennedy, state
librarian. Richmond [Bottom] 1906.

> 38 p. front., fold. map. 8°.   **V**

3324. WINCHESTER, VA. HANDLEY FUND, Board of trustees of the. Report . . . 1913— Winchester, Va., 1914—

ports., plates. 8°.
Includes Report of librarian of the Handley library.
BP: 1920; **H**: 1918; **V**: 1913, 15, 17, 19-20.

Other Source Material

3325. ANDERSON, HENRY W. The education of kings; an address . . . delivered before the State normal schools of Virginia, May, 1916. [n. p., 1916?]

52 p. 8°. **V, VU**
Concerning the education of the individual in relation to society as a whole.

3326. BOYD, THOMAS M., ed. Virginia bar examinations. Annotated . . . Containing examinations propounded by the Virginia Board of law examiners, June 1910 *et seq.,* arranged according to subject classifications of the board. Annotators: T. Munford Boyd . . . Ellsworth Wiltshire . . . T. Nelson Parker . . . Richmond, Va., Appeals press [*ca.* 1925]

2 p. l., 208 p. 8°. **LC**

3327. CURRY, JABEZ L. Address of Hon. J. L. M. Curry, LL.D., before the General assembly of Virginia, Feb. 4, 1892. Richmond, 1892.

10 p. 8°. **USE**
A brief, but pointed, survey of economic conditions in the South since 1865, of Virginia's educational system, and of the needs of the state for improvement in education.

3328. DABNEY, WILLIAM C. An abstract of a course of lectures on the practice of medicine . . . [Charlottesville, Va.] G. W. Olivier [*ca.* 1891]

308 p. 8°. **LC, V**

3329. DREHER, JULIUS D. Endowments: How shall capital be attracted in larger amounts? A paper read before the Educational association of Virginia, at Hollins institute, Roanoke Co., Va., July 15, 1880 . . . Richmond, Jones, 1880.

14 p. 8°. **NYP, VU**
By the president of Roanoke college.

3330. DUKE, RICHARD T. Libraries and their contents; an address delivered . . . at the laying of the cornerstone of the McIntire public library. Charlottesville, Va., Nov. 27, 1919. [n. p., 1919?]

11 p. 8°.   V, VU

3331. EGGLESTON, J[OSEPH] D., jr. Extension work in Virginia—its possibilities and needs. Speech delivered at Charlottesville, Virginia, Aug. 10, 1909, at the annual meeting of the State farmers institute. [n. p., 1909]

8 p. 8°.   USAg

3332. GREEN, WILLIAM. Catalogue of the . . . law and miscellaneous library of the late Hon. William Green . . . To be sold by auction, Jan. 18, 1881, at Richmond, Va. . . . John E. Laughton, jr., auctioneer . . . Richmond. [Richmond, Jones, 1880]

210 p. 8°.   LC, V
Prepared under the supervision of R. A. Brock.

3333. JONES, ANNA L. An abridgment of the Virginia laws concerning education . . . Lynchburg, Va., Bell, 1915.

285, [19] p. 8°.   LC, USE, V, VU, WM

3334. JOYNES, EDWARD S. The best method of teaching the elements of Latin and Greek. A report read before the Educational association of Virginia at its annual session, July, 1870 . . . Richmond, Hazlewood, 1870.

24 p. 8°.   V

3335. LOGAN, THOMAS M. Education and progress, an address delivered before the Educational association of Virginia, July 6, 1876 . . . [n. p., 1876]

16 p. 8°.   V

3336. McILWAINE, RICHARD. Addresses and papers bearing chiefly on education . . . Richmond, Va., Whittet & Shepperson [ca. 1908]

184 p. 8°.   LC, USE, V
Include papers on: Some essentials in the improvement of our public schools; Local taxation for public schools under the present state constitution; Relation of the citizen to the public schools; The family and the school; etc.

3337. MAPHIS, CHARLES G. Educational preparedness . . . [New York? 1917]

11 p. 4°.   **USE, V, VU**

"Annual address of the president of the Virginia state teachers association." Reprint from *School and society*, V, no. 111, p. 151-161.

Virginia's educational needs as regards financial support, supervision, administration, teaching staff, etc.

3338. ———. A tentative report to the Virginia Education commission on a mill tax for the educational system of the state. Charlottesville, Va., Michie, 1910.

29 p. 8°.   **VU**

3339. PAINTER, FRANKLIN V. Educational needs of Virginia. An address delivered before the Botetourt normal college, June, 1906, by Prof. F. V. N. Painter . . . [n.p., 1906]

4 p. 4°.   **V**

3340. SINTON, RICHARD B. Catalogue of the library of the late Richard B. Sinton, of Richmond, Va.; an important collection of books on Virginia, including many very rare items . . . To be sold at auction, Oct. 24-26, 1906, by the Merwin-Clayton sales co. [n.p., 1906?]

75 p. 8°.   **V**

3341. SWANSON, CLAUDE A. Address of Governor C. A. Swanson at the [Virginia] educational conference, November, 1906. [Richmond, 1906]

15 p. 8°.   **V**

Emphasizes the fundamental importance of well equipped superintendents and teachers to further education.

3342. TAYLOR, D. W. Virginia state bar questions and answers . . . Charlottesville, Va., Anderson [*ca.* 1905]

2 p. l., 3-189 p. 8°.   **LC**

3343. THOMAS BALCH LIBRARY, Leesburg, Va. . . . Addresses delivered at the presentation exercises on the 13th of May, 1922; letter in the New York daily tribune 13th May, 1865; charter; list of officers. Leesburg, Loudoun County, Va., 1923.

2 p. l., 58 p., 2 l. front. (port.) plate. 8°.   **LC**

3344. WADDEY, EVERETT, CO., Richmond. Specimens of type for

book printing, used in the printing house of the Everett Waddey
co., Richmond, Va. . . . Richmond, 1907.

138 p. 8°.   V

3345. WALLACE, CHARLES M. Catalogue of the valuable private library of Mr. Charles M. Wallace of Richmond, Virginia. Pts.
1 & 2: Americana . . . To be sold at auction Oct. 19-29,
1909, by the Merwin-Clayton sales co., New York [n. p., 1909?]

2 v. 8°.   V

3346. WYNNE, THOMAS H. Catalogue of the . . . library collected by the late Hon. Thos. W. Wynne, of Richmond, Va. . . .
rich in works relating to the history of Virginia, and in the local
history of . . . Richmond, Va., and in Confederate States
printed, and in books relating to the late war. The whole to be
sold at auction, in . . . Richmond, Va. . . . by J. Thompson Brown . . . [Richmond, Va.] Richmond dispatch [1875]

2 p. l., 158 p. 8°.   LC, V
Includes some state documents, 1865-75. Sale commenced July 14,
1875.

3347. YOUNG MEN'S CHRISTIAN ASSOCIATIONS. RICHMOND, VA. LI-
BRARY. . . . Catalogue of library . . . [Richmond, Va.,
Clemmitt, 18-?]

24 p. 12°.   LC

Secondary Works

3348. ALDERMAN, EDWIN A., *et al.* J. L. M. Curry; a biography,
by Edwin Anderson Alderman and Armistead Churchill Gordon.
New York & London, Macmillan, 1911.

xx p., 1 l., 468, p. front. (port.) 8°.   H, LC, V, VU
Ed. of 1903.   H, LC
Authoritative biography based on Curry mss., with many quotations
therefrom.

3349. DAVIS, ARTHUR K. "Education in Virginia": its distinctive
qualities to-day achieved through a noble and historic past . . .
[Petersburg, Va.] 1912.

[6] p. 8°.   NYP, USE, V, VU
"An article prepared by request for the *Times-dispatch* of Richmond,
Virginia, and published in the annual school section; republished with
additions in the Petersburg *Index-appeal*."

3350. GEE, WILSON, *et al.* . . . A statistical study of Virginia [by] Wilson Gee . . . and John J. Corson, 3rd . . . [Charlottesville] Pub. by the Institute for research in the social sciences, University, Va. [Michie] December, 1927.

> 201 p. tables, diagrs. 8°. (University of Virginia. Institute for research in the social sciences. *Institute Monograph,* no. 1)   **LC, V, VU**
>
> Analysis and comparison of Virginia's rank in education, industry, finance, etc., with that of other states. Based upon census figures for 1920-26, with state and county tables.

3350a. HEATWOLE, CORNELIUS J. A history of education in Virginia . . . New York, Macmillan, 1916.

> xviii p., 1 l., 382 p. 8°. (Home and school ser., ed. by P. Monroe)
>
> A condensed survey of the development of education in its various aspects, with chapters on public education, institutions for higher learning, education of women, Negro schools, etc.

3351. HENNEMAN, JOHN B. Historic elements in Virginia education and literary effort. A paper read before the Virginia historical society, Monday, Dec. 21, 1891 . . . [n. p., 1892]

> 22 p. 8°. (Reprint from *Collections of the Virginia historical society,* XI, 1892)
>
> Contains tables showing counties of Virginia and other states from which students come to William and Mary college, Hampden-Sidney college, and Washington and Lee university.

3352. KNIGHT, EDGAR W. Reconstruction and education in Virginia . . . [Durham, N. C., 1916]

> 36 p. 8°. (Reprint from *South Atlantic quarterly,* XV, 1 & 2; Jan. & Apr., 1916)   **NYP, USE, V, VU**
>
> A reliable account, based on state documents and newspapers, of the struggle to establish a public school system during the reconstruction period, and of the work of William H. Ruffner.

3353. PEARSON, CHARLES C. William Henry Ruffner: reconstruction statesman of Virginia. [n. p., 1921?]

> 24 p. 8°. (Reprint from *South Atlantic quarterly,* XX, 1 & 2; Jan. & Apr., 1921)
>
> Concerning the development of the public school system in Virginia.

3354. [2902] ROBERTSON, ALEXANDER F. Alexander Hugh Holmes Stuart, 1807-1891; a biography . . . Richmond [*ca.* 1925]

Periodicals

3355. The ALBEMARLE stamp collector. Vol. 1-   ; 1914— Keswick, Va., Albemarle stamp co., 1914—

12°.-8°.   **NYP**: I-IX, 7 (Sept., 1914-July, 1923).

3356. MISCELLANEOUS literary, scientific and historical notes, queries, and answers. For teachers, pupils, practical and professional men. Vol. 1-[?]   Norfolk, Va., 1882-[?]

8°. monthly.   **V**: I, 8-9 (Feb.-Mar., 1883).
N. B. Webster, ed.

3357. SOUTHERN philatelist. Vol. 1-   ; Nov., 1924— Richmond, Va., 1924—

8°. monthly.   **V**: I, 1-5 (Nov., 1924-Mar., 1925).

3358. TIMES-DISPATCH, Richmond, Va.   Annual educational number.   [Richmond, Va., 190-?—

illus. (incl. ports.) f°.   **LC**: 1907-09.

3359. The VIRGINIA philatelist. Vol. 1-   ; 1898— Richmond, Virginia philatelic pub., 1898-19—

8°.   **V**: II-IV (1899-1901).
A stamp collectors' magazine.

3360. The VIRGINIA teacher. Vol. 1-   ; 1920— Harrisonburg, Va., State teachers college, 1920—

illus. 4°. monthly, except Aug. and Sept.
Includes bibliographies.

H: I, 5-7; II, 12; V, 2 (suppl., no. 1), 4 (supple., no. 2); (1920, 21, 24). **LC**: VI-VII (1925-26). **NYP**: V-VI; VII, 1-5 7-10; VIII; (1924-27). **USE**: Feb., 1920-Dec., 1926. **V**: I-VIII; IX, 1-7, 10; X, 1-3; (1920-29). **VU**: III-X (1922-29). **WM**: II-III, V-VI, VIII (1921-22, 24-25, 27).

Directory

3361. YATES, PAUL, pub.   1911 Yates-Fisher school directories, Pennsylvania, Virginia, District of Columbia.   [Chicago, 1911?]

96 p. 16°.   **V**

3. HIGHER EDUCATION

Government Publications and Documents

3362. ADAMS, HERBERT B. . . . The college of William and Mary: a contribution to the history of higher education, with suggestions for its national promotion . . . Washington, Govt., 1887.

89 p. illus., plates. 8°. (In U. S. Bur. of education. *Contributions to American educatonal history,* ed. by Herbert B. Adams, I, 1889)

Issued also as U. S. Bur. of education. *Circulars of information,* 1887, no. 1.

Written when the fortunes of the College were at ebb tide as a result of destruction wrought during the Civil war and the hard times afterwards. Contains suggestions for the removal of the College to Alexandria or Richmond. Includes "A bibliography of the history of William and Mary college," p. 84-88.

3363. ————. . . . Thomas Jefferson and the University of Virginia, . . . with authorized sketches of Hampden-Sidney, Randolph-Macon, Emory-Henry, Roanoke, and Richmond colleges, Washington and Lee university, and Virginia military institute. Washington, Govt., 1888.

308 p. front. (port.) illus., plates. 8°. (In U. S. Bur. of education. *Contributions to American educational history,* ed. by Herbert B. Adams, II)

Issued also as U. S. Bur. of education. *Circulars of information,* 1888, no. 1.

Includes "A bibliography of the history of the University of Virginia," p. 203-216; "Writings of the faculty of the university, 1825-1887," by William P. Trent, p. 218-225; "Present organization and condition of the university," by John B. Minor; etc.

3364. EWELL, BENJAMIN S. Remarks of Benjamin S. Ewell, president of the College of William and Mary, before the Committee of education and labor of the House of representatives, Jan. 24, 1872, in support of the petition of the Board of visitors and governors and the faculty of the institution, praying Congress for relief on account of destruction of buildings and other property during the rebellion. [Washington? 1872?]

9, [1] p. 8°.   H

3365. ————. Remarks of Benjamin S. Ewell, president of the College of William and Mary, in Virginia, before the Committee of education and labor, House of representatives, in support of the petition of the College for an appropriation by Congress because of revolutionary losses, and because of the destruction of its buildings and other property by U. S. troops during the late Civil war —delivered Apr. 1, 1874. [Washington? 1874]

16 p. 8°.   BP, H, LC, NYP

3366. FEDERAL RESERVE BANK OF RICHMOND. Letters to college classes in economics and banking, discussing the practical operations of the federal reserve system. [Richmond] Dec., 1921—

4°. monthly.   H: Dec., 1921-Apr., 1923.

3367. HOAR, GEORGE F. The College of William and Mary, in Virginia. Speech of Hon. George F. Hoar, of Massachusetts, in the House of representatives, Feb. 9, 1872. [Washington, Congressional globe, 1872]

4 p. 8°.   H, LC
A plea to Congress to aid in restoring the college after the destruction wrought by the Civil war.

3368. LORING, GEORGE B. College of William and Mary; speech of Hon. G. B. Loring . . . in the House of representatives, Jan. 10, 1879. Washington, 1879.

8 p. 8°.   H
In support of the bill to re-imburse the college for property destroyed during the Civil war.

3369. U. S. CONGRESS. SENATE. CLAIMS, Committee on. Virginia military institute. Hearing before the Committee on claims, U. S. Senate. Sixty-third Congress, second session, on S. 544, a bill for the relief of the Virginia military institute, of Lexington, Va. [Feb. 7, 1914] Printed for the use of the Committee on claims. Washington, Govt., 1914.

20 p. 8°.   LC
Nathan P. Bryan, chairman.

3370. [101] VIRGINIA. Annual reports of . . . institutions of . . . Virginia . . . Richmond, Va. [1866-19—

Include reports of the Medical college of Virginia, 1881/82-86/87; State teacher's college, Farmville, 1885—   ; University of Virginia, 1865-65/66, 71/72—   ; Virginia military institute, 1865/66, 70/71—   ; Virginia polytechnic institute, 1871/72—
Some reports of educational institutions are to be found in the reports

of the supt. of public instruction. See list in E. G. Swem, *Bibliography of Virginia,* II, 1045 **[36]**

3371. [3289] ———. EDUCATION, State board of. Bulletin . . . Vol. 1-   ; 1918—   Richmond, 1918—

3372. ———. ———. The colored normal school at Lynchburg. [Also, the University normal school]   [Richmond, 1880]

[8] p. 8°.   **BP**

Two circulars, one addressed to the colored, the other to the white teachers of Virginia, by W. H. Ruffner, superintendent of public instruction.

3373. ———. ———. . . . . Matriculation records of standard Virginia colleges, session 1915-16.   [Richmond, 1916]

26 p. 4°.   **V**

3374. [3300] ———. ———. Virginia school report . . . 1st-   ; 1871-19—   Richmond, 1871-19—

3375. [3302] ———. EDUCATIONAL SYSTEM OF VIRGINIA, Commission to survey the. Public education in Virginia . . . Richmond, 1928.

See also items **3303-3304.**

3376. ———. GENERAL ASSEMBLY. LEGISLATIVE INVESTIGATING COMMITTEE FOR THE VIRGINIA POLYTECHNIC INSTITUTE. . . . Report of the . . . committee appointed under authority of the joint resolution approved Feb. 27, 1906.   [Richmond, 1906]

5 p. 8°.   (Its House *Doc.,* no. 2)   **NYP, V**

3377. ———. ———. VIRGINIA MILITARY INSTITUTE INVESTIGATING COMMITTEE. Report . . . July 25, 1906.   [n. p., n. d.]

11 p. 8°.   **V**

The dismissal of certain cadets for insubordination, which led to an inspection of the Institute and improvement in living conditions.

3378. [3306] ———. GOVERNOR, 1926— (Harry F. Byrd). The educational system of Virginia . . . Richmond, 1928.

3379. ———. LAWS, STATUTES, ETC. . . . A bill to authorize and require the rector and visitors of the University of Virginia to establish and maintain a co-ordinate college for women, to be known as the Woman's College in the University of Virginia and to form an integral part of said university. [n. p., 1916?]

8 p. 8°. ([Virginia. General assembly] Senate. *Bill,* no. 62) **VU**

3380. [3311] VIRGINIA. LAWS, STATUTES, ETC. Virginia school laws . . . Richmond [1878-19—

3381. ———. MEDICAL EDUCATION, Commission on. Minority report of the Commission on medical education in Virginia. Submitted to His Excellency, the governor of Virginia, the rector and Board of visitors of the University of Virginia, the chairman and Board of visitors of the Medical college of Virginia . . . [n. p., 1921?]

v, 99 p. 8°. **NYP**

3382. ———. ———. The proper location of the state-supported medical school in Virginia. By Theodore Hough. [Also a brief summary of the argument for University location] Charlottesville, Va., The University, 1921.

80 p. illus., plate, map. 8°. (In University of Virginia. *Alumni bulletin,* 3d. ser., XIV, 1; Jan., 1921) **LC, V, VU, WM**

3383. ———. ———. Report of the Commission on medical education in Virginia to His Excellency, the governor of Virginia, the rector and Board of visitors of the University of Virginia, the chairman and Board of visitors of the Medical College of Virginia. Richmond, Va., 1921.

2 p. l., [3]-87 p. 8°. **LC, V, VU, WM**
Wilbur C. Hall, chairman.
Question whether the state medical school should be located in Richmond or at the University of Virginia.

Other Source Material

Averett college, Danville, Va.

3384. AVERETT COLLEGE. Catalogue. [1st-   ; 1860/61-19— Danville 1860?-19—

plates, ports. 8°. (Jr. col.; women; non-sect.; 1859)
Name changed from Roanoke institute, 1917.
Includes Announcements for succeeding year.
H: 55th (1914/15); **LC:** 41st-42d (1900/01-01/02), summer 1918/19;

USE: 1871/72-76/77, 78/79-81/82, 83/84-84/85, 90/91-93/94, 95/96-99/1900, 08/09-09/10, 12/13-14/15, 17/18-18/19, 20/21, 22/23-25/26; **V**: 1910/11-11/12, 13/14-16/17, 19/20.

Bishop Payne divinity school, Petersburg, Va.

3385. BISHOP PAYNE DIVINITY SCHOOL. Testimonials from bishops and others. [Circular and appeal] [Petersburg, 1902]

6 l. nar. 16°. (Colored; Prot. Episc.; 1878) **NYP**

Blackstone college for girls, Blackstone, Va.

3386. BLACKSTONE COLLEGE FOR GIRLS. Catalogue. [1st- ; 1894/95?-19— n. p., 1895-19—

8°. (Jr. col.; M. E., So.; 1894)
Successor to Blackstone female institute.
USE: 1919/20, 21/22-22/23, 27/28; **V**: 1896/97-98/99, 1906/07, 08/09, 12/13-15/16, 17/18.

3387. CANNON, JAMES, jr. Farewell words to the Class of 1905. Delivered by the principal in the Blackstone institute chapel, Sunday evening, June 3, 1906. [n. p., 1906]

25 p. 16°. **V**

3388. ———. Farewell words to the Class of 1908. Delivered by the principal . . . in the Backstone institute chapel, commencement, 1908. [n. p., 1908]

22 p. 16°. **V**

Bluefield college, Tazewell Co., Va.

3389. BLUEFIELD COLLEGE. Catalogue. [1st- ; 1921/22— n. p., 1922—

8°. (Jr. col.; men; Bapt.; 1921) **USE**: 2d, 4th (1922/23, 24/25).

Bridgewater college, Bridgewater, Va.

3390. BRIDGEWATER COLLEGE. [Book of views. Washington, D. C., n. d.]

24 p. 8°. **USE, V**

3391. [———] Bridgewater college: its past and present. A tribute to the alumni. Elgin, Ill., Brethren pub., 1905.

298 p. illus. 8°. **NYP**

3392. BRIDGEWATER COLLEGE. Bulletin . . . Vol. 1- ; [1912?—n. p., 1912?—

    8°. bi-monthly.
    V: X, 4; XI, 2-3, 5; XII, 2-3; XIII, 2-6; XIV, 1, 5-6; (1921-25); new ser.: II, 1A; III, 1A; IV, 1A; (1926-28).

3393. ———. Catalogue . . . [1st- ; 1880/81?-19— n. p., 1881?-19—

    8°. (Col. & prep.; co-ed.; Church of the Brethren; 1880)
    Includes Announcements for succeeding year.
    H: 1902/03-20/21, 22/23-27/28; **LC:** 1896/97-97/98, 99/1900, 02/03, 04/05-06/07; **USE:** 1889/90, 92/93-98/99, 1900/01-12/13, 22/23-27/28; **V:** 1899/1900-01/02, 04/05-10/11, 12/13-22/23.

Chester institute, Chester, Va.

3394. CHESTER INSTITUTE. Catalogue . . . Bedford City, Va., [18-?—

    8°. (Girls; col. & prep.; non-sect.; 18-?)   **V:** 1895/96.

Culpeper female institute, Culpeper, Va.

3395. CULPEPER FEMALE INSTITUTE. Catalogue . . . Richmond, Va. [18-?—

    8°. (Prep. & col.; non-sect.; 18-?)   **V:** 1874/75, 76/77.

Culpeper female seminary, Culpeper, Va.

3396. CULPEPER FEMALE SEMINARY. Catalogue . . . Charlottesville, Va. [1890?-?]

    8°. (Prep. & col.; non-sect.; 1890?)   **V:** 1893/94-94/95.

Daleville college, Daleville, Va.

3397. DALEVILLE COLLEGE. Catalogue. [1st- ; 1890/91— n. p., 1891?—

    8°. (Jr. col.; co-ed.; Church of the Brethren; 1890)
    USE: 1910/11, 14/15, 18/19, 22/23-23/24; **V:** 1909/10.

Danville college, Danville, Va.

3398. DANVILLE COLLEGE FOR YOUNG LADIES. Catalogue . . . Danville, Waddill [1881?—

    illus. 8°. (M. E., So.; 1881)
    Advertisements in back.
    LC: 1883/84; **V:** 1886/87-87/88, 89/90.

Eastern college, conservatory and academy, Manassas, Va.

3399. EASTERN COLLEGE, CONSERVATORY AND ACADEMY. Book of views. [Charlotte, N. C., Observer, 19-?]

24 p. of illus. 4°. **USE**

3400. ——. Catalogue . . . [1st- ; 1899?-19— n. p., 1899?-19—

8°. (Col. & prep.; non-sect.; 1899)
H: 1902/03, 09/10; **USE:** 1909/10-10/11, 12/13, 17/18, 21/22-23/24;
V: 1914/15.

Elizabeth college, Salem, Va.

3401. ELIZABETH COLLEGE. Catalogue . . . [1st- ; 1897/98-19— n. p., 1898?-19—

8°. (Women; Luth.; 1897)
Founded at Charlotte, N. C.; merged with Roanoke woman's college, Salem, Va., 1915.
NYP: 1915/16, 17/18; **USE:** 1916/17-20/21; **V:** 1915/16.

Emory and Henry college, Emory, Va.

3402. EMORY AND HENRY COLLEGE. Annual catalogue . . . with courses of instruction. Cincinnati, O. [etc., 1839?-19—

illus., fold. plates. 8°. (Co-ed.; M. E., So.; 1838)
Issued as number of *Bulletin* of the college, 1908—
Includes Announcements for succeeding year.
H: 1871/72, 77/78, 88/89-98/99, 1900/01-06/07, 08/09-12/13, 14/15-18/19, 25/26; **LC:** 1868/69-69/70, 88/89, 90/91, 93/94, 95/96-1901/02, 03/04-05/06, 07/08, 17/18; **NYP:** 1872/73, 1910/11; **USE:** 1867/68, 70/71-74/75, 76/77-80/81, 84/85, 89/90-98/99; 1901/02, 03/04-27/28; **V:** 1867/68-68/69, 73/74-75/76, 78/79, 85/86, 87/88-88/89, 90/91, 93/94, 95/96-1902/03, 05/06-07/08, 11/12, 13/14-14/15.

3403. ——. Catalogue of the library of Emory and Henry college, Washington County, Virginia. Printed for the use of the students of the College. Wytheville [Va.] St. Clair, 1869.

39 p. 16°. **LC**

3404. ——. Semi-centennial catalogue and historical register of Emory and Henry college, Washington County, Virginia. 1837-87 . . . Tazewell, Va., Clinch Valley news, 1887.

133, [4] p., 1 l., xxiii p. incl. front. ports. 8°. **LC, USE**

3405. EMORY AND HENRY COLLEGE. CALLIOPEAN SOCIETY. Catalogue of the library of the Calliopean society of Emory and Henry college. Wytheville [Va.] St. Clair, 1872.

46 p. 16°.   LC

3406. ———. HERMESIAN SOCIETY. Catalogue of the Hermesian library of Emory and Henry college, 1872. Bristol [Va.] Bristol news book and job office, 1872.

24 p. 16°.   LC

Episcopal female institute, Winchester, Va.

3407. EPISCOPAL FEMALE INSTITUTE. Announcement, 1874/75-19— Winchester, 1874-19—

8°. (Col. & prep.; Prot. Episc.; 1874)

USE: 1875/76-78/79, 82/83, 84/85-87/88, 89/90, 1906/07; V: 1874/75, 90/91, 94/95, 1903/04, 05/06.

Fairfax Hall, Winchester, Va.

3408. FAIRFAX HALL. Catalogue [1st- ; 1869/70—   Wytheville, Va., etc.] 1869—

8°. (Prep. & col.; women; non-sect.; 1869)

V: 1869/70, 73/74-75/76, 77/78, 79/80, 82/83, 98/99.

3409. ———. Catalogue of the teachers and pupils of Fairfax Hall, Winchester, Va., for ten years, ending June, 1879. Dansville, N. Y., The Advertiser, 1879.

23, [1] p. front. 8°.   V

Fredericksburg college, Fredericksburg, Va.

3410. FREDERICKSBURG COLLEGE. . . . Catalogue. 1893/94-19— [Baltimore, etc.] 1893-19—

plates. 8°. (Col. & prep.; co-ed.; Presbyt.; 1893)
Title varies: . . . Catalogue . . . Prospectus.

On cover: Catalogue . . . including the Kenmore school for young ladies, the Saunders memorial school for boys.

H: 9-11th, 13-15th, 18th (1901/02-03/04, 05/06-07/08, 10/11); LC: 5-6th, 13th (1897/98-98/99, 1905/06); USE: 1896/97-99/1900, 04/05-08/09, 11/12, 13/14; V: 1910/11-12/13, 14/15.

Gladeville college, Wise, Va.

3411. GLADEVILLE COLLEGE. Catalogue . . . Tazewell, Va. [189-?-19—

8°. (Jr. col., prep., & elem.; co.ed.; non-sect.; 189-?)
V: 1905/06.

Hampden-Sidney college, Hampden-Sidney, Va.

3412. HAMPDEN-SIDNEY COLLEGE. Bulletin . . . Vol. 1- ; Mar., 1906— Hampden-Sidney, The College, 1906—

8°. **H:** II-XIX (1907/08-24/25—incompl.). **LC:** III, 4; IV, 3-4; V, 2-3; VI, 2-4; VII, 2, 4; VIII, 2; IX, 2-3; X, 2-3; XI, 3, 5, 7-9; XII, 3; (1908-18); XV-XVIII, 1; XXII, 3; (1920-23, 28). **USE:** VII, 4 (1913); IX, 4 (1917). **V:** I-III; V, 2-4; VI, 2-4; VII, 2-4; VIII, 2-4; IX, 2-3; X, 2-4; XI, 2-4; XII, 2-4; XIII, 2-3; XIV, 1-2, 4; XV, 1-3; XVI, 1-3; XVII, 1-3; (1906-08, 10-22).

3413. ———. . . . Calendar of Board of minutes, 1776-1876, by Alfred J. Morrison. Richmond, Va., Hermitage press, 1912.

186 p. front., ports. 8°.   **H, LC, NYP, USE, V, VU**

3414. ———. Catalogue of the officers and students. Richmond [etc., 18-?-19—

8°. (Men; Presbyt.; 1776)
Issue for 1866/67 includes the "General catalogue," 1776-1866.

BP: 1866/67, 73/74, 75/76; **H:** 1872/73, 77/78, 83/84-85/86, 87/88-1904/05, 06/07, 08/09-24/25, 26/27, **LC:** 1865/66-67/68, 69/70, 85/86, 91/92-92/93, 95/96-96/97, 98/99-1905/06, 09/10-10/11, 12/13-14/15, 16/17-17/18; **NYP:** 1867/68, 73/74-75/76, 77/78, 79/80-81/82, 91/92-92/93; **USE:** 1865/66, 69/70-1927/28; **V:** 1874/75-1927/28.

3415. ———. Circular. [Hampden-Sidney, Va., 1874]

16 p. 16°.
                                                          BP

3416. ———. Class-letters, Class of '94, Hampden-Sidney college; ed. by John I. Armstrong. Hampden-Sidney college [Richmond, Va., Whittet & Shepperson] May, 1905.

37 p. 8°.   **V**
Letters from alumni regarding their work and experience since graduation; with some notes on conditions at the college since 1899.

3417. ———. General catalogue of the officers and students of

Hampden-Sidney college, Virginia.   1776-1906.   Richmond, Va.,
Whittet & Shepperson [1908]

> 246 p. diagrs. 8°.   (Its *Bulletin,* III, 4; Nov., 1908)
>
> **LC, NYP, USE, V, WM**
>
> Two 10-year supplements issued: 1907-16 (1917); and 1917-26 (1928).

3418. HAMPDEN-SIDNEY COLLEGE. [Prospectus] [n. p., n. d.]

> [5] p. 4°.   **BP**

3419. HOOPER, THOMAS W. Unconscious influence: an address de-
livered before the Union and Philanthropic societies . . .
Hampden-Sidney college, Va. June 12, 1889. Pub. by order of
Union society. Richmond, Va., Whittet & Shepperson, 1889.

> p. [25]-40. 8°.   **V**
>
> On the influence of college life at Hampden-Sidney on her alumni.

3420. LINGLE, WALTER L. Union seminary cemetery at Hampden-
Sidney . . . [Richmond, Richmond press, 1919?]

> 16 p. front., plates. 8°.   **LC, V**
>
> Restoration of the cemetery, with names of faculty of Hampden-Sid-
> ney who are buried there.

3421. [3336] McILWAINE, RICHARD. Addresses and papers
. . . Richmond [*ca.* 1908]

3422. ———. Hampden-Sidney college; its relation and services to
the Presbyterian church, and to the cause of education and religion: a discourse preached at the Second Presbyterian church
. . . Richmond, Virginia, Feb. 5, 1888. Richmond, Va., Whittet & Shepperson, 1888.

> 19 p. 8°.   **V**

3423. PRYOR, ROGER A. The religious and the secular culture. An
address before the alumni of Hampden-Sidney college, Virginia,
delivered 12th June, 1873 . . . New York, Evening post,
1873.

> 26 p. 8°.   **USE, VU**

3424. THORNTON, WILLIAM M. The demands of modern life upon
the school. An address before the Society of alumni of Hampden-
Sidney college, . . . June 11, 1890. Wytheville, Va., St.
Clair, 1890.

> 16 p. 8°.   **NYP**

3425. WOOL, THEODORE J. Address delivered before the student body of Hampden-Sidney college, at the opening exercises of the college, Sept. 14, 1910. Portsmouth, Va., 1911.

21 p. 8°.   **V**

Concerning the opportunities of college life.

Hampton college, Hampton, Va.

3426. HAMPTON COLLEGE. [Announcement]   [Philadelphia, etc., 190-?—

8°. (Col. & prep.; women; non-sect.; 190-?)

LC: 1907/08; **V:** 1902/03, 06/07, 09/10.

Hartshorn memorial college, Richmond, Va.

3427. HARTSHORN MEMORIAL COLLEGE. Annual catalogue of the officers and students. 1st- ; 1883/84-19— Richmond, Va. [1883?-19—

illus. (port.) plates. 8°. (Colored; men; Bapt.; 1883)

H: 15th (1897/98); **LC:** 6th, 19-20th, 23d (1888/89, 1901/02-02/03, 05/06); **USE:** 1883/84-98/99, 1906/07, 09/10-10/11, 15/16, 21/22; **V:** 1899/1900-03/04, 05/06, 07/08.

Hollins college, Hollins, Va.

3428. HOLLINS COLLEGE. Annual catalogue. Roanoke, Va. [18-?-19—

plates (part fold.) ports., map. 8°. (Women; non-sect.; 1842)

Known as Valley union seminary, to 1855; Hollins institute, 1855-1911; Hollins college, 1911—

Title varies: Annual register and announcement; Annual catalogue . . .

H: 1894/95-1907/08, 09/10-10/11, 12/13-13/14, 15/16-27/28; **LC:** 1864/67-67/68, 70/71, 72/73, 88/89, 90/91, 93/94, 1902/03-04/05, 08/09, 17/18, 26/27; **NYP:** 1905/06, 07/08, 14/15, 17/18; **USE:** 1867/68, 70/71, 72/73-77/78, 79/80-1923/24, 25/26-27/28; **V:** 1864/67, 78/79, 91/92-98/99, 1900/01-27/28.

3429. ———. Bulletin of information . . . [n. p., 19-?—

8°.   **V:** 1910.

3430. ———. Testimonials. [n. p., 1868?]

6 p. 8°.   **LC**

Recommendations by men in public life in Virginia.

3431. HOLLINS COLLEGE. Valedictory. Closing remarks of the superintendent, to the young ladies of Hollins institute. June 26, 1872. [n. p., 1872]

    8 p. 12°.   **V**

3432. ——. [Views of Hollins institute. 1911] [n. p., 1911?]

    12 p. 16°.   **V**

3433. ——. MUSIC, School of. [Catalogue] [n. p., 19-?—

    8°.   **USE**: 1909/10-10/11; **V**: 1910/11.

3434. [MERTIUS, EMMA A., *et al.*] Shakespeare prize examination. In Hamlet. Hollins institute, Va. 1881. [By Emma A. Mertius and Hannah Wilson. Papers forwarded to the "New Shakspere society" of England in competition for the prize offered for the encouragement of the study of Shakespeare in schools.] [Botetourt Springs, Va.?] 1881.

    34 p. 8°.   **H**
    Questions by Horace H. Furness of Philadelphia.

3435. THOM, WILLIAM T. Shakespeare and Chaucer examinations. Ed., with some remarks on the class-room study of Shakespeare . . . Boston, Ginn, 1888.

    346 p. 16°.   **LC, VU**
    Examination papers by pupils of Hollins institute, Va.
    2d enlarged edit.; 1st edit. pub. under title: *Two Shakespeare examinations* (1883).

3436. ——. Two Shakespeare examinations: with some remarks on the class-room study of Shakespeare . . . Boston, Ginn, Heath & co., 1883.

    154 p. 12°.   **LC, VU**

Lynchburg college, Lynchburg, Va.

3437. LYNCHBURG COLLEGE. Catalogue . . . with announcements . . . [1st- ; 1903/04— n. p., 1903?—

    front. (port.) 12°.-8°. (Col. & prep.; co-ed; Disciples of Christ; 1903) Founded as Virginia Christian college; became Lynchburg college, 1919.
    H: 1910/11, 19/20-26/27; **LC**: 1924/25; **USE**: 1904/05, 07/08-09/10, 13/14, 15/16-18/19; **V**: 1911/12.

3438. ———. Charter and by-laws. [n. p., 1921]

    35 p. 8°.   **H**

Marion college, Marion, Va.

3439. MARION COLLEGE. Catalogue . . . [n. p., 1874?-19—

    8°. (Jr. col.; women; non-sect.; 1873)
    Founded as Marion female college.
    USE: 1873/74-99/1900, 06/07, 08/09, 17/18, 19/20-22/23; **V**: 1901/02-02/03.

Martha Washington college, Abingdon, Va.

3440. MARTHA WASHINGTON COLLEGE. Annual catalogue of Martha Washington college and conservatory of music. Pulaski, Va. [1860?-19—

    plates. 8°. (Jr. col.; women; non-sect.; 1860)
    LC: 1890/91, 1902/03, USE: 1869/70, 71/72, 75/76-76/77, 78/79, 86/87, 88/89, 90/91, 92/93-99/1900, 07/08, 09/10-10/11, 12/13, 14/15, 16/17, 21/22, 23/24, 25/26; **V**: 1908/09-09/10, 11/12, 13/14-14/15.

3441. ———. Announcements of the Abingdon state summer school, Martha Washington college, Abingdon, Va. June 23rd to July 20th, 1915. [Bristol, Tenn., King, 1915]

    15 p. 8°.   **V**

3442. ———. Views. [Lynchburg, Dulaney-Boatright, n. d.]

    2 v. 14 & 17 plates. 8°.   **V**

3443. ———. Views. [Richmond, Whittet & Shepperson, 19-?]

    34 p. of illus. 4°.   **USE**

Mary Baldwin seminary, Staunton, Va.

3444. MARY BALDWIN SEMINARY. Catalogue . . . Roanoke [etc.] 1896-19—

    plates. 8°. (Jr. col. & prep.; women; non-sect.; 1842)
    Founded as Augusta female seminary; became Mary Baldwin seminary, 1896.
    USE: 1923/24-26/27; **V**: 1896/97, 1905/06-15/16, 17/18-23/24, 27/28.

Medical college of Virginia, Richmond, Va.

3445. JOHNSTON, GEORGE B., *et al.* Reply of George Ben Johnston

and Christopher Tompkins to A protest against the use of state
funds for professional education, by Stuart McGuire . . . as
presented to the Committee on education of the Constitutional convention. [n. p., 1901?]

27 p. 8°.   V

Argument over the proposal that the State grant an appropriation to
assist professional education in the Medical college of Virginia.

3446. MEDICAL COLLEGE OF VIRGINIA. Catalogue . . . Announcement. Richmond, Va. [18-?-19—

illus. fold. pl. 8°. (Co.-ed.; state; 1838)
Merged with University college of medicine, 1913.
Issued as *Bulletin* of Medical college of Virginia **[3448]**
H: 1868/69, 70/71, 84/85, 1907/08-08/09, 10/11-12/13, 15/16; **LC:**
1895/96, 97/98, 1900/01; **NYP:** 1866/67, 75/76, 83/84-86/87, 88/89-90/91,
1902/03; **V:** 1866/67, 93/94-95/96, 97/98-99/1900, 01/02, 03/04-05/06, 08/09-
09/10, 11/12-27/28.

3447. ———. Bi-monthly bulletin, vol. 1- ; 1896-19— Richmond,
Va., 1896-19—

4°.   **V:** I, 6; II, 1, 4; III, 4-6; IV, 1-6; (1896-1900).

3448. ———. Bulletin . . . Vol. 1- ; 1904— Richmond,
Va., 1904—

plates. 8°. quarterly.
USHy: XVIII, 1, 2—suppl., 3 (1921). **V:** I-XX; XXI, 5; XXII,
1-4, & suppls., 6; XXIII, 2-3, 4—suppls. 1-6; XXIV, 1 & suppl., 2-7;
XXV, 3; 1904-28). **VU:** XVIII, 1—suppl.; XX, 3; (1921, 23).

3449. ———. A protest against the use of state funds for professional education. Argument and stenographic report of discussion before the Committee on education of the Constitutional
convention of Virginia [1901-02] . . . [Richmond, Whittet &
Shepperson, 1902]

69 p. 8°.   VU

Includes statements of Drs. Stuart McGuire, L. M. Cowardin, George
B. Johnston, Christopher Tompkins, J. A. Hodges.

3450. ———. The response of the Board of visitors of the Medical college of Virginia to the invitation of the Commission on
medical education in Virginia "to make any contribution of facts
. . . pertinent to the subject of . . . the best organization of medical education in Virginia." [n. p., 192-?]

51 p. incl. plan, maps. front. 4°.   V

Advocating Richmond as the location of the state supported medical
school.

3451. ———. Scrapbook of clippings, mostly from Richmond newspapers, 1911-13, relating to medical colleges and hospitals in Richmond, the merger of the University college of medicine and the Medical college of Virginia, and Pres. S. C. Mitchell. [1911-13]

[107] p. illus. f°. **V**

3452. ———. DENTISTRY, Dept. of. Catalogue . . . Announcements. Richmond, Va., [18-?-19—

illus. 8°. (Issued as no. of *Bulletin* of the University college of medicine)
Announcements are for succeeding year.
LC: 1905/06-06/07; **V:** 1895/96-96/97.

3453. ———. MEDICINE, Dept. of. Catalogue . . . Announcements. Richmond, Va., [18-?-19—

8°. (Issued as no. of *Bulletin* of the University college of medicine)
V: 1895/96-96/97; 1909/10.

3454. ———. PHARMACY, Dept. of. Catalogue . . . Announcements. Richmond, Va. [18-?-19—

illus. 8°. (Issued as no. of *Bulletin* of the University college of medicine)
LC: 1905/06-08/09; **V:** 1895/96-96/97, 1909/10.

Norfolk college for young ladies, Norfolk, Va.

3455. NORFOLK COLLEGE. Catalogue . . . Announcement . . . Norfolk, Barron [187-?-?]

8°. (Col. & prep.; non-sect.; 187-?)
NYP: 1890/91; **USE:** 1880/81, 83/84-85/86, 87/88-89/90; **V:** 1895/96-97/98.

Piedmont business college, Lynchburg, Va.

3456. PIEDMONT BUSINESS COLLEGE. Catalogue . . . Lynchburg [1887?-19—

8°. (Bus. & stenog.; 1887) **V:** 1907/08(?)

Protestant Episcopal theological seminary in Virginia, Alexandria, Va.

3457. PACKARD, JOSEPH. Recollections of the old chapel. A discourse delivered at the consecration of the new chapel of the The-

ological seminary of the Diocese of Virginia . . . June 23,
1881. Philadelphia, Matlack & Harvey, 1881.

24 p. illus. (front.) 8°.   H, VU

3458. PROTESTANT EPISCOPAL THEOLOGICAL SEMINARY. Brief in
support of the petition of sundry persons for the relief of the trustees of the Episcopal seminary in Virginia. [n. p., 1875?]

14 p. 8°.   LC
Argument of the seminary that the Federal government make compensation for rent due and damage suffered, 1861-65, while the buildings were occupied by U. S. troops.

3459. ———. Catalogue of the officers, students, and alumni . . .
Fairfax County, Va. [18-?-19—

8°. (Men; 1823)
H: 1892/93-93/94, 1903/04, 05/06, 16/17-17/18; V: 1880/81.

3460. ———. Semi-centennial celebration of the Theological seminary of the Protestant Episcopal church in the Diocese of Virginia,
held on the 24th and 25th days of September, 1873. Baltimore
[Innes] 1873.

108 p. front., plate. 8°.   V
Includes addresses by Joseph Packard, C. W. Andrews, Philip Slaughter, and E. D. Dalrymple.

3461. ———. . . . The Theological seminary in Virginia, Alexandria, Virginia. Its centennial, 1823-1923 . . . [Richmond,
Va., Whittet & Shepperson, 1923]

24 p. illus. (incl. ports.) 4°.   LC, V
A well illustrated pamphlet of the seminary's old and new plant, its
faculty and distinguished alumni, centennial fund, etc.

Randolph-Macon college, Ashland, Va.

3462. JARVIS, THOMAS J. Address delivered by Hon. Thos. J. Jar-
vis, governor of North Carolina, before the Society of alumni of
Randolph-Macon college, June 15th, 1881. Pub. by the Society.
Richmond, Johns & Goolsby, 1881.

20 p. 8°.   USE
The theme of the address is: Work and service.

3463. RANDOLPH-MACON COLLEGE. Catalogue . . . Richmond
[18-?-19—

8°. (Men; M. E., So.; 1832)
H: 1872/73-73/74, 82/83, 88/89-89/90, 91/92, 93/94-1903/04, 06/07-

10/11, 12/13-14/15, 16/17-27/28; **LC**: 1888/89, 93/94, 95/96-96/97, 98/99-1903/04, 05/06, 07/08-10/11, 12/13-26/27; **NYP**: 1870/71, 72/73, 77/78, 88/89-90/91, 96/97-98/99, 1901/02-02/03, 04/05, 10/11-11/12, 14/15, 21/22, 23/24; **USE**: 1870/71-71/72, 73/74-75/76, 77/78-78/79, 82/83-1908/09, 10/11, 12/13-14/15, 16/17, 18/19-19/20, 21/22-25/26; **V**: 1877/78, 83/84-84/85, 89/90-90/91, 96/97, 98/99-1914/15, 17/18-26/27, 28/29.

3464. ———. Convention in the interests of Randolph-Macon college [held at Richmond, Va., Apr. 8, 9, 1874] [n. p., 1874]

2, 8 p. 8°. **BP**

3465. ———. Illustrated booklet, Randolph-Macon college, Ashland, Va. [Richmond, Va., Waddey, 1906?]

45, [1] p. illus. (incl. plan) fold. plate. 8°. **LC, V**

3466. ———. Illustrated booklet. Randolph-Macon college, Ashland, Va. [n. p., 19-?]

52 p. illus. 8°. **LC**
"Designed to supplement the catalogue."

3467. ———. Pictorial Randolph-Macon. [Ashland? n. d.]

[4] p. illus. 13 plates. 14 1/2 x 22 cm. **USE, V**

3468. ———. Randolph-Macon system illustrations. [Lynchburg, Va., Bell, 190-?]

1 l., 20 plates. 4 1/2 x 21 1/2 cm. **USE**

3469. ———. The Randolph-Macon system. Its relation to the church and the Carnegie foundation. Pub. by direction of the Board of trustees. [n. p., 1908]

63 p. 8°. **V**

Randolph-Macon woman's college, Lynchburg, Va.

3470. Randolph-Macon woman's college. Book of views. Lynchburg, Va. [Bell, n. d.]

unp. illus. 12°. **V**

3471. ———. Bulletin . . . Vol. 1- ; 1915— Lynchburg, 1915—

illus. 8°. quarterly.
BP: IX, 1 (1922). **H**: I-VIII, X, XII-XIV (1914/15-21/22, 23/24, 25/26-27/28). **LC**: II, 4; IX, 3-4; X, 1, 3-4; XI, 1, 3-4; XII, 1; XIII, 1; (1916, 23-27). **USE**: I, 1-2, 4; V, 4; IX, 1, 3-4; X, 1, 3; XI, 3-4; XII, 1; XIII, 1; (1914/15, 20, 23/24-26/27). **V**: I-II, 3; III, 4; IV, 1;

V, 5; IX, 1, 3; X, 3-XII; XIII, 1, 3-4; XIV, 1, 3-4; XV, 1. **VU: IX, 3** (1923).

3472. RANDOLPH-MACON WOMAN'S COLLEGE. Catalogue . . . Announcements. [1st-   ; 1893/94—   ] Lynchburg, Va., 1893-19—

> plates. 8°. (M. E., So.; 1893)
> Announcements are for succeeding year.
> **H**: 1914/15-21/22, 23/24, 25/26-27/28; **LC**: 1893/94-94/95, 1904/05, 17/18; **NYP**: 1910/11, 13/14-27/28; **USE**: 1893/94-94/95, 1905/06-26/27; **V**: 1905/06-07/08, 09/10-11/12, 13/14-28/29.

3473. ————. Home life at Randolph-Macon women's college, Lynchburg, Virginia. [Lynchburg, Va., Brown-Morrison, 1909?]

> 27, [4] p. incl. illus., plates, ports. 4°.   **USE, V**

Rappahannock institute, Tappahannock, Va.

3474. RAPPAHANNOCK INSTITUTE. Catalogue . . . [n. p., 18-?—

> 8°. (Prep. & col.; girls; non-sect.; 18-?)   **V**: 1894/95.

Richmond City normal school, Richmond, Va.

3475. RICHMOND CITY NORMAL SCHOOL. . . . Catalogue . . . Richmond, Va. [19-?—

> plates. 8°. (Estab., 19-?)   **LC, USAg**: 1914; **V**: 1913-15.

Richmond university, Richmond, Va.

3476. BOATWRIGHT, FREDERIC W. Achievements of Richmond college alumni now resident in Richmond. [Richmond, 1905]

> 3 p. 8°.   **V**

3477. BROADUS, JOHN A. College education for men of business: a familiar essay, written at the request of the trustees of Richmond college . . . Richmond, Ryland, 1875.

> 24 p. 12°.   **LC, V, VU**
> Arguments in favor of a college education, and certain objections answered. Appended are a list of Richmond college faculty and a summary of expenses for one session of 9 months.

3478. GREEN, WILLIAM. Address to the law class of Richmond college . . . delivered Oct. 10, 1870. Richmond, Fergusson & Rady, 1870.

> 20 p. 8°.   **VU**
> Advice to the young lawyers.

3479. HARRIS, H. H. Richmond college; alumni address, 1891. [Richmond, Hill] 1891.

15 p. 8°.   **V**
A survey of the development of the college, changes in student body and faculty, and activity of alumni.

3480. RICHMOND COLLEGE historical papers . . . Ed. by D. R. Anderson . . . Vol. 1-2, no. 1. June, 1915-1917. Richmond, Va., 1915-17.

3 nos. 8°. annual.
H, LC, NYP, V, WM: I-II, 1; **VU:** I, 1.

3481. RICHMOND UNIVERSITY. Annual report of the president . . . [Richmond, Va., 18-?-19—

8°.   **H:** 1925; **USE:** 1927; **V:** 1915, 19, 26-28.

3482. ———. Annual report of the treasurer . . . [Richmond, Va., 18-?-19—

8°.   **LC:** 1921-23; **USE:** 1923, 27; **V:** 1882, 1915.

3483. ———. . . . Bulletin . . . Vol. 1- ; 1899/1900-19— Richmond, 1899-19—

plates. 16°.-8°. quarterly.
H: XXVIII, 2, 4; XXIX, 2, 4; (1927-28). **LC:** VII, 2 (1905). **V:** IX, 2; XII, 3; XIV, 3; XVI, 3; XX, 2; XXI, 1; XXII, 1-3; XXIII, 1-4; XXIV, 1-4; XXV, 2-4; XXVI, 1-3, 5; XXVII, 2-4; XXVIII, 2-4; XXIX, 2, 4; XXX, 2; (1907-29).

3484. ———. Catalogue . . . with announcements . . . Richmond, Va. [18-?-19—

plates. 16°.-8°. (Men; Bapt.; 1832)
Issued as no. of its *Bulletin*, 1900—   **[3483]**
University includes Westhampton college for women **[3491]**
H: 1870/71-71/72, 89/90, 92/93, 94/95-1901/02, 05/06-12/13, 14/15-26/27; **LC:** 1866/67, 68/69, 70/71, 72/73, 93/94, 95/96-98/99, 1901/02-04/05, 06/07, 13/14, 17/18; **NYP:** 1872/73, 83/84-84/85; **USE:** 1866/67-67/68, 69/70-72/73, 74/75-78/79, 80/81-89/90, 91/92-1911/12, 15/16-19/20, 22/23-25/26, 27/28; **V:** 1894/95, 97/98-98/99, 1900/01-01/02, 04/05-26/27; **WM:** 1884/85.

3485. ———. Dedication of Jeter memorial hall. Address by Rev. J. B. Thomas . . . Remarks of the chairman of the Jeter memorial committee and the president of the trustees, Richmond college, June 18, 1884. Richmond [Va.] Jones, 1884.

30 p., 1 l. front. 8°.   **H, LC, NYP, USE, V**

3486. RICHMOND UNIVERSITY. [Descriptive pamphlets] [Richmond, Whittet & Shepperson, n. d.]

    var. pag. 8°.   **LC**

3487. ———. Greater Richmond college; an appeal and a prospect . . . Richmond, Dietz, 1908.

    [14] p. 8°.   **V**

3488. ———. Memorial of James Thomas, jr. Addresses by John A. Broadus . . . and officers of the college, on the formal opening of the Museum and art hall, Richmond college, Sept. 22, 1887. Richmond, 1888.

    79 p. 8°.   **H, LC, NYP, USE**
    Describes the work of Broadus in furthering the cause of higher education in Virginia after the Civil war.

3489. ———. Roll of students of Richmond college, 1865 to 1905. With list of graduates, 1849-1861. Richmond, Va., Whittet & Shepperson, 1905.

    72 p., 1 l. 8°. (Its *Bulletin*, VII, 2)   **LC**
    Preface signed: F. W. Boatwright.

3490. ———. LAW SCHOOL. Catalogue . . . Richmond, Va. [18-?-19—

    8°. (Estab., 1870)
    Issued as no. of Richmond college *Bulletin*, 19-?— **[3483]**
    V: 1907/08, 09/10-10/11, 12/13-17/18, 19/20-26/27.

3491. WESTHAMPTON COLLEGE, Richmond, Va. Catalogue . . . 1st- ; 1914/15— Richmond, 1914—

    8°. (Co-ord. for women; Bapt.; 1914)
    H: 1915/16, 17/18, 20/21, 26/27-27/28; USE: 1914/15-20/21, 22/23-25/26, 27/28; V: 1913/14-15/16, 17/18-25/26.

Roanoke college, Salem, Va.

3492. DREHER, JULIUS D. Roanoke college, Salem, Va. [n. p., 1884]

    [4] p. 4°.   **BP**

3493. EATON, JOHN. An address on scholarly workers: their spirit and methods . . . Delivered before the literary societies of Roanoke college . . . June 10, 1879. Washington, Judd & Detweiler, 1879.

    18 p. 8°.   **BP, V, VU**

3494. POTTER, CLARKSON N. Address before the literary societies of Roanoke college, Virginia . . . June 12, 1878. Washington, D. C., Darby & Duvall, Pub. for the societies, 1878.

29 p. 8°. **BP, LC, NYP, VU**

On the need of limiting legislation and the patronage.

3495. ROANOKE COLLEGE. Addresses at the inauguration of Julius D. Dreher as president of Roanoke college, Salem, Virginia. Oct. 17, 1879. Pub. by order of the trustees. [Boston, Wood] 1879.

62 p. 8°. **BP, H, LC, NYP, V**

Addresses by C. P. Krauth, J. J. Moorman, and inaugural by Pres. Dreher.

3496. ————. Bulletin . . . Vol. 1- ; 1911— Salem, Roanoke college, 1911—

8°. quarterly.

H: I, 2; XV, 3; XVI, 3; (1911, 26, 27). **LC:** I, 2, 4 (1911-12). **USE:** I-II, 3; III, 1-2; IV, 2-3; V, 3; VI, 3; VII, 3; VIII, 4; IX, 3; XI, 3-4; XII, 2, 4; XIII, 4; XIV, 3; XV, 3; XVI, 3; XVII, 2; (1911-28). **V:** I, 1-2, 4; II, 1-4; III, 1-2; IV, 1-4; V, 1-2; VI, 2-3; VII, 2, 4; VIII, 1-2; IX, 1/2; XVI, 1-2; (1911-20, 27).

3497. ————. Catalogue of the officers and students . . . 1st- ; 1853/54— with announcements . . . Wytheville, Va. [etc., 1854-19—

plates. 8°. (Men; Luth.; 1853)

Announcements are for the succeeding year.

BP: 1872/73, 81/82; **H:** 1870/71, 72/73, 74/75-75/76, 77/78, 80/81-81/82, 85/86-86/87, 89/90-91/92, 93/94, 95/96-1910/11, 14/15-16/17, 18/19-26/27; **LC:** 1866/67-67/68, 69/70, 88/89, 90/91-1905/06, 17/18; **NYP:** 1874/75, 76/77, 79/80, 81/82-82/83, 88/89, 92/93, 95/96, 97/98-99/1900, 02/03-04/05, 09/10; **USE:** 1867/68, 70/71-74/75, 76/77-79/80, 81/82-1916/17, 20/21-27/28; **V:** 1877/78-78/79, 81/82, 83/84, 1910/11-11/12, 14/15-17/18, 19/20-23/24; **VU:** 1878/79.

3498. ————. Catalogue of the alumni of Roanoke college, 1853-1893. Salem, Va., 1893.

14, [1] p. 8°. **H, NYP, USE**

3499. ————. 1853-1903. Semi-centennial celebration and commencement of Roanoke college, June 7-11, 1903. Salem, Va., Pub. by the College, 1903.

217 p. incl. front., plates, ports. 8°. **H, LC**

Appendix contains notes on the building fund, with list of subscriptions, and on the alumni association and general association.

3500. ROANOKE COLLEGE. Lewis centennial hall, for the library, museum, and public exercises of Roanoke college. [n. p., 1875?]

[4] p. 8°.   USE

3501. ———. Quarto-centennial anniversary of Roanoke college, 1853-1878. [Circular] [Salem, Va., Register print., 1878]

[4] p. 8°.   USE

3502. ———. Roanoke college, Salem, Va. Founded 1853. No endowment . . . Additional buildings needed . . . [n. p., 1876?]

[4] p. 8°.   USE

3503. ———. Views. [Salem, Va., Salem print., n. d.]

12 illus. 8°.   NYP, V

3504. WARNER, CHARLES D. The work laid upon the southern college. An address before the literary societies of Roanoke college, Salem, Virginia, June 12, 1883. [Salem? 1883]

7 p. 8°.   BP

3505. WELLS, S. C. Memorial address; delivered at the opening of the Bittle memorial hall, Roanoke college, Salem, Va., Oct. 19, 1879 . . . Gettysburg, Wible, 1880.

34 p. 8°. (Reprint from *Lutheran quarterly*, Oct., 1880)

BP, USE, V, VU

3506. WISE, HENRY A. Address . . . before the literary societies of Roanoke college, Salem, Va., June 17, 1873. Baltimore, Ehler [1873]

16 p. 8°.   NYP

St. John's academy, Alexandria, Va.

3507. ST. JOHN'S ACADEMY. Catalogue . . . Alexandria, Va. [18-?-?]

8°. (Col. & prep. [milit.]; men; Prot. Episc.; 1839?)
V: 1872/73-79/80, 84/85-90/91.

3508. ———. Plan of discipline and instruction. [n. p., n. d.]

8 p. 8°.   V

Shenandoah college, Reliance, Va.

3509. SHENANDOAH COLLEGE. Catalogue . . . and announcements. Reliance, Va. [1883?-19—

    illus., plates. 16°.-8°. (Col. & prep.; co-ed.; non-sect.; 1883)
    Announcements are for the succeeding year.
    H: 1901/02; LC: 1900/01, 04/05, 06/07; USE: 1924/25, 26/27; V:
    1904/05-05/06.

Shenandoah collegiate institute, Dayton, Va.

3510. SHENANDOAH COLLEGIATE INSTITUTE. Bulletin, vol. 1-25
[1899/1900?]-1923/24; new ser., vol. 1- ; 1924— [n. p.,
1899?-19—

    8°.   H: XVII, 1 (1915); new ser., V, 1 (1928). V: XVII, 1-2.

3511. ———. [Catalogue] [n. p., 1875?-19—

    8°. (Jr. col.; co-ed.; non-sect.; 1875)
    H: 1914/15; V: 1884/85-85/86, 89/90, 91/92-92/93, 94/95, 96/97-
    98/99, 1902/03.

3512. ———. What others think of Shenandoah. [n. p., 1916]
    [28] p. 16°.   **V**
    Testimonials regarding the school.

Shoemaker college, Gate City, Va.

3513. SHOEMAKER COLLEGE. Catalogue . . . Gate City, Va.
[1897?-19—

    ports., plates. 8°. (Col. & prep.; co-ed.; non-sect.; 1897)
    LC: 1904/05; V: 1903/04-04/05.

South Boston female institute, South Boston, Va.

3514. SOUTH BOSTON FEMALE INSTITUTE. Catalogue . . . [n. p.,
1884?—

    8°. (Col. & prep.; non-sect.; 1884)   V: 1893/94-95/96.

Southern college, Petersburg, Va.

3515. SOUTHERN COLLEGE. . . . Catalogue . . . [1st-   ;
1863/64?-19—   Petersburg?   1864?-19—

illus. 4°. (Jr. col. & prep.; women; non-sect.; 1863)
Founded as Southern female college.
Includes Announcement for succeeding year.
LC: 34th, 36th, 41st (1897/98, 99/1900, 03/04); USE: 1866/67-68/69,
74/75-79/80, 81/82-82/83, 86/87-87/88, 89/90, 93/94-1900/01, 18/19, 21/22,
23/24; V: 1910/11-11/12, 13/14.

3516. ———. Souvenir booklet, Jamestown exhibit. [n. p., 1907?]

[23] p. illus. 8°.   V

Southwest Virginia institute, Bristol, Va.

3517. SOUTHWEST VIRGINIA INSTITUTE. Catalogue . . . [Bris-
tol, etc., 1884?-19—

8°. (Col. & prep.; women; Bapt.; 1884)
Located at Glade Springs, Va., 1884-93; at Bristol, 1893-19—
LC: 1886/87; V: 1886/87-87/88, 89/90-91/92, 94/95, 1901/02.

Staunton female seminary, Staunton, Va.

3518. STAUNTON FEMALE SEMINARY. Catalogue . . . [Staunton,
1870?-]

8°. (Col. & prep.; Luth.; 1870)
USE: 1875/76, 77/78, 79/80, 81/82-83/84, 85/86-96/97; V: 1890/91.

Stonewall Jackson institute, Abingdon, Va.

3519. STONEWALL JACKSON INSTITUTE. Catalogue . . . [n. p.,
18-?-19—

8°. (Jr. col.; women; Presbyt.; 1868)
USE: 1908/09-09/10, 13/14-18/19, 20/21, 23/24-25/26, 27/28; V:
1890/91-93/94, 95/96, 98/99, 1901/02, 03/04-05/06, 07/08, 10/11, 12/13,
14/15.

Stuart normal college, Stuart, Va.

3520. STUART NORMAL COLLEGE. Annual catalogue . . . with announcement. Lynchburg, Va. [18-?—

8°. (Co-ed.; non-sect.; 18-?)   LC: 1893/94.

Suffolk collegiate institute, Suffolk, Va.

3521. SUFFOLK COLLEGIATE INSTITUTE. Catalogue . . . [n. p., 1870?—

8°. (Col. & prep.; women; non-sect.; 1869)
USE: 1876/77-86/87, 88/89-89/90; **V:** 1874/75-76/77, 78/79, 80/81, 83/84, 87/88-88/89, 93/94-94/95.

Sullins college, Bristol, Va.

3522. SULLINS COLLEGE. Announcements of Sullins college for young ladies . . . Catalogue . . . [Pulaski, Va., 1870?-19—

8°. (Jr. col.; M. E., So.; 1869)
LC: 1902/03; **USE:** 1906/07, 09/10-10/11, 17/18-20/21, 22/23-23/24, 25/26-26/27.

3523. ———. Sullins college, "Virginia park." [Views] [Bristol? Va., 1919?]

32 plates. 4°.   **USE**

Sweet Briar college, Sweet Briar, Va.

3524. SWEET BRIAR COLLEGE. [Announcement] [n. p., 19—

8°.   **H:** 1915/16; **V:** 1905(?)

3525. ———. Bulletin . . . Vol. 1- ; 1917/18— [Sweet Briar, Va., 1917—

8°. **H:** I, 1; II, 2; III, 2; IV, 2; V, 2; VI, 2; VII, 2; VIII, 3; IX, 2; X, 1; XI, 2; (1917-28). **NYP:** II, 2 (1919). **USE:** IX, 1 (1925).

3526. ———. [Prospectus and] views. [Lynchburg? 1904]

2 v. in 1. plates. 8°.   **BP**

3527. ———. Requirements for admission. Sweet Briar institute. Sweet Briar, Amherst County, Virginia. 1st ed. [n. p.] 1905.

20 p. 8°.   **BP, V**
2d ed., 1906: 21 p.   **LC, V**

3528. ———. Sweet Briar institute. [n. p., 1904?]

15, [1] p. 8°.   **LC**
Descriptive pamphlet, sketching the history, equipment, policy, etc., of the institution.

3529. SWEET BRIAR COLLEGE. Views. Sweet Briar institute. [n. p., 1906?]

1 p. l., 17 plates. 8°.　　　　　　　　　　　　　　　　　**LC**
Ed. of 1901.　　　　　　　　　　　　　　　　　　　　　**NYP**
Eds. of [1904?] and 1906.　　　　　　　　　　　　　　**USE**
Ed. of [n. d.]　　　　　　　　　　　　　　　　　　　　**V**

3530. ———. Year book. 1st ; 1906/07— [Lynchburg, Va., 1906—

8°. (Women; non-sect.; 1901)
Founded as Sweet Briar institute; includes also Sweet Briar academy, the preparatory dept.
BP: 1906/07; **H:** 1909/10-12/13, 14/15-15/16, 17/18-28/29; **LC:** 1906/07-08/09, 18/19; **NYP:** 1911/12-12/13, 15/16; **USE:** 1907/08-27/28; **V:** 1906/07, 08/09-16/17, 18/19-19/20, 21/22-23/24, 25/26-28/29.

Tazewell college, Tazewell, Va.

3531. TAZEWELL COLLEGE. Annual catalogue . . . with announcements. Tazewell, Va. [1891?-19—

8°. (Col. & prep.; co-ed.; non-sect.; 1891)　　　　**LC:** 1897/98.

Union theological seminary, Richmond, Va.

3532. DABNEY, ROBERT L. Syllabus and notes of the course of systematic and polemic theology, taught in Union theological seminary, Virginia. Published by the students. Richmond, Shepperson & Graves, 1871.

vi, 303, 323 p. 8°.　　　　　　　　　　　　　　　　**LC, V**

3533. [429] [McCORMICK, CYRUS H.] [Personal papers of the Cyrus H. McCormick family, 1865-*ca.* 1910]

Includes ms. letters, notes, etc., regarding affairs in Union theological seminary during the reconstruction period.

3534. UNION THEOLOGICAL SEMINARY. . . . Bulletin . . . [1st ser., 190-?-19-?] 2d ser., vol. 1- ; July, 1923— Richmond, Va. [190-?—

16°.-8°. quarterly.
V: Nov., 1907; Jan., Nov., 08; Jan., Mar., 12. 2d ser.: I, 1, 4; II, 2, 5-6; III, 3; IV, 1-3; (1923-27).

3535. ———. . . . . Catalogue . . . Richmond [etc., 18-?-19—

8°. (Men; Presbyt.; 1812)
Founded at Hampden-Sidney, Va.
H: 1901/02-07/08, 09/10-19/20, 22/23, 24/25, 26/27; **McC:** 1877/78; **V:** 1869/70-70/71, 73/74-1922/23.

3536. ———. Centennial general catalogue of the trustees, officers, professors and alumni of Union theological seminary in Virginia, 1807-1907. Ed. by Walter W. Moore and Tilden Scherer. Richmond, Va., Whittet & Shepperson [1908]

189 p. front., plates, ports. 8°.   **LC, USE, V, WM**

Based on a former general catalogue comp. by Rev. Benjamin M. Smith (1884), before the removal of the seminary from Hampden-Sidney to Richmond.

3537. ———. A general catalogue of the officers and alumni . . . 1823/24-1883/84 . . . Baltimore, Sun, 1884.

92 p. 8°.   **V**

3538. ———. General catalogue of the trustees, officers, professors and alumni of Union theological seminary in Virginia, 1807-1924. Ed. by Walter W. Moore, William R. Miller, and John A. Lacy. Richmond, Whittet & Shepperson, 1924.

203 p. 8°.   **V**

3539. ———. Septuagesimal celebration of Union theological seminary in Virginia. 1824-1894. Richmond, Whittet & Shepperson, 1894.

76 p. 8°.   **V**

University of Virginia, Charlottesville, Va.

3540. ALDERMAN, EDWIN A. [Addresses, essays, etc., of President Edwin Anderson Alderman in the University of Virginia. Charlottesville, etc., 1888-1928]

11 v. of bound pamphlets. 8°.   **VU**

3541. ———. Freedom of the mind. Address . . . to the graduating class, finals of 1927, University of Virginia . . . [Charlottesville? 1927]

[4] p. 8°.   **V**

3542. ———. Magnanimitas. Address . . . to the graduating classes, finals of 1926, University of Virginia . . . [Charlottesville, Michie, 1926]

[4] p. illus. 8°.   **V**

3543. ———, *et al.* "An alumnus is a devoted son of a good mother"; definition by Edwin A. Alderman [and] an elaboration, by Tom

Williamson, '08.   Pub. by the Alumni secretary's office, University
of Virginia, May, 1916.   [University, Va., 1916]
[4] p. 8°.   V

3544. Bayard, Thomas F.   Address . . . before the literary societies of the University of Virginia, at Charlottesville, Va., . . .
July 2, 1873.   [Charlottesville, Chronicle, 1873?]
23 p. 8°.   VU

3545. Benedict, Charles J.   Class poem, University of Virginia,
1916.   [n. p., 1916]
16 p. 16°.   V
A sonnet series.

3546. Bruce, William C.   Mr. Lodge and his distribution of ability
in the U. S.   Address before the Society of alumni of the University of Virginia.   Charlottesville, Chronicle, 1893.
26 p. 8°.   LC, V, VU

3547. Buchanan, B. F.   An abstract of the letters relating to Mr.
George W. Miles, in connection with the presidency of the University of Virginia.   Prepared by Mr. B. F. Buchanan, chairman of a
committee appointed by the alumni of the University residing in
Smyth County, Virginia.   [Roanoke, Va., Stone, n. d.]
26 p. 8°.   V

3548. Dabney, Richard H.   University of Virginia . . . [New
York? 1897?]
[12] p. illus. (incl. ports.) 4°.   BP, LC, NYP, V, VU
Description of the University, its plant and system of education in
the 'nineties, by a member of the faculty.

3549. [Doswell, Sallie J., et al.]   Guide to the University of Virginia, by Sallie J. Doswell and John S. Patton.   [n. p., 19-?]
56 p. illus., diagr. 8°.   VU
Advertisements in back.

3550. ———.   Installation of the first president of the University of
Virginia, Dr. E. A. Alderman, April 13, 1905.   [n. p., n. d.]
72, [10] p. illus. 8°.   H, V, VU
Programme of installation, addresses, etc.

3551. Dudley, Thomas U.   An address before the Society of alumni
of the University of Virginia, July 2, 1879, by the Rt. Rev.

Thomas U. Dudley. Pub. by order of the Society. Charlottesville, Chronicle, 1879.

28 p. 8°.   V, VU

"Freedom" and "thoroughness", the watchwords of the University, and their significance to her students.

3552. FENNER, CHARLES E. Old faiths, true faiths. A plea for the commonplace. An address delivered before the Society of alumni of the University of Virginia . . . June 30, 1886 . . . Pub. by the Society . . . Lynchburg, Bell, 1886.

19 p. 8°.   VU

3553. FITZHUGH, THOMAS. Our alma mater in Texas and the Southwest. A study made at the request of the Bulletin committee of the University of Virginia . . . Lynchburg, Va., Bell, 1897.

15 p. 4°.   VU

Activity of Virginia alumni in the Southwest, with an alphabetical list by states.

3554. FONTAINE, WILLIAM M. Introductory lecture by Wm. M. Fontaine, M. A., professor of geology and natural history, University of Virginia; with a short account of the Lewis Brooks' museum of natural history. Charlottesville, Va., Chronicle, 1879.

48 p. 8°.   LC, USE, VU

Concerning the origin and founding of the museum, with a description of its collections.

3555. GAITHER, FRANCES O. The shadow of the builder, by Frances O. J. Gaither, the centennial pageant of the University of Virginia, as presented on the night of June first, 1921. [Charlottesville, Va., Surber Arundale, *ca.* 1921]

36 p. 8°.   LC, USE, V, VU

3556. [GARNETT, JAMES M.] . . . The elective system of the University of Virginia. [n. p., 1886?]

17 p. 8°. (Reprint from *Andover review,* Apr., 1886)

                                              BP, H, LC, NYP, VU

Signed: James M. Garnett.

Sketch of the organization and machinery of the University, showing how the elective system functions; a valuable summary of this system in the 'eighties.

3557. GRAVES, JOHN T. "The reign of the demagogue." Delivered before the literary societies of the University of Virginia, June 15,

1893 . . . Published by the Washington and Jefferson societies. [Charlottesville] Chronicle, 1893.

31 p. 8°.   **LC, VU**
Exemplifies the oratory of the literary society during the 'nineties.

3558. HERBERT, HILARY A. An address delivered before the Society of alumni of the University of Virginia . . . June 29, 1887 . . . Pub. by . . . order of the Society of alumni. Lynchburg, Bell, 1887.

15 p. 8°.   **VU**
Contains some notes on the University after 1865.

3559. HOLLIDAY, FREDERICK W. The higher education, the hope of American republicanism. Annual address delivered before the Society of alumni of the University of Virginia, June 29, 1876 . . . Winchester [Va.] Times, 1876.

52 p. 12°.   **V, VU**

3560. HORNER, FREDERICK. Autographs of the University of Virginia, 1892-93 . . . New York, Moss, 1892.

30 p. incl. front., illus. ports. 8°.   **LC, VU, WM**
Description of the University, its organizations, income, scholarships, etc., with portraits of professors and officials. First pub. in 1850.

3561. [HOUGH, THEODORE] Supplementary statement to special bulletin of medical education at the University of Virginia, by Theodore Hough, acting-dean, Dept. of medicine. Dec. 1, 1916. [n. p., 1916?]

[4] p. 8°.   **VU**

3562. HUNT, SAMUEL F. Conscience in public life. An address delivered before the Washington and Jefferson literary societies of the University of Virginia, on commencement day . . . July 3, 1879. Charlottesville, Chronicle, 1880.

30 p. 8°.   **VU**

3563. HUNTER, ROBERT M. Address to the alumni of the University of Virginia at Charlottesville, by Hon. R. M. T. Hunter on Wednesday, June 30, 1875. Pub. by request of the Society of alumni. Richmond, Goode, 1875.

17 p. 8°.   **NYP, USE, V, VU**
The principles on which Jefferson founded the University, and a plea that they be upheld.

3564. JOHNSON, JOHN L. To every loyal son of the University of Virginia. [Prospectus of the University memorial] Baltimore, 1872.

33 p. port. 8°.
List of University men who lost their lives in the Civil war; a preliminary publication to a planned "Memorial volume."

3565. KENT, CHARLES W. Literature and life: being the lecture delivered upon the inauguration of the work of the Linden-Kent memorial school of English literature in the University of Virginia . . . Richmond, Whittet & Shepperson, 1894.

32 p. 8°.   V, VU
"Historical note on the study of English at the University of Virginia," signed W. M. T., p. [27]-32.

3566. LILE, WILLIAM M. Notes to [vol.] 1 Minor's Institutes, (4th ed.) Prepared for the use of the students of the junior class at the University of Virginia . . . [Charlottesville, Va., Michie] 1899.

2 p. l., 299, x p. 8°.   LC

3567. ———. Study of cases, head-noting; supplementary to Wambaugh's Study of cases. Some practical hints for the beginner in the making of a brief, prepared for the use of the students of the Law school of the University of Virginia . . . 3d ed., 1927. [University, Va.] Virginia law review association [ca. 1927]

53 p. 8°.   LC

3568. LUCAS, DAN B. Semi-centennial ode . . . before the Society of alumni, of the University of Virginia . . . Charlottesville, Chronicle, 1875.

7 p. 8°.   VU

3569. McKIM, RANDOLPH H. The relations of the state to the university. An address delivered before the Society of the alumni of the University of Virginia, June 15, 1898, by Rev. Randolph H. McKim, D.D., of Washington, D. C. [Charlottesville, Va., University of Virginia] 1898.

36 p. 8°. (University of Virginia. *Alumni bulletin*, V, June, 1898)
LC, V, VU
The significance of the University in the life of the state; with some reference to contemporary conditions.

3570. MALLET, JOHN W. Chemistry applied to the arts. A lecture delivered before the University of Virginia, May 30, 1868 . . . Lynchburg, Schaffter & Bryant, 1868.

38 p. 8°.   LC, V

3571. MAPHIS, CHARLES G., *et al.,* comp. "Songs" of the University of Virginia summer school, by Charles G. Maphis and Aden L. Fillmore. [n. p., *ca.* 1915]

53, [2], p. music. 4°.   VU

3572. MORROW, JOHN A. Virginia, hail, all hail! An alma mater song of Virginia. Pub. by the Alumni association of the University of Virginia. University, Va., 1923.

3 p. music. 4°.   VU

3573. NAPTON, WILLIAM B. An address delivered before the Society of alumni of the University of Virginia, June 29, 1871. Charlottesville, Chronicle, 1871.

30 p. 8°.   V

3574. NICOLL, DE LANCEY. Address delivered to the graduates of the University of Virginia, at the commencement exercises on June 14th, 1916 . . . [n. p., n. d.]

15 p. 8°.   VU

3575. [PAGE, JAMES M.] Ninth annual letter to the alumni [of the University of Virginia] [n. p., 1912?]

19 p. 8°. (Reprint from *Alumni bulletin,* Apr., 1912)   VU
Signed: James M. Page.
Outline of progress and prospects of the university.

3576. ———. Per capita cost of educating students at the proposed woman's college. [Charlottesville, Michie, n. d.]

10 p. 8°.   VU
In favor of the proposed woman's college at the University of Virginia rather than elsewhere.

3577. ———. The successful student. By J. M. Page, dean. [n. p., 19-?]

[4] p. 8°.   VU
Advice to freshmen entering the University of Virginia.

3578. ———. The unsuccessful student . . . [n. p., 19-?]

[4] p. 8°.   VU
Advice to freshmen in the University of Virginia.

3579. [211] PAGE, JOHN R. Report of John R. Page, . . . professor of agriculture, zoölogy and botany, in the University of Virginia. Charlottesville, 1885.

3580. PATTON, JOHN S., *et al.* The University of Virginia: glimpses of its past and present . . . Prepared by John S. Patton and Sallie J. Doswell. [Lynchburg, Va., Bell, *ca.* 1900]

    96 p. illus. (incl. ports.) 8°.   **H, LC, USE, V, VU**
    Ed. of [1900?]: 82 p., 1 l.   **NYP**
    "Primarily designed to afford information," this volume contains a description of the buildings and campus, with bits of history interwoven, and notes on the faculty and student life.

3581. PENDLETON, GEORGE H. Address . . . before the literary societies of the University of Virginia, at Charlottesville, Virginia, . . . June 29, 1870. Charlottesville, Intelligencer, 1870.

    18 p. 8°.   **VU**

3582. PETERS, WILLIAM E. Outlines of lectures, delivered to the Latin classes of the University of Virginia . . . [Charlottesville, Va., Anderson, 1885]

    2 p. l., 335 numb. l. 4°.   **LC**
    Eds. of 1884 and 1894.   **VU**

3583. ———. Outlines of lectures, delivered to the senior Latin class of the University of Virginia. Printed by J. B. Lippincott for Henry L. Massie, University of Virginia [1875]

    173 p. 8°.   **V, VU**

3584. POTT, WILLIAM S. The honor system from a student's point of view. [n. p., n. d.]

    55 p. 8°. (Reprint from *Alumni bulletin,* Apr., 1913)   **VU**
    How the honor system functions in the University of Virginia.

3585. PRESTON, JOHN S. Virginia. Address before the Washington and Jefferson literary societies of the University of Virginia. June 30, 1868 . . . Lynchburg, Schaffter & Bryant, 1868.

    25 p. 8°.   **VU**

3586. QUARLES, W[ILLIAM] A. Oration delivered before the Society of alumni of the University of Virginia, by Gen'l W. A. Quarles, of Tennessee, June 27, 1872. Subject—True manhood. Clarksville, Tobacco leaf book and job office, 1872.

    28 p. 8°.   **LC**
    The declamation shed some light upon social and intellectual interests in the early 'seventies.

3587. RIVES, WILLIAM C., jr.   An address delivered before the Society of alumni of the University of Virginia, July 1, 1869 . . . Pub. by order of the Society. Richmond, Gary, Clemmitt & Jones, 1869.

34 p. 8°.   **LC, VU**
On "the relation of recent changes to the interests and the duties of the people of Virginia."

3588. ――――.   William Barton Rogers . . .   An address delivered before the Society of the alumni of the University of Virginia, on commencement day, June 27, 1883 . . . Cambridge, University press, 1883.

32 p. 8°.   **VU**

3589. ROBINSON, MORGAN P.   The burning of the rotunda; being a sketch of the partial destruction of the University of Virginia, 1895 . . . Centennial ed. Richmond, Va., Mitchell [ca. 1921]

30 p. incl. front. plates. 8°.   **H, LC, NYP, USE, V, VU, WM**
Ed. of 1905.   **H, LC**
Pub. originally in *University of Virginia magazine*, Oct., 1905 **[4011]**
Written the night after the disaster by an eye-witness and participant in fighting the fire. An interesting and authentic account.

3590. RODMAN, WALTER S.   A further report concerning salaries and salary scales at the University of Virginia, supplementing the resolutions of May 1, 1928. [n. p.] 1929.

57 p. tables. 8°.   **VU**

3591. [SMITH, C. ALPHONSO]   The student body at the University of Virginia. [n. p., 19-?]

8 p. 12°.   **VU**
Characteristic traits of the student body.

3592. SOUTHALL, JAMES C.   Opening of the Lewis Brooks museum at the University of Virginia, June 27th, 1878. Address on man's age in the world. By Jas. C. Southall . . . With introductory remarks of Hon. A. H. H. Stuart, rector. Richmond, Printed by order of the Board of visitors, 1878.

58, [2] p. 8°.   **H, LC, NYP, USG, V, VU, WM**
Introductory remarks concerning Lewis Brooks and the donation of the museum.

3593. STEVENSON, JOHN W.   An address delivered before the Society

of the alumni of the University of Virginia, June 30, 1870 . . . .
Pub. by order of the Society. Charlottesville, Chronicle, 1870.

20 p. 8°.   V, WM
Reveals indirectly something of the social turmoil through which the
state was passing.

3594. STUART, ALEXANDER H. The recent revolution; its causes and
its consequences, and the duties and responsibilities which it has
imposed on the people, and especially the young men, of the South.
Address of Alexander H. H. Stuart. Delivered before the literary
societies of the University of Virginia, June 29, 1866. Richmond,
Examiner, 1866.

26 p. 8°.   LC, V

3595. SWANN, THOMAS. Address . . . before the alumni of the
University of Virginia, July 3d, 1873. Pub. by the Society of the
alumni. Charlottesville, Jeffersonian, 1874.

22 p. 8°.   V
Reveals the effect of the Civil war on Virginia.

3596. THORNTON, WILLIAM M. The genesis of the honour system.
An address before the Council and students of the Marion military
institute . . . [n. p., 1904?]

20 p. plates (incl. front.) 8°.   V, VU
Address delivered Apr. 13, 1904, on the development of the honor system at the University of Virginia.

3597. ———. Honour system at the University of Virginia in origin
and use. [n. p., n.d.]

18 p. 8°. (Reprint from *Sewanee review,* Nov., 1906)   VU

3598. THURMAN, ALLEN G. Address delivered . . . before the
literary societies of the University of Virginia, at Charlottesville,
Va. . . . June 26th, 1872. Washington, Polkinhorn, 1872.

19 p. 8°.   BP, LC, VU

3599. TUNSTALL, ROBERT B. The duty of the state to higher education . . . Published by Central committee, Institutions of
higher education in Virginia, Richmond, Va. Richmond [19-?]

8 p. 8°.   V
With special reference to the University of Virginia.

3600. UNIVERSITY OF VIRGINIA. Addresses commemorative of James

L. Cabell, delivered at the University of Virginia, July 1, 1890.
Pub. by the faculty. Charlottesville, Va., Chronicle & Brand, 1890.

40 p. 8°.   **V, VU**

Addresses by W. S. Forbes, G. T. Harrison, and Stephen Smith, the
last dealing particularly with Dr. Cabell's scientific work and connection
with the National board of health.

3601. University of Virginia. Addresses on the honor system at
the University of Virginia. [Charlottesville, Michie, 1914?]

55 p. 8°.   **V**

3602. ———. Alphabetical list of alumni of the University of Virginia. [Charlottesville? 1910]

139 p. 8°.   **VU, WM**

3603. ———. [Barbour-Page foundation lectures, 1907— New
York, 1909—

8°. Lectures of 1907, 11, 12, 24, 29 not pub.

Silas W. Mitchell, *Some literary reminiscences,* 1907 (not pub.). Basil L.
Gildersleeve, *Hellas and Hesperia; or, The vitality of Greek studies in America,* 1908 (1909). Charles W. Eliot, *The conflict between individualism and
collectivism in a democracy,* 1909 (1910). Thomas R. Lounsbury, *The early
literary career of Robert Browning,* 1910 (1911). William H. Welch, *The
development of medicine as a science,* 1911 (not pub.). James Bryce, *Ancient
democracy,* 1912 (not pub.). Arthur T. Hadley, *Undercurrents in American
politics,* 1914 (1915). William H. Taft, *The presidency, its duties, its powers, its opportunities, and its limitations,* 1915 (1916). Archibald C. Coolidge,
The origins of the Triple Alliance, 1916 (1917). John H. Wigmore, *Problems of law, its past, present and future,* 1917 (1920). William R. Thayer,
The art of biography, 1920 (1920). Thomas N. Page, *Dante and his influence,* 1922 (1922). John H. Finley, *The making and the mission of America,* 1924 (not pub.). Alexander F. Whyte, *Asia in the twentieth century,*
1926 (1926). Alfred N. Whitehead, *Symbolism, its meaning and effect,* 1927
(1927). Walter Lippmann, *American inquisitors, a commentary on Dayton and Chicago,* 1928 (1928). William E. Dodd, *The statecraft of Woodrow Wilson,* 1929 (not pub.).

3604. ———. Catalogue . . . 1825-19— Charlottesville, Va.
[etc., 1838-19—

plates, plans. 12°.-8°. (State; men; 1819)

None pub., 1862-65.

Issued as no. of *University of Virginia record,* 1907—

Title varies: Catalogue of the officers and matriculates; Catalogue of
the officers and students; Annual announcements, with a catalogue of
the officers and students.

BP: 1865/66-74/75, 76/77, 79/80-81/82, 92/93-93/94, 96/97-97/98,
99/1900-12/13, 26/27-27/28; **H:** 1865/66-72/73, 75/76-1913/14, 15/16-

17/18, 20/21-21/22, 23/24, 26/27-27/28; **LC**: 1865/66-74/75, 76/77-86/87, 88/89-1928/29; **NYP**: 1866/67-98/99, 1900/01-18/19, 21/22-27/28; **USE**: 1865/66-77/78, 79/80-1927/28; **V**: 1865/66-83/84, 85/86-97/98, 99/1900-28/29; **VU**: 1865/66-1928/29; **WM**: 1901/02-05/06, 09/10-12/13, 14/15-17/18.

3605. ———. [Catalogue of the Austin library. 188-?]

113 p. 4°. MSS. **VU**

3606. ———. Catalogue of exhibits at the Jamestown ter-centennial exposition, 1607-1907. Charlottesville, University, 1907.

15 p. 8°. **V, VU**

3607. ———. The centennial of the University of Virginia, 1819-1921 ; the proceedings of the centenary celebration, May 31 to June 3, 1921 . . . New York & London, Putnam, 1922.

xi, 235 p. front., plates, ports., facsims. 4°.
Editorial committee: John C. Metcalf, chairman, Fiske Kimball, Bruce Williams, Robert H. Webb, James S. Wilson.
Includes programmes, speeches, and text of centennial pageant.

3608. ———. Ceremonies of the alumni of the University of Virginia who served in the World war in dedication of a tablet memorial to their comrades who died in service. The Rotunda, June 1st at 3 o'clock, 1921. [n. p., 1921]

16 p. front. 8°. **H, VU**

3609. ———. . . . Circular of information. [Charlottesville, Va., 19—

8°. (*University of Virginia record,* new ser., II-VI)
LC: 1915/16-17/18; **NYP, V, VU**: 1915/16-17/18, 19/20-20/21.

3610. ———. . . . Courses passed and degrees conferred . . . Charlottesville, Va., 19—

8°. (*University of Virginia record,* II-VII; new ser., I-III)
LC: 1916; **NYP**: 1906; **V, VU**: 1908-16.

3611. ———. Decennial catalogue of visitors, faculty, officers, and students, 1874-1884. Richmond, Whittet & Shepperson, 1889.

93 p. 8°. **NYP, VU**

3612. ———. Deed of trust. University of Virginia to Virginia trust company. [n. p., 1896]

29 p. 8°. **VU**

3613. ———. The delayed pledging agreement, being a statement

of the stand of thirteen fraternities with regard to pledging first
year men. University of Virginia. [n. p., n.d.]

[10] p. 12°.   VU

3614. UNIVERSITY OF VIRGINIA. Facts and conclusions concerning
the proposed co-ordinate college for women. [n. p., 191-?]

8 p. 8°.   VU

Arguments in favor of the proposed woman's college.

3615. ———. [Faculty] correspondence respecting the admission of
women to the University of Virginia. [n. p., 1894?]

31 p. 8°.   VU

3616. ———. [Fifteenth amendment debated by Virginia and Penn-
sylvania] Cambridge, Mass., 1905.

p. 9-10. 8°. (In *Both sides* [intercollegiate debating journal] I, 1,
Jan., 1905)   VU

The brief of each team.

3617. ———. Graduating exercises [programme] . . . 3 June
1921. [n. p., 1921]

[7] p. 8°.   V

3618. ———. [Hymns for general assembly and vesper service.
n. p., n. d.]

15 p. music. 8°.   VU

3619. ———. List of books, nucleus for the library of Madison
Hall . . . 1905. [Tarrytown, Tarrytown news print., 1905]

31 p. 8°.   VU

3620. ———. [Miscellaneous announcements, programmes, etc.
Charlottesville, 18-?-19-?]

var. pag. & sizes.   LC

3621. ———. . . . . The one hundredth anniversary of the founding of the University of Virginia, May 31st to June 3d [1921.
Programme of centennial exercises. Boston, Merrymount press,
1921]

[23] p. 4°.   V

Programme and invitation bound together.

3622. ———. Phelps-Stokes fellowship papers. [Charlottesville,
Michie, 1915—

8 v. 8°.   H, LC, NYP, USL, V, VU

Studies of economic, political, and social conditions among the Ne-

groes of Virginia. See items **278, 1131, 1388, 1825, 1846, 2342, 2351.**
Include also *Lectures and addresses on the Negro in the South,* by A. H.
Stone, U. B. Phillips, *et al.*

3623. ———. Programme of exercises on the public day, Wednesday, June 27, 1888 [and list of students receiving distinctions, certificates of proficiency, diplomas as graduates, professional degrees,
and academic degrees] [n. p., 1888]

6, [2] p. 8°. **V**

3624. ———. The Raven book. Vol. I . . . University of
Virginia. [Philadelphia, Wright] 1905.

74 p. illus. 4°. **VU**
Origin and organization, objects and aims, of the Raven society;
roster of the Society and biographical sketches.

3625. ———. Register of certificates issued by the University of
Virginia in favor of Thomas Jefferson Randolph, trustee for Mrs.
Martha Randolph. Also receipts for interest on stock issued by
the University in favor of Mrs. Martha Randolph. 1837-81.

MSS. f°. **V**

3626. ———. A sketch of the University of Virginia. Richmond,
Va., Whittet & Shepperson, 1885.

42 p. 8°.
Description of the university organization, discipline, system of
courses, buildings and equipment, endowments and annual income, and
necessary expenses of a student for 9 months.

3627. ———. A sketch of the University of Virginia, together with
a catalogue of the professors and instructors, the graduates in law
and medicine, and the masters and bachelors of arts, etc., since the
foundation of the institution. Charlottesville, Chronicle, 1880.

66 p. 8°. **H, V**

3628. ———. Some facts about the University of Virginia. [Char-
lottesville, Michie] 1916.

11 p. 8°. **VU**
Notes on student enrollment, state support, living expenses, etc.

3629. ———. Some objections to the proposed co-ordinate woman's
college at the University of Virginia. Lynchburg, Va., Dulaney-
Boatwright [1914]

64 p. 8°. **LC**
Reprint of letters, editorials, and articles published in Virginia news-

papers and university magazines, in opposition to the proposed woman's college; with counter-proposals to afford higher education for women in the state.

3630. UNIVERSITY OF VIRGINIA. A statement of accomplishment and of recent growth. Charlottesville, University, 1907.

21 p. charts. 8°.   H, NYP, V, VU

Reprint in part from *The University of Virginia in the life of the nation* [3642]

3631. ———. . . . Statement of conditions and needs of the university. [1918] Charlottesville, Va., The University [1917]

23 p. 8°. (*Universtiy of Virginia record.* Extension series, III, 4)

USE, V, VU

3632. ———. A statement of growth. Charlottesville, Va., The University, 1906.

unp. 8°. (Its *Alumni bulletin,* new ser., VI, 2)   NYP, V, VU

3633. ———. A statement relative to the establishment of a church at the University of Virginia, with special reference to the care of the Episcopal students at that institution. Charlottesville, Va., 1908.

16 p. illus. (front.) 8°.   VU

3634. ———. Student life at the University of Virginia. [Charlottesville, Michie, 1927?]

14 p. illus. (incl. ports.) 8°.   USE, VU

Running title: The University and the new student.

3635. ———. Students of the University of Virginia. A semi-centennial catalogue with brief biographical sketches. Baltimore, Harvey [*ca.* 1878]

[167] p. 4°.   USE, V, VU

3636. ———. Training for war at the University of Virginia. [Charlottesville, Michie, 1917?]

8 p. illus. 8°.   VU

"War courses" offered at the University.

3637. ———. The university and the student. [n. p., 192-?]

14 p. illus. 4°.   VU

Student life and activities at the University.

3638. ———. University location of medical schools; collected papers, University of Virginia. [Charlottesville, Va., 1922?]

[465] p. illus., plates. 8°.   LC, V, VU

Papers on medical education in Virginia, the university hospital, financial aspects of the location of the medical school, clinical aspects, attitude of the medical profession in Virginia, etc.

3639. ———. The University of Virginia and medical education. 1. A communication from President Alderman . . . 2. Resolutions of the Board of visitors, passed on June 23, 1921. [n. p., 1921?]

 16 p. 8°.   V

3640. ———. The University of Virginia centennial endowment fund. [n. p., 1921]

 32 p. illus. 8°.   V

3641. ———. University of Virginia honor code. 1924. [n. p., 1924]

 1 l. 4°.   VU

3642. ———. The University of Virginia in the life of the nation; academic addresses delivered on the occasion of the installation of Edwin Anderson Alderman as president of the University of Virginia, Apr. 13th, year of Our Lord 1905. For the sister universities: East: Archibald Cary Coolidge. North: Nicholas Murray Butler. South: Walter Barnard Hill. West: Richard Henry Jesse. Inaugural address: Edwin Anderson Alderman. [Charlottesville? Va., 1905?]

 121 p. 8°.

3643. ———. University of Virginia in the service of the republic . . . a partial roster of eminent alumni. [Charlottesville, Va., Surber-Arundale, 1921?]

 31, [1] p. 12°.   L'C, V, VU

3644. ———. . . . The University of Virginia in women's education. [Charlottesville? Va., 1923?]

 7 p. 8°.   USE

3645. ———. University of Virginia. Photo-gravures. [Charlottesville? *ca.* 1895]

 2 p. l., 20 plates (incl. ports.) 12½ x 17 cm.   LC
 Pictures of the buildings, the faculty, and of Monticello.

3646. ———. The University of Virginia record . . . Vol. 1-7, 1907-13/14; new ser., vol. 1- ; 1914/15— Charlottesville, Va., The University, 1907—

 8°. monthly, during school year.
 BP: I (1907/08). H: new ser., X, 5; XI, 5, 7; XII, 4-8; XIII, 4, 7;

XIV, 5; (1924-28). **LC**: I-VII; new ser., I-XV (incompl.). **NYP**:
I; II, 1-2, 4; III, 1-5; IV, 2-5; V, 1-3, 5; VI, 1-5; VII, 2-5. New ser.,
I, 1-8; II, 3; III, 3; IV, 4; V, 4; VIII, 4, 10; IX-XV (incompl.). **V**:
I, 1-9; II, 1, 3-4; III, 2-5; IV, 1-5; V, 3; VI, 1; VII, 2-5. New ser., I,
1-2, 7, 9; III, 2-3, 6; IV, 1-6, 8; V, 1, 3, 5-6; VI, 1-2, 4-5, 9; VII, 1-2, 4;
VIII, 1-2, 5; IX, 1-2, 5-6; 9-10, 12; X, 1-2, 5-6; XI, 1, 3-4, 7; XII, 1 &
suppl., 2-8; XIII-XV. **VU**: I-VII; new ser., I-XV.

3647. UNIVERSITY OF VIRGINIA. The University of Virginia record.
Extension series. Vol. 1-   ; Sept., 1915—   Charlottesville, Va.,
The University, 1915—

  8°. monthly.
  Includes the Economic and social surveys of Virginia counties, ed.
by Wilson Gee, 1922—   **[1834]**

  H: I, 5; II, 1, 3-4, 6-10; III, 1, 3; IV, 1-5, 7; V, 1-2; VII, 2; VIII,
7; X, 11-12; XI, 5; XII, 1, 12; (1916-28). **LC**: I-XII (incompl.).
NYP: II, 3; X, 3, 8; XI, 5, 8, 12; XII, 5-7. **USE**: I, 1-2, 4; II, 1, 3-4,
6-9; III, 1-4; IV, 3-7; V, 2, 4, 7-8, 10; VI, 1-3, 5-6; VII, 1-4, 6, 8; VIII,
4-6, 8; IX, 1, 3-4, 9, 11; X, 1-6, 8, 10; XI, 5, 7, 10; XII, 1, 5-7, 11; XIII,
7; XIV, 7. **USL**: II, 3; VII, 2; IX, 10; X, 10, 12; XI, 8; XII, 5, 7;
XIII, 9. **V**: I, 1-7; II, 1, 3-10; III, 1-4; IV, 1-5; V, 1-2, 4, 6, 8, 10; VI,
1-3, 6; VII, 1-3, 6, 8-9; VIII, 2, 4-12; IX, 1-12; X-XI; XII, 1-8, 11-12.
VU: I-XIII.

3648. ———. Why should I go to college? [Charlottesville, Va.,
Michie, 1917?]

  8 p. illus. 8°.   **VU**
  On the relation of college training to the World war.

3649. ———. ALUMNI. The centennial and alumni endowment
funds . . . [Charlottesville, Michie, n. d.]

  14, [2] p. 16°.   **V**

3650. ———. ———. . . . . Charter, constitution, etc. [of the Society of alumni of the University of Virginia] Charlottesville,
Chronicle, 1875.

  p. [8]-20. 8°. (In D. B. Lucas, *Semi-centennial ode* . . . **[3568]**)
                                                                    VU

3651. ———. ———. A Christmas report [by Lewis D. Crenshaw,
alumni secretary. Dec. 22, 1916, n. p., n. d.]

  16 p. 8°.   **VU**
  Report on the activity of the Alumni association.

3652. ———. ———. Circular no. 2 of the Executive committee of the Society of alumni of the University of Virginia, with a sketch of its history. Charlottesville, Chronicle, 1873.

19 p. 8°.   NYP, VU

3653. ——. ——. . . . Class of 1908. [Annual record] 1st- ; 1909— Charlottesville, Michie, 1909—

12°.   VU: 1st-4th (1909-12).

3654. ——. ——. Class of 1910 of the University of Virginia after three years. April, 1913. [Charlottesville, Michie, 1913?]

38 p. 12°.   V, VU
List of class members and letters from many of them concerning their activities since graduation.

3655. ——. ——. Class of 1910 of the University of Virginia after five years . . . 1915. [Charlottesville, Michie 1915]

12°.   V, VU

3656. ——. ——. Class of 1910 of the University of Virginia after six years . . . 1916. [Charlottesville, Michie, 1916]

95 p. 12°.   V, VU

3657. ——. ——. . . . Class of 1911 of the University of Virginia [Fourth annual record] [n. p., 1915]

50 p. 16°.   V

3658. ——. ——. . . . Class of 1912 of the University of Virginia. [Second annual record] April, 1914. [n. p., 1914]

75 p. 16°.   V

3659. ——. ——. Endowment of the University of Virginia. Circular of the Executive committee of the Society of alumni . . . Charlottesville, Chronicle, 1872.

8 p. 8°.   V, VU
Proposal of alumni to raise an endowment for scholarships and professorships. Report dated Nov. 15, 1872.

3660. ——. ——. Guide map of the University of Virginia and chronological history of Albemarle County. Arranged and distributed by McLane Tilton, secretary [of] the Alumni association . . . [Charlottesville, Michie, 1926?]

sheet. 47 x 32 cm.   V, VU

3661. ——. ——. Law class of 1902. Names, addresses, and occupations. Nashville, Tenn., Pub. by the secretary [1903]

16 p. 16°.   VU

3662. UNIVERSITY OF VIRGINIA. ALUMNI. Medical alumni association of the University of Virginia. Directory, April, 1917. Pub. by the Alumni secretary's office, University of Virginia. [University? Va.] 1917.

104 p. 12°.   **NYP, USE, V, VU**

Geographical list (by states and cities) and alphabetical.

3663. ———. ———. Medical alumni of the University of Virginia, July, 1899.

58 p. MSS. 4°.   **VU**

3664. ———. ———. Medical class of '99 [Record] New Haven, Conn. [etc., 19-?—

12°.-8°.   **VU**: 190-?, 1910.

3665. ———. ———. New York alumni association [Constitution and minutes] 1870.

12 p. MSS. 4°.   **VU**

3666. ———. ———. [Roll of living alumni in positions of distinction with brief allusion to others. Roanoke, Stone, 1904?]

[20] p. folder. 12°.   **V**

3667. ———. ATHLETIC ASSOCIATION, General. Rules governing athletics at the University of Virginia. [n. p., 1912?]

38, [6] p. 12°.   **VU**

3668. ———. BURSAR. Report . . . University, Va. [18-?-19—

8°. annual.

USE: 1913/14, 21/22-22/23; **V**: 1917/18, 22/23-23/24; **VU**: 1909/10-27/28.

3669. ———. CHEMISTRY, School of. Announcement . . . Charlottesville, The University [19—

8°.   **USE**: 1919/20.

3670. ———. ———. Department of industrial chemistry, civil and mining engineering, and agriculture. 1872. Charlottesville, Va., 1872.

8 p. 8°.   **BP**

3671. ———. ———. Notes of work by students of practical chemistry in the laboratory . . . London [187-?-18-?]

8°.   **NYP**: no. 9 (1880).

3672. ———. COLONNADE CLUB. Charter, by-laws, officers, members. April, 1910. [n. p., 1910?]

64 p. 16°. **H**
Ed. of 1911: 71 p. **NYP**

3673. ———. ———. A list of "lost" alumni of the University of Virginia . . . Sept., 1912. [n. p., 1912?]

48 p. 8°. **NYP, V**
Russell Bradford, secretary.

3674. ———. EDUCATION, Dept. of. The Curry memorial department of education. Announcements . . . Charlottesville, The University, 19—

8°. (*University of Virginia record,* new ser., VIII-   ; 1921/22—
USE: 1919/20, 26/27; **V, VU**: 1921/22-27/28.

3675. ———. ENGINEERING, Dept. of. . . . Catalogue . . . Announcements. Charlottesville, Va. [18-?-19—

8°. (*University of Virginia record,* IV-VI; new ser., I-   ; 1910-11—
LC: 1907/08, 14/15-17/18, 19/20, 22/23-28/29; **NYP**: 1889/90, 1914/15, 24/25-26/27; **USE**: 1889/90, 1920/21, 25/26; **V**: 1887/88, 1907/08, 10/11, 13/14, 16/17-28/29; **VU**: 1910/11-28/29.

3676. ———. EXTENSION, Div. of. Announcement of extension courses offered by the University of Virginia . . . Charlottesville, The University, 19—

8°. (*University of Virginia record.* Extension series, XI, 1; XII, 2)
V, VU: 1926/27-27/28.

3677. ———. ———. Announcement of extension courses in Richmond . . . [Richmond? Va., 19—

8°. **V**: 1927.

3678. ———. ———. Annual report, 1925— Charlottesville, The University, 1926—

8°. (*University of Virginia record.* Extension series, XI, 3)
V, VU: 1925/26.

3679. ———. ———. University extension lectures. Charlottesville, The University, 19—

8°. **LC**: 1915/16; **USE**: 1915/16-16/17, 25/27.

3680. ———. ———. The Virginia Institute of citizenship and government, University, Virginia . . . [University, Va., Extension division, 1927]

163 p. 8°. (*University of Virginia record.* Extension series, XI, 12; June, 1927)   **NYP, V, VU**

3681. UNIVERSITY OF VIRGINIA. FACULTY. Annual report of the faculty . . . June 4, 1894. [n. p., 1894?]

20 p. 8°.   **VU**
Includes Report on education of women at the University.

3682. ———. ———. Correspondence respecting the admission of women to the University of Virginia. [1893-94. n. p., n. d.]

31 p. 4°.   **VU**
Letters collected by the Faculty committee from educational leaders in the U. S.

3683. ———. ———. [Faculty committee] minority report on the admission of women to the academic schools. [n. p., 1894?]

4 p. 8°.   **VU**

3684. ———. ———. Report of the Committee of the faculty on the admission of women to the academic schools. [n. p., 1894?]

[7] p. 8°.   **VU**
In favor of admission of women to certain schools in the University.

3685. ———. GRADUATE CLUB. The constitution, amendments and minute book of the Graduate club of the University of Virginia, from May 14, 1900 to [Mar. 15, 1904]

74 p. 4°. MSS.   **VU**

3686. ———. GRADUATE STUDIES, Dept. of. . . . Catalogue . . . Announcements. Charlottesville, Va., 19—

8°. (*University of Virginia record,* VI-VII; new ser., I- ; 1912/13—)
LC: 1914/15-17/18, 26/27-28/29; **NYP:** 1912/13-28/29 (incompl.); **USE:** 1919/20; **V:** 1913/14-28/29 (incompl.); **VU:** 1912/13-28/29.

3687. ———. HIGH SCHOOL DEBATING COMMITTEE OF THE WASHINGTON AND JEFFERSON SOCIETIES. . . . Selected arguments, bibliographies, etc., for the use of the Virginia high school and athletic league, comp. by the High school committee of the Washington and Jefferson literary societies, and ed. by John S. Patton . . . [Charlottesville] The University [1915]

1 p. l., p. [101]-126. 8°. (*University of Virginia record.* Extension series, I, 3; Nov., 1915)   **LC, USE, V, VU**
On compulsory education in Virginia.

3688. ———. HOSPITAL. Annual report. Charlottesville, Va., 19—

8°.   **V**: 1921; **VU**: 1914-20, 23.

3689. ———. ———. SCHOOL FOR NURSES. Circular of information
. . . Charlottesville, Va., 19—

illus. 8°.   **VU**: 1912/13.

3690. ———. INSTITUTE FOR RESEARCH IN THE SOCIAL SCIENCES.
Institute monograph no. 1- University, Va., The Institute, 1927—

tables, diagrs. 8°.

1. Wilson Gee and John J. Corson 3d, *A statistical study of Virginia* (1927)
[3350] 2. Frank W. Hoffer, *Counties in Transition* . . . (1929) **[1840]**
3. Wilson Gee and John J. Corson 3d, *Rural depopulation in certain* . . .
areas of Virginia (1929) **[279]** 4. Charles N. Hulvey and William H.
Wandel, *Life insurance in Virginia* (1929). 5. Lester J. Cappon, *Bibliography of Virginia history since 1865* (1930). 6. Wilson Gee and William
H. Stauffer, *Rural and Urban living standards in Virginia* (1929).
7. Floyd N. House, Frank W. Hoffer, Robert H. Barker, and Charles C.
Rodeffer, *Fort Lewis: a community in transition* (1930). 8. Wylie Kilpatrick, *The government of the Virginia County* (1930). 9. Abraham Berglund, George T. Starnes, and Frank T. de Vyver, *Labor in the industrial
South* (1930).

3691. ———. ———. . . . . Research program, 1927-28— University, Va., University of Virginia [1928—

8°.   **V**: **VU**: 1927/28-28/29.

3692. ———. INSTITUTE OF PUBLIC AFFAIRS. . . . Addresses delivered at the general sessions . . . held at the University of
Virginia, Aug. 8-20, 1927. Charlottesville, 1927.

viii, 251 p. illus. 8°. (Its *Summer quarter bulletin,* I, 8; Oct. 1, 1927
[3720])   **H, V, VU**

3693. ———. ———. . . . . Announcement and program . . .
University, Va., The University, 1927—

illus., 8°. (In its *Summer quarter bulletin,* I, 6; *et seq.*)
                                     H, V, VU : 1927-28.

Programs "designed to advance the popular understanding of current public questions."

3694. ———. JEFFERSON SOCIETY. Constitution and by-laws . . .
As revised and published by order of the Society, Nov., 1927
. . . [n. p.] 1927.

21 p. 16°.   **VU**

3695. University of Virginia. Latin, School of. Bulletin . . . Studies in philology, no. 1-10. Charlottesville, Anderson, 1908- [20?]

10 v. 8°. No more pub.?
BP: IV (1909); H: III-VI, VIII-IX (1909-10, 15, 17); LC,NYP, VU: I-X.

3696. ――――. Law, Dept. of. Catalogue . . . Announcements . . . Charlottesville, Va. [18-?-19―

8°. (*University of Virginia record,* new ser., I- ; 1914/15-)
BP: 1871/72; LC: 1909/10, 14/15-17/18, 19/20-28/29; McC: 1880/81; NYP: 1914/15-28/29 (incompl.); V: 1895/96, 1914/15-28/29 (incompl.); VU: 1914/15-28/29.

3697. ――――. ――――. Catalogue of students, summer law class, 1884. [Charlottesville? 1884?]

[7] p. 8°.   LC

3698. ――――. ――――. Examination for degree. Junior course. June 15, 1875.

MSS. 3 f°.   HL
In the handwriting of John B. Minor and bound with his *Synopsis,* etc.

3699. ――――. ――――. Intermediate examination. Junior class. Feb. 24, 1875.

MSS. 4 f°.   HL
In the handwriting of John B. Minor.

3700. ――――. ――――. Intermediate examination. Senior class. Mar. 23, 1875.

MSS. 4 f°.   HL
In the handwriting of John B. Minor.

3701. ――――. ――――. Summer law lectures. Catalogue [and] announcements for [the following year] Charlottesville, 1899-19―

12°.   LC: 1899/1900.

3702. ――――. ――――. [William H. White foundation lectures] [New York, etc., 1925―

8°. Lectures of 1923/24, 26/27, not pub.   VU
Roscoe Pound, *Codification.* 1923/24. Newton D. Baker, *Progress and the constitution.* 1924/25 (1925). Henry M. Bates, *Modern developments in the law.* 1926/27. Junius Parker, *Some Aspects of French law.* 1927/28 (1928). Samuel Williston, *Some modern tendencies in the law.* 1928/29 (1929).

3703. ———. LEANDER McCORMICK OBSERVATORY. Publications of the Leander McCormick observatory of the University of Virginia . . . Vol. 1-   ; 1883-19— Charlottesville, University press, 1883-19—

plates, tables. 8°.-4°.
Vol. IV issued as *Memoir* of National academy of sciences, XXII, 1.
LC: I, 1-7; II, 1-7; III-IV, 1 (1883-1927). **V**: I, 1-2, 4-7; II, 1-7; III-IV. **VU**: I-IV.

3704. ———. ———. Report of the director of the Leander McCormick observatory of the University of Virginia . . . [Charlottesville, 1887]

8°. Report year ends June 1. No more pub.   **LC, VU**: 1886-87.
Ormond Stone, director.

3705. [28] ———. LIBRARY. The Byrd library . . . Comp. by John S. Patton . . . Charlottesville, 1914.

3706. ———. ———. . . . The library, an invitation . . . by John S. Patton, librarian. [Charlottesville, Va., Michie, 1926]

[11] p. 16°.   **LC, V, VU**
Description of the various collections of books in the University library, with some notes on the classification used.

3707. ———. LOUISIANA ALUMNI ASSOCIATION. Annual dinner of the Louisiana alumni association of the University of Virginia, anniversary of the birth of Thomas Jefferson, New Orleans, La., April 13, 1907 . . . [New Orleans, 1907]

[3] p. illus. (port.) 8°.   **LC**

3708. ———. MEDICINE, Dept. of. Catalogue . . . Announcements . . . Charlottesville, The University [18-?-19—

8°. (*University of Virginia record,* VI, 1912/13; new ser., I-   , 1914/15—   )
BP: 1872/73; **LC**: 1870/71, 99/1900-00/01, 06/07, 12/13, 14/15-17/18, 19/20-20/21, 22/23-28/29; **NYP**: 1869/70-70/71, 72/73-73/74, 86/87, 89/90, 95/96, 1914/15; **USE**: 1917/18, 20/21; **V**: 1907/08, 14/15-28/29 (incompl.); **VU**: 1912/13, 14/15-28/29.

3709. ———. ———. Medical education at the University of Virginia. Special bulletin. Charlottesville, The University [n. d.]

30 p. illus. 8°.   **V**
Signed: R. H. Whitehead, dean, Dept. of medicine.

3710. UNIVERSITY OF VIRGINIA. PHILOSOPHICAL SOCIETY. . . .
Bulletin . . . Humanistic series . . . Charlottesville, The
University [1910-12]

> 2 nos. 8°.   BP: I, 2; **H, LC, NYP, V, VU, WM:** I, 1-2.

3711. ———. ———. . . . Bulletin . . . Scientific series . . .
Charlottesville, The University, 1910-[15?]

> 24 nos. plates. 8°. No more pub.?
> BP: 6-9; **H:** 1-23; **LC:** 1-24; **NYP:** 1-16, 18-19, 21-23; **USAg:** 10;
> **USG:** 1-5, 7-8, 10-12, 14, 16-23; **V, VU:** 1-24; **WM:** 1-23.

3712. ———. ———. . . . Proceedings of the Philosophical society. Reports of the proceedings of the scientific, medical and
humanistic sections of the Society. Charlottesville, Va., University of Virginia, 1910-[15?]

> 8°. (University of Virginia publications)
> BP: 1910/11; **H, LC:** 1910/11-11/12; **NYP:** 1909/10-14/15; **USG:**
> 1911/12; **V:** 1910/11-12/13; **VU:** 1909/10-14/15; **WM:** 1910/11-11/12.

3713. ———. PHILOSOPHY, Corcoran school of. Announcements
. . . Charlottesville, The University, 19—

> 8°.   NYP: 1922/23

3714. ———. RECTOR. Reply of the rector and visitors to the remonstrance on recent changes in the requirements for the degree
of master of arts. [Prepared by W. G. McCabe] Charlottesville,
1892.

> 60 p. 8°.   **H, NYP, VU**
> Contains also the "Remonstrance."

3715. ———. ———. Reports of the rector and the proctor for session 1904/05. Charlottesville, University of Virginia, 1905.

> 21 p. 8°.   **V**

3716. ———. ———. To the alumni and friends of the University
of Virginia . . . [signed] J. Marshal Hanger, president of
the Society of alumni . . . Memorial of the rector and visitors of the University of Virginia relative to the McCormick tel-
escope . . . 1877. [n. p., 1877?]

> 16 p. 8°. No title-page.   **VU**

3717. ———. RURAL LIFE CONFERENCE. . . . Rural life conference held at the University of Virginia summer school . . .

1909—[21?] Charlottesville, Va., University of Virginia, 1909—[21?]

plates. 8°. (In *Alumni bulletin* of the University of Virginia, IV-IX (no. 4 of each vol.), 1911-16)

BP: 1911-16; H: 1911, 13, 15-16; LC: 1909, 11-16; NYP: 1911-16; USAg: 1909-14, 16, 19, 21; USE: 1909-16, 19-21; V: 1911-16; VU: 1909-16, 19-21; WM: 1911-16.

3718. ———. SUMMER SCHOOL. [Announcement] Charlottesville, Va., 1908—

illus. 8°. (*University of Virginia record,* I-VII; new ser., I- ; 1908-)

LC: 1910, 13, 15-20, 26-28; NYP: 1908, 10-11, 15; USE: 1918, 22, 24, 26; V: 1908-28 (incompl.); VU: 1908-28.

3719. ———. ———. . . . Preliminary announcement. Charlottesville, Va., 1915—

illus. 8°. (*University of Virginia record,* new ser., II-IV, [no. 2 of each vol.])

Not pub. in 1916.

LC: 1915, 17-19; USE: 1919; V: 1917-18; VU: 1915, 17-19.

3720. ———. ———. Summer quarter bulletin . . . Vol. 1- ; 1927— Charlottesville, University of Virginia, 1927—

illus. 8°. H: I, 6-8; II, 4; (1927-28). V: I, 1-2, 4-9; II, 4. VU: I-II.

3721. ———. ———. Views. [n. p., 1909—

illus. 4°.   VU: 1909-10.

3722. ———. TEUTONIC LANGUAGES, School of. University of Virginia monographs . . . ed. by James A. Harrison. New York, Barnes, 1901-[04?]

6 nos. 8°. No more pub.?   H: 2-3, 5; LC: 2-3, 5-6.

3723. ———. VISITORS, Board of. Annual report . . . Richmond, Va. [18-?—

8°. H: 1876, 86/87, 89/90-92/93; V: 1876/77, 80/81-81/82; VU: 1878/79, 87/88, 89/90-90/91.

3724. ———. ———. Report of the Special committee of the Board of visitors of the University of Virginia on the expediency of having an executive head of the University. [n. p., 1897?]

13 p. 8°.   VU

Includes Minority report of the committee.

3725. UNIVERSITY OF VIRGINIA. WASHINGTON SOCIETY. Catalogue of the Washington literary society of the University of Virginia . . . Richmond, Goode, 1866.

50 p. 8°.   V, VU

3726. [WEAVER, WILLIAM D.] Types of schools for the higher education of women. [Charlottesville?] 1918.

7 p. 8°.   BP, USE, VU

Signed: W. D. Weaver. Feb. 7, 1918.
Brief sketch of the development of the co-ordinate college idea, and a proposal that co-ordinate education for women be established in connection with the University of Virginia.

3727. WHY a co-ordinate college at Charlottesville affiliated with the University of Virginia rather than a separate college.   [n. p., n. d.]

8 p. 8°.   VU

3728. WILDE, ADNA G. In and about the University of Virginia . . . [Lynchburg, Bell, *ca.* 1910]

[35] p. illus. 18 x 23½ cm.   LC, USE

Views of the University grounds, buildings, etc.

3729. WILLIAMS, JOHN L. In behalf of the old degrees of the University of Virginia. [Richmond, News leader, Sept. 23, 1907]

[6] l. pasted clippings. 12°.   VU

A plea for the humanistic studies in the University.

3730. WILLIAMS, JOHN S. The University of Virginia and the development of Thomas Jefferson's educational ideas; speech of Hon. John Sharp Williams delivered at the St. Louis meeting of the Association of state universities, June 28, 1904. [Charlottesville? Va., 1904]

16 p. plates. 8°.   LC, V, VU

Discussion of such subjects as the honor system, equality of opportunity for all students, the "sturdy conservatism" of the University, etc.

3731. WILSON, ALBERT F., comp. Songs of the University of Virginia. New York, Hinds, Noble & Eldridge [*ca.* 1906]

viii, 86 p. music. 4°.   H

3732. [WOMEN'S COMMITTEE INTERESTED IN THE ESTABLISHMENT OF A STATE COLLEGE FOR WOMEN AT THE UNIVERSITY OF VIRGINIA. The co-ordinate college at Charlottesville affiliated with the University of Virginia. Strode bill, 1910. Early-Rison bill, 1912.

Proposed bill, 1914. Expert evidence as to the social and educational efficiency of this type of institution and its need by the people of Virginia. Letter of the President of the U. S. . . . [Charlottesville, 1913]

136 p. 8°. **LC, USE, VU**

Mrs. B. B. Munford, chairman.

3733. YOUNG MEN'S CHRISTIAN ASSOCIATIONS. UNIVERSITY OF VIRGINIA. Students' hand book. [Charlottesville, 18-?-19—

illus., plans (fold.) 16°. **LC**: 1884/85-88/89.

Valley female college, Winchester, Va.

3734. VALLEY FEMALE COLLEGE. Register of pupils and announcements. Winchester, Va. [18-?-19—

plates. 8°. (Col. & prep.; M. E., So.; 1878/79) **LC**: 1900/01.

Virginia college for young women, Roanoke, Va.

3735. VIRGINIA COLLEGE FOR YOUNG WOMEN. Annual announcement . . . catalogue . . . [Roanoke? 189-?-19—

8°. (Jr. col.; non-sect.; 1892)
NYP: 1913/14-15/16; **USE**: 1909/10-11/12, 13/14-18/19, 20/21-23/24, 25/26; **V**: 1910/11, 12/13-13/14.

3736. ———. Scenes about Virginia college, Roanoke, Virginia. [Roanoke? Va., 1912?]

[11] p., 14 plates. 18 x 26 cm. **USE, V**

Virginia intermont college, Bristol, Va.

3737. VIRGINIA INTERMONT COLLEGE. Annual [catalogue] [Bristol? 188-?-19—

8°. (Jr. col.; women; Bapt.; 1883)
Successor to Virginia institute for young women.
USE: 1911/12, 16/17-20/21, 22/23-25/26, 27/28; **V**: 1912/13, 14/15.

3738. ———. [Views] [Bristol, Tenn., King, 1919?]

32 p. incl. plates. 4°. **USE**

3739. ———. Virginia intermont college (chartered as Virginia in-

stitute), Bristol, Va.; a flourishing school for young women . . .
Lynchburg, Bell [1913]

    40 p. incl. plates. 8°.   **V**
    Ed. of [1912?]   **USE**
    Ed. of 1914.   **V**

3740. VIRGINIA INTERMONT COLLEGE. FINE ARTS DEPT. [Announce-
ment] [Bristol? 19-?—

    8°.   **USE**: 1918/19-19/20.

Virginia mechanics' institute, Richmond, Va.

3741. CALISCH, EDWARD N. The promotion and encouragement of
manufactures, the mechanic and useful arts; an address delivered
before the Virginia mechanics' institute, May 16, 1899. Richmond,
Hill, 1899.

    14 p. 8°.   **V**

3742. KENT, CHARLES W. "Stand four-square." An address delivered before the Virginia mechanics' institute . . . Richmond,
Va., . . . May 12th, 1903 . . . Also introductory remarks
by Wyndham R. Meredith . . . [Richmond, Fergusson] 1903.

    20 p. 8°.   **V, VU**
    The necessity of a well balanced education; with some reference to
an educational conference held at Capon Springs.

3743. THURSTON, R. H. The mechanic arts and modern education;
an address delivered before the Virginia mechanics' institute . . .
May 18th, 1894. Richmond, Jones, 1894.

    23 p. 12°.   **V**

3744. VIRGINIA MECHANICS' INSTITUTE. Bulletin . . . Richmond [18-?-19—

    8°.   **V**: 1907, 10.

3745. ——. Catalogue . . . [1st- ; 1885/86—   ] Richmond [1886?-19—

    illus., plates. 8° (Night school of technology; men; 1854)
    H: 19th (1902/03); **V**: 1906/07-10/11, 12/13, 14/15-15/16, 17/18-
28/29.

Virginia military institute, Lexington, Va.

3746. EDWARDS, MURRAY F., *et al.*, ed. The V. M. I. muse; being a collection of poems written at odd times by cadets, alumni and friends of the Institute, comp. and ed., by Major Murray French Edwards, '07, and Captain Benjamin Franklin Crowson, '10. [Lynchburg, Va., Dulaney-Boatwright, *ca.* 1914]

164 p. incl. port. 12°.   **LC, VU**

3747. KEMPER, JAMES L. Jackson-Hope medals. Address of Gov. J. L. Kemper of Virginia on the first award of the Jackson-Hope medals to Cadet L. H. Strother . . . and Cadet E. M. Davison . . . as the first and second honor graduates of the Virginia military institute, July 3, 1877. [n. p., 1877]

36 p. 8°.   **VU**

3748. LETCHER, JOHN. Address on the re-inauguration of the bronze statue of George Washington at the Virginia military institute, Sept. 10, 1866 . . . Richmond, Whig [1866]

20 p. 8°.   **LC, NYP, V**
Portrays the aftermath of the Civil war, as felt at V. M. I.

3749. MORGAN, JOHN T. Address to the graduating class of the Virginia military institute, on the third day of July, 1868, by Gen. J. T. Morgan . . . Richmond, Nye, 1868.

26 p. 8°.   **LC**

3750. OTEY, PETER J. Response of Hon. Peter J. Otey, at the Alumni banquet, June, 1896 [Virginia military institute] to the toast, "The war cadets." [n. p., 1896?]

9 p. 8°.   **LC**
Speech preliminary to the presentation of a portrait of C. R. Norris, one of the "War cadets" of 1861-65.

3751. PATTON, JOHN M. Address delivered before the Society of alumni of the Virginia military institute, July 4th, 1871 . . . Wytheville [Va.] St. Clair, 1871.

26 p. 8°.   **BP, V, VU**
2d edit.: Richmond, Whig, 1873. 23 p.   **McC, V, VU**

3752. SMITH, FRANCIS HENNEY. Gymnastic and technical education in the Virginia military institute, Lexington, Va. An introductory lecture on the resumption of academic exercises in the institution, Sept. 5th, 1871 . . . New York, Van Nostrand, 1871.

27 p. 8°.   **H, USE**

3753. SMITH, FRANCIS HENNEY. Introductory address to the corps of cadets of Virginia military institute on the resumption of the academic exercises, Sept. 10, 1866. Richmond, Whig [*ca.* 1866]

    13 p. 8°.   **BP, LC, NYP, V, VU**
    "The inner life of the V. M. I. cadet; its responsibilities and its privileges."

3754. ———. Memorial of the Academic board of the Virginia military institute. [n. p., n. d.]

    12 p. 8°.   **V**
    Petition to the Virginia legislature to give some of the Congressional land grant to V. M. I., "for the benefit of agriculture and the mechanic arts."

3755. ———. The Virginia military institute, its building and rebuilding, by Major-General Francis H. Smith . . . Lynchburg, Bell, 1912.

    277 p. front. (port.) plates. 8°.   **LC, USE, V, VU**
    The author, superintendent of V. M. I. throughout the reconstruction period until 1890, gives a clear picture of the problems met during that time, in the mingling of politics and education. Based largely on his annual reports and recollections.

3756. SMITH, FRANCIS HENRY. Address before graduating class of Virginia military institute, July 4, 1900. Roanoke, Stone, [n. d.]

    14 p. 8°.   **V**
    "Why the young men of the South should be hopeful."

3757. STEPHENS, JAMES I., comp. The Virginia military institute scrap book; a collection of poems and prose pieces contained in the cadet poetry books and "The Cadet, V. M. I.," together with much original matter . . . Lexington, Globe, 1891.

    96 p. 8°.   **V**

3758. VIRGINIA MILITARY INSTITUTE. Alphabetical list of graduates, 1839 to 1898. Lynchburg, Bell [1898?]

    35 p. 12°.   **H, V**
    Ed. of 1910: 46 p.   **BP**

3759. ———. Annual report . . . [1st- ; 1839/40-19—   ] Lexington, Va. [1840?-19—

    8°. (State; men; 1839)
    Report year ends in June.
    Pub. also in Virginia. Annual reports of . . . institutions of
. . . Virginia, 1865/66, 70/71— **[3370]**

LC: 77th-83d, 86-88th (1915/16-21/22, 24/25-26/27); **USE**: 1917/18, 22/23, 24/25-26/27; **V**: 1864/65-66/67, 81/82, 95/96, 98/99, 1901/02, 03/04-07/08, 15/16-16/17, 20/21, 24/25-27/28; **VMI**: 1839/40-1928/29.

3760. ———. [Circular] [Baltimore, Kelly & Piet, 1866?]

4 p. 4°. LC

3761. ———. Circular [July 7, 1882] [Philadelphia, Times, 1882?]

[4] p. 8°. V

3762. ———. In memoriam. Francis H. Smith, father and founder of the Virginia military institute . . . 1812 . . . [-] 1890. [New York, Knickerbocker press] 1890.

25 p. 8°. McC, V
"A true copy from the records of the Academic board of the Virginia military institute."

3763. ———. In memoriam. John Mercer Brooke, born in Tampa, Florida, Dec. 18, 1826; died at Virginia military institute, Lexington, Virginia, Dec. 14, 1906. [New York, N. Y., and Winchester, Va., Eddy press, 1906]

16 p. 8°. LC, USE, V
Contains brief mention of Brooke's professorship of physics and astronomy at V. M. I., 1865-99.

3764. ———. In memoriam. Matthew Fontaine Maury . . . Born in Spottsylvania County, Virginia, Jan. 14, 1806. Died at Virginia military institute, Lexington, Vᵃ., Feb. 1, 1873 . . . [Lexington?] 1873.

32 p. 8°. BP, LC, V, VU, WM
Includes a sketch of his life and services at V. M. I.

3765. ———. Official register . . . Lynchburg, Va. [etc., 18-?-19—

plates. 12°.-8°.
H: 1866/67, 91/92-94/95, 96/97-1900/01, 05/06-08/09, 13/14-14/15, 17/18-18/19, 20/21, 23/24; **LC**: 1865/66-67/68, 73/74-74/75, 90/91-1909/10, 12/13-13/14, 15/16, 17/18, 24/25-26/27; **NYP**: 1870/71, 72/73, 1909/10-10/11, 17/18, 25/26; **USE**: 1874/75, 1907/08, 09/10-10/11, 12/13-16/17, 18/19-27/28; **V**: 1865/66-68/69, 70/71, 72/73-74/75, 77/78-81/82, 83/84-89/90, 91/92-1901/02, 03/04-06/07, 08/09, 10/11-26/27; **VMI**: 1865/66-1928/29; **VU**: 1878/79.

3766. ———. [Prospectus] Baltimore, Kelly & Piet [1866?]

[4] p. 4°. LC
Signed: Francis H. Smith, supt.

3767. VIRGINIA MILITARY INSTITUTE. Regulations for the Virginia military institute, at Lexington, Virginia. (Rev.) Lynchburg, Bell, 1887.

xiv, 81 p. 8°.   LC, USE

Regulations regardnig organization, admission of cadets, uniform, course of instruction, examinations, discipline, etc.

3768. ———. Report of the Board of visitors . . . Richmond, 1839-19—

8°.   H: 1867; **LC:** 1867, 73/74; **VMI:** 1839-1929.

3769. ———. Roster of graduates of the Virginia military institute, 1842-1919, with brief biographical notes. World war edition. Comp. by the official historiographer [Joseph R. Anderson] of the . . . Institute. [Richmond, Whittet & Shepperson] 1920.

109 p. 4°.   **V, VMI**

3770. ———. Superintendent's report to the Board of visitors in the case of Cadet Sweet. [n. p.] 1915.

21 p. 8°.   **V**

Involving hazing at V. M. I.

3771. ———. Views. [Lynchburg, Bell, 1915?]

[30] p. of illus. 16 x 23 cm.   **LC, V**

Ed. of [19-?]: 24 illus.   **USE**

3772. ———. ALUMNI ASSOCIATION. New Market day at V. M. I. Celebrating the thirty-ninth anniversary of the battle of New Market and unveiling of Ezekiel's statue: Virginia mourning her dead. [Roanoke, Va., Stone, 1903]

84 p. front., illus. (facsim.) 3 port. 8°.   **LC, V**

Each article has special title-page.

Contains addresses by J. N. Upshur, H. Conrad, and J. S. Wise.

3773. ———. ———. RICHMOND (VA.) CHAPTER. . . . Constitution and roll 1910-1911. [Richmond, Mitchell & Hotchkiss, 1911]

15 p. 8°.   **V**

Comp. by Jennings C. Wise.

3774. ———. COMMITTEE ON DEGREES. Report . . . to the Academic board of the Virginia military institute. Lexington, Va., May 29, 1913.

13 p. 16°.   **V**

3775. WISE, JENNINGS C. A comparison of the academic system of

the Virginia military institute with that of other institutions.
[Lynchburg, Dulaney-Boatwright, n. d.]

13 p. 8°. **V**

3776. ———. Notes on the Virginia military institute: The academic situation, 1917. Richmond, Saunders, 1917.

14 p. 8°. **V**

Advocating proper balance between the military and academic functions of V. M. I., the standardization of entrance requirements, and increase of permanent faculty.

3777. ———. A special report to the Board of visitors of the Virginia military institute on the history of agricultural education in Virginia and the Virginia military institute as a school of agriculture, including a sketch of the physical survey of Virginia by the School of applied science; by Colonel Jennings C. Wise, professor of law, economic and political science, V. M. I. [Lexington?] 1914.

34 p. 8°. **LC, USAg, USE, V**

Includes presentation of claims of V. M. I. under the Morrill Act, as opposed to Hampton normal and agricultural institute and V. P. I., which received land grants and became agricultural colleges.

3778. ———. V. M. I. papers . . . Pub. privately by the author for his friends . . . [Lynchburg, Va., Dulaney-Boatwright, n. d.]

53 p. 8°. **VMI, VU**

Dedicated to V. M. I., the papers are concerned with life and education at the Institute.

Virginia polytechnic institute, Blacksburg, Va.

3779. APPEAL from a judgment of the Board of visitors of the Virginia polytechnic institute, affirming a judgment of the faculty, refusing to allow William B. Christian, Rowland P. Eubank and Julian M. Salley to matriculate . . . Also a statement of Judge George L. Christian . . . Also a letter from Senator John W. Daniel . . . [Richmond, 1906?]

72 p. 8°. **V, VU**

Concerning hazing at V. P. I.

3780. BRAXTON, ALLEN C. Address . . . to the graduating

class of the Virginia polytechnic institute at Blacksburg, Va., on
June 17th, 1903. Lynchburg, Bell, 1903.

16 p. 8°.   **V, VPI**

3781. [BROWN, JOHN T.] The present condition and outlook at the
Virginia polytechnic institute and the necessity for the appropriation asked for buildings and equipment and for an increase of annuity including a statement of moneys expended. Memorial submitted for the Board of visitors. [Blacksburg? 1906?]

20 p. 8°.   **USE, V**
Signed: John Thompson Brown.

3782. DABNEY, CHARLES W., jr. The old college and the new. An
address delivered at the commencement of the Virginia polytechnic institute, Blacksburg, Virginia, June 24, 1896. [n. p.] Privately printed, 1896.

16 p. 8°.   **VU**

3783. NORFOLK & WESTERN RAILWAY. AGRICULTURAL AND INDUS-
TRIAL DEPT. The trip of a college on wheels. Virginia polytechnic
institute and Norfolk & western railway better farming special.
Issued by Agricultural and industrial department N & W ry.
Roanoke, Virginia [Stone, n. d.]

69 p. illus. 8°.   **HB, USAg**

3784. VIRGINIA POLYTECHNIC INSTITUTE. . . . The alumni register . . . Blacksburg, Va. [18-?-19—

8°. Issued as no. of Bulletin of V. P. I. [19-?— [**3787**]
Title varies: Alumni record; Alumni number [of Bulletin]
LC: 1905-06, 08-11, 15; **NYP**: 1912, 14-15; **USE**: 1905, 11-15; **VPI**:
1891, 1906, 08, 10-20.

3785. ———. . . . . Announcements. Roanoke, Va. [18-?-19—

8°. **H**: 1908/09, 20/21; **LC**: 1906/07-07/08, 26/27-27/28; **NYP**:
1899/1900; **V**: 1900/01, 05/06; **VPI**: 1891, 92/93-95/96, 98/99-1907/08,
09/10-28/29.

3786. ———. Appropriations asked for and reasons therefor.
Blacksburg, 1916.

8°.   **VPI**
Memorial presented to the General assembly of Virginia.

3787. ———. Bulletin . . . vol. 1- ; 1908— Blacksburg, 1908—

plates, ports. 8°. quarterly.

H: I-II, 2; III-VI; VII, 1-2, 4; VIII, 1-2; IX, 1; X, 2; XI, 2; XII, 2; XIII, 3; XIV, 3; XV, 3-4; XVI, 4; XVII, 4; XVIII, 4; XX, 2; XXII, 3; (1908-29). **LC:** 1908-10, 26 (incompl.). **NYP:** II, 2-3; III, 2; IV, 2, 4; V, 1-2, 4; VI, 2, 4; VII, 1; VIII, 1-3; IX, 1; X, 2; XII, 2; (1909-19). **USAg:** XI, 1, 4; XV, 1; XVII, 2. **USE:** I, 2; II, 2, 4; III, 2; IV, 1-4; V, 2-4; VI, 1, 4; VII, 1, 3-4; VIII, 1, 3; IX, 1; X, 2, 4; XI, 2; XII, 2; XIII, 2-3; XIV, 2-3; XV, 2-3; XVI, 3-4; XVII, 4; XVIII, 4; XIX, 3-4; XX, 2, extra 3, 4; XXI, 1, 5. **USL:** May, 1923. **V:** I-VII; VIII, 1, 3; IX, 1 (suppl.); X, 1-2; XIII, 2; XV, 1, 3-5; XVI, 6; XVII, 1, 4; XVIII, 1, 6; XIX-XXI; XXII, 1, extra 4; XXIII, 3. **VPI:** I-XXII. **VU:** XXI, 6 (July, 1928).

3788. ———. Catalogue . . . 1st- ; 1872/73-19— [Richmond] 1873-19—

12°. (State agric. & engin. col.; men; 1872)

Title varies: Catalogue of the officers and students of the Virginia agricultural and mechanical college.

Catalogue for 1890/91 not pub.

H: 1872/73-73/74, 1907/08-18/19, 20/21-24/25; **LC:** 1872/73, 74/75, 93/94, 95/96, 1900/01-06/07, 14/15, 17/18, 26/27; **NYP:** 1872/73, 97/98, 99/1900-00/01, 02/03, 05/06-06/07, 08/09-12/13, 14/15-16/17, 18/19, 24/25, 26/27; **USAg:** 1872/73, 74/75-75/76, 77/78, 81/82, 83/84, 87/88-89/90, 91/92, 93/94-99/1900, 01/02-20/21, 22/23-25/26, 27/28; **USE:** 1872/73-84/85, 86/87-89/90, 93/94, 95/96, 99/1900-27/28; **V:** 1881/82, 83/84-84/85, 86/87-89/90, 91/92-97/98, 99/1900-00/01, 02/03-16/17, 20/21-23/24, 25/26-27/28; **VPI:** 1872/73-1928/29.

3789. ———. Honor list . . . Blacksburg, Va., 1892-19—

8°. **VPI:** 1891/92, 97/98, 99/1906, 07/08-10/11, 12/13-15/16.

3790. ———. The present condition and outlook at the Virginia polytechnic institute and the necessity for the appropriation asked for buildings and equipment and for an increase of annuity including a statement of moneys expended. Memorial submitted for the Board of visitors. [n. p., 1902]

20 p. 8°. **V, VPI**

Ed. of 1905. **V, VPI**

3791. ———. Regulations . . . Blacksburg [18-?-19—

8°. **V:** 1901, 03, 06, 08-11; **VPI:** 1878, 80, 1901-02, 03-04, 07-11, 13, 15, 21-22, 25, 28.

3792. VIRGINIA POLYTECHNIC INSTITUTE. Report . . . Richmond, 1873-19—

8°. Pub. also in Virginia. Annual reports of . . . institutions of . . . Virginia, 1871/72-19— **[3370]**
H: 1872/73; **USAg**: 1872/73, 81/82, 90/91.

3793. ———. Rules and regulations for the government of the president, professors, and other officers and students of the Virginia agricultural and mechanical college. [n. p., 188-?]

17 p. 8°.   **USE**

3794. ———. Summer school . . . announcement. Blacksburg, Va., 19—

8°.   **USAg**: 1915, 21; **VPI**: 1921-26.

3795. ———. Virginia agricultural and mechanical college. Its history and organization. [n. p., 1872]

36 p. 8°.   **H, LC, NYP, V, VPI**
A discussion of scientific engineering, mechanical, and agricultural schools in Europe and America, with application to the situation at Blacksburg; proposed courses of instruction, and equipment needed.

3796. ———. ENGINEERING EXPERIMENT STATION. Bulletin no. 1- ; March, 1923— Blacksburg, Va., 1923—

tables, diagrs. 8°.   **NYP**: 2 (1926); **V, VPI**: 1-4 (1923-28).

3797. ———. ENGINEERING EXTENSION DIVISION. Bulletin no. 1- ; Oct., 1924— Blacksburg, Va., 1924—

illus., tables, diagrs. 8°. quarterly.
V: 1-15 (1924-28); **VPI**: 1-17 (1924-28).

3798. ———. EXTENSION DIVISION. Agricultural club letter. Vol. 1- ; May/June, 1918— [Blacksburg, Va., 1918—

illus. f°. bi-monthly.
USAg: I-II; III, 1-4, 6-11; IV-IX; (1918-27). **V**: II, 6; IV, 4-11; X, 9-12; XI, 1-11. **VPI**: I-XI.

3799. ———. ———. [Circular] E-1- Blacksburg, Va. [192-?—

illus. 8°.
USAg: E-107, 127, 131, 210; **V**: E-27, 39 (1926, 28); **VPI**.

3800. ———. ———. Extension bulletin no. 1- ; 1915— Blacksburg, Va., 1915—

8°. **USAg**: 1-69, 71-98, 105; **V**: 1-4, 7-8, 10-19, 21-23, 25-48, 50-60, 63, 65-67, 71, 74-78, 81-102, 104-106; **VU**: 3, 8, 12, 19, 27, 30, 34, 36, 39, 71-78, 81-82; **VPI**: 1-110 (1915-29).

3801. ———. ———. Three years of extension work in agriculture and home economics in Virginia; a report of the Virginia agricultural and mechanical college and polytechnic institute from July 1, 1916 to May 15, 1919. Blacksburg, Va., 1919.

148 p. 8°.   USAg, WM

3802. ———. GERMAN CLUB. . . . Constitution. Rev. ed. [Blacksburg, Home print., 19-?]

11 p. 16°.   LC

3803. ———. PRESIDENT. . . . Report of the president. 1919/20— Blacksburg, 1920—

plates, diagrs. 8°. (In its *Bulletin*)

Report, 1872/73-1917/18, made to Board of visitors and printed in *Report* of Supt. of public instruction [3300] No formal report received for 1885/86.

LC: 1919/20-26/27; USE: 1919/20-24/25; VPI: 1872-74, 92, 1919/20-26/27.

3804. ———. VIRGINIA TECH DAIRY CLUB. . . . Report, 1st- ; 1924— Blacksburg, 1924—

8°.   VPI: 1st-5th (1924-28).

3805. ———. VISITORS, Board of. Report of the Executive committee for the Board of visitors . . . Richmond, Va. [1872-19—

8°. Reports for 1872-77, 82, 84-1918 printed in *Report* of Supt. of public instruction [3300]

USAg: 1877/78; VPI: 1876/77, 78/79-80/81, 82/83.

3806. WALKER, GILBERT C. Address of Gov. Gilbert C. Walker, at the commencement of the Virginia agricultural and mechanical college, July 9, 1873. Plan of instruction, expenses, &c., of the college. Richmond, Enquirer, 1873.

16 p. 8°.   H, LC, NYP, USAg, VPI

3807. YOUNG MEN'S CHRISTIAN ASSOCIATIONS. VIRGINIA POLYTECHNIC INSTITUTE. Student's handbook of the Virginia polytechnic institute. Pub. by the Y. M. C. A. [Blacksburg, Va., 1895-19—

12°.   VPI: 1st-33d ed. (1895-1928/29).

Virginia state teachers' colleges.

3808. Culpeper, Va. . . . Reasons why a normal school should be located here. [n. p., n. d.]

7 p. 8°.   V

3809. State Peabody summer normal schools. [Circular, no. 1-? n. p., 18-?-?]

8°.   H: 133, 147 (May, 1896, & May, 1897).

3810. State summer institute for white teachers, Luray, Va. Session 1915, June 23d to July 20th. State examination will be held July 21st, 22d, and 23d. Luray, Va., Page news and courier [1915]

22 p. 8°.   V

3811. State summer normal institute, Martinsville, Va. Announcements . . . [n. p., 1909?—

8°. (Women; 1909?)   V: June 22-July 23, 1915.
Advertisements in back.

3812. State summer school for teachers, Covington, Va. Announcement . . . Under the direction of the State board of education . . . [Covington, Covington daily Virginian, 19—]

illus. 8°.   V: 10th (1915).

3813. Virginia state summer institute, Big Stone Gap, Va. Announcements . . . [n. p., 19—

8°.   V: 1908.

3814. Virginia state summer normal institute, Chase City, Va. Annual session . . . [1st- ; 1908—] Chase City, 1908—

8°.   V: 8th (1915).

3815. Virginia state summer normal school, Norfolk, Va. State summer school for tidewater Virginia. [Announcement. n. p., 19—

illus. 8°. Advertisements in back.   V: 1915.

3816. Virginia state teachers' college, Farmville, Va. [Announcement folder] [Lynchburg, Va., Bell, 191-?]

2 l. illus. 8°.   NYP

3817. ———. Bulletin . . . Vol. 1, no. 1- ; Sept., 1914— Farmville, State college, 1914—

8°. quarterly.

H: I-XIII (only no. 4 of each) (1915-27/28). LC: I, 1-4; V, 2; XII, 3; XIII, 1, 3; XIV, 1; (1914, 19, 26-28). **NYP:** I; II, 4; III; IV, 1, 4; V, 4; VI, 4; VII, 4; VIII, 4. **USE:** I, 1-2; VIII, 1. **V:** I, 1-3; II, 1; IV, 2; V, 2; VI, 2; VIII, 1; IX, 2; X, 2-3; XI, 3; XII, 3; XIII, 1, 3; XIV, 3.

3818. ———. Catalogue . . . [Richmond, 188-?-19—

plates. 8°. (Women; 1884)

H: 1915/16-27/28; LC: 1891/92, 1902/03, 05/06, 16/17-27/28; **NYP:** 1906/07-08/09, 11/12-28/29; **V:** 1897/98-99/1900, 02/03-15/16, 17/18-28/29.

3819. ———. . . . The course of study for the kindergarten and elementary grades of the training school. Farmville, Va., State normal school for women, 1914.

294 p. 8°. (Its *Bulletin*, I, 1) **LC, NYP, USE, V**
Appendix I: Typical special day. programs.—Appendix II: Sources of songs, games, poems and stories.

3820. ———. The lighter side of our school life. [Farmville? 1911]

4 l. nar. 8°. **NYP**

3821. ———. Special days in the Training school work of the kindergarten and elementary grades; selected and arranged by the Training school faculty of the State female normal school, Farmville, Virginia. Farmville, Va., The State female normal school [*ca.* 1913]

62 p. 8°. **LC, USE, V**

3822. ———. . . . Spelling: I. Theory of spelling instruction. II. Types of spelling lessons. Farmville, Va., The State normal school for women, 1915.

57 p. 8°. (Its *Bulletin*, I, 2) **LC, NYP, USE, V**

3823. ———. State normal school, Farmville, Virginia. Views. [Lynchburg, Va., Bell, n. d.]

32 p. incl. plates. 14½ x 22½ cm. **H, USE, V**
Ed. of 1908 & [n. d.] **V**
Ed. of [1918]: Richmond. 17 plates. **USE**

3824. VIRGINIA STATE TEACHERS' COLLEGE, Farmville, Va. CON-
SERVATORY OF MUSIC. [Announcement] Farmville, 19—
8°.   NYP: 1911/12, 13/14-14/15.

3825. ———. SUMMER SCHOOL. State summer normal and school
of elementary methods. Farmville, June 30th to July 27th, 1909.
[n. p., 1909]
22 p. 12°.   V

3826. VIRGINIA STATE TEACHERS' COLLEGE, Fredericksburg, Va.
. . . Bulletin, vol. 1- ; 1914/15— [Richmond, 1914—
8°. quarterly?
H: II, 2; VIII, 5; (1915, 23). LC: VIII, 4. USE: VII, 4; VIII,
4; X, 4. V: I; II, 2; VIII, 5; IX, 1-2, 4; X, 1-2, 4-5; XI, 1, 3; XII, 1-2,
4; XIII, 1-2.

3827. ———. Catalogue . . . 1st- ; 1911/12— [Richmond,
1912—
8°. (Women; 1911)
H: 1915/16, 22/23; V: 1912/13-15/16, 22/23-23/24, 25/26-26/27.

3828. ———. State summer school and school of elementary methods . . . 1914— [n. p., 1914—
8°.   V: 1914.

3829. VIRGINIA STATE TEACHERS' COLLEGE, Harrisonburg, Va. An-
nual catalogue . . . [1908/09—] Harrisonburg, Va., 1909—
8°. (Women; 1908)
Called State normal and industrial school for women, to 1924.
Includes register and announcements.
H: 1915/16, 24/25-25/26; NYP: 1912/13; V: 1924/25, 26/27-27/28;
VU: 1908-09.

3830. ———. Home demonstration work in Virginia. A record of
the short course at the Normal school, Aug., 1915, with papers by
those in attendance. Harrisonburg, Va. [1915]
30 p. 4 plates. 8°. (Its *Normal bulletin,* VII, 4)   USAg

3831. ———. Normal bulletin . . . Vol. 1- ; Feb., 1909—
Harrisonburg, 1909—
plates. 8°. quarterly.
H: VIII, 4 & suppl. (1915-16). USAg: VII, 4. V: I-VII; VIII,
1, 3-6; IX-X; XI, 1, 3.

3832. ———. Practical work for rural schools. Suggestions for lessons in housekeeping, home nursing, cooking, sewing, and handwork. Preliminary announcement of summer quarter. Harrisonburg [1914]

47 p. plates. 8°.   **USAg**

3833. VIRGINIA STATE TEACHERS' COLLEGE, Petersburg, Va. Catalogue . . . Petersburg [188-?-19—

'8°. (Colored; 1883)
H: 1886/87, 90/91-92/93, 1907/08, 15/16, 18/19; LC: 1891/92, 97/98-99/1900, 04/05-06/07, 22/23-26/27, **NYP**: 1886/87, 1910/11, 12/13; **V**: 1915/16, 19/20, 23/24, 25/26-26/27.

3834. VIRGINIA STATE TEACHERS' COLLEGE, East Radford, Va. Bulletin . . . vol. 1- ; July, 1913— East Radford, 1913—

8°. (Women; 1913?)
Includes annual catalogue.
USE: II, 2; III, 4; (1914-15). **V**: I-IV; V, 2, 4; VI, 3-4; VII, 3-4; VIII, 1-3; IX, 1, 3-5; X, 1-2, 5; XI, 1-2, 5-7; XII, 2-5; XIII, 1-10; XIV, 1-4; XV, 1-3; (1913-28).

3835. ———. Evidence and arguments before a sub-committee of the Radford state normal school Board of trustees at Radford, Dec. 16, 1913, in the case of charges preferred against R. J. Noell by the editor of the Radford record. [Radford, 1913]

77 p. 8°.   **V**

Virginia theological seminary and college, Lynchburg, Va.

3836. VIRGINIA THEOLOGICAL SEMINARY AND COLLEGE. Catalogue . . . [Lynchburg, 18-?-19—

8°. (Colored; co-ed.; Bapt.; 1888)
H: 1892/93; **NYP**: 1908/09, 15/16; **V**: 1899/1900.

Virginia union university, Richmond, Va.

3837. MORGAN, THOMAS J. Virginia union university. What it signifies. New York, Amer. Baptist home missionary society [1900]

12 p. illus. 8°.   **NYP**

3838. VIRGINIA UNION UNIVERSITY. Annual catalogue . . . Richmond, Va. [1866?-19—

plates. 8°. (Colored; theol. & prep.; men; Bapt.; 1865)

Consolidation of Richmond institute **[4388]**, Richmond theological seminary, and Wayland seminary, Washington, D. C.

LC: 1899/1900, 01/02-03/04, 06/07, 17/18; **USE:** 1899/1900-20/21, 22/23-27/28; **V:** 1875/76-76/77, 85/86, 1899/1900-22/23.

Washington and Lee university, Lexington, Va.

3839. ADAMS, CHARLES F. Lee's centennial; an address by Charles Francis Adams, delivered at Lexington, Virginia, Saturday, Jan. 19, 1907, on the invitation of the president and faculty of Washington and Lee university. [Boston? 1907]

76 p. 8°.   BP, LC, NYP,V

Includes a sketch of Lee's educational work, 1865-70.

3840. ANDERSON, HENRY W. An American citizen. An address . . . before the literary societies and graduating class of Washington and Lee unviersity and in presenting a memorial tablet to Charles Francis Adams. June, 1916. [n. p., 1916?]

74 p. front. (port.) 8°.   VU

Depicts Adams' kindly feeling towards Virginia and the South. (Cf. item **3839**)

3841. CENTENNIAL ORGANIZATION FOR THE BETTER ENDOWMENT OF WASHINGTON AND LEE UNIVERSITY . . . Report of the meetings held in Independence hall, Philadelphia, Oct. 10th, 1876, and June 8th, 1881 . . . New York, Evening post, 1882.

ii, [2], 88 p. 8°.   LC, McC, NYP, USE, V

3842. [2395] [DAVIDSON papers] [Papers of James D. Davidson and his son, Charles A., of Lexington, Va., 1865-85]

3843. HOGE, MOSES D. The memories, hopes and duties of the hour: a historic discourse, delivered at Washington and Lee university, Lexington, Virginia, June 15, 1886 . . . pub. by the Board of trustees. Richmond, Va., Whittet & Shepperson, 1886.

28 p. 8°.   BP, LC

Contains some mention of the movement for a larger endowment for the University.

3844. HOLLAND, R. A. Integrity of character, the proper aim of education; an address before the literary societies of Washington college, Lexington, Va., . . . June 24th, 1869. Baltimore, Murphy, 1869.

23 p. 8°.   V

3845. JOHNSTON, WILLIAM P. Address before the literary societies of Washington and Lee university, Lexington, Va. . . .June 25, 1879. [n. p., n. d.]

10 p. 8°.   USE, V

The ideals and accomplishments of the University and its alumni.

3846. MACCORKLE, WILLIAM A. An address, delivered June 17, 1908 . . . before the literary societies of Washington and Lee university, Lexington, Va. New York & London, Putnam, 1908.

1 p. l., 71 p. 12°.   LC, V

Concerning the patriotism of the South.

3847. [429] [MCCORMICK, CYRUS H.] [Personal papers of the Cyrus H. McCormick family, 1865-*ca*.1910]

3848. TAYLOR, JOSEPH W. Address before the literary societies of Washington and Lee university, . . . June 22, 1871 . . . Baltimore, Murphy, 1871.

52 p. 8°.   BP, V

"A plea for the conversion of Washington and Lee university into a memorial university by the people of the South . . . to the memory of Robert E. Lee."

3849. WASHINGTON AND LEE UNIVERSITY. The alumni directory and service record of Washington and Lee university. Compiled by the Alumni office and edited by Verbon E. Kemp. Lexington, Va., The Alumni [*ca.* 1926]

604, [2] p. ports., plates. 8°.   H, WL

3850. ———. Alumni register . . . Lexington, Pub. by the University [18-?-19—

8°.   H: 1910, 12; V: 1910, 12; WL: 1869, 1912, 26.

3851. ———. Annual report . . . of [the] president. Lexington, Va. [18-?-19—

8°.   BP: 1897/98; H: 1917, 21-28; LC, V: 1897/98; WL: 1911-28.

3852. ———. Bulletin . . . vol. 1- [1902?— Lexington, etc., 1902?—

8°. Includes Alumni bulletin and Catalogue.

H: XXV, 1-5, 7, 9-20; XXVI, 1 5, 7 12, 14-15; XXVII, 1-9, 11-12, 14-18; XXVIII, 2-3; (1926-29). LC: XIII, 1; XVI, 1; XVIII, 16; XXI, 3; XXII, 4, 8, 10; XXIII, 2, 22; XXV, 4, 9, 19; XXVII, 4, 8;

(1914-28). **McC**: VI, 3. **USE**: I, 2; II-XVI (only no. 1 of each);
IX, 4; X, 4; XVII, 1, 12, 19; XVIII, 5, 13-14; XIX, 1, 8-9, 14, 16; XX, 1,
5-6, 15, 20-21, 24; XXI, 1, 3-4, 6, 12-14, 16-18, 22-23; XXII, 1, 3-4, 7-10,
12-13, 18, 20-21; XXIII, 1, 4, 9-10, 13, 21, 23-24; XXIV, 4, 6; XXV, 5, 9;
XXVI, 5, 9. **V**: July of 1901, 08, 09, 11, 12; 1913 (Feb., Apr., July, Aug.,
Dec.); XVI, 6C; XVII, 1C, 2A, 13, 16-20; XVIII, 3, 7, 10-11, 15-18; XIX,
3, 5-6, 16; XX, 7, 12, 15, 19-21, 23; XXI, 3-6, 10-11, 13; XXII, 1, 3-4, 8, 10,
14-15, 21; XXIII, 1-2, 4, 22-23; XXIV, 2, 4, 6, 15, 22; XXV, 4, 9, 14,
19; XXVII, 4, 8, 18, 21; XXVIII, 2-5; (1917-28/29). **WL**: XIX-
XXVIII (1920-28).

3853. WASHINGTON AND LEE UNIVERSITY. Catalogue . . . Richmond [etc., 18-?-19—

> plates. 12°.-8°. (Men; non-sect.; 1749)
>
> Called Washington academy; then Washington college, to 1870.
> Pub. in its *Bulletin* [1902?—   **[3852]**
>
> **BP**: 1870/71-74/75, 81/82, 83/84, 85/86-90/91, 92/93-93/94, 98/99-
> 1900/01; **H**: 1865/66-66/67, 68/69-1927/28; **LC**: 1866/67-69/70, 71/72-
> 77/78, 83/84-91/92, 93/94-95/96, 97/98-1917/18, 19/20, 24/25, 26/27-27/28;
> **McC**: 1875/76-76/77, 80/81, 83/84, 89/90, 93/94; **NYP**: 1865/66, 68/69-
> 78/79, 82/83-89/90, 91/92-95/96, 97/98-1903, 04/05-07/08, 09/10-19/20,
> 21/22-27/28; **USE**: 1866/67-75/76, 78/79-1927/28; **V**: 1866/67-85/86,
> 87/88-1919/20, 22/23-26/27; **WL**: 1865/66-1928/29.

3854. ———. Catalogue of the alumni of Washington college, Virginia, for the year 1869. Baltimore, Murphy, 1869.

> 74, [2] p. 8°.   **BP, H, LC, USE, V**

3855. ———. Catalogue of the officers and alumni of Washington
and Lee university, Lexington, Virginia, 1749-1888. Pub. by order of the Board of trustees. Baltimore, Murphy, 1888.

> 245 p. 8°.

3856. ———. The charter and laws, and trustees and faculty of
Washington college at Lexington, Va., A. D. 1865. Richmond,
Wynne, 1865.

> 24 p. 8°.   **H, V**

3857. ———. The charter and laws of Washington college, Lexington, Va. Revised, A. D. 1866. Staunton, Spectator, 1866.

> 13 p. 8°.   **H, USE**
> Eds. of 1893 and 1918.   **H**

3858. ———. Correspondence between a committee of the Alumni
of Washington and Lee university, and the presiding officials of

certain American colleges and universities. [Lexington, Va.? 1903?]

15 p. 8°.   BP
Concerning alumni representation on the Board of trustees.

3859. ———. . . . Historical papers, no. 1-6; 1890-1904 . . . Baltimore, 1890-1904.

6 v. plates, ports, plans. 8°. No. 6 pub. in Lynchburg, Va.
Include the history of the college, historical addresses, sketches of trustees and alumni, etc.
BP: 1-4; H, LC: 1-6; NYP: 1-3, 5-6; USE, V, VU, WL, WM: 1-6.

3860. ———. The inauguration of William Lyne Wilson, LL.D. as president of Washington and Lee university, Lexington, Va., Sept. 15, 1897. Lynchburg, Va., Bell [1897]

49 p. 8°.   BP, H, NYP, USE
Introductory remarks by W. McLaughlin; addresses by H. C. Cameron, J. H. Kirkland, D. C. Gilman, and W. L. Wilson. The addresses contain some evidence on educational conditions in Virginia and the South.

3861. ———. Kappa alpha memorial hall. [Lexington, 1903]

8 p., 2 l. 8°.   LC
Plans for building a hall at Washington and Lee university to memorialize the founding of Kappa alpha fraternity in 1865; with certificate for charter, resolution of Board of trustees, and subscription blanks.

3862. ———. . . . Summer bulletin. Lexington, Va., The University, 1904-24.

illus. (incl. port., plan) 8°. (In its *Bulletin* [3852])
No more pub. after 1924.
LC: 1904-05; McC, V: 1907; WL: 1904-24.

3863. ———. Treasurer's report . . . Lexington, Va. [1911—

8°. (Printed with President's report [3851])
H: 1916/17, 20/21-27/28; USE: 1910/11-12/13, 14/15-15/16; WL: 1910/11-27/28.

3864. ———. ENGINEERING, School of. . . . Engineering bulletin . . . new ser., vol. 1- ; 1902— [Lynchburg, 1902—

plates. 12°. quarterly.
LC: IV, 4 (Oct., 1905); V: III, 4 (Oct., 1904); WL: III (1904).

3865. ———. LAW DEPT. Catalogue of the alumni of the Lexington law school, and of its successor, the Law department of Wash-

ington and Lee university. 1849-1881. Lynchburg, Virginian,
1881.

40 p. 8°.   H, USE

3866. WASHINGTON AND LEE UNIVERSITY. LAW DEPT. . . . Law
bulletin . . . [1st ser., 18-?-1901?] new ser., vol. 1- ;
1902— [Lynchburg, Va., etc., 18-?-19—

plates. 12°. quarterly.
LC: new ser., V, 2 (1906). WL: 1874, 95-1914, 20, 22-28.

3867. ———. ———. [Law catalogue] Lexington, Va. [18-?-19—

8°. (Men; 1866)
Successor to Lexington law school.
Pub. in Washington and Lee university. *Bulletin* [190-?—   [3852]
LC: 1921/22; V: 1901/02, 04/05-05/06; WL: 1873/74, 94/95-1913/14,
19/20, 21/22-27/28.

3868. ———. NEW YORK ALUMNI ASSOCIATION. Proceedings upon
the organization of the New York alumni association of Washington and Lee university. New York, Evening post [1881]

44 p. 8°.   USE, V

Wayland seminary and college, Richmond, Va.

3869. WAYLAND SEMINARY AND COLLEGE. Catalogue . . . [Rich-
mond, Va., 18-?-19-?]

8°. (Colored; prep. & col.; co-ed.; Bapt.; 1865)
Founded in Washington, D. C., 1865; moved to Richmond, 1899.
V: 1898/99.

William and Mary college, Williamsburg, Va.

3870. BOWEN, CLARENCE W. Baccalaureate address delivered before
the faculty and students of the College of William and Mary, at
the 222d annual commencement at Williamsburg, Virginia, June
10, 1915 . . . [New York, De Vinne, 1915]

20 p. 8°.   LC, V, WM

3871. EWELL, BENJAMIN S. Address to the students of the College
of William and Mary by President . . . Ewell, at the commencement, July 4th, 1873. Baltimore, Murphy, 1873.

12 p. 12°.   H, V

3872. ———. Report and address of Benjamin S. Ewell, the president of the College of William and Mary, at their convocation in Richmond, on the 18th day of April, 1879. Richmond, Va., Randolph & English, 1879.

    15 p. 8°.   **VU**

3873. [GILMAN, DANIEL C., *et al.*] Address [by D. C. Gilman] and poem [by A. C. Gordon] delivered before the Phi beta kappa society of the College of William and Mary at Williamsburg, Va., Dec. 5, 1906 . . . Richmond, Jones, 1907.

    15 p. 8°.   **H, V**

"The significance of a liberal education."

3874. HUGHES, ROBERT W. "The ideal student." Address . . . before the Society of alumni of the College of William and Mary, on the occasion of the 198th commencement exercises of that institution. June 30th, 1892. Richmond, Daily record, 1892.

    23, [1] p. 8°.   **V, VU**

3875. MONTAGUE, ROBERT L. Address of Hon. Robert L. Montague, delivered before the Society of alumni of William and Mary college, Williamsburg, Va., on the 4th of July, 1870. Norfolk, Va., The Society, 1871.

    20 p. 8°.   **LC**

The duty and responsibility of the College in restoring Virginia and the South in their economic, social, and educational aspects; an indirect attack upon the evils of Republican reconstruction.

3876. MUNFORD, BEVERLEY B. "Our times and the men for our times." Address . . . before the Association of the alumni of the College of William and Mary . . . July 4, 1889. Richmond, Fergusson, 1889.

    30 p. 8°.   **V**

3877. PHI BETA KAPPA. Report of the public exercises held in connection with the Ninth triennial council of the United chapters of Phi beta kappa at William and Mary college, Williamsburg, Va., Sept. 11, 1907, together with the proceedings of the Council. Somerville, N. J., Unionist gazette assoc. [1907?]

    47 p. illus., front. 8°. (Phi beta kappa publications. New ser., no. 6)
                                       V

3878. PHI BETA KAPPA. To honor the fifty founders of Phi beta kappa. A memorial. [Williamsburg, Va., 1924]

14 p. 16°.   **BP**
Concerning a permanent memorial to be located at the College of William and Mary, where the society originated.

3879. RANDOLPH, A. M. Address by Rev. A. M. Randolph, A. M., before the Alumni at the 182d commencement of William and Mary college, Williamsburg, Va. Published by request of the Alumni. Baltimore, Turnbull, 1875.

20 p. 8°.   **V**

3880. SEMPLE, HENRY C. Address . . . to the Society of the alumni of William and Mary college. July 4th, 1890. Washington, D. C., Judd & Detweiler [1890]

24 p. 8°.   **LC, USE, V**
Some account of the struggles and vicissitudes of the College after 1865, and of the introduction of the normal school system.

3881. SWEM, EARL G. Description of the mace of William and Mary college . . . Williamsburg, Va. For sale by the Library of William and Mary college, 1926.

[4] p. illus. 8°.   **LC, V, WM**
The mace was presented to the College by alumni and students in 1923.

3882. ———. Portraits in the library and chapel of William and Mary college . . . [Williamsburg, Va.] For sale by the Library, 1926.

8 p. 8°.   **H, LC, V, WM**

3883. TYLER, LYON G. College of William and Mary. Letter from its president, Hon. Lyon G. Tyler. The plan of reorganization and the special work proposed—reasons why William and Mary was selected as the site for a normal school. [Williamsburg, Va., Long, 1889]

7 p. 8°.   **LC, V**

3884. ———. Farewell address of Lyon Gardiner Tyler . . . president (1888-1919) of the College of William and Mary, Williamsburg, Virginia, delivered in the college chapel, at the close of the final exercises, June 10, 1919. [Richmond, Richmond press, 1919?]

38 p., 1 l., incl. front. (port.) 16°.   **BP, LC, NYP, V**

3885. ————. The Mattey Whaley model and practice school of William and Mary college. Richmond, Va., Whittet & Shepperson, 1895.

18 p. illus. 8°. **BP, H**

3886. WATTS, J. ALLEN. Address . . . before the Society of alumni of the College of William and Mary, on the occasion of the celebration of the 200th anniversary of the charter of the College . . . June 21, 1893. Roanoke, Stone, 1893.

26 p. 8°. **V**

3887. WELLFORD, BEVERLY R. An address, delivered before the Phoenix and Philomathean literary societies of the College of William and Mary. Richmond, Whittet & Shepperson, 1896.

21 p. 8°. **V**

The story of Virginia's part in the secession movement retold, upholding the traditions of the Old South.

3888. WILLIAM AND MARY COLLEGE. Annual report . . . Richmond [18-?-19—

8°. Report year ends June 30.

Printed also in *Report* of Supt. of public instruction, 1889-19— **[3300]** H: 1911/12; LC: 1888/89-89/90; NYP: 1888/89-89/90, 1911/12; USC: 1888/89; WM: 1865/66-1928/29.

3889. ————. Bulletin . . . vol. 1- ; 1907— [Williamsburg? Va., 1907—

8°. Issued irreg.

BP: IX, 2; XVI-XX; (1916, 24-27). H: I, 3; II, 3-4; III, 2, 4, 6; IV, 1; V, 1; VI, 1-5; VII, 1-4; VIII, 1-2; IX, 1-2, 4; X, 1-2, 4; XI, 1-3; XII, 1, 4; XIII, 1; XIV, 1, 8-9; XV, 1; XVI, 1; XVII, 1; XVIII, 1, 4; XIX, 1, 6; XX, 1, 4; XXI, 1-2; XXII, 1. LC: IX, 4; X, 4; XI, 2-3; XX, 4, 6-7; XXI, 3-5; (1915-17, 27-28). McC: XIX, 4 (1926). USE: III, 2-5; IV-IX (only no. 1 of each); X, 1-4; XI-XII, XIV-XVI (only no. 1 of each); XVII, 1-2; XVIII, 1, 5; XIX, 6; XX, 1; XXI, 1. V: Jan., Apr., Oct., 1907; Jan., Apr., Nov., 08; Apr., July, Oct., 09; Oct., 10; Jan., Oct., 11; May, Oct., 12; Jan., Apr., May, Oct., 13; Jan., May, Oct., 14 & 15; Apr., Oct., 16; Apr., May, Oct., 17; Jan., Apr., Oct., 18; Jan., Apr., 19; XIII, 2, 9; XVII, 2, 13; XVIII, 2, 5; XIX, 3-4; XX, 1-4, 6-7; XXI, 1-2, 5; XXII, 1; (1920-28). WM: I-XXII.

3890. ————. Catalogue . . . announcements . . . Richmond [etc., 18-?-19—

illus., plates, ports. 8°. (State; co-ed.; 1693)

Title varies: Catalogue of the officers and students; Catalogue and course of studies.

Catalogue pub. in 1866 covers the sessions 1860/61 and 1865/66.

BP: 1865/66, 88/89, 90/91, 93/94; **H**: 1889/90-1904/05, 06/07-27/28; **LC**: 1865/66, 88/89, 91/92, 94/95-97/98, 1900/01-03/04, 05/06-07/08, 09/10-13/14, 17/18, 21/22, 24/25-26/27; **NYP**: 1865/66, 89/90-97/98, 99/1900-05/06, 07/08-16/17, 18/19-22/23, 24/25, 27/28; **USE**: 1895/96-1903/04, 08/09-17/18, 19/20-23/24, 25/26-27/28; **V**: 1865/66, 89/90-1927/28; **WM**: 1865/66-1928/29.

3891. WILLIAM AND MARY COLLEGE. Catalogue of the alumni and alumnae, 1865-1923. [Williamsburg, 1923]

159 p. 8°.   (In its *Bulletin*, XVIII, 5 **[3889]**) **BP, H, USE, V, WM**

3892. ———. Citizenship creed, 1922. Marshall-Wythe school of government and citizenship, of the College of William and Mary. 3d edit. [n. p.] 1922.

[4] p. 12°.   **VU**

3893. ———. Historical sketch of the College of William and Mary in Virginia. Richmond, Gary & Clemmitt, 1866.

20 p. 8°. (With its *Catalogue,* 1866 **[3890]**) **BP, H, LC, NYP, V, WM**

3894. ———. Proceedings at the formal installation of Julian Alvin Carroll Chandler as president of the College of William and Mary in Virginia, Oct. 19, 1921. [New York, Morning star press] 1921.

1 p. l., 50 p. 8°.   **V, WM**

3895. ———. Programme of the colonial pageant, Williamsburg, Virginia, 4 July 1921, campus of William and Mary college, 3:30 P. M. [Williamsburg, Ferguson, 1921]

[6] p. illus. 8°.   **V, VU**

3896. ———. A roll of fame. [n. p., 1920?]

8 p. 16°.   **V**

Distinguished alumni of the college.

3897. ———. The romance and renaissance of the College of William and Mary. [Richmond, Va., Whittet & Shepperson, 1924?]

8°.   **H**

3898. ———. Souvenir programme. Community celebration and John Marshall pageant, College of William and Mary campus, Williamsburg, Va., July 4th, 1922. Joint auspices College of

William and Mary, the churches and civic organizations of Williamsburg. [Williamsburg, Va., 1922]

32 p. illus., plates. 8°. **BP**

3899. ———. Two hundredth anniversary of the charter of the College of William and Mary. 1693. 1893. [Richmond, Whittet & Shepperson, 1894]

3 p. l., [5]-49 p. 8°. **BP, H, LC, NYP, V**
"Edited by Lyon G. Tyler."
Programme of celebration, addresses, officers of the college, etc.

3900. ———. Vital facts about Jamestown, Yorktown, Williamsburg, College of William and Mary. Prepared by the students of the College of William and Mary in honor of the attendance of the President of the U. S. and distinguished educators at the formal installation of Dr. J. A. C. Chandler as president of the college, Oct. 19, 1921. [Williamsburg, Va., 1921]

[3] p. 8°. **USE**

3901. ———. ALUMNI ASSOCIATION. Addresses delivered at the unveiling of the tablet erected by the Alumni to the memory of Benjamin Stoddard Ewell, College chapel, June 21, 1899. Richmond, Whittet & Shepperson, 1899.

16 p. 8°. **H**
B. S. Ewell, president of the College, 1854-1888.

3902. ———. ———. Constitution . . . [n. p., n. d.]
6 p. 16°. **V**

3903. ———. RICHMOND DIVISION. The first year of the School of social work and public health; selected newspaper articles and editorials . . . June 24, 1918. [Richmond, 1918?]

14 p. port. 8°. **V**

3904. ———. ———. [Richmond school of social work and public health] Bulletin, vol. 1, no. 1- ; May 1, 1925— Richmond, Va., 1925—

8°. "Pub. at least 4 times a year."
Includes Catalogue of Richmond school . . .
LC: III, 1 (May, 1927); **V, WM:** I-III (1925-28).

3905. ———. ———. Richmond school of social work and public health . . . Catalogue . . . Richmond [1918?—

8°. (In its *Bulletin,* 1925/26— **[3904]**)

LC: 1927/28; **V**: 1918/19, 20/21-22/23, 24/25-27/28; **WM**: 1918/19-27/28.

3906. WILLIAM AND MARY COLLEGE. RICHMOND DIVISION. Richmond, Va. School of social work and public health. Should the South's first school of public health nursing and social work be established on a permanent basis? . . . Richmond, School of social work . . . [n. d.]

2 circulars. 8°.   **V**

The Woman's college, Richmond, Va.

3907. THE WOMAN'S COLLEGE. . . . Catalogue. Richmond, Va. [18-?-19—

illus. 8°. (Prep. & col.; non-sect.; 1854)
    LC: 1902/03; **USE**: 1896/97-97/98, 1905/06, 08/09; **V**: 1896/97, 99/1900, 01/02-06/07, 08/09-09/10, 11/12, 13/14.

Young ladies' college, Buena Vista, Va.

3908. YOUNG LADIES' COLLEGE. Catalogue . . . [Staunton, etc., 18-?-?]

8°. (Non-sect.; 186-?)   **V**: 1894/95.
    Located at Staunton, 18-?-1882?; at Luray, 1883?-93; at Buena Vista, 1894-?

Secondary Works

3909. ANDERSON, JOSEPH R. The V. M. I. and her sons—in the past. A paper read . . . before Washington chapter, Virginia military institute alumni assosiation . . . at New Willard hotel, Mar. 15, 1904. Pub. by V. M. I. [n. p., 1904?]

10 p. 8°.   **V**
Leading alumni of V. M. I., with a compilation of V. M. I. men in the various professions and occupations.

3910. ———. The V. M. I.—her past. Address . . . delivered before the Richmond chapter, Virginia military institute alumni association, on the 71st anniversary of the founding of the Institute, Nov. 11, 1910. [n. p., Pub. by V. M. I., 1910]

12 p. 8°.   **NYP, V**

3911. BARRINGER, PAUL B. A history of the Medical department of the University of Virginia; its system of education, and its results. [An address delivered before the students and alumni of the Medical dept. of the University of Virginia, Oct. 25th, 1887. n. p., n. d.]

10 p. 8°.   **VU**
Includes a sketch of the Dept. since 1865.

3912. ———, ed. University of Virginia; its history, influence, equipment and characteristics, with biographical sketches and portraits of founders, benefactors, officers and alumni; editorial staff, historical: Paul Brandon Barringer . . . James Mercer Garnett . . . biographical: Rosewell Page . . . illustrated . . . New York, Lewis pub., 1904.

2 v. front. (v. 1) illus., ports., plans, facsim. 4°.
                                        NYP, USE, V, VU, WM
Based mainly on university records and publications. Chs. 13-16 on the period since 1865 treat such subjects as faculty changes, the woman question, the president question, student life and activity, alumni, etc. Vol. II is biographical.

3913. BRUCE, PHILIP A. History of the University of Virginia, 1819-1919; the lengthened shadow of one man . . . Centennial ed. . . . New York, Macmillan [ca. 1920-22]

5 v. fronts. (incl. ports.) 8°.
The standard, definitive history of the University, in the characteristic readable style of the author. Vols. III-V on the periods since the Civil war: reconstruction and expansion, 1865-95; restoration, 1895-1904; the presidency, 1904-19. Bibliography listed for each period.

3914. COREY, CHARLES H. Historical sketch of the Richmond institute, founded at Richmond, Va., in 1867, one of the seven institutions sustained by the American Baptist home mission society, for the education of teachers and preachers among the freedmen of the South . . . Richmond, Clemmitt & Jones, 1876.

31, [1] p. illus. 8°.   **NYP, USE, WM**

3915. ———. A history of the Richmond theological seminary, with reminiscences of thirty years' work among the colored people of the South. By Charles H[enry] Corey . . . with an introduction by W. W. Landrum, D.D. Richmond, Va., Randolph, 1895.

240 p. front., illus., plates, ports. 12°.   **BP, H, USE, V, VU**
Portrays the early history of the Seminary and its predecessors with vividness; includes many letters, reports, etc., quoted. Valuable information on social and educational conditions—much of it source material.

3916. CRENSHAW, LEWIS D. A history of the quinquennial reunion of the Class of 1908, University of Virginia, June 14-18, 1913 . . . Roanoke, Stone [1915]

139 p. front., illus., plate. 8°.   V, VU
Material collected from various members of the class; written in a humorous vein.

3917. CROWSON, BENJAMIN F., comp. English fundamentals, supplementary material, compiled for the fourth class, Virginia military institute . . . Lexington, Va., B. F. Crowson [ca. 1926]

296 p. 12°.   LC, USE
Text-book of English grammar, spelling, etc.

3918. CULBRETH, DAVID M. The University of Virginia; memories of her student-life and professors . . . New York and Washington, Neale, 1908.

501 p. incl. front. plates, ports. 8°.   BP, H, LC, USE, V, VU, WM

3919. DAVIS, JOHN S. History of the medical department of the University of Virginia, 1825-1914. [n. p., n. d.]

22 p. illus. 8°. (Reprint from *Alumni bulletin,* University of Virginia, July, 1914)   VU
Based on official records of the dept.

3920. FISHER, MILES M., ed. Virginia union university and some of her achievements . . . Twenty-fifth anniversary, 1899-1924. [Richmond, Brown, ca. 1924]

110 p., 1 l. incl. front., illus., ports. 4°.   LC
Historical sketch of the University and its antecedents, followed by a description of its achievements, student activities, etc.

3921. GILMAN, DANIEL C. University problems in the U. S. . . . New York, Century, 1898.

5 p. l., 319 p. 8°.   H, LC, VU
Includes a sketch of Washington and Lee university.

3922. GOODWIN, WILLIAM A., ed. History of the Theological seminary in Virginia and its historical background [edited by] Rev. Wm. A. R. Goodwin . . . Centennial ed. New York, Gorham, 1923-[24]

2 v. fronts., plates, ports. 8°.   LC, V, VU, WM
The authoritative history of the seminary, based on reliable source material, in large part the records of the institution; a collaboration by men connected with the Seminary. Contains biographical sketches of

alumni, articles on alumni association, benefactors, the Episcopal high
school, etc.

3923. GORDON, ARMISTEAD C. Memories and memorials of William
Gordon McCabe . . . Richmond, Va., Old Dominion press,
1925.

> 2 v. fronts., ports., facsim. 8°.   **LC, NYP, V, VU**
> Consists largely of quotations from McCabe's writings and correspond-
> ence and reveals his importance in secondary and higher education and
> in the field of letters. Valuable contribution to the educational history
> of Virginia.

3924. HODGES, WILLIAM T. The problem of student accounting and
guidance in six Virginia colleges. Harvard university, 1925.

> xii, 137 p. typew. 4°. (Thesis, Harvard university)   **H**
> Study, based on official records, of student elimination from William
> and Mary college, University of Virginia, Virginia military institute, Vir-
> ginia polytechnic institute, Washington and Lee university, and Univer-
> sity of Richmond.

3925. IRBY, RICHARD. History of Randolph-Macon college, Virginia. The oldest incorporated Methodist college in America.
. . . Richmond, Va., Whittet & Shepperson [189-?]

> 331 p. front., illus., plates, ports. 8°.   **H, LC, RM, USE, V**
> Based on the records of the college, with long quotations therefrom.
> Author was on the Board of trustees after the Civil war. Narrative
> proper is carried to 1886.

3926. LEE MEMORIAL FUND. Robert E. Lee, soldier, patriot, educator; with special reference to his life and services at Washington
and Lee university, Lexington, Va. Pub. for the Lee memorial
fund . . . [Philadelphia, Patterson & White, *ca.* 1921]

> [31] p. illus. (incl. ports., facsim.) 8°.   **H, LC, V**
> Includes an account of Lee's presidency at Washington and Lee uni-
> versity; with notes on the Lee memorial at Lexington, Va.

3927. McILWAINE, HENRY R. History of the library at the College
of William and Mary. [Address . . . May 14, 1909] [n. p.,
n. d.]

> 15 p. 8°.   **VU**

3928. McILWAINE, RICHARD. Does college education pay? [By
Richard McIlwaine, Hampden-Sidney, Va. n. p., 189-?]

> [4] p. 8°.   **VU**
> An answer in the affirmative, based on records of Hampden-Sidney
> college.

3929. MOORE, WALTER W. Appreciations and historical addresses . . . [Richmond, Presbyterian committee of publication, 1914?]

167, [6] p. front., ports. 8°.   LC, V

Includes essays on Moses Drury Hoge; The centennial celebration of Union seminary; The first fifty years of Union seminary.

3930. NICHOLS, EDWARD W. Fifty years of service, and other papers. By E. W. Nichols, superintendent emeritus, Virginia military institute, Nov., 1926. Lexington, Rockbridge, 1926.

58, 77, 28 p., 2 l., 53 p. incl. tables (part fold) diagrs., ports. 8°.   V

Pt. I: V. M. I., 1839-1874, historical and traditional. Pt. II; 50 years of service, V. M. I., 1874-1924. Pt. III: Courses of instruction, 1839-1924. Pt. IV: . . . Training of officers at home and abroad.

3931. PATTON, JOHN S. The University of Virginia in the World war . . . [Charlottesville? 1927?]

71 p. illus. (incl. ports.) 8°.   LC, V, VU

Based mainly on contemporary periodical literature of the University; includes lists of distinguished alumni and students in the war.

Ed. of 1922.   VU

3932. ———, et al., ed. Jefferson's university; glimpses of the past and present of the University of Virginia . . . Editors: John S. Patton, Sallie J. Doswell, Lewis D. Crenshaw. [Charlottesville, Va., Michie, ca. 1915]

97, [3] p. illus. (incl. ports.) 8°.   H, LC, NYP, USE, VU

Includes chapters on buildings and equipment, societies and publications, athletics, alumni, etc.

3933. RYLAND, GARNETT. The old Richmond college; an address delivered at commencement, June 9, 1914 . . . [n. p.] 1914.

[18] p. illus. 8°.   VB

Historical sketch of the "first great epoch . . . of Richmond college [which] came to an end in June, 1914."

3934. SMITH, WILLIAM R. Charles Lewis Cocke, founder of Hollins college . . . Boston, Badger [ca. 1921]

161 p. front., plates, ports. 8°.   LC, NYP, V

Based on the college records and personal reminiscences, this biography affords an interesting and enlightening picture of education for women in Virginia during the second half of the 19th century.

3935. [SMYTH, E. A., comp.] A brief history of the Virginia agricultural and mechanical college and polytechnic institute, 1872-1922.

With the exception of the supplement, the contents were prepared by Prof. E. A. Smyth. [Blacksburg, The Institute, 1922]

71 p. illus. (incl. ports.) plan. 8°. (V. P. I., *Bulletin,* XV, 4; May, 1922)   **USE, V, VPI**

3936. TYLER, LYON G. The College of William and Mary in Virginia: its history and work. 1693-1907 . . . Richmond, Va., Whittet & Shepperson, 1907.

96 p. front., illus. (incl. ports., facsims.) 8°.   **LC, V, WM**
Based on college records and other reliable source material, this sketch by the president discusses the system of instruction since 1865, organizations, officers, etc.

3937. ——. . . . The College of William and Mary: its work, discipline and history, from its foundation to the present time . . . [Williamsburg? Va., 1917]

38 p. (College of William and Mary. *Bulletin,* X, 4) **H, LC, USE, WM**

3938. ——. Williamsburg, the old colonial capital . . . Richmond, Va., Whittet & Shepperson [*ca.* 1907]

285 p. illus. (incl. ports., maps, facsims.) 2 fold. plans (incl. front.) 8°.
Contains brief notes on the College of William and Mary at the beginning of the 20th century.

3939. U. S. ARTILLERY SCHOOL, Fort Monroe, Va. Historical sketch of the U. S. Artillery school . . . from 1867 to 1887, extracted from the annual report of the commanding officer for 1887. Ft. Monroe, Va., 1887.

34 p. 8°.   **USE**

3940. [3244] VIRGINIA POLYTECHNIC INSTITUTE. Virginia polytechnic institute in the World war. Blacksburg, Va., 1927.

3941. WADDELL, JOSEPH A. History of the Mary Baldwin seminary (originally Augusta female seminary) from 1842 to 1905 inclusive. 1905. [Staunton, Augusta print., 1908]

[85] p. front. (port.) 8°.   V
The narrative, quite strictly chronological, is based mainly on the records of the school.

3942. WALKER, CORNELIUS. The life and correspondence of Rev. William Sparrow, D.D., late professor of systematic divinity and evidences, in the Episcopal theological seminary of Virginia . . . Philadelphia, Hammond, 1876.

viii, [17]-433 p. front. (port.) 8°.   V

Contains some information on the seminary during the decade following the Civil war.

3943. WILLIAM AND MARY COLLEGE. The history of the College of William and Mary from its foundation, 1660, to 1874. Richmond, Randolph & English, 1874.

183, [1] p., 1 l. 8°.   **BP, H, LC, USE, V, VU, WM**
Comp. by the faculty.
Includes "Catalogue of the College . . . from its foundation to 1874," p. [74]-168.

3944. ———. The history of the College of William and Mary, from its foundation, 1693 to 1870. Baltimore, Murphy, 1870.

162 p. 8°.   **BP, H, LC, NYP, USE, V**
Includes General catalogue to 1870; also "Catalogue of the College . . . from its foundation to 1870," p. 64-147.

3945. WISE, JENNINGS C. Personal memoir of the life and services of Scott Shipp . . . [Lexington? Va.] 1915.

56 p. ports. (incl. front.) 8°.   **LC, NYP, V, VU, WM**
Shipp's long association with Virginia military institute throws light upon educational problems in Virginia since 1865. The author is full of praise for his subject.

Periodicals

3946. AGREVIEW, Pub. by the Agricultural education dept., Virginia polytechnic institute. Blacksburg, Va., 1926-28.

mimeog. bi-monthly.   **VPI**
Discont. pub., Aug., 1928.

3947. ARGONAUT . . . issued by the junior class, Lynchburg college. Lynchburg, Va., 1922—

illus., plates (part. col.) ports. 4°. annual.   **LC, USE:** 1922.

3948. ASSOCIATION record; a report of the religious work in the University of Virginia. Pub. by the Y. M. C. A. of the University. Vol. 1- ; 1903—   [Charlottesville, 1903—

illus. 8°.   **V:** I-V (1903-07).

3949. The BIG tent. Vol. 1, nos. 1-10. University of Virginia, Charlottesville, Va., Mar. 12-June 10, 1914.

10 nos. illus. f°.   **VU**
Lewis Dabney, ed. "Official trumpet of the [alumni] re-union movement."

3950. The BLUESTOCKING, published by the junior class, Mary Baldwin college . . . Vol. 1- ; 1923/24— Staunton, Va. [1924—

col. front., illus. (part col., incl. ports.) 4°. annual.
LC, USE: III-IV (1925/26-26/27).

3951. The BOMB, Virginia military institute . . . Vol. 1- [1874?-19— Lexington, Va., 1874?-19—

illus. (incl. ports.) 4°. annual.
Discont. pub., 1884-94.
LC, USE: XXXIX, XL (1923-24); V: XXXI, XL (1915, 24); VMI: I- XLV (1874?-1929).

3952. BRIAR patch, pub. by the senior and junior classes of Sweet Briar college. Sweet Briar, Va. [19—

4°. annual.   USE: 1914/15.

3953. The BUGLE. [Pub. annually by the Corps of cadets of the Virginia polytechnic institute] Vol. 1- ; 1895-19— Blacksburg, Va. [1895-19—

illus. (part. col.) plates (part. col.) ports. 4°.
LC: XIV, XXIV, XXIX-XXX, XXXIII-XXXIV (1908, 18, 23-24, 27-28); NYP: III, V (1897, 99); USE: 1918, 23-24; V: 1904-05; VPI: 1895-1928.

3954. The CADET, a . . . magazine of science, literature, and art. Pub. by the literary societies of Virginia military institute. [1st ser., vol. 1- ?; 1870-?] New ser., vol. 1- ; 1907— [Lexington, Va.] 1870-19—

8°.-f°. monthly.
V: 1st ser., II-III (1870-71). New ser.: I, 9-13, 15; II, 1; VII, 15; IX, 2-5, 7-30, 32; X, 1-2, 10-25; (1908-16). VMI: new ser., I-XXII (1907-28/29).

3955. The CALYX . . . Vol. 1- ; 1895-19— published annually by the students of Washington and Lee university. [Lexington, Va., 1895-19—

illus. (part col., incl. ports.) 4°.
LC: XXX-XXXIII (1924-27); NYP: 1901; USE: 1914, 24, 26-27; V: 1915; VU: 1900; WL: 1895-1928.

3956. The CAMEO . . . Martha Washington college . . . senior class . . . Vol. 1- ; 1909/10— Abingdon, Va., 1910—

illus., plates, ports. 4°. annual.
LC: XVI, XVIII (1924/25, 26/27).

3957. Cargoes. Pub. by Hollins college. Vol. 1- [1910/11—n. p., 1910—

> 4°. monthly during college year. A literary magazine.
> **V:** XV, 1-6; XVI, 1-7; XVII, 1-6; (1924/25-26/27).

3958. The Cavalier [pub. by the students of the University of Virginia] Vol. 1, no. 1- ; May, 1920— Lynchburg, 1920—

> illus. 4°. monthly during school year. Humor magazine.
> Originally called The Virginia reel, 1920-29.
> **NYP:** III, 1-10 (1922/23); **VU:** I-X (1920/21-29/30).

3959. Chapter chats. Pub. by the State board of education with the Dept. of agricultural education of the Virginia polytechnic institute co-operating. Blacksburg, Va., 1928—

> bi-monthly. Alternates with Virginia news letter [4019]
> **VPI:** 1928-29.

3960. The Chisel, published by the students of the Woman's college, Richmond, Va. Vol. 1- [1894-19—] Richmond, 1894-19—

> 8°. quarterly.
> **V:** XIV, 3; XVI, 1-4; XVII, 1-4; XVIII, 1-4; XIX, 1-3; XXI, 2-3; (1907-12).

3961. Cohee; published by Virginia polytechnic institute, Blacksburg, Va., 1897-98.

> monthly? Ceased pub., June, 1898.
> **VPI:** Dec., 1897; June 22, 1898.

3962. College topics. Vol. 1- [1889/90?-19—] Charlottesville, Va., University of Virginia [1889?-19—

> f°. tri-weekly during college year.
> "Official publication of the General athletic association."
> **V:** XIX-XX (Jan., 1908-June, 09); **VU:** II-XLI (1890/91-1929/30).

3963. Colonial echo . . . published by the students of William and Mary college. [Williamsburg, Va., 1903—

> illus. (part. col.) plates, ports. 4°. annual.
> **LC:** 1926; **USE:** 1914, 26; **V:** 1905, 07-15, 17, 19, 21-22, 24.

3964. Corks and curls . . . Ed. by the Greek letter fraternities. University of Virginia. Vol. 1- ; 1888-19— Charlottesville, Va. [1888-19—

> illus., plates, ports. 4°. annual.
> **LC:** IV, VI-VIII, XIII (1891, 93-95, 1900); **NYP:** 1888, 94-95,

1915, 22; **USE**: 1895, 1914; **V**: 1888-93, 96-1900, 02-04, 06, 15, 17, 25-26; **VU**: 1888-1929.

3965. Elizabeth chronicle. Vol. 1- [Published by Elizabeth college, Salem, Va.] Charlotte [N. C.] 1898—

8°.-4°.   **NYP**: I, 1-2 (1898).

3966. The Emory and Henry bulletin, vol. 1- Emory, Va., 1907—

8°. Issued 8 times yearly by Emory and Henry college.
H: II, 6; III, 4; IV, 3; V, 3; VI, 1; VIII-XII (only no. 1 of each); XIX, 2; (1909-19, 26). **V**: I, 5 (Dec., 1907).

3967. Extension division news, vol. 1- ; Nov., 1918— Blacksburg, Va. [Pub. by Extension division, Virginia polytechnic institute] 1918—

f°. monthly.
USAg: I, 1-9, 11-12; II-IX. **V**: IV, 7, 9-12; V, 1-8, 10-12; VI, 1-8, 10-12; VII-X; XI, 1, 3-5; (1923-29). **VPI**: I-XI.

3968. Extension topics. Pub. by the Extension division, University of Virginia. Vol. 1- ; 1926— [University, Va.] 1926—

f°. leaf. quarterly. None pub., 1928/29.
V: I, 2-3; II, 2; (1926-27). **VU**: I-III; (1926/27-29/30).

3969. The Firing line. [Pub. by the students of Virginia polytechnic institute] Vol. 1- ; 1913— Blacksburg, 1913—

ports., plates. 8°.
V: I; **VPI**: I, 1-7 (Nov., 1913-May, 14).

3970. Grapurchat: pub. by the Virginia State teachers' college, East Radford, Va. Vol. 1- ; 1920/21— [n. p., 1920—

monthly.   **V**: VIII, 9 (June, 1928).

3971. Gray jacket. [1st ser.] vol. 1, no. 1 (July, 1875); 2d ser., vol. 1, nos. 1-2 (Feb.-Mar., 1884); 3d ser., vol. 1-14 (1892/93-1905/06); 4th ser., vol. 11-13 (1906/07-08/09). Blacksburg, Va., Pub. monthly by the Maury and Lee literary societies, Virginia polytechnic institute, 1875, 1884, 1892-1909.

19 v. 8°. No more pub.
V: I, 1; III, 1-3, 8-9; 4th ser.; I, 6, 9-10; II, 8; IV, 1-2; VII, 2-5, 7; VIII, 1, 6; IX, 9; X, 6-7, 9; XI, 1, 3-5, 7; XII, 1-8; XIII, 1-7; XIV, 1-2. **VPI**: 1st-4th ser.

3972. The Hampden-Sidney magazine. Vol. 1- ; 1883/84-19—

Pub. by the literary societies of Hampden-Sidney college [n. p., 1883-19—

8°. **H**: XII, 2, 5-6. **NYP**: VIII, 1. **V**: XXIV, 1; XLII, 2; (1906, 24).

3973. The HELIANTHUS . . . published by the junior and senior classes of Randolph-Macon women's college. [Lynchburg, 19—

4°. annual. **USE**: 1914; **LC**: 1928.

3974. HOLLINS alumnae quarterly. Hollins college. Vol. 1, no. 1- ; 1926/27— [n. p., 1926—

4°. **V**: I, 1-II, 3 (1926/27-27).

3975. The HOLLINS magazine. Pub. by the Euzelian and Euepian literary societies of Hollins institute. Vol. 1- [n. p.] 1910—

8°. monthly.
H: I, 7 (Apr., 1911); **V**: I-XI, XIII-XIV (1910-24).

3976. IN ole Virginny . . . published by the student body, Virginia college . . . Vol. 1- ; 1913— Roanoke, Va. [1913—

4°. annual. **LC**: XVI (1928).

3977. The KALEIDOSCOPE, published by the students of Hampden-Sidney college, Virginia . . . Vol. 1- ; 1893-19— [Buffalo, etc., 1893-19—

illus., plates (part col.) 8°.
LC: II, VIII-X, XII-XIII, XV-XX, [XXI], XXIV-XXVI, XXXIV (1894, 1900-02, 06-07, 09-19, 28); **NYP**: 1894-97; **USE**: 1902, 14; **V**: 1893-94, 96, 1900-03, 06-23.

3978. MADISON HALL notes. [Pub. by the Young men's Christian association] University of Virginia. Vol. 1-13; 1905/06-19/20. University, Va., 1905-20.

4°. weekly, Sept. to June. No more pub. **VU**: I-XIII.

3979. The MESSENGER. [Pub. by the Philologian and Mu sigma rho societies of Richmond college, Richmond, Va.] Vol. 1, no. 1- ; Richmond [1875?-19—

plates. 8°. monthly.
H: XII, 2; XXV, 1-4, 6; LI, 4; (1886, 98/99, 1925). **NYP**: XX, 5-6; XXI, 1-5; XXII, 4; XXIV, 7; XXV, 1-3; (1894-99). **V**: VIII, 5-6, 8-9; IX, 1, 3-4; XXI, 8; XXV, 2; XXVI, 4; XXXI, 1, 2/3, 4/5, 7-9; XXXIV, 3; XXXV, 3, 5-7; XXXVI, 2; XXXIX, 7; XL, 1-2; XLI, 1-2; XLII, 2-8; XLIII, 2-8; XLIV, 1; XLVIII, 6; L, 4-6; LI, 1-7; LII, 1-7; LIII, 1-7; LIV, 1.

3980. MICROCOSM. Roanoke college, Salem, Va. New York [1870?- ?]

8°.   **LC:** 1869/70; **USE:** 1871/72.

3981. NEW yellow journal (an ancient tradition) [University of Virginia] Vol. 1- ; 1927— [University, Va., 1927—

f°. annual.   **VU:** 1927.

3982. NEW YORK alumni bulletin, pub. by the New York association of alumni of the University of Virginia. Vol. 1-[?] 1912-[?] New York, 1912—

illus. 4°. monthly?   **VU:** I, 2 (May 1, 1912).

3983. The PHI beta kappa key . . . William and Mary number, Mar., 1912 . . . [Somerville, N. J.? 1912]

45 p. illus. 8°. (Vol. 1, no. 7)   **H, V**

3984. RANDOLPH-MACON COLLEGE monthly. Vol. 1- [Ashland? Va., 1879?-19—

8°. **NYP:** Apr., 1882. **V:** IV, 7; V, 7-9; VII, 1, 3; VIII, 2, 7; XXVII, 1-5, 7; XXVIII, 1-2, 5; XXIX, 1-8; XXX, 2-3, 5; XXXIV, 5; (Apr., 1882, 83-87, 1904-08, 12).

3985. [RANDOLPH-MACON woman's college] Alumnae bulletin . . . Vol. 1- ; 1907/08— [Lynchburg? 1907—

8°. quarterly?   **H, LC:** XVIII, 1 (Nov., 1924).

3986. The RAWENOCH, published by the student body of Roanoke college. Vol. 1- Salem, Va. [1900?—

4°. annual.   **LC:** XXIX (1928).

3987. The RECORD of the Hampden-Sidney alumni association. Vol. 1, no. 1- ; Oct., 1926— [Hampden-Sidney, Va., 1926—

illus. 4°. quarterly.
LC: I, 1-4; II, 1; (1926-27). **V:** I-III, 2; (1926-29).

3988. The RING-TUM phi. Vol. 1- Washington and Lee university, Lexington, Va., Rockbridge news print. [1898?-19—

f°. weekly.
H: III, 12 (1900). **V:** XX, 2, 7-24, 26-30; XXI, 1-3; 11-24, 26-29; XXII, 1-17, 19; (1917-19).

3989. ROANOKE collegian. Vol. 1- Roanoke college, Salem, Va. [1877?-19—

4°. monthly, Nov. to June.
BP: VIII-IX; X, 1, 3-5; XI, 2, 4; XII, 1, 9; XIII, 1, 3-4; XIV, 1,

8; XV, 1-3; (1881-87). **H**: III, 10; V, 8; VI, 2; VII, 3, 9-10; VIII, 1, 10; IX, 1-3, 10; X, 9; XI, 1-2, 9; XII, 1-2, 9; XIII, 1; XIV, 1, 8; XV, 1, 3-4, 9; XVI, 1, 7; XVII, 1; XIX, 4, 8; XXI, 4; XXIII, 1-3, 6, 8; XXIV, 1; (1879, 82-97). **NYP**: VI, 2, 4; XV, 1; XVI, 1; XIX, 4; XXI, 4; XXII, 1; XXIII, 4; XXIV, 1, 4, 8; XXV, 5; XXVI, 1, 4, 8; XXVII, 5; XXXI, 3-4; XXXII, 1; XXXVIII, 3; (1879, 88-89, 93, 95, 97-1901, 05, 12).

3990. The ROENTGEN rays, published by the junior class of Roanoke college. Salem, Va. [19—

illus. (incl. ports.) 4°. annual.   **USE**: 1914.

3991. SAMPLER . . . published by [the] senior class of Sullins college. Bristol, Va. [19—

illus. (incl. ports.) 4°. annual.   **LC**: 1925-26; **USE**: 1926.

3992. The SCHOOLMA'AM, published by the students of the State teachers' college. Harrisonburg, Va. [19—

4°. annual.   **LC**: 1928; **V**: 1910-15, 20-23.

3993. The SEMI-ANNUAL. [Pub. by the Euzelian and Euepian literary societies of Hollins institute] Vol. 1- [Roanoke, Va., 1886?- ?]

8°.   **H**: XII (1897); **USE**: 1896.

3994. The SKIRMISHER; pub. by the Virginia polytechnic institute, Blacksburg, Va. Vol. 1-2, no. 1; Oct., 1910-Mar., 1912. Blacksburg, 1910-12.

8°. Issued irreg. No more pub.   **VPI**

3995. The SNIPER; published by the Virginia military institute. Lexington, Va., 1924—

quarterly?   **VMI**: 1924/25-28/29.

3996. The SOUTHERN collegian. Vol. 1- ; 1868-19— [Lexington, Va., 1868-19—

8°. monthly during school year, by students of Washington and Lee university.

H: XIX, 5-8; XX, 3, 5; XXVII, 2-3; XXXII, 8; XLI, 3; XLII, 5; XLV, 5. **LC**: XXXVII (1904/05). **McC**: XIV, 6; XIX, 8. **NYP**: XI, 1-4, 6; XII-XIV, 6; XV, 1-3, 5-7; XVI, 1, 3-7; XIX, 8; XXVI, 3-6; XXXII, 1; XXXIV, 2; XXXVI, 7; XLI, 5; (1878-1909). **V**: XV, 8; XVI, 4-5, 7; XVII, 6-8; XVIII, 1-2; XIX, 1, 5, 8; (1883-87). **WL**: I-XXXIII; XXXIV, 5; XXXV, 1-2; XXXVI-XXXVII, XLII-XLVI; XLVII, 4; XLVIII, 4; XLIX, 1-2; (1868-1900/01; Feb., Oct.-Nov., 02; 03/04-04/05, 09/10-13/14; Apr., 15; Apr., Nov.-Dec., 16).

3997. The . . . SPHINX, published by the senior class of Emory and Henry college. Vol. 1- [Emory, Va., 1916—

illus. (part. col.) plates, ports. 4°. annual.
LC: XI, XIII; (1926, 28).

3998. The SPIDER, pub. by the junior class, Richmond college. Vol. 1- [Richmond, Va., 1903?—

illus. (incl. ports.) 4°. annual.
USE: XII (1914); **V:** 1912-16, 18.

3999. The SPINSTER. Ed. by the students of Hollins institute. [Hollins, Va., 1898-19—

fronts., illus., plates, ports. 4°. annual.
USE: 1914, 17; **V:** 1898-1921, 23-27.

4000. SUMMER school items, University of Virginia, Charlottesville, Va. [1908?—

8°. weekly during summer school.   **VU:** [I-II] 1908-09.

4001. SUMMER school news. [Pub. by the students of the University of Virginia during the first term of summer quarter] New ser., vol. 1- [University, Va.] 1911—

illus. f°. semi-weekly.   **VU:** I-XVIII (1911-28).
Title varies: Summer school item, I-II (1911-12).
Continuation of *College topics* **[3962]** during summer session.

4002. TECHGRAM. Vol. 1- ; Jan., 1923— Blacksburg, Va., Virginia polytechnic institute, 1923—

9 x 16 cm. semi-monthly, Jan.-Apr.; monthly, May-Dec.
V: III, 16; IV-VII, 6; (1925-29). **VPI:** I-VII (1923-29).

4003. The TIE; pub. by the V. M. I. club of Richmond. Vol. 1- [1922?— Richmond, 1922?—

monthly?   **V:** VII, 3 (Oct., 1928).

4004. The TIGER; pub. by the students of Hampden-Sidney college. Vol. 1- [n. p., 192-?—

Issued irreg.   **V:** IX-X (1927-29).

4005. UNION-HARTSHORN journal. Pub. by Virginia union university and Hartshorn memorial college. Richmond, Va. Vol. 1- Richmond [1899?-19—

8°. quarterly?   **V:** XIII, 1 (Nov., 1912).

4006. The UNION seminary magazine. Pub. by the Union theological seminary in Virginia. Vol. 1-   Richmond [1889?-19—

8°. quarterly.
Title varies: Union seminary review.
V: I; II, 2-3; III, 2-4; IV, 1, 3-4; V; VI, 1, 3-4; VII-XI, 3; XII, 2, 4; XIII, 3-4; XV; XVI, 2; XVII, 1-2; XVIII, 4; XIX-XL; (1888/89-1929).

4007. [UNIVERSITY of Virginia] Alumni bulletin . . . [1st ser.] vol. 1-7; 1894-1900. New ser., vol. 1-7; 1901-07. 3d ser., vol. 1-17; 1908-24. Charlottesville, Va., University of Virginia press, 1894-1924.

31 v. plates. 8°. quarterly. No more pub.
BP: 1st ser.: II, 3-4; III-VI, 1. New ser.: VII. 3d ser.: I-II, IV-IX. **H**: 1st ser.: I-III, 2; IV, 2, 4; V, 1-2, 4; VI, 1. New ser.: I, 2-4; II, 2-4; III, 2-4; IV, 2-3; V, 5; VII, 2. 3d ser.: III, 3; IV, 4; VI, 4-5; VIII, 1-5; IX, 4; X, 2-5; XII, 1, 3-5; XIII, 2-5; XIV, 1, 3-4; XV, 1, 3-4; XVI-XVII. **LC**: 1st ser.: I-VII. New ser.: I-III; V, 2, 5; VII, 1-2, 4. 3d ser.: I-XVII. **NYP**: 1st ser.: I-VII. New ser.: I-IV; V, 3, 5; VII. 3d ser.: I-XI; XII, 1-2, 4-5; XIII; XIV, 1, 3-4; XV-XVII. **USE**: 1st ser.: I-IV. 3d ser.: II; III, 3; IV, 4; V, 4; VI, 2, 4; VII, 4; VIII, 1-4; IX, 1, 4; X, 1; XI-XII, 1. **V**: 1st ser.: I, 1, 3-4; II, 1-4; III-V; VI, 1-2. New ser.: I-IV; V, 1-5; VI, 1-2, 2a, 2b; VII, 1, 1a, 1b, 2-4. 3d ser.: I-VII; VIII, 1-2, 4-5; IX-XII; XIII, 1, 3, 4/5; XIV, 1, 3-4; XV-XVII. **VU**: complete file. **WM**: 3d ser.: II-XVII.

4008. UNIVERSITY of Virginia alumni news. Vol. 1-   ; 1913— Charlottesville, Va., 1913—

illus. 8°.
Pub. fortnightly during college year by the General alumni association.
LC: IV-VII, X-XI (1915/16-18/19, 21/22-22/23). **NYP**: I, 1-7; II, 1-17, 19-20; III, 1-4, 6, 8-20; IV, 1-3. **V**: I, 1-7; II, 1, 3, 5, 7-20; III, 1-2, 4-20; IV-VII; VIII, 1-11, & suppls. to 5, 9, 11; IX, 1-11, & suppls. to 3, 6, 10; X, 1-12 & suppl. to 6; XI-XVII. **VU**: I-XVII. **WM**: XII-XIII.

4009. UNIVERSITY of Virginia extension news. Vol. 1-   ; 1923/ 24— University, Va., 1923—

var. siz. bi-weekly. Vol. V, nos. 21-22 not pub.
V: IV, 13, 15, 18; V, 4, 6-7, 12-20, 23-26; VI, 1-10, 12-15, 21; (1927-28/29). **VU**: I-VII; (1923/24-29/30).

4010. UNIVERSITY of Virginia journal of engineering, vol. 1- University, Va. [1920?—

illus. 4°. monthly.
V: VI, 1-3, 5-8; VII, 2-9; (1925/26-26/27. **VU**: I-IX.

4011. UNIVERSITY of Virginia magazine. Vol. 1-87. Lynchburg [etc.] 1856-1928.

87 v. 4°. monthly during school year.
Title varies: The Virginia university magazine, 1856-92.
Succeeded by The Virginia spectator **[4022]**
H: VI, 3-7; VII, 4-6; VIII, 1-2, 4-7; XXX, 5-7; XXXI, 1-4, 6-8; XXXVIII, 1-4; (1868-70, 87-88, 94-95). **LC:** VI; XXII-XXIV; XXXII-XXXIV; XLII, 3, 8; LII-LVII; (1867/68, 82/83-84/85, 88/89-90/91, 98/99, 1908/09-13/14). **NYP:** XII, 5; XV, 5; XXXVIII, 4-9; XXXIX, 2, 4-5; L, 1; LVI, 2-3, 5, 7-8; LVII, 1-8; LVIII, 1-3, 6-7; LIX; (1895-1916). **V:** XI, 7; XIV, 1; XLIV; XLIX, LI, LXII, LXVI-LXX, LXXII (scattered nos.); LXXVI, 1-2, 6-8; LXXVII, 1, 4, 7-8; LXXVIII, 1-4; LXXIX, 1-4/5; LXXX, 1-7; LXXXI, 1-9; (1873, 84/85, 89-1913). **VU:** I-LXXXVII.

4012. [3982] [UNIVERSITY of Virginia] New York alumni bulletin . . . New York, 1912—

4013. The UNIVERSITY of Virginia news letter, published bi-weekly for the Bureau of extension of the University of Virginia. [1st ser.] vol. 1-3; 1918/19-20/21. New ser., vol. 1- ; 1925/26— University, Va., 1918-21, 1925—

f°. bi-weekly. None pub., 1920-24.
H: 1st ser.: I, 1, 3-20, 22-23; II (incompl.); III, 1-18, 21; (1918/19-20/21). **LC:** 1st ser.: I, 1 (Nov., 1918). New ser.: I, 1-12; II, 1-18; III, 1-19; (1925-27). **V:** 1st ser.: I, 1-20; II, 1-21, 23-24, 26; III, 1-2, 4-11, 13-17, 20-21. New ser.: I, 1-12; II, 1-16, 18; III-V. **VU:** complete file.

4014. V. M. I. alumni news. Pub. by Virginia military institute . . . Vol. 1, no. 1- [Sept., 1924— n. p., 1924—

8°. quarterly.
V: III, 3-4 (Mar.-June, 1927); **VMI:** I-VI (1924/25-28/29).

4015. The V. N. & I. I. gazette. Published by the Virginia normal and industrial institute, Ettrick, Va. Vol. 1- [1894-19— n. p., 1894?-19—

monthly.   **V:** XVIII, 2; XXI, 4; (1911, 15).

4016. V. P. I. alumnus. Vol. 1, no. 1- ; Sept., 1928— Blacksburg, Virginia polytechnic institute, 1928—

8°. quarterly.   **VPI:** I (1928/29).

4017. V. P. I. skipper. Vol. 1, no. 1- ; Dec., 1927— Blacksburg, Virginia polytechnic institute, 1927—

4°. Issued irreg. Humor magazine.   **VPI:** I-II (1927/28-28/29)

4018. VIM. Virginia mechanics' institute, Vol. 1- ; Jan., 1927— Richmond, Va., 1927—

4°. Issued 9 times a year.
V: I-III; (1927-29). VU: I, 2-9; II, 1-8; (1927-29).

4019. VIRGINIA news letter. Pub. by the State board of education with the Dept. of agricultural education of Virginia polytechnic institute co-operating. Blacksburg, Va., 1919—

bi-monthly. Alternates with Chapter chats [3959]
VPI: 1919-29.

4020. The VIRGINIA normal and industrial institute gazette. Vol. 1- Petersburg, Va. [189-?-19—

quarterly?
V: XVIII, 2; XXI, 4; XXIII, 2-4; XXIV, 1, 3-4; XXV, 4; XXVI, 1-4; XXVII, 1, 3; XXVIII, 4-5; XXIX, 1-2; XXX, 1-2; Jan., 1925; Jan., Nov., 26; XXXII, 1-2, 5; XXXIII, 1.

4021. The VIRGINIA seminary magazine. Theological seminary, Va. Vol. 1- ; 1888/89-[?] [n. p., 1888- ?]

plates, ports. 8°. monthly, Nov. to July.
NYP: IV, 7-9; V, 1-9; (1891-92). V: I; II, 1-8; III; IV, 1-3, 6-7, 9; V; (1888/89-92/93).

4022. The VIRGINIA spectator; published by the students of the University of Virginia. Vol. 88 [vol. 1]- ; Dec., 1927— Lynchburg, Bell, 1927—

4°.-8°. monthly during school year.
Successor to University of Virginia magazine [4011]
VU: I-III (1927/28-29/30).

4023. The VIRGINIA tech. Vol. 1- ; Oct. 21, 1901 [i. e. 1903]— [Blacksburg, Va.] Virginia polytechnic institute [1903—

illus. f°. weekly during school year.
LC: I-III (Oct. 21, 1901-May 18, 1904). NYP: VI, 16 (Jan., 1909).
V: I, 1-29; II 3-6, 8-11, 13, 17-20, 22-24; III, 3-7, 9-26; IV, 1, 4, 9, 18, 21, 24-25; V, 1-26; VI, 2-3; VII, 3; VIII, 2-3, 6; IX, 2, 5, 7; XII, 13; XIII, 3-5, 7-8, 10-11; XVI, 1-12, 14-23; XXVI, 22; (1903-29). VPI: I-XXVI.

4024. VIRGINIA tech engineer. Vol. 1- ; Nov., 1923— Blacksburg, Virginia polytechnic institute, 1923—

quarterly.   VPI: I-IV (1923/24-28/29).

4025. The VIRGINIAN . . . edited by the student body of the State teachers college. Vol. 1- ; 1902— Farmville, Va. [1902—
illus. (part col.) plates, ports. 4°. annual.
LC: XXVI (1927); V: IV (1905).

4026. The WASHINGTON AND LEE news-letter. Vol. 1- ; Apr., 1918— Lexington, Va., Pub. by the University, 1918—
semi-monthly.   H: I, 1-4 (Apr.-May, 1918). V: I, 1-3.

4027. The WILLIAM AND MARY college monthly. Vol. 1-12; 1891-1903. [Published by the students of William and Mary college, Williamsburg, Va. n. p., 1891-1903]
8°. Title varies: William and Mary college bi-monthly.
Succeeded by William and Mary literary magazine, 1903— **[4029]**
V: Jan., Mar., Apr., Dec., 1891; Jan., Apr., Nov., Dec., 96; May, 97; Jan.-June, 1901; Feb., Oct., Dec., 02; Jan., Mar., Apr., 03. WM: I-XII.

4028. WILLIAM AND MARY college quarterly historical magazine . . . vol. 1-27; July, 1892-Apr., 1919. 2d ser., vol. 1- ; Jan., 1921— Williamsburg, Va., William and Mary college [etc.] 1892-19—
illus., plates, ports, maps (part fold.) facsims., tables. 8°.
Vols. 4-27 have imprint: Richmond, Va., 1895-1920.
Title varies: William and Mary college quarterly historical papers, 1892-94; William and Mary college quarterly historical magazine, 1894-19—
Editors: L. G. Tyler, 1892-1919; J. A. C. Chandler, E. G. Swem, 1921—

4029. The WILLIAM AND MARY literary magazine. [Pub. by the students of William and Mary college, Williamsburg, Va.] Vol. 1- ; 1903— Pulaski [etc.] 1903—
8°. monthly.
Successor to The William and Mary college monthly **[4027]**
H: XVIII, 1-5; XIX, 1-5; XXIX, 4; (1910/11-11/12, 22). NYP: XVI, 5; XX, 4-5; XXVII, 1; (1907, 13, 19). V: Nov., 1903; Nov., Dec., 06; Jan.-May, Nov., Dec., 07; Feb.-May, Nov., Dec., 08; Feb., Mar., May, 09; Jan., 11; Dec., 23. WM: I-XVII, XIX-XXXIV; (1903/04-18/19, 20/21-28/29).

4030. YE scandal sheet [University of Virginia summer school] Vol. 1, no. 1- [1928—] University, Va., 1928—
4°.   VU: I, 1.

4031. The YELLOW jacket . . . Edited by the literary societies of Randolph-Macon college. Vol. 1- [1899-19-? n. p., 1899-19-?]

4°.   **V**: II (1900).

4032. The YELLOW journal. Vol. 1- ; 1916— University of Virginia [1916—

f°. Pub. once a year, "every now and then by the social, political and scholastic outcasts of the University."
VU: V-XIII (1920-28).

3. ELEMENTARY AND SECONDARY EDUCATION

Government Publications and Documents

4033. ACCOMAC COUNTY, VA. PUBLIC SCHOOLS. . . . Jamestown school exhibit. Catalogue . . . [n. p., 1907]

6 p. 8°.   **V**

4034. ALEXANDRIA, VA. SUPT. OF PUBLIC SCHOOLS. Annual report . . . 1st- ; 1871/72-19— Alexandria, 1872-19—

8°. **H**: 30th (1899/1900); **LC**: 19th, 28th, 34th, 36-38th (1888/89, 97/98, 1901/02, 03/04, 05/06-07/08); **NYP**: 1878/81-81/82, 87/88-99/1900; **USE**: 1871/72-80/81, 82/83-87/88, 89/90-92/93, 94/95-1907/08, 11/12-12/13.

4035. BRISTOL, VA.-TENN. EDUCATION, Board of. Annual report . . . Bristol [18-?-19—

12°.-8°. None pub., 1896/97-1901/02.
USE: 1893/94, 96/97, 1902/03.

4036. ———. SCHOOL BOARD. Annual report . . . Bristol [19—

diagrs. 8°.   **USE**: 1916/17.

4037. CLARKSVILLE, VA. PUBLIC SCHOOLS. Catalogue of Clarksville graded and high school . . . 1st- ; 1914/15— [n. p., 1914?—

illus. 8°. Advertisements in back.   **V**: 6th (1919/20).

4038. COEBURN, VA. PUBLIC SCHOOLS. General regulations and course of study . . . Big Stone Gap, Va., Wise print. [19—

8°.   **V**: 1907/08.

4039. HARRISONBURG, VA. PUBLIC SCHOOLS. Catalogue of . . . graded and high schools . . . Harrisonburg, Va. [18-?-19—

8°.   V: 1897/98.

4040. HENRICO COUNTY, VA. DIVISION SUPT. OF SCHOOLS. . . . Annual report of the industrial work of the colored schools . . . 1st- ; 1908/09— [Richmond, Fergusson, 1909?—

illus. 8°.   H: 3d (1910/11).

4041. JOHN, WALTON C. . . . Hampton normal and agricultural institute; its evolution and contribution to education as a federal land-grant college, prepared under the direction of Walton C. John, U. S. Bureau of education, with an introduction by William Howard Taft, chief justice of the U. S. Washington, Govt., 1923.

v, 118 p. front., plates. 8°. ([U. S.] Bur. of education. *Bulletin,* 1923, no. 27)

4042. LEXINGTON, VA. PUBLIC SCHOOLS. Announcements of Lexington high school . . . Lexington, Va. [19—

16°.   V: 1906/07.

4043. LYNCHBURG, VA. SCHOOL BOARD. Report . . . 1875/76— [Lynchburg, 1876-19—

8°.   USE: 1875/76.

Contains course of study and rules and regulations.

4044. MANCHESTER, VA. SCHOOL BOARD. Report . . . Manchester, Va. [18-?-19—

8°.   USE: 1898/99-1902/03.

4045. MARION, VA. PUBLIC SCHOOLS. Catalogue of Marion high school . . . [n. p., 1875?-19—

8°.   V: 1888/89, 91/92.

4046. MONTEREY, VA. PUBLIC SCHOOLS. Announcement of Monterey high school . . . [n. p., 1906—

8°.   V: 1906/07.

4047. NELSON COUNTY, VA. PUBLIC SCHOOLS. Catalogue of Norwood high school . . . [n. p., 187-?-19—

8°. H: 1874/75; USE: 1871/72-77/78, 80/81-81/82, 83/84; V: 1871/72-77/78, 80/81-82/83.

4048. NEW MARKET, VA. PUBLIC SCHOOLS. Catalogue of New Market high school . . . New Market [189-?-19—

8°.   V: 1899/1900.

4049. NEWPORT, VA. PUBLIC SCHOOLS. Catalogue of Newport high school . . . [n. p.,1892?-19—

8°.   V: 1891/92.

4050. NEWPORT NEWS, VA. PUBLIC SCHOOLS. Annual report of the Board of school trustees . . . Newport News [19—

plates. 8°.
H: 1921/22; **USE:** 1910/11, 21/22; **V, WM:** 1921/22.

4051. ———. ———. Catalogue of Newport News high school . . . [Newport News, 19—

8°.   V: 1908/09.

4052. ———. ———. The Newport News high school aim, scope, and methods. Newport News, Va., Franklin [n. d.]

23 p. tables. 8°.   V

4053. NORFOLK, VA. PLAYGROUND COMMISSION. Annual report . . . 1st- ; 1913— Norfolk, 1913—

illus. 8°.   **USE:** 1913.

4054. ———. SCHOOL BOARD. Course of study for elementary schools, kindergarten to sixth grade, inclusive. By the teaching and supervisory staff of elementary schools, Norfolk, Va. Norfolk, 1923.

431 p. illus., tables, diagrs. 8°.   H

4055. ———. ———. Course of study in the public schools of the city of Norfolk, Va., together with the rules, regulations and by-laws of the city School board. [Norfolk] Barron, 1901.

41 p. 8°.   H

4056. ———. ———. Directory of public schools of Norfolk, Virginia . . . [Norfolk, 19—

16°.   USE: 1923/24.

4057. ———. ———. Physical education and recreation. Health education. [n. p., 192-?]

123 p. diagrs., music. 8°.   H
Course of study for elementary schools.

4058. ――――. ――――. Prospectus of the public schools. Norfolk, Barron, 1896.

32 p. 8°   H

Organization, rules and regulations, and curricula of grammar and high schools.

4059. ――――. ――――. The public schools of Norfolk, Va. A brief description. [Norfolk? 1925]

51 p. illus. 8°.   H

4060. ――――. ――――. The public schools of the city of Norfolk, Va., 1906-1907. Norfolk, Wilkinson, 1907.

64 p. 8°.   V

Includes description of course of study in grammar and high schools.

4061. ――――. ――――. Report of the Board of school trustees . . . [Norfolk, 18-?-19—

illus. 8°. Report year irreg.

H: 1900/01, 22/23; **USE**: 1872-74/75, 76/77, 78/79-79/80, 81/82-82/83, 1906/07.

4062. PALMYRA, VA. PUBLIC SCHOOLS. Catalogue of Central high school, Palmyra, Va. . . . Charottesville [18-?-19—

8°.   V: 1888/89.

4063. PETERSBURG, VA. EDUCATION, Board of. Annual report . . . 1st- ; 1868/69— [Petersburg, 1869-19—

8°.   H: 1868/69-69/70.

4064. ――――. PUBLIC SCHOOLS. Course of study . . . Petersburg high school. 1921-22. [Petersburg? 1921]

4 p. 4°.   H

4065. ――――. ――――. Outline of course of study . . . elementary schools. Petersburg, Va., 1918.

7, [1] p. 8°.   H

4066. PORTSMOUTH, VA. SCHOOL BOARD. Annual report . . . [Portsmouth, Va., 19—

8°. biennial, 1915/17-19/21.

H: 1919/21-22/23; **NYP**: 1912/13, 17/18; **USE**: 1910/11-12/13, 14/15-15/17, 19/21.

4067. ――――. ――――. Courses of study . . . [n. p., 19—

8°.   H: 1910, 20.

4068. RICHMOND, VA. SCHOOL BOARD. Annual report of the superintendent of the public schools of the city of Richmond, Va., for
1870-19—   ; 1st-   Richmond, 1870-19—

fold. tables. 8°.

Report year varies: 1st, for fiscal year ending Jan. 31, 1870; 2d, July,
1870-Feb. 1, 1871; 3d-   , 1870/71—   for current scholastic year.

Title varies: Annual report of the Board of education . . . and the
superintendent of public schools; Annual report of the School board . . .

Reports for 1875/76 and 76/77 are both called 8th annual report.

Supts.: A. Washburn, 1869-70; J. H. Binford, 1870-76; J. H. Peay,
jr., 1876-82; E. M. Garnett, 1882-86; J. B. Cary, 1886-89; W. F. Fox,
1889-1909; J. A. C. Chandler, 1909-19; A. H. Hill, 1919—

H: 1870/71-73/74, 75/76-77/78, 79/80-83/84, 88/89, 90/91, 92/93,
95/96-97/98, 1903/04-05/06, 14/15-17/18, 19/20, 21/22-22/23, 24/25; LC:
20th, 33d-35th, 37-39th, 43d-58th (1888/89, 1901/02-03/04, 05/06-07/08,
11/12-26/27); NYP: 1893/94, 1906/07, 11/12-22/23; USE: 1870-1908/09,
10/11-18/19, 21/22-26/27; V: 1870/71, 85/86, 1907/08, 10/11-11/12, 22/23-
26/27; VU: 1924/25; WM: 1915/16, 17/18-18/19, 20/21-24/25.

4069. ——. ——. Course of study in English . . . for elementary and jurnior high schools . . . Richmond, Saunders,
1917.

367 p. 8°. (Its *Circular,* 17)   WM

4070. ——. ——. Course of study. Junior high school. Richmond, Va., 1924.

148 p. 8°.   WM

4071. ——. ——. Intermediate examination . . . Richmond
[18-?

8°.   V: 1885, 87.

4072. ——. ——. John Marshall high school . . . Catalogue
. . . Richmond, Pub. by the School board [19—

ports, plates. 8°.   V: 1912/13.

4073. ——. ——. John Marshall night high school . . . Commencement . . . Programme [1921] [Richmond? Va., 1921]

[12] p. fold. 4°.   V

4074. ——. ——. Outline of graded course of studies pursued
in the primary, grammar, and high schools in the city of Richmond, with rules, regulations, and by-laws of the city School
board. Richmond, 1871-19—

8°. Outline for 1871, 76, in its *Annual report* **[4068]**

H: 1906; USE: 1887, 89, 98, 1900.

4075. ——. ——. . . . . Report of war activities, 1917-1918 . . . Richmond, School board, 1918.

24 p. illus. 8°. **USE**

4076. ——. ——. Rules and regulations for the government of the Richmond public schools with the By-laws of the School board of the city of Richmond, Va. Rev. and printed Aug., 1907. [Richmond, Va., Flanhart, 1907]

96 p. fold. table. 16°. **H, USE**
Ed. of 1920. **H**

4077. ——. ——. . . . . Supplementary word lists for use in the elementary schools. 1911. [Richmond? 1911?]

42 p. 8°. (Its *Circular,* 4) **V**

4078. ——. VOCATIONAL EDUCATION SURVEY. . . . Vocational education survey of Richmond, Va. August, 1915. Washington, Govt., 1916.

333 p. fold. tables. 8°. (U. S. Bur. of labor statistics. *Bulletin,* whole no. 162. Miscell. ser., 7) **H, HB, USC, USL, V, VU**
At head of title: U. S. Dept. of labor. Bur. of labor statistics. Royal Meeker, commissioner . . .
"The Executive committee of the National society for the promotion of industrial education arranged with the Richmond Board of education to make [this survey]"
Issued also as *House doc.,* 1445, U. S. 63d Cong., 3d sess.

4079. ROANOKE, VA. PUBLIC SCHOOLS. Catalogue of Roanoke high school . . . [Roanoke? 1891?-19—

8°. (Estab., 1891) **V:** 1900/01, 05/06.

4080. ——. ——. Courses of study, elementary, junior and senior grades. Rev. & comp., 1926.

69 p. typed mimeog. 4°. **H**

4081. ——. ——. Rules and regulations . . . [Roanoke? n. d.]

6 p. typed mimeog. 4°. **H**

4082. ROCKINGHAM COUNTY, VA. BOARD OF EDITORS. The public schools of Rockingham County, Virginia. Educational report and history of schools of county. Harrisonburg, News-record [1915?]

5 p. l., 112 p. illus. (incl. ports.) 8°. **USE, V**

4083. SUSSEX COUNTY, VA. SUPERVISOR OF INDUSTRIAL WORK OF THE COLORED SCHOOLS. . . . Annual report . . . 1909/10— Richmond, Fergusson [1910—

illus. 8°.   H, NYP: 2d (1910/11).

4084. U. S. EDUCATION, Bur. of. . . . Survey of the schools of Alexandria, Virginia. Washington, Govt., 1924.

iii, 62 p. 8°. (Its *Bulletin,* 56)
W. S. Deffenbaugh, director of the survey.
A study of the school population, instruction and courses of study, teaching staff, intelligence tests, health, building programme, financial support, etc.; with findings and recommendations.

4085. [3283] VIRGINIA. Annual reports of officers, boards, and institutions of . . . Virginia . . . Richmond, Va. [1866-19—

4086. ———. AUDITOR. The public free schools. A statement by the auditor . . . [Richmond, 1878]

18 p. tables. 8°.   BP, H
Financing the public school system, and weaknesses of the method used.

4087. [1978] ———. DEAF AND BLIND, School for the, Staunton . . . Report . . . Richmond and Charlottesville [1867-19—

See also items **1979-1980.**

4088. [1981] ———. DEAF AND BLIND CHILDREN (COLORED), State school for, Newport News. . . . Annual report . . . Hampton, Va., 1909—

See also item **1982.**

4089. ———. EDUCATION, State board of. Annual report of the public high schools of Virginia [1912/13—] Richmond [1913—

8°. Issued as no. of its *Bulletin,* 1916/17—   **[3289]**
H: 1914/15, 16/17, 20/21-22/23; LC: 1915/16-17/18, 22/23-25/26; NYP: 1914/15-15/16; USE: 1914/15-20/21, 22/23-26/27; V: 1916/17-22/23; VU: 1917/18, 20/21, 23/24-24/25.

4090. ———. ———. Beautifying our schools. More attractive grounds and exteriors. [Richmond, 1911]

[20] p. illus. 8°.   H, LC, NYP, USE, USL, V

4091. [3289] ———. ———. Bulletin . . . Vol. 1- ; 1918— Richmond, 1918—

See also items **3290-3299.**

4092. ———. ———. Bulletin issued jointly by the Department of public instruction, the State university, the Co-operative education association of Virginia . . . [n. p.] 1911.

3 v. 8°. USE, V, VU

Ser. 1, no. 1. Literary societies in the public schools; organization. no. 2. . . . Parliamentary forms and rules. no. 3. . . . Questions for debate, arguments and references.

4093. ———. ———. County school fairs in Virginia. Issued by Dept. of public instruction of Virginia. J. D. Eggleston, superintendent. March, 1912. [Richmond? Va., 1912]

1 p. l., 55 p. illus. 8°. USAg, USE, V, VU
Ed. of Dec., 1912. USE
Ed. of 1913. NYP

4094. ———. ———. Course of study for the elementary schools of Virginia. 2d ed. Oct., 1909, Dept. of public instruction . . . [Richmond? Va.] 1909.

22, [2] p. incl. tables, 8°. USE

4095. ———. ———. "The high school club" . . . with which is [sic] printed . . . three chapters from Life questions of school boys, by Jeremiah W. Jenks . . . Issued by the Dept. of public instruction . . . and Co-operative education association of Virginia. [n. p., 191-?]

19 p. illus. 8°. V

4096. ———. ———. How to standardize the one and two teacher schools of Virginia . . . Richmond, Bottom, 1915.

28 p. illus., plate, plans. 8°. V

4097. ———. ———. . . . Official syllabus of Bible study for high school pupils; approved and authorized by the State board of education, Richmond, Virginia, Aug. 29, 1916. [Charlottesville, The University, 1916]

48 p., 1 l. 8°. (*University of Virginia record.* Extension series, II, 1; Sept., 1916) H, LC, USE, V, VU

4098. ———. ———. Play and athletics for Virginia public schools. Rev. Nov., 1916 . . . Issued by Dept. of public instruction of Virginia, assisted by University of Virginia, William and Mary college, State female normal school, Farmville . . . [and others] Richmond, Bottom, 1916.

95 p. illus. (incl. music) diagrs. 8°. USE, V

Planned and ed. by T. S. Settle; with bibliography.
Ed. of 1913.   NYP, USAg

4099. VIRGINIA. EDUCATION, State board of.   Public lectures and
entertainments for rural high schools . . .   [Richmond, 1911?]
8 p. 8°.   LC

4100. ———. ———. The school and citizens league bulletin . . .
The "school beautiful" number, Mar. 10, 1910.   [Richmond, 1910]
8 p. 8°.   LC

4101. ———. ———. School and civic league bulletin. I. How to
organize a league. II. How to make league meetings a success.
III. What constitutes a successful league. Issued by the Dept. of
public instruction. Richmond, Bottom, 1913.
25 p. 8°.   USE

4102. ———. ———. Special day programme bulletin for use in Virginia public schools and community leagues. Issued and distributed
by the Dept. of public instruction and the Co-operative education
association in co-operation with the state departments of health,
highways, agriculture, dairy and food, charities and corrections,
Virginia polytechnic institute. Richmond, Bottom, 1916.
2 p. l., 174 p. 8°.   USE, V

4103. ———. ———. Standard of requirements for high schools.
1906. [Richmond] 1907.
8°.   USE

4104. ———. ———. . . . State course of study [for] high schools
of Virginia . . .   Richmond, Bottom, 19—
8°. (In its *Bulletin*, 1924—   )
H, LC, USE: 1924; V: 1915/16, 24; VU: 1924.

4105. ———. ———. State course of study for normal training high
schools. Virginia, 1915 . . .   Richmond, Bottom, 1915.
65 p. 8°.   USE, V

4106. ———. ———. . . . State course of study for rural and elementary schools of Virginia . . .   Richmond, Bottom, 19—
illus. 8°. (In its *Bulletin*, V, 4 [1923]; IX, 1, suppl. 1 [1927])
H: 1916, 23, 27; LC: 1927; USE: 1923, 27; V, VU: 1923.

4107. ———. ———. Text-books for the primary and grammar grades of the public schools of Virginia. Adopted, June 24, 1904. Richmond, Jones, 1904.

130 p. 8°. (Its *Circular,* 256)   **H, NYP, V**

4108. ———. ———. Virginia public school exhibit at Jamestown exposition, 1907. [n. p., n. d.]

8 p. tables. 8°.   **VU**

Brief notes on educational progress in Virginia.

4109. [3300] ———. ———. Virginia school report . . . 1st- ; 1871-19— Richmond, 1871-19—

4110. [3302] ——— EDUCATIONAL SYSTEM OF VIRGINIA, Commission to survey the. Public education in Virginia . . . Richmond, 1928.

See also items **3303-3304.**

4111. ———. GENERAL ASSEMBLY. HAMPTON NORMAL AND AGRICULTURAL INSTITUTE, Committee to investigate the condition of. Report . . . Feb. 13, 1873. [Richmond? 1873?]

8 p. 8°.   **WM**

4112. ———. ———. SENATE. A bill to establish and maintain an efficient system of public free schools. [Richmond, 190-?]

88 p. 8°. (*Senate bill,* 355)   **USE**

4113. ———. ———. ———. . . . . A bill to establish and maintain an uniform system of public free schools. [Richmond? 1871?]

31 p. 8°. (*Senate bill,* 150)   **USE, V**

4114. ———. GOVERNOR, 1894-98 (Charles T. O'Ferrall). Virginia school book question. Richmond, Hill [1895]

17 p. table. 8°.   **H**

Reply to an attack upon the method of choosing textbooks and making contracts for their purchase.

4115. ———. HIGH SCHOOLS, Supervisor of. Annual report of the public high schools of Virginia. 1st- ; 1913— Richmond, Bottom [1913?—

8°. Issued by the Supt. of public instruction.

Title varies: Inspector of high schools, 1913-17; Supervisor of high schools, 1918—

Pub. in Virginia. State board of education. *Bulletin,* 1918—
[3289]
V: 1915-19/20, 22/23-23/24.

4116. VIRGINIA. HIGH SCHOOLS, Supervisor of. Record of the
graduates of the public high schools of Virginia . . .
1917/18— Richmond, Bottom, 1918—

8°. (In Virginia. State board of education. *Bulletin,* 1918—   **[3289]**

4117. [1996] ———. HOME AND INDUSTRIAL SCHOOL FOR GIRLS,
Chesterfield County. Annual report . . . Richmond, 1915—

4118. [1997] ———. INDUSTRIAL SCHOOL FOR COLORED GIRLS,
Peake. . . . Annual report . . . [Peake? Va., 1916?—

4119. ———. LAWS, STATUTES, ETC. An act to incorporate the
Hampton normal and agricultural institution. Approved June 4,
1870. [n. p., 1870?]

3 p. 8°.   **LC**

4120. ———. ———. . . . Acts relating to public schools. Passed
at the session of 1871-72. [Richmond? 1872]

13 p. 8°. (*Circular,* 70)   **USE, VU**

4121. ———. ———. Virginia compulsory attendance law. [n. p.,
192-?]

4 p. 8°.   **VU**
Concerning compulsory school attendance.

4122. [3311] ———. ———. Virginia school laws . . . Richmond [1878-19—

See also items **3308-3310.**

Other Source Material

4123. ABINGDON ACADEMY, Abingdon, Va.   Catalogue . . .
[Bristol, Va.-Tenn., etc., 18-?-19—

8°. (Prep.; boys; non-sect.; 18-?)
Founded as Abingdon male academy.
V: 1875/76, 96/97, 98/99-99/1900, 01/02.

4124. ———. Prospectus . . . [n. p., n. d.]

[3] p. 8°.   **V**

4125. ACADEMY OF THE VISITATION, Wytheville, Va. [Announcement] [n. p., 18-?-19—

8°. (Girls; Rom. Cath.; 1868) V: 1902/03, 04/05.
Founded at Abingdon; removed to Wytheville, 1902.

4126. AERY, WILLIAM A. Hampton institute. Aims, methods, and results. Hampton institute, Hampton, Va., 1923.

26 p. typew. mimeog. 4°. H, USAg, USE

4127. AGRICULTURAL HIGH SCHOOL, Appomattox, Va. Announcement of Tenth congressional district agricultural high school . . . Lynchburg, Bell [19—

illus., ports. 8°. (Boys; 1908) USAg: 1917; V: 1912/13.

4128. AGRICULTURAL HIGH SCHOOL, Driver, Va. Bulletin of the Agricultural high school, Second congressional district of Virginia, Driver, Va., and list of prizes and catalogue for school fair of Second congressional district, to be held at Suffolk, Va., Dec. 2-7, 1912. [Norfolk, Burke & Gregory, 1913]

81 p. 8°. V

4129. AGRICULTURAL HIGH SCHOOL, Middletown, Va. Announcement of Seventh congressional district agricultural high school, 1915-16. [n. p., 1915]

19, [11] p. illus. 8°. USAg

4130. ALEXANDRIA ACADEMY, Alexandria, Va. Catalogue . . . Alexandria [18-?-?]

8°. (Prep.; boys; non-sect.; 185-?) V: 1872/73, 74/75.

4131. [ALEXANDRIA] SCHOOL FOR YOUNG LADIES, Alexandria, Va. [Announcement. n. p., n. d.]

[10] p. obl. 4°. V
Mrs. Frances B. Ewing, principal.

4132. ALLEGHANY INSTITUTE, Clifton Forge, Va. Catalogue . . . [n. p., 19—

8°. (Prep.; co-ed.; non-sect.; 1901) V: 1902/03.

4133. [AMERICAN MISSIONARY ASSOCIATION] Report upon the Hampton normal & agricultural institute at Hampton, Virginia. [n. p., 1869]

11 p. fold. plate. 8°. BP, LC
Report made by Mark Hopkins, Alexander Hyde, B. G. Northrop,

and James A. Garfield, who visited the Institute under the auspices of the American missionary association.

Includes *Report* of the farm manager, and *Statement* by the principal. Reprint from *American missionary,* Aug., 1869.

4134. ARMSTRONG, Mrs. MARY F., *et al.* Hampton and its students. By two of its teachers, Mrs. M. F. Armstrong and Helen W. Ludlow. With fifty cabin and plantation songs, arranged by Thomas P. Fenner . . . New York, Putnam, 1874.

255, [1] p. fold. front., illus. 8°.
Valuable source material on the early history of Hampton and its system of education. [Pt. 2] Interior views of the school and the cabin, by the Negroes. [Pt. 3] Hampton students in the North.

4135. [————] ed. Hampton institute. 1868 to 1885. Its work for two races. Hampton, Va., Normal school press, 1885.

34 p. 8°.   **LC, USE**
[1] The story of the school, by M. F. A. [2] Hampton's Indian students at home, by Helen W. Ludlow. [3] Does civilization civilize? by Elaine Goodale. Pt. 2 shows the effects of Hampton training on the Indians in their native environment.

4136. ARMSTRONG, SAMUEL C. Education for life, by Samuel Chapman Armstrong, founder of Hampton institute, with an introduction by Francis Greenwood Peabody . . . and a biographical note by Helen W. Ludlow . . . [Hampton, Va., Hampton normal and agricultural institute press, 1913]

54 p. incl. front. (port.) 12°.   **H, LC, NYP, USE, V**
"Sayings and teachings of General Armstrong," including his first Annual report (1870).
Ed. of 1914.   **H, NYP**

4137. ————. . . . The founding of the Hampton institute . . . [Boston, Directors of the Old South work, 1904]

16 p. 8°. (*Old South leaflets* [Gen. ser., VI] no. 149)
                                                                  BP, H, LC, V, WM
"From the chapter prepared by General Armstrong in 1890 for the volume 'Twenty-two years' work of the Hampton institute.' " **[4274]**

4138. ————. Ideas on education expressed by Samuel Chapman Armstrong . . . [Hampton, Va.] Issued for the Armstrong league of Hampton workers by the Hampton institute press, 1908.

37 p. 8°.   **H, USE, VU**

4139. ————. Indian education in the East, at Hampton, Va., and

Carlisle, Pa., an address in Boston, October, 1880. Hampton, Va., Normal press, 1880.

8 p. 8°.   BP

4140. ———. The Indian question, by S. C. Armstrong, principal of Hampton institute . . . [Hampton] Normal school press, 1883.

36 p. 16°.   LC

Includes a report on the results of Indian education at Hampton, Va., by Rev. Thomas L. Riggs of Dakota, and by George Bushotter, an Indian. Also a statement concerning the relation of the Hampton school with the government.

4141. ———. A paper read at the anniversary meeting of the American missionary association, held in Syracuse, N. Y., Oct. 24, 1877 . . . [Hampton] Normal school press, 1877.

7 p. 8°.   V

On the value of education in improving the Negro's status and making him an asset to society.

4142. ARMSTRONG ASSOCIATION, New York. The work and influence of Hampton. Proceedings of a meeting held in New York City Feb. 12, 1904, under the direction of the Armstrong association. With the addresses of Mr. Andrew Carnegie, chairman; President Charles W. Eliot; Dr. H. B. Frissell; and Dr. Booker T. Washington. [New York, Lehmaier press, 1904]

38 p. 8.

Concerning the progress of Negro education in the South, with special reference to Hampton institute.

4143. AUGUSTA FEMALE SEMINARY, Staunton, Va. Catalogue . . . [n. p., 18-?-95?]

8°. (Prep.; non-sect.; 1842)

Became Mary Baldwin seminary **[3444]** in 1896.

H: 1892/93; **USE**: 1873/74-76/77, 79/80, 83/84-84/85, 86/87-89/90; **V**: 1891/92, 95/96.

4144. AUGUSTA MILITARY ACADEMY, Fort Defiance, Va. Catalogue . . . [n. p., 18-?-19—

8°. (Boys; non-sect.; 1865)

V: 1896/97, 1910/11, 13/14-14/15, 22/23.

4145. BELLE HAVEN INSTITUTE, Alexandria, Va. Catalogue . . . [Alexandria? 18-?-?]

8°. (Prep.; girls; non-sect.; 1859)   **V**: 1878/79-79/80.

4146. BELLEVUE HIGH SCHOOL, Bellevue, Va. Announcements . . .
[n. p., 18-?-19—
illus. 8°.   V: 1899/1900.

4147. ———. Catalogue . . . [Roanoke, Va., 18-?-19—
front., plates. 8°. (Boys; non-sect.; 1866)
H: 1873/74-74/75, 89/90-90/91; **LC**: 1907/08; **V**: 1877/78, 82/83-
83/84, 86/87-91/92, 94/95, 99/1900.

4148. BELMONT SEMINARY, Bedford City, Va. Catalogue . . .
[n. p., 18-?-?]
8°. (Prep.; girls; non-sect.; 1882)
V: 1877/78, 82/83-83/84, 86/87-91/92, 94/95.

4149. BENEDICTINE MILITARY COLLEGE, Richmond, Va. Catalogue
. . . Richmond, Va. [1912?—
8°. (Boys; Rom. Cath.; 1911)
USE: 1915/16, 21/22, 25/26; **V**: 1912/13, 22/23-25/26.

4150. BERKLEY MILITARY INSTITUTE, Berkley, Va. Announcement
. . . Catalogue . . . [n. p., 1895?-19—
8°. (Co-ed.; non-sect.; 1894)   **V**: 3d (1896/97).

4151. BERRYVILLE HIGH SCHOOL, Berryville, Va. Catalogue . . .
[Berryville, 18-?-19—
8°. Advertisements in back.   **V**: 1899/1900.

4152. BETHEL ACADEMY, Fauquier County, Va. Catalogue . . .
[n. p., 186-?-19—
8°. (Prep. & milit.; non-sect.; 1866)
V: 1873/74, 75/76-79/80, 81/82-83/84, 87/88-89/90, 91/92-94/95, 96/97,
1901/02.

4153. BLACKSTONE MILITARY ACADEMY, Blackstone, Va. Catalogue
. . . [n. p., 1893?-19—
8°. (Prep.; boys; Presbyt.; 1893)
Founded as Hoge military academy, to 19-?
USE: 1923/24-24/25; **V**: 1895/96, 98/99, 1901/02.

4154. BON AIR SCHOOL, Bon Air, Va. Catalogue . . . [n. p.,
1893?—
8°. (Prep.; girls; M. E., So.; 1893?)   **V**: 1893/94.

4155. BOWLING GREEN ACADEMY, Bowling Green, Va. Announcement. [n. p., n. d.]

28 p. 12°. (Prep.; boys) **V**

4156. BOWLING GREEN FEMALE SEMINARY, Bowling Green, Va. Catalogue . . . Richmond [186-?-?]

8°. (Prep.; M. E., So.; 1867) **V:** 1882/83.

4157. BOYDTON ACADEMIC AND BIBLE INSTITUTE, Boydton, Va. Catalogue . . . Boydton, Va. [1880?-19—

front. 8°. (Colored; co-ed.; non-sect.; 1879) **V:** 1907/08.

4158. BRENTSVILLE SEMINARY, Brentsville, Prince William County, Va. Catalogue . . . [n. p., 1879?-?]

8°. (Prep.; co-ed.; non-sect.; 1879) **V:** 1885/86-86/87.

4159. ———. Program of commencement. June 25, 1885. [n. p., 1885]

[4] p. 8°. **V**

4160. [3390] BRIDGEWATER COLLEGE, Bridgewater, Va. [Book of views. Washington, D. C., n. d.]

See also items **3391-3393.**

4161. BROOKLYN ARMSTRONG ASSOCIATION. [To the members of the Brooklyn Armstrong association. Change of membership plan. Report of the secretary. Report of the treasurer. Brooklyn, 19—

sq. 16°. **NYP:** 1912/13-13/14.

4162. BROWN'S UNIVERSITY SCHOOL, near Charlottesville, Va. [Catalogue. n. p., 1893?-19—

illus. 8°. (Prep.; boys; non-sect.; 1893?) **V:** 1904/05.

4163. CAMPBELL COUNTY SCHOOL FAIR. Sixth annual exhibition . . . To be held at Rustburg, Va., Friday, Oct. 17, 1913. Lynchburg, Bell [1913]

86 p. fold. map. 8°. **V**

4164. CEDAR BLUFF HIGH SCHOOL, Cedar Bluff, Va. Announcement . . . Tazewell, Va. [18-?-19—

8° **V:** 1899/1900-00/01.

4165. CENTRAL FEMALE INSTITUTE, Gordonsville, Va. Catalogue . . . [n. p., 18-?-?]

8°. (Prep.; non-sect.; 18-?) **V:** 1886/87.

4166. CHAMBERLAYNE SCHOOL, Richmond, Va. [Catalogue] Richmond [1911?—

8°. (Prep.; boys; non-sect.; 1910)
V: 1911/12, 13/14-15/16, 19/20-23/24.

4167. CHARLOTTESVILLE FEMALE SEMINARY, Charlottesville, Va. Catalogue . . . [Charlottesville, 1890?-19-?]

8°. (Prep.; non-sect.; 1889)   V: 1893/94.

4168. CHATHAM EPISCOPAL INSTITUTE, Chatham, Va. Catalogue . . . [n. p., 1895?-19—

8°. (Prep.; girls; 1894)   H: 1898/99; V: 1901/02, 08/09.

4169. CHESAPEAKE MALE AND FEMALE ACADEMY, Irvington, Va. Catalogue . . . 1st-   ; 1889/90-19— Irvington [1890?-19—

8°. (Prep.; co-ed.; non-sect.; 1889)   V: 6-7th (1894/95-95/96).

4170. [3394] CHESTER INSTITUTE. Catalogue . . . Bedford City, Va. [18-?—

4171. CHICHESTER, E. L. Hampton sketches; Johnson of Hampton . . . Hampton, Va., The Institute press, 1911.

[7] p. 16°.   USE
"This sketch has appeared in the 'Utica press,' the 'Boston Transcript,' the 'Youth's companion,' and the 'Southern workman.' "

4172. CHURCH, J. W. The crucible, a southerner's impression of Hampton . . . Hampton, Press of the Institute, 1910.

[14] p. illus. 12°.   H, LC, NYP, USAg, USE, V, VU
A favorable impression of Hampton's work and its wide influence for good.

4173. ———. The regeneration of Sam Jackson . . . Hampton, Va., Press of the Institute, 1911.

19 p. incl. illus., ports. 12°.   LC, USE, VU
"Sam Jackson" typifies the average Negro whom Hampton trains and educates for a useful life.

4174. CHURCHLAND ACADEMY, Churchland, Va. Catalogue . . . [Charlottesville, etc., 18-?-19—

8°. (Prep.; co-ed.; non-sect.; 18-?)   V: 1893/94, 95/96.

4175. CLAREN'S SCHOOL FOR GIRLS, near Alexandria, Va. Catalogue . . . [n. p., 18-?-?]

8°. (Non-sect.; 1877)   V: 1886/87, 89/90.

4176. CLAY HILL ACADEMY, Millwood, Va. [Announcement] Richmond, Va. [etc., 1889?-19—

8°. (Prep.; boys; non-sect.; 1888)
V: 6th, 10-11th (1893/94, 98/99-99/1900).

4177. CLIFTON FORGE NORMAL AND INDUSTRIAL INSTITUTE. Catalogue . . . [n. p., 19—

8°. (Colored; 19-?) H: 1910/11-11/12.

4178. ———. [Miscellaneous notices, etc. n. p., 191-?]

var. pag. & size. LC

4179. CLUSTER SPRINGS ACADEMY, Black Walnut, Va. Catalogue . . . Richmond [etc., 18-?-19—

8°. (Prep.; boys; Presbyt.; 1865)
H: 1914/15; V: 1892/93-95/96, 1900/01-02/03, 04/05-07/08, 09/10-14/15.

4180. CLUSTER SPRINGS HIGH SCHOOL, Black Walnut, Va. Catalogue . . . [n. p., 1893-19—

8°. (Boys; Presbyt.; 1892)
V: 1892/93-95/96, 1900/01-02/03, 04/05, 06/07, 09/10.

4181. COLLEGIATE SCHOOL FOR GIRLS, Richmond, Va. [Catalogue] 1915/16— Richmond, 1915—

8°. (Prep.; non-sect.; 1915) V: 1915/16, 23/24.

4182. CONQUEST, EDWIN P. The organization of school cadet corps . . . [Richmond, Va., 1916]

44 p. front., plates. 8°. V

4183. CO-OPERATIVE EDUCATION COMMISSION OF VIRGINIA. Universal education. [Richmond? 19-?]

45 p. 8°. V, VU
On the "supreme educational problem" in Virginia—the elementary rural school.

4184. CO-OPERATIVE SCHOOL FOR GIRLS AND YOUNG WOMEN, Bedford City, Va. Catalogue . . [n. p., 1898?-19—

illus. (plates) map. 8°. (Prep.; non-sect.; 1898) V: 1908/09.

4185. COVE ACADEMY, Covesville, Albemarle County, Va. Announcement . . . Richmond, Whittet & Shepperson [1896?-19—

8°. (Prep.; boys; non-sect.; 1895) V: 1895/96.

4186. [3395] CULPEPER FEMALE INSTITUTE, Culpeper, Va. Catalogue . . . Richmond, Va. [18-?—

4187. [3396] CULPEPER FEMALE SEMINARY, Culpeper, Va. Catalogue . . . Charlottesville, Va. [1890?-?]

4188. DANVILLE MILITARY INSTITUTE, Danville, Va. [Catalogue . . .] Danville, Va., 1891-19—

     8°. (Boys; non-sect.; 1890)   **V**: 1891/92, 95/96.

4189. ———. [Prospectus] . . . A classical, scientific and business boarding school, with military training . . . Danville, Va., Bell, Dance & co., 1890.

     23 p. front. 8°.   **V**

4190. The DEMOCRATIC view of the free schoolbook question in Virginia, Richmond, Sullivan [1905]

     16 p. 8°.   **V**
     Excerpts from Virginia newspapers favoring the purchase of school books by the local communities rather than by the State, and the purchase of books for Negro children by Negroes.

4191. DENNY, GEORGE H. Expert supervision; [address] delivered before the Virginia educational conference, Nov. 26, 1908. [n. p., 1909]

     16 p. 8°.   **V**
     The necessity for well trained and equipped superintendents of schools in Virginia.

4192. DUBLIN INSTITUTE, Dublin, Pulaski County, Va. Catalogue . . . [Roanoke, Stone, 19—

     8°. (Prep.; co-ed.; non-sect.; 190-?)   **V**: 1905/06.

4193. DUNN, FANNIE W. Educative seat work. With an appendix containing a discussion of a schedule for a two-room school, and references and addresses for helpful books and materials. By Fannie W. Dunn, supervisor of rural schools, State normal school. Pub. by State female normal school, Farmville, Va. [ca. 1912]

     77 p. 8°.   **V**

4194. [3399] EASTERN COLLEGE, CONSERVATORY AND ACADEMY, Manassas, Va. Book of views. [Charlotte, N. C., 19-?]

     See also item **3400.**

4195. EASTERN SHORE ACADEMY, Onancock, Va. Catalogue . . . [n. p., 18-?—

8°. (Prep.; co-ed.; non-sect.; 1877)
Founded as Onancock academy; became Eastern Shore academy, 1892(?).
H: 1890/91, 92/93; V: 1887/88-90/91, 92/93.

4196. EDGE HILL SCHOOL, Keswick Depot, Va. Catalogue . . . n. p., [18-?-?]

8°. (Girls; non-sect.; *ante* 1881) V. 1883/84.

4197. ELK CREEK ACADEMY, Ursus, Va. Catalogue . . . [n. p., 18?-19—

8°. (Prep.; co-ed.; non-sect.; 18-?) V: 1899/1900.

4198. [3407] EPISCOPAL FEMALE INSTITUTE, Winchester, Va. Announcement . . . Winchester, 1874-19—

4199. EPISCOPAL HIGH SCHOOL, Fairfax County, Va. Catalogue . . . Washington, D. C., & Baltimore [18-?-19—

8°. (Boys; 1839)
H: 1881/82-86/87, 88/89-93/94; LC: 1872/73, 74/75, 93/94; NYP: 1895/96; V: 1870/71-96/97, 98/99-1905/06, 07/08-15/16, 18/19-22/23, 24/25-26/27.

4200. ———. Regulations . . . [n. p., 18-?—

8°. V: 1873, 77.

4201. EVERETT, JOSEPH W. Virginia's public schools . . . [Richmond, Whittet & Shepperson] 1915.

[30] p. front., illus. 8°. USE, V
Educational advancement in Virginia, as exhibited by modern school buildings, boys' and girls' clubs, fairs, athletics, medical inspection, the Co-operative education association, etc.

4202. [3408] FAIRFAX HALL, Winchester, Va. Catalogue . . . [Wytheville, Va., etc.] 1869—

See also item **3409**.

4203. FAIRVIEW ACADEMY, Simmonsville, Va. Announcement, . . . Annual session . . . [1st- ; 1887/88— n. p., 1887—

8°. (Prep.; boys, 1887?) V: 9th (1895/96).

4204. FANCY HILL CLASSICAL SCHOOL, Fancy Hill, Va. Catalogue
. . . [n. p., 18-?-?]

8°. (Prep.; boys; 18-?)   H: 1882/83.

4205. FAUQUIER FEMALE INSTITUTE, Warrenton, Va. Catalogue
. . . [Warrenton, etc., 186-?-19—

8°. (Non-sect.; 1859)
USE: 1911/12, 24/25; **V**: 1885/86, 87/88-92/93, 96/97-97/98, 1900/01-
01/02, 03/04.

4206. FISHBURNE MILITARY SCHOOL, Waynesboro, Va. Catalogue
and prospectus . . . [n. p., 1880?-19—

8°. (Boys; non-sect.; 1880)
H: 1899/1900; **V**: 1891/92-93/94, 97/98, 1900/01, 04/05-05/07.

4207. FORK UNION MILITARY ACADEMY, Fork Union, Va. Catalogue . . . [Lynchburg, Bell, 1897?-19—

illus. (plates) 8°. (Boys; 1897)
USE: 1922/23-23/24; **V**: 1907/08-08/09, 11/12, 14/15-15/16, 18/19,
21/22-23/24.

4208. FORT LOUDOUN SEMINARY, Winchester, Va. [Catalogue]
[Winchester, 1905?—

8°. (Prep.; girls; 1905)   **V**: 1907/08.

4209. ———. Why Fort Loudoun is a good school. From the students' standpoint, from a theme upon a series of "Why's" given in
1910. [n. p., 191-?]

13 p. 8°.   **H**

4210. FRANKLIN ACADEMY, Franklin, Va. Catalogue . . . [1st- ;
1889/90-19—   ] Portsmouth [etc., 1890?-19—

8°. (Prep.; milit.; boys; non-sect.; 1889?)
V: 1890/91, 95/96-97/98, 1900/01.

4211. FRANKLIN FEMALE SEMINARY, Franklin, Va. Catalogue
. . . Raleigh, N. C. [etc., 1895?-19—

illus. (plates) 8°. (Prep.; non-sect.; 1895)
V: 1902/03-03/04, 05/06.

4212. **[3410]** FREDERICKSBURG COLLEGE, Fredericksburg, Va. . . .
Catalogue. 1893/94-19—   [Baltimore, etc.] 1893-19—

4213. FRISSELL, HOLLIS B. The aim and methods of Hampton. An address delivered . . . Feb. 12, 1904. New York, Armstrong assoc. [1904]

12 p. 8°. **BP**

4214. FRISSELL, SYDNEY D. Hampton's message . . . [Hampton, Va., Press of the Hampton normal and agricultural institute, 1914]

22 p. incl. front., illus. 12°. **LC, USAg, USE**
The constructive work being done at Hampton—a plea for further financial aid.

4215. GALAX HIGH SCHOOL, Galax, Va. Catalogue . . . [n. p., 1907?—

8°. (Co-ed.; non-sect.; 1906)
V: 1st-2d, 4th (1906/07-07/08, 09/10).

4216. GENERAL EDUCATION BOARD. The Handley fund, Winchester, Va.; a report to the Board of Handley trustees. New York, General education board, 1918.

3 p. l., v-vi, 77 p. plates, tables (1 fold.) 8°. **LC, USE, V**
Ed. of 1919. **BP, LC, NYP, USAg**
Report advising that the Handley bequest to the city of Winchester be used "to co-operate with the people of Winchester in establishing a system of superior public schools." Contains survey of the people, industry, and schools of the city.

4217. GENERAL SURVEY COMMITTEE. Synopsis of recommendations for vocational education for Richmond made by the General survey committee for consideration at the eighth annual convention of the National society for the promotion of industrial education held at Richmond, Virginia, Dec. 9-12, 1914. New York City, N. Y., National society for the promotion of industrial education [1914]

29 p. 8°. **USE, V**

4218. GILMER'S (MRS.) SCHOOL FOR YOUNG LADIES, Roanoke, Va. Catalogue . . . [Roanoke? 18-?-?]

12°. (Non-sect.; 18-?) **V: 1892/93.**

4219. [3411] GLADEVILLE COLLEGE. Catalogue . . . Tazewell, Va., [189-?-19—

4220. GLOUCESTER ACADEMY, near Gloucester C. H., Va. Catalogue . . . [n. p., 18-?-19—

8°. (Prep.; boys; non-sect.; 187-?) **V: 1906/07.**

4221. GOLD'S (MISS LAURA W.) SCHOOL, Berryville, Va. [Announcement. n. p., 1895?]

11 p. 12°.   (Non-sect.; 1895)   V

4222. GORDONSVILLE FEMALE INSTITUTE, Gordonsville, Va. Catalogue . . . [n. p., 1878?- ?]

8°. (Non-sect.; 1878)   V: 1878/79, 80/81, 83/84, 85/86-86/87.
Successor to Culpeper female institute [3395]

4223. ———. Circular of the Board of trustees . . . [n. p., 1878]

3 p. 8°.   V
Concerning the establishment of the Institute, with Dr. William R. Vaughan as principal.

4224. GRACE INDUSTRIAL SCHOOL AND FARM, Alleghany parish, Diocese of southern Virginia. How the call came . . . [Covington, Va., 1911]

14 p., 1 l., 8°.   NYP
Cover-title: A call from our mountains.

4225. GREENWOOD SCHOOL FOR BOYS, Greenwood Depot, Va. Catalogue . . . [n. p., 1890?-19—

8°. (Prep.; non-sect.; 1889)   V: 1892/93-95/96.

4226. GROTON, MASS. FIRST PARISH. Hampton normal and agricultural institute . . . A public meeting in the interest of the Institute will be held in the Congregational church, Groton, Mass. . . . Mar. 1, 1899 . . . [Groton? 1899]

1 l. 8°.   LC

4227. [3426] HAMPTON COLLEGE, Hampton, Va. [Announcement] [Philadelphia, etc., 190-?—

4228. HAMPTON NORMAL AND AGRICULTURAL INSTITUTE, Hampton, Va. Annual reports . . . [Hampton, Va., 1870?-19—

plates. 8°. Report year ends June 30.
Title varies: Report of the Hampton normal and agricultural institute, 1873-74.
BP: 1873/74-81/82, 83/84-86/87, 88/89-93/94, 99/1900-06/07, 13/14-15/16; H: 1870, 73/74, 75/76-88/89, 90/91-91/92, 93/94-94/95, 97/98; LC: 1873/74-74/75, 76/77, 80/81, 82/83-83/84, 85/86, 87/88, 89/90, 92/93-93/94, 96/97-1903/04, 14/15-15/16, 18/19, 25/26; NYP: 1877/78, 79/80, 81/82-82/83; 84/85-89/90; V: 1877/78, 82/83-84/85, 87/88-89/90, 91/92, 93/94, 95/96-1920/21.

4229. ———. [An appeal to the friends of the Institute in the hope of increased aid] Hampton, 1879.

30 p. 8°. **NYP**

4230. ———. . . . Bulletin, no. 1-[?] Hampton, Va., 1895-[?]

8°. No. more pub.? **USAg:** no. 1 (May, 1895).

4231. ———. . . . Catalogue. Hampton, Va., 1871-19—

illus., plates, ports., plans. 8°. (Colored; co-ed.; 1868)
Title varies: Annual catalogue . . ., 1900/01—
Issued as no. of the *Hampton bulletin,* 1905— **[4240]**
Catalogues for 1872/73-73/74 issued in one pamphlet; also 1893/94-94/95.
BP: 1870/71-76/77, 79/80, 81/82, 83/84, 85/86-89/90, 91/92-96/97, 1912/13-25/26; **H:** 1870/71-71/72, 74/75-75/76, 80/81-83/84, 85/86-86/87, 88/89-89/90, 92/93, 96/97-1927/28; **LC:** 1870/71-73/74, 81/82-1921/22, 23/24-24/25; **NYP:** 1870/71, 75/76, 79/80, 82/83-83/84, 87/88-89/90, 93/94-1925/26; **USAg:** 1887/88-89/90, 91/92-92/93, 95/96-1927/28; **USE:** 1870/71-89/90, 1910/11-11/12, 15/16, 19/20-27/28; **V:** 1878/79, 88/89-89/90, 93/94-1922/23; **VU:** 1920/21-21/22.

4232. ———. Circular . . . [Hampton, Va., 18-?-19—

illus., ports., plates. 8°. **BP:** 1874/75, 79, 1905.

4233. ———. Congressional land scrip. Hampton normal and agricultural institute. Letters of R. W. Hughes, a trustee, and Gen. S. C. Armstrong, superintendent of the Hampton institute. Richmond, Gillis, 1872.

12 p. 8°. **BP, LC, V**
Claims of Hampton to a portion of the land scrip at the disposal of the General assembly, for the benefit of agricultural colleges.

4234. ———. . . . Cooking course . . . by Amelia Avery Cooke. Hampton, Va., Press of the Institute, 1912.

23 p., 8 l. 8°. **LC**

4235. ———. A decade (1893-1903) of the Hampton school . . . Hampton, Hampton institute press, 1903.

unp. illus. 12°. **V**

4236. ———. . . . Emancipation day at Hampton institute. [Hampton? 1911?]

broadside. 24 x 21 cm. **LC**

4237. ———. . . . Every-day life at Hampton. [n. p., 1922]

[16] p. illus. 12°. **USE**

4238. HAMPTON NORMAL AND AGRICULTURAL INSTITUTE, Hampton, Va. Every-day life at the Hampton normal and agricultural institute. Hampton, Va., Press of the Institute, 1909.

32 p. illus. 8°.   **BP, LC, USE, V**
Ed. of 1907.   **H, USAg**
Depicts the wide range of activities in which Hampton students are engaged.

4239. ———. From the beginning; reprinted from articles by Gen. S. C. Armstrong and Helen W. Ludlow in "22 years' work of Hampton institute." Hampton, Va., Normal school press [189-?]

20 p. 12°. (See item **4274**)   **BP, LC, NYP, VU**

4240. ———. The Hampton bulletin . . . Vol. 1- [1905—] Hampton, Va., The Institute [1905—

8°. Includes the Catalogue of the Institute.
BP: I, 3; II, 3; IV, 3; V, 3; VI, 3; VII, 3; VIII, 7; (1905-06, 08-12).
H: I, 1-2, 4; II, 1; III, 1, 4; IV, 1, 4; V, 1-2, 4; VI, 1-2, 4; VII, 1-2, 5; VIII, 3, 5, 8; IX, 1, 5-6; X, 2, 5; XI, 1-3, 6; XII, 2, 5; XIII, 1-5; XIV, 2-6; XV, 2-5; XVI, 1-5; XVII, 1-3, 6; XVIII, 1-4, 6; XIX, 1-3, 6; XX, 2-4; XXI, 2, 4, 6; XXII, 1; XXIII, 1, 4; XXIV, 1. LC: IX, 2, 6; XIII, 4; XIV, 1, 5; XVI, 1; (1913, 17-18, 20). USAg: IX, 6; XIII, 4; XIV, 1; XIX, 4. USE: V, 3; VIII, 7; IX, 6; XIV, 5; XVII, 4; XVIII, 1, 4; XX, 3. V: XI, 3; XII; XIII, 1, 4-5; XV, 1; XVI, 1; XVII, 1, 4; XVIII, 1-4; XIX; XX, 2-3; XXI, 2-3; XXII, 1-3; XXIII, 3; XXIV, 1, 3. VU: XXVII, 1.

4241. ———. Hampton graduates at work . . . [Hampton, Press of the Institute, 1920]

[12] p. illus. 12°.   **BP, USAg, USE, V**

4242. ———. Hampton in war time . . . [Hampton, Press of the Institute, 1918]

23 p. incl. front., illus. 8°.   **BP, LC, NYP, USAg, V, VU**
Includes extracts from letters of Hampton men in the service of the U. S.

4243. ———. Hampton institute. 1868 to 1885. Its work for two races. Hampton, Normal school press, 1885.

34 p. 12°.   **BP, H, V**
Ed. of 1884: 73 p. 8°.   **NYP**

4244. ———. Hampton leaflets . . . [1st ser.] no. 1-9; 1902-05. New ser., vol. 1-11[?] 1905-[12?] Rev. ser., vol. 1-[?] 1912— Hampton, Va., Hampton institute press, 1902—

illus., plates. 8°. monthly.
Issued monthly for teachers by the trustees of the . . . Institute.

BP: 1st ser., 1-3, 5-9. New ser., I-V. **H**: New ser., I, 1, 3, 9-11; II, 7-8; III, 1, 4-6, IV, 1, 3-4, 6; V, 1, 3, 6, 8, 10; VI, 2-5, 7-12; VII, 1-9, 11 & suppl. Rev. ser., 102-103. **LC**: New ser., I-IV; V, 1-9, 11-12; VI, 1, 3-5, 8, 11-12; VII, 1; XI, 9. Rev. ser., VI, 6-9, 12; VII, 1, 1a, 2-4, 6; (1905-15). **USAg**: New ser., I-VIII, 1. Rev. ser., 102-117. **USE**: New ser., III, 4; VI, 12; VII, 1-2, 7-9, 12. Rev. ser., 102-105, 108-110. **V**: New ser., I, 1-3, 10-12; II, 3-4, 6, 8-9, 11-12; III-V; VI, 7-9, 12; VII, 1-4, 9-11, & suppl. to 11, 12; VIII, 1. Rev. ser., 102-106, 108-110, 113, 119.

4245. ———. Hampton men and women. [n. p., 1921 ?]

[12] p. illus. 12°. **VU**

4246. ———. Hampton normal and agricultural institute and its work for Negro and Indian youth. [Hampton] Institute press, 1898.

15, [1] p. illus., fold. plate. 16°. **BP, H, LC**
Ed. of 1889. **LC**
Ed. of 1900. **BP**

4247. ———. Hampton normal and agricultural institute, founded by General S. C. Armstrong in 1868, Hampton, Virginia. H. B. Frissell, principal. [Hampton, Va., Hampton institute press, 1902]

31 p. illus. 8°. **LC**
Cover-title: Then and now at Hampton institute, 1868-1902.

4248. ———. The Hampton normal and agricultural institute, Hampton, Va. . . . Hampton, Va. Hampton institute press, 1905.

15, [1] p. 8°. **LC**
Ed. of 1900. **H**
Descriptive pamphlet of the buildings, equipment, and courses at Hampton; with recommendations by distinguished Americans.

4249. ———. . . . . Hampton normal and agricultural institute. Its reply to a new attack on eastern schools. [Hampton? Va., 1890]

20 p. 8°. **BP, H, LC, USE**
Signed: S. C. Armstrong, principal.
Refutation of charges that most of the Indians at Hampton die or lose all interest and affection for their own people; with testimony by Indian students and visitors.

4250. ———. The Hampton normal and agricultural institute opened April, 1868. Incorporated by special act of the General assembly of Virginia in 1870. Hampton, Va., Normal school press, 1879.

30 p. 8°. **BP, H**

4251. HAMPTON NORMAL AND AGRICULTURAL INSTITUTE, Hampton, Va. Hampton papers, no. 1-[?] Hampton, Va., 1898-[?]

illus. 16°.   No more pub.?   NYP, USAg: no. 1.

4252. ———. Hampton sketches. Hampton, Va., The Institute press, 1911.

4 nos. 16°.   LC
Sketches of individual students to illustrate the character of training at Hampton.

4253. ———. Hampton summer normal institute papers. [Hampton, Va., 1901]

1 no. 8°.   No more pub.?   LC
A. O. Stafford, *Negro ideals* (July, 1901).

4254. ———. Hampton tracts for the people. Sanitary series, no. 1-11. Hampton, Va., The Institute, 1878-79.

11 nos. 16°.   No more pub.?   LC: 3-6, 9-11; **NYP:** 3, 5.

4255. ———. How Hampton is teaching college agriculture . . . prepared, Sept. 26, 1921, by the staff of the agricultural school . . . [Hampton, 192-?]

28 numb. 1. illus. 4°. mimeog.   USAg

4256. [186] ———. How to know the best layers in a flock of hens . . . Hampton, Va., 1920.

4257. ———. Indian education at Hampton. [Hampton? n. d.]

15 p. illus. 16°.   LC, USE
Ed. of 1881: 16 p. 8°.   BP, H

4258. ———. The Jamestown exposition and Hampton institute. [Hampton, Va., Hampton institute press, 1907]

[24] p. illus. (map) 16°.   USE

4259. ———. . . . Letter from the Secretary of the interior, in response to Senate resolution of Feb. 28, 1891, forwarding report made by the Hampton institute regarding its returned Indian students . . . [Washington, Govt., 1891]

87 p. plates (1 fold.) fold. maps. 8°. ([U. S.] 52d Cong., 1st sess. Senate. *Exec. doc.,* 31)   USE

4260. ———. [Miscellaneous announcement, etc.] [Hampton, Va., 18-? -19—

var. pag. & size.   BP, LC, NYP

4261. ———. Mr. Taft's new trust. Hampton, Va., Press of the Institute, 1909.

17 p. 16°.   USE

"Address . . . made in Carnegie Hall, New York, under the auspices of the Armstrong association by Hon. William H. Taft, president elect, in aid of Hampton institute, . . . Feb. 23, 1909."

4262. ———. The need for Hampton . . . [Hampton, Va. The Institute, 1915]

[12] p. front., illus., plate. 12°.   BP, LC, USAg

The reason for Hampton's existence and its service to the Negro.

4263. ———. Notes on agriculture. Hampton, Va., Hampton institute, 1904.

98 p. illus. 8°.   USAg

4264. ———. [Out from cabin and tepee. Hampton, Hampton institute press, 1900]

32 p. illus. 16°.   LC

4265. ———. Report of the principal . . . 1868/69-19— Richmond [etc., 1869-19—

illus., port. 8°.

Title varies: Report upon the Hampton normal and agricultural institute; Annual report.

Issued as no. of the *Hampton bulletin*, 1905(?)—   **[4240]**

BP: 1871/72-72/73, 74/75, 79/80, 83/84; **H:** 1874/75, 79/80-80/81, 83/84, 86/87-90/91, 92/93-93/94, 97/98, 1900/01-01/02, 04/05, 08/09-11/12, 15/16-19/20, 21/22-24/25; **LC:** 1871/72, 73/74, 75/76-77/78, 81/82, 87/88-88/89, 98/99-1903/04, 05/06-1916/17, 18/19, 22/23-23/24, 25/26-26/27; **NYP:** 1874/75, 76/77, 79/80, 83/84, 88/89, 90/91-1912/13, 14/15-19/20, 25/26; **USAg:** 1887/88, 89/90, 98/99, 1900/01-01/02, 03/04-23/24, 25/26-26/27; **USE:** 1917/18, 20/21-24/25; **V:** 1877/78, 82/83-84/85, 87/88-89/90, 91/92, 93/94, 95/96-1920/21; **V:** 1910/11, 20/21-21/22, 23/24.

4266. ———. Report of the treasurer . . . Hampton, Va. [18-?-19—

8°. Report year ends June 30.

Printed as appendix to the Catalogue.

Title varies: Reports; Annual reports; Principal's report.

H: 1904/05, 06/07-24/25, 26/27; **LC:** 1872/73, 82/83, 1904/05-18/19; **NYP:** 1904/05-21/22, 25/26; **USE:** 1908/09, 17/18-18/19; **VU:** 1921/22.

4267. ———. Report [by Pres. Hopkins, Mr. Hyde, Secretary Northrup, and Gen. Garfield. With report by the former manager, and statement by the principal. Hampton, 1870]

11 p. 8°. (See item **4133**)

4268. [188] HAMPTON NORMAL AND AGRICULTURAL INSTITUTE, Hampton, Va. [Report of meeting of the Farmers' conference . . . June 22-25, 1920]

4269. ———. Some results of Hampton's work. [Hampton, Va., The Institute press, 1915]

> 30 p., 1 l. illus. 8°.   **H, LC**
> Pictures and brief sketches of what certain representative Hampton graduates have accomplished.

4270. ———. Some results of Hampton's work, land buying, home-making, business enterprises, farming, trades, industrial schools, missionary work, professional work, etc. [Hampton, The Institute press, 1909]

> 34 p. illus. (incl. ports.) 8°.   **USE, V, VU**
> Ed. of 1915.   **USE**

4271. ———. Suggestions for special gifts and legacies. [Hampton, Va., 1919]

> [8] p. 16°.   **BP, H, V**

4272. ———. . . . Summer session for teachers. [Hampton? 19—

> 8°. **LC**: 1909, 11, 17-20, 22, 26; **USAg**: 1917-23; **V**: 1903, 15-16, 18-23.

4273. ———. . . . Ten years' work for Indians at the Hampton normal and agricultural institute, at Hampton, Virginia. [Hampton, 1888]

> 2 p. l., 80 p. illus. 8°.   **BP, H, LC, NYP, USE**
> "Edited and partly written by Miss Helen Ludlow."
> Valuable source material, with an introduction by S. C. Armstrong and letters from Indian graduates and outside testimony.

4274. ———. Twenty-two years' work of the Hampton normal and agricultural institute at Hampton, Virginia. Records of Negro and Indian graduates and ex-students, with historical and personal sketches and testimony on important race questions from within and without, to which are added . . . some of the songs of the races gathered in the school. Illustrated with views and maps. Hampton, Normal school press, 1893.

> v. p., 1 l., 520, [8] p. fold. front., fold. maps. 8°.
>   **BP, H, LC, NYP, USE, V**
> Ed. of 1891.   **H, LC**
> "Songs of two races, from 'Cabin and plantation songs as sung by the Hampton students'" (with music): [7] p. at end.

4275. ———. Visitors' handbook. [Hampton, 19—

map. 12°. BP: 1926.

4276. ———. What Hampton graduates are doing in land-buying, in home-making, in business, in teaching, in agriculture, in establishing schools, in the trades, in church and missionary work, in the professions, 1868-1904. [Hampton, Va., Hampton institute press, 1904?]

98, [1] p. illus. (incl. ports.) 8°. BP, LC, V

4277. ———. What some men have said of Hampton students. [Hampton, Institute press, 19-?]

[8] p. illus. 16°. USE, V

4278. ———. The work and workers of the Hampton normal and agricultural institute, Hampton, Va. [Hampton, Va., 1902?]

29, [1] p. 8°. LC, V
Catalogue of the departments, with courses offered; also statistics of the school, 1868-1902.
Ed. of 1903: 21, [1] p. 8°. BP
Ed. of 1909: [14] p. 12°. USE

4279. ———. ARMSTRONG LEAGUE OF HAMPTON WORKERS. Memories of old Hampton; historical papers published by "The Armstrong league of Hampton workers." Hampton institute, Printed by the students, 1894.

74 p. 16°. BP, V
Ed. of 1909. H

4280. ———. BOSTON COMMITTEE. [Annual statement . . . n. p., 19—

16°. BP: 1914; H: 1910-11.

4281. ———. ———. A brief sketch of the record of the American Negro and Indian in the Great war. Report . . . [Boston, 1919]

12 p. 8°. BP, H

4282. ———. ———. Report of a Hampton teacher on visiting one of his recent pupils. [Boston, 1921?]

[4] p. 12°. BP

4283. ———. LIBRARY. Finding-list of books and pamphlets in the library of the Hampton normal and agricultural institute, Hampton, Va., 1892. Hampton, Va., Normal school press, 1892.

1 p. l., 75 p. 8°.   **USE, V**

4284. HAMPTON NORMAL AND AGRICULTURAL INSTITUTE, Hampton, Va. NATIONAL HAMPTON ASSOCIATION. National Hampton association notes, 1916. [Hampton? Va.] 1916.

15 p. 8°.   **USE**
"Brief notes on the growth and accomplishment of the Hampton clubs and associations."

4285. ———. NATURE STUDY BUREAU. Animal-industry leaflet. No. 1-4. Hampton, 1903-04.

4 nos. 8°.   **NYP**

4286. ———. ———. Children's nature-study leaflet. No. 1-9[?] Hampton, Va., 1902-03.

9 nos. 8°. No more pub.?
BP: 1-2; **LC:** 1-4, 7-9; **NYP, USAg:** 1-3; **USE:** 7.

4287. ———. ———. Hampton agricultural leaflet. No. 1-9. Hampton, Va., 1902-04.

9 nos. 8°.   **BP:** 1-3, 5-9; **LC, NYP, USAg:** 1-9.
Combined in 1905 with other leaflets of the Institute to form *Hampton leaflets,* new ser. **[4244]**

4288. ———. ———. Hampton nature-study leaflet . . . issued for teachers, no. 1-17. Hampton, Va., 1901-04.

17. nos. illus. 8°.   **BP, NYP:** 1-17; **USAg;** 1-12, 15-16.
Succeeded by *Hampton leaflets,* 1905— **[4244]**

4289. ———. ———. Preliminary leaflet on school gardening. Issued for teachers . . . [School gardening. Fall work, by John B. Peirce] Hampton, Va., 1903.

8°.   **NYP**

4290. ———. TRADE SCHOOL. [Publications] no. 1-8. Hampton, 1913-16.

8 nos. illus. 8°.   **NYP**

4291. HAMPTON ROADS MILITARY ACADEMY, Newport News, Va. Announcement and catalogue; Hampton Roads military academy (Newport News military academy). Newport News, Franklin, 19—

illus. 8°. Advertisements in back.   **LC,** 1901/02.

4292. HAMPTON TRAINING SCHOOL FOR WOMEN AND DIXIE HOSPITAL, Hampton, Va. . . . Annual report . . . Hampton, Va. [1892-19—

12°. (Estab., 1891)
NYP: 1893/94-95/96, 99/1900, 15/16, 17/18-18/19; USC: 1891/92-1901/02; V: 1904/05, 12/13.

4293. HANOVER ACADEMY, Taylorsville, Va. Catalogue . . . [n. p., 18-?-?]

8°. (Prep.; boys; non-sect.; 1851?)
V: 1872/73, 74/75, 77/78, 80/81, 82/83, 85/86-86/87.

4294. HAWKINS CHAPEL INSTITUTE, Rural Retreat, Va. Catalogue . . . [Wytheville, Va., etc., 18-?-?]

8°. (Prep.; co-ed.; non-sect.; 18-?)
V: 1891/92-92/93, 95/96, 97/98.

4295. HIGH POINT ACADEMY, Grant, Va. Catalogue . . . Eona, Va., 19—

8°. (Prep.; co-ed.; non-sect.)   V: 1903/04.

4296. [3428] HOLLINS COLLEGE, Hollins, Va. Annual catalogue. Roanoke, Va. [18-?-19—

See also items 3429-3436.

4297. HOMESTEAD SCHOOL FOR GIRLS, Hot Springs, Va. [Announcement. n. p., 19—

8°. (Prep.; non-sect.)   H: 1917/18.

4298. HOOVER'S SELECT HIGH SCHOOL, Staunton, Va. Catalogue . . . Staunton [1878?-19—

8°. (Milit.; boys; non-sect.; 1877)   V: 1879/80.

4299. INGLESIDE SEMINARY, Burkeville, Va. Catalogue . . . [n. p., 1893?-19—

8°. (Prep.; colored; girls; Presbyt.; 1892)   V: 1892/93-97/98.

4300. INGRAM INSTITUTE, Ingram, Va. Catalogue . . . [n. p., 189-?-19—

8°. (Co-ed.; non-sect.; 1892)   V: 1892/93, 94/95.

4301. JACKSONVILLE FEMALE INSTITUTE, Floyd C. H., Va. [Announcement . . . n. p., 18—

12°.   H: 1880/81.

4302. JEFFERSON SCHOOL FOR BOYS. Catalogue . . . Charlottesville, 19—

12°. (Non-sect.; 190-?)   **V**: 1905/06.

4303. JONES, THOMAS J. Social studies in the Hampton curriculum
. . . Hampton, Hampton institute press, 1906.

32 p. incl. diagrs. 8°.   **H, LC, NYP**
Reprint from the *Southern workman.*
The practical nature of the material used in courses in government
and economics at Hampton.

4304. JONESVILLE INSTITUTE, Jonesville, Va. Catalogue . . .
[n. p., 18- ?-19—

8°. (Co-ed.; non-sect.)   **V**: 1901/02-02/03, 04/05.
Called Jonesville academy, *ante* 1902.

4305. KENMORE UNIVERSITY HIGH SCHOOL, Amherst C. H., Va.
[Catalogue] [Lynchburg, 1873 ?- ?]

8°. (Prep.; non-sect.; 1872)
H: 1874/75; **V**: 1875/76-76/77, 78/79-79/80, 83/84.

4306. KESWICK SCHOOL FOR BOYS, Cobham, Va. Catalogue . . .
[Charlottesville, 18- ?—

8°. (Prep.; non-sect.; 1890?)   **V**: 1891/92.

4307. KEYSVILLE MISSION INDUSTRIAL SCHOOL, Keysville, Va. Catalogue . . . Lynchburg [1898 ?-19—

8°. (Colored; co-ed.; Bapt.; 1898)   **V**: 1906/07.

4308. KLEINBERG FEMALE HOME SCHOOL, Rockfish Depot, Nelson
County, Va. Catalogue . . . [Charlottesville, 1881 ?-19—

8°. (Non-sect.; 1881)   **V**: 1890/91-91/92, 94/95.

4309. LEACHEWOOD SEMINARY, Norfolk, Va. Catalogue . . .
[Norfolk ? 187 ?-19—

8°. (Prep.; girls; non-sect.; 1871)
H: 1908/09; **V**: 1880/81, 1903/04, 06/07-07/08.

4310. LEESBURG ACADEMY, Leesburg, Va. Catalogue . . . [n. p.,
188- ?-19—

8°. (Public management; co-ed.; 1886?)   **V**: 1897/98-98/99.

4311. LEXINGTON HIGH SCHOOL, Lexington, Va. Catalogue . . .
[Lexington ? Va., 19—

8°.   **V**: 1906/07.

4312. LOCUST DALE ACADEMY, Madison County, Va. Catalogue
. . . [1st- ; 1858?— n. p., 1859?-19—

8°. (Prep.; milit.; non-sect.; 1858)
V: 18-19th, 21st, 24th, 40th, 42d-44th, 52d (1874/75-75/76, 77/78, 80/81,
96/97, 98/99-1900/01, 08/09).

4313. LOUDOUN VALLEY ACADEMY, Hamilton, Va. Catalogue . . .
[n. p., 1869?-?]

8°. (Prep.; co-ed.; non-sect.; 1868)   V: 1869/70.

4314. ———. Circular . . . [n. p., 18-?-?]

8°.   V: 1872/73.

4315. LOUISA HOME SCHOOL, Louisa C. H., Va. Catalogue . . .
[n. p., 18-?-?]

8°. (Co-ed.; non-sect.; 18-?)   V: 1884/85.
Mrs. Joseph B. Winston, principal.

4316. LURAY FEMALE INSTITUTE, Luray, Va. Catalogue . . .
[Luray? Va., 1890?-19—

8°. (Prep. & col.; girls; non-sect.; 1889)   V: 1889/90-90/91.

4317. LYNCHBURG ACADEMY, Lynchburg, Va. Catalogue . . .
[Lynchburg? Va., 188-?-19—

8°. (Prep.; girls; non-sect.; 1883)   ·   V: 1889/90.

4318. ———. [Circular. n. p., n. d.]

4 p. 8°.   H

4319. LYNCHBURG CLASSICAL AND COMMERCIAL SCHOOL, Lynchburg,
Va. Catalogue . . . Lynchburg, Va. [1869-?]

8°.   V: 1868/69.

4320. [3437] LYNCHBURG COLLEGE, Lynchburg, Va. Catalogue
. . . [n. p., 1903—

4321. [McALLISTER, W. H.] A sketch of Boydton institute. Nov.,
1904. [n. p., 1904]

8 p. illus. 12°.   V
Condensed from an article by the author in *Living truths.*

4322. McCONNELL, JOHN P. The relation of high schools and colleges to the improvement of rural life. An address delivered before the Association of secondary schools and colleges of Virginia.
[Pulaski, Va., Smith, n. d.]

11 p. 12°.   V

4323. McGaheysville high school, McGaheysville, Va. Catalogue . . . [n. p., 1907?—

    8°. Successor to Oak Hill academy **[4362]**   **V**: 1907/08.

4324. McGuire, Hunter. Official report of History committee of Grand camp C[onfederate] V[eterans], Dept. of Virginia, 1899. Richmond, Hill, 1899.

    16 p. 8°.   **V**
    Campaign against northern text books which, according to the Confederate veterans, do injustice to the South. (See also item **2492**)

4325. McGuire's university school, Richmond, Va. Catalogue . . . Richmond, Va. [186-?-19—

    8°. (Prep.; boys; non-sect.; 1865)
    H: 1908/09; **V**: 1900/01-01/02, 03/04-04/05, 16/17-17/18.

4326. Mahone, William. An assassin-like blow at the public schools [in Virginia] by Bourbon managers. [Petersburg, Va., 1885]

    3 p. 8°.   **BP**
    A protest against the diversion of school funds to the State treasury.

4327. [Manassas industrial school, Manassas, Va.] A battleground school. A colored woman's work in uplifting Negro boys and girls. The story of the Manassas industrial school for colored youth. [n. p., 1903?]

    11 p. 8°.   **BP, LC, NYP**
    Reprint from New York *Evening post:* "Jennie Dean's efforts among her own people."

4328. ———. [Catalogue . . . n. p., 189-?-19—

    illus., plan. 8°. (Prep. & indust.; colored; co-ed.; non-sect.; 1894)
    H: 1903/04, 08/09; **LC**: 1908/09; **NYP**: 1902/03-03/04, 06/07, 08/09, 10/11, 14/15; **V**: 1914/15.

4329. ———. Financial statement and donors' list . . . for the year . . . Manassas, Va., 19—

    illus. 8°. Title varies.
    H: 1906/07-07/08; **LC**: 1904/05, 08/09; **NYP**: 1906/07, 12/13.

4330. Manassas institute, Manassas, Va. Catalogue . . . [n. p., 1890?-19—

    8°. (Prep.; co-ed.; non-sect.; 1889)
    V: 1894/95, 1900/01, 03/04.

4331. MARGARET ACADEMY, Onancock, Va. Catalogue . . . Richmond, Va. [18-?-19—

8°. (Prep.; co-ed.; non-sect.; 1786)
H: 1894/95-96/97; V: 1893/94-94/95, 96/97.

4332. MARX, ELLIE M. Citizenship training in elementary schools . . . Norfolk, Va., The Henry Clay home and school league [*ca.* 1926]

4 p. l., [3]-134 p. plates. 12°.   H, LC, V, WM
A description of the Henry Clay school, Norfolk, Va.,—"a little democracy in which the pupils are responsible members, their activities being based upon the curriculum and the various organizations of school life."

4333. [3444] MARY BALDWIN SEMINARY, Staunton, Va. Catalogue . . . Roanoke [etc.] 1896-19—

4334. MAYO, AMORY D. . . . Education in southwestern Virginia. 1890-91. By Rev. A. D. Mayo, M. A. Washington, Govt., 1894.

1 p. l., 881-921 p. 8°.   BP, LC, NYP, USC, USE, V
Reprint of chap. 24 of the *Report* of the U. S. Commissioner of education for 1890-91.
Reveals strikingly the backwardness of public education in this section of Virginia, especially in elementary schools.

4335. MEADOWBROOK SCHOOL, Leesburg, Va. [Announcement. n. p., 19—

illus., map. 8°. (Prep.; boys; non-sect.; 19-?)   LC: 1912/13.
Continuation of the University school, Washington, D. C., established in 1891.

4336. MERRILL FEMALE SCHOOL, Richmond, Va. Catalogue . . . Richmond, Jones [18-?-?]

8°. (Prep.; girls; non-sect.; 18-?)   V: 1889/90.

4337. MILLER, EDWARD A. Elementary agriculture for Virginia schools . . . Lessons outlined by months. Richmond, State dept. of public instruction [1918]

143 p. illus., diagrs. 8°.   USAg, V
Prepared by the States relation service, U. S. Dept. of agriculture, in co-operation with the Virginia Dept. of public instruction and the Virginia agricultural and mechanical college.

4338. [MILLER, SAMUEL]   Extract of so much of the will of Samuel Miller as relates to the Miller manual labor school of Albemarle. [Also] an act . . . to establish the Manual labor school provided for in the 25th clause of said will.   [n. p., n. d.]

15 p. 8°.   V

4339. MILLER MANUAL LABOR SCHOOL OF ALBEMARLE, Crozet, Va. [Catalogue . . . Charlottesville, Va., 1879?-19—

plates. 8°.   (Tech.; co-ed.; 1878)
H: 1884/85, 87/88, 96/97; **LC**: 1900/01; **V**: 1900/01, 02/03; **VU**: 1880/81.

4340. ———. Miller manual labor school of Albemarle.   [n. p., n. d.]

15 p. 8°.   **V, VU**
Contains text of will of Samuel Miller (1859); also act of 1874 establishing the school.

4341. ———. The Miller manual labor school of Albemarle. Crozet, Virginia. June, 1892.   [Charlottesville, Va., Jeffersonian, 1892]

99 p. front., plates, fold. plans. 8°.   **USE**
Includes "The last will and testament of Samuel Miller."

4342. ———. The Miller school of Albemarle . . . [Charlottesville, Michie] 1901.

184 p. 8°.   V
Contains description of the Miller fund, courses of instruction, buildings, and catalogue for 1900-01.

4343. MITCHELL, SAMUEL C. A southern man's estimate of Hampton institute . . . Hampton, Institute press, 1908.

1 p. l., [5]-13, [1] p. 16°.   **USE**
Address delivered at the 40th anniversary of Hampton institute; reprint from *Southern workman,* June, 1908.

4344. MOTON, ROBERT R. An apostle of good will. Founder's day address, Robert R. Moton, principal of Tuskegee institute. [Hampton, Va., Press of the Institute, 1917]

1 p. l., 7 p. 8°.   **LC, NYP, USE, VU**
Emphasizes the spirit of good will between Negroes and whites which Hampton seeks to promote.

4345. MOUNT CRAWFORD ACADEMY, Mount Crawford, Va. Catalogue . . . [n. p., 188-?-19—

8°.   (Prep.; co-ed.; non-sect.; 1885?)   **V**: 1893/94.

4346. MOUNT PISGAH ACADEMY, Culpeper C. H., Va. Catalogue
. . . Richmond, Va. [1873?-?]

8°. (Prep.; girls; 1872)   V: 1884/85.

4347. MOUNT WELCOME HIGH SCHOOL, near Mitchell's Station, Culpeper County, Va. Catalogue . . . Charlottesville [etc., 18-?-?]

8°. (Boys; non-sect.; 18-?)   V: 1886/87-88/89.

4348. MUNFORD, THOMAS T. Address . . . to the graduates and corps of cadets of Marion institute, May 23d, 1916. [n. p., 1916?]

[8] p. illus. 8°.   V

4349. NANSEMOND INDUSTRIAL INSTITUTE, Suffolk, Va. Annual catalogue . . . Richmond, Reformer print., 1908—

illus., front. 8°. (Co-ed.; colored; 1908)   V: 1908/09.

4350. NANSEMOND SEMINARY, Suffolk, Va. Catalogue . . . [n. p., 1878?-19—

8°. (Prep.; girls; Prot. Episc.; 1877)   V: 1895/96.

4351. NATIONAL EDUCATION ASSOCIATION. DEPT. OF SUPERINTENDENCE. The public schools of Richmond, Virginia. Richmond, Richmond press [1914]

24 p. 12°.   H
Contains a directory of schools, school board and officers, administration and organization of schools.

4352. NEW LONDON ACADEMY, Bedford Springs, Va. Catalogue
. . . Lynchburg [etc., 18-?-19—

8°. (Prep.; boys, then co-ed.; non-sect.; 1795)
Became public high school, 1887.
V: 1885/86, 88/89, 95/96, 97/98-98/99.

4353. NOLLEY'S SCHOOL, Richmond, Va. Catalogue . . . [Richmond, 189-?-19—

8°. (Prep.; boys; non-sect.; 189-?)   V: 1903/04, 07/08-08/09.

4354. NORFOLK ACADEMY, Norfolk, Va. Catalogue of the trustees, officers and students . . . [Norfolk, Va., 18-?-19—

8°. (Prep.; boys; non-sect.; 1804)
H: 1888/89-90/91, 93/94, 96/97-98/99, 1900/01-01/02, 03/04-06/07, 08/09; V: 1882/83, 85/86-87/88, 91/92, 93/94-95/96, 1901/02, 03/04, 05/06, 07/08-13/14, 24/25-25/26, 28/29.

4355. NORFOLK ACADEMY, Norfolk, Va.   Laying of the corner stone of the Norfolk academy, Norfolk, Virginia, Saturday, May 31, 1924.   Exercises in connection   . . .   [n. p., 1924]

[16] p. 8°.   **VU**

4356. ———.   Norfolk academy; a trial list of the alumni, revised and corrected to May 15, 1927.   Comp. & issued at the instance of the Board of trustees.   Norfolk, 1927.

67 p. incl. front. 12°.   **LC, WM**

4357. ———.   JUNIOR DEPT.   [Catalogue]   Norfolk, Keyser-Doherty, 19—

illus. 8°.   **V:** 1927/28.

4358. [3455] NORFOLK COLLEGE, Norfolk, Va.   Catalogue . . . Norfolk, [187-?-?]

4359. NORFOLK MISSION COLLEGE, Norfolk, Va.   Annual catalogue . . .   Norfolk [188-?-19—

plates, port. 8°.   (Prep.; co-ed.; United Presbyt.; 1883)
Title varies: Catalogue of the officers and students . . .
L'C: 1894/95, 97/98, 1906/07; **V:** 1900/01.

4360. NORWOOD HIGH SCHOOL, Nelson County, Va.   Catalogue . . .   [1st- ; 1866/67—   Richmond, etc., 1867?—

8°.   (Prep. & col.; boys; non-sect.; 1865)
Advertisements in back.
Title varies: Catalogue . . .   Norwood high school and college, 1876/77—
V: 1871/72-77/78, 81/82-83/84.

4361. ———.   A historical sketch of Norwood high school and college, Nelson County, Virginia.   Richmond, Whittet & Shepperson, 1881.

25, [6] p. 8°.   Advertisements in back.   **V**
Includes testimonials and lists of professors and students.

4362. OAK HILL ACADEMY, McGaheysville, Va.   Catalogue . . . [n. p., 1882?-1906?]

8°.   (Prep.; co-ed.; non-sect.; 1881)   **V:** 1897/98, 1905/06.
Succeeded by McGaheysville high school, 190-? **[4323]**

4363. OAKLAND MALE AND FEMALE HIGH SCHOOL, Doe Hill, Va.   Catalogue . . .   Staunton, 1873—

8°.   (Estab., 1872)   **V:** 1872/73.

4364. OLD POINT COMFORT COLLEGE, Fort Monroe, Va. Catalogue . . . [n. p., 1899?-19—

plates. 8°. (Prep.; boys; Rom. Cath. [Xaverian bros.]; 1898)
BP: 1901/02; V: 1905/06.

4365. OXFORD ACADEMY, Floyd C. H., Va. Catalogue . . . [n. p., 18-?-19—

8°. (Prep.; co-ed.; non-sect.; 18-?) V: 1894/95.

4366. PAEONIAN SPRINGS HIGH SCHOOL, Paeonian Springs, Va. Catalogue . . . Woodstock, Va. [etc., 1904?—

8°. (Establ., 1903) V: 1906/07-07/08.

4367. PANTOPS ACADEMY, near Charlottesville, Va. Catalogue . . . [n. p., 187-?-?]

8°. (Prep.; boys; non-sect.; 1877?) V: 1881/82-82/83, 85/86.

4368. PATE, MCCALL. Hand-book of general information for men under instruction in the Artificer school, Dept. of C. & R., Navy yard, Norfolk, Va. Comp. and arranged by Chief carpenter McCall Pate, U. S. N. Annapolis, Md., U. S. naval institute, 1908.

88 p. diagrs. 16°. LC
On cover: The naval artificer's hand-book, 1908.

4369. PETERSBURG ACADEMY, Petersburg, Va. Announcement . . . [Petersburg? Va., 19—

8°. V: 1908/09.

4370. PHILLIPS AND WEST SCHOOL FOR GIRLS, Norfolk, Va. Catalogue . . . [Norfolk? Va., 18-?-19—

12°. (Prep.; girls; non-sect.; 18-?) V: 1895/96, 1905/06, 09/10.

4371. PIEDMONT FEMALE INSTITUTE, Charlottesville, Va. Catalogue . . . [Charlottesville? Va., 18-?-?]

8°. (Non-sect.; 1851?) V: 1874/75, 76/77, 79/80-81/82.

4372. PLATT'S (MRS. W. H.) SCHOOL FOR GIRLS, Petersburg, Va. Catalogue . . . [Petersburg, Va., 18-?-19—

8°. (Non-sect.; 18-?) V: 1891/92.

4373. PORTSMOUTH ACADEMY, Portsmouth, Va. Catalogue . . . [Portsmouth? Va., 18-?-19—

8°. (Prep.; boys; non-sect.; 1868) V: 1895/96, 1900/01-01/02.

4374. PORTSMOUTH SEMINARY, Portsmouth, Va. Catalogue . . .
[n. p., 18-?-?]

12°. (Girls; non-sect.; 18-?)   **V**: 1889/90.

4375. POTOMAC ACADEMY, Alexandria, Va. Catalogue . . . and
prospectus of study for the academic year . . . [Alexandria,
1870?-19—

8°. (Prep.; boys; non-sect.; 1869)
Prospectus is for year following date of Catalogue.
LC: 1877/78, 87/88; **V**: 1872/73-88/89, 90/91-1909/10.

4376. PRINCE EDWARD ACADEMY, Worsham, Va. Catalogue . . .
[n. p., 187-?-?]

8°. (Prep.; boys; non-sect.; 1874)
NYP: 1877/78, 79/80-81/82; **V**: 1877/78.

4377. [PURYEAR, BENNET] The public school in its relation to the
Negro. By Civis. Republished by request, from the Southern
planter and farmer. Richmond, Clemmitt & Jones, 1877.

39 p. 8°.   **H, LC, V**
Arguments against a public school system supported by the State,
with particular reference to evils in educating the Negro.

4378. RANDOLPH-MACON ACADEMY, Bedford City, Va. Catalogue
. . . [n. p., 1891?-19—

8°. (Milit; M. E., So.; 1890)
V: 1890/91, 92/93, 1904/05, 06/07, 08/09.

4379. ———. Decennial catalogue . . . [n. p., 19—

8°.   **V**: 1900.

4380. RANDOLPH-MACON ACADEMY, Front Royal, Va. Catalogue
. . . [Winchester? Va., etc., 1893?-19—

8°. (Milit.; non-sect.; 1892)
BP: 1893/94; **NYP**: 1893/94, 1909/10-10/11; **V**: 1892/93-1906/07,
08/09, 14/15, 18/19-20/21, 23/24, 25/26-27/28.

4381. ———. Randolph-Macon academy at Front Royal, the county
seat of Warren County in the northern end of the Shenandoah
Valley of Virginia. [Lynchburg, Bell, n. d.]

47 p. incl. plates, front. (port.) 8°.   **V**
Ed. of 1928.   **V**

4382. Randolph-Macon institute, Danville, Va. Catalogue . . .
[1st- ; 1897/98-19—   Danville? Va., 1898?-19—

8°. (Prep.; girls; M. E., So.; 1897)
NYP: 1905/06, 09/10, 15/16; USE: 1904/05, 09/10; V: 1904/05-
05/06, 07/08, 09/10.

4383. [3474] Rappahannock institute, Tappahannock, Va. . . .
Catalogue . . . [n. p., 18-?—

4384. Richmond academy, Richmond, Va. Catalogue . . .
[Richmond? Va., 19—

8°.   V: 1903/04-14/15.

4385. [Richmond] Academy of the visitation, Richmond, Va.
Announcement . . . [n. p., n. d.]

sheet. 4°. (Girls; Rom. Cath.)   H

4386. Richmond female institute, Richmond, Va. Catalogue
. . . Richmond, Va. [18-?-?]

8°. (Prep. & col.; non-sect.; 1853)
USE: 1867/68, 69/70, 71/72, 75/76; V: 1876/77.

4387. [Richmond] Franklin street school, Richmond, Va. Catalogue . . . Richmond, Va., Whittet & Shepperson [188-?-
19—

12°. (Prep.; boys; non-sect.; 188-?)   V: 1890/91-91/92.

4388. Richmond institute, Richmond, Va. Catalogue of the officers and students . . . for the academic year . . . Richmond, Clemmitt & Jones [etc., 186-?-?]

8°. (Colored; Bapt.; 1865)
Merged into Virginia union university [3838]
NYP: 1876/77; V: 1874/75-76/77; WM: 1877/78-85/86.

4389. ———. Historical sketch . . . [Richmond? 1876]

unp. 8°.   V

4390. Riverview seminary, Wood, Va. Catalogue . . . [n. p.,
1889?-?]

8°. (Prep.; co-ed.; non-sect.; 1888)   V: 1890/91-91/92.

4391. Robinson, Charles M. Fairfield and Varina districts, Henrico County. School housing survey. 1924. Charles M. Robin-

son, school architects, A. C. Cooper, division superintendent. Richmond, Va., Hill [*ca.* 1924]

16 p. diagrs., map. 8°.   H

4392. ROBINSON, CHARLES M. Portsmouth, Virginia, public schools; report and survey of school housing conditions. Copyrighted, Charles M. Robinson, school architects, Portsmouth public schools. Richmond, Va., Hill, 1921.

18 p. diagrs. 8°.   LC, USE, V

4393. ROOSEVELT, THEODORE. Address . . . at Hampton institute [Decoration day, 1906] [Hampton, Va., Hampton press, 1906]

[15] p. illus. 8°.   BP, NYP

4394. RUFFIN, FRANK G. The cost and outcome of Negro education in Virginia. Respectfully addressed to the white people of the state. Richmond, Waddey, 1889.

20 p. 8°.   BP, H, NYP, V

4395. RUFFNER, WILLIAM H. [Addresses, pamphlets, public documents, and miscellaneous matter on the subject of public education in Virginia. Collected by W. H. Ruffner, supt. of public instruction. Richmond, etc., 188-]

2 v. var. pag. 8°.   V

4396. ———. The public free school system. Mr. Dabney answered by Mr. Ruffner. [n. p., 1876?]

43 p. 8°.   USE, WM
Reply to Rev. R. L. Dabney's articles in the *Planter and farmer* attacking education of the Negro and the public school system generally. Reprints from Richmond *Enquirer.*

4397. RURAL RETREAT HIGH SCHOOL, Rural Retreat, Va. Catalogue . . . [n. p., 19—

8°. (Estab., 1900)   V: 1906/07-07/08.

4398. RUSSELL COLLEGE, Lebanon, Va. Annual catalogue . . . Norton, Va. [1894?-19—

8°. (Prep.; co-ed.; non-sect.; 1893)
LC: 1895/96; V: 1893/94-95/96, 98/99.

4399. ———. Prospectus . . . Announcements for 1893-94. Bristol, Tenn., King, 1893.

12 p. 8°. **V**

4400. RYLAND INSTITUTE, Berkley, Va. Catalogue . . . [n. p., 1890?-?]

8°. (Girls; non-sect.; 1889) **V**: 1890/91, 92/93, 94/95-95/96. Founded at Suffolk, Va.

4401. ST. ANNE'S SCHOOL, Charlottesville, Va. . . . Catalogue . . . Charlottesville [18-?-19—

8°. (Prep.; girls; Prot. Episc.; 187-?) Formed in 1910 by consolidation of Albemarle female institute and Rawlings institute.

USE: 1889/90-91/92, 94/95-95/96; **V**: 1879/80, 89/90, 95/96, 1906/07, 10/11-11/12.

4402. ———. A day at St. Anne's. A church school for girls near the University of Virginia. Charlottesville, Va. [19-?]

[12] p. illus. 16° **VU**

4403. [3507] ST. JOHN'S ACADEMY, Alexandria, Va. Catalogue . . . Alexandria, Va. [18-?-?]

4404. ST. MARY'S ACADEMY, Alexandria, Va. [Announcement. n. p., 18-?-?]

8°. (Prep.; girls; Rom. Cath.; 1869, re-opened 1882) **V**: 1882/83, 89/90.

4405. ST. MARY'S MALE ACADEMY, Norfolk, Va. . . . Curriculum of studies . . . conducted by the Xaverian brothers . . . [Norfolk, Va? n. d.]

[4] p. 8°. (Rom. Cath.; date?) **V**

4406. ST. PAUL NORMAL AND INDUSTRIAL SCHOOL, Lawrenceville, Va. . . . Annual report of the principal . . . 1st- ; 1888/89-19— [Roanoke? 1889-19—

8°. **BP**: 10th (1897/98); **H**: 4th (1891/92); **LC**: 15th (1902/03); **NYP**: 1895/96, 98/99, 1906/07-07/08; **V**: 1923/24.

4407. ———. Catalogue . . . Lawrenceville, Va. [1889?-19—

plates. 8°. (Prot. Episc.; 1888) **H**: 1889/90, 91/92, 96/97, 1901/02; **LC**: 1902/03; **NYP**: 1915/16.

4408. St. Paul normal and industrial school, Lawrenceville, Va. [Circular] [n. p.] 1897.

12°.   NYP

4409. ———. The Saint Paul bulletin. Vol. 1- [1906—] Lawrenceville, Va. [1906—

illus. 8°. quarterly.
H: V, 2-3 (1913). **V:** VIII, 1-2; XVIII, 4; XIX, 4; XXII, 2-3; (1915, 24-25, 28).

4410. St. Paul's female school, Petersburg, Va. Catalogue . . . [Petersburg? Va., 187-?-?]

8°. (Prep.; 187-?)   **V:** 1889/90 & [n. d.]

4411. St. Timothy's home school, Herndon, Va. Catalogue . . . [n. p., 18-?-?]

8°. (Boys; Prot. Episc., 18-?)   **V:** 1874/75.

4412. A School and home for homeless boys. Alleghany County, Virginia. [Lynchburg, Bell, 19-?]

[24] p. illus. 4°.   **V**

4413. Scott, Rhea C., comp. . . . Things that all county school children should know and do, by the children of the schools of Rockingham County, Va. [Harrisonburg, Va., Rockingham pub., 1913]

14 p. 8°. (*Rockingham school bulletin,* Jan., 1913)   **V**

4414. Sears, Barnas. Education: an address delivered to the Constitutional convention, State of Virginia, . . . Jan. 23, 1868, by Rev. Dr. Sears. Richmond, New nation, 1868.

18 p. 8°.   **V**
Arguments in favor of "free schools for the whole people," revealing indirectly Virginia's lack of public education.

4415. Semple, F. A. A plan of the property of the Hampton normal and agricultural institute at Hampton, Virginia. Surveyed by F. A. Semple. S. C. A[rmstrong] . . . 1876. [Hampton, 1876]

18 3/8 x 28 1/2 in. No. scale.   **BP**

4416. Seven Islands school, Buckingham County, Va. Catalogue . . . [n. p., 18-?-?]

8°. (Prep.; boys; non-sect.; 18-?)   **V:** 1893/94, 99/1900.
Philip B. Ambler, principal.

4417. SHARON COLLEGE SCHOOL, Sharon Springs, Effna, Va. Catalogue . . . [n. p., 18-?-1903?]

8°. (Prep.; co-ed.; non-sect.; 18-?)   V: 1897/98-98/99.
Closed, 1904.

4418. [3509] SHENANDOAH COLLEGE, Reliance, Va. Catalogue . . . Reliance, Va. [1883?-19—

4419. SHENANDOAH VALLEY ACADEMY, Winchester, Va. [Catalogue] [Staunton, Va., 1896?-19—

illus. 8°. (Milit.; boys; 1895)
L'C: 1912/13; V: 1880/81, 83/84-84/85, 1908/09.

4420. [3513] SHOEMAKER COLLEGE, Gate City, Va. Catalogue . . . Gate City, Va. [1897?-19—

4421. SOLDIERS' MEMORIAL SOCIETY, Boston. Report on free white schools at Richmond. [Richmond, 1866]

8 p. 8°.   BP, H
Ed. of 1867.   H

4422. [3514] SOUTH BOSTON FEMALE INSTITUTE, South Boston, Va. Catalogue . .   [n. p., 1884?—

4423. [3515] SOUTHERN COLLEGE, Petersburg, Va. . . . Catalogue . . . [Petersburg? 1864?-19—

4424. SOUTHERN FEMALE INSTITUTE, Richmond, Va. Catalogue . . . Richmond [18-?-?]

8°. (Prep.; non-sect.; 1854)   V: 1866/67, 75/76.
Founded at Fredericksburg, Va.

4425. SOUTHERN SEMINARY, Buena Vista, Va. Catalogue . . . [n. p., 186-?-19—

8°. (Prep. & col.; girls; M. E., So.; 1867)   V: 1904/05.

4426. SOUTH-SIDE ACADEMY, Chase City, Va. Catalogue . . . [n. p., 1890?-19—

plates. 8°. (Prep.; co-ed.; Bapt.; 1889)
V: 1896/97-99/1900, 09/10.

4427. SOUTHSIDE FEMALE INSTITUTE, Burkeville, Va. Catalogue . . . Richmond, Va. [189-?-19—

8°. (Prep. & col.; non-sect.; 1890?)   V: 1894-95.
Closed during 1904.

4428. [3517] SOUTHWEST VIRGINIA INSTITUTE, Bristol, Va. Catalogue . . . [Bristol, etc., 1884?-19—

4429. STAUNTON BAPTIST FEMALE INSTITUTE, Staunton, Va. Catalogue . . . [Staunton? Va., 1871-?]
8°. (Estab., 1870?)   **V**: 1870/71-71/72.

4430. [3518] STAUNTON FEMALE SEMINARY, Staunton, Va. Catalogue . . . [Staunton, 1870?-?]

4431. STAUNTON MALE ACADEMY, Staunton, Va. Catalogue . . . [Staunton? Va., 18-?-?]
8°. (Prep.; non-sect.; 18-?)   **V**: 1889/90.

4432. STAUNTON MILITARY ACADEMY, Staunton, Va. Catalogue . . . [Staunton? Va., 1873?-19—
8°. (Boys; non-sect.; 1872)
H: 1909/10; **USE**: 1917/18; **V**: 1892/93-95/96, 98/99-99/1900, 03/04.

4433. ———. [Circular, 1894-95] [Staunton?] Daily news, 1894.
41 p. plates. 16°.   **BP**

4434. STUART HALL, Staunton, Va. [Announcement . . . Virginia female institute . . . Staunton, 18-?-19—
illus., plates. 12°.   **V**: 1899/1900.

4435. ———. Catalogue . . . Staunton [18-?-19—
illus., plates. 8°. (Prep.; girls; Prot. Episc.; 1843)
Founded as Virginia female institute; became Stuart hall, 1907.
H: 1880/81; **USE**: 1874/75, 77/78, 82/83-83/84, 85/86-89/90; **V**: 1894/95, 97/98-98/99, 1900/01-05/06, 09/10.

4436. ———. Commencement program . . . Virginia female institute . . . [Staunton? Va., 18-?-?]
8°.   H: June, 1869.

4437. STUYVESANT SCHOOL, Warrenton, Va. [Catalogue . . . Baltimore, Industrial print, 1913—
illus. 8°. (Prep.; boys; 1912)   H: 1912/13-13/14; **LC**: 1914/15.

4438. [3521] SUFFOLK COLLEGIATE INSTITUTE, Suffolk, Va. Catalogue . . . [n. p., 1870—

4439. SUFFOLK MILITARY ACADEMY, Suffolk, Va. Catalogue . . . [n. p., 1877?-?]

8°. (Boys; non-sect.; 1876) **V**: 1883/84.

4440. SUMMERVILLE HOME SCHOOL FOR GIRLS, near Gloucester C. H., Va. Catalogue . . . [n. p., 189-?-?]

8°. (Non-sect.; 18-?) **V**: 1893/94.
Removed from Baltimore, Md., 1893.

4441. SWEET BRIAR ACADEMY, Sweet Briar, Va. [Announcement . . . Lynchburg, 1906—

12°. (Prep. dept. of Sweet Briar college [3524-3530]) **V**: 1915/16.

4442. TAFT, WILLIAM H. Armstrong and world freedom, founder's day address by Hon. William Howard Taft . . . president of Hampton's board of trustees. [Hampton? Va., 1918]

1 p. l., [5]-14 p. 8°. **BP, H, NYP, USE, V, VU**
Reprint from *Southern workman,* Mar., 1918.

4443. [3531] TAZEWELL COLLEGE, Tazewell, Va. Annual catalogue . . . Tazewell, Va. [1891?-19—

4444. TAZEWELL FEMALE SEMINARY, Tazewell, Va. Catalogue . . . 1st- ; 1886/87-19— [n. p., 1887-19—

8°. (Non-sect.; 1886) **V**: 4-5th (1889/90-90/91).

4445. TAZEWELL HIGH SCHOOL, Tazewell, Va. Announcement . . . [n. p., 1874?-19—

8°. (Estab., 1874) **V**: 33d-34th (1906/07-07/08).

4446. TEMPERANCE INDUSTRIAL AND COLLEGIATE INSTITUTE, Claremont, Va. Catalogue . . . [n. p., 1893?-19—

8°. (Prep.; colored; co-ed.; non-sect.; 1892) **V**: 1906/07.

4447. TENNEY, JOHN E. A manual for the use of church and mission schools of the Southern union conference of Seventh-day adventists . . . [Nashville, Tenn., Ft. Worth, Tex., etc.] Southern publishing association, 1907.

2 p. l., [3]-70 p. 12°. **LC**
Contains sections on plan of organization, relation of church to school, school room suggestions, text books, the relation of the Adventist to public schools, etc.

4448. THOM, PEMBROKE L. Address delivered at the joint final celebration of the Fairfax and Blackford literary societies of the Episcopal high school of Virginia. June 24th, 1884 . . . Baltimore, King [1884?]

11 p. 8°.   V

4449. THOM, WILLIAM T. Secondary education in Virginia. [Nor-
folk, 1881]

14 p. 8°.   BP, NYP

4450. THOMAS, A[LSEN] F. Primary education and the race problem; an address to the people of Virginia . . . Lynchburg,
Moose [1904?]

26 p. 8°.   LC, V
Caption title: Shall the country children of Virginia be educated?

4451. THORNTON, WILLIAM M. The school and the commonwealth,
the center of our larger hope. An address to the graduates of the
Richmond city high school, June 15, 1903 . . . [Richmond,
Williams, 1903]

21 p. port. 8°.   V, VU

4452. THYNE INSTITUTE, Chase City, Va. Catalogue . . . [n. p.,
18-?-19—

8°. (Prep.; colored; co-ed.; Presbyt.; 18-?)
V: 1883/84, 86/87, 1905/06.

4453. UNIVERSITY OF VIRGINIA. . . . Literary societies in secondary schools. Part I. Organization. Part II. Parliamentary
forms and rules. Part III. Questions for debate—arguments and
references. [Charlottesville] The University, 1915.

75 p. 8°. (*University of Virginia record.* Extension series, [I] 1)
                                                     LC, USE, V, VU
At head of title: . . . The Virginia high school literary and athletic league.
"The University of Virginia, through its Extension bureau, is repub-
lishing in this one bulletin, with some modifications, three bulletins,
which were issued jointly in 1911 by the University, the Department of
public instruction, and the Co-operative education association of Virginia." **[4092]**

4454. ———. The Virginia high school literary and athletic league
. . . [Charlottesville] The University, 1915—

8°. (*University of Virginia record.* Extension series, I, 1, 3; II, 2;
III, 2; IV, 1/5; V, 1, 4, 9; VI, 5; VII, 1; VIII, 1, 3; IX, 4, 6; X, 1-2;
XI, 2; XII, 3, 8; XIII, 2, 4; XIV, 4; [1915-29])

4455. UNIVERSITY SCHOOL, Petersburg, Va. Catalogue . . . [Petersburg? Va., 1866?-19—

8°. (Prep.; boys; non-sect.; 1865)
H: 1877/78, 79/80-81/82, 89/90, 91/92, 96/97-98/99; V: 1874/75, 77/78-79/80, 82/83, 84/85-88/89, 90/91, 92/93.

4456. [3734] VALLEY FEMALE COLLEGE, Winchester, Va. Register of pupils . . . Winchester, Va. [18-?-19—

4457. VALLEY HIGH SCHOOL, Spotswood, Va. Catalogue . . . Staunton, Va. [18-?-19—

8°. (Co-ed.; estab., 18-?) V: 1898/99.

4458. VALLEY SEMINARY, Waynesboro, Va. Catalogue . . . [n. p., 1888-19—

8°. (Prep.; girls; non-sect.; 1887)
McC: 1892/93; V: 1887/88-88/89, 90/91.

4459. VIRGINIA INSTITUTE, Bristol, Va. Annual of the Virginia institute with Conservatory of music and art for young women . . . with announcements. Knoxville, Tenn. [1885?-19—

illus. (incl. port.) 8°. (Prep.; Bapt.; 1884)
LC: 1902/03; USE: 1908/09-09/10.

4460. VIRGINIA MANUAL LABOR SCHOOL FOR COLORED BOYS, Hanover, Va. Biennial report . . . 1st- [n. p., 19-?—

8°. V: 12-13th (1921/23-23/25).

4461. VIRGINIA MIDLAND ACADEMY, near Culpeper, Va. Catalogue . . . [n. p., 1886-19—

8°. (Prep.; boys; non-sect.; 1885) V: 1886/87.

4462. VIRGINIA RANDOLPH ELLETT SCHOOL, Richmond, Va. The Virginia Randolph Ellett school . . . a country day school for girls, Westhampton, Richmond. [Announcement] 1917-1918. [Richmond? 1917]

[12] p. front., plate. 12°. V

4463. [3838] VIRGINIA UNION UNIVERSITY, Richmond, Va. Annual catalogue . . . Richmond, Va. [1866?-19—

4464. WARRENTON COUNTRY SCHOOL FOR YOUNG GIRLS, Warrenton, Va. [Announcement . . . n. p., 19—

8°. H: 1918/19(?)

4465. WARTBURG SEMINARY, Graham, Va. Catalogue . . . [n. p., 1889?-19—

8°. (Prep.; co-ed.; Luth.; 1888)   **V**: 1893/94-95/96.

4466. [3869] WAYLAND SEMINARY AND COLLEGE, Richmond, Va. Catalogue . . . [Richmond, Va., 18-?-19—

4467. WEBSTER INSTITUTE, Norfolk, Va. Catalogue . . . [Norfolk? Va., 1870?-?]

8°. (Prep.; boys; non-sect.; 1869)   **V**: 1874/75, 76/77, 78/79.

4468. ———. Catalogue, circular, and brief historical sketch of the Webster institute, nos. 45 & 47 Charlotte Street, Norfolk, Va. . . . Centennial year. Norfolk, Va., Landmark book & job, 1876.

8 p. 8°.   **V**

4469. WESLEYAN FEMALE INSTITUTE, Staunton, Va. Catalogue . . . [Staunton? Va., 18-?-?]

8°. (M. E., So.; 1849?)
V: 1872/73, 74/75, 79/80, 82/83-83/84, 90/91, 94/95-95/96.

4470. WEST CENTRAL ACADEMY, Mt. Clinton, Va. Catalogue . . . [n. p., 1892?-?]

8°. (Prep.; co-ed.; non-sect.; 1891)   **V**: 1894/95-96/97.

4471. WEST POINT ACADEMY, West Point, Va. Catalogue . . . West Point, Va., 1893-19—

8°. (Prep. & milit.: boys; non-sect.; 1893)   **V**: 1893/94-94/95.

4472. WEST POINT FEMALE SEMINARY, West Point, Va. Annual catalogue . . . [n. p., 18-?-19—

8°. (Prep.; non-sect.; date?)   **V**: 1901/02.

4473. WESTMINSTER SCHOOL, Richmond, Va. Announcement . . . Richmond, 1900?—

illus., plates. 12°. (Women; Presbyt.; 1900)   **V**: 1906/07-09/10.

4474. WILLIAMSBURG FEMALE INSTITUTE, Williamsburg, Va. Catalogue . . . [Williamsburg, Va., 19—

8°. (Prep.; Presbyt.; 190-?)   **V**: 1909/10-10/11.

4475. [3907] THE WOMAN'S COLLEGE, Richmond, Va. . . . Catalogue. Richmond, Va. [18-?-19—

4476. WOODBERRY FOREST SCHOOL, Orange, Va. Catalogue . . .
[Charlottesville? Va., 1890?-19—
8°. (Prep.; boys; non-sect.; 1889)
H: 1905/06; V: 1902/03-07/08, 09/10.

4477. WOODLAWN ACADEMY, Woodlawn, Va. Catalogue . . .
[n. p., 1887?-?]
8°. (Prep.; co-ed.; non-sect.; 1886) V: 1892/93.

4478. WOODLAWN SEMINARY, Gordonsville, Va. Catalogue . . .
[n. p., 1879?-19—
8°. (Prep.; girls; non-sect.; 1878) V: 1902/03-03/04, 05/06.

4479. WYTHEVILLE SEMINARY, Wytheville, Va. Catalogue . . .
[Wytheville? Va., 1887?-19—
8°. (Prep.; girls; non-sect.; 1886) V: 1889/90.

4480. YELVERTON HOME SCHOOL FOR GIRLS, The Plains, Va. Catalogue . . . [n. p., 18-?-?]
8°. (Prep.; non-sect.; 187-?) V: 1875/76.

Secondary Works

4481. BALDWIN, C. C. Moral maxims for schools and families
. . . 3d ed. This book is used in the Public free schools of
Virginia . . . Petersburg, D'Arcy, Paul, 1876.
16 p. 12°. McC

4482. BROWN, SARA A. School attendance of children fourteen and
fifteen years of age in Virginia in 1925. New York, National
child labor committee [1926]
8 p. tables. 8°. (National child labor committee. *Publication,* 330)
USL, V

4483. CARTER, FRANKLIN. General Armstrong's life and work.
Founder's day address, 1902 . . . [Hampton, Va., Press of
the Hampton normal and agricultural institute, 1913]
15, [1] p. illus. (incl. ports.) 8°. LC, NYP, USE, V, VU

4484. COMBS, MORGAN L. Efficiency in relation to size of high
schools in Virginia. Harvard University, 1927.
195 p. typew. 4°. (Thesis, Harvard university. Graduate school of
education) H

4485. DEARBORN, WALTER F., *et al.* Psychological and educational tests in the public schools of Winchester, Virginia. A report to the city School board and the Handley board of trustees of an investigation conducted by Dr. W. F. Dearborn . . . and Dr. Alexander Inglis . . . [Charlottesville, The University, 1922]

54 p. incl. tables. 8°. (*University of Virginia record.* Extension series, VI, 6; Jan., 1922)   **USE, V, VU**

4486. FURST, CLYDE B., *et al.* Retiring allowances for officers and teachers in Virginia public schools. New York, Carnegie foundation, 1926.

vi, 70 p.   (Carnegie foundation for the advancement of teaching, *Bulletin,* 17)   **BP**

4487. HOKE, KREMER J. Placement of children in the elementary grades . . . Washington, Govt., 1916.

93 p., 1 l. diagrs. 8°.   **BP, LC, USE, V**
Thesis (Ph.D.)—Columbia university, 1916.
Pub. also as U. S. Bur. of education, *Bulletin,* 3, under title: "Placement of children in the elementary grades; a study of the schools of Richmond, Va."
A study of the progress of both white and Negro children, their acceleration and retardation by grades and ages, etc.

4488. KINSOLVING, ARTHUR B. The story of a southern school; the Episcopal high school of Virginia . . . Baltimore, Norman, Remington, 1922.

4 p. l., 13-330, [5] p. front., plates, ports. 8°.   **LC, USE, V, VU**
An interesting account, based on mss. and documents of the school and upon personal reminiscences of alumni, teachers, and others.

4489. A LIFE well lived; in memory of Robert Curtis Ogden. [Hampton, Va., Hampton institute press, 1914]

26 p. front. (port.) 8°.   **H, LC, USE**
Addresses by F. G. Peabody, S. C. Mitchell, and W. H. Taft on Ogden's services to education in the South during his membership on the Board of trustees of Hampton institute, 1874-1913.

4490. [1385] MAGRUDER, FRANK A. . . . Recent administration in Virginia . . . Baltimore, Johns Hopkins, 1912.

4491. MERRIMAN, DANIEL. Armstrong, the Christian soldier . . . Founder's day address, 1906. [Hampton, Va.] 1906.

11 p. 4°.   **LC**

4492. [NEWLIN, MARGARET] Memoir of Mary Anna Longstreth, by an old pupil. With a sketch of her work for Hampton. By Helen W. Ludlow. Philadelphia, Lippincott, 1886.

> 224 p. front. 12°.   **LC, V**
> Preface signed: Margaret Newlin.
> Contains an account of the aid given to Hampton institute by Mary A. Longstreth, a Quaker, through her school in Philadelphia, p. 181-216.

4493. NORWOOD HIGH SCHOOL, Norwood, Va. A historical sketch of Norwood high school and college, Nelson County, Va. . . . Richmond, Whittet & Shepperson, 1881.

> 25, [7] p. 8°. Advertisements in back.   **LC, V**
> Sketches of faculty members (with excerpts from testimonials) and list of students.

4494. OGDEN, ROBERT C. . . . Samuel Chapman Armstrong; a sketch . . . New York, Chicago [etc.] Fleming H. Revell [ca. 1894]

> 40 p. 12°.   **BP, H, LC, NYP, V**
> "Memoranda" written by Gen. Armstrong, at end of sketch.

4495. [PAYNE, BRUCE R.] Five years of high school progress in Virginia. [Charlottesville? Va., 1911]

> 55 p. tables. 8°.   **H, NYP, USE, V, VU**
> Tables for 5 years, 1905/06-09/10, taken from reports of local school officials, showing number of teachers, enrollment, appropriations, etc.
> Ed. of 1910.   **NYP**

4496. ———. Virginia high schools. A table showing number of pupils taking each subject. Session 1909-10. [n. p., 1910?]

> 14 p. tables. 4°.   **VU**

4497. PEABODY, Francis G. Education for life; the story of Hampton institute, told in connection with the fiftieth anniversary of the foundation of the school . . . Garden City, New York, Doubleday, Page, 1918.

> xxiv, 393, [1] p. front., illus. (maps, facsims.) plates, ports., diagrs. 8°.
>   **BP, H, LC, USE, V, VU, WM**
> Authoritative, well written history of Hampton institute, based on mss. and printed records of the school, with emphasis upon its great principals, Armstrong and Frissell.

4498. ———. Founder's day at Hampton; an address in memory of

Samuel Chapman Armstrong . . . Jan. 30, 1898. Boston and New York, Houghton, Mifflin, 1898.

2 p. l., 3-31, [1] p. front. (port.) 12°.   **BP, H, LC, NYP**
Eulogy of Armstrong and the Hampton creed.

4499. RICHMOND, VA. PUBLIC SCHOOLS. Richmond, Virginia, 1914; a brief sketch of its history, industrial life, government, and educational facilities, by the sixth and seventh year pupils of the public schools. [Richmond, 1914]

94 p. front., illus. 8°.   **V**
"Presented to the Dept. of superintendence of the National educational association, by the pupils . . ."

4500. ST. PAUL NORMAL AND INDUSTRIAL SCHOOL, Lawrenceville, Va. . . . Thirty-eight years, 1887 to 1925 . . . The St. Paul normal and industrial school, Lawrenceville, Va. [Norfolk, Guide, 1925]

[7] p. illus. 8°.   **V**

4501. SMITHEY, W. R., ed. Secondary education in Virginia . . . [no. 1]- University, Va., University of Virginia Extension division, 1927—

8°. (*University of Virginia record.* Extension series, XI, 10; XII, 4; XIII, 3, 6, 8, 11; XIV, 5, 7; Apr., 1927-Jan., 30—in progress)

4502. TALBOT, MRS. EDITH (A.) Samuel Chapman Armstrong; a biographical study, by Edith Armstrong Talbot. New York, Doubleday, Page, 1904.

vi p., 3 l., 3-301 p. front., plates, ports. 8°.   **BP, H, LC, NYP, V**
An interesting, straightforward account, by Armstrong's daughter, without any attempt to be laudatory; contains many quotations from his speeches and writings.

4503. TOMLINSON, EVERETT T., *et al.* A leader of freemen; the life story of Samuel Chapman Armstrong, brevet brigadier-general, U. S. A., by Everett T. and Paul G. Tomlinson. Army and navy ed. Philadelphia, American Sunday-school union [*ca.* 1917]

86 p. front., ports. 16°.   **LC**
Based in large part upon Mrs. Talbot's biography of Armstrong [4502] and upon material obtained at Hampton.

4504. WARREN, HENRY P. General Samuel Chapman Armstrong; founder's day address, 1913 . . . [Hampton, Va., Hampton institute press, 1913]

13 p. 8°. (Reprint from *Southern workman*)   **LC, NYP**

Periodicals

4505. The BEACON . . . published by the senior class of the Newport News high school, 1927— Newport News, Va., 1927—
illus. (incl. ports.) plates. 4°. annual.   **LC:** 1927.

4506. BELLEVUE high school nondescript. Vol. 1- [n. p., 1895?-19—
8°. monthly.   **V:** V, 5 (May-June, 1899).

4507. The CHARLES Citian. Vol. 1- ; 1926— Charles City, Va., Pub. annually by the senior class of Charles City high school. [Richmond, William Byrd, 1926—
illus. (incl. ports.) 4°.   **V:** I (1926).

4508. The CRITIC. Vol. 1- [1901?—] Pub. on the fifteenth of each month by the students of the Lynchburg high school. Lynchburg, Va. [1901?—
4°. monthly.   **V:** VI, 9 (Jan., 1907).

4509. HIGH school messenger. Manchester, Va. Vol. 1, no. 1- ; Oct., 1908— Manchester, Va., 1908—
8°. quarterly.
V: I, 1; II, 5-6; (Oct., 1908; Feb., Apr., 10).

4510. The HIGH school student [pub. by the Newport News high school] Vol. 1- ; 1903/04— Newport News, Va. [1903—
illus. 8°. monthly during school year.   **V:** IV, 6 (Apr., 1907).

4511. JOHN MARSHALL record. Vol. 1- ; 1909/10— Richmond, Va. [1909—
8°. monthly during school year.   **V:** VI, 4 (Jan.-Feb., 1915).

4512. The MARSHALLITE. Pub. by the students of John Marshall high school, Richmond, Va. Richmond, Va. [1911?—
4°. annual.   **V:** 1912, 17, 19, 21-22, 24, 28.

4513. MAURY news. Pub. by the Maury high school, Norfolk, Va. Vol. 1- Norfolk, Va. [1921?—
f°. weekly.   **H:** VII, 7; IX, 2; (Nov. 23, 1927, Oct. 11, 1928).

4514. The MONTHY chronicle. Vol. 1- [1887/88-19—] Pub.

by the literary societies of the Episcopal high school, Alexandria,
Va. [Alexandria, Va., 1887?—

8°. monthly during school year.
V: XXVIII, 1-3, 6-9; XXIX, 1-9; XXX, 1-9; XXXI, 1-7; XXXII,
1-8; XXXIII, 2-3; (1916-21).

4515. Mosaics . . . [Pub. by the Virginia female institute,
Staunton, Va.] Roanoke [etc. 18-?-19—

illus., plates, ports. 4°. annual.   V: 1900, 02-03.

4516. The Signet. Pub. by the students of Richmond academy,
Richmond, Va. Vol. 1-   Richmond, 1908—

illus., plates, ports. 4°. annual.   V: 1908, 11, 13.

4517. The Southern missioner. Pub. monthly by the St. Paul normal and industrial school. Vol. 1- [1891?-19—] Lawrenceville, Va., The School [1891?-19—

8°.   V: XXXV, 6, 10, 12; XXXVI, 4, 6; (1925-26).

4518. [2358] The Southern workman. [Vol. 1-   ; 1873?-19—]
Hampton, Va. [1873?-19—

4519. [2069] The Virginia guide, published at the Virginia school
for the deaf and blind. Vol. 1-   Staunton, Va. [18-?-19—

4520. Virginia high school bulletin . . . Vol. 1-   University,
Va., The University of Virginia, 1915—

8°. quarterly.
Charles G. Maphis, ed.
H: II, 1; III, 2; IV, 1; (1916-18). V: I, 1-4; II, 2-4; III, 1-3. VU:
I, 1-4; II, 2-4; III, 1-2; IV, 1; V, 1.

4521. The Warwick, Morrison, Va. Pub. by the students of Morrison high school. [n. p., 19—

illus. 4°. annual.   WM: 1926.
Advertisements in back.

Directory

4522. Virginia teachers' directory [1900] Compiled and published
by J. S. Gruver. Reliance, Va., Cutting & Wallihan [1900]

68 p. 12°.   LC, USE
Contains list of public school teachers, by counties and cities.

5. PROFESSIONAL AND LEARNED SOCIETIES

Government Publication and Documents

4523. CO-OPERATIVE EDUCATION ASSOCIATION OF VIRGINIA. Community league bulletin, giving plan of organization, constitution and by-laws, suggestions for the work of each committee by the Co-operative education association of Virginia . . . Issued jointly by state departments of health, education, highways, agriculture, dairy and food, charities and corrections, Virginia polytechnic institute. Richmond, Bottom, 1916.

48 p. illus. 8°.   **USE, USL**
Ed. of 1918.   **USE**

4524. GUY, GEORGE W. . . . The Coöperative education association of Virginia . . . Washington, Govt., 1924.

iv, 23, [1] p. illus. 8°. ([U. S.] Bur. of education. *Bulletin,* 1923, no. 53)   **BP, H, LC, USE, USL, V, VU**
At head of title: Dept. of the interior . . .
Organization and work of the Association, with text of its constitution.

Other Source Material

4525. APPALACHIAN SCHOOL IMPROVEMENT FOUNDATION. Semiannual report . . . [Emory, Va., 19—

nar. 16°.   **NYP:** 1912.

4526. ASSOCIATION FOR THE PRESERVATION OF VIRGINIA ANTIQUITIES. Charter, constitution and by-laws of the Association for the preservation of Virginia antiquities, Richmond, Va. . . . Richmond, Jones, 1901.

16 p. 8°.   **H, LC, NYP, V ,VU**

4527. ———. Notes on a journey on the James, together with a guide to old Jamestown. Comp. for A. P. V. A. by William G. Stanard . . . [Richmond, 1913]

24 p. fold. map. 14 x 18 cm.   **LC, NYP, V**
Contains some mention of the work of the Association at Jamestown.

4528. ———. . . . Officers and board for 1919. Richmond, Va., Whittet & Shepperson, 1919.

22, [2] p. 12°.   **VU**

4529. ASSOCIATION FOR THE PRESERVATION OF VIRGINIA ANTIQUITIES. Programme. Celebration of the ter-centennial (1607-1907) at Jamestown Island, Virginia . . . May 13, 1907. [n. p., 1907]

[2] p. 8°.   LC

4530. ———. The report of the president of the Association for the preservation of Virginia antiquities to the annual meeting . . . also the report of the Jamestown committee. Richmond, 1915.

16°.   LC, NYP, V, VU

4531. ———. PRINCE EDWARD CHAPTER. LAND MARK COMMITTEE. Prince Edward County, Virginia, historical places worthy of appropriate marking. [Farmville? 1927]

16 p. illus. (incl. port.) 12°.   LC

4532. ———. ———. ———. Report . . . [Farmville, Va., 19—

illus., port. 12°.   V: 1926-27.
Report for 1926 reprinted from *Farmville herald,* Mar. 4, 1927.

4533. ASSOCIATION OF DIVISION SCHOOL SUPERINTENDENTS OF VIRGINIA. . . . Proceedings of superintendents' conference . . . [Richmond? 19—

8°.   USE: 1916-17.

4534. ASSOCIATION OF ENGINEERS OF VIRGINIA. . . . Constitution and rules, list of members, Jan. 1st, 1893 . . . Roanoke, Va., Stone [1893]

8 p. 8°.   LC

4535. ———. Proceedings . . . 1st- ; 1891-19— Roanoke, Va. [etc.] 1891-19—

8°.   NYP, V: 1891.

4536. ———. Transactions . . . 1891/93— Roanoke, Va., Stone [1891?—

8°.   NYP, USAg, V: 1891/93.

4537. BLACK, W. M. The value of a library commission. [n. p., 1910]

[4] p. 8°. (Reprint from *Public libraries,* Feb., 1910)   V, VU
"Presidential address before the Virginia library association, Nov. 25, 1910."

4538. BRYAN, BELLE S. [Circular letter to the Association for the preservation of Virginia antiquities.] [n. p., 1905]

2 l. 8°. LC

4539. CENTRAL COMMITTEE OF THE INSTITUTIONS OF HIGHER EDUCATION IN VIRGINIA. Bulletin, no. 1- ; 1925— Richmond, Va. [1925—

8°. V: 1-[3]

4540. CHARITABLE ASSOCIATION OF LEARNING, NO. 1, Sussex County, Va. Constitution . . . Ratified and adopted Feb. 28, 1880. Petersburg, Ege, 1880.

8 p. 8°. V

4541. CONFEDERATE MEMORIAL LITERARY SOCIETY, Richmond, Va. Catalogue of the Confederate museum, of the Confederate memorial literary society . . . Richmond, Va. Richmond, Jones, 1898.

218 p. 8°. NYP, VU
Ed. of 1905: 300 p. front. LC, NYP, V, VU
Material arranged by state. Contains also the constitution and by-laws of the Society.

4542. CONFERENCE OF VIRGINIA HIGH SCHOOL PRINCIPALS. . . . Proceedings of . . . annual conference. Charlottesville [1919?—

8°. (*University of Virginia record.* Extension series . . .)
LC, VU: 6th (1924).

4543. CO-OPERATIVE EDUCATION ASSOCIATION OF VIRGINIA. Annual report . . . [Richmond? 1906?—

illus. 8°. Report year ends Dec. 31.
Full title: Annual report of the Co-operative education association of Virginia . . . with selected reports of school and civic leagues and roll of contributing and active members of the association.
H: 1912; LC: 1910/11, 12, 25; NYP: 1921, 22/23, 27; USAg: 1912, 15/16, 22, 27; USE: 1910/11-12, 14/15-17/18, 19/20-27; V: 1910/11, 12, 14-27; VU: 1917/18, 21/22-23/24; WM: 1922-25, 27.

4544. ———. Bulletin . . . [Richmond? 19—

8°. USE: 1913; V: 1912-18, 27.

4545. ———. Community league bulletin; how to organize a league. Constitution and by-laws. Suggestions to committee. The community league; a citizens' organization through which all the citizens of a community can co-operate . . . Dr. J. P. McConnell, president. J. H. Montgomery, director. Richmond [1926?]

16 p. 8°.   USE

4546. CO-OPERATIVE EDUCATION ASSOCIATION OF VIRGINIA. High and elementary school co-operative league bulletin for Virginia public schools . . . Richmond, Richmond press, 1917.

19 p. 8°.   USE

4547. ———. . . . Junior community league bulletin . . . [Richmond? 1922]

29 p. illus. 8°.   USE

4548. ———. Junior community league handbook . . . [Richmond, Va., 1927]

72 p. illus. (incl. ports., facsims., charts) 8°.   USAg, V
Suggestions for organization and activities of Junior community leagues in local schools; with "program helps" and references for preparing programs.

4549. ———. . . . Junior community league pageant. Prepared and presented by Henrico County schools, Mr. A. C. Cooper, supt. Under auspices of Co-operative education association of Virginia. At the Virginia educational conference, Richmond . . . Charlottesville, University of Virginia [1923]

18 p. illus. 8°. (*University of Virginia record.* Extension series, VII, 8; Apr., 1923)   USE, V, VU

4550. ———. Proceedings of . . . annual session . . . 1st- ; 1904— [Charlottesville, 1904—

8°.   USE, V: 2d (1905).

4551. [———] Reports from Citizens' leagues. [Richmond? 19—
8°.   V: 1908-09, 11-12.

4552. ———. School clubs for Virginia boys and girls; handbook of information. Pub. by the Dept. of public instruction. [Richmond? n. d.]

[22] p. 12°.   V

4553. ———. A successful state-wide project in community co-operation over a period of nearly a quarter of a century, 1904-26, under the Co-operative education association of Virginia, State council of rural agencies . . . [Richmond, 1926?]

12 p. 8°.   USE, V

4554. [CO-ORDINATE COLLEGE LEAGUE. CENTRAL COMMITTEE] The co-ordinate college. Its relation to public education in Virginia. Richmond, Va., Whittet & Shepperson, 1917.

24 p. 8°. **VU**

4555. EDUCATIONAL ASSOCIATION OF VIRGINIA. Minutes . . . 1st- ; 1866— Richmond, 1866—

8°. **USE:** 1st-4th (1866-70); **V:** 1866-73; **VU:** 1866, 73.

4556. ———. Reports and other papers delivered before the Educational association of Virginia, at its anniversary in Lynchburg, July, 1867. Pub. by order of the Association. [n. p., n. d.]

67 p. 8°. **H, VU**

4557. EGGLESTON, J. D. Prince Edward County, Virginia. Historical places worthy of appropriate marking. Preliminary report of J. D. Eggleston, chairman of the Land mark committee of Prince Edward chapter, Association for the preservation of Virginia antiquities. [n. p., 1927?]

8 l. illus. 8°. (Reprint from *Farmville herald,* March 4, 1927) **VU**

4558. FAUQUIER HISTORICAL SOCIETY, Warrenton, Va. Bulletin . . . [no. 1] Aug., 1921— Richmond, Va., 1921—

front., plates, ports., maps, fold. plan. 8°.
NYP, V: 1-4 (1921-24); **WM:** 1-3.

4559. HALL, JOHN L. Introductory address, delivered at the Jamestown celebration, held May 13, 1895. [n. p., 1895?]

8 p. 8°. **V**

Celebration under the auspices of the College of William and Mary and the Association for the preservation of Virginia antiquities.

4560. HAMPTON NEGRO CONFERENCE. Annual report . . . 1st- ; 1897-19— Hampton, Va., Hampton institute press [1898-19—

illus. 8°. (In *Hampton bulletin,* 1905?— **[4240]**)
BP: 1898-1903, 05-06, 08-12; **H:** 1897-1912; **NYP:** 1897-1913; **USAg:** 9-16th (1905-12); **USC:** 1898-99, 1901-08; **USE:** 1909, 12; **V:** 1903, 09-10, 12; **VU:** 1898-99, 1901-12.

4561. HOAR, GEORGE F. The Virginia state bar association. Annual address by Hon. George F. Hoar, of Massachusetts. "Relation of the American bar to the state." Delivered at the tenth annual meeting held at hotel Chamberlin, Fort Monroe, Virginia, July 5th, 6th and 7th, 1898. Richmond, Williams, 1898.

30 p. port. 8°. **LC, NYP**

4562. JAMESTOWN DENTAL CONVENTION, 1907. Revised program for the Jamestown dental convention to be held in Convention hall, Exposition grounds, Norfolk, Va. . . . Sept. 10, 11, 12, 1907. [Norfolk? Va., 1907]

37, [1] p., 1 l. 16°.   LC

4563. JEFFERSON CLUB, Richmond, Va. Catalogue of the Jefferson club library . . . Librarian: Miss May Lee Myers. Richmond, Virginia, Feb., 1911. Richmond, Ezekiel, 1911.

125 p. 8°.   LC, V

4564. [2041] JOHNSTON, GEORGE B. Value to the public of state medical societies . . . [Richmond, Va., 1897]

4565. KENT, CHARLES W. The preservation of the past. An address delivered before the Association for the preservation of Virginia antiquities . . . Mar. 14, 1901 . . . Richmond, Jones, 1901.

16 p. 8°.   V, VU

4566. McGUIRE, HUNTER. Address . . . Delivered on 23d day of June, 1897, at the Virginia military institute, in the presence of a vast audience, upon the occasion of the inauguration of the Stonewall Jackson memorial building. Pub. by the Virginia military institute. Lynchburg, Va., Bell, 1897.

22 p. 8°.   LC, NYP, V

4567. [MAPHIS, CHARLES G.] . . . The Jewish Chautauqua society and the University of Virginia. Charlottesville, Va., The University [1917]

p. [123]-148. 8°. *University of Virginia record.* Extension series, II, 6-7; Feb-Mar., 1917)   H, USE, V, VU
How the Society is promoting education in Virginia.

4568. MEDICAL SOCIETY OF VIRGINIA. The organization and proceedings of the first session of the Medical society of Virginia, held in Richmond, Nov. 2d and 3d, 1870, to which is appended a copy of the constitution and by-laws, and an alphabetical register of fellows. Lynchburg, Virginian, 1870.

116 p. 8°.   V

4569. ⸺. Transactions of the . . . annual session . . . 1st- ; 1870-19— Lynchburg [etc.] 1870-19—

illus. 8°.

BP: 1875-82; **LC**: 2-3d, 8-9th, 15th, 19th, 22d, 25-26th (1871-72, 77-78, 84, 88, 91, 94-95); **NYP**: 1892, 94; **V**: 1870-1915; **VU**: 1900-12, 14; **WM**: 1900-15.

4570. NEGRO ORGANIZATION SOCIETY. Report of the work of the School improvement leagues of Virginia . . . [Norfolk, 1917—

tables. 8°. Report year ends June 30. H: 1916/17.

4571. NEGRO TEACHERS' ASSOCIATION AND SCHOOL IMPROVEMENT LEAGUE OF VIRGINIA. Annual report . . . [n. p., 19—

8°. USE: 1913.

4572. NEWPORT NEWS PUBLIC LIBRARY ASSOCIATION. Annual report of the trustees . . . [Newport News? 19—

8°. V: 1924/25.

4573. NORFOLK LIBRARY ASSOCIATION. Catalogue of the library of the Norfolk library association, with an historical sketch, containing the charter, constitution, by-laws and regulations of the institution. Norfolk, Va., Landmark, 1875.

87, [1] p. 8°. LC, V, VU

4574. PROTESTANT EPISCOPAL EDUCATION SOCIETY IN VIRGINIA. . . . The act of incorporation, by-laws, and rules and regulations. Alexandria, Bell's, 1905.

15 p. 12°. V

4575. [PUBLIC SCHOOL PROTECTIVE LEAGUE OF VIRGINIA] Virginia schools, their progress and their needs. Richmond, Va., Ancient and accepted Scottish rite of freemasonry, 1923.

23 p. 8°. V

Treats such subjects as high school progress, illiteracy, compulsory education, etc.

4576. RICHMOND BAR ASSOCIATION. Catalog of books. [Richmond, Va.] 1901.

8 p. 8°. V

4577. ⸺. [Report] Richmond, Waddey [18-?-19—

8°. V: 1894, 99, 1909, 20.

4578. RICHMOND EDUCATION ASSOCIATION, Richmond, Va. Annual
report . . . 1st- ; 1900/01— Richmond, Va., 1901—

8°. **H**: 1902/03, 06/07-07/08, 09/10-11/12, 13/14-15/16; **LC**: 1907/08,
14/15-15/16; **USE**: 1900/01-10/11, 13/14; **V**: 1901/02-16/17.

4579. RICHMOND KINDERGARTEN ASSOCIATION. Annual report
. . . 1st- ; 1910— Richmond, 1910—

8°.   **V**: 2d (1911).

4580. RYLAND, ROBERT. The Virginia Baptist education society.
The society—the seminary—the college. An address . . . Introduction by Charles H. Ryland . . . Library, Richmond
college. [Richmond? Va.] 1891.

24 p. 8°.   **V**

4581. SEABOARD MEDICAL ASSOCIATION OF VIRGINIA AND NORTH
CAROLINA. Transactions . . . [1st- ; 1896-19— n. p.,
1896?-19—

8°.   **V**: 7th, 9-13th (1902, 04-07).

4582. SHOCKOE HILL LITERARY SOCIETY, Richmond, Va. Constitution and by-laws of the Shockoe Hill literary society . . . Organized Sept. 6th, 1866. Adopted Feb. 1st, 1869 . . . Richmond, Gary, Clemmitt & Jones, 1869.

16 p. 16°.   **V**

4583. SOUTHERN WOMAN'S EDUCATIONAL ALLIANCE, Richmond, Va.
Report . . . 1st- [1914/15?—] Richmond [1915?—

8°. biennial, 1921—
Organized in 1914 as the Virginia bureau of vocations for women;
name changed in 1921.
V: 1918/19, 21, 21/23, 24/25.

4584. [2231] STANARD, MARY N. Jamestown and the Association
for the preservation of Virginia antiquities . . . [Richmond,
1903?]

4585. STEARNES, R. C. . . . The year's progress—1915. Address delivered Nov. 24, before the Virginia educational conference, by R. C. Stearnes, state superintendent of public instruction.
[Richmond, 1916]

29 p. 8°.   **USE**

4586. Tri-state medical association of the Carolinas and Virginia. Transactions of the . . . annual session . . . [n. p., 189-?-19—

8°.   V: 1899-1914; **WM**: 1900, 02, 04-06, 08-17.

4587. Virginia academy of science. Announcement of the . . . annual meeting of the Virginia academy of science, together with the Virginia section of the American chemical society . . . 1st- [1923?— Richmond, etc., 1923?—

8°. Advertisements in back.

LC: 3d-4th (1925-26); **V**: 1926-27; **VU**: 1926.

4588. ————. . . . Organization and proceedings. 1923/24— Richmond, Va. [1924—

8°. **BP**: 1923/24; **H**: 1923/24-27/28; **LC, NYP, USG, V**: 1923/24-26/27; **VU**: 1923/24-27/28; **WM**: 1923/24-24/25, 26/27.

4589. ————. Program of the . . . annual meeting . . . [n. p., 1923?—

8°.   **H**: 6th (1928); **LC**: 6-7th (1928-29).

4590. Virginia association of colleges and schools for girls. Minutes of the . . . annual meeting . . . [1st- ; 1907?— n. p., 1907?—

8°.   **USE**: 11th (1917).

4591. Virginia chemists' club. Proceedings . . . Vol. 1- ; 1908— Richmond, Richmond press, 1908—

diagrs. 8°.   **H**: II (1909/10); **V**: I-II (1908-09/10)

4592. Virginia conference of county and city superintendents of public free schools. Proceedings . . . [1st]- ; 1883-19— Richmond [1883-19—

8°. Title varies.

H: 2-3d, 15th (1884-85, 97); **USE**: 1883-85, 97.

4593. Virginia education association. Annual convention . . . [1st- ; 1907?— Richmond, 1907?—

12°.   **V**: 21st (1927).

4594. ————. Digest of the proceedings of the conference of District J, Virginia education association, held at the University of

Virginia, Apr. 9 & 10, 1926. University, Va., University of Virginia, 1927.

[361]-406 p. 8°. (*University of Virginia record.* Extension series, XI, 7; Jan., 1927) **USE, V, VU**

4595. VIRGINIA EDUCATIONAL CONFERENCE. Some pressing educational needs of Virginia. Measures advocated by the Committee of 25 appointed by the Virginia educational conference . . . Richmond, Saunders, 1916.

[8] p. 8°. **VU**

4596. VIRGINIA HIGH SCHOOL PRINCIPALS. . . . Proceedings of . . . annual conference . . . [1st- ; 1919?— Charlottesville, 1919?—

8°. (*University of Virginia record.* Extension series . . .) **USE, V, VU**: 1925.

4597. VIRGINIA HISTORICAL SOCIETY, Richmond, Va. [Circular letter] Richmond, 1881.

2 p. 29 x 22½ cm. Dated July 20. **BP, LC**
Announcement of new headquarters and programme of the Society.

4598. ———. [Circulars. 1870-78. n. p., 1870-78]

var. pag. 8°. **V**

4599. ———. Collections of the Virginia historical society, vol. 1; new series, vol. 1-11. [Richmond, The Society, 1833-92]

12 v. in 11. plates, 3 front. (ports.) fold. map, fold. plan, facsim. 8°. No more pub.
The place of the Collections is supplied by the *Virginia magazine of history and biography,* 1893-19— **[4654]**

4600. ———. A list of portraits, engravings, etc., in the library of the Virginia historical society. Richmond, The Society, 1894.

7 p. 8°. **BP, NYP, V**

4601. ———. Monthly meeting, Nov. 30, 1877. [Richmond, 1877]

clipping from Richmond *Dispatch,* Dec. 8, 1877. **BP**

4602. ———. Organization of the Virginia historical society; officers and members; with a list of its publications. Richmond, Va., Virginia historical society, 1881.

22 p., 1 l. 8°. **BP, H, LC, NYP, V, VU**
Ed. of 1894. **NYP, V**

4603. ———. Presentation of an oil painting of Captain William Gordon McCabe to Virginia historical society by the Alumni of McCabe's University school. [Richmond, 1926]

13 p. port. 8°.   **V**

4604. ———. Proceedings at . . . annual meeting . . . Richmond [1882?-1901?]

8°. Proceedings for 1891 in its *Collections,* XI [**4599**]; for 1893-1901 in *Virginia magazine of history and biography,* I-IX [**4654**]
BP: 1882; H: 1891, 93-1901; LC: 1882, 91, 93-1901; NYP, V, VU, WM: 1882, 93-1901.

4605. ———. Publications of the . . . Society. [Richmond, 1926]

10 p. 8°.   **H, NYP, V**

4606. ———. Souvenir guide-book to the building of the Society, the war residence of Gen. Robert E. Lee, Richmond, Virginia. [Richmond, 1896?]

[6] p. 8°.   **H**

4607. ———. The Virginia historical society to Virginians and friends of Virginia. [Richmond, 1878]

1 l. 4°.   **LC**
An appeal for subscriptions for a building.

4608. VIRGINIA MUSIC TEACHERS STATE ASSOCIATION. Report of the annual conference . . . 1st- ; 1920— Richmond [1920?—

illus. 8°. Advertisements in back.   **WM:** 6th (1925).

4609. VIRGINIA PHARMACEUTICAL ASSOCIATION. Proceedings . . . 1st- ; 1882-19— Lynchburg [1882?-19—

illus. 8°. Advertisements in front and in back.
LC: 13-15th, 19th (1894-96, 1900); USAg: 1882-1901, 10; V: 1894, 1906-08, 10.

4610. VIRGINIA PRESS ASSOCIATION. Souvenir-historical program, sixth mid-winter meeting of the Virginia press association . . . Richmond, Virginia . . . Jan. 25-26, 1924. [Richmond, Federal press, 1924]

7 p. 8°.   **V**

4611. VIRGINIA STATE BAR ASSOCIATION. Charter, constitution and by-laws, code of ethics. 1919. [n. p., n. d.]

38 p. 12°.   **V**

4612. VIRGINIA STATE BAR ASSOCIATION. Delegates and alternates to the convention of the bar of Virginia . . . The Cavalier, Virginia Beach, Aug. 4, 1927. [n. p., 1927?]

[4] p. 8°.   V

4613. ———. . . . Prefatory statement. Proceedings of the convention held at Virginia Beach, July 5th and 6th, 1888. Constitution and by-laws of the association; names of officers and standing committees; roll of members, and proposed code of ethics. Richmond, Va., Waddey, 1888.

68 p., 1 l. 8°.   HL, LC, NYP, V

4614. ———. . . . Program . . . [of annual convention] [n. p., 19—

8°.   V: 1920.

4615. ———. Report of the 1st- annual meeting of the Virginia state bar association . . . 1889-19— Richmond, Va., Richmond press [etc., 1889?-19—

fronts., plates, ports. 8°.
Editors: E. C. Massie, 1897-1904; J. B. Minor, 1905-23; C. M. Chichester, 1924—
HL: 1889-1927; LC: 1st-30th, 32d-38th (1889-1918, 20-26); NYP: 1889-1910, 24-27; V: 1889-1916, 18-27; VU: 1889-1928; WM: 1889-1927.

4616. ———. Report of committee on amendment of practice . . . Aug. 5, 1908. Richmond, Richmond press [1908?]

13 p. 8°.   V

4617. Report of the committee on international arbitration presented to the ninth annual meeting . . . 1897. Richmond, 1897.

14 p. 8°.   NYP

4618. ———. Report of the Special committee on the organization of the bar, to be presented to the . . . association at its 38th annual meeting, Aug. 4, 1926. [n. p., 1926]

75 p. 8°.   V

4619. ———. Report of the Special committee on the Torrens system of land registration. Aug., 1903. [n. p., 1903?]

24 p. 8°.   V

4620. VIRGINIA STATE DENTAL ASSOCIATION. Preliminary program . . . annual meeting . . . [n. p., 1870?-19—

8°.   V: 59th (1928).

4621. ———. Program of the 1st- annual convention . . . . Hampton [etc., 1870?-19—

illus., ports. 8°.   **V:** 1909, 11-12, 17-18, 25, 27.

4622. VIRGINIA STATE DENTAL SOCIETY. Proceedings . . . [n. p., 19-?—

8°.   **V:** 1911 (reprint from *Dental summary,* Toledo, Ohio).

4623. VIRGINIA STATE TEACHERS' ASSOCIATION. Annual bulletin . . . 1st- ; 1901- Salem, Va., 1901—

8°.   **USE:** 2d-6th (1902, 05-08); **V:** 1908.

4624. ———. . . . Annual proceedings . . . Announcements, Virginia educational conference . . . Salem, Va., 19—

illus. 8°.
Proceedings for 1913-16 pub. as its *Quarterly,* I-III **[4658]**
USE: 1908-09, 11-16; **V:** 1909-16; **VU:** 1910/11; **WM:** 1910/11-12/13.

4625. ———. Constitution and by-laws of the Virginia state teachers' association. Approved at annual meeting held in Staunton, Virginia. July 30-31, 1901. Norfolk, Va., Donaldson, 1901.

16 p. 16°.   **USE**

4626. ———. What do you pay your teachers? Forty states in the Union pay their teachers higher salaries than does Virginia . . . Issued by the Virginia state teachers' association . . . and the Co-operative education association of Virginia . . . [n. p., 1914?]

15 p. 8°.   **USE**

Secondary Works

4627. CONFEDERATE MEMORIAL LITERARY SOCIETY. . . . In memoriam sempiternam. Confederate museum, Richmond, Va., 1896. [Richmond, Waddey, 1896]

98 p. incl. front., illus. 12°.   **BP, H, LC, V**
Edited by Mrs. A. W. Garber.
An account of the Confederate museum.

4628. HAMILTON, ALEXANDER. . . . Memorial of Hon. John Randolph Tucker, presented and read at the ninth annual meeting [of the Virginia state bar association] held at the Hot Springs of Virginia, Aug. 3, 4 and 5, 1897 . . . Richmond, Goode, 1897.

23 p. 8°.   **LC**

Sketch of J. R. Tucker, distinguished in education, law, and politics in Virginia and in Congress.

4629. The JOHN P. BRANCH historical papers of Randolph-Macon college. Published annually by the Department of history. Vol. [1]-5, no. 2; June, 1901-1918. Richmond, Va., 1901-18.

5 v. 8°.

No. 1 pub. by the Randolph-Macon historical society.

Running title: Randolph-Macon historical papers.

4630. [3480] RICHMOND COLLEGE historical papers . . . Vol. 1-2, no. 1 . . . Richmond, Va., 1915-17.

4631. ST. ELIZABETH'S HOSPITAL, Richmond, Va. Clinics and collected papers of St. Elizabeth's hospital, Richmond, Virginia . . . contributed by the staff . . . St. Louis, Mosby, 1922.

1 v. illus. 8°.   **LC, V**

Periodicals

4632. ANNALS of mathematics. Vol. 1-   Charlottesville, Va., 1884-99; Salem, Mass., 1899-19—

illus., tables. 4°. bi-monthly.

Pub. under auspices of University of Virginia, 1894-June, 1899 (v. 1-12).

BP, H: I-XII, XIII-XLI (1884/85-1928/29); **LC:** I-XXIV, XXXVIII-XL (1884/85-1910/11, 24/25-26/27); **NYP, USG:** I-XII, XIII-XLI.

4633. ASSOCIATION FOR THE PRESERVATION OF VIRGINIA ANTIQUITIES. Yeare booke of the Association for the preservation of Virginia antiquities . . . Richmond, 1896-19—

fronts., illus., plates, ports., fold. map, plan, facsim. 8°.

Imprint varies. None pub., 1912/13-18.

H: 1896, 98, 1900-01, 05-10, 11/12; **LC:** 1896, 98-1911/12, 19-26/27; **NYP:** 1905-11/12, 19-26/27; **V:** 1896, 98-1900, 04-11/12, 19-20, 23-26/27; **VU:** 1896/97, 98-99, 1900/01-04, 05-08, 19, 20/21, 23, 26/27; **WM:** 1896, 99, 1900-12, 20.

4634. ASSOCIATION OF ENGINEERS OF VIRGINIA. Journal . . . [New York, 1895-98]

8 v. illus., plates, ports., maps, plans, tables, diagrs. 8°. (In *Journal of the Association of engineering societies,* XIV-XXI, 1895-98) **H, LC, NYP**

4635. ATLANTIC educational journal. Vol. 1-6 [1898?-1903] Richmond, St. Louis [etc., 1898?]-1903.

> 6 v. illus. (incl. ports.) 4°. monthly.
> P. P. Claxton, ed.
> Merged into the *Teachers' institute,* New York.
> H: V, 10; VI, 5; (1902-03). **LC**: IV, 7-VI, 7 (1901-03).

4636. The COMMUNITY league news. Pub. by the Co-operative education association of Virginia. Vol. 1- [1918?—] Richmond [1918?—

> illus. 4°. monthly.
> **NYP**: III, 9; IV, 2-12; V; VI, 2-5, 11; VII-XII; (1920-28/29). **V**: VIII-XII (1925-29).

4637. CONFEDERATE MEMORIAL LITERARY SOCIETY. Year book . . . of the Confederate memorial literary society . . . 1st- ; 1907— Richmond, Va. [1908—

> 8°. None pub., 1917-19.
> Annual reports and membership included.
> Reports for 1905 and 1906 were published in the Richmond *Times-dispatch,* Dec., 1905, and Dec., 1906.
> Fourth issue [1910/11] incorrectly dated 1911/12.
> **BP**: 1st, 3d-4th (1907, 09-10); **H**: 1st-10th, (1907-16, 20); **LC, NYP**: 1907-16; **V**: 1907-16, 20-26; **VU**: 1907, 09-14/15, 16; **WM**: 1907, 09-15.

4638. The EDUCATIONAL journal of Virginia. [Vol. 1-22; 1869/70?-91?] Richmond, Jones [1869?-91?]

> 22 v. 8°. monthly. No more pub.?
> Superseded by *The Virginia school journal,* 1892— **[4657]**
> **H**: I, 5-6; IV, 9; VIII, 7, 9-12; IX, 1-2, 5-[12]; X, 1-3, 5-12; XI, 2-3, 5-7, 9-12; XII, 2-5, 7-11; XIII-XXII. **LC**: VII, XI-XXII (1875/76, 80-91). **V**: I-XIX, XXI-XXII.

4639. The LOWER Norfolk County Virginia antiquary. Ed. by Edward W. James. Vol. 1-5; 1895-1906. [n. p., 1895-1906]

> 5 v. 8°. **BP**: I-V. **H**: I-III; IV, 3. **V, VU, WM**: I-V.

4640. NATURALIST'S companion. Pub. in the interests of the Virginia collector's club. Vol. 1-[?] Wytheville, Va. [1882?-?]

> 4°. monthly.   **LC**: I, 3-4, 8, 10 (Mar.-Dec., 1882).

4641. The OLD Dominion journal of medicine and surgery, vol. 1- ; 1903— Richmond, Old Dominion pub. [1903—

> 8°. monthly.
> **V**: II, 3-6; III, 3, 5-6, 9-11; IV, 1, 4, 6, 10; V, 2, 8, 12; VII, 1, 3; IX; X, 3-6; XI, 1, 4, 6; XII, 3-4, 6; XIII-XVII; XXI, 6; XXII, 1-2; (1903-16). **WM**: IX-XV.

4642. The RICHMOND and Louisville medical journal.   Vol. 1-[16?]
Richmond, Va., 1866-82.

> 16 v. 8°. monthly?
> Called *Richmond medical journal,* I-V; became *Gaillard's medical journal,*
> New York, 1882.
> E. G. Gaillard, ed.
> **BP:** I-VI (1866-71); **NYP:** I-XIV, XVI (1866-79, 81).

4643. RICHMOND journal of practice; a monthly review of medicine
and surgery. Ed. by John F. Winn, M. D. Vol. 1-   Richmond,
Va., 1886-19—

> 8°. monthly. **V:** XVII, 9, 11-12; XVIII, 8, 12; XIX, 2-4; XXI, 7-8;
> (1903-07).

4644. The SOUTHERN clinic; a monthly journal of medicine, surgery and new remedies   . . .   Vol. 1-   [1878?-19—   ] Richmond, Va. [1878?-19—

> 8°. monthly.
> **V:** XXII; XXIV, 6, 10-12; XXV, 1-5, 7-12; XXVI-XXVII, 2;
> XXVIII-XXXIII; XXXIV, 2-7; XXXV, 2, 5, 7, 11-12; XXXVII, 10-12;
> XXXVIII-XLII, 9; (1899-1919).

4645. TYLER'S quarterly historical and genealogical magazine   . . .
Vol. 1-   ; July, 1919—   Richmond, Va., Whittet & Shepperson
[etc.] 1920—

> port. 8°. quarterly.   **H, LC, V, VU, WM:** I-XII (1919-30).
> L. G. Tyler, ed.

4646. The VIRGINIA educational journal. [n. p., 186-?]

> 3 p. 12°. (Virginia Dept. of public instruction. *Circular,* 83 **[3290]**)
> Signed: W. H. Ruffner, supt. of public instruction.

4647. The VIRGINIA historical magazine. Vol. 1, no. 1-3; July,
1891-Jan., 1892. Richmond, Va. [etc.] 1891-92.

> 54 p., 1 l. col. plate. 8°. quarterly. No more pub.   **LC, V**
> Jefferson Wallace, ed.

4648. VIRGINIA hospital bulletin. A quarterly journal of medicine
and surgery published by the staff of the Virginia hospital, Richmond. Vol. 1-[?] [Richmond, 1904-?]

> 8°. quarterly.   **V:** I-II, 1 (1904-05).

4649. The VIRGINIA journal of education. Vol. 1-   ; Oct., 1907—
Richmond, Va. [J. A. C. Chandler] 1907—

> illus. 8°. monthly during school year.
> Editors: J. A. C. Chandler, 1907-08/09; R. L. Blanton, 1909/10-12/13;

J. W. Everett, 1913/14-17/18; W. C. Blakey & A. B. Chandler, jr., 1918/19-20/21; W. T. Sanger, 1921/22-Sept., 22; C. J. Heatwole, Oct., 1922—

H: III; XVIII, 5; XX, 5; XXI, 6-7; (1909/10, 27-28). **LC**: I-III, VIII, X; (1907-10, 14/15, 16/17). **NYP**: XVII, 1-4, 6-XXI. **USE**: I, 1, 3-XXII. **V, VU**: I-XXII (1907-29). **WM**: I-XX.

4650. The VIRGINIA law journal, vol. 1-17; 1877-93. Richmond, 1877-93.

17 v. 8°. monthly, I-XIII; weekly, XIV-XVII. No more pub.
HL, V, VU: I-XVII.

4651. The VIRGINIA law register . . . Vol. 1-20; 1895/96-1915. New ser., vol. 1- ; 1915— Charlottesville, Va., Michie, 1896-19—

8°. **HL, LC, V, VU**: complete file to 1929/30; **WM**: I-XIII, XVII-XX; new ser., I-VIII.
Editors: Richard T. W. Duke, A. R. Michie, Frank D. Moore.

4652. VIRGINIA law review, vol. 1- ; Oct., 1913— University, Va., The Virginia law review association, 1914—

8°. monthly, Oct.-May.
Vol. 8 is "Cumulative index, 1913-1922."
HL, LC, V, VU: complete file to 1929/30; **WM**: III-V, XII.

4653. VIRGINIA libraries. Vol. 1- ; April, 1928— Richmond, Virginia State library, Extension division, 1928—

8°. quarterly. **NYP**: I; **V, VU**: I-II (1928-30).

4654. The VIRGINIA magazine of history and biography, published quarterly by the Virginia historical society . . . Vol. 1- ; July, 1893-19— Richmond, The Society [1893-19—

plates, ports., facsims. 8°.
Editors: P. A. Bruce, 1893-98; W. G. Stanard, 1899-19—

4655. VIRGINIA medical monthly. Vol. 1-22; 1874-96. New ser., vol. 1-21; 1896-1916/17. [Old ser., vol. 44- ; 1917/18— Richmond. Va., 1874-19—

8°. monthly, 1874-96, 1917— ; issued semi-monthly, as new ser., 1896-1917, under title: Virginia medical semi-monthly.
BP: I-X (1874-84). **H**: new ser., XVIII, 3 (1913). **USAg**: new ser., I-XI; XII, 2-21; XIII, 1-10, 12; XIV-XXI; (1896-1917). [Old ser.], XLIV, 20-XLV; XLVI, 1-2, 4-5, 9-12; XLVII, 1, 3-4, 6, 8, 10-12; XLVIII, 1-5, 7-10, 12; XLIX-L; LI, 1-4, 6, 8-12; LII; (1918/26). **USH**: IV, XII-XIII; (1877, 85/86-86/87). New ser., I-III (1896/97-98/99). [Old ser.], XLVII-LIV (1920/21-27/28). **USHy**: new ser., I (incompl.),

XI, XIV, XVII-XVIII, XX-XXI; (1896, 1906, 09, 12-13, 15/16-16/17).
V: I, 19-24; II, 7-8, 10, 24; VI, 18, 20, 22; VII, 1-3, 7-10, 12-13, 15-16,
19-20, 22-24; VIII, 1-8, 12-18; IX, 1-18; XI, XIII-XIV; XVII (no. 8
wanting); XVIII, 2-4, 6-10, 12, 14-16, 18-24; XIX; XX, 1, 23; XXI, 1-2,
4, 12, 24; XXII, 1-18; XLIV, 19-20; XLV-LV. **VU**: XIII, 8, 10. New
ser., X, 5-6; XII, 1-4, 11-12, 14-19; XIII, 2-11, 13-20, 22, 24; XIV; XV,
1-22, 24; XVI-XVII; XVIII, 1-16, 18-20, 22-24; XIX-XXI. [Old ser.],
XLIV-LV. **WM**: VI, IX-X (1879/80, 82/83-83/84). New ser., VII,
VIII.

4656. The VIRGINIA pharmacist; pub. by the Virginia pharmaceutical association and the Board of pharmacy. Vol. 1- ; Sept.,
1916—   Richmond, Va., 1916—

> illus., fold. plate. 8°. monthly.
> Editors: Albert Bolenbaugh *et al.,* 1916—
> **LC**: I-IX (1916-25). **V**: I, 1-8, 10-12; II-XIII. **WM**: VI-XI.

4657. The VIRGINIA school journal. Vol. 1-[?]; Jan., 1892-[190-?
Richmond, 1892-190-?]

> illus., ports., diagrs. 4°. monthly, except July and Aug.
> Official organ of the State dept of public instruction and the Educa-
> tional association of Virginia.
> Supersedeas *The Educational journal of Virginia* **[4638]**
> **USE**: I-XIV, 6 (Jan., 1892-June, 1905). **V**: 1892-1902. **WM**:
> 1893-99.

4658. VIRGINIA state teachers' quarterly, vol. 1- ; 1915—   Richmond, Virginia state teachers' association, 1915—

> 8°. quarterly.
> Includes *Proceedings* of Virginia state teachers' association **[4624]**; also
> Announcements of the Virginia educational conference.
> **USE**: I, 2-3; II, 2-3; (1915-16). **V**: I-IV, 1.

4659. **[3360]** The VIRGINIA teacher. Vol. 1- ; 1920—   Harrisonburg, Va., 1920—

4660. **[4028]** WILLIAM AND MARY college quarterly historical magazine . . . Williamsburg, Va., 1892-19—

PART VII. RELIGIOUS

Bibliography

See above, Pt. I: *Bibliography*.

Source Material

4661. ABINGDON AND WARE PARISHES, Gloucester County, Va. Parish register, 1830-1916.
photostat prints of MSS.   **V**

4662. ALEXANDRIA, VA. CHRIST CHURCH. Centenary services held in Christ church, Alexandria, Va. Nov. 20th & 21st, 1873. Alexandria, Pub. by the Vestry [n. d.]
24 p. 8°.   **V**
Ed. of 1888: 30 p.   **H**

4663. An APPEAL for the brotherhood [of the Protestant Episcopal church of the Diocese of Virginia] By a layman. Richmond, Clemmitt & Jones, 1877.
8 p. 8°.   **V**

4664. BAPTISTS. VIRGINIA. ACCOMAC ASSOCIATION. Minutes of the . . . Accomac Baptist association. [n. p., 1865-19—
8°. (Organized, 1809)   **VB**: 1865-67, 69-1929.

4665. ——. ——. ALBEMARLE ASSOCIATION. Minutes of the . . . Albemarle Baptist association. [Charlottesville? Va., 1865-19—
8°. (Organized, 1791)   **VB**: 1865-1929.

4666. ——. ——. APPOMATTOX ASSOCIATION. Minutes of the . . . Appomattox Baptist association. [n. p., 1865-19—
8°. (Organized, 1805)   **VB**: 1865-1929.

4667. ——. ——. AUGUSTA ASSOCIATION. Minutes of the . . . annual session of the Augusta Baptist association. Staunton, Va. [1876?-19—
8°. (Organized, 1876; no meeting, 1917)
V: 32d (1907); **VB**: 1876-1929.

4668. ——. ——. BLACKWATER ASSOCIATION. Minutes of the . . . annual session of the Blackwater Baptist association, 1907— Petersburg, Va. 1907—
8°. (Organized, 1907)   **V**: 1st, 3d (1907, 09); **VB**: 1907-29.

4669. BAPTISTS. VIRGINIA. BLUE RIDGE ASSOCIATION. Minutes of the . . . annual meeting of the Blue Ridge Baptist association. Salem, Va. [1865-19—

8°. (Organized, 1858)   **V:** 51st (1909); **VB:** 1865-67, 69-1929.

4670. ———. ———. CLINCH VALLEY ASSOCIATION. Minutes of the . . . annual meeting of the Clinch Valley Baptist association. Gate City, Va. [1865-19—

8°. (Organized, 1856?)
V: 53d (1909); **VB:** 1868-78, 80-98, 1900-07, 09, 11-12, 14, 16, 21, 23-29.

4671. ———. ———. CONCORD ASSOCIATION. Minutes of the . . . annual session of the Concord Baptist association. Farmville, Va. [1865-19—

8°. (Organized, 1833)   **V:** 76th (1909); **VB:** 1865-1929.

4672. ———. ———. DAN RIVER ASSOCIATION. Minutes of the . . . Dan River Baptist association. [Danville? Va., 1866-19—

8°. (Organized, 1839)   **VB:** 1866-1929.
Minutes for 1865 not printed.

4673. ———. ———. DOVER ASSOCIATION. Minutes of the . . . annual session of the Dover Baptist association. Richmond, Va. [1865-19—

8°. (Organized, 1783)
V: 86th, 117-118th, 124-126th, 128-130th, 132-133d, 137-139th, 142-143d, 145-146th (1869, 1900-01, 07-09, 11-13, 15-16, 20-22, 25-26, 28-29); **VB:** 1865-1929.

4674. ———. ———. GENERAL ASSOCIATION. Address of the Memorial committee of the Baptist General association of Virginia. [Staunton, Va., 1872]

16 p. 8°.   **V**

4675. ———. ———. ———. A memorial addressed by the Baptist General association of Virginia to the General assembly of Virginia, 1926, against the compulsory reading of the Bible in the public schools . . . [n. p., 1926?]

7 p. 8°.   **VB**

4676. ———. ———. ———. Minutes of the . . . annual session of the Baptist General association of Virginia. [n. p., 1865-19—

8°. (Organized, 1823)
On cover: The Virginia Baptist annual.
V: 1874, 1909, 11, 13-17, 20-28; **VB:** 1865-1929.

4677. ———. ———. ———. Report of the Educational board . . . [Portsmouth, Va.? 19—

8°. USE: 1916/17.

4678. ———. ———. GOSHEN ASSOCIATION. Minutes of the . . . session of the Goshen Baptist association. Richmond, Va. [1865-19—

8°. (Organized, 1792) **V:** 118th (1910); **VB:** 1865, 67-1929.

4679. ———. ———. HERMON ASSOCIATION. Minutes of the . . . session of the Hermon Baptist association, 1902— Kenbridge, Va., 1902—

8°. (Organized, 1902) **V:** 4th, 8th (1905, 09); **VB:** 1902-29.

4680. ———. ———. JAMES RIVER ASSOCIATION. Minutes of the . . . annual session of the James River Baptist association. Salem, Va. [1865-19—

8°. (Organized, 1832)
V: 74-75th, 77th (1906-07, 09); **VB:** 1866-1929.

4681. ———. ———. KETOCTON ASSOCIATION. Minutes of the . . . annual meeting of the Ketocton association of regular Baptists . . . [n. p., 1890-19—

8°. (Organized, 1767?) **VB:** 1890-1929.
1890 is 124th meeting of the old Ketocton association.

4682. ———. ———. LEBANON ASSOCIATION. Minutes of the . . . annual session of the Lebanon Baptist association. [n. p., 1865-19—

8°. (Organized, 1846) **V:** 62d (1907); **VB:** 1865-1929.

4683. ———. ———. MIDDLE DISTRICT ASSOCIATION. Minutes of the . . . Middle district association. [n. p., 1865-19—

8°. (Organized, 1783?) **VB:** 1865-1929.

4684. ———. ———. NEW LEBANON ASSOCIATION. Minutes of the . . . New Lebanon Baptist association. [n. p., 1875?-19—

12°. (Organized, 1875)
V: 1906; **VB:** 1875-76, 78-1907, 09, 11-28.

4685. ———. ———. NEW RIVER ASSOCIATION. Minutes of the . . . New River Baptist association. [n. p., 1871-19—

8°. (Organized, 1871) **VB:** 1871-1912, 14, 16-17, 20-29.

4686. BAPTISTS. VIRGINIA. PENINSULA ASSOCIATION. Minutes of the . . . annual session of the Peninsula Baptist association, 1904— Gloucester, Va., 1904—

8°. (Organized, 1904)   V: 4th, 6th (1907, 09); VB: 1904-29.

4687. ——. ——. PETERSBURG ASSOCIATION. Minutes of the . . . Petersburg Baptist association. [Petersburg? Va., 1907—

8°. (Organized, 1906)   V, VB: 1st-23d (1907-29).

4688. ——. ——. PIEDMONT ASSOCIATION. Minutes of the . . . Piedmont Baptist association. [n. p., 1903—

8°. (Organized, 1903)   VB: 1903-29.

4689. ——. ——. PORTSMOUTH ASSOCIATION. Minutes of the . . . Portsmouth Baptist association. [Portsmouth? Va., 1865-19—

8°. (Organized, 1791)
V: 114th, 116th (1904, 06); VB: 1865-1929.

4690. ——. ——. POTOMAC ASSOCIATION. Minutes of the . . . annual meeting of the Potomac Baptist association. Charlottesville, Va. [etc., 1865-19—

8°. (Organized, 1856)
LC: 7-9th, 13-14th, 16-17th, 20th, 22-23d, 28-29th, 31st (1865-69, 71-72, 75, 77-78, 83-84, 86); V: 55th (1910); VB: 1865-1929.

4691. ——. ——. POWELLS RIVER ASSOCIATION. Minutes of the . . . annual session of the Powells River Baptist association. [n. p., 1894-19—

12°. (Organized, 1894)
V: 16th (1909); VB: 1894-1908, 11-12, 14-16, 18, 20-29.

4692. ——. ——. RAPPAHANNOCK ASSOCIATION. Minutes of the . . . annual session of the Rappahannock Baptist association. Baltimore, Md. [1865-19—

8°. (Organized, 1843)
V: 64-65th, 68th (1906-07, 10); VB: 1865-1929.

4693. ——. ——. RICHMOND COUNCIL. Annual report of the Baptist council of Richmond and vicinity . . . [Richmond, 1903?—

8°.   V: 1924.

4694. ——. ——. Roanoke association. Minutes of the . . . annual session of the Roanoke Baptist association. Danville, Va. [1865-19—

8°. (Organized, 1788)   V: 119-120th (1906-09); VB: 1865-1929.

4695. ——. ——. Shenandoah association. Minutes of the . . . annual session of the Shenandoah Baptist association. Front Royal, Va. [1883?-19—

8°. (Organized, 1882)   V: 23d, 27th (1905, 09); VB: 1882-1929.

4696. ——. ——. Shiloh association. Minutes of the . . . session of the Shiloh Baptist association. Culpeper, Va. [1865-19—

8°. (Organized, 1792)
V: 112th (1906); VB: 1865-67, 68 (MS.), 69-1929.

4697. ——. ——. State convention. Minutes of the . . . annual session of the Virginia Baptist state convention . . . Portsmouth, Va. [etc., 18-?-19—

8°.   V: 1885.

4698. ——. ——. State Sunday school convention. Minutes of the . . . annual session of the . . . convention and Baptist young people's union . . . [n. p., 1879?-19—

8°. (Organized, 1879?)   V: 31st-33d (1900-02).

4699. ——. ——. Strawberry association. Minutes of the . . . session of the Strawberry association. Bedford City, Va. [1865-19—

8°. (Organized, 1776)
V: 129-130th, 133d (1906-07, 10); VB: 1865-1929.

4700. ——. ——. Valley association. Minutes of the . . . session of the Valley Baptist association. Salem, Va. [etc., 1865-19—

8°. (Organized, 1841)   V: 1906-07, 09, 23-24; VB: 1865-1929.

4701. ——. ——. Woman's missionary union. Report of the annual meeting . . . [n. p., 1900—

8°. (Organized, 1889)   V: 1909-12; VB: 1900-01, 04-11, 13-28.

4702. ——. ——. (Colored) Banister association. Minutes of the . . . Banister Baptist association. [n. p., 1872?-19—

8°. (Organized, 1872)   VB: 1874-75, 83.

4703. BAPTISTS. VIRGINIA. (COLORED) BEAVER CREEK ASSOCIATION. Minutes of the . . . Beaver Creek Baptist association. [n. p., 1869-19—

8°. (Organized, 1869)   VB: 1869.

4704. ———. ———. (———) BETHANY ASSOCIATION. Minutes of the . . . Bethany Baptist association. [n. p., 1881-19—

8°. (Organized, 1881)   VB: 1881, 89, 92.

4705. ———. ———. (———) BLUESTONE ASSOCIATION. Constitution and rules of decorum . . . Oct. 1st and 2d, 1870. Clarksville, Va., Roanoke Valley, 1871.

9 p. 8°.   VB

4706. ———. ———. (———). Minutes of the . . . Bluestone Baptist association. [n. p., 18- ?-19—

8°.   VB: 1871-75.

4707. ———. ———. (———) BLUESTONE SUNDAY SCHOOL CONVENTION. Minutes of the . . . annual session of the Bluestone Baptist Sunday school convention. Boydton, Va. [1886?-19—

8°. (Organized, 1886?)   V: 14th (1899).

4708. ———. ———. (———) CEDAR GROVE ASSOCIATION. Minutes of the . . . Cedar Grove Baptist association. [n. p., 1868?-19—

8°. (Organized, 1868)   VB: 1873.

4709. ———. ———. (———) GENERAL ASSOCIATION. Proceedings . . . Richmond, Baptist press [1899?-19—

8°. (Organized, 1899?)   V: 2d (1900).

4710. ———. ———. (———) HASADIAH ASSOCIATION. Minutes of the . . . Hasadiah Baptist association. [n. p., 1874-19—

8°. (Organized, 1874)   VB: 1874-75, 79.

4711. ———. ———. (———). Minutes of the formation of the Hasadiah Baptist association of South side Virginia, in the city of Lynchburg, Va., May 11th and 12th, 1874 . . . Petersburg, Ege, 1874.

10 p. 8°.   VB

4712. ———. ———. (———) HARMONY ASSOCIATION. Minutes of the . . . annual session of the Harmony Baptist association. [n. p., 1879?-19—

8°. (Organized, 1879?)   **V**: 21st (1899).

4713. ———. ———. (———) LOTT CAREY FOREIGN MISSIONARY CONVENTION. Annual report of the corresponding secretary of the Lott Carey Baptist foreign missionary convention . . . [n. p., 19—

8°.   **VB**: 1914, 22/23.

4714. ———. ———. (———). Proceedings . . . [n. p., 19—

8°.   **VB**: 1900, 11, 23-24.

4715. ———. ———. (———) MACEDONIA ASSOCIATION. Minutes of the . . . annual session of the Macedonia Baptist association. [n. p., 1877?-19—

8°. (Organized, 1877?)   **V**: 31st, 34th (1907, 10).

4716. ———. ———. (———) MATTAPONI ASSOCIATION. Minutes of the . . . annual session of the Mattaponi Baptist association. Richmond [1879?-19—

8°. (Organized, 1879?)   **V**: 30th (1908).

4717. ———. ———. (———) MATTAPONI SUNDAY SCHOOL CONVENTION. Minutes of the . . . annual session of the Mattaponi Baptist Sunday school convention. Richmond, Va. [1885?-19—

12°.-8°. (Organized, 1885?)   **V**: 23d, 25th (1908, 10).

4718. ———. ———. (———) MT. PLEASANT SUNDAY SCHOOL ASSOCIATION. Minutes of the . . . annual session of the Mt. Pleasant Baptist Sunday school association. [n. p., 1899?-19—

8°. (Organized, 1899?)   **V**: 10th (1908).

4719. ———. ———. (———) NORFOLK UNION ASSOCIATION. Minutes of the . . . annnual session of the Norfolk, Virginia, union Baptist association. Richmond, Va. [1864?-19—

8°. (Organized, 1864?)
V: 37th (1900); **VB**: 1868-69, 71, 73-75, 79-80, 82.

4720. ———. ———. (———) NORTHERN VIRGINIA ASSOCIATION. Minutes of the . . . Northern Virginia Baptist association. [n. p., 1878-19—

8°. (Organized, 1878)   **VB**: 1878.

4721. BAPTISTS. VIRGINIA. (COLORED) PAMUNKEY ASSOCIATION.
Minutes of the annual session of the Pamunkey Baptist association. Richmond, Va., 1901—

8°. (Organized, 1900?)   V: 1st-3d (1900-02).
Title varies: Proceedings and constitution, 1900, 02.

4722. ———. ———. (———) PEAKS OF OTTER ASSOCIATION. Minutes of the . . . Peaks of Otter Baptist association. [n. p.,
1902?—

8°. (Organized, 1902)   VB: 1919.

4723. ———. ———. (———) RAPPAHANNOCK UNION SUNDAY SCHOOL
CONVENTION. Minutes of the . . . annual session of Rappahannock union Sunday school convention. Richmond, Va. [1875?-
19—

8°. (Organized, 1875?)   V: 26th (1900).

4724. ———. ———. (———) RIVERSIDE ASSOCIATION. Minutes of
the . . . annual session of the Riverside Baptist association.
[n. p., 1896?-19—

8°. (Organized, 1896?)   V: 15th (1910).

4725. ———. ———. (———) SHILOH ASSOCIATION. Minutes of the
. . . annual session of the Shiloh Baptist association. [Rich-
mond, Va., 1866?-19—

8°. (Organized, 1866?)
V: 31st (1896); VB: 1868-75, 83, 91, 1922, 24.

4726. ———. ———. (———) SOUTHSIDE RAPPAHANNOCK ASSOCIA-
TION. Minutes of the . . . Southside Rappahannock association. [n. p., 1878?-19—

8°. (Organized, 1878)   VB: 1916, 21, 24-27.

4727. ———. ———. (———) STAR OF THE EAST ASSOCIATION. Minutes of the . . . Star of the East Baptist association. [n. p.,
1911?—

8°. (Organized, 1911)   VB: 1915, 17, 21, 23-26.

4728. ———. ——— (———) STATE CONVENTION. Annual report of
the Foreign mission board of the Baptist state convention of Virginia, embracing the work of the first foreign mission district of
the U. S., made at Lexington, Va., May 12th, 1886. [n. p., 1886?]
[4] p. 8°.   VB

4729. ——. ——. (——) STATE SUNDAY SCHOOL CONVENTION. Minutes of the . . . State Sunday school convention and Baptist young people's union. [Richmond? Va., 1870?-19—

8°. (Organized, 1870?)

V: 33d (1902); VB: 1872-74, 78, 80, 82-85, 87, 95, 1925, 27.

4730. ——. ——. (——) SUNNYSIDE SUNDAY SCHOOL CONVENTION. Minutes of the . . . annual session of the Sunnyside Sunday school convention. Richmond, Va., 1900—

8°. (Organized, 1900) V: 1st (1900).

4731. ——. ——. (——) TUCKAHOE ASSOCIATION. Minutes of the . . . annual session of the Tuckahoe Baptist association. Richmond, Va. [1895?-19—

8°. (Organized, 1895?) V: 11th (1905).

4732. ——. ——. (——) VALLEY ASSOCIATION. Minutes of the . . . Valley Baptist association. [n. p., 1866?-19—

8°. (Organized, 1866). VB: 1869-70, 72-75.

4733. ——. ——. (——) WAYLAND BLUE RIDGE ASSOCIATION. Minutes of the . . . annual session of the Wayland Blue Ridge Baptist association. Richmond, Va. [1891?-19—

8°. (Organized, 1890?) V: 11-12th (1900-01).

4734. ——. ——. (——) WOMEN'S MISSIONARY AND EDUCATIONAL ASSOCIATION. Minutes of the . . . annual session . . . Richmond [etc., 1901?—

8°. (Organized, 1901?) V: 10th (1910).

4735. ——. ——. (PRIMITIVE) CORRESPONDING MEETING. Minutes of the . . . annual meeting . . . [n. p., 18-?—

8°. VB: 1866-67.

4736. ——. ——. (——) COUNTRY LINE ASSOCIATION. Minutes of the . . . Country line Baptist association. [n. p., 18-?—

8°. VB: 1874.

4737. ——. ——. (——) EASTERN DISTRICT ASSOCIATION. Minutes of the . . . Eastern district [Baptist] association . . . [n. p., 18-?-19—

8°. VB: 1888.

4738. BAPTISTS. VIRGINIA. (PRIMITIVE) EBENEZER ASSOCIATION.
Minutes of the . . . Ebenezer Baptist association. [n. p.,
18-?-19—

8°.   VB: 1872, 75, 98.

4739. ——. ——. (——) KEHUKEE ASSOCIATION. Minutes of the
. . . Kehukee Baptist association. [n. p., 18-?-19—

8°.   VB: 1880, 86.

4740. ——. ——. (——) KETOCTON ASSOCIATION. Minutes of
the . . . Ketocton Baptist association. [n. p., 18-?-19—

8°.   VB: 1873-75, 81.

4741. ——. ——. (——) McCLURE BAPTIST CHURCH, Dickenson
County, Va. Minutes of the McClure primitive Baptist church in
Dickenson County, Virginia. Book one. Nov., 1849-Feb., 1884.
[Clintwood, Va., 1926]

[60] p. typew. 4°.
"Copied by H[etty] J. S[utherland] and E. J. S[utherland?], Clint-
wood, Virginia, Jan. 26, 1926."

4742. ——. ——. (——) MAYO ASSOCIATION. Minutes of the
Mayo primitive Baptist association . . . [n. p., 18-?-19—

8°.   VB: 1869, 74, 1915.

4743. ——. ——. (——) NEW RIVER ASSOCIATION. Minutes of
the . . . New River [old school] Baptist association. [n. p.,
18-?-19—

8°.   VB: 1873, 76, 88, 1915.

4744. ——. ——. (——) PATTERSON'S CREEK ASSOCIATION. Minutes of the . . . Patterson's Creek Baptist association. [n. p.,
18-?—

8°.   VB: 1875.

4745. ——. ——. (——) PIG RIVER ASSOCIATION. Minutes of
the . . . Pig River Baptist association. [n. p., 18-?—

8°.   VB: 1868-69, 71, 74-75.

4746. ——. ——. (——) ST. CLAIR'S BOTTOM ASSOCIATION.
Minutes of the . . . St. Clair's Bottom Baptist association.
[n. p., 19—

8°.   VB: 1907.

4747. ———. ———. (———) SMITH'S RIVER ASSOCIATION. Minutes of the . . . Smith's River Baptist association. [n. p., 18-?-19—

    8°.   **VB:** 1888, 1901, 15.

4748. ———. ———. (———) STAUNTON RIVER ASSOCIATION. Minutes of the . . . Staunton River Baptist association. [n. p., 18-?-19—

    8°.   **VB:** 1869, 74-75, 92-96, 98, 1900-04, 06-07.

4749. ———. ———. (———) STONY CREEK ASSOCIATION. Minutes of the . . . Stony Creek regular primitive Baptist association. [n. p., 19—

    8°.   **VB:** 1913.

4750. ———. ———. (———) THREE FORKS OF POWELL'S RIVER ASSOCIATION. Minutes of the . . . Three forks of Powell's River Baptist association. [n. p., 19—

    8°.   **VB:** 1915.

4751. ———. ———. (———) VALLEY ASSOCIATION. Minutes of the . . . Valley primitive Baptist association. [n. p., 18-?-19—

    8°.   **VB:** 1890.

4752. ———. ———. (———) WASHINGTON ASSOCIATION. Minutes of the Washington district primitive Baptist association, 1811-1897. [Clintwood, Va., 1928]

    2 v. in 1. tables. typew. 4°.   **V**
    "This book copied by Hetty Jean Sutherland."

4753. ———. ———. (———). Minutes of the . . . Washington primitive Baptist association. [n. p., 18-?-19—

    8°.   **VB:** 1900.

4754. BARRETT, ROBERT S. The churchman's scrap-book, by Rev. Robert S. Barrett . . . Richmond, Baughman, 1879.

    48 p. 16°.   **V**
    On the nature and characteristics of the Protestant Episcopal church.
    Ed. of 1885.   **V**

4755. BARTON, W. S. Diocese of Virginia. Remarks on some of the proposed canons. [n. p., 1881?]

    24 p. 8°.   **VU**
    Important changes proposed, and comments upon them.

4756. BATH PARISH, Dinwiddie County, Va.   Parish register, 1827-97.
photostat prints of MSS.   V

4757. BIBLE SOCIETY OF VIRGINIA.   Annual report, with proceedings
of the annual meeting . . . Richmond [18-?-19—
   8°.   **V:** 1872, 87, 90-91, 93-1901, 03-05.
   Pub. after 1905 in *Report* of American Bible society.

4758. BLEDSOE, A. C., comp.   Devotional hymns, compiled by Rev.
A. C. Bledsoe . . . of the Virginia [Methodist] conference.
Richmond, Fergusson & Rady, 1875.
   96, v p. 12°.   V
   101 hymns (without music), "many of the best and most popular
   . . ., old and new," to promote the "Service of Song" by the congregation.

4759. BROADDUS, WILLIAM.   Centennial sermon of Potomac Baptist
association of Virginia. [Alexandria?] Pub. by the acting board,
1867.
   58 p. 12°.   **LC, NYP**
   Some account of the Association and the new constitution adopted
   in 1866.

4760. BROADUS, JOHN A.   Sermons and addresses . . . Richmond, Va., Johnson, 1886.
   ix, 445 p. front. (port.) 8°.   V
   2d ed.: 1887.   **LC**

4761. BRUTON PARISH, James City County, Va.   Parish register,
1868-1908.
   photostat prints of MSS.   V

4762. ———.   Vestry book, 1827-89.
   photostat prints of MSS.   V

4763. BRYAN, JOSEPH.   Christian stewardship. An address delivered
before the Y. M. C. A. of Richmond college on Feb. 20, 1908.
Richmond, Jones, 1909.
   18 p. 8°.   V

4764. BYRD [PRESBYTERIAN] CHURCH, Goochland County, Va.   Byrd
church records, 1811-91.
   MSS.   V

4765. CHARLOTTESVILLE, VA. PRESBYTERIAN CHURCH.   Program of
services held on March 4th, 1928, in celebration of Dr. George

Laurens Petrie's fifty years' administration in this church, 1878-1928. Charlottesville, Michie [n. d.]

38 p. 8°.   VU

4766. CHENAULT, FRED R. The Broad Street Methodist Episcopal church, South, and community house. Richmond, Virginia. By Rev. Fred R. Chenault, D.D., the pastor. Richmond, Va., Whittet & Shepperson, 1923.

112 p. illus., ports. (front.) 12°.   RM

Emphasis upon contemporary life in the church and its activities; with testimonials by former pastors, elders, laymen, etc.

4767. CHRISTIAN BAPTISTS. VIRGINIA. EASTERN VIRGINIA SUNDAY SCHOOL CONVENTION. Proceedings of the . . . annual session . . . Richmond, Va. [1877?-19—

8°.   V: 27th (1903).

4768. CONSER, SOLOMON L. Virginia after the war. An account of three years' experience in reorganizing the Methodist Episcopal church in Virginia at the close of the Civil war . . . Indianapolis, Baker-Randolph litho. & eng. co., 1891.

82 p. 8°.   LC, VU.

A conversational narrative based upon the author's experiences and written more then 20 years after the events occurred; sheds light upon religious and social conditions in Virginia during the early years of reconstruction.

4769. COOL SPRING BAPTIST CHURCH, Atlee, Va. Manual of the Cool Spring Baptist church, Atlee, Hanover County, Va. [Richmond, Beverly & Gayle, 19-?]

22 p. illus. (front.) 16°.   VB

4770. CUMBERLAND PRESBYTERIAN CHURCH, Cumberland County, Va. Congregation book, 1844-66.

MSS.   V

4771. DABNEY, ROBERT L. Ecclesiastical relation of Negroes. Speech . . . in the Synod of Virginia, Nov. 9, 1867; against the ecclesiastical equality of Negro preachers in our church, and their right to rule over white Christians. Richmond, Printed at office of the "Boys' and girls' monthly", 1868.

16 p. 8°.   V, VU

4772. DABNEY, ROBERT L.   Sacred rhetoric; or, a course of lectures on preaching.   Delivered in the Union theological seminary of the General assembly of the Presbyterian church in the U. S. in Prince Edward, Va.   Richmond, Presbyterian committee of publication, 1870.

361 p. 12°.   **LC, NYP, V**

4773. DASHIELL, T. G.   A pastor's recollections.   By Rev. T. G. Dashiell, rector of St. Mark's church, Richmond, Virginia.   New York, Appleton, 1875.

208 p. 12°.   **LC, NYP, V, VU**

Some account of pastoral work in Richmond after the Civil war.

4774. [2395] [DAVIDSON papers] [Papers of James D. Davidson and his son, Charles A., of Lexington, Va., 1865-85]

4775. DISCIPLES OF CHRIST. VIRGINIA. TIDEWATER CONVENTION.   Minutes of the . . . Tidewater convention . . . [n. p., 18-?-19—

plates, ports. 8°.   **V:** 1881-86, 1903-15.

4776. DOWD, WILLIS B.   Three measures of meal . . . Boston, Riverdale press, Brookline, 1910.

38 p. col. front., plates. 12°.   **LC, NYP**

In part concerning St. John's Episcopal church, Richmond.

4777. DUNAWAY, T[HOMAS] S.   Personal memoirs; sermons and addresses, by T. S. Dunaway, with an introduction by Hon. J. L. M. Curry.   Lynchburg, Bell, 1900.

xiv, 383 p. 8°.   **V, VB, VU**

Chaps. 6 & 7 deal with the author's Baptist ministry in Virginia after the Civil war and shed light upon the condition of the church until the late 'nineties.

4778. DUNN, JOSEPH B.   In the service of the King; a parson's story.   New York & London, Putnam, 1915.

ix, 158 p. 8°.   **LC, V**

Concerning the ministry and problems of a Presbyterian parson in rural and urban Virginia.

4779. FAUNTLEROY, THOMAS T., jr.   Argument . . . before a military commission sitting in Winchester, Va., Aug. 1, 1867. [n. p., 1867?]

8 p. 8°.   **VU**

Controversy between the M. E. church and the M. E. church, South, over property claimed by both since the Civil war.

4780. GOODWIN, WILLIAM A. Bruton parish church restored and its historic environments, by Rev. Wm. A. R. Goodwin . . . [Petersburg, Va.] 1907.

205 p. incl. front., illus., plates, plans, facsims. 8°.

BP, LC, NYP, V, VD, VU, WM

Includes brief account of the modern church as restored, and the services held after the restoration.

4781. GUNTER, BENJAMIN T. Address: made Aug. 14, 1890 . . . at the Accomack Baptist association, Virginia, held with the Pungoteague church; the centennial year of that church. 1890. Baltimore, Weishampel [1890?]

16 p. 8°.   **VB**

4782. HOGE, MOSES D. The perfection of beauty, and other sermons by the Rev. Moses D. Hoge . . . with a lecture on "The success of Christianity an evidence of its divine origin," delivered at the University of Virginia. Richmond, Va., Presbyterian committee of publication, 1904.

335 p. front. (port.) plate. 8°.   **LC, NYP, V**

4783. HOPKINS, MARK. "What hath God wrought?" [Sermon . . . delivered May 20th, 1886, at the dedication of the Memorial church . . . to the Hampton normal and agricultural institute. Hampton, Va., Institute press, 1886.

37 p. 12°.   **NYP**

4784. IMMANUEL [PROTESTANT EPISCOPAL] CHURCH, Hanover County, Va. Immanuel church records, 1815-1926.

photostat prints of MSS.   **V**

4785. INGLE, JAMES A. Address delivered before the Young men's Christian association of the University of Virginia, Sunday, 27 June, 1886 . . . [Charlottesville? 1886?]

4 p. 8°.   **LC**

Review of work done by the University Y. M. C. A. during the current year.

4786. INTERNATIONAL ORDER OF THE KING'S DAUGHTERS AND SONS. VIRGINIA. Minutes of the . . . meeting . . . Richmond, Va., 19—

8°.   **V: 1908, 10.**

Religious and charitable organization.

4787. JOHNS, JOHN. Addresses, delivered at the 78th annual council of the Protestant Episcopal church in Virginia . . . Richmond, Clemmitt & Jones, 1873.

32 p. 8°.   V, VD, VU

4788. JORDAN, HARVEY E. The call of science to the church. [Lecture delivered before the Y. M. C. A. of the University of Virginia, 1912. n. p., n. d.]

p. 266-288. 8°. (Reprint from the *Open court*)   V, VU

4789. KRATZIG, HENRY H., comp. The voice of Norfolk; radio messages from the city's foremost preachers; compiled by Henry H. Kratzig . . . introduction by Ira S. D. Knight . . . New York, Chicago [etc.] Revell [*ca.* 1929]

xiii, 153, [1] p. 8°.   LC, V

4790. LACY, WILLIAM S. William Sterling Lacy: memorial, addresses, sermons . . . Richmond, Va., Presbyterian committee of publication [*ca.* 1900]

198 p., 1 l. front. (port.) 8°.   LC, V
Rev. Lacy was pastor in Norfolk, 1888-98. Memorial by Rev. J. P. Smith, p. 5-12.

4791. LEXINGTON, VA. GRACE MEMORIAL CHURCH. In memoriam. Rev. William Nelson Pendleton, D.D., rector of Grace memorial church, Latimer parish, Diocese of Virginia. Died Jan. 15, 1883. Minutes adopted by wardens and vestry, Jan. 20th, 1883. [Lexington? Va., 1883?]

5 l. 12°.   V

4792. LYNCHBURG, VA. ST. PAUL'S CHURCH. Memorial exercises to our soldier dead. Lynchburg, Va. [1921?]

15 p. 12°.   V

4793. LYNNHAVEN PARISH, Princess Anne County, Va. Vestry book of Lynnhaven parish . . . 1723-1892.

photostat prints of MSS.   V

4794. [429] [McCORMICK, CYRUS H.] [Personal papers of the Cyrus H. McCormick family, 1865-*ca.* 1910]

4795. [3422] McILWAINE, RICHARD. Hampden-Sidney college; its relation and services to the Presbyterian church . . . Richmond, Va., 1888.

4796. ———. Memories of three score years and ten . . . New York and Washington, Neale, 1908.

4 p. l., vii-xiv, [11]-383 p. front., ports. 8°.   L'C, V, VU

The experiences of a Presbyterian clergyman in Virginia during the Civil war and reconstruction (at Farmville and Lynchburg, to 1872), later as president of Hampden-Sidney college (1883-1904), and as a member of the constitutional convention of 1901-02; told in simple, direct language.

4797. McKIM, RANDOLPH H. In memoriam. Good men a nation's strength, a sermon preached on the occasion of the death of General Robert E. Lee, in Christ church, Alexandria, Va., Oct. 16, 1870, by the rector . . . Pub. by unanimous request of the vestry . . . Baltimore, Murphy, 1870.

16 p. 8°.   LC, NYP, V, VU

4798. MATTAPONY BAPTIST CHURCH, King and Queen County, Va. . . . Records, 1854-75.

photostat prints of MSS.   V

4799. MAYO, WAT T., *et al.* A sketch of Yeocomico church (built 1706) in Cople parish, Westmoreland County, Va. With a reference to the bicentennial celebration on July 15, 1906, and the movement to raise an endowment fund for the preservation of the church. By W. T. Mayo, W. R. Crabbe [and] S. D. Cox, Committee of the congregation. [Washington, D. C., Sudworth, 1906]

[20] p. illus. (incl. ports.) 8°.   V

4800. METHODIST EPISCOPAL CHURCH. VIRGINIA CONFERENCE. Official minutes . . . Petersburg, Va. [etc., 1869?-19—

8°. (Organized, 1869?)
LC: 12th-20th, 23d, 25-39th (1880-88, 91, 93-1906).

4801. METHODIST EPISCOPAL CHURCH, SOUTH. BALTIMORE CONFERENCE. Minutes of the . . . session, Baltimore annual conference . . . Baltimore, Md. [1866-19—

tables. 8°.   RM: 1868-94, 1902-29.
Includes part of Virginia.

4802. ———. VIRGINIA CONFERENCE. Minutes of the . . . session of the Virginia annual conference . . . Richmond, Norfolk [etc., 1866-19—

tables. 8°.
Sessions numbered from that of 1796 thru Conference of 1879; from 1880-19—, numbered from General Conference of 1784.

Editors: P. A. Peterson, 187-?-77; A. G. Brown, 1878-87; B. F. Lips-comb, 1888-19-?
Title varies: Virginia conference annual, 1915—
LC: 1923; RM: 1868-1904, 06-1929; V: 1879/84, 99; VU: 79th, 81st-85th, 98-99th, 101st-118th, 120th-122d (1873, 75-79, 80-81, 83-1900, 02-04).

4803. METHODIST EPISCOPAL CHURCH, SOUTH. VIRGINIA CONFER-ENCE. ROCKINGHAM DISTRICT CONFERENCE. Minutes of the . . . session of the Rockingham district conference . . . Staunton, Va. [1873?-19—

illus. 8°. (Organized, 1873?)   RM: 34th (1906).
1901 includes Proceedings and papers of the . . . Epworth league conference.

4804. ———. ———. WOMAN'S FOREIGN MISSIONARY SOCIETY. Min-utes of the . . . annual session . . . Petersburg [etc., 1879?-19—

8°. (Organized, 1879?)   V: 24th (1902).

4805. ———. ———. WOMAN'S HOME MISSION SOCIETY. Annual report . . . [n. p., 1891-?19—

8°. (Organized, 1891?)   V: 15th, 17-20th (1905, 07-10).

4806. ———. ———. WOMAN'S MISSIONARY SOCIETY. . . . An-nual report of the Woman's missionary society of the Virginia conference . . . [Richmond, 1915?—

8°. (Organized, 1915?)   V: 13-15th (1927-29).

4807. MOFFETT, W. W. Correspondence between W. W. Moffett and . . . the [Richmond] Times-dispatch, concerning its ed-itorial of Apr. 16th, 1903, referring to Rev. John R. Moffett . . . [Roanoke, Va., 1924]

53 p. illus., front. (port.) typew. 4°.   VB
Signed: "W. W. Moffett, Roanoke, Va., July 14, 1924."
Concerning Rev. J. R. Moffett's connection with the prohibition move-ment in Danville, Va., during the 'nineties. (See item 2063)

4808. NEVE, FREDERICK W. Light in dark places. An account of mission school work in the mountains of Greene County, Virginia. [Ivy Depot, Va., 190-?]

16 p. plates. obl. 24°.   NYP

4809. NORFOLK, VA. ST. LUKE'S AFRICAN UNION METHODIST PROTESTANT CHURCH. Souvenir program, fiftieth anniversary ex-ercises . . . 1911. Norfolk, New century print. [1911?]

[9] p. ports. 4°.   V

4810. Norton, George H. The interpretation of scripture. A discourse delivered before the associate alumni of the Theological seminary of the Protestant Episcopal church of the Diocese of Virginia, June 21, 1871 . . . Pub. by the alumni. Washington, M'Gill & Witherow, 1871.

23 p. 8°.   VU

4811. O'keefe, Matthew. The key to true Christianity; being a series of letters addressed to Rev. J. D. Blackwell, d.d., pastor of the Cumberland M. E. church, Norfolk, Va., by Rev. M. O'Keefe, pastor of the Catholic church, Norfolk, Va., pending a discussion on the "Bible as a divine revelation." During the months of July, August, September, and October, 1873 . . . Philadelphia, Kildare, 1874.

vi, 7-151, 42 p. 8°.   LC, V

4812. Old Donation church; erected 1736; mother church erected 1633. [Norfolk, Atlantic coast print.] 1911.

14 p. front. 16°.   V

"Issued by the Association for restoring Old Donation."

4813. Orkney Springs, Va. Shrine of the transfiguration. The shrine of the transfiguration, Orkney Springs, Va. . . . [Richmond, Whittet & Shepperson, 1925]

39, [1] p. incl. illus., ports. 4°.   V, VU

Description of Episcopalian shrine, and sermon preached at its consecration, by Rev. Churchill G. Chamberlayne.

4814. Packard, Joseph. Recollections of a long life . . . Edited by Rev. Thomas J. Packard. Washington, D. C., Adams, 1902.

4 p. l., 5-364 p. plates, 2 ports. (incl. front.) 8°.   LC, V, VU

The scattered notes on the period since 1865 by this Episcopalian clergyman deal mostly with the Episcopal Theological seminary at Alexandria, Va.

4815. Patton, John M. Argument . . . in respect to the validity of ministerial orders in the Council of the Diocese of Virginia, at Alexandria, May 18, 1876. Richmond, Clemmitt & Jones, 1876.

34 p. 8°.   V

4816. PETERKIN, JOSHUA.   Observations on the doctrine of divine Providence. By . . . [the] rector of St. James church, Richmond, Va.   Richmond, Medical journal print., 1867.

37 p. 16°.   **V**

4817. PITT, R. H.   Soul liberty; some of its implications . . . An address delivered at the Baptist General asssociation of Virginia, Nov. 12, 1925, under the auspices and at the request of the Virginia Baptist historical society.   Nashville, Sunday school board Southern Baptist convention [1925?]

12 p. 16°.   **VB**
Part of the campaign against the bill compelling Bible reading in the public schools of Virginia.

4818. PLEASANTS, EDWIN.   Historical sketch of the Third Presbyterian church, Richmond, Va.   Read by the author . . . at the celebration of the seventy-fifth anniversary of its organization, May 22, 1910, with some account of the commemorative events. Richmond, Va., Whittet & Shepperson [1910?]

29 p. 8°.   **LC**
Annals of the church, written by one of the oldest members, evidently as recollections; no sources are quoted.

4819. PRESBYTERIAN CHURCH IN THE U. S. APPALACHIA, Synod of. ABINGDON, Presbytery of.   Minutes of the Presbytery of Abingdon . . . Richmond, Va. [etc., 1865-19—

8°. semi-annual. (Re-organized, 1866)
LC: 82d, 84th-91st, 93-101st, 103d-107th, 110-119th, 121st-123d (1907-20, 21-28); **UT**: 1865-1929; **V**: 1903-06; **VU**: 1921-29.

4820. ———.   VIRGINIA, Synod of.   Minutes of the Synod of Virginia . . . Wytheville [etc., 1865-19—

8°. tables. annual. (Organized, 1788)
LC: 1868; **UT**: 1865-1929; **V**: 1873, 75, 99, 1910, 13, 15-17.

4821. ———. ———.   CHESAPEAKE, Presbytery of.   Minutes of the Presbytery of Chesapeake . . . [Richmond? 1869?-1911]

8°. semi-annual. (Organized, 1868)   **UT**: 1868-1911.
Merged with Maryland presbytery to form Potomac presbytery, 1912.

4822. ———. ———.   EAST HANOVER, Presbytery of.   Minutes of the Presbytery of East Hanover . . . Richmond, Va. [1865-19—

tables 8°. semi-annual. (Organized as the Presbytery of Hanover, 1758; East Hanover organized, 1829)
UT: 1865-1929; **V**: 1913-14; **VU**: 1927-28.

4823. ——. ——. LEXINGTON, Presbytery of. Minutes of the Presbytery of Lexington . . . [Richmond? Va., 1865-19—

8°. semi-annual. (Organized, 1786)   **UT**: 1865-1929.

4824. ——. ——. MARYLAND, Presbytery of. Minutes of the Presbytery of Maryland . . . [Richmond? Va., 1878?-1911]

8°. semi-annual. (Organized, 1878)   **UT**: 1878-1911.
Merged with Chesapeake presbytery to form Potomac presbytery, 1912.

4825. ——. ——. MONTGOMERY, Presbytery of. Minutes of the Presbytery of Montgomery . . . [Richmond? Va., 1865-19—

8°. semi-annual. (Organized, 1843)   **UT**: 1865-1929.

4826. ——. ——. NORFOLK, Presbytery of. Manual of Norfolk presbytery, Synod of Virginia. Revised and adopted Apr., 1926. [n. p., n. d.]

26 p. 12°.   **VU**

4827. ——. ——. ——. Minutes of the Presbytery of Norfolk . . . [Richmond? Va., 1895?-19—

8°. semi-annual. (Organized, 1894)
UT: 1894-1929; **V**: 1904, 06-07.

4828. ——. ——. POTOMAC, Presbytery of. Manual of the Presbytery of Potomac. Revised edition, 1927 . . . [Pulaski, Va., Smith, 1927?]

28 p. 12°.   **VU**

4829. ——. ——. ——. Minutes of the Presbytery of Potomac . . . [Richmond? Va., 1866-19—

8°. semi-annual. (Organized, 1911)   **UT**: 1912-29.
Formed by consolidation of Chesapeake and Maryland presbyteries.

4830. ——. ——. ROANOKE, Presbytery of. Minutes of the Presbytery of Roanoke . . . [Richmond? Va., 1865-19—

8°. semi-annual. (Organized, 1858)   **UT**: 1865-1929.

4831. PRESBYTERIAN CHURCH IN THE U. S. VIRGINIA, Synod of. WEST HANOVER, Presbytery of. Minutes of the Presbytery of West Hanover . . . [Richmond? Va., 1865-19—

8°. semi-annual. (Organized, 1829)   **UT**: 1865-1929.

4832. ———. ———. WINCHESTER, Presbytery of. Minutes of the Presbytery of Winchester . . . [Richmond? Va., 1865-19—

8°. semi-annual. (Organized, 1794)
UT: 1865-1929; **VU**: 1914-15, 17, 19-29.

4833. PROTESTANT EPISCOPAL CHURCH IN THE U. S. A. COMMISSION FOR WORK AMONG THE COLORED PEOPLE. Report of the Commission . . . [Washington? D. C., 1897]

8 p. 8°.   **LC**
Schedule of appropriations and work being done, with special reference to religious and industrial education in Virginia, North Carolina, and Tennessee.

4834. ———. SOUTHERN VIRGINIA, Diocese of. . . . Handbook, 1924. Published in connection with the church's program for 1925 . . . Portsmouth, Va., Shepherd [1924]

31 p. 8°.   **VD**

4835. ———. ———. Journal of the . . . annual council . . . Norfolk, Va., 1893-19—

8°. (Organized, 1893)
V: 1st-3d, 8th, 10-18th, 21st-35th (1893-95, 1900, 02-10, 13-27); **VD**: 1893-1929.

4836. ———. ———. Reports and proceedings of the Southern Virginia branch of the Woman's auxiliary to the Board of missions. Friday, June 3, 1904. [n. p., 1904]

18 p. tables. 8°.   **VD**

4837. ———. ———. Questions and answers on the church's program for 1925 in the Diocese of Southern Virginia. Pub. for the Church program committee, Norfolk, Va. [1925?]

14 p. 16°.   **VD**

4838. ———. SOUTHWESTERN VIRGINIA, Diocese of. Journal of the . . . annual council . . . Roanoke, Va., 1919—

8°. (Organized, 1919)
V: 1st, 2d & suppl., 3d-8th (1919-26); **VD**: 1919-29.

4839. ———. VIRGINIA, Diocese of. Altar cloths and flowers: a review. Richmond, Randolph & English [1880]

  28 p. 8°. BP

  Refers to a circular letter of the Bishop of Virginia forbidding the use of such on special occasions.

4840. ———. ———. Journal of the . . . annual council . . . Richmond, Va. [1865-19—

  8°. (Organized, 1796?)

  LC: 70th-72d, 74-75th, 77-79th, 81st-86th, 89th-91st, 101st, 103d, 109th, 114th-133d (1865-67, 69-70, 72-74, 76-81, 84-86, 96, 98, 1904, 09-28); **V:** 1865, 68-1928; **VD:** 1865-1929; **VU:** 1880, 90, 1910-11; **WM:** 1909-10, 12.

4841. ———. ———. Journal of the Special council of the Protestant Episcopal church in the Diocese of Virginia, held in St. Paul's church, Alexandria, on Wednesday, Dec. 16th, 1908. Richmond, Jones, 1908.

  18 p. 8°. LC

4842. ———. ———. [Miscellaneous Mss.. pamphlets, and clippings on Episcopal churches and parishes in Virginia. 18-?-19-?]

  var. pag. & size, arranged by counties. VD

4843. ———. ———. On the incompatibility of theater-going and dancing with membership in the Christian church; an address of the clergy of the convocation of the Valley of Virginia to the people of their respective parishes. Philadelphia, Leighton, 1872.

  31 p. 8°. H

4844. ———. ———. Report on federal relations presented to the Eighty-third annual Council of the Diocese of Virginia. [n. p., 1877]

  20 p. 8°. BP

4845. ———. ———. Revised constitution and canons of the Protestant Episcopal church in the Diocese of Virginia. Richmond, Jones, 1904.

  24 p. 8°. VD

4846. ———. ———. The story of the budget. Where does my dollar go? Bird's-eye view of program of Diocese of Virginia for 1928. [Richmond, Va.? 1928]

  [20] p. diagrs. 8°. VD

4847. PROTESTANT EPISCOPAL CHURCH IN THE U. S. A. VIRGINIA, Diocese of. A survey of the Diocese of Virginia. 1919. Issued by Virginia Diocesan committee, Nation-wide campaign. Richmond, Va. [1919]

14 p. 4°. VD

4848. ——. ——. Then and now; a comparison of figures of the work of the Diocese of Virginia in 1923 as compared with 1918-1919. Richmond, Va., Pub. by the Board of apportionment, The Church house of the Diocese of Virginia, 1923.

8 p. 8°. VD

4849. ——. ——. COLONIAL CHURCHES, Commission on. Minutes of the Commission . . . 1912.

9 p. 8°. MS. book. VD

4850. ——. ——. ——. Report . . . 1913. [n. p., 1913?]

7 p. 8°. V, VD

Information as to location and present ownership of sites on which stood colonial churches.

4851. ——. ——. SOCIAL SERVICE COMMISSION. Present opportunities for constructive leadership, particularly in the country. Report of the Social service commission of the Diocese of Virginia to the Diocesan council, 1914. [n. p., 1914?]

12 p. 12°. V

4852. ——. ——. SUNDAY SCHOOL COMMISSION. Annual report . . . to the Diocesan council . . . Richmond, Va. [1907?—

8°. V: 1st (1907).

4853. RICHMOND, VA. BETHLEHEM EVANGELICAL CHURCH. Order of services in connection with the 50th anniversary celebration of the dedication of Bethlehem Evangelical church, Richmond, Va. 25-August-27th, 1918. Richmond, Dietz [1918]

[12] p. ports., plate. 8°. V

4854. ——. CHURCH OF THE HOLY TRINITY. Year book . . . [Richmond? Va., 18-?-19—

8°. V: 1897-99, 1903-05, 07-11.

4855. ——. CONGREGATION BETH AHABAH. Year book . . . [Richmond, Va., 1910?—

8°. V: no. 19 (1927/28).

4856. ———. FIRST BAPTIST CHURCH. [Miscellaneous pamphlets, 1870-1916]

var. pag. & size.   **VB**

4857. ———. ———. Pastor's annual letter to the First Baptist church of Richmond, Virginia. [Richmond, 19—

16°.-12°.   **V**: 1909-11, 13-14, 16.

4858. ———. FIRST PRESBYTERIAN CHURCH. Manual for members . . . Pub. by order of the session. Richmond, Shepperson & Graves, 1870.

28 p. 8°.   **V**

4859. ———. ———. . . . . Proceedings of the celebration of the 80th anniversary of its organization, May 1, 1892. Richmond, Whittet & Shepperson [1892]

[63] p. front., plates, ports. 8°.   **V**

4860. ———. FOURTH PRESBYTERIAN CHURCH. The Fourth Presbyterian church . . . Richmond, Va., 1887. Richmond, Whittet & Shepperson [1887?]

25 p. 12°.   **V**

4861. ———. GRACE STREET BAPTIST CHURCH. A manual of the Grace Street Baptist church of Richmond, Va. . . . Richmond, Va., Adkins & co., 1897.

76 p. front., illus., ports. 16°.   **V**

4862. ———. ———. [Miscellaneous pamphlets, 1867-1927]

var. pag. & size.   **VB**

4863. ———. ———. Report of Committee on constitution and by-laws. [1910] [Richmond, 1911]

16 p. 8°.   **V**

4864. [———. OLD MARKET HALL PRESBYTERIAN SUNDAY SCHOOL] A talk with my class. By a teacher at the Old market hall Sunday school. Richmond, Whittet & Shepperson, 1885.

79 p. front. 16°.   **V**

4865. ———. ST. JOHN'S PROTESTANT EPISCOPAL CHURCH. Commemoration of the 150th anniversary of the erection of St. John's

. . . church, Henrico parish, Richmond, Va., June 10th, 1741-1891. [n. p., 1891?]

24 p. 16°.   **V**

4866. RICHMOND, VA. ST. JOHN'S PROTESTANT EPISCOPAL CHURCH. The order of service for the centennial anniversary of the inauguration of George Washington as president of the U. S., Apr. 30, 1789 . . . [Richmond, Ware, Duke & Taylor, 1889]

11 p. 12°.   **V**

4867. ———. ST. MARY'S [GERMAN CATHOLIC] CHURCH. Annual financial statement . . . [Richmond? 19—

8°.   **NYP**: 1903-04.

4868. ———. ———. Annual statement of the building committee . . . [Richmond? 19—

8°.   **NYP**: 1903.

4869. ———. ———. Manual and directory . . . [Richmond, Whittet & Shepperson, 19—

8°.   **NYP**: 1903/04.

4870. ———. ST. PAUL'S [PROTESTANT EPISCOPAL] CHURCH. Year book . . . Richmond [18-?—

8°.   **V**: 1888-89.

4871. ———. SECOND BAPTIST CHURCH. [Miscellaneous pamphlets, 1880-1927]

var. pag. & size.   **VB**

4872. ———. SECOND PRESBYTERIAN CHURCH. [Bulletin . . . Richmond? Va., 19—

8°.   **V**: 1914-18 (incompl.).

4873. ———. ———. . . . . Commemoration of 45 years of service by the Rev. Moses Drury Hoge . . . , as pastor of the Second Presbyterian church of the city of Richmond. Richmond, Va., Whittet & Shepperson [1890]

143 .p. 8°.   **NYP, V, VU**

4874. ———. ———. Fifty years a pastor. An account of the observance of the semi-centennial anniversary of the installation of

Rev. Moses Drury Hoge, D.D., LL.D., in the pastorate of the Second Presbyterian church, Richmond, Va. Richmond, 1895.

vi, [1], 156 p. front. (port.) 8°.   NYP, V, VU
Contains a sketch of Hoge's life and a detailed account of the celebration.

4875. ———. ———. Manual of the . . . church, Rev. Moses D. Hoge, D.D., pastor. Containing historical sketch from 1845 to 1883 . . . Richmond, Marquess, 1883.

60 p. front. (port.) 16°.   V

4876. ———. ———. Memorial service, Feb. 5, 1899, in memory of Rev. Moses D. Hoge, D.D., LL.D., for fifty-four years pastor of the Second Presbyterian church, Richmond, Virginia . . . [Richmond, Va., Whittet & Shepperson, 1899]

[8] p. incl. port. 12°.   V

4877. RUEBUSH, WILL H., *et al.,* comp. Exalted praise; a superior collection of gospel songs . . . By Will H. Ruebush, Samuel W. Beazley, James H. Ruebush, G. L. Shirley, Curtis Taylor [and] Julius S. Rushing . . . Dayton, Va., Ruebush-Kieffer [*ca.* 1924]

151 hymns (with music). 8°.   V

4878. SHALL we have an assistant bishop; or, shall we divide? . . . By a clergyman. Richmond, Baughman, 1878.

27 p. 8°.   VU
Addressed to the clergy and laity of the Diocese of Virginia; the need for more espiscopal supervision.

4879. SMITH, E. R., comp. Handbook of the Baltimore conference, Methodist Episcopal church, South, containing map, historical notes, etc. Baltimore, King, 1871.

134 p. map, tables. 8°.   LC, RM

4880. SOUTH FARNHAM PARISH, Essex County, Va. Vestry book, 1739-1876.

photostat prints of MSS.   V

4881. SPARROW, WILLIAM. Our times and our duties; an address delivered at the annual commencement of the Theological seminary of the Protestant Episcopal church of the Diocese of Virginia, June 27, 1872. Philadelphia [1872]

34 p. 8°.   V

On the trend of religious thought and the divided state of the Christian church.

4882. STAUNTON, VA. FIRST PRESBYTERIAN CHURCH. Handbook of the First Presbyterian church . . . compiled by the Committee on printing. [Staunton, Ross] 1903.

114 p. 8°.   V

4883. TROSTLE, J. A. Timber Ridge Presbyterian church, Rockbridge County, Virginia. Handbook and historical sketch . . . [Roanoke, Stone, 1906]

46 p. plates. 8°.   NYP

4884. TUCKER, BEVERLEY D. The continuity of the church. A plea for endowment. Sermon preached in St. Paul's church, Elizabeth River parish, Norfolk, Va. . . . Apr. 1st, 1906. Norfolk, 1906.

11 p. 8°.   BP, NYP

4885. ———. . . . The restoration at Bruton, the court church of colonial Virginia . . . Sermon . . . Williamsburg, Va., 1905.

20 p. 8°.   NYP, WM

Introduction by A. M. Randolph, bishop of the Diocese of southern Virginia; Statement relative to the history and condition of the church, by W. A. R. Goodwin.

4886. [UNIVERSITY OF VIRGINIA] A statement relative to the erection of St. Paul's memorial church at the University of Virginia; with special reference to the care of the Episcopal students at that institution. University, Virginia, 1913.

23 p. illus., plans. 8°.   VD, VU

4887. VAUGHAN, C[LEMENT] R. Sermons; apologetic, doctrinal and miscellaneous . . . Richmond, Va., Presbyterian committee of publication [1902]

363 p. 8°.   LC, V

4888. [274] [WALKER FAMILY diary. Walker's Creek, Rockbridge County, Va., 1865-19—

4889. WALLIS, SAMUEL A. Sermon preached at the re-opening of Pohick church, Fairfax County, Virginia, after its restoration, on Advent Sunday, Dec. 2, 1906, by the . . . rector of that church, 1881 to 1894. Alexandria, Bell, 1907.

16 p. illus. (front.) 8°. VD

4890. WHITE, WILLIAM S. Rev. William S. White, D.D., and his times. (1800-1873). An autobiography. Ed. by his son, Rev. H. M. White . . . Richmond, Va., Presbyterian committee of publication, 1891.

284 p. front. (port.) 8°. LC, V, VU
Chaps. 14-15 deal with his brief ministry in Virginia after 1865; these chapters not purely autobiographical.

4891. [WILLIAMSBURG, VA. BRUTON PARISH CHURCH] Memorials to be placed in Bruton parish church, Williamsburg, Virginia, to some of the distinguished statesmen, and parish vestrymen, of the colonial and revolutionary period, who worshipped in the building . . . [Petersburg, Va., Franklin, 1906]

30 p., 1 l., incl. front., plan. 8°. LC, NYP
Some account of the expense involved, financial support obtained, etc.

4892. ———. ———. 300th anniversary of the departure of the colony from England which landed at Jamestown, Va., May 14, 1607 . . . to be observed in Bruton parish church . . . Dec. 20th, 1906 . . . [Williamsburg, Va., 1906?]

8 p., 1 l., 8°. NYP

4893. WOMAN'S CHRISTIAN TEMPERENCE UNION OF VIRGINIA. Annual report . . . [n. p., 1883?-19—

8°. V: 20th (1902).

4894. [2509] YOUNG MEN'S CHRISTIAN ASSOCIATION. VIRGINIA. Report of the annual convention . . . Staunton, Va. [etc., 1875?-19—

See also items 2510-2511.

Secondary Works

4895. BARTON, OTTO S. Elizabeth River parish. An historical paper read at the celebration of the fiftieth anniversary of the consecration of the present building of Christ church, Norfolk, Va., on Sunday, Nov. 10th, 1878 . . . Pub. by request of the vestry. Norfolk, Virginian, 1878.

28 p. 8°.   **V, VU**

4896. BURROWS, J. L. Centennial discourse. Dover Baptist association—1783-1883. [Richmond? Va., Virginia Baptist historical society, 1883]

19 p. 8°.   **VB**

Scattered notes on the churches since 1865.

4897. BUTT, ISRAEL L. History of African Methodism in Virginia; or, Four decades in the Old Dominion, by Rev. Israel L. Butt . . . introduction by Rev. Benjamin F. Lee . . . Hampton, Va., Hampton institute press, 1908.

252 p. plate, 3 ports. (incl. front.) 8°.   **LC, V**

Contains sketches of the meetings of the Virginia conference, 1867-1906, based upon Conference *Minutes* and personal recollections; also biographical sketches of members of the conference.

4898. CARTER, ANNE J. Recollections of the early history of the Presbyterian church of Fredericksburg, Virginia. Fredericksburg, Kishpaugh, 1906.

20 p. illus. 12°.   **V**

Appendix contains list of church officers to 1906.

4899. [DANVILLE, VA. FIRST PRESBYTERIAN CHURCH. COMMITTEE ON CHURCH HISTORY] A brief history of the First Presbyterian church, published on the occasion of the 100th anniversary of its founding. 1826-1926. Danville, Townes, 1926.

61 p. illus. 8°.   **VD**

4900. DASHIELL, T. G. Digest of the proceedings of the conventions and councils in the Diocese of Virginia. Richmond, Jones, 1883.

viii, 431 p. 8°.   **BP, H, V, VD, VU, WM**

4901. [DAVIS, MRS. MARY S.] . . . Centennial celebration, First Baptist church, Lynchburg, Va. . . . [Lynchburg, Bell, 1915?]

40 p. incl. table. front. (ports.) 8°.   **V**

At head of title: 1815[-]1915.

Contains also historical sketches of other Baptist churches in Lynchburg.

4902. DREWRY, PATRICK H. The story of a church; a history of Washington street church (Methodist Episcopal church, South)

at Petersburg, Virginia, 1773-1923 . . . [Petersburg, Va.,
Plummer, *ca.* 1923]

240 p. incl. front., illus., plates. 8°.   **LC, NYP, RM, V, VU, WM**

Based to a large extent upon reliable source material, with lists of pastors and stewards, and biographical sketches. Chap. 7 contains much of
value on the period since 1865.

4903. DUNAWAY, T. S. Life and writings of Rev. Addison Hall
. . . Philadelphia, Bible & publication society [1872?]

viii, 239 p. front. (port.) 12°.   **V**

Contains a few notes on Hall's Baptist ministry after the Civil war,
until his death in 1871. His writings are of the *ante bellum* period.

4904. EARNEST, JOSEPH B. The religious development of the Negro
in Virginia . . . Charlottesville, Va., Michie, 1914.

233 p. 8°.   **H, LC, V, VU**

Thesis (Ph.D.)—University of Virginia.

An objective, unbiased monograph, based upon source material of a
controversial and factual nature, wide correspondence and personal investigation by the author; about half of the study treats the period
since 1865.

List "of names of some of the more prominent Negro ministers of
Virginia," p. 205-233.

4905. ELAM BAPTIST CHURCH, Charles City County, Va. 1810.
1910. History of Elam Baptist church, Charles City Co., Va.
Published on its one hundredth anniversary. Richmond, Va., Reformer electric print., 1910.

35 p. incl. illus., ports. 8°.   **V**

The leading events and accomplishments of this colored church since
1865 are related in chap. 5.

4906. FISHER, GEORGE D. History and reminiscences of the Monumental church, Richmond, Va., from 1814 to 1878 . . . Richmond, Whittet & Shepperson, 1880.

xvi, 508 p., 2 l. front., ports. 8°.

Based mainly upon the annual vestry and parochial reports, with long,
quotations therefrom. Material on the *post bellum* period reveals the
Episcopal church's attitude on prevailing public questions involving the
South.

4907. FITZGERALD, O. P., *et al.* Eminent Methodists. Twelve book-

lets in one book, by O. P. Fitzgerald and C. B. Galloway. Nashville, Tenn., Pub. house of M. E. church, South, 1897.

375 p. 16°.   **RM**
Contains scattered information on leaders in the M. E. church, South,
after 1865.

4908. Foster, Bertram G. A history of St. John's Protestant Episcopal church and the parish of Langley in Fairfax County, Virginia . . . [Washington] 1917.

2 p. l., 24 p. plates, ports., map. 8°.   **LC, V, VD**
Based upon recollections of church members and church records.

4909. Funkhouser, Abram P. History of the church of the United
brethren in Christ, Virginia conference, by Rev. A. P. Funkhouser
. . . comp. by Oren F. Morton . . . [Dayton, Va., Ruebush-Kieffer, 1921]

[6], 304 p. front. (port.) 8°.   **H, VD, VU**
Chap. 13: The church in recent times, by O. F. Morton; also list of
preachers, biographical sketches, relation of the church to education, and
digest of conference minutes to 1921.

4910. Gilbert, David M. The Lutheran church in Virginia, 1776-
1876. A historical discourse delivered before the Evangelical Lutheran synod of Virginia, at its 47th convention, held in Strasburg, Shenandoah County, Virginia, Aug. 3-8, 1876 . . . New
Market, Henkel, 1876.

iv, [1], 6-43, 14 p. illus. 8°.   **NYP**

4911. ———. The praises of the Lord in the story of our fathers.
A historical discourse, delivered in Grace Evangelical Lutheran
church, Winchester, Virginia, on Sunday morning, May 13, 1877,
by Rev. D. M. Gilbert, pastor. Pub. by the congregation. New
Market, Va., Henkel, 1877.

iv, [5]-33 p. 8°.   **LC, NYP**
Brief notes on the church since 1865, and on its renovation.

4912. Gill, Robert E. History of the Phoenix Bible class of High
street M. E. (South) Sunday school, Petersburg, Va. [n. p.,
1906]

110 p. plates, ports. 8°.   **V**
By the teacher of the class; based upon records and reminiscences.

4913. Goodwin, Edward L. The colonial church in Virginia, with
biographical sketches of the first six bishops of the Diocese of

Virginia, and other historical papers, together with brief biographical sketches of the colonial clergy of Virginia, by the Rev. Edward Lewis Goodwin . . . with a foreword by the Rt. Rev. William Cabell Brown . . . and introduction by the Rev. G. MacLaren Brydon. Milwaukee, Morehouse pub. co.; London, Mowbray & co. [ca. 1927]

xxiv, 342, [2] p. front., plates, ports. 8°.
Biographical sketches include the period since 1865.

4914. ———. Historical address on the thirtieth anniversary of the consecration of St. Mark's church, Richmond, Virginia. [n. p., n. d.]

15 p. 12°. **VD**
Contains a sketch of the church since 1865.

4915. ———. The Right Rev. Robert Atkinson Gibson. Memorial address delivered before the Council of the Diocese of Virginia, May 21, 1919. [Richmond] Pub. by the Diocesan council [1919?]

[12] p. front. (port.) 4°. **VD**

4916. ———, et al., comp. A report upon the parish lines of the parishes in the Diocese of Virginia (1905); revised and enlarged by G. M. Brydon, 1927.

photostat prints of typew. copy. **V**

4917. GOODWIN, WILLIAM A. Bruton church, Williamsburg, Virginia; brief historical notes, by Revd. W. A. R. Goodwin, A. M., rector of Bruton church . . . [Williamsburg] 1903.

2 p. l., [5]-16 p. front., plates. 8°. **H, LC, VD**
Includes some incidental information on the church at the end of the 19th century.

4918. ———. Historical sketch of Bruton church, Williamsburg, Virginia . . . [Petersburg, Va., Franklin] 1903.

183 p. front., illus., plates, facsim. 8°.

4919. GULLINS, W[ILLIAM] R. The heroes of the Virginia annual conference of the A. M. E. church. Smithfield, Va., 1899.

40 p. port. 8°. **LC**

4920. HALSEY, DON P., jr. Centenary of St. Paul's church, Lynchburg, Virginia: historical address . . . [n. p.] 1922.

22 p. 8°. **V**
Sketch of events during the ministry of successive rectors.

4921. HAMILTON, CHARLES H. Religious education in relation to rural life in Virginia . . . Distributed by the Virginia council of religious education . . . Bridgewater, Va. [1929]

33, [3] p. maps, tables, diagrs. 8°.   LC, V, VPI, VU
Based upon Virginia agricultural experiment station, *Bulletin,* 267 (1929) **[4922]**

4922. ――――, *et al.* The rôle of the church in rural community life in Virginia, by Charles H. Hamilton and William E. Garnett. Blacksburg, Va., Agricultural experiment station, 1929.

191 p. illus. maps, tables, diagrs. 8°. (Virginia agricultural experiment station, *Bulletin,* 267; June, 1929)   LC, V, VPI, VU
A valuable study revealing the influence of the rural church upon the intellectual and social as well as the religious life of the community.

4923. HATCHER, ELDRIDGE B. William E. Hatcher, D.D. . . . a biography by his son Eldridge B. Hatcher. Richmond, Hill [1915?]

[xiii], 696 p. illus., ports., 8°.   LC, V, VB, VU
The life of this leading Baptist clergyman as portrayed in his letters and in the recollections of his friends and associates. Contains chapters interspersed on the church in Virginia, 1866-1912.

4924. HATCHER, WILLIAM E. Life of J[eremiah] B[ell] Jeter . . . Baltimore, Wharton, 1887.

vi, 508 p. front. (port.) 8°.   V, VB
Scattered notes on religious conditions (especially on Baptists) and some reference to economic problems in Virginia during the 'seventies and 'eighties.

4925. ――――. *et al.,* ed. Sketch of the life and writings of A[bram] B[urwell] Brown, . . . professor of English in Richmond college, Virginia. Edited by Dr. and Mrs. Wm. E. Hatcher . . . Baltimore, Wharton, 1886.

x, [11]-351 p. front. (port.) 8°.   LC, V, VB, VU
Compilation of excerpts from Brown's writings and articles on his life by men with whom he was associated in work among Virginia Baptists.

4926. HEFFELFINGER, JACOB. Kecoughtan old and new; or, Three hundred years of Elizabeth City parish . . . An address, delivered July 19th, in St. John's church, Hampton, Virginia, on the occasion of the 300th anniversary of the occupation of the parish by the English. [Hampton, Va., Houston print., 1910?]

56 p. 2 plates. 8°.   LC, NYP, V
What was accomplished under successive rectors of St. John's; based mostly upon church records.

4927. History of the Ashland Baptist church, Ashland, Virginia. 1858 to 1908. [n. p., n. d.]

16 p. 16°.   VB

4928. A History of the Mennonite conference of Virginia and its work, with a brief biographical sketch of its founders and organizers as arranged and formulated by a committee appointed for this work by the conference session held at the Warwick River church, May 13th and 14th, 1910. Scottdale, Penn., Mennonite pub. house, 1910.

117 p. 8°.   H, VU
Consists mostly of summaries of conference minutes, 1860-1910.

4929. Hoge, Peyton H. Moses Drury Hoge: life and letters. By his nephew, Peyton Harrison Hoge. Richmond, Va., Presbyterian committee of publication [1899]

ix, [1] p., 1 l., 518 p. front., plates, ports., facsims. 8°.
                                               BP, LC, NYP, V, VU
Based mainly upon family papers and Presbyterian church records.

4930. Huddle, William P. History of the Hebron Lutheran church, Madison County, Virginia, from 1717 to 1907. By Rev. W. P. Huddle, pastor. New Market, Va., Henkel, 1908.

xi, 115, [1] p. front., plates, ports. 8°.   LC, NYP, V, VU
Includes notes on the church's development since 1865.

4931. Hundley, W[illiam] T., ed. History of Mattaponi Baptist church, King and Queen County, Virginia . . . Richmond, Va., Appeals press; Cumnor, Va., For sale by C. C. Vaughan [1928]

xiv, 561 p. illus., ports. (front.), facsim. 8°.   H, LC, V, VU
Based largely upon the church minute books, in part reprinted; contains also memoirs of Hundley. Detailed account of the church's development since 1865.

4932. Johnson, Asa. A history of Clay Street M. E. church (South), Richmond, Virginia. 1844-1918. Richmond, Whittet & Shepperson, 1919.

22 p. 16°.   V
Sketch of events during the various pastorates.

4933. Johnson, Thomas C. The life and letters of Robert Lewis Dabney. By Thomas Cary Johnson. Richmond, Va., Presbyterian committee of publication [1903]

xvi, 585 p. plates, 2 ports. (incl. front.) tables. 8°. H, LC, NYP, V, VU
Consists in large measure of the correspondence of this Presbyterian

clergyman; sheds much light upon religious and educational conditions, through Dabney's long connection with Hampden-Sidney college.

4934. JONES, REUBEN, *et al.* History of the Virginia Portsmouth Baptist association, from its beginning in 1791 to the division in 1906. By Rev. Reuben Jones, D.D. Revised and enlarged by Rev. George J. Hobday.

8 pts. 8°. MSS.   **VB**
Contents: 1. Preface. 2. List of original churches and comparison of past and present constitutions and rules of order. 3. History of the Association, 1791-1906. 4. History of the churches. 5. Sketches of the lives of deceased ministers who were connected with the Association. 6. Deceased prominent laymen who were connected with the Association. 7. List of ministers raised up in the Association. 8. Historical table of the places of holding meetings of the Association.
Almost purely a chronology, based upon the minutes and other records of the Association.

4935. KEARFOTT, MRS. C. P. Historical sketch of the First Baptist church, Martinsville, Virginia . . . 1884-1927. [n. p., 1927?]

23 p. illus. 12°.   **VB**
Read at the dedication, Apr. 10, 1927.

4936. KEILEY, A[NTHONY] M. Memoranda of the history of the Catholic church, Richmond, Va., since the revolution, reported to the 4th annual convention of the Catholic benevolent union of Virginia . . . Norfolk, Virginian, 1874.

20 p. 8°.   **V**
Brief notes and statistics on the period since 1865.

4937. LAFFERTY, JOHN J. Sketches and portraits of the General conference of the Methodist Episcopal church, South. Held in Richmond, Va., May, 1886. By Rev. John J. Lafferty, with an introduction by Bishop H. N. McTyeire, D.D. Richmond, Va., Christian advocate office, 1886.

4 p. l., 102 p. front., plates (ports.) 4°.   **RM, V**

4938. ———. Sketches and portraits of the Virginia conference . . . Richmond, Va., Christian advocate, 1890.

496 p. illus., plates, ports. 4°.   **RM, VU**
20th cent. ed., 1901: 7 p. l., [7]-496 p. illus.   **RM, V, VU**

4939. ———. Sketches of the Virginia conference, Methodist Episcopal church, South . . . With introduction by Bishop David S. Doggett. Richmond, Christian advocate, 1880.

viii, 208 p. ports. 4°.   **RM, V, VU**
Ed. of 1884.   **RM**

4940. LINDSAY, JOHN S. Hamilton parish, 1730-1876. An anniversary discourse, delivered by the rector, Rev. John S. Lindsay, in St. James' church, Warrenton, Va., on the eighth Sunday after Trinity, Aug. 6, 1876. Baltimore, Sherwood, 1876.

15 p. 8°.　　　　　　　　　　　　　　　　　　　　LC, V
Some account of the condition of the parish in the 'seventies.

4941. LOVING, J. W. A brief history of Lyles Baptist church, Fluvanna County, Virginia, for the 150 years of its existence. Wichita Falls, Tex., 1925.

64 p. 16°.　　　　　　　　　　　　　　　　　　　　VB

4942. LYNCHBURG, VA. FIRST BAPTIST CHURCH. Centennial celebration, First Baptist church, Lynchburg, Virginia. 1815-1915. [n. p., 1915?]

40 p. front., illus. 8°.　　　　　　　　　　　　　　　VU
Contains historical sketch of the church under its various ministers; and of the Sunday school, church societies, etc.

4943. [McKIM, RANDOLPH H.] Washington's church. An historical sketch of old Christ church, Alexandria, Virginia, together with a brief description of the centenary services therein, Nov. 20th and 21st, 1873. Alexandria, Va. [Bell] 1886.

30 p., 1 l. 8°.　　　　　　　　　　　　　　　　　BP, LC
Ed. of 1877.　　　　　　　　　　　　　　　　　　V
Ed. of 1888.　　　　　　　　　　　　　　　H, NYP, VU
Ed. of 1894.　　　　　　　　　　　　　　　　　NYP

4944. [MAGRI, FRANCIS J.] The Catholic church in the city and diocese of Richmond. By a priest of the diocese. Richmond, Va., Whittet & Shepperson [ca. 1906]

150 p. front., plates, ports. 8°.　　　　　　　　　　LC, V
The development of the church under successive bishops; based in part upon the records of the diocese.

4945. MATHEWS, JAMES T., jr. The romance of old Christ chvrch, Alexandria, Virginia . . . [Washington, D. C., Park press, ca. 1926]

31, [1] p. mounted illus. 8°.　　　　　　　　　　　LC, V

4946. [MINNIGERODE, Rev. Charles F. E.] presbyter of the Diocese of Virginia. Entered into the Paradise of God, Oct. 13, 1894. This tribute to his memory is issued Oct., 1895. New York, Pott [1895]

23 p. plates (ports.) 8°.　　　　　　　　　　　　　V

4947. MONTAGUE, ROBERT L.   Sketch of the history of Glebe Landing Baptist church of Middlesex County, Va.   Address delivered at its 150th anniversary, Sunday, Oct. 1, 1922 . . . Richmond, Richmond press, 1927.

> 47 p. front. 8°.   **V**
> Brief sketches of successive pastors and their work.

4948. MOORE, ERNEST W., comp.   History of St. John's P. E. church, Richmond, Va., erected 1741. 3d ed. . . . [Richmond, Trevvett, Christian & co., 1924]

> 46 p. illus. (port.) 16°.   **LC, V**
> 2d ed.   **NYP**
> Composed to a large extent of extracts from J. S. Moore's *Annals of Henrico parish* . . .   **[4949]**

4949. MOORE, JOSIAH S., ed.   Annals of Henrico parish, by Rt. Rev. L. W. Burton . . . History of St. John's P. E. church . . . A complete roster of the vestries, from 1741 to 1904. List of communicants, marriages, baptisms, deaths and burials, together with the inscriptions upon the tombstones.   Records of the parish of Henrico in their entirety, with their quaint and antique language and entries, from the original vestry book, from 1730 to 1773, with notes by Dr. R. A. Brock. . . . Oration of Rt. Rev. A. M. Randolph, and the address of Hon. Wm. Wirt Henry, delivered in the church on its 150th anniversary, in 1891.   Ed. and comp. by J. Staunton Moore . . . [Richmond, Williams, *ca.* 1904]

> 4 p. l., [3]-541 p., 2 l., [3]-221 p. plates, ports. 8°.
> Some of the articles have special title-pages.

4950. MOORE, L. W.   A history of the Middle district Baptist association [of Virginia], by Rev. L. W. Moore, with an introduction by Rev. W. E. Hatcher.   Richmond, Virginia Baptist historical society, 1886.

> 118 p. tables. 8°.   **V, VB**
> Scattered notes on the churches since 1865.

4951. NEWPORT NEWS, VA. TRINITY EVANGELICAL LUTHERAN CHURCH.   History of Trinity evangelical Lutheran church of Newport News, Virginia, prepared in celebration of the twenty-fifth anniversary, held Nov. 28th to Dec. 2d, 1923 . . . Newport News, Va., The Church cabinet by order of the council, 1923.

90 p., 1 l., front., plate, ports. 8°. **LC, V, WM**
Based mostly upon church records, supplemented by recollections and mss. of church members.

4952. NORFOLK, VA. FIRST PRESBYTERIAN CHURCH. The church on the Elizabeth River: A memorial of the 210th anniversary of the First Presbyterian church of Norfolk, Va., 1682-1892. By order of the session. Richmond, Whittet & Shepperson [1892?]

4 p., 4 l., [9]-80 p. front., ports. 12°. **V, VU**
Contains sketches of the pastors, sabbath schools, anniversary sermons, roster of pastors, etc.

4953. [OGDEN, MORRIS M.] A Virginia village. Historical sketch of Falls Church and the old colonial church. Falls Church, Va., Newell, 1904.

3 p. l., 112 p. incl. illus., port. 8°. **LC**
Advertisements in back.
Contains a review of economic, religious, and social conditions of the town since the Civil war.

4954. PELL, EDWARD L., ed. A hundred years of Richmond methodism, as told at the centennial celebration of 1899. Richmond, Idea pub. [1899?]

24 p. front., plates (ports.) 12°. **NYP, RM, V, VU, WM**
Considerable material on conditions in the church at the close of the century; with biographical sketches.

4955. PROTESTANT EPISCOPAL CHURCH IN THE U. S. A. VIRGINIA, Diocese of. Addresses and historical papers before the centennial council . . . at its meeting in St. Paul's and St. John's churches in Richmond, May 20-24, 1885. Philip Slaughter, comp. New York, Whittaker, 1885.

iv p., 1 l., 195 p. 8°. **V, VD, VU, WM**
Contains only meager information on the diocese since 1865.

4956. RANDOLPH, EDWIN A. The life of Rev. John Jasper, pastor of Sixth Mt. Zion Baptist church, Richmond, Va.; from his birth to the present time, with his theory on the rotation of the sun . . . Richmond, Va., Hill, 1884.

xii, 167 p. front. (port.) 12°. **LC, V**
Sheds considerable light upon religious life among the Negroes and

upon their churches after the Civil war; with excerpts from contemporary newspapers.

4957. RICHMOND, VA. SECOND BAPTIST CHURCH. Historical sketch of the Young men's society, Second Baptist church, Richmond, Virginia. [Richmond, Va., Ware & Duke, 1911]

27 p. 12°.   **LC, NYP, V**

4958. ROBERTSON, ARCHIBALD T. Life and letters of John Albert Broadus . . . Philadelphia, American Baptist publication society, 1901.

xiv, 462 p. 3 port. (incl. front.) 2 fold. facsims. 8°.
                                                          LC, V, VB, VD, VU
John A. Broadus, 1827-1895, a Baptist minister.

4959. ROBINSON, EDWARD W. Historic sketch of the Southside Rappahannock Baptist association, the Raikes Sunday school convention and Women's missionary convention [colored] [n. p., 1927?]

52 p. front. (port.) 12°.   **VB**
Sketch of officers, scope of operations, and accomplishments of the Association, 1877-1927.

4960. SEMPLE, ROBERT B., *et al.* A history of the rise and progress of the Baptists in Virginia . . . Revised and extended by G. W. Beale, Richmond, Va. [Richmond?] Pitt & Dickinson, 1894.

536 p. 12°.   **V, VB, VU**

4961. SLAUGHTER, PHILIP. A history of Bristol parish, Virginia. With genealogies of families connected therewith, and historical illustrations. 2d ed. Richmond, Randolph & English, 1879.

xx, 237 p. front. 12°.   **BP, LC, V**
Brief notes on the period since 1865.

4962. ———. History of St. George's parish, in the county of Spotsylvania, and Diocese of Virginia . . . Ed. by R. A. Brock, with a biography of the author, and a continuation, embracing the history of St. George's and Trinity churches to the present time. Richmond, Va., Randolph & English, 1890.

xix, 78 p. front. (port.) plate. 12°.

4963. ———. A history of St. Mark's parish, Culpeper County, Virginia, with notes of old churches and old families, and illus-

trations of the manners and customs of the olden time . . .
[Baltimore, Innes] 1877.

> x, 200 p. illus., fold. map. 12°.   **LC, NYP, V, VD, VU**
> Brief notes on the period since 1865.
> Ed. of 1900.   **BP**

4964. ———. The history of Truro Parish in Virginia . . . ;
ed. with notes and addenda by Rev. Edward L. Goodwin . . .
Philadelphia, Jacobs [1908]

> 2 p. l., v, 164, [5] p. front., plates, fold. plan, fold. facsim. 8°.
>   **LC, V, VD, VU, WM**
> Contains brief sketches of the later history of Pohick church and of
> Zion church during the 19th century.

4965. SMITH, HUGH C. History of the Virginia Appomattox Baptist association, 1804-1904.

> MSS.   **VB**
> Largely in the form of notes, taken from the *Minutes* of the Association.

4966. SQUIRES, WILLIAM H. The rise of the Presbyterian church
in Tidewater Virginia . . . Norfolk, Va. [1919?]

> 6, [1] p. 8°.   **BP, H, LC, V, VU**
> Brief sketch of the churches before and since 1865.

4967. STANARD, MRS. MARY M. A brief historical sketch of the
Monumental church [Richmond, Va.] 1814-1924 . . . [Richmond, 1926]

> [8] p. plates. 12°.   **V**

4968. ———. John Brockenbrough Newton, a biographical sketch.
By Mary Newton Stanard. [Richmond, Va., 1924]

> 60, [1] p. front., plates, ports. 8°.   **BP, LC, VU**
> Reprint from *Virginia churchman,* 1924 **[5002]**
> By the daughter of this Episcopalian clergyman.

4969. STICKLEY, E. E. An address entitled The rise and progress
of the Disciples of Christ in the Valley district of Virginia; delivered . . . before the Valley district convention, at Walnut Springs, Va., Aug. 16, 1899. Woodstock, Va., Grabill, 1900.

> 16 p. 8°.   **V**
> Brief notes on the churches since 1865.

4970. STONER, W. S.   St. Paul's Episcopal church, Norfolk, Virginia . . . Norfolk, Nusbaum [1903]

14 p. illus. 8°.   LC, NYP
Incidental information on the church during the latter part of the 19th century.

4971. SYDNOR, THOMAS L., ed. . . . Living epistles, the old guard in the present happy meetings . . . edited and published by T. L. Sydnor . . . Danville, Va., 1924.

xiv, 255, [10] p. illus. (ports.) 12°.   LC, NYP, V
Brief biographical sketches of participants in the meetings of the Semi-centennial session of the Virginia Baptist general association held in Richmond, June, 1873, and the Centennial session on Nov. 12, 1923.

4972. TAYLOR, FRANCES L.   History of the Episcopal church on the Eastern Shore of Virginia, 1608-1924 . . . Pub. by Church school institute of the Eastern Shore of Virginia. Cape Charles, Va., 1924.

25 p. 8°.   WM
Brief notes on the period since 1865.

4973. TAYLOR, GEORGE B.   Life and letters of Rev. George Boardman Taylor, D.D., by George Braxton Taylor. Lynchburg, Va., Bell, 1908.

4 p. l., [7]-413 p. plates, ports. (incl. front.) 8°.   LC, V, VB, VU
Some account of the Baptist church in Virginia during the latter decades of the 19th century and Taylor's part in its development; with many quotations from letters.

4974. ———.   Virginia Baptist ministers . . . [3d series] With a foreword by Rev. Wm. E. Hatcher, D.D. Lynchburg, Va., Bell, 1912.

425 p. 8°.   LC, V, VB, VU
4th series, 1913: 428 p.   LC, VB
5th series, 1915: 525 p. (With a foreword by Rev. George W. Mc-Daniel, D.D.)   LC, NYP, VB

4975. TAYLOR, J. J.   Daniel G[ray] Taylor [1821-1890], a country preacher. Louisville, Ky., Baptist book concern, 1893.

139 p. front. (port.) 8°.   VB
Brief notes on the Baptist church in Virginia after 1865.

4976. [2063] THOMPSON, S. H.   The life of John R. Moffett . . . Salem, Va., 1895.

4977. TUPPER, HENRY A. First century of the First Baptist church of Richmond, Va. Richmond, McCarthy, 1880.

360 p. front. 12°. **BP, NYP, V**
Contains sketches of the various ministers, their pastorates, and the celebration of the centenary in 1880.

4978. TURPIN, JOHN B. A brief history of the Albemarle Baptist association, . . . with an introduction by Wm. W. Landrum. Richmond, Virginia Baptist historical society [1891]

88 p. 12°. **V, VB**
Discourse delivered at the centennial session of the Association, 1891.

4979. VAN DEVANTER, J[AMES] N. History of the Augusta church from 1737 to 1900. Staunton, Va., Ross, 1900.

71, [1] p., 1 l. incl. front., illus., port. 8°. **LC, NYP, V, VU**
Material on the history of this Presbyterian church since 1865 is in the form of biographical sketches of the ministers; also a chapter on the 150th anniversary of the church.

4980. VAUGHAN, C[LEMENT] R. Memorial sketch of the late William B. Morton, ruling elder in the Church of Roanoke, in the county of Charlotte, Va. Written to aid ruling elders . . . Richmond, Va., Presbyterian committee of publication, 1886.

35 p. 16°. **V, VU**

4981. WILLIAMSON, ROBERT. A brief history of the origin and progress of the Baptists on the Eastern Shore of Virginia, embracing an account of the Accomack association and sketches of the churches . . . Baltimore, Weishampel, 1878.

91, [3] p. tables. 8°. **V, VB**

4982. WORSLEY, LIZZIE, comp. Old St. James Episcopal church, Leesburg, Virginia. 1760-1897. Leesburg, Va., Washingtonian print. [1897?]

62 p. front. 8°. **VD**
Contains notes on the church since 1865.

Periodicals

4983. ASSOCIATION record; a report of the religious work in the University of Virginia. Vol. 1-7; June, 1903-09. Pub. by the Y. M. C. A. of the University. [Charlottesville, Va., 1903-09]

7 nos. illus. 8°. annual. No more pub.
NYP: IV-VI (1906-08); **V**: I-V (1903-07); **VU**: I-VII (1903-09).

4984. ATLANTIC missionary. Vol. 1-[?] Gordonsville, Va. [1880?-?]

f°. weekly.   LC: III-IV (Jan. 11, 1882-May 23, 1883).
Earlier title: Virginia missionary.

4985. The BLUE RIDGE Baptist, vol. 1- Martinsville, Va., 1894-19—

f°. monthly.   VB: I-IV (1894-1900)— incompl.

4986. The CHRISTIAN examiner. Vol. 1- ; Jan. 1, 1868— Richmond, Va., Clemmitt [etc.] 1868—

f°. monthly, 1868-70; semi-monthly, 1871-72; weekly, 1873—
Editors: W. H. Clemmitt, 1868(?)-78; J. Z. Tyler, 1878-(?).
Organ of the Disciples of Christ.
LC: I-XI (1868-78); V: I-IV (1868-71).

4987. The DIOCESAN record. Vol. 1- [Pub. by the Diocese of southern Virginia, Protestant Episcopal church] Norfolk, Va., 1917—

illus. 4°. monthly, except Aug.
V: VIII, 10-12; IX, 1-3, 7-11; X, 1-11; XI-XIII; (1924-29). VD:
current nos. only.

4988. The IDEAL; [published by] the Young men's society of the Second Baptist church of Richmond, Va. Richmond, Va., 19—

f°. monthly.   NYP: Oct.-Dec., 1913; Mar., 14.

4989. LOTT CAREY herald; published in the interests of home and foreign [Baptist colored] missions. Vol. 1- [1908?— Richmond, Lott Carey foreign mission society [1908?—

illus. 8°. monthly.   VB: XIII, 12; XIX, 10; (1920, 26).

4990. LUTHERAN visitor. Vol. 1- Harrisonburg, Va., 1866—

8°. monthly?   V: 1866.

4991. The MISSIONARY, vol. 1-44; Sept., 1868-1911. Richmond, Va., Whittet & Shepperson, 1868-1911.

44 v. illus. 8°. monthly.   UT: I (1868); XVIII (1884/85).
Succeeded by The Missionary survey [4992]

4992. The MISSIONARY survey, vol. 1- ; Nov., 1911— Richmond, Va., Presbyterian committee of publication, 1911—

illus. 8°. monthly.
Formed by union of the Missionary and the Home mission herald,
Nov., 1911.
Editor: W. C. Smith, 1911—
LC: I-IV, VI-VII (1911-15, 16-17); UT: I-XIX (1911-29).

4993. MONUMENTAL messenger, vol. 1- Richmond, Va., Pub. by the Monumental [Episcopal] church, Richmond [1891?-19—

4°. monthly.

V: VIII-IX, XII-XXIII; XXIV, 1-6; XXX, 5; (1898-99, 1902-15, 21).

4994. OUR mountain work, in the Diocese of Virginia [Protestant Episcopal church] Charlottesville, Va., 19—

illus. 4°. monthly. **VD:** scattered nos.
W. R. Mason, ed.

4995. The PARISH leaflet, St. Mark's parish, Culpeper County, Va. No. 1- [n. p., 1913—

8°. Issued irreg. **V:** 1-5, 47-50 (1913-15, 28-29).

4996. The PARISH register. Richmond, Pub. by St. Paul's church, Richmond, Va., 19—

8°. monthly.

V: Apr., 1909; Oct., 12; Mar., 13; June, 15; Oct., 16; Jan., 20; Apr., June, 22; Nov., 23; Jan., Apr., 24; Oct., 25; summer, 28.

4997. PINE STREET Sunday school bulletin. Vol. 1- Richmond, Va. [Pub. by the Pine Street Baptist church, 1905?—

8°. monthly. **V:** VII, 6 (June, 1911).

4998. The PROTESTANT Episcopal review. Vol. 1- Published . . . [by the Episcopal seminary] Theological Seminary P. O., Fairfax Co., Va., & Richmond [1887?-19—

8°. monthly, Oct.-July.
Successor to Virginia seminary magazine.

LC: X-XIII (1896-1900). **V:** VI, 3-4; IX, 8; X, 1-2, 4, 7; XII, 5, 9; XIII, 4-5, 8; (1893, 96/97, 99-1900).

4999. The RELIGIOUS herald . . . Richmond, Va., 1828-19—

f°. weekly; Baptist.

LC: I-XIV, LXXIV-XCIX (1865-79, 1901-26); **VB:** 1828-1929.

5000. RICHMOND Christian advocate, vol. 1-38 [1867?]-1903; new ser., vol. 1- ; 1904— Richmond, Va. [Pub. by the Virginia conference, M. E. church, South, 1867?-19—

illus. (incl. ports.) f°. weekly.

Issued as Baltimore and Richmond Christian advocate, 18-?-19-?; absorbed the Southern Methodist recorder, Jan., 1904.

Editors: J. J. Lafferty, S. K. Cox, *et al.*

LC: VIII-XXVI (incompl., 1874-91); XXVII-XXXI, XXXIII-

XXXVI (1892-97, 98, 1900-01). New ser.: I-III, VI-IX (1904-12).
NYP: XXII-XXXVIII (1887-1903). New ser.: I-VI, VIII (1904-09,
11). **RM**: XXIX-XXXVIII (1894-1903). New ser.: I-XIX, XXI-
XXVII (1904-19, 21-29). **V**: new ser.: IX-XV (incompl.); XVI-
XXVII; (1911-17, 18-29).

5001. SOUTHWESTERN Episcopalian, vol. 1- [Pub. by the Diocese of
southwestern Virginia, Protestant Episcopal church]   Staunton,
Va., 1921—

illus. 4°. monthly.
V: V, 1-7, 9-12; VI, 1-6, 8-12; VII-IX; (1925/26-28/29). **VD**: current nos. only.

5002. The VIRGINIA churchman.   Pub. by the Protestant Episcopal
church, Diocese of Virginia. Vol. 1- [1885?-19—] Richmond,
Va. [1885?-19—

illus. f°.-4°. monthly, except Aug. & Sept.
Title varies: Our diocesan work, 1885?-1920; Forward, Nov., 1920-
Jan., 1922; The Virginia churchman, Feb., 1922—
V: XXIX, 2-7, 9-10 (1913); XXXVIII-XLV (1922-29). **VD**:
I-XLV (1885-1929). **VU**: XXXIX, 4-6, 10; XL, 1-2; XLIII, 7; XLIV,
2, 4. **WM**: XXXVIII-XLI.

5003. VIRGINIA men and boys; official magazine of the State executive committee, Virginia Y. M. C. A. Vol. 1- Richmond, Va.
[1910?—

8°. monthly?   **V**: IV-VI (1913-15).

For further references on Religious history, see below, Pt. VIII: *Local
History;* Pt. IX: *Biography.* See also Pt. II, § 8: *Public Welfare and
Regulation.*

PART VIII. LOCAL HISTORY

Bibliography

5004. [16] KENNEDY, JOHN P. Calendar of transcripts, including the annual report of the Dept. of archives and history . . . Richmond, 1905.

5005. [26] NEW YORK. PUBLIC LIBRARY. List of works in the New York public library relating to Virginia. [New York, 1907]

5006. [28] PATTON, JOHN S. The Byrd library. A collection of Virginiana in the library of the University of Virginia . . . Charlottesville, 1914.

5007. [34] STANARD, WILLIAM G. The Virginia archives . . . Washington, 1904.

5008. [36] SWEM, EARL G. . . . A bibliography of Virginia . . . Richmond, 1916-17.

5009. [45] VIRGINIA HISTORICAL SOCIETY. Catalogue of the manuscripts in the collection of the Virginia historical society . . . Richmond, 1901.

Secondary Works

5010. [ADDINGTON, ROBERT M.] A syllabus of Scott County history. Prepared for use in the schools. Gate City, Va., Boatright, 1915.

> 15 p. 12°.   **V**

5011. BAGBY, ALFRED. King and Queen County, Virginia . . . New York & Washington, Neale, 1908.

> 4 p. l., [7]-402 p. front., plates, ports., maps. 8°.
>
> **BP, H, LC, V, VU, WM**
>
> Events since 1865 are briefly related, with a description of the resources of the county.

5012. BELL, LANDON C. The old free state; a contribution to the history of Lunenburg County and southside Virginia . . . Richmond, Va., William Byrd press [*ca.* 1927]

> 2 v. illus. (plan) plates, maps (part fold.) facsim., diagrs. 8°.
>
> Vol. II contains a chapter on politics after the Civil war which betrays the sectional bias of the author; a general lack of historical judgment

is evident throughout the work. Includes a chapter on Dr. L. A. Boswell and his work on the aeroplane.

5013. BROCKETT, F[RANKLIN] L., *et al.* A concise history of the city of Alexandria, Va., from 1669 to 1883, with a directory of reliable business houses in the city, by F. L. Brockett and Geo. W. Rock. Alexandria, Va., Gazette, 1883.

> 140 p. front. (fold. map) 8°.   **H, LC, V**
> Advertisements, p. 74-140.

5014. BURRELL, CHARLES E. A history of Prince Edward County, Virginia, from its formation in 1753, to the present; compiled mainly from original records and personally contributed articles. With a brief sketch of the beginnings of Virginia, a summary of the history of the county seat, and a special chapter on the churches of the county . . . Richmond, Va., Williams, 1922.

> 408 p. front., plates, ports., map. 8°.   **H, LC, NYP, V, VU**
> Little discrimination is shown by the author in his handling of historical materials.

5015. BURTON, H[ARRISON] W. The history of Norfolk, Virginia. A review of important events and incidents which occurred from 1736 to 1877; also a record of personal reminiscences and political, commercial, and curious facts. By H. W. Burton, "Harry Scratch" [*pseud.*] . . . Norfolk, Va., Virginian, 1877.

> vi, 264 p. incl. front. 8°.
> A chronological account, with many clippings from newspapers; sheds some light upon economic and social conditions during the 'seventies.

5016. CARRINGTON, MRS. WIRT J. A history of Halifax County (Virginia) . . . Richmond, Va., Appeals press, 1924.

> 525 p. front., plates. 8°.   **BP, LC, NYP, V, VU, WM**
> Contains a few scattered notes on the period since 1865, mostly concerning church records.

5017. CARTMELL, THOMAS K. Shenandoah Valley pioneers and their descendants. A history of Frederick County, Virginia (illustrated) from its formation in 1738 to 1908. Comp. mainly from original records of old Frederick County, now Hampshire, Berkeley, Shenandoah, Jefferson, Hardy, Clarke, Warren, Morgan and Frederick . . . [Winchester, Va., Eddy, 1909]

> vii, 587 p. front., plates. 4°.   **BP, H, LC, NYP, V, VU**

5018. CHANDLER, JULIAN A. . . . Makers of Virginia history . . . New York, Atlanta [etc.] Silver, Burdett [1904]

347 p. front. (map) illus. 12°. (Stories of the states)

LC, V, VU, WM

Designed as a history and supplementary reader for children; only the last chapter (on W. H. Ruffner) deals to any extent with the period since 1865.

5019. CHRISTIAN, WILLIAM A. Lynchburg and its people . . . Lynchburg, Bell, 1900.

463 p. front., plates, ports. 8°.

A purely chronological history, with biographical sketches interspersed. The author cites no authorities and is by no means unbiased.

5020. ———. Richmond, her past and present. Richmond, Va., Jenkins, 1912.

618, vi p. illus., map. 8°.

Chronological history, with biographical sketches interspersed.

5021. CLEMENT, MAUD C. The history of Pittsylvania County, Virginia. Lynchburg, Va., Bell, 1929.

ix, 340 p. front., ports., fold. maps, facsim. 8°. LC, V, VU

Contains brief account of events since 1865.

5021a. COOKE, JOHN E. . . . Virginia; a history of the people . . . Boston, New York [etc.] Houghton, Mifflin, 1883.

1 p. l., xxi, 523 p. map. 12°. (American commonwealths, ed. by Horace E. Scudder)   BP, LC, NYP, V, WM
Ed. of 1884.   H, NYP, USAg, VU
Ed. of 1891.   BP, LC
Ed. of 1892.   NYP
Ed. of 1895.   BP
Ed. of 1896.   NYP
Ed. of 1897.   BP, VU
Ed. of 1899.   H
Ed. of 1903: 2 p. l., xxi, 535 p. map. 12°.   H, LC, NYP, USC, V, WM

Based upon reliable sources throughout; brief treatment of the period since 1865.

5022. DALBY, J. A. A history of Old Point Comfort and Fortress Monroe, Va., from 1608 to Jan. 1st, 1881, with sketches of Hampton normal school, National soldiers' home, and the Hygeia hotel, by J. Arnold Dalby. Norfolk, Va., Landmark, 1881.

91 p. 12°. Advertisements in back.   LC

5023. DICKINSON, SALLY B., comp. A summary of Virginia history
. . . Farmville, Va., Herald, 1910.

66 p. 8°.   LC, VU, WM
A series of chronologies under such headings as charters and constitutions, wars, religious life, education, etc.

5024. DUNN, JOSEPH B. History of Nansemond County, Va. [n. p.,
n. d.]

71 p. illus., map. 8°.   LC, NYP, V, VU
Includes a brief summary of conditions in the early 20th century, with
a description of Dismal swamp and the U. S. government's reclamation
project. Advertisements in front and back.

5025. EARLY, RUTH H. Campbell chronicles and family sketches,
embracing the history of Campbell County, Virginia, 1782-1926
. . . Lynchburg, Va., Bell, 1927.

xxii, 554 p., 1 l. illus. (incl. ports.) 8°.   LC, NYP, V, VU, WM
Material is arranged topically and poorly organized; many direct quotations from the sources.

5026. [2345] EZEKIEL, HERBERT T., et al. History of the Jews of
Richmond, 1769-1917 . . . Richmond, 1917.

See also item **2346.**

5027. GARNETT, WILLIAM C. Tidewater tales, by Professor William C. Garnett of Essex. Dunnsville, Va., Tidewater pub. [ca.
1927]

237, [2] p. front., plates, ports. 8°.   LC, V, VU
An historical and descriptive account of Essex County, Va.

5028. GOLD, THOMAS D., et al. History of Clarke County, Virginia,
and its connection with the War between the states, with illustra-
tions of colonial homes and of Confederate officers, by Thos D.
Gold; with sketches by Dr. H. C. Sommerville, Geo. H. Burwell,
Geo. B. Harrison, A. Moore, jr. and M. W. Jones. [Berryville,
Va., Hughes, ca. 1914]

337, [1] p. plates, ports. 8°.   LC, NYP, V, VU
Scattered notes on the development of the county since 1865.

5029. GOOLRICK, JOHN T. Historic Fredericksburg; the story of an
old town . . . Richmond, Va., Whittet & Shepperson [ca.
1922]

200 p. front., plates. 8°.   BP, LC, NYP, V, VU, WM
Contains laudatory sketches of "Men of modern times" and an account of the celebration of Fredericksburg's 200th anniversary (1921).

5030. HARMAN, JOHN N. Annals of Tazewell County, Virginia, from 1800 to 1922 . . . Richmond, Va., Hill, 1922-25.

2 v. fronts., illus., plates, ports. 8°. BP, LC, NYP, V, VU, WM
Vol. II: 1853-1924; material arranged topically, but undigested; needs to be checked for accuracy.

5031. HEAD, JAMES W. History and comprehensive description of Loudoun County, Virginia . . . [Washington, D. C.] Park view press [ca. 1909]

186 p. front. (port.) 8°. LC, NYP, V, VU
In 3 parts: descriptive, statistical, historical; based upon reliable sources.

5032. HILL, JUDITH P. A history of Henry County, Virginia, with biographical sketches of its most prominent citizens and genealogical histories of half a hundred of its oldest families . . . Martinsville, Va., 1925.

332 p., 1 l. plates, ports. 8°. LC, NYP, V, VU, WM
Poorly organized, without any references to sources, this history is full of information, colored by the author's pride in her people.

5033. HISTORICAL sketch of Bedford County, Virginia. 1753. 1907. [Lynchburg, Va., Bell, 1907]

121 p. front. (fold. map) illus. 8°. LC, V, WM
Economic and social conditions during the first decade of the 20th century are described in detail, but the material on the earlier history of the county is of little value.

5034. HISTORY of Virginia . . . Chicago & New York, The American historical society, 1924.

6 v. illus., plates, ports., fold. maps. 4°.
Vol. III: Virginia since 1861, by R. L. Morton. Vols. IV-VI: Virginia biography, by special staff of writers.
A scholarly, well balanced account, based mainly upon source material, treating economic, social, and educational, as well as political developments.

5035. JACK, GEORGE S., et al. History of Roanoke County, by George S. Jack; History of Roanoke city and history of the Norfolk & western railway company, by E. B. Jacobs. [Roanoke, Va., Stone, ca. 1912]

255 p. illus. (incl. ports.) 4°. LC, V, WM
Chiefly valuable for their contemporary account of conditions in industry, education, etc. The historical sections are based mainly upon secondary material.

5036. JOHNSTON, DAVID E. A history of middle New River settlements and contiguous territory . . . Huntington, W. Va., Standard print., 1906.

> 500, xxxi p. front., plates, ports. 8°.   LC, V, VU, WM
> A poorly written chronicle of events in which the author does not always distinguish between fact and fiction. The narrative centers about Mercer County, W. Va. Chap. 8 treats the period, 1866-1905.

5037. LAMB, ROBERT W., ed. Our twin cities of the nineteenth century: (Norfolk and Portsmouth) their past, present and future . . . Norfolk, Va., Barcroft, 1887-88.

> 312 p. front., illus., plates, port. 8°.   BP, LC, NYP, V
> The historical matter is presented in the form of annals. Special emphasis on the period since 1865 with a detailed picture of activities during the 'eighties. Well illustrated; advertisements, p. [201]-306.

5038. LICHTENSTEIN, GASTON. History of the Jews of Richmond. Their progress and prospects . . . Chicago, Ill., Bloch & Newman [1913]

> 32 p. illus. (incl. ports.) f°.   H, LC, V
> Special issue of the *Reform advocate,* Mar. 8, 1913.
> The Jews as a factor in Richmond's economic, political, and social life; with a description of the city.

5039. McALLISTER, HUGH M. Historical sketch of Alleghany County, Virginia, . . . published in the Clifton Forge review, Aug.-Sept., 1902, and here collected for Robert L. Parrish, esq. [with four other newspaper extracts relative to Alleghany County] Richmond, 1910.

> 18 p. front. (port.) 8°.   V

5040. McALLISTER, JEAN G. A brief history of Bath County, Virginia. Prepared . . . under the auspices of the County school board and the Board of supervisors . . . [Staunton, McClure] 1920.

> 23 p. 12°.   V

5041. McCAULEY, WILLIAM, ed. History of Roanoke County, Salem, Roanoke City, Virginia, and representative citizens. Ed. and comp. by William McCauley . . . 1734-1900. Chicago, Biographical publishing co., 1902.

> 560 (*i. e.* 556) p. incl. plates, ports., map. 4°.   LC, NYP
> Based largely upon secondary material, except the articles on contemporary conditions.

5042. MAGILL, MARY T. History of Virginia for the use of schools . . . Baltimore, Turnbull, 1873.

> viii, 258 p. incl. illus., map. 12°   LC, NYP, USE, V
> Ed. of 1884.   V
> Ed. of 1887.   H
> Ed. of 1889: Lynchburg, Bell; 374 p.   V
> Ed. of 1890.   NYP, USE
> Ed. of 1904.   NYP
> Ed. of 1914: xii, 324 p.   LC, USE, VU

The author has "adopted the familiar style of a 'story-teller';" with brief list of reference books at end.

5043. ———. Magill's first book in Virginia history . . . Lynchburg, Bell [*ca.* 1908]

> 217 p. front. (port.) illus., ports. 12°.   V

5044. ———. Stories from Virginia history, for the young . . . Prepared especially for use in schools as an introduction to the study of the history of Virginia. Lynchburg, Bell [1897]

> 217 p. incl. front. (port.) illus. 12°.   LC, NYP

5045. MAURY, DABNEY H. A young people's history of Virginia and Virginians . . . Richmond, Johnson, 1896.

> 246 p. front., illus., port. 12°.   LC, V
> Ed. of 1904: 248 p. front., illus., map, 8°.   LC, NYP
> Written with patriotic motives, the book is unbalanced, most space being given to wars and their achievements. Brief account of Virginia's condition after the Civil war.

5046. MORTON, OREN F. Annals of Bath County, Virginia . . . Staunton, Va., McClure, 1917.

> vi, 208 p. front. (fold. map) 8°.   H, LC, NYP, V, VU, WM
> Includes a brief sketch of the county in the 20th century and a chapter on Alleghany County.

5047. ———. A centennial history of Alleghany County, Virginia . . . Dayton, Va., Ruebush, 1923.

> 3 p. l., 226, [6] p. front. (double map) 8°.   H, LC, NYP, V, VU, WM
> Based upon documentary records of Alleghany and its parent counties, state archival material, questionnaires answered by citizens, and personal interviews.
> "Alleghany soldiers in the World war," p. [173]-192.

5048. ———. A handbook of Highland County and a supplement to

Pendleton and Highland history . . . Monterey, Va., Highland recorder, 1922.

[4], 109 p. plates, ports. 8°.   **H, LC, NYP, V, VU**
Description of the resources and activities of the county, and a chapter on "Pendleton and Highland in the World war."

5049. MORTON, OREN F. A history of Highland County, Virginia . . . Monterey, Va., The author [1911]

419 p. plates, 2 maps (incl. fold. front.) 8°.
Based to a large extent upon county and state records, information on the period since 1865 is scattered throughout under various topical headings.

5050. ———. A history of Rockbridge County, Virginia . . . Staunton, Va., McClure, 1920.

4 p. l., 574 p. front., plates, ports. 8°.
Some information under various topical headings to be found on the period since 1865. Pt. II is genealogical.

5051. ———. The story of Winchester in Virginia, the oldest town in the Shenandoah Valley . . . Strasburg, Va., Shenandoah pub., 1925.

336 p. incl. front. plate, ports. 8°.
Based equally upon source and secondary material, the book treats the period since 1865 in a very cursory fashion; too strictly chronological, without generalizations.

5052. NORRIS, J. E., ed. History of the lower Shenandoah Valley counties of Frederick, Berkeley, Jefferson and Clarke, their early settlement and progress to the present time; geological features; a description of their historic . . . localities; cities, towns and villages; portraits of some of the prominent men, and biographies of many of the representative citizens . . . Chicago [etc.] Warner, 1890.

viii, [9]-812 p. incl. illus., plates, ports. front. 8°.   **LC, NYP, V, VU**
Conditions since 1865 briefly treated, by counties.

5053. [NORVELL, WATKINS] Richmond, Virginia: colonial, revolutionary, confederate and the present. 1896. [Richmond, Va., Brown, 1896]

1 p. l., [40] p. illus., plate. obl. 8°.   **H, LC, NYP**
Historic spots of Richmond as seen at the end of the 19th century.

5054. [4952] [OGDEN, MORRIS M.] A Virginia village. Historical sketch of Falls Church . . . Falls Church, Va., 1904.

5055. PAGE, ROSEWELL. Hanover County in war time; a community history. [n. p., 1925?]

> 11 p. 8°.   V
> How the World war affected the county and its activities.

5056. ———. Hanover County; its history and legends . . . [Richmond, *ca.* 1926]

> 4 p. l., 153 p. front., plates, ports. 8°.   LC, NYP, V, VU, WM
> A mediocre account of the history and contemporary condition of the county, with little discrimination shown in the use of the materials at hand.

5057. PENDLETON, WILLIAM C. History of Tazewell County and southwest Virginia, 1748-1920 . . . Richmond, Va., Hill, 1920.

> xvi, 700 p. incl. front., illus., ports. 8°.   BP, LC, NYP, V, VU
> Based upon material in state and local archives; the period since 1865 is treated relatively briefly.

5058. ———. Political history of Appalachian Virginia, 1776-1927 . . . Dayton, Va., Shenandoah press, 1927.

> xiv p., 1 l., 613 p. incl. front., illus., (incl. ports.) 8°.
>   H, LC, V, VU, WM
> More than half the book is devoted to the period since 1865; virtually a political history of the state, with special reference to the attitude of the Appalachian region towards public questions. Many excerpts from speeches quoted. The author deplores the movement towards increasing centralization.

5059. PEYTON, JOHN L. History of Augusta County . . . Staunton, Va., Yost, 1882.

> vii, 387, [7] p. 8°.
> Basing his narrative only partially upon source material, the author "pretends to no originality." Material on the period since 1865 is meager and scattered.

5060. QUINN, SILVANUS J. The history of the city of Fredericksburg, Virginia. Prepared and printed by authority of the Common council thereof, under the direction of its Committee on publication . . . Richmond, Va., Hermitage press, 1908.

> 6, [2], 7-349 p. front., plates, ports. 8°.   BP, H, LC, NYP, V, VU
> Conditions of city life since 1865 briefly discussed.

5061. SCOTT, WILLIAM W. A history of Orange County, Virginia, from its formation in 1734 (o. s.) to the end of reconstruction in 1870; compiled mainly from original records, with a brief sketch

of the beginnings of Virginia, a summary of local events to 1907,
and a map . . . Richmond, Va., Waddley, 1907.

292 p. front., plates, double map. 8°.
Only a superficial treatment of the period since 1865.

5062. SMITH, MARGARET V. Virginia, 1492-1892; a brief review of
the discovery of the continent of North America, with a history of
the executives of the colony and of the commonwealth of Virginia
. . . Washington, Lowdermilk, 1893.

xxi p., 1 l., 459 p. plates, ports. (incl. front.) map. 8°.

BP, H, LC, NYP, V

Includes brief sketches of successive governors, 1865-92; also excerpts from the report of the Virginia Commissioner of agriculture on
the resources and industry of the state.

5063. SMITHEY, ROYALL B. History of Virginia; a brief text book
for schools . . . New York, Cincinnati [etc.] American book
co. [1898]

276 p. incl. front. (port.) illus. 8°.   **LC, NYP, V, VU, WM**
Ed. of [ca. 1915]: 292 p. illus., double map. 12°.   **LC**

5064. SOUTH-WEST Virginia and the Valley, historical and biographical. Illustrated. Roanoke, Va., Smith, 1892.

507 p. incl. ports. 12°.   **LC, V, VU**
Arrangement of material by cities, counties, and districts. "For much
of the historical matter the publishers are under obligations to Mr.
Thomas Bruce."

5065. STANARD, MRS. MARY N. Richmond, its people and its story
. . . Philadelphia & London, Lippincott, 1923.

xix, [1], 238, [1] p. front., plates, ports., map. facsim. 8°.
Contains 2 chapters on reconstruction and the new Richmond (after
the Civil war).

5066. STEWART, WILLIAM H. History of Norfolk County, Virginia,
and representative citizens . . . 1637-1900. Chicago, Ill., Biographical pub. co., 1902.

1042 p. illus., ports., map. 4°.   **NYP, V, VU**
Typical county history, with emphasis on political and military events
and biographical sketches.

5067. SUMMERS, LEWIS P. History of southwest Virginia, 1746-
1786, Washington County, 1777-1870 . . . Richmond, Va.,
Hill, 1903.

921 p. incl. front. (port.) illus., plate, map. 8°.
A mass of material from reliable sources, but poorly organized and

indexed; by a native of southwest Virginia who seeks to give his section its due credit. Emphasis upon political and military events, but little on the period since 1865.

5068. SYDENSTRICKER, EDGAR, *et al.* School history of Virginia, by Edgar Sydenstricker and Ammen L. Burger. Lynchburg, Va., Dulaney-Boatright, 1914.

xi, [2], 14-362 p. incl. front. (port.) illus. 12°.   **LC, V, VU, WM**
Contains "Reading references for the use of teachers," verso of p. xi.

5069. TYLER, LYON G., comp. History of Hampton and Elizabeth City County, Virginia . . . Hampton, Va., Board of Supervisors of Elizabeth City County, 1922.

56 p. 8°.   **H, LC, NYP, V, VU, WM**
Includes brief summary of "Hampton after the [Civil] war," p. 53-56.

5070. WADDELL, JOSEPH A. Annals of Augusta County, Virginia, with reminiscences illustrative of the vicissitudes of its pioneer settlers; biographical sketches . . . a diary of the war, 1861-'5, and a chapter on reconstruction . . . Richmond, Jones, 1886.

vii, 374 p. maps (incl. front.) 8°.   **BP, H, LC, V, VU**

5071. ――――. Annals of Augusta County, Virginia . . . with a supplement . . . Richmond, Va., Randolph & English, 1888.

vii, 460 p. maps (incl. front.) 8°.   **H, LC, NYP, V**
Includes a chapter on the aftermath of the Civil war (excerpts from a diary).
2d ed., rev.: Staunton, Va., Caldwell, 1902. x, 545 p.
      LC, NYP, V, WM

5072. [WALSH, GRACE] Lynchburg from 1756 to 1870. An outline for school children . . . [Lynchburg, Va., Brown-Morrison] 1924.

21 p. 16°.   **V**

5073. WAYLAND, JOHN W. A history of Rockingham County, Virginia . . . Dayton, Va., Ruebush-Elkins, 1912.

4 p. l., v-vii, [2], 10-466, [7] p. front., illus., plates, ports., maps (part fold.) facsims. 8°.
Poorly organized, a mixture of topical and chronological arrangement, with scattered notes on conditions since 1865.

5074. WAYLAND, JOHN W.   A history of Shenandoah County, Virginia   .   .   .   Strasburg, Va., Shenandoah pub. co., 1927.

> 874 p. illus. (incl. ports., maps, plan) 8°.   **H, LC, NYP, V, VU, WM**
> Material poorly organized, with no attempt at generalizations.   Events since 1865 are treated briefly, with scattered notes on churches, schools, and the press.

5075. ——.   A history of Virginia for boys and girls   .   .   .   New York, Macmillan, 1920.

> ix, 374 p. incl. front., illus. (incl. ports., maps) 12°.   **LC, V**
> Pt. VI: "Progress and promise"—Virginia since 1865, with some mention of economic life, education, and the World war.
> Ed. of 1924.   **NYP**

5076. WINGFIELD, MARSHALL.   A history of Caroline County, Virginia, from its formation in 1727 to 1924.   Compiled from original records and authoritative sources and profusely illustrated   .   .   .   to which is appended "A discourse of Virginia," by Edward Maria Wingfield   .   .   .   Richmond, Va., Trevvet Christian, 1924.

> xv, [1], 528 p. incl. front. (port.) illus. 8°.
> The material, poorly organized, covers only superficially the period since 1865.

5077. WOODS, EDGAR.   Albemarle County in Virginia; giving some account of what it was by nature, of what it was made by man, and of some of the men who made it   .   .   .   [Charlottesville, Va., Michie, 1901]

> iv, 412 p. 8°.   **BP, H, LC, NYP, V, VU**
> Resources and industry at the opening of the 20th century are described.

5078. [WRIGHT, THOMAS R.]   .   .   .   Perpetuation of local history in Virginia.   (Written for the Manufacturers' record) [Baltimore, 1907]

> 15 p. 8°.   **LC**
> Report of progress of the movement to make the county court-houses historical museums.   List of memorial portraits by counties reprinted from Wright's ms. copy.

5079. [——] comp. .   .   .   Westmoreland County, Virginia .   .   . a short chapter and bright day in its history; addresses delivered by Lawrence Washington, esq., Rev. Randolph Harrison McKim   .   .   .   and Rev. George Wm. Beale   .   .   .   at Montross, Va.,

May 3, 1910 . . . Richmond, Va., Whittet & Shepperson, 1912.

153, xi p. front., plates, ports., facsims. 8°.

H, LC, NYP, V, VU, WM

A compilation of extracts from various sources on the history and economic and social progress of Virginia, principally of Westmoreland County.

5080. YOWELL, CLAUDE L. A history of Madison County, Virginia . . . Strasburg, Va., Shenandoah pub., 1926.

203 p. incl. front. (port.) illus. 8°. H, LC, NYP, V, VU, WM

Little discrimination shown by the author in the use of source and secondary works; material on the period since 1865 is scattered throughout.

Periodicals

5081. [4633] ASSOCIATION FOR THE PRESERVATION OF VIRGINIA ANTIQUITIES. Yeare booke . . . Richmond, 1896-19—

5082. [4639] The LOWER Norfolk County Virginia antiquary . . . Vol. 1-5 . . . [n. p., 1895-1906]

5083. [4645] TYLER's quarterly historical and genealogical magazine . . . Vol. 1- Richmond, Va., 1920—

5084. [4647] The VIRGINIA historical magazine . . . Richmond, Va., 1891-92.

5085. [4654] The VIRGINIA magazine of history and biography . . . Vol. 1- Richmond [1893-19—

5086. [4028] WILLIAM AND MARY college quarterly historical magazine . . . Williamsburg, Va., 1882-19—

For further references on Local history, see above, Pt. VI, § 5: *Professional and Learned Societies.* See also Pt. IX: *Biography.*

PART IX. BIOGRAPHY

Bibliography

5087. [26] NEW YORK. PUBLIC LIBRARY. List of works in the New York public library relating to Virginia. [New York, 1907]

5088. [28] PATTON, JOHN S. The Byrd library. A collection of Virginiana in the library of the University of Virginia . . . Charlottesville, 1914.

5089. [36] SWEM, EARL G. . . . A bibliography of Virginia . . . Richmond, 1916-17.

Government Publications and Documents

5090. U. S. CONGRESS. . . . John Warwick Daniel (late a senator from Virginia) Memorial addresses. Delivered in the Senate and the House of representatives of the U. S. Proceedings in the Senate, Feb. 20, 1911. Proceedings in the House, June 24, 1911. Comp. under the direction of the Joint committee on printing. Washington [Govt.] 1911.

158 p. port. 8°. (61 Cong., 3 sess. Senate. *Doc.*, 876)   **LC, V**

5091. ——. ——. . . . Memorial addresses on the life and character of John S. Barbour (a senator from Virginia), delivered in the Senate and House of representatives, Feb. 3 and 25, 1893. Published by order of Congress. Washington, Govt., 1893.

93 p. front. (port.) 8°. (53 Cong., 2 sess. Senate. *Miscell. doc.*, 64)
LC, V
Concerning Barbour's career in law and politics in Virginia and Congress.

5092. ——. ——. Memorial addresses on the life and character of Peter J. Otey, late a representative from Virginia, delivered in the House of representatives and Senate, 57th Congress, 1st session. Washington, Govt., 1902.

100 p. front. (port.) 8°.   **LC, V**

5093. ——. ——. . . . Memorial addresses on the life and character of Richard Alsop Wise (late a representative from Virginia), delivered in the House of representatives and Senate, 56th Congress, 2d session. Washington, Govt., 1901.

51 p. port. 8°. (56 Cong., 2 sess. House. *Doc.*, 524)   **LC**

5094. ———. ———. . . . Thomas Staples Martin (late a senator from Virginia) Memorial addresses delivered in the Senate and the House of representatives of the U. S., 66th Congress. Proceedings in the Senate Apr. 10, 1920. Proceedings in the House Feb. 13, 1921. Prepared under the direction of the Joint committee on printing. Washington, Govt., 1922.

106 p. port. 8°. (66 Cong., 3 sess. Senate. *Doc.*, 425) LC

5095. ———. ———. HOUSE. . . . Francis Rives Lassiter (late a representative from Virginia) Memorial addresses delivered in the House of representatives of the U. S., 61st Congress, 2d session. Proceedings in the House, May 8, 1910. Proceedings in the Senate, Dec. 7, 1909. Comp. under the direction of the Joint committee on printing. Washington [Govt.] 1911.

44 p. port. 8°. (61 Cong., 3 sess. House. *Doc.*, 1509) LC

5096. ———. ———. SENATE. Obsequies. John S. Barbour, late a senator from the state of Virginia. In the Senate of the U. S., Monday, May 16, 1892. Washington [Govt.] 1892.

13 p. 8°. LC

5097. VIRGINIA. GENERAL ASSEMBLY. Exercises in respect to the memory of Woodrow Wilson, former president of the U. S., held in the hall of the House of delegates by the General assembly of Virginia. Wednesday, Feb. 6, 1924 . . . [n. p., William Byrd press [1924]

[22] p. ports. 4°. LC,V

5098. ———. ———. Thomas Staples Martin. [Richmond, Va., 1920]

[2] p. port. on cover. 4°. V
Resolution of the General assembly (1920) on the death of Senator Martin.

5099. ———. GOVERNOR, 1910-14 (William H. Mann). In memoriam John Warwick Daniel. Born Sept. 5, 1842, died June 29, 1910. [Proclamation by the Governor of Virginia, June 30, 1910] [n. p., 1910]

2 p. port., facsim. 4°. V

5100. ———. SECRETARY OF THE COMMONWEALTH. In memoriam. John Warwick Daniel, born Sept. 5, 1842. Died June 29, 1910. [n. p., 1910]

1 l., 1 port. 4°. NYP

Other Source Material

5101. [2377] ANDREWS, MRS. MARIETTA M. Memoirs of a poor relation . . . New York [*ca.* 1927]

5102. [1564] CLUVERIUS, THOMAS J. My life, trial and conviction. Richmond, 1887.

5103. CONWAY, MONCURE D. Autobiography, memories, and experiences of Moncure Daniel Conway. Boston & New York, Houghton Mifflin, 1904.

> 2 v. fronts., plates, ports., facsims. 8°.   **BP, H, LC, V, VU**
> Vol. II, on the period since 1865, contains only brief mention of Virginia, since most of the author's life was spent abroad.

5104. [4773] DASHIELL, T. G. A pastor's recollections . . . New York, 1875.

5105. [4777] DUNAWAY, T[HOMAS] S. Personal memoirs . . . Lynchburg, 1900.

5106. [4778] DUNN, JOSEPH B. In the service of the King; a parson's story. New York & London, 1915.

5107. EGGLESTON, GEORGE C. Recollections of a varied life . . . New York, Holt, 1910.

> viii, 354 p. front. (plate) 8°.   **BP, LC, NYP, V, VU**
> The author's career in letters and publishing, with interesting comments on contemporary literary men of Virginia and the U. S.

5108. [2782] GOODE, JOHN. Recollections of a lifetime . . . New York & Washington, 1906.   .

5109. [2798] LANGSTON, JOHN M. From the Virginia plantation to the national capital . . . Hartford, 1894.

5110. [4796] McILWAINE, RICHARD. Memories of three score years and ten . . . New York & Washington, 1908.

5111. [1335] MASSEY, JOHN E. Autobiography of John E. Massey . . . New York & Washington, 1909.

5112. [1611] MOORE, JOSIAH S. Reminiscences, letters, poetry, and miscellanies. Richmond, 1903.

5113. [2430] MOORE, SALLIE A. Memories of a long life in Virginia . . . Staunton, Va. [1920]

5114. [2816] MUNFORD, BEVERLEY B. Random recollections. [n. p., 1905]

5115. [2818] O'FERRALL, CHARLES T. Forty years of active service . . . New York & Washington, 1904.

5116. [4814] PACKARD, JOSEPH. Recollections of a long life . . . Washington, Adams, 1902.

5117. [1428] PORTER, DUVAL, ed. Men, places and things . . . [Danville] 1891.

5118. TERHUNE, MRS. MARY V. Marion Harland's autobiography; the story of a long life. New York & London, Harper's, 1910.
ix, 497 p. 8°.   **BP, LC, V, VU**
Only casual mention of Virginia, since the author's life after 1865 was spent in the North and abroad.

5119. [4890] WHITE, WILLIAM S. Rev. William S. White, D.D., and his times. (1800-1873) . . . Richmond, 1891.

Secondary Works

5120. ADAM, GRAEME M. The life of General Robert E. Lee . . . ; the life-career and military achievements of the great southern general, with a record of the campaigns of the Army of northern Virginia . . . New York, Burt [*ca.* 1905]
iv, iii-iv, 321 p. front. (port.) plates. 12°. (Burt's library of the world's best books)   **LC, NYP**
Chaps. 20 & 21 on Lee's presidency of Washington college and his influence for good will between North and South.

5121. [3348] ALDERMAN, EDWIN A., *et al.* J. L. M. Curry; a biography . . . New York & London, 1911.

5122. ALLAN, MRS. ELIZABETH (P.) The life and letters of Margaret Junkin Preston, by Elizabeth Preston Allan. Boston & New York, Houghton, Mifflin, 1903.
4 p. l., 378 p., 1 l. front. (port.) 8°.   **BP, H, LC, NYP, V, VU**
The letters from 1865 to 1897, quoted at length to show her literary interests, reveal also the status of education and literature in Virginia and the South.

5123. ANDERSON, ARCHER. Robert Edward Lee. An address delivered at the dedication of the monument to General Robert Edward Lee at Richmond, Virginia, May 29, 1890 . . . Pub. by the Lee monument association. Richmond, Jones, 1890.

45 p. 8°.   **BP, H, LC, NYP, V, VU**

5124. BAKER, RAY S. Woodrow Wilson; life and letters . . . Garden City, N. Y., Doubleday, Page, 1927—

fronts., plates, ports., facsims. 8°. (In progress)
The authoritative life of Wilson; scholarly and well written. Vol. I, chap. 5, deals with his life at the University of Virginia, 1879-80.

5125. [2382] BEALE, CYRUS W., comp. Kappa alphas in Richmond, Virginia . . . [Richmond] 1915.

5126. BEAR, HARRY. Life and character of Dr. George Fish Keesee . . . [Philadelphia, 1925]

4 p. incl. port. 8°.   **V**
Reprint from *The Dental cosmos,* July, 1925. Read before the Virginia state dental association at Staunton, Apr. 28, 1925.

5127. BEATY, JOHN O. John Esten Cooke, Virginian . . . New York, Columbia university, 1922.

viii p., 1 l., 173 p. 8°. (Columbia university studies in English and comparative literature)   **H, LC, NYP, V, VU**
Pub. also as thesis (Ph.D.)—Columbia university, 1921.
Based on mss. and printed sources. Chaps. 4-5 deal with the author's life after 1865, with an estimate of his writings.

5128. [2757] BELL, JOHN W. Memoirs of Gov. William Smith of Virginia . . . New York, 1891.

5129. BOND, CHRISTIANA. Memories of General Robert E. Lee . . . Baltimore, Norman, Remington, 1926.

4 p. 1., 11-52 p. front. (port.) plates. 12°.   **H, LC, NYP**
Reprint from *South Atlantic quarterly.*
Sheds light upon Lee's character and his influence for amity between North and South during reconstruction.

5130. BRADFORD, GAMALIEL. Lee the American . . . Boston & New York, Houghton Mifflin, 1912.

xvi, 324 p., 1 l. front., ports., facsim. 8°.
Rev. ed., 1927: xxvi, 324 p.
Chap. 11: Lee after the war.

5131. BROCK, ROBERT A. . . . Virginia and Virginians; eminent Virginians, executives of the colony of Virginia, from Sir Thomas Smyth to Lord Dunmore. Executives of the state of Virginia, from Patrick Henry to Fitzhugh Lee. Sketches of Gens. Ambrose Powell Hill, Robert E. Lee, Thos. Jonathan Jackson, Commodore Maury. By Dr. R. A. Brock, secretary of the Virginia historical society . . . With portraits and illustrations. Richmond & Toledo, Hardesty, 1888.

2 v. 8°.   BP, H, LC, V, VU, WM

5132. BRUCE, PHILIP A. . . . Robert E. Lee . . . Philadelphia, Jacobs [1907]

380 p. front. (port.) 12°. (American crisis biographies, ed. by E. P. Oberholtzer)
Chap. 11 on Lee's life after the Civil war.

5133. ———. The Virginia Plutarch . . . Chapel Hill, University of North Carolina, 1929.

2 v. fronts., plates, ports., fold. map. 8°.
Vol. II contains sketches of Robert E. Lee, Woodrow Wilson, and Walter Reed (on the period since 1865), written in the characteristic, delightful style of the author.

5134. CASKIE, JAQUELIN A. Life and letters of Matthew Fontaine Maury . . . Richmond, Va., Richmond press, 1928.

191 p. ports. (incl. front.) 8°.   H, LC, VU, WM
Brief notes on Maury's life in Virginia after the Civil war.

5135. CLARKE, PEYTON N. Old King William homes and families; an account of some of the old homesteads and families of King William County, Virginia, from its earliest settlement . . . Louisville, Morton, 1897.

4 p. l., 211 p. front. (port.) plate. 4°.   H, LC, NYP, V, VU, WM

5136. CLEMENS, WILLIAM M., ed. Famous Virginians, eminent men of the Old Dominion with date and place of birth and death . . . Pompton Lakes, N. J., Clemens, 1921.

14 p. 8°.   LC, NYP, V, VU
List of names, arranged alphabetically.

5137. COOKE, JOHN E. A life of Gen. Robert E. Lee . . . New York, Appleton, 1871.

vi, 577 p. plates, ports. (incl. front.) maps. 8°.

BP, H, LC, NYP, V, VU

Ed. of 1875.   BP
Ed. of 1883.   BP, H
Ed. of 1893: New York, Dillingham. vi, 501 p.   V
Ed. of 1899.   LC

5138. DANIELS, JOSEPHUS. The life of Woodrow Wilson, 1856-1924 . . . Philadelphia, Chicago [etc.] Winston [ca. 1924]

4 p. l., 5-381 p. front., plates, ports. 8°.

5139. DODD, WILLIAM E. Woodrow Wilson and his work . . . Garden City, N. Y., Doubleday, Page, 1920.

xiv, 369 [1] p. front. (port.) illus. (maps) 8°.

5140. [4903] DUNAWAY, T. S. Life and writings of Rev. Addison Hall . . . Philadelphia [1872?]

5141. EATON, WILLIAM D., *et al.* Woodrow Wilson, his life and work; a complete story of the life of Woodrow Wilson, teacher, historian, philosopher, and statesman, including his great speeches, letters, and messages . . . By William Dunseath Eaton and Harry C. Read . . . [Chicago, Peterson] 1919.

769 p. incl. plates, ports., plan, map, col. front. 8°.

5142. EMINENT and representative men of Virginia and the District of Columbia in the nineteenth century. With a concise historical sketch of Virginia, by Hon. William Wirt Henry, and of the District of Columbia, by Ainsworth R. Spofford . . . Madison, Wis., Brant & Fuller, 1893.

6, [9]-600 p. incl. 55 port. 4°.   LC, NYP, V, VU
The biographical sketches are mostly of professional men.

5143. [4907] FITZGERALD, O. P., *et al.* Eminent Methodists . . . Nashville, 1897.

5144. FRETZ, ABRAHAM J. A brief history of Bishop Henry Funck and other Funk pioneers, and a complete genealogical family register, with biographies of their descendants from the earliest avail-

able records to the present time. With portraits and other illustrations . . . With an introduction by John F. Funk . . .
Elkhart, Ind., Mennonite pub., 1899.

874 p. front., plates, ports. 8°. **BP, LC**

5145. GILMAN, BRADLEY. Robert E. Lee . . . New York, Macmillan, 1915.

ix, 205 p. ports. (incl. front.) plates. 12°. (True stories of great
Americans) **H, LC, NYP**
The narrative of Lee's life after the Civil war and of his services to
Washington college is enlivened by numerous incidents revealing his
character.

5146. [5029] GOOLRICK, JOHN T. Historic Fredericksburg . . .
Richmond [ca. 1922]

5147. GORDON, ARMISTEAD C. Virginian portraits; essays in biography . . . Staunton, Va., McClure, 1924.

8 p. l., 137, [7] p. 8°. **LC, NYP, V, VU, WM**
Includes sketches of W. J. Robertson, W. G. McCabe, and T. N.
Page. No authorities cited.

5148. [3923] ———. Memories and memorials of William Gordon
McCabe . . . Richmond, 1925.

5149. ———. William Gordon McCabe; a brief memoir . . .
Richmond, Old Dominion press, 1920.

11 p. front. (port.) 8°. **V, VU**

5150. [4919] GULLINS, W[ILLIAM] R. The heroes of the Virginia
annual conference of the A. M. E. church. Smithfield, Va., 1899.

5151. HALE, WILLIAM B. Woodrow Wilson; the story of his life
. . . Garden City, N. Y., Doubleday, Page, 1912.

[16], 3-233, p. front. (port.) 8°.

5152. HAMILTON, JOSEPH G., et al. The life of Robert E. Lee for
boys and girls, by J. G. de Roulhac Hamilton and Mary Thompson
Hamilton . . . Boston & New York, Houghton Mifflin, 1917.

xi p., 2 l., 209, [1] p. front., ports. 8°. **BP, LC, NYP**
Chap. 14 on Lee's work at Washington college and his influence
on the *post bellum* South.

5153. HANDY, HENRY B., ed. The social recorder of Virginia, edited
by Henry Brantly Handy; with an historical introduction by Ham-

ilton James Eckenrode, Ph.D.   Richmond, The Social recorder of
Virginia [*ca.* 1928]

xiv p., 1 l., 212 p. 8°.   **LC, NYP, V, VU**
A cyclopedia of contemporary Virginians of note; very incomplete,
though including some Virginians residing in other states.

5154. HARDESTY's historical and geographical encyclopedia . . .
Special Virginia ed. giving a history of the Virginias, biographical
sketches of eminent Virginians, written by R. A. Brock . . .
New York, Richmond [etc.] H. H. Hardesty & co., 1884.

430 p. incl. plates, maps, front. plates, ports. f°.   **LC, V**
The "History of the Virginians" (p. [305]-334) and the chapter
"Eminent Virginians" (p. [335]-392) are mainly identical with R. A.
Brock, *Virginia and Virginians* (1888) **[5131]**   Contains little material
on the period since 1865.

5155. [4923] HATCHER, ELDRIDGE B. William E. Hatcher, D.D.
. . . a biography . . . Richmond [1915?]

5156. [4924] HATCHER, WILLIAM E. Life of J[eremiah] B[ell]
Jeter . . . Baltimore, 1887.

5157. [4925] ———, *et al.* Sketch of the life and writings of
A[bram] B[urwell] Brown . . . Baltimore, 1886.

5158. [4929] HOGE, PEYTON H. Moses Drury Hoge: life and letters . . . Richmond [1899]

5159. HUNTER, ROBERT W. General Fitzhugh Lee. A speech delivered on Fitzhugh Lee day at the Jamestown exposition . . .
[n. p.] 1908.

6 p. 8°. (Clippings from Richmond *Times-Dispatch,* Jan. 5, 1908)   **V**

5160. IN memoriam. General Robert E. Lee. Ceremonies at Winchester, Va., Jan. 19, 1871. Oration by Col. F. W. M. Holliday.
Poem by Daniel B. Lucas. Winchester, Times, 1871.

60 p. 8°.   **VU**

5161. IN memoriam. Robert Lewis Dabney, born Mar. 5, 1820, died
Jan. 3, 1898 . . . Knoxville, University of Tennessee, 1899.

41 p. front. (port.) plates (ports.) 4°.   **NYP, V**

5162. IN memoriam. William Green, LL.D. Proceedings of a meeting of the bench and bar to commemorate his virtues and abilities.

Held at Richmond, Va., Nov. 18, 1880. Richmond, Randolph & English [1881]

8 p. 8°. (Reprint from *Virginia law journal,* Jan., 1881) **V**

5163. JETT, DORA C. Minor sketches of major folk and where they sleep; the old masonic burying ground, Fredericksburg, Va. . . . Richmond, Old Dominion press, 1928.

xiii, 128 p. incl. front., plates, port. 12°. **LC, V, VU**

5164. [4933] JOHNSON, THOMAS C. The life and letters of Robert Lewis Dabney . . . Richmond [1903]

5165. JOHNSTON, FREDERICK, comp. Memorials of old Virginia clerks, arranged alphabetically by counties, with complete index of names, and dates of service from 1634 to the present time . . . Lynchburg, Bell, 1888.

v, [7]-405 p. incl. facsims. ports. 8°.
Based upon court records, with many quotations therefrom.

5166. JONES, JOHN W. Life and letters of Robert Edward Lee, soldier and man . . . New York & Washington, Neale, 1906.

9, [xi]-xii, [13]-486 p. front., ports. 8°.

5167. ———. Personal reminiscences, anecdotes, and letters of Gen. Robert E. Lee . . . (Published by authority of the Lee family, and of the faculty of Washington and Lee university.) New York, Appleton, 1874.

xvi, 509 p. front., plates, ports. 8°. **BP, H, LC, NYP, V**
Ed. of 1876. **NYP**

5168. [2880] ———. Virginia's next governor, Gen. Fitzhugh Lee . . . New York [1885]

5169. KING, JOSEPH L. Dr. George William Bagby; a study of Virginian literature, 1850-1880 . . . New York, Columbia university, 1927.

ix, 193 p., 1 l. 8°.
Based on mss. and printed sources, this well written biography portrays the man in relation to his times. Chaps. 7-9 reveal the obstacles to literary work after the Civil war and the achievements of Bagby.

5170. [4937] LAFFERTY, JOHN J. Sketches and portraits of the General conference of the Methodist Episcopal church, South. Held in Richmond, Va., May, 1886 . . . Richmond, 1886.

5171. [4938] LAFFERTY, JOHN J. Sketches and portraits of the Virginia conference . . . Richmond, 1890.

See also item **4939.**

5172. LAWRENCE, DAVID. The true story of Woodrow Wilson . . . New York, Doran [*ca.* 1924]

x p., 1 l., 13-368 p. front. (port.) 8°.

5173. LEE, FITZHUGH. . . . General Lee. By Fitzhugh Lee, his nephew . . . New York, Appleton, 1894.

433 p. front. (port.) maps (2 fold.) 12°. (Great commanders, ed. by J. G. Wilson)   **BP, H, LC, NYP, V**

5174. LEE, ROBERT E. Last will and testament . . . Pub. by the Lee museum committee, Washington and Lee university, Lexington, Va. [n. p., 1928]

[4] p. facsim. 4°.   **VU**

5175. LEE, ROBERT E., jr. Recollections and letters of General Robert E. Lee. By his son, Captain Robert E. Lee. With photogravure portraits. New York, Doubleday, Page, 1904.

xii p., 1 l., 461 p. front. (port.) plates (ports) 8°.
Valuable source material on Lee's work as president of Washington and Lee university and his influence in rebuilding the South.
Ed. of 1909.   **NYP**

5176. ———. Recollections and letters of General Robert E. Lee, by his son, Captain Robert E. Lee; introduction by Gamaliel Bradford . . . concluding with new and previously unpublished material gathered by Dr. William Taylor Thom. Garden City, N. Y., Doubleday, Page, 1924.

xix, 471 p. front., plates, ports.

5177. [3926] LEE MEMORIAL FUND. Robert E. Lee, soldier, patriot, educator . . . [Philadelphia, *ca.* 1921]

5178. LEWIS, CHARLES L. Matthew Fontaine Maury, the pathfinder of the seas . . . Annapolis, U. S. naval institute, 1927.

xvii, 264 p. plates, ports. 8°.   **H, LC, VU, WM**
Based on the Maury mss. Chaps. 15 on "His last years in Virginia" portrays his work at V. M. I. and on behalf of the development of the South.

5179. LITZ, FRANCIS A. Father Tabb; a study of his life and works, with uncollected and unpublished poems . . . Baltimore, Johns Hopkins, 1923.

> 4 p. l., 303 p. front. (port.) 8°. **BP, LC, NYP, V**
> An interesting, readable study of Father Tabb's character and work, based on the Tabb mss. and a thorough understanding and appreciation of his poetry.

5180. LONG, ARMISTEAD L. Memoirs of Robert E. Lee; his military and personal history, embracing a large amount of information hitherto unpublished . . . together with incidents relating to his private life subsequent to the war, collected and edited with the assistance of Marcus J. Wright . . . New York, Philadelphia [etc.] Stoddart, 1886.

> 1 p. l., 707 p. front., illus., plates, ports., maps (3 fold.) facsim. 8°.
> **BP, H, LC, McC, NYP, V**

5181. LONG, CHARLES M. Virginia county names; two hundred and seventy years of Virginia history . . . New York & Washington, Neale, 1908.

> 207, [1] p. incl. tables. fold. map. 12°. **BP, LC, NYP, V, VU**
> Chap. 15 contains a brief description of the Jamestown exposition, 1907.

5182. McCABE, JAMES D. Life and campaigns of General Robert E. Lee . . . Atlanta, Ga., Philadelphia, Pa. [etc.] National publishing co. [1870]

> 732 p. front. (port.) fold. maps. 8°. **H, LC**
> First pub. in 1867. Contains chapters on Lee's last years and his influence for harmony between North and South. Appendix H: Report of examination of Lee by the congressional Committee on reconstruction, 1866.

5183. McKIM, RANDOLPH H. The soul of Lee, by one of his soldiers . . . New York [etc.] Longmans, Green, 1918.

> xi, 258 p. front. 8°. **BP, H, LC, NYP**
> Chap. 11 on Lee's life after the Civil war; based largely upon previous biographies.

5184. MASON, EMILY V. Popular life of Gen. Robert E. Lee . . . Dedicated by permission to Mrs. Lee. Illustrated with 17 original designs by Professor Volck . . . Baltimore, Murphy, 1872.

> xi, [13]-432 p. front. (port.) illus. plates. 12°. **H, LC, V, VU**
> Ed. of 1874. **BP, NYP**

5185. [2813] MEMORIAL of Col. John B. Baldwin, of Staunton, Virginia. [Staunton, 1874]

5186. [4494] OGDEN, ROBERT C. . . . Samuel Chapman Armstrong; a sketch . . . New York, Chicago [*ca.* 1894]

5187. PAGE, ROSEWELL. Thomas Nelson Page; a memoir of a Virginia gentleman, by his brother, Rosewell Page . . . New York, Scribner's, 1923.

> vi p., 1 l., 210 p. front. (port.) plate. 12°.
> A sympathetic biography, with quotations from Page's letters.

5188. PAGE, THOMAS N. Robert E. Lee, man and soldier . . . New York, Scribner's, 1911.

> xviii, 734 p. front. (port.) 9 maps (2 fold.) 8°.
> Based for the most part on source material. Chaps. 26-27 on Lee's life after the Civil war. An enlargement of the author's *Robert E. Lee the southerner* (1908) **[5189]**

5189. ———. Robert E. Lee the southerner . . . with portrait. New York, Scribner's, 1908.

> xiii, 312 p. front. (port.) 12°.   **BP, LC, NYP, V**
> Emphasis upon Lee the man rather than the soldier. Chaps. 16-17 on his life after the Civil war.

5190. PATTESON, SARGENT S. . . . The Supreme court of appeals of Virginia . . . Boston, 1893.

> 3 pts. 4°. (In *The Green bag,* V, 310-329, 361-373, 407-422; July-Sept., 1893)   **V, VU**
> Biographical sketches of the judges.

5191. PORTER, DUVAL. Official Virginia; a composition of sketches of the public men of Virginia at the present time. Richmond, Whittet & Shepperson, 1920.

> 208 p. front., ports. 12°.   **V, VU**
> Brief sketches of state officers and members of the House of delegates and the Senate of Virginia.

5192. [4956] RANDOLPH, EDWIN A. The life of Rev. John Jasper . . . Richmond, 1884.

5193. RILEY, FRANKLIN L., ed. General Robert E. Lee after Appomattox . . . New York, Macmillan, 1922.

> xiv p., 2 l., 250 p. front., plates, ports, 8°.
> A composite work consisting of contemporary records and letters of

alumni and faculty of Washington and Lee university who knew Lee during his presidency of the college.

5194. [2902] ROBERTSON, ALEXANDER F. Alexander Hugh Holmes Stuart, 1807-1891; a biography . . . Richmond [*ca.* 1925]

5195. [4958] ROBERTSON, ARCHIBALD T. Life and letters of John Albert Broadus . . . Philadelphia, 1901.

5196. SCOTT, MRS. LEONORA C. The life and letters of Christopher Pearse Cranch, by his daughter Leonora Cranch Scott. Boston & New York, Houghton Mifflin, 1917.

    xii, 395, [1] p. front., illus., plates, ports. 8°.   **BP, H, LC, NYP**

5197. SHEPHERD, HENRY E. Life of Robert Edward Lee . . . New York & Washington, Neale, 1906.

    280 p. front., plates, ports. 8°.   **BP, H, LC**
    A laudatory character study, dealing excessively in superlatives. Pt. 5: Lee at Lexington.

5198. SLAUGHTER, PHILIP. A brief sketch of the life of William Green, LL.D. jurist and scholar, with some personal reminiscences of him, by Philip Slaughter . . . also, a historical tract of Judge Green, and some curious letters upon the origin of the proverb, "Vox populi, vox Dei." Richmond, Jones, 1883.

    131 p. 8°.   **H, LC, V, VU**
    William Green, 1806-80, a Virginia lawyer.

5199. [3934] SMITH, WILLIAM R. Charles Lewis Cocke, founder of Hollins college . . . Boston [*ca.* 1921]

5200. [4968] STANARD, MRS. MARY N. John Brockenbrough Newton, a biographical sketch . . . [Richmond, 1924]

5201. STEWART, WILLIAM H. Virginia, 1607-1907 . . . Illustrated by Lucy Redd Wise. [Portsmouth, Va., Fiske, *ca.* 1906]

    22 l. illus. 4°.   **LC, NYP, V, VU**
    Eulogy of Virginia's famous men.

5202. [4971] SYDNOR, THOMAS L., ed. Living epistles, the old guard in the present happy meetings . . . Danville, 1924.

5203. TABB, JENNIE M. Father Tabb, his life and work; a memorial,

by his niece, Jennie Masters Tabb; introduction by Dr. Charles Alphonso Smith . . . Boston, Mass., Stratford, 1921.

2 p. l., xi, 174 p. front., plates, ports., facsims. 8°.

BP, H, LC, NYP, V

A laudatory, uncritical biography, poorly written, with many quotations from Tabb's poetry.

5204. [4502] TALBOT, MRS. EDITH (A.) Samuel Chapman Armstrong; a biographical study . . . New York, 1904.

5205. [4973] TAYLOR, GEORGE B. Life and letters of Rev. George
Boardman Taylor . . . Lynchburg, 1908.

5206. [4974] ———. Virginia Baptist ministers . . . Lynchburg, 1912.

5207. [4975] TAYLOR, J. J. Daniel G[ray] Taylor, a country
preacher . . . Louisville, 1893.

5208. [2063] THOMPSON, S. H. The life of John R. Moffett
. . . Salem, Va., 1895.

5209. THORNTON, WILLIAM M. . . . John Warwick Daniel.
Address delivered at the unveiling of Ezekiel's statue of Senator
Daniel, at Lynchburg, Va., May 26, 1915 . . . Washington,
Govt., 1915.

16 p. 8°. ([U. S.] 64 Cong., 1 sess. Senate. *Doc.,* 17)   LC, VU

5210. [4503] TOMLINSON, EVERETT T., *et al.* . . . The life
story of Samuel Chapman Armstrong . . . Philadelphia [*ca.*
1917]

5211. TRENT, WILLIAM P. Robert E. Lee . . . Boston, Small,
Maynard, 1899.

5 p. l., [ix]-xviii p., 1 l., 135 p. front. (port.) 16°. (Beacon biograph-
ies, ed. by M. A. DeWolfe Howe)
The author has "drawn freely upon the larger biographies of . . .
Lee." Pt. VII: brief sketch of Lee's life after the Civil war.

5212. TUNIS, ALLYN B., ed. Press reference book of prominent Virginians, dedicated to the Fourth estate . . . Richmond, Va.,
Virginia newspaper writers association, 1916.

93 p., 1 l., incl. illus. (ports.) plate. 4°.   LC, V
Brief biographical notes accompanying photographs.

5213. [2911] TURPIN, JOHN B. John E. Massey; a memorial address . . . Charlottesville [1904]

5214. TYLER, LYON G., ed. Encyclopedia of Virginia biography, under the editorial supervision of Lyon Gardiner Tyler . . . New York, Lewis historical pub. co., 1915.

> 5 v. fronts., ports. 4°.   **H, LC, NYP, V, VU, WM**
> In vols. I-III the biographies are arranged under various topical headings, including "prominent Virginians"; in vols. IV-V the sketches are unclassified and not even arranged alphabetically. The editor assumes no responsibility for any of the sketches.

5215. ———. Men of mark in Virginia, ideals of American life; a collection of biographies of the leading men in the state. Lyon G. Tyler . . . editor-in-chief . . . Washington, D. C., Men of mark pub. co., 1906-09.

> 5 v. ports. 8°.   **H, LC, V, VU, WM**
> Biographies of contemporary Virginians only; well edited.

5216. VALENTINE, ELIZABETH G. Dawn to twilight; work of Edward V. Valentine, by Elizabeth Gray Valentine . . . Richmond, Va., William Byrd press, 1929.

> 201 p. front., plates, ports., facsim. 8°.   **LC, V, VU**
> Contains brief sketch of the artist's life and comments on his works of art.

5217. [4980] VAUGHAN, C[LEMENT] R. Memorial sketch of the late William B. Morton . . . Richmond, 1886.

5218. [3942] WALKER, CORNELIUS. The life and correspondence of Rev. William Sparrow . . . Philadelphia, 1876.

5219. WHIPPLE, WAYNE. The heart of Lee . . . Philadelphia, Jacobs [ca. 1918]

> 224 p. front. (port.) 12°.   **H, LC, NYP**
> Chap. 8 on Lee's presidency of Washington college, with many incidents illustrating his character.

5220. WHITE, HENRY A. Robert E. Lee and the Southern confederacy, 1807-1870 . . . New York [etc.] Putnam, 1902.

> 1 p. l., xiii, 467 p. front., plates, ports., maps (part fold.) fold. facsim.
> 12°. (Heroes of the nations, ed. by E. Abbott)   **BP, H, LC**
> First published, 1897.   **NYP**
> Based upon original sources, with many quotations from letters, official documents, etc.

5221. WHITE, WILLIAM A. Woodrow Wilson, the man, his times and his task . . . Boston & New York, Houghton Mifflin, 1924.

> xviii, 527 p. front., plates, ports. 8°.

5222. WHITEHEAD, ALBERT C. Two great southerners: Jefferson Davis and Robert E. Lee . . . New York, Cincinnati [etc.] American book co. [*ca.* 1912]

> 190 p. illus. (incl. ports.) 12°.   **LC**
> Eulogistic in tone; written especially for children. Chap. 11 on Lee's presidency of Washington college.

5223. [2913] WILLIAMS, DANIEL B. A sketch of the life and times of Capt. R. A. Paul . . . Richmond [*ca.* 1885]

5224. WILLIAMSON, MRS. MARY L. The life of Gen. Robert E. Lee, for children, in easy words. Illustrated . . . Richmond, Va., Johnson [1895]

> 183 p. incl. front., illus., ports., facsims. maps. 12°.   **LC, V**
> Ed. of [1898]   **NYP**
> Includes chapters on Lee as president of Washington college and on the Lee Monument associations and memorials.

5225. ———. Life of Robert E. Lee . . . Richmond, Atlanta [etc.] Johnson [1918]

> 172 p. incl. front., illus., ports. 12°.   **LC**
> Chap. 6: The college president; chap. 8: The people's hero.

5226. [3945] WISE, JENNINGS C. Personal memoir of the life and services of Scott Shipp . . . [Lexington? Va.] 1915.

> For further references on Virginia biography, see above, Pt. VIII: *Local History.*

PART X. LITERATURE AND ART

Bibliography

5227. [6] [GORDON, ARMISTEAD C.] A bibliography of the published writings of Armistead C. Gordon, . . . 1923. [Staunton, 1923]

5228. [9] HOLT, GUY. A bibliography of the writings of James Branch Cabell . . . Philadelphia, 1924.

5229. [15] JOHNSON, MERLE D. A bibliographic check-list of the works of James Branch Cabell, 1904-1921 . . . New York, 1921.

5230. [27] NEWMAN, CAROL M. Virginia literature . . . June, 1903. [n. p., n. d.]

5231. [29] PAUL, MRS. KATHERINE S. A partial list of Virginia authors and their works . . . [n. p., 1892]

5232. [41] THOMAS, ELLA M. Virginia women in literature . . . Richmond, 1902.

5233. [50] WEGELIN, OSCAR. A bibliography of the separate writings of John Esten Cooke . . . Metuchen, N. J., 1925.

Government Publications and Documents

5234. VIRGINIA. COMMISSION ON PRESENTATION OF A COPY OF HOUDON'S STATUE OF WASHINGTON TO FRANCE. The presentation by the people of Virginia of a copy of Houdon's statue of George Washington to the people of the Republic of France. Report of the commissioners. Richmond, Bottom, 1912.

3 p. l., [3]-65 p. front., plates, ports. 8°.   **LC, V**
James Mann, chairman.

5235. ———. COMMISSION TO PRESENT TO THE UNITED KINGDOM OF GREAT BRITAIN AND IRELAND A COPY OF HOUDON'S STATUE OF GEORGE WASHINGTON. The presentation by the people of Virginia . . . Presented at Trafalgar Square, Thursday, June 30, 1921. Richmond, Bottom, 1922.

55 p. illus., ports. 8°.   **V**
Text without illustrations issued as Virginia. General assembly, 1922. House. *Doc.,* 6.

5236. VIRGINIA. STATE LIBRARY. Catalog of portraits and statuary in the Virginia State library, by Edward S. Evans, assistant librarian; John P. Kennedy, state librarian. Richmond [Bottom] 1906.

8 p. front. 8°.   **LC, NYP, V, VU**

5237. ———. ———. A list of the portraits and pieces of statuary in the Virginia State library, with biographical notes. Compiled by Earl G. Swem, assistant librarian. Richmond, Bottom, 1913.

p. [21]-43. 8°. (In its *Bulletin*, VI, 2; Apr., 1913 **[3316]**)
2d ed.: 1920. (In *ibid.*, XIII, 1-2) Preface signed: H. R. McIlwaine, state librarian.

Other Source Material

5238. ABBOTT, FRANCIS H., comp. Eight Negro songs (from Bedford County, Virginia). Ed. by Alfred J. Swan. New York, Enoch [*ca.* 1924]

47 p. f°.   **H, LC**
With one exception these are songs of amusement rather than spirituals.

5239. ART work of Richmond; published in nine parts. W. H. Parrish pub. co., 1897.

9 pts. plates. 4°.   **V**
Historical description of points of interest in Richmond; beautifully illustrated.

5240. BERNHARD, WILLIAM J. Jurgen in lino-cuts . . . [New York] Priv. print., 1926.

5 p. l., 13 col. plates. col. front. (port.) f°.   **LC**
Illustrations of J. B. Cabell's novel, *Jurgen* **[5358]**

5241. BROCK, ROBERT A. A list of the portraits in oil, engravings, etc., in the rooms of the Westmoreland club, chiefly the property of the Virginia historical society . . . Richmond, 1888.

4 p. 16°.   **V**

5242. BURLIN, MRS. NATALIE (C.) . . . Hampton series Negro folk-songs, recorded by Natalie Curtis Burlin . . . New York, Boston, Schirmer [*ca.* 1918-19]

4 v. music. 12°.   **LC, VU**
Bks. I-II: Spirituals; bks. III-IV: Work- and play-songs. For male

quartette. Each volume has a foreword; each song is accompanied by descriptive notes. Material (typewritten and autographed music) used by author in preparation of these songs is in Music division of **LC**.

5243. [4541] CONFEDERATE MEMORIAL LITERARY SOCIETY. Catalogue of the Confederate museum, of the Confederate memorial literary society . . . Richmond, 1898.

5244. [5103] CONWAY, MONCURE D. Autobiography, memories, and experiences . . . Boston & New York, 1904.

5245. DAUGHTERS OF THE AMERICAN REVOLUTION. OLD DOMINION CHAPTER. Catalogue of loan exhibition under the auspices of Old Dominion chapter, D. A. R., benefit of Virginia historical society, April, 1897. [Richmond, 1897?]

93 p. 8°. Advertisements interspersed. **LC, V, VU**

5246. DAVIS, ARTHUR K., jr. Traditional ballads of Virginia, collected under the auspices of the Virginia folk-lore society . . . Cambridge, Mass., Harvard university press, 1929.

xviii, 634 p. plates, ports., fold. map, music. 8°.
Collection of ballads begun under the direction of C. Alphonso Smith. A priceless volume of folk literature.

5247. [DAWSON, ARTHUR] Catalogue of the paintings in the John Barton Payne collection, given . . . to the commonwealth of Virginia. Richmond, 1921.

32 p. front., plates. 8°. **V**

5248. DETT, ROBERT N., ed. Religious folk-songs of the Negro as sung at Hampton institute, edited by R. Nathanial Dett . . . Hampton, Va., Hampton institute press, 1927.

xxvii, 236, [1], ii, xiii p. music. 8°. **LC, NYP**
Contains some hitherto unpublished melodies from the editor's own collection; arrangement by subject. The introduction by the editor is an enlightening exposition of the innate religious character of the Negro spirituals and their significance.

5249. EMERGENCY COMMITTEE ORGANIZED TO PROTEST AGAINST THE SUPPRESSION OF JAMES BRANCH CABELL'S "JURGEN." Jurgen and the censor; report of the Emergency committee . . . New York, Priv. print., 1920.

77 p. 8°. (Cf. item **5358**) **NYP**

5250. FENNER, THOMAS P., *et al.,* comp. Cabin and plantation songs as sung by the Hampton students, arranged by Thomas P. Fenner, Frederic G. Rathbun and Miss Bessie Cleaveland . . . 3d ed., enl. by the addition of forty-four songs . . . New York & London, Putnam, 1901.

> vi, 166 p. 8°.   LC, V, VU
> Includes a few songs "from Indian and other nationalities."
> For ed. of 1874, see Armstrong and Ludlow, *Hampton and its students,*
> p. 171 ff. **[4134]**   LC, V
> Ed. of 1880: 255 p.   LC, V
> Ed. of 1891: 127 p.   LC, V

5251. ———. Religious folk songs of the Negro as sung on plantations . . . New edit. Hampton, Va., Institute press, 1916.

> vi, 178 p. music. 8°.   H, NYP
> Arranged by the musical directors of Hampton institute from the original edition by T. P. Fenner.
> Ed. of 1924.   VU

5252. HOLT, GUY., ed. Jurgen and the law; a statement with exhibits, including the court's opinion, and the brief for the defendants on motion to direct an acquittal . . . New York, McBride, 1923.

> 78 p. 8°. (Cf. item **5358**)   LC, NYP
> People of the state of New York against Guy Holt, Robert M. McBride & co., and Robert M. McBride for having in possession with intent to sell, a book called *Jurgen,* by James Branch Cabell, in violation of section 1141 of the Penal law, concerning obscene prints and articles. In the Court of general sessions for the county of New York.

5253. KENT, CHARLES W., *et al.,* ed. The book of the Poe centenary; a record of the exercises at the University of Virginia, Jan. 16-19, 1909, in commemoration of the one hundredth birthday of Edgar Allan Poe; ed. by Charles W. Kent . . . and John S. Patton . . . [Charlottesville, Va.] University of Virginia, 1909.

> 2 p. l., 211 p. 12°.   BP, LC, V, VU

5254. ———. The unveiling of the bust of Edgar Allan Poe in the library of the University of Virginia, Oct. 7th, 1899; being an account of Poe's connection with the University of Virginia, the origin and history of the Poe memorial association . . . comp.

and ed. by Charles W. Kent . . . Lynchburg, Va., Bell [1901]

101 p. front., plates, ports., facsims. 8°.   **BP, LC, V, VU**
"The Poe library at the University of Virginia. American and English editions," p. [93]-96.

5255. LIGHTFOOT, MRS. N. M. A few minutes [of the Virginia writers club] [Richmond, William Byrd press, 1923?]

22 p. 8°.   **V**

5256. MASSIE, EUGENE C. Virginia, a state song: words and music by Eugene C. Massie. Arlington, N. J., Ashmall [*ca.* 1914]

[2] p. 8°.   **V**

5257. METCALF, JOHN C., *et al.,* ed. The enchanted years; a book of contemporary verse, dedicated by poets of Great Britain and America to the University of Virginia on the occasion of its one hundredth anniversary; ed. by John Calvin Metcalf . . . and James Southall Wilson . . . New York, Harcourt, Brace, 1921.

ix, 157 p. 12°.   **BP, LC, NYP, V, VU**
The University, its founder and distinguished men are the subjects of many of the poems.

5258. **[1611]** MOORE, JOSIAH S. Reminiscences, letters, poetry, and miscellanies . . . Richmond, 1903.

5259. [NEGRO melodies] A collection of Negro melodies. Rough draft; fragments of words and music. Songs and hymns ranging from *ante bellum* days to 1912. Also a sketch of the Negro as an originator of poetry and song. Presented by Charles M. Wallace, jr., of Richmond.

1 book of music; and loose leaves.   **V**

5260. **[2455]** [POLLOCK, GEORGE F.] Story of the sylvan play and Indian pageant . . . [Washington, D. C., 1916]

5261. **[1634]** RICHMOND ART CLUB. Art movement. [n. p., 1914]

5262. ———. Catalogue . . . [Richmond? 19—
8°.   **V**: 1912-14.

5263. RICHMOND ART CLUB. Richmond in 1915; [a calendar with] drawings by members of the Art club of Richmond. [n. p., 1914]

7 l. illus. 4°.   V

5264. [RICHMOND] EVERY MONDAY CLUB. Year book . . . [Richmond, Va., 19—

16°.   V: 1909/10, 18/19, 27/28.
A literary club.

5265. [RICHMOND] WOMAN'S CLUB. Catalog, loan exhibition of old portraits, Woman's club auditorium, Feb. 21-26, 1927. [Richmond, Dietz, 1927]

[7] p. 8°.   V

5266. [5118] TERHUNE, MRS. MARY V. Marion Harland's autobiography . . . New York & London, 1910.

5267. VALENTINE MUSEUM, Richmond, Va. Annual report . . . [Richmond, 1899?-19—

8°. **BP**: 1899; **LC, NYP**: 1899-1900, 02, 04, 06; **USAg**: 1906; **V**: 1899-1900, 02, 06.

5268. ———. A collection of rare books, early engravings, original sketches, illuminations, china, tapestries, casts from ancient, renaissance, and modern marbles and bronzes, an extensive exhibit of archeological objects, especially of the aborigines of Virginia and North Carolina. [Richmond, 1898?]

96 p. illus. obl. 24°.   NYP, V

5269. ———. [A description and catalog of] the Valentine museum, Eleventh and Clay streets, Richmond, Virginia. [Richmond, 1910]

96 p. 16°.   V

5270. ———. Description of casts in the Valentine museum from original marbles and bronzes. Richmond, Va., 1898.

120, iv p. plates. 8°.   LC, NYP, V
The catalogue of a compilation from well-known writers, collected chiefly by Mary M. P. Newton.

5271. ———. . . . Opening address of the president, act of incorporation, constitution, by-laws and catalogue of collections. Nov. 21, 1898. Richmond, Va., 1898.

58 p. front., plates. 8°.   LC, NYP, V, VU

5272. ———. Report of the exploration of the Hayes' Creek Mound, Rockbridge County, Va. [explored Sept., 1901, by Edward P. Valentine, for the Valentine museum, Richmond, Va.] Richmond, Va., Valentine museum [1903]

1 p. l., 6 plates., diagr. 4°. LC, NYP, V
Description of Indian mound and its contents.

5273. VIRGINIA FOLK-LORE SOCIETY. . . . Bulletin, no. 1- ; 1913— [Charlottesville, 1913?—

12°. Report year ends Dec. 1.
H: 2-12 (1914-24); LC: 12 (1924); NYP: 9, 12 (1921, 24); V: 1-5, 7-12 (1913-17, 19-24); VU: 1-12 (1913-24).

5274. ———. Popular ballads of Virginia, collected by the Virginia folk-lore society under the direction of the late Professor C. Alphonso Smith. Copied at the expense of the Child memorial fund from the manuscripts edited by Professor Arthur Kyle Davis, jr., 1926.

826 p. typew. f°. (Cf. item **5246**) H

5275. VIRGINIA LEAGUE OF FINE ARTS AND HANDICRAFTS, Atelier, Va. [Report] [n. p., 19—

8°. V: 1921-22.

5276. WASHINGTON AND LEE UNIVERSITY. Catalogue of the G. W. C. Lee collection of oil paintings. [n. p., n. d.]

[6] p. port. 8°. H

5277. YOUNG WOMAN'S LITERARY CLUB, Ashland, Va. [Program . . . n. p., 1908?—

16°. V: 1909/10, 11/12, 14/15.

Works of Virginia Men of Letters[1]

5278. ALLMOND, MARCUS B. (1851- ?) Agricola; an idyl. Louisville, Morton, 1885.

16 p. 24°. LC

5279. ———. Estelle; an idyl of old Virginia. Louisville, Morton, 1884.

54 numb. l. 16°. H, LC, NYP
Ed. of 1896: 3 p. l., 9-56 numb. l. front., plate. 12°. LC, V, VU

---

1. Not including biographies, histories, sermons, and travelogues of other states and countries.

5280. ALLMOND, MARCUS B. Fairfax, my lord; a narrative poem. Louisville, The author, 1892.

> 4 p. l., 128 p. front. (port.) illus. 12°.   **H, LC, VU**
> 2d ed.: 1892.   **LC**

5281. AMIS, MRS. E. H. Camping on the Blue Ridge near the "Lick Log" tunnel . . . Richmond, Va., Presbyterian committee of publication [1896]

> 106 p. front., plates. 12°.   **LC, V**

5282. ANDREWS, MRS. MARIETTA M. (1869-19) The cross triumphant; a pageant of the church in England and America . . . [Washington, D. C., Columbian, 1921]

> 28 p. 8°.   **LC**

5283. ———. Out of the dust; verses . . . New York, Dutton, 1920.

> x p., 1 l., 91 p. incl. front., illus. 8°.   **LC**

5284. ———. Songs of a mother; a book of verses. New York, Dutton [ca. 1917]

> 79 p. incl. front., illus. 12°.   **LC**

5285. ———. The voice of the wildflowers; a fantasy. [Washington, D. C., ca. 1922]

> 12 p. 8°.   **LC**

5286. BACON, SUSIE L. Of many moods. By Bona. [pseud.] Richmond, Va. [1886]

> [3]-18 p. f°.   **LC**

5287. ———. A siren's son. Chicago, Kerr, 1895.

> 192 p. 8°.   **LC**

5288. BAGBY, GEORGE W. (1828-83) Meekins's twinses, a perduck-shun uv Mozis Addums [pseud.] Richmun, Westun, Jonsun & kumpny, 1887.

> 16 p. 8°.   **H, LC, V, VU**

5289. ———. The old Virginia gentleman, and other sketches; ed. with an introduction by Thomas Nelson Page. New York, Scribner's, 1910.

> xxix, [1], 312 p. front. (port.) 8°.   **BP, LC, V, VU**
> Ed. of 1911.   **H, NYP**

5290. ———. Original letters of Mozis Addums to Billy Ivvins. New and rev. ed., with introduction and notes. Richmond, Clemmitt & Jones, 1878.

118 p. 17 x 14 cm. (First pub., 1857) H, LC, V

5291. ———. Selections from the miscellaneous writings of Dr. George W. Bagby. Richmond, Va., Whittet & Shepperson, 1884-85.

2 v. front., port. 8°.

5292. ———. . . . . What I did with my fifty millions. By Moses Adams [*pseud.*] Ed. from posthumous ms. of Caesar Maurice. Philadelphia, Lippincott, 1874.

128 p. 12°.

5293. [BARNUM], MRS. FRANCES C. (BAYLOR) (1848-1920) Behind the Blue Ridge. A homely narrative. Philadelphia, Lippincott, 1887.

313 p. 12°. LC, NYP, V

5294. ———. Claudia Hyde, a novel. Boston & New York, Houghton Mifflin, 1894.

442 p. 12°. LC, NYP, VU
Ed. of 1895. VU

5295. ———. A Georgian bungalow. Boston & New York, Houghton Mifflin, 1900.

iv, 121 p. front., plates. 8°. LC, NYP

5296. ———. Juan and Juanita. Boston, Ticknor, 1888.

276 p. incl. illus., plates. front. 8°. LC, V
Ed. of 1900. VU
Ed. of 1915. BP
Ed. of 1926: Boston, Houghton Mifflin. 5 p. l., 300 p. LC

5297. ———. The ladder of fortune. Boston & New York, Houghton Mifflin, 1899.

2 p. l., 352 p. 12°. LC, NYP, V, VU

5298. ———. Miss Nina Barrow. New York, Century, 1897.

4 p. l., 243 p. front. 12°. LC, VU

5299. [BARNUM], MRS. FRANCES C. (BAYLOR) On both sides. A novel. Philadelphia, Lippincott [1886]

478 p. 12°.   H, LC, NYP, V, VU
Ed. of 1887.   LC
Ed. of 1893.   NYP
Ed. of 1895.   NYP

5300. ———. A shocking example, and other sketches. Philadelphia, Lippincott, 1889.

364 p. 12°.   LC, NYP, V

5301. BARTLEY, JAMES A. (1830- ?) New poems. Charlottesville, Va., Jeffersonian, 1883.

48 p. 14½ x 9½ cm.   BP, LC

5302. ———. Poems. Charlottesville, Jeffersonian, 1882.

95, [1] p. 8°.   H, LC, V, VU

5303. ———. Virginia: with other poems. [Charlottesville, Jeffersonian, 1883]

32 p. 8°.   LC

5304. BEALE, MRS. MARIE T. (1849- ?) Jack O'Doon; a novel. New York, Holt, 1894.

1 p. l., 277 p. front. 16 x 10 cm.   LC

5305. BLACKWELL, JAMES D. The poetical works of James De Ruyter Blackwell. In three volumes. New York, Hale, 1879-84.

2 v. 12°. No more pub.   BP, H, LC, NYP, VU

5306. BLAIR, LOUISA C., et al. Nathaniel Bacon, a play in four acts. By Louisa Coleman Blair and Robert F. Williams. Richmond, Va., Hermitage, 1907.

3 p. l., [5]-96 p. front., plates. 8°.   LC, V

5307. BOISSEAU, STERLING. Scenes of childhood. A poem. Richmond, Va., Whittet & Shepperson [ca. 1909]

[12] p. illus. 12°.   V

5308. ———. The Union movement, and other poems. Richmond, Jenkins [ca. 1913]

47 p. illus., front. 12°.   LC

5309. BOONE, HENRY B. The career triumphant. New York, Appleton, 1903.

    vi, 279 p. 12°.   **H, LC, NYP, VU**

5310. ———, *et al.* Eastover court house; a novel, by H. B. Boone and Kenneth Brown. New York & London, Harper, 1901.

    3 p. l., 317 p. 12°.   **H, LC, NYP, V, VU**

5311. ———. The Redfields succession; a novel, by H. B. Boone and Kenneth Brown. New York & London, Harper, 1903.

    3 p. l., 318 p. 12°.   **LC, NYP, V**

5312. BOSHER, MRS. KATE L. (1865-19) "Bobbie." Richmond, Va., Johnson, 1899.

    134 p. incl. front., illus., plate. 8°.   **LC, V**
    Ed. of [*ca.* 1905]: Philadelphia, Altemus. 128 p.   **L:C**

5313. ———. His friend Miss McFarlane; a novel. New York & London, Harper [1919]

    3 p. l., 377 p. front. 12°.   **LC, V, VU**

5314. ———. The house of happiness. New York & London, Harper, 1913.

    4 p. l., 7-304 p. col. front. 12°.   **LC, NYP, V, VU**

5315. ———. How it happened. New York & London, Harper, 1914.

    3 p. l., 163 p. front., plate. 12°.   **LC, V**

5316. ———. Kitty Canary; a novel. New York & London, Harper [1918]

    3 p. l., 189 p. col. front. 12°.   **LC, V**

5317. ———. The man in lonely land. New York & London, Harper, 1912.

    4 p. l., 181 p. front. 12°.   **LC, V**

5318. ———. Mary Cary "frequently Martha." New York & London, Harper, 1910.

    4 p. l., 167 p. col. front. 12°.   **H, LC, NYP, V, VU**

5319. ———. Miss Gibbie Gault; a story. New York & London, Harper, 1911.

    4 p. l., 325 p. front. 12°.   **LC, NYP, V, VU**

5320. BOSHER, MRS. KATE L.   People like that; a novel.   New York
& London, Harper [1916]
  2 p. l., 299 p. front., plate. 12°.   LC, NYP, VU

5321. ———.   When love is love; a novel.   New York & Washington, Neale, 1904.
  318 p. 8°.   LC

5322. BOUVE, MRS. PAULINE C.   Lamp-light fairy tales and other
stories . . .   New York, Grosset & Dunlap [*ca.* 1923]
  4 p. l., 321 p. col. front., illus. 8°.   LC

5323. ———.   Tales of the Mayflower children . . .   Boston,
Jones [1927]
  xiv, 280 p. col. front., plate. 8°.   LC

5324. ———.   Their shadows before; a story of the Southampton
insurrection.   Boston, Small, Maynard, 1899.
  3 p. l., [3]-202 p. 12°.   LC

5325. BOWERS, CHARLES W.   Newspaper waste basket, and other
poems.   Highland Springs, Va., 1906.
  47 p. 16°.   V

5326. BOYD, MRS. LUCINDA (R.)   The sorrows of Nancy.   Richmond, Flanhart, 1899.
  95 p. front. 12°.   LC, V, VU

5327. BRECKINRIDGE, MRS. JULIA A.   In dead earnest.   New York,
Smith, 1878.
  239 p. 12°.   A novel.   LC, V

5328. BROADDUS, ANNIE M. (1867-97)   Poems.   [n. p., n. d.]
  152 p. front. (port.) 12°.   V
  C. A. Rominger, ed.

5329. BRUCE, PHILIP A. (1856-19   )   Pocahontas and other sonnets.   Norfolk, Va., 1912.
  2 p. l., xxx p. 12°.   H, LC, NYP, V, VU

5330. BRUCE, T. SEDDON, jr.   Maggie O'Leary, and other poems.
[Richmond, Va.? 1908?]
  ·39 p. 16°.   V

5331. BRUCE, WILLIAM C. (1860-19) Below the James; a plantation sketch. New York, Neale, 1918.

157 p. front. 12°.   **H, LC, V, VU**
Ed. of 1927.   **BP, V**

5332. ———. Selections from the speeches, addresses, and political writings of William Cabell Bruce. Baltimore, Sun, 1927.

2 p. l., [3]-292 p. front. (port.) 8°.   **LC, V, VU**

5333. BRYAN, EMMA L. 1860-1865. A romance of the Valley of Virginia. [Harrisonburg, Va., Taliaferro, *ca.* 1892]

228 p. 8°.   **H, LC, NYP**

5334. BRYCE, CLARENCE A. Kitty Dixon, belle of the South Anna; a wee bit of love and war. [Richmond, Va., "Southern clinic" press, 1907]

4 p. l., [7]-102 p. front., plates. 16°.   **LC, V**
"A Jamestown-year souvenir of 'old Virginia'."

5335. ———. "Ups and downs" of a Virginia doctor. By his life-long and personal friend, Clarence A. Bryce, M.D. Ashland, Va., Ashland print., 1904.

4 p. l., 137 p. plates. 12°.   **LC, V**

5336. BUCKLEY, RICHARD W. The last of the Houghtons, a novel. New York & Washington, Neale, 1907.

280 p. 12°.   **LC**

5337. BURGWYN, COLLINSON P. The Huguenot lovers; a tale of the Old Dominion. Richmond, Pub. by the author, 1889.

4 p. l., 219 p. 12°.   **BP, H, LC, NYP, V**

5338. ———. The lost diamond. A play in one scene and one tableau. Richmond, Randolph, 1894.

23 p. 8°.   **H, V**

5339. CABELL, ISA C. Seen from the saddle . . . with an introduction by Charles Dudley Warner. New York, Harper, 1893.

vi, 161 p. front. 16°. (Harper's black & white series)   **BP, LC, V**

5340. CABELL, JAMES B. (1879-19) Beyond life; dizain des demiurges. New York, McBride, 1919.

4 p. l., 366 p. 12°.   **H, LC, NYP, V, VU**
Ed. of 1921.   **LC**
Ed. of 1924.   **BP**

5341. CABELL, JAMES B. The certain hour (Dizain des poëtes). New York, McBride, 1916.

253 p. 8°.   **LC, NYP**
Ed. of 1920.   **LC, V, VU**
Ed. of 1923.   **BP**

5342. ———. Chivalry. New York & London, Harper, 1909.

vi p., 3 1., 223, [1] p. col. front., col. plates. 8°.   **LC, NYP, V, VU**

5343. ———. Chivalry; dizain des reines . . . with an introduction by Burton Rascoe . . . [Rev. & enl.] New York, McBride, 1921.

xv, 281 p. illus. 8°.   **LC, V**
Ed. of 1926.   **BP, LC**

5344. ———. The cords of vanity. New York, Doubleday, Page, 1909.

xx, 341 p. col. front. 8°.   **BP, LC, VU**

5345. ———. The cords of vanity; a comedy of shirking . . . with an introduction by Wilson Follett. New York, McBride, 1920.

9 p. 1., 330 p. 12°.   **H, LC, NYP, V**

5346. ———. The cream of the jest; a comedy of evasions. New York, McBride, 1917.

xv, 280 p. incl. front. 8°.   **LC, NYP, V**
Ed. of 1921.   **LC**
Ed. of 1924.   **VU**
Ed. of 1927: with introduction by Harold Ward. . . . xviii p., 2
1., 3-243 p. front., illus., plates. 8°.   **BP, H, LC**

5347. ———. Domnei; a comedy of woman-worship. New York, McBride, 1920.

viii, 218 p. 8°.   **LC, NYP, V, VU**
Ed. of 1925.   **BP**

5348. ———. The eagle's shadow. New York, Doubleday, Page, 1904.

xi, 256 p. front., plates. 8°.   **BP, LC, NYP, V**

5349. ———. The eagle's shadow; a comedy of purse-strings, with an introduction by Edwin Björkman. [Rev. ed.] New York, McBride, 1923.

xv, 280 p. 8°.   **LC, V, VU**

5350. ——. Figures of earth; a comedy of appearances. New York, McBride, 1921.

xvi, 356 p. 8°.   BP, H, LC, NYP, V
Ed. of 1924.   VU
Ed. of 1925: xxi, 274 p. illus., plates.   H, LC, NYP

5351. ——. From the hidden way, being 75 adaptations in verse. New York, McBride, 1916.

187 p. 8°.   BP, LC, NYP

5352. ——. From the hidden way, dizain des échoes. New York, McBride, 1924.

x, 212 p. 8°   LC, V, VU
Ed. of 1925.   BP

5353. ——. Gallantry; an 18th century dizain in ten comedies with an afterpiece. New York & London, Harper, 1907.

6 p. l., 3-333, [1] p. col. front., col. plates. 8°.   LC, NYP, V, VU

5354. ——. Gallantry: Dizain des fêtes galantes . . . with an introduction by Louis Untermeyer. New York, McBride, 1922.

xxii, 342 p. 8°.   BP, H, LC, NYP, V

5355. ——. The high place: a comedy of disenchantment. New York, McBride, 1923.

viii p., 2 l., 312 p. front., illus., plates. 8°.   LC
Ed. of 1923: viii, 312 p. 8°.   H, LC, NYP, V, VU

5356. ——. The jewel merchants; a comedy in one act. New York, McBride, 1921.

63 p. 8°.   BP, LC, NYP, V

5357. ——. The judging of Jurgen. Chicago, Bookfellows, 1920.

13, [1] p. 8°.   BP, LC, V

5358. ——. Jurgen; a comedy of justice. New York, McBride, 1919.

8 p. l., 9-368 p. 8°.   LC, V, VU
Ed. of 1921: London, John Lane. With introduction by Hugh Wal-
pole. xvii, 325, [2] p. illus., plates. 8°.   BP, LC
Ed. of 1922.   H, LC, V
Ed. of 1923.   LC

5359. CABELL, JAMES B. The line of love: Dizain des mariages. New York & London, Harper, 1905.

290 p. 8°.   **LC, NYP, V, VU**
Ed. of 1921: New York, McBride. With an introduction by H. L. Mencken. xv, 261 p. 8°.   **BP, LC, V**
Ed. of 1926.   **LC**

5360. ———. The lineage of Lichfield; an essay in eugenics. New York, McBride, 1922.

4 p. l., 7-46 p. 8°.   **BP, LC, NYP, V**

5361. ———. The majors and their marriages. Richmond, Hill [1915]

4 p. l., 13-188 p. 8°.   **BP, LC, NYP, V**

5362. ———. The music from behind the moon; an epitome. New York, John Day, 1926.

5 p. l., 3-54 p., 1 l. incl. front., plates, 4°.   **LC, NYP, V**

5363. ———. The rivet in grandfather's neck; a comedy of limitations. New York, McBride, 1915.

368 p. 8°.   **LC, V**
Ed. of 1920.   **NYP**
Ed. of 1921.   **H, LC, VU**

5364. ———. The silver stallion; a comedy of redemption. New York, McBride, 1926.

4 p. l., vii-xii p., 2 l., 3-358 p. 8°.   **BP, H, LC, V, VU**
Ed. of [1928]: xxv, [1], 359 p. front., illus., plates. 8°.   **LC**

5365. ———. Something about Eve; a comedy of fig-leaves. New York, McBride, 1927.

ix p., 2 l., 3-364 p. 8°.   **H, LC, V**

5366. ———. The soul of Melicent. New York, Stokes [1913]

5 p. l., 3-216 p. col. front., col. plates. 8°.   **LC, V**

5367. ———. Straws and prayer-books; dizain des diversions. New York, McBride, 1924.

5 p. l., 3-302 p. 8°.   **BP, LC, NYP, V**

5368. ———. Taboo; a legend retold from the Dirghic of Saevius Nicanor, with prolegomena, notes, and a preliminary memoir. New York, McBride, 1921.

40 p. 8°.   **LC, V**

5369. ———. The way of Ecben. New York, McBride, 1929.

209 p. illus. 8°.   LC

5370. ———. The white robe, a saint's summary. New York, Mc-Bride [1928]

[95] p. incl. plates. 4°.   LC, V

5371. CALDWELL, MRS. WILLIE W. (1860-19) Donald McElroy, Scotch Irishman. Philadelphia, Jacobs [ca. 1918]

351 p. front., plate. 8°.   LC

5372. ———. The tie that binds; a story of the North and the South. Franklin, O., Editor pub. co., 1895.

111 p. 16°.   LC
Ed. of 1904.   VU

5373. CAPLON, MILTON. Some class. A book of funny laughs. Richmond, Va., Caplon print. [19-?]

32 p. 16°.   V

5374. CARRINGTON, MARY C. Pilgrim paths. Cedar Rapids, Ia., Torch press [ca. 1929]

95 p. 12°. Poems.   LC, VU

5375. CARTER, WILLIAM P. Echoes from the glen in divers keys. New York, Grafton [1904]

x, 138 p. front. (port.) 16°.   LC, NYP, VU

5376. CASTLEMAN, VIRGINIA C. (1864-19) Between whiles; a war tramp's musings. [Washington, D. C., Sheiry, ca. 1919]

28 p. 8°. Poems.   LC

5377. ———. A child of the covenant. Milwaukee, Young churchman, 1894.

220 p. front. 12°.   LC

5378. ———. Pocahontas; a poem. New York, Broadway [ca. 1907]

4 p. l., ii, 44 p. front. (port.) 8°.   LC, V, VU

5379. ———. Roger of Fairfield. New York & Washington, Neale, 1906.

269 p. front., plate. 12°.   LC, NYP, V

5380. CHESTERMAN, EVAN R. The bobcat of Jump Mountain, by Elliott Whitney [*pseud.*] illustrated by Harry W. Armstrong. Chicago, Reilly & Lee [*ca.* 1920]

224 p. front. 8°. (The boy's big game series)   LC, V

5381. ———. The crazy elk of Terrapin swamp . . . Chicago, Reilly & Lee [1921]

224 p. front. 8°. (The boy's big game series)   V

5382. ———. The lady dragon of Dancing Point . . . Chicago, Reilly & Lee [*ca.* 1922]

256 p. incl. front. 8°. (The boy's big game series)   LC, V

5383. ———. Things mundane, as observed by . . . Evan R. Chesterman. New York, Neale, 1912.

152 p. 12°.   LC, V

5384. CHRISTIAN, WILLIAM A. Marah; a story of old Virginia. Richmond, Jenkins, 1903.

386 p. front., plate. 12°.   LC, V

5385. CLARK, EMILY. Stuffed peacocks. New York & London, Knopf, 1927.

5 p. l., 3-227 p. front., plates. 12°.   BP, LC, NYP, V, VU

5386. CLARKSON, HENRY M. (1835-1915) Songs of love and war. Manassas, Va., Manassas journal, 1898.

2 p. l., 158 p. port. 12°.   LC, V, VU
2d ed.: vii, 9-198 p. front. (port.) 8°.   LC, V

5387. CLAYTOR, GRAHAM (1852-?) Among the hills: or, Scenes in Piedmont Virginia, and other poems. Richmond, Va., Randolph & English, 1886.

4 p. l., 11-94 p. 18 x 14 cm.   H, LC, V, VU

5388. ———. Otterdale: or, Pen pictures of farm life, and other poems. Richmond, Randolph & English, 1885.

72 p. front. 18 x 14 cm.   H, LC, NYP, V, VU

5389. ———. Pleasant Waters: a story of southern life and character. Philadelphia, Lippincott, 1888.

215 p. 12°.   LC, NYP

5390. ———. Wheat and tares. A novel. Philadelphia, Lippincott, 1889.

    2 p. l., 7-273 p. 12°.   **LC, NYP**

5391. COLEMAN, CHARLES W. (1862-19) Westward, ho! [a poem, pub. by the Association for the preservation of Virginia antiquities] [Richmond, 1913]

    p. 23-24. 14 x 18 cm. (See item **4527**)

5392. CONWAY, MONCURE D. (1832-1907) Moncure D. Conway; addresses and reprints, 1850-1907; published and unpublished works representing the literary and philosophical life of the author. Boston & New York, Houghton Mifflin, 1909.

    xv, 444 p., 1 l. front. (port.) 8°.

5393. ———. Consequences. London, Scott [1875]

    15 p. 12°.   **H, LC, NYP**

5394. ———. The criminal's ascension; a discourse given Mar. 2d, 1879. [London, Waterlow, 1879]

    20 p. 16°.   **LC**

5395. ———. Earthward pilgrimage. New York, Holt, 1870.

    2 p. l., x, [2], [19]-406 p. 8°.   **BP, NYP**
    Ed. of 1874.   **H, V, VU**

5396. ———. Idols and ideals, with an essay on Christianity. New York, Holt, 1877.

    2 p. l., 214, 137 p. 12°.   **BP, H, LC, NYP**

5397. ———. My pilgrimage to the wise men of the East. Boston & New York, Houghton Mifflin, 1906.

    viii p., 1 l., 416 p. front., plates, ports., facsims. 8°.

        BP, H, LC, NYP, VU

5398. ———. A necklace of stories. London, Chatto & Windus, 1880.

    viii, 206 p., 1 l. incl. illus., plates. 12°.   **BP, LC**

5399. ———. Pine and palm, a novel. New York, Holt, 1887.

    2 p. l., 348 p. 12°.   **LC, NYP, V**

5400. ———. Prisons of air. New York, Lovell [*ca.* 1891]

    270 p. 12°.   **LC, V**

5401. CONWAY, MONCURE D. The wandering Jew. New York, Holt, 1881.

4 p. l., [3]-292 p. 12°.   **BP, H, LC, NYP**

5402. COOKE, JOHN E. (1830-86) Beatrice Hallam. A novel. New York, Dillingham [n. d.]

[13]-332 p. 12°.   **LC, V, VU**

5403. ———. Bonnybel Vane. Embracing the history of Henry St. John, gentleman. New York, Harper, 1883.

xv, [17]-503 p. 12°.   **BP, H, LC**

First pub. in 1859 as *Henry St. John.*

5404. ———. Canolles: the fortunes of a partisan of '81. Detroit, Smith, 1877.

313 p. 12°.

5405. ———. Captain Ralph. A sequel to Beatrice Hallam. New York, Dillingham [n. d.]

[3]-282 p. 12°.   **LC, V, VU**

5406. ———. Col. Ross of Piedmont. A novel. New York, Dillingham [188-?]

245 p. 12°.   **LC, NYP, V, VU**

5407. ———. Doctor Vandyke. A novel. New York, Appleton, 1872.

142 p. front., plates. 8°.   **H, LC, NYP, V, VU**

5408. ———. Fairfax; or, The master of Greenway court. A chronicle of the valley of the Shenandoah. New York, Carleton; London, Low, 1868.

vii, [9]-405 p. 12°.   **H, LC, NYP, V**

5409. ———. . . . . Fanchette. By one of her admirers. Boston, Osgood, 1883.

iv, 369 p. 12°.   **LC, NYP**

5410. ———. Hammer and rapier. New York, Dillingham [*ca.* 1898]

2 p. l., 11-307 p. 12°.
Ed. of [*ca.* 1870]   **BP, H, NYP, VU**
Ed. of 1888.   **V**

5411. ———. The heir of Gaymount: a novel. New York, Van Evrie, Horton, 1870.

91 p. 8°.   **LC, NYP**

5412. ———. Her majesty the queen. A novel. New York, Dillingham, 1901.

v, 7-330 p. 12°.   **LC, V, VU**
Ed. of 1873.   **H, VU**
Ed. of 1895.   **NYP**

5413. ———. Hilt to hilt. From the mss. of Colonel Surry of Eagle's Nest. New York, Dillingham [ca. 1896]

2 p. l., [2]-270 p. 12°.   **LC, V, VU**
Ed. of 1869.   **BP, H, NYP, VU**

5414. ———. Justin Harley: a romance of old Virginia. New York, Boston [etc.] To-day print., 1874.

301 p. front., plates. 12°.   **LC, VU**

5415. ———. Justin Harley: a romance of old Virginia. Philadelphia, Claxton, Ramsen & Haffelfinger, 1875.

301 p. front., plates. 12°.   **NYP, V**

5416. ———. Leather and silk. New York, Dillingham [n. d.]

408 p. 12°.   **LC, V, VU**

5417. ———. Lord Fairfax; or, The master of Greenway court. New York, Dillingham, 1892.

1 p. l., [9]-405 p. 12°.   **LC, VU**
Ed. of 1888.   **NYP**
Ed. of 1896.   **LC, V**

5418. ———. The Maurice mystery. New York, Appleton, 1885.

245 p. 12°.   **H, LC, NYP, VU**

5419. ———. Miss Bonnybel. New York, Dillingham [n. d.]

[xi]-503 p. 12°.   **LC, V, VU**

5420. ———. Mr. Grantley's idea. New York, Harper, 1879.

1 p. l., [7]-154 p. 16°. (Harper's half-hour series, CIII)   **LC, VU**

5421. ———. Mohun; or, The last days of Lee and his paladins. Final memoirs of a staff officer serving in Virginia. From the

mss. of Col. Surry of Eagle's Nest. [*pseud.*] New York, Huntington, 1869.

509 p. plates. 12°.   **BP, LC, NYP, V, VU**
Ed. of 1889.   **NYP, VU**
Ed. of [*ca.* 1896]   **LC, V**

5422. COOKE, JOHN E. My lady Pokahontas. A true relation of
Virginia. Writ by Anas Todkill, puritan and pilgrim. [*pseud.*]
With notes by John Esten Cooke. Boston, Houghton Mifflin, 1885.
vi, 190 p. 12°.

5423. ———. Out of the foam. A novel. New York, Carleton
[etc.] 1871.

viii, 9-340 p. 12°.   **H, LC, VU**
Ed. of [*ca.* 1900]: N. Y., Dillingham.   **LC, V**

5424. ———. Pretty Mrs. Gaston, and other stories. New York,
Judd [*ca.* 1874]

288 p. incl. front. 12°.   **H, LC, VU**

5425. ———. Professor Pressensee, materialist and inventor: a
story. New York, Harper, 1878.

1 p. l., [7]-133 p. 16°.   **H, LC, NYP, VU**

5426. ———. Surry of Eagle's Nest; or, The memoirs of a staff
officer serving in Virginia, ed. from the mss. of Col. Surry . . .
New York, Huntington, 1869.

2 p. l., [9]-484 p. front., plates. 12°.   **LC, VU**
Ed. of 1866.   **BP, NYP**
Ed. of 1894.   **H, LC**
Ed. of 1898.   **V**

5427. ———. The Virginia Bohemians; a novel. New York, Harper, 1880.

1 p. l., [7]-233 p. 8°.   **BP, LC, NYP, VU**

5428. ———. The Virginia comedians; or, Old days in the Old Dominion. New York, Appleton, 1883.

2 v. in 1. 12°. (First pub., 1854)   **H, LC, NYP, V**

5429. ———. Westbrooke Hall. A novel. New York, Dillingham,
1891.

viii, [9]-340 p. 12°.   **V**

5430. COOPER, CHARLES W. . . . The musings of Myron. New Market, Va., Henkel, 1880.

50 p. 8°. **V, VU**

Poems, a few of which were written after 1865.

5431. COTTEN, SALLIE S. The white doe; the fate of Virginia Dare, an Indian legend. Philadelphia, Lippincott, 1901.

3 p. l., 5-89 p. front., plates, map. 8°.

5432. CRANCH, CHRISTOPHER P. (1813-92) Ariel and Caliban, with other poems. Boston & New York, Houghton Mifflin, 1887.

vi, 232 p. 12°. **BP, H, LC, NYP**

5433. ———. The bird and the bell. Boston, Osgood, 1866.

xiii, 327 p. 8°. **LC**

5434. ———. The bird and the bell, with other poems. Boston, Osgood, 1875.

x p., 2 l., 317, [9] p. 12°. **BP, H, LC, NYP, VU**
Ed. of 1890. **BP**

5435. ———. The last of the huggermuggers; a giant story. Boston, Lee & Shepard, 1889.

iv, 70 p. plate, illus. 12°. **NYP**

5436. ———. Satan: a libretto. Boston, Roberts, 1874.

2 p. l., [5]-36 p. 16°. **BP, H, LC**

5437. DABNEY, VIRGINIUS (1835-94) Gold that did not glitter. A novel. Philadelphia, Lippincott, 1889.

254 p. 12°. **LC, V, VU**

5438. ———. The story of Don Miff, as told by his friend John Bouche Whacker. A symphony of life. 2d edit. Philadelphia, Lippincott, 1886.

492 p. 4 plates. 8°.

5439. DAINGERFIELD, MRS. NETTIE G. (1844-19) Frescati, a page from Virginia history. New York & Washington, Neale, 1909.

71 p. 12°. **LC, NYP, V, VU**

5440. ———. Our mammy, and other sketches. Lexington, Ky., 1906.

5 p. l., 11-143 p. front., plate. 8°. **LC, V**

5441. DAINGERFIELD, MRS. NETTIE G. That dear old sword [a story] Richmond, Presbyterian committee of publication [1903]

99 p. front., plate. 8°.   **BP, LC, V**

5442. DANDRIDGE, DANSKE. Joy, and other poems. New York & London, 1888.

vi, 110 p. 16°.   **LC**
Ed. of 1900: x, 206 p. 12°.   **LC, V**   ·

5443. ———. Rose Brake; poems . . . New York, Putnam, 1890.

vi, 110 p. 16°.   **LC**

5444. DAVIS, DANIEL W. Idle moments; containing Emancipation and other poems . . . with an introduction by Hon. John H. Smythe, LL.B., ex-U. S. minister to Liberia. Baltimore, The educator of Morgan college print., 1895.

81 p. plates, port. 16°.   **LC, V**

5445. ———. Weh down souf, and other poems. Cleveland, Helman-Taylor, 1897.

vi, 7-136 p. front., plate. 12°.   **LC, V**

5446. DAVIS, MARY D. She waited patiently. Lynchburg, Bell, 1900.

270 p. 12°. A novel.   **LC, V**

5447. [DAY, MRS. W. C.] The blended flags. [Danville, Va., Dance, *ca.* 1898]

46 p. 8°. Poems.   **V, VU**

5448. DE JARNETTE, MRS. EVELYN M. Ole Virginny yarns. Vol. 1, no. 1; Jan., 1893. Portsmouth, Va., Whitehurst [1893]

43 p. 8°.   **V**

5449. DOWNING, MRS. FRANCES M. (1835-94) Nameless. A novel. Raleigh, N. C., Smith, 1865.

2 p. 1., viii, [9]-232 p. 12°.   **LC**

5450. ———. Pluto: being the sad story and lamentable fate of the fair Minthe. Raleigh, Nichols, Gorman & Neathery, 1867.

35 p. 8°. Poems.   **LC**

5451. DUKE, RICHARD T. Colonial Virginia; a poem delivered . . . at a meeting of the Society of colonial dames of Virginia in Richmond, Va., Apr. 18, 1899. [Richmond? 1899]

4 l. 8°. **LC, V, VU**

5452. ———. In my library, and other poems . . . with foreword by Armistead C. Gordon. Charlottesville, Michie, 1927.

viii, 64 p. front. (port.) 12°. **LC, NYP, V, VU**

5453. EGGLESTON, GEORGE C. (1839-1911) American war ballads and lyrics. New York & London, Putnam [1889?]

2 v. in 1. front., illus. 12°. **H, LC, NYP, V, VU**

5454. ———. The bale marked circle X; a blockade-running adventure. Boston, Lothrop [1902]

376 p. front., plate. 8°. **BP, LC**

5455. ———. The big brother; a story of Indian war. New York, Putnam, 1875.

182 p. front., plate. 8°. **H, LC, NYP**
Ed. of 1887. **NYP**
Ed. of 1890. **V**
Ed. of 1899. **VU**

5456. ———. Blind alleys; a novel of nowadays. Boston, Lothrop, Lee & Shepard [1906]

2 p. l., [3]-414 p. front., plate. 8°. **LC**

5457. ———. Camp Venture; a story of the Virginia mountains. Boston, Lothrop [ca. 1901]

4 p. l., 11-401 p. front., plate. 12°. **LC, V, VU**

5458. ———. A captain in the ranks, a romance of affairs. New York, Barnes, 1904.

x, 337 p., col. front. 12°. **BP, LC, V, VU**

5459. ———. Captain Sam; or, The boy scouts of 1814. New York, Putnam, 1876.

2 p. l., [7]-212 p. plates. 8°. **LC**
Ed. of 1889. **V**
Ed. of 1899. **VU**

5460. ———. A Carolina cavalier; a romance of the American revolution. Boston, Lothrop [ca. 1901]

448 p. incl. front. plate. 12°. **LC, V**

5461. Eggleston, George C.   A daughter of the South, a war's-end romance.   Boston, Lothrop [1905]

v, 403 p. front., plate. 8°.   H, LC, NYP, VU

5462. ———.   Dorothy South; a love story of Virginia just before the war.   Boston, Lothrop [1902]

453 p. front., plate. 12°.   LC, NYP, VU

5463. ———.   Evelyn Byrd.   Boston, Lothrop [1904]

438 p. incl. map, front. plate. 8°.   BP, LC, V, VU

5464. ———.   Irene of the mountains; a romance of old Virginia.   Boston, Lothrop, Lee & Shepard [1909]

3 p. l., 347 p. front., plate. 8°.   LC, V

5465. ———.   Jack Shelby; a story of the Indiana backwoods.   Boston, Lothrop, Lee & Shepard [1906]

viii p., 1 l., 338 p. incl. front., plate. 12°.   LC, NYP

5466. ———.   Joe Lambert's ferry . . .   With other stories of the frontier and early settlers.   Boston, Lothrop [*ca.* 1883]

[150] p. front., plate. 12°.   LC

5467. ———.   Juggernaut; a veiled record.   New York, Fords, Howard & Hulbert, 1891.

2 p. l., 343 p. 12°.   LC, NYP, VU
Ed. of [1903]:   Boston, Lothrop.   V

5468. ———.   The last of the flatboats; a story of the Mississippi and its interesting family of rivers.   Boston, Lothrop [*ca.* 1900]

382 p. front., plate, map. 12°.   LC, NYP

5469. ———.   Long Knives; the story of how they won the West.   Boston, Lothrop, Lee & Shepard [1907]

2 p. l., [iii], 2 p., 1 l., 393 p. front., plate. 12°.   LC

5470. ———.   Love is the sum of it all; a plantation romance.   Boston, Lothrop, Lee & Shepard [1907]

5 p. l., 387 p. front., plate. 8°.   LC

5471. ———.   A man of honor.   New York, Judd [*ca.* 1873]

3 p. l., 9-222 p. front., illus. 12°.   H, LC, NYP

5472. ——. The master of Warlock; a Virginia war story. Boston, Lothrop [1903]

    5 p. l., 11-433 p. front., plate. 8°.   **BP, LC, NYP, V**

5473. ——. Red Eagle and the wars with the Creek Indians of Alabama. New York, Dodd, Mead [1878]

    346 p. 12°.   **BP, NYP, V**
    Ed. of 1890.   **NYP**

5474. ——. Running the river; a story of adventure and success. New York, Barnes, 1904.

    vi p., 1 l., 295 p. front., illus., plates. 12°.   **LC**

5475. ——. The signal boys; or, Captain Sam's company. New York, Putnam, 1878.

    2 p. l., 218 p. front. (map) plate. 8°.   **LC**
    Ed. of 1890.   **V**
    Ed. of 1898.   **VU**

5476. ——. Southern soldier stories. New York, London, Macmillan, 1898.

    xi, 251 p. plates (incl. front.) 12°.

5477. ——. Two gentlemen of Virginia; a novel of the old régime in the Old Dominion. Boston, Lothrop, Lee & Shepard [1908]

    5 p. l., 456 p. front., plates. 8°.   **LC, VU**

5478. ——. The Warrens of Virginia, a novel . . . founded on the play by William C. De Mille. New York, Dillingham [ca. 1908]

    344 p. front., plate. 8°.   **LC, V**

5479. ——. Westover of Wanalah; a story of love and life in old Virginia. Boston, Lothrop, Lee & Shepard [1910]

    vi p., 1 l., 451 p. front., plates. 12°.   **LC, NYP, VU**

5480. ——. What happened at Quasi; the story of a Carolina cruise. Boston, Lothrop, Lee & Shepard [1911]

    6 p. l., 368 p. front., plate. 12°.   **LC**

5481. ——. The wreck of the Red Bird; a story of the Carolina coast. New York, Putnam, 1882.

    vii, 216 p. plates. (incl. front.) 8°.   **LC**
    Ed. of 1891.   **V**
    Ed. of 1898.   **VU**
    Ed. of 1903.   **LC**

5482. EGGLESTON, JOSEPH W. Tuckahoe; an old-fashioned story of an old-fashioned people. New York & Washington, Neale, 1903.

x, 305 p. front., plate. 12°.   LC, V, VU

5483. EGGLESTON, RICHARD B. Kitty Knight, by Ralph Conkley [*pseud.*] Richmond, Va., Whittet & Shepperson, 1913.

313 p. incl. front. 12°.   A novel.   LC, V

5484. [ELLETT, ANDREW L.] Virginia, by an absent Virginian . . . Jamestown edit. . . . Newport News, Willett, Patton & Lee [1907?]

[31] p. illus., ports. 8°.   A poem.   LC, VU

5485. EWELL, ALICE M. (1860-19) The heart of old Virginia; with illustrations by Sue Berkeley Alrich. New York & Washington, Neale, 1907.

27 l. illus. 8°.   A poem.   H, LC, V

5486. FARRAR, FERDINANDO R. Rip van Winkle, or the Virginian that slept ten years: a lecture . . . Delivered more than 60 times . . . Richmond, Nye, 1869.

18 p. 8°.   LC, NYP, V

5487. FERGUSON, MRS. EMMA H. Courage and loyalty, a novel. Cincinnati, Editor pub., 1898.

3 p. l., 195 p. 12°.   LC, V

5488. FESTETITS, MRS. KATE N. (1837-?) Doris Selwyn; or a girl's influence. Philadelphia, American Baptist publication society [*ca.* 1887]

3 p. l., 5-335 p. front., plates. 12°.   LC

5489. ———. Eunice and Laura; or, The right use of prayer. Philadelphia, Amer. Baptist pub. soc. [*ca.* 1885]

3 p. l., 5-320 p. front., plates. 12°.   LC

5490. ———. Florry Forrester; or, Three dreadful days. Philadelphia, Amer. Baptist pub. soc. [*ca.* 1886]

2 p. l., 3-320 p. front., plates. 12°.   LC

5491. ———. The flower mission, and what grew out of it. Philadelphia, New York, Amer. Baptist pub. soc. [*ca.* 1879]

viii, 9-224 p. incl. front. plates. 12°.   LC

5492. ———. From post to pillar. Philadelphia, Amer. Baptist pub. soc. [*ca.* 1889]

   3 p. l., 5-304 p. front., plates. 12°.   **LC**

5493. ———. In mother's place; or, The Jay family. Philadelphia, New York, Amer. Baptist pub. soc. [*ca.* 1879]

   385 p. front., plates. 12°.   **LC**

5494. ———. Irma. The little musician. Philadelphia, Amer. Baptist pub. soc. [*ca.* 1885]

   2 p. l., 3-249 p. front., plates. 12°.   **LC**

5495. ———. Leslie Rossiter: what she was born for. Philadelphia, Amer. Baptist pub. soc. [*ca.* 1891]

   3 p. l., 5-318 p. front., plates. 12°.   **LC**

5496. ———. The old academy; how the church was rebuilt. Philadelphia, Amer. Baptist pub. soc. [*ca.* 1890]

   3 p. l., 5-288 p. front., plates. 12°.   **LC**

5497. ———. Picnics and parties; or, Aunt Sally's experiences. Philadelphia, Amer. Baptist pub. soc. [*ca.* 1880]

   224 p. front., plates. 12°.   **LC**

5498. ———. Stephen Hardee. Philadelphia, Amer. Baptist pub. soc. [*ca.* 1897]

   279 p. front., plates. 12°.   **LC**

5499. ———. "That horrid Sarah." Philadelphia, Amer. Baptist pub. soc. [*ca.* 1879]

   2 p. l., 3-206 p. front., plates. 12°.   **LC**

5500. FIREY, SAMUEL M. (1835-19) Poems. Roanoke, Hammond, 1904.

   282, [2] p. front. (port.) 16°.   **H, LC, NYP, VU**

5501. FLEMING, LUCY R. Alice Withrow; or, The summer at home. New York, Crowell, 1886.

   241 p. front. 12°.   **LC, V**

5502. FLOYD, NICHOLAS J. (1828-?) The last of the cavaliers; or, The phantom peril. A historical romance. New York, Broadway [*ca.* 1904]

   xi p., 1 l., 427 p. front. (port.) plates. 12°.   **V**

5503. FLOYD, NICHOLAS J. Thorns in the flesh. (A romance of the war and Ku-Klux periods) A voice of vindication from the South in answer to "A fool's errand" [1] and other slanders. Philadelphia, New York, Hubbard, 1884.

> 607 p. incl. illus., plates, ports., front. 8°.   **LC, V**
> Ed. of 1886.   **H**

5504. FOSDICK, GERTRUDE C. Out of Bohemia. A story of Paris student life. New York, Richmond print., 1894.

> 3 p. l., 236 p. front., illus., 12°.   **LC, V**

5505. FOWLKES, MARY E. D. Poems by Hyde Fowlkes. [Burkeville, Va.] New York, Cosmopolitan, 1911.

> 82 p. 12°.   **LC, V**

5506. FRITH, GILBERT R. Ode to Virginia. Richmond, Va., West, Johnston, 1885.

> 18 p. illus. 12°.   **LC, NYP, V**

5507. GARBER, MRS. VIRGINIA A. The Armistead family, 1635-1910. Richmond, Whittet & Shepperson, 1910.

> 319 p. col. front., illus. 8°.   **LC, NYP, V**

5508. ———. Pocahontas. New York, Broadway pub. [*ca.* 1906]

> 4 p. l., iii, 39 p. col. front. (port.) illus., map. 8°.   **LC, NYP, V, VU**

5509. GARDENER, HELEN H.[2] (1858-1925) Facts and fictions of life. Boston, Arena, 1895.

> 301 p. port. 12°.   **NYP**

5510. ———. Is this your son, my lord? a novel. Boston, Arena, 1890.

> 2 p. l., 257 p. front. (port.) 8°.   **LC**

5511. ———. Men, women and gods, and other lectures. New York, Truth seeker co. [1885]

> 2 p. l., viii-xiv, 174 p. 8°.   **NYP**

5512. ———. Pray you, sir, whose daughter? Boston, Arena, 1892.

> x, 183 p. 12°.   **BP, NYP**

---

1. Cf. item **2330**.
2. Author's full name: Helen Hamilton (Chenoweth) Gardener; later, Mrs. Smart.

5513. ———. Pulpit, pew and cradle. New York, Truth seeker co. [1892]

  30 p. 12°.   **H, NYP**

5514. ———. Pushed by unseen hands. Boston, Arena [1890]

  303 p. 12°.   **NYP**

5515. ———. A thoughtless yes. New York, Belford [*ca.* 1890]

  231 p. 8°.   **LC, NYP**

5516. ———. An unofficial patriot. Boston, Arena, 1894.

  3 p. l., 351 p. front. (port.) 8°.   **BP, H, LC, NYP**

5517. [GARNETT, JUDITH L.] (1862-?) Who? which? and what? By X. Q. C. Richmond, Va., West, Johnston, 1885.

  1 p. l., [9]-77 p. 12°.   **V**

5518. GLASGOW, ELLEN A. (1874-19) The ancient law. New York, Doubleday, Page, 1908.

  viii, 485 p. 8°.   **H, LC, NYP, V, VU**

5519. ———. Barren ground. Garden City, N. Y., Doubleday, Page, 1925.

  3 p. l., 3-511 p. 8°.   **H, LC, NYP, V, VU**

5520. ———. The battleground. New York, Doubleday, Page, 1902.

  viii, 512 p. front., plates. 8°.   **H, LC, NYP, V, VU**
  Ed. of 1903.   **BP**
  Ed. of 1905.   **V**

5521. ———. The builders. Garden City, N. Y., Doubleday, Page, 1919.

  vi, 379 p. 8°.   **LC, NYP, V, VU**

5522. ———. The deliverance; a romance of the Virginia tobacco fields. New York, Doubleday, Page, 1904.

  vii, 543 p. front., plates. 8°.   **H, LC, NYP, V, VU**

5523. ———. The descendant; a novel. New York, Harper, 1897.

  3 p. l., 276 p. 12°.   **H, LC, VU**
  Eds. of 1900 & 1905.   **V**

5524. ———. The freeman, and other poems. New York, Doubleday, Page, 1902.

  3 p. l., 9-56 p. 8°.

5525. GLASGOW, ELLEN A. Life and Gabriella; the story of a woman's courage. New York, Doubleday, Page, 1916.

4 p. l., 3-529 p. front. 8°.   LC, NYP, V, VU

5526. ———. The miller of Old Church. New York, Doubleday, Page, 1911.

3 p. l., vi, 432 p. 8°.   LC, NYP, V, VU

5527. ———. One man in his time. New York, Doubleday, Page, 1922.

vi, 379 p. 8°.   LC, NYP, V, VU

5528. ———. Phases of an inferior planet [a novel] New York & London, Harper, 1898.

4 p. l., 3-324 p. 12°.   LC, NYP, V, VU

5529. ———. The romance of a plain man. New York, Macmillan, 1909.

vi, 464 p. 8°.   BP, LC, NYP, V
Ed. of 1922: Garden City & Toronto, Doubleday, Page.   LC
Ed. of 1924.   VU
Ed. of 1926, with introduction by Hugh Walpole.   LC

5530. ———. The romantic comedians. Garden City, N. Y., Doubleday, Page, 1926.

3 p. l., 346 p. 8°.   LC, V, VU

5531. ———. The shadowy third, and other stories. Garden City, N. Y., Doubleday, Page, 1923.

4 p. l., 3-291 p. col. front. 8°.   H, LC, NYP, V, VU

5531a. ———. They stooped to folly; a comedy of morals. New York, Doubleday, Doran, 1929.

6 p. l., 3-351 p. 8°.   LC, VU

5532. ———. Virginia. Garden City, N. Y., Doubleday, Page, 1913.

vii, 526 p. front. 8°.   LC, NYP, V, VU

5533. ———. The voice of the people. New York, Doubleday, Page, 1900.

4 p. l., 344 p. 8°.   BP, LC, NYP, V
Ed. of 1902: ix, 444 p. illus. (incl. front.)   BP, H, LC, V, VU
Ed. of 1922: 3 p. l., 344 p. front. 8°.   LC

5534. ———. The wheel of life. New York, Doubleday, Page, 1906.

4 p. 1., 3-474 p. 8°. **BP, LC, NYP, V, VU**

5535. GORDON, ARMISTEAD C. (1855-19), *et al.* Befo' de war; echoes in Negro dialect, by A. C. Gordon and Thomas Nelson Page. New York, Scribner, 1888.

vi p., 2 1., 131 p. 12°. **BP, H, LC, NYP, V**

5536. ———. Envion, and other tales of old and new Virginia. London, New York [etc.] Neely, 1899.

171 p. 8°. (Neely's authors' library, no. 16) **V, VU**
Reprinted from various periodicals.

5537. ———. Flandroe's Mogul. New York, Scribner, 1893.

195 p. incl. front., illus. 16°. (Stories of the railway) **LC**

5538. ———. For truth and freedom; poems of commemoration. Staunton, Va., Shultz, 1898.

50 p. 16°. **LC, V, VU**
Ed. of 1910: New York & Washington, Neale. 73 p. **LC, NYP**

5539. ———. The gift of the morning star; a story of Sherando. New York & London, Funk & Wagnalls, 1905.

vi, 373 p. front. 8°. **LC, V, VU**

5540. ———. The ivory gate. New York & Washington, Neale, 1907.

58 p. 8°. Poems. **LC, NYP, V, VU**

5541. ———. Maje; a love story. New York, Scribner, 1914.

5 p. 1., 119 p. front., plates. 8°. **H, LC, V, VU**

5542. ———. Ommirandy; plantation life at Kingswill. New York, Scribner, 1917.

x, 295 p. front., plates. 8°. **LC, V, VU**

5543. ———. Robin Aroon, a comedy of manners. New York & Washington, Neale, 1908.

222 p. 12°. **LC, V, VU**

5544. ———. The western front, a little calendar of the great war. [Staunton] Priv. print., 1928.

5 p. 1., 13-58, [2] p. 8°. Poems. **LC, V**

5545. GORDON, ARMISTEAD C., jr., ed. Virginian writers of fugitive verse . . . New York, White [*ca.* 1923]

   3 p. l., v-xv, 404 p. 8°.

5546. GORDON, JAMES L. (1860-1904) Ballads of the sunlit years. New York, North American press, 1904.

   84 p. 12°.   **LC, V, VU**

5547. [GORDON, W. F.] The secession of Virginia. By a Virginian. Louisa, Va., News press, 1897.

   30 p. front. (port.) plates, ports. 8°. A poem.   **V**

5548. [GORDON, WILLIAM S.] Recollections of the old Quarter. Lynchburg, Va., Moose bros., 1902.

   3 p. l., 142 p. front., plates. 12°.   **H, LC, V**
Fictitious sketches, for the most part in Negro dialect.

5549. GREENE, WILLIAM B. Cloudrifts at twilight. New York, Putnam, 1888.

   8°. Poems.   **BP, H**

5550. ———. A legend of old Virginia. [London, Eyre & Spottiswoode] 1891.

   14 p., 1 l. 12°.   **V**

5551. ———. Thought sketches. London [Eyre & Spottiswoode] 1887.

   30 p. 12°. Poems.   **H**

5552. ———. Three vows. New York, Putnam, 1881.

   [5], 130 p. 4°.   **H, NYP**

5553. GREENWAY, JOHN R. Here and there. A collection of reprinted pieces from the *Religious herald* and other periodicals, by J. R. G. Together with unpublished poems by the same author. Richmond, Va., Brady [1892]

   2 p. l., [7]-46 p., 1 l. 12°.   **LC, V**

5554. GREGORY, EDWARD S. (1843-84) Bonnibell, and other poems. Lynchburg, Va., Bell, 1880.

   266, [2] p. 16°.   **H, LC, NYP, V**

5555. ———. A book of sonnets, by a Virginian . . . Lynchburg, Va., Johnson & Schaffter, 1867.

   31 p. 12°.   **V**

5556. ———. Lenore, and other poems: original and translated. Lynchburg, Bell, 1883.

268 p. 8°. NYP, VU

5557. ———. Love lies bleeding. A charade. Lynchburg, Va., Schaffter & Bryant [1867?]

8 p. 12°. VU

5558. HALL, JOHN L. Judas, a drama in five acts. Williamsburg, Va., Jones, 1894.

87 p. 12°. H, V

5559. HANCOCK, ELIZABETH H., *et al.* The betrayal; a novel, by Walter Neale and Elizabeth H. Hancock. New York & Washington, Neale, 1910.

500 p. 8°. LC, V, VU

5560. ———. Betty Pembroke. New York & Washington, Neale, 1907.

309 p. 12°. LC, V, VU

5561. HARRISON, CONSTANCE C.[1] (1846-1920) Alice in Wonderland; a play for children in three acts. New York, De Witt [*ca.* 1890]

35 p. illus. 12°. LC, NYP
Ed. of 1898. BP, H

5562. ———. The anglomaniacs. New York, Century, 1899.

4 p. l., 216 p. incl. plates. front. 12°. LC, NYP, VU
Ed. of 1890. H, NYP, V

5563. ———. A bachelor maid. New York, Century, 1894.

3 p. l., 244 p. incl. plates. front. 8°. LC, V, VU

5564. ———. Bar Harbor days. New York, Harper, 1887.

4 p. l., 181 p. front., plates. 8°. LC, NYP, V

5565. ———. Behind a curtain. A monologue, in one act. New York, De Witt [*ca.* 1892]

6 p. illus. 12°. LC

5566. ———. Belhaven tales; Crow's Nest; Una and King David. New York, Century, 1892.

5 p. l., 212 p. front., plates. 8°. LC, NYP, V, VU

---

1. Same as Mrs. Burton Harrison.

5567. HARRISON, CONSTANCE C.   Bric-a-brac stories.   New York, Scribner, 1885.

xi, 299 p. front., plates. 12°.   LC

5568. ———.   The Carcellini emerald, with other tales.   Chicago & New York, Stone, 1899.

4 p. l., 3-314 p. front., plates. 8°.   LC, VU

5569. ———.   The Carlyles; a story of the fall of the Confederacy. New York, Appleton, 1905.

3 p. l., 283 p. 8°.   LC, NYP

5570. ———.   The circle of a century.   New York, Century, 1899.

4 p. l., 225 p. 8°.   LC, VU

5571. ———.   The count and the congressman.   New York, Cupples & Leon [ca. 1908]

300 p. front., plates. 8°.   H, LC, NYP

5572. ———.   A daughter of the South, and shorter stories.   New York, Cassell [ca. 1892]

2 p. l., 281 p. 8°.   LC, NYP, V

5573. ———.   An edelweiss of the Sierras; Golden-rod, and other tales.   New York, Harper, 1892.

3 p. l., [3]-209 p. 12°.   LC, NYP, V

5574. ———.   An errant wooing.   New York, Century, 1895.

v, 258 p. front., plates. 8°.   LC, VU

5575. ———.   Flower de Hundred; the story of a Virginia plantation.   New York, Cassell [ca. 1890]

4 p. l., 301 p. 8°.   H, LC, NYP, V, VU
Ed. of 1899: New York, Century.   LC

5576. ———.   Golden-rod, an idyl of Mount Desert.   New York, Harper, 1880.

115 p. 16°.   LC
Ed. of 1879.   BP, H, NYP

5577. ———.   Good Americans.   New York, Century, 1898.

4 p. l., 220 p. 8°.   LC, VU

5578. ———.   Latter-day sweethearts.   New York & London, Authors and newspapers assoc., 1906.

[7]-323 p. 12°   LC, NYP
Ed. of 1907: 323 p. incl. col. front., facsim.   LC, VU

5579. ———. The merry maid of Arcady, His lordship, and other stories. Boston, London, New York, Lamson, Wolffe, 1897.

4 p. l., 3-348 p. front., plates. 12°.   **LC, NYP, V, VU**

5580. ———. The mouse-trap. A comedietta, in one act. New York, De Witt [*ca.* 1892]

14 p. illus. 12°.   **H, LC**

5581. ———. The old-fashioned fairy book. New York, Scribner, 1884.

xxi, 343 p. incl. front., illus., plates. 16°.   **LC**
Ed. of 1887.   **NYP**

5582. ———. A princess of the hills; an Italian romance. Boston, Lothrop [*ca.* 1901]

5 p. l., 13-306 p. front., plates. 12°.   **LC, NYP**

5583. ———. Short comedies for amateur players, as given at the Madison Square and Lyceum theatres, New York, by amateurs. New York, De Witt [1889]

3 p. l., ii, 116 p. illus. 12°.   **H, LC**
Ed. of 1892.   **H**

5584. ———. A son of the Old Dominion. Boston, Lamson, Wolffe, 1897.

355 p. 12°.   **NYP**

5585. ———. The story of Helen Troy. New York, Harper, 1881.

202 p. 12°.   **LC, NYP**
Ed. of 1909.   **LC**

5586. ———. Sweet bells out of tune. New York, Century, 1893.

3 p. l., 231 p. incl. front., plates. 8°.   **H, LC, NYP, VU**

5587. ———. Sylvia's husband. New York, Appleton, 1904.

2 p. l., 221 p. 12°.   **LC, NYP**

5588. ———. Tea at four o'clock. A drawing-room comedy, in one act. New York, De Witt [*ca.* 1892]

29 p. illus. 12°.   **LC**

5589. ———. A triple entanglement. Philadelphia, Lippincott, 1899.

272 p. front., plates. 12°.   **LC, V**
Ed. of 1900.   **NYP**

5590. HARRISON, CONSTANCE C. Two strings to her bow. A comedy in two acts, New York, De Witt [*ca.* 1892]

36 p. illus. 12°.   **LC, NYP**

5591. ———. The unwelcome Mrs. Hatch. A drama of every day. New York, Burgoyne, 1901.

70 p. 8°.   **LC**

Ed. of 1903: 2 p. l., 191 p. 12°.   **LC**

5592. ———. A Virginia cousin, and Bar Harbor tales. Boston & New York, Lamson, Wolffe, 1895.

3 p. l., 3-202 p. front. (port.) 16°.   **LC, V, VU**

Ed. of 1899.   **VU**

5593. ———. The well-bred girl in society. Philadelphia, Curtis; New York, Doubleday & McClure [*ca.* 1898]

vii, 213 p. front. (port.) 16°.   **BP, H, LC, NYP**

Ed. of 1904.   **H**

5594. HARRISON, HENRY S. (1880-19) . . . Andrew Bride of Paris. Boston & New York, Houghton Mifflin, 1925.

4 p. l., 215 p. front., plates. 8°.   **LC, V**

5595. ———. Angela's business. Boston, Houghton Mifflin, 1915.

375 p. front., plates. 12°.   **LC, V**

5596. ———. Captivating Mary Carstairs, by Henry Second [*pseud.*] Boston, Small, Maynard [*ca.* 1910]

viii, 346 p. front. 12°.   **LC, V**

5597. ———. Queed; a novel. Boston & New York, Houghton Mifflin, 1911.

x, 430 p. 12°.   **LC, V**

5598. ———. Saint Teresa, a novel. Boston & New York, Houghton Mifflin, 1922.

3 p. l., 3-455, [1] p. 12°.   **LC, V**

5599. ———. V. V.'s eyes. Boston & New York, Houghton Mifflin, 1913.

x p., 2 l., 508, [2] p. front., plate. 12°.   **LC, V**

Ed. of [1913]: New York, Grosset & Dunlap.   **LC**

5600. ———. When I come back. Boston & New York, Houghton, Mifflin, 1919.

4 p. l., 3-68, [2] p. 8°. **LC, V**

5601. HATCHETT, MAMIE L. Myra: a novel. Richmond, Va., Randolph & English, 1884.

vii, [9]-249 p. 8°. **LC, V**

5602. HAW, MARY J. The Beechwood tragedy. A tale of the Chickahominy. Richmond, Randolph & English, 1889.

241 p. 8°. **LC**
Enlargement of story pub. first in *Magnolia weekly*, 1863.

5603. HODGKIN, JAMES B. Southland stories. Manassas, Va., Journal press, 1903.

175 p. 12°. **V**

5604. HOGE, PEYTON H. (1858-19) The divine tragedy; a drama of the Christ . . . New York, Chicago [etc.] Revell [*ca.* 1905]

146 p. 8°. Poetry. **LC**

5605. HOLCOMBE, WILLIAM H. (1825-93) In both worlds. Philadelphia, Lippincott, 1870.

387 p. 12°. **BP, LC**
Ed. of 1875. **BP**

5606. ———. A mystery of New Orleans: solved by new methods [a novel] Philadelphia, Lippincott, 1890.

332 p. 12°. **LC, NYP**
Ed. of 1892. **LC**

5607. ———. Our children in heaven. Philadelphia, Lippincott, 1868.

318 p. 8°. **BP, LC**
Ed. of 1875. **NYP**

5608. ———. The sexes here and hereafter. Philadelphia, Lippincott, 1869.

277 p. 8°. **BP, LC, NYP**

5609. ———. Southern voices: poems. Philadelphia, Lippincott, 1872.

164 p. 12°. **BP, H, LC, NYP, V**

5610. HOPE, JAMES B. (1829-87)   Arms and the man; a metrical
address, recited on the 100th anniversary (Oct. 19, 1881) of the
surrender of Lord Cornwallis at Yorktown.   Norfolk, Landmark,
1882.

104 p. 8°.   **H, LC, NYP, V**

5611. ———. An elegaic ode [to Annie Carter Lee]   Richmond,
Examiner, 1866.

29 p. 16°.   **BP, LC, NYP, V**

5612. ———. Under the empire; or, The story of Madelon.   Norfolk, Hope, 1878.

211 p. 12°.   **LC**

5613. ———. A wreath of Virginia bay leaves.   Poems of James
Barron Hope.   Selected and edited by his daughter, Janey Hope
Marr.   Richmond, Johnston, West, 1895.

159 p. ports. (incl. front.) plates. 12°.   **V, VU**

5614. HOUSTON, A. C.   Hugh Harrison (a mulatto).   Richmond,
Va., Randolph & English, 1890.

67 p. 12°.   **H, V**

5615. IDYLS of the lawn; with designs by D. Smith, and a preface
by Chas. W. Kent.   Roanoke, Va., Stone, 1899.

1 p. l., x, 130 p. plate. 16°.   **LC, V, VU**

Undergraduate tales selected from the *University of Virginia magazine.*

5616. IVES, CORA S.   The princess of the moon.   A Confederate
fairy story.   Written by a lady of Warrenton, Va.   [Baltimore,
Sun] 1869.

72 p. front. 16°.   **V**

5617. ———. Queen Floradine of Flowerland.   New York, Young,
1900.

46 p. front., plates. 16°.   **LC**

5618. JOHNSON, GEORGE S.   Ballads of the seasons.   New York,
Aberdeen [*ca.* 1910]

4 p. l., 100 p. illus. 8°.   **LC, V**

5619. ———. Poems for the people.   New York, Broadway [*ca.*
1910]

126 p. front. (port.) 8°.   **LC, V**

5620. Johnston, Mary (1870-19) Admiral of the ocean-sea. London, Butterworth, 1923.

> 9-319 p. front. (double map) 8°.   **LC**
> American edit. has title: *1492* **[5628]**

5621. ———. Audrey. Boston & New York, Houghton Mifflin, 1902.

> 4 p. 1., 418 p. plates (incl. front.) 8°.   **H, LC, NYP, V, VU**

5622. ———. By order of the company. [London] Constable, 1900.

> 447 p. 8°.   **LC, NYP**
> American edit. has title: *To have and to hold* **[5641]**

5623. ———. Cease firing. Boston & New York, Houghton Mifflin, 1912.

> viii p., 1 1., 457, [1] p. col. front., col. plates. 8°. **H, LC, NYP, V, VU**

5624. ———. Croatan. Boston, Little, Brown, 1923.

> vi, 298 p. 8°.   **LC, NYP, V, VU**

5625. ———. The exile. Boston, Little, Brown, 1927.

> 3 p. 1., [3]-276 p. 8°.   **LC, V, VU**

5626. ———. Foes; a novel. New York & London, Harper [1918]

> 3 p. 1., 358 p. 8°.   **LC, NYP, V**

5627. ———. The fortunes of Garin. Boston & New York, Houghton Mifflin, 1915.

> 3 p. 1., 375 p. col. front. 8°.   **LC, NYP, V, VU**

5628. ———. 1492. Boston, Little, Brown, 1922.

> 3 p. 1., 315 p. 8°.   **LC, NYP, V**
> English edit. has title: *Admiral of the ocean-sea* **[5620]**

5629. ———. The goddess of reason. Boston & New York, Houghton Mifflin, 1907.

> viii, 234 p., 1 1. 8°. A drama.

5630. ———. The great valley. Boston, Little, Brown, 1926.

> 3 p. 1., 3-317 p. 8°.   **LC, NYP, V, VU**

5631. ———. Hagar. Boston & New York, Houghton Mifflin, 1913.

> vi, 390 p. 8°.   **H, LC, V, VU**

5632. Johnston, Mary. Lewis Rand. Boston & New York, Houghton Mifflin, 1908.

 viii, 510 p. col. front., plates. 8°.   **H, LC, NYP, V, VU**

5633. ———. The long roll. Boston & New York, Houghton Mifflin, 1911.

 x, 683 p. col. front., plates. 8°.   **H, LC, NYP, V, VU**

5634. ———. Michael Forth. New York & London, Harper [*ca.* 1919]

 2 p. l., 363 p. 8°.   **LC, NYP, V, VU**

5635. ———. Prisoners of hope; a tale of colonial Virginia. Boston & New York, Houghton Mifflin, 1898.

 vi, 378 p. front. 8°.   **H, LC, NYP**
 Ed. of 1899.   **LC, VU**
 Ed. of 1900.   **LC**
 Ed. of 1902.   **NYP, V**
 Ed. of [1922?]: New York, Grosset & Dunlap.   **LC**

5636. ———. Silver cross. Boston, Little, Brown, 1922.

 3 p. l., 289 p. 8°.   **LC, NYP, V, VU**

5637. ———. Sir Mortimer, a novel. New York & London, Harper, 1904.

 3 p. l., 349 p. col. front., plates. 8°.   **H, LC, NYP, V, VU**

5638. ———. The slave ship. Boston, Little, Brown, 1924.

 3 p. l., 330 p. 8°.   **LC, V, VU**

5639. ———. The status of woman, a letter to the Richmond Times-dispatch, Dec. 11, 1909. Richmond, Va., Equal suffrage league of Virginia [1909?]

 16 p. 16°.   **LC, NYP**

5640. ———. Sweet Rocket. New York & London, Harper [*ca.* 1920]

 2 p. l., 194 p. 8°.   **LC, V, VU**

5641. ———. To have and to hold. Boston & New York, Houghton Mifflin, 1900.

 vi, 403 p. plates (incl. front.) 8°.
 Ed. of [19-?]
 English edit. has title: *By order of the company* **[5622]**

5642. ——. The wanderers. Boston & New York, Houghton Mifflin [1917]

    3 p. l., 426 p. 8°.   **H, LC, NYP, V, VU**

5643. ——. The witch. Boston & New York, Houghton Mifflin, 1914.

    v, 441 p. incl. col. front. 8°.   **H, LC, NYP, V, VU**

5644. JORDAN, MRS. CORNELIA J. (1830-98) Echoes from the cannon. Ed. by Theresa J. Ambler. Buffalo, Moulton, 1899.

    4 p. l., vii, 9-207 p. front. (port.) 8°.   **LC**

5645. ——. Richmond: her glory and her graves. A poem. In 2 parts. Richmond, Richmond medical journal print., 1867.

    xxxix p. 8°.   **BP, LC, NYP, V**

5646. ——. Useful maxims for a noble life; or, Fireside counsels to a daughter, by a Virginia mother. Lynchburg, Virginian, 1884.

    25 p. 16°.   **LC**

5647. KIEFFER, ALDINE S. (1840-1904) Hours of fancy: or Vigil and vision. Dayton, Va., Ruebush, Kieffer, 1881.

    237 p. front. (port.) 12°. Poems.   **BP, LC, V**

5648. KILBY, L. CLAY. Vernon Lonsdale. Philadelphia, The author, 1876.

    269 p. 12°. A novel.   **LC, V, VU**

5649. KINSOLVING, MRS. SALLY B. (1876-19) David and Bathsheba, and other poems. Baltimore, Norman, Remington, 1922.

    7 p. l., 3-104 p. 8°.   **LC, V**

5650. ——. Depths and shallows. Baltimore, Norman, Remington, 1921.

    5 p. l., 67 p. 12°. Poems.

5651. KOINER, ANNA V. Echoes from the land of the golden horseshoe. New Market, Va., Henkel, 1897.

    70 p. plate. 8°.   **V**

5652. ——. Footprints in the wilderness. Lynchburg, Bell, 1892.

    66, [1] p. 12°.   **V**

5653. LANE, ELINOR M. (*d.* 1909)   All for the love of a lady.   New York, Appleton, 1906.

    8 p. 1., 3-87 p. front., illus., plate. 8°.   LC

5654. ———.   The apple-tree cottage.   New York & London, Harper, 1910.

    3 p. 1., 51 p. col. front., col. plate. 12°.   LC

5655. ———.   Katrine, a novel.   New York, Harper, 1909.

    viii p., 2 1., 314 p. front. 8°.   LC

5656. ———.   Mills of God; a novel.   New York, Appleton, 1901.

    xi, 337 p. front., ports. 12°.   LC, NYP
    Ed. of 1910.   BP

5657. ———.   Nancy Stair; a novel.   New York, Appleton, 1904.

    xii, 385 p. front., facsim. 8°.   LC, NYP
    Ed. of 1905.   LC, NYP
    Ed. of 1910.   LC

5658. LANGHORNE, MRS. ORRA.   Aunt Pokey's son; a story of the new South.   [Lynchburg, Bell, 1890]

    16 p. 8°.   V

5659. LATIMER, MRS. ELIZABETH W. (1822-1904)   . . .   Amabel; or, Amor omnia vincit.   A novel.   New York, Harper [1882]

    78 p. 8°.   LC

5660. ———.   My wife and my wife's sister.   Boston, Roberts, 1881.

    vi, [7]-319 p. 12°.   Pub. anonymously.   LC

5661. ———.   The prince incognito.   Chicago, McClurg, 1902.

    vii, 9-320 p. 8°.   LC

5662. ———.   . . .   Princess Amélie.   A fragment of autobiography.   Boston, Roberts. 1883.

    322 p. 12°.   Pub. anonymously.   H, LC

5663. ———.   Salvage.   Boston, Roberts, 1880.

    293 p. 12°.   Pub. anonymously.   LC

5664. LEE, GEORGE T.   A Virginia feud; the story of a mountain lassie.   New York & Washington, Neale, 1908.

    341 p. 12°.   LC

5665. ———. The Puritan maid; a poem. New York, Broadway pub. [*ca.* 1904]

    iii p., 1 l., v-x, 132 p. front., plate. 12°.   **V**

5666. LITTLETON, JESSE T. (1856-19) The story of Captain John Smith and Pocahontas; a souvenir of the Jamestown exposition. Nashville, Dallas, Pub. house of M. E. church, South, 1907.

    94 p. 12°.   **L/C**

5667. LUCAS, DANIEL B. (1836-1909) Dramatic works . . . , ed. by Charles W. Kent and Virginia Lucas. With a critical introduction by C. F. Tucker Brooke. University of Virginia edit. . . . Boston, Badger [*ca.* 1913]

    x p., 3 l., 9-271 p. front. 8°.   **H, LC, NYP**

5668. ———. The land where we were dreaming, and other poems, ed. by Charles W. Kent and Virginia Lucas. With a critical introduction by Charles W. Kent. University of Virginia edit. Boston, Badger [*ca.* 1913]

    2 p. l., x, [4] p., 2 l., 13-252 p. front. (port.) 8°.   **H, LC, NYP, V, VU**

5669. ———. The maid of Northumberland, a dramatic poem. New York, Putnam, 1879.

    184 p. 8°.   **BP, H, NYP**

5670. ———, *et al.* The wreath of Eglantine, and other poems. Baltimore, Kelly, Piet, 1869.

    169 p. illus. 8°.   **BP, LC, NYP, V, VU**
    Written in part by Virginia Lucas.

5671. LUCAS, VIRGINIA (1871-19) . . . June; a year book of sonnets. Strasburg, Va., Shenandoah pub., 1927.

    96 p. incl. front. 8°.   **LC, NYP, V, VU**

5672. LIONS CLUB, Lynchburg, Va. Lasting lyrics, by Lynchburgers. Lynchburg, The Lions club [19-?]

    21 p. 8°.   **LC, V, VU**
    "Every poem . . . has been reprinted . . . , approved by critics unbiased by local claims, and applauded by audiences far from its native city."
    With biographical sketches of the authors: Bransford Vawter, Dr. H. Grey Latham, H. C. Featherston, Edward S. Gregory, Mrs. Cornelia J. M. Jordan, and Dr. W. W. Smith.

5673. McCABE, JAMES D. (1842-83) The night-express. Philadelphia, Stoddart, 1879.

153 p. 12°.   LC

5674. ————. Planting in the wilderness; or, The pioneer boys. A story of frontier life. Boston, Lee & Shepard, 1870.

256 p. plate. 16°.   BP, H, LC

5675. McCARTHY, CARLTON. Our distinguished fellow citizen. Richmond, Hill, 1890.

169 p. incl. front., plates. 12°.   LC, NYP, V

5676. McCLELLAND, MARGARET G. (*d.* 1895) Broadoaks [a novel] St. Paul, Price-McGill [*ca.* 1893]

268 p. front., plate. 8°.   LC, V

5677. ————. Burkett's lock. New York, Cassell [1889]

279 p. 12°.   LC, NYP, V

5678. ————. Eleanor Gwynn. New York, U. S. book co. [1890]

150 p. 12°.   LC, V

5679. ————. Jean Monteith. New York, Holt, 1887.

2 p. l., 252 p. 12°.   LC, NYP, V

5680. ————. Madame Silva [also The ghost of Dred Power] New York, Cassell [*ca.* 1888]

2 p. l., 320 p. 12°.   LC, NYP, V

5681. ————. Mammy Mystic. New York, Merriam [*ca.* 1895]

242 p. front. 16°.   LC, V

5682. ————. Manitou Island [a novel] New York, Holt, 1892.

vi, 294 p. 12°.   LC, V

5683. ————. ? A nameless novel. New York, Moore [1891]

iv, [5]-248 p. 12°.   LC

5684. ————. Oblivion; an episode. New York, Holt, 1885.

vi, 290 p. 12°.   LC, NYP, V

5685. ————. "Old Ike's memories" . . . Richmond, West, 1884.

16 p. 12°. Poetry.   V, VU

5686. ———. The old post-road. New York, Merriam [*ca.* 1894]
163 p. front. 16°.   LC, NYP

5687. ———. Princess [a novel] New York, Holt, 1886.
2 p. l., 297 p. 12°.   LC, NYP

5688. ———. St. John's wooing; a story. New York, Harper, 1895.
2 p. l., 175 p. front., plate. 16°.   LC, NYP

5689. ———. A self-made man [a novel] Philadelphia, 1887.
p. [193]-284. 8°. (In *Lippincott's magazine,* XXXIX)   H, LC, NYP

5690. ———. Ten minutes to twelve. Philadelphia, 1889.
p. 1-64. 8°. (In *Lippincott's magazine,* XLIV)   H, LC, NYP

5691. ———. White heron. Philadelphia, 1892.
p. 1-76. 8°. (In *Lippincott's magazine,* L)   H, LC, NYP

5692. ———. The wonder-witch. Philadelphia, 1894.
p. 713-779. 8°. (In *Lippincott's magazine,* LIII)   H, LC, NYP

5693. McCORMICK, VIRGINIA T. (1873-19) Charcoal and chalk.
Norfolk, Va., Atlantic coast print., 1926.
xiv, 89 p. front., illus. 8°. Sketches and poems.   NYP, V

5694. ———. Jericho's Christmas. Norfolk, Atlantic coast print.
[n. d.]
22 p. 12°.   VU

5695. ———. Star-dust and gardens. [Norwood, Mass., Plimpton
press] 1920.
3 p. l., 77 p. 8°. Poems.   LC, V, VU

5696. ———. Voices of the wind. New York, White, 1924.
5 p. l., 3-88 p. 12°. Poems.   LC, V

5697. MACK, FLORA L. Old Jamestown, an historical poem. [Rich-
mond, Dietz, 1906]
16 p. 8°.   V, VU

5698. MAGILL, MARY T. (1830-99) The Holcombes. A story of
Virginia home-life. Philadelphia, Lippincott, 1871.
viii, 9-290 p. 8°.   BP, LC, NYP, V, VU
Ed. of 1893.   V

5699. MAGILL, MARY T. Under the pruning-knife. A story of southern life. Philadelphia, Presbyterian board of pub. [*ca.* 1888]
332 p. front. 12°.   **LC, V**

5700. ———. Women, or, Chronicles of the late war. Baltimore, Turnbull, 1871.
xvii, 393 p. 12°.

5701. MAGRUDER, JULIA (1854-1907) Across the chasm. New York, Scribner, 1885.
2 p. l., 310 p. 12°.   **LC, NYP, VU**
Ed. of 1901.   **NYP**

5702. ———. At anchor. A novel. Philadelphia, 1887.
p. [1]-78. 8°. (In *Lippincott's magazine,* XL)   **H, LC, NYP**

5703. ———. A beautiful alien. Boston, Badger, 1900.
223 p. front. 12°.   **LC, NYP, VU**

5704. ———. The child Amy. [New York] Lothrop [*ca.* 1894]
3 p. l., 302 p. incl. plates. 8°.   **LC, VU**

5705. ———. Dead selves. Philadelphia, 1897.
p. 289-385. 8°. (In *Lippincott's magazine,* LIX)   **LC, VU**

5706. ———. A heaven-kissing hill. [A novel] Chicago & New York, Stone, 1899.
2 p. l., 159 p. plate. 16°.   **LC, NYP, VU**

5707. ———. Her husband; the mystery of a man. Boston, Small, Maynard [*ca.* 1911]
3 p. l., 474 p. col. front., plate. 8°.   **LC**

5708. ———. Honored in the breach. Philadelphia, 1888.
p. 287-389. 8°. (In *Lippincott's magazine,* XLI)   **H, LC**

5709. ———. Labor of love; a story for boys. Boston, Lothrop [*ca.* 1898]
144 p. front., plate. 8°.   **LC, VU**

5710. ———. A magnificent plebeian. New York, Harper, 1888.
228 p. 12°.   **LC, NYP, V, VU**

5711. ———. A manifest destiny. New York, Harper, 1900.
2 p. l., 225 p. front., plate. 12°.   **LC, NYP, V, VU**

5712. ———. Miss Ayr of Virginia, and other stories. Chicago, Stone, 1896.

4 p. l., 395 p. 12°.   LC, NYP, V

5713. ———. The Princess Sonia. New York, Century, 1895.

5 p. l., 225 p. front., illus., plate. 8°.   LC, NYP, V, VU

5714. ———. A realized ideal. Chicago & New York, Stone, 1898.

2 p. l., 135 p. 12°.   H, LC, VU
Ed. of 1906: New York, Duffield.   NYP

5715. ———. Struan. Boston, Badger, 1899.

2 p. l., 330 p. 12°.   LC, NYP, VU

5716. ———. A sunny southerner. Boston, Page, 1901.

4 p. l., 194 p. front., plate. 12°.   BP, LC

5717. ———. The violet. New York, London, Longmans, Green, 1896.

5 p. l., 210 p. front., plate. 8°.   LC, NYP, V, VU

5718. MARR, FRANCES H. (1835-?) Heart-life in song. Baltimore, Turnbull, 1874.

165 p. 12°.   V
2d edit.: Richmond, Randolph & English, 1883. vii, [9]-183 p.
                                                                  LC, V, VU

5719. ——— ———. Virginia, and other poems. Philadelphia, Sherman, 1881.

2 p. l., viii, 9-152 p. 12°.   LC, V, VU

5720. MAYO, JOSEPH. Woodbourne: a novel of the revolutionary period in Virginia and Maryland. Part 1. Baltimore, Piet, 1884.

1 v. 8°.   LC, NYP, V
Ed. of 1884, in 2 pts.: Baltimore pub. co.   V

5721. [1611] MOORE, JOSIAH S. Reminiscences, letters, poetry
. . . Richmond, 1903.

5722. MORAN, JEANNIE W.[1] (1842-?) Miss Washington, of Virginia. A semi-centennial love-story. Richmond, The author, 1889.

vi, 77 p. 12°.   LC, V
Ed. of 1893: Philadelphia, Lippincott. 97 p. illus.   BP, LC

---

1. Same as Mrs. B. F. Moran.

5723. Moran, Jeannie W. Twin souls. Boston, Christopher [*ca.* 1922]

    80 p. 8°.   **LC, NYP**

5724. Moran, W. H. From school-room to bar; a novel. Philadelphia, Lippincott, 1892.

    304 p. 12°.   **LC, V, VU**

5725. Morgan, James B. Song-sermons, and other poems. Richmond, Va., Whittet & Shepperson, 1892.

    109 p. front. (port.) 12°.   **V**

5726. Morton, Oren F. (1857-1926) Land of the laurel; a story of the Alleghanies. Morgantown, W. Va., Acme, 1903.

    240 p. plate. 8°.   **LC**

5727. ———. Under the cottonwoods; a sketch of life on a prairie homestead. Morgantown, W. Va., Acme, 1900.

    3 p. l., [5]-318 p. front. 12°.   **LC, V**

5728. Munford, George W. (1803-82) The jewels of Virginia; a lecture delivered in Richmond . . . Richmond, Gary & Clemmitt, 1867.

    50 p. 8°.   **LC, NYP, V**

5729. ———. The two parsons . . . [and other stories] With a biographical sketch of the author. Richmond, Sleight, 1884.

    viii, [9]-592 p. 8°.   **H, NYP, V**

5730. Nelson, James P. (1849-?) Balla, and other Virginia stories. Richmond, Bell, 1914.

    225 p. 12°.   **LC, V**
    Reprinted in part from *Harper's weekly.*

5731. Newberry, Samuel H. Eagle oak, and other poems. Richmond, Va., Waddey, 1906.

    426 p. plates, ports. (incl. front.) 8°.   **LC, V**

5732. ———. Eureka, a prose poem; a new theory, the solution of the riddle of the universe, which solves the riddle of life. New York, Washington, Broadway pub. [*ca.* 1911]

    59 p. ports. (incl. front.) 8°.   **LC, NYP, V**

5733. Owen, Nellie H. (1854-1916) Short stories and poems. Richmond, Va., Whittet & Shepperson [*ca.* 1909]

    129 p. 8°.   **LC, V**
    2d ed. [1927: Richmond, Standard print.] 112 p.   **LC, V**

5734. PAGE, THOMAS N. (1853-1922) The novels, stories and poems of Thomas Nelson Page. [Plantation ed.] New York, Scribner, 1906.

> 18 v. fronts., plates, ports., maps. 8°.

5735. ———. Among the camps; or, Young people's stories of the war, New York, Scribner, 1891.

> 7 p. l., 163 p. incl. front., plate. 8°.   **LC, V, VU**
> Ed. of 1902.   **LC**
> Ed. of 1916.   **H**
> Ed. of 1920.   **NYP**

5736. [5535] ———. Befo' de war . . . New York, 1888.

5737. ———. Bred in the bone. New York, Scribner, 1904.

> 5 p. l., 274 p. front., plate. 8°.   **H, LC, NYP, V, VU**

5738. ———. The burial of the guns. New York, Scribner, 1894.

> 3 p. l., 258 p. 12°.   **BP, LC, NYP, V, VU**
> Ed. of 1900.   **NYP**
> Ed. of 1916.   **H**

5739. ———. A captured Santa Claus. New York, Scribner, 1902. 1902.

> 4 p. l., 81 p. front., plate. 8°.   **H, LC, V, VU**
> Ed. of 1923.   **NYP**

5740. ———. The coast of Bohemia [poems] New York, Scrib-

> ix, 126 p. 8°.

5741. ———. Elsket, and other stories. New York, Scribner, 1891.

> vii, 208 p. 12°.   **LC, NYP, V, VU**
> Ed. of 1916.   **H**

5742. ———. Gordon Keith. New York, Scribner, 1903.

> ix, 548 p. front., plate. 8°.   **H, LC, NYP, V, VU**
> Ed. of 1909.   **LC**

5743. ———. In ole Virginia; or, Marse Chan, and other stories. New York, Scribner, 1887.

> 4 p. l., 230 p. 12°.   **LC, NYP, V, VU**
> Ed. of 1889: London.   **BP**
> Ed. of 1890: New York. 5 p. l., 239 p. plates.   **LC**
> Ed. of 1892.   **NYP**

Ed. of 1896: ix, 275 p. plates.   **LC, NYP**
Ed. of 1910: 5 p. l., 230 p. port.   **LC**
Ed. of 1916.   **H**

5744. PAGE, THOMAS N. John Marvel, assistant. New York, Scribner, 1909.

viii, 573 p. front., plate. 8°.   **H, LC, NYP, V**
Ed. of 1919.   **LC**

5745. ———. The land of the spirit. New York, Scribner, 1913.

viii p., 3 l., 3-257 p. front., plate. 8°.   **H, LC, NYP, V**

5746. ———. Meh lady. A story of the war. New York, Scribner, 1893.

70 p., 6 l. 4°.   **BP, NYP**

5747. ———. Marse Chan; a tale of old Virginia. New York, Scribner, 1885.

180 p. 12°. (Stories by American authors, IX)   **H, LC, V**
Ed. of 1892: 4 p. l., 53 p. illus. 8°.   **LC, VU**
Ed. of 1900.   **NYP**

5748. ———. The old gentleman of the black stock. New York, Scribner, 1897.

3 p. l., 137 p. 16°.   **H, LC, NYP, V, VU**
Ed. of 1900: viii p., 2 l., 169 p. illus. 12°.   **BP, H, LC**
Ed. of 1901.   **LC, NYP**

5749. ———. On Newfound River. New York, Scribner, 1891.

3 p. l., 240 p. 12°.   **LC, NYP, V**
Ed. of 1906: 6 p. l., 3-286 p. col. plates. 8°.   **H, LC, NYP, VU**

5750. ———. The Page story book, ed. by Frank T. Spaulding and Catherine T. Bryce. New York, Scribner, 1906.

xii, 125 p. front. (port.) plates. 12°.   **LC, V**
Ed. of 1918.   **NYP**

5751. ———. Pastime stories. New York, Harper, 1894.

x, 220 p. plates. 12°.   **LC, V**
Ed. of 1898: New York, Scribner.   **H, LC, NYP**
Ed. of 1901.   **LC, VU**
Ed. of 1912.   **H**

5752. ———. Polly; a Christmas recollection. New York, Scribner, 1894.

3 p. l., 49 p. front., plate. 8°.   **LC, NYP, V, VU**

5753. ——. The red riders. New York, Scribner, 1924.

ix, 338 p. 8°.   **H, LC, V**
Ed. of 1927.   **NYP**

5754. ——. Red Rock; a chronicle of reconstruction. New York, Scribner, 1898.

xv, 584 p. front., plate. 12°.   **H, LC, NYP, V**
Ed. of 1899.   **LC, VU**
Eds. of 1901 & 1909.   **NYP**
Eds. of 1907 & 1925.   **V**

5755. ——. Santa Claus's partner. New York, Scribner, 1899.

4 p. l., 176 p. col. plate. 12°.

5756. ——. The shepherd who watched by night. New York, Scribner, 1913.

[10] p. illus. 8°. (Reprint from *Scribner's magazine*)   **LC**
Ed. of 1916: 3 p. l., 3-39 p. front. 12°.   **LC, NYP, V, VU**

5757. ——. The stranger's pew. New York, Scribner, 1914.

3 p. l., 21 p. front. 12°.   **H, LC, V, VU**

5758. ——. Tommy Trot's visit to Santa Claus. New York, Scribner, 1908.

4 p. l., 94 p. col. front., col. plate. 8°.   **H, LC**
Ed. of 1922.   **NYP**

5759. ——. Two little Confederates. New York, Scribner, 1888.

4 p. l., 156 p. incl. plate. front. 8°.   **LC, NYP, V**
Ed. of 1889.   **LC**
Ed. of 1896.   **NYP**
Ed. of 1911.   **V**
Ed. of 1923: 5 p. l., 169 p. incl. front. 8°.   **LC**

5760. ——. Two prisoners. New York, Russell, 1898.

82 p. incl. front. 8°.   **LC, V**
Ed. of 1903: 82 p. col. plates. 8°.   **H, LC, NYP**

5761. ——. Unc' Edinburg, a plantation echo. New York, Scribner, 1895.

3 p. l., 53 p. incl. plate. front. 8°.   **LC, NYP**

5762. ——. Under the crust. New York, Scribner, 1907.

v p., 2 l., 3-307 p. front., plate. 8°.   **H, LC, NYP, V, VU**

5763. PARSONS, HENRY C. (1840-94) The reaper, and other poems. New York, 1884.

> 4 p. l., 13-61 p. incl. plates, front. 8°.   **BP, H, LC, NYP, VU**

5764. PARSONS, KATHARINE L. Poems. By K. L. P. Richmond, Randolph & English, 1889.

> vii, [5]-94 p. 12°.   **V**

5765. PATTON, ABEL. "Har Lampkins;" a narrative of mountain life on the borders of the two Virginias. New York, London [etc.] Abbey press [1901]

> 1 p. l., 5-192 p. 8°.   **LC, NYP**
> The characters and principal features of the story are true.

5766. [PAYNE, A. W.] Original poems and spicy lectures by yours truly. [Shadwell, Va.? 1899]

> 101 p. 12°.   **LC**

5767. ———. Poetical blizzards! The adventures of a lost gosling, by yours truly. [Charlottesville, Jeffersonian, 1890?]

> 32 p. 8°.   **VU**

5768. PEYTON, JOHN L. (1824-96) Tom Swindel; or, The adventures of a boomer. Staunton, Va., Bolen, 1893.

> 2 p. l., [3]-136 p. 16°.   **H, LC, NYP, V, VU**

5769. PICKETT, LASALLE C.[1] (1848-19-?) The bugles of Gettysburg. Chicago, Browne, 1913.

> 163 p. front. 12°.   **H, LC, NYP, V**

5770. ———. Digging through to Manila [poem] Washington, B. S. Adams, 1905.

> 11 l. front., plate. 8°.   **LC**

5771. ———. Ebil eye. Washington, Neale, 1901.

> 166 p. front. (port.) plate. 16°.   **LC, NYP**

5772. ———. Jinny. Washington, Neale, 1901.

> vii, 9-172 p. front. (port.) plate. 16°.   **LC, NYP**

5773. ———. Kunnoo sperits and others. Washington, Neale, 1900.

> xix, 21-174 p. front. (port.) plate. 16°.   **LC, NYP**

---

1. Same as Mrs. G. E. Pickett.

5774. ———. Yule log. Washington, Neale, 1900.

vii, 9-164 p. front. (port.) plate. 12°.   **LC, NYP**

5775. PORTER, DUVAL (1844-19   ) The lost cause, and other poems. 1st ed. Danville, Va., Blair & Boatwright, 1897.

96 p. 8°.   **V**
Ed. of 1914: Danville, Townes. 3 p. l., 150 p.   **LC, NYP, V**

5776. ———. Poems. Lynchburg, Bell, 1875.

vii, 275 p. 12°.   **LC**

5777. ———. Sunset poems. Richmond, Va., Lewis [1923?]

[vii], 180 p. front., ports., plate. 8°.   **V**

5778. POWERS, WILLIAM D. (1849-1924) Uncle Isaac; or, Old days in the South. A remembrance of the South. Richmond, Johnson, 1899.

3 p. l., 11-245 p. incl. front., plate. 12°.
Written for the most part in verse.

5779. PRESTON, MRS. MARGARET J. (1820-97) Aunt Dorothy; an old Virginia plantation-story. New York, Randolph [*ca.* 1890]

92 p. front., illus. 12°.   **LC, NYP, VU**

5780. ———. Beechenbrook; a rhyme of the war. Baltimore, Kelly & Piet, 1867.

106 p. 12°.
Ed. of 1866.   **H, NYP**
Ed. of 1868.   **V**

5781. ———. Cartoons [poems] Boston, Roberts, 1875.

2 p. l., vi, [7]-240 p. 12°.   **BP, H, LC, V**
Ed. of 1881.   **BP, V, VU**

5782. ———. Centennial poem for Washington and Lee university, Lexington, Virginia, 1775-1885. New York & London, Putnam, 1885.

1 p. l., 24 numb. l. 12°.   **H, LC, NYP, USE, V**

5783. ———. Chimes for church-children. Philadelphia, Presbyterian board of pub. [*ca.* 1889]

111 p. 16°.   **LC, V, VU**

5784. ———. Colonial ballads, sonnets, and other verse. Boston & New York, Houghton Mifflin, 1887.

xi, 222 p., 1 l., [223]-259 p. 12°.   **BP, LC, V, VU**

5785. PRESTON, MRS. MARGARET J. For love's sake; poems of faith and comfort. New York, Randolph [1886]

142, [1] p. 12°.   NYP, V

5786. ———. Old song and new. Philadelphia, Lippincott, 1870.

312 p. 12°.   BP, H, LC

5787. ———. Semi-centennial ode for the Virginia military institute, Lexington, Virginia, 1839-1889 (written at the request of the Board of visitors). New York & London, Putnam, 1889.

1 p. l., 26 numb. l. 12°.   H, LC, USE

5788. PRESTON, R. A. Memoria in aeterna, and other poems. Bristol, Tenn.-Va., King, 1908.

34 p. front. (port.) plate, ports. 4°.   V

5789. PRICE, MRS. ANNA L. The old church, and other poems . . . 1850-1921. Marlinton, W. Va., Times book co. [*ca.* 1921]

138 p. front. (port.) 8°.   LC, V

5790. PRYOR, SARA A.[1] (1830-1912) The colonel's story. New York, Macmillan, 1911.

4 p. l., 3-387 p. 8°.   LC, V, VU

5791. PULLIAM, DAVID L. (1857-19) Lays of a southern minstrel. Richmond, Va., William Byrd, 1924.

423 p. front. (port.) 8°.   LC, V

5792. ———. The signet; or, The love of Queen Elizabeth. A play in five acts. Richmond, Johns & Goolsby, 1884.

52 p. 12°.   V

5793. PUTNAM, SALLIE A. (1845?-?) Kenneth, my king. A novel. New York, Carleton, 1873.

2 p. l., [vii]-viii, [1], 10-417 p. 12°.   NYP

5794. ———, ed. The southern amaranth. A carefully selected collection of poems growing out of and in reference to the late war. New York, Wilcox, 1869.

3 p. l., [v]-xii, [3]-651 p. 8°.   BP, LC, NYP

---

1. Same as Mrs. R. A. Pryor.

5795. RANDOLPH, INNES (1837-87) The grasshopper, a tragic cantata. Baltimore, Sutro [*ca.* 1878]

14 p. illus., music. 8°.   **H**

5796. ———. Poems [ed. by Harold Randolph] Baltimore, Williams & Wilkins [*ca.* 1898]

2 p. l., [vii], 13-76 p. front. (port.) 12°.   **H, V**

5797. RAYMOND, WALTER M. Citronaloes. A novel. Richmond, Randolph & English, 1888.

2 p. l., [7]-158 p. 12°.   **LC, NYP**

5798. ———. Rebels of the new South. Chicago, Kerr [*ca.* 1904]

294 p. plate. 8°.   **LC, NYP**

5799. ———. Two men and some women [a novel] New York, Abbey press [*ca.* 1900]

2 p. l., vi, 7-160 p. port. 8°.   **LC, V**

5800. ———. Where the James flows; the story of a perfect palship. New York, Hitchcock, 1927.

3 p. l., 250 p. 8°.   **LC**

5801. READE, WILLOUGHBY. Waifs, gathered on the banks of silent streams; and verses. [n. p., *ca.* 1881]

60 p. 8°.   **V**

5802. ———. When hearts were true. New York & Washington, Neale, 1907.

140 p. 12°.   **LC**

5803. RIVES, HALLIE E.[1] (1876-19) The Valiants of Virginia. Indianapolis, Bobbs-Merrill [*ca.* 1912]

5 p. l., 432 p. col. front., col. plates. 8°.   **LC, VU**

5804. ROBINS, MRS. SALLY N. Scuffles. New York, Harriman, 1912.

207 p. front., plates. 12°.   **LC, V**

5805. ———. A man's reach. Philadelphia & London, Lippincott, 1916.

333 p. col. front., col. plates. 12°.   **LC**

---

1. Same as Mrs. Post Wheeler.

5806. ROBINSON, MRS. MARTHA H. Helen Erskine. Philadelphia, Lippincott, 1870.

    255 p. 12°. A novel.   **LC**

5807. ROEBUCK, GEORGE E. Beatrice; the story of a mountain girl. Richmond, Va., Mitchell-Rudd, 1910.

    45 p. front. 16°.   **V**

5808. RUSSELL, CHARLES W. Iranian rest and other lyrics. Teheran, Persia, Pharos, A.D. 1912 A.H. 1330.

    37 l. 8°.   **LC, V**

5809. ——. Poems . . . New York, Neale, 1921.

    183 p. front. (port.) 8°.   **LC, V**

5810. RUSSELL, FRANCES E. A quaint spinster. Boston, Roberts, 1895.

    119 p. 12°.   **LC**

5811. RYALS, JOHN V. Yankee doodle Dixie; or, Love the light of life. An historical romance, illustrative of life and love in an old Virginia country home . . . Richmond, Waddey, 1890.

    vii, [9]-532 p. 8°.   **LC, V, VU**

5812. RYLAND, CALLY T. (1871-19) Aunt Jemimy's maxims. New York, Broadway pub. [*ca.* 1907]

    2 l., 69 p. 12°.   **LC, V**

5813. ——, *et al.* Daphne and her lad, by M. J. Lagen and Cally Ryland. New York, Holt, 1904.

    5 p. l., 237 p. front. 12°.   **LC, NYP, V**

5814. ——, *et al.* Sulky Sue, by Caroline Wise and Cally Ryland. Richmond, Va. [*ca.* 1921]

    1 p. l., 36 p. 16°. Poetry.   **LC, V**

5815. ——. The taming of Betty. Boston, Lee & Shepard, 1904.

    4 p. l., 228 p. front., plates. 12°.   **LC, V**

5816. SADDLE and song. A collection of verses made at Warrenton, Va., during the winter of 1904-1905 . . . Philadelphia & London, Lippincott, 1905.

    200 p. front., plates. 8°.   **LC, V**

5817. Salyards, Joseph H. Idathea. A poem. New Market, Va., Henkel, Calvert, 1875.

308 p. 16°. **LC, NYP, V, VU**

5818. Seawell, Molly E. (1860-1916) The Berkeleys and their neighbors. New York, Amercian news [*ca.* 1888]

232 p. 8°. **LC, NYP, V**
Rev. ed., 1892: New York, Appleton. **LC**

5819. ———. Betty at Fort Blizzard. Philadelphia & London, Lippincott, 1916.

223 p. incl. illus., plates. 8°. **LC**

5820. ———. Betty's Virginia Christmas. Philadelphia & London, 1914.

5 p. l., 9-213 p. col. front., illus. 8°. **LC**

5821. ———. A boy of 1775. New York & London, Harper, 1907.

viii, 220 p. front., plates. 12°. (Strange stories of the revolution) **LC**

5822. ———. Boys on the railroad. New York & London, Harper, 1909.

5 p. l., 212 p. front., plate. 12°. **LC**

5823. ———. The chateau of Montplaisir. New York, Appleton, 1906.

4 p. l., 245 p. front., plate. 8°. **LC, NYP**

5824. ———. Children of destiny. New York, Appleton, 1893.

341 p. 12°. **LC, V**
Ed. of [1903]: Indianapolis, Bobbs-Merrill. **LC, NYP**

5825. ———. Decatur and Somers. New York, Appleton, 1894.

3 p. l., 169 p. front., plate. 8°. **LC, NYP**

5826. ———. Despotism and democracy; a study in Washington society and politics. New York, McClure, Phillips, 1903.

vi, 311 p. 8°. A novel. **LC, NYP**
Ed. of 1904. **NYP**

5827. ———. The diary of a beauty; a story. Philadelphia & London, Lippincott, 1915.

212 p. front., plate. 8°. **LC**

5828. SEAWELL, MOLLY E. An Englishman's home. London, Sampson Low, Marston, 1909.

vii, 157 p. 12°.   **BP**

5829. ———. The fortunes of Fifi. Indianapolis, Bobbs-Merrill [1903]

4 p. l., 238 p. col. front., col. plate. 8°.   **LC**

5830. ———. Francezka. Indianapolis, Bobbs-Merrill [1902]

5 p. l., 466 p. front., plate 8°.   **LC, NYP, V**

5831. ———. The great scoop. Boston, Page, 1903.

144 p. incl. front. plates. 8°.   **LC**

5832. ———. Hale-Weston. A novel. Philadelphia, 1889.

p. [1]-105. 8°. (In *Lippincott's magazine,* XLIII)   **H, LC**

5833. ———. The history of Lady Betty Stair [a novel] New York, Scribner, 1897.

3 p. l., 144 p. plates. (incl. front.) 12°.   **LC**
Ed. of 1899.   **VU**
Ed. of 1908.   **V**

5834. ———. The house of Egremont; a novel. New York, Scribner, 1900.

vi, 515 p. front., plate. 8°.   **LC, VU**
Ed. of 1901.   **NYP**
Ed. of 1907.   **BP**

5835. ———. The imprisoned midshipmen. New York, Appleton, 1908.

5 p. l., 245 p. col. front., col. plates. 8°.   **LC, NYP**

5836. ———. The jugglers; a story. New York, Macmillan, 1911.

vii, 193 p. col. front. 12°.   **LC, NYP**

5837. ———. The ladies' battle. New York, Macmillan, 1911.

v, 7-119 p. 12°.   **BP, H, LC, NYP, V**
Eds. of 1912 & 1913.   **NYP**

5838. ———. The last duchess of Belgarde. New York, Appleton, 1908.

6 p. l., 121 p. col. front., illus. 12°.   **LC, NYP**

5839. ———. Laurie Vane, and other stories. Boston & Chicago, Wilde [*ca.* 1901]

152 p. front., plates. 12°. **LC**

5840. ———. Little Jarvis. New York, Appleton, 1890.

64 p. front., plate. 8°. **LC, NYP**
Ed. of 1893. **V**
Ed. of 1908. **NYP**

5841. ———. The lively adventures of Gavin Hamilton. New York & London, Harper, 1899.

4 p. l., front., plate. 12°. **LC, V**

5842. ———. The lost battle. New York, Macmillan, 1911.

119 p. 12°. **V**

5843. ———. The loves of the Lady Arabella. New York & London, Macmillan, 1898.

viii, 244 p. front., plates. 8°. **LC, V**
Ed. of 1906: Indianapolis, Bobbs-Merrill. 243 p. **LC, NYP**

5844. ———. Maid Marian, and other stories. New York, Appleton, 1891.

237 p. 12°. **LC, NYP**

5845. ———. The marriage of Theodora. New York, Dodd, Mead, 1910.

4 p. l., 392 p. col. front. 8°. **LC**

5846. ———. Midshipman Paulding. New York, Appleton, 1891.

133 p. front., plate, port. 8°. **LC, V**

5847. ———. Mrs. Darrell, by Foxcroft Davis [*pseud.*] New York, London, Macmillan, 1905.

3 p. l., 391 p. front., plate. 8°. **LC, NYP**

5848. ———. Papa Bouchard. New York, Scribner, 1901.

xi, 261 p. incl. front., illus. 12°. **LC, NYP, V**

5849. ———. Paul Jones. New York, Appleton, 1893.

viii, 166 p. front., plates, ports. 8°. **LC, V**

5850. ———. Quarter deck and fok'sle; stories of the sea. Boston, Wilde [*ca.* 1895]

272 p. front., plates. 12°. **LC, V**

5851. SEAWELL, MOLLY E. The Rock of the Lion. New York & London, Harper, 1898.

    3 p. l., 353 p. illus. 12°.   **LC**

5852. ———. The secret of Toni. New York, Appleton, 1907.

    vi, 330 p. front., plate. 8°.   **LC**

5853. ———. The son of Columbus. New York & London, Harper, 1912.

    5 p. l., 236 p. front., plates. 8°.   **LC**

5854. ———. The sprightly romance of Marsac. New York, Scribner, 1896.

    xii p., 1 l., 194 p. incl. front., illus. 12°.   **LC, NYP, V, VU**

5855. ———. A strange, sad comedy. New York, Century, 1896.

    2 p. l., 281 p. front. 8°.   **LC, V**

5856. ———. Throckmorton; a novel. New York, Appleton, 1890.

    304 p. 12°.   **LC, NYP, V**

5857. ———. Through thick and thin, and The midshipmen's mess; a soldier-story and a sailor-story. Boston, Lothrop, 1893.

    5 p. l., 215 p. incl. front., plate. 8°.   **LC, V**

5858. ———. The victory. New York, Appleton, 1906.

    5 p. l., 405 p. front., plate. 8°.   **LC, V**

5859. ———. A Virginia cavalier. New York, Harper, 1897.

    3 p. l., 349 p. front., plate. 12°.   **LC, V**
    Ed. of 1903.   **LC, V**

5860. ———. The whirl; a romance of Washington society, by Foxcroft Davis [*pseud.*] New York, Dodd, Mead, 1909.

    3 p. l., 306 p. col. front., plate. 8°.   **LC, NYP**

5861. [SHAW, ANNIE R.] Two families and two aims in life. New York, Warren, Broughton & Wyman [1872]

    372 p. plate. 16°. Pub. anonymously.   **LC**

5862. ———. The white chrysanthemum. A story. Boston, Warren [1871]

    389 p. plate. 16°. Pub. anonymously.   **LC**

5863. SHAW, JANE R. Letty Sterling: or the more excellent way. New York, Warren, Broughton & Wyman [1872]

    381 p. plate. 16°.   **LC**

5864. ——. Margaret's old home: a tale of Christian love. Boston, Warren [1871]

    364 p. plate. 16°.   **LC**

5865. ——. The neighbor's house. Boston, Warren & Blakeslee, 1869.

    400 p. plate. 16°.   **L'C**

5866. ——. The new commandment; or, Ella's ministry. Boston, Amer. tract society, 1869.

    378 p. plate. 16°.   **LC**

5867. SHEFFEY, MIRIAM. The spirit-mother, and other poems. New York, Broadway pub. [*ca.* 1905]

    62 p. 8°.   **LC, V**

5868. SLEDD, BENJAMIN (1864-?) From cliff and scaur. A collection of verse. New York & London, Putnam, 1897.

    100 p. 12°.   **H, NYP, VU**

5869. ——. The watchers of the hearth. Boston, Gorham, 1902.

    84 p. 16°. (The Arcadian library, I) Poetry.   **H, LC, NYP, VU**

5870. [SMITH, JAMES P.] Bright side idyls every week of the year. Richmond, Va., Central Presbyterian [1904]

    143, [2] p. front. 8°.   **V**

5871. SMITH, MRS. MARY S. (1834-?) Lang syne; or, The wards of Mount Vernon; a tale of the revolutionary era. New York, Alden, 1889.

    133 p. 8°.   **LC, NYP, V, VU**
    Ed. of 1890.   **H**

5872. SNEAD, GEORGIE T. Beneath Virginia skies. New York, Scott-Thaw, 1904.

    2 p. l., 343 p. front., plate. 12°.   **LC, V**

5873. ——. Joy bells; lyrics of hope and other poems. New York, Gorham, 1909.

    32 p. 21 x 10½ cm.   **LC**

5874. SNEAD, GEORGIE T. The story of Agatha Ann. Philadelphia, Winston, 1913.

121 p. front. 8°.   **LC**

5875. SOUTHWORTH, MRS. EMMA D. E. N. (1819-99) Allworth Abbey. Philadelphia, Peterson [*ca.* 1865]

2 p. l., 421 p. 12°.   **LC**

5876. ———. The artist's love. Philadelphia, Peterson [*ca.* 1872]

2 p. l., 21-479 p. 12°.   **LC**

5877. ———. Brandon Coyle's wife; a sequel to "A skeleton in the closet." New York, Bonner's, 1893.

2 p. l., 7-411 p. plate. 8°.   **LC**

5878. ———. The bride of Llewellyn. Rahway, N. J., Mershon [190-?]

1 p. l., [1], 6-255 p. 12°.   **NYP**

5879. ———. The bride's fate. A sequel to "The changed brides." Philadelphia, Peterson [1869]

488 p. 12°.   **LC, NYP**

5880. ———. Broken pledges. A story of noir et blanc. Philadelphia, Peterson [1891]

19-266 p. 12°.   **LC**

5881. ———. The changed brides. Philadelphia, Peterson [1869]

2 p. l., 21-503 p. 12°.   **LC**
Ed. of [1884]   **LC**
Ed. of [190-?]: New York, Grosset & Dunlap.   **NYP**

5882. ———. The Christmas guest. A collection of stories. Philadelphia, Peterson, 1870.

2 p. l., 19-338 p. 12°.   **LC**

5883. ———. The coral lady; or, The bronzed beauty of Paris. Philadelphia, Alexander [*ca.* 1867]

19-78 p. incl. plates. 8°.   **LC**

5884. ———. Cruel as the grave. Philadelphia, Peterson [*ca.* 1871]

19-372 p. 12°.   **LC**

5885. ———. The curse of Clifton; or, The widowed bride. Philadelphia, Peterson [*ca.* 1886]

15-467 p. 12°.   **LC**

5886. ———. David Lindsay; a sequel to "Gloria." New York, Bonner's, 1891.

2 p. l., [7]-469 p. plates. 12°. **LC, NYP**
Ed. of [1905]: New York, Burt. 390 p. 12°. **LC**

5887. ———. "Em," a novel. New York, Bonner's 1892.

2 p. l., 7-368 p. plates. 12°. **LC**

5888. ———. Em's husband. A novel. New York, Bonner's, 1892.

2 p. l., 7-395 p. plates. 12°. **LC**

5889. ———. Fair play; or, The test of the lone isle. Philadelphia, Peterson [1868]

670 p. 12°. **LC, NYP**

5890. ———. Fallen pride; or, The mountain girl's love. Philadelphia, Peterson [1868]

467 p. 12°. **LC**

5891. ———. The family doom; or, The sin of a countess. Philadelphia, Peterson, 1869.

350 p. 12°. **LC**
Ed. of 1888. **LC**

5892. ———. The fatal secret . . . and other stories by her sister, Mrs. Frances Henshaw Baden. Philadelphia, Peterson [1877]

2 p. l., 374 p. 12°. **LC**

5893. ———. For woman's love. A novel. New York, Bonner's, 1890.

1 p. l., 486 p. front., plates. 12°. **LC**

5894. ———. The fortune seeker. Philadelphia, Peterson [ca. 1886]

2 p. l., 498 p. 12°. **LC**

5895. ———. Gertrude Haddon. "Only a girl's heart." 3d ser. New York, Bonner's, 1894.

2 p. l., 416 p. plates. 12°. **LC**

5896. ———. The gipsy's prophecy; or, The bride of an evening. New York, Lupton [ca. 1886]

1 p. l., 23-455 p. 8°. **NYP**

5897. SOUTHWORTH, MRS. EMMA D. E. N. Gloria. A novel. New York, Bonner's, 1891.

    2 p. l., 348 p. plates. 12°.   **LC, NYP**

5898. ———. The hidden hand; a novel. Chicago, Donohue [190-?]

    1 p. l., [5]-270 p. 8°.   **LC**
    Ed. of [1920?]: New York, Burt. 238 p.   **LC**

5899. ———. How he won her. A sequel to "Fair play." Philadelphia, Peterson [1869]

    2 p. l., 512 p. 12°.   **L'C**

5900. ———. India, the pearl of Pearl River. New York, Federal book [1888]

    1 p. l., 23-402 p. 12°.   **NYP**

5901. ———. Ishmael; or, In the depths. New York, Fenno [1904]

    vi, 549 p. front., plates. 8°.   **LC**
    Ed. of n. d.: New York, Burt.   **V**
    Ed. of [190-?]: New York, Hurst. 440 p. 16°.   **NYP**

5902. ———. A leap in the dark. A novel. New York, Bonner's [1890]

    3 p. l., 556 p. front. 12°.   **LC, NYP**

5903. ———. Lilith. A sequel to "The unloved wife." New York, Bonner's, 1891.

    2 p. l., 399 p. plates. 12°.   **LC, NYP**

5904. ———. Little Nea's engagement; a sequel to "Nearest and dearest." New York, Street & Smith [ca. 1908]

    1 p. l., [283]-572 p. 12°.   **LC**

5905. ———. The lost heir of Linlithgow. Philadelphia, Peterson [ca. 1872]

    1 p. l., [21]-570. 12°.   **LC, NYP**

5906. ———. The lost lady of Lone. New York, Bonner's [1894?]
    561 p. incl. front., plates. 12°.   **NYP**

5907. ———. The maiden widow, a novel. Philadelphia, Peterson, 1870.

    1 p. l., 313 p. 12°. Sequel to "The family doom."   **NYP**
    Ed. of [ca. 1888]   **LC**
    Ed. of [1898]: New York, Lupton.   **LC**

5908. ———. Miriam, the avenger; or, The missing bride. Philadelphia, Peterson [187-?]

    19-635 p. front. (port.) 12°.   **NYP**

5909. ———. The mystery of Dark Hollow. Philadelphia, Peterson [*ca.* 1875]

    1 p. l., 366 p. 12°.   **LC, NYP**

5910. ———. Nearest and dearest. A novel. New York, Bonner's [*ca.* 1889]

    3 p. l., 572 p. front. 12°.   **LC**

5911. ———. A noble lord. The sequel to "The lost heir of Linlithgow." Philadelphia, Peterson [*ca.* 1872]

    1 p. l., [19]-428 p. 12°.   **LC**
    Eds. of [190-?] and [191-?] Rahway and New York.   **NYP**

5912. ———. Only a girl's heart, a novel. New York, Bonner's, 1893.

    2 p. l., 453 p. plates. 8°.   **LC**

5913. ———. The prince of darkness. A romance of the Blue Ridge. Philadelphia, Peterson [*ca.* 1869]

    1 p. l., [19]-370 p. 12°.   **LC, NYP**
    Ed. of [1897]: New York, Lupton.   **LC**

5914. ———. The Red Hill tragedy. A novel. Philadelphia, Peterson [1877]

    1 p. l., 19-266 p. 12°.   **LC**

5915. ———. The rejected bride, "Only a girl's heart." 2d ser. New York, Bonner's, 1894.

    2 p. l., 7-445 p. plates. 8°.   **LC**

5916. ———. Self-raised; or, From the depths. Philadelphia, Peterson, 1876.

    658 p. 12°.   **NYP**
    Ed. of [1904]: New York, Fenno. iv, 499 p. illus. 8°.   **LC**

5917. ———. A skeleton in the closet; a novel. New York, Bonner's [1898]

    2 p. l., 7-381 p. 12°.   **LC**

5918. ———. Sybil Brotherton. A novel. Philadelphia, Peterson [*ca.* 1879]

    1 p. l., 19-168 p. 16°.   **LC**

5919. Southworth, Mrs. Emma D. E. N.   The test of love ("The trail of the serpent") 3d & last ser.   New York, Street & Smith [*ca.* 1907]

> 1 p. l., [5]-301 p. 12°.   **LC**

5920. ———.   Tried for her life.   A sequel to "Cruel as the grave." Philadelphia, Peterson [1871]

> 1 p. l., 19-356 p. 12°.   **LC, NYP**
> Ed. of [1899]:   New York, Lupton.   **LC**

5921. ———.   The two sisters; or, Virginia and Magdalene.   Philadelphia, Peterson [*ca.* 1875]

> 1 p. l., 23-497 p. 12°.   **LC**
> Ed. of [190-?]:   Chicago, Donohue.   306 p. 12°.   **NYP**

5922. ———.   Unknown; or, The mystery of Raven Rocks.   New York, Bonner's [*ca.* 1889]

> 3 p. l., 592 p. front. 12°.   **LC, NYP**
> Ed. of [189-?]   **BP**

5923. ———.   The unloved wife; a novel.   New York, Bonner's, 1891.

> 2 p. l., 374 p. plate. 12°.   .   **LC**

5924. ———.   Victor's triumph.   Philadelphia, Peterson [1874]

> 1 p. l., 19-348 p. 12°.   **LC, NYP**

5925. ———.   Vivia; or, The secret of power.   Philadelphia, Peterson [*ca.* 1875]

> 2 p. l., 25-540 p. 12°.   **LC, NYP**

5926. Spiers, Mrs. Mary B.   The giant of the Blue Ridge, and other poems.   Washington, Neale, 1903.

> 96 p. front. (port.) 12°.   **LC, NYP**
> Ed. of 1916.   **BP**

5927. Stabler, Mrs. Jennie L. (*d.* 1882) Left to herself.   By Jennie Woodville [*pseud.*]   Philadelphia, Lippincott, 1872.

> 311 p. 12°.   **LC**
> Ed. of 1874, with title: *Edith's mistake.*   **LC,V**

5928. Stanard, Mrs. Mary M.   The dreamer; a romantic rendering of the life story of Edgar Allan Poe.   Richmond, Va., Bell, 1909.

> 375 p. 8°.
> Ed. of 1925:   Philadelphia & London, Lippincott.   381 p. illus.

5929. STANTON, HENRY T. (1834-98)   A graduate of Paris. Washington, Morrison [*ca.* 1889]

166 p. 12°.   L'C

5930. ———. Jacob Brown, and other poems.   Cincinnati, Clarke, 1875.

vii, 8-155 p. 12°.   NYP

5931. ———. The moneyless man, and other poems.   Baltimore, Turnbull, 1871.

159 p. 12°.   BP, LC, VU
Ed. of 1884: Cincinnati, Clarke.   183 p. 8°.   V

5932. ———. Poems of the Confederacy, being selections from the writings of H. T. Stanton.   Louisville, Morton, 1900.

46 p. front. (port.) 8°.   LC, NYP, V

5933. ———. The poetical works of H. T. Stanton.   Cincinnati, Clarke, 1901.

vi, 7-337 p. 8°.   LC

5934. ———. Social fetters; or, Within a shadow.   Washington, Morrison, 1889.

100 p. 12°.   LC

5935. STEVENS, THOMAS W. (1880-19)   Book of words, the pageant of Virginia . . . Richmond, Virginia historical pageant association, 1922.

144 p. 8°.   BP, LC, V, VU, WM
Presented at Richmond, in May, 1922.

5936. STEWART, ROBERT A.   The boy scouts of the air at Cape Peril. Chicago, Reilly & Lee [*ca.* 1921]

256 p. front. 8°.   LC, V

5937. ———. The boy scouts of the air in Dismal Swamp, by Gordon Stuart [*pseud.*]   Chicago, Reilly & Lee [*ca.* 1920]

224 p. front. 8°.   LC, V

5938. ———. The boy scouts of the air on Baldcrest.   Chicago, Reilly & Lee [*ca.* 1922]

225 p. front. 8°.   LC, V

5939. ———. Golden stairs.   Richmond, Dietz, 1923.

[28] p. 8°.   Poetry.   H, LC, NYP, V

5940. STEWART, ROBERT A.   Knights of the golden horseshoe, and other lays.   Richmond, Evans, 1909.

    4 p. l., 45 p. 8°.   **H, LC, NYP, V, VU**

5941. ———.   Masks and motley.   [Richmond, 1925]

    47 l. typew. 4°.   Poetry.   **V**

5942. STILES, LEILA C.   (1875-95)   After-glow.   Richmond, Va., Whittet & Shepperson, 1898.

    2 p. l., 5-117 p. front., port. 12°.   **V**
    Biographical sketch of author, p. 9-31.

5943. [SWANK, WILLIAM A.?]   The judgeship.   A tale of the times.   By S. P. Q.   Norfolk, Va., 1884.

    10 p. 8°.   Poetry.   **V**

5944. SWARTZ, JOEL.   Dreamings of the waking heart.   With other poems.   Harrisburg, Pa., 1877.

    8°.   **H**

5945. ———.   Poems.   Philadelphia, Coates, 1901.

    xv, 237 p. front. (port.) plate. 8°.   **LC**

5946. ———.   Wedlock in Eden, in verse.   Philadelphia, Patterson & White, 1902.

    23 p. front. (port.) 12°.   **LC**

5947. TABB, JOHN B.   (1845-1909)   Child verse; poems grave and gay.   Boston, Small, Maynard, 1899.

    7 p. l., 78 p. 8°.   **BP, LC, NYP, V**
    Ed. of 1900.   **VU**

5948. ———.   Later lyrics.   New York & London, Lane, 1902.

    xi, 138 p. 16°.   **H, LC, NYP, V**
    Ed. of 1910.   **BP**

5949. ———.   Later poems.   New York, Kennerley, 1910.

    117 p. 12°.   **BP, LC, NYP**

5950. ———.   Lyrics.   Boston, Copeland & Day; London, Lane, 1897.

    3 p. l., v-xi, 187 p. 16°.
    Ed. of 1909.   **BP**
    Ed. of 1911.   **V**

5951. ———. An octave to Mary. Baltimore, Murphy, 1893.

14 1., front. 18 x 28½ cm.   **L'C, VU**
Ed. of 1897: New York, Mansfield. 27 1. front.   **NYP**

5952. ———. Poems. Boston & London, Lane, 1895.

1 p. 1., xi, 172 p. 16°.   **BP, H, V**
Eds. of 1883, '94, and '96.   **BP**
Ed. of 1897.   **BP, H, VU**
Ed. of 1899.   **NYP**
Ed. of 1903.   **LC**
Ed. of 1911.   **V**

5953. ———. The poetry of Father Tabb, ed. by Francis A. Litz. New York, Dodd, Mead, 1928.

xvi p., 2 1., 3-492 p. front. (port.) 8°.   **BP, H, LC, V**

5954. ———. Quips and quiddits, ques for the qurious. Boston, Small, Maynard, 1907.

[112] p. illus. 8°.   **LC, NYP**

5955. ———. The rosary in rhyme. [Boston, Small, Maynard] 1904.

4 p. 1., 58, [3] p. illus. 16°.   **LC**
Ed. of 1916.   **BP, NYP**

5956. ———. A selection from the verses of John B. Tabb, made by Alice Maynell. Boston, Small, Maynard, 1907.

xi (*i.e.* 9), 120 p. 12°.   **BP, LC, VU**
Ed. of 1907: London, Burne & Oates.   **V**

5957. ———. Two lyrics. [Boston, Craftsman's guild, 1900]

10 1. 12°.   **BP, LC, NYP**

5958. TERHUNE, MRS. MARY V. (1831-1922) At last. A novel. By Marion Harland [*pseud.*] New York, Carleton, 1870.

vi, [7]-360 p. 12°.   **LC**
Ed. of 1898: New York, Dillingham.   **LC, NYP**

5959. ———. Bits of common sense series. New York, Home topics pub. [1899]

4 v. 16°.   **LC**

5960. ———. The Carringtons of High Hill; an old Virginia chronicle. New York, Scribner, 1919.

3 p. 1., 308 p. 12°.   **LC, NYP, V**

5961. TERHUNE, MRS. MARY V. The Christmas holly. New York, Sheldon, 1867.

vii, 86 p. front., plate. 8°.   H, LC

5962. ———. Helen Gardner's wedding-day; or, Col. Floyd's wards. A battle summer. New York, Carleton, 1870.

382 p. 12°.   LC

5963. ———. The distractions of Martha. New York, Scribner, 1906.

5 p. l., 223 p. front., plate. 12°.   LC, V

5964. ———. Dr. Dale; a story without a moral. New York, Dodd, Mead, 1900.

vi, 408 p. 8°.   LC, NYP

5965. ———. From my youth up. New York, Carleton, 1874.

3 p. l., 390 p. 12°.   H, LC, NYP
Ed. of 1875.   V

5966. ———. A gallant fight. New York, Dodd, Mead [1888]

2 p. l., 414 p. 12°.   LC, V

5967. ———. Hannah More. New York & London, Putnam, 1900.

2 p. l., xiv, 238 p. front., plates, ports. 12°.   BP, LC, NYP

5968. ———. The hidden path. New York, Dillingham, 1898.

433 p. 12°.   LC

5969. ———. His great self. Philadelphia, Lippincott, 1892.

355 p. 8°.   LC, NYP, V

5970. ———. In our county; stories of old Virginia life. New York & London, Putnam, 1901.

ix, 465 p. front., plates. 8°.   LC, V

5971. ———. Jessamine. A novel. New York, Carleton, 1873.

3 p. l., x, 387 p. 12°.   LC, NYP

5972. ———. Judith, a chronicle of old Virginia. Philadelphia, New York [etc.] 1883.

2 p. l., 391 p. front., plates. 12°.   LC, VU

5973. ———. A long lane. New York, Hearst's international library co., 1915.

5 p. l., 363 p. col. front. 8°.   LC

5974. ———. Looking westward. New York, Scribner, 1914.
4 p. 1., 28 p. front. (port.) 12°. **BP, LC, NYP**

5975. ———. Miriam. New York, Carleton, 1874.
549 p. 12°. **NYP**

5976. ———. Mr. Wayt's wife's sister. New York, Cassell [ca. 1894]
2 p. 1., 314 p. 12°. **LC**

5977. ———. More than kin. Philadelphia, 1892.
p. [549]-632. 8°. (In *Lippincott's magazine,* XLIX) **H, LC**

5978. ———. My little love. New York, Carleton, 1876.
4 p. 1., [11]-396 p. 12°. **LC, NYP**

5979. ———. An old-field school-girl. New York, Scribner, 1897.
4 p. 1., 208 p. front., plate. 12°. **LC, V**

5980. ———. Phinnie's temptation. A novel. New York, Carleton, 1869.
2 p. 1., 396 p. 12°. **LC**
Ed. of 1870. **NYP**
Ed. of 1897: New York, Dillingham. **LC**

5981. ———. The royal road; or, Taking him at his word. New York, Randolph [1894]
377 p. 8°. **LC**

5982. ———. Ruby's husband. New York, Sheldon, 1869.
392 p. 12°. **LC, NYP**
Ed. of 1876. **V**
Ed. of 1896: New York, Dillingham. **LC**

5983. ———. Ruth Bergen's limitations; a modern auto-da-fe. New York, Chicago, Revell, 1897.
3 p. 1., 123 p. 12°. **LC, V**

5984. ———. Stepping-stones. New York, Street & Smith [ca. 1890]
207 p. front., illus. 8°. **LC**

5985. ———. Sunnybank. New York, Sheldon, 1866.
415 p. 12°. **LC, NYP**
Ed. of 1889: New York, Dillingham. **LC**

5986. TERHUNE, MRS. MARY V. True as steel. A novel. New York, Carleton, 1876.

350 p. 12°.   **V**
Ed. of 1872.   **LC, NYP**
Ed. of 1886.   **LC**

5987. ———. When grandmamma was fourteen. Boston, Lothrop [1905]

399 p. front., plate. 8°.   **LC, V**

5988. ———. When grandmamma was new; the story of a Virginia childhood. Boston, Lothrop [1899]

305 p. illus., plate. 12°.   **LC, V**

5989. ———. With the best intentions; a midsummer episode. New York, Scribner, 1890.

2 p. l., 303 p. 12°.   **LC**
Ed. of 1901.   **NYP**

5990. THOMPSON, JOHN R. (1823-73) Poem read before the Society of alumni, University of Virginia, July 1, 1869. Richmond, Clemmitt & Jones, 1870.

12 p. 8°.   **VU**

5991. ———. Poems . . . with biographical introduction by John S. Patton . . . University of Virginia ed. . . . New York, Scribner, 1920.

lxii p., 1 l., 248 p. front. (port.) 8°.   **BP, LC, NYP, V, VU**

5992. THORNTON, JAMES D. Chorronessee, and other tales. Norfolk, Va., Journal, 1868.

vi p., 1 p. l., [9]-212 p. 12°.   **V**

5993. THRUSTON, MRS. LUCY M. (1862-19) Called to the field; a story of Virginia in the Civil war. Boston, Little, Brown, 1906.

ix, 340 p. 8°.   **LC**

5994. ———. A girl of Virginia. Boston, Little, Brown, 1902.

4 p. l., 306 p. front., plate. 8°.   **LC, NYP, V**

5995. ———. Jack and his island; a boy's adventures along the Chesapeake in the War of 1812. Boston, Little, Brown, 1902.

5 p. l., 304 p. front., plate. 12°.   **BP, LC**

5996. ———. Jenifer. Boston, Little, Brown, 1907.

4 p. l., 298 p. front. plate. 8°.   **LC**

5997. ———. Mistress Brent; a story of Lord Baltimore's colony in 1638. Boston, Little, Brown, 1901.

    4 p. l., 352 p. front., plate. 8°.   **LC**

5998. ———. Where the tide comes in [a novel] Boston, Little, Brown, 1904.

    4 p. l., 391 p. front., plate. 8°.   **LC, V**

5999. TOMPKINS, ELLEN W. The egotistical I. New York, Dutton [*ca.* 1913]

    5 p. l., 172 p. 12°.   **BP, LC, V**

6000. ———. The enlightenment of Paulina; a novel. New York, Dutton [*ca.* 1917]

    4 p. l., 335 p. 12°.   **LC, V**

6001. TROUBETZKOY, AMELIE R. C. (1863-19) According to St. John. New York, Lovell [*ca.* 1891]

    3 p. l., 352 p. front., plate. 12°.   **BP, LC, NYP, V, VU**

6002. ———. As the wind blew; poems. New York, Stokes [*ca.* 1920]

    xii, 229 p. front. (port.) 8°.   **BP, H, LC, NYP, V**

6003. ———. Athelwold. New York, Harper, 1893.

    4 p. l., 118 p. plates. (incl. front.) 12°.

6004. ———. Augustine the man. London, New York, Lane, 1906.

    5 p. l., 83 p. front. (port.) 8°.   **H, LC, NYP, V, VU**

6005. ———. Barbara Dering. A sequel to "The quick or the dead?" Philadelphia, Lippincott, 1893.

    285 p. 12°.   **LC, NYP, VU**

6006. ———. A brother to dragons, and other old-time tales. New York, Harper, 1888.

    4 p. l., 230 p. 12°.   **H, LC, NYP, V, VU**

6007. ———. A damsel errant. Philadelphia, Lippincott, 1898.

    211 p. front., plates. 16°.   **LC, V**

6008. ———. The ghost garden, a novel. New York, Stokes [*ca.* 1918]

    2 p. l., 299 p. front. 8°.   **LC, NYP, V, VU**

6009. Troubetzkoy, Amélie R. C.   The golden rose; the romance of a strange soul. New York & London, Harper, 1908.

    4 p. 1., 225 p. 8°.   **H, LC, NYP, V**

6010. ———. Herod and Marianne. A tragedy. Philadelphia, Lippincott, 1888.

    p. [303]-462. 8°.   (In *Lippincott's magazine,* Sept., 1888)

                                               H, NYP, V, VU

6011. ———. Hidden house. Philadelphia & London, Lippincott, 1912.

    151 p. front. 8°.   **LC, VU**

6012. ———. Love-in-a-mist; a comedy in three acts. New York & London, French [*ca.* 1927]

    96 p. plates. 8°.   **LC, NYP**

6013. ———. Pan's mountain. New York & London, Harper, 1910.

    4 p. 1., 287 p. 8°.   **LC, NYP, V, VU**

6014. ———. The queerness of Celia. New York, Stokes, 1926.

    4 p. 1., 307 p. 8°.   **LC, NYP, V**

6015. ———. The quick or the dead? A study. Philadelphia, 1888.

    p. [431]-522. 8°.   (In *Lippincott's magazine,* XLI)

6016. ———. The sea-woman's cloak, and November eve, two plays. Cincinnati, Kidd [*ca.* 1923]

    156 p. 8°.

6017. ———. Seléné [a poem] New York & London, Harper, 1905.

    3 p. 1., 88 p. 8°.

6018. ———. Shadows of flames; a novel. New York, Stokes [1915]

    4 p. 1., 590 p. col. front. 8°.   **LC, NYP, V, VU**

6019. ———. Tanis, the sand-digger. New York, Town topics pub., 1893.

    2 p. 1., 187 p. 8°.   **H, LC, NYP, V, VU**

6020. ———. Trix and Over-the-moon. New York & London, Harper, 1909.

    4 p. 1., 164 p. front., plates. 8°.   **LC, VU**

6021. ———. Virginia of Virginia; a story. New York, Harper, 1888.

    2 p. 1., 222 p. incl. illus. front. 12°.   **LC, NYP, V, VU**

6022. ———. The witness of the sun. Philadelphia, Lippincott, 1889.

    2 p. 1., 7-248 p. front. (port.) 12°.   **H, LC, NYP, V, VU**

6023. ———. World's end. New York, Stokes [1914]

    3 p. 1., 425 p. front., plates. 8°.   **LC, NYP, V, VU**

6024. TUCKER, BEVERLEY D. (1846-19) Confederate memorial verses. Norfolk, Pub. by Pickett-Buchanan chapter, United daughters of the Confederacy [1904?]

    36 p. 8°.   **LC, V**

6025. ———. My three loves; the poems of B. D. Tucker. New York & Washington, Neale, 1910.

    106 p. 12°.   **LC, NYP, V, VU**

6026. TUCKER, HARRY. The man about town; short stories, philosophical reflections [etc.] [Richmond, Va., Saunders, 1902]

    142, [1] p. front. (port.) 12°.   **V**
    Reprinted from Richmond *Evening leader.*

6027. TUNSTALL, NANNIE W. "No. 40." A romance of Fortress Monroe and the Hygeia. Richmond, Va., McCarthy, 1884.

    111 p. front. 12°.   **LC, VU**
    2d ed., 1884.   **V**
    3d ed., 1890: Richmond, Randolph & English.   **LC, NYP, V**

6028. TUNSTALL, MRS. VIRGINIA H. A white sail set. New York, Vinal, 1927.

    5 p. 1., 67 p. 8°. Poetry.   **LC, NYP, VU**

6029. TYLER, ODETTE[1] (1872-19) Boss. New York & London, Transatlantic pub., 1896.

    215 p. 12°.   **H, LC**
    Ed. of 1897: New York & London, Continental pub.   **LC**

---

1. Same as Mrs. Elizabeth Lee (Kirkland) Shepard.

6030. URNER, CLARENCE H. (1856-19) Poems. Richmond, Va., 1924.

42 l. 4°. Title-page typew.   **V**
Poems clipped from periodicals.

6031. ———. The thrush. New Market, Va., Henkel, 1927.

88 p. 12°. Poetry.   **LC, V, VU**

6032. VALENTINE, BENJAMIN B. (1862-1919) Ole marster, and other verses. Richmond, Va., Whittet & Shepperson, 1921.

117 p. 12°.   **BP, H, LC, NYP, V**

6033. ———. [Poems] [n. p., n. d.]

Printed on post cards.   **V**

6034. WALL, HENRY. Fashion: a humorous and satirical poem. In two parts. Richmond, Va., West & Johnson, 1870.

22 p. 8°.   **LC, NYP, V**

6035. WALL, MARY V. The daughter of Virginia Dare. New York & Washington, Neale, 1908.

194 p. 8°. A novel.   **LC, V**

6036. WARD, MRS. LYDIA A. (1845-1924) Lincoln and Washington . . . verses by L. A. Coonley [Ward] . . . For the story hour . . . in primary and intermediate grades. Chicago, Flannagan [1899?]

90, [6] p. incl. plates, ports. 8°.   **LC**

6037. ———. Love songs. [Chicago, Windtryst] 1898 [i. e. 1899]
59 p. 16°.   **LC**

6038. ———. The melody of childhood. New York, White, 1921.

7 p. l., 166 p. front. (port.) 12°.   **LC**

6039. ———. The melody of life. New York, White, 1921.

7 p. l., 145 p. front. (port.) 12°. Poetry.   **LC**

6040. ———. The melody of love. New York, White, 1921.

7 p. l., 178 p. front. 12°.   **LC**

6041. ———. Our flag with the stars and stripes. A patriotic cantata for school and choir. New York, Church, 1896.

82 p. 12°.   **LC**

6042. ———. Singing verses for children. Words by L. A. Coonley [Ward] New York, London, Macmillan, 1897.

[82] p. illus. 4°. **LC, NYP**

6043. ———. Susan B. Anthony . . . Love's rosary. [n. p., 1900]

[4] p. 8°. A poem. **LC**

6044. ———. Under the pines, and other verses. Chicago, Way & Williams, 1895.

vii, [9]-104 p. 12°. **LC, NYP**

6045. WARREN, B. C. Arsareth; a tale of the Luray Caverns. New York, Lovell [ca. 1893]

3 p. l., [5]-273 p. 8°. **L'C, V, VU**

6046. WAYLAND, JOHN W. (1872-19) Whispers of the hills. New Market, Va., Henkel, 1928.

104 p. 12°. Poems. **LC, NYP, V**

6047. WHITTET, ROBERT (1829-?) The brighter side of suffering, and other poems. Richmond, Va., Whittet & Shepperson [1882]

3 p. l., [3]-384 p. 12°. **LC, V**

6048. ———. Sonnets, mostly on Scripture themes, with a few other poems. Richmond, Whittet & Shepperson, 1900.

1 p. l., xiv, 324 p. 8°. **LC, NYP, V**

6049. WILLIAMS, FLORA M. Who's the patriot? A story of the southern Confederacy. Louisville, Ky., Courier-Journal, 1886.

288 p. illus. (incl. port.) 12°. **H, LC, NYP, V**

6050. WILSON, RICHARD H. (1870-19) Mazel, by Richard Fisquill [*pseud.*] Chicago, Stone, 1902.

3 p. l., 321 p. 8°. **LC, VU**

6051. ———. The Venus of Cadiz; an extravaganza. New York, Holt, 1905.

323 p. 8°. **LC, VU**

6052. WINSTON, NANNIE B. The regeneration of Helen Galbraith; or, waters that pass away. New York, Dillingham [1901]

322 p. 12°. (Dillingham's American authors' library, LXXVI) **LC**
Ed. of 1899. **LC, V**

6053. WINSTON, MRS. ROSALIE B. Pilate's question; or, What is truth? Richmond, Va., Walford, 1885.

134 p. 16°. Poetry.   **V**

6054. WINTERBURN, FLORENCE H. (1858-19) Liberty Hall, a story for girls. New York & London, Harper [1916]

3 p. l., 299 p. front., plates. 12°.   **LC**

6055. ———. Southern hearts. New York, Lupton, 1900.

5 p. l., 13-406 p. front. 12°.   **LC, V**

6056. WISE, JOHN S. (1846-19) Diomed; the life, travels and observations of a dog. Boston, London [etc.] Lamson, Wolffe, 1897.

vi, 330 p. illus. 8°.   **BP, H, LC, NYP, V**
Ed. of 1899: New York, Macmillan.   **H, LC**
Ed. of 1905.   **NYP**

6057. ———. The lion's skin; a historical novel and a novel history. New York, Doubleday, Page, 1905.

xv, 3-404 p. 8°.   **LC, NYP, V**

6058. WOOD, ANNA C. Diana Fontaine. A novel. By Algernon Ridgeway [*pseud.*] Philadelphia, Lippincott, 1891.

v, 306 p. 12°.   **LC, NYP**

6059. ———. Idyls and impressions of travel, from the note-books of two friends. New York & Washington, Neale, 1904.

x, 264 p. 8°.   **BP, LC**

6060. WOOD, THOMAS L., comp. Arcade echoes. Selected poems from the Virginia university magazine, 1859-1890. Collected and arranged by Thomas L. Wood. Philadelphia, Lippincott, 1890.

125 p. 16°.   **LC, NYP, V**
Ed. of 1894.   **LC, V, VU**

6061. WORMELEY, CARTER W. Poems. New York, Broadway pub. [1904]

1 p. l., iv, 73 p. front. (port.) 12°.   **LC, V**

6062. WREN, MARGARET B. (1853-88) Echoes from the heart. Richmond, Va., Whittet & Shepperson, 1887.

259 p. 8°. Poetry.   **V, VU**

Secondary Works

6063. **[5122]** ALLAN, MRS. ELIZABETH (P.)   The life and letters of Margaret Junkin Preston . . .   Boston & New York, 1903.

6064. **[5127]** BEATY, JOHN O.   John Esten Cooke . . .   New York, 1922.

6065. BREGENZER, DON M., *et al.,* ed.   A round-table in Poictesme; a symposium, edited by Don Bregenzer and Samuel Loveman . . .   Cleveland, Priv. print. by members of the Colophon club, 1924.

> xi, [1], 126 p. 8°.   LC, V
> Published as an appreciation of James Branch Cabell's contribution to creative literature.

6066. COOPER, FREDERIC T.   Some American story tellers . . .   New York, Holt, 1911.

> vii p. 2 l., 338 p. ports. (incl. front.) 8°.
> Includes an essay on Ellen Glasgow.

6067. COVER, JAMES P.   Notes on Jurgen . . .   New York, McBride, 1928.

> x p., 2 l., 3-115 p. 8°.   LC, V

6068. COX, MRS. KATHERINE C.   Some facts regarding the Houdon statue of Washington in the capitol at Richmond, Virginia.   Richmond, Dietz, 1924.

> 15 p. illus. 12°.   V

6069. CURTIS, ELIZABETH S. . . .   Suggestions to teachers, notes and study helps . . .   for *Queed* by Henry Sydnor Harrison.   Boston, New York [etc.]   Houghton, Mifflin [*ca.* 1928]

> iv, [431]-458 p. 12°.   (Riverside literature series)   LC

6070. FIELD, LOUISE M.   Ellen Glasgow, novelist of the old and the new South.   An appreciation . . .   together with a critical essay and an index to her works . . .   Garden City, N. Y., Doubleday, Page [*ca.* 1923]

> 20 p. front. (port.) 12°.   (Little biographies of great writers series)
>   V

6071. [FINN, *Sister* Mary P.]   John Bannister Tabb, the priest-

poet, by M. S. Pine [*pseud.*] . . . Washington, D. C., Pub.
for the Georgetown Visitation convent, 1915.

153 p. front. (port.) 8°.   H, BP, LC, NYP, V

Sketch of Tabb's life and analysis of his poetic style, with many quotations from his works, by an enthusiastic admirer.

6072. [5545] GORDON, ARMISTEAD C., jr., ed. Virginian writers
of fugitive verse . . . New York, [*ca.* 1923]

6073. HENKEL, ELON O. Memorial address on the life and character of Joseph Salyards. New Market, Va., Henkel, 1893.

31, [1] p. front. (port.) 8°.   V, VU

6074. HUBBELL, JAY B. Virginia life in fiction . . . Dallas,
1922.

3 p. l., 5-79 p. 8°.   H, LC, NYP, V, VU

Thesis (Ph.D.), Columbia university, 1922.
Chap. 6 on "Modern Virginia."

6075. JOHNSON, ROBERT U., *et al.* Commemorative tributes to
[Thomas Nelson] Page, by Robert Underwood Johnson; [Wood-
row] Wilson, by Bliss Perry; . . . prepared for the American academy of arts and letters, 1924. [New York] American
academy of arts and letters, 1925.

2 p. l., 24 p. 12°. (Academy publication, 50)   LC, NYP

6076. [5169] KING, JOSEPH L. Dr. George William Bagby . . .
New York, 1927.

6077. [5179] LITZ, FRANCIS A. Father Tabb; a study of his life
and works . . . Baltimore, 1923.

6078. ———. Father Tabb; a study of his poetry . . . Baltimore, Litz print., 1924.

2 p. l., 123-193, 284-288 p., 1 l. 8°.   BP, H, LC, NYP

Thesis (Ph.D.), Johns Hopkins university, 1921.
Based on the same author's *Father Tabb; a study of his life and works*
[5179] Appendix contains hitherto unpublished poems of Tabb.

6079. McCABE, WILLIAM G. John R. Thompson, poet and editor,
1823-1873; an address delivered at the University of Virginia,
June 12, 1899. [n. p., n. d.]

17 p. 8°.   V

6080. [McRAE, SHERWIN] Washington: his person as represented
by the artists. The Houdon statue, its history and value . . .

Published by order of the Senate of Virginia. [Richmond] Walker, 1873.

23 p. 8°. ([Virginia] Senate, Doc., XXI) **LC, V, VU**

6081. MANN, DOROTHEA L., *et al.* Ellen Glasgow . . . with critical essays and bibliography. Garden City, N. Y., Doubleday, Page, 1927.

1 p. l., 42, [4] p. front. (port.) illus. 8°. **LC, V**
Ellen Glasgow portrayed as an exponent of realism in southern literature. Essays by J. B. Cabell, Joseph Collins, and Carl Van Vechten.

6082. MENCKEN, HENRY L. James Branch Cabell . . . New York, McBride, 1927.

32 p. front. (port.) facsim. 12°. **H, LC, NYP, V**
In praise of Cabell's iconoclasm and fine literary qualities; with brief reviews of his books.

6083. [5187] PAGE, ROSEWELL. Thomas Nelson Page; a memoir . . . New York, 1923.

6084. PAGE, THOMAS N., ed. The old Virginia gentleman, and other sketches, by George W. Bagby; ed. with an introduction by Thomas Nelson Page. New York, Scribner, 1910.

xxix, [1], 312 p. front. (port.) 8°. **H, LC, V, VU, WM**
The introduction is a characterization of Bagby and his writings; with a sketch of his life by E. S. Gregory.

6085. PAINTER, FRANKLIN V. Poets of Virginia . . . Richmond, Atlanta [etc.] Johnson [*ca.* 1907]

336 p. front., ports. 8°. **BP, LC, V, VU, WM**
Pt. V: "Second national period," 1870-1906.
Brief biographical sketches and criticism of poetry.

6086. PRICE, THOMAS R. John Bannister Tabb. A study of his poetry. A paper prepared for the Woman's club of Richmond, Va., 18 March 1895. Boston [Copeland] 1896.

[1], 12 p. 8°. **BP**

6087. [5196] SCOTT, MRS. L. C. The life and letters of Christopher Pearse Cranch . . . Boston & New York, 1917.

6088. SHEWMAKE, EDWIN F. English pronunciation in Virginia . . . [Davidson? N. C., 1928]

45 p. 8°. **LC, VU**
Thesis (Ph.D.), University of Virginia, 1920.
A study of the historical background of Virginia pronunciation, its use in literature, and a comparison of Virginia and standard pronunciation.

6089. [5203] TABB, JENNIE M. Father Tabb, his life and work
. . . Boston, 1921.

6090. [5216] VALENTINE, ELIZABETH G. Dawn to twilight; work
of Edward V. Valentine . . . Richmond, 1929.

6091. VAN DOREN, CARL C. James Branch Cabell . . . New
York, McBride, 1925.

> 3 p. l., 87 p. double map. 8°. (Modern American writers, I)
> Critical essay on Cabell's novels and short stories, with emphasis on
> his romantic qualities.

6092. WALPOLE, HUGH. The art of James Branch Cabell . . .
with an appendix of individual comment upon the Cabell books.
New York, McBride, 1920.

> 32 p., 1 l. front. (port.) 12°.   **BP, LC, NYP, V**

6093. WAYLAND, JOHN W. Joseph Funk, father of song in northern
Virginia . . . Dayton, Va., Ruebush-Kieffer [1911]
> [12] p. illus. (incl. ports.) 4°.   **H, LC, V**
> Reprint from the *Pennsylvania German,* XII, 10; Oct., 1911, p. 580-594.
> With the copy in **LC** are bound 2 nos. of the *Musical million* **[6097]:**
> XXXIX, 8 (Aug., 1908), the Kieffer memorial number; and XLII, 7
> (Aug., 1911), containing a history of the Ruebush-Kieffer publishing co.,
> by O. F. Morton.

Periodicals

6094. The BLACK swan. Vol. 1- ; 1927/28— Richmond, 1927—
> 8°. monthly. A literary magazine.
> **V:** I, 2-11; II-III; (1927-29).

6095. The LYRIC. Vol. 1- ; 1921—   Norfolk, Va., 1921—
> 12°. monthly. A poetry magazine.
> Virginia T. McCormick, ed.
> **LC:** II-IX (1922-29). **V:** III, 1, 3-12; IV; V, 1-8, 10-12; VI-IX.

6096. The MUSICAL advocate and singer's friend. Vol. 1-[?] July,
1859-[68?] Singer's Glen, Va., J. Funk & sons, 1859-[68?]
> 4(?) v. illus. (music) 8°. monthly. No more pub.?
> Title varies: The Southern musical advocate and singer's friend.
> Editors: J. Funk & sons; A. S. Kieffer; W. S. Rohr.
> **LC:** I, 1-12; IV, 1-12; (1859/60, 68).

6097. The MUSICAL million, vol. 1-   a journal of music, poetry, and chaste home literature.   Dayton, Va.   [1870?-19—

illus., music. 8°. monthly.
LC: XXXIX, 8; XLII, 7; (Aug. of 1908, 11). **V:** XLIV, 10 (Oct., 1913).

6098. The OLD DOMINION.   A monthly magazine of literature, science and art.   Vol. 1-[?]   Richmond, Va., M. W. Hazlewood [1867?-?]

8°.   Title varies: Seminary magazine, 1869; The Old Dominion and Virginia historical register, Dec., 1871.
Editors: M. W. Hazlewood, G. W. James.
LC: IV-VI (1870-72). **V:** IV, 4-12; V, 1-8, 10-12; VI, 1-2, 5, 8, 12; VII, 1-2; (1870-73). **VU:** IV, 2-12; V, 1-2, 4-12; VI, 1-12; VII, 1-12; (1870-73).

6099. The REVIEWER.   Vol. 1-   ; Feb. 15, 1921—   Richmond, Va., 1921-24; Chapel Hill, N. C., University of North Carolina, 1925—

8°.   semi-monthly, Feb.-Aug., 1921; monthly, Oct., 1921-July, 1922; quarterly, Oct., 1922—
No number issued for Sept., 1921.
Editors: Emily Clark, *et al.*, 1921-24; Paul Green, 1925—
H: I-V; **LC:** I-III, V; (1921-23, 25).

6100. The RICHMOND eclectic.   A monthly magazine of foreign literature, religious and secular.   Edited by Rev. Moses D. Hoge and Rev. William Brown.   Vol. 1-3.   Richmond, Va.   [1866]-67.

3 v. 8°.   **H, LC** (incompl.), **V, VU**
Caption title: The Richmond eclectic magazine.
I-II contains 6 nos. each; III contains 2 nos.
Superseded by the New eclectic magazine of Baltimore (later the Southern magazine).

6101. RICHMOND literary miscellany.   Vol. 1-[?]   Richmond, Va., 1883-[?]

8°.   monthly. **V:** I, 1 (May, 1883); **VU:** I (1883/84).
A. S. Morton, ed.

6102. The VIRGINIA magazine.   Vol. 1-[?]   Lynchburg, Va. [1908?-?]

8°.   monthly.   A literary magazine.
V: I, 2-5 (Jan.-Apr., 1909).

6103. The VIRGINIA quarterly review.   A national journal of discussion. Vol. 1-   ; Apr., 1925—   Charlottesville, University of Virginia, 1925—

8°. quarterly. Only 3 nos. in v. 1.
James S. Wilson, ed., 1925—

For further references on Literature and Art, see above, Pt. II, § 7: *Urban Development,* especially under Petersburg and Richmond. See also Pt. VI, § 5: *Professional and Learned Societies.*

PART XI. NEWSPAPERS

Bibliography

6104. [25] MINOR, MRS. KATE P., *et al.* . . . A list of newspapers in the Virginia state library, Confederate museum and Valentine museum . . . Richmond, 1912.

Abingdon, Va.

6105. ABINGDON STANDARD.
V: Jan. 23, Oct. 16, 1879.

6106. ABINGDON VIRGINIAN.
V: July 25, 1879.

Alexandria, Va.

6107. ALEXANDRIA GAZETTE. (daily)
LC: Jan. 17, 1865-Mar. 7, 1866; 1901-30. V: Nov. 30, 1878; Aug. 11, 1879; 1905-30.

Amherst Court House, Va.

6108. AMHERST ENTERPRISE. (weekly)
V: July 17, Aug. 7, 28, Sept. 4, 11, 18, 1879.

Ashland, Va.

6109. HERALD PROGRESS. (weekly)
V: 1925-26.

Bedford, Va.

6110. BEDFORD SENTINEL.
V: May 2, 1879.

Boydton, Va.

6111. MECKLENBURG DEMOCRAT. (weekly)
V: Mar. 10, Apr. 14, Dec. 14, 21, 1881; Jan. 11, Mar. 29, Apr. 12, May 17, June 21, Sept. 27, Oct. 11, Nov. 8, 1882.

Bristol, Va.-Tenn.

6112. BRISTOL NEWS.
    V: Sept. 11, 1877.

Cape Charles, Va.

6113. EASTERN SHORE NEWS. (weekly)
    V: Apr. 6, 1923-Dec. 19, 1924.

Charlottesville, Va.

6114. CHRONICLE, Charlottesville. (semi-weekly; Dem.)
    VU: 1867-69.

6115. JEFFERSONIAN REPUBLICAN. (weekly & semi-weekly)
    V: Nov. 27, 1889. **VU**: Apr. 10, 1873-Oct. 29, 1879; Nov. 12, 1879-
Mar. 28, 1888; Mar. 25, 1892-Feb. 1, 1893; Feb. 10, 1893-Mar. 2, 1894.

6116. PROGRESS, The Daily. (Dem.)
    V: 1905-30. **VU**: Jan.-July, 1896; 1909-30.

6117. The VIRGINIA ADVOCATE. (weekly)
    V: Oct. 21, 1880.

6118. VIRGINIA LEGIONNAIRE. (monthly; Amer. legion)
    V: Jan., 1925-July, 1926 (July, 1925, not pub.).

Clarksville, Va.

6119. CLARKSVILLE VIRGINIAN.
    V: Sept. 20, 1883.

Clifton Forge, Va.

6120. The VALLEY VIRGINIAN. (weekly; non-part.)
    Removed from Staunton, Va., 1891 (cf. item **6233**).
    LC: May 14, 1891-Mar. 15, 1894.

Crewe, Nottoway Co., Va.

6121. NOTTOWAY RECORD. (weekly)
    V: 1925-27.

Culpeper, Va.

6122. CULPEPER TIMES.
V: Apr. 23, 1880.

Danville, Va.

6123. DANVILLE REGISTER. (daily)
V: 1905-30.

6124. The SIXTH CORPS. (daily; estab., Apr., 1865)
LC: Apr. 27, May 1-4, 9-10, 1865.

Dillwyn, Buckingham Co., Va.

6125. VIRGINIA UNION FARMER. (weekly)
V: 1926-27.

Eastville, Va.

6126. EASTERN SHORE HERALD. (weekly)
Combined with *Accomac news* in 1925 and title changed to *Eastern Shore news* **[6152]** pub. in Onancock, Va.
V: Oct. 1904-24.

Fredericksburg, Va.

6127. LEDGER, The Fredericksburg. (semi-weekly)
LC: Jan. 16, 1866.

6128. The NEWS. (semi-weekly)
V: May 20, 24, 27, 31, June 3, 7, 10, 14, 17, 21, 24, 28, July, 1, 8, 1886.

6129. The STAR. (daily)
Title varies: Free Lance-Star, Jan.-Sept., 1926.
LC: Sept. 19, 1894; **V**: 1905-30.

6130. The VIRGINIA HERALD. (semi-weekly)
LC: Jan. 15, 22, Feb. 26, Sept. 17, 1866.

Hamilton, Va.

6131. The LOUDOUN TELEPHONE. (weekly; Repub.; estab., 1878)
LC: Jan. 7, 1881-Apr. 28, 1893; May 4, 1894-Apr. 24, 1896.

Hampton, Va.

6132. The TRUE SOUTHERNER.   (weekly; Repub.; estab., 1865)
WM: Nov. 24, 1865-Apr. 19, 1866.

Harrisonburg, Va.

6133. ROCKINGHAM REGISTER.   (weekly; Dem.)
LC: Nov. 4, 1869-Oct. 17, 1873; Nov. 14, 1878-June 23, 1881. V:
1866-1906. VU: 1866-68, 75 (incompl.); 1876-77; 1878, 81 (incompl.);
1882; 1883 (incompl.); 1884; 1886-87 (incompl.); Nov. 1, 1889-June 1, 1906.

Herndon, Fairfax Co., Va.

6134. NEWS OBSERVER.   (weekly)
V: 1925-27.

Hopewell, Va.

6135. DAILY NEWS.
V: Nov., 1915-June, 1916.

6136. DAILY PRESS.
V: May-June, 1916; 1917.

Lynchburg, Va.

6137. DEMOCRATIC CAMPAIGN.
V: Nov. 12, 1883.

6138. The NEWS.   (daily; Dem.; estab., Jan., 1866)
LC: 1898. V: 1905-22, 25-26.

6139. PRESS, The Lynchburg.   (weekly)
LC: Sept. 18, 1869.

6140. REPUBLICAN, Lynchburg.   (daily)
LC: May 6-Oct. 31, 1875.

6141. TRI-WEEKLY NEWS.
V: Feb. 21, 1873.

Manchester, Va.

6142. COURIER, Manchester. (weekly)
V: May 29, June 5, 12, 29, July 3, 17, 24, Aug. 14, 28, 1875.

6143. LEADER, Manchester.
V: Nov. 2, 1894.

Newport News, Va.

6144. DAILY PRESS.
V: 1920-30.

Norfolk, Va.

6145. DAY BOOK, The Norfolk. (daily; estab., Oct. 3, 1857)
Title varies: The Day book, Oct. 5, 1857-Nov. 2, 1866.
LC: July 25, 1865-Nov. 2, 1866; Apr. 9-Nov. 18, 1869.

6146. LANDMARK, The Norfolk. (daily; Dem.)
LC: Jan. 1, 1887-Dec. 31, 1896; July 1-Dec. 31, 1897. V: Jan. 20, 1892; 1905-22.
Continued as Virginian-pilot and Norfolk landmark [6150]

6147. OLD DOMINION, The Norfolk. (daily)
LC: Apr. 20-Nov. 3, 1866.

6148. OUR DAY. (weekly)
V: Mar. 3-17, 31, Apr. 14, May 5-19, 1866.

6149. POST, The Norfolk. (daily; estab., June 22, 1865)
LC: June 22, 1865-Apr. 5, 1866. (No more pub.)

6150. VIRGINIAN-PILOT. (daily; Dem.)
Consolidation of Norfolk Virginian (estab., 1865) and Daily pilot, Mar., 1898.
LC: Aug. 2, 1899-1930; V: 1905-30.

Norton, Va.

6151. CRAWFORD WEEKLY. (mid-week & week-end editions)
V: Apr. 30, May 14, 21, June 3, 10, Aug. 6-Oct. 26, Nov. 23, 26, 30, Dec. 5, 10, 14, 17, 21, 1921; 1922-23, 25-26.

Onancock, Va.

6152. EASTERN SHORE NEWS. (weekly)

Consolidation of Accomac news and Eastern Shore herald **[6126]**, 1925.

V: 1926-27.

Orange Court House, Va.

6153. NATIVE VIRGINIAN. (weekly)

V: Nov. 15, 1867-Nov. 5, 1869; Nov. 12, 1869-May 13, 1870 (incompl.).

Petersburg, Va.

6154. INDEX, Petersburg. (daily)

NYP: 1870-July 22, 1873 (incompl.). **V:** May 8, 1866-Jan. 18, 1867 (incompl.); Feb. 8, Mar. 7, Apr. 25, May 23, 28, July 2, 1870.

6155. INDEX AND APPEAL. (daily)

NYP: Mar., 1873-75 (incompl.).

6156. INDEX APPEAL. (daily, except Mon.)

Title changed to Progress-index appeal, 1892; to Progress-appeal, 1894.

NYP: 1883 (incompl.). **V:** 1892-1902 (incompl.); 1905-30.

6157. NEWS, Daily.

V: June 22, 1865.

6158. TIMES, Weekly.

V: Aug. 22, 1868.

6159. The VIRGINIA CITIZEN. (weekly; Repub.; estab., May 1, 1876)

WM: May 1-Oct. 28, 1876.

Portsmouth, Va.

6160. TIDEWATER TIMES.

V: Mar. 29, 1880.

Pulaski, Va.

6161. SOUTHWEST TIMES. (daily)

V: Sept.-Dec., 1916 (incompl.); Jan., 1917-Apr., 1918; Oct.-Dec., 1919 (except Dec. 13); 1920-26 (except Feb. 7, 1923); Jan.-Apr. 1, 1927.

Richmond, Va.

6162. The CAMPAIGN. (weekly)

V: Mar. 8, 22, May 10, June 21, July 5, 12, 19, 1884; Sept. 5, 26, Oct. 3, 17, 1885.

6163. CATHOLIC VISITOR.

V: Apr. 5, 1884.

6164. [1854] The CAVALIER. (weekly)

6165. CENTRAL PRESBYTERIAN. (weekly)

Became Presbyterian of the South, 1909.
V: Sept. 28, 1865; Mar. 19, 26, 1879; 1880-82.

6166. CHRISTIAN OBSERVER AND FREE CHRISTIAN COMMONWEALTH. (weekly; Presbyt.)

V: May 11, 1870.

6167. The COMMERCIAL.

V: Aug. 28, 1869.

6168. COMMERCIAL AND TOBACCO LEAF.

V: May 25, June 8, 1885.

6169. The COMMONWEALTH. (daily; Dem.; estab., 1880)

Discont. publication, July 28, 1880.
William L. Royall, ed.
LC, NYP: Jan. 30-July 28, 1880; **V**: Jan. 30-July 28, 1880 (incompl.).

6170. The CONSERVATIVE.

V: Nov. 7, 1872.

6171. The CRITIC. (weekly; estab., 1887)

Editors: James Hudson, C. A. Woolfolk.
V: Sept. 12, Oct. 3, 10, Nov. 7-28, Dec. 19, 26, 1887; Jan. 9, 1888-90 (incompl.). **WM**: Oct., 1887-Mar., 1890 (incompl.).

6172. DEMOCRAT, The. (daily)

V: Sept. 25, 1890-Jan. 23, 1891 (incompl.).

6173. DISPATCH, The Evening. (daily)

V: Sept. 27, Oct.-Dec., 1920; 1921-Nov. 9, 1923. (No more pub.)

6174. DISPATCH, The Richmond. (daily; Dem.)

Title varies: The Daily dispatch, 1862-June 30, 1884.
Combined with The Times **[6213]** to form The Richmond times-dispatch **[6216]**, 1903.

LC: June 1, 1870-Aug. 31, 1899; Jan. 2, 1900-Dec. 31, 1902. **NYP**: 1872-74 (incompl.). **V**: Jan. 3-Apr. 1, Dec., 1865; Jan.-Dec., 1866 (incompl.); 1867-Jan. 25, 1903.

6175. DISPATCH, The Weekly.

V: Mar.-Dec., 1899.

6176. ENQUIRER, The Daily Richmond.   (Dem.; estab., 1844)

Combined with The Daily Richmond examiner **[6180]** to form The Daily enquirer and examiner, July 15, 1867 **[6177]**
    LC: Mar. 3, Apr. 10, 25, 1866-July 13, 1867. **V**: Jan. 28, Feb. 9, Oct. 30-Dec. 30 (incompl.); Feb. 1-Dec. 31, 1866 (incompl.). **VU**: Oct. 30, 1865-Dec. 31, 1866 (incompl.).

6177. ENQUIRER AND EXAMINER, The Daily.   (Dem.; estab., July 15, 1867)

Consolidation of The Daily Richmond enquirer **[6176]** and The Daily Richmond examiner **[6180]** Continued as The Richmond enquirer **[6178]**
    LC, V: July 15, 1867-June 30, 1869.

6178. ENQUIRER, The Richmond.   (daily; Dem.)

Continuation of The Daily enquirer and examiner **[6177]**
    LC: Feb. 27, 1871-Aug. 31, 1876; Dec. 2, 1876-Nov. 28, 1877. **V**: 1869-77 (incompl.).

6179. EVERY SATURDAY JOURNAL.   (weekly)

V: June 6, July 4, 1885; Oct. 9, 1886; Sept. 29, 1888.

6180. EXAMINER, The Daily Richmond.

Combined with The Daily Richmond enquirer **[6176]** to form The Daily enquirer and examiner, July 15, 1867 **[6177]**
    LC: May 14-Nov. 3, 1866. **V**: Jan. 2-Mar. 31, 1865 (incompl.); Dec. 12, 23, 27, 29, 1865; Apr. 10, 28, May 5, 10, Oct. 13, Nov. 5-6, 1866; Feb. 8, Apr. 20, 1867.

6181. EXCHANGE REPORTER.

V: Dec. 12, 1891.

6182. GUIDE, The Weekly.

V: Sept. 18, 1871.

6183. GUIDE AND NEWS, The.

V: May 22-23, June 7, 1876.

6184. INDEPENDENT REPUBLICAN.   (weekly)

V: Mar. 20, Apr. 10, 17, May 1, 8, 22, 29, June 5-26, 1869.

6185. INDEPENDENT VIRGINIAN.

> **V:** Oct. 25, Nov. 7, 1921.

6186. The INDUSTRIAL SOUTH. (weekly; non-part.; estab., 1881)

> **LC:** Aug. 13, 1880-Dec. 20, 1884. **V:** July 30, 1881-July 25, 1885 (incompl.).

6187. The JEWISH RECORD. (weekly)

> **NYP, V:** Sept. 19, 1909-Oct. 14, 1910.

6188. JOURNAL, Richmond. (weekly)

> **V:** Apr. 24, May 8, 1886; Feb. 12-26, Mar. 5, 26, May 14, Oct. 1, Nov. 19, 1887.

6189. JOURNAL, Richmond evening. (daily)

> **V:** June, 1905-Sept., 1920. (No more pub.)

6190. LABOR HERALD, Richmond. (weekly)

> Title varies: Square deal, 1916-20; Richmond labor journal, 1921-24. **V:** 1916-Sept., 1924.

6191. LEADER, The Evening. (daily; Dem.; estab., 1896)

> Estab. as evening edit. of The Richmond times; discont. when the Dispatch and the Times united (1903) and the News-leader took the place of the evening edit. of both papers.
> **LC:** July 1-Dec. 31, 1898; **V:** Nov. 30, 1896-Jan. 24, 1903 (incompl.).

6192. LITERARY PASTIME.

> **V:** Aug. 8, 1868.

6193. MONDAY COMMERCIAL. (weekly)

> **V:** July 2, 1883.

6194. The NEW NATION. (daily)

> **V:** Jan. 4-Oct. 23, 1867 (incompl.); Jan. 23-Nov. 14, 1868 (incompl.).

6195. The NEW NATION. (weekly)

> **V:** Mar. 22, 1866-Dec. 18, 1868 (incompl.).

6196. [6173] NEWS, The Richmond. (daily)

> Evening edit. of The Dispatch, beginning Oct., 1899, and consolidated with The Leader **[6191]**, 1903.

6197. NEWS, The Evening. (daily)

> **V:** Apr. 28, Dec. 9-10, 29, 1868; Apr. 20-Dec. 6, 1869 (incompl.); Jan. 6-Dec. 5, 1870 (incompl.); July 19, 1871; July 7, 1873.

6198. NEWS-LEADER, The Richmond. (daily)

Consolidation of The Richmond news and The Evening leader [6191]
V: 1903-22, 25-30.

6199. PLANET, Richmond. (weekly; col.)

H: Aug., 1890-92; Apr., 1893-97; 1901-Sept., 04; Aug., 1905-Aug.,
06; 07-08, 10, 12-Aug., 13. V: June 8, 1889; 1895-June 29, 1901 (incompl.); May 12, July-Dec. (except Nov. 3), 1917; 1918-30.

6200. RECORD, The Daily.

V: Apr., 1916-30.

6201. REFORMER, The.

V: Feb. 13, 1886.

6202. The RELIGIOUS HERALD. (weekly; Bapt.)

V: Oct. 19, 1865-1882 (incompl.); Jan. 24, Sept. 4, 1884; May 21, 28,
June 18, 1885; Feb. 13, Sept. 17, 1896; 1908-14; 1915-16 (incompl.); 1917;
1918-20 (incompl.); 1921-29.

6203. The REPUBLIC. (daily)

H: May 10-Dec. 21, 1865 (incompl.). NYP: July-Dec., 1865 (incompl.). V: May 10-Dec. 4, 1865 (incompl.); Jan. 10-Apr. 14, 1866 (incompl.).

6204. The SOUTHERN INTELLIGENCER. (weekly)

V: Jan. 26-Oct. 18, 1880 (incompl.).

6205. SOUTHERN OPINION. (weekly)

LC: July 27, 1867-Nov. 21, 1868. V: June 15, 1867-May 1, 1869 (incompl.). WM: June 15, 1867-Apr. 10, 1869 (incompl.).

6206. STANDARD, The Richmond. (weekly; Dem.; estab., 1878)

H: 1879-81 (incompl.). LC: Sept. 7, 1878-Feb. 12, 1882. V: Sept.
7, 1878-Feb. 18, 1882 (incompl.). WM: Sept., 1879-Jan., 1882 (incompl.).

6207. STAR, The Richmond. (daily)

V: Aug. 31, 1893-Oct. 23, 1896 (incompl.).

6208. The STATE. (daily; Dem.; estab., 1876)

Title varies: The Richmond state, July 11-Sept. 15, 1897.
Discont. pub., Nov. 20, 1897.
LC: Dec. 20, 1877-Nov. 20, 1897. V: Mar. 20, 1876; Aug. 7, 1877;
1878-Nov. 20, 1897.

6209. STATE FAIR GAZETTE.

V: Oct. 31, 1877.

6210. STATE JOURNAL, Daily.

V: Dec. 16, 1868; Feb. 18, May 10, 31, June 15, 1869; Jan. 5, Feb. 3, 8, Mar. 17-18, Apr. 14, 20, 25-26, May 5, 23, 25, July 9, 22, 25, 27-28, Sept. 1-2, Oct. 6, Nov. 4, 1870; Apr. 6, May 26, July 17, 1871; Jan. 2, 1874.

6211. SUN, The. (daily)

V: Jan. 27, 1879.

6212. TELEGRAM, Evening.

V: Apr. 11, 1878.

6213. TIMES, The Daily. (Dem.)

Combined with the Richmond dispatch [6173] to form The Richmond times-dispatch [6216], 1903.

H: Dec., 1889-Mar., 1891 (incompl.). LC: Dec. 1, 1893-Dec. 31, 1902. V: 1886-Jan. 25, 1903 (incompl.).

6214. TIMES, The Daily Richmond. (Dem.; estab., 1865)

Discont. pub., June 10, 1867; absorbed by the Daily dispatch [6173]

H: Apr., 1865-Mar., 1866 (incompl.). LC: Apr. 21, 1865-June 10, 1867. NYP: May, 1865-June, 1867 (incompl.). V: May 2, 1865-June 10, 1867 (incompl.). WM: May 13-July 27, 1865.

6215. TIMES, The Weekly.

V: 1889-90, 93-1902.

6216. TIMES-DISPATCH, The Richmond. (daily; Dem.)

Consolidation of The Daily times [6213] and the Richmond dispatch [6173], 1903.

LC, V: Jan. 1, 1903-30. VU: 1905-30.

6217. TIMES-DISPATCH, Weekly.

V: 1903-05, 08.

6218. TRUTH, The Evening.

V: June-Aug., 1887.

6219. The VIRGINIA DEMOCRAT. (weekly; estab., Dec. 5, 1925)

V: Dec. 5, 1925-May 8, 1926.

6220. The VIRGINIA GAZETTE.

V: Mar. 4, Apr. 4, 1892.

6221. The VIRGINIA STAR. (weekly; col.)

V: May 11, Dec. 14, 1878; Mar. 27, 1880; Apr. 30, Aug. 27, 1881; Nov. 11, 18, Dec. 9, 16, 23, 1882.

6222. The VIRGINIA TRIBUNE.

> **V:** Sept. 16, 1922.

6223. VIRGINIAN, The Richmond. (daily, except Sun., 1910-Mar. 29, 1912)

> Merged with Richmond evening journal **[6189]**, 1920.
> **V:** 1910-May 15, 1920.

6224. VIRGINISCHE ZEITUNG.

> **V:** Apr., 1915-30.

6225. WHIG, The Richmond. (daily; Dem.)

> Title varies: Daily Richmond Whig, 1865-67; Richmond daily Whig, 1868-85.
> Publication suspended, Dec. 23, 1885-Jan. 26, 1886.
> **LC:** Jan.-May (incompl.), July 4, Oct. 24, 30, 1865; Apr. 10, 1866; Apr. 13, 1867-Dec. 31, 1868; Jan.-Feb. (incompl.), Mar. 1, 1869-Dec. 31, 1874; Mar. 1, 1879-Jan. 18, 1887; Jan. 1-Dec. 23, 1888 (Oct. 3, Exposition edit.). **NYP:** Jan. 20, Feb. 14, 21, Mar. 10, 20-21, 23, 1865; July, 1866-Dec., 1867 (incompl.); 1881-82 (incompl.); 1883-86. **V:** 1865-74 (incompl.); Mar. 4, Sept. 1, 20, Oct. 4-5, 12, 14, 18-19, 21, Nov. 1, Dec. 8, 1875; 1876-88.

Roanoke, Va.

6226. The ROANOKE TIMES. (daily; Dem.; estab., 1886)

> **LC:** Jan. 1, 1898-June 30, 1900; **V:** 1905-30.

Salem, Va.

6227. REGISTER, The Weekly.

> **V:** May 16, 1879.

6228. TIMES, The Roanoke. (weekly; estab., June 8, 1866)

> **LC:** June 15, 1866-Dec. 21, 1871 (incompl.); Jan. 2, 1873-Dec. 23, 1875.

South Boston, Va.

6229. HALIFAX GAZETTE. (weekly)

> **V:** 1925-30.

Staunton, Va.

6230. DISPATCH AND NEWS, Staunton. (daily)

> **V:** 1905-11.

6231. NEWS LEADER, Staunton. (daily)

> **V:** 1925-26.

6232. SPECTATOR, The Staunton.
McC: 1884-86, 88-90. **V:** 1865-81 (incompl.).

6233. The VALLEY VIRGINIAN. (weekly; non-part.)
Removed to Clifton Forge, Va., May 14, 1891 (cf. item **6120**).
Publication suspended, Apr. 23-May 14, 1891.
LC: May 26, 1881-May 27, 1884; Apr. 1, 1886-Apr. 23, 1891. **V:** 1865-81 (incompl.).

6234. VINDICATOR, The Staunton. (weekly)
V: 1865-81 (incompl.).

Warrenton, Va.

6235. FAUQUIER LAND JOURNAL. (monthly; estab., 1868)
V: Oct., 1868.

6236. WARRENTON TRUE INDEX.
V: Feb. 18, 1871 (suppl. only).

West Point, Va.

6237. WEST POINT STAR.
V: Jan. 17, 1889.

Williamsburg, Va.

6238. The VIRGINIA GAZETTE. (weekly; non-part.)
V: Mar. 4, Apr. 4, 1892. **WM:** Feb. 18-July 1, 1869.

6239. WILLIAMSBURG GAZETTE AND JAMES CITY ADVERTISER. (weekly)
V: Mar. 31, Apr. 7, 14, May 5, Sept. 29, Oct. 6-27, Nov. 3-17, Dec. 1-15, 1886.

Winchester, Va.

6240. NEWS, The Winchester. (weekly)
V: Sept. 1, 15, 22, Oct. 13, 27, 1865; Jan. 12, Mar. 23, 30, 1866.

6241. STAR, Winchester evening. (daily)
V: 1905-22, 25-26.

Woodstock, Va.

6242. SHENANDOAH HERALD. (weekly)
V: Mar. 5, 1879.

INDEX

[The numbers refer to items, not to pages]

Agriculture & immigration, Dept. of.
Annual report, 112
Bulletin, 113, 123
Chemistry, Committee on analytical & agricultural, 117
Descriptive pamphlets, 118-119, 121-122
Farmer's bulletin, 114
Farms for sale, 120
Fertilizers, Analyses of, 110-111
Geological survey, 362
Handbook, 115
Highways, Description of, 2076
Leaflet, 116
Statistics, Div. of, 138-140
Test farm, 141
Truck experiment station, 150
Agronomy, Amherst Co., 61
Airplanes, 5012
Airports, 601, 1652
Airway bulletin, 601
Aitken, Robert, 1417
Albemarle agricultural society, 177
Albemarle & Chesapeake canal co., 717
Albemarle & Pantego r. r. co., 827
Albemarle area. Soils, 96
Albemarle Baptist assoc., 4665, 4978
Albemarle circuit court, 647
Albemarle club of colonial dames, 1411
Albemarle County. Agricultural society, 156, 177
County commissioner, 1759
Daughters of the American revolution, 1411
Description, 1415, 1759, 1811, 5077
Directories, 1885, 1915
Economic & social survey, 1834-1835
Education, 1811
Geography, 1811, 1847
Guide books, 1411, 1759, 1811
Historic homes, 2285. *See also* Monticello
History, 1811, 3660, 5077
Mining, 521
Negro farmers, 278
Reconstruction, 2780
Schools, 4338-4343, 4367, 4401
United daughters of the Confederacy, 2496, 2538
Albemarle female institute, Charlottesville, 4401
Albemarle home-coming celebration, 1415
Albemarle stamp collector (period.), 3355
Alderman, E. A., 30, 1417, 2374, 3348, 3540-3543, 3550, 3639, 3642
Alexander, Charles, 1760
Alexander, F. W., 2449
Alexander family, 183

Alexandria (city). Annexation to District of Columbia, 2919
Auditor, 2917
Centennial celebration, 2918
Charter, 2923
Churches, 2841, 4662, 4797, 4841, 4943, 4945
Civic improvement, 1824
Conference of colored people, 2767
Council, 2918-2919
Debt, 2921
Democratic convention, 8th dist. (1878), 3159
Description, 1401, 1404-05, 1824
Directories, 1874-1878, 2917, 5013
Economic progress, 1402
Guide book, 1401
Harbor, 622
History, 1401-1402, 1404-1405, 5013
Mayor, 2917, 2920-2921
Ordinances, 2917, 2922-2923
Schools, Private, 3457-3461, 3507-3508, 4084, 4130-4131, 4145, 4175, 4375, 4404
Schools, Public, 4034, 4084
Ship building, 518
Washington memorial, 1399-1400
Washington monument assoc., 1403
Alexandria academy, 4130
Alexandria & Fairfax passenger ry. co., 1071
Alexandria & Fredericksburg ry. co., 718-719, 957, 1078
Alexandria & Washington ry. co., 720, 1078
Alexandria canal, 619
Alexandria chamber of commerce, 1404
Alexandria County. Abington Park, 1742
Board of supervisors, 1761
Description, 1761
Directories, 1877, 1879
Soils, 96
Alexandria gazette, 860, 6107
Alexandria hospital, 1397
Alexandria school for young ladies, 4131
Alexandria water co., 1398
Alfalfa, 59, 230
Allan, Mrs. E. P., 5122
Allan, W., 2421
Allan-Onley, Mary, 2375
Alleghany car trust, 721, 874
Alleghany County. Description, 1744, 5046
Farmers' manufacturing co., 406
History, 5039, 5046-5047
Iron ore property, 417
Schools, 4412
Springs, 479

Alleghany institute, Clifton Forge, 4132
Alleghany Mts. Fiction, 5726
Alleghany Springs, Montgomery Co., 383, 386
Allen, E. H., 2521
Allen, George, 275
Allen, H. C., 1136
Allen, S. B., 600
Allison & Addison's hand book, 290
Allmond, M. B., 5278-5280
Almanacs, 290, 293, 303, 1912, 1930, 2557-2560, 2566-2567
Alpin, L. C., 2138
Alpin hotel, Hot Springs, 2138
Alrich, Sue B., 5485
Alwood, W. B., 60, 145
Ambler, P. B., 4416
Ambler, Theresa J., 5644
Amelia County, 1782, 1895
American academy of arts & letters. Publications, 6075
American academy of polit. & soc. science. *Annals,* 1148
American Bapt. home mission society, 3914
American Bible society, 4757
American bond-funding and banking assoc., 1220
American breeder & planter (period.), 291
American cheap transportation assoc., 980
American chemical society. Va. section, 4587
American climatological assoc. *Transactions,* 2037
American commonwealths series, 5021a
American crisis biographies series, 5132
American digest system, 5, 33
American expeditionary forces, France. Virginians in, 3229, 3236-3238
American federation of labor. Va. branch. *See* Va. fed. of labor
American forestry assoc., 336
American fruit grower (period.), 292
American geographical society. *Bulletin,* 2355
American historical assoc. *Annual report* (1903), 34
American illustrating co., Richmond, 1542
American institute of banking. Richmond chapter, 1296, 1394
American institute of mining engineers. *Transactions,* 431
American issue (period.). Va. edition, 2064
American legion. Charlottesville & Albemarle post, no. 74, 1412
 Richmond posts, 3219, 3254
 Va. dept., 3221, 3248, 6118
American legion directory, 3254

American legion year book committee, 3248
American missionary (period.), 4133
American missionary assoc., 4133, 4141
American nat'l bank, Richmond, 1297
American news co., 2158
American scenic & historic preservation soc., 2376
American soc. of mechanical engineers, 1545
American tel. & tel. co., 722
American tobacco co., 277
American white orpington club, 157
American wool & cotton reporter, 158
Amherst County. Agric. engineering, 61
 Board of supervisors, 1762
 Club work, Boys' & girls', 61
 Livestock, 61
 Resources, 1762, 2328
Amherst Co. agric. advisory council, 61
Amherst Court House (town). Kenmore univ. high school, 4305
Amherst enterprise (period.), 6108
Amis, Mrs. E. H., 5281
Ammen, S. Z., 2085
Anderson, Archer, 2030, 5123
Anderson, B. G., 78
Anderson, D. R., 3480
Anderson, H. W., 2785, 2858, 3325, 3840
Anderson, J. P., 2201
Anderson, J. R., 3242, 3769, 3909-3910
Anderson, M. J., 1940
Anderson, Mary, 1105
Anderson, W. A., 1546, 2635
Andover review (period.), 3556
Andrews, C. W., 3460
Andrews, Mrs. M. M., 2377, 5282-5285
Annals of mathematics (period.), 4632
Annual reports of Va., 101, 1968, 1971-1973, 1981, 1986-1987, 1996-1997, 2017, 2020, 2373
Anthony, Susan B., 6043
Appalachian mines & indust. record (period.), 542
Appalachian power co., Bluefield, W. Va., 387, 478
Appalachian region, 1812, 2173, 5058, 5765
Appalachian school improvement foundation, 4525
Apples, 90, 133, 136, 205, 228, 262, 271, 1053
Appleton, J. H., 1517
Appomattox Bapt. assoc., 4666, 4965
Appomattox County. Soils, 96
Appomattox Co. agric. advisory board, 62
Appomattox Court House (town), 1406
 Agric. high school, 4127
Appomattox land co., 1406
Appropriations, State, 1213, 1219

[The numbers refer to items, not to pages]

Arbitration, Internat'l. Report of committee of state bar assoc., 4617
Arbitration, R. R. employees, 1122
Arcadian library series, 5869
Archives. W. G. Stanard's report (1903), 34
Archives & history, Va. dept. of. Report (1905), 16
Argonaut (period.), 3947
Argyll, J. G. (Duke of), 2086
Arlington & Fairfax ry. co., 1082
Arlington County, 1880-1881, 3044
Arlington estate, 2159, 2262, 2282
Armistead, J. C., 3034
Armistead family, 5507
Armistice day celebration, 3219-3220
Armor plants, 327, 1525, 1651a
Armstrong, H. W., 5380
Armstrong, J. I., 3416
Armstrong, Mrs. M. F., 4134-4135
Armstrong, S. C., 2358, 4136-4141, 4233, 4239, 4247, 4249, 4273, 4415, 4442, 4483, 4491, 4494, 4497-4498, 4502-4504
Armstrong, W. N., 388
Armstrong assoc., N. Y., 4142, 4261
Armstrong league of Hampton workers, 4138, 4279
Army of northern Va., 1581, 2818, 5120
Army of northern Va. assoc., 2387, 2417, 2422
Arnold, B. W., 277
Art clubs, 1634, 5262-5263, 5275
Art periodicals, 6098
Art schools. *See* Schools
Art work of Richmond, 5239
Artificer school, Norfolk navyyard, 4368
Arts, Fine. *See* Paintings; Portraits; Statuary
Ashe, W. W., 313-314, 333
Ashland (town), 1794, 1894, 3462-3469
Ashland Bapt. church, 4927
Associated rys. of Va. & the Carolinas, 723
Association for restoring Old Donation church, Norfolk, 4812
Association for the preservation of Va. antiquities, 2231, 2384, 2485, 4526-4530, 4538, 4559, 4565, 4584, 4633, 5391
  Prince Edward chapter, 4531-4532, 4557
Association of division school superintendents of Va., 4533
Association of engineers of Va., 1726, 4534-4536, 4634
Association of secondary schools & colleges of Va., 4322
Association of state universities, 3730

Association record (period.), 3948, 4983
Aston, A. C., 3223
Atlantic & Danville ry. co., 724-728
Atlantic & northeastern r. r. co., 875
Atlantic coast line assoc., 729-730, 899
Atlantic coast line r. r. co., 636, 656, 723, 729, 731-732, 817, 862, 899, 939, 2087
  Traffic dept., 1096
Atlantic coast line r. r. co. of Va., 732-733, 862, 899
Atlantic coastal trunk line r. r., 745
Atlantic deeper waterways assoc., 781
Atlantic educational journal (period.), 4636
Atlantic missionary (period.), 4984
Atlantic, Mississippi & Ohio r. r. co., 734-735, 750, 823, 841, 979, 1006, 2088
Atlantic seaboard ry., 802
Atlantic trust co., 830, 934
Atlee (town), 4769
Attachment, Law of, 2866, 2904
Attorney general. Prohibition enforcement, Div. of, 2020
Attorneys, City. *See* name of city
Auditor of public accounts. Annual reports, 1179, 1194
  Baltimore & Ohio r. r. co., Taxation of, 600
  Circular letter to r. rs., 645,
  Constitutional convention vouchers, 1203
  County supervisors, Powers & duties of, 3139
  Disbursements, 1186, 1190, 1204
  Fidelity companies' reports, 1196, 1235
  Guaranty companies' reports, 1196, 1235
  Indemnity companies' reports 1196, 1235
  Insurance companies' reports, 1197, 1234-1235
  Judges & officers, List of, 2639-2640
  Licenses, State, 1198
  Pensions, 1200, 1202, 1243-1244, 1261
  Public schools, Financing of, 4086
  Railroad property valuation, 646
  Revenue commissioners, Instructions, to, 1189, 1192
  Taxation, 1139, 1157, 1187-1189, 1192-1193, 1199, 1201, 1257
  Trust companies' reports, 1196, 1235
Auditor of public accounts, Second, 1162-1166, 1179, 1195, 3283
Auditors, City. *See* name of city
Augusta Bapt. assoc., 4667
Augusta church, Augusta Co., 4979
Augusta County. Caves, 2127, 2177, 2205

[The numbers refer to items, not to pages]

Augusta County—cont'd
Dairying, 71
Description, 1733
Economic & social survey, 1823, 1834, 1836
History, 5059, 5070-5071
Iron mining, 403
Kaolin mining, 413
Treasurer, 2924
Augusta Co. agric. advisory council, 63
Augusta female seminary, Staunton, 3444, 4143
Augusta military academy, Fort Defiance, 4144
Austin, W. L., 98
Automobile clubs, 736, 1576
Automobiles. *See* Motor vehicles
Avary, Mrs. M. L., 2378
Averett college, Danville, 3384

BACON, SUSIE L., 5286-5287
Baden, Mrs. F. H., 5892,
Bagby, Alfred, 5011
Bagby, B. B., 1744
Bagby G. W., 2756, 5169, 5288-5292, 6084
Baggarly, F. C., 2472
Bagley, T. P., 1747
Bail, Law of, 2866, 2904
Bailey, J. M., 389
Baker, H. P., 315
Baker, J. B., 1085
Baker, N. D., 3702
Baker, R. S., 5124
Baker, W. W., 1763, 2685
Balch (Thomas) library, Leesburg, 3343
Baldwin, C. C., 4481
Baldwin, I. P., 2812
Baldwin, J. B., 2813
Baldwin, R. T., 1040
Ball, Emma R. (Mrs. C. B.), 2089
Ballads, 5246, 5274
Ballot, Short, 2783, 2821
Ballot counting, 1154
Baltimore agricultural aid soc., 2379
Baltimore & Ohio r. r. co., 600, 783, 992, 2169, 2194
Baltimore & Richmond Christian advocate (period.), 5000
Baltimore & Va. r. r. co., 737
Baltimore & Va. steamboat co., 738-739,
Baltimore sun (period.), 2532
Baltimore trust & guarantee co., 445
Banister Bapt. assoc. (col.), 4702
Bank examiner, State, 1339
Bank legislation, 1211, 1241, 1254, 1258, 1320
Bank of North America & trust co., 740
Bank of Va., Richmond, 1150
Bankers trust co., N. Y., 741-742
Banking associations, 1368-1370

Banking division. *See* Corporation commission, State
Banking progress, 365
Banking systems, Rural, 1138
Banking systems, State, 1161
Bankruptcy laws, 2624, 2718
Banks, B. A., 3003
Banks, City, 1382
Banks. Federal reserve bank of Richmond, 1140-1144, 1160, 1391a
Banks, National, 1210, 1351, 1382
Banks, Real estate, 1346
Banks, State, 1208, 1210-1211, 1320, 1382
Banks, Taxation of, 1187
Baptist churches. *See* Churches
Baptist general assoc., 4674-4677, 4817, 4971
Baptist general assoc. (col.), 4709
Baptist home for aged women, Richmond, 2535
Baptist young people's union, 4698
Baptists, 4903, 4923-4925, 4958, 4960, 4973-4975, 4981
Associations, 4580, 4664-4701, 4896, 4934, 4950, 4965, 4971, 4978, 4981
Education societies, 4580
Periodicals, 4985, 4988-4989, 4997, 4999, 6202
State convention, 4697
State Sunday school convention, 4698
Baptists (col.). Associations, 4702-4734, 4959
State convention, 4728
State Sunday school convention, 4729
Baptists (primitive). Associations, 4735-4753
Corresponding meeting, 4735
Baptists, Christian, 4767
Bar associations, 4561, 4576-4577, 4611-4619, 4628
Bar examinations, 2676, 3326, 3342
Bar, State, 2676, 2849, 3342, 4561, 4611-4619, 5162
Barbour, B. J., 159
Barbour, J. S., 2802, 5091, 5096
Barbour bill, 1147
Barbour-Page lectures. *See* Univ. of Va.
Barger. D. H., 988
Barker, R. H., 3690
Barksdale, C. C., 1210
Barley, 253
Barnes' brief history of the U. S., Criticism of, 2475
Barnum, Mrs. F. C., 5293-5300
Barret, B. T., 771
Barrett, R. S., 4754
Barrett's directory of Alexandria, 1874
Barrie, George, 2090
Barrie, Robert, 2090

[The numbers refer to items, not to pages]

Barringer, P. B., 1835, 3911-3912
Barrows, J. S., 316
Barry, Herbert, 2381
Bartley, J. A., 5301-5303
Barton, O. S., 4895
Barton, R. T., 2859
Barton, W. S., 4755
Base hospitals. *See* U. S. army
Baseball, 1633
Bassler, R. S., 526
Batchelder, Roger, 3224
Bates, H. M., 3702
Bath County. Board of supervisors, 5040
  Healing Springs, 401, 405, 416, 440, 459
  History, 5040, 5046
  Hot springs, 384, 418-419, 428, 2040, 2108, 2173
  School board, 5040
  Wallawhatoola water, 523
  Warm Sulphur springs, 428, 524
Bath parish, Dinwiddie Co., 4756
Battlefields, 1431, 1549-1550, 1557, 1572, 1595, 1626-1627, 2106, 2168, 2425
Bay shore terminal co., 583
Bayard, T. F., 1378, 3544
Baylor, J. B., 390
Bayne, Howard, 4, 2136
Bayonet, The (period.), 3255
Beach, S. F., 2855
Beacon, The (period.), 4505
Beacon biographies series, 5211
Beale, C. W., 2382
Beale, E. I., 2091
Beale, G. W., 4960, 5079
Beale, Mrs. M. T., 5304
Bear, Harry, 5126
Beard, J. W., 1936
Beaty, J. O., 5127
Beaver Creek Bapt. assoc. (col.), 4703
Beazeley, S. W., 4877
Beck, J. B., 2585
Beck, Thomas, 160
Bedford (city). Directory, 1889
  Schools, 4148, 4378-4379, 4184
Bedford area. Soils, 96
Bedford County. Description, 1764, 1787, 2328, 5033
  History, 1817, 5033
  Negro songs, 5238
Bedford Co. pageant, 1817
Bedford sentinel (period.), 6110
Bedford Springs P. O. New London academy, 4352
Beets, 209
Bell, J. W., 2757
Bell, Jeremiah, 4924
Bell, L. C., 5012
Belle Haven institute, Alexandria, 4145
Bellevue high school, 4146-4147

Bellevue high school nondescript (period.), 4506
Belmont seminary, Bedford City, 4148
Benedict, C. J., 3545
Benedictine military college, Richmond, 4149
Benevolent & protective order of Elks. *See* Elks.
Bennett, A. L., 1835
Bennett, F. P., 158
Bennett, H. H., 64
Bennett, R. H., 2065
Bennoch, Francis, 1298
Benson, C. H., 2383
Benton, L. D., 2113
Bercaw, Louise O., 1-2,
Berglund, Abraham, 3690
Berkeley, C. N., 161
Berkeley, Edmund, 1732
Berkeley, F. B., 3323
Berkley (city). Description, 1494
  Directories, 1906, 1908
  Schools, Private, 4400
  Water company, 1540
Berkley military institute, 4150
Bernard, R. S., 1895
Bernhard, W. J., 5240
Berries, 253
Berryville (town). Schools, 4221
Berryville high school, 4151
Best, Mrs. E. L., 1105
Beth Ahabah (synagogue), Richmond, 1610, 4855
Bethany Bapt. assoc. (col.), 4704
Bethel academy, Fauquier Co., 4152
Bethlehem Evangel. church, Richmond, 4853
Better Newport News assoc., 1468
Betts, C. W., 1437
Bevier, Isabel, 2306
Beyer, Edward, 2094
Bibb, A. P., & co., 1413
Bible, Discussion on, 4811
Bible reading in public schools, 4675, 4817
Bible society of Va., 4757
Bible study in high schools, 4097
Bibliographies of Va., 1-2, 6, 8-9, 15, 25-26, 28-30, 35-40, 42-43, 45-50, 987, 1177, 3318
Biddle, T. A., 958, 960
Big Lick (town), 3127
Big Stone Gap (town). State summer institute, 3813
Big Stone Gap coal field, 317
Big Stone Gap herald (period.), 2202
Big Stone Gap improvement co., 2202
Big tent, The (period.), 3949
Billings, C. K., 171
Bi-monthly guild (period.), 1391
Binford, J. H., 4068

Biographical dictionaries. *See* Dictionaries

Biographical sketches, 1407, 1428, 1574, 1689, 2279-2280, 2282, 3588, 3624, 3912, 3922, 4483, 4489, 4491, 4494, 4498, 4504, 4628, 4897, 4902, 4909, 4913, 4928, 4934, 4954, 4962, 4971, 4974, 4979, 5019-5020, 5032, 5034, 5052, 5064, 5066, 5070, 5942, 6070-6071, 6073. *See also* Pt. IX.

Biographical sketches (col.), 2059, 2325

Bishop, C. R., 1520

Bishop, W. B., 440

Bishop Payne divinity school, Petersburg, 3385

Bitting, S. T., 278

Bittle memorial hall, Roanoke college, 3505

Björkman, Edwin, 5349

Black, J. S., 2583, 2585

Black, James, 2078

Black, W. M., 4537

Black Forest farm, 225

Black swan, The (period.), 6094

Black Walnut (town). Schools, 4179-4180

Blackburn, J. W., 2028

Blackford, C. M., 743, 2966, 3249

Blackstone college for girls, 3386-3388

Blackstone institute. *See* Blackstone college

Blackstone military academy, 4153

Blackwater Bapt. assoc., 4668

Blackwell, J. D., 4811, 5305

Blair, Louisa C., 5306

Blair, W. R., 82

Blair & co., 498

Blakey, A. R., 1268-1269

Blakey, W. C., 4649

Bland County. Land for sale, 175
  Resources, 393, 407

Blanton, R. L., 4649

Bledsoe, A. C., 4758

Blind, Assoc. of workers for the, 2050

Blind, Books for the, 3315

Blind, Commission for the, 1963-1964

Blind, Legislative commission for the, 1965

Blind, Schools for the, 1962, 1978-1982, 2069

Blossom, A. C., 3053

Blow, Mrs. A. A., 2384

Blue Ridge Mts. Description, 2192, 2224, 2375
  Fiction, 5281, 5293, 5913, 5926
  Fruit growing, 73

Blue Ridge Baptist, The (period.), 4985

Blue Ridge Bapt. assoc., 4669

Blue Ridge iron co., 391

Blue Ridge rod & gun club, 2385

Blue sky law, 1356

Bluefield (city). Directory, 1944

Bluefield college, Tazewell Co., 3389

Bluestocking, The (period.), 3950

Bluestone Bapt. assoc. (col.), 4705-4706

Bluestone Bapt. Sunday school convention (col.), 4707

Boatwright, F. W., 3476, 3489

Bohannon, A. W., 1820

Bohannan, J. G., 806

Boisseau, Sterling, 5307-5308

Bolenbaugh, Albert, 4656

Bolling, C. E., 3073

Bolster, R. H., 333

Bomb, The (period.), 3951

Bon Air land & improvement co., 2212

Bon Air school, 4154

Bona (pseud.). *See* Bacon, Susie L.

Bond, Christiana, 5129

Bond, J. F., 321

Bondholders' committee, N. Y., 1299-1302

Bondholders, Corp. of foreign, 1310, 1312, 1361

Bonsteel, J. A., 65

Books, Rare, 5268

Boone, H. B., 5309-5311

Booth, E. G., 744

Borst, Addison, 1430

Borum, S. R., 1500

Bosher, Mrs. K. L., 5312-5321

Bossom, A. C., 3053

Boston transcript, 4171

Boswell (pseud.). *See* Johnson, W. B.

Boswell, L. A., 5012

Boteler, C. G., 1761

Botetourt County, 417, 1322

Botetourt normal college, 3339

Both sides (period.), 3616

Boundaries, Description of, 2292

Boundaries, Md. & Va., 2599, 2912
  Bibliography, 42
  Board of arbitrators on, 2583-2585, 2754
  Eastern Shore, Joint committee on (1867), 2606
  Md. commissioner for surveying & marking, 2603
  Pocomoke Sound, Governors' correspondence on, 2607
  Pocomoke Sound, Md. commission on (1916), 2605
  Pocomoke Sound, Md. commissioner on (1898), 2604
  Potomac River, Report on, 2609, 2754
  Tangier Sound, Md. commission on (1916), 2605
  Tangier Sound, Md. commissioner on (1898), 2604
  Va. commission on (1870-1874), 2586, 2643-2646
  Va. commissioner on (1888), 2642

[The numbers refer to items, not to pages]

Boundaries, N. C. & Va., 2646
Boundaries, Tenn. & Va., 2626, 2646
Boutwell, W. R., 1481
Bouvé, Mrs. P. C., 5322-5324
Bowen, C. W., 3870
Bowers, C. W., 1673, 5325
Bowers, G. M., 342
Bowles, B. F., 392
Bowles, R. K., 2558, 2567
Bowling Green academy, 4155
Bowling Green female seminary, 4156
Bowman, S. W., 1094
Boy scouts, Winchester, 1867
Boyd, C. R. 393, 1765
Boyd, Mrs. L. R., 5326
Boyd, T. M., 3326
Boyd's directories, 1875-1876, 1928
Boydton academic & Bible institute, 4157, 4321
Boykin, Maury, 745
Boy's big game series, 5380-5382
Boys' club work, 61, 4201
Bradfield, W., 321
Bradford, Gamaliel, 5130, 5176
Bradford, J. H., 1224, 1227-1228
Bradford, Russell, 3673
Bradford, S. S., 215
Bradley, A. G., 2386
Bradley, J. H., 1821, 2487
Brady, T. J., 2803
Bragg, G. F., 2860
Braithwaite, S. N., 1301, 1361
Brakemen's organization, 671, 674
Branch, J. P., 4629
Branch, Thomas, & co., 1322
Braxton, A. C., 746, 2758-2759, 3780
Breckinridge, Mrs. J. A., 5327
Breckinridge, W. C., 2387
Bregenzer, D. M., 6065
Brenaman, J. N., 2861
Brentsville seminary, 4158-4159
Brethren, Church of the, 4909
  Schools. *See* Colleges; Schools
Briar patch (period.), 3952
Bridges, Highway, 685, 687
Bridgewater college, 3390-3393
Briquetting tests, 382
Bristol (city). Board of trade, 1408
  Business conditions, 1407-1408
  City clerk, 2925
  Directories, 1882-1883
  Education, Board of, 4035-4036
  Industrial resources, 1407-1408
  Schools, Private, 3517, 3522-3523, 3737-3740, 4459
  Treasurer, 2925
Bristol-Goodson. *See* Bristol
Bristol news, 6112
Bristol parish, 4961
Bristow, M. E., 1209
British bondholders, 1163

Broad St. M. E. church, Richmond, 4766
Broaddus, Annie M., 5328
Broaddus, William, 4759
Broadus, J. A., 3477, 3488, 4760, 4958
Brock, R. A., 1547, 2476, 3332, 4949, 4962, 5131, 5154, 5241
Brockett, F. L., 1822, 5013
Brodell, A. P., 66
Brooke, C. F., 5667
Brooke, J. M., 3763
Brooke, W. T., 2997
Brooklyn Armstrong assoc., 4161
Brooks, Lewis, 3554
Brooks, S. A., 1745
Brown, A. B., 4925
Brown, A. G., 4802
Brown, Alexander, & sons, 812
Brown, J. C., 1378
Brown, J. T., 3346, 3781
Brown, J. W., 747, 1040, 1303-1305, 1326
Brown, Kenneth, 5310-5311
Brown, M. C., 2965
Brown, Mrs. Mary C., 2097
Brown, N. C., 321
Brown, R. M., 10
Brown, Sara A., 4482
Brown, W. C., 4913
Brown, W. H., 2342
Brown, William, 6100
Brown bros. & co., N. Y., 812, 1378
Brown's university school, Charlottesville, 4162
Browne, W. W., 2059
Browne-Smith, Mrs. M. A., 2059
Bruce, P. A., 2315, 3913, 4654, 5132-5133, 5329
Bruce, T. S., jr., 5330
Bruce, Thomas, 2098, 5064
Bruce, W. C., 3546, 5331-5332
Brunswick County, 1766, 1895
Brunswick times-gazette, 2032
Bruton parish, James City Co., 4761-4762, 4780
Bruton parish church, Williamsburg, 4780, 4885, 4891-4892, 4917-4918
Bryan, Belle S., 4538
Bryan, Emma L., 5333
Bryan, Helen, 1105
Bryan, Joseph, 2084, 4763
Bryan, N. P., 3369
Bryant, R. C., 321
Bryce, C. A., 5334-5335
Bryce, Catherine T., 5750
Bryce, James, 3603
Brydon, G. M., 4913, 4916
Buchanan, B. F., 3547
Buchanan, J. L., 3300
Buchanan & Clifton Forge ry. co., 579, 748
Buchanan County. Resources, 393, 426, 460, 482

Buck, J. L., 1130
Buckingham County. Mineral resources, 412, 456
Seven Islands school, 4416
Buckley, R. W., 5336
Buckley, William, 2517
Budget, City. *See* name of city
Budget, County, 1224, 1227
Budget, Div. of the, 1224, 1227-1228
Budget, State, 1217-1219, 1221, 1223, 1228, 1373, 2675
Budgets of state officers, 1180
Buell, P. B., 162
Buena Vista (town), 1409-1410, 3908, 4425
Buena Vista plaster & mining co., 394
Buffalo Lithia Springs, Mecklenburg Co., 2031
Buford, E. P., 2032
Buford, Pattie, 2316
Bugle, The (period.), 3953
Building & loan associations, 1209, 1342, 1349, 1363, 2325
Building stone, 537, 1765
Buildings, State, 1340, 1674
Bumgarner, S. C., 2760
Bureau of economics & public efficiency, 3165
Bureau of municipal research, N. Y.
City government surveys, 3154-3156
County govt. in Va., 3153
State govt., 2761
Burford, W. B., 1548
Burger, A. L., 5068
Burgess, Mrs. M. A., 1549-1551
Burgwyn, C. P., 1463, 1556, 5337-5338
Burke, R. E., 2587
Burkeville (town). Schools, 4299, 4427
Burks, E. C., 2720
Burks, M. P., 2747, 2862, 2877
Burlin, Mrs. N. C., 5242
Burrell, C. E., 5014
Burrows, J. L., 4896
Burton, H. W., 5015
Burton, L. W., 4949
Burton, P. J., 1552
Burt's library of the world's best books, 5120
Burwell, G. H., 5028
Bushotter, George, 4140
Business men, Laws prepared for, 2867, 2873
Business schools. *See* Schools
Butler, B. F., 2786
Butler, N. M., 3642
Butt, I. L., 4897
Button, Joseph, 1249
Buxton, S. R., 2976
Byrd, A. H., 28
Byrd, H. F., 365, 676, 749, 1223-1225, 2687, 2702-2712, 3146, 3306

Byrd library, Univ. of Va., 28
Byrd Presbyt. church, Goochland Co., 4764
CABELL, G. C., 2592
Cabell, I. C., 5339
Cabell, J. B., 9, 15, 5240, 5248, 5252, 5340-5370, 6065, 6081-6082, 6091-6092
Cabell, J. L., 384, 3600
Cabell, J. M., 3225
Cabell, N. F., 37, 39
Cabell, R. E., 2033
Cadet, The (period.), 3954
Cafeterias, 1569
Caldwell, F. P., 2863
Caldwell, M. P., 2872
Caldwell, Mrs. W. W., 5371-5372
Calendar of Va. state papers, 3
Calhoun, D. A., 1468
Calisch, E. N., 3741
Callahan, C. H., 1399
Calliopean society, Emory & Henry college, 3405
Calyx, The (period.), 3955
Cameo, The (period.), 3956
Cameron, H. C., 3860
Cameron, W. E., 2267
Camp Lee. *See* Lee, Camp
Camp Stuart. *See* Stuart, Camp
Campaign (period.), Richmond, 6162
Campbell, Agnes H., 1105
Campbell, H. D., 396
Campbell, J. L., 163, 395-396
Campbell, M. R., 317
Campbell & co., 1918
Campbell County, 96, 1837, 5025
Campbell Co. agric. advisory board, 67
Campbell Co. school fair, 4163
Canal companies. Annual reports to Va., 987
Canals, 427, 507, 561-562, 565-568, 570-577, 582, 602-605, 608, 619, 621, 637, 662, 690-691, 714, 717, 747, 752-753, 764, 781-783, 795, 801-803, 980, 987
Canby, E. S., 2841, 3186-3187
Cannon, James, Jr. 3387-3388
Cantonments, 1954
Canvassers, State board of, 2635
Cape Charles City, 196
Capital invested in Va., 1367
Capitol, State, 3, 421, 1580, 1674, 1826, 2195, 2885, 3108
Caplon, Milton, 5373
Cappon, L. J., 3690
Carbonate, 422
Cargoes (period.), 3957
Carleton, G. W., 2787
Carlin, C. C., 1174
Carlin, Leo, 2864
Carlville (town), 2867, 2873
Carlville trust co., 2873

Carne, W. F., 2923
Carnegie, Andrew, 4142
Carnegie foundation. Randolph-Macon college relations, 3469
Carnegie foundation for advancement of teaching. *Bulletin,* 4486
Caroline County, 1768, 5076
Caroline Co. agric. advisory council, 68
Carpenter, H. W., 1853
Carrico, J. H., 2620
Carrington, Mary C., 5374
Carrington, J. C., 1769
Carrington, T. M., 1560
Carrington, Mrs. W. J., 5016
Carroll County. Resources, 393
Carruthers, E. I., 2930
Carter, Anne J., 4898
Carter, E. E., 321
Carter, Franklin, 4483
Carter, W. P., 5375
Cartmell, T. K., 5017
Cary, Clarence, 1378
Cary, Hunsdon, 2762
Cary, J. B., 4068
Cary & Whitridge, *law firm,* N. Y., 1378
Caskie, Jaquelin A., 5134
Casselman & co., 164
Castleman, Virginia C., 5376-5379
Catawba tuberculosis sanatorium, 2049
Catholic benevolent union of Va., 4936
Catholic churches. *See* Churches
Catholic periodicals, 6163
Catholic university of America. Theses, 1086
Catholic visitor (period.), Richmond, 6163
Catlett, C. M., 1823, 1834
Cato, M. P., 165-166
Caton, H. B., 1307, 2763
Caton, J. R., 1307, 2763
Cattle, 149, 152-153, 1808
Cavalier, The (period.), Fort Monroe, 1855
Cavalier, The (period.), Richmond, 1854
Cavalier, The (period.), Univ. of Va., 3958, 4612
Cavanagh, Catherine F., 1824
Caves, 2085, 2093, 2097, 2099, 2113, 2122-2123, 2126-2127, 2133, 2171-2172, 2175, 2177, 2196, 2205, 2216, 2222-2223, 2243, 2266
Cedar Bluff high school, 4164
Cedar Grove Bapt. assoc. (col.), 4708
Cedar works, Richmond, 462
Cement, 423, 526
Cemeteries, 1437, 1444, 1554, 1575, 1596, 1730, 1736, 3420
Censors, State board of. *See* Motion picture censorship
Central American trade, 917

Central committee of the institutions of higher education, 4539
Central female institute, Gordonsville, 4165
Central high school, Palmyra, 4062
Central lunatic asylum for colored insane. *See* Central state hospital
Central Presbyterian (period.), Richmond, 6165
Central r. r. of Ga. Lease by Richmond & Danville r. r. co., 607
Central state hospital, Petersburg, 1962, 1966
Central trust co. of N. Y., 452, 494, 499, 877, 885, 887, 894, 922-923, 1038-1039, 1064
Central union trust co. of N. Y., 500, 1057
Central Virginia, 2228
Central Va. mining & manufacturing co., 397
Cereals. *See* Grain
Certificates, W. Va. debt, 1377-1378
Chamberlayne, C. G., 4813
Chamberlayne, J. H., 2764
Chamberlayne school, Richmond, 4166
Chamberlin hotel, Old Point Comfort, 1384, 1443, 1446
Chancery, Commissioners in. Laws concerning, 2888, 2907
Chandler, A. B., jr., 4649
Chandler, J. A. C., 2268, 2424, 2865, 3894, 3900, 4028, 4068, 4649, 5018
Chapman, G. S., 2100
Chapter chats (period.), 3959
Charitable assoc. of learning, Sussex Co., 4540
Charitable organizations, 1391, 2034, 2044-2045, 2050-2055, 2068, 4786. *See also* names of cities
Charities & correction, Nat'l conferences of, 1961, 2035, 2045
Charities & correction, State board of, 1962, 1967-1973, 2001, 2005, 2010, 2012, 2023, 4102, 4523
Charities & correction, Va. conference of, 2052-2054
Charles citian, The (period.), 4507
Charles City County. Churches, 4905
  Directory, 1098
  Physiography, 1098
  Ruthville community, 2344
  Soils, 1098
  Taxes, 1193
Charles City high school, 4507
Charles field, Richmond, 601
Charlotte County. Board of supervisors, 1769
  Churches, 4980
  Description, 1769, 1786
  Guide book, 1786

Charlotte County—cont'd
History, 1769, 1786
Test farm, 141
Tobacco, 66
Charlottesville (city). Auditor, 2928
Building code, 1886
Charter, 2930
Churches, 4765, 4994
Clubs, 2532
Crime, 2525
Debt, 2928
Description, 1413-1414, 1418, 1420, 1759
Directories, 1884-1887
Gas works, Supt. of, 2929
George Rogers Clark monument, 1417
Guide books, 1411, 1759, 1885
Lewis-Clark monument, 1419
Library, McIntire public, 3271, 3330
Licenses, Taxes on, 2927, 2931
Monticello hotel, 1418
Negroes, 1846
Ordinances, 2930-2932
Schools, Private, 4162, 4167, 4302, 4371, 4401-4402
Social conditions, 1412, 1414-1415, 1420
Street improvement bonds, 2926
Water supply, 538
Water works, 2933-2934
Charlottesville & Albemarle ry. co., 751
Charlottesville chamber of commerce, 1414
Charlottesville chronicle (period.), 6114
Charlottesville female seminary, 4167
Charlottesville home-coming commit-tees, 1415
Charlottesville public health & nurse assoc., 1416
Charters. Extension of, 2796
Method & cost of obtaining, 1206
Charters, City. See name of city
Chase City, 199, 3814, 4426, 4452
Chataigne, J. H., 1098, 1917
Chataigne & Boyd pub. co., 1906
Chataigne & co., J. H., 2554
Chataigne & Gillis Richmond directory, 1928
Chataigne's directories, 1874, 1877, 1903, 1906, 1917, 1928, 2554
Chatham (city). Directory, 1889
Chatham Episc. institute, 4168
Chaucer examinations, Hollins institute, 3435
Chautauqua, Jewish, 4567
Chemical associations, 4587, 4591
Chemical industries, 472
Chenault, F. R., 4766
Chesapeake agric. fair assoc., 196

Chesapeake & Ohio and Hocking Valley employes' magazine, 1088, 1092
Chesapeake & Ohio canal co., 582, 714, 752-753, 783
Chesapeake & Ohio employes' magazine, 1088
Chesapeake & Ohio hospital assoc., Rich-mond, 1555
Chesapeake & Ohio r. r. co., 410, 465, 471, 755, 1020, 1519, 2101-2102
Chesapeake & Ohio ry. co., 289, 558, 636, 647, 656, 680, 754-759, 852, 870, 962, 994, 2092, 2103-2108, 2115-2216
Industrial dept., 167, 398
Passenger dept., 2109-2110
Real estate dept., 168, 2111
Safety first bulletin, 1092
Chesapeake & Ohio ry. directory, 1098
Chesapeake & Potomac telephone co., 649, 760-761, 1008, 1086
Directories, 1889, 1894, 1904
Chesapeake Bay. Description, 2090, 2165, 2238, 2270
Fiction, 5995
Fish & oysters, 325, 388
Chesapeake City. Directory, 1903
Chesapeake male & female academy, Irvington, 4169
Chesapeake presbytery, 4821, 4824
Chester institute, 3394
Chesterfield chronicle (period.), 1320
Chesterfield County. Description, 1463, 1763, 1770, 1775
Directories, 1895, 1902
History, 1775
Home & indust. school for girls, 1996
Soils, 96
Chesterfield land & improvement co., 1556
Chesterman, E. R., 3293, 5380-5383
Chesterman, W. D., 1557-1558, 2112
Chichester, C. M., 4615
Chichester, E. L., 4171
Chickahominy River. Drainage, 525
Fiction, 5602
Chickering, J. W., 2113
Child labor, 1104, 1113, 1125, 4482
Child memorial fund, 5274
Child welfare, 1974, 1994-1995, 2034, 2051-2052, 2055, 2062, 2068, 4053
Child welfare, Bur. of, 1994-1995
Children's code commission, 1974
Children's home society of Va., 2034
Childs, B. G., 1825
Chilton, W. E., 2588
Chisel, The (period.), 3960
Chisolm bros., 1559
Chittenden, A. K., 321
Chittenden, L. E., 1308
Chowan & southern r. r. co., 817

[The numbers refer to items, not to pages]

Christ church, Alexandria, 4662, 4797, 4943, 4945
Christ church, Norfolk, 4895
Christian, F. W., 669
Christian, G. L., 1560, 1826-1827, 2391, 2766, 3779
Christian, W. A., 5019-5020, 5384
Christian, W. B., 3779
Christian church. *See* Disciples of Christ
Christian examiner (period.), 4986
Christian federation, 2065
Christian observer & free Christian commonwealth (period.), 6166
Church, G. H., 1063
Church, J. W., 4172-4173
Church, M. E., 1761, 1781
Church of the Holy Trinity, Richmond, 4854
Churches, Bapt., 4769, 4777, 4781, 4798, 4856-4857, 4861-4863, 4871, 4896, 4901, 4927, 4931, 4934-4935, 4941-4942, 4947, 4950, 4957, 4977
Churches, Bapt. (col.) 4905, 4956
Churches, Bapt. (primitive), 4741
Churches, Catholic, 4811, 4867-4869, 4936, 4944
Churches, Colonial, 2278, 4849-4850, 4913, 4953
Churches, Disciples of Christ, 4969
Churches, Jewish, 1610, 4855
Churches, Lutheran, 4853, 4910-4911, 4930, 4951
Churches, Mennonite, 4928
Churches, M. E., South, 4766, 4768, 4811, 4902, 4932, 4954
Churches, Meth. Prot. (col.), 4809
Churches, Presbyt., 1449, 4764-4765, 4770, 4818, 4858-4860, 4872-4876, 4882-4883, 4898-4899, 4952, 4966, 4979-4980
Churches, Prot. Episc., 4662-4663, 4773, 4776, 4780, 4784, 4791-4792, 4799, 4812, 4816, 4841-4842, 4849-4850, 4854, 4865-4866, 4870, 4884-4886, 4889, 4891-4892, 4895, 4906, 4908, 4913-4914, 4917-4918, 4920, 4926, 4940, 4943, 4945, 4948-4949, 4953, 4961-4964, 4967, 4970, 4972, 4982
Churchland academy, 4174
Churchman's scrap-book, 4754
Cities, Acts relating to, 3152
Cities, World war activity of, 3215, 3217
Citizens' committee on consolidation & simplification in state & local govts., 2647
Citizen's military training camp, Ft. Eustis, 3263
Citizens' rapid transit co., Richmond, 3104
Citizenship, 2853-2854, 2876, 2900, 4332

Citizenship creed, 3892
City managers. *See* name of city
City planning, 1711-1712, 1726, 1841
City Point (town). Directory, 1897
City tresaurers, 1255
Civic associations, 3155-3158, 4100-4102, 4523, 4543, 4545, 4547-4549, 4551, 4553
Civic sentinel (period.), 2064-2065
Civil law, 2877-2878, 2897
Civil war battles, Reminiscences of, 3241
Civil war roster, 3235
Claiborne, H. A., 1383
Claiborne, J. G., 1771-1772
Claiborne, J. H., 2388
Claims of Va. against U. S., 1150-1151, 1173-1174, 1176
Clam industry, Laws relating to, 371
Claremont (town). Temperance indust. & colleg. institute, 4446
Claren's school for girls, Alexandria, 4175
Clark, E. C., pub., 1562
Clark, E. D., 321
Clark, Emily, 5385, 6099
Clark, George Rogers, 1417, 2252
Clark, Taliaferro, 1950
Clark, W. B., 318
Clarke, P. N., 5135
Clarke County. Econ. & social survey, 1834, 1853
  History, 5028, 5052
Clarkson, H. M., 5386
Clarksville. Public schools, 4037
Clarksville Virginian (period.), 6119
Claxton, P. P., 4635
Clay Hill academy, Millwood, 4176
Clay St. M. E. church, Richmond, 4932
Clays, 526
Clayton, H. D., 1175
Claytor, Graham, 5387-5390
Cleaveland, Bessie, 5250
Clemens, W. M., 5136
Clement, Maud C., 5021
Clemmitt, W. H., 4986
Clergyman (pseud.), 1309
Clerks of court, 1248, 5165
Clifton Forge (city). Alleghany institute, 4132
  Description, 2210
  Directories, 1888
Clifton Forge normal & indust. institute, 4177-4178
Clifton Forge review (period.), 5039
Climate, 97, 119, 244, 262, 332, 1786, 1790, 1811, 2037, 2072, 2080, 2120, 2134, 2209, 2234, 2290, 2292
Clinch Valley, 434
Clinch Valley Bapt. assoc., 4670
Clinch Valley news, Tazewell, 989
Clos, J. H., 1755

Club work, Boys' & girls', 61, 4201
Cluster Springs academy, Black Walnut, 4179
Cluster Springs high school, Black Walnut, 4180
Cluverius, T. J., 1564, 1570
Coal, Analyses of, 316, 347
Coal, Tariff on, 1372
Coal, Transportation of, 970-971, 1009, 1056
Coal mines, 513, 522, 970-971, 1003
    Safety of employees, 1112
Coal products, 503
Coal resources, 317, 338, 347, 393, 400, 410, 421-422, 424, 434, 439, 442, 447, 465, 470, 482-484, 503, 513, 531, 537, 1396
Coal trade, Ches. & Ohio r. r., 471, 759
Coal trade, Virginian ry., 804, 1060
Coalitionists, Republican party, 2826
Cobb, W. W., 3226
Cobham P. O. Keswick school for boys, 4306
Cochran, A. B., 1137
Cochran, H. G., 2982
Cocke, C. L., 3934
Cocke, E. R., 2819
Cocke, W. B., 1773
Code, Business man's, 1318, 2590, 2760
Code, Commissions to revise the, 2648-2648a
Code, Index (Hurst's) to (1887-1914), 14
Code of 1849, 2724
Code of 1860, 2724, 2866
Code of 1870, 2002
Code of 1873, 2719, 2893, 2903
Code of 1887, 698, 1250, 1255, 2718, 2720, 2722, 2903, 2907
    Howard's index to, 2721
Code of 1904, 2723-2724, 2735-2736
Code of 1906, 371
Code of 1918, 2724, 2744, 2877
Code of 1919, Statutes subsequent to, 2610
Code of 1924, 2725, 2733
Code, Pollard's biennial (1908), 2735
Codes, City. See name of city
Codes, Shepard's citations of, 2906
Coe, W. R., 1063
Coeburn. Public schools, 4038
Coghlan, P. G., 1645
Cohee (period.), 3961
Coinage, Gold standard, 2857
Coke, 513, 1003, 1372
Cole, E. F., 169
Coleman, C. W., 5391
Coleman, G. P., 762
Coleman, W. D., 1306

College topics (period.), 3962
Colleges, Agricultural. See Virginia Polytechnic Institute
    Baptist, 3389, 3427, 3476-3491, 3517, 3737-3740, 3836-3838, 3869
    Brethern, Church of the, 3390-3393, 3397
    Central committee on higher education, 4539
    Co-ed., 3390-3393, 3410-3411, 3437-3438, 3445-3454, 3509-3513, 3520, 3531, 3779-3807, 3836, 3869-3906
    Colored, 3385, 3427, 3836-3838, 3869, 3914-3915
    Co-ordinate, 4554
    Disciples of Christ, 3437-3438
    Endowments for, 3329
    Hazing at, 3770, 3779
    Literary societies in, 3405-3406, 3419, 3493-3494, 3504, 3506, 3544, 3557, 3562, 3581, 3585, 3594, 3598, 3687, 3694, 3725, 3840, 3844-3846, 3848, 3887, 3954, 3971-3972, 3975, 3979, 3993, 4029, 4031
    Lutheran, 3401, 3492-3506, 3518
    Men's, 3385, 3389, 3412-3425, 3427, 3457-3469, 3476-3490, 3492-3508, 3532-3733, 3741-3778, 3837-3868
    Methodist, 3386-3388, 3398, 3402-3406, 3462-3473, 3522-3523, 3734.
    Military. See Va. Military Institute; Va. Polytechnic Institute
    Presbyterian, 3410, 3412-3425, 3519, 3532-3539
    Prot. Episc., 3385, 3407, 3457-3461, 3507-3508, 3922, 3942, 4021, 4810, 4814, 4881
    Rural life improvement through, 4322
    Women's, 3384, 3386-3388, 3394-3396, 3398, 3401, 3407-3409, 3426, 3428-3436, 3439-3444, 3455, 3470-3475, 3490, 3514-3519, 3521-3530, 3734-3740, 3808-3835, 3907-3908
    Women's, Assoc. of, 4590
    See also Schools
Collegiate school for girls, Richmond, 4181
Collins, Joseph, 6081
Collins, W. G., 1879, 1892
Collinson, John, 750, 1310
Colonial dames of America, 1411, 2436-2442
Colonial echo (period.), 3963
Colonial Virginia, 2115
Colonnade club. See Univ. of Va.
Colored orphan asylum & indust. school, Lynchburg, 1456
Colored state fair, Richmond, 2317

Columbia university. Studies in history, economics & public law, 1087
Studies in English & comparative literature, 5127
Theses, 540, 1087, 4487, 5127, 6074
Columbian exposition (1892), Va. at, 2083
Colvin, H. T., 1114, 1116, 1135
Combs, M. L., 4484
Comeback, The (period.), 3256
Commerce, Domestic, 991, 1053, 1808, 1858, 2080, 2292, 2294
Commerce, Foreign, 1045, 1053, 2080, 2292, 2294
Commercial, The (period.), Richmond, 6167
Commercial & tobacco leaf (period.), 6168
Commercial law, 1318, 2760, 2867, 2872-2873
Commercial trust co., 763
Commercio americano (1928), Va. state chamber of commerce, 1053
Commission on colonial churches, 4849-4850
Commission to present Washington statue to France, 5234
Commission to present Washington statue to Great Britain & Ireland, 5235
Commissioners in other states, Laws concerning, 2739
Committee of nine on reconstruction (1869), 2843
Commonwealth, The (period.), Richmond, 6169
Commonwealth club, Richmond, 1565
Community league news, The, 4636
Community leagues, 4545, 4547-4549, 4551
Community life campaign, 2056
Compensation insurance. *See* Workmen's compensation
Concord Bapt. assoc., 4671
Conductors. *See* Railroad conductors
Confederate memorial assoc., 2391
Confederate memorial day, 2389, 2538, 3295
Confederate memorial institute, Richmond, 1604, 1827, 2391
Confederate memorial literary society, 3295, 4541, 4627, 4637
Confederate memorial verses, 6026
Confederate memorials, 1730, 1737, 1751, 2425, 2478, 2491, 2497, 2507, 2538
Confederate museum, Richmond, 4541, 4627
Newspapers in, List of, 25
Confederate pensions, 1200, 1202, 1244
Confederate soldiers' & sailors' monument assoc., 1567-1568

Confederate veterans. *See* United Confed. veterans
Conference of boards of visitors of Va. state institutions, 1975
Conference of Va. high school principals, 4542
Conference to consider question of tax reform, 1311
Congress. *See* United States
Congressional apportionment, 2596, 2650
Congressional district, Second, 2587, 2598, 4128
Congressional district, Third, 2752
Congressional district, Fourth, 2589, 2593, 2601-2602, 2755
Congressional district, Fifth, 2620
Congressional district, Seventh, 2614, 2621, 4129
Congressional district, Eighth, 3159
Congressional district, Tenth, 4127
Congressional record, 670, 2619
Conkley, Ralph (pseud.). *See* Eggleston, R. B.
Conley, W. G., 1181
Connor, J. V., 1086
Conquest, E. P., 4182
Conrad, H., 3772
Conser, S. L., 4768
Conservation & development, State commission on, 350
Conservation of resources, 350-360, 545, 547, 554
Conservative, The (period.), Richmond, 6170
Consolidation & simplification of govt., Committee on, 2761, 3153
Constitution (1864), 2806
Constitution (1867), 2627, 2649-2656, 2664, 2720, 2796, 2861, 2870
Amendments to, 2715, 2901
Constitution (1902), 1318, 2657-2660, 2683, 2723-2724, 2728, 2735-2736, 2796, 2861, 2869, 2909, 3311
Amendments to, 2658, 2715
Amendments to, Commission to suggest (1927), 2629-2632
Amendments proposed, 2611, 2661-2662, 2703-2706, 2711, 2730
Constitutional convention (1867-68), 1203, 2663-2668, 2861, 2901, 4414
Constitutional convention (1901-02), 1976, 2657, 2669-2672, 2759, 2782, 2814, 2846, 2858, 2861, 2884, 2901
Corporations, Committee on, 792, 2758
Democratic members, Conference of, 2800
Directory, 2916
Education, Committee on, 3449
Revision & adjustment, Committee on, 2673
Constitutional convention (1928), 2850

Davidson papers, 2395
Davies, A. B., 1888
Davies' directory of Clifton Forge, 1888
Davis, A. K., 3215, 3349
Davis, A. K., jr., 5246, 5274
Davis, C. H., 1138
Davis, D. W., 2059, 5444-5445
Davis, Eugene, 597
Davis, Foxcroft (pseud.). *See* Seawell, Molly E.
Davis, J. J., 1104
Davis, J. S., 3919
Davis, Jane E., 2269
Davis, Jefferson, 1563, 1607, 2372, 2486, 5222
Davis, Mary D., 5446
Davis, Mrs. M. S., 4901
Davis, R. B., jr., 2867
Davis, Westmoreland, 174, 677-678, 978, 1975, 2845
Davison, E. M., 3747
Dawson, Arthur, 5247
Day, R. F., 1090, 2191
Day, Mrs. W. C., 5447
Day book (period.), Norfolk, 2839, 6145
Dayton (town). Shenandoah collegiate institute, 3510-3512
D-Barker (period.), 3257
Deaf & Blind (col.), State school for, Newport News, 1981-1982
Deaf, dumb & blind, Schools for the, 1962, 1978-1980, 2069
Dean, Jennie (col.), 4327
Dearborn, W. F., 4485
Debt, Public, 1165, 1179, 1195, 1214-1215, 1237, 1251-1252, 1294, 1299, 1303-1306, 1322-1323, 1335, 1345-1346, 1353, 1355, 1360, 1376, 1380-1381, 1386-1387, 2782, 2811, 2851, 2880
  Bondholders, 1163, 1298-1302, 1310, 1312, 1347, 1361
  Claim against U. S., 1175
  Coupon cases, 1153, 1172, 1178, 1355, 2794
  Coupons, 1149, 1155, 1355
  Funding of, 1137, 1162, 1171, 1220, 1310, 1322-1323, 1330. 1376, 1381
  Laws concerning, 1156, 1181, 1236, 1251-1252, 1301
  Readjusters, 1154, 1314, 1332, 1335, 1386-1387, 2597, 2765, 2771, 2799, 2816, 2835, 2851, 2860, 2911, 2913
  Repudiation of, 1147, 1169, 1308-1309, 1316-1317, 1333, 1352, 1362, 2794
  Settlement of, 1136, 1152, 1236-1237, 1295

Debt controversy (*Va. v. W. Va.*), 1177, 1181, 1285-1293, 1315, 1334, 1377-1378, 1380, 1384, 1386-1387, 2818
Debts, City. *See* name of city
Deck, P. A., 1830, 1834
Deffenbaugh, W. S., 4084
De Jarnette, Mrs. E. M., 5448
Delaware, Md. & Va. r. r. co., 769-770
Delaware state & peninsula directory, 2555-2556
Delaware state publishing co., 2556
De Mille, W. C., 5478
Democrat, The (period.), Richmond, 6172
Democratic campaign (period.), Lynchburg, 6137
Democratic convention. Va., 8th Congress. dist. (1878), 3159
Democratic mirror (period.), Leesburg, 1784
Democratic party, 1320, 2615, 2756, 2762, 2791, 2804, 2839, 2843
  State central committee, 2774
  State conventions, 2772-2773
Dempsey, S. W., 604
Denny, G. H., 4191
Dental associations, 4562, 4620-4622, 5126
Dental cosmos (period.), 5126
Dental examiners, State board of, 1983
Dental summary (period.), 4622
Dentistry, 1983, 3452
Dett, R. N., 5248
Detwiler, Sadie C., 1831
de Vyver, F. T., 3690
Dialect in Va., 2519
Dickenson County. Bapt. church, 4741
  Resources, 393, 426, 482
Dickinson, Sally B., 5023
Dictionaries, Biographical, 4919, 4937-4939, 5136, 5142, 5147, 5153-5154, 5163, 5214-5215
Dictionary digest, Va. & W. Va. cases, 2863
Dietz, August, 1655
Diggs, Isaac, 771, 1747
Dillingham's American authors' library, 6052
D'Invilliers, E. V., 434-436
Dinwiddie, M. L., 2118
Dinwiddie County. Bath parish, 4756
  Description, 1810
  Directory, 1895
Diocesan record (period.), 4987
Directories. American legion, 3254
  Builders', 1886, 1901
  Business, 1875, 1877, 1880, 1885, 1902-1903, 1910, 1914, 1921, 1925, 1928, 1931, 1934, 1948, 2552-2554, 2561, 2565, 5013

[The numbers refer to items, not to pages]

[The numbers refer to items, not to pages]

Ebenezer community (col.), 2344
Eberle, Frank, 1482
Eby, J. B., 531
Echols, Edward, 2685
Eckenrode, H. J., 2868, 5153
Eclectic geographies. Va. supplement, 2275
Economic conditions. *See* Virginia, description; Financial conditions; Resources; Social Conditions.
Economy & efficiency, Commission on, 2675
Edge Hill school, Keswick Depot, 4196
Education. Addresses on, 2084, 3325, 3335-3336
  Agricultural, 248, 281, 301, 3301, 3777, 3779-3807
  City boards of. *See* names of cities
  Compulsory, 4575
  Conference for, in the South, 1264
  County, 1761, 1776, 1811, 1823, 1830, 1832, 1835, 1842, 1845, 1848-1850, 1852-1853, 5035-5074
  County boards of. *See* name of county
  Extension work, 3331
  Health, 4057, 4084, 4098, 4201
  History of, 3349, 3350a, 3352-3353, 5023, 5034
  Laws concerning. *See* School legislation
  Negro. *See* Negroes
  Periodicals, 3360, 4635-4636, 4638, 4646, 4649, 4657-4658
  Public, 3348, 3350a, 3923, 4334, 4449, 4501, 4554, 4567, 4575, 5075
    Addresses on, 3336, 4395, 4414, 4450-4451
    Survey of (1927), 3302-3304
  Reconstruction period. *See* Reconstruction
  Religious, 4909, 4921, 4933
  Secondary. *See* Education, Public
  State board of
    Agricultural education, Div. of, 3301
    Bulletin, 3289, 3300, 3311, 4089, 4104, 4106, 4115-4116
    Circulars, 3290-3291, 4107
    Colleges, Publications concerning, 3373
    Elementary schools, Publications concerning, 4094, 4096, 4102, 4106-4107. *See also* Education, State bd. of, Public schools
    High schools, Publications concerning, 4089, 4095, 4097, 4099, 4103-4105. *See also* Education, State bd. of, Public schools
    Illiteracy in Va., 3293
    Memorial day annual (1912), 3295
    Normal schools, Publications concerning, 3372, 4105

Education, State board of—cont'd.
    Periodicals, 3959, 4019
    Public schools, Publications concerning, 3294, 3299, 4090, 4092-4093, 4098, 4100-4102, 4108
    Regulations, 3296, 3308
    Regulations for examination of teachers, 3297
    State summer school for teachers, Covington, 3812
    Supt. of public instruction, Report of, 3283, 3288, 3298, 3300, 4585, 4646
    Survey of efforts to improve public education, 3292
    Virginia news letter, 4019
    State dept. of, 1991, 4523
    Statistics on, 3350-3351
    Vocational, 250, 4078, 4217
Education commission. Public schools, Survey of (1919), 3287
  Public schools, Survey of (1920-1921), 3286
  Report on mill tax by C. G. Maphis (1910), 3285
  Report to general assembly (1912), 3284
Educational advantages. *See* Cultural advantages
Educational assoc. of Va., 4555-4556, 4657
  Addresses, 3329, 3334-3335
Educational associations, 4523-4525, 4533, 4539-4540, 4542-4556, 4567, 4570-4571, 4574-4575, 4578-4580, 4583, 4585, 4590, 4592-4596, 4608, 4623-4626, 4636, 4657-4658
Educational board, Gen. Bapt. assoc., 4677
Educational commission. Report of survey (1928), 3302
Educational development since 1902, 1385
Educational institutions, 2234
Educational journal of Va., 4638, 4657
Educational system, 119, 3285, 3305-3306, 3327, 3337, 3339, 3341
Educational system of Va., Commission to survey the, 3302-3304, 3318
Edwards, M. F., 3745
Effna P. O. Sharon college school, 4417
Eggleston, G. C., 5107, 5453-5481
Eggleston, J. D., 3300, 3331, 4093, 4557
Eggleston, J. W., 5482
Eggleston, R. B., 5483
Elam, W. C., 1314
Elam Bapt. church, Charles City Co., 4905
Election of 1876, 2782, 2815
Election of 1911, 3160
Election of 1921, 2785

[The numbers refer to items, not to pages]

Election campaign, of 1872, 2792
Election campaign of 1884-85, 6162
Election campaign of 1887, 2851
Election campaign of T. S. Martin (1911), 2807
Election (senatorial) campaign of 1922, 2845
Election districts, 2688
Election laws, 2650, 2717, 2727, 2738, 2740, 2820
Elections. Contested, 2587, 2589, 2591-2593, 2595, 2598, 2600-2602, 2608, 2614, 2617-2618, 2620-2621, 2752-2753, 2755
   National, 2618-2619
   Plural voting in, 2814
   Primary, 2898
   Registration of voters for, 2669, 2727, 2734, 2796
Electric light companies, 807-813, 821, 955, 1025
Electric railroads. *See* Railroads, Electric
Elementary community civics. Va. supplement, 2876
Eliot, C. W., 3603, 4142
Elizabeth chronicle (period.), 3965
Elizabeth City County. Directory, 1098
   History, 5069
   Physiography, 1098
   Soils, 1098
Elizabeth City parish, 4926
Elizabeth college, Salem, 3401, 3965
Elizabeth iron co., 403
Elizabeth River, 612, 614, 641, 4952
Elizabeth River district, 2024
Elizabeth River parish, 4895
Elk Creek academy, Ursus, 4197
Elks (fraternity). Richmond lodge, 2520
Ellett, A. L., 5484
Ellinger, William, 404
Elliott, C. G., 3014
Elliott's Knob, 2205
Ellis, S. G., 1302
Ellis, T. H., 568
Elmwood cemetery, Norfolk, 2389
Elmwood nurseries, 180
Emancipation club of Roanoke, 2340
Emancipation club of Salem, 2340
Emerson, C. E., jr., 3121
Emory & Henry college, Emory, 3363, 3402-3406
   Periodicals, 3966, 3997
Emporia (town), 1953
Emporia land & investment co., 504
Employment in Richmond, 1100-1102
Enabling act, 2638
Enchanted years (poetry, Univ. of Va.), 5257
Endless Caverns, 2097, 2123, 2133
Endlich, F. M., 446

Engineering, 3675, 3796-3797, 3864. *See also* Schools, Technical
   Agricultural, Amherst Co., 61
Engineering associations, 4534-4536, 4634
Engineering periodicals, 4634
Engineers, City. *See* name of city
Engineers' assoc. of Va., 3126
Engineers' soc. of western Pa., 528
English pronunciation in Va., 6088
Engravings, 5241, 5268
Enquirer & examiner, The daily, Richmond, 6176-6177
Entomologist, State, 143-145
Entomology, 107, 143-144
Epes, J. F., 2589, 2593, 2595, 2753
Epileptics, 1962, 1985, 2036, 2039
Episcopal female institute, Winchester, 3407
Episcopal high school, Fairfax Co., 3922, 4199-4200, 4448, 4488, 4514
Episcopal theological seminary, Alexandria, 4814
Episcopal. *See also* Protestant Episcopal
Equal suffrage league of Va., 2777-2778, 2822, 5639
Equitable trust co. of N. Y., 496-497, 1065
Equity procedure, 2864, 2872, 2905
Essex County. Description, 1814, 5027
   Finances, 2944
   Oyster records, 351
   South Farnham Parish, 4880
Essex Co. agric. advisory council, 70
Estates, Country, 2161, 2169, 2213
Eubank, J. L., 405
Eubank, R. P., 3779
Eugenics, 1995
European agent of immigration, for Va., 2072
European emigrants, 2072, 2078-2079, 2183
European trade, 784
Evans, C. A., 2378
Evans, E. S., 1572, 5236
Evans, T. J., 2667
Everett, J. W., 4201, 4649
Every Saturday journal, Richmond, 6179
Ewell, Alice M., 5485
Ewell, B. S., 3364-3365, 3871-3872, 3901
Ewell, Representative, 978
Ewing, Mrs. F. B., 4131
Exchange bank, Richmond, 1150
Exchange reporter (period.), Richmond, 6181
Excise, State bd. of commissioners of, 1212
Exhibits, Mineral, at U. S. Centennial, Philadelphia, 447, 532
Expenditures, State, 1366, 1373
Expositions, 447, 2211, 2247. *See also* Jamestown exposition

Express companies, 663, 665, 878
Extension division news (period.), Va.
  polytechnic institute, 3967
Extension topics (period.), Univ. of
  Va., 3968
Extension work, Educational, 3331
Ezekiel, H. T., 1573, 2345-2346
Ezekiel, Mordecai, 71
Ezekiel's statues, 2616, 3772, 5209

FAHRNEY, ELIZABETH, 1835
Fairfax County. Board of supervisors,
  1781
  Churches, 4889, 4908
  Description, 1781, 2213
  Directories, 1877, 1892
  Economic & social survey, 1834, 1849
  Episcopal high school, 4199-4200
  Farming, 72
  Geography, 1831
  History, 1781
  Soils, 96
Fairfax Hall, Winchester, 3408-3409
Fairs. County, 170, 196, 199, 201, 214,
  223-224, 245, 247
  School. *See* School fairs
  State, 260-261, 264-265, 286, 296, 2317,
    6209
Fairview academy, Simmonsville, 4203
Falls Church (town), 2039, 2945, 3272,
  4953
Fancy Hill classical school, 4204
Farm & household almanac for Va. &
  N. C., 2558
Farm life, 251
Farm machinery, 307, 430
Farm management, 165-166
Farm statistics, 140
Farmer, The (period.), 294
Farmers. Directory of, 1885
  Laws concerning, 282, 2867, 2873
Farmers' alliance co-operative manufac-
  turing co., 406
Farmers' bank, Richmond, 1150
Farmers' conference, 188
Farmers' convention of Va., 181
Farmers' council of Va. & N. C., 182
Farmers' educational & co-operative un-
  ion, 1119
Farmers' 4H club, Madison Co., 2709
Farmers' gazette & indust. index (pe-
  riod.), 295
Farmers' loan & trust co., 776, 1066
Farms for sale. 120, 160, 162, 164, 167-
  168, 175, 183, 189, 193, 203, 229-231,
  244, 276, 458, 1788
Farmville. Negroes, 2305
  State teachers' college, 3816-3825
Farmville & Powhatan r. r. co., 696, 777-
  778
Farmville herald, 4532, 4557

Farr, R. R., 3300
Farrar, F. R., 1782, 5486
Farrow, E. S., 407
Fashions, 2543
Fauntleroy, T. T., jr., 4779
Fauquier County. Bethel academy, 4152
  Directories, 1877
  Farms, 160
  Gold mining, 446
  History, 1783
  Politics, 2806
  Springs, 408-409
Fauquier female institute, Warrenton,
  4205
Fauquier historical society, 4558
Fauquier land journal, 6235
Fauquier White Sulphur Springs, 408-
  409
Faure, J. P., 1164, 1166
Fayerdale ore & lumber corp., 1043
Featherston, H. C., 5672
Federal court cases (Va. debt), 1172
Federal farm loan board, 1344
Federal government, Virginia's relations
  with. Letter of Gov. Kemper, 3168
Federal reporter, 1172, 2906
Federal reserve bank of Richmond, 1140-
  1144, 1160, 1357
  Letters to college classes, 3366
  Monthly review, 1391a
Federal reserve system, 1142, 3366
Fee commission, State, 1348
Fee system, 1348
Feeble-minded, 1969, 1971, 1985, 2006,
  2039
Feeding stuffs funds, 284
Fenner, C. E., 3552
Fenner, T. P., 4134, 5250-5251
Ferebee, E. E., 1832, 1834
Ferguson, Mrs. E. H., 5487
Ferguson, M., 287
Ferneyhough, J. G., 153
Ferry, B. A., & co., 1470
Fertilizers, 110-111, 147, 200, 238, 253,
  284, 486
Fess, S. D., 606
Festetits, Mrs. K. N., 5488-5499
Fidelity companies, 1196, 1235, 1249
Field, Louise M., 6070
Field artillery assoc., of Va., 3253
Fillmore, A. L., 3571
Filtration plants, 1426, 1517
Finance, Dept. of, 709
Financial conditions, 1298, 1385, 1391a,
  2711, 3350
Finley, J. H., 3603
Finn, *Sister* M. B., 6071
Fire departments, City. *See* name of
  city
Firemen's associations, 1574, 2058
Firey, S. M., 5500

Fredericksburg (city)—cont'd.
  Schools, Private, 3410, 4424
  State teachers' college, 3826-3828
Fredericksburg & Gordonsville r. r. co.,
  779
Fredericksburg & Rappahannock r. r.
  co., 780
Fredericksburg chamber of commerce,
  1433
Fredericksburg college, 3410
Fredericksburg ledger, The (period.),
  6127
Fredericksburg memorial park assoc.,
  1431
Fredericksburg Presbyt. church, 4898
Free lance-star (period.), Fredericks-
  burg, 1434, 6129
Freedman's friend (period.), 2357
Freeman, A. W., 1710, 2060
Freeman, D. S., 1145, 1576
Freeman, E. A., 2125
Freeman, J. C., 781
Freemasons.   Alexandria-Washington
  lodge no. 22, 1400, 1822
  Grand lodge, 2396, 2399-2401
  Grand royal arch chapter, 2402
  Henrico union lodge, no. 130, Rich-
    mond, 2528
  Loge Française, no. 53, Richmond,
    2536
  Meridian lodge, no. 284, 2404, 2524
  Richmond lodge, no. 10, 1696
  Royal arch chapter, no. 3, Richmond,
    2529
  See also Knights templar
Freight rates. *See* Railroads, Rates
French, S. B., 782
Fretz, A. J., 5144
Frissell, H. B., 2306, 4142, 4213, 4247,
  4497
Frissell, S. D., 4214
Frith, G. R., 5506
Froehling, Henry, 532
Front Royal (town). Randolph-Macon
  academy, 4380-4381
Fruit grower, The (period.), 292
Fruit-growing, 73, 169, 176, 205, 253,
  1746, 1764, 1811
  Bibliography, 2
  Catalogues, 180, 191
  Periodicals, 292, 298, 306
  Societies, 257, 268-271
Frye-Atwood geographical series. Va.
  supplement, 2291
Fulkerson, Abraham, 1316-1317
Fuller, Mabel C., 1833
Fullerton, William, 185
Funding assoc. of the U. S. A. (ltd.),
  1310
Funck, Henry, 5144
Funk, J., & sons, 6096

Funk, Joseph, 6093
Funk, W. C., 72
Funk family, 5144
Funkhouser, A. P., 4909
Furlow, H. W., 1114
Furness, H. H., 3434
Furniture made in penitentiary, 380
Furst, C. B., 4486

GAILLARD, E. G., 4642
Gaillard's medical journal, 4642
Gaines, Elizabeth V., 3161
Gaines, R. H., 117
Gaines, R. V., 1786
Gaither, F. O., 3555
Galax high school, 4215
Gallagher, Charles, 412
Galloway, C. B., 4907
Galt, James, 2078
Game & fish conservationist (period.),
  545
Game and inland fisheries, Commission
  of, 358-360, 372, 376, 2605
Game & inland fisheries, State dept. of,
  See Commission of
Game laws, 373, 376-377, 508-509
Game preserves, 231
Gammack, F. S., 186
Gannett, Henry, 2070
Garber, Mrs. A. W., 4627
Garber, Mrs. V. A., 5507-5508
Gardener, Helen H. (Mrs. Smart),
  5509-5516
Gardens, Historic, 2144
Garfield, J. A., 4133, 4267
Garnett, A. Y., 2037
Garnett, C. B., 1318, 2590
Garnett, E. M., 4068
Garnett, G. T., 2842
Garnett, J. M., 3556, 3912
Garnett, Judith L., 5517
Garnett, T. S., 1581
Garnett, W. C., 5027
Garnett, W. E., 4922
Garrett, J. W., 783
Garrett, Robert, 1040
Gas companies, 807-810, 1718-1719, 2992
Gas works, City. *See* name of city
Gasoline tax, 1246, 1331
Gate City. Shoemaker college, 3513
Gazeteers, 1918, 2070, 2554, 2561
Gee, Wilson, 279-280, 1823, 1830, 1832,
  1834-1835, 1842, 1845, 1848-1850,
  1852-1853, 3350, 3647, 3690
Gee aitch 43 (period.), 3258
Geisinger, J. F., 3228
Genealogical periodicals, 4639, 4645
Genealogy, 2543, 4961, 4963, 5025, 5032,
  5050, 5135, 5144, 5507
General assembly.   Addresses,   1139,
  1159, 3306, 3327

[The numbers refer to items, not to pages]

[The numbers refer to items, not to pages]

Goode, T. F., 2031
Goodwin, E. L., 4913-4916, 4964
Goodwin, W. A. R., 3922, 4780, 4885, 4917-4918
Goolrick, C. O., 2783
Goolrick, J. T., 5029
Gordon, A. C., 6, 1419, 1732, 3348, 3873, 3923, 5147, 5149, 5452, 5535-5544
Gordon, A. C., jr., 5545, 6072
Gordon, F. R., 1741
Gordon, J. L., 2784, 5546
Gordon, James, & co., 784
Gordon, W. F., 5547
Gordon, W. S., 5548
Gordonsville (town), 1894, 4165, 4478
Gordonsville female institute, 4222-4223
Gorman, A. P., 783
Goshen Bapt. assoc., 4678
Gosport. U. S. Navy yard, 3180
Gosson, L. C., 2407
Gould, H. P., 73
Government
   City, 3154-3158, 3166, 3189-3174, 3177-3179, 3279
     Laws concerning, 3014-3016, 3019, 3152
   County, 1184-1185, 1191, 3146, 3153, 3161
   Local, 1921, 2647, 2746, 3165
   State, 1921, 2080, 2565, 2707, 2709, 2824, 2853, 2871, 2884
     Consolidation of, 2647, 2702, 2711-2712, 2714, 2746, 2761
     Economy & efficiency, 2675
     Personnel of, 2701
     Textbooks on, 2869-2870, 2876, 2882-2883, 2896, 2908-2909
Government appeal agents, 3197, 3213
Government officials. Local, 2733, 2737, 2760, 2878
   State, 1180, 5191
Governor, 1864-65 (William Smith), 2757
Governor, 1865-68 (F. H. Peirpont), 2451, 2838, 2875, 5062
Governor, 1869-73 (G. C. Walker), 1233, 2697, 3305, 5062
Governor, 1874-78 (J. L. Kemper), 364, 1220, 2414, 2584, 3145, 3167-3168, 3747, 5062
Governor, 1878-82 (F. W. M. Holliday), 1251, 5062
Governor, 1894-98 (C. T. O'Ferrall), 4114
Governor, 1898-1902 (J. H. Tyler), 2084, 2699
Governor, 1906-10 (C. A. Swanson), 2372, 2700, 3341
Governor, 1910-14 (W. H. Mann), 2684, 5099

Governor, 1914-18 (H. C. Stuart), 1117, 2026, 2685
Governor, 1918-22 (Westmoreland Davis), 677-678, 978, 1217-1219, 1975
Governor, 1922-26 (E. L. Trinkle), 1221-1222, 2686, 2701, 2785, 3207
Governor, 1926-30 (H. F. Byrd), 365, 1223-1225, 2687, 2702-2712, 3146, 3153, 3306
Governors. Executive papers, 2694
   Messages, proclamations, etc., 1263, 2695-2712
Governors' conference (1922). Address of E. L. Trinkle, 1221
Gracchussary rhyme book, 281
Grace Episc. church, Richmond. Ladies' aid society, 2408
Grace Evangel. Luth. church, Winchester, 4911
Grace indust. school & farm, Alleghany Co., 4224
Grace memorial church, Lexington, 4791
Grace St. Bapt. church, Richmond, 4861-4863
Graham, W. A., 2583
Graham (town), 1944, 4465
Grain, 92-93, 221, 236, 239, 253
Grand army of the Republic. Andrew (J. A.) post, Mass., 2409
   Kearney (Phil.) post, no. 10, Richmond, 2383
   Lincoln post, no. 11, Newark, N. J., 2383
   Wilkes (Aaron) post, N. J., 2407, 2410
Grand Caverns, 2126
Grand fountain united order of true reformers (col.), 2059
Grange. See Va. state grange
Granite, 463
Grant, C. W., 2685
Grant, E. W., 3159
Grant, U. S., 2792, 3240
Grant, U. S., jr., 848
Grant P. O. High Point academy, 4295
Grapurchat (period.), 3970
Grape growing, 60, 191, 298, 1764
Grass, 195, 208, 253
Grasty, J. S., 515
Grattan, Charles, 2081
Grattan, P. R., 17, 31, 2747, 2750
Graves, C. A., 2877
Graves, H. S., 321
Graves, J. T., 3557
Gray jacket (period.), 3971
Graybill, W. M., 2871
Grayson County, 393, 1765
Grayson Co. agric. advisory board, 74
Great Britain, Emigrants from, 2078-2079

[The numbers refer to items, not to pages]

[The numbers refer to items, not to pages]

Harrison, H. S., 5594-5600, 6069
Harrison, J. A., 3722
Harrison, R. L., 28, 1378
Harrison, Randolph, 112
Harrison, Susie B., 25
Harrison, T. W., 2614, 2874
Harrisonburg (city). Description, 1351, 1448-1449
  Massanetta mineral springs, 437
  Rockingham national bank, 1351
  Schools, Public, 4039
  State teachers' college, 3360, 3829-3832, 3992
Harrisonburg daily news, 1448
Harrisonburg daily news-record, 1321
Hart, A. B., 2447
Hart, Harris, 3286, 3300
Hartford city guard at Manassas, 3227
Hartshorn memorial college, Richmond, 3427, 4005
Harvard university. Theses, 3924, 4484
Harwood, W. R., 2520
Hasadiah Bapt. assoc. (col.), 4710-4711
Haswell, J. R., 525
Hatcher, E. B., 4923
Hatcher, Orie L., 1123
Hatcher, W. E., 4923-4925, 4950, 4974
Hatcher, Mrs. W. E., 4925
Hatchett, Mamie L., 5601
Hatfield, H. D., 1292-1293
Haupt, Herman, 415
Haw, Mary J., 5601
Hawkins, R. W., 2790
Hawkins Chapel institute, Rural Retreat, 4294
Hawthorne, Hildegarde, 2132
Haxall, B. B., 2078
Haxall, B. W., 598
Hay, James, 2595
Hayes, J. M., jr., 2596
Hayes' Creek Mound, Rockbridge Co., 5272
Hayes-Tilden election, 2618
Hazlewood, M. W., 6098
Head, J. W., 5031
Heads up (period.), 3260
Healing Springs, Bath Co., 385, 401, 405, 416, 440, 459
Health. Dept. of, 1962, 1986-1995, 4102, 4523
  Public, 1336, 1416, 1804, 2047-2049, 3903-3906
  State board of. *See* Dept. of
Health agencies, 1685
Health departments, City. *See* names of cities
Heard, J. L., 1146
Heartman, C. F., 50
Heaton, Henry, 1830, 1834
Heatwole, C. J., 3350a, 4649

Hebron Luth. church, Madison Co., 4930
Heffelfinger, Jacob, 4926
Heindl, J. J., 3076, 3108
Heinrich, Elizabeth Jeffries, 2821
Heitmann, John, 2521
Helianthus (period.), 3973
Hellier, C. E., 426
Helper, H. A., 1457
Helper, H. R., 2780
Henderson, Archibald, 1417
Henderson, D. B., 2826
Henderson, F. M., 1784
Henkel, D. S., 2133
Henkel, E. O., 6073
Henneman, J. B., 3351
Henning, Julia R., 2273
Henrico County. Board of supervisors, 1792
  Description, 1780, 1792
  Directories, 1098
  Guide book, 1792
  History, 1792
  Physiography, 1098
  Property rented to U. S. army, 1779
  Public schools, 4040, 4391, 4549
  Soils, 96, 1098
Henrico farmers club, 190
Henrico parish, 4949
Henrico ry. co., 3101
Henry, R. L., 2360
Henry, W. W., 1147, 4949, 5142
Henry Clay school, Norfolk, 4332
Henry County, 1424, 5032
Henry Second (pseud.). *See* Harrison, H. S.
Herald-progress (period.), Ashland, 1789, 6109
Herbert, H. A., 1122, 3558
Herdener, E. B., 2521
Hermesian society, Emory & Henry college, 3406
Hermitage country club, Richmond, 1584
Hermon Bapt. assoc., 4679
Herndon (town). St. Timothy's home school, 4411
Heroes of the nations series, 5220
Hetzel, Susan R., 1839
Heuser, H. M., 1793
Higginson, Lee, & co., 794
High Point academy, Grant, 4295
High school messenger (period.), 4509
High school student, The (period.), 4510
High schools. *See* Schools
High St. M. E. church, South, Petersburg, 4912
Highland County, 5048-5049
Highway commission, State. Act establishing, 693
  Annual report, 643, 684
  Bridge specifications, 685, 687
  Bulletin, 686

[The numbers refer to items, not to pages]

Highway commission, State—cont'd.
Bulletin for public schools & community leagues, 4102, 4523
Highway routes, Description of, 688
Highways, Specifications for, 689
Road laws, 702, 705
Highways. *See* Roads
Hildebrand, S. F., 325
Hill, A. H., 4068
Hill, A. P., 1585, 5131
Hill, B. H., 2597
Hill, Judith P., 5032
Hill, Lysander, 2855
Hill, W. B., 3642
Hill monument assoc., Richmond, 1585
Hill's directories, 1882, 1905, 1908, 1917, 1928, 2559, 2916
Hill's southern almanac, 2559
Hill's Va. & N. C. southern almanac, 2559
Hillyard, M. B., 2134
Hilton (town), 399
Hine, W. F., 2992
Hines, W. D., 632-633
Hinsdale, W. R., 417
Hinton, W. E., jr., 2600, 3162-3163
Hirschberg, John, 1114
Historical markers, 4531-4532, 4557
Historical periodicals, 4028, 4633, 4639, 4645, 4647, 4654
Historical societies, 4526-4532, 4538, 4557-4559, 4565, 4597-4607, 4629, 4633, 4654
History. City, 4952, 5013, 5019-5020, 5022, 5029, 5035, 5037-5038, 5051, 5053, 5060, 5064-5065, 5069, 5072
County, 5010-5012, 5014-5017, 5021, 5024-5025, 5027-5028, 5030-5033, 5035, 5039-5041, 5046-5050, 5052, 5055-5057, 5059, 5061, 5064, 5066-5067, 5069-5071, 5073-5074, 5076-5080
Local, Perpetuation of, 5078
State, 2128, 2139, 2192, 2194, 2276, 2292, 2294, 2388, 2531, 2879, 3346, 3356, 5018, 5021a, 5023, 5034, 5042-5045, 5058, 5062-5063, 5068, 5075-5076, 5142, 5154, 5181
Hoag, D. T., 848
Hoar, G. F., 3367, 4561
Hobart, W. F., 424
Hobday, G. J., 4934
Hodges, J. A., 3449
Hodges, LeRoy, 806, 1844, 3164-3165
Hodges, W. T., 3924
Hodgkin, J. B., 5603
Hocing, J. B., 2202
Hoffer, F. W., 1840-1841, 3690
Hoge, M. D., 2414, 3843, 3929, 4782, 4873-4876, 4929, 6100
Hoge, P. H., 2136, 4929, 5604
Hoge, W. S., jr., 1761

Hoge military academy. *See* Blackstone military academy
Hogg's Equity procedure, 2864
Hogs, 84, 153
Hoke, K, J., 4487
Holcombe, W. H., 5605-5609
Holden, R. J., 526
Holladay, A. R., 669
Holladay mine, 515
Holland, C. W., jr., 1834, 1842
Holland, N. L., 1834, 1842
Holland, R. A., 3844
Holliday, F. W., 3559, 5160
Hollins college, 3329, 3428-3436, 3934
Periodicals, 3957, 3974-3975, 3993, 3999
Hollins institute. *See* Hollins college
Hollywood cemetery, Richmond, 1554, 1596, 1843
Holmes, J. T., 1586
Holsinger, S. D., 3166
Holstein-Friesian cattle, 149
Holt, Guy, 9, 5252
Homans, G. M., 321
Home & indust. school for girls, Chesterfield Co., 1996
Home & school series, 3350a
Home mission herald (period.), 4992
Homes, Historic, 2278, 2285, 2532, 5028, 5135. *See also* Monticello; Mt. Vernon
Homestead hotel, Hot Springs, 418
Homestead school for girls, Hot Springs, 4297
Hood, W. T., & co., 191
Hoof & mouth disease, 153
Hooper, T. W., 3419
Hoover's select high school, Staunton, 4298
Hope, J. B., 5610-5613
Hopewell (city). Directory, 1897
Hopkins, Mark, 4133, 4267, 4783
Horner, Frederick, 3560
Horses, 222, 1659
Horsley, J. R., 381
Horticulture, 61, 107, 213, 294
Horton, A. H., 324
Horton, H. L., 417
Hosmer, R. S., 321
Hospitals, 1397, 1423, 1484, 1555, 1624, 1630-1631, 1671, 1675, 3055, 3223, 3228, 3256-3258, 3260-3261, 3451, 3688-3689, 4292, 4631, 4648. *See also* U. S. Army—Base hospitals, Debarkation hospitals, General hospitals
Hot Springs P. O. Convention meetings at, 1356, 2041, 2848, 4628
Homestead school for girls, 4297
Hotel Alpin, 2138

[The numbers refer to items, not to pages]

Independent Virginian (period.), Richmond, 6185
Index appeal (period.), Petersburg, 1521, 3349, 6156
Index & appeal (period.), Petersburg, 6155
Indian music. *See* Music
Indian pageant, 2455
Indian place-names, 2519
Indian relics, 5268, 5272
Indians. Education. *See* Hampton normal & agric. institute
Industrial commission, 366-368, 1109, 1115
Industrial resources, 204, 289, 295, 331-332, 381, 398, 410, 990, 1407-1408, 1441, 1457
Industrial review (period.), 843
Industrial school for colored girls, Peake, 1997
Industrial societies, 1513
Industrial South, The (period.), Richmond, 557, 6186
Industrial surveys, 520
Industrial towns, Committee on, 399
Industrial wastes, 333
Industry. *See* Manufacturing
Inebriates, Laws concerning, 2006
Infantry
  1st regiment. Co. A, 3232
    Co. E, 3249
  5th regiment, 2517
  11th regiment. Co. G, 3249
Ingersoll, Ernest, 2141-2142
Ingle, J. A., 4785
Ingle, William, 1140, 1144
Ingleside seminary, Burkeville, 4299
Inglis, A. J., 3286, 4485
Ingram institute, 4300
Inheritance law, 2874
Injunction, Law of, 2866
Insane, 2006, 2035
  Commissioner of hospitals for, 1962, 1998
Insane asylums, 1689, 1962, 1966, 1984, 1998-1999, 2002, 2025, 2027-2029, 2035
Inspection laws, 284, 1354
Institute for research in the social sciences. *See* Univ. of Va.
Institution for the deaf, dumb & blind. *See* Va. school for the deaf & blind
Institutions, State, 1180, 1367, 1975
Instruction. Dept. of public, 3311, 4092-4095, 4098, 4101-4102, 4646, 4657
  Supt. of public. *See* Education, State board of
Insurance. Bureau of, 1197, 1229-1232, 1249, 1260
  Compensation. *See* Workmen's compensation

Insurance—cont'd.
  Fire, 1231-1232, 1340-1341, 1350, 1371, 1383, 1392
  Life, 1231-1232, 1268-1270, 1328-1329, 1359, 1364-1365, 1392, 3690
Insurance advocate (periodicals), 1392-1393
Insurance commissioner, 1229, 1249
Insurance companies, 1197, 1231-1232, 1364-1365, 1371, 1383, 1391, 1395, 2395
  Laws concerning, 1234-1235, 1249, 1260
Intelligence tests, 4084
Intermont hotel, Covington, 2143
Internal improvements, 711, 987, 2080
International brotherhood of maintenance of way employees, 1122
International order of Good Templars. *See* Good Templars
International order of the King's daughters & sons, 4786
International trust co., Boston, Mass., 505
Investment opportunities, 244
Irby, Richard, 3925
Iron, Tariff on, 1372
Iron age (period.), 527
Iron-clad oath, 2622, 2841
Iron Gate (town), 406
Iron industry, 389, 403, 420, 513, 521, 970-971, 1003, 1056
Iron resources, 379, 391, 393, 400, 403, 410, 417, 420-421, 431-436, 439, 447, 465, 470, 483, 517, 526-528, 532, 1396
Irvington P. O. Chesapeake male & female academy, 4169
Isaacs, I. J., 1408
Isaacs & co., W. B., 1151
Isle of Wight County. Description, 1802
  Financial condition, 2951
  Oyster records, 351
  Taxes, 1193
Ives, Cora S., 5616-5617

Jack, G. S., 5035
Jackson, E. B., 1401
Jackson, E. H., 1384
Jackson, J. C., 2064
Jackson, T. J. (Stonewall), 5131
Jackson (Stonewall) monuments, 1546, 1682, 2260, 2414, 4566
Jacksonville female institute, Floyd C. H., 4301
Jacobs, E. B., 1717, 5035
Jails, 1968, 2005
James, A. W., 2011, 2022, 2066
James, B. O., 2738
James, E. W., 4639
James, G. W., 1637, 6098

[The numbers refer to items, not to pages]

James, G. W., jr., 2547

James City County. Bruton parish, 4761
Directory, 1098
Physiography, 1098
Soils, 1098

James River. Description, 1757, 2112, 2165, 2210, 2250, 2265, 4527
Drainage, 322-323, 3077
Fiction, 5331, 5800
History, 2139-2140, 2191, 2250
Improvement of, 570-577, 579, 589-594, 602-603, 608, 672, 791, 800, 918, 990, 1556
Oyster industry, 342, 388
Shipbuilding advantages, 961
Survey of, 640
Trades waste in, 3077

James River & Kanawha canal. *See* James River & Kanawha co.

James River & Kanawha co., 561-562, 570-577, 579-580, 594, 597-598, 602-603, 608, 621, 639, 690-691, 747-748, 764, 782, 795, 801-803, 980, 1087

James River Bapt. assoc., 4680

James River basin. Physiography, 540

James River coal co., 422

James River construction co., 507, 1026

James River garden club, 2144

James River improvement co., 791

James River Valley immigration society, 2319

James Valley. Description, 2192, 2265
Geology, 395, 527-528
Iron resources, 379, 527-528
Resources, 395, 469

Jamestown. Celebration at, 3268-3269, 4892
Description, 1550, 2129, 2269, 4527
History, 1748, 2129, 2236-2237, 3900, 5697
Preservation of, 2231, 2236, 4527, 4530
Prot. Episc. pilgrimage to, 2203

Jamestown aeronautical congress, 2148

Jamestown association, Woman's 2298

Jamestown bulletin, 2298

Jamestown celebration (1895), 2130, 2485, 4559

Jamestown dental convention, 4562

Jamestown exposition (1907), 1404, 1440, 1482, 1485, 2075, 2145-2158, 2237, 2241, 2287, 2298-2300, 2588, 4108, 4258, 4529, 5159, 5181
School exhibits, 3606, 4033, 4108, 4258
Souvenirs, 5666
Va. pamphlets distributed at, 1404-1405, 1440, 1485, 1524, 1717, 1793, 1800, 1802, 1808, 1810, 2264, 3516

Jamestown magazine, 2299

Jamestown official photograph corp., 2155-2158

Jamestown portland cement corp., 423

Jamestown ter-centennial (period), 2300

Jamestown ter-centennial commission, 2075, 2150-2151, 2153, 2287

Jarman, H. D., 2930

Jarvis, J. F., 2159

Jarvis, T. J., 3462

Jarvis' Mt. Vernon & Arlington album, 2159

Jasper, John, 4956

Jay, John, 2817

Jefferson, Thomas, 2289, 2295, 3363, 5257

Jefferson club, Richmond, 1610, 4563

Jefferson club association, St. Louis, 2160

Jefferson hotel, Richmond, 1591

Jefferson memorial & interstate good roads convention, 578

Jefferson memorial foundation, 2208, 2289, 2537

Jefferson realty corp., Richmond, 1590

Jefferson school for boys, Charlottesville, 4302

Jeffersonian republican (period.), Charlottesville, 6115

Jeffress, T. D., 1760

Jenkins, C. J., 2583, 2585

Jenks, J. W., 4095

Jesse, R. H., 3642

Jeter, W. H., & co., 193

Jeter memorial committee, 3485

Jeter memorial hall, Richmond university, 3485

Jett, Dora C., 2161, 5163

Jewett, H. C., 592

Jewish Chautauqua society, 4567

Jewish churches. *See* Churches

Jewish record, The (period.), Richmond, 6187

Jews, 1610, 2345-2346, 4855, 5038
Directories, 1909, 1937

Jobbing, 549, 1367

John, W. C., 4041

John Marshall high school, Richmond, 4072-4073, 4512

John Marshall record (period.), 4511

Johns, John, 4787

Johns Hopkins university. Studies in historical & political science, 277, 1385, 2865, 2868, 2884
Theses, 531, 537, 2912, 6078

Johnson, Asa, 4932

Johnson, B. T., 714, 1152, 1322-1323

Johnson, Eleanor S., 1486

Johnson, Ella W., 3271

Johnson, G. S., 5618-5619

Johnson, J. L., 3564

Johnson, L. E., 194, 792-793, 988

Johnson, M. D., 15

Johnson, Marmaduke, 2667

Johnson, R. U., 6075
Johnson, Reverdy, 1285
Johnson, T. C., 4933
Johnson, W. B., 2879
Johnston, D. E., 5036
Johnston, Elizabeth B., 2162
Johnston, Frederick, 5165
Johnston, G. B., 2041, 3445, 3449, 4564
Johnston, J. W., 576, 579
Johnston, Mary, 5620-5643
Johnston, W. P., 3845
Jones, Anna L., 3333
Jones, B. M., 968
Jones, C. W., 1487-1488
Jones, H. S., 2856
Jones, I. D., 2586, 2599
Jones, J. E., 2163
Jones, J. W., 2417, 2475, 2880, 5166-5167
Jones, M. W., 5028
Jones, Meriwether, 424
Jones, Reuben, 4934
Jones, T. J., 4303
Jones, T. W., 1522
Jonesville academy. *See* Jonesville institute
Jonesville institute, 4304
Jordan, B. L., 2320
Jordan, Mrs. C. J., 5644-5646, 5672
Jordan, H. E., 4788
Jordan's White Sulphur Springs, Frederick Co., 425
Jorgensen, Joseph, 2600
Journal of agriculture, 296
Journal of commerce, 1858
Journal of the assoc. of engineering societies, 4634
Joynes, E. S., 3334
Joynes, L. S., 1593
Judges, 1233, 5162, 5190
  List of, 2639-2640
Judicial circuit, 13th, 2842
Judicial dictionary digest, Va. & W. Va. cases, 2863
Judson, S. C. 1461
Jurgen (novel), 5240, 5249, 5252, 5357-5358, 6067
Juries, law of instructions to, 2897
Juvenile & domestic relations courts, 2012, 3093
Juvenile laws, 2011-2012
Juvenile protective society of Va., 1594

KALEIDOSCOPE, THE (period.), 3977
Kanawha River, 324, 561, 621, 672
Kanawha Valley, 439
Kaolin mining, 413
Kappa alpha fraternity, 2382, 3861
Kearfott, Mrs. C. P., 4935
Kecoughtan, 1905, 4926
Keefer, J. I., 2164
Keeler, G. A., 1443

Keep the cadence (period.), 3261
Keesee, G. F., 5126
Kehukee Bapt., assoc. (primitive), 4739
Keiley, A. M., 4936
Keiley, C. R., 1489
Keim, De B. R., 2165-2166
Keithly, K. A., 77
Kellogg, J. B., 2167
Kemp, V. E., 3849
Kemper, J. L., 364, 1220, 2414, 2698, 3145, 3168, 3747
Kemper, K., 2921
Kenmore school for young ladies, Fredericksburg, 3410
Kenmore university high school, Amherst C. H., 4305
Kennedy, J. P., 16, 3323, 5236
Kennedy, R. E., 1834, 1845
Kent, C. W., 3565, 3742, 4565, 5253-5254, 5615, 5667-5668
Kerbey, J. O., 2168
Kern, Margaret E., 2276
Kernodle, Mrs. L. W., 1523, 1595
Keswick P. O., 3355, 4196
Keswick school for boys, Cobham, 4306
Ketocton Bapt. assoc., 4681
Ketocton Bapt. assoc. (primitive), 4740
Keysville mission indust. school, 4307
Kieffer, A. S., 5647, 6096
Kilby, L. C., 5648
Kilpatrick, Wylie, 3690
Kimball, Fiske, 3607
Kimberly, W. H., 1442
Kindergartens, 3819, 3821, 4054, 4579
King, Grace E., 2277
King, J. L., 5169
King, J. T., 2169
King & Queen County. Churches, 4798, 4931
  Description, 1816, 5011
  Economic & social survey, 1834, 1848
  History, 5011
  Taxes, 1193
King William County. Description, 1098, 1747, 1796
  Directory, 1098
  History, 5135
  Soils, 1098
King's daughters & sons, Internat. order of the, 4786
Kinsolving, A. B., 4488
Kinsolving, Mrs. S. B., 5649-5650
Kirkland, J. H., 3860
Kishpaugh, R. A., 1436
Kissel, Kinnicutt & co., 794, 1067
Kleinberg female home school, Rockfish, 4308
Kleybolte, Rudolphe & co., 998
Kline, H. E., 222
Knight, C. L., 1846
Knight, E. W., 3352

[The numbers refer to items, not to pages]

[The numbers refer to items, not to pages]

[The numbers refer to items, not to pages]

[The numbers refer to items, not to pages]

Lutheran churches. *See* Churches
Lutheran quarterly, 3505
Lutheran visitor (period), 4990
Lybrook, A. M., 2799
Lyles Bapt. church, Fluvanna Co., 4941
Lynchburg (city). Armor plant, 327
  Building code, 1901
  Charters, 2957, 2964-2966
  Churches, 4792, 4901, 4920, 4942
  City manager, 2958
  Code, 2956, 2964-2965
  Colleges, 3456, 3470-3473, 3836
  Colored orphan asylum & indust. school, 1456
  Council, 2959-2961
  Daniel (J. W.) statue, 2616, 5209
  Description, 1421, 1457, 1459, 1461, 2210, 2959
  Directories, 1889, 1900-1901
  Engineering dept., 2962
  Health dept., 2963
  History, 2965, 5019, 5072
  Lions club, 5672
  Negroes, 1825, 1846, 4711
  Odd Fellows home of Va., 1460
  Official reports, 2954-2956
  Ordinances, 2964-2967
  Political corruption, 1855
  School board, 4043
  Taxes, 2967
  Views, 1421, 1461
  Water dept., 2968
Lynchburg academy, 4317-4318
Lynchburg & Danville r. r. co., 859, 1076
Lynchburg bar association, 2850
Lynchburg chamber of commerce, 1459
Lynchburg classical & commercial school, 4319
Lynchburg college, 3437-3438, 3947
  Periodical, 3947
Lynchburg high school, 4508
Lynchburg home guard, Annals of, 3249
Lynchburg press, The, 6139
Lynchburg Republican (period.), 6140
Lynching, 2412
Lynnhaven parish, Princess Anne Co., 4793
Lyons, James, 795, 1330
Lyric (period.), 6095

McAdams, T. B., 796
McAllister, H. M., 5039
McAllister, J. G., 5040
McAllister, J. T., 428, 2173, 2349
McAllister, W. H., 4321
McAlpine, W. J., 3028
McBain, H. L., 2882-2883
McBride, R. M., & co., 5252
McCabe, J. D., 5182, 5673-5674

McCabe, W. G., 3714, 3923, 4603, 5147, 5149, 6079
McCabe's university school, 4603
McCarthy, Carlton, 1599, 3049-3050, 5675
McCauley, William, 5041
McClelland, Margaret G., 5676-5692
McClure Bapt. church, Dickenson Co., 4741
McComas, F. W., 1834, 1852
McConnell, J. P., 2350, 4322, 4545
MacCorkle, W. A., 3846
McCormick, C. H., 429-430, 4794
McCormick, Virginia T., 5693-5696, 6095
McCormick reaper co., 430
McCreath, A. S., 431-436
McCue murder, Charlottesville, 2525
McCulloch, Catherine W., 2777
McDanel, R. C., 2884
McDaniel, G. W., 4974
McDonald, J. J., 2424
McDonald, James, 3206
McDonald, M., 379
Macedonia Bapt. assoc. (col.), 4715
McGaheysville (town), 4323, 4362
McGee, W. J., 2283
McGuire, H. H., 2413, 4324, 4566
McGuire (Hunter) memorial assoc., 2413
McGuire, Stuart, 3445, 3449
McGuire's university school, Richmond, 4325
Machen, L. H., 375, 706, 1263, 1265, 2015, 2742-2743, 2801, 3204
McHugh, C. A., 3127
McIlwaine, H. R., 3927, 5237
McIlwaine, Richard, 2800, 3336, 3422, 3928, 4796
McIntire, P. G., 1417
McIntire public library, Charlottesville, 3330
Mack, Flora L., 5697
Mackall, B. F., 609
McKelway, A. J., 1125
McKenney, W. R., 3278
McKenney, W. R., free library, Petersburg, 3278
Mackenzie, A., 617
Mackey, Crandal, 1761
McKim, R. H., 3569, 4797, 4943, 5079, 5183
McLaughlin, W., 3860
McLean, Mr., 1269-1270
McLean, F. H., 1600
McMahon, J. R., 285
McNeill, W. A., 1331
McNess, G. T., 78
McRae, Sherwin, 2885, 6080
McTyeire, H. N., 4937
Maddux, H. C., 409, 2174
Maddux, Martin, 2174

Madison County. Churches, 4930
  Description, 1809, 2709
  History, 5080
  Politics, 2806
  Schools, Private, 4312
Madison Hall notes (period.), 3978
Magdalen assoc., Richmond, 1601
Magie, H. M., 228
Magill, Mary T., 5042-5044, 5698-5700
Magnolia weekly, 5602
Magri, F. J., 4944
Magruder, F. A., 1385
Magruder, Julia, 5701-5717
Maher, N. D., 675
Mahone, William, 750, 797, 824, 1154,
  1314, 1332, 1352, 2597, 2756, 2765,
  2771, 2774, 2781, 2799, 2802-2804,
  2830-2831, 2835-2836, 2851, 2860,
  3230, 4326
Mahone's brigade. Reunion (1876), 3230
Mahood, Alexander, 2691
Mains, B. W., 2410
Mallet, J. W., 476, 3570
Manassas (town). Army manoeuvres
  (1904), 3227, 3240
  Description, 1462
  Eastern college, conservatory & acad-
  emy, 3399-3400
Manassas battlefield Confed. park, 2425
Manassas Gap r. r. co., 859
Manassas hotel, 2841
Manassas industrial school, 4327-4329
Manassas institute, 4330
Manassas journal, 1462
Manchester (city). Charters, 2971
  Consolidation with Richmond, 1707,
  3172
  Description, 1463-1465, 2972
  Directories, 1878, 1902, 1928
  Finances, 2969-2970
  Health, Board of, 2973
  Industries, Committee of, 2972
  Ordinances, 2971
  School board, 4044
  Street railways, 1044, 1046-1049
  Transportation, 1044, 1046, 1465
Manchester anti-consolidation league,
  3172
Manchester board of trade, 1464
Manchester courier (period.), 6142
Manchester high school, 4509
Manchester leader (period.), 6143
Manhattan trust company, 834
Manchester water power mortgage, 875
Mann, Dorothea L., 6081
Mann, H. C., 1524
Mann, James, 5234
Mann, W. H., 1277, 1344, 2684, 5099
Manny, T. B., 79
Manufacturers' record, 365, 1490, 5078

Manufacturing. Addresses on, 402
  Capital invested in, 1367
  Companies, miscell., 406, 420, 443, 447,
  469-470, 504-505
  Description, 206, 990, 999, 1765, 2080,
  2134-2135, 2188, 2210, 2234-2235,
  2972, 3350, 5035, 5062, 5077
  Directories, 559-560
  Govt. reports on, 328, 365-369
  History of, 2294
  Periodicals, 295, 298, 542, 549-550,
  555, 557
Manuscripts. Calendar of Va., 3
  Virginia historical society, 45
  Virginia state library, Check-list, 16,
  38-39
Maphis, C. G., 3285, 3337, 3571, 4520,
  4567
Maps of Va. Library of Congress, 40
  State library, 40
Margaret academy, Onancock, 4331
Margolin, L., 321
Marine r. r. & coal co., Alexandria, 2805
Marion college, 3439
Marion female college, 3439
Marion high schools, 4045
Marion military institute, 3596, 4348
Markets, Div. of, Dept. of Agric., 77,
  90, 130, 132-137, 154
  Bulletin, 131
  Report, 135
Marquis, Don, 2233
Marr, Frances H., 5718-5719
Marr, Janey H., 5613
Marsh, M. C., 333
Marshall, A. J., 2806
Marshall, Charles, 2426
Marshall, H. S., 1604
Marshall, R. B., 329-330
Marshall, R. C., 3175
Marshall, William, 1333
Marshallite, The (period.), 4512
Martha Washington college, 3440-3443,
  3956
Martin, Mr., 1176
Martin, T. S., 2807, 5094, 5098
Martin, W. B., 17
Martinsville. Churches, 4935
  Schools, 3811
Marvin, C. F., 81
Marx, Ellie M., 4332
Mary Baldwin seminary, 3444, 3941,
  3950, 4143
Mary Washington associations, 1839
Maryland. Court of appeals, 582
  Governor, 2607
Maryland-Va. boundaries. *See* Bounda-
  ries
Maryland, Delaware & Va. r. r. co., 739,
  798-799
Maryland presbytery, 4821, 4824

Maryland trust co., 810, 813
Mason, Emily V., 5184
Mason, J. M., 1334
Mason, J. W., 1292
Mason, Lucy R., 1126
Mason, O. T., 2175
Mason, W. R., 4994
Masonic cemetery, Fredericksburg, 5163
Masonic grand lodges, 2396
Masonic home of Va., Richmond 1605-
1606
Masonic publications, 2545-2546, 2550
Masonic review (period.), 2545
Masonic temple assoc., 2401
Masons. *See* Freemasons
Massachusetts field artillery at Manas-
sas (1904), 3240
Massanetta mineral springs, Harrison-
burg, 437
Massey, J. E., 646, 714, 1155, 1335, 2608,
2911, 3300, 3309
Massie, E. C., 197-198, 2808, 2887, 4615,
5256
Massie, H. L., 3583
Mastin, J. T., 1973
Mathematics, Annals of (period.), 4632
Mathews, E. B., 2609
Mathews, J. T., jr., 4945
Mathews County. Oyster records, 351
Mathewson, E. H., 78
Matoaca manufacturing co., 504
Mattaponi Bapt. assoc. (col.), 4716
Mattaponi Bapt. church, King & Queen
Co., 4798, 4931
Mattaponi Bapt. Sunday school conven-
tion (col.), 4717
Matthews, Ellen N., 1104
Matthews, J. M., 18-19, 2747, 2888
Maurice, Caesar, 5292
Maury, D. H., 5045
Maury, M. F., 331-332, 438-439, 820,
2284, 2427, 3764, 5131, 5134, 5178
Maury, R. L., 332
Maury high school, Norfolk, 4513
Maury news (period.), 4513
Maury's manual of geography, 2283-
2284
Maximum car limit bill, 671
May, C. W., 1181
Mayflower's log (period.), 2176
Mayhew, Odie, 1835
Maynell, Alice, 5956
Mayo, A. D., 4334
Mayo, Joseph, 2810, 5720
Mayo, W. R., 1491
Mayo, W. T., 4799
Mayo Bapt. assoc. (primitive), 4742
Mayors. *See* names of cities
Mead, E. C., 2285
Meadowbrook school, Leesburg, 4335
Mechanic arts, 294-295, 402

Mechanics, Laws prepared for, 1250,
2867, 2873
Mechanics' assoc. of Danville, 2481
Mecklenburg County. Buffalo Lithia
Springs, 2031
Description, 1760, 1788
History, 1760
Industry, 1799
Lands for sale, 1788
South Hill enterprise (period.), 1799
Taxes, 1193
Mecklenburg Co. agric. advisory board,
80
Mecklenburg Co. agric. fair, 199
Mecklenburg Democrat (period.), Boyd-
ton, 6111
Medical advisory boards, 3197, 3213
Medical associations, 1336, 1685, 2041,
4568-4569, 4581, 4586
Medical college of Va., Richmond, 1624,
3370, 3381, 3445-3454
Alumni society addresses, 2448
U. S. Base hospital, no. 45, 3228
Medical education
Commission on. Medical college of
Va., 3450
Reports, 3381-3383
See also Medical college of Va.;
Univ. of Va.
Medical examiners, Board of, 3312
Medical practice, Lectures on, 3328
Medical periodicals, 4641-4644, 4648,
4655
Medical register (period.), 2041
Medical society of Va., 1336, 2041,
4568-4569
Meeker, Royal, 4078
Meekins, G. W., 2811
Mencken, H. L., 5359, 6082
Mennonites, 4928
Mercantile trust & deposit co. of Balti-
more, 953
Merchandising, 441, 549-551, 1367, 2325
Merchants & planters savings bank,
Richmond, 1337
Merchants' trust co., N. Y., 935
Meredith, W. R., 1127, 1156, 3742
Merrill, H. G., 321
Merrill female school, Richmond, 4336
Merrimac anthracite coal corp., 442
Merriman, Daniel, 4491
Mertius, Emma A., 3434
Merwin-Clayton sales co., 3340, 3345
Messenger, The (period.), 3979
Metcalf, J. C., 3607, 5257
Methodist Episc. church. Va. confer-
ence, 4800
Methodist Episc. church, South. Balti-
more conference, 4801, 4879
Biographical sketches, 4907

Methodist Episc. church, South—cont'd.
Claims against M. E. church, 4779
General conference, 4937
Periodicals, 5000
Randolph-Macon college relations, 3469
Re-organization after Civil war, 4768
Rockingham district conference, 4803
Virginia conference, 4758, 4768, 4802-4806, 4897, 5000
Biographies, 4838-4839
Woman's foreign missionary society, 4804
Woman's home mission society, 4805
Woman's missionary society, 4806
Methodist Episc. church (col.). *See* African Meth. Episc. church
Methodist Episc. churches. *See* Churches
Methodist Episc. schools. *See* Colleges; Schools
Methodist Prot. churches. *See* Churches
Michie, A. R., 4651
Michie, T. J., 20-24, 2747, 2750
Microcosm (period.), 3980
Middendorf, Oliver & co., 944
Middle district Bapt. assoc., 4683, 4950
Middlesex County. Churches, 4947
Oyster records, 351
Middletown. Agric. high school, 4129
Midwives, 1994
Miles, G. M., 2084
Miles, G. W., 3547
Military board of Va., 3265
Military hospitals, 3225, 3228, 3256-3258, 3260-3261
Military laws, 3204, 3207
Military records, Secretary of, 3211
Militia, 3194, 3206, 3209, 3212, 3243, 3253
Milk, Artificial mothers', 225
Millboro Depot, Bath Co., 523
Miller, Assoc. Judge, 582
Miller, E. A., 4337
Miller, E. H., 1943, 1949
Miller, J. M., 1173-1174
Miller, Mrs. L. K., 1847
Miller, Samuel, 4338, 4340-4341
Miller, W. R., 3538
Miller & Rhoads monthly record, 1133
Miller manual labor school of Albemarle, 4338-4342
Millhiser, Charles, 1610
Milligan, J. F., 1911
Milling. *See* Lumber
Mills, Hilda K., 1600
Millwood (town). Clay Hill academy, 4176
Mineral production, 362-363
Mineral resources, 119, 362, 389, 393, 395, 400, 407, 410, 420-421, 432-436, 447, 460-461, 465, 469-470, 472, 482, 519, 526, 532, 537, 1043, 1396, 1765, 1776, 1782, 1811, 2080, 2134, 2209

Mines, 119, 396-397, 403, 412-413, 417, 420, 424, 446, 483-484, 516-517, 522, 542, 557, 970, 1009, 1043, 1056, 1367, 2188
Minnigerode, C. F., 4946
Minor, B. B., 2476
Minor, J. B., 2877, 2889-2890, 3363, 3698-3700, 4615
Minor, J. F., 1128
Minor, Mrs. Kate P., 25
Minor, R. C., 1338, 2814, 2877, 2891
Minor's institutes of common & statute law, 2903, 3566
Miscellaneous literary, scientific & historical notes, queries, & answers (period.), 3356
Missionary, The (period.), 4991
Missionary periodicals, 4984, 4989, 4991-4992, 4994
Missionary societies. Bapt., 4701
Baptist (col.), 4713-4714, 4728, 4734, 4959, 4989
Methodist Episc., South, 4804-4806
Protestant Episc., 4836
Missionary survey (period.), 4992
Mitchell, Broadus, 800
Mitchell, John, jr., 2325
Mitchell, S. C., 3451, 4343, 4489
Mitchell, S. W., 3603
Mitchell's Station, Culpeper Co. Mt. Welcome high school, 4347
Modern American writers series, 6091
Modern farming (period.), 297
Moffett, J. R., 2063, 2936, 4807
Moffett, W. W., 4807
Mohler, J. L., 2177
Monday commercial (period.), Richmond, 6193
Money claimed from U. S. by Va., 1150-1151, 1173-1174, 1176
Monroe, P., 3350a
Monroe, T. M., 802
Monroe County. Land for sale, 175
Monsees, C. H., 2286
Montague, A. J., 2620
Montague, J. G., 1854
Montague, R. L., 3875, 4947
Monterey high school, 4046
Montezuma development & trust co., 443
Montgomery, J. H., 4545
Montgomery County. Alleghany springs, 383, 386
Resources, 393, 442, 1800
Soils, 96
Montgomery presbytery, 4825
Monthly chronicle, The, 4514
Monthly weather review, 81
Monticello area. Geology, 534
Monticello association, 2428
Monticello estate, 1411, 1418, 2160, 2170, 2208, 2289, 2293, 2295, 2360-2363, 2376, 2428, 2537, 3645

[The numbers refer to items, not to pages]

Monticello farmer & grape grower (period.), 298
Monticello graveyard assoc. *See* Monticello assoc.
Monticello hotel, Charlottesville, 1418
Monticello papers, 2537
Montross, (town), 5079
Monumental church, Richmond, 4906, 4967, 4993
Monumental messenger (period.), 4993
Monuments. *See* name of city; name of individual
Moomaw, B. C., jr., 130
Moomaw, C. B., 3127
Moore, A., jr., 5028
Moore, C. L., 1157
Moore, Carrie P., 2429
Moore, E. W., 4948
Moore, F. D., 4651
Moore, G. B., 2065
Moore, H. F., 342
Moore, J. S., 1611, 2528-2529, 4949, 5721
Moore, L. W., 4950
Moore, R. W., 2252
Moore, Sallie A. (Mrs. J. H.), 2430
Moore, W. L., 81
Moore, W. W., 3536, 3538, 3929
Moore House, Yorktown, 458
Moore St. indust. institution, Richmond, 1612-1614
Moorman, J. J., 444, 3495
Moral maxims for schools & families, 4481
Moran, Jeannie W. (Mrs. B. F.), 5722-5723
Moran, W. H., 5724
Morgan, J. B., 5725
Morgan, J. T., 1751, 3749
Morgan, T. J., 3837
Morris, Gouverneur, 445
Morris, R. F., 477
Morrison, A. J., 286, 1801, 3413
Morrison, Andrew, 1615-1617
Morrison, E. M., 1802
Morrison, R. F., 1803
Morrison high school, 4521
Morrissett, C. H., 1158, 1224, 2006, 2610-2612, 2728, 2744, 3207
Morrisville. Sugar production, 155
Morrow, J. A., 3572
Morticians, 2501
Morton, A. S., 6101
Morton, J. H., 446
Morton, O. F., 4909, 5046-5051, 5726-5727, 6093
Morton, R. L., 2351, 2892, 5034
Morton, W. B., 4980
Morton trust co., 1004
Mosaics (period.), 4515
Mosby, J. S., 2815
Mosquitoes, Extermination of, 3088

Moss, W. W., 1339
Motion picture censorship, Div. of, 2016
Moton, R. R., 4344
Motor vehicle commissioner, 700-701, 707-708
Motor vehicles. Division of, 709, 1246
Laws concerning, 700-701, 704
Report (form) to State corp. commission, 655
Mount Clinton P. O. West central academy, 4470
Mount Crawford academy, 4345
Mount Pisgah academy, Culpeper C. H., 4346
Mount Pleasant Sunday school assoc. (col.), 4718
Mount Vernon, Alexandria & Washington ry. co., 1082
Mount Vernon avenue assoc., 609, 1176, 2206, 2262
Mount Vernon estate, 609, 2089, 2118-2119, 2159, 2162-2164, 2166-2167, 2179-2180, 2200, 2206, 2244, 2263, 2277, 2279-2282, 2288, 2296, 2431, 2435
Board of visitors to, 2373
Mount Vernon ladies' assoc., 2089, 2162, 2179-2180, 2277, 2288, 2431-2435, 2483
Mount Vernon memorial highway, 606
Mount Weather observatory, 81-82
Mount Welcome high school, Culpeper Co., 4347
Mountain Lake, Giles Co., 2199
Mu sigma rho society, Richmond college, 3979
Mundie, J. R., 1834, 1848
Munford, B. B., 2816, 3876
Munford, Mrs. B. B., 3732
Munford, G. W., 2719, 2893, 5728-5729
Munford, T. T., 4348
Municipal journal & engineer (period.), 3177
Munn, Anderson & Munn, 3247
Murphy, Daniel, 1618
Murphy, L. S., 321
Murray, K. F., 1510
Museums, 4541, 4627, 5078, 5267-5272
Music. College, 3571-3572, 3618, 3731
Folk, 5246, 5250, 5274
Indian, 4274, 5250
Negro, 4134, 4274, 5238, 5242, 5248, 5250-5251, 5259
Northern Va., 6093
Sacred, 4877, 5248, 5251, 5259
Musical advocate & singer's friend (period.), 6096
Musical education, 3399-3400, 3433
Musical million, The (period.), 6093, 6097

Musical organizations, Richmond, 1531-1532, 1662, 1684, 1700, 4608
Musical periodicals, 6096-6097
Mustard, H. S., 1804
Mutual assurance society of Va., 1340-1341, 1383
Mutual building fund assoc., 1342
Mycology, 107
Myers, May L., 4563

NANSEMOND COUNTY. History, 5024
Negroes, 2344
Oyster record, 351
Nansemond indust. institute, Suffolk, 4349
Nansemond River, 618
Nansemond seminary, Suffolk, 4350
Napton, W. B., 3573
National academy of sciences, 3703
National board of health, 3600
National board of trade, 801-803
National child labor committee, 1125, 4482
National city bank, N. Y., 794
National city co., N. Y., 804-805
National confer. of charities & correction, 1961, 2035, 2045
National confer. on state parks, 2220
National editorial assoc., 2100, 2137
National education assoc. Dept. of superintendence, 4351, 4499
National exposition of chemical industries, 472
National guard. Year book, 3243
National home for disabled volunteer soldiers, 1437, 1444, 2043
National soc. for the promotion of indust. education, 4078, 4217
National soc. of colonial dames of America, 2436-2442
National soldiers' home, 3261, 5022
National state & city bank, Richmond, 1382
National woman's party, 2894-2895
Native Virginian (period.), Orange C. H., 6153
Natural Bridge, 2117, 2181-2182, 2196, 2207, 2219, 2223
Natural Bridge national forest, 473
Naturalist's companion (period.), 4640
Nature study, 4285-4286, 4288
Naval artificer's hand-book, 4368
Naval training stations. *See* U. S., Navy dept.
Navigation, Inland, 603, 611, 673, 764, 781
Navy life (period.), 3262
Neale, Walter, 5559
Neely's authors' library series, 5536
Neeson, James, 2637
Negotiable instruments law, 2732

Negro evidence, 2779
Negro ideals (period.), 4253
Negro organization society, 4570
Negro reformatory assoc. of Va., 1955-1957, 2045
Negro teachers' assoc. & school improvement league of Va., 4571
Negroes. Artisans, 1131
Charitable institutions, 3068
Citizenship, 2767
Deaf & blind school, 1981-1982
Delinquents, 1955-1957, 2045
Economic & social status, 1825, 2305-2306, 2315-2316, 2325, 2327, 2342, 2344, 2349-2350
Education, 1429, 2342, 2798, 3914-15, 4141-4142, 4299, 4377, 4394, 4396, 4450. *See also* Schools, colored; Colleges, colored, espec. Hampton normal & agric. institute
Fairs, 2317
Farming, 89, 241, 247, 278-279
Farmville, 2305
Hampton conference, 4560
Hampton normal & agric. institute (*q. v.*)
Insane, 1962, 1966
Living conditions, 1846, 2305-2306
Lynchburg, 1825
Music (*q. v.*)
Organizations, 1507, 1684, 2321-2322, 2326a, 2336-2338, 2340, 2767
Orphan asylums, 1456
Political status of, 1387, 2350-2351, 2798, 2804, 2846, 2913, 3167-3168
Presbyterian church, 4771
Protestant Episc. church work among, 4833
Reconstruction period, 2315, 2327, 2330, 2350-2351, 2356, 2798, 2868
Religion, 4897, 4904, 4919, 4956, 4959. *See also* names of churches
Riots. *See* Race riots
Schools, 1456, 1612-1614, 1997, 3350a, 3838, 3869, 4040, 4083, 4177, 4190, 4270, 4290, 4299, 4307, 4327-4329, 4349, 4388, 4446, 4452, 4460, 4487, 4570-4571. *See also* Hampton normal & agric. institute
Suffrage, 2623, 2762, 2767, 2776, 2846
Taxation of, 1388
Temperance & reform movement, 2059
Vocations, 1130-1131
Negroes in oyster industry, Litwalton, 339
Nelson, J. C., 1945
Nelson, J. P., 5730
Nelson, Knute, 605
Nelson, W. A., 2609
Nelson County. Description, 1772
Schools, 4047, 4360-4361, 4493

[The numbers refer to items, not to pages]

[The numbers refer to items, not to pages]

Norfolk & western ry. co.—cont'd
  793, 840-844, 952, 1009, 1018, 1061,
  1089, 1099, 2172, 2190, 2302, 5035
  Agricultural & indust. dept., 202-
  206, 552, 3783
  Virginia resorts pamphlets, 2188-2189,
  2235
Norfolk area. Soils, 96
Norfolk bar, 1146
Norfolk-Beaufort Inlet waterway, 611
Norfolk board of trade, 1497
Norfolk board of trade & business
  men's assoc., 1493-1496
Norfolk chamber of commerce, 1491,
  1497-1505, 1518, 3174
Norfolk college, 3455
Norfolk committee, Louisville, Ky., 581
Norfolk County. History, 1805, 5066
  Oyster records, 351
  Politics, 3175
Norfolk County conspiracy, 3175
Norfolk County water co., 3026
Norfolk creosoting co., 453
Norfolk day book (period.), 2839, 6145
Norfolk election district, 2839
Norfolk emancipation assoc., 1507
Norfolk heat, light & power co., 583
Norfolk landmark, The (period.), 6146
Norfolk-ledger-dispatch (period.), 789
Norfolk library assoc., 4573
Norfolk merchants' & mechanics' ex-
  change, 1509
Norfolk mission college, 4359
Norfolk naval recruit (period.), 3262
Norfolk Old Dominion, The (period.),
  6147
Norfolk, Portsmouth & Newport News
  co., 826
Norfolk post, The (period.), 6149
Norfolk potato conference, 184
Norfolk presbytery, 4826-4827
Norfolk railway & light co., 821
Norfolk southern r. r. co., 627, 827, 833,
  845-851
Norfolk terminal & transportation co.,
  852
Norfolk terminal ry. co., 853-855
Norfolk tidewater terminal, 856
Norfolk union Bapt. assoc. (col.), 4719
Norfolk, Va. Beach & southern r. r. co.,
  815, 830, 857-858
Norfolk Virginian (period.), 6150
Norfolk Virginian annual, The, 1912
Norris, C. R., 3750
Norris, J. E., 5052
North River P. O., 1350
North River Valley. Resources, 469
Northampton Co. Directory, 2557
  Economic & social survey, 1834, 1842
  Oyster records, 351
  Soils, 96

Northern Neck, 2071
Northern Va. Agric. resources, 242
  Farms for sale, 162
Northern Va. Bapt. assoc. (col.), 4720
Northrop, B. G., 4133, 4267
Northumberland County. Description,
  2071
  Oyster records, 351
Northwest territory, Va. claims for re-
  lease of, 1384, 2588
Norton, G. H., 4810
Norton, W. J., 1049
Norvell, Watkins, 5053
Norwood high school, Nelson Co., 4047,
  4360-4361, 4493
Nottoway County. World war roster,
  3226
Nottoway record (period.), Crewe, 978,
  6121
Nowitzky, G. I., 1512
Nuckols, R. R., 3178
Nurseries, Plant, 180, 191
Nurses, 1416, 1622-1623, 2004, 3689,
  3906, 4292
Nussman, Mabel, 1835
Nut growing, 1746

OAK HILL ACADEMY, McGaheysville,
  4323, 4362
Oakland male & female high school,
  Doe Hill, 4363
Oakwood memorial assoc., 2454
Oats, 253
Oberholtzer, E. P., 5132
Oberlin college. Laboratory bulletin,
  533
Ocean View (resort), 1515
"O. D." (period.), 3263
Odd-fellows. Grand united order of
  District grand lodge (col.), 2326a
Odd-fellows. Independent order of,
  2521
  Grand encampment, 2551
  Grand lodge, 2443, 2551
  Rebekah assembly, 2551
Odd Fellows home of Va., Lynchburg,
  1460
Odell, J. T., 481
O'Ferrall, C. T., 2621, 2818, 4114
Ogden, M. M., 4953
Ogden, R. C., 4489, 4494
O'Keefe, Matthew, 4811
Old Colony trust co., 423
Old Dominion & Va. historical register
  (period.), 6098
Old Dominion hospital, Richmond, 1624
Old Dominion industrial corp., 1746
*Old Dominion journal of medicine &
  surgery,* 2060, 4641
Old Dominion land co., 1479-1480
Old Dominion magazine, 2885, 6098

[The numbers refer to items, not to pages]

Patton, J. S., 28, 2289, 2532, 3549, 3580, 3687, 3706, 3931-3932, 5253, 5991
Paul, John, 1314, 2614, 2621
Paul, Katherine S., 29
Paul, R. A. (col.), 2913
Payne, A. W., 5766-5767
Payne, B. R., 4495-4496
Payne, J. B., 5247
Peabody, F. G., 4136, 4489, 4497-4498
Peake (town), 1997
Peaks of Otter, 1787
Peaks of Otter Bapt. assoc. (col.), 4722
Peanuts, 95, 253
Pearson, C. C., 1386, 3353
Pearson, J. S., 1781
Peatross, R. W., 2982
Peay, J. H., jr., 4068
Pegram battalion assoc., 3241
Peirpont, F. H., 2451, 2838, 2875
Pell, E. L., 4954
Pendleton, Edmund, 1322
Pendleton, G. H., 3581
Pendleton, W. C., 5057
Pendleton, W. N., 4791
Peninsula Bapt. assoc., 4686
Peninsula horticultural society, 213
"Peninsula" of Va., 1903, 2091, 2269
Penitentiary, State, 660, 2003, 2017-2018
    Industrial dept., 380
Pen-Mar, 2216
Pennsylvania stockholders of Richmond, Fredericksburg & Potomac r. r., 958, 960
Pennsylvania co., 1364
Pennsylvania German (period.), 6093
Pennsylvania r. r. co., 769-770, 807, 973, 2114, 2196-2197
Pensions, 1200, 1202, 1244, 2161
People's party (1897), 2819
Peple, C. A., 1142
Perry, Bliss, 6075
Peterkin, Joshua, 4816
Peters, J. S., 1834, 1850, 2021
Peters, W. E., 3582-3583
Petersburg. Camp Lee, 3247, 3264
    Central state hospital, 1966
    Charter, 3034-3035, 3145, 3167-3168
    Churches, 4902, 4912
    Code, 3035
    Confederate veterans, A. P. Hill camp, no. 6, 2489
    Council, 3031, 3034
    Directories, 1878, 1914, 1917-1918, 1920-1921, 1933
    Economic & social conditions, 1521, 1524, 1528-1529, 1534, 1844, 2374
    Education, Board of, 4063
    Fort Mahone monument, 1537
    Government, 1921, 3164
    Guide books, 1523, 1528-1529, 1534

Petersburg—cont'd.
    Health dept., 3032-3033
    History, 1918
    Library, W. R. McKenney, 3278
    Negroes, 3167
    Ordinances, 3034-3036
    Political conditions, 3162-3163
    Schools. Private, 3385, 3515-3516, 4369, 4372, 4410, 4455
        Public, 4064-4065
    State teachers' college, 3833
    Streets, 1921, 3030
    Tax ordinances, 3036
    Transportation, 1465
    Treasurer, 3037
    Views, 1522-1523
    Visit of W. H. Taft (1909), 1537
    Woman's club, 1538
Petersburg academy, 4369
Petersburg armor plant committee, 1525
Petersburg Bapt. assoc., 4687
Petersburg benevolent mechanic assoc., 1526
Petersburg bur. of governmental research. Bulletin, 3164
Petersburg chamber of commerce, 1344, 1525, 1527-1529, 1844, 3247
Petersburg daily post, 3162-3163
Petersburg index (period.), 6154
Petersburg land bank committee, 1344
Petersburg musical assoc., 1531-1532
Petersburg r. r. co., 563, 587, 733, 862-863, 899
Petersburg telephone co., 864
Peterson, Agnes L., 1105
Peterson, P. A., 4802
Petrie, G. L., 4765
Pettee, W. E., 275
Peyton, Jeannie S., 334
Peyton, John L., 5059, 5768
Pharmaceutical associations, 4609
Pharmaceutical periodicals, 4656
Pharmacy, 3454
    Board of, 4656
Phelps, E. J., 1301, 1378
Phelps-Stokes fellowship papers. See Univ. of Va.
Phi beta kappa, 3873, 3877-3878
Phi beta kappa key (period.), 3983
Philadelphia trust co., 1719
Philanthropic society, Hampden-Sidney college, 3419
Philately. See Stamp collecting
Philip, J. B., 2201
Phillips, J. J., 2452
Phillips, J. W., 2410
Phillips, L. C., 2897
Phillips, U. B., 3622
Phillips & West school for girls, Norfolk, 4370

Philologian society, Richmond college, 3979
Phoebus, Harrison, 1445
Phoebus (town). Directory, 1905
Phosphate, 195
Physicians, 1336, 1685, 2448
Physiography of Va., 540, 1098, 1757, 1786, 1793, 2292, 3777
Pickett, Lasalle C. (Mrs. G. E.), 5769-5774
Pidgeon, Mary E., 2062, 2820-2821, 2898, 2900
Piedmont agric. society, 185, 214-215
Piedmont air line r. r., 723, 2215
Piedmont & Arlington life insurance co., 1268-1270
Piedmont Bapt. assoc., 4688
Piedmont business college, Lynchburg, 3456
Piedmont directory co., 1943, 1949
Piedmont female institute, Charlottesville, 4371
Piedmont gold belt chartered co., 456
Piedmont r. r. co., 865
Piedmont region, 73, 279, 298, 535, 537, 1413, 1764, 2100, 2228
Fiction, 5387
Pierce, Mildred B., 1855
Pig River Bapt. assoc. (primitive), 4745
Pilot, The (period.), 1090
Pilot, Daily (period.), Norfolk, 6150
Pilotage, 978, 1045
Pinchbeck, R. B., 1131
Pine, M. S. (pseud.), See Finn, Sister M. B.
Pine St. African Meth. Episc. church, Suffolk, 2326a
Pine St. Sunday school bulletin, 4997
Pine trees, 314, 337, 454
Pinners Point, 612
Pipe, Concrete, 1953
Pitt, R. H., 4817
Pittsylvania County. Geography, 1833
History, 5021
Industrial survey, 1424
Soils, 96
Plains, The (town). Yelverton home school for girls, 4480
Plankton studies of Potomac River, 1951
Plant pathology, 108, 143-144
Planter & farmer (period.), 4396
Plaster, 394
Plasterco P. O., 394
Platt, J. H., 2615
Platt v. Goode, 2591, 2617
Platt's (Mrs. W. H.) school for girls, Petersburg, 4372
Pleasants, Edwin, 4818
Plecker, W. A., 1446, 2290

Plumbing, 502, 2932, 3018
Pocahontas (town). Directory, 1944
Pocomoke Sound, 364, 2604-2605, 2607
Poe, E. A., 5253-5254, 5928
Poe memorial association, 5254
Poets, 27, 29, 41, 1611, 5278, 5282, 5301, 5305, 5307, 5325, 5328-5330, 5378, 5386-5387, 5391, 5430, 5432, 5442, 5444, 5447, 5451, 5453, 5485, 5500, 5505-5506, 5524, 5535, 5545-5546, 5549, 5554, 5609-5610, 5615, 5618, 5645, 5647, 5649, 5668-5672, 5693, 5697, 5718, 5725, 5731-5734, 5763-5764, 5766, 5775-5778, 5780-5789, 5794-5796, 5801, 5808, 5816-5817, 5867-5870, 5873, 5926, 5930, 5944-5957, 5990, 6024, 6030-6034, 6036, 6046-6048, 6059-6062, 6085
Pohick Episc. church, Fairfax Co., 4889, 4964
Poindexter, Charles, 1626-1627
Police department, City. See names of cities
Polish emigration land co. in Va., 2328
Political cancer, A (pamphlet), 3175
Political conditions, 1385, 2769, 2775, 2782, 2790, 2802-2803, 2811, 2816, 2818, 2823-2824, 2858, 2911, 3162-3163, 3175, 5034, 5058, 5066-5067
Mahone, Wm., campaign, 2765, 2771, 2774, 2781, 2804, 2830-2831, 2835-2836, 2851, 2860
See also Reconstruction
Political corruption, 1856, 2615, 2771, 2774, 2825
Political parties. See Democratic party; Populist; Republican party
Polk, R. L., & co.'s directories, 1944, 1946
Pollard, E. A., 2198, 2453
Pollard, E. B., 2822
Pollard, H. R., 2453-2454, 2823, 3049-3050, 3099
Pollard, J. G., 2636, 2638, 2722-2724, 2729, 2735-2736, 2738
Pollard, R. N., 1318, 2590
Pollard, Thomas, 84-85, 109, 112
Pollock, Edward, 1427, 1454, 1461, 1487, 1534, 1539, 1738
Pollock, G. F., 2455
Poor. Laws concerning, 2010
Overseers of the, 2019
Poor houses, County, 2022
Population. Agricultural, 279
Distribution of, 2292, 2355
Populist club, Swansboro, 1320
Populist platform, 1320
Port authority, State, 710
Port Norfolk electric ry. co., 826
Porter, Duval, 1428, 5191, 5775-5777
Porter, J. J., 803, 1798

[The numbers refer to items, not to pages]

Porterfield, G. T., 2199
Portraits, 3882, 5236-5237, 5241, 5265
Ports. *See* Harbors
Portsmouth. Accountant-auditor, 3038
  Commerce, 1494, 1539
  Directories, 1904, 1906, 1908, 1910
  Economic & social conditions, 1494,
    1509, 1539
  Guide books, 1481, 1485, 1515-1516
  Harbor, 586, 596, 623, 682-683
  History, 1485, 5037
  Mayor, 3039
  Official reports, 3039
  Ordinances, 3040-3043
  Plumbing ordinances, 3040
  Schools. Private, 4373-4374
    Public, 4066-4067, 4392
  Surveyor, City, 3040
  Tax ordinances, 3041
Portsmouth academy, 4373
Portsmouth Bapt. assoc., 4689, 4934
Portsmouth, Berkley & Suffolk water
  co., 1540
Portsmouth business men's assoc., 457
Portsmouth seminary, 4374
Post office clerks, State federation of,
  2504
Post offices, List of Va., 1903, 2565
Potatoes, 79, 184
Potomac (town), 3044
Potomac academy, Alexandria, 4375
Potomac Bapt. assoc., 4690, 4759
Potomac, Fredericksburg & Piedmont r.
  r. co., 861
Potomac gardens, inc., 2200
Potomac presbytery, 4821, 4824, 4828-
  4829
Potomac River, 322-323, 427, 536, 616-
  617, 619. 1951, 2165, 2201, 2297,
  2609, 2754, 2805
Potomac River basin, 333
Pott, W. S., 3584
Potter, C. N., 3494
Poulson, H. N., 3016-3017
Poultry, 157, 186
Pound, Roscoe, 3702
Powder & explosives, 1134
Powell, E. A., 1714
Powell, T. N., 2856
Powells River Bapt. assoc., 4691
Power, R. B., 458
Power companies, 478, 664, 933-935,
  987, 1025, 1044, 1046-1049, 1425,
  3101, 3105
Powers, W. D., 5778
Powhatan's Village, 2276
Pratt, A. S., 467
Prentis, R. R., 2629, 2632
Presbyterian church, 429, 4890, 4929,
  4933, 4966
  Appalachia synod, 4819

Hampden-Sidney college relations,
  3422
Periodicals, 4991-4992, 6165-6166
Presbyteries, 4819, 4821-4832
Virginia synod, 4820
  Negroes in, 4771
  See also Union theolog. seminary
Presbyterian churches. *See* Churches
Presbyterian orphans' home, Lynchburg,
  2044
Presbyterian schools. *See* Colleges;
  Schools
President's conference committee on r.
  rs., 866
Press, 5074-5075
Press, Daily, Hopewell, 6136
Press, Daily, Newport News, 1469, 6144
Press associations, 4610
Press reference book of prominent Vir-
  ginians, 5212
Preston, J. S., 3585
Preston, Mrs. M. J., 5122, 5779-5787
Preston, R. A., 5788
Price, Mrs. A. L., 5789
Price, H. L., 287
Price, T. R., 6086
Price, T. R. & co., 419
Price Mountain coal lands, Montgomery
  Co., 442
Prices of merchandise, 392, 441
Prince Edward academy, Worsham, 4376
Prince Edward area. Soils, 96
Prince Edward County. Description,
  1807
  Historic places in, 4557
  History, 5014
  Taxes, 1193
Prince William County, 1877, 2425, 4158
Princess Anne County. Economic &
  social survey, 1832, 1834
  Health, Board of, 3045
  Oyster records, 351
Princess Anne hotel, Va. Beach, 2184
Printing, 1655, 3313, 3344
Printing, Supt. of public, 3283, 3313
Prison assoc. of Va., 1958-1961
Prison farms, 1972
Prison system, 1958-1961
Private welfare administration, 1840-
  1841
Pro querente; "P. Q." (period.), 549
Probation laws, 1970
Procter, J. R., 163, 2202
Progress-appeal (period.), Petersburg,
  6156
Progress-index appeal (period.), Peters-
  burg, 6156
Progress, The daily (period.), Char-
  lottesville, 1420, 6116

Railroads—cont'd.
Car service, 659, 671, 674-675, 1013-1015
Charters, 400, 563-564, 583, 587, 873, 884, 904, 921
Clubs, 937
Consolidation of, 658, 680, 797, 824, 827, 836, 985, 1076, 1078, 1082
Construction of, 506
Corporate history, 628
Demurrage, 659
Director general of rrs., Agreements & settlements, 629-630
Electric, 507, 583, 662, 751, 785-786, 826, 938, 1025, 1071-1075, 1082-1083, 1465
Employees, Rules governing, 928-929, 938
Equipment trust agreements, 632-633, 740-742, 763, 776, 788, 889, 1065
Freight claims, 1024
Freight classification, 657, 666-668
Full crew bill, 674-675
Guide books, 2169, 2186, 2227, 2235
Laws concerning, 564, 692, 694-698, 758, 771, 884, 921
Leases, 726, 874, 890-891
Loading facilities, 1067
Maximum car limit bill, 671, 675
Mortgages, 728, 757, 778-779, 810, 812-813, 829-831, 834, 840, 848, 854, 873, 875, 885, 889, 894, 898, 922-923, 934-935, 953, 976, 996, 1004-1005, 1038-1040, 1057, 1064, 1066, 1080
Property taxation, 662
Property valuation, 646, 662
Rates, 636, 652-654, 657, 670, 797, 962, 991, 1055
Regulation of, 564, 651, 746
Schedules, 660, 713, 794, 844, 905, 2169
Stockholders, Proceedings of, 820, 859-860, 865, 901, 984, 1022, 1036, 1077, 1081
Storage rules, 659
Street, 933-935, 1044, 1046-1049, 3101, 3104-3105
Taxation of, 600, 656, 662, 673, 715, 793
Terminal facilities, 905, 939, 1067-1070
Terminal lines, 907-914, 939-943, 981, 1068-1070
Traffic reports, 765
Train service, 674-675
Valuation reports, 624-625, 646, 662, 849-850
Virginia's interest in Richmond, Fredericksburg & Potomac r. r., 669
Wage dispute, 1122
Warning devices, 695
Yards, 1067

Railroads & the people, 967
Randall, J. C., 1948
Randall, R. H., co., 3114
Randall's business directory of Winchester, 1948
Randolph, A. M., 3879, 4885, 4949
Randolph, C. J., 1834, 1849
Randolph, E. A., 4956
Randolph, Harold, 5796
Randolph, Innes, 5795-5796
Randolph, J. C., 2418
Randolph, Mrs. Martha, 3625
Randolph, T. J., 3625
Randolph-Macon academy, Bedford City, 4378-4379
Randolph-Macon academy, Front Royal, 4380-4381
Randolph-Macon college, Ashland, 1794, 3363, 3462-3469, 3925, 4031, 4629
Randolph-Macon college monthly, 3984
Randolph-Macon institute, Danville, 4382
Randolph-Macon historical papers, 4629
Randolph-Macon historical society, 4629
Randolph-Macon system, 3468-3469
Randolph-Macon woman's college, Lynchburg, 3470-3473, 3973, 3985
Ransom, M. W. 784,
Rappahannock Bapt. assoc., 4692
Rappahannock County, 1803, 2806
Rappahannock institute, Tappahannock, 3474
Rappahannock River, Timber along, 315
Rappahannock union Bapt. Sunday school convention (col.), 4723
Rappahannock Valley. Farms, 230
Rascoe, Burton, 5343
Rathbun, F. G., 5250
Raven book, Univ. of Va., 3624
Rawenoch, The (period.), 3986
Rawlings institute. *See* St. Anne's school
Raymond, W. M., 5797-5800
Rayner, Isidor, 1174
Read, H. C., 5141
Reade, Willoughby, 5801-5802
Reading, Pa. *Times & dispatch,* 2266
Readjusters. *See* Debt, Public
Real estate, 258-259, 309-312, 552, 1406, 1590, 1628, 3128
Real estate bank of Va., 1346
Real estate trust co., Richmond, 1628
Reavis, J. R., 2206
Reconciliation between North & South, 2517, 2810, 3227, 3240, 5129, 5152, 5182
Reconstruction. Congressional committee on examination of R. E. Lee, 5182
Economic, 159, 161, 185, 192, 233-234, 392, 429, 438, 441, 580, 915-916,

[The numbers refer to items, not to pages]

Richmond (city)—cont'd.

Annual city reports, 3046, 3094
Armor factory location, 1651a
Attorney, City, 3049-3050, 3099
Auditor, 3056
Banks, 939, 1140-1144, 1150-1151, 1160, 1296-1297, 1319, 1337, 1382, 1394, 3363
Baptist council, 4693
Baptist home for aged women, 2535
Battlefields, 1549-1550, 1557, 1572, 1595, 1626-1627
Biographical sketches, 1698
Building inspector, 3057
Building ordinances, 3095-3096
Buildings, Public, 3053, 3108
Cafeteria, Mrs. Cook's, 1569
Capitol building. *See* Capitol, State
Cemeteries, 1554, 1575, 1596, 1843, 3055
Charitable organizations, 1587, 1594, 1600-1603, 1605-1606, 1612-1614, 1635, 2535, 3054-3055, 3068-3069
Charities, Public, 3109
Charter, 3058-3059, 3098-3100, 3106
Child welfare, 1594
Church Hill, 3076
Churches, 1579, 1610, 1932, 2408, 3422, 4766, 4773, 4818, 4853-4876, 4906, 4914, 4932, 4936, 4948-4949, 4954-4957, 4967, 4977, 4988, 4993, 4996-4997
City hall, 1553
City limits, Extension of, 3066
Civic association, 3155-3158
Clubs & societies, 736, 937, 1565-1566, 1571, 1576, 1578-1579, 1584, 1594, 1596, 1601, 1607, 1610, 1634, 1637, 1654-1655, 1658-1659, 1662, 1677, 1684, 1700-1706, 1709, 1843, 1934, 2144, 4003, 4541, 4563, 4582-4583, 5241, 5262-5265, 6086
Code (1885), 3062, 3103
Code (1910), 3099
Code (1924), 3102
Collector, 3060
Colleges & universities, 3427, 3445-3454, 3476-3491, 3837-3838, 3869, 3907
Commerce, 551, 579, 759, 781, 800, 917-918, 1547, 1561, 1597, 1637, 1641, 1698, 1708, 1858
Community recreation assoc., 1566
Comptroller, 3061-3061a
Confederate museum, 4541, 4627
Confederate organizations, 2407, 2409
Confederate veterans. R. E. Lee camp, no. 1, 2383
Confederate veterans' reunions, 2484, 2486-2488

Richmond (city)—cont'd.

Convention facilities, 1588
Conventions, meetings, at, 261, 677, 749, 1028-1030, 1119-1120, 1311, 1975, 2035, 2051-2052, 2057, 2465, 2650, 2652-2653, 2663-2673, 4217, 4549, 4568
Council, 3062-3077
    Health dept., Special committee to investigate, 3071
    Manual, 3063
    Printing & claims, Committee on, 3070
    Rules, 3064
    Yorktown centennial, Resolutions on, 2393
Court record, 1925
Credit men's assoc., 1672
Crime, 1564, 1570, 2452
Department stores, 1133
Description, 1542, 1550-1551, 1558, 1561, 1569, 1572, 1586, 1595, 1617-1618, 1625-1627, 1632, 1646-1651, 1668, 1674, 1676, 1678, 1690, 1695, 1697-1698, 1757, 2196-2197, 2210, 2265, 3082, 3114, 4499, 4606, 5038, 5065, 5239
Directories, 1878, 1894, 1909, 1913-1914, 1925, 1928-1934
Distance from county courthouses, 713
Economic & social conditions, 1542, 1611, 1616, 1618, 1620, 1641, 1646, 1672, 1676, 1690, 1697-1698, 1709, 2410, 2457-2458, 5038
Economic geology, 319
Education, 1698, 3358, 4217, 4578
Electrical dept., 3078
Employment, Public. Annual report, 3079
Employment bureau, 1100-1102
Engineer, City, 3080-3082
Equal suffrage league, 2822
Federal reserve bank organization committee, 1160
Fire dept., 3083
Fire prevention, Bur. of, 3084
Fire protection, 1574, 1670
Franchises, 3062, 3103
Fraternal organizations, 1578-1579, 2382, 2520, 2528-2529, 2534
Gas works, 3052, 3085
Government surveys, 3155-3158, 3178
Grand army of the republic. Phil. Kearney post, no. 10, 2383
Grand army of the republic visit Andrew (J. A.) post, 2409
Wilkes (A.) post, 2407, 2410
Guide books, 1550-1551, 1557, 1572, 1576, 1595, 1599, 1617-1618, 1626-1627, 1665, 1673, 1695, 1757
Harbor, 593, 990, 1556

Richmond (city)—cont'd.

Health agencies, 1593, 1685
Health dept., 2048, 3071, 3086-3092
History, 1547, 1549, 1615, 1627, 1673-1674, 1690, 1698, 1757, 3346, 4499, 5020, 5053, 5065
Home for needy Confederate women, 1587
Hospitals, 1555, 1624, 1630-1631, 1671, 1675, 1966, 3055, 3068-3069, 3451, 4631, 4647
Hotels, 1311, 1588, 1591, 1673
Industry, 549-550, 990, 1547, 1556, 1558, 1561, 1597, 1620, 1637, 1641, 1646, 1651, 1698, 1708, 4499
Jefferson Davis monument fund, 1563
Jews, 1610, 1909, 2345-2346, 5038
Joint committee on improvement of James River, 591
Juvenile & domestic relations court, 2012, 3093
Lee camp soldiers' home, 2014, 2030
Libraries. Private, 3332, 3340, 3345-3347
Public, 3279-3281, 3314-3323
Living conditions, 1699
Male orphan asylum, 1602-1603
Manchester, Consolidation with, 1707, 3172
Manufacturing. See Industry
Masonic temple, Plans to build, 2401
Mayor, 3094
Medical organizations, 1685
Memorial to Congress on James River, 589
Military district, First, 3192
Monuments, 1546, 1554, 1563, 1567-1568, 1581, 1585, 1607-1608, 1679, 1682, 2413-2414, 2426, 2486, 5123, 6068
Moore St. indust. institution, 1612-1614
Music organizations, 1662, 1684, 1700
Negroes, 1684, 1846
New York news letter, Richmond number, 1621
Nurses settlement, 1622-1623
Oakwood memorial assoc., 2454
Ordinances, 3095-3106
Physicians, 1685
Police court, 1552, 1594
Police dept., 3107
Politics, 1856, 2668, 2825, 5038
Poor, 3068-3069
Port commission, 592
Post office, 1628
Public interests, Board of, 579
Public service companies, 933-935, 3105
Public utilities, Dept. of, 3110
Public utility ordinances, 3101, 3104-3105
Public welfare dept., 3109, 3111-3112

Richmond (city)—cont'd.

Public works dept., 593, 3113-3114
Religious life, 1611, 1865
Retreat for the sick, 1630-1631
Sanitation. See Health dept.
School board, 4068-4078
School of present day politics, 2858
Schools. Private, 1612-1614, 3475, 3532-3539, 3741-3745, 3837-3838, 3869, 3907, 4149, 4166, 4181, 4325, 4336, 4353, 4384-4389, 4424, 4462, 4473
Public, 4351, 4421, 4451, 4473, 4487, 4499, 4511-4512
See also School board
Seal of city, 3065
Sewerage, 3081
Sinking fund, 3049-3050, 3115
Social agencies, 1600, 1932
Social life, 1854, 1857, 1863, 1865, 1873, 2543
Southern Bell tel. & tel. co. v. City of Richmond, 634-635
Street cleaning dept., 3116
Street railways, 1044, 1046-1049, 1465, 3101, 3104-3105
Streets, 1047, 3072, 3081, 3101
Survey, Topographic, 3114
Tax laws, 3102
Taxes, Capitation, 3176
Telephone & telegraph companies, 634-635, 1933, 3072
Terminal facilities, 1556
Theatres, 1673
Tobacco trade, 479
Treasurer, 3117, 3176
Typhoid fever, 2060
Views, 261, 1542, 1545, 1548, 1550-1551, 1557, 1559, 1583, 1589, 1595, 1619, 1626-1627, 1632, 1661, 1667, 1673, 1676, 1686, 1690, 5263
Virginia historical pageant, 1688, 5935
Virginia mechanics' institute, 3741-3745
Virginia volunteers, 3212
Vocational education survey, 4078, 4217
Water supply, 1670
Water works, 3073-3077, 3118
World war, 3228
Young men's Christian assoc., 1865, 3347
Richmond (period.), 1861
Richmond academy, 4384, 4516
Richmond academy of the visitation, 4385
Richmond air junction, 601
Richmond amateur base ball commission, 1633

[The numbers refer to items, not to pages]

Richmond & Alleghany r. r. co., 598, 721, 748, 868-875, 962, 986, 2209-2211
Richmond & Danville r. r. co., 461, 607, 766, 865, 876-895, 908, 910-911, 1034, 2212-2215
Richmond & eastern ry. co., 896
Richmond & Henrico ry. co., 3101
Richmond & Louisville medical journal, 4642
Richmond & Mecklenburg r. r. co., 897-898
Richmond & Newport News ry. co., 772
Richmond & Norfolk society blue book, 1913
Richmond & Petersburg r. r. co., 697, 715, 733, 862, 899-901
Richmond & Rappahannock ry. co., 902
Richmond & southwestern ry. co., 474, 903-905
Richmond & trans-Alleghany narrow gauge ry. co., 906
Richmond & West Point terminal ry. & warehouse co., 907-914, 981
Richmond & York River r. r. co., 915-916, 947, 1745
Richmond art club, 1634, 5262-5263
Richmond associated charities, 1635-1636
Richmond bar assoc., 4576-4577
Richmond cedar works, 462
Richmond chamber of commerce, 1637-1653
 Addresses, 967, 1560, 1598, 1707
 Air port committee, 1652
 Conference for trade with Latin America, 917
 James River improvement, 918
 Railroad corporation taxation, 673
 Oyster convention, 455
 Tax reform conference, 1311
 Traffic manager, 1653
Richmond Christian advocate (period.), 5000
Richmond circuit court, 597
Richmond City normal school, 3475
Richmond club, 1654
Richmond club of printing house craftsmen, 1655
Richmond coal field, 424
Richmond college. *See* Richmond university
Richmond college historical papers, 3480
Richmond commercial club, 1637
Richmond County. Immigration, 2071
 Oyster records, 351
 Taxes, 1193
Richmond daily Whig, 6225
Richmond dispatch, The (period.), 390 1322, 4601, 6173
Richmond eclectic (period.), 6100
Richmond education association, 4578

Richmond enquirer, The (period.), 568, 4396, 6178
Richmond enquirer, The daily, 6176
Richmond evening journal, 1656, 6189
Richmond every Monday club, 5264
Richmond examiner, The daily, 568, 6176, 6180
Richmond exchange for women's work, 1129
Richmond exposition, 1798, 1815
Richmond female institute, 4386
Richmond, Fredericksburg & Potomac and Richmond & Petersburg connection r. r. co., 931
Richmond, Fredericksburg & Potomac r. r. co., 632, 658, 669, 715, 719, 744, 919-930, 939, 957-960, 1078
Richmond grain exchange, 221
Richmond granite co., 463
Richmond Grays, 3232-3234
Richmond gun club, 1658
Richmond horse show assoc., 1659
Richmond hotel, 1311, 1588
Richmond Howitzer monument, 1680
Richmond Howitzers, 3252
Richmond ice co., 464
Richmond institute, 3838, 3914, 4388-4389
Richmond journal, 6188
Richmond journal of practice, 4643
Richmond kindergarten assoc., 4579
Richmond labor herald, 6190
Richmond labor journal, 6190
Richmond Light infantry blues, 2479, 3235
Richmond literary miscellany (period.), 6101
Richmond medical journal, 4642
Richmond mercantile & manufacturing journal, 550
Richmond modes & manners (period.), 1863
Richmond Mozart assoc., 1662
Richmond municipal airport, 601
Richmond-New York steamship co., 932
Richmond News, The, 6173
Richmond News-leader, The, 1348, 6191, 6198
Richmond passenger & power co., 933-935, 3105
Richmond, Petersburg & Carolina r. r. co., 936, 964
Richmond planet (period., col.), 6199
Richmond r. r. club, 937
Richmond ry. & electric co., 938
Richmond school of social work & public health. *See* William & Mary college, Richmond div.
Richmond society blue book, 1929
Richmond special horse sale co., 222
Richmond standard, The (period.), 6206
Richmond star, The (period.), 6207

[The numbers refer to items, not to pages]

[The numbers refer to items, not to pages]

Roanoke chamber of commerce, 1716-1717, 1841, 1866
Roanoke college, 3363, 3492-3506
  Periodicals, 3980, 3986, 3989-3990
Roanoke collegian (period.), 3989
Roanoke conference on law reform, 2788
Roanoke County. Crop pest inspection, 145
  History, 5035, 5041
  Hollins institute, 3329
Roanoke evening world, 2788
Roanoke fair, 223
Roanoke gas & water co., 1718
Roanoke gas light co., 1719
Roanoke high school, 4079
Roanoke hospital assoc., 1720
Roanoke indust. & agric. assoc., 223
Roanoke institute, 3384
Roanoke Presbyt. church, Charlotte Co., 4980
Roanoke presbytery, 4830
Roanoke ry. & electric co., 955
Roanoke River, 322-323
Roanoke roofing & metal cornice co., 466
Roanoke telephone co., 954
Roanoke times, The (daily), 2204, 6226
Roanoke times, The (weekly), 6228
Roanoke traction & light co., 955
Roanoke Valley, 1727
Roanoke water works co., 1721, 1724
Roanoke woman's college, 3401
Roaring Fork r. r. co., 956
Roaring Run iron ore property, 417
Roberts, G. B., 888, 957
Roberts, J. K., 537
Robertson, A. F., 2902
Robertson, A. T., 4958
Robertson, Andrew, 532
Robertson, John, 2834
Robertson, J. C., 1670
Robertson, W. J., 2583, 5147
Robins, Mrs. S. N., 5804-5805
Robinson, C. M., 4391-4392
Robinson, Conway, 958-959
Robinson, E. W., 4959
Robinson, Leigh, 1680
Robinson, Mrs. M. H., 5806
Robinson, M. P., 3589
Robinson, Moncure, 958, 960
Robinson, R. B., (col.), 2322
Rock, G. W., 5013
Rock Enon springs & baths, 467
Rockbridge Alum Springs, 411, 468
Rockbridge building fund assoc., 1349
Rockbridge company, 469
Rockbridge County. Description, 2182, 2328
  Health administration, 1804
  History, 5050
  Indian mound, 5272
  Presbyterian church, 4883

Rockbridge County—cont'd.
  Water, 539
Rockbridge Co. agric. advisory board, 87
Rockfish Depot. Kleinberg female home school, 4308
Rockingham County. Board of editors, 4082
  Dairying, 71
  Description, 1351, 1448
  Economic & social survey, 1834, 1850
  Geography, 1838
  History, 5073
  Schools, 4082, 4413
Rockingham district conference. *See* M. E. Church, So.
Rockingham home mutual fire insurance co., 1350
Rockingham national bank, Harrisonburg, 1351
Rockingham register (period.), Harrisonburg, 6133
Rockingham school bulletin, 4413
Rodeffer, C. C., 3690
Rodman, W. S., 3590
Roebuck, G. E., 5807
Roentgen rays (period.), 3990
Rogers, H. H., 1063
Rogers, W. B., 335, 3588
Rohr, W. S., 6096
Roman Catholic schools. *See* Colleges; Schools
Rominger, C. A., 5328
Roosevelt, Theodore, 4393
Rosemont development co., Washington, D. C., 1743
Rosser, Elizabeth W. (Mrs. T. L.), 2461
Rosser, T. L., 224
Rossiter, W. S., 806
Rough Ashlar (period.), 2546
Rouss, C. B., 2391
Routt, L. P., 477
Rowell, W. W., 375
Rowland, W. H., 551
Royal land co. of Va., 470
Royall, W. L., 31, 1161, 1352-1353, 1387, 2330, 6169
Ruebush, J. H., 4877
Ruebush, W. H., 4877
Ruebush-Kieffer publishing co., 6093
Ruediger, F. E., 2605
Ruffin, E. S., jr., 3020
Ruffin, F. G., 961-962, 1162-1166, 1354, 2835-2836, 4394
Ruffin, F. G., jr., 291
Ruffner, W. H., 3298, 3300, 3310, 3352-3353, 3372, 4395-4396, 4646, 5018
Runner, G. A., 88
Rural agencies, Council of, 2056
Rural banking, 1138
Rural depopulation, 279
Rural economic conditions, 159, 278-280

Rural health administration, 1804
Rural life, 2111, 2375, 2464, 3717, 4322, 4921-4922
Rural Retreat high school, 4397
Rural road improvement league, 963
Rural social welfare. *See* Public welfare
Rushing, J. S., 4877
Russell, C. W., 5808-5809
Russell, Frances E., 5810
Russell college, Lebanon, 4398-4399
Russell County. Resources, 393
Russell Fork basin, 338
Rustburg (town). Campbell Co. school fair, 4163
Ruthville community (col.), 2344
Ryals, J. V., 5811
Ryan, M. J., 1821
Rye, 253
Ryland, C. H., 4580
Ryland, Cally T., 5812-5815
Ryland, Garnett, 3933
Ryland, Robert, 4580
Ryland institute, Berkley, 4400

SAFE DEPOSIT & TRUST CO. of Baltimore, 1080
Safety first bulletin (period.), 1088, 1092
St. Anne's school, Charlottesville, 4401-4402
St. Clair, G. E., 988
St. Clair's Bottom Bapt. assoc. (primitive), 4746
St. Elizabeth's hospital, Richmond, 1671, 4631
St. George's church, Spotsylvania Co., 4962
St. George's parish, Spotsylvania Co., 4962
St. James Episc. church, Leesburg, 4982
St. James Episc. church, Richmond, 4816
St. James Episc. church, Warrenton, 4940
St. John, I. M., 471
St. John's academy, Alexandria, 3507-3508
St. John's Episc. church, Fairfax Co., 4908
St. John's Episc. church, Hampton, 4926
St. John's Episc. church, Richmond, 4776, 4865-4866, 4948-4949, 4955
St. Louis exposition, 1904. Va. commission, 532
St. Luke's African union Meth. Prot. church, Norfolk, 4809
St. Mark's Episc. church, Richmond, 4773, 4914
St. Mark's parish, Culpeper Co., 4963, 4995
St. Mary's academy, Alexandria, 4404

St. Mary's (German Cath.) church, Richmond, 4867-4869
St. Mary's male academy, Norfolk, 4405
St. Paul (town), 3129-3130
St. Paul normal & indust. school, Lawrenceville, 4406-4409, 4500, 4517
St. Paul's church, Lynchburg, 4792
St. Paul's Episc. church, Alexandria, 4841
St. Paul's Episc. church, Norfolk, 4884, 4970
St. Paul's Episc. church, Richmond, 4870, 4955, 4996
St. Paul's female school, Petersburg, 4410
St. Paul's memorial church, Univ. of Va., 4886
St. Timothy's home school, Herndon, 4411
St. Vincent De Paul hospital, 1484
Salaries of state officials, 1186, 1190
Sale, Edith T., 2144
Sale, W. W., 3207
Salem (town). Bonds, 3131
    Citizen's executive committee, 1727
    Colleges, 3401, 3492-3506
    Description, 1727-1728
    Directory, 1940
    Emancipation club, 2340
    History, 1729, 5041
    Transportation, 1727
Salem improvement committee, 1728
Salley, J. M., 3779
Salomon, William, & co., 482
Salyards, J. H., 5817, 6073
Sampler (period.), 3991
Sams, C. W., 2903-2904
Samuel, W. H., 2664
San José scale, 144-145
Sanders, H. R., 1851
Sands, A. H., 2667, 2905
Sands, O. J., 1672
Sands, W. H., 1167
Sanger, W. T., 4649
Sanitation, 1744, 1951-1952, 1954, 1991, 2037, 3001, 3091
Sapp, C. P., 1510
Sarg, J. F., 225
Sargeant, W. H., 3274
Saunders, C. W., 1673
Saunders, E. W., 2620
Saunders, J. R., 2685
Saunders, W. H., 2788
Saunders memorial school for boys, 3410
Saxby, H., 2217
Scarborough, W. S., 89
Scharf, J. T., 2218
Scherer, Paul, 226-227
Scherer, Tilden, 3536
Schofield, J. M., 2462, 2627, 2667-2668, 2787, 2837

[The numbers refer to items, not to pages]

School & citizens league bulletin, 4100
School & civic league bulletin, 4101
School & home for homeless boys, Alleghany Co., 4412
School & society (period.), 3337
School attendance, 4482
School cadet corps, 4182
School clubs, 4095, 4201, 4552
School directories, 3361, 4056
School exhibits, 4033, 4108
School fairs, 3299, 4093, 4128, 4163, 4201
School improvement foundation, 4525
School improvement leagues (col.), 4570-4571
School leagues, 4100-4102, 4332, 4453-4454, 4543, 4546-4549, 4575
School legislation, 3307-3311, 3333, 4112-4113, 4119-4121
School superintendents, 3341, 4191, 4351, 4533, 4592. *See also* names of cities & counties
Schoolma'am, The (period.), 3992
Schools. Agricultural, 4127-4129, 4224. *See also* Hampton normal & agric. institute
  Art, 3740, 4459
  Baptist, 3517, 4426, 4429, 4459
  Baptist (col.), 3838, 3869, 4307, 4388-4389, 4466
  Brethren, Church of the, 3390-3393
  Business, 3456, 4319
  Disciples of Christ, 3437
  Elementary. *See* Schools, Public
  Engineering, 3779-3807, 3864
  High. Agricultural, 4127-4129
    Courses of study, 4037, 4039, 4042, 4045-4049, 4051-4052, 4062, 4064, 4069-4070, 4072, 4074, 4079, 4097, 4103-4105, 4146-4147, 4151, 4164, 4215, 4311, 4366, 4397, 4445
    Efficiency in relation to size, 4484
    Inspector of. *See* Schools, Supervisor of
    Principals, 4542, 4596
    Private, 4047, 4180, 4215, 4298, 4305, 4323, 4347, 4360-4361, 4363, 4448, 4457, 4488, 4493, 4514
    Progress of, (1905-1910), 4495, 4575
    Publications, 4505-4514, 4520-4521
    Rural life improvement, 4322
    Statistics of pupils, 4496
    Supervisor of, 4115-4116
  Industrial, 1959, 1962, 1996, 4224, 4338-4342, 4368, 4406-4409, 4500, 4517
  Industrial (col.), 1131, 1456, 1612-1614, 1997, 4177-4178, 4270, 4290, 4307, 4327-4329, 4349, 4446, 4460
  Law, 3478, 3490, 3696-3702, 3865-3867
  Lutheran, 3518, 4465

Schools—cont'd.
  Medical, 3445-3454, 3708-3709
  Methodist Episc., 3734, 4154, 4156, 4378-4379, 4382, 4425, 4469
  Military, 3507-3508, 3939, 4144, 4149-4150, 4152-4153, 4188-4189, 4206-4207, 4210, 4291, 4298, 4312, 4348, 4368, 4378-4381, 4419, 4432-4433, 4439, 4471
  Mountain, 4424, 4808
  Music, 3399-3400, 4459
  Normal, 3325, 3339, 3808-3832, 3834-3835, 3880, 4105, 4177-4178, 4406-4409, 4500, 4517
  Normal (col.), 3372, 3833. *See also* Hampton normal & agric. institute
  Presbyterian, 3410, 4153, 4179-4180, 4359, 4473-4474
  Presbyterian (col.), 4299, 4452
  Private. Boys, 3922, 4047, 4123-4124, 4130, 4152-4153, 4155, 4162, 4166, 4176, 4179-4180, 4185, 4188-4189, 4199-4200, 4203-4204, 4206-4207, 4210, 4220, 4225, 4293, 4298, 4302, 4306, 4312, 4325, 4335, 4347, 4352-4357, 4360-4361, 4364, 4367, 4373, 4375-4376, 4378-4379, 4381-4382, 4387, 4411-4412, 4416, 4419, 4431-4433, 4437, 4439, 4448, 4455, 4461, 4467-4468, 4471, 4476, 4488
    Co-ed., 3390-3393, 3410-3411, 3437, 3509, 3513, 3531, 4132, 4150, 4158-4159, 4169, 4174, 4192, 4195, 4197, 4215, 4294-4295, 4300, 4304, 4310, 4313-4315, 4330-4331, 4338-4342, 4345, 4347, 4352, 4359, 4362-4363, 4365, 4390, 4398-4399, 4417, 4426, 4465, 4470, 4477
    Girls, 3394-3396, 3407-3408, 3426, 3428-3436, 3444, 3455, 3474, 3514-3515, 3517-3518, 3521, 3524-3530, 3734, 3907, 4125, 4143, 4145, 4148, 4154, 4156, 4165, 4167-4168, 4175, 4181, 4184, 4196, 4205, 4208-4209, 4211, 4218, 4221-4223, 4297, 4301, 4308-4309, 4316-4317, 4336, 4350, 4370-4372, 4374, 4382, 4385-4386, 4400-4402, 4404, 4410, 4424-4425, 4427, 4429, 4434-4436, 4440-4441, 4444, 4456, 4458-4459, 4462, 4464, 4469, 4472-4474, 4478-4480, 4590
    Literary societies, 4448
    Publications, 4515-4517
  Private (col.). Boys, 3838, 4460
    Co-ed., 3869, 4157, 4307, 4327-4329, 4349, 4446, 4452
    Girls, 4292, 4299
  Protestant Episc., 3408, 3507-3508, 4168, 4199-4200, 4224, 4350, 4401-4402, 4406-4409, 4411, 4434-4436, 4448, 4488, 4500, 4514, 4517

[The numbers refer to items, not to pages]

Sharon college school, Sharon Springs, Effna, 4417
Shaw, A. F., 3238
Shaw, Annie R., 5861-5862
Shaw, C. P., 969
Shaw, Jane R., 5863-5866
Sheep, 85, 158
Sheet metal works, Roanoke, 466
Sheffey, J. P., 1812
Sheffey, Miriam, 5867
Sheltering arms free hospital, Richmond, 1675
Shenandoah Alum Springs, 476
Shenandoah Bapt. assoc., 4695
Shenandoah college, Reliance, 3509
Shenandoah collegiate institute, Dayton, 3510-3512
Shenandoah County. Description, 1813
  History, 5017, 5074
  Springs, 476, 2174, 2193, 2218
Shenandoah herald, Woodstock, 1813, 6242
Shenandoah iron & coal co.'s r. r., 970-971
Shenandoah iron, lumber, mining & manufacturing co., 420
Shenandoah lumber co.'s r. r., 972
Shenandoah national park, 340-341, 519, 2220, 2252
Shenandoah River terrace, 64
Shenandoah Valley. Agriculture, 2222
  Apples, 228
  Caves, 2085, 2093, 2097, 2099, 2113, 2122-2123, 2171-2172, 2175, 2196, 2216, 2222-2223, 2243
  Churches, 4843, 4969
  Dairying, 71
  Description, 2096, 2098, 2100, 2141-2142, 2146, 2169, 2221-2224, 2228, 2258-2261, 5052
  Fiction, 5333, 5408
  Guide books, 2169, 2261
  History, 2097, 2258, 2260-2261, 5017, 5051-5052, 5064
  Merchants' account books, 441
  Resorts, 2116, 2189
  Resources, 415, 420, 431
  Views, 2258, 2260-2261
Shenandoah Valley academy, Winchester, 4419
Shenandoah Valley & Ohio r. r. co., 2221
Shenandoah Valley apple lands co., 228
Shenandoah Valley fruit growers' assoc., 257
Shenandoah Valley r. r. co., 415, 431-433, 973-977, 2098, 2223, 2254, 2266
  Passenger dept., 2141
Shepard, Mrs. E. L. *See* Tyler, Odette
Shepard, Frank, 2906

Shepard's Va. citations & annotations, 2906
Shepherd, H. E., 5197
Sheriff, B. R., 1906, 1921
Sheriff & Chataigne's directories, 1906, 1928
Sheriff & co.'s directories, 1906, 1921, 1928
Sheriffs, List of, 2640
Sherman, W. T., 3187
Sherrard, T. H., 321
Shethar, Samuel, 874
Shewmake, E. F., 6088
Shewmake, O. L., 1357
Shiloh Bapt. assoc., 4696
Shiloh Bapt. assoc. (col.), 4725
Ship building, Alexandria, 518
Ship building, James River, 961
Ship building, Newport News, 448-452, 1103
Shipp, Scott, 3945
Shirley, G. L., 4877
Shockoe Hill cemetery, 3055
Shockoe Hill literary society, Richmond, 4582
Shoemaker college, Gate City, 3513
Showell, Virginia, 1814
Shrine of the transfiguration, Orkney Springs, 4813
Shroeder, W. C., 325
Shrubs, 191
Signet, The (period.), 4516
Silver mining, 412
Simmons, R. E., 336
Simmonsville. Fairview academy, 4203
Simplification & economy of state & local govt., Commission on, 2746
Simpson, Benjamin, 1428
Sinking fund, Commissioners of the, 1156, 1164, 1166, 1179, 1195, 1267, 1306
Sinton, R. B., 3340
Sixth corps, The (period.), Danville, 6124
Sixth Mt. Zion Bapt. church, Richmond, 4956
Skeen, Lyman, 538
Skirmisher, The (period.), 3994
Skyland (town), 2220, 2224, 2455
Slate mining, 396, 521
Slater, J. F., fund, 1513
Slater, William, 2225
Slaughter, Philip, 3460, 4961-4964, 5198
Sledd, Benjamin, 5868-5869
Sleeping car companies, 663
Smart, Mrs. *See* Gardener, Helen H.
Smith, A., 2907
Smith, B. M., 3536
Smith, C. A., 3591, 5203, 5246, 5274
Smith, D., 5615
Smith, E. E., 2226, 2291

Stone, Ormond, 3704
Stone, R. W., 338
Stone. *See* Building stone
Stone printing & manufacturing co., 2235
Stone tavern, 2532
Stoneman, George, 2787
Stoner, W. S., 4970
Stoner, Winifred S., 2236
Stonewall Jackson institute, Abingdon, 3519
Stony Creek Bapt. assoc. (primitive), 4749
Stony Man camp, 2455
Stony Man Peak, 2224
Stories by American authors series, 5747
Stories of the railway series, 5537
Stovall, J. T., 2592
Strange stories of the revolution series, 5821
Strasburg & Harrisonburg r. r., 600
Strawberries, 253
Strawberry Bapt. assoc., 4699
Stringfellow gold mine, Fauquier Co., 446
Strother, L. H., 3747
Stuart, A. H., 1360, 2480, 2843, 2902, 3592, 3594
Stuart, Gordon (pseud.). *See* Stewart, R. A.
Stuart, H. C., 285, 2685
Stuart, J. E. B., 1581
Stuart, Camp, 3256
Stuart hall, Staunton, 4434-4436, 4515
Stuart normal college, 3520
Sturdivant, N. A., 2667
Stuyvesant school, Warrenton, 4437
Suffolk (city). Confederate monument, 1737
  Description, 1738, 1740
  Directories, 1904, 1943
  Odd-fellows' (col.) meeting, 2326a
  School fair, 4128
  Schools, Private, 3521, 4349-4350, 4400, 4439
  Water supply, 1540
Suffolk & Carolina ry. co., 997
Suffolk collegiate institute, 3521
Suffolk military academy, 4439
Suffrage, 1154, 2638, 2783-2784, 2800, 2804, 2814, 2821, 2840, 2861, 2884
  Negro. *See* Negroes
  Women's. *See* Women's suffrage
Suffrage cases, 2635
Sugar production, 155
Sullins college, Bristol, 3522-3523, 3991
Summer school items (period.), 4000
Summer school news (period.), 4001
Summer schools. *See* Schools
Summers, L. P., 5067
Summerville home school for girls, Gloucester C. H., 4440

Sun, The (period.), Richmond, 6211
Sunday school commission, Diocese of Va., 4852
Sunday schools. Baptist, 4698, 4942, 4997
  Baptist (col.), 4707, 4717-4718, 4723, 4729-4730, 4959
  Christian Bapt., 4767
  Methodist Episc., South, 4912
  Presbyterian, 4864, 4952
  Protestant Episc., 4852
Sunnyside Bapt. Sunday school convention (col.), 4730
Superintendent of public instruction. *See* Education, State bd. of
Supervisors, Boards of, 2737, 3139. *See also* names of counties
Supreme court of appeals, Va. *See* Court of appeals
Surface, G. T., 2292, 2355
Surry, Col., of Eagle's Nest (pseud.). *See* Cooke, J. E.
Surry County, 1820
Surry Co. Negro farmers' fair assoc., 247
Sussex County. Description, 1773
  Charitable assoc. of learning, 4540
  Schools (col.), 4083
Sutherland, E. J., 4741
Sutherland, Hetty J., 4741, 4752
Sutherland, Howard, 427
Sutherlin, W. T., 2481
Swaim, R. D., 3240
Swan, A. J., 5238
Swank, W. A., 5943
Swann, Thomas, 3595
Swansboro (town). Populist club, 1320
Swanson, C. A., 2237, 2363, 2372, 2588, 2700, 2844-2845, 3181, 3341
Swarts, G. T., 1517
Swartz, Joel, 5944-5946
Sweet Briar academy, 3530, 4441
Sweet Briar college, 3524-3530, 3952
Sweet Briar institute. *See* Sweet Briar college
Sweet Chalybeate Springs, 479
Swem, E. G., 25, 35-40, 101, 987, 1177, 2681, 2694, 3881-3882, 4028, 5237
Sydenstricker, Edgar, 1389, 5068
Sydnor, T. L., 4971
Syme, B. C., 3035

Tabb, J. B. (Father Tabb), 5179, 5203, 5947-5957, 6071, 6078, 6086
Tabb, Jennie M., 5203
Taft, W. H., 1537, 3603, 4041, 4261, 4442, 4489
Talbot, Mrs. E. A., 4502-4503
Talcott, T. M., 886
Taliaferro, W. B., 1169, 1214
Tangier Sound, 2604-2605

[The numbers refer to items, not to pages]

Test farm, Dept. of agric., Charlotte Co., 141
Test oath in Va., 2622, 2841
Thayer, W. R., 3603
Theological schools. *See* Schools
Third Presbyt. church, Richmond, 4818
Thom, P. L., 4448
Thom, W. T., 339, 3435-3436, 4449, 5176
Thomas, A. F., 1170, 2046, 2846, 4450
Thomas, Ella M., 41
Thomas, J. B., 3485
Thomas, James, jr., 3488
Thomas, W. E., 3120, 3125
Thomas Jefferson memorial foundation. *See* Jefferson
Thomas S. Martin rally, 2807
Thompson, J. R., 5990-5991, 6079
Thompson, S. H., 2063
Thornrose cemetery, Staunton, 1730, 1736
Thornton, Edward (Sir), 1361
Thornton, J. D., 5992
Thornton, W. M., 177, 2616, 3424, 3596-3597, 4451, 5209
Thorp v. Epes, 2589, 2595, 2753
Thostle, J. A., 4883
Three forks of Powell's River Bapt. assoc. (primitive), 4750
Thruston, Mrs. L. M., 5993-5998
Thurman, A. G., 3598
Thurston, J. M., 2620
Thurston, R. H., 3743
Thyne institute, Chase City, 4452
Tibbets, L. C., 2847
Tidal waters, Pollution of, 1952
Tidewater & western r. r. co., 777
Tidewater ry. co., 1058
Tidewater tales, 5027
Tidewater times (period.), Portsmouth, 6160
Tidewater trail (period.), 2067
Tidewater Va. Agriculture, 83
  Climate, 2037, 2290
  Depopulation in, 279
  Description, 2100, 2106, 2109, 2161, 2228, 2424
  Guide-book, 2264
  Negroes, 2344
  Presbyterian churches, 4966
Tie, The (period.), 4003
Tierney, D., 321
Tiger, The (period.), 4004
Tilton, McLane, 3660
Timber, Creosoted, 453
Timber resources, 315, 321, 420, 426, 460-461, 469-470, 481, 998, 1765, 1776
Timber Ridge Presbyt. church, Rockbridge, 4883
Times, The daily, Richmond, 390, 6213
Times, The weekly, Richmond, 6215
Times, Weekly, Petersburg, 6158

Times-dispatch, Weekly, Richmond, 6217
Tobacco growers' co-operative assoc. of Va., N. C., & S. C., 302
Tobacco growing, 66, 78, 88, 173, 216-219a, 237, 240-241, 253, 277, 287, 297, 302, 1764
Tobacco industry, 277
Tobacco trade of Richmond, 480
Tochman, G., 2072, 2079
Tod, J. K., 1378
Todkill, Anas (pseud.). *See* Cooke, J. E.
Tomkins, Calvin, 595
Tomlinson, E. T., 4503
Tomlinson, P. G., 4503
Tompkins, Christopher, 3445, 3449
Tompkins, Ellen W., 5999-6000
Topography, 1811, 2091, 3114
Torrens system, 197-198, 220, 2887, 4619
Towles, W. B., 2031
Townes, J. W., jr., 2276
Towns, Acts relating to, 3152
Townsend, G. A., 2286, 2293
Trachoma, 1950
Tractors. *See* Farm machinery
Trade schools. *See* Schools, Industrial
Trademarks, Laws protecting, 2713
Traffic laws, 704
Trail, The (period.), 1867
Training camps. Citizen's, 3263
  World war, 2013
Transportation, 119, 244, 307, 438, 1765, 1785
Travelers' protective assoc. of America, 2294
Treasurer, State, 1179, 1283, 1308, 1347, 1362
Treasurers. City, 1255. *See also* names of cities
  County, Laws concerning, 1255
  List of, 2640
Treasury, State, 1190, 4326
Trench & camp (period.), 3255, 3264
Trent, W. P., 3363, 5211
Trice, T. R., 6086
Tri-city r. r. system, 1465
Trinity Episc. church, Spotsylvania Co., 4962
Trinity Evangel. Luth. church, Newport News, 4951
Trinkle, E. L., 1221-1222, 2686, 2701, 2785, 3207
Tri-state medical assoc. of the Carolinas & Va., 4586
Tri-state tobacco grower, 302
Tri-weekly news, Lynchburg, 6141
Trostle, J. A., 4883
Troubetzkoy, Amélie R., 6001-6023
Truck crops, 65, 83, 180, 253, 299
Truck farms, 1104, 1746

[The numbers refer to items, not to pages]

[The numbers refer to items, not to pages]

U. S. Census, Bur. of, 98, 328, 1265
U. S. Children's bureau, 1104, 1994-1995
U. S. Circuit court. 4th circuit, 94
Eastern dist. of Va., 597-599, 1149, 1172
Western dist. of Va., 600, 1149, 1172
U. S. Commerce, Dept. of. Secretary, Aeronautics branch, 601
U. S. Congress. Admission of Va. to, 2832
Annexation of Alexandria to District of Columbia, 2919
Dismal Swamp canal co., Memorial of, 566
James River, Appropriation requested for, 589
Memorial addresses, 5090-5095
Reconstruction acts, 3189-3190
Reconstruction committee, 5182
Representation apportionment for Va., 2596, 2650
Southern issues during the 'nineties, 2818
Washington memorial medallions, 1403
See also U. S. House of representatives; U. S. Senate
U. S. 40 Congress, 2 sess. Senate Exec. doc., 2627
U. S. 41 Congress, 2 sess. House Miscell. doc., 2622
3 sess. House Exec. doc., 562, 608, 639
U. S. 42 Congress, 3 sess., 561
U. S. 45 Congress, House, 2600
2 sess. House Exec. doc., 637
2 sess. Miscell. doc., 1151
U. S. 47 Congress, 1 sess. Exec. doc., 640
2 sess. House, 2592
2 sess. Senate Report, 2367
U. S. 48 Congress, 1 sess. House Miscell. doc., 2608
U. S. 49 Congress, 2 sess. Senate Report, 1176
U. S. 51 Congress, 1 sess. House Exec. doc., 609
U. S. 52 Congress, 1 sess. Senate Exec. doc., 4259
U. S. 53 Congress, 2 sess. Senate Miscell. doc., 5091
U. S. 56 Congress, 2 sess. House Doc., 5093
U. S. 57 Congress, 1 sess., 5092
House, 2602, 2755
U. S. 59 Congress, 1 sess. House Doc., 614-615
2 sess. House Doc., 611
U. S. 60 Congress, 1 sess. House Doc., 617
1 sess. Senate Bills, 1174
1 sess. Senate Report, 1176
2 sess. House Doc., 616

U. S. 60 Congress—cont'd.
2 sess. House Report, 1173
2 sess. Senate Doc., 2075
U. S. 61 Congress, 1 sess. House, 2620
2 sess. House Doc. 610, 612
3 sess. House Doc., 5095
3 sess. Senate Doc., 536, 1138, 5090
U. S. 62 Congress, 2 sess. House Doc., 786, 1074, 1083
2 sess. Senate, 2362
2 sess. Senate Doc., 2588
3 sess. House Doc., 1083
U. S. 63 Congress, 2 sess. Senate, 3369
3 sess. House Doc., 4078
U. S. 64 Congress, 1 sess. Senate Doc., 2616, 5209
2 sess. Senate, 2363
U. S. 66 Congress, 3 sess. Senate Doc., 5094
U. S. 68 Congress, 1 sess., 604
1 sess. Doc., 641
U. S. 69 Congress, 1 sess. House Report, 340
1 sess. Senate Report, 341
U. S. 70 Congress, 1 sess. House Doc., 613
1 sess. Senate Report, 606
U. S. District court. Va. (Eastern dist.), 2624-2625
U. S. Education, Bur. of, 3362, 4084
Bulletin, 1991, 4041, 4084, 4487, 4524
Circulars of information, 3282, 3362-3363
Contributions to American educational history, 3362-3363
U. S. Education, Commissioner of, 4334
U. S. Engineer dept., 608-619
Chief of engineers, 609-617, 620-621, 640
Rivers & harbors, Bd. of engineers for, 610-612, 614-615, 622-623
U. S. Fisheries, Bur. of. Bulletins, 325, 343
Documents, 342
Statistical bulletin, 343
U. S. Fisheries, Commission of, 351-352
U. S. Forest service, 314, 336, 344-346
Forestry laws leaflets, 334
U. S. Fuel-testing plant, Norfolk, 316, 382
U. S. Game & inland fisheries, Commission of, 358-359
U. S. Geological survey. Bulletin, 316-320, 326, 329-330, 338, 382, 2070
Water-supply paper, 322-324, 333
U. S. House of representatives, 2587, 2589, 2592, 2598, 2600, 2617-2619
Banking & currency, Committee on, 1161
Claims, Committee on, 1173-1174
Commerce, Committee on, 571, 602-603, 605

[The numbers refer to items, not to pages]

Virginia agric. advisory council, 251
Virginia agric. & mechanical college.
See Va. polytechnic institute
Virginia agric. & mechanical society, 2333
Virginia air line ry. co., 994-996
Virginia Alberene corporation, 1364-1365
Virginia & Carolina coast r. r. co., 481, 997-998
Virginia & Carolinas insurance directory, 1395
Virginia & Kentucky coal fields corp., 482
Virginia & Kentucky r. r., 999
Virginia & Kentucky ry. co., 1000-1001
Virginia & N. C. southern almanac, 2559
Virginia & southwestern ry. co., 513, 741-742, 788, 1002-1005, 1122
Virginia & southwestern ry. co. Maintenance of way dept., 1122
Virginia & Tennessee coal & iron co., 434, 445, 483
Virginia & Tennessee r. r. co., 692, 735, 1006-1007
Virginia & Tennessee telephone co., 1008
Virginia & the Carolinas illustrated, 232
Virginia angora co., 252
Virginia anthracite coal & ry. co., 1009-1010
Virginia anthracite coal co., 484
Virginia anti-saloon league, 2065
Virginia anti-tuberculosis assoc., 2047-2049
Virginia artillery. Pegram battalion, 3241
Virginia assoc. for the common good, 1366-1367
Virginia assoc. of colleges & schools for girls, 4590
Virginia assoc. of workers for the blind, 2050
Virginia bankers' assoc., 1368-1370
Virginia bankers' convention, 250
Virginia Bapt. annual, 4676
Virginia Bapt. education society, 4580
Virginia Bapt. historical society, 4817, 4896
Virginia Beach, 1515, 2037, 2184, 2245, 4613
Virginia Beach development co., 414
Virginia Blue Ridge ry. co., 1011-1012
Virginia board of trade, 197, 969, 1339, 1491, 2246
Virginia briefs, 718
Virginia bureau of vocations for women. See Southern woman's educational alliance
Virginia business directory & gazeteer, 2561

Virginia canal co., 691
Virginia car service assoc., 1013-1015
Virginia-Carolina & southern ry. co., 1016-1017
Virginia-Carolina chemical co., 200, 253, 303, 485-501
Virginia-Carolina ry. co., 1016, 1018-1019
Virginia-Carolina supply co., 502
Virginia central r. r. co., 1020-1022
Virginia central ry. co., 1023
Virginia chemists' club, 4591
Virginia child welfare conference, 2051-2052
Virginia children's home finder (period.), 2068
Virginia children's home society, 2068
Virginia Christian college, Lynchburg, 3437
Virginia churchman (period.), 4968, 5002
Virginia citizen, The (period.), Petersburg, 6159
Virginia claim conference, 1024
Virginia club, Norfolk, 1511
Virginia club woman (period.), 2549
Virginia coal products corp., 503
Virginia collector's club, 4640
Virginia college for young women, Roanoke, 3735-3736, 3976
Virginia committee on training-camp activities, 2013
Virginia conference annual (M. E. church, So.), 4802, 4897
Virginia conference of charities & correction, 2053-2054
Virginia conference of county & city supts. of public free schools, 4592
Virginia conference of social work, 2055
Virginia consolidated milling co., 504-505
Virginia constitutional convention directory (1901-02), 2916
Virginia construction co., 506
Virginia corporation digest, 771
Virginia council of defense, 3204
Virginia council of religious education, 4921
Virginia council of rural agencies, 2056
Virginia crop improvement assoc., 254-255
Virginia dahlia society, 256
Virginia dairymen's assoc., 174
Virginia debt commission, 1292
Virginia decisions, Court of appeals, 2852
Virginia democrat, The (period.), Richmond, 6219
Virginia democratic state organization, 2773

[The numbers refer to items, not to pages]

[The numbers refer to items, not to pages]

War history commission. Publications, 3214-3217
War history commission news letter (period.), 3267
War memorial commission, 3218
Ward, Harold, 5346
Ward, Mrs. L. A., 6036-6044
Ware parish, Gloucester Co., 4661
Warehouse book, 1284
Warehouses, 907-918, 981
Warm Sulphur Springs, Bath Co., 428, 524
Warner, C. D., 2255, 3504, 5339
Warner, P. L., 1834, 1853
Warren, B. C., 6045
Warren, G. H., 525
Warren, H. P., 4504
Warren County, 5017
Warrenton (town). Churches, 4940
  Fauquier historical society, 4558
  Schools, 4205, 4437, 4464
  Verses written at, 5816
Warrenton country school for young girls, 4464
Warrenton true index (period.), 6236
Warrock-Richardson almanacks, 2567
Wartburg seminary, Graham, 4465
Warwick, The (period.), 4521
Warwick County. Directory, 1098
  Oyster records, 351
  Physiography, 1098
  Soils, 1098
Warwick River Mennonite church, 4928
Washburn, A., 4068
Washington, B. T. (col.), 4142
Washington, Lawrence, 5079
Washington, D. C. Annexation of Alexandria to, 2919
  Virginia suburbs, 1741-1743
  Directories, 1945-1946
Washington academy. *See* Washington & Lee university
Washington, Alexandria & Mt. Vernon ry. co., 1071-1072, 1075, 1082, 2227
Washington & Arlington ry. co., 1075
Washington & Lee historical papers, 3859
Washington & Lee news-letter (period.), 4026
Washington & Lee university, 429, 2395, 3363, 3839-3868, 3921, 3924, 3926
  Addresses, 2824, 3839-3840, 3843-3846, 3848, 3859-3860
  Alumni, 3849-3850, 3854-3855, 3868
  Centennial poem, 5782
  Description, 3921
  Engineering, School of, 3864
  Kappa alpha memorial hall, 3861
  Law department, 3865-3867
  Lee, R. E., at. *See* Lee, R. E.

Washington & Lee university—cont'd.
  Lee monument, 2421
  Lee museum committee, 5174
  Paintings, G. W. C. Lee collection of, 5276
  Periodicals, 3955, 3988, 3996, 4026
  Students, Geog. distribution of, 3351
  Summer school, 3862
Washington & Ohio r. r. co., 2256
Washington & Old Dominion ry. co., 786, 1073-1074
Washington, Arlington & Falls Church ry. co., 1075, 1082
Washington Bapt. assoc. (primitive), 4752-4753
Washington City, Va. midland & great southern r. r. co., 859, 1034, 1076-1077, 2257
Washington college. *See* Washington & Lee university
Washington County. Resources, 393, 1790
  History, 5067
Washington district Bapt. assoc. (primitive), 4752-4753
Washington herald, The, 1402
Washington masonic national memorial assoc., 1399
Washington memorial, Alexandria, 1399-1400
Washington memorial medallions, 1403
Washington monument assoc., 1403
Washington southern ry. co., 633, 656, 720, 929, 1078-1081
Washington statue, Va. military institute, 3748
Washington St. church, Petersburg, 4902
Washington-Va. ry. co., 1071, 1082-1083
Water companies, 664, 1398, 1540, 1718, 1721, 1724, 3026
Water composition, Rockbridge Co., Va., 539
Water power, 378, 381, 387, 420, 507, 536, 1463, 1776, 1785
Water power & development commission, 381
Water supply, 322-324, 333,, 538-539, 1776, 1785, 3028
Water works, City. *See* names of cities
Waterways, Inland, 611, 764, 781. *See also* James River & Kanawha co.
Watkins, J. B., 1775
Watson, T. L., 362, 526
Watson, W. A., 2506
Watson, Mrs. W. A., 2506
Watts, J. A., 3886
Watts, L. L., 1964
Waverly (town). Directory, 1894
Wayland, J. W., 2258-2261, 5073-5075, 6046, 6093

[The numbers refer to items, not to pages]

William & Mary college—cont'd.
  Model & practice school, 3885
  Periodicals, 3963, 4027-4029
  Phi beta kappa, 3873, 3877-3878, 3983
  Richmond division, 3903-3906
  School of present day politics, 2858
  Students, Geog. distribution of, 3351
William & Mary college monthly, 4027
William & Mary college quarterly historical magazine, 4028
William & Mary college quarterly historical papers, 4028
William & Mary literary magazine, 4029
William Byrd hotel, Richmond, 1588
Williams, Ashby, 1379
Williams, Bruce, 3607
Williams, C. U., 1294
Williams, D. B., 2340, 2913
Williams, E. G., 3068-3069
Williams, Flora M., 6049
Williams, Franklin, jr., 1781
Williams, G. G., 1378
Williams, George, jr. (col.), 2325
Williams, J. L., 3729
Williams, J. S., 3730
Williams, J. W., 51, 2596, 2681
Williams, R. F., 5306
Williams, S. W., 716
Williamsburg (city).   Bruton parish
  church, 4780, 4885, 4891-4892, 4917-
  4918
  Celebration at (1919), 2369
  Description, 1550, 1748-1749
  Directories, 1894
  Distances from Va. courthouses, 713
  History, 1748, 3900
Williamsburg business men's assoc., 1749
Williamsburg female institute, 4474
Williamsburg gazette & James City advertiser, 6239
Williamson, A. W., 321
Williamson, Mrs. M. L., 5224-5225
Williamson, Robert, 4981
Williamson, Tom, 3543
Willis, Bailey, 333
Williston, Samuel, 3702
Wills, Laws concerning, 2874
Wilmer, A. P., 1396
Wilson, A. F., 3731
Wilson, C. E., 2602, 2755
Wilson, F. T., 2366
Wilson, Hannah, 3434
Wilson, J. G., 5173
Wilson, J. P., jr., 1832, 1834
Wilson, J. S., 3607, 5257, 6102
Wilson, R. H., 6050-6051
Wilson, R. T., 666, 1245
Wilson, W. L., 3860
Wilson,   Woodrow,   3603, 5097, 5124,
  5133, 5138-5139, 5141, 5151, 5172,
  5221, 6075

Wilson's landing, 2265
Wilstach, Paul, 2295-2297
Wilton estate, Albemarle Co., 276
Wiltshire, Ellsworth, 3326
Winchester (city).   Centennial, 1750
  Charter, 3152
  Churches, 4911
  Confederate memorial, 1751
  Council, 3150
  Description, 1752-1754, 4216
  Directories, 1948-1949
  Handley fund, 3150, 3324, 4216, 4485
  History, 1752, 5051
  Library, Handley, 3324
  Memorial exercises for R. E. Lee, 5160
  Ordinances, 3151-3152
  Schools,   Private,   3407-3409,   3734,
    4208-4209, 4419
  Schools, Public, 4216, 4485
  Va. state bar assoc. meeting, 2612
Winchester & Potomac r. r., 600
Winchester & Strasburg r. r., 600
Winchester board of trade, 1753
Winchester chamber of commerce, 1754
Winchester evening star (period.), 6241
Winchester news, The, 6240
Winchester presbytery, 4832
Window, R. R., 1084
Wingfield, E. M., 5076
Wingfield, Marshall, 5076
Winn, J. F., 4643
Winslow, E. E. 614-615
Winslow, Mary N., 1105
Winston, Mrs. J. B., 4315
Winston, Nannie B., 6052
Winston, Mrs. R. B., 6053
Winterburn, Florence H., 6054-6055
Wise, Caroline, 5814
Wise, G. D., 2752
Wise, H. A., 1380, 3235, 3506
Wise, J. C., 3247, 3773, 3775-3778, 3945
Wise, J. S., 2507, 2608, 3772, 6056-6057
Wise, Kate E., 2264
Wise, Lucy R., 5201
Wise, R. A., 2587, 2598, 2826, 5093
Wise (town).   Gladeville college, 3411
Wise   County.   Biographical   sketches,
  1819
  Description, 393, 434, 460, 1819
  Economic & social survey, 1834, 1845
  Lands, Report on, 460
  Resources, 393, 426, 460, 531, 1819
Woman labor, 1104-1105, 1123, 1126,
  1129
Woman voter of Va. (period.), 2915
Woman's auxiliary to Episc. board of
  missions, 4836
Woman's Bapt. missionary union, 4701
Woman's Christian temperance union of
  Va., 4893
Woman's college, Richmond, 3907, 3960

[The numbers refer to items, not to pages]